UNIFORM CRIME REPORTS

for the United States

1993

SUMMARY

CRIME INDEX

CRIMES CLEARED

PERSONS ARRESTED

HOMICIDE PATTERNS - PAST AND PRESENT

LAW ENFORCEMENT PERSONNEL

PRINTED ANNUALLY

Federal Bureau of Investigation
U.S. Department of Justice
Washington, D.C. 20535

APPENDICES

ADVISORY:

Committee on Uniform Crime Records
International Association of Chiefs of Police;
Committee on Uniform Crime Reporting
National Sheriffs' Association;
Criminal Justice Information Services Data Providers Advisory Policy Board

For sale by the U.S. Government Printing Office
Superintendent of Documents, Mail Stop: SSOP, Washington, DC 20402-9328
ISBN 0-16-045321-6

PREFACE

Fifty years ago America was caught up in the Second World War. In those difficult times, there was the fear of losing family and friends and even democracy itself. Today Americans are focused on different kinds of fears—crime and violence—that have become a part of everyday life. The fear of crime has settled over communities everywhere, challenging our sense of safety and law enforcement's resources. This fear alters the way we perceive ourselves, our society, and law enforcement.

Reducing crime, as well as the fear it causes, poses a significant challenge. It will require careful planning, based on accurate, detailed, and timely information, along with extensive cooperation of local, state, and federal law enforcement agencies. The National Incident-Based Reporting System (NIBRS) was designed to provide that information, enabling law enforcement to understand and analyze crime more effectively. As NIBRS implementation becomes more and more widespread and the partnership among local, state, and federal law enforcement grows stronger, more information for critical decisions affecting law enforcement priorities and future crime prevention programs will be available.

This publication is a product of the long-standing cooperation among members of the law enforcement community. While it contains important crime information, it also demonstrates law enforcement's ability to work together for a common purpose. The Uniform Crime Reporting Program is continually changing in an effort to enhance and maintain that relationship so law enforcement can meet each and every challenge in the years to come.

CRIME FACTORS

Each year when *Crime in the United States* is published, many entities—news media, tourism agencies, and others with an interest in crime in our Nation—compile rankings of cities and counties based on their Crime Index figures. These simplistic and/or incomplete analyses often create misleading perceptions which adversely affect cities and counties, along with their residents. Assessing criminality and law enforcement's response from jurisdiction to jurisdiction must encompass many elements, some of which, while having significant impact, are not readily measurable nor applicable pervasively among all locales. Geographic and demographic factors specific to each jurisdiction must be considered and applied if crime assessment is to approach completeness and accuracy. There are several sources of information which may assist the responsible researcher. The U.S. Bureau of the Census data, for example, can be utilized to better understand the makeup of a locale's population. The transience of the population, its racial and ethnic makeup, its composition by age and gender, education levels, and prevalent family structures are all key factors in assessing and better understanding the crime issue.

Local chambers of commerce, planning offices, or similar entities provide information regarding the economic and cultural makeup of cities and counties. Understanding a jurisdiction's industrial/economic base, its dependence upon neighboring jurisdictions, its transportation system, its economic dependence on nonresidents (such as tourists and convention attendees), its proximity to military reservations, etc., all help in better gauging and interpreting the crime known to and reported by law enforcement.

The strength (personnel and other resources) and the aggressiveness of a jurisdiction's law enforcement agency are also key factors. While information pertaining to the number of sworn and civilian law enforcement employees can be found in this publication, assessment of the law enforcement emphases is, of course, much more difficult. For example, one city may report more crime than a comparable one, not because there is more crime, but rather because its law enforcement agency through proactive efforts identifies more offenses. Attitudes of the citizens toward crime and their crime reporting practices, especially concerning more minor offenses, have an impact on the volume of crimes known to police.

It is incumbent upon all data users to become as well educated as possible about how to categorize and quantify the nature and extent of crime in the United States and in any of the over 16,000 jurisdictions represented by law enforcement contributors to this Program. Valid assessments are only possible with careful study and analysis of the various unique conditions affecting each local law enforcement jurisdiction.

Historically, the causes and origins of crime have been the subjects of investigation by varied disciplines. Some factors which are known to affect the volume and type of crime occurring from place to place are:

Population density and degree of urbanization with size of locality and its surrounding area.

Variations in composition of the population, particularly youth concentration.

Stability of population with respect to residents' mobility, commuting patterns, and transient factors.

Modes of transportation and highway system.

Economic conditions, including median income, poverty level, and job availability.

Cultural factors and educational, recreational, and religious characteristics.

Family conditions with respect to divorce and family cohesiveness.

Climate.

Effective strength of law enforcement agencies.

Administrative and investigative emphases of law enforcement.

Policies of other components of the criminal justice system (i.e., prosecutorial, judicial, correctional, and probational).

Citizens' attitudes toward crime.

Crime reporting practices of the citizenry.

The Uniform Crime Reports give a nationwide view of crime based on statistics contributed by state and local law enforcement agencies. Population size is the only correlate of crime utilized in this publication. While the other factors listed above are of equal concern, no attempt is made to relate them to the data presented. *The reader is, therefore, cautioned against comparing statistical data of individual reporting units from cities, counties, metropolitan areas, states, or colleges and universities solely on the basis of their population coverage or student enrollment.*

Data users are cautioned against comparisons of crime trends presented in this report and those estimated by the National Crime Victimization Survey (NCVS), administered by the Bureau of Justice Statistics. Because of differences in methodology and crime coverage, the two programs examine the Nation's crime problem from somewhat different perspectives, and their results are not strictly comparable. The definitional and procedural differences can account for many of the apparent discrepancies in results from the two programs. Appendix IV, "The Nation's Two Crime Measures," contains a detailed description of the NCVS and UCR.

CONTENTS

SECTION I

Summary of the Uniform Crime Reporting Program

The Uniform Crime Reporting (UCR) Program is a nationwide, cooperative statistical effort of over 16,000 city, county, and state law enforcement agencies voluntarily reporting data on crimes brought to their attention. During 1993, law enforcement agencies active in the UCR Program represented over 245 million United States inhabitants or 95 percent of the total population as established by the Bureau of the Census. The coverage amounted to 97 percent of the United States population living in Metropolitan Statistical Areas (MSAs), 86 percent of the population in cities outside metropolitan areas and in rural counties.

Since 1930, the FBI has administered the Program and issued periodic assessments of the nature and type of crime in the Nation. While the Program's primary objective is to generate a reliable set of criminal statistics for use in law enforcement administration, operation, and management, its data have over the years become one of the country's leading social indicators. The American public looks to UCR for information on fluctuations in the level of crime, while criminologists, sociologists, legislators, municipal planners, the press, and other students of criminal justice use the statistics for varied research and planning purposes.

Historical Background

Recognizing a need for national crime statistics, the International Association of Chiefs of Police (IACP) formed the Committee on Uniform Crime Records in the 1920s to develop a system of uniform police statistics. Establishing offenses known to law enforcement as the appropriate measure, the Committee evaluated various crimes on the basis of their seriousness, frequency of occurrence, pervasiveness in all geographic areas of the country, and likelihood of being reported to law enforcement. After studying state criminal codes and making an evaluation of the recordkeeping practices in use, the Committee in 1929 completed a plan for crime reporting which became the foundation of the UCR Program.

Seven offenses were chosen to serve as an Index for gauging fluctuations in the overall volume and rate of crime. Known collectively as the Crime Index, these offenses included the violent crimes of murder and non-negligent manslaughter, forcible rape, robbery, and aggravated assault and the property crimes of burglary, larceny-theft, and motor vehicle theft. By congressional mandate, arson was added as the eighth Index offense in 1979.

During the early planning of the Program, it was recognized that the differences among criminal codes precluded a mere aggregation of state statistics to arrive at a national total. Further, because of the variances in punishment for the same offenses in different state codes, no distinction between felony and misdemeanor crimes was possible. To avoid these problems and provide nationwide uniformity in crime reporting, standardized offense definitions by which law enforcement agencies were to submit data, without regard for local statutes, were formulated. The definitions used by the Program are set forth in Appendix II of this publication.

In January, 1930, 400 cities representing 20 million inhabitants in 43 states began participating in the UCR Program. Congress enacted Title 28, Section 534, of the U.S. Code authorizing the Attorney General to gather crime information that same year. The Attorney General, in turn, designated the FBI to serve as the national clearinghouse for the data collected. Since that time, data based on uniform classifications and procedures for reporting have been obtained from the Nation's law enforcement agencies.

Advisory Groups

Providing vital links between local law enforcement and the FBI in the conduct of the UCR Program are the IACP and the National Sheriffs' Association (NSA). The IACP's Committee on Uniform Crime Records, as it has since the Program began, represents the thousands of police departments nationwide. The NSA's Committee on Uniform Crime Reporting, established in June, 1966, encourages sheriffs throughout the country to participate fully in the Program. Both committees serve in advisory capacities concerning the UCR Program's operation.

To function in an advisory capacity concerning UCR policy and provide suggestions on UCR data usage, a Data Providers' Advisory Policy Board (APB) was established in August, 1988. The Board operated until 1993 when a new Board to address all FBI criminal justice information services was approved. The new Board will continue the work of the former APB but will also consider policy issues concerning the National Crime Information Center and FBI identification services.

The Association of State Uniform Crime Reporting Programs and committees on UCR within individual state law enforcement associations are also active in promoting interest in the UCR Program. These organizations foster widespread and more intelligent use of uniform crime statistics and lend assistance to contributors when the needs arise.

Redesign of UCR

While throughout the years the UCR Program remained virtually unchanged in terms of the data collected and disseminated, a broad utility had evolved for UCR by the 1980s. Recognizing the need for improved statistics, law enforcement called for a thorough evaluative study that would modernize the UCR Program. The FBI fully concurred with the need for an updated Program and lent its complete support, formulating a comprehensive three-phase redesign effort. The Bureau of Justice Statistics (BJS), the Department of Justice agency responsible for funding criminal justice information projects, agreed to underwrite the first two phases. Conducted by an independent contractor, these phases were structured to determine what, if any, changes should be made to the current Program. The third phase would involve implementation of the changes identified. Abt Associates Inc. of Cambridge, Massachusetts, overseen by the FBI, BJS, and a Steering Committee comprised of prestigious individuals representing a myriad of disciplines, commenced the first phase in 1982.

During the first phase, the historical evolution of the Program was examined. All aspects of the Program, including the objectives and intended user audience, data items, reporting mechanisms, quality control, publications and user services, and relationships with other criminal justice data systems, were studied.

Early in 1984, a conference on the future of UCR, held in Elkridge, Maryland, launched the second phase of the study, which would examine potential futures for UCR and conclude with a set of recommended changes. Attendees at this conference reviewed work conducted during the first phase and discussed the potential changes that should be considered during phase two.

Findings from the evaluation's first phase and input on alternatives for the future were also major topics of discussion at the seventh National UCR Conference in July, 1984. Overlapping phases one and two was a survey of law enforcement agencies.

Phase two ended in early 1985 with the production of a draft "Blueprint for the Future of the Uniform Crime Reporting Program." The study's Steering Committee reviewed the draft report at a March, 1985, meeting and made various recommendations for revision. The Committee members, however, endorsed the report's concepts.

In April, 1985, the phase two recommendations were presented at the eighth National UCR Conference. While various considerations for the final report were set forth, the overall concept for the revised Program was unanimously approved. The joint IACP/NSA Committee on UCR also issued a resolution endorsing the Blueprint.

The final report, the "Blueprint for the Future of the Uniform Crime Reporting Program," was released in the summer of 1985. It specifically outlined recommendations for an expanded, improved UCR Program to meet informational needs into the next century. There were three recommended areas of enhancement to the UCR Program. First, reporting of offenses and arrests would be made by means of an incident-based system. Second, collection of data would be accomplished on two levels. Agencies in level one would report important details about those offenses comprising the current Crime Index, their victims, and arrestees. Law enforcement agencies covering populations of over 100,000 and a sampling of smaller agencies would be included in level two, which would collect expanded detail on all significant offenses. The third proposal involved introducing a quality assurance program.

One of the first actions taken by the FBI to begin implementation was to award a contract for the development of new offense definitions and data elements for the redesigned system. The work involved: (a) revision of the definitions of certain Index offenses; b) identification of additional significant offenses to be reported; (c) refining definitions for both; and (d) development of data elements (incident details) for all UCR offenses in order to fulfill the requirements of incident-based reporting versus the current summary reporting.

Concurrent with the preparation of the data elements, the FBI studied the various state systems to select an experimental site for implementation of the redesigned Program. In view of its long-standing incident-based Program and well-established staff dedicated solely to UCR, the South Carolina Law Enforcement Division (SLED) was chosen. The SLED agreed to adapt its existing system to meet the requirements of the redesigned Program and collect data on both offenses and arrests relating to the newly defined offenses.

To assist SLED in conducting the pilot project, offense definitions and data elements developed under the private contract were put at the staff's disposal. Also, FBI automated data processing personnel developed "Automated Data Capture Specifications" for use in adapting the state's data processing procedures to incorporate the revised system. The BJS supplied funding to facilitate software revisions needed at the state level. Testing of the new Program was completed in late 1987.

Following the completion of the pilot project conducted by SLED, the FBI produced a draft set of guidelines for an enhanced UCR Program. Law enforcement executives from around the country were then invited to a conference in Orange Beach, Alabama, where the guidelines were presented for final review.

During the conference, three overall endorsements were passed without dissent. First, that there be established a new, incident-based national crime reporting system; second, that the FBI manage this Program; and third, that an Advisory Policy Board composed of law enforcement executives be formed to assist in the direction and implementation of the new Program.

Information about the redesigned UCR Program, called the National Incident-Based Reporting System or NIBRS, is contained in four documents produced subsequent to the Orange Beach Conference. Volume 1, *Data Collection Guidelines,* contains a system overview and descriptions of the offenses, offense codes, reports, data elements, and data values used in the system. Volume 2, *Data Submission Specifications,* is for the use of state and local systems personnel who are responsible for preparing magnetic tapes/floppy disks/etc., for submission to the FBI. Volume 3, *Approaches to Implementing an Incident-Based Reporting (IBR) System,* is for use by computer programmers, analysts, etc., responsible for developing a state or local IBR system which will meet NIBRS' reporting requirements. Volume 4, *Error Message Manual,* contains designations of mandatory and optional data elements, data element edits and error messages.

A NIBRS edition of the UCR Handbook has been produced to assist law enforcement agency data contributors implementing NIBRS within their departments. This document is geared toward familiarizing local and state law enforcement personnel with the definitions, policies, and procedures of NIBRS. It does not contain the technical coding and data transmission requirements presented in Volumes 1 through 4.

NIBRS will collect data on each single incident and arrest within 22 crime categories. For each offense known to police within these categories, incident, victim, property, offender, and arrestee information will be gathered when available. The goal of the redesign is to modernize crime information by collecting data presently maintained in law enforcement records; the enhanced UCR Program is, therefore, a byproduct of current records systems. The integrity of UCR's long-running statistical series will, of course, be maintained.

It became apparent during the development of the prototype system that the level one and level two reporting proposed in the "Blueprint" may not be the most practical approach. Many state and local law enforcement administrators indicated that the collection of data on all pertinent offenses could be handled with more ease than could the extraction of selected ones. While "Limited" participation, equivalent to the "Blueprint's" level one, will remain an option, it appears that most reporting jurisdictions, upon implementation, will go immediately to "Full" participation, meeting all NIBRS data submission requirements.

The pace of NIBRS implementation will be commensurate with the resources, abilities, and limitations of the contributing law enforcement agencies. The FBI was able to accept NIBRS data as of January, 1989, and nine state-level UCR Programs (Colorado, Idaho, Illinois, Iowa, North Dakota, South Carolina, Utah, Vermont, and Virginia) are now supplying data in the NIBRS format. An additional 18 state agencies, as well as three local law enforcement agencies in non-Program states and one federal agency (the FBI), have submitted test tapes or disks containing the expanded data. Seventeen other state UCR Programs and agencies in the District of Columbia and Guam are in various stages of planning and development. Test tapes for six of these states, the District of Columbia, and Guam are expected during 1994.

Recent Developments

STATE UCR PROGRAMS — UCR welcomed two states to the ranks of state-level programs, Louisiana and Nevada. In 1993, the Louisiana Commission on Law Enforcement and the Nevada Highway Patrol each commenced collection of UCR data from local law enforcement within their respective states. With their addition, there are now state Programs in 44 states and the District of Columbia.

HATE CRIME STATISTICS — The Hate Crime Statistics Act, passed by the U.S. Congress and signed by the President in April, 1990, mandates a data collection of crimes motivated by religious, ethnic, racial, or sexual-orientation prejudice. Collection commenced January 1, 1991, and the UCR Program has distributed hate crime *Data Collection Guidelines* and *Training Guides* to city, county, and state law enforcement agencies. Training sessions have been held across the Nation to educate federal, state, and local law enforcement agencies in the hate crime reporting procedures. The first annual hate crime publication, which contained 1992 statistics, has been produced, and a 1993 issue is planned for late 1994. Participation continues to grow; 1993 submissions were received from 6,840 law enforcement agencies covering 56 percent of the U.S. population.

VIOLENCE AGAINST POLICE OFFICERS — A "Violence Against Law Enforcement Officers" study funded by a grant from the National Institute of Justice is now underway. It will examine 40 selected incidents of serious assault by *cutting instrument or firearm* where the victim officer *survived* the incident. Extensive interviews of victim officers and convicted assailants are now being conducted, and a special report is planned for 1995. The report will attempt to answer questions raised in the earlier report, *Killed in the Line of Duty.*

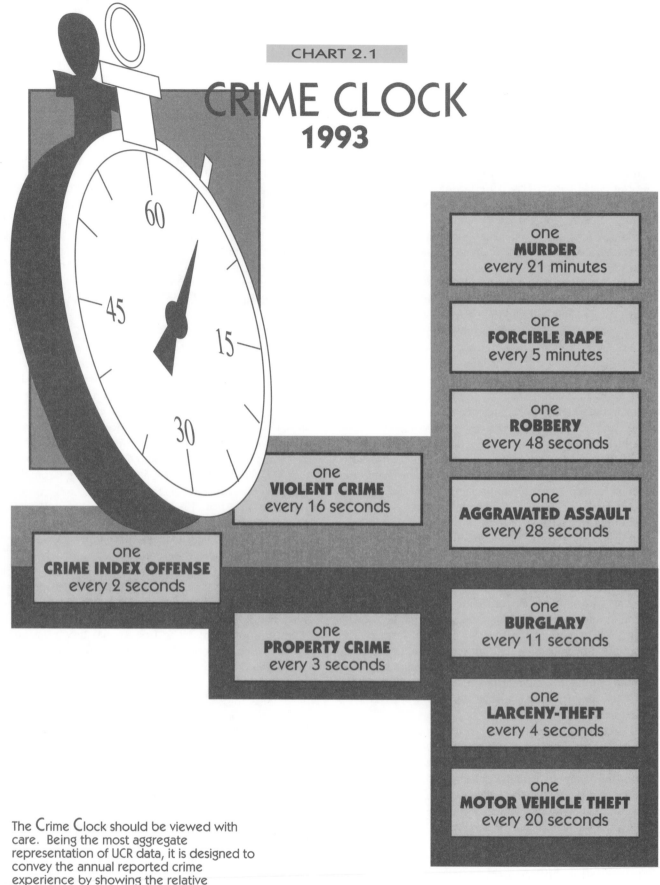

CHART 2.1

CRIME CLOCK
1993

one
MURDER
every 21 minutes

one
FORCIBLE RAPE
every 5 minutes

one
ROBBERY
every 48 seconds

one
AGGRAVATED ASSAULT
every 28 seconds

one
VIOLENT CRIME
every 16 seconds

one
CRIME INDEX OFFENSE
every 2 seconds

one
PROPERTY CRIME
every 3 seconds

one
BURGLARY
every 11 seconds

one
LARCENY-THEFT
every 4 seconds

one
MOTOR VEHICLE THEFT
every 20 seconds

The Crime Clock should be viewed with care. Being the most aggregate representation of UCR data, it is designed to convey the annual reported crime experience by showing the relative frequency of occurrence of the Index Offenses. This mode of display should not be taken to imply a regularity in the commission of the Part I Offenses; rather, it represents the annual ratio of crime to fixed time intervals.

SECTION II
Crime Index Offenses Reported

CRIME INDEX TOTAL

DEFINITION

The Crime Index is composed of selected offenses used to gauge fluctuations in the overall volume and rate of crime reported to law enforcement. The offenses included are the violent crimes of murder and nonnegligent manslaughter, forcible rape, robbery, and aggravated assault and the property crimes of burglary, larceny-theft, motor vehicle theft, and arson.

TREND

Year	Number of offenses[1]	Rate per 100,000 inhabitants[1]
1992	14,438,191	5,660.2
1993	14,140,952	5,482.9
Percent change	–2.1	–3.1

[1]Does not include arson. See page 57.

The Crime Index total dropped 2 percent to 14.1 million offenses in 1993, the second consecutive year of decline. In the rural and the suburban counties, the Index was also down 2 percent from 1992, while the cities collectively registered a 3-percent decrease. This downward trend was evident in all city population groups, with those having a million or more inhabitants showing the largest decrease, 5 percent. Five- and 10-year percent changes showed the 1993 national experience was 1 percent lower than the 1989 level but 19 percent higher than the 1984 total.

Geographically, the largest volume of Crime Index offenses was reported in the most populous Southern States, which accounted for 38 percent of the total. Following were the Western States with 25 percent, the Midwestern States with 21 percent, and the Northeastern States with 17 percent. The regions showed Crime Index decreases ranging from 1 to 4 percent during 1993 as compared to 1992. (See Table 4.)

As in previous years, Crime Index offenses occurred most frequently in August and least often in February.

Table 2.1 – Crime Index Total by Month, 1989-1993
[Percent distribution]

Months	1989	1990	1991	1992	1993
January	8.2	8.3	7.9	8.3	8.0
February	7.2	7.4	7.4	7.8	6.9
March	8.2	8.2	8.1	8.2	8.1
April...................	7.8	7.9	8.0	8.0	7.9
May	8.5	8.3	8.4	8.3	8.2
June	8.5	8.3	8.5	8.4	8.6
July...................	9.2	8.9	9.1	9.0	9.1
August................	9.3	9.1	9.2	9.0	9.2
September..............	8.4	8.4	8.4	8.4	8.4
October	8.7	8.7	8.7	8.5	8.6
November	8.1	8.2	8.0	8.0	8.1
December	7.9	8.6	8.3	8.1	9.1

Rate

Crime rates relate the incidence of crime to population. In 1993, there were an estimated 5,483 Crime Index offenses for each 100,000 in United States population. The Crime Index rate was highest in the Nation's metropolitan areas and lowest in the rural counties. (See Table 2.) The national 1993 Crime Index rate fell 3 percent from 1992 and 4 percent from the 1989 level. It was 9 percent above the 1984 rate.

Regionally, the Crime Index rates ranged from 6,220 in the West to 4,613 in the Northeast. The 2-year percent changes (1993 versus 1992) showed declines in all regions. (See Table 4.)

Nature

The Crime Index is composed of violent and property crime categories, and in 1993, 14 percent of the Index offenses reported to law enforcement were violent crimes and 86 percent, property crimes. Larceny-theft was the offense with the highest volume, while murder accounted for the fewest offenses. (See Chart 2.4.)

Property estimated in value at $15.3 billion was stolen in connection with all Crime Index offenses, with the largest losses due to theft of motor vehicles; jewelry and precious metals; and televisions, radios, stereos, etc. Law enforcement agencies nationwide recorded a 34-percent recovery rate for dollar losses in connection with stolen property. The highest recovery percentages were for stolen motor vehicles, consumable goods, livestock, clothing and furs, and firearms. (See Table 24.)

Law Enforcement Response

Law enforcement agencies nationwide recorded a 21-percent clearance rate for the collective Crime Index offenses in 1993 and made an estimated 2.8 million arrests for Index crimes. Crimes can be cleared by arrest or by exceptional means when some element beyond law enforcement control precludes the placing of formal charges against the offender. The arrest of one person may clear several crimes, or several persons may be arrested in connection with the clearance of one offense.

The Index clearance rate has remained relatively stable throughout the past 10-year period. As in 1993, the clearance rates in both 1989 and 1984 were 21 percent.

Arrests for Index crimes dropped 2 percent in 1993 when compared to 1992. Adult arrests for Index crimes were down 3 percent, and those of juveniles declined 1 percent. Arrests of males decreased 3 percent for the 2-year period, while those of females increased less than 1 percent.

Considering the individual offenses composing the Index, only murder and aggravated assault showed increases in arrest totals from 1992 to 1993. Decreases for the remaining Index offenses ranged from 1 percent for robbery and arson to 5 percent for burglary.

As in past years, larceny-theft arrests accounted for the highest volume of Crime Index arrests at 1.5 million. (See Table 29.)

CRIME INDEX

CHART 2.2

VARIATION FROM MONTHLY AVERAGE
1993

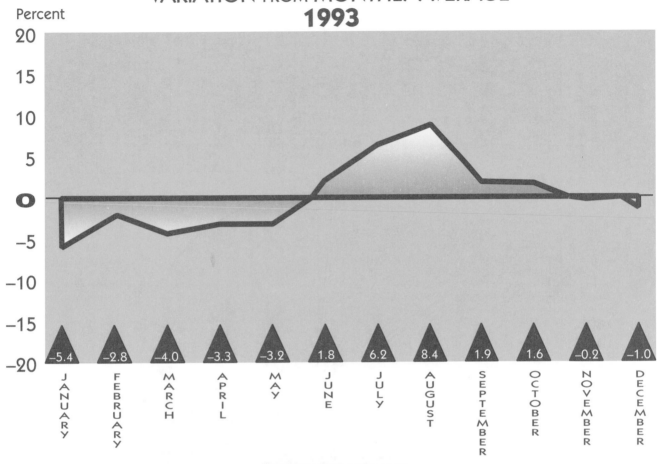

CHART 2.3

PERCENT CHANGE FROM 1989

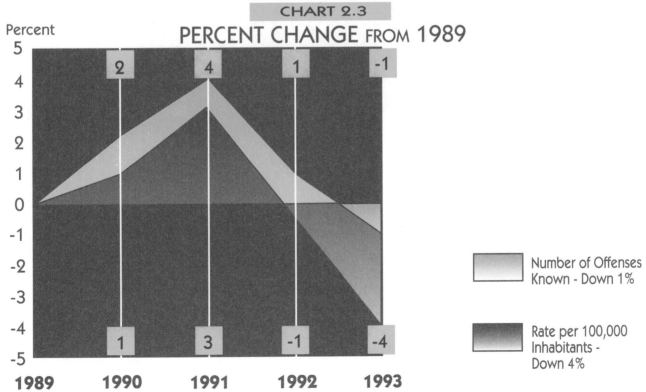

Number of Offenses
Known - Down 1%

Rate per 100,000
Inhabitants -
Down 4%

CHART 2.4

CRIME INDEX OFFENSES

1993
Percent Distribution

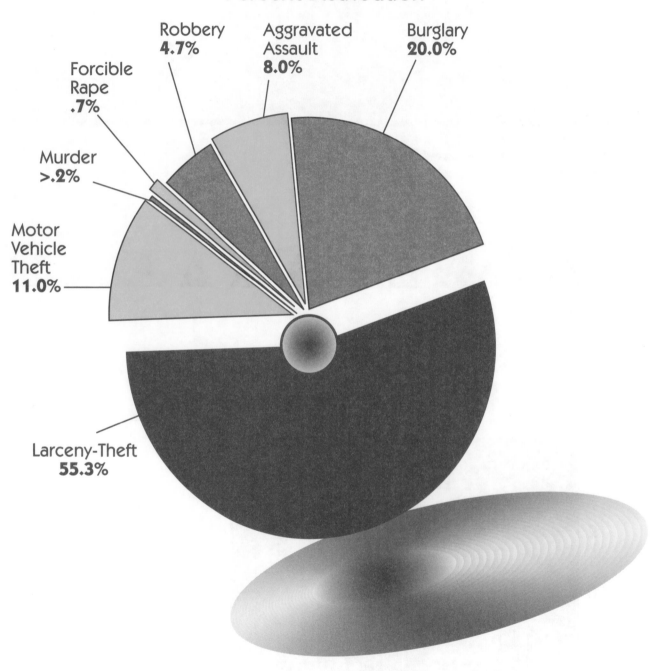

Robbery
4.7%

Aggravated
Assault
8.0%

Burglary
20.0%

Forcible
Rape
.7%

Murder
>.2%

Motor
Vehicle
Theft
11.0%

Larceny-Theft
55.3%

CHART 2.5

REGIONAL VIOLENT
AND PROPERTY CRIME RATES
1993

per 100,000 inhabitants

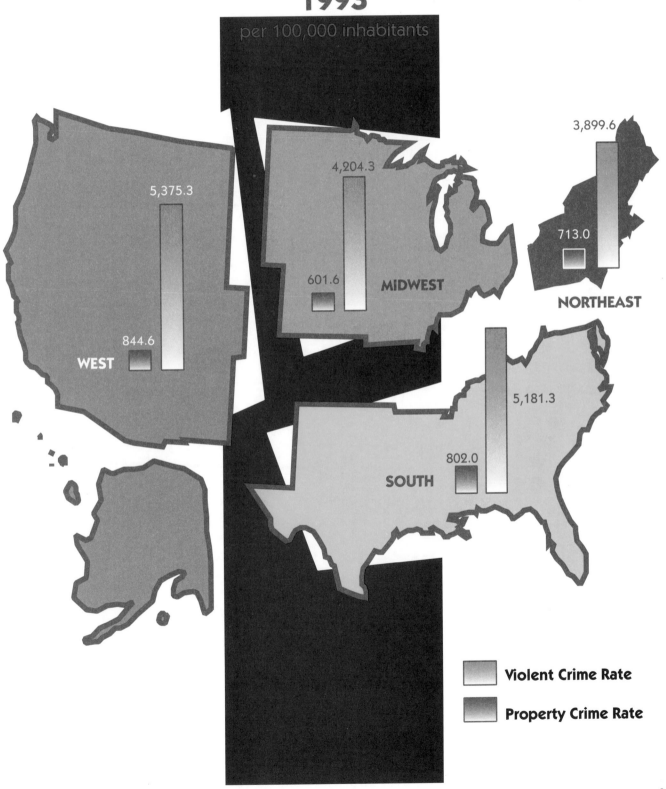

5,375.3

844.6

WEST

4,204.3

601.6

MIDWEST

3,899.6

713.0

NORTHEAST

5,181.3

802.0

SOUTH

Violent Crime Rate

Property Crime Rate

VIOLENT CRIME TOTAL

DEFINITION

Violent crime is composed of four offenses: murder and nonnegligent manslaughter, forcible rape, robbery, and aggravated assault. All violent crimes involve force or threat of force.

	Year	Number of offenses	Rate per 100,000 inhabitants
TREND			
1992	....	1,932,274	757.5
1993	....	1,924,188	746.1
	Percent change.........	−.4	−1.5

Violent crimes reported to law enforcement during 1993 exceeded 1.9 million offenses, showing a decrease of less than 1 percent from 1992. The annual estimated total was 17 percent above the 1989 level, and 51 percent above that of 1984. From 1992 to 1993, rural counties recorded an increase of 1 percent, while suburban counties experienced virtually no change. The Nation's cities collectively recorded a 1-percent decrease.

Regionally, the South, the most populous region, accounted for 37 percent of all violent crimes reported in 1993. Lesser volumes of 25 percent for the West and 19 percent for both the Midwest and Northeast were recorded. Three of the four regions registered decreases in the numbers of violent crimes reported from 1992 to 1993. The West and Northeast recorded decreases of 1 and 2 percent, respectively, and the Midwestern States experienced a decline of less than 1 percent. The Southern States registered a 1-percent increase. (See Table 4.)

Violent crimes occurred more frequently in July. The lowest total was experienced in the month of February. (See Chart 2.2.)

Table 2.2 – Violent Crime Total by Month, 1989-1993

[Percent distribution]

Months	1989	1990	1991	1992	1993
January	8.0	7.9	7.6	8.0	8.0
February	6.9	6.9	7.0	7.6	6.7
March	7.9	7.8	7.8	8.1	8.2
April.	7.9	7.8	7.8	8.3	8.0
May	8.4	8.5	8.6	8.7	8.4
June	8.4	8.8	8.7	8.5	8.7
July.	9.2	9.5	9.2	9.0	9.3
August.	9.0	9.1	9.5	8.9	9.1
September.	8.8	8.8	8.8	8.5	8.4
October	9.1	8.5	8.8	8.6	8.6
November	8.4	7.9	8.0	7.8	7.8
December	8.2	8.4	8.2	8.0	8.9

Rate

A violent crime rate of 746 per 100,000 inhabitants was registered nationally in 1993. Two-, 5-, and 10-year trends showed the 1993 rate was 2 percent lower than the 1992 rate, 13 percent above the 1989 rate, and 38 percent above the 1984 figure. The violent crime rate was highest in the Nation's cities, which collectively registered 975 offenses per 100,000 population. The suburban counties' rate was 461, and for rural counties, it was 233.

The Western States registered the highest overall violent crime rate per 100,000 inhabitants, 845, and the Midwestern States the lowest, 602. Among the geographic regions, the Northeast experienced a rate decline of 3 percent; the West, 2 percent; and the Midwest and South each 1 percent. (See Table 4.)

Nature

Aggravated assaults accounted for 59 percent of the violent crimes reported to law enforcement during 1993. Robberies comprised 34 percent; forcible rapes, 5 percent; and murders, 1 percent.

While data concerning weapons used in connection with forcible rape are not collected, firearms were the weapons used in 32 percent of all murders, robberies, and aggravated assaults, collectively, in 1993. Knives or cutting instruments were used in 15 percent; other dangerous weapons in 23 percent, and personal weapons (hands, fists, feet, etc.) in 30 percent. The proportion of violent crimes committed with firearms has increased in recent years. In 1989, firearms were employed in the commission of 27 percent of violent offenses.

Law Enforcement Response

The 1993 violent crime clearance rate was 44 percent, down from 45 percent in 1992. Among the violent offenses, the clearance rates ranged from 66 percent for murder to 24 percent for robbery.

There were an estimated 754,110 persons arrested for violent crime in 1993. Violent crime arrests accounted for 6 percent of the total arrests for all offenses and 27 percent of those for Index crimes. Males made up 87 percent of all violent crime arrestees and whites, 53 percent. (See Tables 42 and 43.)

Total arrests for violent crimes rose 1 percent from 1992 to 1993. Adult arrests showed a less than 1-percent decline, while juvenile arrests (under age 18) increased 6 percent. Overall violent crime arrests remained virtually unchanged in the Nation's cities, while increasing 1 percent in suburban counties and 7 percent in rural counties from 1992 to 1993. (See Section IV, Persons Arrested.)

VIOLENT CRIME

CHART 2.6

VARIATION FROM MONTHLY AVERAGE
1993

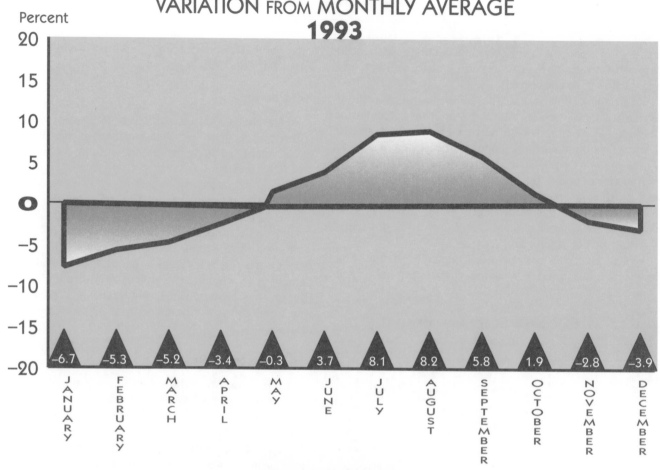

Percent

JANUARY −6.7
FEBRUARY −5.3
MARCH −5.2
APRIL −3.4
MAY −0.3
JUNE 3.7
JULY 8.1
AUGUST 8.2
SEPTEMBER 5.8
OCTOBER 1.9
NOVEMBER −2.8
DECEMBER −3.9

CHART 2.7

PERCENT CHANGE FROM 1989

Percent

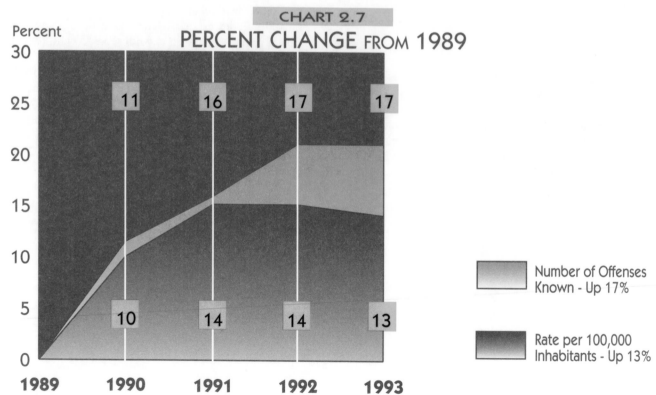

Number of Offenses
Known - Up 17%

Rate per 100,000
Inhabitants - Up 13%

1989   1990   1991   1992   1993

MURDER AND NONNEGLIGENT MANSLAUGHTER

DEFINITION

Murder and nonnegligent manslaughter, as defined in the Uniform Crime Reporting Program, is the willful (nonnegligent) killing of one human being by another.

The classification of this offense, as for all other Crime Index offenses, is based solely on police investigation as opposed to the determination of a court, medical examiner, coroner, jury, or other judicial body. Not included in the count for this offense classification are deaths caused by negligence, suicide, or accident; justifiable homicides; and attempts to murder or assaults to murder, which are scored as aggravated assaults.

─── TREND ───		
Year	Number of offenses	Rate per 100,000 inhabitants
1992	23,760	9.3
1993	24,526	9.5
Percent change	+3.2	+2.2

The total number of murders in the United States during 1993 was estimated at 24,526. Monthly figures show that more persons were murdered in the month of December in 1993, while the fewest were killed in February. (See Table 2.3.)

Table 2.3 – Murder by Month, 1989-1993
[Percent distribution]

Months	1989	1990	1991	1992	1993
January	8.1	7.9	8.0	8.1	8.1
February	7.1	7.0	7.0	7.5	6.7
March	7.8	8.0	7.7	8.2	7.9
April.....................	7.9	7.4	7.8	8.0	7.6
May	7.8	8.1	8.1	8.5	7.8
June	8.2	8.4	8.6	7.9	8.6
July......................	9.1	9.6	9.1	9.1	9.3
August...................	9.0	9.3	9.4	9.1	9.2
September................	8.8	9.2	8.8	8.7	8.3
October	8.9	8.8	8.6	8.0	8.4
November	8.5	7.6	7.8	8.1	8.2
December	8.7	8.8	9.0	8.8	9.8

When viewing the regions of the Nation, the Southern States, the most populous region, accounted for 41 percent of the murders. The Western States reported 23 percent; the Midwestern States, 19 percent; and the Northeastern States, 17 percent. Among the regions, the Northeast experienced a 5-percent increase; the South and West each recorded 4-percent increases; and the Midwest registered a less than 1-percent increase. (See Table 4.)

The murder volume was up 3 percent nationwide in 1993 over 1992. In the Nation's cities overall, murder increased 4 percent, with the greatest increase – 10 percent – registered in cities with populations of 100,000 to 249,999. The greatest decrease – 6 percent – was recorded in cities with populations of 10,000 to 24,999. The suburban counties recorded a 2-percent rise in the murder volume and the rural counties, a 3-percent increase for the 2-year period. (See Table 12.)

The accompanying chart reveals a 14-percent rise nationally in the murder counts from 1989 to 1993. The 10-year trend showed the 1993 total 31 percent above the 1984 level.

Rate

Up 2 percent over the 1992 rate, the national murder rate in 1993 was 10 per 100,000 inhabitants. Five- and 10-year trends showed the 1993 rate was 9 percent higher than in 1989 and 20 percent above the 1984 rate.

On a regional basis, the South averaged 11 murders per 100,000 people; the West, 10 per 100,000; and the Midwest and Northeast, 8 per 100,000. Compared to 1992, murder rates in 1993 increased in three of the four geographic regions. The Midwest experienced no change. (See Table 4.)

The Nation's metropolitan areas reported a 1993 murder rate of 11 victims per 100,000 inhabitants. In the rural counties and in cities outside metropolitan areas, the rate was 5 per 100,000.

Nature

Supplemental data provided by contributing agencies recorded information for 23,271 of the estimated 24,526 murders in 1993. Submitted monthly, the data consist of the age, sex, and race of both victims and offenders; the types of weapons used; the relationships of victims to the offenders; and the circumstances surrounding the murders.

Based on this information, 77 percent of the murder victims in 1993 were males; and 87 percent were persons 18 years of age or older. Forty-eight percent were aged 20 through 34 years. Considering victims for whom race was known, an average of 51 of every 100 were black, 46 were white, and the remainder were persons of other races.

Table 2.4 – Murder Victims by Race and Sex, 1993

Race of Victims	Sex of Victims			
	Total	Male	Female	Unknown
Total White Victims	10,709	7,764	2,945	....
Total Black Victims	11,795	9,642	2,151	2
Total Other Race Victims ...	563	417	146	....
Total Unknown Race	204	126	36	42
Total Victims[1]	23,271	17,949	5,278	44

[1]Total murder victims for whom supplemental data were received.

MURDER

CHART 2.8

VARIATION FROM MONTHLY AVERAGE
1993

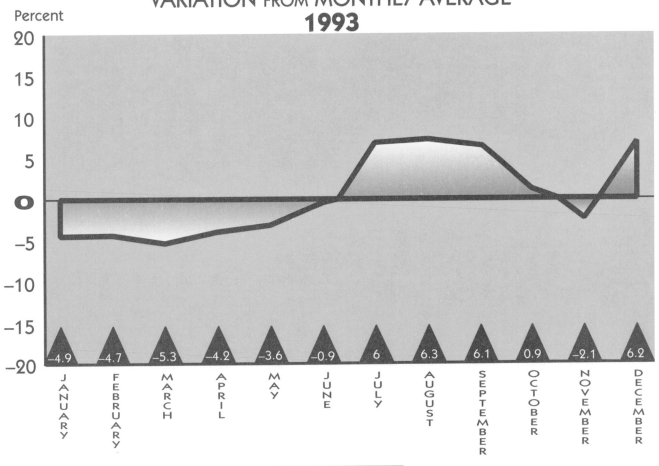

Percent

JANUARY	−4.9
FEBRUARY	−4.7
MARCH	−5.3
APRIL	−4.2
MAY	−3.6
JUNE	−0.9
JULY	6
AUGUST	6.3
SEPTEMBER	6.1
OCTOBER	0.9
NOVEMBER	−2.1
DECEMBER	6.2

CHART 2.9

PERCENT CHANGE FROM 1989

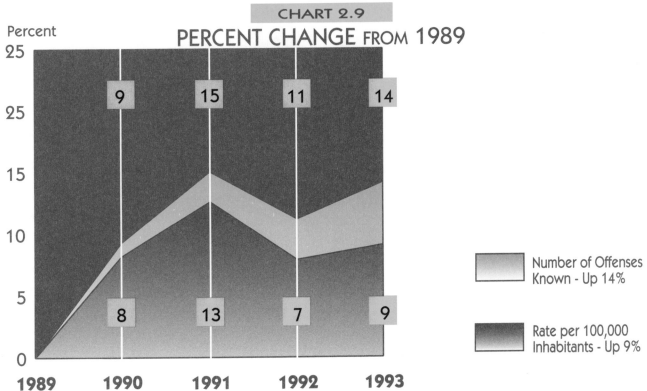

Percent

9   15   11   14

8   13   7   9

1989   1990   1991   1992   1993

Number of Offenses
Known - Up 14%

Rate per 100,000
Inhabitants - Up 9%

Table 2.5 — Age, Sex, and Race of Murder Victims, 1993

Age	Total	Sex			Race			
		Male	Female	Unknown	White	Black	Other	Unknown
Total............................	23,271	17,949	5,278	44	10,709	11,795	563	204
Percent distribution	100.0	77.1	22.7	.2	46.0	50.7	2.4	.9
Under 18[1].........................	2,697	1,933	761	3	1,187	1,411	81	18
18 and over[1]......................	20,250	15,800	4,441	9	9,387	10,266	473	124
Infant (under 1)	272	150	120	2	135	118	10	9
1 to 4	459	258	200	1	217	225	16	1
5 to 9	173	84	89	....	101	61	10	1
10 to 14	387	258	129	....	185	194	8	....
15 to 19	3,084	2,652	432	....	1,125	1,857	81	21
20 to 24	4,355	3,667	684	4	1,597	2,656	78	24
25 to 29	3,466	2,729	736	1	1,451	1,921	74	20
30 to 34	3,083	2,338	745	....	1,444	1,541	86	12
35 to 39	2,318	1,767	550	1	1,143	1,108	56	11
40 to 44	1,620	1,226	394	....	800	753	52	15
45 to 49	1,077	825	252	....	649	389	28	11
50 to 54	717	549	166	2	443	244	21	9
55 to 59	465	352	112	1	299	149	13	4
60 to 64	393	285	108	....	253	130	9	1
65 to 69	319	210	109	....	209	102	7	1
70 to 74	292	171	121	....	194	93	4	1
75 and over........................	467	212	255	....	329	136	1	1
Unknown............................	324	216	76	32	135	118	9	62

[1]Does not include unknown ages.

Table 2.6 — Age, Sex, and Race of Murder Offenders, 1993

Age	Total	Sex			Race			
		Male	Female	Unknown	White	Black	Other	Unknown
Total	26,239	16,859	1,742	7,638	7,669	10,357	392	7,821
Percent distribution	100.0	64.3	6.6	29.1	29.2	39.5	1.5	29.8
Under 18[1]	2,631	2,490	138	3	863	1,688	62	18
18 and over[1]	14,404	12,843	1,547	14	6,347	7,672	314	71
Infant (under 1)	....	....	....	....	....	....	....	....
1 to 4	....	....	....	....	....	....	....	....
5 to 9	2	1	1	....	1	1	....	....
10 to 14	319	284	34	1	127	180	10	2
15 to 19	4,650	4,428	219	3	1,490	3,014	117	29
20 to 24	4,233	3,913	316	4	1,546	2,580	88	19
25 to 29	2,459	2,160	297	2	1,052	1,336	60	11
30 to 34	1,763	1,494	268	1	915	800	40	8
35 to 39	1,246	1,029	216	1	650	570	19	7
40 to 44	832	711	120	1	473	340	14	5
45 to 49	541	456	85	....	319	209	11	2
50 to 54	349	292	57	....	230	114	5	....
55 to 59	218	192	26	....	132	83	2	1
60 to 64	162	142	20	....	100	55	6	1
65 to 69	100	91	9	....	58	38	4	....
70 to 74	67	59	8	....	50	17	....	....
75 and over	94	81	9	4	67	23	....	4
Unknown	9,204	1,526	57	7,621	459	997	16	7,732

[1]Does not include unknown ages.

16

Table 2.7 – Victim/Offender Relationship by Age, 1993
[Single Victim/Single Offender]

Age of Victim	Age of Offender			
	Total	Under 18	18 and over	Unknown
Total.....................	11,721	1,200	9,768	753
Under 18..................	1,426	399	958	69
18 and over..............	10,191	791	8,731	669
Unknown.................	104	10	79	15

Supplemental data were also reported for 26,239 murder offenders in 1993. Of those for whom sex and age were reported, 91 percent were males, and 85 percent were persons 18 years of age or older. Seventy-seven percent were aged 15 through 34 years. Of offenders for whom race was known, 56 percent were black, 42 percent were white, and the remainder were persons of other races.

Data based on incidents involving one victim and one offender showed that in 1993, 94 percent of the black murder victims were slain by black offenders, and 84 per-

cent of the white murder victims were killed by white offenders. Likewise, males were most often slain by males (88 percent in single victim/single offender situations). These same data showed, however, that 9 of every 10 female victims were murdered by males.

As in previous years, firearms were the weapons used in approximately 7 of every 10 murders committed in the United States. Of those murders for which weapons were reported, 57 percent were by handguns, 5 percent by shotguns, and 3 percent by rifles. Other or unknown types of firearms accounted for another 5 percent of the total murders. Among the remaining weapons, cutting or stabbing instruments were employed in 13 percent of the murders; blunt objects (clubs, hammers, etc.) in 4 percent; personal weapons (hands, fists, feet, etc.) in 5 percent; and other dangerous weapons, such as poison, explosives, etc., in the remainder. A state-by-state breakdown of weapons used in connection with murder is shown in Table 20.

Table 2.8 – Victim/Offender Relationship by Race and Sex[1], 1993
[Single Victim/Single Offender]

Race of Victim	Race of Offender				Sex of Offender		
	White	Black	Other	Unknown	Male	Female	Unknown
Total White Victims	4,686	849	58	55	5,057	536	55
Total Black Victims	304	5,393	18	67	4,985	730	67
Total Other Race Victims	61	40	137	2	210	28	2
Total Unknown Race	11	17	1	22	27	2	22

Sex of Victim	Race of Offender				Sex of Offender		
	White	Black	Other	Unknown	Male	Female	Unknown
Total Male Victims	3,469	4,869	153	93	7,487	1,004	93
Total Female Victims	1,582	1,413	60	31	2,765	290	31
Total Unknown Sex	11	17	1	22	27	2	22

[1]Data based on 11,721 victims.

Past years' statistics on relationships of victims to offenders showed that over half of murder victims knew their killers. However, in the last few years (1990 through 1993) the relationship percentages have shifted. (Refer to Section V, Homicide Patterns: Past and Present.) In 1993, 47 percent of murder victims were either related to (12 percent) or acquainted with (35 percent) their assailants. Fourteen percent of the victims were murdered by strangers, while the relationships among victims and offenders were unknown for 39 percent of the murders. Among all female murder victims in 1993, 29 percent were

slain by husbands or boyfriends. Three percent of the male victims were killed by wives or girlfriends.

Arguments resulted in 29 percent of the murders during the year. Nineteen percent occurred as a result of felonious activities such as robbery, arson, etc., while another 1 percent were suspected to have been the result of some type of felonious activity. Three percent of the murders were committed during brawls while offenders were under the influence of alcohol or narcotics. Table 2.14 shows murder circumstances for the past 5 years.

Table 2.9 – Murder, Type of Weapons Used, 1993

[Percent distribution by region]

Region	Total all weapons[1]	Firearms	Knives or cutting instruments	Unknown or other dangerous weapons	Personal weapons (hands, fists, feet, etc.)
Total	100.0	69.6	12.7	12.7	5.0
Northeastern States	100.0	68.2	14.4	11.9	5.5
Midwestern States	100.0	69.7	11.3	12.9	6.0
Southern States	100.0	69.8	12.4	13.3	4.5
Western States	100.0	70.0	13.1	12.1	4.8

[1]Because of rounding, percentages may not add to totals.

Table 2.10 – Murder Victims, Type of Weapons Used, 1989-1993

Weapons	1989	1990	1991	1992	1993
Total	18,954	20,273	21,676	22,716	23,271
Total Firearms	11,832	13,035	14,373	15,489	16,189
Handguns	9,013	10,099	11,497	12,580	13,252
Rifles	865	746	745	706	754
Shotguns	1,173	1,245	1,124	1,111	1,059
Other guns	34	25	30	42	38
Firearms-not stated	747	920	977	1,050	1,086
Knives or cutting instruments	3,458	3,526	3,430	3,296	2,957
Blunt objects (clubs, hammers, etc.)	1,128	1,085	1,099	1,040	1,024
Personal weapons (hands, fists, feet, etc.)[1]	1,050	1,119	1,202	1,131	1,164
Poison	11	11	12	13	9
Explosives	16	13	16	19	26
Fire	234	288	195	203	217
Narcotics	17	29	22	24	22
Drowning	60	36	40	29	23
Strangulation	366	312	327	314	329
Asphyxiation	101	96	113	115	113
Other weapons or weapons not stated	681	723	847	1,043	1,198

[1]Pushed is included in personal weapons.

Table 2.11 – Murder Victims – Weapons Used, 1993

Age	Total	Firearms	Knives or cutting instruments	Blunt objects (clubs, hammers, etc.)	Personal[1] weapons (hands, fists, feet, etc.)	Poison	Explosives	Fire	Narcotics	Strangulation	Asphyxiation	Other[2] weapon or weapon not stated
Total	23,271	16,189	2,957	1,024	1,164	9	26	217	22	329	113	1,221
Percent distribution[3]	100.0	69.6	12.7	4.4	5.0	....	.1	.9	.1	1.4	.5	5.2
Under 18[4]	2,697	1,637	180	107	417	1	5	53	7	38	50	202
18 and over[4]	20,250	14,373	2,742	895	728	8	21	156	15	287	62	963
Infant (under 1)	272	15	5	17	147	....	....	5	4	3	19	57
1 to 4	459	57	13	38	223	1	....	28	1	7	19	72
5 to 9	173	74	27	6	20	....	2	12	....	6	6	20
10 to 14	387	278	38	17	13	....	1	7	1	7	4	21
15 to 19	3,084	2,650	227	53	28	....	3	4	1	24	5	89
20 to 24	4,355	3,594	388	79	70	1	4	12	2	40	5	160
25 to 29	3,466	2,609	476	96	67	....	1	14	2	52	7	142
30 to 34	3,083	2,136	472	113	118	1	3	29	3	50	8	150
35 to 39	2,318	1,549	370	121	93	....	2	13	2	49	6	113
40 to 44	1,620	1,060	271	95	94	....	3	10	3	18	3	63
45 to 49	1,077	704	154	81	45	....	1	20	....	12	3	57
50 to 54	717	423	107	67	41	2	3	9	....	12	3	50
55 to 59	465	263	73	44	30	....	....	4	1	7	4	39
60 to 64	393	203	83	38	24	2	....	11	....	5	3	24
65 to 69	319	152	59	37	24	2	....	10	....	6	3	26
70 to 74	292	114	64	35	31	....	1	4	....	13	1	29
75 and over	467	129	95	65	77	....	2	17	2	14	13	53
Unknown	324	179	35	22	19	....	....	8	....	4	1	56

[1]Pushed is included in personal weapons.
[2]Includes drownings.
[3]Because of rounding, percentages may not add to totals.
[4]Does not include unknown ages.

Table 2.13 – Murder Circumstances by Weapon, United States, 1993

Circumstances	Total murder victims	Total firearms	Handguns	Rifles	Shotguns	Other guns or type not stated	Knives or cutting instruments	Blunt objects (clubs, hammers, etc.)	Personal weapons (hands, fists, feet, etc.)	Poison	Pushed or thrown out window	Explosives	Fire	Narcotics	Drowning	Strangulation	Asphyxiation	Other
Total[1]	23,271	16,189	13,252	754	1,059	1,124	2,957	1,024	1,161	9	3	26	217	22	23	329	113	1,198
Felony type total	4,451	3,222	2,833	102	161	126	416	231	175	1		1	141	8	4	79	25	148
Rape	116	15	14		1		29	20	24							13	5	10
Robbery	2,301	1,748	1,552	34	96	66	243	137	75	1			1	1		40	5	50
Burglary	179	88	62	9	12	5	28	31	11				1		2	3	1	14
Larceny-theft	32	20	17		2	1	3	1	2									6
Motor vehicle theft	61	42	34	1	2	5	9	4	1									5
Arson	151	9	6			3	2	2					131			2	2	3
Prostitution and commercialized vice	17	3	3				7	2								2		3
Other sex offenses	25	5	4			1	3	6	4							5	1	1
Narcotic drug laws	1,287	1,153	1,025	50	34	44	68	16	15				3	6	1	7	2	16
Gambling	10	10	9			1												
Other - not specified	272	129	107	8	13	1	24	12	43			1	5	1	1	7	9	40
Suspected felony type	144	85	68	6	2	9	16	5	9	1		1	4			8	2	13
Other than felony type total	12,235	8,424	6,689	558	706	471	1,871	496	765	5	3	20	40	12	13	119	58	409
Romantic triangle	439	320	263	16	25	16	79	9	14							4		13
Child killed by babysitter	33						1	1	28							1		2
Brawl due to influence of alcohol	381	211	153	29	19	10	104	23	35				1			1	1	5
Brawl due to influence of narcotics	262	214	168	8	13	25	24	8	7							3		6
Argument over money or property	445	318	256	20	32	10	68	25	21							4	2	7
Other arguments	6,292	4,284	3,525	254	390	115	1,242	271	251		2	8	23		3	76	10	122
Gangland killings	147	131	96	13	8	14	2	6	1			1	1					5
Juvenile gang killings	1,147	1,093	937	72	39	45	37	9	5								1	2
Institutional killings	15	2	1			1	6	1	3							2		1
Sniper attack	7	7	5	2														
Other - not specified	3,067	1,844	1,285	144	180	235	308	143	400	5	1	11	15	12	10	28	44	246
Unknown	6,441	4,458	3,662	88	190	518	654	292	212	2		4	32	2	6	123	28	628

[1]Total murder victims for whom supplemental homicide data were received.

19

Table 2.12 — Murder Circumstances by Relationship,[1] 1993

Circumstances	Total	Husband	Wife	Mother	Father	Son	Daughter	Brother	Sister	Other Family	Acquaintance	Friend	Boyfriend	Girlfriend	Neighbor	Stranger	Unknown Relationship
Total[2]	23,271	335	928	133	173	334	248	175	38	361	6,217	859	256	603	207	3,259	9,145
Felony type total	4,451	9	21	9	12	23	21	1	4	40	1,097	90	4	19	52	1,333	1,716
Rape	116		2				2			2	34	6			7	32	30
Robbery	2,301	1	2		6					20	412	39	1	4	27	959	830
Burglary	179	1	1		1				3	3	42	3			5	54	66
Larceny-theft	32									1	6	1				15	8
Motor vehicle theft	61										8		1	2		32	18
Arson	151	1	3	4		1	4				28	2		2	3	29	74
Prostitution and commercialized vice	17										3					5	9
Other sex offenses	25	1		1			1	1		2	5	1		1	3	3	9
Narcotic drug laws	1,287		2		3		1			5	479	32	1		1	151	610
Gambling	10										8					1	1
Other - not specified	272	5	11	4	2	22	13			7	72	6		10	6	52	61
Suspected felony type	144		2				1			3	22			1	2	19	94
Other than felony type total	12,235	301	826	97	147	283	205	158	30	284	4,542	698	239	529	136	1,558	2,202
Romantic triangle	439	22	65			2		1	1	5	178	27	16	64	2	33	24
Child killed by babysitter	33					2				1	30						
Brawl due to influence of alcohol	381	10	16		1	7		9		11	154	53	9	8	10	62	31
Brawl due to influence of narcotics	262	3		2	2			1		2	114	11	2	2	2	34	88
Argument over money or property	445	4	8	4	6	1	1	7	3	13	265	40	5	7	15	35	31
Other arguments	6,292	218	536	50	98	75	41	114	13	192	2,308	447	183	365	78	759	815
Gangland killings	147		1								61	5				29	51
Juvenile gang killings	1,147										627	9				205	306
Institutional killings	15										10					2	3
Sniper attack	7															3	4
Other - not specified	3,067	44	200	41	40	196	163	26	13	60	795	106	26	83	29	396	849
Unknown	6,441	25	79	27	14	28	21	16	4	34	556	71	13	54	17	349	5,133

[1] Relationship is that of victim to offender.

[2] Total murder victims for whom supplemental homicide data were received.

20

Table 2.14 — Murder Circumstances, 1989-1993

	1989	1990	1991	1992	1993
Total[1].....................	18,954	20,273	21,676	22,716	23,271
Felony type total:.........	4,049	4,209	4,636	4,917	4,451
Rape.................	131	152	132	138	116
Robbery.............	1,728	1,871	2,226	2,266	2,301
Burglary..............	212	202	197	212	179
Larceny-theft..........	18	28	32	41	32
Motor vehicle theft......	37	55	53	66	61
Arson	165	152	138	148	151
Prostitution and commercialized vice...	12	27	20	32	17
Other sex offenses	58	50	47	34	25
Narcotic drug laws	1,402	1,367	1,353	1,302	1,287
Gambling.............	23	11	33	20	10
Other - not specified	263	294	405	658	272
Suspected felony type	150	148	210	280	144
Other than felony type total.................	10,270	10,889	11,220	11,244	12,235
Romantic triangle.......	385	407	314	334	439
Child killed by babysitter	24	34	32	36	33
Brawl due to influence of alcohol	432	533	500	429	381
Brawl due to influence of narcotics	306	242	254	253	262
Argument over money or property	551	514	520	483	445
Other arguments.......	5,736	6,044	6,108	6,066	6,292
Gangland killings.......	56	104	206	137	147
Juvenile gang killings....	542	679	840	813	1,147
Institutional killings......	22	16	19	18	15
Sniper attack..........	49	41	12	33	7
Other - not specified	2,167	2,275	2,415	2,642	3,067
Unknown	4,485	5,027	5,610	6,275	6,441

[1]Total number of murder victims for whom supplemental homicide information was received.

Table 2.15 — Murder Circumstances by Victim Sex, 1993

	Total Murder Victims[1]	Male	Female	Unknown
Total[1]	23,271	17,949	5,278	44
Felony type total:..............	4,451	3,610	839	2
Rape......................	116	10	106	....
Robbery...................	2,301	1,950	351	....
Burglary...................	179	119	60	....
Larceny-theft	32	23	9	....
Motor vehicle theft	61	50	11	....
Arson	151	83	68	....
Prostitution and commercialized vice	17	2	15	....
Other sex offenses...........	25	13	12	....
Narcotic drug laws...........	1,287	1,180	105	2
Gambling..................	10	10	....	....
Other - not specified........	272	170	102	....
Suspected felony type	144	89	55	....
Other than felony type total	12,235	9,191	3,032	12
Romantic triangle	439	257	182	....
Child killed by babysitter	33	17	16	....
Brawl due to influence of alcohol	381	339	42	....
Brawl due to influence of narcotics	262	221	40	1
Argument over money or property..................	445	378	67	....
Other arguments	6,292	4,698	1,590	4
Gangland killings...........	147	136	11	....
Juvenile gang killings	1,147	1,055	92	....
Institutional killings	15	14	1	....
Sniper attack...............	7	5	2	....
Other - not specified........	3,067	2,071	989	7
Unknown....................	6,441	5,059	1,352	30

[1]Total number of murder victims for whom supplemental homicide information was received.

Law Enforcement Response

The clearance rate for murder continued to be higher than for any other Crime Index offense. Law enforcement agencies nationwide recorded a 66-percent clearance rate for 1993. Eighty percent of murders in rural counties and 65 percent of those in suburban counties and in the Nation's cities were cleared. Of the city population groups, those with populations under 10,000 reported the most successful clearance rate, 76 percent. (See Table 25.)

Geographically, the South, the most populous region, registered the highest murder clearance rate, 71 percent. Following were the Northeastern States with 66 percent, the Midwestern States with 61 percent, and the Western States with 59 percent.

Persons under 18 years of age accounted for 9 percent of the willful killings cleared by law enforcement nationally. Only persons in this young age group accounted for 10 percent of clearances in the Nation's cities, 8 percent of those in the suburban counties, and 7 percent of the rural county clearances. This proportion of juvenile involvement was lower than for any other Index offense.

An estimated 23,400 arrests for murder were made in 1993. Fifty-seven percent of the arrestees in 1993 were under 25 years of age. The 18- to 24-year age group accounted for 41 percent of the total. (See Table 38.)

Ninety-one percent of those arrested were males and 9 percent, females. Blacks comprised 58 percent of the total arrestees for murder in 1993. Whites made up 41 percent, and the remainder were of other races.

Compared to the 1992 level, the 1993 murder arrest total increased 4 percent. Arrests of persons aged 18 and over increased 2 percent, and those of younger persons were up 14 percent. During the same 2-year period, female arrests increased 1 percent and male arrests rose by 4 percent.

Long-term trends indicate the 1993 murder arrest total was 11 percent above the 1989 level and 25 percent higher than the 1984 figure.

Justifiable Homicide

Certain willful killings are classified as justifiable or excusable, based on law enforcement investigation. In Uniform Crime Reporting, justifiable homicide is defined as and limited to the killing of a felon by a law enforcement officer in the line of duty, or the killing of a felon, during the commission of a felony, by a private citizen. These offenses are tabulated independently and are not included in the murder counts.

In 1993, the justifiable homicide total was 811, up 5 percent from the 1992 total of 769 and 28 percent higher than the 1989 total of 636. Of the justifiable homicides in 1993, 455 involved law enforcement officers and 356 were by private citizens. Data on weapons used in connection with justifiable homicide showed that handguns were the weapons used most often. (See Tables 2.16 and 2.17.)

Table 2.16 — Justifiable Homicide by Weapon, Law Enforcement,[1] 1989-1993

Year	Total	Total fire-arms	Hand-guns	Rifles	Shot-guns	Fire-arms type not specified	Knives or other cutting instru-ments	Other danger-ous weapons	Personal weapons
1989	363	360	299	15	42	4	....	2	1
1990	385	382	345	8	19	10	....	2	1
1991	367	361	319	10	25	7	1	3	2
1992	418	411	357	22	21	11	4	1	2
1993	455	451	391	22	26	12	....	2	2

[1]The killing of a felon by a law enforcement officer in the line of duty.

Table 2.17 — Justifiable Homicide by Weapon, Private Citizen,[1] 1989-1993

Year	Total	Total fire-arms	Hand-guns	Rifles	Shot-guns	Fire-arms type not specified	Knives or other cutting instru-ments	Other danger-ous weapons	Personal weapons
1989	273	236	178	22	34	2	23	9	5
1990	328	276	210	20	39	7	39	9	4
1991	331	296	243	15	25	13	29	4	2
1992	351	311	264	20	24	3	31	5	4
1993	356	311	251	16	33	11	28	10	7

[1]The killing of a felon, during the commission of a felony, by a private citizen.

FORCIBLE RAPE

DEFINITION

Forcible rape, as defined in the Program, is the carnal knowledge of a female forcibly and against her will. Assaults or attempts to commit rape by force or threat of force are also included; however, statutory rape (without force) and other sex offenses are excluded.

	TREND	
Year	Number of offenses	Rate per 100,000 inhabitants
1992	109,062	42.8
1993	104,806	40.6
Percent change	−3.9	−5.1

The estimated 104,806 forcible rapes reported to law enforcement agencies across the Nation during 1993 was down 4 percent from the 1992 volume. The 1993 total showed the first decline in forcible rape since 1987 and was the lowest since 1990.

Geographically, 39 percent of the forcible rape total in 1993 was accounted for by the most populous Southern States, 25 percent by the Midwestern States, 23 percent by the Western States, and 14 percent by the Northeastern States. Two-year trends showed that all regions experienced declines ranging from 1 percent in the South to 7 percent in the Midwest and West. (See Table 4.)

Monthly totals show the greatest numbers of forcible rapes were reported during the summer months. (See Table 2.18.)

Table 2.18 – Forcible Rape by Month, 1989-1993
[Percent distribution]

Months	1989	1990	1991	1992	1993
January	7.4	7.6	7.1	7.0	7.7
February	6.3	6.7	7.0	7.6	6.9
March	7.7	7.9	7.9	8.6	8.5
April	8.3	8.1	8.3	8.5	8.2
May	8.6	9.1	9.2	8.9	8.9
June	8.9	9.0	9.2	8.7	9.2
July	10.0	9.6	9.5	9.4	9.7
August	9.5	9.4	9.7	9.6	9.3
September	8.8	9.1	8.8	8.7	8.3
October	8.9	8.4	8.6	8.4	8.1
November	8.3	7.7	7.8	7.6	7.5
December	7.3	7.4	6.8	7.0	7.7

Rate

By Uniform Crime Reporting definition, the victims of forcible rape are always female. In 1993, an estimated 79 of every 100,000 females in the country were reported rape victims, a rate decrease of 6 percent from 1992. The 1993 female forcible rape rate was, however, 5 percent higher than the 1989 rate.

In 1993, there were 84 victims per 100,000 females in MSAs, 76 per 100,000 females in cities outside metropolitan areas, and 49 per 100,000 females in rural counties. Although MSAs record the highest rape rates, they have shown the smallest change over the past 10 years. During this time, the greatest rate increase was shown in cities outside metropolitan areas, 90 percent. Rural counties recorded a 44-percent rate rise, while MSAs showed a lesser increase, 6 percent.

Regionally, in 1993, the highest female rape rate was in the Southern States, which recorded 88 victims per 100,000 females. Following were the Western States with a rate of 84, the Midwestern States with 83, and the Northeastern States with 55. Over the last 10 years, regional increases in

the female forcible rape rate were 30 percent in the Midwest, 21 percent in the South, and 4 percent in the Northeast. A 3-percent decrease was reported in the West. All regions showed declines, 1992 versus 1993.

Nature

Rapes by force constitute the greatest percentage of total forcible rapes, 87 percent of the 1993 experience. The remainder were attempts or assaults to commit forcible rape. The number of rapes by force decreased 3 percent in 1993 from the 1992 volume, while attempts to rape decreased 12 percent.

As for all other Crime Index offenses, complaints of forcible rape made to law enforcement agencies are sometimes found to be false or baseless. In such cases, law enforcement agencies "unfound" the offenses and exclude them from crime counts. The "unfounded" rate, or percentage of complaints determined through investigation to be false, is higher for forcible rape than for any other Index crime. In 1993, 8 percent of forcible rape complaints were "unfounded," while the average for all Index crimes was 2 percent.

Law Enforcement Response

Nationwide, as well as in the cities, over half of the forcible rapes reported to law enforcement were cleared by arrest or exceptional means in 1993. Rural and suburban county law enforcement agencies cleared a slightly higher percentage of the offenses brought to their attention than did city law enforcement agencies. (See Table 25.)

Geographically, clearance rates for the regions were lowest in the Western States and highest in the Southern States. (See Table 26.)

Of the total clearances for forcible rape in the country as a whole, 14 percent involved only persons under 18 years of age. The percentage of juvenile involvement varied by community type, ranging from 13 percent in the Nation's cities to 20 percent in suburban counties. (See Table 28.)

Law enforcement agencies made an estimated 38,420 arrests for forcible rape in 1993. Of the forcible rape arrestees, about 3 of every 10 were in the 18- to 24-year age group. Over half of those arrested were white. (See Tables 38 and 43.)

The number of arrests for forcible rape fell 2 percent nationwide from 1992 to 1993. A decrease of 4 percent was experienced in the Nation's cities, and a 1-percent decline was recorded in the suburban counties. Forcible rape arrests were up 10 percent in the rural counties for the 2-year period. (See Tables 44, 50, and 56.)

FORCIBLE RAPE

CHART 2.10

VARIATION FROM MONTHLY AVERAGE
1993

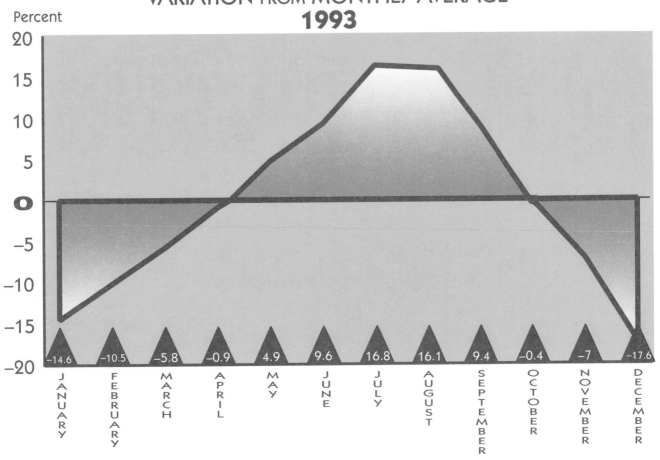

Percent

JANUARY	-14.6
FEBRUARY	-10.5
MARCH	-5.8
APRIL	-0.9
MAY	4.9
JUNE	9.6
JULY	16.8
AUGUST	16.1
SEPTEMBER	9.4
OCTOBER	-0.4
NOVEMBER	-7
DECEMBER	-17.6

CHART 2.11

PERCENT CHANGE FROM 1989

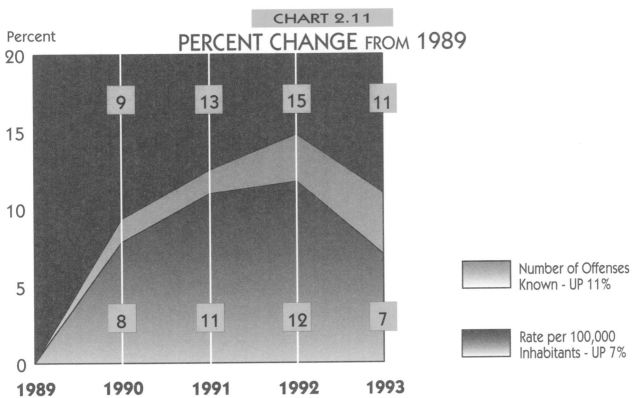

Percent

Number of Offenses
Known - UP 11%

Rate per 100,000
Inhabitants - UP 7%

1989   1990   1991   1992   1993

ROBBERY

DEFINITION

Robbery is the taking or attempting to take anything of value from the care, custody, or control of a person or persons by force or threat of force or violence and/or by putting the victim in fear.

		TREND	
Year	Number of offenses	Rate per 100,000 inhabitants
1992	672,478	263.6
1993	659,757	255.8
Percent change	−1.9	−3.0

Reported robberies in 1993 were estimated at 659,757 offenses, accounting for 5 percent of all Index crimes and 34 percent of the violent crimes. During the year, robberies occurred most frequently in December and least often in February.

Table 2.19 – Robbery by Month, 1989-1993
[Percent distribution]

Months	1989	1990	1991	1992	1993
January	8.8	8.7	8.7	9.0	8.8
February	7.4	7.3	7.5	8.0	7.1
March	8.0	8.1	8.0	8.1	8.3
April	7.3	7.2	7.4	7.8	7.4
May	7.6	7.7	7.8	7.9	7.5
June	7.6	7.8	7.8	7.9	8.1
July	8.4	8.5	8.4	8.4	8.7
August	8.6	8.8	8.8	8.6	8.8
September	8.6	8.6	8.5	8.3	8.4
October	9.2	8.9	9.2	8.7	9.0
November	9,0	8.7	8.7	8.3	8.5
December	9.3	9.6	9.2	9.0	9.4

Compared to 1992 levels, the 1993 robbery volume decreased 2 percent nationally, in the Nation's cities, and in the suburban counties. It declined 1 percent in the rural counties. This downward trend was also evident in most city population groups. The largest decline—4 percent—was experienced in cities with a million or more inhabitants. (See Table 12.)

Distribution figures for the regions showed that the most populous region, the Southern States, accounted for 32 percent of all reported robberies. (See Table 3.) Two-year trends show the number of robberies in 1993 was down in all regions as compared to 1992. The declines were 4 percent in the Northeast, 2 percent in the West, and 1 percent in the Midwest and South.

Chart 2.13 depicts the national trend in the robbery volume, as well as the robbery rate, for the years 1989-1993. In 1993, the number of robbery offenses was 14 percent higher than in 1989 and 36 percent above the 1984 total.

Rate

The national robbery rate in 1993 was 256 per 100,000 people, 3 percent lower than in 1992. In metropolitan areas, the 1993 rate was 312; in cities outside metropolitan areas, it was 71; and in the rural areas, it was 16. With 955 robberies per 100,000 inhabitants, the highest rate was recorded in cities with a million or more inhabitants. (See Table 16.) A comparison of 1992 and 1993 regional robbery rates per 100,000 inhabitants showed the Northeastern and Western States' rates of 323 and 283, respectively, down 4 percent; and the rates of 204 in the Midwest and 236 in the South each down 2 percent.

Nature

In 1993, a total estimated national loss of $538 million was attributed to robberies. The value of property stolen during robberies averaged $815 per incident, down from $840 in 1992. Average dollar losses in 1993 ranged from $449 taken during robberies of convenience stores to $3,308 per bank robbery. (See Table 23.) The impact of this violent crime on its victims cannot be measured in terms of monetary loss alone. While the object of a robbery is to obtain money or property, the crime always involves force or threat of force, and many victims suffer serious personal injury.

As in previous years, robberies on streets or highways accounted for more than half (55 percent) of the offenses in this category. Robberies of commercial and financial establishments accounted for an additional 22 percent, and those occurring at residences, 10 percent. The remainder were miscellaneous types. A comparison of 1992 and 1993 robbery totals by type showed robberies of convenience stores were down 8 percent; gas or service station robberies dropped 6 percent; and street/highway robberies declined 2 percent. Increases of 2 percent or less were recorded for the other categories. (See Table 23.)

Table 2.20 – Robbery, Percent Distribution, 1993
[By region]

	United States Total	North-eastern States	Mid-western States	Southern States	Western States
Total[1]	100.0	100.0	100.0	100.0	100.0
Street/highway	54.7	61.2	61.2	50.1	50.8
Commercial house	12.5	10.0	10.3	12.7	15.7
Gas or service station	2.3	2.0	2.9	2.3	2.5
Convenience store	5.3	2.4	4.2	7.7	5.6
Residence	10.3	10.2	8.9	12.6	8.0
Bank	1.8	1.4	1.2	1.4	2.9
Miscellaneous	13.1	12.7	11.3	13.1	14.5

[1]Because of rounding, percentages may not add to totals.

ROBBERY

CHART 2.12

VARIATION FROM MONTHLY AVERAGE
1993

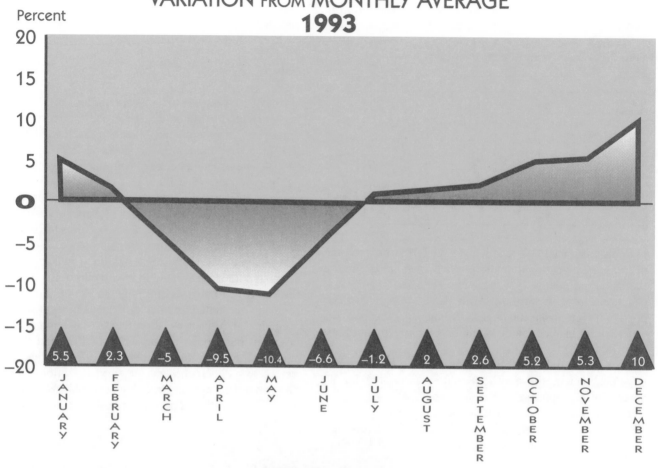

Percent

20
15
10
5
0
−5
−10
−15
−20

JANUARY	FEBRUARY	MARCH	APRIL	MAY	JUNE	JULY	AUGUST	SEPTEMBER	OCTOBER	NOVEMBER	DECEMBER
5.5	2.3	−5	−9.5	−10.4	−6.6	−1.2	2	2.6	5.2	5.3	10

CHART 2.13

PERCENT CHANGE FROM 1989

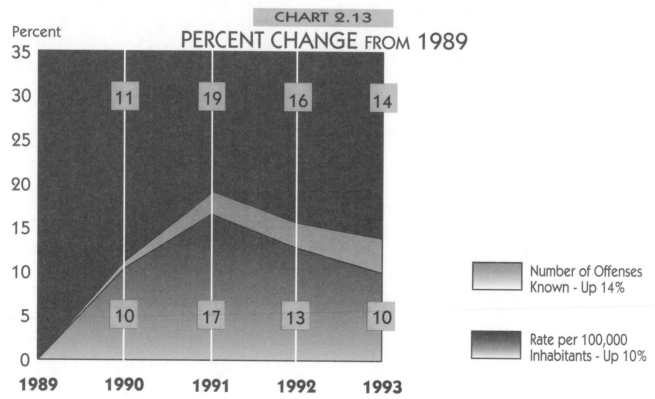

Percent

35
30
25
20
15
10
5
0

	1990	1991	1992	1993
Number of Offenses	11	19	16	14
Rate per 100,000	10	17	13	10

1989   1990   1991   1992   1993

Number of Offenses Known - Up 14%

Rate per 100,000 Inhabitants - Up 10%

Table 2.21 – Robbery, Percent Distribution, 1993

[By population group]

	Group I (60 cities, 250,000 and over; population 41,790,000)	Group II (126 cities, 100,000 to 249,999; population 18,637,000)	Group III (327 cities, 50,000 to 99,999; population 22,485,000)	Group IV (604 cities, 25,000 to 49,999; population 20,932,000)	Group V (1,427 cities, 10,000 to 24,999; population 22,420,000)	Group VI (5,683 cities under 10,000; population 19,486,000)	County agencies (3,521 agencies; population 70,605,000)
Total[1]	100.0	100.0	100.0	100.0	100.0	100.0	100.0
Street/highway	61.7	54.5	50.6	44.5	38.0	25.6	35.9
Commercial house	11.3	12.5	14.1	14.4	14.7	13.1	15.9
Gas or service station	1.6	2.4	3.1	3.6	4.9	3.2	4.0
Convenience store	3.0	6.7	7.7	8.2	10.3	9.6	10.4
Residence	9.7	9.9	9.3	10.0	11.0	10.3	15.1
Bank	1.4	1.9	2.3	2.7	2.8	2.3	2.5
Miscellaneous	11.4	12.0	12.9	16.6	18.1	36.0	16.2

[1]Because of rounding, percentages may not add to totals.

Forty-two percent of robberies in 1993 were committed with firearms. Strong-armed tactics were used in 38 percent, knives or cutting instruments were used in 10 percent, and other dangerous weapons in the remainder. A comparison of 1992 and 1993 robbery totals by weapon showed those by knives or cutting instruments dropped 8 percent; those by strong-arm tactics decreased 6 percent; and those by other dangerous weapons were down 4 percent. Robberies by firearms showed the only increase, up 4 percent since 1992. A state-by-state breakdown of weapons used in robberies in 1993 is shown in Table 21.

Table 2.22 – Robbery, Type of Weapons Used, 1993

[Percent distribution by region]

Region	Total all weapons[1]	Armed			
		Fire-arms	Knives or cutting instruments	Other weapons	Strong-armed
Total	100.0	42.4	10.0	9.5	38.2
Northeastern States	100.0	36.7	13.5	8.9	41.0
Midwestern States	100.0	46.9	6.9	9.8	36.3
Southern States	100.0	47.1	8.1	8.3	36.6
Western States	100.0	40.3	10.1	11.3	38.2

[1]Because of rounding, percentages may not add to totals.

Law Enforcement Response

The 1993 national robbery clearance rate was 24 percent. In the Nation's cities, the clearance rate was 23 percent, and in the suburban counties, 25 percent. The highest robbery clearance rate—39 percent—was registered by rural county law enforcement agencies. (See Table 25.) Regional robbery clearance percentages ranged from 19 percent in the Midwest to 27 percent in the South. (See Table 26.)

Nationally, persons under the age of 18, exclusively, were the offenders in 17 percent of all 1993 robbery clearances. This age group accounted for 20 percent of the suburban county clearances, 16 percent in the Nation's cities, and 13 percent of those by rural county agencies.

Arrests for robbery declined 1 percent nationwide and in cities during 1993 when compared to 1992. For the same 2-year period, the number of persons arrested for robbery was down 7 percent in the suburban counties and 4 percent in the rural counties.

Sixty-two percent of all robbery arrestees in 1993 were under 25 years of age, and 91 percent were males. Sixty-two percent of those arrested were black, 36 percent were white, and the remainder were of other races.

The total number of robbery arrests was up 9 percent during the 5-year period, 1989-1993. For the same time-span, arrests of males for robbery also rose 9 percent, and female arrests increased 11 percent. Juvenile arrests rose 37 percent, and those of persons 18 years of age and older increased 1 percent.

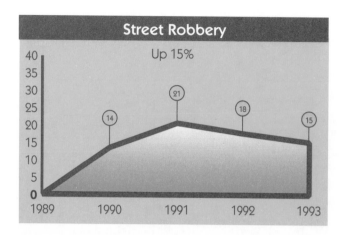

Street Robbery
Up 15%

Values: 1989: 0, 1990: 14, 1991: 21, 1992: 18, 1993: 15

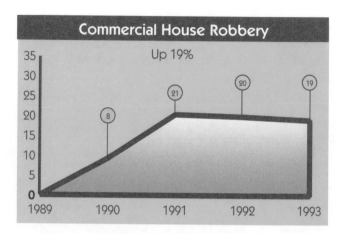

Commercial House Robbery
Up 19%

Values: 1989: 0, 1990: 8, 1991: 21, 1992: 20, 1993: 19

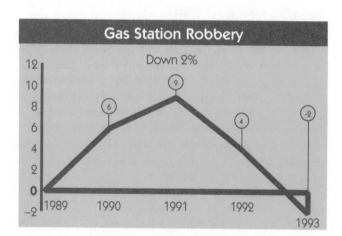

Gas Station Robbery
Down 2%

Values: 1989: 0, 1990: 6, 1991: 9, 1992: 4, 1993: -2

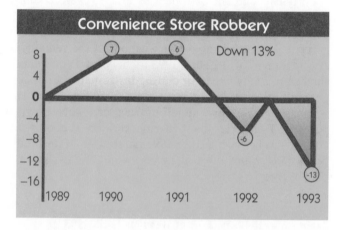

Convenience Store Robbery
Down 13%

Values: 1989: 0, 1990: 7, 1991: 6, 1992: -6, 1993: -13

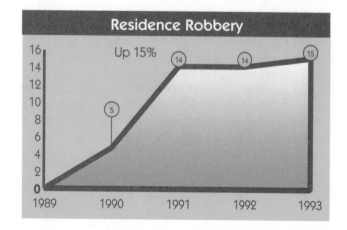

Residence Robbery
Up 15%

Values: 1989: 0, 1990: 5, 1991: 14, 1992: 14, 1993: 15

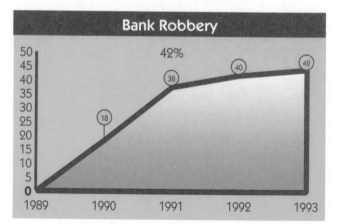

Bank Robbery
42%

Values: 1989: 0, 1990: 18, 1991: 38, 1992: 40, 1993: 42

30

AGGRAVATED ASSAULT

DEFINITION

Aggravated assault is an unlawful attack by one person upon another for the purpose of inflicting severe or aggravated bodily injury. This type of assault is usually accompanied by the use of a weapon or by means likely to produce death or great bodily harm. Attempts are included since it is not necessary that an injury result when a gun, knife, or other weapon is used which could and probably would result in serious personal injury if the crime were successfully completed.

TREND		
Year	Number of offenses	Rate per 100,000 inhabitants
1992	1,126,974	441.8
1993	1,135,099	440.1
Percent change	+.7	−.4

Totaling an estimated 1,135,099 offenses nationally, aggravated assaults in 1993 accounted for 59 percent of the violent crimes. Geographic distribution figures show that 40 percent of the aggravated assault volume was accounted for by the most populous Southern Region. Following were the Western Region with 25 percent, the Midwestern Region with 19 percent, and the Northeastern Region with 16 percent. Among the regions, only the Northeast registered a decline in the number of reported aggravated assaults. (See Table 4.)

The 1993 monthly figures show that the greatest number of aggravated assaults was recorded during July, while the lowest volume occurred during February.

Table 2.23 – Aggravated Assault by Month, 1989-1993
[Percent distribution]

Months	1989	1990	1991	1992	1993
January	7.5	7.4	6.9	7.3	7.5
February	6.6	6.7	6.6	7.3	6.5
March	7.9	7.8	7.7	8.0	8.1
April	8.1	8.2	8.1	8.7	8.3
May	8.9	9.0	9.1	9.2	8.9
June	8.9	9.4	9.3	8.9	9.1
July	9.6	10.1	9.7	9.4	9.6
August	9.2	9.3	9.9	9.1	9.2
September	8.8	8.9	9.0	8.6	8.3
October	9.1	8.3	8.6	8.5	8.5
November	7.9	7.4	7.6	7.6	7.4
December	7.5	7.5	7.6	7.4	8.6

In 1993, aggravated assaults were up 1 percent nationwide as compared to 1992. For the same time period, cities collectively experienced an increase of less than 1 percent in the aggravated assault volume. Percent changes among the city population groupings ranged from 4-percent increases in cities with 100,000 to 249,999 inhabitants and in those with 500,000 to 999,999 to a 2-percent decline in cities with 1,000,000 or more inhabitants. The suburban counties registered a 1-percent increase and the rural counties, a 2-percent rise for the 2-year period. (See Table 12.)

Five- and 10-year trends for the country as a whole showed aggravated assaults up 19 percent over the 1989 level and 66 percent over the 1984 experience. (See Table 1.)

Rate

Down less than 1 percent from the 1992 rate, there were 440 reported victims of aggravated assault for every 100,000 people nationwide in 1993. The rate was 15 percent higher than in 1989 and 52 percent above the 1984 rate.

Higher than the national average, the rate in metropolitan areas was 486 per 100,000 in 1993. Cities outside metropolitan areas experienced a rate of 389, and rural counties, a rate of 176.

Regionally, the aggravated assault rates ranged from 510 per 100,000 people in the South to 348 per 100,000 in the Midwest. Compared to 1992, 1993 aggravated assault rates were down 1 percent in the Northeast and West and less than 1 percent in the South. Rates in the Midwest showed a less than 1-percent increase. (See Table 4.)

Nature

In 1993, 31 percent of the aggravated assaults were committed with blunt objects or other dangerous weapons. Of the remaining weapon categories, personal weapons such as hands, fists, and feet were used in 26 percent of the offenses; firearms in 25 percent; and knives or cutting instruments in the remainder.

From 1992 to 1993, assaults with knives or cutting instruments fell 1 percent and those with personal weapons (hands, fists, and feet) declined 3 percent. Those involving blunt objects or other dangerous weapons showed virtually no change. Similar to the murder experience, those with firearms increased 5 percent. State-by-state totals for weapons used in assaults during 1993 are shown in Table 22.

Table 2.24 – Aggravated Assault, Type of Weapons Used, 1993
[Percent distribution by region]

Region	Total all weapons[1]	Fire-arms	Knives or cutting instruments	Other weapons (clubs, blunt objects, etc.)	Personal weapons
Total	100.0	25.1	17.6	31.0	26.3
Northeastern States	100.0	17.2	21.1	32.3	29.4
Midwestern States	100.0	28.2	16.8	31.7	23.3
Southern States	100.0	26.8	18.5	31.2	23.5
Western States	100.0	24.7	13.6	27.9	33.8

[1]Because of rounding, percentages may not add to totals.

AGGRAVATED ASSAULT

CHART 2.15

VARIATION FROM MONTHLY AVERAGE
1993

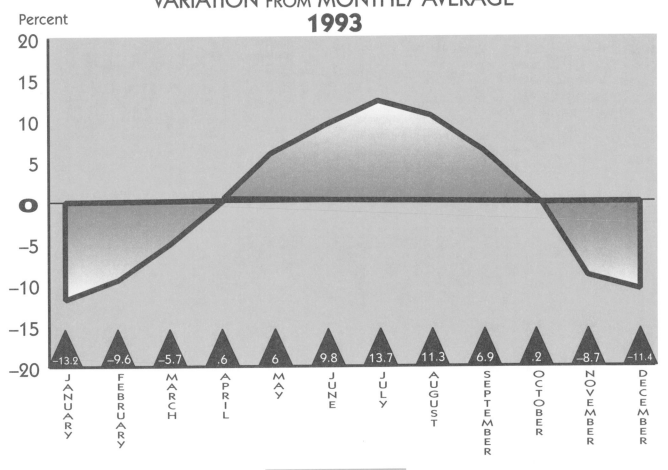

Percent

JANUARY	FEBRUARY	MARCH	APRIL	MAY	JUNE	JULY	AUGUST	SEPTEMBER	OCTOBER	NOVEMBER	DECEMBER
-13.2	-9.6	-5.7	.6	6	9.8	13.7	11.3	6.9	.2	-8.7	-11.4

CHART 2.16

PERCENT CHANGE FROM 1989

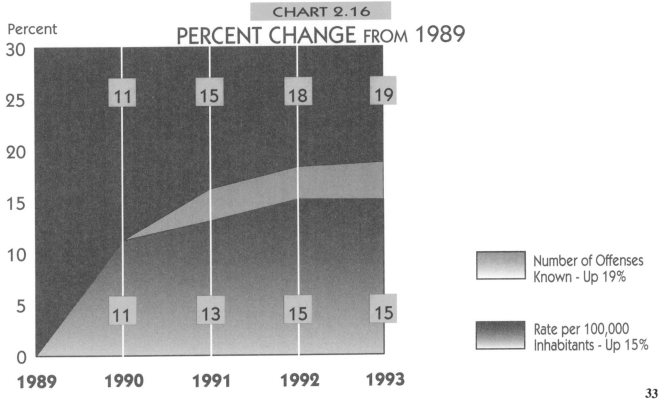

Percent

	1989	1990	1991	1992	1993
Number of Offenses Known - Up 19%		11	15	18	19
Rate per 100,000 Inhabitants - Up 15%		11	13	15	15

33

Law Enforcement Response

During 1993, law enforcement agencies nationwide recorded a 56-percent aggravated assault clearance rate. The cities collectively reported 54 percent cleared, while the suburban and rural county law enforcement agencies cleared 59 and 62 percent, respectively. Among the city groupings, those with populations under 10,000 recorded the highest clearance rate, 63 percent. (See Table 25.)

Regional clearance percentages for aggravated assault were 58 percent in the West, 57 percent in the South, 55 percent in the Northeast, and 50 percent in the Midwest.

Thirteen percent of the clearances reported nationally and in cities involved only persons under age 18. Persons in this age group were identified as the assailants in 14 percent of the clearances in the suburban counties and 10 percent of those in the rural counties.

The estimated 518,670 persons arrested for aggravated assault in 1993 represented two-thirds of all arrestees for violent crimes. Whites comprised 58 percent of the arrestees; blacks, 40 percent; and all other races, the remainder. Eighty-four percent of the arrestees were males and 16 percent, females.

Total arrests for aggravated assault were up 1 percent in 1993 from the 1992 total. During this 2-year period, arrests of persons under age 18 were up 6 percent, and arrests of adults increased 1 percent. A comparison of 1989 and 1993 figures showed increases of 15 percent for total arrests, 37 percent for juvenile arrests, and 12 percent for adult arrests.

PROPERTY CRIME TOTAL

DEFINITION

Property crime includes the offenses of burglary, larceny-theft, motor vehicle theft, and arson. The object of these offenses is the taking of money or property, but there is no force or threat of force against the victims.

TREND		
Year	Number of offenses[1]	Rate per 100,000 inhabitants[1]
1992	12,505,917	4,902.7
1993	12,216,764	4,736.9
Percent change	−2.3	−3.4

[1]Does not include arson. See page 57.

The estimated property crime total decreased to 12.2 million reported offenses in 1993, the lowest total since 1987. The 1993 volume was 2 percent lower than the 1992 level. (See Table 1.).

Regional property crime declines were 5 percent in the Northeast, 3 percent in the Midwest, 2 percent in the South, and 1 percent in the West. All city population groups also showed property crime decreases, with the greatest drop (5 percent) in cities with populations of 1 million or more. Rural and suburban county law enforcement agencies each recorded 2-percent decreases in their property crime totals during 1993. (See Table 12.)

As in previous years, 1993 monthly figures show more property crime occurred in August, while the lowest total was reported in February.

Table 2.25 – Property Crime Total by Month, 1989-1993
[Percent distribution]

Months	1989	1990	1991	1992	1993
January	8.2	8.3	7.9	8.4	8.0
February	7.2	7.4	7.4	7.8	6.9
March	8.2	8.2	8.2	8.2	8.1
April	7.8	7.9	8.0	8.0	7.9
May	8.5	8.2	8.3	8.2	8.1
June	8.5	8.2	8.4	8.4	8.6
July	9.2	8.9	9.1	9.0	9.1
August	9.3	9.1	9.2	9.1	9.2
September	8.4	8.3	8.4	8.4	8.4
October	8.6	8.7	8.7	8.5	8.6
November	8.1	8.2	8.0	8.0	8.1
December	7.9	8.6	8.4	8.1	9.1

Rate

In 1993, there were an estimated 4,737 property crimes for every 100,000 United States inhabitants. The 1993 property crime rate was 3 percent lower than the 1992 rate and 7 percent under the 1989 rate but 5 percent above the 1984 rate.

Geographically, the 1993 property crime rate declined in all regions. The rates of 5,375 per 100,000 in the West and 5,181 in the South were each down 3 percent. The rate of 4,204 in the Midwest represented a 4-percent decrease; and the Northeast's rate of 3,900, a 5-percent decline.

Property crime rates for 1993 were 5,193 in metropolitan areas, 4,799 in cities outside metropolitan areas, and 1,749 in rural counties. By population group, the highest rate — 8,510 — was recorded in cities with populations from 250,000 to 499,999. (See Table 16.)

Nature

Total dollar losses due to property crime were estimated at $14.8 billion in 1993, down from $15.2 billion in 1992. The average loss per offense in 1993 was $1,212, as compared to $1,217 in 1992.

In 1993, larceny-theft accounted for 64 percent of all property crime. Burglary accounted for 23 percent and motor vehicle theft for 13 percent. Although arson is excluded from the property crime offense and clearance tabulations because of its lower national coverage, it accounted for another 95,764 offenses reported by 11,860 agencies. An average of $16,616 was lost per arson in 1993, based on data from 11,743 law enforcement agencies. The average loss per arson in 1993, although slightly down from the 1992 average, was largely influenced by arson damages in forested areas of California. While the fires spread and destroyed various properties, their points of origin were in the forest.

Regionally, 38 percent of property crime was accounted for by the Southern States, 25 percent by the Western States, 21 percent by the Midwestern States, and 16 percent by the Northeastern States.

Law Enforcement Response

Property crimes generally have lower clearance rates than violent crimes, and in 1993, the overall property crime clearance rate was 17 percent, as compared to 44 percent for violent crime. Geographically the Midwest's 1993 property crime clearance rate equalled the Nation's, 17 percent. In two of the four regions, the South and West, property crime clearance rates of 18 percent were recorded. The Northeast recorded a lesser rate of 16 percent. (See Table 26.)

Twenty-three percent of the property crimes cleared by law enforcement nationwide and in cities in 1993 involved only young people under age 18. The juvenile percentage was 24 percent in suburban counties and 21 percent in rural counties. (See Table 28.)

The estimated 2.1 million persons arrested for property crimes in 1993 accounted for 15 percent of all arrestees. The volume of property crime arrests in 1993 was 3 percent below the 1992 level and 6 percent lower than the 1989 total but 13 percent above the 1984 experience. Compared to 1992 totals, juvenile and adult property crime arrests in 1993 declined 2 and 4 percent, respectively, nationwide. (See Tables 32, 34, and 36.)

In 1993, 74 percent of all property crime arrestees were males. Sixty-four percent of the total were white, and 33 percent were under age 18.

PROPERTY CRIME

CHART 2.17

VARIATION FROM MONTHLY AVERAGE
1993

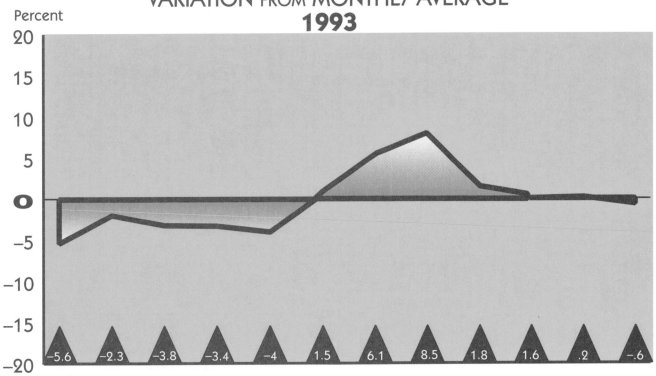

Percent

−5.6	−2.3	−3.8	−3.4	−4	1.5	6.1	8.5	1.8	1.6	.2	−.6

CHART 2.18

PERCENT CHANGE FROM 1989

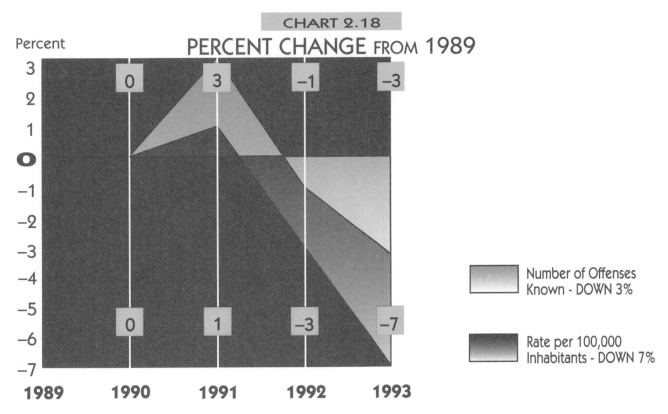

Percent

Number of Offenses
Known - DOWN 3%

Rate per 100,000
Inhabitants - DOWN 7%

1989   1990   1991   1992   1993

BURGLARY

DEFINITION

The Uniform Crime Reporting Program defines burglary as the unlawful entry of a structure to commit a felony or theft. The use of force to gain entry is not required to classify an offense as burglary. Burglary in this Program is categorized into three subclassifications: forcible entry, unlawful entry where no force is used, and attempted forcible entry.

Year	Number of offenses	Rate per 100,000 inhabitants
1992	2,979,884	1,168.2
1993	2,834,808	1,099.2
Percent change	−4.9	−5.9

TREND

An estimated 2,834,808 burglaries occurred in the United States during 1993. These offenses accounted for 20 percent of the Crime Index total and 23 percent of the property crimes.

Distribution figures for the regions showed the highest burglary volume occurred in the most populous Southern States, accounting for 41 percent of the total. The Western States followed with 24 percent, the Midwestern States with 19 percent, and the Northeastern States with 16 percent.

In 1993, the greatest number of burglaries was recorded during December, while the lowest count was reported in February. (See Table 2.26.)

Table 2.26 – Burglary by Month, 1989-1993
[Percent distribution]

Months	1989	1990	1991	1992	1993
January	8.8	8.8	8.1	8.6	8.3
February	7.3	7.5	7.3	7.7	6.9
March	8.2	8.1	8.1	8.2	8.2
April	7.7	7.8	7.9	7.8	7.7
May	8.4	8.1	8.3	8.2	8.0
June	8.3	7.9	8.2	8.1	8.4
July	9.2	8.9	9.2	9.0	9.0
August	9.3	9.0	9.2	9.0	9.1
September	8.6	8.3	8.6	8.4	8.5
October	8.5	8.5	8.6	8.3	8.4
November	8.1	8.3	8.0	8.2	8.1
December	7.8	8.7	8.6	8.3	9.3

Nationwide, the burglary volume dropped 5 percent in 1993 from the 1992 total. By population group, decreases were registered in all city groupings; the largest decrease was in cities with populations of 250,000 and over, which showed a 7-percent decline. (See Table 12.)

Geographically, all four regions of the United States reported decreases in burglary volumes during 1993 as compared to 1992. Both the Northeastern States and the Midwestern States experienced 6-percent declines. The Southern States showed a 5-percent decrease; and the Western States reported the smallest change, a 2-percent decline.

Longer term national trends show burglary down 11 percent from the 1989 volume and 5 percent below the 1984 level.

Rate

A burglary rate of 1,099 per 100,000 inhabitants was registered nationwide in 1993. The rate was 6 percent lower than in 1992 and 13 percent below the 1984 rate. In 1993, for every 100,000 in population, the rate was 1,182 in the metropolitan areas, 993 in the cities outside metropolitan areas, and 633 in the rural counties.

Regionally, the burglary rate was 1,286 in the Southern States, 1,221 in the Western States, 900 in the Midwestern States, and 878 in the Northeastern States. A comparison of 1992 and 1993 rates showed decreases of 7 percent in the South and Midwest, 6 percent in the Northeast, and 4 percent in the West.

Nature

Two of every 3 burglaries in 1993 were residential in nature. Sixty-eight percent of all burglaries involved forcible entry, 24 percent were unlawful entries (without force), and the remainder were forcible entry attempts. Offenses for which time of occurrence was reported were evenly divided between day and night.

Burglary victims suffered losses estimated at $3.4 billion in 1993, and the average dollar loss per burglary was $1,185. The average loss for residential offenses was $1,189, while for nonresidential property, it was $1,179. Compared to 1992, the 1993 average loss for both residential and nonresidential property declined. Both residential and nonresidential burglary volumes also showed declines from 1992 to 1993, 4 and 6 percent, respectively. (See Table 23.)

Law Enforcement Response

Nationwide in 1993, a 13-percent clearance rate was recorded for burglaries brought to the attention of law enforcement agencies across the country. Geographically, in the South, the clearance rate was 15 percent; in the Northeast, 13 percent; in the West, 12 percent; and in the Midwest, 11 percent.

Rural county law enforcement agencies cleared 16 percent of the burglaries in their jurisdictions. Agencies in suburban counties cleared 14 percent, and those in cities, 13 percent.

BURGLARY

CHART 2.19

VARIATION FROM MONTHLY AVERAGE
1993

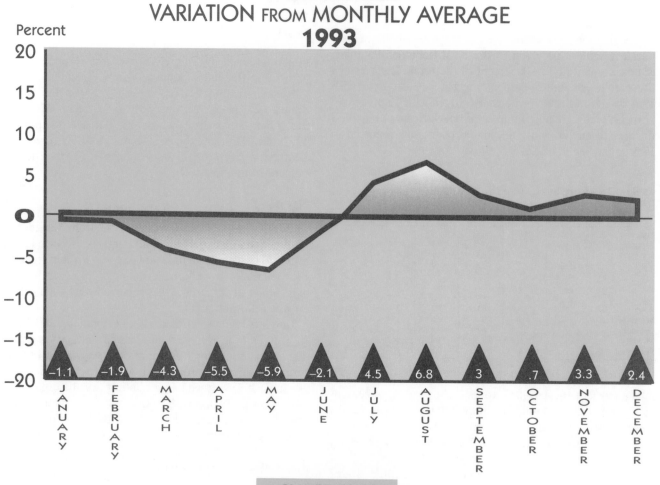

Percent

JANUARY	FEBRUARY	MARCH	APRIL	MAY	JUNE	JULY	AUGUST	SEPTEMBER	OCTOBER	NOVEMBER	DECEMBER
−1.1	−1.9	−4.3	−5.5	−5.9	−2.1	4.5	6.8	3	.7	3.3	2.4

CHART 2.20

PERCENT CHANGE FROM 1989

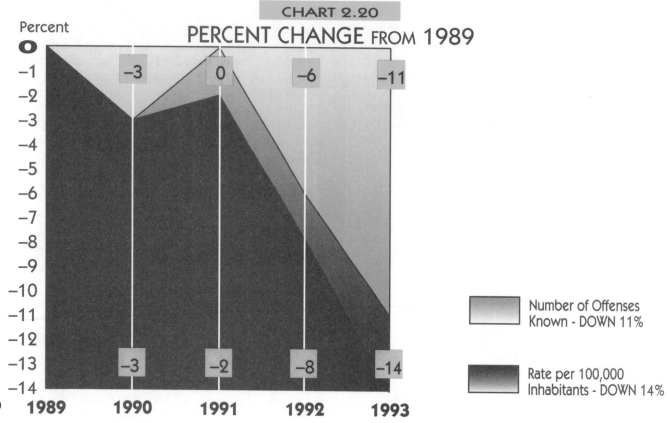

Percent

Number of Offenses
Known - DOWN 11%

Rate per 100,000
Inhabitants - DOWN 14%

1989   1990   1991   1992   1993

−3   0   −6   −11

−3   −2   −8   −14

BURGLARY Percent Change from 1989

CHART 2.21

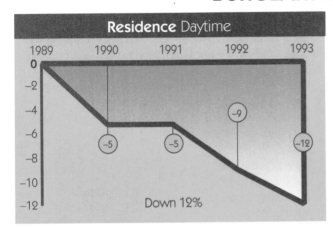

Residence Daytime

Down 12%

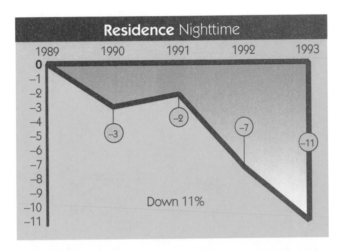

Residence Nighttime

Down 11%

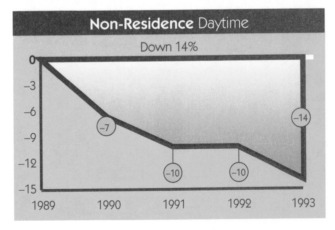

Non-Residence Daytime

Down 14%

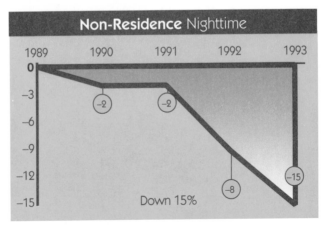

Non-Residence Nighttime

Down 15%

Adults were involved in 79 percent of all burglary offenses cleared; the remaining 21 percent involved only young people under 18 years of age. Persons under age 18 accounted for 20 percent of the burglary clearances in cities, and 22 percent of those in both rural and suburban counties. The highest degree of juvenile involvement was recorded in the Nation's smallest cities (under 10,000 in population) where young persons under 18 years of age accounted for 27 percent of the clearances. (See Table 28.)

In the UCR Program, several persons may be arrested in connection with the clearance of one crime, or the arrest of one individual may clear numerous offenses. The latter is often true in cases of burglary, for which an estimated 402,700 arrests were made in 1993. Arrest trends between 1992 and 1993 show total burglary arrests were down 5 percent. Arrests of persons under 18 years of age decreased 4 percent, while those of adults were down 6 percent. For the same 2-year time period, total burglary arrest trends showed decreases of 6 percent in cities and suburban counties, and less than a 1-percent increase in the rural counties.

Ninety percent of the burglary arrestees during 1993 were males, and 63 percent of the total were under 25 years of age. Among all burglary arrestees, whites accounted for 67 percent, blacks for 31 percent, and other races for the remainder.

LARCENY-THEFT

DEFINITION

Larceny-theft is the unlawful taking, carrying, leading, or riding away of property from the possession or constructive possession of another. It includes crimes such as shoplifting, pocket-picking, purse-snatching, thefts from motor vehicles, thefts of motor vehicle parts and accessories, bicycle thefts, etc., in which no use of force, violence, or fraud occurs. In the Uniform Crime Reporting Program, this crime category does not include embezzlement, "con" games, forgery, and worthless checks. Motor vehicle theft is also excluded from this category inasmuch as it is a separate Crime Index offense.

TREND		
Year	*Number of offenses*	*Rate per 100,000 inhabitants*
1992	7,915,199	3,103.0
1993	7,820,909	3,032.4
Percent change	−1.2	−2.3

Larceny-theft, estimated at 7.8 million offenses during 1993, comprised 55 percent of the Crime Index total and 64 percent of the property crimes. Similar to the experience in previous years, larceny-thefts were recorded most often during August and least frequently in February.

Table 2.27 – Larceny-Theft by Month, 1989-1993
[Percent distribution]

Months	1989	1990	1991	1992	1993
January	8.0	8.2	7.8	8.2	7.7
February	7.2	7.4	7.5	7.8	6.8
March	8.2	8.2	8.2	8.3	8.0
April	8.0	7.9	8.1	8.1	8.0
May	8.6	8.3	8.4	8.2	8.2
June	8.7	8.3	8.5	8.5	8.7
July	9.2	8.9	9.2	9.1	9.2
August	9.5	9.1	9.3	9.1	9.3
September	8.3	8.2	8.3	8.4	8.3
October	8.6	8.7	8.7	8.6	8.6
November	8.0	8.1	7.9	7.9	8.0
December	7.7	8.4	8.2	8.0	9.1

When viewed geographically, the Southern States, the most populous region, recorded 38 percent of the larceny-theft total. The Western States recorded 24 percent; the Midwestern States, 22 percent; and the Northeastern States, 15 percent. (See Table 3.)

Compared to 1992, the 1993 volume of larceny-thefts decreased 1 percent in the Nation and in rural and suburban counties and 2 percent in all cities collectively. Similar to the national experience, city population groups ranging from 50,000 to 999,999 inhabitants experienced 1-percent declines in their 1993 larceny volumes; the remaining population groups recorded 2-percent decreases.

Regionally, larceny volumes dropped in the Northeast, 3 percent; in the Midwest, 2 percent; and in the West, 1 percent. The number of larceny-thefts in the South showed no change.

The 5- and 10-year national trends indicated larceny was down 1 percent when compared to the 1989 total but up 19 percent above the 1984 level.

Rate

The 1993 larceny-theft rate was 3,032 per 100,000 U.S. inhabitants. The rate was 2 percent lower than in 1992 and 4 percent under the 1989 level. When compared to 1984, the rate showed an increase of 9 percent. The 1993 rate was 3,289 per 100,000 inhabitants of metropolitan areas; 3,582 per 100,000 population in cities outside metropolitan areas; and 1,006 per 100,000 people in the rural counties. (See Tables 1 and 2.)

For all regions, the larceny-theft rate per 100,000 inhabitants declined from 1992 levels. The rate in the Northeast was 2,358, down 4 percent; the rates of 3,360 in the West and 2,850 in the Midwest dropped 3 percent; and the South's rate of 3,339 was down 1 percent. (See Table 4.)

Nature

During 1993, the average value of property stolen due to larceny-theft was $504, up from $483 in 1992. When the average value was applied to the estimated number of larceny-thefts, the loss to victims nationally was $3.9 billion for the year. This estimated dollar loss is considered conservative since many offenses in the larceny category, particularly if the value of the stolen goods is small, never come to law enforcement attention. Losses in 23 percent of the thefts reported to law enforcement in 1993 ranged from $50 to $200, while in 37 percent, they were over $200.

Losses of goods and property reported stolen as a result of pocket-picking averaged $411; purse-snatching, $341; and shoplifting, $109. Thefts from buildings resulted in an average loss of $831; from motor vehicles, $531; and from coin-operated machines, $208. The average value loss due to thefts of motor vehicle accessories was $303 and for thefts of bicycles, $241. (See Table 23.)

Thefts of motor vehicle parts, accessories, and contents made up the largest portion of reported larcenies – 37 percent. Also contributing to the high volume of thefts were shoplifting, accounting for 15 percent; thefts from buildings, 13 percent; and bicycle thefts, 6 percent. The remainder was distributed among pocket-picking, purse-snatching, thefts from coin-operated machines, and all other types of larceny-thefts. Table 2.28 presents the distribution of larceny-theft by type and geographic region.

Table 2.28 – Larceny Analysis by Region, 1993
[Percent distribution]

	United States Total	North- eastern States	Mid- western States	Southern States	Western States
Total[1]	100.0	100.0	100.0	100.0	100.0
Pocket-picking	.9	3.3	.4	.5	.5
Purse-snatching	.9	1.7	.9	.7	.6
Shoplifting	15.4	13.5	14.1	15.0	17.8
From motor vehicles (except accessories)	23.4	21.9	20.4	21.0	29.8
Motor vehicle accessories	13.9	13.8	15.3	15.1	11.3
Bicycles	6.1	7.0	6.0	5.2	7.1
From buildings	13.2	18.5	15.5	10.7	12.1
From coin-operated machines	.8	1.1	.7	.7	.7
All others	25.5	19.1	26.7	31.0	20.1

[1]Because of rounding, percentages may not add to totals.

LARCENY-THEFT

CHART 2.22

VARIATION FROM MONTHLY AVERAGE
1993

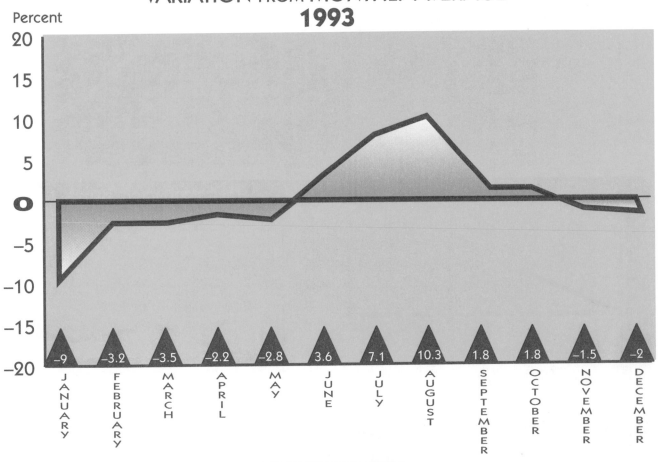

Percent

JANUARY	−9
FEBRUARY	−3.2
MARCH	−3.5
APRIL	−2.2
MAY	−2.8
JUNE	3.6
JULY	7.1
AUGUST	10.3
SEPTEMBER	1.8
OCTOBER	1.8
NOVEMBER	−1.5
DECEMBER	−2

CHART 2.23

PERCENT CHANGE FROM 1989

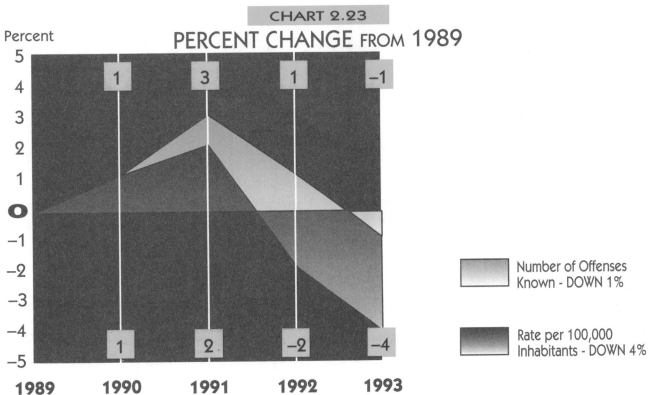

Percent

1989 1990 1991 1992 1993

Number of Offenses
Known - DOWN 1%

Rate per 100,000
Inhabitants - DOWN 4%

45

LARCENY/THEFT Percent Change from 1989

CHART 2.24

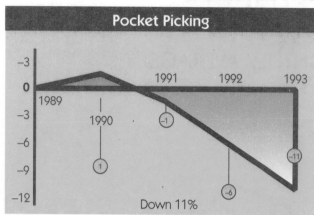

Pocket Picking

Down 11%

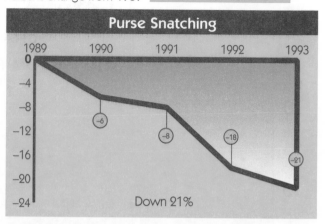

Purse Snatching

Down 21%

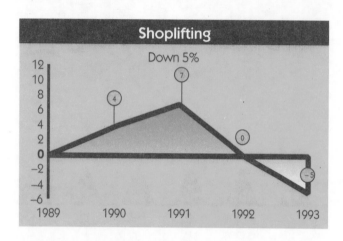

Shoplifting

Down 5%

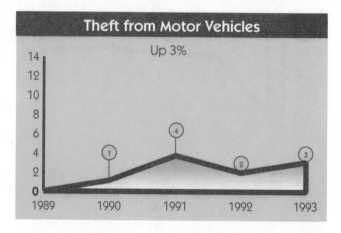

Theft from Motor Vehicles

Up 3%

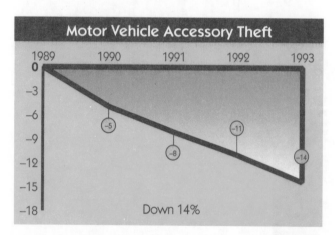

Motor Vehicle Accessory Theft

Down 14%

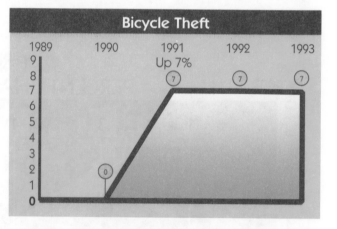

Bicycle Theft

Up 7%

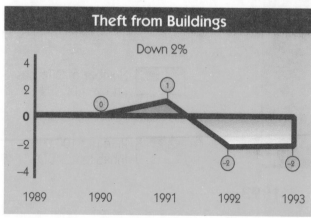

Theft from Buildings

Down 2%

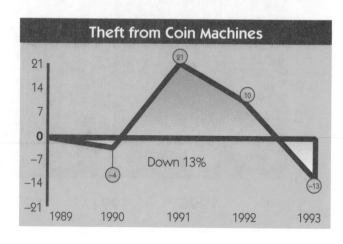

Theft from Coin Machines

Down 13%

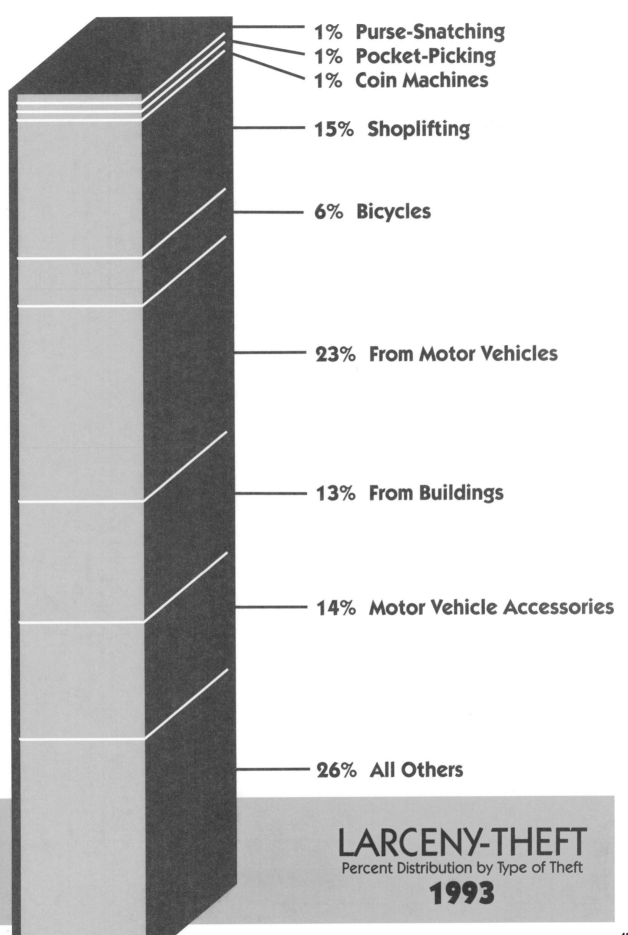

CHART 2.25

1% Purse-Snatching

1% Pocket-Picking

1% Coin Machines

15% Shoplifting

6% Bicycles

23% From Motor Vehicles

13% From Buildings

14% Motor Vehicle Accessories

26% All Others

LARCENY-THEFT
Percent Distribution by Type of Theft
1993

Law Enforcement Response

A 20-percent larceny-theft clearance rate was recorded nationally and in cities collectively during 1993. The highest rate, 25 percent, was reported by law enforcement agencies in cities from 10,000 to 24,999 in population. Suburban and rural counties recorded 17-percent and 18-percent clearance rates, respectively.

Geographically, law enforcement agencies in the Western Region cleared 21 percent of the larceny offenses brought to their attention, while the Midwestern Region recorded a clearance rate of 20 percent. The Northeastern and Southern Regions each recorded clearance rates of 19 percent. (See Table 26.)

Twenty-four percent of the larceny-theft clearances nationally and in cities involved only offenders under 18 years of age. Twenty-five percent of those in suburban counties and 20 percent of those in rural counties were accounted for by persons in this age group.

Between 1992 and 1993, the total number of persons arrested for larceny dropped 3 percent. By gender, arrests for males and females declined 4 and 1 percent, respectively. During this same period, adult arrests were down 4 percent, and those of persons under 18 years of age, down 1 percent.

Considering a longer timeframe, larceny-theft arrests declined 3 percent for the 5-year period, 1989-1993. Arrests of adults were down 7 percent, and those of juveniles, up 5 percent. During this 5-year timespan, female arrests rose 3 percent, while male arrests declined 6 percent.

Larceny-theft not only comprised the largest portion of Crime Index offenses reported to law enforcement, but this offense also accounted for 52 percent of the arrests for Index crimes and 70 percent of those for property crimes in 1993. Forty-four percent of the larceny arrests were of persons under 21 years of age, and 31 percent of the arrestees were under 18. Females, who were arrested for this offense more often than for any other in 1993, comprised 33 percent of all larceny-theft arrestees.

Whites accounted for 65 percent of the total larceny-theft arrestees, blacks for 33 percent, and all other races for the remainder.

MOTOR VEHICLE THEFT

DEFINITION

Defined as the theft or attempted theft of a motor vehicle, this offense category includes the stealing of automobiles, trucks, buses, motorcycles, motorscooters, snowmobiles, etc. The definition excludes the taking of a motor vehicle for temporary use by those persons having lawful access.

	TREND	
Year	*Number of offenses*	*Rate per 100,000 inhabitants*
1992	1,610,834	631.5
1993	1,561,047	605.3
Percent change	−3.1	−4.1

An estimated total of 1,561,047 thefts of motor vehicles occurred in the United States during 1993. These offenses comprised 13 percent of all property crimes. The regional distribution of motor vehicle thefts showed 32 percent of the volume was in the Southern States, 29 percent in the Western States, 22 percent in the Northeastern States, and 18 percent in the Midwestern States.

The 1993 monthly figures show that the greatest numbers of motor vehicle thefts were recorded during the months of July and August, while the lowest count was in February.

Table 2.29 — Motor Vehicle Theft by Month, 1989-1993
[Percent distribution]

Months	1989	1990	1991	1992	1993
January	8.3	8.5	8.3	8.8	8.5
February	7.3	7.6	7.5	7.9	7.3
March	8.1	8.4	8.2	8.2	8.2
April	7.5	7.9	7.8	7.8	7.8
May	8.0	8.1	8.1	8.1	7.9
June	8.2	8.1	8.2	8.2	8.4
July	8.8	8.8	8.7	8.8	8.9
August	9.0	8.8	8.9	8.9	8.9
September	8.5	8.4	8.3	8.2	8.4
October	9.0	8.8	8.7	8.6	8.6
November	8.7	8.3	8.5	8.3	8.3
December	8.5	8.4	8.8	8.2	8.8

The number of motor vehicle thefts nationally fell 3 percent from 1992 to 1993. The largest decline was experienced in cities with populations of 1 million or more, 8 percent. During the same period, increases occurred in the suburban counties, 1 percent, and the rural counties, 2 percent.

Geographically, three regions experienced motor vehicle theft decreases, while the Western Region showed a 1-percent increase. (See Table 4.)

The accompanying chart shows that the volume of motor vehicle thefts in 1993 remained virtually unchanged when compared to the 1989 volume.

Rate

The 1993 national motor vehicle theft rate — 605 per 100,000 people — was 4 percent lower than in 1992 and 1989. The 1993 rate was 38 percent above the 1984 rate.

For every 100,000 inhabitants living in MSAs, there were 721 motor vehicle thefts reported in 1993. The rate in cities outside metropolitan areas was 224 and in rural counties, 110. As in previous years, the highest rates were in the Nation's most heavily populated municipalities, indicating that this offense is primarily a large-city problem. For every 100,000 inhabitants in cities with populations over 250,000, the 1993 motor vehicle theft rate was 1,509. The Nation's smallest cities, those with fewer than 10,000 inhabitants, recorded a rate of 240 per 100,000.

Among the regions, the motor vehicle theft rates ranged from 794 per 100,000 people in the Western States to 454 in the Midwestern States. The Northeastern States' rate was 664 and the Southern States' rate, 556. All regions registered rate decreases from 1992 to 1993. (See Table 4.)

An estimated average of 1 of every 126 registered motor vehicles was stolen nationwide during 1993. Regionally, this rate was greatest in the Northeast and West where 1 of every 98 motor vehicles registered was stolen. The other two regions reported lesser rates — 1 per 141 in the South and 1 per 178 in the Midwest.

Nature

During 1993, the estimated value of motor vehicles stolen nationwide was nearly $7.5 billion. At the time of theft, the average value per vehicle stolen was $4,808. The recovery percentage for the value of vehicles stolen was higher than for any other property type. Relating the value of vehicles stolen to the value of those recovered resulted in a 62-percent recovery rate for 1993.

Seventy-nine percent of all motor vehicles reported stolen during the year were automobiles, 15 percent were trucks or buses, and the remainder were other types.

Table 2.30 — Motor Vehicle Theft, 1993
[Percent distribution by region]

Region	Total[1]	Autos	Trucks and buses	Other vehicles
Total[1]	100.0	79.2	15.4	5.5
Northeastern States	100.0	92.3	4.6	3.2
Midwestern States	100.0	82.1	11.8	6.1
Southern States	100.0	75.2	18.0	6.8
Western States	100.0	72.5	22.0	5.5

[1]Because of rounding, percentages may not add to totals.

MOTOR VEHICLE THEFT

CHART 2.26

VARIATION FROM MONTHLY AVERAGE
1993

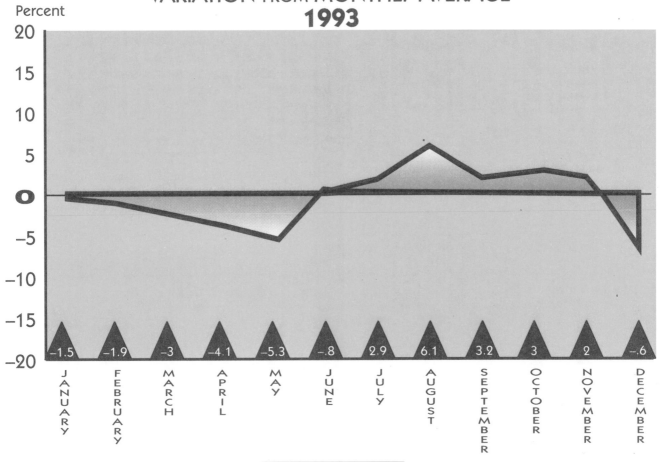

Percent

JANUARY	FEBRUARY	MARCH	APRIL	MAY	JUNE	JULY	AUGUST	SEPTEMBER	OCTOBER	NOVEMBER	DECEMBER
-1.5	-1.9	-3	-4.1	-5.3	-.8	2.9	6.1	3.2	3	2	-.6

CHART 2.27

PERCENT CHANGE FROM 1989

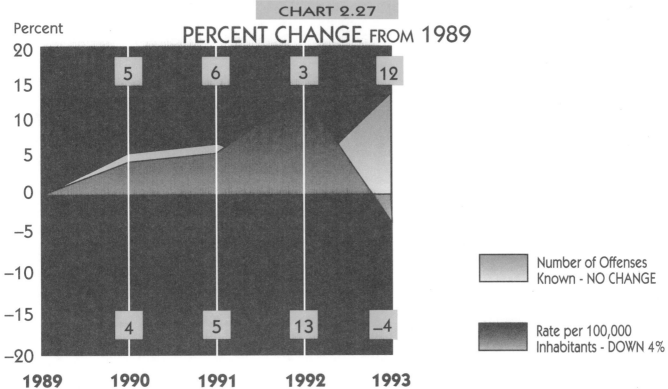

Percent

Number of Offenses
Known - NO CHANGE

Rate per 100,000
Inhabitants - DOWN 4%

1989   1990   1991   1992   1993

51

Law Enforcement Response

Law enforcement agencies nationwide recorded a 14-percent motor vehicle theft clearance rate for 1993. Those in cities cleared 13 percent; those in suburban counties cleared 16 percent; and rural county agencies cleared 33 percent.

Regional clearance percentages for motor vehicle theft were 17 percent in the Southern States, 15 percent in the Midwestern States, 12 percent in the Western States, and 10 percent in the Northeastern States.

Persons in the under-18 age group accounted for 25 percent of the motor vehicle thefts cleared both nationally and in cities. They comprised 23 percent of the clearances in the suburban counties and 21 percent of those in the rural counties.

During 1993, law enforcement agencies nationwide made an estimated 195,900 arrests for motor vehicle theft. Males accounted for 88 percent of those arrested. Fifty-seven percent were white, 40 percent were black, and the remainder were of other races.

A large proportion of motor vehicle theft arrestees was accounted for by the younger segment of the population. In 1993, 61 percent of all persons arrested for this offense were under 21 years of age, and those under 18 comprised 45 percent of the total. Between 1992 and 1993, overall arrests of persons under age 18 were down 3 percent. Within this age range, arrests of males decreased 4 percent, while those of females were up 8 percent.

Total motor vehicle theft arrests were down 3 percent in 1993 from the previous year. For longer timeframes, total vehicle theft arrests in 1993 were 12 percent lower than in 1989 but 62 percent above the 1984 level.

ARSON

———— DEFINITION ————

Arson is defined by the Uniform Crime Reporting Program as any willful or malicious burning or attempt to burn, with or without intent to defraud, a dwelling house, public building, motor vehicle or aircraft, personal property of another, etc.

Only fires determined through investigation to have been willfully or maliciously set are classified as arsons. Fires of suspicious or unknown origins are excluded.

A total of 95,764 arson offenses was reported by 11,860 law enforcement agencies across the country; these agencies furnished from 1 to 12 months of reports during 1993. Of these reporting agencies, 11,743 provided the detailed information—type of structure, estimated monetary value of the property damaged, etc.—from which the tables on the accompanying pages were tabulated. Further information regarding arson offenses and trends is presented in Tables 12 through 15 and arson clearances in Tables 25 through 28. Since only 9,146 agencies, covering 74 percent of the United States population, submitted reports for all 12 months of the year, the data user should be aware that, while conservative indicators, the figures do not represent the Nation's total arson experience.

The number of arson offenses reported nationally and overall in the Nation's cities decreased 5 percent in 1993 as compared to the 1992 total. Changes in counts for the Nation's cities ranged from a 1-percent increase in cities with populations between 500,000 and 999,999 to an 11-percent decline in those with populations of 1,000,000 or more. The rural and suburban counties registered declines of 6 and 8 percent, respectively. (See Table 12.)

Geographically, arson decreased 10 percent in the Northeast, 7 percent in the West, 6 percent in the Midwest, and 1 percent in the South.

By property type nationally, the number of arsons of mobile property and structures declined 7 percent. Those of all other property increased 4 percent. (See Table 15.)

Caution is recommended when viewing arson trend information. The percent change figures may have been influenced by improved arson reporting procedures. It is expected that year-to-year statistical comparability will improve as collection continues.

Table 2.31—Arson Rate, Population Group, 1993
[9,146 agencies; 1993 estimated population 191,161,033; rate per 100,000 inhabitants]

Group	Rate
Total	45.9
Total cities	53.7
Group I (cities 250,000 and over)	85.5
(cities 1,000,000 and over)	89.0
(cities 500,000 to 999,999)	77.1
(cities 250,000 to 499,999)	87.1
Group II (cities 100,000 to 249,999)	63.1
Group III (cities 50,000 to 99,999)	40.5
Group IV (cities 25,000 to 49,999)	33.8
Group V (cities 10,000 to 24,999)	26.3
Group VI (cities under 10,000)	28.4
Suburban counties	33.9
Rural counties	18.8
Suburban area	31.3

Rate

Since population coverage for arson data is lower than for the other Crime Index offenses, arson rates per 100,000 inhabitants are tabulated independently. Based on figures from law enforcement agencies supplying 12 months of statistics for all Index crimes, including arson, the 1993 rates are shown in Table 2.31.

The rates ranged from 89 per 100,000 inhabitants in cities with populations over 1 million to 19 per 100,000 rural county inhabitants. The suburban counties and all cities collectively recorded rates of 34 and 54 per 100,000 inhabitants, respectively. Overall, the 1993 national arson rate was 46 per 100,000 population.

Regionally, the highest arson rate was registered in the Western States with 55 offenses per 100,000 population. Following were the Midwestern States with a rate of 47 per 100,000, the Northeastern States with 44 per 100,000, and the Southern States with 39 per 100,000.

Nature

As in previous years, structures were the most frequent targets of arsonists in 1993 and comprised 52 percent of the reported incidents. Twenty-six percent of the arsons were directed at mobile property (motor vehicles, trailers, etc.), while other types of property (crops, timber, etc.) accounted for 22 percent.

Table 2.32—Arson, Type of Property, 1993
[11,743 agencies; 1993 estimated population 201,989,000]

Property classification	Number of offenses	Percent distribution[1]
Total	82,348	100.0
Total structure	42,867	52.1
Single occupancy residential	17,795	21.6
Other residential	7,516	9.1
Storage	3,753	4.6
Industrial/manufacturing	681	.8
Other commercial	4,968	6.0
Community/public	5,049	6.1
Other structure	3,105	3.8
Total mobile	21,617	26.3
Motor vehicles	20,094	24.4
Other mobile	1,523	1.8
Other	17,864	21.7

[1]Because of rounding, percentages may not add to totals.

Residential property was involved in 59 percent of the structural arsons during the year, with 42 percent of such offenses directed at single-family dwellings. Nineteen percent of all targeted structural property was either uninhabited or abandoned at the time the arson occurred.

Motor vehicles comprised 93 percent of all mobile property at which arsons were directed.

Table 2.33—Arson, Structures Not in Use, 1993
[11,743 agencies; 1993 estimated population 201,989,000]

Type of structure	Number of offenses	Percent not in use
Total	42,867	18.7
Single occupancy residential	17,795	23.2
Other residential	7,516	13.3
Storage	3,753	23.8
Industrial/manufacturing	681	22.9
Other commercial	4,968	13.1
Community/public	5,049	8.3
Other structure	3,105	25.4

The monetary value of property damaged due to reported arsons averaged $16,616 per incident in 1993. The overall average for all types of structures was $16,468. Mobile properties averaged $4,107 per incident, and other targets averaged $32,114.

The value of other targets was largely influenced by arsons in forested areas of California. While the fires spread and destroyed various properties, their points of origin were in the forest.

Table 2.34—Arson, Monetary Value of Property Damaged, 1993
[11,743 agencies; 1993 estimated population 201,989,000]

Property classification	Number of offenses	Average damage
Total	82,348	$16,616
Total structure	42,867	16,468
Single occupancy residential	17,795	13,575
Other residential	7,516	13,110
Storage	3,753	17,698
Industrial/manufacturing	681	71,993
Other commercial	4,968	33,959
Community/public	5,049	12,474
Other structure	3,105	6,034
Total mobile	21,617	4,107
Motor vehicles	20,094	3,729
Other mobile	1,523	9,094
Other	17,864	32,114

Law Enforcement Response

The national 1993 arson clearance rate was 15 percent. Agencies in cities with fewer than 10,000 inhabitants showed the highest rate, clearing 24 percent of the arson offenses brought to their attention. Rural county law enforcement agencies cleared 21 percent; those in suburban counties, 19 percent; and in cities, 14 percent. (See Table 25.)

Regionally, the Southern States recorded a clearance rate of 20 percent; the Western States, 15 percent; and the Northeastern and Midwestern States, 13 and 12 percent, respectively.

Forty-four percent of all 1993 arson clearances involved only young people under age 18, a higher percentage of juvenile involvement than for any other Index crime.

Juveniles accounted for 42 percent of structural arson clearances, 26 percent of the clearances for arsons of mobile property, and 58 percent of those of all other property.

Table 2.35—Arson Offenses Cleared by Arrest,[1] 1993
[11,743 agencies[2]; 1993 estimated population 201,989,000]

Property classification	Number of offenses	Percent cleared by arrest
Total	82,348	17.7
Total structure	42,867	22.1
Single occupancy residential	17,795	22.6
Other residential	7,516	22.9
Storage	3,753	16.9
Industrial/manufacturing	681	12.5
Other commercial	4,968	15.6
Community/public	5,049	33.1
Other structure	3,105	17.9
Total mobile	21,617	8.8
Motor vehicles	20,094	8.2
Other mobile	1,523	16.8
Other	17,864	18.1

[1]Includes offenses cleared by exceptional means.
[2]To be included in this table, it was necessary that arson clearances be reported by property classification.

By population grouping, juveniles were the offenders in 46 percent of the city, 41 percent of the suburban county arson clearances, and 25 percent of those in the rural counties.

Tables 2.35 and 2.36 show clearance data only for those 11,743 law enforcement agencies which were able to furnish breakdowns by type for the structural and mobile classifications. As can be seen, the highest clearance rate (33 percent) was recorded for offenses in which community or public structures were involved, while the lowest rate (8 percent) was registered for motor vehicles.

Table 2.36—Arson Offenses Cleared by Arrest[1] of Persons under 18 Years of Age, 1993
[11,743 agencies[2]; 1993 estimated population 201,989,000]

Property classification	Total clearances	Percent under 18
Total	14,610	44.0
Total structure	9,465	42.6
Single occupancy residential	4,022	34.5
Other residential	1,722	33.9
Storage	635	57.0
Industrial/manufacturing	85	38.8
Other commercial	775	29.7
Community/public	1,670	68.4
Other structure	556	52.2
Total mobile	1,906	27.0
Motor vehicles	1,650	25.0
Other mobile	256	39.5
Other	3,239	58.4

[1]Includes offenses cleared by exceptional means.
[2]To be included in this table, it was necessary that arson clearances be reported by property classification.

The estimated number of arrests for arson during 1993 totaled 19,400. Forty-nine percent of the arrestees were under 18 years of age and 66 percent were under 25. Males comprised 85 percent of all arson arrestees. Seventy-five percent of those arrested were white, 24 percent were black, and the remainder were of other races.

Trends for 1992 versus 1993 show national arson arrests decreased 1 percent and in suburban counties, 6 percent.

An increase of 1 percent occurred in the Nation's cities, and no change was shown in rural counties.

Nationwide, arrests of juveniles were up 2 percent, while adult arrests showed a 3-percent decrease from 1992 to 1993. During the same period, male arrests for arson declined 2 percent and female arrests rose 8 percent. The 1993 arson arrest total for all ages was 8 percent higher than the 1989 level and 2 percent above the 1984 level.

Crime Index Tabulations

This Section's tabular portions present data on crime in the United States as a whole; geographic divisions; individual states; Metropolitan Statistical Areas; cities, towns, and counties; and college and university campuses. Also furnished in the following tables are national averages for the value of property stolen in connection with Crime Index offenses; further breakdowns by type for the robbery, burglary, larceny-theft, and arson classifications; information on the types of weapons used; and data on the type and value of property stolen and recovered.

Although the total number of crimes occurring throughout the Nation is unknown, information on those reported to law enforcement gives a reliable indication of criminal activity. In reviewing the tables in this report, it must be remembered, however, that many factors can cause the volume and type of crime to vary from place to place. Even though population, one of these factors, is used in computing crime rates, all communities are affected to some degree by seasonal or transient populations. Since counts of current, permanent population are used in their construction, crime rates do not account for short-term population variables, such as an influx of day workers, tourists, shoppers, etc. A further discussion of various factors contributing to the amount of crime in a given area is shown on page *iv* of this publication.

National data can serve as a guide for the law enforcement administrator in analyzing the local crime count, as well as the performance of the jurisdiction's law enforcement agency. The analysis, however, should not end with a comparison based on data presented in this publication. It is only through an appraisal of local conditions that a clear picture of the community crime problem or the effectiveness of the law enforcement operation is possible.

National estimates of volume and rate per 100,000 inhabitants for all Crime Index offenses covering the past two decades are set forth in Table 1, "Index of Crime, United States, 1974-1993."

Table 2, "Index of Crime, United States, 1993," shows current year estimates for MSAs, rural counties, and cities and towns outside metropolitan areas. See Appendix III for the definitions of these community types.

Provided in Table 3, "Index of Crime, Regional Offense and Population Distribution, 1993," are data showing the geographical distribution of estimated Index crimes and population. When utilizing figures presented on a regional basis in this publication, the reader is cautioned to consider each region's proportion of the total United States population. For example, although the Southern States accounted for the largest volume of Crime Index offenses in 1993, they also represented the greatest regional population.

Note

The collection of statistics on arson as a Crime Index offense began in 1979. However, 1993 annual figures are not available for inclusion in tables presenting statistics for the total United States. Arson totals reported by individual law enforcement agencies are displayed in Tables 8 through 11. Two-year arson trends are shown in Tables 12 through 15.

Table 1. — Index of Crime, United States, 1974-1993

Population[1]	Crime Index total[2]	Modified Crime Index total[3]	Violent crime[4]	Property crime[4]	Murder and non-negligent man-slaughter	Forcible rape	Robbery	Aggra-vated assault	Burglary	Larceny-theft	Motor vehicle theft	Arson[3]
					Number of Offenses							
Population by year:												
1974-211,392,000	10,253,400		974,720	9,278,700	20,710	55,400	442,400	456,210	3,039,200	5,262,500	977,100	
1975-213,124,000	11,292,400		1,039,710	10,252,700	20,510	56,090	470,500	492,620	3,265,300	5,977,700	1,009,600	
1976-214,659,000	11,349,700		1,004,210	10,345,500	18,780	57,080	427,810	500,530	3,108,700	6,270,800	966,000	
1977-216,332,000	10,984,500		1,029,580	9,955,000	19,120	63,500	412,610	534,350	3,071,500	5,905,700	977,700	
1978-218,059,000	11,209,000		1,085,550	10,123,400	19,560	67,610	426,930	571,460	3,128,300	5,991,000	1,004,100	
1979-220,099,000	12,249,500		1,208,030	11,041,500	21,460	76,390	480,700	629,480	3,327,700	6,601,000	1,112,800	
1980-225,349,264	13,408,300		1,344,520	12,063,700	23,040	82,990	565,840	672,650	3,795,200	7,136,900	1,131,700	
1981-229,146,000	13,423,800		1,361,820	12,061,900	22,520	82,500	592,910	663,900	3,779,700	7,194,400	1,087,800	
1982-231,534,000	12,974,400		1,322,390	11,652,000	21,010	78,770	553,130	669,480	3,447,100	7,142,500	1,062,400	
1983-233,981,000	12,108,600		1,258,090	10,850,500	19,310	78,920	506,570	653,290	3,129,900	6,712,800	1,007,900	
1984-236,158,000	11,881,800		1,273,280	10,608,500	18,690	84,230	485,010	685,350	2,984,400	6,591,900	1,032,200	
1985-238,740,000	12,431,400		1,328,800	11,102,600	18,980	88,670	497,870	723,250	3,073,300	6,926,400	1,102,900	
1986-241,077,000	13,211,900		1,489,170	11,722,700	20,610	91,460	542,780	834,320	3,241,400	7,257,200	1,224,100	
1987-243,400,000	13,508,700		1,484,000	12,024,700	20,100	91,110	517,700	855,090	3,236,200	7,499,900	1,288,700	
1988-245,807,000	13,923,100		1,566,220	12,356,900	20,680	92,490	542,970	910,090	3,218,100	7,705,900	1,432,900	
1989-248,239,000	14,251,400		1,646,040	12,605,400	21,500	94,500	578,330	951,710	3,168,200	7,872,400	1,564,800	
1990-248,709,873	14,475,600		1,820,130	12,655,500	23,440	102,560	639,270	1,054,860	3,073,900	7,945,700	1,635,900	
1991-252,177,000	14,872,900		1,911,770	12,961,100	24,700	106,590	687,730	1,092,740	3,157,200	8,142,200	1,661,700	
1992-255-082,000	14,438,200		1,932,270	12,505,900	23,760	109,060	672,480	1,126,970	2,979,900	7,915,200	1,610,800	
1993-257,908,000	14,141,000		1,924,190	12,216,800	24,530	104,810	659,760	1,135,100	2,834,800	7,820,900	1,561,000	
Percent change: number of offenses:												
1993/1992	-2.1		-.4	-2.3	+3.2	-3.9	-1.9	+.7	-4.9	-1.2	-3.1	
1993/1989	-.8		+16.9	-3.1	+14.1	+10.9	+14.1	+19.3	-10.5	-.7	-.2	
1993/1984	+19.0		+51.1	+15.2	+31.2	+24.4	+36.0	+65.6	-5.0	+18.6	+51.2	
					Rate per 100,000 Inhabitants							
Year:												
1974	4,850.4		461.1	4,389.3	9.8	26.2	209.3	215.8	1,437.7	2,489.5	462.2	
1975	5,298.5		487.8	4,810.7	9.6	26.3	220.8	231.1	1,532.1	2,804.8	473.7	
1976	5,287.3		467.8	4,819.5	8.8	26.6	199.3	233.2	1,448.2	2,921.3	450.0	
1977	5,077.6		475.9	4,601.7	8.8	29.4	190.7	247.0	1,419.8	2,729.9	451.9	
1978	5,140.3		497.8	4,642.5	9.0	31.0	195.8	262.1	1,434.6	2,747.4	460.5	
1979	5,565.5		548.9	5,016.6	9.7	34.7	218.4	286.0	1,511.9	2,999.1	505.6	
1980	5,950.0		596.6	5,353.3	10.2	36.8	251.1	298.5	1,684.1	3,167.0	502.2	
1981	5,858.2		594.3	5,263.9	9.8	36.0	258.7	289.7	1,649.5	3,139.7	474.7	
1982	5,603.6		571.1	5,032.5	9.1	34.0	238.9	289.2	1,488.8	3,084.8	458.8	
1983	5,175.0		537.7	4,637.4	8.3	33.7	216.5	279.2	1,337.7	2,868.9	430.8	
1984	5,031.3		539.2	4,492.1	7.9	35.7	205.4	290.2	1,263.7	2,791.3	437.1	
1985	5,207.1		556.6	4,650.5	7.9	37.1	208.5	302.9	1,287.3	2,901.2	462.0	
1986	5,480.4		617.7	4,862.6	8.6	37.9	225.1	346.1	1,344.6	3,010.3	507.8	
1987	5,550.0		609.7	4,940.3	8.3	37.4	212.7	351.3	1,329.6	3,081.3	529.4	
1988	5,664.2		637.2	5,027.1	8.4	37.6	220.9	370.2	1,309.2	3,134.9	582.9	
1989	5,741.0		663.1	5,077.9	8.7	38.1	233.0	383.4	1,276.3	3,171.3	630.4	
1990	5,820.3		731.8	5,088.5	9.4	41.2	257.0	424.1	1,235.9	3,194.8	657.8	
1991	5,897.8		758.1	5,139.7	9.8	42.3	272.7	433.3	1,252.0	3,228.8	659.0	
1992	5,660.2		757.5	4,902.7	9.3	42.8	263.6	441.8	1,168.2	3,103.0	631.5	
1993	5,482.9		746.1	4,736.9	9.5	40.6	255.8	440.1	1,099.2	3,032.4	605.3	
Percent change: rate per 100,000 inhabitants:												
1993/1992	-3.1		-1.5	-3.4	+2.2	-5.1	-3.0	-.4	-5.9	-2.3	-4.1	
1993/1989	-4.5		+12.5	-6.7	+9.2	+6.6	+9.8	+14.8	-13.9	-4.4	-4.0	
1993/1984	+9.0		+38.4	+5.4	+20.3	+13.7	+24.5	+51.7	-13.0	+8.6	+38.5	

[1]Populations are Bureau of the Census provisional estimates as of July 1, except 1980 and 1990 which are the decennial census counts.

[2]Because of rounding, the offenses may not add to totals.

[3]Although arson data are included in the trend and clearance tables, sufficient data are not available to estimate totals for this offense.

[4]Violent crimes are offenses of murder, forcible rape, robbery, and aggravated assault. Property crimes are offenses of burglary, larceny—theft, and motor vehicle theft. Data are not included for the property crime of arson.

Complete data for 1993 were not available for the states of Illinois and Kansas; therefore, it was necessary that their crime counts be estimated. See "Offense Estimation," page 376 for details.

All rates were calculated on the offenses before rounding.

Table 2. — Index of Crime, United States, 1993

Area	Population[1]	Crime Index total	Modified Crime Index total[2]	Violent crime[3]	Property crime[3]	Murder and non-negligent man-slaughter	Forcible rape	Robbery	Aggra-vated assault	Burglary	Larceny-theft	Motor vehicle theft	Arson[2]
United States Total	257,908,000	14,140,952		1,924,188	12,216,764	24,526	104,806	659,757	1,135,099	2,834,808	7,820,909	1,561,047	
Rate per 100,000 inhabitants		5,482.9		746.1	4,736.9	9.5	40.6	255.8	440.1	1,099.2	3,032.4	605.3	
Metropolitan Statistical Area	204,951,864												
Area actually reporting[4]	96.6%	12,158,473		1,725,319	10,433,154	21,514	86,573	634,848	982,384	2,377,910	6,594,975	1,460,269	
Estimated totals	100.0%	12,389,557		1,746,540	10,643,017	21,712	88,611	639,413	996,804	2,423,097	6,741,385	1,478,535	
Rate per 100,000 inhabitants		6,045.1		852.2	5,192.9	10.6	43.2	312.0	486.4	1,182.3	3,289.3	721.4	
Cities outside metropolitan areas	21,233,685												
Area actually reporting[4]	85.8%	997,708		94,508	903,200	979	7,319	13,391	72,819	185,845	675,069	42,286	
Estimated totals	100.0%	1,126,113		107,112	1,019,001	1,117	8,297	15,137	82,561	210,809	760,531	47,661	
Rate per 100,000 inhabitants		5,303.4		504.4	4,799.0	5.3	39.1	71.3	388.8	992.8	3,581.7	224.5	
Rural Counties	31,718,451												
Area actually reporting[4]	85.6%	561,222		62,093	499,129	1,470	7,141	4,576	48,906	179,631	288,150	31,348	
Estimated totals	100.0%	625,282		70,536	554,746	1,697	7,898	5,207	55,734	200,902	318,993	34,851	
Rate per 100,000 inhabitants		1,971.1		222.4	1,749.0	5.4	24.9	16.4	175.7	633.4	1,005.7	109.9	

[1]Populations are Bureau of the Census provisional estimates as of July 1, 1993, and are subject to change.

[2]Although arson data are included in the trend and clearance tables, sufficient data are not available to estimate totals for this offense.

[3]Violent crimes are offenses of murder, forcible rape, robbery, and aggravated assault. Property crimes are offenses of burglary, larceny-theft, and motor vehicle theft. Data are not included for the property crime of arson.

[4]The percentage representing area actually reporting will not coincide with the ratio between reported and estimated crime totals, since these data represent the sum of the calculations for individual states which have varying populations, portions reporting, and crime rates.

Complete data were not available for 1993 for the states of Illinois and Kansas; therefore, it was necessary that their crime counts be estimated. See "Offense Estimation," page 376 for details.

Table 3. — Index of Crime, Regional Offense and Population Distribution, 1993

Region	Population	Crime Index total	Modified Crime Index total[1]	Violent crime[2]	Property crime[2]	Murder and non-negligent man-slaughter	Forcible rape	Robbery	Aggra-vated assault	Burglary	Larceny-theft	Motor vehicle theft	Arson[1]
United States Total[3]	**100.0**	**100.0**		**100.0**	**100.0**	**100.0**	**100.0**	**100.0**	**100.0**	**100.0**	**100.0**	**100.0**	
Northeastern States	19.9	16.8		19.0	16.4	17.1	13.9	25.1	16.0	15.9	15.5	21.8	
Midwestern States	23.7	20.8		19.1	21.0	19.0	24.6	18.9	18.7	19.4	22.3	17.8	
Southern States	34.7	37.8		37.3	37.9	41.2	38.5	32.0	40.2	40.6	38.2	31.9	
Western States	21.7	24.7		24.6	24.7	22.7	22.9	24.1	25.1	24.1	24.1	28.5	

[1]Although arson data are included in the trend and clearance tables, sufficient data are not available to estimate totals for this offense.

[2]Violent crimes are offenses of murder, forcible rape, robbery, and aggravated assault. Property crimes are offenses of burglary, larceny-theft, and motor vechicle theft. Data are not included for the property crime of arson.

[3]Because of rounding, percentages may not add to totals.

Complete data were not available for 1993 for the states of Illinois and Kansas; therefore, it was necessary that their crime counts be estimated. See "Offense Estimation," page 376 for details.

Table 4. — Index of Crime: Region, Geographic Division, and State, 1992-1993

Area	Year	Population[1]	Crime Index total		Modified Crime Index total[2]		Violent crime[3]		Property crime[3]		Murder and non-negligent manslaughter	
			Number	Rate per 100,000	Number	Rate per 100,000	Number	Rate per 100,000	Number	Rate per 100,000	Number	Rate per 100,000
United States Total[4,5]	1992	255,082,000	14,438,191	5,660.2			1,932,274	757.5	12,505,917	4,902.7	23,760	9.3
	1993	257,908,000	14,140,952	5,482.9			1,924,188	746.1	12,216,764	4,736.9	24,526	9.5
Percent change			-2.1	-3.1			-.4	-1.5	-2.3	-3.4	+3.2	+2.2
Northeast	1992	51,118,000	2,472,428	4,836.7			373,913	731.5	2,098,515	4,105.2	4,007	7.8
	1993	51,355,000	2,368,814	4,612.6			366,162	713.0	2,002,652	3,899.6	4,203	8.2
Percent change			-4.2	-4.6			-2.1	-2.5	-4.6	-5.0	+4.9	+5.1
New England	1992	13,200,000	609,045	4,614.0			70,581	534.7	538,464	4,079.3	467	3.5
	1993	13,230,000	586,245	4,431.2			71,125	537.6	515,120	3,893.6	542	4.1
Percent change			-3.7	-4.0			+.8	+.5	-4.3	-4.6	+16.1	+17.1
Connecticut	1992	3,281,000	165,787	5,052.9			16,252	495.3	149,535	4,557.6	166	5.1
	1993	3,277,000	152,392	4,650.4			14,949	456.2	137,443	4,194.2	206	6.3
Percent change			-8.1	-8.0			-8.0	-7.9	-8.1	-8.0	+24.1	+23.5
Maine	1992	1,235,000	43,516	3,523.6			1,616	130.9	41,900	3,392.7	21	1.7
	1993	1,239,000	39,077	3,153.9			1,558	125.7	37,519	3,028.2	20	1.6
Percent change			-10.2	-10.5			-3.6	-4.0	-10.5	-10.7	-4.8	-5.9
Massachusetts	1992	5,998,000	300,071	5,002.9			46,727	779.0	253,344	4,223.8	214	3.6
	1993	6,012,000	294,224	4,893.9			48,393	804.9	245,831	4,089.0	233	3.9
Percent change			-1.9	-2.2			+3.6	+3.3	-3.0	-3.2	+8.9	+8.3
New Hampshire	1992	1,111,000	34,225	3,080.6			1,397	125.7	32,828	2,954.8	18	1.6
	1993	1,125,000	32,681	2,905.0			1,550	137.8	31,131	2,767.2	23	2.0
Percent change			-4.5	-5.7			+11.0	+9.6	-5.2	-6.3	+27.8	+25.0
Rhode Island	1992	1,005,000	46,009	4,578.0			3,965	394.5	42,044	4,183.5	36	3.6
	1993	1,000,000	44,990	4,499.0			4,017	401.7	40,973	4,097.3	39	3.9
Percent change			-2.2	-1.7			+1.3	+1.8	-2.5	-2.1	+8.3	+8.3
Vermont	1992	570,000	19,437	3,410.0			624	109.5	18,813	3,300.5	12	2.1
	1993	576,000	22,881	3,972.4			658	114.2	22,223	3,858.2	21	3.6
Percent change			+17.7	+16.5			+5.4	+4.3	+18.1	+16.9	+75.0	+71.4
Middle Atlantic	1992	37,918,000	1,863,383	4,914.2			303,332	800.0	1,560,051	4,114.3	3,540	9.3
	1993	38,125,000	1,782,569	4,675.6			295,037	773.9	1,487,532	3,901.7	3,661	9.6
Percent change			-4.3	-4.9			-2.7	-3.3	-4.6	-5.2	+3.4	+3.2
New Jersey	1992	7,789,000	394,463	5,064.4			48,745	625.8	345,718	4,438.5	397	5.1
	1993	7,879,000	378,257	4,800.8			49,390	626.9	328,867	4,174.0	418	5.3
Percent change			-4.1	-5.2			+1.3	+.2	-4.9	-6.0	+5.3	+3.9
New York	1992	18,119,000	1,061,489	5,858.4			203,311	1,122.1	858,178	4,736.3	2,397	13.2
	1993	18,197,000	1,010,176	5,551.3			195,352	1,073.5	814,824	4,477.8	2,420	13.3
Percent change			-4.8	-5.2			-3.9	-4.3	-5.1	-5.5	+1.0	+.8
Pennsylvania	1992	12,009,000	407,431	3,392.7			51,276	427.0	356,155	2,965.7	746	6.2
	1993	12,048,000	394,136	3,271.4			50,295	417.5	343,841	2,853.9	823	6.8
Percent change			-3.3	-3.6			-1.9	-2.2	-3.5	-3.8	+10.3	+9.7

See footnotes at end of table.

Table 4.—Index of Crime: Region, Geographic Division, and State, 1992-1993

Forcible rape		Robbery		Aggravated assault		Burglary		Larceny-theft		Motor vehicle theft		Arson[2]	
Number	Rate per 100,000	Number	Rate per 100,000	Number	Rate per 100,000	Number	Rate per 100,000	Number	Rate per 100,000	Number	Rate per 100,000	Number	Rate per 100,000
109,062	42.8	672,478	263.6	1,126,974	441.8	2,979,884	1,168.2	7,915,199	3,103.0	1,610,834	631.5		
104,806	40.6	659,757	255.8	1,135,099	440.1	2,834,808	1,099.2	7,820,909	3,032.4	1,561,047	605.3		
-3.9	-5.1	-1.9	-3.0	+.7	-.4	-4.9	-5.9	-1.2	-2.3	-3.1	-4.1		
15,089	29.5	171,704	335.9	183,113	358.2	477,880	934.9	1,248,896	2,443.2	371,739	727.2		
14,567	28.4	165,648	322.6	181,744	353.9	450,993	878.2	1,210,771	2,357.6	340,888	663.8		
-3.5	-3.7	-3.5	-4.0	-.7	-1.2	-5.6	-6.1	-3.1	-3.5	-8.3	-8.7		
4,221	32.0	19,633	148.7	46,260	350.5	132,990	1,007.5	322,352	2,442.1	83,122	629.7		
4,149	31.4	18,644	140.9	47,790	361.2	122,421	925.3	313,046	2,366.2	79,653	602.1		
-1.7	-1.9	-5.0	-5.2	+3.3	+3.1	-7.9	-8.2	-2.9	-3.1	-4.2	-4.4		
884	26.9	6,918	210.9	8,284	252.5	36,372	1,108.6	89,463	2,726.7	23,700	722.3		
800	24.4	6,447	196.7	7,496	228.7	32,052	978.1	85,876	2,620.6	19,515	595.5		
-9.5	-9.3	-6.8	-6.7	-9.5	-9.4	-11.9	-11.8	-4.0	-3.9	-17.7	-17.6		
294	23.8	288	23.3	1,013	82.0	10,156	822.3	29,966	2,426.4	1,778	144.0		
329	26.6	264	21.3	945	76.3	8,909	719.0	26,945	2,174.7	1,665	134.4		
+11.9	+11.8	-8.3	-8.6	-6.7	-7.0	-12.3	-12.6	-10.1	-10.4	-6.4	-6.7		
2,166	36.1	11,059	184.4	33,288	555.0	64,318	1,072.3	141,610	2,361.0	47,416	790.5		
2,006	33.4	10,563	175.7	35,591	592.0	60,220	1,001.9	136,548	2,271.3	49,063	816.1		
-7.4	-7.5	-4.5	-4.7	+6.9	+6.7	-6.4	-6.6	-3.6	-3.8	+3.5	+3.2		
424	38.2	367	33.0	588	52.9	6,909	621.9	23,754	2,138.1	2,165	194.9		
499	44.4	307	27.3	721	64.1	5,795	515.1	23,153	2,058.0	2,183	194.0		
+17.7	+16.2	-16.3	-17.3	+22.6	+21.2	-16.1	-17.2	-2.5	-3.7	+.8	-.5		
311	30.9	950	94.5	2,668	265.5	10,529	1,047.7	24,052	2,393.2	7,463	742.6		
286	28.6	1,011	101.1	2,681	268.1	10,409	1,040.9	24,101	2,410.1	6,463	646.3		
-8.0	-7.4	+6.4	+7.0	+.5	+1.0	-1.1	-.6	+.2	+.7	-13.4	-13.0		
142	24.9	51	8.9	419	73.5	4,706	825.6	13,507	2,369.6	600	105.3		
229	39.8	52	9.0	356	61.8	5,036	874.3	16,423	2,851.2	764	132.6		
+61.3	+59.8	+2.0	+1.1	-15.0	-15.9	+7.0	+5.9	+21.6	+20.3	+27.3	+25.9		
10,868	28.7	152,071	401.1	136,853	360.9	344,890	909.6	926,544	2,443.5	288,617	761.2		
10,418	27.3	147,004	385.6	133,954	351.4	328,572	861.8	897,725	2,354.7	261,235	685.2		
-4.1	-4.9	-3.3	-3.9	-2.1	-2.6	-4.7	-5.3	-3.1	-3.6	-9.5	-10.0		
2,392	30.7	22,216	285.2	23,740	304.8	75,508	969.4	206,686	2,653.6	63,524	815.6		
2,215	28.1	23,319	296.0	23,438	297.5	76,738	974.0	195,876	2,486.1	56,253	714.0		
-7.4	-8.5	+5.0	+3.8	-1.3	-2.4	+1.6	+.5	-5.2	-6.3	-11.4	-12.5		
5,152	28.4	108,154	596.9	87,608	483.5	193,548	1,068.2	495,708	2,735.8	168,922	932.3		
5,008	27.5	102,122	561.2	85,802	471.5	181,709	998.6	481,166	2,644.2	151,949	835.0		
-2.8	-3.2	-5.6	-6.0	-2.1	-2.5	-6.1	-6.5	-2.9	-3.3	-10.0	-10.4		
3,324	27.7	21,701	180.7	25,505	212.4	75,834	631.5	224,150	1,866.5	56,171	467.7		
3,195	26.5	21,563	179.0	24,714	205.1	70,125	582.0	220,683	1,831.7	53,033	440.2		
-3.9	-4.3	-.6	-.9	-3.1	-3.4	-7.5	-7.8	-1.5	-1.9	-5.6	-5.9		

Table 4. — Index of Crime: Region, Geographic Division, and State, 1992-1993 — Continued

Area	Year	Population[1]	Crime Index total		Modified Crime Index total[2]		Violent crime[3]		Property crime[3]		Murder and non-negligent manslaughter	
			Number	Rate per 100,000	Number	Rate per 100,000	Number	Rate per 100,000	Number	Rate per 100,000	Number	Rate per 100,000
Midwest[4,5]	1992	60,713,000	3,020,703	4,975.4			368,675	607.2	2,652,028	4,368.1	4,642	7.6
	1993	61,070,000	2,934,920	4,805.8			367,384	601.6	2,567,536	4,204.3	4,654	7.6
Percent change	.....	....	-2.8	-3.4			-.4	-.9	-3.2	-3.7	+.3	....
East North Central[4,5]	1992	42,753,000	2,195,617	5,135.6			286,868	671.0	1,908,749	4,464.6	3,666	8.6
	1993	43,017,000	2,130,716	4,953.2			284,458	661.3	1,846,258	4,291.9	3,584	8.3
Percent change	.....	....	-3.0	-3.6			-.8	-1.4	-3.3	-3.9	-2.2	-3.5
Illinois[4]	1992	11,631,000	670,564	5,765.3			113,664	977.3	556,900	4,788.1	1,322	11.4
	1993	11,697,000	657,129	5,617.9			112,260	959.7	544,869	4,658.2	1,332	11.4
Percent change	.....	....	-2.0	-2.6			-1.2	-1.8	-2.2	-2.7	+.8	....
Indiana	1992	5,662,000	265,375	4,686.9			28,791	508.5	236,584	4,178.5	464	8.2
	1993	5,713,000	255,090	4,465.1			27,941	489.1	227,149	3,976.0	430	7.5
Percent change	.....	....	-3.9	-4.7			-3.0	-3.8	-4.0	-4.8	-7.3	-8.5
Michigan[5]	1992	9,437,000	529,472	5,610.6			72,672	770.1	456,800	4,840.5	938	9.9
	1993	9,478,000	516,788	5,452.5			75,021	791.5	441,767	4,661.0	933	9.8
Percent change	.....	....					-3.3		-3.7		-.5	-1.0
Ohio	1992	11,016,000	513,952	4,665.5			57,935	525.9	456,017	4,139.6	724	6.6
	1993	11,091,000	497,465	4,485.3			55,915	504.1	441,550	3,981.2	667	6.0
Percent change	.....	....	-3.2	-3.9			-3.5	-4.1	-3.2	-3.8	-7.9	-9.1
Wisconsin	1992	5,007,000	216,254	4,319.0			13,806	275.7	202,448	4,043.3	218	4.4
	1993	5,038,000	204,244	4,054.1			13,321	264.4	190,923	3,789.7	222	4.4
Percent change	.....	....	-5.6	-6.1			-3.5	-4.1	-5.7	-6.3	+1.8	....
West North Central[4,5]	1992	17,960,000	825,086	4,594.0			81,807	455.5	743,279	4,138.5	976	5.4
	1993	18,054,000	804,204	4,454.4			82,926	459.3	721,278	3,995.1	1,070	5.9
Percent change	.....	....	-2.5	-3.0			+1.4	+.8	-3.0	-3.5	+9.6	+9.3
Iowa	1992	2,812,000	111,275	3,957.1			7,816	278.0	103,459	3,679.2	44	1.6
	1993	2,814,000	108,239	3,846.4			9,159	325.5	99,080	3,521.0	66	2.3
Percent change	.....	....	-2.7	-2.8			+17.1	+17.1	-4.2	-4.3	+50.0	+43.8
Kansas[4]	1992	2,523,000	134,222	5,319.9			12,888	510.8	121,334	4,809.1	151	6.0
	1993	2,531,000	125,924	4,975.3			12,564	496.4	113,360	4,478.8	161	6.4
Percent change	.....	....	-6.2	-6.5			-2.5	-2.8	-6.6	-6.9	+6.6	+6.7
Minnesota[5]	1992	4,480,000	205,664	4,590.7			15,144	338.0	190,520	4,252.7	150	3.3
	1993	4,517,000	198,125	4,386.2			14,778	327.2	183,347	4,059.0	155	3.4
Percent change	.....	....							-3.8	-4.6	+3.3	+3.0
Missouri	1992	5,193,000	264,694	5,097.1			38,448	740.4	226,246	4,356.7	547	10.5
	1993	5,234,000	266,694	5,095.4			38,963	744.4	227,731	4,351.0	590	11.3
Percent change	.....	....	+.8	....			+1.3	+.5	+.7	-.1	+7.9	+7.6
Nebraska	1992	1,606,000	69,444	4,324.0			5,598	348.6	63,846	3,975.5	68	4.2
	1993	1,607,000	66,162	4,117.1			5,450	339.1	60,712	3,778.0	63	3.9
Percent change	.....	....	-4.7	-4.8			-2.6	-2.7	-4.9	-5.0	-7.4	-7.1
North Dakota	1992	636,000	18,465	2,903.3			530	83.3	17,935	2,820.0	12	1.9
	1993	635,000	17,909	2,820.3			522	82.2	17,387	2,738.1	11	1.7
Percent change	.....	....	-3.0	-2.9			-1.5	-1.3	-3.1	-2.9	-8.3	-10.5
South Dakota	1992	711,000	21,322	2,998.9			1,383	194.5	19,939	2,804.4	4	.6
	1993	715,000	21,151	2,958.2			1,490	208.4	19,661	2,749.8	24	3.4
Percent change	.....	....	-.8	-1.4			+7.7	+7.1	-1.4	-1.9	+500.0	+466.7

See footnotes at end of table.

Forcible rape		Robbery		Aggravated assault		Burglary		Larceny-theft		Motor vehicle theft		Arson[2]	
Number	Rate per 100,000	Number	Rate per 100,000	Number	Rate per 100,000	Number	Rate per 100,000	Number	Rate per 100,000	Number	Rate per 100,000	Number	Rate per 100,000
27,639	**45.5**	**125,878**	**207.3**	**210,516**	**346.7**	**585,107**	**963.7**	**1,777,622**	**2,927.9**	**289,299**	**476.5**		
25,831	**42.3**	**124,558**	**204.0**	**212,341**	**347.7**	**549,398**	**899.6**	**1,740,711**	**2,850.4**	**277,427**	**454.3**		
-6.5	**-7.0**	**-1.0**	**-1.6**	**+.9**	**+.3**	**-6.1**	**-6.7**	**-2.1**	**-2.6**	**-4.1**	**-4.7**		
21,314	49.9	103,718	242.6	158,170	370.0	416,472	974.1	1,262,257	2,952.4	230,020	538.0		
19,733	45.9	101,117	235.1	160,024	372.0	391,402	909.9	1,240,107	2,882.8	214,749	499.2		
-7.4	-8.0	-2.5	-3.1	+1.2	+.5	-6.0	-6.6	-1.8	-2.4	-6.6	-7.2		
4,312	37.1	47,973	412.5	60,057	516.4	125,306	1,077.3	359,618	3,091.9	71,976	618.8		
4,046	34.6	44,584	381.2	62,298	532.6	118,788	1,015.5	360,730	3,084.0	65,351	558.7		
-6.2	-6.7	-7.1	-7.6	+3.7	+3.1	-5.2	-5.7	+.3	-.3	-9.2	-9.7		
2,398	42.4	6,921	122.2	19,008	335.7	53,907	952.1	157,181	2,776.1	25,496	450.3		
2,234	39.1	6,845	119.8	18,432	322.6	48,677	852.0	154,016	2,695.9	24,456	428.1		
-6.8	-7.8	-1.1	-2.0	-3.0	-3.9	-9.7	-10.5	-2.0	-2.9	-4.1	-4.9		
7,550	80.0	20,902	221.5	43,282	458.6	98,257	1,041.2	299,486	3,173.5	59,057	625.8		
6,740	71.1	22,601	238.5	44,747	472.1	93,143	982.7	290,333	3,063.2	58,291	615.0		
		+8.1	+7.7	+3.4	+2.9	-5.2	-5.6	-3.1	-3.5	-1.3	-1.7		
5,739	52.1	21,925	199.0	29,547	268.2	104,357	947.3	299,774	2,721.3	51,886	471.0		
5,444	49.1	21,373	192.7	28,431	256.3	97,394	878.1	295,880	2,667.7	48,276	435.3		
-5.1	-5.8	-2.5	-3.2	-3.8	-4.4	-6.7	-7.3	-1.3	-2.0	-7.0	-7.6		
1,315	26.3	5,997	119.8	6,276	125.3	34,645	691.9	146,198	2,919.9	21,605	431.5		
1,269	25.2	5,714	113.4	6,116	121.4	33,400	663.0	139,148	2,762.0	18,375	364.7		
-3.5	-4.2	-4.7	-5.3	-2.5	-3.1	-3.6	-4.2	-4.8	-5.4	-15.0	-15.5		
6,325	35.2	22,160	123.4	52,346	291.5	168,635	938.9	515,365	2,869.5	59,279	330.1		
6,098	33.8	23,441	129.8	52,317	289.8	157,996	875.1	500,604	2,772.8	62,678	347.2		
-3.6	-4.0	+5.8	+5.2	-.1	-.6	-6.3	-6.8	-2.9	-3.4	+5.7	+5.2		
528	18.8	1,113	39.6	6,131	218.0	21,197	753.8	77,788	2,766.3	4,474	159.1		
686	24.4	1,517	53.9	6,890	244.8	20,562	730.7	73,148	2,599.4	5,370	190.8		
+29.9	+29.8	+36.3	+36.1	+12.4	+12.3	-3.0	-3.1	-6.0	-6.0	+20.0	+19.9		
1,042	41.3	3,277	129.9	8,418	333.7	32,639	1,293.7	80,526	3,191.7	8,169	323.8		
1,016	40.1	3,128	123.6	8,259	326.3	28,655	1,132.2	76,538	3,024.0	8,167	322.7		
-2.5	-2.9	-4.5	-4.8	-1.9	-2.2	-12.2	-12.5	-5.0	-5.3	....	-.3		
1,840	41.1	4,906	109.5	8,248	184.1	39,859	889.7	134,750	3,007.8	15,911	355.2		
1,588	35.2	5,092	112.7	7,943	175.8	38,147	844.5	129,727	2,872.0	15,473	342.6		
		+3.8	+2.9	-3.7	-4.5	-4.3	-5.1	-3.7	-4.5	-2.8	-3.5		
1,895	36.5	11,783	226.9	24,223	466.5	57,127	1,100.1	143,288	2,759.3	25,831	497.4		
1,894	36.2	12,654	241.8	23,825	455.2	53,673	1,025.5	145,392	2,777.8	28,666	547.7		
-.1	-.8	+7.4	+6.6	-1.6	-2.4	-6.0	-6.8	+1.5	+.7	+11.0	+10.1		
504	31.4	911	56.7	4,115	256.2	11,477	714.6	49,144	3,060.0	3,225	200.8		
447	27.8	890	55.4	4,050	252.0	10,662	663.5	46,811	2,912.9	3,239	201.6		
-11.3	-11.5	-2.3	-2.3	-1.6	-1.6	-7.1	-7.2	-4.7	-4.8	+.4	+.4		
148	23.3	50	7.9	320	50.3	2,487	391.0	14,498	2,279.6	950	149.4		
149	23.5	53	8.3	309	48.7	2,370	373.2	14,073	2,216.2	944	148.7		
+.7	+.9	+6.0	+5.1	-3.4	-3.2	-4.7	-4.6	-2.9	-2.8	-.6	-.5		
368	51.8	120	16.9	891	125.3	3,849	541.4	15,371	2,161.9	719	101.1		
318	44.5	107	15.0	1,041	145.6	3,927	549.2	14,915	2,086.0	819	114.5		
-13.6	-14.1	-10.8	-11.2	+16.8	+16.2	+2.0	+1.4	-3.0	-3.5	+13.9	+13.3		

Table 4. — Index of Crime: Region, Geographic Division, and State, 1992-1993 — Continued

Area	Year	Population[1]	Crime Index total — Number	Crime Index total — Rate per 100,000	Modified Crime Index total[2] — Number	Modified Crime Index total[2] — Rate per 100,000	Violent crime[3] — Number	Violent crime[3] — Rate per 100,000	Property crime[3] — Number	Property crime[3] — Rate per 100,000	Murder and non-negligent manslaughter — Number	Murder and non-negligent manslaughter — Rate per 100,000
South	1992	88,143,000	5,424,811	6,154.6			713,565	809.6	4,711,246	5,345.0	9,761	11.1
	1993	89,438,000	5,351,303	5,983.3			717,267	802.0	4,634,036	5,181.3	10,113	11.3
Percent change			-1.4	-2.8			+.5	-.9	-1.6	-3.1	+3.6	+1.8
South Atlantic	1992	45,061,000	2,896,666	6,428.3			390,742	867.1	2,505,924	5,561.2	4,795	10.6
	1993	45,738,000	2,896,819	6,333.5			398,635	871.6	2,498,184	5,461.9	4,961	10.8
Percent change				-1.5			+2.0	+.5	-.3	-1.8	+3.5	+1.9
Delaware	1992	689,000	33,406	4,848.5			4,280	621.2	29,126	4,227.3	32	4.6
	1993	700,000	34,105	4,872.1			4,801	685.9	29,304	4,186.3	35	5.0
Percent change			+2.1	+.5			+12.2	+10.4	+.6	-1.0	+9.4	+8.7
District of Columbia[6]	1992	589,000	67,187	11,407.0			16,685	2,832.8	50,502	8,574.2	443	75.2
	1993	578,000	67,979	11,761.1			16,888	2,921.8	51,091	8,839.3	454	78.5
Percent change			+1.2	+3.1			+1.2	+3.1	+1.2	+3.1	+2.5	+4.4
Florida	1992	13,488,000	1,127,360	8,358.2			162,827	1,207.2	964,533	7,151.0	1,208	9.0
	1993	13,679,000	1,142,338	8,351.0			164,975	1,206.0	977,363	7,145.0	1,224	8.9
Percent change			+1.3	-.1			+1.3	-.1	+1.3	-.1	+1.3	-1.1
Georgia	1992	6,751,000	432,430	6,405.4			49,496	733.2	382,934	5,672.3	741	11.0
	1993	6,917,000	428,367	6,193.0			50,019	723.1	378,348	5,469.8	789	11.4
Percent change			-.9	-3.3			+1.1	-1.4	-1.2	-3.6	+6.5	+3.6
Maryland	1992	4,908,000	305,503	6,224.6			49,085	1,000.1	256,418	5,224.5	596	12.1
	1993	4,965,000	303,187	6,106.5			49,540	997.8	253,647	5,108.7	632	12.7
Percent change			-.8	-1.9			+.9	-.2	-1.1	-2.2	+6.0	+5.0
North Carolina	1992	6,843,000	397,047	5,802.2			46,600	681.0	350,447	5,121.2	723	10.6
	1993	6,945,000	392,555	5,652.3			47,178	679.3	345,377	4,973.0	785	11.3
Percent change			-1.1	-2.6			+1.2	-.2	-1.4	-2.9	+8.6	+6.6
South Carolina	1992	3,603,000	212,327	5,893.1			34,029	944.5	178,298	4,948.6	373	10.4
	1993	3,643,000	215,060	5,903.4			37,281	1,023.4	177,779	4,880.0	377	10.3
Percent change			+1.3	+.2			+9.6	+8.4	-.3	-1.4	+1.1	-1.0
Virginia	1992	6,377,000	274,118	4,298.5			23,907	374.9	250,211	3,923.6	564	8.8
	1993	6,491,000	267,135	4,115.5			24,160	372.2	242,975	3,743.3	539	8.3
Percent change			-2.5	-4.3			+1.1	-.7	-2.9	-4.6	-4.4	-5.7
West Virginia	1992	1,812,000	47,288	2,609.7			3,833	211.5	43,455	2,398.2	115	6.3
	1993	1,820,000	46,093	2,532.6			3,793	208.4	42,300	2,324.2	126	6.9
Percent change			-2.5	-3.0			-1.0	-1.5	-2.7	-3.1	+9.6	+9.5
East South Central	1992	15,529,000	712,653	4,589.2			104,409	672.3	608,244	3,916.8	1,511	9.7
	1993	15,717,000	711,722	4,528.4			100,720	640.8	611,002	3,887.5	1,611	10.3
Percent change			-.1	-1.3			-3.5	-4.7	+.5	-.7	+6.6	+6.2
Alabama	1992	4,136,000	217,889	5,268.1			36,052	871.7	181,837	4,396.4	455	11.0
	1993	4,187,000	204,274	4,878.8			32,676	780.4	171,598	4,098.4	484	11.6
Percent change			-6.2	-7.4			-9.4	-10.5	-5.6	-6.8	+6.4	+5.5
Kentucky	1992	3,755,000	124,799	3,323.5			20,107	535.5	104,692	2,788.1	216	5.8
	1993	3,789,000	123,509	3,259.7			17,530	462.7	105,979	2,797.0	249	6.6
Percent change			-1.0	-1.9			-12.8	-13.6	+1.2	+.3	+15.3	+13.8
Mississippi	1992	2,614,000	111,944	4,282.5			10,763	411.7	101,181	3,870.7	320	12.2
	1993	2,643,000	116,775	4,418.3			11,467	433.9	105,308	3,984.4	357	13.5
Percent change			+4.3	+3.2			+6.5	+5.4	+4.1	+2.9	+11.6	+10.7
Tennessee	1992	5,024,000	258,021	5,135.8			37,487	746.2	220,534	4,389.6	520	10.4
	1993	5,099,000	267,164	5,239.5			39,047	765.8	228,117	4,473.8	521	10.2
Percent change			+3.5	+2.0			+4.2	+2.6	+3.4	+1.9	+.2	-1.9
West South Central	1992	27,554,000	1,815,492	6,588.9			218,414	792.7	1,597,078	5,796.2	3,455	12.5
	1993	27,983,000	1,742,762	6,227.9			217,912	778.7	1,524,850	5,449.2	3,541	12.7
Percent change			-4.0	-5.5			-.2	-1.8	-4.5	-6.0	+2.5	+1.6
Arkansas	1992	2,399,000	114,233	4;761.7			13,831	576.5	100,402	4,185.2	259	10.8
	1993	2,424,000	116,612	4,810.7			14,381	593.3	102,231	4,217.5	247	10.2
Percent change			+2.1	+1.0			+4.0	+2.9	+1.8	+.8	-4.6	-5.6
Louisiana	1992	4,287,000	280,647	6,546.5			42,209	984.6	238,438	5,561.9	747	17.4
	1993	4,295,000	294,061	6,846.6			45,600	1,061.7	248,461	5,784.9	874	20.3
Percent change			+4.8	+4.6			+8.0	+7.8	+4.2	+4.0	+17.0	+16.7
Oklahoma	1992	3,212,000	174,464	5,431.6			20,005	622.8	154,459	4,808.8	210	6.5
	1993	3,231,000	171,058	5,294.3			20,512	634.8	150,546	4,659.4	273	8.4
Percent change			-2.0	-2.5			+2.5	+1.9	-2.5	-3.1	+30.0	+29.2
Texas	1992	17,656,000	1,246,148	7,057.9			142,369	806.3	1,103,779	6,251.6	2,239	12.7
	1993	18,031,000	1,161,031	6,439.1			137,419	762.1	1,023,612	5,677.0	2,147	11.9
Percent change			-6.8	-8.8			-3.5	-5.5	-7.3	-9.2	-4.1	-6.3

See footnotes at end of table.

Table 4. — Index of Crime: Region, Geographic Division, and State, 1992-1993 — Continued

Forcible rape		Robbery		Aggravated assault		Burglary		Larceny-theft		Motor vehicle theft		Arson[2]	
Number	Rate per 100,000	Number	Rate per 100,000	Number	Rate per 100,000	Number	Rate per 100,000	Number	Rate per 100,000	Number	Rate per 100,000	Number	Rate per 100,000
40,631	**46.1**	**212,328**	**240.9**	**450,845**	**511.5**	**1,215,309**	**1,378.8**	**2,986,605**	**3,388.4**	**509,332**	**577.8**		
40,387	**45.2**	**210,872**	**235.8**	**455,895**	**509.7**	**1,149,850**	**1,285.6**	**2,986,483**	**3,339.2**	**497,703**	**556.5**		
-.6	**-2.0**	**-.7**	**-2.1**	**+1.1**	**-.4**	**-5.4**	**-6.8**	**.........**	**-1.5**	**-2.3**	**-3.7**		
20,379	45.2	124,407	276.1	241,161	535.2	644,286	1,429.8	1,609,647	3,572.2	251,991	559.2		
19,587	42.8	126,250	276.0	247,837	541.9	622,717	1,361.5	1,613,636	3,528.0	261,831	572.5		
-3.9	-5.3	+1.5	....	+2.8	+1.3	-3.3	-4.8	+.2	-1.2	+3.9	+2.4		
591	85.8	1,042	151.2	2,615	379.5	6,598	957.6	20,419	2,963.6	2,109	306.1		
539	77.0	1,307	186.7	2,920	417.1	6,244	892.0	20,853	2,979.0	2,207	315.3		
-8.8	-10.3	+25.4	+23.5	+11.7	+9.9	-5.4	-6.9	+2.1	+.5	+4.6	+3.0		
215	36.5	7,459	1,266.4	8,568	1,454.7	10,721	1,820.2	30,663	5,205.9	9,118	1,548.0		
324	56.1	7,107	1,229.6	9,003	1,557.6	11,534	1,995.5	31,495	5,449.0	8,062	1,394.8		
+50.7	+53.7	-4.7	-2.9	+5.1	+7.1	+7.6	+9.6	+2.7	+4.7	-11.6	-9.9		
7,310	54.2	49,482	366.9	104,827	777.2	254,755	1,888.8	598,093	4,434.3	111,685	828.0		
7,359	53.8	48,913	357.6	107,479	785.7	251,063	1,835.4	603,784	4,413.9	122,516	895.7		
+.7	-.7	-1.1	-2.5	+2.5	+1.1	-1.4	-2.8	+1.0	-.5	+9.7	+8.2		
3,057	45.3	16,863	249.8	28,835	427.1	97,402	1,442.8	246,619	3,653.1	38,913	576.4		
2,448	35.4	17,154	248.0	29,628	428.3	90,423	1,307.3	246,849	3,568.7	41,076	593.8		
-19.9	-21.9	+1.7	-.7	+2.8	+.3	-7.2	-9.4	+.1	-2.3	+5.6	+3.0		
2,278	46.4	21,054	429.0	25,157	512.6	55,520	1,131.2	165,244	3,366.8	35,654	726.4		
2,185	44.0	21,582	434.7	25,141	506.4	56,246	1,132.8	163,471	3,292.5	33,930	683.4		
-4.1	-5.2	+2.5	+1.3	-.1	-1.2	+1.3	+.1	-1.1	-2.2	-4.8	-5.9		
2,455	35.9	12,784	186.8	30,638	447.7	113,117	1,653.0	217,717	3,181.6	19,613	286.6		
2,379	34.3	13,364	192.4	30,650	441.3	105,270	1,515.8	220,071	3,168.8	20,036	288.5		
-3.1	-4.5	+4.5	+3.0	+.1	-1.4	-6.9	-8.3	+1.1	-.4	+2.2	+.7		
2,072	57.5	6,148	170.6	25,436	706.0	49,669	1,378.6	116,186	3,224.7	12,443	345.4		
1,905	52.3	6,825	187.3	28,174	773.4	47,695	1,309.2	117,553	3,226.8	12,531	344.0		
-8.1	-9.0	+11.0	+9.8	+10.8	+9.5	-4.0	-5.0	+1.2	+.1	+.7	-.4		
2,008	31.5	8,787	137.8	12,548	196.8	45,217	709.1	185,506	2,909.0	19,488	305.6		
2,083	32.1	9,216	142.0	12,322	189.8	43,338	667.7	181,104	2,790.1	18,533	285.5		
+3.7	+1.9	+4.9	+3.0	-1.8	-3.6	-4.2	-5.8	-2.4	-4.1	-4.9	-6.6		
393	21.7	788	43.5	2,537	140.0	11,287	622.9	29,200	1,611.5	2,968	163.8		
365	20.1	782	43.0	2,520	138.5	10,904	599.1	28,456	1,563.5	2,940	161.5		
-7.1	-7.4	-.8	-1.1	-.7	-1.1	-3.4	-3.8	-2.5	-3.0	-.9	-1.4		
6,456	41.6	24,310	156.5	72,132	464.5	173,629	1,118.1	373,772	2,406.9	60,843	391.8		
6,441	41.0	25,009	159.1	67,659	430.5	167,903	1,068.3	381,773	2,429.0	61,326	390.2		
-.2	-1.4	+2.9	+1.7	-6.2	-7.3	-3.3	-4.5	+2.1	+.9	+.8	-.4		
1,704	41.2	6,819	164.9	27,074	654.6	49,053	1,186.0	117,801	2,848.2	14,983	362.3		
1,471	35.1	6,677	159.5	24,044	574.3	45,578	1,088.6	111,878	2,672.0	14,142	337.8		
-13.7	-14.8	-2.1	-3.3	-11.2	-12.3	-7.1	-8.2	-5.0	-6.2	-5.6	-6.8		
1,209	32.2	3,273	87.2	15,409	410.4	27,378	729.1	69,186	1,842.5	8,128	216.5		
1,301	34.3	3,425	90.4	12,555	331.4	28,041	740.1	69,745	1,840.7	8,193	216.2		
+7.6	+6.5	+4.6	+3.7	-18.5	-19.2	+2.4	+1.5	+.8	-.1	+.8	-.1		
1,166	44.6	3,254	124.5	6,023	230.4	33,533	1,282.8	58,851	2,251.4	8,797	336.5		
1,125	42.6	3,683	139.3	6,302	238.4	33,985	1,285.8	62,467	2,363.5	8,856	335.1		
-3.5	-4.5	+13.2	+11.9	+4.6	+3.5	+1.3	+.2	+6.1	+5.0	+.7	-.4		
2,377	47.3	10,964	218.2	23,626	470.3	63,665	1,267.2	127,934	2,546.5	28,935	575.9		
2,544	49.9	11,224	220.1	24,758	485.5	60,299	1,182.6	137,683	2,700.2	30,135	591.0		
+7.0	+5.5	+2.4	+.9	+4.8	+3.2	-5.3	-6.7	+7.6	+6.0	+4.1	+2.6		
13,796	50.1	63,611	230.9	137,552	499.2	397,394	1,442.2	1,003,186	3,640.8	196,498	713.1		
14,359	51.3	59,613	213.0	140,399	501.7	359,230	1,283.7	991,074	3,541.7	174,546	623.8		
+4.1	+2.4	-6.3	-7.8	+2.1	+.5	-9.6	-11.0	-1.2	-2.7	-11.2	-12.5		
990	41.3	3,011	125.5	9,571	399.0	26,214	1,092.7	66,288	2,763.2	7,900	329.3		
1,028	42.4	3,027	124.9	10,079	415.8	26,646	1,099.3	67,767	2,795.7	7,818	322.5		
+3.8	+2.7	+.5	-.5	+5.3	+4.2	+1.6	+.6	+2.2	+1.2	-1.0	-2.1		
1,813	42.3	11,636	271.4	28,013	653.4	58,574	1,366.3	152,938	3,567.5	26,926	628.1		
1,817	42.3	12,182	283.6	30,727	715.4	58,768	1,368.3	163,334	3,802.9	26,359	613.7		
+.2	....	+4.7	+4.5	+9.7	+9.5	+.3	+.1	+6.8	+6.6	-2.1	-2.3		
1,556	48.4	4,376	136.2	13,863	431.6	43,678	1,359.8	94,180	2,932.1	16,601	516.8		
1,592	49.3	3,935	121.8	14,712	455.3	39,903	1,235.0	95,111	2,943.7	15,532	480.7		
+2.3	+1.9	-10.1	-10.6	+6.1	+5.5	-8.6	-9.2	+1.0	+.4	-6.4	-7.0		
9,437	53.4	44,588	252.5	86,105	487.7	268,928	1,523.2	689,780	3,906.8	145,071	821.7		
9,922	55.0	40,469	224.4	84,881	470.8	233,913	1,297.3	664,862	3,687.3	124,837	692.3		
+5.1	+3.0	-9.2	-11.1	-1.4	-3.5	-13.0	-14.8	-3.6	-5.6	-13.9	-15.7		

Table 4. — Index of Crime: Region, Geographic Division, and State, 1992-1993 — Continued

Area	Year	Population[1]	Crime Index total Number	Crime Index total Rate per 100,000	Modified Crime Index total[2] Number	Modified Crime Index total[2] Rate per 100,000	Violent crime[3] Number	Violent crime[3] Rate per 100,000	Property crime[3] Number	Property crime[3] Rate per 100,000	Murder and non-negligent manslaughter Number	Murder and non-negligent manslaughter Rate per 100,000
West	1992	55,108,000	3,520,249	6,387.9			476,121	864.0	3,044,128	5,523.9	5,350	9.7
	1993	56,044,000	3,485,915	6,220.0			473,375	844.6	3,012,540	5,375.3	5,556	9.9
Percent change	.....	....	-1.0	-2.6			-.6	-2.2	-1.0	-2.7	+3.9	+2.1
Mountain	1992	14,381,000	864,572	6,011.9			80,979	563.1	783,593	5,448.8	946	6.6
	1993	14,776,000	876,127	5,929.4			87,082	589.3	789,045	5,340.0	950	6.4
Percent change			+1.3	-1.4			+7.5	+4.7	+.7	-2.0	+.4	-3.0
Arizona	1992	3,832,000	269,335	7,028.6			25,706	670.8	243,629	6,357.8	312	8.1
	1993	3,936,000	292,513	7,431.7			28,142	715.0	264,371	6,716.7	339	8.6
Percent change	.....	....	+8.6	+5.7			+9.5	+6.6	+8.5	+5.6	+8.7	+6.2
Colorado	1992	3,470,000	206,770	5,958.8			20,086	578.8	186,684	5,379.9	216	6.2
	1993	3,566,000	197,085	5,526.8			20,229	567.3	176,856	4,959.5	206	5.8
Percent change	.....	....	-4.7	-7.2			+.7	-2.0	-5.3	-7.8	-4.6	-6.5
Idaho	1992	1,067,000	42,639	3,996.2			3,003	281.4	39,636	3,714.7	37	3.5
	1993	1,099,000	42,258	3,845.1			3,097	281.8	39,161	3,563.3	32	2.9
Percent change	.....	....	-.9	-3.8			+3.1	+.1	-1.2	-4.1	-13.5	-17.1
Montana	1992	824,000	37,872	4,596.1			1,400	169.9	36,472	4,426.2	24	2.9
	1993	839,000	40,188	4,790.0			1,489	177.5	38,699	4,612.5	25	3.0
Percent change	.....	....	+6.1	+4.2			+6.4	+4.5	+6.1	+4.2	+4.2	+3.4
Nevada	1992	1,327,000	82,324	6,203.8			9,247	696.8	73,077	5,506.9	145	10.9
	1993	1,389,000	85,842	6,180.1			12,157	875.2	73,685	5,304.9	144	10.4
Percent change	.....	....	+4.3	-.4			+31.5	+25.6	+.8	-3.7	-.7	-4.6
New Mexico	1992	1,581,000	101,723	6,434.1			14,781	934.9	86,942	5,499.2	141	8.9
	1993	1,616,000	101,260	6,266.1			15,024	929.7	86,236	5,336.4	130	8.0
Percent change	.....	....	-.5	-2.6			+1.6	-.6	-.8	-3.0	-7.8	-10.1
Utah	1992	1,813,000	102,589	5,658.5			5,267	290.5	97,322	5,368.0	54	3.0
	1993	1,860,000	97,415	5,237.4			5,599	301.0	91,816	4,936.3	58	3.1
Percent change	.....	....	-5.0	-7.4			+6.3	+3.6	-5.7	-8.0	+7.4	+3.3
Wyoming	1992	466,000	21,320	4,575.1			1,489	319.5	19,831	4,255.6	17	3.6
	1993	470,000	19,566	4,163.0			1,345	286.2	18,221	3,876.8	16	3.4
Percent change	.....	....	-8.2	-9.0			-9.7	-10.4	-8.1	-8.9	-5.9	-5.6
Pacific	1992	40,726,000	2,655,677	6,520.8			395,142	970.2	2,260,535	5,550.6	4,404	10.8
	1993	41,269,000	2,609,788	6,323.8			386,293	936.0	2,223,495	5,387.8	4,606	11.2
Percent change	.....	....	-1.7	-3.0			-2.2	-3.5	-1.6	-2.9	+4.6	+3.7
Alaska	1992	587,000	32,693	5,569.5			3,877	660.5	28,816	4,909.0	44	7.5
	1993	599,000	33,352	5,567.9			4,557	760.8	28,795	4,807.2	54	9.0
Percent change	.....	....	+2.0	....			+17.5	+15.2	-.1	-2.1	+22.7	+20.0
California	1992	30,867,000	2,061,761	6,679.5			345,624	1,119.7	1,716,137	5,559.8	3,921	12.7
	1993	31,211,000	2,015,265	6,456.9			336,381	1,077.8	1,678,884	5,379.1	4,096	13.1
Percent change	.....	....	-2.3	-3.3			-2.7	-3.7	-2.2	-3.3	+4.5	+3.1
Hawaii	1992	1,160,000	70,899	6,112.0			2,998	258.4	67,901	5,853.5	42	3.6
	1993	1,172,000	73,566	6,277.0			3,061	261.2	70,505	6,015.8	45	3.8
Percent change	.....	....	+3.8	+2.7			+2.1	+1.1	+3.8	+2.8	+7.1	+5.6
Oregon	1992	2,977,000	173,289	5,820.9			15,189	510.2	158,100	5,310.7	139	4.7
	1993	3,032,000	174,812	5,765.6			15,254	503.1	159,558	5,262.5	140	4.6
Percent change	.....	....	+.9	-1.0			+.4	-1.4	+.9	-.9	+.7	-2.1
Washington	1992	5,136,000	317,035	6,172.8			27,454	534.5	289,581	5,638.3	258	5.0
	1993	5,255,000	312,793	5,952.3			27,040	514.6	285,753	5,437.7	271	5.2
Percent change	.....	....	-1.3	-3.6			-1.5	-3.7	-1.3	-3.6	+5.0	+4.0
Puerto Rico[7]	1992		128,874				32,286		96,588		864	
	1993		121,029				26,336		94,693		948	
Percent change	.....		-6.1				-18.4		-2.0		+9.7	

[1]Populations are Bureau of the Census provisional estimates as of July 1 and are subject to change.

[2]Although arson data are included in the trend and clearance tables, sufficient data are not available to estimate totals for this offense.

[3]Violent crimes are offenses of murder, forcible rape, robbery, and aggravated assault. Property crimes are offenses of burglary, larceny-theft, and motor vehicle theft. Data are not included for the property crime of arson.

[4]Complete data for 1993 were not available for the states of Illinois and Kansas; therefore, it was necessary that their crime counts be estimated. See "Offense Estimation," page 376 for details.

[5]Forcible rape figures furnished by the state-level Uniform Crime Reporting (UCR) Programs administered by the Michigan State Police and Minnesota Department of Public Safety were not in accordance with national UCR guidelines. The 1993 forcible rape totals for Michigan and Minnesota were estimated using the national rate of forcible rapes when grouped by like agencies. See "Offense Estimation," page 376 for details. No percent changes are shown for Michigan and Minnesota for the forcible rape, violent crime, and Crime Index total categories because the figures are not comparable.

[6]Includes offenses reported by the Zoological Police.

[7]The 1993 Bureau of Census population estimate for Puerto Rico was not available prior to publication; therefore, no population or rates per 100,000 inhabitants are provided. Data for Puerto Rico are not included in totals.

Offense totals are based on all reporting agencies and estimates for unreported areas.

Table 4. — Index of Crime: Region, Geographic Division, and State, 1992-1993 — Continued

Forcible rape		Robbery		Aggravated assault		Burglary		Larceny-theft		Motor vehicle theft		Arson[2]	
Number	Rate per 100,000	Number	Rate per 100,000	Number	Rate per 100,000	Number	Rate per 100,000	Number	Rate per 100,000	Number	Rate per 100,000	Number	Rate per 100,000
25,703	**46.6**	**162,568**	**295.0**	**282,500**	**512.6**	**701,588**	**1,273.1**	**1,902,076**	**3,451.5**	**440,464**	**799.3**		
24,021	**42.9**	**158,679**	**283.1**	**285,119**	**508.7**	**684,567**	**1,221.5**	**1,882,944**	**3,359.8**	**445,029**	**794.1**		
-6.5	**-7.9**	**-2.4**	**-4.0**	**+.9**	**-.8**	**-2.4**	**-4.1**	**-1.0**	**-2.7**	**+1.0**	**-.7**		
6,646	46.2	18,195	126.5	55,192	383.8	165,364	1,149.9	545,241	3,791.4	72,988	507.5		
6,421	43.5	19,162	129.7	60,549	409.8	165,027	1,116.9	547,845	3,707.7	76,173	515.5		
-3.4	-5.8	+5.3	+2.5	+9.7	+6.8	-.2	-2.9	+.5	-2.2	+4.4	+1.6		
1,647	43.0	5,867	153.1	17,880	466.6	54,095	1,411.7	158,053	4,124.6	31,481	821.5		
1,488	37.8	6,412	162.9	19,903	505.7	57,684	1,465.5	172,689	4,387.4	33,998	863.8		
-9.7	-12.1	+9.3	+6.4	+11.3	+8.4	+6.6	+3.8	+9.3	+6.4	+8.0	+5.1		
1,641	47.3	4,180	120.5	14,049	404.9	37,853	1,090.9	131,169	3,780.1	17,662	509.0		
1,633	45.8	4,160	116.7	14,230	399.0	36,011	1,009.8	124,787	3,499.4	16,058	450.3		
-.5	-3.2	-.5	-3.2	+1.3	-1.5	-4.9	-7.4	-4.9	-7.4	-9.1	-11.5		
339	31.8	229	21.5	2,398	224.7	7,934	743.6	30,023	2,813.8	1,679	157.4		
388	35.3	186	16.9	2,491	226.7	7,350	668.8	29,795	2,711.1	2,016	183.4		
+14.5	+11.0	-18.8	-21.4	+3.9	+.9	-7.4	-10.0	-.8	-3.6	+20.1	+16.5		
210	25.5	222	26.9	944	114.6	5,306	643.9	29,243	3,548.9	1,923	233.4		
234	27.9	272	32.4	958	114.2	5,992	714.2	30,641	3,652.1	2,066	246.2		
+11.4	+9.4	+22.5	+20.4	+1.5	-.3	+12.9	+10.9	+4.8	+2.9	+7.4	+5.5		
833	62.8	4,397	331.3	3,872	291.8	17,108	1,289.2	46,714	3,520.3	9,255	697.4		
846	60.9	4,724	340.1	6,443	463.9	17,293	1,245.0	46,137	3,321.6	10,255	738.3		
+1.6	-3.0	+7.4	+2.7	+66.4	+59.0	+1.1	-3.4	-1.2	-5.6	+11.0	+5.9		
990	62.6	2,202	139.3	11,448	724.1	23,896	1,511.4	57,072	3,609.9	5,974	377.9		
842	52.1	2,237	138.4	11,815	731.1	22,966	1,421.2	56,723	3,510.1	6,547	405.1		
-14.9	-16.8	+1.6	-.6	+3.2	+1.0	-3.9	-6.0	-.6	-2.8	+9.6	+7.2		
823	45.4	1,014	55.9	3,376	186.2	16,045	885.0	76,964	4,245.1	4,313	237.9		
829	44.6	1,090	58.6	3,622	194.7	14,708	790.8	72,603	3,903.4	4,505	242.2		
+.7	-1.8	+7.5	+4.8	+7.3	+4.6	-8.3	-11.0	-5.7	-8.0	+4.5	+1.8		
163	35.0	84	18.0	1,225	262.9	3,127	671.0	16,003	3,434.1	701	150.4		
161	34.3	81	17.2	1,087	231.3	3,023	643.2	14,470	3,078.7	728	154.9		
-1.2	-2.0	-3.6	-4.4	-11.3	-12.0	-3.3	-4.1	-9.6	-10.3	+3.9	+3.0		
19,057	46.8	144,373	354.5	227,308	558.1	536,224	1,316.7	1,356,835	3,331.6	367,476	902.3		
17,600	42.6	139,517	338.1	224,570	544.2	519,540	1,258.9	1,335,099	3,235.1	368,856	893.8		
-7.6	-9.0	-3.4	-4.6	-1.2	-2.5	-3.1	-4.4	-1.6	-2.9	+.4	-.9		
579	98.6	640	109.0	2,614	445.3	5,170	880.7	20,728	3,531.2	2,918	497.1		
502	83.8	733	122.4	3,268	545.6	4,893	816.9	21,201	3,539.4	2,701	450.9		
-13.3	-15.0	+14.5	+12.3	+25.0	+22.5	-5.4	-7.2	+2.3	+.2	-7.4	-9.3		
12,761	41.3	130,897	424.1	198,045	641.6	427,491	1,384.9	968,534	3,137.8	320,112	1,037.1		
11,766	37.7	126,436	405.1	194,083	621.8	414,182	1,327.0	945,407	3,029.1	319,295	1,023.0		
-7.8	-8.7	-3.4	-4.5	-2.0	-3.1	-3.1	-4.2	-2.4	-3.5	-.3	-1.4		
440	37.9	1,151	99.2	1,365	117.7	13,006	1,121.2	50,544	4,357.2	4,351	375.1		
394	33.6	1,214	103.6	1,408	120.1	13,310	1,135.7	51,912	4,429.4	5,283	450.8		
-10.5	-11.3	+5.5	+4.4	+3.2	+2.0	+2.3	+1.3	+2.7	+1.7	+21.4	+20.2		
1,580	53.1	4,507	151.4	8,963	301.1	32,945	1,106.7	109,274	3,670.6	15,881	533.5		
1,554	51.3	3,930	129.6	9,630	317.6	31,072	1,024.8	110,878	3,656.9	17,608	580.7		
-1.6	-3.4	-12.8	-14.4	+7.4	+5.5	-5.7	-7.4	+1.5	-.4	+10.9	+8.8		
3,697	72.0	7,178	139.8	16,321	317.8	57,612	1,121.7	207,755	4,045.1	24,214	471.5		
3,384	64.4	7,204	137.1	16,181	307.9	56,083	1,067.2	205,701	3,914.4	23,969	456.1		
-8.5	-10.6	+.4	-1.9	-.9	-3.1	-2.7	-4.9	-1.0	-3.2	-1.0	-3.3		
433		24,242		6,747		35,415		42,315		18,858			
401		18,181		6,806		33,636		43,468		17,589			
-7.4		-25.0		+.9		-5.0		+2.7		-6.7			

Table 5. — Index of Crime, State, 1993

Area	Population	Crime Index total	Modified Crime Index total[1]	Violent crime[2]	Property crime[3]	Murder and non-negligent man-slaughter	Forcible rape	Robbery	Aggra-vated assault	Burglary	Larceny-theft	Motor vehicle theft	Arson[1]
ALABAMA													
Metropolitan Statistical Area	2,822,961												
Area actually reporting	99.5%	163,712		25,535	138,177	376	1,175	6,037	17,947	35,757	89,954	12,466	
Estimated totals	100.0%	164,545		25,660	138,885	377	1,180	6,061	18,042	35,924	90,441	12,520	
Cities outside metropolitan areas	576,104												
Area actually reporting	94.0%	28,269		5,184	23,085	56	185	494	4,449	5,431	16,645	1,009	
Estimated totals	100.0%	30,076		5,516	24,560	60	197	526	4,733	5,778	17,709	1,073	
Rural	787,935												
Area actually reporting	83.1%	8,017		1,246	6,771	39	78	75	1,054	3,219	3,096	456	
Estimated totals	100.0%	9,653		1,500	8,153	47	94	90	1,269	3,876	3,728	549	
State Total	**4,187,000**	**204,274**		**32,676**	**171,598**	**484**	**1,471**	**6,677**	**24,044**	**45,578**	**111,878**	**14,142**	
Rate per 100,000 inhabitants		4,878.8		780.4	4,098.4	11.6	35.1	159.5	574.3	1,088.6	2,672.0	337.8	
ALASKA													
Metropolitan Statistical Area	250,720												
Area actually reporting	100.0%	16,140		2,213	13,927	23	212	568	1,410	1,880	10,660	1,387	
Cities outside metropolitan areas	159,225												
Area actually reporting	85.4%	8,722		1,066	7,656	13	100	116	837	1,088	5,886	682	
Estimated totals	100.0%	10,218		1,249	8,969	15	117	136	981	1,275	6,895	799	
Rural	189,055												
Area actually reporting	100.0%	6,994		1,095	5,899	16	173	29	877	1,738	3,646	515	
State Total	**599,000**	**33,352**		**4,557**	**28,795**	**54**	**502**	**733**	**3,268**	**4,893**	**21,201**	**2,701**	
Rate per 100,000 inhabitants		5,567.9		760.8	4,807.2	9.0	83.8	122.4	545.6	816.9	3,539.4	450.9	
ARIZONA													
Metropolitan Statistical Area	3,331,808												
Area actually reporting	98.3%	263,949		25,680	238,269	310	1,355	6,119	17,896	51,694	154,340	32,235	
Estimated totals	100.0%	266,756		25,888	240,868	314	1,372	6,155	18,047	52,297	156,064	32,507	
Cities outside metropolitan areas	302,131												
Area actually reporting	94.8%	18,624		1,396	17,228	11	56	206	1,123	3,253	12,926	1,049	
Estimated totals	100.0%	19,650		1,473	18,177	12	59	217	1,185	3,432	13,638	1,107	
Rural	302,061												
Area actually reporting	100.0%	6,107		781	5,326	13	57	40	671	1,955	2,987	384	
State Total	**3,936,000**	**292,513**		**28,142**	**264,371**	**339**	**1,488**	**6,412**	**19,903**	**57,684**	**172,689**	**33,998**	
Rate per 100,000 inhabitants		7,431.7		715.0	6,716.7	8.6	37.8	162.9	505.7	1,465.5	4,387.4	863.8	
ARKANSAS													
Metropolitan Statistical Area	1,084,180												
Area actually reporting	99.6%	74,179		10,480	63,699	160	671	2,253	7,396	15,441	42,787	5,471	
Estimated totals	100.0%	74,424		10,499	63,925	160	673	2,258	7,408	15,480	42,960	5,485	
Cities outside metropolitan areas	525,324												
Area actually reporting	99.9%	29,819		2,791	27,028	52	192	669	1,878	6,975	18,545	1,508	
Estimated totals	100.0%	29,857		2,794	27,063	52	192	670	1,880	6,984	18,569	1,510	
Rural	814,496												
Area actually reporting	100.0%	12,331		1,088	11,243	35	163	99	791	4,182	6,238	823	
State Total	**2,424,000**	**116,612**		**14,381**	**102,231**	**247**	**1,028**	**3,027**	**10,079**	**26,646**	**67,767**	**7,818**	
Rate per 100,000 inhabitants		4,810.7		593.3	4,217.5	10.2	42.4	124.9	415.8	1,099.3	2,795.7	322.5	
CALIFORNIA													
Metropolitan Statistical Area	30,165,785												
Area actually reporting	99.9%	1,965,979		330,735	1,635,244	4,027	11,410	125,734	189,564	401,118	918,421	315,705	
Estimated totals	100.0%	1,966,516		330,808	1,635,708	4,028	11,413	125,759	189,608	401,229	918,696	315,783	
Cities outside metropolitan areas	428,342												
Area actually reporting	98.7%	28,961		3,094	25,867	22	164	495	2,413	6,122	17,459	2,286	
Estimated totals	100.0%	29,350		3,135	26,215	22	166	502	2,445	6,204	17,694	2,317	
Rural	616,873												
Area actually reporting	100.0%	19,399		2,438	16,961	46	187	175	2,030	6,749	9,017	1,195	
State Total	**31,211,000**	**2,015,265**		**336,381**	**1,678,884**	**4,096**	**11,766**	**126,436**	**194,083**	**414,182**	**945,407**	**319,295**	
Rate per 100,000 inhabitants		6,456.9		1,077.8	5,379.1	13.1	37.7	405.1	621.8	1,327.0	3,029.1	1,023.0	

See footnotes at end of table.

Table 5. — Index of Crime, State, 1993 — Continued

Area	Population	Crime Index total	Modified Crime Index total[1]	Violent crime[2]	Property crime[3]	Murder and non-negligent man-slaughter	Forcible rape	Robbery	Aggra-vated assault	Burglary	Larceny-theft	Motor vehicle theft	Arson[1]
COLORADO													
Metropolitan Statistical Area	2,907,385			18,219	147,801	179	1,438	4,035	12,567	31,101	101,755	14,945	
Area actually reporting	99.9%	166,020		18,219	147,801	179	1,438	4,035	12,567	31,101	101,755	14,945	
Estimated totals	100.0%	166,120		18,229	147,891	179	1,438	4,037	12,575	31,117	101,823	14,951	
Cities outside metropolitan areas	301,092												
Area actually reporting	98.9%	20,703		1,240	19,463	10	111	96	1,023	2,872	15,905	686	
Estimated totals	100.0%	20,941		1,254	19,687	10	112	97	1,035	2,905	16,088	694	
Rural	357,523												
Area actually reporting	99.5%	9,977		743	9,234	17	83	26	617	1,980	6,843	411	
Estimated totals	100.0%	10,024		746	9,278	17	83	26	620	1,989	6,876	413	
State Total	**3,566,000**	**197,085**		**20,229**	**176,856**	**206**	**1,633**	**4,160**	**14,230**	**36,011**	**124,787**	**16,058**	
Rate per 100,000 inhabitants		5,526.8		567.3	4,959.5	5.8	45.8	116.7	399.0	1,009.8	3,499.4	450.3	
CONNECTICUT													
Metropolitan Statistical Area	3,019,247			14,266	132,508	202	735	6,382	6,947	30,553	82,868	19,087	
Area actually reporting	100.0%	146,774		14,266	132,508	202	735	6,382	6,947	30,553	82,868	19,087	
Cities outside metropolitan areas	66,818												
Area actually reporting	100.0%	2,354		143	2,211	1	19	26	97	542	1,499	170	
Rural	190,935												
Area actually reporting	100.0%	3,264		540	2,724	3	46	39	452	957	1,509	258	
State Total	**3,277,000**	**152,392**		**14,949**	**137,443**	**206**	**800**	**6,447**	**7,496**	**32,052**	**85,876**	**19,515**	
Rate per 100,000 inhabitants		4,650.4		456.2	4,194.2	6.3	24.4	196.7	228.7	978.1	2,620.6	595.5	
DELAWARE													
Metropolitan Statistical Area	582,465			4,011	24,823	25	412	1,217	2,357	4,868	17,860	2,095	
Area actually reporting	99.9%	28,834		4,011	24,823	25	412	1,217	2,357	4,868	17,860	2,095	
Estimated totals	100.0%	28,846		4,012	24,834	25	412	1,217	2,358	4,870	17,869	2,095	
Cities outside metropolitan areas	29,163												
Area actually reporting	100.0%	2,315		225	2,090	....	23	38	164	408	1,634	48	
Rural	88,372												
Area actually reporting	100.0%	2,944		564	2,380	10	104	52	398	966	1,350	64	
State Total	**700,000**	**34,105**		**4,801**	**29,304**	**35**	**539**	**1,307**	**2,920**	**6,244**	**20,853**	**2,207**	
Rate per 100,000 inhabitants		4,872.1		685.9	4,186.3	5.0	77.0	186.7	417.1	892.0	2,979.0	315.3	
DISTRICT OF COLUMBIA[4]													
Metropolitan Statistical Area	578,000			16,888	51,091	454	324	7,107	9,003	11,534	31,495	8,062	
Area actually reporting	100.0%	67,979		16,888	51,091	454	324	7,107	9,003	11,534	31,495	8,062	
Cities outside metropolitan areas	NONE												
Rural	NONE												
State Total	**578,000**	**67,979**		**16,888**	**51,091**	**454**	**324**	**7,107**	**9,003**	**11,534**	**31,495**	**8,062**	
Rate per 100,000 inhabitants		11,761.1		2,921.8	8,839.3	78.5	56.1	1,229.6	1,557.6	1,995.5	5,449.0	1,394.8	
FLORIDA													
Metropolitan Statistical Area	12,714,931			157,579	933,335	1,148	6,862	47,747	101,822	236,927	576,852	119,556	
Area actually reporting	99.7%	1,090,914		157,579	933,335	1,148	6,862	47,747	101,822	236,927	576,852	119,556	
Estimated totals	100.0%	1,094,254		157,976	936,278	1,151	6,878	47,867	102,080	237,625	578,776	119,877	
Cities outside metropolitan areas	222,437												
Area actually reporting	91.2%	17,275		2,411	14,864	18	98	501	1,794	3,838	10,093	933	
Estimated totals	100.0%	18,937		2,643	16,294	20	107	549	1,967	4,207	11,064	1,023	
Rural	741,632												
Area actually reporting	100.0%	29,147		4,356	24,791	53	374	497	3,432	9,231	13,944	1,616	
State Total	**13,679,000**	**1,142,338**		**164,975**	**977,363**	**1,224**	**7,359**	**48,913**	**107,479**	**251,063**	**603,784**	**122,516**	
Rate per 100,000 inhabitants		8,351.0		1,206.0	7,145.0	8.9	53.8	357.6	785.7	1,835.4	4,413.9	895.7	

See footnotes at end of table.

Table 5.—Index of Crime, State, 1993—Continued

Area	Population	Crime Index total	Modified Crime Index total[1]	Violent crime[2]	Property crime[3]	Murder and non-negligent man-slaughter	Forcible rape	Robbery	Aggra-vated assault	Burglary	Larceny-theft	Motor vehicle theft	Arson[1]
GEORGIA													
Metropolitan Statistical													
Area....................	4,726,261												
Area actually reporting	97.1%	327,806		38,074	289,732	578	1,900	15,007	20,589	66,610	187,657	35,465	
Estimated totals...............	100.0%	336,080		38,743	297,337	588	1,942	15,268	20,945	68,230	192,801	36,306	
Cities outside metropolitan areas.....	832,395												
Area actually reporting	87.2%	49,989		6,204	43,785	87	221	1,245	4,651	9,723	31,892	2,170	
Estimated totals...............	100.0%	57,330		7,115	50,215	100	253	1,428	5,334	11,151	36,575	2,489	
Rural......................	1,358,344												
Area actually reporting	90.4%	31,616		3,763	27,853	91	229	414	3,029	9,987	15,803	2,063	
Estimated totals...............	100.0%	34,957		4,161	30,796	101	253	458	3,349	11,042	17,473	2,281	
State Total....................	**6,917,000**	**428,367**		**50,019**	**378,348**	**789**	**2,448**	**17,154**	**29,628**	**90,423**	**246,849**	**41,076**	
Rate per 100,000 inhabitants		6,193.0		723.1	5,469.8	11.4	35.4	248.0	428.3	1,307.3	3,568.7	593.8	
HAWAII													
Metropolitan Statistical													
Area....................	875,455												
Area actually reporting	100.0%	56,405		2,501	53,904	31	286	1,085	1,099	9,296	40,148	4,460	
Cities outside metropolitan areas.....	39,321												
Area actually reporting	100.0%	2,708		85	2,623	2	16	18	49	639	1,890	94	
Rural......................	257,224												
Area actually reporting	100.0%	14,453		475	13,978	12	92	111	260	3,375	9,874	729	
State Total....................	**1,172,000**	**73,566**		**3,061**	**70,505**	**45**	**394**	**1,214**	**1,408**	**13,310**	**51,912**	**5,283**	
Rate per 100,000 inhabitants		6,277.0		261.2	6,015.8	3.8	33.6	103.6	120.1	1,135.7	4,429.4	450.8	
IDAHO													
Metropolitan Statistical													
Area....................	329,652												
Area actually reporting	100.0%	15,403		1,123	14,280	8	126	87	902	2,583	10,957	740	
Cities outside metropolitan areas.....	385,988												
Area actually reporting	98.9%	19,322		1,221	18,101	13	163	82	963	2,980	14,346	775	
Estimated totals...............	100.0%	19,536		1,235	18,301	13	165	83	974	3,013	14,504	784	
Rural......................	383,360												
Area actually reporting	98.3%	7,198		727	6,471	11	95	16	605	1,725	4,262	484	
Estimated totals...............	100.0%	7,319		739	6,580	11	97	16	615	1,754	4,334	492	
State Total....................	**1,099,000**	**42,258**		**3,097**	**39,161**	**32**	**388**	**186**	**2,491**	**7,350**	**29,795**	**2,016**	
Rate per 100,000 inhabitants		3,845.1		281.8	3,563.3	2.9	35.3	16.9	226.7	668.8	2,711.1	183.4	
ILLINOIS[5]													
State Total....................	**11,697,000**	**657,129**		**112,260**	**544,869**	**1,332**	**4,046**	**44,584**	**62,298**	**118,788**	**360,730**	**65,351**	
Rate per 100,000 inhabitants		5,617.9		959.7	4,658.2	11.4	34.6	381.2	532.6	1,015.5	3,084.0	558.7	
INDIANA													
Metropolitan Statistical													
Area....................	4,092,015												
Area actually reporting	82.4%	184,190		21,481	162,709	323	1,734	6,027	13,397	34,488	108,485	19,736	
Estimated totals...............	100.0%	209,462		23,475	185,987	343	1,918	6,380	14,834	38,931	125,266	21,790	
Cities outside metropolitan areas.....	569,788												
Area actually reporting	62.2%	17,491		1,385	16,106	14	93	209	1,069	3,026	12,101	979	
Estimated totals...............	100.0%	28,140		2,229	25,911	23	150	336	1,720	4,868	19,468	1,575	
Rural......................	1,051,197												
Area actually reporting	44.0%	7,691		984	6,707	28	73	57	826	2,145	4,082	480	
Estimated totals...............	100.0%	17,488		2,237	15,251	64	166	129	1,878	4,878	9,282	1,091	
State Total....................	**5,713,000**	**255,090**		**27,941**	**227,149**	**430**	**2,234**	**6,845**	**18,432**	**48,677**	**154,016**	**24,456**	
Rate per 100,000 inhabitants		4,465.1		489.1	3,976.0	7.5	39.1	119.8	322.6	852.0	2,695.9	428.1	

See footnotes at end of table.

Table 5. — Index of Crime, State, 1993 — Continued

Area	Population	Crime Index total	Modified Crime Index total[1]	Violent crime[2]	Property crime[3]	Murder and non-negligent man-slaughter	Forcible rape	Robbery	Aggra-vated assault	Burglary	Larceny-theft	Motor vehicle theft	Arson[1]
IOWA													
Metropolitan Statistical Area	1,233,430												
Area actually reporting	92.1%	68,333		6,876	61,457	44	505	1,390	4,937	12,640	45,022	3,795	
Estimated totals	100.0%	71,790		7,110	64,680	44	530	1,412	5,124	13,361	47,365	3,954	
Cities outside metropolitan areas	686,357												
Area actually reporting	78.5%	20,330		1,207	19,123	13	80	69	1,045	3,161	15,253	709	
Estimated totals	100.0%	25,900		1,538	24,362	17	102	88	1,331	4,027	19,432	903	
Rural	894,213												
Area actually reporting	77.9%	8,220		398	7,822	4	42	13	339	2,473	4,949	400	
Estimated totals	100.0%	10,549		511	10,038	5	54	17	435	3,174	6,351	513	
State Total	2,814,000	108,239		9,159	99,080	66	686	1,517	6,890	20,562	73,148	5,370	
Rate per 100,000 inhabitants		3,846.4		325.5	3,521.0	2.3	24.4	53.9	244.8	730.7	2,599.4	190.8	
KANSAS[5]													
Metropolitan Statistical Area	1,383,986												
Estimated totals	100.0%	86,024		9,368	76,656	131	723	2,855	5,659	19,534	50,361	6,761	
Cities outside metropolitan areas	690,844												
Estimated totals	100.0%	32,250		2,465	29,785	22	221	236	1,986	6,527	22,166	1,092	
Rural	456,170												
Estimated totals	100.0%	7,650		731	6,919	8	72	37	614	2,594	4,011	314	
State Total	2,531,000	125,924		12,564	113,360	161	1,016	3,128	8,259	28,655	76,538	8,167	
Rate per 100,000 inhabitants		4,975.3		496.4	4,478.9	6.4	40.1	123.6	326.3	1,132.2	3,024.0	322.7	
KENTUCKY													
Metropolitan Statistical Area	1,776,748												
Area actually reporting	99.7%	80,339		10,886	69,453	88	659	2,887	7,252	17,006	46,914	5,533	
Estimated totals	100.0%	80,599		10,918	69,681	88	660	2,893	7,277	17,053	47,082	5,546	
Cities outside metropolitan areas	632,000												
Area actually reporting	94.5%	23,670		3,128	20,542	25	189	343	2,571	4,665	14,616	1,261	
Estimated totals	100.0%	25,051		3,310	21,741	26	200	363	2,721	4,937	15,469	1,335	
Rural	1,380,252												
Area actually reporting	96.9%	17,299		3,199	14,100	131	427	164	2,477	5,861	6,968	1,271	
Estimated totals	100.0%	17,859		3,302	14,557	135	441	169	2,557	6,051	7,194	1,312	
State Total	3,789,000	123,509		17,530	105,979	249	1,301	3,425	12,555	28,041	69,745	8,193	
Rate per 100,000 inhabitants		3,259.7		462.7	2,797.0	6.6	34.3	90.4	331.4	740.1	1,840.7	216.2	
LOUISIANA													
Metropolitan Statistical Area	3,175,397												
Area actually reporting	92.7%	232,949		35,367	197,582	767	1,357	11,024	22,219	46,380	127,448	23,754	
Estimated totals	100.0%	246,992		37,149	209,843	787	1,440	11,409	23,513	48,940	136,016	24,887	
Cities outside metropolitan areas	362,493												
Area actually reporting	66.0%	19,862		3,313	16,549	15	112	353	2,833	3,843	12,023	683	
Estimated totals	100.0%	30,111		5,023	25,088	23	170	535	4,295	5,826	18,227	1,035	
Rural	757,110												
Area actually reporting	57.9%	9,823		1,986	7,837	37	120	138	1,691	2,318	5,266	253	
Estimated totals	100.0%	16,958		3,428	13,530	64	207	238	2,919	4,002	9,091	437	
State Total	4,295,000	294,061		45,600	248,461	874	1,817	12,182	30,727	58,768	163,334	26,359	
Rate per 100,000 inhabitants		6,846.6		1,061.7	5,784.9	20.3	42.3	283.6	715.4	1,368.3	3,802.9	613.7	
MAINE													
Metropolitan Statistical Area	455,139												
Area actually reporting	100.0%	17,936		877	17,059	7	144	200	526	3,619	12,666	774	
Cities outside metropolitan areas	437,860												
Area actually reporting	98.1%	14,595		429	14,166	1	93	50	285	2,670	10,922	574	
Estimated totals	100.0%	14,874		437	14,437	1	95	51	290	2,721	11,131	585	
Rural	346,001												
Area actually reporting	100.0%	6,267		244	6,023	12	90	13	129	2,569	3,148	306	
State Total	1,239,000	39,077		1,558	37,519	20	329	264	945	8,909	26,945	1,665	
Rate per 100,000 inhabitants		3,153.9		125.7	3,028.2	1.6	26.6	21.3	76.3	719.0	2,174.7	134.4	

See footnotes at end of table.

Table 5.—Index of Crime, State, 1993 — Continued

Area	Population	Crime Index total	Modified Crime Index total[1]	Violent crime[2]	Property crime[3]	Murder and non-negligent man-slaughter	Forcible rape	Robbery	Aggra-vated assault	Burglary	Larceny-theft	Motor vehicle theft	Arson[1]
MARYLAND													
Metropolitan Statistical Area	4,607,671												
Area actually reporting	99.9%	287,276		47,379	239,897	618	2,031	21,279	23,451	52,694	153,884	33,319	
Estimated totals	100.0%	287,326		47,385	239,941	618	2,031	21,281	23,455	52,703	153,915	33,323	
Cities outside metropolitan areas	91,305												
Area actually reporting	100.0%	9,106		1,175	7,931	3	70	198	904	1,627	5,984	320	
Rural	266,024												
Area actually reporting	100.0%	6,755		980	5,775	11	84	103	782	1,916	3,572	287	
State Total	**4,965,000**	**303,187**		**49,540**	**253,647**	**632**	**2,185**	**21,582**	**25,141**	**56,246**	**163,471**	**33,930**	
Rate per 100,000 inhabitants		6,106.5		997.8	5,108.7	12.7	44.0	434.7	506.4	1,132.8	3,292.5	683.4	
MASSACHUSETTS													
Metropolitan Statistical Area	5,722,022												
Area actually reporting	87.8%	255,631		42,993	212,638	220	1,741	9,983	31,049	52,169	115,781	44,688	
Estimated totals	100.0%	280,389		46,389	234,000	229	1,881	10,478	33,801	57,345	128,297	48,358	
Cities outside metropolitan areas	277,720												
Area actually reporting	56.0%	7,678		1,090	6,588	2	69	47	972	1,602	4,600	386	
Estimated totals	100.0%	13,711		1,947	11,764	4	123	84	1,736	2,861	8,214	689	
Rural	12,258												
Area actually reporting	100.0%	124		57	67	....	2	1	54	14	37	16	
State Total	**6,012,000**	**294,224**		**48,393**	**245,831**	**233**	**2,006**	**10,563**	**35,591**	**60,220**	**136,548**	**49,063**	
Rate per 100,000 inhabitants		4,893.9		804.9	4,089.0	3.9	33.4	175.7	592.0	1,001.7	2,271.3	816.1	
MICHIGAN[6]													
Metropolitan Statistical Area	7,834,641												
Area actually reporting	97.0%				385,317	895		22,163	41,406	79,241	250,615	55,461	
Estimated totals	100.0%				395,833	902		22,430	42,227	80,941	258,355	56,537	
Cities outside metropolitan areas	612,312												
Area actually reporting	96.3				20,945	6		97	919	3,061	17,259	625	
Estimated totals	100.0%				21,743	6		101	954	3,178	17,916	649	
Rural	1,031,047												
Area actually reporting	100.0%				24,191	25		70	1,566	9,024	14,062	1,105	
State Total	**9,478,000**	**516,788**		**75,021**	**441,767**	**933**	**6,740**	**22,601**	**44,747**	**93,143**	**290,333**	**58,291**	
Rate per 100,000 inhabitants		5,452.5		791.5	4,661.0	9.8	71.1	238.5	472.1	982.7	3,063.2	615.0	
MINNESOTA[6]													
Metropolitan Statistical Area	3,132,045												
Area actually reporting	99.9%				143,702	130		4,981	6,829	29,391	101,172	13,139	
Estimated totals	100.0%				143,845	130		4,982	6,833	29,414	101,283	13,148	
Cities outside metropolitan areas	518,578												
Area actually reporting	99.5%				22,561	6		77	531	3,111	18,384	1,066	
Estimated totals	100.0%				22,667	6		77	533	3,126	18,470	1,071	
Rural	866,377												
Area actually reporting	100.0%				16,835	19		33	577	5,607	9,974	1,254	
State Total	**4,517,000**	**198,125**		**14,778**	**183,347**	**155**	**1,588**	**5,092**	**7,943**	**38,147**	**129,727**	**15,473**	
Rate per 100,000 inhabitants		4,386.2		327.2	4,059.0	3.4	35.2	112.7	175.8	844.5	2,872.0	342.6	
MISSISSIPPI													
Metropolitan Statistical Area	811,396												
Area actually reporting	78.4%	46,812		4,533	42,279	130	424	2,140	1,839	12,695	24,126	5,458	
Estimated totals	100.0%	52,250		5,028	47,222	148	540	2,268	2,072	14,757	26,595	5,870	
Cities outside metropolitan areas	682,810												
Area actually reporting	65.7%	32,324		2,901	29,423	78	201	727	1,895	8,452	19,500	1,471	
Estimated totals	100.0%	49,182		4,414	44,768	119	306	1,106	2,883	12,860	29,670	2,238	
Rural	1,148,794												
Area actually reporting	30.1%	4,614		609	4,005	27	84	93	405	1,915	1,865	225	
Estimated totals	100.0%	15,343		2,025	13,318	90	279	309	1,347	6,368	6,202	748	
State Total	**2,643,000**	**116,775**		**11,467**	**105,308**	**357**	**1,125**	**3,683**	**6,302**	**33,985**	**62,467**	**8,856**	
Rate per 100,000 inhabitants		4,418.3		433.9	3,984.4	13.5	42.6	139.3	238.4	1,285.8	2,363.5	335.1	

See footnotes at end of table.

Table 5. — Index of Crime, State, 1993 — Continued

Area	Population	Crime Index total	Modified Crime Index total[1]	Violent crime[2]	Property crime[3]	Murder and non-negligent man-slaughter	Forcible rape	Robbery	Aggra-vated assault	Burglary	Larceny-theft	Motor vehicle theft	Arson[1]
MISSOURI													
Metropolitan Statistical													
Area..........................	3,573,206												
Area actually reporting	95.1%	223,776		34,348	189,428	510	1,514	12,245	20,079	43,700	119,105	26,623	
Estimated totals...............	100.0%	229,210		34,801	194,409	515	1,552	12,350	20,384	44,799	122,519	27,091	
Cities outside metropolitan areas.....	484,787												
Area actually reporting	89.8%	22,079		1,993	20,086	19	171	212	1,591	3,630	15,611	845	
Estimated totals...............	100.0%	24,582		2,218	22,364	21	190	236	1,771	4,042	17,381	941	
Rural...........................	1,176,007												
Area actually reporting	58.5%	7,551		1,138	6,413	32	89	40	977	2,828	3,214	371	
Estimated totals...............	100.0%	12,902		1,944	10,958	54	152	68	1,670	4,832	5,492	634	
State Total..................	**5,234,000**	**266,694**		**38,963**	**227,731**	**590**	**1,894**	**12,654**	**23,825**	**53,673**	**145,392**	**28,666**	
Rate per 100,000 inhabitants		5,095.4		744.4	4,351.0	11.3	36.2	241.8	455.2	1,025.5	2,777.8	547.7	
MONTANA													
Metropolitan Statistical													
Area..........................	201,157												
Area actually reporting	88.5%	13,650		355	13,295	7	53	140	155	2,357	10,188	750	
Estimated totals...............	100.0%	14,238		362	13,876	8	54	143	157	2,503	10,596	777	
Cities outside metropolitan areas.....	206,726												
Area actually reporting	90.8%	13,406		422	12,984	2	59	94	267	1,362	11,095	527	
Estimated totals...............	100.0%	14,765		465	14,300	2	65	104	294	1,500	12,220	580	
Rural...........................	431,117												
Area actually reporting	96.2%	10,763		637	10,126	14	111	24	488	1,914	7,530	682	
Estimated totals...............	100.0%	11,185		662	10,523	15	115	25	507	1,989	7,825	709	
State Total..................	**839,000**	**40,188**		**1,489**	**38,699**	**25**	**234**	**272**	**958**	**5,992**	**30,641**	**2,066**	
Rate per 100,000 inhabitants		4,790.0		177.5	4,612.5	3.0	27.9	32.4	114.2	714.2	3,652.1	246.2	
NEBRASKA													
Metropolitan Statistical													
Area..........................	812,979												
Area actually reporting	100.0%	45,117		4,613	40,504	45	319	812	3,437	7,080	30,898	2,526	
Cities outside metropolitan areas.....	380,514												
Area actually reporting	94.3%	14,572		543	14,029	7	77	59	400	2,079	11,485	465	
Estimated totals...............	100.0%	15,460		576	14,884	7	82	63	424	2,206	12,185	493	
Rural...........................	413,507												
Area actually reporting	100.0%	5,585		261	5,324	11	46	15	189	1,376	3,728	220	
State Total..................	**1,607,000**	**66,162**		**5,450**	**60,712**	**63**	**447**	**890**	**4,050**	**10,662**	**46,811**	**3,239**	
Rate per 100,000 inhabitants		4,117.1		339.1	3,778.0	3.9	27.8	55.4	252.0	663.5	2,912.9	201.6	
NEVADA													
Metropolitan Statistical													
Area..........................	1,178,234												
Area actually reporting	98.3%	76,425		10,670	65,755	140	770	4,646	5,114	15,281	40,653	9,821	
Estimated totals...............	100.0%	77,010		10,738	66,272	141	774	4,652	5,171	15,425	40,970	9,877	
Cities outside metropolitan areas.....	40,928												
Area actually reporting	48.4%	1,310		68	1,242	....	8	9	51	323	848	71	
Estimated totals...............	100.0%	2,707		141	2,566	....	17	19	105	667	1,752	147	
Rural...........................	169,838												
Area actually reporting	67.8%	4,156		867	3,289	2	37	36	792	815	2,317	157	
Estimated totals...............	100.0%	6,125		1,278	4,847	3	55	53	1,167	1,201	3,415	231	
State Total..................	**1,389,000**	**85,842**		**12,157**	**73,685**	**144**	**846**	**4,724**	**6,443**	**17,293**	**46,137**	**10,255**	
Rate per 100,000 inhabitants		6,180.1		875.2	5,304.9	10.4	60.9	340.1	463.9	1,245.0	3,321.6	738.3	
NEW HAMPSHIRE													
Metropolitan Statistical													
Area..........................	662,979												
Area actually reporting	91.6%	18,983		852	18,131	15	232	249	356	3,406	13,066	1,659	
Estimated totals...............	100.0%	20,569		930	19,639	16	256	262	396	3,660	14,181	1,798	
Cities outside metropolitan areas.....	321,495												
Area actually reporting	86.0%	9,625		462	9,163	1	186	35	240	1,574	7,289	300	
Estimated totals...............	100.0%	11,191		537	10,654	1	216	41	279	1,830	8,475	349	
Rural...........................	140,526												
Area actually reporting	92.3%	851		77	774	6	25	4	42	282	459	33	
Estimated totals...............	100.0%	921		83	838	6	27	4	46	305	497	36	
State Total..................	**1,125,000**	**32,681**		**1,550**	**31,131**	**23**	**499**	**307**	**721**	**5,795**	**23,153**	**2,183**	
Rate per 100,000 inhabitants		2,905.0		137.8	2,767.2	2.0	44.4	27.3	64.1	515.1	2,058.0	194.0	

See footnotes at end of table.

Table 5. — Index of Crime, State, 1993 — Continued

Area	Population	Crime Index total	Modified Crime Index total[1]	Violent crime[2]	Property crime[3]	Murder and non-negligent man-slaughter	Forcible rape	Robbery	Aggra-vated assault	Burglary	Larceny-theft	Motor vehicle theft	Arson[1]
NEW JERSEY													
Metropolitan Statistical													
Area............................	7,879,000												
Area actually reporting	100.0%	378,257		49,390	328,867	418	2,215	23,319	23,438	76,738	195,876	56,253	
Cities outside metropolitan areas.....	NONE												
Rural	NONE												
State Total......................	**7,879,000**	**378,257**		**49,390**	**328,867**	**418**	**2,215**	**23,319**	**23,438**	**76,738**	**195,876**	**56,253**	
Rate per 100,000													
inhabitants		4,800.8		626.9	4,174.0	5.3	28.1	296.0	297.5	974.0	2,486.1	714.0	
NEW MEXICO													
Metropolitan Statistical													
Area............................	905,587												
Area actually reporting	80.1%	58,735		8,857	49,878	65	443	1,848	6,501	12,571	32,416	4,891	
Estimated totals...............	100.0%	65,244		9,821	55,423	73	536	1,925	7,287	14,513	35,578	5,332	
Cities outside metropolitan areas.....	417,267												
Area actually reporting	63.7%	19,624		2,690	16,934	30	139	161	2,360	4,253	12,101	580	
Estimated totals...............	100.0%	30,830		4,226	26,604	47	218	253	3,708	6,682	19,011	911	
Rural	293,146												
Area actually reporting	61.2%	3,174		598	2,576	6	54	36	502	1,084	1,306	186	
Estimated totals...............	100.0%	5,186		977	4,209	10	88	59	820	1,771	2,134	304	
State Total......................	**1,616,000**	**101,260**		**15,024**	**86,236**	**130**	**842**	**2,237**	**11,815**	**22,966**	**56,723**	**6,547**	
Rate per 100,000													
inhabitants		6,266.1		929.7	5,336.4	8.0	52.1	138.4	731.1	1,421.2	3,510.1	405.1	
NEW YORK													
Metropolitan Statistical													
Area............................	16,694,219												
Area actually reporting	99.5%	962,293		190,892	771,401	2,379	4,677	101,650	82,186	170,610	450,269	150,522	
Estimated totals...............	100.0%	965,026		191,156	773,870	2,381	4,689	101,753	82,333	171,088	452,007	150,775	
Cities outside metropolitan areas.....	645,563												
Area actually reporting	97.3%	24,929		2,137	22,792	9	160	287	1,681	4,135	18,089	568	
Estimated totals...............	100.0%	25,617		2,195	23,422	9	164	295	1,727	4,249	18,589	584	
Rural	857,218												
Area actually reporting	100.0%	19,533		2,001	17,532	30	155	74	1,742	6,372	10,570	590	
State Total......................	**18,197,000**	**1,010,176**		**195,352**	**814,824**	**2,420**	**5,008**	**102,122**	**85,802**	**181,709**	**481,166**	**151,949**	
Rate per 100,000													
inhabitants		5,551.3		1,073.5	4,477.8	13.3	27.5	561.2	471.5	998.6	2,644.2	835.0	
NORTH CAROLINA													
Metropolitan Statistical													
Area............................	4,605,749												
Area actually reporting	98.5%	288,692		35,856	252,836	543	1,839	11,333	22,141	73,671	163,974	15,191	
Estimated totals...............	100.0%	291,549		36,122	255,427	547	1,856	11,394	22,325	74,530	165,561	15,336	
Cities outside metropolitan areas.....	698,993												
Area actually reporting	93.3%	57,238		6,442	50,796	85	246	1,436	4,675	13,850	34,708	2,238	
Estimated totals...............	100.0%	61,376		6,908	54,468	91	264	1,540	5,013	14,851	37,217	2,400	
Rural	1,640,258												
Area actually reporting	98.0%	38,821		4,063	34,758	144	254	421	3,244	15,565	16,940	2,253	
Estimated totals...............	100.0%	39,630		4,148	35,482	147	259	430	3,312	15,889	17,293	2,300	
State Total......................	**6,945,000**	**392,555**		**47,178**	**345,377**	**785**	**2,379**	**13,364**	**30,650**	**105,270**	**220,071**	**20,036**	
Rate per 100,000													
inhabitants		5,652.3		679.3	4,973.0	11.3	34.3	192.4	441.3	1,515.8	3,168.8	288.5	
NORTH DAKOTA													
Metropolitan Statistical													
Area............................	263,878												
Area actually reporting	100.0%	11,083		348	10,735	1	100	35	212	1,360	8,755	620	
Cities outside metropolitan areas.....	144,877												
Area actually reporting	91.3%	4,224		88	4,136	3	25	13	47	403	3,567	166	
Estimated totals...............	100.0%	4,627		95	4,532	3	27	14	51	442	3,908	182	
Rural	226,245												
Area actually reporting	95.6%	2,102		76	2,026	7	21	4	44	543	1,347	136	
Estimated totals...............	100.0%	2,199		79	2,120	7	22	4	46	568	1,410	142	
State Total......................	**635,000**	**17,909**		**522**	**17,387**	**11**	**149**	**53**	**309**	**2,370**	**14,073**	**944**	
Rate per 100,000													
inhabitants		2,820.3		82.2	2,738.1	1.7	23.5	8.3	48.7	373.2	2,216.2	148.7	

See footnotes at end of table.

Table 5. – Index of Crime, State, 1993 – Continued

Area	Population	Crime Index total	Modified Crime Index total[1]	Violent crime[2]	Property crime[3]	Murder and non-negligent man-slaughter	Forcible rape	Robbery	Aggra-vated assault	Burglary	Larceny-theft	Motor vehicle theft	Arson[1]
OHIO													
Metropolitan Statistical													
Area.....................	9,021,939												
Area actually reporting	78.6%	381,058		48,054	333,004	591	4,411	19,633	23,419	75,282	215,799	41,923	
Estimated totals..............	100.0%	444,590		52,249	392,341	625	4,918	20,817	25,889	86,244	260,141	45,956	
Cities outside metropolitan areas.....	754,302												
Area actually reporting	68.3%	24,031		1,625	22,406	12	220	322	1,071	4,033	17,392	981	
Estimated totals..............	100.0%	35,162		2,377	32,785	17	322	471	1,567	5,901	25,449	1,435	
Rural......................	1,314,759												
Area actually reporting	63.4%	11,230		817	10,413	16	129	54	618	3,328	6,524	561	
Estimated totals..............	100.0%	17,713		1,289	16,424	25	204	85	975	5,249	10,290	885	
State Total................	**11,091,000**	**497,465**		**55,915**	**441,550**	**667**	**5,444**	**21,373**	**28,431**	**97,394**	**295,880**	**48,276**	
Rate per 100,000													
inhabitants		4,485.3		504.1	3,981.2	6.0	49.1	192.7	256.3	878.1	2,667.7	435.3	
OKLAHOMA													
Metropolitan Statistical													
Area.....................	1,942,398												
Area actually reporting	100.0%	127,642		15,481	112,161	186	1,254	3,479	10,562	28,044	70,907	13,210	
Cities outside metropolitan areas.....	662,928												
Area actually reporting	99.8%	32,840		3,719	29,121	51	230	381	3,057	7,998	19,480	1,643	
Estimated totals..............	100.0%	32,919		3,728	29,191	51	231	382	3,064	8,017	19,527	1,647	
Rural......................	625,674												
Area actually reporting	100.0%	10,497		1,303	9,194	36	107	74	1,086	3,842	4,677	675	
State Total................	**3,231,000**	**171,058**		**20,512**	**150,546**	**273**	**1,592**	**3,935**	**14,712**	**39,903**	**95,111**	**15,532**	
Rate per 100,000													
inhabitants		5,294.3		634.8	4,659.4	8.4	49.3	121.8	455.3	1,235.0	2,943.7	480.7	
OREGON													
Metropolitan Statistical													
Area.....................	2,123,172												
Area actually reporting	99.8%	133,864		13,048	120,816	107	1,139	3,569	8,233	22,651	82,785	15,380	
Estimated totals..............	100.0%	134,113		13,062	121,051	107	1,141	3,573	8,241	22,691	82,961	15,399	
Cities outside metropolitan areas.....	420,325												
Area actually reporting	95.6%	27,423		1,151	26,272	10	168	287	686	4,646	20,360	1,266	
Estimated totals..............	100.0%	28,698		1,204	27,494	10	176	300	718	4,862	21,307	1,325	
Rural......................	488,503												
Area actually reporting	100.0%	12,001		988	11,013	23	237	57	671	3,519	6,610	884	
State Total................	**3,032,000**	**174,812**		**15,254**	**159,558**	**140**	**1,554**	**3,930**	**9,630**	**31,072**	**110,878**	**17,608**	
Rate per 100,000													
inhabitants		5,765.6		503.1	5,262.5	4.6	51.3	129.6	317.6	1,024.8	3,656.9	580.7	
PENNSYLVANIA													
Metropolitan Statistical													
Area.....................	10,222,866												
Area actually reporting	96.0%	346,084		46,118	299,966	766	2,747	20,934	21,671	59,211	190,886	49,869	
Estimated totals..............	100.0%	357,019		47,140	309,879	774	2,809	21,195	22,362	60,837	198,129	50,913	
Cities outside metropolitan areas.....	761,248												
Area actually reporting	87.5%	18,667		1,609	17,058	6	140	225	1,238	2,820	13,441	797	
Estimated totals..............	100.0%	21,341		1,839	19,502	7	160	257	1,415	3,224	15,367	911	
Rural......................	1,063,886												
Area actually reporting	100.0%	15,776		1,316	14,460	42	226	111	937	6,064	7,187	1,209	
State Total................	**12,048,000**	**394,136**		**50,295**	**343,841**	**823**	**3,195**	**21,563**	**24,714**	**70,125**	**220,683**	**53,033**	
Rate per 100,000													
inhabitants		3,271.4		417.5	2,853.9	6.8	26.5	179.0	205.1	582.0	1,831.7	440.2	
PUERTO RICO[7]													
Metropolitan Statistical													
Area.....................													
Area actually reporting	100.0%	107,379		23,905	83,474	885	320	17,303	5,397	28,585	38,171	16,718	
Cities outside metropolitan areas.....													
Area actually reporting	100.0%	13,650		2,431	11,219	63	81	878	1,409	5,051	5,297	871	
Total.....................		**121,029**		**26,336**	**94,693**	**948**	**401**	**18,181**	**6,806**	**33,636**	**43,468**	**17,589**	

See footnotes at end of table.

Table 5. — Index of Crime, State, 1993 — Continued

Area	Population	Crime Index total	Modified Crime Index total[1]	Violent crime[2]	Property crime[3]	Murder and non-negligent man-slaughter	Forcible rape	Robbery	Aggra-vated assault	Burglary	Larceny-theft	Motor vehicle theft	Arson[1]
RHODE ISLAND													
Metropolitan Statistical													
Area........................	918,339												
Area actually reporting......	100.0%	41,389		3,544	37,845	38	261	950	2,295	9,708	21,840	6,297	
Cities outside metropolitan areas.....	81,661												
Area actually reporting	100.0%	3,580		472	3,108	1	25	61	385	699	2,243	166	
Rural..........................													
Area actually reporting	100.0%	21		1	20	....	....	....	1	2	18	....	
State Total....................	**1,000,000**	**44,990**		**4,017**	**40,973**	**39**	**286**	**1,011**	**2,681**	**10,409**	**24,101**	**6,463**	
Rate per 100,000													
inhabitants		4,499.0		401.7	4,097.3	3.9	28.6	101.1	268.1	1,040.9	2,410.1	646.3	
SOUTH CAROLINA													
Metropolitan Statistical													
Area........................	2,543,765												
Area actually reporting	100.0%	160,955		26,441	134,514	251	1,408	5,391	19,391	34,443	90,107	9,964	
Cities outside metropolitan areas.....	313,633												
Area actually reporting	98.9%	23,953		5,269	18,684	42	169	812	4,246	4,740	13,019	925	
Estimated totals...............	100.0%	24,223		5,328	18,895	42	171	821	4,294	4,794	13,166	935	
Rural..........................	785,602												
Area actually reporting	100.0%	29,882		5,512	24,370	84	326	613	4,489	8,458	14,280	1,632	
State Total....................	**3,643,000**	**215,060**		**37,281**	**177,779**	**377**	**1,905**	**6,825**	**28,174**	**47,695**	**117,553**	**12,531**	
Rate per 100,000													
inhabitants		5,903.4		1,023.4	4,880.0	10.3	52.3	187.3	773.4	1,309.2	3,226.8	344.0	
SOUTH DAKOTA													
Metropolitan Statistical													
Area........................	234,211												
Area actually reporting	98.3%	9,981		872	9,109	6	197	74	595	1,623	7,092	394	
Estimated totals...............	100.0%	10,220		888	9,332	6	200	75	607	1,656	7,273	403	
Cities outside metropolitan areas.....	190,367												
Area actually reporting	84.1%	6,534		296	6,238	3	59	20	214	1,155	4,861	222	
Estimated totals...............	100.0%	7,774		353	7,421	4	70	24	255	1,374	5,783	264	
Rural..........................	290,422												
Area actually reporting	71.5%	2,259		178	2,081	10	34	6	128	642	1,330	109	
Estimated totals...............	100.0%	3,157		249	2,908	14	48	8	179	897	1,859	152	
State Total....................	**715,000**	**21,151**		**1,490**	**19,661**	**24**	**318**	**107**	**1,041**	**3,927**	**14,915**	**819**	
Rate per 100,000													
inhabitants		2,958.2		208.4	2,749.8	3.4	44.5	15.0	145.6	549.2	2,086.0	114.5	
TENNESSEE													
Metropolitan Statistical													
Area........................	3,394,091												
Area actually reporting	87.1%	206,195		31,829	174,366	399	2,065	10,420	18,945	43,149	105,417	25,800	
Estimated totals...............	100.0%	219,285		33,208	186,077	415	2,194	10,620	19,979	46,547	112,669	26,861	
Cities outside metropolitan areas.....	595,968												
Area actually reporting	82.5%	24,207		2,976	21,231	32	166	399	2,379	5,176	14,625	1,430	
Estimated totals...............	100.0%	29,342		3,608	25,734	39	201	484	2,884	6,274	17,727	1,733	
Rural..........................	1,108,941												
Area actually reporting	51.1%	9,478		1,140	8,338	34	76	61	969	3,824	3,726	788	
Estimated totals...............	100.0%	18,537		2,231	16,306	67	149	120	1,895	7,478	7,287	1,541	
State Total....................	**5,099,000**	**267,164**		**39,047**	**228,117**	**521**	**2,544**	**11,224**	**24,758**	**60,299**	**137,683**	**30,135**	
Rate per 100,000													
inhabitants		5,239.5		765.8	4,473.8	10.2	49.9	220.1	485.5	1,182.6	2,700.2	591.0	
TEXAS													
Metropolitan Statistical													
Area........................	15,127,913												
Area actually reporting	99.9%	1,058,762		124,314	934,448	1,937	9,055	39,424	73,898	207,218	606,672	120,558	
Estimated totals...............	100.0%	1,058,998		124,338	934,660	1,937	9,057	39,428	73,916	207,263	606,823	120,574	
Cities outside metropolitan areas.....	1,310,738												
Area actually reporting	99.7%	69,152		8,598	60,554	107	473	820	7,198	14,916	42,887	2,751	
Estimated totals...............	100.0%	69,288		8,613	60,675	107	473	821	7,212	14,946	42,972	2,757	
Rural..........................	1,592,349												
Area actually reporting	100.0%	32,745		4,468	28,277	103	392	220	3,753	11,704	15,067	1,506	
State Total....................	**18,031,000**	**1,161,031**		**137,419**	**1,023,612**	**2,147**	**9,922**	**40,469**	**84,881**	**233,913**	**664,862**	**124,837**	
Rate per 100,000													
inhabitants		6,439.1		762.1	5,677.0	11.9	55.0	224.4	470.8	1,297.3	3,687.3	692.3	

See footnotes at end of table.

Table 5.—Index of Crime, State, 1993—Continued

Area	Population	Crime Index total	Modified Crime Index total[1]	Violent crime[2]	Property crime[3]	Murder and non-negligent man-slaughter	Forcible rape	Robbery	Aggra-vated assault	Burglary	Larceny-theft	Motor vehicle theft	Arson[1]
UTAH													
Metropolitan Statistical													
Area..........................	1,440,962												
Area actually reporting	98.7%	80,932		4,737	76,195	48	673	1,035	2,981	12,044	60,311	3,840	
Estimated totals...............	100.0%	81,867		4,780	77,087	48	680	1,042	3,010	12,183	61,030	3,874	
Cities outside metropolitan areas.....	217,667												
Area actually reporting	95.3%	10,799		444	10,355	7	84	34	319	1,559	8,369	427	
Estimated totals...............	100.0%	11,335		466	10,869	7	88	36	335	1,636	8,785	448	
Rural........................	201,371												
Area actually reporting	100.0%	4,213		353	3,860	3	61	12	277	889	2,788	183	
State Total.................	**1,860,000**	**97,415**		**5,599**	**91,816**	**58**	**829**	**1,090**	**3,622**	**14,708**	**72,603**	**4,505**	
Rate per 100,000													
inhabitants		5,237.4		301.0	4,936.3	3.1	44.6	58.6	194.7	790.8	3,903.4	242.2	
VERMONT													
Metropolitan Statistical													
Area..........................	113,634												
Area actually reporting	62.3%	4,780		95	4,685	1	34	13	47	893	3,659	133	
Estimated totals...............	100.0%	7,667		153	7,514	2	55	21	75	1,432	5,869	213	
Cities outside metropolitan areas.....	199,095												
Area actually reporting	22.1%	2,163		71	2,092	2	25	6	38	326	1,695	71	
Estimated totals...............	100.0%	9,768		321	9,447	9	113	27	172	1,472	7,654	321	
Rural........................	263,271												
Area actually reporting	95.4%	5,195		176	5,019	10	58	4	104	2,034	2,766	219	
Estimated totals...............	100.0%	5,446		184	5,262	10	61	4	109	2,132	2,900	230	
State Total.................	**576,000**	**22,881**		**658**	**22,223**	**21**	**229**	**52**	**356**	**5,036**	**16,423**	**764**	
Rate per 100,000													
inhabitants		3,972.4		114.2	3,858.2	3.6	39.8	9.0	61.8	874.3	2,851.2	132.6	
VIRGINIA													
Metropolitan Statistical													
Area..........................	5,028,934												
Area actually reporting	100.0%	235,277		21,442	213,835	437	1,747	8,899	10,359	36,756	160,030	17,049	
Cities outside metropolitan areas.....	414,000												
Area actually reporting	100.0%	16,355		1,143	15,212	21	134	170	818	2,229	12,380	603	
Rural........................	1,048,066												
Area actually reporting	100.0%	15,503		1,575	13,928	81	202	147	1,145	4,353	8,694	881	
State Total.................	**6,491,000**	**267,135**		**24,160**	**242,975**	**539**	**2,083**	**9,216**	**12,322**	**43,338**	**181,104**	**18,533**	
Rate per 100,000													
inhabitants		4,115.5		372.2	3,743.3	8.3	32.1	142.0	189.8	667.7	2,790.1	285.5	
WASHINGTON													
Metropolitan Statistical													
Area..........................	4,271,558												
Area actually reporting	99.5%	260,366		23,645	236,721	227	2,633	6,681	14,104	46,170	169,402	21,149	
Estimated totals...............	100.0%	261,765		23,725	238,040	227	2,647	6,702	14,149	46,375	170,418	21,247	
Cities outside metropolitan areas.....	499,098												
Area actually reporting	96.7%	36,183		2,335	33,848	16	484	437	1,398	5,447	26,444	1,957	
Estimated totals...............	100.0%	37,408		2,414	34,994	17	500	452	1,445	5,631	27,340	2,023	
Rural........................	484,344												
Area actually reporting	100.0%	13,620		901	12,719	27	237	50	587	4,077	7,943	699	
State Total.................	**5,255,000**	**312,793**		**27,040**	**285,753**	**271**	**3,384**	**7,204**	**16,181**	**56,083**	**205,701**	**23,969**	
Rate per 100,000													
inhabitants		5,952.3		514.6	5,437.7	5.2	64.4	137.1	307.9	1,067.2	3,914.4	456.1	
WEST VIRGINIA													
Metropolitan Statistical													
Area..........................	760,354												
Area actually reporting	100.0%	26,128		2,191	23,937	56	204	555	1,376	5,983	16,327	1,627	
Cities outside metropolitan areas.....	278,369												
Area actually reporting	99.4%	9,488		701	8,787	9	81	124	487	1,568	6,832	387	
Estimated totals...............	100.0%	9,548		706	8,842	9	82	125	490	1,578	6,875	389	
Rural........................	781,277												
Area actually reporting	100.0%	10,417		896	9,521	61	79	102	654	3,343	5,254	924	
State Total.................	**1,820,000**	**46,093**		**3,793**	**42,300**	**126**	**365**	**782**	**2,520**	**10,904**	**28,456**	**2,940**	
Rate per 100,000													
inhabitants		2,532.6		208.4	2,324.2	6.9	20.1	43.0	138.5	599.1	1,563.5	161.5	

See footnotes at end of table.

Table 5. — Index of Crime, State, 1993 — Continued

Area	Population	Crime Index total	Modified Crime Index total[1]	Violent crime[2]	Property crime[3]	Murder and non-negligent man-slaughter	Forcible rape	Robbery	Aggra-vated assault	Burglary	Larceny-theft	Motor vehicle theft	Arson[1]
WISCONSIN													
Metropolitan Statistical													
Area..........................	3,438,606												
Area actually reporting	99.9%	159,229		11,382	147,847	202	1,000	5,533	4,647	24,577	106,775	16,495	
Estimated totals...............	100.0%	159,410		11,388	148,022	202	1,000	5,535	4,651	24,601	106,917	16,504	
Cities outside metropolitan areas.....	613,883												
Area actually reporting	99.3%	28,029		1,053	26,976	7	145	133	768	3,097	22,917	962	
Estimated totals...............	100.0%	28,221		1,060	27,161	7	146	134	773	3,118	23,074	969	
Rural.........................	985,511												
Area actually reporting	100.0%	16,613		873	15,740	13	123	45	692	5,681	9,157	902	
State Total....................	**5,038,000**	**204,244**		**13,321**	**190,923**	**222**	**1,269**	**5,714**	**6,116**	**33,400**	**139,148**	**18,375**	
Rate per 100,000													
inhabitants		4,054.1		264.4	3,789.7	4.4	25.2	113.4	121.4	663.0	2,762.0	364.7	
WYOMING													
Metropolitan Statistical													
Area..........................	139,815												
Area actually reporting	100.0%	6,949		398	6,551	....	65	44	289	1,201	5,082	268	
Cities outside metropolitan areas.....	206,014												
Area actually reporting	99.6%	10,009		634	9,375	6	65	30	533	1,268	7,753	354	
Estimated totals...............	100.0%	10,047		636	9,411	6	65	30	535	1,273	7,783	355	
Rural.........................	124,171												
Area actually reporting	100.0%	2,570		311	2,259	10	31	7	263	549	1,605	105	
State Total....................	**470,000**	**19,566**		**1,345**	**18,221**	**16**	**161**	**81**	**1,087**	**3,023**	**14,470**	**728**	
Rate per 100,000													
inhabitants		4,163.0		286.2	3,876.8	3.4	34.3	17.2	231.3	643.2	3,078.7	154.9	

[1]Although arson data were included in the trend and clearance tables, sufficient data are not available to estimate totals for this offense.

[2]Violent crimes are offenses of murder, forcible rape, robbery, and aggravated assault.

[3]Property crimes are offenses of burglary, larceny-theft, and motor vehicle theft. Data are not included for the property crime of arson.

[4]Includes offenses reported by the Zoological Police.

[5]Complete data were not available for the states of Illinois and Kansas; therefore, it was necessary that their crime counts be estimated. See "Offense Estimation," page 376 for details.

[6]Forcible rape figures furnished by the state-level Uniform Crime Reporting (UCR) Programs administered by the Michigan State Police and the Minnesota Department of Public Safety were not in accordance with national UCR guidelines. The 1993 forcible rape totals for Michigan and Minnesota were estimated using the national rate of forcible rapes when grouped by like agencies. Therefore, only the state totals are shown. See "Offense Estimation," page 376 for details.

[7]The 1993 Bureau of the Census population estimate for Puerto Rico was not available prior to publication; therefore, no population or rates per 100,000 inhabitants are provided.

Table 6. — Index of Crime, Metropolitan Statistical Areas, 1993

Metropolitan Statistical Area	Population	Crime Index total	Modified Crime Index total[1]	Violent crime[2]	Property crime[3]	Murder and non-negligent man-slaughter	Forcible rape	Robbery	Aggra-vated assault	Burglary	Larceny-theft	Motor vehicle theft	Arson[1]
Abilene, Tx. M.S.A.	**122,927**												
(Includes Taylor County.)													
City of Abilene	110,222	5,474		890	4,584	8	75	134	673	1,089	3,323	172	
Total area actually reporting	100.0%	5,758		915	4,843	8	80	137	690	1,177	3,479	187	
Rate per 100,000 inhabitants		4,684.1		744.3	3,939.7	6.5	65.1	111.4	561.3	957.5	2,830.1	152.1	
Akron, Oh. M.S.A.[5]	**667,989**												
(Includes Portage and Summit Counties.)													
City of Akron[5]	225,040				14,085	19	204	840		3,367	8,675	2,043	
Total area actually reporting	80.5%	26,784		2,867	23,917	21	273	996	1,577	4,947	16,397	2,573	
Estimated total	100.0%	30,547		3,116	27,431	24	307	1,069	1,716	5,684	18,934	2,813	
Rate per 100,000 inhabitants		4,573.0		466.5	4,106.5	3.6	46.0	160.0	256.9	850.9	2,834.5	421.1	
Albany, Ga. M.S.A.	**117,680**												
(Includes Dougherty and Lee Counties.)													
City of Albany	81,328	9,377		1,128	8,249	22	55	473	578	2,767	4,957	525	
Total area actually reporting	99.3%	10,178		1,160	9,018	22	56	483	599	3,018	5,450	550	
Estimated total	100.0%	10,242		1,165	9,077	22	56	485	602	3,029	5,493	555	
Rate per 100,000 inhabitants		8,703.3		990.0	7,713.3	18.7	47.6	412.1	511.6	2,573.9	4,667.7	471.6	
Albuquerque, N.M. M.S.A.	**629,814**												
(Includes Bernalillo, Sandoval, and Valencia Counties.)													
City of Albuquerque	407,286	39,025		6,696	32,329	50	259	1,552	4,835	8,199	20,552	3,578	
Total area actually reporting	81.9%	43,955		7,441	36,514	52	320	1,593	5,476	9,295	23,386	3,833	
Estimated total	100.0%	47,537		8,021	39,516	57	378	1,631	5,955	10,462	24,977	4,077	
Rate per 100,000 inhabitants		7,547.8		1,273.6	6,274.2	9.1	60.0	259.0	945.5	1,661.1	3,965.8	647.3	
Alexandria, La. M.S.A.	**131,041**												
(Includes Rapides Parish.)													
City of Alexandria	49,133	5,937		1,774	4,163	21	23	117	1,613	758	3,119	286	
Total area actually reporting	99.4%	9,008		2,394	6,614	26	59	129	2,180	1,408	4,743	463	
Estimated total	100.0%	9,068		2,402	6,666	26	59	131	2,186	1,418	4,780	468	
Rate per 100,000 inhabitants		6,920.0		1,833.0	5,087.0	19.8	45.0	100.0	1,668.2	1,082.1	3,647.7	357.1	
Altoona, Pa. M.S.A.	**131,894**												
(Includes Blair County.)													
City of Altoona	52,708	1,566		163	1,403	....	16	40	107	417	888	98	
Total area actually reporting	100.0%	3,170		263	2,907	1	26	47	189	730	1,968	209	
Rate per 100,000 inhabitants		2,403.4		199.4	2,204.0	.8	19.7	35.6	143.3	553.5	1,492.1	158.5	
Amarillo, Tx. M.S.A.	**195,405**												
(Includes Potter and Randall Counties.)													
City of Amarillo	164,234	13,868		1,129	12,739	11	89	208	821	2,739	9,351	649	
Total area actually reporting	100.0%	14,798		1,202	13,596	12	104	213	873	2,974	9,911	711	
Rate per 100,000 inhabitants		7,573.0		615.1	6,957.9	6.1	53.2	109.0	446.8	1,522.0	5,072.0	363.9	
Anchorage, Ak. M.S.A.	**250,720**												
(Includes Anchorage Borough.)													
City of Anchorage	250,720	16,140		2,213	13,927	23	212	568	1,410	1,880	10,660	1,387	
Total area actually reporting	100.0%	16,140		2,213	13,927	23	212	568	1,410	1,880	10,660	1,387	
Rate per 100,000 inhabitants		6,437.5		882.7	5,554.8	9.2	84.6	226.5	562.4	749.8	4,251.8	553.2	
Ann Arbor, Mi. M.S.A.[4]	**503,897**												
(Includes Lenawee, Livingston and Washtenaw Counties.)													
City of Ann Arbor[4]	110,277				5,393	2		129	336	1,101	4,032	260	
Total area actually reporting	98.5%				19,430	16		427	1,433	3,957	14,307	1,166	
Estimated total	100.0%				19,770	16		436	1,460	4,012	14,557	1,201	
Rate per 100,000 inhabitants					3,923.4	3.2		86.5	289.7	796.2	2,888.9	238.3	
Anniston, Al. M.S.A.	**117,781**												
(Includes Calhoun County.)													
City of Anniston	27,436	4,286		971	3,315	12	36	142	781	1,049	2,089	177	
Total area actually reporting	100.0%	6,536		1,394	5,142	17	60	171	1,146	1,531	3,346	265	
Rate per 100,000 inhabitants		5,549.3		1,183.6	4,365.7	14.4	50.9	145.2	973.0	1,299.9	2,840.9	225.0	
Appleton-Oshkosh-Neenah, Wi. M.S.A.	**329,973**												
(Includes Calumet, Outagamie and Winnebago Counties.)													
City of:													
Appleton	69,078	2,691		45	2,646	2	9	11	23	372	2,187	87	
Oshkosh	56,799	3,304		88	3,216	5	19	7	57	479	2,625	112	
Neenah	24,178	854		43	811	....	2	6	35	104	665	42	
Total area actually reporting	100.0%	11,585		1,351	11,234	7	46	34	264	1,688	9,168	378	
Rate per 100,000 inhabitants		3,510.9		106.4	3,404.5	2.1	13.9	10.3	80.0	511.6	2,778.4	114.6	

See footnotes at end of table.

Table 6. — Index of Crime, Metropolitan Statistical Areas, 1993 — Continued

Metropolitan Statistical Area	Population	Crime Index total	Modified Crime Index total[1]	Violent crime[2]	Property crime[3]	Murder and non-negligent man-slaughter	Forcible rape	Robbery	Aggra-vated assault	Burglary	Larceny-theft	Motor vehicle theft	Arson[1]
Asheville, N.C. M.S.A.	**200,605**												
(Includes Buncombe County.)													
City of Asheville	63,791	5,268		456	4,812	9	44	142	261	1,148	3,311	353	
Total area actually reporting......	91.4%	7,467		608	6,859	15	54	163	376	1,834	4,551	474	
Estimated total	100.0%	8,107		665	7,442	16	58	175	416	2,036	4,899	507	
Rate per 100,000 inhabitants.....		4,041.3		331.5	3,709.8	8.0	28.9	87.2	207.4	1,014.9	2,442.1	252.7	
Athens, Ga. M.S.A.	**154,465**												
(Includes Clarke, Madison and Oconee Counties.)													
City of Athens	89,016	7,133		719	6,414	13	50	240	416	1,284	4,653	477	
Total area actually reporting......	86.6%	8,717		841	7,876	16	60	250	515	1,660	5,646	570	
Estimated total	100.0%	9,754		923	8,831	17	65	283	558	1,892	6,247	692	
Rate per 100,000 inhabitants.....		6,314.7		597.5	5,717.2	11.0	42.1	183.2	361.2	1,224.9	4,044.3	448.0	
Atlanta, Ga. M.S.A.	**3,225,549**												
(Includes Barrow, Bartow, Carroll, Cherokee, Cobb, Coweta, DeKalb, Douglas, Fayette, Forsyth, Fulton, Gwinnett, Henry, Newton, Paulding, Pickens, Rockdale, Spalding, and Walton Counties.)													
City of Atlanta.................	402,877	69,914		16,281	53,633	203	492	6,045	9,541	13,168	31,249	9,216	
Total area actually reporting......	97.3%	239,099		29,321	209,778	387	1,336	11,722	15,876	47,125	134,325	28,328	
Estimated total	100.0%	244,965		29,800	215,165	394	1,367	11,907	16,132	48,216	138,057	28,892	
Rate per 100,000 inhabitants.....		7,594.5		923.9	6,670.6	12.2	42.4	369.1	500.1	1,494.8	4,280.1	895.7	
Altantic City, N.J. M.S.A.	**328,721**												
(Includes Atlantic and Cape May Counties.)													
City of Atlantic City	37,539	11,142		1,317	9,825	10	46	643	618	1,268	8,146	411	
Total area actually reporting......	100.0%	27,936		2,750	25,186	22	184	1,022	1,522	5,185	18,954	1,047	
Rate per 100,000 inhabitants.....		8,498.4		836.6	7,661.8	6.7	56.0	310.9	463.0	1,577.3	5,766.0	318.5	
Augusta-Aiken, Ga.-S.C. M.S.A.	**451,500**												
(Includes Columbia, McDuffie, and Richmond Counties, Ga., and Aiken and Edgefield Counties, S.C.)													
City of:													
Augusta, Ga.	45,412	4,481		375	4,106	15	18	209	133	1,259	2,314	533	
Aiken, S.C.	22,677	1,400		163	1,237	2	9	41	111	263	889	85	
Total area actually reporting......	100.0%	21,834		2,920	18,914	58	192	794	1,876	5,529	11,069	2,316	
Rate per 100,000 inhabitants.....		4,835.9		646.7	4,189.1	12.8	42.5	175.9	415.5	1,224.6	2,451.6	513.0	
Austin-San Marcos, Tx. M.S.A.	**918,765**												
(Includes Bastrop, Caldwell, Hays, Travis, and Williamson Counties.)													
City of:													
Austin	502,018	51,468		3,011	48,457	37	271	1,555	1,148	8,453	35,647	4,357	
San Marcos..................	30,074	1,644		146	1,498	2	19	33	92	303	1,112	83	
Total area actually reporting......	100.0%	69,684		4,853	64,831	55	502	1,748	2,548	12,666	46,890	5,275	
Rate per 100,000 inhabitants.....		7,584.5		528.2	7,056.3	6.0	54.6	190.3	277.3	1,378.6	5,103.6	574.1	
Bakersfield, Ca. M.S.A.	**593,687**												
(Includes Kern County.)													
City of Bakersfield	198,908	15,614		1,871	13,743	27	39	568	1,237	3,650	8,498	1,595	
Total area actually reporting......	98.5%	38,268		5,149	33,119	73	174	1,157	3,745	9,781	19,709	3,629	
Estimated total	100.0%	38,805		5,222	33,583	74	177	1,182	3,789	9,892	19,984	3,707	
Rate per 100,000 inhabitants.....		6,536.3		879.6	5,656.7	12.5	29.8	199.1	638.2	1,666.2	3,366.1	624.4	
Baltimore, Md. M.S.A.	**2,457,276**												
(Includes Baltimore City and Anne Arundel, Baltimore, Carroll, Harford, Howard, and Queen Anne's Counties.)													
City of Baltimore...............	732,968	91,920		21,945	69,975	353	668	12,376	8,548	17,901	41,451	10,623	
Total area actually reporting......	100.0%	178,776		33,322	145,454	423	1,221	15,632	16,046	34,072	91,733	19,649	
Rate per 100,000 inhabitants.....		7,275.4		1,356.1	5,919.3	17.2	49.7	636.2	653.0	1,386.6	3,733.1	799.6	
Bangor, Me. M.S.A.	**67,623**												
(Includes part of Penobscot and Waldo Counties.)													
City of Bangor	32,223	1,612		72	1,540	2	18	20	32	162	1,314	64	
Total area actually reporting......	100.0%	2,399		85	2,314	2	22	24	37	289	1,933	92	
Rate per 100,000 inhabitants.....		3,547.6		125.7	3,421.9	3.0	32.5	35.5	54.7	427.4	2,858.5	136.0	

See footnotes at end of table.

Metropolitan Statistical Area	Population	Crime Index total	Modified Crime Index total[1]	Violent crime[2]	Property crime[3]	Murder and non-negligent manslaughter	Forcible rape	Robbery	Aggravated assault	Burglary	Larceny-theft	Motor vehicle theft	Arson[1]
Barnstable-Yarmouth, Ma. M.S.A.......	**137,118**												
(Includes part of Barnstable County.)													
City of:													
Barnstable...................	41,609	2,179		776	1,403	2	22	29	723	609	666	128	
Yarmouth	21,514	1,028		100	928	....	9	9	82	280	592	56	
Total area actually reporting......	94.2%	5,653		1,121	4,532	2	39	49	1,031	1,586	2,677	269	
Estimated total	100.0%	5,937		1,161	4,776	2	41	55	1,063	1,645	2,820	311	
Rate per 100,000 inhabitants.....		4,329.8		846.7	3,483.1	1.5	29.9	40.1	775.2	1,199.7	2,056.6	226.8	
Baton Rouge, La. M.S.A.	**548,361**												
(Includes Ascension, East Baton Rouge, Livingston and West Baton Rouge Parishes.)													
City of Baton Rouge	225,544	36,527		6,822	29,705	74	177	1,866	4,705	7,543	18,156	4,006	
Total area actually reporting......	94.8%	52,019		8,014	44,005	102	264	2,152	5,496	10,596	28,470	4,939	
Estimated total	100.0%	54,047		8,284	45,763	105	274	2,210	5,695	10,934	29,722	5,107	
Rate per 100,000 inhabitants.....		9,856.1		1,510.7	8,345.4	19.1	50.0	402.0	1,038.5	1,993.9	5,420.2	931.3	
Beaumont-Port Arthur, Tx. M.S.A.....	**377,093**												
(Includes Hardin, Jefferson and Orange Counties.)													
City of:													
Beaumont	117,766	12,577		1,466	11,111	23	200	683	560	2,610	6,939	1,562	
Port Arthur..................	70,589	5,538		985	4,553	8	18	246	713	1,404	2,401	748	
Total area actually reporting......	99.4%	26,919		3,177	23,742	42	299	1,093	1,743	5,965	14,942	2,835	
Estimated total	100.0%	27,048		3,189	23,859	42	300	1,095	1,752	5,989	15,025	2,845	
Rate per 100,000 inhabitants......		7,172.8		845.7	6,327.1	11.1	79.6	290.4	464.6	1,588.2	3,984.4	754.5	
Bellingham, Wa. M.S.A..............	**140,914**												
(Includes Whatcom County.)													
City of Bellingham	56,499	4,326		197	4,129	2	45	44	106	689	3,179	261	
Total area actually reporting......	100.0%	7,428		344	7,084	3	82	61	198	1,470	5,251	363	
Rate per 100,000 inhabitants.....		5,271.3		244.1	5,027.2	2.1	58.2	43.3	140.5	1,043.2	3,726.4	257.6	
Benton Harbor, Mi. M.S.A.[4]	**162,208**												
(Includes Berrien County.)													
City of Benton Harbor[4]	13,106				1,700	5		160	654	663	880	157	
Total area actually reporting.....	100.0%				9,032	11		286	1,237	2,211	6,310	511	
Rate per 100,000 inhabitants.....					5,568.2	6.8		176.3	762.6	1,363.1	3,890.1	315.0	
Bergen-Passaic,N.J., M.S.A.	**1,300,853**												
(Includes Bergen and Passaic Counties.)													
City of Passaic	57,389	3,726		606	3,120	3	17	382	204	583	1,864	673	
Total area actually reporting	100.0%	48,913		4,690	44,223	43	207	2,083	2,357	9,295	27,882	7,046	
Rate per 100,000 inhabitants		3,760.1		360.5	3,399.5	3.3	15.9	160.1	181.2	714.5	2,143.4	541.6	
Binghamton, N.Y. M.S.A..............	**267,981**												
(Includes Broome and Tioga Counties.)													
City of Binghamton............	52,306	3,133		145	2,988	3	18	62	62	329	2,653	6	
Total area actually reporting......	100.0%	8,787		569	8,218	6	61	92	410	1,495	6,607	116	
Rate per 100,000 inhabitants......		3,279.0		212.3	3,066.6	2.2	22.8	34.3	153.0	557.9	2,465.5	43.3	
Birmingham, Al. M.S.A...............	**869,321**												
(Includes Blount, Jefferson, St. Clair and Shelby Counties.)													
City of Birmingham	268,768	31,776		6,678	25,098	121	297	1,706	4,554	6,628	14,926	3,544	
Total area actually reporting.....	99.2%	54,249		9,906	44,343	167	449	2,358	6,932	11,361	27,495	5,487	
Estimated total	100.0%	54,663		9,969	44,694	168	452	2,370	6,979	11,444	27,736	5,514	
Rate per 100,000 inhabitants.....		6,288.0		1,146.8	5,141.3	19.3	52.0	272.6	802.8	1,316.4	3,190.5	634.3	
Bismarck, N.D. M.S.A...............	**86,183**												
(Includes Burleigh and Morton Counties.)													
City of Bismarck	51,400	2,269		44	2,225	....	7	3	34	369	1,773	83	
Total area actually reporting.....	100.0%	3,203		151	3,052	1	29	5	116	489	2,432	131	
Rate per 100,000 inhabitants.....		3,716.5		175.2	3,541.3	1.2	33.6	5.8	134.6	567.4	2,821.9	152.0	
Bloomington, In. M.S.A.	**112,184**												
(Includes Monroe County.)													
City of Bloomington	62,100	2,826		515	2,311	....	20	10	485	354	1,797	160	
Total area actually reporting	100.0%	4,204		542	3,662	....	27	15	500	591	2,873	198	
Rate per 100,000 inhabitants		3,747.4		483.1	3,264.3	....	24.1	13.4	445.7	526.8	2,561.0	176.5	
Boise, Id. M.S.A....................	**329,652**												
(Includes Ada and Canyon Counties.)													
City of Boise..................	139,868	7,683		617	7,066	3	72	48	494	1,204	5,538	324	
Total area actually reporting.....	100.0%	15,403		1,123	14,280	8	126	87	902	2,583	10,957	740	
Rate per 100,000 inhabitants......		4,672.5		340.7	4,331.8	2.4	38.2	26.4	273.6	783.6	3,323.8	224.5	

See footnotes at end of table.

Table 6. — Index of Crime, Metropolitan Statistical Areas, 1993 — Continued

Metropolitan Statistical Area	Population	Crime Index total	Modified Crime Index total[1]	Violent crime[2]	Property crime[3]	Murder and non-negligent man-slaughter	Forcible rape	Robbery	Aggra-vated assault	Burglary	Larceny-theft	Motor vehicle theft	Arson[1]
Boston, Ma.-N.H. M.S.A.	**3,393,227**												
(Includes part of Bristol, Essex, Middlesex, Plymouth, Suffolk and Worcester Counties, Ma., and part of Rockingham County, N.H.)													
City of Boston, Ma	553,870	55,555		10,843	44,712	98	480	4,081	6,184	7,982	24,798	11,932	
Total area actually reporting......	92.3%	155,138		25,097	130,041	141	1,009	6,686	17,261	28,319	73,849	27,873	
Estimated total	100.0%	164,388		26,366	138,022	145	1,061	6,871	18,289	30,253	78,525	29,244	
Rate per 100,000 inhabitants......		4,844.6		777.0	4,067.6	4.3	31.3	202.5	539.0	891.6	2,314.2	861.8	
Boulder-Longmont, Co. M.S.A.	**245,117**												
(Includes Boulder County.)													
City of:													
Boulder	88,111	5,817		183	5,634	1	20	40	122	947	4,398	289	
Longmont	56,219	2,697		104	2,593	3	30	20	51	466	2,044	83	
Total area actually reporting......	100.0%	12,323		577	11,746	6	98	79	394	2,249	8,965	532	
Rate per 100,000 inhabitants......		5,027.4		235.4	4,792.0	2.4	40.0	32.2	160.7	917.5	3,657.4	217.0	
Brazoria, Tx. M.S.A.	**207,861**												
(Includes Brazoria County.)													
Total area actually reporting......	100.0%	7,013		635	6,378	7	87	87	454	1,436	4,393	549	
Rate per 100,000 inhabitants......		3,373.9		305.5	3,068.4	3.4	41.9	41.9	218.4	690.8	2,113.4	264.1	
Bremerton, Wa. M.S.A.	**215,355**												
(Includes Kitsap County.)													
City of Bremerton	42,569	2,343		267	2,076	....	43	63	161	366	1,573	137	
Total area actually reporting......	100.0%	8,521		655	7,866	3	104	132	416	1,637	5,805	424	
Rate per 100,000 inhabitants......		3,956.7		304.1	3,652.6	1.4	48.3	61.3	193.2	760.1	2,695.5	196.9	
Bridgeport, Ct. M.S.A.	**452,865**												
(Includes part of Fairfield and New Haven Counties.)													
City of Bridgeport	136,865	13,599		2,540	11,059	60	72	1,560	848	3,653	3,820	3,586	
Total area actually reporting......	100.0%	25,132		3,004	22,128	67	101	1,778	1,058	5,897	10,837	5,394	
Rate per 100,000 inhabitants......		5,549.6		663.3	4,886.2	14.8	22.3	392.6	233.6	1,302.2	2,393.0	1,191.1	
Brockton, Ma. M.S.A.	**246,237**												
(Includes part of Bristol, Norfolk and Plymouth Counties.)													
City of Brockton	89,473	6,895		1,156	5,739	15	54	328	759	1,816	2,089	1,834	
Total area actually reporting......	81.8%	10,418		1,586	8,832	15	61	371	1,139	2,556	3,916	2,360	
Estimated total	100.0%	12,010		1,805	10,205	16	70	403	1,316	2,889	4,720	2,596	
Rate per 100,000 inhabitants......		4,877.4		733.0	4,144.4	6.5	28.4	163.7	534.4	1,173.3	1,916.9	1,054.3	
Brownsville-Harlingen-San Benito, Tx. M.S.A.	**284,168**												
(Includes Cameron County.)													
City of:													
Brownsville..................	107,838	11,393		1,097	10,296	17	28	281	771	2,209	7,291	796	
Harlingen...................	52,984	4,971		429	4,542	6	3	65	355	834	3,325	383	
San Benito	22,030	1,519		127	1,392	1	12	14	100	251	1,044	97	
Total area actually reporting......	100.0%	21,371		1,965	19,406	31	55	388	1,491	4,591	13,349	1,466	
Rate per 100,000 inhabitants......		7,520.6		691.5	6,829.1	10.9	19.4	136.5	524.7	1,615.6	4,697.6	515.9	
Bryan-College Station, Tx. M.S.A.	**127,620**												
(Includes Brazos County.)													
City of:													
Bryan......................	57,657	4,368		512	3,856	2	54	87	369	853	2,719	284	
College Station..............	56,777	2,280		128	2,152	....	19	25	84	405	1,622	125	
Total area actually reporting......	100.0%	7,697		660	7,037	3	77	113	467	1,433	5,164	440	
Rate per 100,000 inhabitants......		6,031.2		517.2	5,514.0	2.4	60.3	88.5	365.9	1,122.9	4,046.4	344.8	
Buffalo-Niagara Falls, N.Y. M.S.A.	**1,201,686**												
(Includes Erie and Niagara Counties.)													
City of:													
Buffalo	324,855	31,871		6,041	25,830	76	295	2,898	2,772	7,597	12,714	5,519	
Niagara Falls	62,002	4,938		445	4,493	3	39	207	196	1,068	2,932	493	
Total area actually reporting......	99.8%	63,386		9,059	54,327	88	445	3,516	5,010	13,233	32,584	8,510	
Estimated total	100.0%	63,495		9,070	54,425	88	445	3,521	5,016	13,251	32,656	8,518	
Rate per 100,000 inhabitants......		5,283.8		754.8	4,529.1	7.3	37.0	293.0	417.4	1,102.7	2,717.5	708.8	
Canton-Massillon, Oh. M.S.A.	**401,855**												
(Includes Carroll and Stark Counties.)													
City of:													
Canton.....................	85,326	7,280		1,035	6,245	11	82	537	405	1,700	3,910	635	
Massillon...................	31,397	1,368		83	1,285	2	11	35	35	260	926	99	
Total area actually reporting......	93.7%	18,263		1,861	16,402	18	177	835	831	4,128	10,931	1,343	
Estimated total	100.0%	18,911		1,903	17,008	18	183	848	854	4,269	11,355	1,384	
Rate per 100,000 inhabitants......		4,705.9		473.6	4,232.4	4.5	45.5	211.0	212.5	1,062.3	2,825.6	344.4	

See footnotes at end of table.

Table 6. — Index of Crime, Metropolitan Statistical Areas, 1993 — Continued

Metropolitan Statistical Area	Population	Crime Index total	Modified Crime Index total[1]	Violent crime[2]	Property crime[3]	Murder and non-negligent man-slaughter	Forcible rape	Robbery	Aggra-vated assault	Burglary	Larceny-theft	Motor vehicle theft	Arson[1]
Charleston-North Charleston, S.C. M.S.A.	**534,445**												
(Includes Berkeley, Charleston, and Dorchester Counties.)													
City of:													
Charleston	82,203	6,661		989	5,672	12	35	340	602	1,071	4,091	510	
North Charleston.............	75,204	9,323		1,537	7,786	9	98	430	1,000	1,484	5,472	830	
Total area actually reporting.....	100.0%	34,565		5,044	29,521	43	306	1,159	3,536	6,613	20,449	2,459	
Rate per 100,000 inhabitants.....		6,467.5		943.8	5,523.7	8.0	57.3	216.9	661.6	1,237.4	3,826.2	460.1	
Charleston, W.V. M.S.A...............	**254,300**												
(Includes Kanawha and Putnam Counties.)													
City of Charleston	57,430	6,754		769	5,985	16	51	290	412	1,293	4,238	454	
Total area actually reporting.....	100.0%	11,022		1,031	9,991	26	80	326	599	2,361	6,813	817	
Rate per 100,000 inhabitants.....		4,334.3		405.4	3,928.8	10.2	31.5	128.2	235.5	928.4	2,679.1	321.3	
Charlotte-Gastonia-Rock Hill, N.C.-S.C. M.S.A.........................	**1,230,964**												
(Includes Cabarrus, Gaston, Lincoln, Mecklenburg, Rowan and Union Counties, N.C., and York County, S.C.)													
City of:													
Charlotte, N.C	422,862	49,758		9,725	40,033	122	356	3,227	6,020	10,691	26,370	2,972	
Gastonia, N.C	57,985	6,138		894	5,244	19	25	304	546	1,386	3,590	268	
Rock Hill, S.C	44,876	4,094		965	3,129	6	23	120	816	710	2,270	149	
Total area actually reporting.....	99.9%	89,523		14,820	74,703	204	575	4,220	9,821	21,484	48,540	4,679	
Estimated total	100.0%	89,577		14,826	74,751	204	575	4,222	9,825	21,496	48,574	4,681	
Rate per 100,000 inhabitants......		7,277.0		1,204.4	6,072.6	16.6	46.7	343.0	798.2	1,746.3	3,946.0	380.3	
Charlottesville, Va. M.S.A.............	**136,484**												
(Includes Albemarle, Fluvanna and Greene Counties and Charlottesville City.)													
City of Charlottesville...........	41,173	2,752		285	2,467	....	25	80	180	384	1,934	149	
Total area actually reporting.....	100.0%	5,916		399	5,517	3	51	96	249	901	4,314	302	
Rate per 100,000 inhabitants.....		4,334.6		292.3	4,042.2	2.2	37.4	70.3	182.4	660.2	3,160.8	221.3	
Chattanooga, Tn.-Ga. M.S.A.	**438,176**												
(Includes Hamilton and Marion Counties, Tn.; Catoosa, Dade, and Walker Counties, Ga.)													
City of Chattanooga, Tn.	155,140	16,338		3,032	13,306	38	154	709	2,131	3,144	7,907	2,255	
Total area actually reporting.....	94.6%	23,162		3,567	19,595	44	190	788	2,545	4,739	12,047	2,809	
Estimated total	100.0%	23,953		3,652	20,301	45	197	802	2,608	4,931	12,501	2,869	
Rate per 100,000 inhabitants......		5,466.5		833.5	4,633.1	10.3	45.0	183.0	595.2	1,125.3	2,853.0	654.8	
Cheyenne, Wy. M.S.A.................	**76,880**												
(Includes Laramie County.)													
City of Cheyenne................	53,033	2,666		108	2,558	....	22	17	69	258	2,224	76	
Total area actually reporting.....	100.0%	3,199		162	3,037	....	40	24	98	329	2,612	96	
Rate per 100,000 inhabitants.....		4,161.0		210.7	3,950.3	....	52.0	31.2	127.5	427.9	3,397.5	124.9	
Chico-Paradise, Ca. M.S.A............	**190,302**												
(Includes Butte County.)													
City of:													
Chico........................	41,122	2,941		197	2,744	1	33	47	116	601	1,983	160	
Paradise	26,377	822		67	755	....	....	3	64	245	472	38	
Total area actually reporting.....	100.0%	9,549		836	8,713	6	82	135	613	2,660	5,482	571	
Rate per 100,000 inhabitants......		5,017.8		439.3	4,578.5	3.2	43.1	70.9	322.1	1,397.8	2,880.7	300.0	
Cincinnati, Oh.-Ky.-In. M.S.A.........	**1,571,218**												
(Includes Brown, Clermont, Hamilton and Warren Counties, Oh.; Boone, Campbell, Gallatin, Grant, Kenton and Pendleton Counties, Ky.; and Dearborn and Ohio Counties, In.)													
City of Cincinnati, Oh	366,591	30,923		5,621	25,302	39	449	2,327	2,806	6,154	17,085	2,063	
Total area actually reporting.....	89.0%	70,617		8,647	61,970	56	796	3,079	4,716	12,672	45,596	3,702	
Estimated total	100.0%	75,947		9,012	66,935	59	840	3,175	4,938	13,669	49,219	4,047	
Rate per 100,000 inhabitants.....		4,833.6		573.6	4,260.1	3.8	53.5	202.1	314.3	870.0	3,132.5	257.6	

See footnotes at end of table.

Table 6. — Index of Crime, Metropolitan Statistical Areas, 1993 — Continued

Metropolitan Statistical Area	Population	Crime Index total	Modified Crime Index total[1]	Violent crime[2]	Property crime[3]	Murder and non-negligent man-slaughter	Forcible rape	Robbery	Aggra-vated assault	Burglary	Larceny-theft	Motor vehicle theft	Arson[1]
Clarksville-Hopkinsville, Tn.-Ky. M.S.A.	**180,407**												
(Includes Christian County, Ky., and Montgomery County, Tn.)													
City of:													
Clarksville, Tn	85,637	4,728		1,061	3,667	1	90	112	858	901	2,627	139	
Hopkinsville, Ky	31,174	1,814		274	1,540	3	18	57	196	424	1,035	81	
Total area actually reporting......	99.6%	7,873		1,564	6,309	7	115	185	1,257	1,676	4,355	278	
Estimated total	100.0%	7,906		1,568	6,338	7	115	186	1,260	1,682	4,376	280	
Rate per 100,000 inhabitants......		4,382.3		869.1	3,513.2	3.9	63.7	103.1	698.4	932.3	2,425.6	155.2	
Colorado Springs, Co. M.S.A.	**433.461**												
(Includes El Paso County.)													
City of Colorado Springs	304,438	19,608		1,555	18,053	19	265	389	882	3,645	13,391	1,017	
Total area actually reporting......	99.9%	23,556		1,959	21,597	24	288	424	1,223	4,491	15,921	1,185	
Estimated total	100.0%	23,593		1,963	21,630	24	288	425	1,226	4,497	15,946	1,187	
Rate per 100,000 inhabitants......		5,442.9		452.9	4,990.1	5.5	66.4	98.0	282.8	1,037.5	3,678.8	273.8	
Columbia, Mo. M.S.A.	**117,862**												
(Includes Boone County.)													
City of Columbia................	73,683	4,708		439	4,269	1	30	108	300	571	3,532	166	
Total area actually reporting......	100.0%	6,004		542	5,462	2	43	120	377	781	4,478	203	
Rate per 100,000 inhabitants......		5,094.1		459.9	4,634.2	1.7	36.5	101.8	319.9	662.6	3,799.4	172.2	
Columbia, S.C. M.S.A.	**477,627**												
(Includes Lexington and Richland Counties.)													
City of Columbia................	99,929	12,363		2,204	10,159	22	94	666	1,422	2,090	7,316	753	
Total area actually reporting......	100.0%	33,083		5,393	27,690	50	321	1,441	3,581	6,793	18,611	2,286	
Rate per 100,000 inhabitants......		6,926.5		1,129.1	5,797.4	10.5	67.2	301.7	749.7	1,422.2	3,896.6	478.6	
Columbus, Ga.-Al. M.S.A.	**278,325**												
(Includes Chattahoochee, Harris, and Muscogee Counties, Ga., and Russell County, Al.)													
City of Columbus, Ga	190,331	12,266		1,163	11,103	32	49	451	631	2,309	7,752	1,042	
Total area actually reporting......	99.7%	15,193		1,550	13,643	38	87	505	920	3,131	9,252	1,260	
Estimated total	100.0%	15,262		1,555	13,707	38	87	507	923	3,142	9,299	1,266	
Rate per 100,000 inhabitants......		5,483.5		558.7	4,924.8	13.7	31.3	182.2	331.6	1,128.9	3,341.1	454.9	
Columbus, Oh. M.S.A.	**1,401,383**												
(Includes Delaware, Fairfield, Franklin, Licking, Madison, and Pickaway Counties.)													
City of Columbus................	646,933	56,322		7,146	49,176	105	658	3,887	2,496	13,055	29,051	7,070	
Total area actually reporting......	85.1%	77,510		9,115	68,395	113	832	4,332	3,838	16,938	43,308	8,149	
Estimated total	100.0%	84,262		9,561	74,701	117	887	4,458	4,099	18,127	47,996	8,578	
Rate per 100,000 inhabitants......		6,012.8		682.3	5,330.5	8.3	63.3	318.1	292.5	1,293.5	3,424.9	612.1	
Corpus Christi, Tx. M.S.A.	**369,485**												
(Includes Nueces and San Patricio Counties.)													
City of Corpus Christi	271,654	27,416		2,225	25,191	34	194	509	1,488	4,600	18,919	1,672	
Total area actually reporting......	100.0%	30,981		2,586	28,395	44	248	527	1,767	5,750	20,800	1,845	
Rate per 100,000 inhabitants......		8,384.9		699.9	7,685.0	11.9	67.1	142.6	478.2	1,556.2	5,629.5	499.3	
Cumberland, Md.-W.V. M.S.A.	**102,409**												
(Includes Allegany County, Md., and Mineral County, W.V.)													
City of Cumberland, Md	24,135	1,477		270	1,207	....	5	15	250	222	934	51	
Total area actually reporting......	100.0%	2,905		426	2,479	2	15	26	383	490	1,867	122	
Rate per 100,000 inhabitants......		2,836.7		416.0	2,420.7	2.0	14.6	25.4	374.0	478.5	1,823.1	119.1	
Dallas, Tx. M.S.A.	**2,751,065**												
(Includes Collin, Dallas, Denton, Ellis, Henderson, Kaufman, and Rockwall Counties.)													
City of Dallas...................	1,042,619	110,799		18,176	92,623	317	1,000	7,420	9,439	20,975	54,183	17,465	
Total area actually reporting......	100.0%	200,577		26,035	174,542	403	1,623	8,979	15,030	38,948	111,455	24,139	
Rate per 100,000 inhabitants......		7,290.9		946.4	6,344.5	14.6	59.0	326.4	546.3	1,415.7	4,051.3	877.4	

See footnotes at end of table.

Table 6. — Index of Crime, Metropolitan Statistical Areas, 1993 — Continued

Metropolitan Statistical Area	Population	Crime Index total	Modified Crime Index total[1]	Violent crime[2]	Property crime[3]	Murder and non-negligent manslaughter	Forcible rape	Robbery	Aggravated assault	Burglary	Larceny-theft	Motor vehicle theft	Arson[1]
Danbury, Ct. M.S.A.	**162,590**												
(Includes part of Fairfield, and Litchfield Counties.)													
City of Danbury	65,257	3,524		172	3,352	1	12	71	88	546	2,405	401	
Total area actually reporting	100.0%	5,496		232	5,264	3	17	79	133	960	3,807	497	
Rate per 100,000 inhabitants		3,380.3		142.7	3,237.6	1.8	10.5	48.6	81.8	590.4	2,341.5	305.7	
Danville, Va. M.S.A.	**110,979**												
(Includes Pittsylvania County and Danville City.)													
City of Danville	54,383	2,303		211	2,092	10	24	78	99	388	1,622	82	
Total area actually reporting	100.0%	3,231		290	2,941	17	51	95	127	650	2,146	145	
Rate per 100,000 inhabitants		2,911.4		261.3	2,650.1	15.3	46.0	85.6	114.4	585.7	1,933.7	130.7	
Dayton-Springfield, Oh. M.S.A.	**968,224**												
(Includes Clark, Greene, Miami and Montgomery Counties.)													
City of:													
Dayton	184,352	19,637		2,922	16,715	49	269	1,475	1,129	4,303	9,473	2,939	
Springfield	70,868	6,527		1,059	5,468	6	59	208	786	963	4,048	457	
Total area actually reporting	95.9%	49,255		5,222	44,033	75	560	2,104	2,483	9,253	29,648	5,132	
Estimated total	100.0%	50,787		5,325	45,462	76	571	2,132	2,546	9,478	30,755	5,229	
Rate per 100,000 inhabitants		5,245.4		550.0	4,695.4	7.8	59.0	220.2	263.0	978.9	3,176.4	540.1	
Daytona Beach, Fl. M.S.A.	**427,877**												
(Includes Flagler and Volusia Counties.)													
City of Daytona Beach	65,573	7,524		1,367	6,157	12	90	349	916	1,848	3,599	710	
Total area actually reporting	100.0%	25,272		3,388	21,884	22	240	644	2,482	6,659	13,422	1,803	
Rate per 100,000 inhabitants		5,906.4		791.8	5,114.6	5.1	56.1	150.5	580.1	1,556.3	3,136.9	421.4	
Decatur, Al. M.S.A.	**136,793**												
(Includes Lawrence and Morgan Counties.)													
City of Decatur	51,041	4,152		276	3,876	8	27	86	155	725	2,889	262	
Total area actually reporting	98.6%	4,862		330	4,532	14	30	93	193	933	3,308	291	
Estimated total	100.0%	4,975		347	4,628	14	31	96	206	956	3,374	298	
Rate per 100,000 inhabitants		3,636.9		253.7	3,383.2	10.2	22.7	70.2	150.6	698.9	2,466.5	217.8	
Denver, Co. M.S.A.	**1,757,721**												
(Includes Adams, Arapahoe, Denver, Douglas and Jefferson Counties.)													
City of Denver	498,402	39,796		5,252	34,544	74	393	1,863	2,922	9,128	17,858	7,558	
Total area actually reporting	100.0%	107,059		12,862	94,197	132	800	3,278	8,652	20,288	61,612	12,297	
Rate per 100,000 inhabitants		6,090.8		731.7	5,359.0	7.5	45.5	186.5	492.2	1,154.2	3,505.2	699.6	
Des Moines, Ia. M.S.A.	**408,171**												
(Includes Dallas, Polk and Warren Counties.)													
City of Des Moines	195,485	15,505		902	14,603	9	84	271	538	1,986	11,763	854	
Total area actually reporting	93.6%	21,859		1,156	20,703	10	106	288	752	3,038	16,565	1,100	
Estimated total	100.0%	22,650		1,214	21,436	10	113	292	799	3,221	17,077	1,138	
Rate per 100,000 inhabitants		5,549.1		297.4	5,251.7	2.4	27.7	71.5	195.8	789.1	4,183.8	278.8	
Detroit, Mi. M.S.A.[4]	**4,330,568**												
(Includes Lapeer, Macomb, Monroe, Oakland, St. Claire and Wayne Counties.)													
City of Detroit[4]	1,020,062				93,971	579		13,591	12,999	23,092	42,818	28,061	
Total area actually reporting	95.1%				224,636	679		17,089	23,697	44,191	136,305	44,140	
Estimated total	100.0%				234,223	686		17,332	24,446	45,741	143,361	45,121	
Rate per 100,000 inhabitants					5,408.6	15.8		400.2	564.5	1,056.2	3,310.4	1,041.9	
Dothan, Al. M.S.A.	**134,860**												
(Includes Dale and Houston Counties.)													
City of Dothan	55,435	4,787		707	4,080	4	33	115	555	835	2,965	280	
Total area actually reporting	99.2%	6,423		1,052	5,371	8	43	142	859	1,140	3,900	331	
Estimated total	100.0%	6,484		1,061	5,423	8	43	144	866	1,152	3,936	335	
Rate per 100,000 inhabitants		4,807.9		786.7	4,021.2	5.9	31.9	106.8	642.1	854.2	2,918.6	248.4	
Dubuque, Ia. M.S.A.	**87,612**												
(Includes Dubuque County.)													
City of Dubuque	58,804	2,721		180	2,541	....	43	14	123	527	1,876	138	
Total area actually reporting	100.0%	3,211		219	2,992	....	62	14	143	727	2,107	158	
Rate per 100,000 inhabitants		3,665.0		250.0	3,415.1	....	70.8	16.0	163.2	829.8	2,404.9	180.3	
Duluth-Superior, Mn.-Wi. M.S.A.[4]	**243,527**												
(Includes St. Louis County, Mn., and Douglas County, Wi.)													
City of:													
Duluth, Mn.[4]	86,368				4,393	6		53	221	859	3,266	268	
Superior, Wi	27,639				1,850	1		15	43	347	1,403	100	
Total area actually reporting	100.0%				9,083	11		77	337	2,163	6,397	523	
Rate per 100,000 inhabitants					3,729.8	4.5		31.6	138.4	888.2	2,626.8	214.8	

See footnotes at end of table.

Table 6. – Index of Crime, Metropolitan Statistical Areas, 1993 – Continued

Metropolitan Statistical Area	Population	Crime Index total	Modified Crime Index total[1]	Violent crime[2]	Property crime[3]	Murder and non-negligent man-slaughter	Forcible rape	Robbery	Aggra-vated assault	Burglary	Larceny-theft	Motor vehicle theft	Arson[1]
Dutchess County, N.Y. M.S.A		**264,128**											
(Includes Dutchess County.)													
Total area actually reporting......	98.2%	7,826		893	6,933	14	37	253	589	1,552	5,039	342	
Estimated total	100.0%	8,000		911	7,089	14	38	260	599	1,581	5,153	355	
Rate per 100,000 inhabitants......		3,028.8		344.9	2,683.9	5.3	14.4	98.4	226.8	598.6	1,950.9	134.4	
Eau Claire, Wi. M.S.A...............	**141,145**												
(Includes Chippewa and Eau Claire Counties.)													
City of Eau Claire	58,492	2,939		85	2,854	....	....	8	77	550	2,201	103	
Total area actually reporting......	97.8%	4,894		125	4,769	....	11	14	100	925	3,653	191	
Estimated total	100.0%	5,021		129	4,892	....	11	15	103	942	3,753	197	
Rate per 100,000 inhabitants......		3,557.3		91.4	3,465.9	....	7.8	10.6	73.0	667.4	2,659.0	139.6	
Elkhart-Goshen, In. M.S.A	**160,863**												
(Includes Elkhart County.)													
City of:													
Elkhart	44,709	4,305		226	4,079	3	58	122	43	789	3,114	176	
Goshen	24,647	1,148		108	1,040	1	13	6	88	160	845	35	
Total area actually reporting......	100.0%	7,806		818	6,988	4	90	144	580	1,388	5,298	302	
Rate per 100,000 inhabitants......		4,852.6		508.5	4,344.1	2.5	55.9	89.5	360.6	862.8	3,293.5	187.7	
El Paso, Tx. M.S.A..................	**640,839**												
(Includes El Paso County.)													
City of El Paso..................	554,515	46,738		6,109	40,629	47	281	1,561	4,220	5,643	29,440	5,546	
Total area actually reporting......	100.0%	50,163		6,607	43,556	55	340	1,629	4,583	6,397	31,373	5,786	
Rate per 100,000 inhabitants......		7,827.7		1,031.0	6,796.7	8.6	53.1	254.2	715.2	998.2	4,895.6	902.9	
Enid, Ok. M.S.A....................	**56,818**												
(Includes Garfield County.)													
City of Enid	45,441	3,763		416	3,347	1	31	37	347	717	2,486	144	
Total area actually reporting......	100.0%	3,928		420	3,508	2	31	37	350	775	2,584	149	
Rate per 100,000 inhabitants......		6,913.3		739.2	6,174.1	3.5	54.6	65.1	616.0	1,364.0	4,547.9	262.2	
Erie, Pa. M.S.A....................	**280,843**												
(Includes Erie County.)													
City of Erie....................	109,749	5,474		837	4,637	7	59	426	345	999	3,261	377	
Total area actually reporting......	99.9%	9,614		1,088	8,526	8	103	458	519	1,821	6,117	588	
Rate per 100,000 inhabitants......		3,423.3		387.4	3,035.9	2.8	36.7	163.1	184.8	648.4	2,178.1	209.4	
Estimated total	100.0%	9,673		1,086	8,587	8	104	458	516	1,836	6,160	591	
Rate per 100,000 inhabitants......		3,444.3		386.7	3,057.6	2.8	37.0	163.1	183.7	653.7	2,193.4	210.4	
Eugene-Springfield, Or. M.S.A	**296,820**												
(Includes Lane County.)													
City of:													
Eugene	118,390	8,697		470	8,227	3	64	166	237	1,381	6,471	375	
Springfield	47,215	3,644		251	3,393	2	20	51	178	624	2,605	164	
Total area actually reporting......	100.0%	16,246		945	15,301	6	134	253	552	3,016	11,538	747	
Rate per 100,000 inhabitants......		5,473.4		318.4	5,155.0	2.0	45.1	85.2	186.0	1,016.1	3,887.2	251.7	
Evansville-Henderson,In.-Ky. M.S.A. ..	**285,569**												
(Includes Posey, Vanderburgh and Warrick Counties, In., and Henderson County, Ky.)													
City of:													
Evansville, In	128,805	7,071		772	6,299	7	43	151	571	1,580	4,359	360	
Henderson, Ky................	26,699	1,878		345	1,533	1	20	12	312	272	1,179	82	
Total area actually reporting......	85.7%	10,627		1,298	9,329	9	76	168	1,045	2,168	6,643	518	
Estimated total	100.0%	11,933		1,400	10,533	10	86	187	1,117	2,417	7,486	630	
Rate per 100,000 inhabitants......		4,178.7		490.2	3,688.4	3.5	30.1	65.5	391.1	846.4	2,621.4	220.6	
Fargo-Moorhead, N.D.-Mn. M.S.A.[4] ...	**158,369**												
(Includes Cass County, N.D., and Clay County, Mn.)													
City of:													
Fargo, N.D....................	77,186	3,872		92	3,780	....	35	16	41	425	3,149	206	
Moorehead, Mn.[4]	33,071				1,639	1	4	44	194	1,386	59		
Total area actually reporting......	100.0%				6,345	1		21	104	797	5,206	342	
Rate per 100,000 inhabitants......					4,006.5	.6		13.3	65.7	503.3	3,287.3	216.0	
Fayetteville, N.C. M.S.A.	**281,740**												
(Includes Cumberland County.)													
City of Fayetteville	77,872	10,189		1,786	8,403	30	92	583	1,081	2,071	5,685	647	
Total area actually reporting......	100.0%	23,321		3,033	20,288	61	195	987	1,790	5,767	12,922	1,599	
Rate per 100,000 inhabitants......		8,277.5		1,076.5	7,201.0	21.7	69.2	350.3	635.3	2,046.9	4,586.5	567.5	

See footnotes at end of table.

Table 6. — Index of Crime, Metropolitan Statistical Areas, 1993 — Continued

Metropolitan Statistical Area	Population	Crime Index total	Modified Crime Index total[1]	Violent crime[2]	Property crime[3]	Murder and non-negligent man-slaughter	Forcible rape	Robbery	Aggra-vated assault	Burglary	Larceny-theft	Motor vehicle theft	Arson[1]
Fayetteville-Springdale-Rogers, Ar. M.S.A.	**228,557**												
(Includes Benton and Washington Counties.)													
City of:													
Fayetteville	46,648	2,139		127	2,012	1	29	14	83	305	1,542	165	
Springdale	33,192	1,468		66	1,402	1	9	13	43	256	1,059	87	
Rogers	27,670	1,559		63	1,496	....	9	10	44	233	1,215	48	
Total area actually reporting	98.1%	7,562		429	7,133	9	70	53	297	1,447	5,298	388	
Estimated total	100.0%	7,807		448	7,359	9	72	58	309	1,486	5,471	402	
Rate per 100,000 inhabitants		3,415.8		196.0	3,219.8	3.9	31.5	25.4	135.2	650.2	2,393.7	175.9	
Fitchburg-Leominster, Ma. M.S.A.	**136,990**												
(Includes part of Middlesex and Worcester Counties.)													
City of:													
Fitchburg	39,060	2,570		628	1,942	1	38	83	506	685	1,050	207	
Leominster	38,379	1,842		157	1,685	4	13	25	115	458	1,082	145	
Total area actually reporting	81.8%	5,433		1,001	4,432	5	68	115	813	1,426	2,592	414	
Estimated total	100.0%	6,315		1,122	5,193	5	73	133	911	1,610	3,038	545	
Rate per 100,000 inhabitants		4,609.8		819.0	3,790.8	3.6	53.3	97.1	665.0	1,175.3	2,217.7	397.8	
Flint, Mi. M.S.A.[4]	**435,436**												
(Includes Genesee County.)													
City of Flint[4]	139,960				14,032	48		1,039	2,507	4,024	7,701	2,307	
Total area actually reporting	98.8%				25,873	54		1,278	3,297	6,247	16,325	3,301	
Estimated total	100.0%				26,108	54		1,284	3,315	6,285	16,498	3,325	
Rate per 100,000 inhabitants					5,995.8	12.4		294.9	761.3	1,443.4	3,788.8	763.6	
Florence, Al. M.S.A.	**135,811**												
(Includes Colbert and Lauderdale Counties.)													
City of Florence	37,304	1,944		225	1,719	4	9	30	182	345	1,308	66	
Total area actually reporting	99.4%	3,678		352	3,326	12	14	35	291	598	2,587	141	
Estimated total	100.0%	3,723		358	3,365	12	14	36	296	607	2,614	144	
Rate per 100,000 inhabitants		2,741.3		263.6	2,477.7	8.8	10.3	26.5	217.9	446.9	1,924.7	106.0	
Florence, S.C. M.S.A.	**119,908**												
(Includes Florence County.)													
City of Florence	31,081	3,457		545	2,912	1	20	180	344	629	2,108	175	
Total area actually reporting	100.0%	8,355		1,254	7,101	17	76	277	884	2,044	4,562	495	
Rate per 100,000 inhabitants		6,967.8		1,045.8	5,922.0	14.2	63.4	231.0	737.2	1,704.6	3,804.6	412.8	
Fort Collins-Loveland, Co. M.S.A.	**203,897**												
(Includes Larimer County.)													
City of:													
Fort Collins	96,055	4,768		389	4,379	1	68	26	294	760	3,447	172	
Loveland	41,505	1,641		168	1,473	....	35	8	125	172	1,246	55	
Total area actually reporting	100.0%	7,985		621	7,364	2	108	41	470	1,233	5,835	296	
Rate per 100,000 inhabitants		3,916.2		304.6	3,611.6	1.0	53.0	20.1	230.5	604.7	2,861.7	145.2	
Fort Lauderdale, Fl. M.S.A.	**1,320,180**												
(Includes Broward County.)													
City of Fort Lauderdale	150,683	25,775		2,350	23,425	31	76	1,270	973	5,822	14,477	3,126	
Total area actually reporting	100.0%	117,550		13,273	104,277	104	533	4,839	7,797	23,520	67,436	13,321	
Rate per 100,000 inhabitants		8,904.1		1,005.4	7,898.7	7.9	40.4	366.5	590.6	1,781.6	5,108.1	1,009.0	
Fort Myers-Cape Coral, Fl. M.S.A.	**357,168**												
(Includes Lee County.)													
City of:													
Fort Myers	47,041	7,846		1,373	6,473	5	39	459	870	1,682	3,672	1,119	
Cape Coral	82,708	4,162		262	3,900	1	12	22	227	1,077	2,588	235	
Total area actually reporting	100.0%	21,628		2,535	19,093	19	187	698	1,631	5,099	11,258	2,736	
Rate per 100,000 inhabitants		6,055.4		709.8	5,345.7	5.3	52.4	195.4	456.6	1,427.6	3,152.0	766.0	
Fort Pierce-Port St. Lucie, Fl. M.S.A.	**269,255**												
(Includes Martin and St. Lucie Counties.)													
City of:													
Fort Pierce	38,086	5,227		964	4,263	10	50	246	658	1,314	2,188	761	
Port St. Lucie	64,383	2,282		198	2,084	3	13	9	173	617	1,322	145	
Total area actually reporting	100.0%	16,135		2,084	14,051	27	128	453	1,476	4,264	8,231	1,556	
Rate per 100,000 inhabitants		5,992.5		774.0	5,218.5	10.0	47.5	168.2	548.2	1,583.6	3,057.0	577.9	
Fort Smith, Ar.-Ok. M.S.A.	**182,651**												
(Includes Crawford and Sebastian Counties, Ar., and Sequoyah County, Ok.)													
City of Fort Smith, Ar	74,875	5,831		521	5,310	4	66	62	389	963	3,956	391	
Total area actually reporting	100.0%	8,397		780	7,617	9	86	70	615	1,670	5,426	521	
Rate per 100,000 inhabitants		4,597.3		427.0	4,170.2	4.9	47.1	38.3	336.7	914.3	2,970.7	285.2	

See footnotes at end of table.

Table 6.—Index of Crime, Metropolitan Statistical Areas, 1993—Continued

Metropolitan Statistical Area	Population	Crime Index total	Modified Crime Index total[1]	Violent crime[2]	Property crime[3]	Murder and non-negligent man-slaughter	Forcible rape	Robbery	Aggra-vated assault	Burglary	Larceny-theft	Motor vehicle theft	Arson[1]
Fort Walton Beach, Fl. M.S.A.	**155,654**												
(Includes Okaloosa County.)													
City of Fort Walton Beach	23,057	1,297		137	1,160	2	16	29	90	247	820	93	
Total area actually reporting	100.0%	5,829		571	5,258	7	36	91	437	1,160	3,778	320	
Rate per 100,000 inhabitants		3,744.8		366.8	3,378.0	4.5	23.1	58.5	280.8	745.2	2,427.2	205.6	
Fort Wayne, In. M.S.A.	**467,750**												
(Includes Adams, Allen, De Kalb, Huntington and Whitley Counties.)													
City of Fort Wayne	175,405	14,857		1,027	13,830	28	130	552	317	2,028	10,016	1,786	
Total area actually reporting	89.3%	19,501		1,463	18,038	40	154	585	684	2,903	12,973	2,162	
Estimated total	100.0%	21,208		1,596	19,612	41	166	609	780	3,210	14,098	2,304	
Rate per 100,000 inhabitants		4,534.0		341.2	4,192.8	8.8	35.5	130.2	166.8	686.3	3,014.0	492.6	
Fort Worth-Arlington, Tx. M.S.A.	**1,538,831**												
(Includes Johnson, Parker and Tarrant Counties.)													
City of:													
Fort Worth	463,373	49,801		6,979	42,822	133	507	2,750	3,589	10,505	26,310	6,007	
Arlington	281,336	20,202		2,259	17,943	7	146	710	1,396	3,977	11,514	2,452	
Total area actually reporting	100.0%	105,885		12,689	93,196	180	987	4,062	7,460	21,369	60,530	11,297	
Rate per 100,000 inhabitants		6,880.9		824.6	6,056.3	11.7	64.1	264.0	484.8	1,388.7	3,933.5	734.1	
Fresno, Ca. M.S.A.	**812,859**												
(Includes Fresno and Madera Counties.)													
City of Fresno	379,977	41,584		5,511	36,073	87	216	2,879	2,329	8,472	14,518	13,083	
Total area actually reporting	100.0%	65,838		8,816	57,022	137	424	3,477	4,778	15,056	25,341	16,625	
Rate per 100,000 inhabitants		8,099.6		1,084.6	7,015.0	16.9	52.2	427.7	587.8	1,852.2	3,117.5	2,045.3	
Gadsden, Al. M.S.A.	**100,556**												
(Includes Etowah County.)													
City of Gadsden	44,333	5,163		1,026	4,137	9	40	187	790	974	2,733	430	
Total area actually reporting	100.0%	6,519		1,184	5,335	13	51	206	914	1,229	3,608	498	
Rate per 100,000 inhabitants		6,483.0		1,177.5	5,305.5	12.9	50.7	204.9	908.9	1,222.2	3,588.1	495.2	
Gainesville, Fl. M.S.A.	**192,158**												
(Includes Alachua County.)													
City of Gainesville	88,024	10,697		1,403	9,294	4	83	368	948	2,313	6,197	784	
Total area actually reporting	98.3%	19,189		2,520	16,669	11	172	568	1,769	4,404	10,908	1,357	
Estimated total	100.0%	19,468		2,553	16,915	11	173	578	1,791	4,462	11,069	1,384	
Rate per 100,000 inhabitants		10,131.2		1,328.6	8,802.7	5.7	90.0	300.8	932.0	2,322.0	5,760.4	720.2	
Galveston-Texas City, Tx. M.S.A.	**232,567**												
(Includes Galveston County.)													
City of:													
Galveston	60,754	6,650		1,060	5,590	24	56	296	684	975	3,844	771	
Texas City	42,542	3,913		293	3,620	4	36	109	144	674	2,565	381	
Total area actually reporting	100.0%	16,474		1,914	14,560	36	156	490	1,232	3,024	9,960	1,576	
Rate per 100,000 inhabitants		7,083.6		823.0	6,260.5	15.5	67.1	210.7	529.7	1,300.3	4,282.6	677.7	
Gary-Hammond, In. M.S.A.	**622,774**												
(Includes Lake and Porter Counties.)													
City of:													
Gary	117,836	11,231		2,484	8,747	105	174	934	1,271	2,555	3,589	2,603	
Hammond	85,074	7,144		1,166	5,978	8	53	281	824	1,148	3,517	1,313	
Total area actually reporting	99.2%	34,923		5,546	29,377	126	304	1,527	3,589	6,195	16,956	6,226	
Estimated total	100.0%	35,182		5,568	29,614	126	306	1,530	3,606	6,230	17,141	6,243	
Rate per 100,000 inhabitants		5,649.2		894.1	4,755.2	20.2	49.1	245.7	579.0	1,000.4	2,752.4	1,002.5	
Glens Falls, N.Y. M.S.A.	**121,523**												
(Includes Warren and Washington Counties.)													
City of Glens Falls	14,277	1,272		269	1,003	....	10	12	247	196	790	17	
Total area actually reporting	100.0%	4,157		519	3,638	2	39	22	456	715	2,830	93	
Rate per 100,000 inhabitants		3,420.8		427.1	2,993.7	1.6	32.1	18.1	375.2	588.4	2,328.8	76.5	
Goldsboro, N.C. M.S.A.	**109,427**												
(Includes Wayne County.)													
City of Goldsboro	43,283	4,208		677	3,531	6	20	207	444	910	2,419	202	
Total area actually reporting	100.0%	6,090		861	5,229	10	30	243	578	1,620	3,299	310	
Rate per 100,000 inhabitants		5,565.4		786.8	4,778.5	9.1	27.4	222.1	528.2	1,480.4	3,014.8	283.3	
Grand Forks, N.D.-Mn. M.S.A.[4]	**103,652**												
(Includes Grand Forks County, N.D. and Polk County, Mn.)													
City of Grand Forks, N.D.	49,409	2,961		61	2,631	....	19	14	28	234	2,202	195	
Total area actually reporting	100.0%				3,890	1		16	108	467	3,142	281	
Rate per 100,000 inhabitants					3,752.9	1.0		15.4	104.2	450.5	3,031.3	271.1	

See footnotes at end of table.

88

Table 6. — Index of Crime, Metropolitan Statistical Areas, 1993 — Continued

Metropolitan Statistical Area	Population	Crime Index total	Modified Crime Index total[1]	Violent crime[2]	Property crime[3]	Murder and non-negligent manslaughter	Forcible rape	Robbery	Aggravated assault	Burglary	Larceny-theft	Motor vehicle theft	Arson[1]
Grand Rapids-Muskegon-Holland, Mi. M.S.A.[4]	**968,826**												
(Includes Allegan, Kent, Muskegon, and Ottawa Counties.)													
City of:													
Grand Rapids[4]	192,121				13,063	33		829	1,793	3,161	8,827	1,075	
Muskegon[4]	41,122				4,354	3		142	451	1,139	2,920	295	
Holland[4]	31,640				1,671	1		7	122	193	1,424	54	
Total area actually reporting	100.0%				42,837	52		1,293	3,741	9,329	30,868	2,640	
Rate per 100,000 inhabitants					4,421.5	5.4		133.5	386.1	962.9	3,186.1	272.5	
Greeley, Co. M.S.A.	**139,826**												
(Includes Weld County.)													
City of Greeley	63,574	4,332		134	4,198	3	20	25	86	675	3,352	171	
Total area actually reporting	99.3%	7,321		412	6,909	6	52	41	313	1,296	5,311	302	
Estimated total	100.0%	7,384		418	6,966	6	52	42	318	1,306	5,354	306	
Rate per 100,000 inhabitants		5,280.8		298.9	4,981.9	4.3	37.2	30.0	227.4	934.0	3,829.0	218.8	
Green Bay, Wi. M.S.A.	**203,170**												
(Includes Brown County.)													
City of Green Bay	101,364	4,702		451	4,251	2	62	46	341	644	3,368	239	
Total area actually reporting	100.0%	7,713		585	7,128	3	85	56	441	1,084	5,696	348	
Rate per 100,000 inhabitants		3,796.3		287.9	3,508.4	1.5	41.8	27.6	217.1	533.5	2,803.6	171.3	
Greensboro-Winston-Salem-High Point, N.C. M.S.A.	**1,096,140**												
(Includes Alamance, Davidson, Davie, Forsythe, Guilford, Randolph, Stokes, and Yadkin Counties.)													
City of:													
Greensboro	192,951	15,303		1,720	13,583	27	105	791	797	3,177	9,657	749	
Winston-Salem	147,098	18,338		2,832	15,506	36	177	1,053	1,566	4,783	9,590	1,133	
High Point	71,879	7,084		934	6,150	12	39	291	592	2,060	3,714	376	
Total area actually reporting	99.5%	66,485		7,660	58,825	115	435	2,523	4,587	17,774	37,656	3,395	
Estimated total	100.0%	66,968		7,715	59,253	116	438	2,539	4,622	17,883	37,954	3,416	
Rate per 100,000 inhabitants		6,109.4		703.8	5,405.6	10.6	40.0	231.6	421.7	1,631.5	3,462.5	311.6	
Greenville, N.C. M.S.A.	**112,149**												
(Includes Pitt County.)													
City of Greenville	47,445	5,560		692	4,868	5	52	244	391	1,322	3,243	303	
Total area actually reporting	99.6%	8,896		1,090	7,806	12	72	284	722	2,454	4,920	432	
Estimated total	100.0%	8,935		1,094	7,841	12	72	285	725	2,463	4,944	434	
Rate per 100,000 inhabitants		7,967.1		975.5	6,991.6	10.7	64.2	254.1	646.5	2,196.2	4,408.4	387.0	
Greenville-Spartanburg-Anderson, S.C. M.S.A.	**863,667**												
(Includes Anderson, Cherokee, Greenville, Pickens, and Spartanburg Counties.)													
City of:													
Greenville	59,697	6,381		1,053	5,328	9	38	254	752	842	4,126	360	
Spartanburg	45,613	6,893		1,565	5,328	10	42	319	1,194	1,158	3,830	340	
Anderson	28,241	2,477		551	1,926	8	15	134	394	568	1,221	137	
Total area actually reporting	100.0%	49,626		9,328	40,298	87	428	1,576	7,237	10,508	27,060	2,730	
Rate per 100,000 inhabitants		5,746.0		1,080.0	4,665.9	10.1	49.6	182.5	837.9	1,216.7	3,133.2	316.1	
Hagerstown, Md. M.S.A.	**126,701**												
(Includes Washington County.)													
City of Hagerstown	37,938	1,954		240	1,714	....	12	57	171	422	1,187	105	
Total area actually reporting	100.0%	3,249		366	2,883	5	27	70	264	755	1,948	180	
Rate per 100,000 inhabitants		2,564.3		288.9	2,275.4	3.9	21.3	55.2	208.4	595.9	1,537.5	142.1	
Harrisburg-Lebanon-Carlisle, Pa. M.S.A.	**604,920**												
(Includes Cumberland, Dauphin, Lebanon and Perry Counties.)													
City of:													
Harrisburg	53,666	4,976		1,144	3,832	13	67	539	525	1,043	2,382	407	
Lebanon	25,364	1,002		76	926	6	11	27	32	155	743	28	
Carlisle	18,999	700		67	633	3	6	36	22	86	518	29	
Total area actually reporting	99.2%	20,098		2,332	17,766	40	162	795	1,335	3,379	13,369	1,018	
Estimated total	100.0%	20,232		2,344	17,888	40	163	798	1,343	3,399	13,458	1,031	
Rate per 100,000 inhabitants		3,344.6		387.5	2,957.1	6.6	26.9	131.9	222.0	561.9	2,224.8	170.4	

See footnotes at end of table.

Table 6.—Index of Crime, Metropolitan Statistical Areas, 1993—Continued

Metropolitan Statistical Area	Population	Crime Index total	Modified Crime Index total[1]	Violent crime[2]	Property crime[3]	Murder and non-negligent man-slaughter	Forcible rape	Robbery	Aggra-vated assault	Burglary	Larceny-theft	Motor vehicle theft	Arson[1]
Hartford, Ct. M.S.A.	**1,053,803**												
(Includes all of Hartford County, Ct. and part of Litchfield, Middlesex, New London, Tolland, and Windham Counties.)													
City of Hartford	131,914	17,927		2,842	15,085	30	99	1,243	1,470	3,628	8,824	2,633	
Total area actually reporting	100.0%	51,024		5,209	45,815	52	253	1,972	2,932	10,395	29,429	5,991	
Rate per 100,000 inhabitants		4,841.9		494.3	4,347.6	4.9	24.0	187.1	278.2	986.4	2,792.6	568.5	
Hickory-Morganton, N.C. M.S.A.	**303,975**												
(Includes Alexander, Burke, Caldwell, and Catawba Counties.)													
City of:													
Hickory	29,134	3,414		338	3,076	3	25	136	174	707	2,214	155	
Morganton	15,676	1,250		89	1,161	....	4	22	63	246	876	39	
Total area actually reporting	99.8%	12,846		1,105	11,741	16	83	263	743	3,409	7,783	549	
Estimated total	100.0%	12,886		1,109	11,777	16	83	264	746	3,418	7,808	551	
Rate per 100,000 inhabitants		4,239.2		364.8	3,874.3	5.3	27.3	86.8	245.4	1,124.4	2,568.6	181.3	
Honolulu Hi. M.S.A.	**875,455**												
(Includes Honolulu County.)													
Total area actually reporting	100.0%	56,405		2,501	53,904	31	286	1,085	1,099	9,296	40,148	4,460	
Rate per 100,000 inhabitants		6,442.9		285.7	6,157.3	3.5	32.7	123.9	125.5	1,061.8	4,586.0	509.4	
Houma, La. M.S.A.	**187,213**												
(Includes Lafourche and Terrebonne Parishes.)													
City of Houma	31,360	1,707		457	1,250	5	14	78	360	296	856	98	
Total area actually reporting	92.4%	6,361		912	5,449	10	44	146	712	1,688	3,402	359	
Estimated total	100.0%	7,367		1,046	6,321	11	49	175	811	1,856	4,023	442	
Rate per 100,000 inhabitants		3,935.1		558.7	3,376.4	5.9	26.2	93.5	433.2	991.4	2,148.9	236.1	
Houston, Tx. M.S.A.[5]	**3,600,764**												
(Includes Chambers, Fort Bend, Harris, Liberty, Montgomery, and Waller Counties.)													
City of Houston[5]	1,724,327				116,110	446	1,109			27,022	61,569	27,519	
Total area actually reporting	100.0%				192,173	571	2,455			45,375	106,262	40,536	
Rate per 100,000 inhabitants					5,337.0	15.9	68.2			1,260.1	2,951.1	1,125.8	
Huntington-Ashland, W.V.-Ky.-Oh. M.S.A.	**317,163**												
(Includes Cabell and Wayne Counties, W.V., Boyd, Carter and Greenup Counties, Ky., and Lawrence County, Oh.)													
City of:													
Huntington, W.V	54,422	3,486		304	3,182	2	61	83	158	787	2,259	136	
Ashland, Ky	24,488	993		126	867	....	7	5	114	193	625	49	
Total area actually reporting	79.3%	7,573		741	6,832	17	89	115	520	1,690	4,732	410	
Estimated total	100.0%	9,393		867	8,526	18	106	151	592	2,072	5,931	523	
Rate per 100,000 inhabitants		2,961.6		273.4	2,688.2	5.7	33.4	47.6	186.7	653.3	1,870.0	164.9	
Huntsville, Al. M.S.A.	**311,694**												
(Includes Limestone and Madison Counties.)													
City of Huntsville	165,252	15,694		2,171	13,523	18	82	320	1,751	2,571	10,002	950	
Total area actually reporting	99.8%	18,655		2,618	16,037	22	102	360	2,134	3,291	11,659	1,087	
Estimated total	100.0%	18,698		2,624	16,074	22	102	361	2,139	3,300	11,684	1,090	
Rate per 100,000 inhabitants		5,998.8		841.9	5,157.0	7.1	32.7	115.8	686.2	1,058.7	3,748.5	349.7	
Jackson, Mi. M.S.A.[4]	**152,438**												
(Includes Jackson County.)													
City of Jackson[4]	38,341					5		74	1,245	359	1,769	154	
Total area actually reporting	97.4%				5,059	7		102	1,534	920	3,856	283	
Estimated total	100.0%				5,237	7		107	1,548	949	3,987	301	
Rate per 100,000 inhabitants					3,435.5	4.6		70.2	1,015.5	622.5	2,615.5	197.5	
Jackson, Ms. M.S.A.	**409,223**												
(Includes Hinds, Madison, and Rankin Counties.)													
City of Jackson	198,227	25,508		2,780	22,728	83	173	1,505	1,019	7,071	11,603	4,054	
Total area actually reporting	91.3%	30,209		3,144	27,065	99	211	1,609	1,225	8,527	14,202	4,336	
Estimated total	100.0%	32,092		3,308	28,784	103	228	1,665	1,312	8,977	15,362	4,445	
Rate per 100,000 inhabitants		7,842.2		808.4	7,033.8	25.2	55.7	406.9	320.6	2,193.7	3,753.9	1,086.2	
Jackson, Tn. M.S.A.	**81,410**												
(Includes Madison County.)													
City of Jackson	51,592	5,982		948	5,034	19	33	266	630	1,264	3,471	299	
Total area actually reporting	100.0%	6,823		1,054	5,769	19	45	262	728	1,516	3,906	347	
Rate per 100,000 inhabitants		8,381.0		1,294.7	7,086.4	23.3	55.3	321.8	894.2	1,862.2	4,797.9	426.2	

See footnotes at end of table.

Table 6. — Index of Crime, Metropolitan Statistical Areas, 1993 — Continued

Metropolitan Statistical Area	Population	Crime Index total	Modified Crime Index total[1]	Violent crime[2]	Property crime[3]	Murder and non-negligent man-slaughter	Forcible rape	Robbery	Aggra-vated assault	Burglary	Larceny-theft	Motor vehicle theft	Arson[1]
Jacksonville, Fl. M.S.A.	**966,411**												
(Includes Clay, Duval, Nassau, and St. Johns Counties.)													
City of Jacksonville	672,310	67,513		11,417	56,096	125	699	3,604	6,989	15,127	31,936	9,033	
Total area actually reporting	98.7%	82,027		13,597	68,430	145	819	3,887	8,746	18,112	40,661	9,657	
Estimated total	100.0%	83,092		13,722	69,370	146	824	3,924	8,828	18,333	41,282	9,755	
Rate per 100,000 inhabitants		8,598.0		1,419.9	7,178.1	15.1	85.3	406.0	913.5	1,897.0	4,271.7	1,009.4	
Jacksonville, N.C. M.S.A.	**146,832**												
(Includes Onslow County.)													
City of Jacksonville	32,084	3,528		310	3,218	3	25	101	181	778	2,292	148	
Total area actually reporting	100.0%	6,736		426	6,310	5	45	137	239	1,794	4,217	299	
Rate per 100,000 inhabitants		4,587.6		290.1	4,297.4	3.4	30.6	93.3	162.8	1,221.8	2,872.0	203.6	
Janesville-Beloit, Wi. M.S.A.	**144,047**												
(Includes Rock County.)													
City of:													
Janesville	54,784	3,826		113	3,713	....	23	26	64	682	2,888	143	
Beloit	36,762	2,216		127	2,089	....	11	70	46	269	1,688	132	
Total area actually reporting	99.1%	7,418		376	7,042	....	43	103	230	1,219	5,486	337	
Estimated total	100.0%	7,472		378	7,094		43	104	231	1,226	5,528	340	
Rate per 100,000 inhabitants		5,187.2		262.4	4,924.8	....	29.9	72.2	160.4	851.1	3,837.6	236.0	
Jersey City, N.J. M.S.A.	**559,129**												
(Includes Hudson County.)													
City of Jersey City	230,298	18,760		4,584	14,176	20	100	2,500	1,964	4,190	6,331	3,655	
Total area actually reporting	100.0%	36,257		6,397	29,860	29	164	3,345	2,859	7,944	14,881	7,035	
Rate per 100,000 inhabitants		6,484.6		1,144.1	5,340.4	5.2	29.3	598.3	511.3	1,420.8	2,661.5	1,258.2	
Johnson City-Kingsport-Bristol, Tn.-Va. M.S.A.	**450,919**												
(Includes Carter, Hawkins, Sullivan, Unicoi and Washington Counties, Tn., Bristol City and Scott and Washington Counties, Va.)													
City of:													
Johnson City, Tn	51,131	2,749		123	2,626	3	13	30	77	530	1,879	217	
Kingsport, Tn	38,399	2,494		223	2,271	2	5	32	184	405	1,728	138	
Bristol, Tn	24,833	1,089		80	1,009	....	15	4	61	198	773	38	
Total area actually reporting	95.9%	12,116		920	11,196	12	94	100	714	2,789	7,611	796	
Estimated total	100.0%	13,157		1,044	12,113	13	102	121	808	2,972	8,290	851	
Rate per 100,000 inhabitants		2,917.8		231.5	2,686.3	2.9	22.6	26.8	179.2	659.1	1,838.5	188.7	
Johnstown, Pa. M.S.A.	**241,842**												
(Includes Cambria and Somerset Counties.)													
City of Johnstown	27,806	1,310		190	1,120	....	19	48	123	296	762	62	
Total area actually reporting	96.6%	3,573		483	3,090	4	53	63	363	901	1,931	258	
Estimated total	100.0%	3,793		503	3,290	4	54	68	377	934	2,077	279	
Rate per 100,000 inhabitants		1,568.4		208.0	1,360.4	1.7	22.3	28.1	155.9	386.2	858.8	115.4	
Joplin, Mo. M.S.A.	**138,638**												
(Includes Jasper and Newton Counties.)													
City of Joplin	41,693	2,901		227	2,674	5	25	55	142	631	1,876	167	
Total area actually reporting	76.0%	4,751		293	4,458	8	39	65	181	1,123	3,094	241	
Estimated total	100.0%	5,585		363	5,222	9	46	78	230	1,309	3,601	312	
Rate per 100,000 inhabitants		4,028.5		261.8	3,766.6	6.5	33.2	56.3	165.9	944.2	2,597.4	225.0	
Kalamazoo-Battle Creek, Mi. M.S.A.[4]	**438,379**												
(Includes Calhoun, Kalamazoo and Van Buren Counties.)													
City of:													
Kalamazoo[4]	81,631				5,883	8		248	1,112	1,308	4,082	493	
Battle Creek[4]	54,688				4,310	8		194	490	1,172	2,867	271	
Total area actually reporting	99.6%				22,292	26		586	2,354	5,363	15,575	1,354	
Estimated total	100.0%				22,373	26		588	2,360	5,376	15,635	1,362	
Rate per 100,000 inhabitants					5,103.6	5.9		134.1	538.3	1,226.3	3,566.5	310.7	
Kenosha, Wi. M.S.A.	**135,181**												
(Includes Kenosha County.)													
City of Kenosha	84,258	4,772		460	4,312	8	53	129	270	859	3,141	312	
Total area actually reporting	100.0%	6,769		569	6,200	9	69	143	348	1,155	4,629	416	
Rate per 100,000 inhabitants		5,007.4		420.9	4,586.4	6.7	51.0	105.8	257.4	854.4	3,424.3	307.7	

See footnotes at end of table.

Table 6. — Index of Crime, Metropolitan Statistical Areas, 1993 — Continued

Metropolitan Statistical Area	Population	Crime Index total	Modified Crime Index total[1]	Violent crime[2]	Property crime[3]	Murder and non-negligent man-slaughter	Forcible rape	Robbery	Aggra-vated assault	Burglary	Larceny-theft	Motor vehicle theft	Arson[1]
Killeen-Temple, Tx. M.S.A.	**259,871**												
(Includes Bell and Coryell Counties.)													
City of:													
Killeen......................	67,884	4,768		543	4,225	6	90	223	224	1,142	2,800	283	
Temple......................	45,990	3,570		618	2,952	5	73	89	451	567	2,089	296	
Total area actually reporting......	99.6%	13,030		1,742	11,288	18	249	358	1,117	2,841	7,699	748	
Estimated total	100.0%	13,093		1,747	11,346	18	249	359	1,121	2,853	7,740	753	
Rate per 100,000 inhabitants......		5,038.3		672.3	4,366.0	6.9	95.8	138.1	431.4	1,097.9	2,978.4	289.8	
Kokomo,In. M.S.A.	**99,536**												
(Includes Howard and Tipton Counties.)													
City of Kokomo	46,405	2,603		227	2,376	1	28	36	162	413	1,882	81	
Total area actually reporting......	83.7%	3,331		413	2,918	2	35	38	338	572	2,232	114	
Estimated total	100.0%	3,929		459	3,470	2	39	46	372	674	2,635	161	
Rate per 100,000 inhabitants......		3,947.3		461.1	3,486.2	2.0	39.2	46.2	373.7	677.1	2,647.3	161.8	
La Crosse, Wi.-Mn. M.S.A.[4]	**119,099**												
(Includes La Crosse County, Wi., and Houston County, Mn.)													
City of La Crosse, Wi	51,809				2,876	....		13	18	183	2,625	68	
Total area actually reporting......	100.0%				4,381	....		15	90	420	3,849	112	
Rate per 100,000 inhabitants......					3,678.5	....		12.6	75.6	352.6	3,231.8	94.0	
Lafayette, La. M.S.A.	**354,604**												
(Includes Acadia, Lafayette, St. Landry, and St. Martin Parishes.)													
City of Lafayette	97,726	8,638		895	7,743	18	50	245	582	1,493	5,869	381	
Total area actually reporting......	90.1%	14,245		1,725	12,520	29	89	326	1,281	2,922	9,002	596	
Estimated total	100.0%	16,735		2,056	14,679	32	101	397	1,526	3,337	10,540	802	
Rate per 100,000 inhabitants......		4,719.3		579.8	4,139.5	9.0	28.5	112.0	430.3	941.0	2,972.3	226.2	
Lafayette, In. M.S.A.	**166.449**												
(Includes Clinton and Tippecanoe Counties.)													
City of Lafayette	45,585	2,509		93	2,416	1	18	19	55	445	1,879	92	
Total area actually reporting......	80.8%	5,734		438	5,296	1	41	35	361	831	4,272	193	
Estimated total	100.0%	7,016		543	6,473	2	50	53	438	1,034	5,151	288	
Rate per 100,000 inhabitants......		4,215.1		326.2	3,888.9	1.2	30.0	31.8	263.1	621.2	3,094.6	173.0	
Lake Charles, La. M.S.A.	**172,146**												
(Includes Calcasieu Parish.)													
City of Lake Charles.............	71,401	4,834		648	4,186	12	30	165	441	940	2,932	314	
Total area actually reporting......	87.9%	10,551		1,487	9,064	16	89	258	1,124	2,186	6,352	526	
Estimated total	100.0%	12,027		1,683	10,344	18	96	300	1,269	2,432	7,264	648	
Rate per 100,000 inhabitants......		6,986.5		977.7	6,008.9	10.5	55.8	174.3	737.2	1,412.8	4,219.7	376.4	
Lakeland-Winter Haven, Fl. M.S.A. ...	**425,061**												
(Includes Polk County.)													
City of:													
Lakeland	73,684	10,515		1,102	9,413	8	45	366	683	2,195	5,805	1,413	
Winter Haven	25,295	3,324		361	2,963	2	18	97	244	608	2,053	302	
Total area actually reporting......	100.0%	37,494		4,184	33,310	35	180	964	3,005	9,184	20,188	3,938	
Rate per 100,000 inhabitants......		8,820.9		984.3	7,836.5	8.2	42.3	226.8	707.0	2,160.6	4,749.4	926.5	
Lancaster, Pa. M.S.A.	**436,325**												
(Includes Lancaster County.)													
City of Lancaster................	57,423	4,485		506	3,979	11	45	273	177	882	2,784	313	
Total area actually reporting......	96.3%	12,021		942	11,079	15	97	351	479	2,108	8,279	692	
Estimated total	100.0%	12,447		981	11,466	15	99	361	506	2,171	8,562	733	
Rate per 100,000 inhabitants......		2,852.7		224.8	2,627.9	3.4	22.7	82.7	116.0	497.6	1,962.3	168.0	
Lansing-East Lansing, Mi. M.S.A.[4]	**438,470**												
(Includes Clinton, Eaton and Ingham Counties.)													
City of:													
Lansing[4]	127,311				7,367	14		302	1,066	1,372	5,295	700	
East Lansing[4]...............	48,739				1,935	2		28	82	252	1,522	161	
Total area actually reporting......	99.5%				19,222	21		424	1,633	3,310	14,588	1,324	
Estimated total	100.0%				19,317	21		426	1,640	3,325	14,658	1,334	
Rate per 100,000 inhabitants......					4,405.5	4.8		97.2	374.0	758.3	3,343.0	304.2	
Laredo, Tx. M.S.A.	**151,386**												
(Includes Webb County.)													
City of Laredo	139,194	10,059		1,053	9,006	21	7	163	862	1,720	6,246	1,040	
Total area actually reporting......	100.0%	10,465		1,104	9,361	21	10	166	907	1,875	6,419	1,067	
Rate per 100,000 inhabitants......		6,912.8		729.3	6,183.5	13.9	6.6	109.7	599.1	1,238.6	4,240.2	704.8	

See footnotes at end of table.

Metropolitan Statistical Area	Population	Crime Index total	Modified Crime Index total[1]	Violent crime[2]	Property crime[3]	Murder and non-negligent manslaughter	Forcible rape	Robbery	Aggravated assault	Burglary	Larceny-theft	Motor vehicle theft	Arson[1]
Las Vegas, Nv.-Az. M.S.A.	**1,007,944**												
(Includes Clark and Nye Counties Nv.; and Mohave County, Az.)													
City of Las Vegas, Nv.	717,441	48,365		7,281	41,084	91	435	3,572	3,183	9,783	23,855	7,446	
Total area actually reporting	98.0%	65,824		9,603	56,221	131	599	4,166	4,707	14,107	32,869	9,245	
Estimated total	100.0%	66,409		9,671	56,738	132	603	4,172	4,764	14,251	33,186	9,301	
Rate per 100,000 inhabitants		6,588.6		959.5	5,629.1	13.1	59.8	413.9	472.6	1,413.9	3,292.4	922.8	
Lawrence, Ma.-N.H. M.S.A.[5]	**295,930**												
(Includes part of Essex County, Ma. and Rockingham County, N.H.)													
City of Lawrence, Ma.[5]	65,700			1,348		3	33	387	925	1,464			
Total area actually reporting	97.0%	13,763		1,795	11,968	7	122	496	1,170	2,687	5,790	3,491	
Estimated total	100.0%	14,075		1,838	12,237	7	124	502	1,205	2,752	5,948	3,537	
Rate per 100,000 inhabitants		4,756.2		621.1	4,135.1	2.4	41.9	169.6	407.2	929.9	2,009.9	1,195.2	
Lawton, Ok. M.S.A.	**121,443**												
(Includes Comanche County.)													
City of Lawton	87,874	6,046		825	5,221	12	62	161	590	1,262	3,635	324	
Total area actually reporting	100.0%	6,384		848	5,536	14	65	165	604	1,351	3,826	359	
Rate per 100,000 inhabitants		5,256.8		698.3	4,558.5	11.5	53.5	135.9	497.4	1,112.5	3,150.4	295.6	
Lewiston-Auburn, Me. M.S.A.	**104,092**												
(Includes part of Androscoggin County.)													
City of:													
Lewiston	38,123	2,517		140	2,377	....	7	48	85	534	1,791	52	
Auburn	23,998	714		17	697	....	3	8	6	116	553	28	
Total area actually reporting	100.0%	4,141		191	3,950	1	19	60	111	874	2,939	137	
Rate per 100,000 inhabitants		3,978.2		183.5	3,794.7	1.0	18.3	57.6	106.6	839.6	2,823.5	131.6	
Lexington, Ky. M.S.A.	**364,218**												
(Includes Bourbon, Clark, Fayette, Jessamine, Scott, and Woodford Counties.)													
City of Lexington	235,094	15,641		2,160	13,481	8	139	558	1,455	3,187	9,684	610	
Total area actually reporting	99.8%	21,150		2,761	18,389	11	208	605	1,937	4,080	13,486	823	
Estimated total	100.0%	21,179		2,765	18,414	11	208	606	1,940	4,085	13,505	824	
Rate per 100,000 inhabitants		5,814.9		759.2	5,055.8	3.0	57.1	166.4	532.6	1,121.6	3,707.9	226.2	
Lincoln, Nb. M.S.A.	**220,404**												
(Includes Lancaster County.)													
City of Lincoln	198,228	13,561		1,125	12,436	4	83	127	911	1,984	10,023	429	
Total area actually reporting	100.0%	15,153		1,158	13,995	7	89	133	929	2,170	11,349	476	
Rate per 100,000 inhabitants		6,875.1		525.4	6,349.7	3.2	40.4	60.3	421.5	984.6	5,149.2	216.0	
Little Rock-North Little Rock, Ar. M.S.A.	**532,157**												
(Includes Faulkner, Lonoke, Pulaski and Saline Counties.)													
City of:													
Little Rock	178,924	28,070		5,887	22,183	68	215	1,136	4,468	5,796	14,306	2,081	
North Little Rock	63,108	7,704		643	7,061	13	71	324	235	1,456	4,732	873	
Total area actually reporting	100.0%	47,281		7,733	39,548	107	390	1,647	5,589	9,571	26,340	3,637	
Rate per 100,000 inhabitants		8,884.8		1,453.1	7,431.6	20.1	73.3	309.5	1,050.3	1,798.5	4,949.7	683.4	
Longview-Marshall, Tx. M.S.A.	**203,855**												
(Includes Gregg, Harrison and Upshur County.)													
City of:													
Longview	74,125	6,147		622	5,525	10	73	198	341	1,317	3,669	539	
Marshall	23,912	1,937		222	1,715	7	18	35	162	368	1,249	98	
Total area actually reporting	100.0%	12,439		1,390	11,049	23	134	287	946	2,892	7,267	890	
Rate per 100,000 inhabitants		6,101.9		681.9	5,420.0	11.3	65.7	140.8	464.1	1,418.7	3,564.8	436.6	
Los Angeles-Long Beach, Ca. M.S.A.	**9,146,057**												
(Includes Los Angeles County.)													
City of:													
Los Angeles	3,525,317	312,789		83,701	229,088	1,076	1,773	38,415	42,437	50,232	119,092	59,764	
Long Beach	443,259	35,630		7,116	28,514	126	200	3,717	3,073	6,780	14,108	7,626	
Total area actually reporting	100.0%	644,758		153,876	490,882	1,944	3,688	65,994	82,250	116,374	248,455	126,053	
Rate per 100,000 inhabitants		7,049.6		1,682.4	5,367.1	21.3	40.3	721.6	899.3	1,272.4	2,716.5	1,378.2	
Louisville, Ky.-In. M.S.A.	**976,668**												
(Includes Bullitt, Jefferson and Oldham Counties, Ky., and Clark, Floyd, Harrison, and Scott Counties, In.)													
City of Louisville	273,564	17,329		2,724	14,605	37	135	1,393	1,159	4,204	8,076	2,325	
Total area actually reporting	92.7%	42,033		5,983	36,050	56	277	1,900	3,750	8,942	23,133	3,975	
Estimated total	100.0%	44,867		6,213	38,654	58	296	1,939	3,920	9,395	25,072	4,187	
Rate per 100,000 inhabitants		4,593.9		636.1	3,957.7	5.9	30.3	198.5	401.4	961.9	2,567.1	428.7	

See footnotes at end of table.

Metropolitan Statistical Area	Population	Crime Index total	Modified Crime Index total[1]	Violent crime[2]	Property crime[3]	Murder and non-negligent man-slaughter	Forcible rape	Robbery	Aggra-vated assault	Burglary	Larceny-theft	Motor vehicle theft	Arson[1]
Lubbock, Tx. M.S.A.	**228,251**												
(Includes Lubbock County.)													
City of Lubbock	191,639	12,353		1,275	11,078	17	136	282	840	2,541	7,927	610	
Total area actually reporting......	100.0%	14,190		1,465	12,725	19	155	287	1,004	2,892	9,175	658	
Rate per 100,000 inhabitants......		6,216.8		641.8	5,575.0	8.3	67.9	125.7	439.9	1,267.0	4,019.7	288.3	
Lynchburg, Va. M.S.A.	**201,399**												
(Includes Lynchburg and Bedford Cities and Amherst, Bedford and Campbell Counties.)													
City of Lynchburg	67,099	3,566		506	3,060	3	45	107	351	560	2,316	184	
Total area actually reporting.	100.0%	6,228		806	5,422	9	82	124	591	1,051	4,085	286	
Rate per 100,000 inhabitants......		3,092.4		400.2	2,692.2	4.5	40.7	61.6	293.4	521.8	2,028.3	142.0	
Macon, Ga. M.S.A.	**304,968**												
(Includes Bibb, Houston, Jones, Peach, and Twiggs Counties.)													
City of Macon	109,537	11,096		914	10,182	20	102	384	408	1,811	7,533	838	
Total area actually reporting......	99.9%	18,906		1,465	17,441	34	125	487	819	3,476	12,739	1,226	
Estimated total	100.0%	18,922		1,466	17,456	34	125	487	820	3,479	12,750	1,227	
Rate per 100,000 inhabitants......		6,204.6		480.7	5,723.9	11.1	41.0	159.7	268.9	1,140.8	4,180.8	402.3	
Madison, Wi. M.S.A.	**376,681**												
(Includes Dane County.)													
City of Madison	196,919	10,616		631	9,985	2	99	316	214	1,606	7,466	913	
Total area actually reporting......	100.0%	17,095		1,112	15,983	3	117	366	626	2,425	12,404	1,154	
Rate per 100,000 inhabitants......		4,538.3		295.2	4,243.1	.8	31.1	97.2	166.2	643.8	3,293.0	306.4	
Manchester, N.H. M.S.A.	**166,876**												
(Includes part of Hillsborough, Merrimack and Rockingham Counties.)													
City of Manchester	98,145	5,480		219	5,261	5	33	140	41	1,277	3,536	448	
Total area actually reporting.....	97.2%	6,990		269	6,721	7	38	152	72	1,544	4,631	546	
Estimated total	100.0%	7,131		276	6,855	7	40	153	76	1,566	4,731	558	
Rate per 100,000 inhabitants......		4,273.2		165.4	4,107.8	4.2	24.0	91.7	45.5	938.4	2,835.0	334.4	
Mansfield, Oh. M.S.A.	**176,573**												
(Includes Crawford and Richland Counties.)													
City of Mansfield	53,563	5,420		1,332	4,088	3	50	128	1,157	1,265	2,613	210	
Total area actually reporting......	79.9%	8,351		1,409	6,942	3	58	144	1,204	1,939	4,646	357	
Estimated total	100.0%	9,475		1,484	7,991	3	67	166	1,248	2,144	5,420	427	
Rate per 100,000 inhabitants......		5,366.1		840.4	4,525.6	1.7	37.9	94.0	706.8	1,214.2	3,069.6	241.8	
McAllen-Edinburg-Mission, Tx. M.S.A.	**429,233**												
(Includes Hidalgo County.)													
City of :													
McAllen	92,028	11,867		718	11,149	8	28	135	547	2,083	7,706	1,360	
Edinburg....................	33,268	2,600		183	2,417	2	7	40	134	452	1,760	205	
Mission	33,394	2,290		70	2,220	....	2	12	56	456	1,562	202	
Total area actually reporting.....	100.0%	32,663		3,218	29,445	40	119	425	2,634	8,016	18,410	3,019	
Rate per 100,000 inhabitants......		7,609.6		749.7	6,859.9	9.3	27.7	99.0	613.7	1,867.5	4,289.0	703.3	
Medford-Ashland, Or. M.S.A.	**157,196**												
(Includes Jackson County.)													
City of:													
Medford	50,517	4,584		281	4,303	1	35	39	206	639	3,471	193	
Ashland.....................	16,908	985		25	960	1	5	11	8	154	772	34	
Total area actually reporting.....	100.0%	8,957		667	8,290	4	86	73	504	1,497	6,344	449	
Rate per 100,000 inhabitants......		5,698.0		424.3	5,273.7	2.5	54.7	46.4	320.6	952.3	4,035.7	285.6	
Memphis, Tn.-Ar.-Ms. M.S.A.	**1,048,342**												
(Includes Fayette, Shelby, and Tipton Counties Tn.; Crittenden County, Ar.; and De Soto County, Ms.)													
City of Memphis, Tn	618,981	62,150		10,113	52,037	198	725	5,366	3,824	15,314	23,434	13,289	
Total area actually reporting.....	88.2%	74,265		11,291	62,974	221	838	5,696	4,536	18,017	30,313	14,644	
Estimated total	100.0%	77,667		11,629	66,038	230	899	5,754	4,746	19,207	31,902	14,929	
Rate per 100,000 inhabitants......		7,408.6		1,109.3	6,299.3	21.9	85.8	548.9	452.7	1,832.1	3,043.1	1,424.1	
Merced, Ca. M.S.A.	**191,038**												
(Includes Merced County.)													
City of Merced..................	60,271	4,759		331	4,428	10	30	121	170	1,376	2,563	489	
Total area actually reporting......	100.0%	10,958		1,183	9,775	21	70	213	879	3,075	5,645	1,055	
Rate per 100,000 inhabitants......		5,736.0		619.2	5,116.8	11.0	36.6	111.5	460.1	1,609.6	2,954.9	552.2	

See footnotes at end of table.

Table 6. — Index of Crime, Metropolitan Statistical Areas, 1993 — Continued

Metropolitan Statistical Area	Population	Crime Index total	Modified Crime Index total[1]	Violent crime[2]	Property crime[3]	Murder and non-negligent man-slaughter	Forcible rape	Robbery	Aggra-vated assault	Burglary	Larceny-theft	Motor vehicle theft	Arson[1]
Miami, Fl. M.S.A.	**2,037,568**												
(Includes Dade County.)													
City of Miami	372,519	69,828		14,502	55,326	127	204	7,082	7,089	12,277	31,871	11,178	
Total area actually reporting	99.6%	274,337		43,437	230,900	367	1,076	18,583	23,411	52,725	135,179	42,996	
Estimated total	100.0%	275,080		43,526	231,554	368	1,080	18,610	23,468	52,880	135,607	43,067	
Rate per 100,000 inhabitants		13,500.4		2,136.2	11,364.2	18.1	53.0	913.3	1,151.8	2,595.3	6,655.3	2,113.6	
Middlesex-Somerset-Hunterdon, N.J. M.S.A.	**1,054,645**												
(Includes Hunterdon, Middlesex, and Somerset.)													
Total area actually reporting	100.0%	36,417		3,050	33,367	16	144	1,122	1,768	7,236	22,624	3,507	
Rate per 100,000 inhabitants		3,453.0		289.2	3,163.8	1.5	13.7	106.4	167.6	686.1	2,145.2	332.5	
Milwaukee-Waukesha, Wi. M.S.A.	**1,453,647**												
(Includes Milwaukee, Ozaukee, Washington, and Waukesha Counties.)													
City of:													
Milwaukee	623,114	50,432		6,014	44,418	157	424	4,022	1,411	8,250	25,553	10,615	
Waukesha	59,705	2,064		84	1,980	1	9	19	55	254	1,618	108	
Total area actually reporting	100.0%	77,854		7,009	70,845	166	515	4,377	1,951	12,090	46,314	12,441	
Rate per 100,000 inhabitants		5,355.8		482.2	4,873.6	11.4	35.4	301.1	134.2	831.7	3,186.1	855.8	
Minneapolis-St. Paul, Mn.-Wi. M.S.A.[4]	**2,648,322**												
(Includes Anoka, Carver, Chisago, Dakota, Hennepin, Isanti, Ramsey, Scott, Sherburne, and Wright Counties, Mn., and Pierce and St. Croix Counties, Wi.)													
City of:													
Minneapolis, Mn.[4]	366,642	40,463		6,481	33,982	58	518	3,178	2,727	9,358	19,952	4,672	
St. Paul, Mn.[4]	271,208	20,382		2,704	17,678	22	242	954	1,486	4,023	11,329	2,326	
Total area actually reporting	99.9%				127,788	116		4,880	6,239	26,182	89,380	12,226	
Estimated total	100.0%				127,931	116		4,881	6,243	26,205	89,491	12,235	
Rate per 100,000 inhabitants					4,830.6	4.4		184.3	235.7	989.5	3,379.2	462.0	
Mobile, Al. M.S.A.	**501,440**												
(Includes Baldwin and Mobile Counties.)													
City of Mobile	204,286	18,567		2,220	16,347	42	122	1,186	870	4,884	9,926	1,537	
Total area actually reporting	99.7%	30,917		4,274	26,643	65	199	1,643	2,367	8,513	15,853	2,277	
Estimated total	100.0%	31,013		4,289	26,724	65	200	1,646	2,378	8,532	15,909	2,283	
Rate per 100,000 inhabitants		6,184.8		855.3	5,329.5	13.0	39.9	328.3	474.2	1,701.5	3,172.7	455.3	
Modesto, Ca. M.S.A.	**399,253**												
(Includes Stanislaus County.)													
City of Modesto	174,054	12,929		1,442	11,487	12	80	356	994	2,555	7,339	1,593	
Total area actually reporting	100.0%	29,358		3,961	25,397	23	193	612	3,133	7,021	15,094	3,282	
Rate per 100,000 inhabitants		7,353.2		992.1	6,361.1	5.8	48.3	153.3	784.7	1,758.5	3,780.6	822.0	
Monmouth-Ocean, N.J. M.S.A.	**1,010,250**												
(Includes Monmouth and Ocean counties.)													
Total area actually reporting	100.0%	35,904		2,661	33,243	23	206	753	1,679	7,258	24,257	1,728	
Rate per 100,000 inhabitants		3,554.0		263.4	3,290.6	2.3	20.4	74.5	166.2	718.4	2,401.1	171.0	
Monroe, La. M.S.A.	**145,451**												
(Includes Ouachita Parish.)													
City of Monroe	56,384	6,787		1,123	5,664	17	29	127	950	1,047	4,357	260	
Total area actually reporting	100.0%	10,000		1,416	8,584	23	42	147	1,204	1,961	6,203	420	
Rate per 100,000 inhabitants		6,875.2		973.5	5,901.6	15.8	28.9	101.1	827.8	1,348.2	4,264.7	288.8	
Montgomery, Al. M.S.A.	**309,452**												
(Includes Autauga, Elmore, and Montgomery Counties.)													
City of Montgomery	194,399	12,310		1,695	10,615	39	87	562	1,007	3,558	5,843	1,214	
Total area actually reporting	99.7%	17,268		2,532	14,736	46	114	635	1,737	4,810	8,530	1,396	
Estimated total	100.0%	17,329		2,541	14,788	46	114	637	1,744	4,822	8,566	1,400	
Rate per 100,000 inhabitants		5,599.9		821.1	4,778.8	14.9	36.8	205.8	563.6	1,558.2	2,768.1	452.4	
Myrtle Beach, S.C. M.S.A.	**154,007**												
(Includes Horry County.)													
City of Myrtle Beach	27,766	5,084		409	4,675	2	31	129	247	996	3,451	228	
Total area actually reporting	100.0%	13,612		1,348	12,264	13	95	322	918	2,954	8,562	748	
Rate per 100,000 inhabitants		8,838.6		875.3	7,963.3	8.4	61.7	209.1	596.1	1,918.1	5,559.5	485.7	

See footnotes at end of table.

Table 6. — Index of Crime, Metropolitan Statistical Areas, 1993 — Continued

Metropolitan Statistical Area	Population	Crime Index total	Modified Crime Index total[1]	Violent crime[2]	Property crime[3]	Murder and non-negligent man-slaughter	Forcible rape	Robbery	Aggra-vated assault	Burglary	Larceny-theft	Motor vehicle theft	Arson[1]
Naples, Fl. M.S.A.	**167,124**												
(Includes Collier County.)													
City of Naples	20,728	1,395		117	1,278	....	7	38	72	308	882	88	
Total area actually reporting.....	100.0%	9,381		1,298	8,083	11	107	305	875	2,512	4,805	766	
Rate per 100,000 inhabitants.....		5,613.2		776.7	4,836.5	6.6	64.0	182.5	523.6	1,503.1	2,875.1	458.3	
Nashua, N.H. M.S.A.	**160,383**												
(Includes part of Hillsborough County.)													
City of Nashua..................	80,435	2,649		68	2,581	3	26	13	26	380	1,935	266	
Total area actually reporting.....	100.0%	4,269		175	4,094	3	71	22	79	656	3,107	331	
Rate per 100,000 inhabitants.....		2,661.8		109.1	2,552.6	1.9	44.3	13.7	49.3	409.0	1,937.2	206.4	
Nashville, Tn. M.S.A.	**1,038,512**												
(Includes Cheatham, Davidson, Dickson, Robertson, Rutherford, Sumner, Williamson, and Wilson Counties.)													
City of Nashville	513,648	55,500		9,164	46,336	87	577	2,709	5,791	9,149	32,456	4,731	
Total area actually reporting.....	83.2%	70,961		10,866	60,095	101	718	2,963	7,084	12,018	42,552	5,525	
Estimated total	100.0%	76,142		11,410	64,732	107	769	3,042	7,492	13,367	45,419	5,946	
Rate per 100,000 inhabitants.....		7,331.8		1,098.7	6,233.1	10.3	74.0	292.9	721.4	1,287.1	4,373.5	572.5	
Nassau-Suffolk, N.Y. M.S.A.	**2,628,063**												
(Includes Nassau and Suffolk Counties.)													
Total area actually reporting.....	99.9%	89,119		7,290	81,829	92	203	3,526	3,469	17,920	48,035	15,874	
Estimated total	100.0%	89,155		7,293	81,862	92	203	3,527	3,471	17,926	48,059	15,877	
Rate per 100,000 inhabitants.....		3,392.4		277.5	3,114.9	3.5	7.7	134.2	132.1	682.1	1,828.7	604.1	
Newark, N.J. M.S.A.	**1,937,773**												
(Includes Essex, Morris, Sussex, Union, and Warren Counties.)													
City of Newark, N.J..............	269,892	38,514		10,222	28,292	96	257	5,892	3,977	6,879	10,420	10,993	
Total area actually reporting.....	100.0%	112,459		19,977	92,482	172	704	10,945	8,156	21,621	45,620	25,241	
Rate per 100,000 inhabitants.....		5,803.5		1,030.9	4,772.6	8.9	36.3	564.8	420.9	1,115.8	2,354.2	1,302.6	
New Bedford, Ma. M.S.A.[5]	**174,609**												
(Includes part of Bristol and Plymouth Counties.)													
City of New Bedford[5]	97,226			1,363		3	59	327	974	2,014	2,237		
Total area actually reporting.....	82.7%	8,512		1,513	6,999	3	63	342	1,105	2,448	3,533	1,018	
Estimated total	100.0%	9,583		1,659	7,924	3	69	363	1,224	2,672	4,075	1,177	
Rate per 100,000 inhabitants.....		5,488.3		950.1	4,538.1	1.7	39.5	207.9	701.0	1,530.3	2,333.8	674.1	
Newburgh, N.Y.-Pa. M.S.A.	**349,972**												
(Includes Orange County, N.Y. and Pike County, Pa.)													
City of Newburgh	26,259	1,715		399	1,316	5	26	142	226	528	735	53	
Total area actually reporting.....	97.9%	11,133		1,311	9,822	13	80	245	973	2,306	7,091	425	
Estimated total	100.0%	11,395		1,339	10,056	13	81	256	989	2,348	7,262	446	
Rate per 100,000 inhabitants.....		3,256.0		382.6	2,873.4	3.7	23.1	73.1	282.6	670.9	2,075.0	127.4	
New Haven-Meriden, Ct. M.S.A.	**562,831**												
(Includes part of Middlesex and New Haven Counties.)													
City of:													
New Haven	123,890	15,553		2,544	13,009	22	130	1,238	1,154	3,417	7,719	1,873	
Meriden.....................	58,549	2,757		189	2,568	1	5	93	90	592	1,676	300	
Total area actually reporting.....	100.0%	32,031		3,314	28,717	28	174	1,547	1,565	6,742	18,469	3,506	
Rate per 100,000 inhabitants.....		5,691.1		588.8	5,102.2	5.0	30.9	274.9	278.1	1,197.9	3,281.4	622.9	
New London-Norwich, Ct.-R.I. M.S.A.	**301,303**												
(Includes part of Middlesex and New London Counties, Ct., and Washington County, R.I.)													
City of:													
New London, Ct.	24,341	1,631		162	1,469	8	11	74	69	339	998	132	
Norwich, Ct.	36,402	1,598		193	1,405	3	37	57	96	395	926	84	
Total area actually reporting.....	100.0%	9,222		883	8,339	16	99	198	570	1,969	5,847	523	
Rate per 100,000 inhabitants.....		3,060.7		293.1	2,767.6	5.3	32.9	65.7	189.2	653.5	1,940.6	173.6	
New Orleans, La. M.S.A.	**1,260,951**												
(Includes Jefferson, Orleans, Plaquemines, St. Charles, St. James, St. John the Baptist, and St. Tammany Parishes.)													
City of New Orleans	491,619	52,773		10,024	42,749	395	298	5,179	4,152	11,184	22,019	9,546	
Total area actually reporting.....	90.7%	101,301		15,835	85,466	465	615	6,891	7,864	19,462	51,417	14,587	
Estimated total	100.0%	107,328		16,551	90,777	475	659	7,047	8,370	20,686	55,034	15,057	
Rate per 100,000 inhabitants.....		8,511.7		1,312.6	7,199.1	37.7	52.3	558.9	663.8	1,640.5	4,364.5	1,194.1	

See footnotes at end of table.

Table 6. — Index of Crime, Metropolitan Statistical Areas, 1993 — Continued

Metropolitan Statistical Area	Population	Crime Index total	Modified Crime Index total[1]	Violent crime[2]	Property crime[3]	Murder and non-negligent man-slaughter	Forcible rape	Robbery	Aggra-vated assault	Burglary	Larceny-theft	Motor vehicle theft	Arson[1]
New York, N.Y. M.S.A.................	**8,619,661**												
(Includes Bronx, Kings, New York, Putnam, Queens, Richmond, Rockland and Westchester Counties, N.Y.)													
City of New York, N.Y...........	7,347,257	600,346		153,543	446,803	1,946	2,818	86,001	62,778	99,207	235,132	112,464	
Total area actually reporting......	99.4%	647,735		160,661	487,074	1,999	2,989	90,255	65,418	106,418	262,832	117,824	
Estimated total	100.0%	649,309		160,804	488,505	2,001	2,996	90,310	65,497	106,706	263,810	117,989	
Rate per 100,000 inhabitants.....		7,532.9		1,865.5	5,667.3	23.2	34.8	1,047.7	759.9	1,237.9	3,060.6	1,368.8	
Norfolk-Virginia Beach-Newport News, Va.-N.C. M.S.A.....................	**1,519,381**												
(Includes Gloucester, Isle of Wight, James City, Mathews, and York Counties; and Chesapeake, Hampton, Newport News, Portsmouth, Poquoson, Suffolk, Virginia Beach and Williamsburg Cities Va., and Currituck County, N.C.)													
City of :													
Norfolk, Va..................	257,617	22,209		2,769	19,440	62	204	1,428	1,075	3,732	13,535	2,173	
Virginia Beach, Va............	423,387	20,516		1,248	19,268	22	181	631	414	3,261	14,812	1,195	
Newport News, Va............	179,975	12,230		2,178	10,052	22	103	719	1,334	2,101	7,267	684	
Total area actually reporting......	100.0%	89,203		9,915	79,288	184	728	4,460	4,543	14,890	57,496	6,902	
Rate per 100,000 inhabitants......		5,871.0		652.6	5,218.4	12.1	47.9	293.5	299.0	980.0	3,784.2	454.3	
Oakland, Ca. M.S.A.................	**2,170,116**												
(Includes Alameda and Contra Costa Counties.)													
City of Oakland	377,037	44,927		9,809	35,118	154	353	4,559	4,743	8,355	18,991	7,772	
Total area actually reporting......	100.0%	159,061		24,685	134,376	312	934	9,832	13,607	30,798	84,235	19,343	
Rate per 100,000 inhabitants......		7,329.6		1,137.5	6,192.1	14.4	43.0	453.1	627.0	1,419.2	3,881.6	891.3	
Ocala, Fl. M.S.A.....................	**211,008**												
(Includes Marion County.)													
City of Ocala	44,556	6,466		877	5,589	4	53	312	508	1,143	4,197	249	
Total area actually reporting......	100.0%	13,057		2,409	10,648	8	191	432	1,778	3,052	7,023	573	
Rate per 100,000 inhabitants......		6,187.9		1,141.7	5,046.3	3.8	90.5	204.7	842.6	1,446.4	3,328.3	271.6	
Odessa-Midland, Tx. M.S.A...........	**238,376**												
(Includes Ector and Midland Counties.)													
City of:													
Odessa......................	95,605	8,848		771	8,077	9	39	146	577	1,969	5,684	424	
Midland.....................	97,039	5,398		448	4,950	6	83	91	268	1,126	3,485	339	
Total area actually reporting......	100.0%	16,294		1,341	14,953	22	146	253	920	3,739	10,362	852	
Rate per 100,000 inhabitants......		6,835.4		562.6	6,272.9	9.2	61.2	106.1	385.9	1,568.5	4,346.9	357.4	
Oklahoma City, Ok. M.S.A............	**991,503**												
(Includes Canadian, Cleveland, Logan, McClain, Oklahoma and Pottawatomie Counties.)													
City of Oklahoma City	457,448	51,335		6,480	44,855	80	515	1,724	4,161	10,000	29,316	5,539	
Total area actually reporting......	100.0%	76,273		8,212	68,061	103	733	2,021	5,355	15,599	45,196	7,266	
Rate per 100,000 inhabitants......		7,692.7		828.2	6,864.4	10.4	73.9	203.8	540.1	1,573.3	4,558.3	732.8	
Olympia, Wa. M.S.A.	**180,410**												
(Includes Thurston County.)													
City of Olympia	37,588	2,924		130	2,794	....	33	37	60	313	2,342	139	
Total area actually reporting......	98.4%	8,413		416	7,997	1	110	72	233	1,520	6,061	416	
Estimated total	100.0%	8,607		427	8,180	1	112	75	239	1,548	6,202	430	
Rate per 100,000 inhabitants......		4,770.8		236.7	4,534.1	.6	62.1	41.6	132.5	858.0	3,437.7	238.3	
Orange County, Ca. M.S.A............	**2,510,193**												
(Includes Orange County.)													
Total area actually reporting......	100.0%	135,212		13,456	121,756	196	546	5,567	7,147	27,418	73,050	21,288	
Rate per 100,000 inhabitants......		5,386.5		536.1	4,850.5	7.8	21.8	221.8	284.7	1,092.3	2,910.1	848.1	
Orlando, Fl. M.S.A...................	**1,323,652**												
(Includes Lake, Orange, Osceola and Seminole Counties.)													
City of Orlando	176,748	21,953		4,140	17,813	15	209	1,107	2,809	4,352	11,655	1,806	
Total area actually reporting......	100.0%	99,448		14,801	84,647	69	749	3,240	10,743	24,269	52,549	7,829	
Rate per 100,000 inhabitants......		7,513.2		1,118.2	6,395.0	5.2	56.6	244.8	811.6	1,833.5	3,970.0	591.5	

See footnotes at end of table.

Table 6. — Index of Crime, Metropolitan Statistical Areas, 1993 — Continued

Metropolitan Statistical Area	Population	Crime Index total	Modified Crime Index total[1]	Violent crime[2]	Property crime[3]	Murder and non-negligent man-slaughter	Forcible rape	Robbery	Aggra-vated assault	Burglary	Larceny-theft	Motor vehicle theft	Arson[1]
Owensboro, Ky. M.S.A.	**89,640**												
(Includes Daviess County.)													
City of Owensboro	53,863	2,975		149	2,826	4	30	53	62	610	2,131	85	
Total area actually reporting	100.0%	3,560		199	3,361	4	36	57	102	821	2,441	99	
Rate per 100,000 inhabitants		3,971.4		222.0	3,749.4	4.5	40.2	63.6	113.8	915.9	2,723.1	110.4	
Panama City, Fl. M.S.A.	**135,954**												
(Includes Bay County.)													
City of Panama City	37,224	3,531		369	3,162	3	23	74	269	631	2,348	183	
Total area actually reporting	89.6%	9,542		901	8,641	9	76	120	696	1,972	6,221	448	
Estimated total	100.0%	10,722		1,040	9,682	10	82	161	787	2,217	6,909	556	
Rate per 100,000 inhabitants		7,886.5		765.0	7,121.5	7.4	60.3	118.4	578.9	1,630.7	5,081.9	409.0	
Philadelphia, Pa.-N.J. M.S.A.	**4,969,334**												
(Includes Bucks, Chester, Delaware, Montgomery, and Philadelphia Counties, Pa., and Burlington, Camden, Gloucester and Salem Counties, N.J.)													
City of Philadelphia, Pa	1,559,534	97,659		19,576	78,083	439	785	11,531	6,821	15,117	39,181	23,785	
Total area actually reporting	98.9%	214,910		32,766	182,144	595	1,530	16,225	14,416	37,808	106,814	37,522	
Estimated total	100.0%	216,429		32,908	183,521	596	1,539	16,261	14,512	38,034	107,820	37,667	
Rate per 100,000 inhabitants		4,355.3		662.2	3,693.1	12.0	31.0	327.2	292.0	765.4	2,169.7	758.0	
Phoenix-Mesa, Az. M.S.A.	**2,393,251**												
(Includes Maricopa and Pinal Counties.)													
City of:													
Phoenix	1,039,369	96,476		11,911	84,565	158	444	3,437	7,872	20,617	48,382	15,566	
Mesa	304,695	24,146		2,335	21,811	6	111	410	1,808	4,664	14,430	2,717	
Total area actually reporting	99.7%	185,800		19,261	166,539	229	878	4,898	13,256	38,862	102,713	24,964	
Estimated total	100.0%	186,384		19,308	167,076	229	881	4,908	13,290	38,976	103,077	25,023	
Rate per 100,000 inhabitants		7,787.9		806.8	6,981.1	9.6	36.8	205.1	555.3	1,628.6	4,307.0	1,045.6	
Pine Bluff, Ar. M.S.A.	**86,325**												
(Includes Jefferson County.)													
City of Pine Bluff	58,397	5,148		867	4,281	16	59	261	531	1,754	2,010	517	
Total area actually reporting	100.0%	5,758		914	4,844	17	69	272	556	1,994	2,294	556	
Rate per 100,000 inhabitants		6,670.1		1,058.8	5,611.4	19.7	79.9	315.1	644.1	2,309.9	2,657.4	644.1	
Pittsburgh, Pa. M.S.A.	**2,423,968**												
(Includes Allegheny, Beaver, Butler, Fayette, and Westmoreland Counties.)													
City of Pittsburgh	368,473	28,613		4,479	24,134	80	226	2,784	1,389	4,611	13,017	6,506	
Total area actually reporting	91.5%	69,918		9,020	60,898	123	627	3,922	4,348	12,713	36,116	12,069	
Estimated total	100.0%	75,414		9,535	65,879	128	659	4,053	4,695	13,530	39,756	12,593	
Rate per 100,000 inhabitants		3,111.2		393.4	2,717.8	5.3	27.2	167.2	193.7	558.2	1,640.1	519.5	
Pittsfield, Ma. M.S.A.	**98,519**												
(Includes part of Berkshire County.)													
City of Pittsfield	47,253	1,859		247	1,612	....	2	29	216	530	956	126	
Total area actually reporting	88.2%	2,478		350	2,128	....	15	30	305	661	1,313	154	
Estimated total	100.0%	2,889		406	2,483	....	17	38	351	747	1,521	215	
Rate per 100,000 inhabitants		2,932.4		412.1	2,520.3	....	17.3	38.6	356.3	758.2	1,543.9	218.2	
Portland, Me. M.S.A.	**233,775**												
(Includes part of Cumberland and York Counties.)													
City of Portland	62,624	4,808		416	4,392	2	61	92	261	1,142	2,978	272	
Total area actually reporting	100.0%	10,254		563	9,691	2	99	114	348	2,240	6,938	513	
Rate per 100,000 inhabitants		4,386.3		240.8	4,145.4	.9	42.3	48.8	148.9	958.2	2,967.8	219.4	
Portland-Vancouver, Or.-Wa. M.S.A.	**1,640,863**												
(Includes Clackamas, Columbia, Multnomah, Wa. and Yamhill Counties, Or. and Clark County, Wa.)													
City of:													
Portland, Or	454,889	51,765		8,445	43,320	58	479	2,305	5,603	7,845	27,016	8,459	
Vancouver, Wa	50,654	4,350		456	3,894	3	43	96	314	629	2,905	360	
Total area actually reporting	99.9%	102,346		11,672	90,674	93	927	3,216	7,436	17,360	59,646	13,668	
Estimated total	100.0%	102,464		11,679	90,785	93	928	3,218	7,440	17,379	59,729	13,677	
Rate per 100,000 inhabitants		6,244.5		711.8	5,532.8	5.7	56.6	196.1	453.4	1,059.1	3,640.1	833.5	

See footnotes at end of table.

Metropolitan Statistical Area	Population	Crime Index total	Modified Crime Index total[1]	Violent crime[2]	Property crime[3]	Murder and non-negligent man-slaughter	Forcible rape	Robbery	Aggra-vated assault	Burglary	Larceny-theft	Motor vehicle theft	Arson[1]
Providence-Fall River-Warwick, R.I.-Ma. M.S.A.	**956,796**												
(Includes part of Bristol, Kent, Newport, Providence and Washington Counties, R.I., and part of Bristol County, Ma.)													
City of:													
Providence, R.I.	159,178	15,162		1,373	13,789	22	114	636	601	4,240	6,433	3,116	
Fall River, Ma.	91,354	5,283		705	4,578	4	57	143	501	1,161	2,673	744	
Warwick, R.I.	86,062	3,960		363	3,597	3	17	35	308	517	2,444	636	
Total area actually reporting	93.9%	41,137		3,560	37,577	36	262	949	2,313	9,665	21,623	6,289	
Estimated total	100.0%	43,218		3,846	39,372	37	274	991	2,544	10,100	22,675	6,597	
Rate per 100,000 inhabitants		4,517.0		402.0	4,115.0	3.9	28.6	103.6	265.9	1,055.6	2,369.9	689.5	
Provo-Orem, Ut. M.S.A.	**282,500**												
(Includes Utah County.)													
City of:													
Provo	93,661	3,695		143	3,552	1	36	18	88	508	2,889	155	
Orem	71,315	3,159		58	3,101	1	11	12	34	386	2,602	113	
Total area actually reporting	96.4%	11,000		377	10,623	3	90	41	243	1,547	8,627	449	
Estimated total	100.0%	11,518		401	11,117	3	94	45	259	1,624	9,025	468	
Rate per 100,000 inhabitants		4,077.2		141.9	3,935.2	1.1	33.3	15.9	91.7	574.9	3,194.7	165.7	
Pueblo, Co. M.S.A.	**127,363**												
(Includes Pueblo County.)													
City of Pueblo	101,424	7,016		1,735	5,281	9	87	165	1,474	1,337	3,640	304	
Total area actually reporting	100.0%	7,776		1,788	5,988	9	92	172	1,515	1,544	4,111	333	
Rate per 100,000 inhabitants		6,105.4		1,403.9	4,701.5	7.1	72.2	135.0	1,189.5	1,212.3	3,227.8	261.5	
Punta Gorda, Fl. M.S.A.	**120,986**												
(Includes Charlotte County.)													
City of Punta Gorda	11,712	471		51	420	1	1	21	28	73	332	15	
Total area actually reporting	100.0%	3,717		385	3,332	6	20	79	280	948	2,179	205	
Rate per 100,000 inhabitants		3,072.3		318.2	2,754.0	5.0	16.5	65.3	231.4	783.6	1,801.0	169.4	
Racine, Wi. M.S.A.	**181,121**												
(Includes Racine County.)													
City of Racine	86,896	6,480		704	5,776	8	18	325	353	1,288	4,014	474	
Total area actually reporting	100.0%	9,316		796	8,520	9	31	366	390	1,754	6,141	625	
Rate per 100,000 inhabitants		5,143.5		439.5	4,704.0	5.0	17.1	202.1	215.3	968.4	3,390.6	345.1	
Raleigh-Durham-Chapel Hill, N.C. M.S.A.	**923,111**												
(Includes Chatham, Durham, Franklin, Johnston, Orange and Wake Counties.)													
City of:													
Raleigh	224,057	15,255		2,030	13,225	27	94	795	1,114	2,947	9,395	883	
Durham	143,172	14,980		1,707	13,273	26	109	848	724	4,851	7,471	951	
Chapel Hill	43,903	2,699		319	2,380	1	15	100	203	516	1,766	98	
Total area actually reporting	99.9%	55,578		5,821	49,757	86	317	2,137	3,281	14,263	32,582	2,912	
Estimated total	100.0%	55,587		5,822	49,765	86	317	2,137	3,282	14,265	32,588	2,912	
Rate per 100,000 inhabitants		6,021.7		630.7	5,391.0	9.3	34.3	231.5	355.5	1,545.3	3,530.2	315.5	
Rapid City, S.D. M.S.A.	**85,853**												
(Includes Pennington County.)													
City of Rapid City	57,617	3,793		258	3,535	1	45	25	187	481	2,912	142	
Total area actually reporting	100.0%	4,521		356	4,165	4	85	28	239	679	3,306	180	
Rate per 100,000 inhabitants		5,266.0		414.7	4,851.3	4.7	99.0	32.6	278.4	790.9	3,850.8	209.7	
Reading, Pa. M.S.A.	**344,635**												
(Includes Berks County.)													
City of Reading	79,377	6,405		937	5,468	6	42	555	334	1,521	3,362	585	
Total area actually reporting	98.3%	11,623		1,302	10,321	11	71	610	610	2,333	7,062	926	
Estimated total	100.0%	11,782		1,317	10,465	11	72	614	620	2,357	7,167	941	
Rate per 100,000 inhabitants		3,418.7		382.1	3,036.5	3.2	20.9	178.2	179.9	683.9	2,079.6	273.0	
Redding, Ca. M.S.A.	**159,209**												
(Includes Shasta County.)													
City of Redding	72,254	4,944		463	4,481	6	62	114	281	1,073	3,066	342	
Total area actually reporting	100.0%	7,893		798	7,095	12	91	149	546	1,915	4,572	608	
Rate per 100,000 inhabitants		4,957.6		501.2	4,456.4	7.5	57.2	93.6	342.9	1,202.8	2,871.7	381.9	
Reno, Nv. M.S.A.	**279,191**												
(Includes Washoe County.)													
City of Reno	145,433	11,571		1,047	10,524	16	129	432	470	1,837	8,006	681	
Total area actually reporting	100.0%	18,079		1,616	16,463	23	191	554	848	3,158	12,212	1,093	
Rate per 100,000 inhabitants		6,475.5		578.8	5,896.7	8.2	68.4	198.4	303.7	1,131.1	4,374.1	391.5	

See footnotes at end of table.

Table 6. — Index of Crime, Metropolitan Statistical Areas, 1993 — Continued

Metropolitan Statistical Area	Population	Crime Index total	Modified Crime Index total[1]	Violent crime[2]	Property crime[3]	Murder and non-negligent man-slaughter	Forcible rape	Robbery	Aggra-vated assault	Burglary	Larceny-theft	Motor vehicle theft	Arson[1]
Richland-Kennewick-Pasco, Wa. M.S.A.	**164,404**												
(Includes Benton and Franklin Counties.)													
City of:													
Richland	34,945	1,072		84	988	....	23	5	56	153	791	44	
Kennewick	46,061	2,962		186	2,776	2	32	24	128	460	2,187	129	
Pasco	22,688	1,595		208	1,387	4	24	42	138	308	931	148	
Total area actually reporting.....	100.0%	7,290		638	6,652	9	107	75	447	1,334	4,918	400	
Rate per 100,000 inhabitants......		4,434.2		388.1	4,046.1	5.5	65.1	45.6	271.9	811.4	2,991.4	243.3	
Richmond-Petersburg, Va. M.S.A.	**909,654**												
(Includes Colonial Heights, Hopewell, Petersburg, and Richmond Cities, and Charles City, Chesterfield, Dinwiddie, Goochland, Hanover, Henrico, New Kent, Powhatan, and Prince George Counties.)													
City of:													
Richmond	205,331	22,142		3,275	18,867	112	174	1,578	1,411	5,081	11,571	2,215	
Petersburg..................	40,719	3,306		551	2,755	11	26	221	293	810	1,720	225	
Total area actually reporting.....	100.0%	51,242		5,262	45,980	158	381	2,282	2,441	10,244	32,077	3,659	
Rate per 100,000 inhabitants......		5,633.1		578.5	5,054.7	17.4	41.9	250.9	268.3	1,126.1	3,526.3	402.2	
Riverside-San Bernardino, Ca. M.S.A.	**2,837,569**												
(Includes Riverside and San Bernardino Counties.)													
City of:													
Riverside....................	241,041	22,147		3,975	18,172	33	131	1,287	2,524	4,975	9,635	3,562	
San Bernardino	174,215	22,312		5,566	16,746	82	129	1,550	3,805	4,740	8,410	3,596	
Total area actually reporting.....	100.0%	204,408		30,924	173,484	414	1,170	8,753	20,587	54,730	87,878	30,876	
Rate per 100,000 inhabitants.....		7,203.6		1,089.8	6,113.8	14.6	41.2	308.5	725.5	1,928.8	3,096.9	1,088.1	
Roanoke, Va. M.S.A.	**229,712**												
(Includes Roanoke and Salem Cities, and Botetourt and Roanoke Counties.)													
City of Roanoke.................	98,221	6,458		565	5,893	11	32	217	305	1,180	4,398	315	
Total area actually reporting.....	100.0%	9,661		763	8,898	15	55	243	450	1,753	6,736	409	
Rate per 100,000 inhabitants.....		4,205.7		332.2	3,873.5	6.5	23.9	105.8	195.9	763.1	2,932.4	178.0	
Rochester, Mn. M.S.A.[4]	**111,693**												
(Includes Olmsted County.)													
City of Rochester[4]...............	74,723				3,245	3		22	94	603	2,454	188	
Total area actually reporting.....	100.0%				3,836	3		22	108	819	2,790	227	
Rate per 100,000 inhabitants......					3,434.4	2.7		19.7	96.7	733.3	2,497.9	203.2	
Rochester, N.Y. M.S.A.	**1,086,478**												
(Includes Genesee, Livingston, Monroe, Ontario, Orleans and Wayne counties.)													
City of Rochester	235,301	25,520		2,704	22,816	64	159	1,638	843	6,340	13,522	2,954	
Total area actually reporting......	99.8%	52,667		3,810	48,857	79	272	1,902	1,557	10,573	33,885	4,399	
Estimated total	100.0%	52,756		3,819	48,937	79	272	1,906	1,562	10,588	33,943	4,406	
Rate per 100,000 inhabitants.....		4,855.7		351.5	4,504.2	7.3	25.0	175.4	143.8	974.5	3,124.1	405.5	
Rocky Mount, N.C. M.S.A............	**139,396**												
(Includes Edgecombe and Nash Counties.)													
City of Rocky Mount	51,201	5,523		674	4,849	14	25	203	432	1,356	3,259	234	
Total area actually reporting.....	98.5%	8,678		983	7,695	22	37	274	650	2,390	4,926	379	
Estimated total	100.0%	8,859		1,003	7,856	22	38	280	663	2,431	5,038	387	
Rate per 100,000 inhabitants......		6,355.3		719.5	5,635.7	15.8	27.3	200.9	475.6	1,744.0	3,614.2	277.6	
Sacramento, Ca. M.S.A...............	**1,433,067**												
(Includes El Dorado, Placer and Sacramento Counties.)													
City of Sacramento	386,732	39,485		4,850	34,635	85	167	2,310	2,288	8,080	18,670	7,885	
Total area actually reporting......	100.0%	100,865		11,544	89,321	159	550	4,101	6,734	23,360	48,184	17,777	
Rate per 100,000 inhabitants......		7,038.4		805.5	6,232.9	11.1	38.4	286.2	469.9	1,630.1	3,362.3	1,240.5	

See footnotes at end of table.

Table 6. — Index of Crime, Metropolitan Statistical Areas, 1993 — Continued

Metropolitan Statistical Area	Population	Crime Index total	Modified Crime Index total[1]	Violent crime[2]	Property crime[3]	Murder and non-negligent man-slaughter	Forcible rape	Robbery	Aggra-vated assault	Burglary	Larceny-theft	Motor vehicle theft	Arson[1]
Saginaw-Bay City-Midland, Mi. M.S.A.[4]	**404,419**												
(Includes Bay, Midland and Saginaw Counties.)													
City of:													
Saginaw[4]	71,048				5,369	22		479	1,586	1,817	3,307	245	
Bay City[4]	39,204				1,858	....		54	186	349	1,392	117	
Midland[4]	39,193				1,087	....		10	46	110	945	32	
Total area actually reporting.....	100.0%				16,936	29		678	2,480	3,713	12,481	742	
Rate per 100,000 inhabitants......					4,187.7	7.2		167.6	613.2	918.1	3,086.2	183.5	
St. Cloud, Mn. M.S.A.[4]	**154,366**												
(Includes Benton and Stearns Counties.)													
City of St. Cloud[4]	50,412				2,839	2		15	68	343	2,344	152	
Total area actually reporting.....	100.0%				4,568	1		16	99	621	3,675	272	
Rate per 100,000 inhabitants......					2,959.2	.6		10.4	64.1	402.3	2,380.7	176.2	
St. Joseph, Mo. M.S.A.	**98,796**												
(Includes Andrew and Buchanan Counties.)													
City of St. Joseph	72,524	5,053		323	4,730	3	33	54	233	866	3,643	221	
Total area actually reporting.....	84.1%	5,210		339	4,871	4	34	54	247	903	3,744	224	
Estimated total	100.0%	5,698		379	5,319	4	37	64	274	999	4,054	266	
Rate per 100,000 inhabitants......		5,767.4		383.6	5,383.8	4.0	37.5	64.8	277.3	1,011.2	4,103.4	269.2	
Salem, Or. M.S.A.	**297,177**												
(Includes Marion and Polk Counties.)													
City of Salem	114,311	9,802		391	9,411	7	67	208	109	1,592	7,122	697	
Total area actually reporting.....	99.2%	18,134		876	17,258	15	131	308	422	3,045	12,742	1,471	
Estimated total	100.0%	18,265		883	17,382	15	132	310	426	3,066	12,835	1,481	
Rate per 100,000 inhabitants......		6,146.2		297.1	5,849.0	5.0	44.4	104.3	143.3	1,031.7	4,319.0	498.4	
Salinas, Ca. M.S.A.	**372,077**												
(Includes Monterey County.)													
City of Salinas	115,936	8,424		1,469	6,955	15	50	560	844	1,327	4,844	784	
Total area actually reporting.....	100.0%	19,188		2,759	16,429	32	115	910	1,702	3,876	11,200	1,353	
Rate per 100,000 inhabitants......		5,157.0		741.5	4,415.5	8.6	30.9	244.6	457.4	1,041.7	3,010.1	363.6	
Salt Lake City-Ogden, Ut. M.S.A......	**1,158,462**												
(Includes Davis, Salt Lake and Weber Counties.)													
City of:													
Salt Lake City	170,380	18,453		1,402	17,051	19	204	498	681	2,823	12,831	1,397	
Ogden	68,028	5,700		400	5,300	6	42	98	254	890	4,156	254	
Total area actually reporting.....	99.3%	69,932		4,360	65,572	45	583	994	2,738	10,497	51,684	3,391	
Estimated total	100.0%	70,349		4,379	65,970	45	586	997	2,751	10,559	52,005	3,406	
Rate per 100,000 inhabitants......		6,072.6		378.0	5,694.6	3.9	50.6	86.1	237.5	911.5	4,489.1	294.0	
San Angelo, Tx. M.S.A.	**101,060**												
(Includes Tom Green County.)													
City of San Angelo	87,793	4,812		463	4,349	8	43	39	373	842	3,333	174	
Total area actually reporting.....	100.0%	5,334		628	4,706	8	55	41	524	926	3,596	184	
Rate per 100,000 inhabitants......		5,278.1		621.4	4,656.6	7.9	54.4	40.6	518.5	916.3	3,558.3	182.1	
San Antonio, Tx. M.S.A.	**1,405,738**												
(Includes Bexar, Comal, Guadalupe and Wilson Counties.)													
City of San Antonio	985,456	97,671		6,725	90,946	220	553	2,979	2,973	17,866	61,284	11,796	
Total area actually reporting.....	100.0%	118,798		8,851	109,947	261	687	3,274	4,629	22,074	74,474	13,399	
Rate per 100,000 inhabitants......		8,450.9		629.6	7,821.3	18.6	48.9	232.9	329.3	1,570.3	5,297.9	953.2	
San Diego, Ca. M.S.A.	**2,627,659**												
(Includes San Diego County.)													
City of San Diego	1,160,603	85,227		13,463	71,764	133	396	4,651	8,283	14,583	37,862	19,319	
Total area actually reporting.....	100.0%	161,878		22,959	138,919	245	803	7,494	14,417	32,027	73,694	33,198	
Rate per 100,000 inhabitants......		6,160.5		873.7	5,286.8	9.3	30.6	285.2	548.7	1,218.8	2,804.5	1,263.4	
San Francisco, Ca. M.S.A.	**1,642,731**												
(Includes Marin, San Francisco, and San Mateo Counties.)													
City of San Francisco	736,377	70,132		13,365	56,767	129	361	8,454	4,421	11,153	34,558	11,056	
Total area actually reporting.....	100.0%	110,022		17,875	92,147	166	559	9,755	7,395	17,814	58,733	15,600	
Rate per 100,000 inhabitants......		6,697.5		1,088.1	5,609.4	10.1	34.0	593.8	450.2	1,084.4	3,575.3	949.6	
San Jose, Ca. M.S.A.	**1,544,156**												
(Includes Santa Clara County.)													
City of San Jose...............	809,528	36,743		5,317	31,426	41	391	1,186	3,699	6,014	21,398	4,014	
Total area actually reporting.....	100.0%	71,654		8,102	63,552	61	590	1,802	5,649	11,806	45,063	6,683	
Rate per 100,000 inhabitants......		4,640.3		524.7	4,115.6	4.0	38.2	116.7	365.8	764.6	2,918.3	432.8	

See footnotes at end of table.

Table 6. – Index of Crime, Metropolitan Statistical Areas, 1993 – Continued

Metropolitan Statistical Area	Population	Crime Index total	Modified Crime Index total[1]	Violent crime[2]	Property crime[3]	Murder and non-negligent man-slaughter	Forcible rape	Robbery	Aggra-vated assault	Burglary	Larceny-theft	Motor vehicle theft	Arson[1]
San Luis, Obispo-Atascadero-Paso Robles, Ca. M.S.A.	222,812												
(Includes San Luis Obispo County.)													
City of:													
San Luis Obispo	41,631	2,146		239	1,907	....	11	32	196	368	1,429	110	
Atascadero	24,093	963		81	882	....	11	13	57	269	574	39	
Paso Robles	17,325	997		167	830	....	16	10	141	286	489	55	
Total area actually reporting.....	100.0%	8,752		1,120	7,632	....	83	92	945	1,949	5,289	394	
Rate per 100,000 inhabitants.....		3,928.0		502.7	3,425.3	....	37.3	41.3	424.1	874.7	2,373.8	176.8	
Santa Barbara-Santa Maria-Lompoc, Ca. M.S.A.	379,359												
(Includes Santa Barbara County.)													
City of:													
Santa Barbara	85,989	5,152		671	4,481	5	44	159	463	938	3,317	226	
Santa Maria	64,767	4,937		513	4,424	1	39	177	296	910	3,270	244	
Lompoc....................	40,556	2,059		195	1,864	1	13	48	133	402	1,376	86	
Total area actually reporting.....	100.0%	18,044		1,973	16,071	12	149	444	1,368	4,311	10,974	786	
Rate per 100,000 inhabitants.....		4,756.4		520.1	4,236.4	3.2	39.3	117.0	360.6	1,136.4	2,892.8	207.2	
Santa Cruz-Watsonville, Ca. M.S.A. ...	233,352												
(Includes Santa Cruz County.)													
City of:													
Santa Cruz	49,334	4,211		474	3,737	3	8	109	354	724	2,793	220	
Watsonville	31,399	2,815		488	2,327	1	12	128	347	399	1,729	199	
Total area actually reporting.....	100.0%	14,048		1,704	12,344	9	57	334	1,304	2,539	9,068	737	
Rate per 100,000 inhabitants.....		6,020.1		730.2	5,289.9	3.9	24.4	143.1	558.8	1,088.1	3,886.0	315.8	
Santa Rosa, Ca. M.S.A.	405,090												
(Includes Sonoma County.)													
City of Santa Rosa	117,746	7,696		632	7,064	7	102	197	326	1,545	5,011	508	
Total area actually reporting.....	100.0%	20,204		2,119	18,085	24	206	347	1,542	4,792	11,967	1,326	
Rate per 100,000 inhabitants.....		4,987.5		523.1	4,464.4	5.9	50.9	85.7	380.7	1,182.9	2,954.2	327.3	
Sarasota-Bradenton, Fl. M.S.A.	506,026												
(Includes Manatee and Sarasota Counties.)													
City of:													
Sarasota	51,660	6,971		1,020	5,951	3	47	441	529	1,596	4,029	326	
Bradenton..................	45,359	4,172		682	3,490	3	31	200	448	1,083	2,099	308	
Total area actually reporting.....	100.0%	34,230		4,726	29,504	20	213	1,127	3,366	8,491	19,073	1,940	
Rate per 100,000 inhabitants.....		6,764.5		933.9	5,830.5	4.0	42.1	222.7	665.2	1,678.0	3,769.2	383.4	
Savannah, Ga. M.S.A.	273,038												
(Includes Bryan, Chatham, and Effingham Counties.)													
City of Savannah	141,861	12,715		1,417	11,298	33	89	831	464	2,868	7,297	1,133	
Total area actually reporting.....	91.3%	18,782		1,962	16,820	38	124	943	857	4,130	11,130	1,560	
Estimated total	100.0%	19,985		2,058	17,927	40	130	982	906	4,398	11,827	1,702	
Rate per 100,000 inhabitants......		7,319.5		753.7	6,565.8	14.6	47.6	359.7	331.8	1,610.8	4,331.6	623.4	
Scranton-Wilkes Barre-Hazleton, Pa. M.S.A.	641,457												
(Includes Columbia, Lackawanna, Luzerne, and Wyoming Counties.)													
City of:													
Scranton	80,098	2,829		231	2,598	2	26	86	117	487	1,870	241	
Wilkes Barre	47,091	1,887		218	1,669	2	21	61	134	359	1,176	134	
Hazleton	25,115	616		28	588	....	5	7	16	222	342	24	
Total area actually reporting.....	86.4%	13,034		1,162	11,872	10	123	225	804	2,602	8,419	851	
Estimated total	100.0%	15,347		1,378	13,969	12	136	280	950	2,946	9,951	1,072	
Rate per 100,000 inhabitants.....		2,392.5		214.8	2,177.7	1.9	21.2	43.7	148.1	459.3	1,551.3	167.1	
Seattle-Bellevue-Everett, Wa. M.S.A.	2,075,927												
(Includes Island, King and Snohomish Counties.)													
City of:													
Seattle.....................	531,274	62,679		7,437	55,242	67	356	2,670	4,344	9,247	39,176	6,819	
Bellevue....................	87,491	4,853		191	4,662	2	32	74	83	641	3,742	279	
Everett.....................	76,760	6,348		407	5,941	4	116	161	126	915	4,565	461	
Total area actually reporting.....	99.8%	142,706		12,350	130,356	114	1,511	4,151	6,574	23,046	93,666	13,644	
Estimated total	100.0%	142,982		12,366	130,616	114	1,514	4,155	6,583	23,087	93,866	13,663	
Rate per 100,000 inhabitants......		6,588.1		569.8	6,018.3	5.3	69.8	191.4	303.3	1,063.8	4,325.0	629.5	
Sheboygan, Wi. M.S.A.	105,984												
(Includes Sheboygan County.)													
City of Sheboygan	50,651	2,842		74	2,768	1	11	22	40	309	2,368	91	
Total area actually reporting.....	100.0%	4,155		123	4,032	1	29	24	69	528	3,379	125	
Rate per 100,000 inhabitants.....		3,920.4		116.1	3,804.3	.9	27.4	22.6	65.1	498.2	3,188.2	117.9	

See footnotes at end of table.

Metropolitan Statistical Area	Population	Crime Index total	Modified Crime Index total[1]	Violent crime[2]	Property crime[3]	Murder and non-negligent manslaughter	Forcible rape	Robbery	Aggravated assault	Burglary	Larceny-theft	Motor vehicle theft	Arson[1]
Sherman-Denison, Tx. M.S.A.	**96,941**												
(Includes Grayson County.)													
City of:													
Sherman	31,766	2,668		232	2,436	1	29	71	131	468	1,817	151	
Denison	21,757	1,720		176	1,544	2	9	27	138	258	1,228	58	
Total area actually reporting	100.0%	5,451		466	4,985	4	48	105	309	1,104	3,635	246	
Rate per 100,000 inhabitants		5,623.0		480.7	5,142.3	4.1	49.5	108.3	318.8	1,138.8	3,749.7	253.8	
Shreveport-Bossier City, La. M.S.A.	**375,630**												
(Includes Bossier, Caddo and Webster Parishes.)													
City of:													
Shreveport	197,379	22,631		2,570	20,061	76	100	842	1,552	4,774	13,784	1,503	
Bossier City	53,071	3,911		588	3,323	9	21	75	483	558	2,550	215	
Total area actually reporting	96.4%	29,464		3,584	25,880	96	155	975	2,358	6,157	17,859	1,864	
Estimated total	100.0%	30,420		3,711	26,709	97	160	1,002	2,452	6,316	18,450	1,943	
Rate per 100,000 inhabitants		8,098.4		987.9	7,110.5	25.8	42.6	266.8	652.8	1,681.4	4,911.7	517.3	
Sioux City, Ia.-Nb. M.S.A.	**117,570**												
(Includes Woodbury County, Ia., and Dakota County, Nb.)													
City of Sioux City, Ia.	82,228	7,333		1,279	6,054	4	61	121	1,093	1,275	4,523	256	
Total area actually reporting	100.0%	8,210		1,333	6,877	4	70	127	1,132	1,477	5,101	299	
Rate per 100,000 inhabitants		6,983.1		1,133.8	5,849.3	3.4	59.5	108.0	962.8	1,256.3	4,338.7	254.3	
Sioux Falls, S.D. M.S.A.	**148,358**												
(Includes Lincoln and Minnehaha Counties.)													
City of Sioux Falls	106,315	4,875		475	4,400	2	103	44	326	735	3,470	195	
Total area actually reporting	97.3%	5,460		516	4,944	2	112	46	356	944	3,786	214	
Estimated total	100.0%	5,699		532	5,167	2	115	47	368	977	3,967	223	
Rate per 100,000 inhabitants		3,841.4		358.6	3,482.8	1.3	77.5	31.7	248.0	658.5	2,673.9	150.3	
South Bend, In. M.S.A.	**252,959**												
(Includes St. Joseph County.)													
City of South Bend	106,971	10,380		1,159	9,221	19	104	459	577	2,606	5,825	790	
Total area actually reporting	100.0%	16,272		1,509	14,763	24	145	534	806	3,722	9,936	1,105	
Rate per 100,000 inhabitants		6,432.7		596.5	5,836.1	9.5	57.3	211.1	318.6	1,471.4	3,927.9	436.8	
Spokane, Wa. M.S.A.	**389,486**												
(Includes Spokane County.)													
City of Spokane	191,511	15,952		1,558	14,394	13	112	354	1,079	2,699	10,965	730	
Total area actually reporting	98.4%	23,448		1,916	21,532	17	178	438	1,283	4,200	16,229	1,103	
Estimated total	100.0%	23,879		1,941	21,938	17	182	445	1,297	4,263	16,542	1,133	
Rate per 100,000 inhabitants		6,130.9		498.3	5,632.6	4.4	46.7	114.3	333.0	1,094.5	4,247.1	290.9	
Springfield, Mo. M.S.A.	**277,899**												
(Includes Christian, Greene and Webster Counties.)													
City of Springfield	146,642	10,907		669	10,238	7	77	136	449	2,094	7,690	454	
Total area actually reporting	91.1%	12,749		747	12,002	7	91	150	499	2,569	8,885	548	
Estimated total	100.0%	13,382		800	12,582	8	96	160	536	2,705	9,274	603	
Rate per 100,000 inhabitants		4,815.4		287.9	4,527.5	2.9	34.5	57.6	192.9	973.4	3,337.2	217.0	
Springfield, Ma. M.S.A.[5]	**539.699**												
(Includes part of Franklin, Hampden and Hampshire Counties.)													
City of Springfield[5]	153,952				11,416	20	120	676		3,140	4,506	3,770	
Total area actually reporting	85.0%				23,345	28	228	962		5,801	12,250	5,294	
Estimated total	100.0%				25,817	29	244	1,019		6,400	13,698	5,719	
Rate per 100,000 inhabitants					4,783.6	5.4	45.2	188.8		1,185.8	2,538.1	1,059.7	
Stamford-Norwalk, Ct. M.S.A.	**329,636**												
(Includes part of Fairfield County.)													
City of:													
Stamford	107,524	5,872		537	5,335	8	22	270	237	1,105	3,503	727	
Norwalk	78,480	4,233		325	3,908	9	10	188	118	840	2,516	552	
Total area actually reporting	100.0%	13,406		951	12,455	18	35	507	391	2,516	8,368	1,571	
Rate per 100,000 inhabitants		4,066.9		288.5	3,778.4	5.5	10.6	153.8	118.6	763.3	2,538.6	476.6	
Steubenville-Weirton, Oh.-W.V. M.S.A.	**142,406**												
(Includes Jefferson County, Oh., and Brooke and Hancock Counties, W.V.)													
City of:													
Steubenville, Oh	22,023	1,196		421	775	2	6	43	370	189	519	67	
Weirton, W.V	22,015	487		52	435	1	3	4	44	115	288	32	
Total area actually reporting	100.0%	2,782		549	2,233	6	13	52	478	606	1,470	157	
Rate per 100,000 inhabitants		1,953.6		385.5	1,568.1	4.2	9.1	36.5	335.7	425.5	1,032.3	110.2	

See footnotes at end of table.

Table 6. — Index of Crime, Metropolitan Statistical Areas, 1993 — Continued

Metropolitan Statistical Area	Population	Crime Index total	Modified Crime Index total[1]	Violent crime[2]	Property crime[3]	Murder and non-negligent man-slaughter	Forcible rape	Robbery	Aggra-vated assault	Burglary	Larceny-theft	Motor vehicle theft	Arson[1]
Stockton-Lodi, Ca. M.S.A.	**509,244**												
(Includes San Joaquin County.)													
City of:													
Stockton	221,867	24,849		3,500	21,349	45	157	1,554	1,744	5,362	12,291	3,696	
Lodi.......................	53,717	3,937		630	3,307	2	29	73	526	638	2,353	316	
Total area actually reporting......	100.0%	43,430		5,559	37,871	65	266	1,932	3,296	9,948	22,256	5,667	
Rate per 100,000 inhabitants......		8,528.3		1,091.6	7,436.7	12.8	52.2	379.4	647.2	1,953.5	4,370.4	1,112.8	
Sumter, S.C. M.S.A.	**106,524**												
(Includes Sumter County, S.C.)													
City of Sumter	42,932	3,230		627	2,603	5	22	179	421	810	1,620	173	
Total area actually reporting......	100.0%	6,680		1,256	5,424	10	59	246	941	2,022	2,996	406	
Rate per 100,000 inhabitants......		6,270.9		1,179.1	5,091.8	9.4	55.4	230.9	883.4	1,898.2	2,812.5	381.1	
Syracuse, N.Y. M.S.A.	**756,865**												
(Includes Cayuga, Madison, Onondaga, and Oswego Counties.)													
City of Syracuse................	163,626	11,115		1,361	9,754	18	79	561	703	2,824	6,358	572	
Total area actually reporting......	99.6%	27,430		2,077	25,353	32	192	687	1,166	6,009	18,344	1,000	
Estimated total	100.0%	27,549		2,090	25,459	32	193	692	1,173	6,028	18,422	1,009	
Rate per 100,000 inhabitants......		3,639.9		276.1	3,363.7	4.2	25.5	91.4	155.0	796.4	2,434.0	133.3	
Tacoma, Wa. M.S.A.	**633,847**												
(Includes Pierce County.)													
City of Tacoma.................	187,895	21,046		3,441	17,605	31	191	1,015	2,204	3,915	11,355	2,335	
Total area actually reporting......	99.5%	42,619		5,577	37,042	57	413	1,443	3,664	8,370	24,868	3,804	
Estimated total	100.0%	42,843		5,589	37,254	57	415	1,446	3,671	8,403	25,031	3,820	
Rate per 100,000 inhabitants......		6,759.2		881.8	5,877.4	9.0	65.5	228.1	579.2	1,325.7	3,949.1	602.7	
Tallahassee, Fl. M.S.A.	**248,840**												
(Includes Gadsden and Leon Counties.)													
City of Tallahassee	132,252	19,426		2,690	16,736	9	137	790	1,754	3,970	10,701	2,065	
Total area actually reporting......	100.0%	26,766		3,847	22,919	18	219	1,017	2,593	6,037	14,096	2,786	
Rate per 100,000 inhabitants......		10,756.3		1,546.0	9,210.3	7.2	88.0	408.7	1,042.0	2,426.1	5,664.7	1,119.6	
Tampa-St. Petersburg-Clearwater, Fl. M.S.A.	**2,137,896**												
(Includes Hernando, Hillsborough, Pasco, and Pinellas Counties.)													
City of:													
Tampa	288,877	45,373		9,379	35,994	43	247	2,965	6,124	8,987	18,534	8,473	
St. Petersburg.................	238,727	23,022		5,173	17,849	19	176	1,599	3,379	4,828	11,729	1,292	
Clearwater	99,547	7,610		1,171	6,439	3	70	212	886	1,502	4,567	370	
Total area actually reporting......	99.9%	162,763		26,146	136,617	130	1,144	6,619	18,253	34,332	85,003	17,282	
Estimated total	100.0%	162,845		26,155	136,690	130	1,144	6,622	18,259	34,349	85,051	17,290	
Rate per 100,000 inhabitants......		7,617.1		1,223.4	6,393.7	6.1	53.5	309.7	854.1	1,606.7	3,978.3	808.7	
Texarkana, Tx.-Texarkana, Ar. M.S.A...	**123,027**												
(Includes Bowie County, Tx., and Miller County, Ar.)													
City of:													
Texarkana, Tx................	32.754	3,224		479	2,745	4	28	102	345	601	1,970	174	
Texarkana, Ar	22,959	3,120		323	2,797	7	21	71	224	433	2,289	75	
Total area actually reporting......	100.0%	7,940		981	6,959	21	66	190	704	1,492	5,120	347	
Rate per 100,000 inhabitants......		6,453.9		797.4	5,656.5	17.1	53.6	154.4	572.2	1,212.7	4,161.7	282.1	
Toledo, Oh. M.S.A.	**619,203**												
(Includes Fulton, Lucas and Wood Counties.)													
City of Toledo.................	331,416	28,461		3,191	25,270	45	357	1,594	1,195	5,502	15,251	4,517	
Total area actually reporting......	99.8%	38,484		3,695	34,789	49	421	1,708	1,517	7,043	22,664	5,082	
Estimated total	100.0%	38,530		3,698	34,832	49	421	1,709	1,519	7,050	22,697	5,085	
Rate per 100,000 inhabitants......		6,222.5		597.2	5,625.3	7.9	68.0	276.0	245.3	1,138.6	3,665.5	821.2	
Trenton, N.J. M.S.A.	**330,159**												
(Includes Mercer County.)													
City of Trenton.................	88,468	7,923		1,753	6,170	11	109	717	916	1,710	2,608	1,852	
Total area actually reporting......	100.0%	17,015		2,133	14,882	19	136	874	1,104	3,030	8,039	3,813	
Rate per 100,000 inhabitants......		5,153.6		646.1	4,507.5	5.8	41.2	264.7	334.4	917.7	2,434.9	1,154.9	
Tucson, Az. M.S.A.	**708,931**												
(Includes Pima County.)													
City of Tucson	426,344	48,945		4,363	44,582	44	314	894	3,111	7,363	32,076	5,143	
Total area actually reporting......	99.0%	64,825		5,304	59,521	65	425	1,075	3,739	9,896	43,209	6,416	
Estimated total	100.0%	65,363		5,347	60,016	65	427	1,084	3,771	10,001	43,545	6,470	
Rate per 100,000 inhabitants......		9,219.9		754.2	8,465.7	9.2	60.2	152.9	531.9	1,410.7	6,142.3	912.6	

See footnotes at end of table.

Table 6.—Index of Crime, Metropolitan Statistical Areas, 1993—Continued

Metropolitan Statistical Area	Population	Crime Index total	Modified Crime Index total[1]	Violent crime[2]	Property crime[3]	Murder and non-negligent man-slaughter	Forcible rape	Robbery	Aggra-vated assault	Burglary	Larceny-theft	Motor vehicle theft	Arson[1]
Tulsa, Ok. M.S.A.	737,648												
(Includes Creek, Osage, Rogers, Tulsa and Wagoner Counties.)													
City of Tulsa...................	378,350	29,354		4,921	24,433	54	339	1,143	3,385	7,196	12,790	4,447	
Total area actually reporting.....	100.0%	40,453		5,909	34,544	63	421	1,254	4,171	10,086	19,057	5,401	
Rate per 100,000 inhabitants.....		5,484.1		801.1	4,683.0	8.5	57.1	170.0	565.4	1,367.3	2,583.5	732.2	
Tuscaloosa, Al. M.S.A.	155,452												
(Includes Tuscaloosa County.)													
City of Tuscaloosa...............	79,664	8,865		1,003	7,862	8	56	282	657	1,093	6,421	348	
Total area actually reporting.....	100.0%	12,496		1,569	10,927	10	77	345	1,137	1,798	8,627	502	
Rate per 100,000 inhabitants.....		8,038.5		1,009.3	7,029.2	6.4	49.5	221.9	731.4	1,156.6	5,549.6	322.9	
Tyler, Tx. M.S.A.	157,425												
(Includes Smith County.)													
City of Tyler	78,384	8,647		933	7,714	9	100	229	595	1,797	5,389	528	
Total area actually reporting.....	100.0%	11,541		1,234	10,307	17	123	266	828	2,699	6,908	700	
Rate per 100,000 inhabitants.....		7,331.1		783.9	6,547.2	10.8	78.1	169.0	526.0	1,714.5	4,388.1	444.7	
Utica-Rome, N.Y. M.S.A.	317,581												
(Includes Herkimer and Oneida Counties.)													
City of:													
Utica	67,173	3,848		273	3,575	14	24	170	65	681	2,634	260	
Rome......................	45,358	906		62	844	....	9	14	39	215	580	49	
Total area actually reporting.....	100.0%	9,669		784	8,885	18	86	204	476	1,990	6,470	425	
Rate per 100,000 inhabitants.....		3,044.6		246.9	2,797.7	5.7	27.1	64.2	149.9	626.6	2,037.3	133.8	
Vallejo-Fairfield-Napa, Ca. M.S.A......	479,963												
(Includes Napa and Solano Counties.)													
City of:													
Vallejo......................	114,866	9,278		1,623	7,655	10	65	599	949	1,802	4,703	1,150	
Fairfield	83,032	5,722		801	4,921	10	46	188	557	828	3,612	481	
Napa	63,929	3,360		390	2,970	3	20	43	324	491	2,268	211	
Total area actually reporting.....	100.0%	27,236		3,730	23,506	31	201	1,016	2,482	5,212	15,810	2,484	
Rate per 100,000 inhabitants.....		5,674.6		777.1	4,897.5	6.5	41.9	211.7	517.1	1,085.9	3,294.0	517.5	
Ventura, Ca. M.S.A.	693,577												
(Includes Ventura County.)													
City of Ventura	95,614	5,012		395	4,617	9	29	139	218	1,271	2,979	367	
Total area actually reporting.....	100.0%	26,937		3,471	23,466	42	185	921	2,323	6,110	14,580	2,776	
Rate per 100,000 inhabitants.....		3,883.8		500.4	3,383.3	6.1	26.7	132.8	334.9	880.9	2,102.1	400.2	
Victoria, Tx. M.S.A...................	78,557												
(Includes Victoria County.)													
City of Victoria	58,517	4,987		576	4,411	4	21	82	469	1,116	3,049	246	
Total area actually reporting.....	100.0%	5,549		612	4,937	4	31	86	491	1,289	3,383	265	
Rate per 100,000 inhabitants.....		7,063.7		779.1	6,284.6	5.1	39.5	109.5	625.0	1,640.8	4,306.4	337.3	
Vineland-Millville-Bridgeton, N.J. M.S.A...........................	139,537												
(Includes Cumberland County.)													
City of:													
Vineland	55,076	4,460		496	3,964	4	46	193	253	971	2,631	362	
Millville....................	26,479	1,652		254	1,398	2	28	69	155	414	907	77	
Bridgeton	19,311	1,946		429	1,517	8	17	135	269	478	987	52	
Total area actually reporting.....	100.0%	8,949		1,330	7,619	21	112	417	780	2,139	4,918	562	
Rate per 100,000 inhabitants.....		6,413.4		953.2	5,460.2	15.0	80.3	298.8	559.0	1,532.9	3,524.5	402.8	
Visalia-Tulare-Porterville, Ca. M.S.A.	334,462												
(Includes Tulare County.)													
City of:													
Visalia	82,154	6,585		664	5,921	3	24	167	470	1,126	4,179	616	
Tulare	36,808	2,056		335	1,721	3	16	75	241	574	979	168	
Porterville.................	31,094	2,520		192	2,328	4	14	50	124	461	1,563	304	
Total area actually reporting.....	100.0%	19,748		2,224	17,524	28	132	408	1,656	4,495	11,053	1,976	
Rate per 100,000 inhabitants.....		5,904.4		664.9	5,239.5	8.4	39.5	122.0	495.1	1,343.9	3,304.7	590.8	
Waco, Tx. M.S.A.....................,	195,325												
(Includes McLennan County.)													
City of Waco..................	106,043	11,254		1,666	9,588	29	141	453	1,043	2,397	6,121	1,070	
Total area actually reporting.....	100.0%	14,894		2,056	12,838	32	168	509	1,347	3,199	8,409	1,230	
Rate per 100,000 inhabitants.....		7,625.2		1,052.6	6,572.6	16.4	86.0	260.6	689.6	1,637.8	4,305.1	629.7	

See footnotes at end of table.

Table 6. — Index of Crime, Metropolitan Statistical Areas, 1993 — Continued

Metropolitan Statistical Area	Population	Crime Index total	Modified Crime Index total[1]	Violent crime[2]	Property crime[3]	Murder and non-negligent man-slaughter	Forcible rape	Robbery	Aggra-vated assault	Burglary	Larceny-theft	Motor vehicle theft	Arson[1]
Washington, D.C.-Md.-Va.-W.V. M.S.A.	4,399,049												
(Includes District of Columbia, Calvert, Charles, Frederick, Montgomery, and Prince Georges Counties, Md.; Alexandria, Fairfax, Falls Church, Fredericksburg, Manassas, and Manassas Park Cities, and Arlington, Clarke, Culpeper, Fairfax, Fauquier, King George, Loudoun, Prince William, Spotsylvania, Stafford, and Warren Counties, Va.; and Berkeley and Jefferson Counties, W.V.)													
City of Washington, D.C	578,000	67,946		16,888	51,058	454	324	7,107	9,003	11,532	31,466	8,060	
Total area actually reporting......	100.0%	240,295		33,935	206,360	696	1,469	14,251	17,519	36,255	143,386	26,719	
Rate per 100,000 inhabitants......		5,462.4		771.4	4,691.0	15.8	33.4	324.0	398.2	824.2	3,259.5	607.4	
Waterbury, Ct. M.S.A.	185,361												
(Includes part of Litchfield and New Haven Counties.)													
City of Waterbury	106,838	8,735		586	8,149	20	39	288	239	1,815	4,957	1,377	
Total area actually reporting......	100.0%	10,911		689	10,222	20	56	303	310	2,191	6,403	1,628	
Rate per 100,000 inhabitants......		5,886.4		371.7	5,514.6	10.8	30.2	163.5	167.2	1,182.0	3,454.3	878.3	
Waterloo-Cedar Falls, Ia. M.S.A.	125,885												
(Includes Black Hawk County.) City of:													
Waterloo	67,387	4,532		442	4,090	9	50	124	259	1,115	2,766	209	
Cedar Falls..................	35,231	1,076		44	1,032	....	9	5	30	121	879	32	
Total area actually reporting......	100.0%	6,205		513	5,692	9	58	130	316	1,369	4,071	252	
Rate per 100,000 inhabitants......		4,929.1		407.5	4,521.6	7.1	46.1	103.3	251.0	1,087.5	3,233.9	200.2	
Wausau, Wi. M.S.A.	138,369												
(Includes Marathon County.)													
City of Wausau.................	38,393	1,503		19	1,484	....	6	9	4	210	1,212	62	
Total area actually reporting......	100.0%	3,680		92	3,588	1	9	14	68	502	2,961	125	
Rate per 100,000 inhabitants......		2,659.6		66.5	2,593.1	.7	6.5	10.1	49.1	362.8	2,139.9	90.3	
Wichita Falls, Tx. M.S.A.	130,603												
(Includes Archer and Wichita Counties.)													
City of Wichita Falls.............	96,887	8,003		831	7,172	9	69	189	564	1,463	5,307	402	
Total area actually reporting......	100.0%	8,751		902	7,849	9	77	192	624	1,618	5,812	419	
Rate per 100,000 inhabitants......		6,700.5		690.6	6,009.8	6.9	59.0	147.0	477.8	1,238.9	4,450.1	320.8	
Williamsport, Pa. M.S.A.	120,995												
(Includes Lycoming County.)													
City of Williamsport	32,469	2,083		101	1,982	2	8	48	43	439	1,477	66	
Total area actually reporting......	95.1%	3,621		199	3,422	2	21	57	119	799	2,457	166	
Estimated total	100.0%	3,780		214	3,566	2	22	61	129	823	2,562	181	
Rate per 100,000 inhabitants......		3,124.1		176.9	2,947.2	1.7	18.2	50.4	106.6	680.2	2,117.4	149.6	
Wilmington, N.C. M.S.A.	185,143												
(Includes Brunswick and New Hanover Counties.)													
City of Wilmington	60,435	6,829		767	6,062	7	38	279	443	1,531	4,156	375	
Total area actually reporting......	76.6%	11,312		1,227	10,085	11	61	310	845	2,564	6,991	530	
Estimated total	100.0%	12,726		1,346	11,380	13	70	333	930	3,040	7,733	607	
Rate per 100,000 inhabitants......		6,873.6		727.0	6,146.6	7.0	37.8	179.9	502.3	1,642.0	4,176.8	327.9	
Worcester, Ma.-Ct. M.S.A.[5]	470,774												
(Includes part of Windham County, Ct., and Hampden and Worcester Counties, Ma.)													
City of Worcester[5]	163,932					12	77	628		3,404	5,221	1,692	
Total area actually reporting......	81.9%				14,145	14	128	653		4,484	7,677	1,984	
Estimated total	100.0%				16,752	15	145	713		5,116	9,204	2,432	
Rate per 100,000 inhabitants......					3,558.4	3.2	30.8	151.5		1,086.7	1,955.1	516.6	
Yakima, Wa. M.S.A.	202,331												
(Includes Yakima County.)													
City of Yakima.................	59,720	7,777		768	7,009	6	65	175	522	1,443	5,164	402	
Total area actually reporting......	98.0%	15,822		1,278	14,544	15	167	229	867	3,506	10,136	902	
Estimated total	100.0%	16,101		1,294	14,807	15	170	233	876	3,547	10,339	921	
Rate per 100,000 inhabitants......		7,957.8		639.5	7,318.2	7.4	84.0	115.2	433.0	1,753.1	5,109.9	455.2	

See footnotes at end of table.

Metropolitan Statistical Area	Population	Crime Index total	Modified Crime Index total[1]	Violent crime[2]	Property crime[3]	Murder and non-negligent man-slaughter	Forcible rape	Robbery	Aggra-vated assault	Burglary	Larceny-theft	Motor vehicle theft	Arson[1]
Yolo, Ca. M.S.A.	**146,290**												
(Includes Yolo County.)													
Total area actually reporting	100.0%	10,658		781	9,877	10	76	173	522	2,105	6,757	1,015	
Rate per 100,000 inhabitants		7,285.5		533.9	6,751.7	6.8	52.0	118.3	356.8	1,438.9	4,618.9	693.8	
Yuba City, Ca. M.S.A.	**131,663**												
(Includes Sutter and Yuba Counties.)													
City of Yuba City	30,723	2,666		210	2,456	2	23	44	141	479	1,774	203	
Total area actually reporting	100.0%	8,012		1,131	6,881	5	66	116	944	1,946	4,332	603	
Rate per 100,000 inhabitants		6,085.2		859.0	5,226.2	3.8	50.1	88.1	717.0	1,478.0	3,290.2	458.0	
San Juan, Puerto Rico M.S.A.[6]		75,946		18,327	57,619	698	209	14,136	3,284	18,933	24,797	13,889	
Total area actually reporting	100.0%												
Aguadilla, Puerto Rico M.S.A.[6]		4,015		509	3,506	11	15	235	248	1,333	1,882	291	
Total area actually reporting	100.0%												
Arecibo, Puerto Rico M.S.A.[6]		4,621		602	4,019	15	10	306	271	1,722	1,835	462	
Total area actually reporting	100.0%												
Caguas, Puerto Rico M.S.A.[6]		8,601		1,911	6,690	84	19	1,237	571	2,901	2,740	1,049	
Total area actually reporting	100.0%												
Mayaguez, Puerto Rico M.S.A.[6]		5,597		871	4,726	31	26	351	463	1,555	2,715	456	
Total area actually reporting	100.0%												
Ponce, Puerto Rico M.S.A.[6]		8,599		1,685	6,914	46	41	1,038	560	2,141	4,202	571	
Total area actually reporting	100.0%												

[1]Although arson data are included in the trend and clearance tables, sufficient data are not available to estimate totals for this offense. Arson data for individual cities are shown in Table 8.

[2]Violent crimes are offenses of murder, forcible rape, robbery, and aggravated assault.

[3]Property crimes are offenses of burglary, larceny-theft, and motor vehicle theft. Data are not included for the property crime of arson.

[4]Forcible rape figures furnished by the state-level Uniform Crime Reporting (UCR) Programs administered by the Michigan State Police and the Minnesota Department of Public Safety were not in accordance with national UCR guidelines. Therefore, the figures were excluded from the forcible rape, violent crime, and Crime Index total categories. However, several Minnesota law enforcement agencies verified and/or adjusted their forcible rape figures to comply with national UCR guidelines and are shown in this table.

[5]Due to reporting changes figures are not comparable to previous years.

[6]The 1993 Bureau of the Census population estimates for the individual Puerto Rico M.S.A.'s were not available prior to publication; therefore, no population or rates per 100,000 inhabitants are provided.

Complete data for 1993 were not available for the states of Illinois and Kansas; therefore, it was necessary that their crime counts be estimated. See "Offense Estimation," page 376 for details.

Table 7. — Offense Analysis, United States, 1989-1993

Classification	1989	1990	1991	1992	1993
Murder..	21,500	23,440	24,700	23,760	24,530
Forcible Rape	94,500	102,560	106,590	109,060	104,810
Robbery:					
Total...	578,330	639,270	687,730	672,480	659,760
Street/highway................................	318,017	360,861	386,552	374,157	360,739
Commercial house	68,173	72,589	80,448	79,717	82,371
Gas or service station.........................	16,355	17,394	17,829	16,752	15,389
Convenience store.............................	36,381	38,643	39,429	35,312	34,811
Residence....................................	56,928	61,733	67,592	67,619	67,902
Bank..	7,932	9,345	11,019	11,121	11,854
Miscellaneous	74,544	78,705	84,863	87,802	86,693
Burglary:					
Total...	3,168,200	3,073,900	3,157,200	2,979,900	2,834,800
Residence (dwelling):	2,096,233	2,034,865	2,088,343	1,972,919	1,883,907
Night..	650,852	648,856	663,991	629,462	591,404
Day..	894,475	889,874	900,149	863,812	827,731
Unknown	550,906	496,135	524,203	479,645	464,772
Nonresidence (store,office,etc.)	1,071,967	1,039,035	1,068,807	1,006,981	950,893
Night..	519,195	491,356	501,437	469,929	440,653
Day..	236,196	262,067	255,946	258,914	242,340
Unknown	316,575	285,612	311,424	278,138	267,900
Larceny-theft (except motor vehicle theft):					
Total...	7,872,400	7,945,700	8,142,200	7,915,200	7,820,900
By type:					
Pocket-picking................................	78,502	81,027	83,132	78,194	72,775
Purse-snatching	89,032	82,875	83,183	74,858	68,447
Shoplifting....................................	1,230,317	1,291,492	1,343,196	1,253,766	1,200,910
From motor vehicles (except accessories)	1,726,688	1,746,830	1,827,508	1,792,386	1,827,643
Motor vehicle accessories	1,227,923	1,183,567	1,150,443	1,107,131	1,090,850
Bicycles......................................	431,634	442,214	475,172	468,584	478,485
From buildings	1,154,833	1,116,898	1,150,443	1,106,809	1,028,997
From coin-operated machines	65,140	62,993	79,325	72,087	61,686
All others....................................	1,868,332	1,937,803	1,949,826	1,961,384	1,991,106
By value:					
Over $200.....................................	2,780,065	2,840,662	2,916,280	2,844,553	2,865,453
$50 to $200...................................	1,928,809	1,893,021	1,930,465	1,874,226	1,829,138
Under $50	3,163,526	3,212,017	3,295,483	3,196,421	3,126,309
Motor Vehicle Theft	1,564,800	1,635,900	1,661,700	1,610,800	1,561,000

Because of rounding, offenses may not add to totals.

Complete data for 1993 were not available for the states of Illinois and Kansas; therefore, it was necessary that their crime counts be estimated. See "Offense Estimation," page 376 for details.

Table 8. — Number of Offenses Known to the Police, Cities and Towns 10,000 and over in Population, 1993

*Arson is shown only if 12 months of arson data were received. Leaders (..) indicate zero data. The Modified Crime Index total is the sum of the Crime Index offenses, including arson.

City by State	Population	Crime Index total	Modified* Crime Index total	Murder and non-negligent man-slaughter	Forcible rape	Robbery	Aggra-vated assault	Burglary	Larceny-theft	Motor vehicle theft	Arson*
ALABAMA											
Alabaster	16,256	109		1	3	2	18	22	56	7	
Albertville	15,821	549		3	7	4	22	166	306	41	
Alexander City	15,218	189	189	4	1	11	36	56	77	4	....
Anniston	27,436	4,286	4,313	12	36	142	781	1,049	2,089	177	27
Athens	17,977	698		2	2	7	94	96	476	21	
Auburn	35,658	2,027		4	14	20	96	409	1,443	41	
Bessemer	33,296	3,957	3,995	10	31	193	651	941	1,689	442	38
Birmingham	268,768	31,776	31,991	121	297	1,706	4,554	6,628	14,926	3,544	215
Cullman	14,815	752		....	3	7	61	114	535	32	
Daphne	12,828	459		....	....	3	15	94	335	12	
Decatur	51,041	4,152	4,161	8	27	86	155	725	2,889	262	9
Dothan	55,435	4,787		4	33	115	555	835	2,965	280	
Enterprise	20,917	996		4	6	19	186	192	558	31	
Eufaula	13,395	641		1	6	12	76	69	468	9	
Fairfield	12,402	1,348		3	11	79	149	199	716	191	
Florence	37,304	1,944		4	9	30	182	345	1,308	66	
Fort Payne	12,617	270		....	2	1	7	62	177	21	
Gadsden	44,333	5,163		9	40	187	790	974	2,733	430	
Hartselle	11,220	132		....	1	2	....	22	101	6	
Homewood	23,620	1,551		2	4	58	26	180	1,106	175	
Hoover	42,841	1,723		2	7	42	37	299	1,205	131	
Hueytown	15,957	615		....	3	18	61	116	356	61	
Huntsville	165,252	15,694	15,755	18	82	320	1,751	2,571	10,002	950	61
Jacksonville	10,575	386	387	....	6	6	39	60	264	11	1
Jasper	13,691	1,146	1,151	....	3	20	157	170	722	74	5
Madison	17,759	455	455	....	2	7	33	73	309	31	....
Mobile	204,286	18,567	18,619	42	122	1,186	870	4,884	9,926	1,537	52
Montgomery	194,399	12,310	12,380	39	87	562	1,007	3,558	5,843	1,214	70
Mountain Brook	20,365	414		....	....	6	3	65	323	17	
Northport	18,861	1,044		....	2	30	142	130	711	29	
Opelika	23,635	2,272		3	17	79	556	434	1,107	76	
Ozark	12,878	791	798	1	5	18	176	80	495	16	7
Pelham	11,194	275	275	1	....	2	5	33	211	23	....
Phenix City	26,863	1,634		2	29	42	165	377	860	159	
Prattville	21,989	1,499	1,502	....	6	34	253	284	878	44	3
Prichard	34,206	4,594		7	36	352	605	1,626	1,529	439	
Saraland	12,114	946		1	1	9	184	120	586	45	
Scottsboro	14,492	778		....	2	9	44	160	528	35	
Selma	24,646	3,379		8	39	84	681	590	1,846	131	
Sheffield	10,761	507	508	2	2	1	20	94	371	17	1
Sylacauga	13,240	685		1	4	19	82	109	445	25	
Talladega	19,293	1,104		4	5	23	115	164	748	45	
Troy	13,611	72	73	1	....	5	3	25	24	14	1
Tuscaloosa	79,664	8,865		8	56	282	657	1,093	6,421	348	
Tuskegee	12,039	1,200	1,203	2	9	18	128	492	521	30	3
Vestavia Hills	20,434	232		....	....	7	....	40	159	26	
ALASKA											
Anchorage	250,720	16,140	16,245	23	212	568	1,410	1,880	10,660	1,387	105
Fairbanks	33,842	2,206	2,208	6	25	80	143	251	1,460	241	2
Juneau	28,894	1,077	1,084	....	12	3	18	128	857	59	7
ARIZONA											
Apache Junction	20,138	1,090	1,096	1	8	5	72	214	729	61	6
Avondale	16,636	1,704	1,720	1	9	23	134	601	794	142	16

Table 8.—Number of Offenses Known to the Police, Cities and Towns 10,000 and over in Population, 1993—Continued

City by State	Population	Crime Index total	Modified* Crime Index total	Murder and non-negligent man-slaughter	Forcible rape	Robbery	Aggra-vated assault	Burglary	Larceny-theft	Motor vehicle theft	Arson*
ARIZONA—Continued											
Bullhead City.........................	25,453	2,273	2,291	1	9	32	185	565	1,296	185	18
Casa Grande	20,495	3,275	3,302	3	15	49	237	589	2,197	185	27
Chandler.............................	102,891	6,651	6,697	....	27	82	167	1,635	4,061	679	46
Douglas..............................	13,614	998	998	....	....	5	18	157	677	141	....
Flagstaff.............................	49,438	4,528	4,531	2	14	41	202	586	3,528	155	3
Gilbert	37,909	1,977	1,986	....	5	13	110	479	1,168	202	9
Glendale.............................	160,403	13,625	13,708	16	79	317	1,013	2,037	8,422	1,741	83
Lake Havasu City.....................	28,815	1,636	1,653	2	4	6	53	294	1,184	93	17
Mesa................................	304,695	24,146	24,232	6	111	410	1,808	4,664	14,430	2,717	86
Nogales..............................	20,091	2,017	2,022	1	4	95	73	578	999	267	5
Paradise Valley......................	12,712	626	626	....	1	7	12	395	169	42	....
Peoria...............................	57,476	2,921	2,933	4	16	31	247	691	1,759	173	12
Phoenix..............................	1,039,369	96,476	96,785	158	444	3,437	7,872	20,617	48,382	15,566	309
Prescott..............................	28,919	1,733	1,748	1	14	16	107	227	1,285	83	15
Prescott Valley.......................	11,049	589	591	....	1	4	71	70	416	27	2
Scottsdale............................	140,740	8,329	8,352	3	29	131	234	1,609	5,362	961	23
Sierra Vista	36,437	1,270	1,278	1	4	12	27	255	871	100	8
Tempe...............................	145,996	12,305	12,361	4	65	244	518	2,073	8,000	1,401	56
Tuscon...............................	426,344	48,945	49,107	44	314	894	3,111	7,363	32,076	5,143	162
ARKANSAS											
Arkadelphia..........................	10,120	314	314	1	....	4	....	24	271	14	....
Benton	20,341	1,138	1,140	....	12	10	80	182	812	42	2
Bentonville...........................	12,392	444	445	....	....	7	9	71	351	6	1
Blytheville...........................	21,186	2,678	2,720	6	18	91	270	774	1,371	148	42
Camden	14,372	966	972	2	8	51	106	189	569	41	6
Conway..............................	30,555	1,784	1,788	1	8	25	58	188	1,429	75	4
El Dorado............................	24,137	1,639	1,642	4	11	47	63	407	1,048	59	3
Fayetteville...........................	46,648	2,139	2,140	1	29	14	83	305	1,542	165	1
Forrest City	13,472	1,547	1,552	....	11	39	128	268	1,030	71	5
Fort Smith	74,875	5,831	5,854	4	66	62	389	963	3,956	391	23
Harrison.............................	10,371	258	259	....	....	2	3	25	194	34	1
Hope................................	10,092	794	798	2	7	25	44	213	474	29	4
Hot Springs	34,074	4,310	4,325	5	25	155	130	1,209	2,556	230	15
Jacksonville	31,028	1,954	1,966	3	17	48	179	278	1,322	107	12
Jonesboro............................	49,226	2,956	2,966	2	29	74	186	793	1,741	131	10
Little Rock...........................	178,924	28,070	28,244	68	215	1,136	4,468	5,796	14,306	2,081	174
Magnolia.............................	11,642	365	369	....	1	18	38	105	184	19	4
North Little Rock.....................	63,108	7,704	7,729	13	71	324	235	1,456	4,732	873	25
Paragould............................	20,012	691	692	1	9	2	8	134	502	35	1
Pine Bluff............................	58,397	5,148	5,194	16	59	261	531	1,754	2,010	517	46
Rogers...............................	27,670	1,559	1,565	....	9	10	44	233	1,215	48	6
Russellville...........................	22,325	1,379	1,380	....	8	7	39	206	1,064	55	1
Searcy...............................	16,746	746	746	....	6	4	4	109	580	43	....
Sherwood	20,335	921	922	1	3	16	36	119	653	93	1
Springdale	33,192	1,468	1,468	1	9	13	43	256	1,059	87	....
Stuttgart.............................	10,620	818	818	2	2	17	39	205	470	83	....
Texarkana............................	22,959	3,120	3,138	7	21	71	224	433	2,289	75	18
Van Buren	16,088	888	889	....	2	3	13	157	665	48	1
West Memphis........................	28,179	1,434	1,434	7	24	121	50	197	797	238	....
CALIFORNIA											
Adelanto.............................	12,188	483	484	....	3	17	43	169	190	61	1
Agoura Hills	22,875	610	612	....	2	10	82	145	278	93	2
Alameda.............................	79,747	5,000	5,046	1	26	239	208	769	3,278	479	46
Albany	16,635	784	784	1	1	42	58	124	467	91	....

Table 8. — Number of Offenses Known to the Police, Cities and Towns 10,000 and over in Population, 1993 — Continued

City by State	Population	Crime Index total	Modified* Crime Index total	Murder and non-negligent man-slaughter	Forcible rape	Robbery	Aggra-vated assault	Burglary	Larceny-theft	Motor vehicle theft	Arson*
CALIFORNIA — Continued											
Alhambra	84,065	3,875	3,908	3	19	311	129	894	1,720	799	33
Anaheim[1]	276,966			33	70	909		3,942	9,145	3,607	74
Antioch	69,812	3,842	3,923	7	21	157	344	865	2,058	390	81
Apple Valley	52,080	2,996	3,020	7	16	66	263	916	1,457	271	24
Arcadia	49,639	2,464	2,485	2	4	96	101	480	1,453	328	21
Arcata	15,196	1,254	1,258	....	8	6	48	169	970	53	4
Arroyo Grande	14,953	627	633	....	5	6	95	116	384	21	6
Artesia	15,652	1,009	1,018	3	3	90	161	261	333	158	9
Atascadero	24,093	963	969	....	11	13	57	269	574	39	6
Atwater	23,914	1,412	1,422	3	7	25	132	407	739	99	10
Auburn	11,138	554	557	....	1	10	34	79	390	40	3
Avenal	11,779	355	364	....	3	3	24	116	192	17	9
Azusa	42,679	2,078	2,090	4	17	101	163	565	883	345	12
Bakersfield	189,908	15,614	15,727	27	39	568	1,237	3,650	8,498	1,595	113
Baldwin Park	71,773	2,619	2,635	8	14	196	224	1,144	290	743	16
Banning	22,536	1,528	1,617	5	8	56	142	406	712	199	89
Barstow	22,354	1,962	1,972	3	22	43	141	447	1,117	189	10
Beaumont	10,507	936	952	1	6	40	99	327	391	72	16
Bell	35,279	1,111	1,114	8	6	166	131	235	283	282	3
Bell Gardens	43,087	2,184	2,194	8	11	214	327	669	562	393	10
Bellflower	65,162	4,645	4,667	4	28	383	729	910	1,454	1,137	22
Belmont	24,857	725	728	....	3	10	29	107	522	54	3
Benicia	26,434	1,070	1,076	....	8	21	42	313	605	81	6
Berkeley	102,156	13,090	13,154	8	35	815	773	2,383	7,915	1,161	64
Beverly Hills	32,435	2,810	2,824	1	8	281	72	472	1,755	221	14
Brawley	21,581	1,490	1,506	1	4	38	174	437	758	78	16
Brea	33,880	2,180	2,196	3	5	51	69	309	1,521	222	16
Buena Park	71,661	4,460	4,474	7	19	203	188	994	2,100	949	14
Burbank	97,310	4,705	4,819	5	16	209	262	665	2,556	992	114
Burlingame	27,514	1,268	1,277	1	4	23	48	139	880	173	9
Calabasas	74,661	559	561	1	4	15	96	165	206	72	2
Calexico	22,379	2,153	2,194	....	3	54	103	424	1,057	512	41
Camarillo	55,372	1,292	1,308	....	13	41	100	263	790	85	16
Campbell	37,131	2,027	2,036	....	17	44	86	320	1,367	193	9
Carlsbad	65,018	3,549	3,557	5	22	96	233	817	1,755	621	8
Carpinteria	13,756	414	417	....	4	7	55	126	203	19	3
Carson	88,004	4,856	4,900	10	28	340	769	940	1,638	1,131	44
Cathedral City	33,913	2,326	2,331	8	19	61	342	754	891	251	5
Ceres	29,036	2,236	2,250	....	9	35	140	455	1,303	294	14
Cerritos	54,074	4,010	4,034	5	10	217	268	797	1,807	906	24
Chico	41,122	2,941	2,966	1	33	47	116	601	1,983	160	25
Chino	63,863	4,035	4,083	8	18	127	466	798	1,933	685	48
Chino Hills	28,336	1,432	1,435	1	7	31	79	412	731	171	3
Chula Vista	146,232	10,170	10,234	14	37	459	573	1,895	4,726	2,466	64
Claremont	33,506	1,887	1,900	3	5	55	60	438	1,086	240	13
Clearlake	12,525	1,356	1,369	1	11	18	191	461	598	76	13
Clovis	55,593	3,168	3,197	2	17	69	156	718	1,844	362	29
Colton	43,485	3,287	3,305	6	15	172	261	803	1,390	640	18
Commerce	12,286	2,029	2,035	1	8	136	176	252	839	617	6
Compton	96,586	6,935	6,963	62	75	969	998	1,601	1,745	1,485	28
Concord	113,840	7,928	7,958	5	44	210	342	1,604	4,845	878	30
Corcoran	14,020	427	438	2	4	12	88	109	178	34	11
Corona	87,223	6,470	6,493	1	28	237	219	1,552	3,099	1,334	23
Coronado	26,319	984	993	3	3	19	48	214	552	145	9
Costa Mesa	97,224	7,587	7,613	5	30	184	225	1,250	4,918	975	26
Covina	45,349	2,666	2,688	10	18	139	141	522	1,274	562	22

See footnotes at end of table.

Table 8. — Number of Offenses Known to the Police, Cities and Towns 10,000 and over in Population, 1993 — Continued

City by State	Population	Crime Index total	Modified* Crime Index total	Murder and non-negligent man-slaughter	Forcible rape	Robbery	Aggra-vated assault	Burglary	Larceny-theft	Motor vehicle theft	Arson*
CALIFORNIA — Continued											
Cudahy	23,512	994	1,000	3	7	69	290	144	319	162	6
Culver City	39,397	2,693	2,694	4	7	305	52	406	1,450	469	1
Cupertino	42,149	1,816	1,832	1	6	43	100	421	1,148	97	16
Cypress	45,046	2,182	2,198	1	7	57	84	423	1,262	348	16
Daly City	94,313	3,486	3,492	7	14	165	362	361	1,932	645	6
Dana Point	37,100	1,500	1,507	2	13	35	123	372	826	129	7
Danville	35,286	688	697	1	1	5	3	156	504	18	9
Davis	47,673	3,014	3,033	1	14	22	30	339	2,415	193	19
Delano	24,634	2,142	2,143	4	14	73	117	435	1,324	175	1
Desert Hot Springs	13,744	1,968	1,980	4	8	60	230	724	792	150	12
Diamond Bar	56,487	1,693	1,707	2	5	67	204	390	702	323	14
Dinuba	14,041	757	758	....	3	10	67	195	409	73	1
Dixon	11,186	652	661	1	3	14	28	93	463	50	9
Downey	96,224	4,229	4,275	3	28	319	167	827	1,728	1,157	46
Duarte	21,726	885	887	1	8	42	128	195	324	187	2
Dublin	25,452	741	743	....	1	16	49	120	494	61	2
East Palo Alto	24,210	1,658	1,695	4	11	194	400	367	388	294	37
El Cajon	93,429	7,406	7,437	8	42	243	540	1,368	4,316	889	31
El Centro	36,518	3,053	3,077	1	18	82	160	818	1,695	279	24
El Cerrito	23,059	1,856	1,865	1	8	139	58	336	1,067	247	9
El Monte	108,028	6,127	6,201	19	45	625	698	1,357	2,184	1,199	74
El Segundo	15,844	1,119	1,125	1	7	33	27	230	647	174	6
Escondido	114,318	8,276	8,309	8	26	215	481	1,490	4,809	1,247	33
Eureka	28,040	3,257	3,295	4	25	66	203	610	2,051	298	38
Fairfield	83,032	5,722	5,772	10	46	188	557	828	3,612	481	50
Fillmore	12,435	425	431	1	7	5	74	124	182	32	6
Folsom	36,035	1,173	1,173	....	4	17	55	226	765	106	....
Fontana	99,642	6,439	6,481	14	79	433	864	1,612	1,988	1,449	42
Foster City	29,357	756	762	1	1	17	36	111	526	64	6
Fountain Valley	54,595	2,903	2,912	3	3	88	57	394	1,971	387	9
Fremont	181,134	7,245	7,295	4	39	135	714	1,584	3,945	824	50
Fresno	379,977	41,584	42,243	87	216	2,879	2,329	8,472	14,518	13,083	659
Fullerton	116,657	7,874	7,905	2	36	260	325	1,385	4,575	1,291	31
Galt	10,803	645	649	....	4	12	99	106	370	54	4
Gardena	51,768	4,040	4,057	7	12	639	437	787	1,201	957	17
Garden Grove	147,366	9,550	9,615	13	33	430	441	1,759	5,075	1,799	65
Gilroy	32,708	2,029	2,107	2	9	40	216	406	1,223	133	78
Glendale	179,488	8,215	8,288	9	30	355	277	1,596	4,501	1,447	73
Glendora	50,174	1,895	1,902	....	13	46	95	474	1,076	191	7
Grand Terrace	11,799	694	694	....	5	19	13	211	306	140	....
Grover City	12,049	461	464	....	9	5	42	119	255	31	3
Hanford	32,900	2,031	2,039	1	5	38	187	327	1,284	189	8
Hawaiian Gardens	13,669	1,087	1,100	3	6	103	213	266	345	151	13
Hawthorne	75,672	7,051	7,132	12	57	895	960	1,126	2,477	1,524	81
Hayward	116,367	8,506	8,561	8	53	399	839	1,737	4,493	977	55
Hemet	39,822	3,764	3,789	1	23	128	233	1,047	1,772	560	25
Hercules	18,963	478	481	1	1	8	54	93	233	88	3
Hermosa Beach	18,562	1,140	1,145	1	3	33	56	281	595	171	5
Hesperia	57,660	2,638	2,656	9	19	65	142	800	1,197	406	18
Highland	38,622	2,368	2,380	4	14	138	191	699	951	371	12
Hillsborough	10,939	124	124	....	....	....	7	29	78	10	....
Hollister	20,446	1,229	1,255	....	1	21	181	240	696	90	26
Huntington Beach	186,948	9,122	9,156	3	38	174	662	1,984	5,042	1,219	34
Huntington Park	56,017	4,628	4,644	9	14	524	291	604	1,186	2,000	16
Indio	38,576	3,206	3,216	13	31	144	189	691	1,671	467	10
Inglewood	112,636	8,402	8,462	45	68	1,329	858	1,561	2,251	2,290	60

112

Table 8. — Number of Offenses Known to the Police, Cities and Towns 10,000 and over in Population, 1993 — Continued

City by State	Population	Crime Index total	Modified* Crime Index total	Murder and non-negligent man-slaughter	Forcible rape	Robbery	Aggra-vated assault	Burglary	Larceny-theft	Motor vehicle theft	Arson*
CALIFORNIA — Continued											
Irvine..............................	120,610	4,538	4,576	1	12	58	70	990	2,957	450	38
La Canada-Flintridge	20,539	404	407	....	....	18	33	113	211	29	3
Lafayette	24,226	633	635	....	1	17	2	192	395	26	2
Laguna Beach.......................	23,813	1,616	1,619	....	5	22	164	412	874	139	3
Laguna Hills	47,965	1,146	1,158	....	3	26	36	220	762	99	12
Laguena Niguel......................	50,493	1,151	1,163	....	8	18	85	310	638	92	12
La Habra	52,632	2,620	2,636	4	17	89	378	452	1,351	329	16
Lake Elsinore	20,578	2,919	2,923	2	10	106	362	871	1,153	415	4
Lake Forest	57,545	1,973	2,000	....	6	37	122	469	1,146	193	27
Lakewood..........................	76,922	4,903	4,932	3	22	274	489	697	2,059	1,359	29
La Mesa	54,116	2,994	2,999	1	10	147	108	679	1,494	555	5
La Mirada	43,912	1,754	1,765	2	9	83	209	404	696	351	11
Lancaster..........................	107,224	6,221	6,327	7	60	263	1,130	1,370	2,375	1,016	106
La Palma	15,848	706	718	1	2	16	41	140	378	128	12
La Puente..........................	38,544	1,843	1,849	8	18	171	456	287	507	396	6
La Quinta..........................	14,343	1,069	1,072	....	3	10	118	429	448	61	3
La Verne...........................	32,210	1,355	1,368	2	2	34	49	381	705	182	13
Lawndale..........................	28,833	2,137	2,157	2	8	218	352	438	689	430	20
Lemoore...........................	14,602	678	680	3	2	5	49	116	453	50	2
Livermore..........................	60,659	3,172	3,187	1	11	36	152	633	2,127	212	15
Lodi...............................	53,717	3,937	3,952	2	29	73	526	638	2,353	316	15
Loma Linda	18,653	1,156	1,158	1	2	30	32	306	527	258	2
Lomita............................	20,258	899	905	....	3	43	222	209	298	124	6
Lompoc............................	40,556	2,059	2,077	1	13	48	133	402	1,376	86	18
Long Beach	443,259	35,630	35,873	126	200	3,717	3,073	6,780	14,108	7,626	243
Los Alamitos	12,043	566	583	....	3	18	22	143	279	101	17
Los Altos	27,231	588	599	....	6	9	15	208	332	18	11
Los Angeles........................	3,525,317	312,789	317,908	1,076	1,773	38,415	42,437	50,232	119,092	59,764	5,119
Los Banos..........................	15,971	1,379	1,379	....	4	19	274	216	793	73	....
Los Gatos..........................	28,460	1,028	1,047	....	5	12	62	253	640	56	19
Lynwood...........................	63,862	4,612	4,671	22	33	676	1,195	771	887	1,028	59
Madera............................	32,561	2,660	2,673	3	23	137	254	488	1,302	453	13
Malibu............................	11,432	615	617	2	8	21	78	134	288	84	2
Manhattan Beach....................	33,805	1,833	1,838	1	5	71	37	559	874	286	5
Manteca...........................	42,903	3,246	3,259	1	15	59	199	501	2,002	469	13
Marina	27,774	923	928	2	9	42	47	226	547	50	5
Martinez...........................	32,670	1,442	1,445	....	13	33	62	421	775	138	3
Marysville..........................	12,941	1,126	1,134	2	8	33	120	160	685	118	8
Maywood	28,120	963	972	6	3	80	149	147	358	220	9
Menlo Park.........................	28,980	1,447	1,456	2	8	68	101	298	887	83	9
Merced	60,271	4,759	4,793	10	30	121	170	1,376	2,563	489	34
Millbrae	21,067	593	596	1	4	27	29	97	369	66	3
Mill Valley	13,536	604	605	....	4	10	24	182	369	15	1
Milpitas	54,314	2,490	2,494	....	18	62	104	408	1,685	213	4
Mission Viejo.......................	76,822	2,636	2,671	3	13	32	142	687	1,539	220	35
Modesto...........................	174,054	12,929	13,213	12	80	356	994	2,555	7,339	1,593	284
Monrovia	37,393	2,247	2,249	1	17	102	246	430	1,105	346	2
Montclair	29,712	3,508	3,513	9	17	180	169	555	1,873	705	5
Montebello.........................	60,985	3,904	3,967	4	30	255	506	565	1,823	721	63
Monterey	32,357	2,119	2,133	....	12	61	189	363	1,380	114	14
Monterey Park......................	59,964	2,892	2,894	6	9	296	209	758	933	681	2
Moorpark	27,639	511	519	1	3	12	53	159	239	44	8
Moraga	16,143	238	238	....	1	6	21	61	139	10	....
Moreno Valley......................	133,456	9,785	9,835	12	58	523	1,089	2,220	4,457	1,426	50
Morgan Hill........................	25,396	1,133	1,152	1	10	19	99	214	704	86	19
Mountain View	67,625	4,232	4,253	2	10	77	183	521	3,090	349	21

Table 8.— Number of Offenses Known to the Police, Cities and Towns 10,000 and over in Population, 1993—Continued

City by State	Population	Crime Index total	Modified* Crime Index total	Murder and non-negligent man-slaughter	Forcible rape	Robbery	Aggra-vated assault	Burglary	Larceny-theft	Motor vehicle theft	Arson*
CALIFORNIA—Continued											
Napa	63,929	3,360	3,439	3	20	43	324	491	2,268	211	79
National City	57,631	5,151	5,185	7	31	327	485	1,002	2,001	1,298	34
Newark	39,057	2,630	2,651	....	12	70	240	310	1,792	206	21
Newport Beach	68,594	3,690	3,730	3	25	42	205	1,060	2,005	350	40
Norco	24,309	1,240	1,255	1	4	29	117	279	554	256	15
Norwalk	98,767	5,234	5,255	6	33	393	757	1,079	1,794	1,172	21
Novato	49,009	1,925	1,941	....	22	29	137	411	1,190	136	16
Oakdale	13,107	762	775	....	4	7	37	161	502	51	13
Oakland	377,037	44,927	45,328	154	353	4,559	4,743	8,355	18,991	7,772	401
Oceanside	141,147	9,007	9,073	18	66	446	969	2,007	3,527	1,974	66
Ontario	140,402	10,784	10,848	19	66	642	846	2,469	4,827	1,915	64
Orange	114,753	6,015	6,057	3	30	234	289	1,444	3,033	982	42
Orinda	17,231	393	395	....	1	6	2	130	247	7	2
Oxnard	146,286	8,631	8,687	16	55	464	908	1,615	4,425	1,148	56
Pacifica	39,032	1,140	1,153	2	10	21	213	166	631	97	13
Pacific Grove	16,773	727	733	2	3	12	75	231	375	29	6
Palmdale	85,293	4,873	4,930	8	49	250	929	1,020	1,871	746	57
Palm Desert	25,110	3,002	3,009	4	4	43	147	888	1,733	183	7
Palm Springs	41,038	4,070	4,152	7	18	155	324	1,189	1,875	502	82
Palo Alto	56,763	3,409	3,424	....	11	61	66	487	2,596	188	15
Palos Verdes Estates	13,625	251	253	....	2	....	12	90	135	12	2
Paradise	26,377	822	828	....	....	3	64	245	472	38	6
Paramount	50,478	3,817	3,843	13	20	369	629	730	1,149	907	26
Pasadena	133,961	9,684	9,735	27	44	834	822	1,797	4,808	1,352	51
Paso Robles	17,325	997	1,007	....	16	10	141	286	489	55	10
Perris	26,192	2,397	2,455	5	17	129	270	699	779	498	58
Petaluma	44,548	1,875	1,888	2	28	28	181	407	1,096	133	13
Pico Rivera	61,364	2,661	2,671	8	18	203	619	478	836	499	10
Piedmont	11,029	460	471	....	....	10	6	125	265	54	11
Pinole	18,316	1,094	1,105	....	2	62	85	225	572	148	11
Pittsburg	50,718	2,969	2,987	2	18	199	235	899	1,353	263	18
Placentia	41,816	1,474	1,509	3	4	44	93	309	773	248	35
Pleasant Hill	32,118	1,998	2,007	....	3	58	109	415	1,266	147	9
Pleasanton	54,771	2,106	2,118	....	4	22	58	346	1,533	143	12
Pomona	141,799	10,196	10,585	40	81	995	1,237	2,282	3,721	1,840	389
Porterville	31,094	2,520	2,522	4	14	50	124	461	1,563	304	2
Port Hueneme	21,421	645	650	3	3	35	71	159	302	72	5
Rancho Cucamonga	112,298	5,391	5,415	4	31	215	143	1,262	2,728	1,008	24
Rancho Palos Verdes	42,796	841	849	1	4	21	117	239	363	96	8
Red Bluff	13,106	1,081	1,090	....	6	16	109	106	769	75	9
Redding	72,254	4,944	4,964	6	62	114	281	1,073	3,066	342	20
Redlands	61,617	3,683	3,699	5	21	150	296	975	1,620	616	16
Redondo Beach	63,432	4,023	4,026	4	17	145	221	849	2,162	625	3
Redwood City	67,900	3,337	3,339	3	15	106	371	513	1,876	453	2
Reedley	16,355	1,005	1,008	2	8	14	99	146	614	122	3
Rialto	81,730	5,137	5,173	10	26	356	767	2,012	1,088	878	36
Richmond	91,079	10,262	10,374	52	82	977	1,752	2,153	3,786	1,460	112
Ridgecrest	28,898	1,215	1,272	3	7	16	181	280	680	48	57
Riverbank	10,458	641	648	1	4	7	84	216	263	66	7
Riverside	241,041	22,147	22,485	33	131	1,287	2,524	4,975	9,635	3,562	338
Rocklin	22,813	760	763	1	7	8	29	177	468	70	3
Rohnert Park	37,995	2,218	2,235	1	12	16	342	757	958	132	17
Rosemead	52,987	2,636	2,646	8	10	265	377	631	893	452	10
Roseville	49,832	3,398	3,425	1	12	56	219	754	1,914	442	27
Sacramento	386,732	39,485	39,649	85	167	2,310	2,288	8,080	18,670	7,885	164
Salinas	115,936	8,424	8,487	15	50	560	844	1,327	4,844	784	63

City by State	Population	Crime Index total	Modified* Crime Index total	Murder and non-negligent man-slaughter	Forcible rape	Robbery	Aggra-vated assault	Burglary	Larceny-theft	Motor vehicle theft	Arson*
CALIFORNIA — Continued											
San Anselmo	11,936	493	496	....	1	5	19	142	312	14	3
San Bernardino	174,215	22,312	22,456	82	129	1,550	3,805	4,740	8,410	3,596	144
San Bruno	40,186	1,932	1,942	....	8	55	52	190	1,409	218	10
San Carlos	27,026	851	851	1	1	24	32	153	586	54	....
San Clemente	43,576	1,389	1,405	3	10	31	99	370	662	214	16
San Diego	1,160,603	85,227	85,472	133	396	4,651	8,283	14,583	37,862	19,319	245
San Dimas	34,650	1,333	1,342	....	7	47	163	322	641	153	9
San Fernando	23,628	1,245	1,249	3	7	113	138	219	454	311	4
San Francisco	736,377	70,132	70,620	129	361	8,454	4,421	11,153	34,558	11,056	488
San Francisco Highway Patrol	....	15		....	....	....	2	....	2	11	
San Francisco State Police	....	295	299	....	1	26	62	24	168	14	4
San Gabriel	37,922	1,638	1,647	4	14	164	132	448	605	271	9
Sanger	17,894	962	966	....	2	8	126	268	453	105	4
San Jacinto	18,702	842	842	1	7	20	101	350	264	99	....
San Jose	809,528	36,743	37,061	41	391	1,186	3,699	6,014	21,398	4,014	318
San Juan Capistrano	27,940	1,148	1,157	....	7	21	88	331	596	105	9
San Leandro	69,637	5,597	5,626	5	25	358	244	851	3,408	706	29
San Luis Obispo	41,631	2,146	2,194	....	11	32	196	368	1,429	110	48
San Marino	13,235	294	298	....	....	17	10	101	151	15	4
San Mateo	87,423	3,494	3,508	3	22	119	245	560	2,136	409	14
San Pablo	26,756	3,072	3,092	12	21	309	362	478	1,460	430	20
San Rafael	49,075	3,037	3,061	2	10	80	182	512	1,943	308	24
San Ramon	37,813	1,061	1,067	....	3	11	18	173	786	70	6
Santa Ana	290,970	19,071	19,563	78	77	1,886	1,149	2,950	8,973	3,958	492
Santa Barbara	85,989	5,152	5,170	5	44	159	463	938	3,317	226	18
Santa Clara	94,950	5,623	5,643	3	28	83	345	835	3,806	523	20
Santa Clarita	119,890	3,900	3,934	4	22	131	619	886	1,770	468	34
Santa Cruz	49,334	4,211	4,244	3	8	109	354	724	2,793	220	33
Santa Fe Springs	16,251	2,407	2,414	3	13	129	197	518	1,008	539	7
Santa Maria	64,767	4,937	4,945	1	39	177	296	910	3,270	244	8
Santa Monica	87,954	10,891	11,028	9	49	716	671	1,511	6,181	1,754	137
Santa Paula	25,783	1,588	1,593	2	10	62	149	517	745	103	5
Santa Rosa	117,746	7,696	7,754	7	102	197	326	1,545	5,011	508	58
Saratoga	29,229	576	578	....	4	13	35	178	332	14	2
Seal Beach	25,200	904	916	1	3	35	22	224	482	137	12
Seaside	39,770	1,498	1,519	6	9	121	215	218	844	85	21
Selma	15,536	1,138	1,150	1	4	30	186	181	486	250	12
Sierra Madre	11,102	172	173	1	....	2	13	43	90	23	1
Simi Valley	104,875	2,868	2,892	....	16	54	185	611	1,632	370	24
South El Monte	20,445	1,241	1,252	4	10	109	217	286	375	240	11
South Gate	89,528	4,922	4,950	11	27	589	387	1,068	1,264	1,576	28
South Lake Tahoe	22,428	1,402	1,407	3	10	29	102	333	851	74	5
South Pasadena	24,949	947	994	....	4	57	26	213	405	242	47
South San Francisco	56,178	2,331	2,352	2	5	78	127	331	1,494	294	21
Stanton	30,620	2,345	2,379	4	9	125	164	636	1,036	371	34
Stockton	221,867	24,849	24,981	45	157	1,554	1,744	5,362	12,291	3,696	132
Suisun City	25,121	997	1,014	1	15	35	55	288	503	100	17
Sunnyvale	119,649	4,989	5,038	3	21	106	170	604	3,566	519	49
Temecula	33,834	1,892	1,899	3	9	53	151	406	950	320	7
Temple City	32,662	1,020	1,031	....	7	50	127	305	403	128	11
Thousand Oaks	108,621	3,226	3,276	3	22	65	251	649	1,892	344	50
Torrance	137,029	8,244	8,298	12	30	430	390	1,582	4,096	1,704	54
Tracy	39,534	2,304	2,315	....	8	27	279	362	1,433	195	11
Tulare	36,808	2,056	2,103	3	16	75	241	574	979	168	47
Turlock	46,210	3,898	3,951	2	24	68	301	833	2,165	505	53
Tustin	53,852	3,321	3,354	2	12	91	98	677	2,104	337	33

Table 8. — Number of Offenses Known to the Police, Cities and Towns 10,000 and over in Population, 1993 — Continued

City by State	Population	Crime Index total	Modified* Crime Index total	Murder and non-negligent man-slaughter	Forcible rape	Robbery	Aggra-vated assault	Burglary	Larceny-theft	Motor vehicle theft	Arson*
CALIFORNIA — Continued											
Twenty-Nine Palms...............	12,600	865	873	1	11	28	87	325	358	55	8
Twin Cities.....................	11,578	802	807	1	....	13	7	206	524	51	5
Ukiah	14,867	1,087	1,094	....	11	15	39	232	758	32	7
Union City......................	55,358	3,005	3,032	1	21	119	166	638	1,793	267	27
Upland	65,329	5,556	5,591	3	26	208	382	1,415	2,793	729	35
Vacaville.......................	78,698	3,544	3,571	1	20	75	266	563	2,401	218	27
Vallejo.........................	114,866	9,278	9,358	10	65	599	949	1,802	4,703	1,150	80
Ventura.........................	95,614	5,012	5,069	9	29	139	218	1,271	2,979	367	57
Victorville.....................	48,639	4,558	4,585	3	24	178	232	1,026	2,390	705	27
Visalia.........................	82,154	6,585	6,598	3	24	167	470	1,126	4,179	616	13
Walnut	30,967	899	907	2	8	32	119	299	346	93	8
Walnut Creek....................	61,641	2,811	2,834	1	10	42	130	544	1,906	178	23
Watsonville.....................	31,399	2,815	2,828	1	12	128	347	399	1,729	199	13
West Covina.....................	99,787	6,267	6,352	5	33	276	350	1,017	3,195	1,391	85
West Hollywood	35,569	4,250	4,270	5	26	485	352	675	1,838	869	20
Westminster.....................	78,984	5,125	5,135	10	11	202	175	1,208	2,554	965	10
West Sacramento	30,241	2,932	2,952	5	19	102	152	791	1,458	405	20
Whittier	81,356	3,808	3,824	5	15	175	243	810	2,066	494	16
Windsor	13,507	657	662	....	4	5	46	131	447	24	5
Woodland........................	41,921	2,048	2,095	2	29	32	184	483	1,020	298	47
Yorba Linda.....................	57,387	1,366	1,389	....	5	20	64	249	888	140	23
Yuba City.......................	30,723	2,666	2,675	2	23	44	141	479	1,774	203	9
Yucaipa	36,706	1,832	1,840	5	5	24	96	628	895	179	8
Yucca Valley	14,062	848	856	1	9	18	60	284	395	81	8
COLORADO											
Arvada	96,050	3,731	3,758	....	19	48	194	618	2,623	229	27
Aurora	246,610	20,367	20,486	19	166	740	3,532	2,909	11,512	1,489	119
Boulder.........................	88,111	5,817	5,835	1	20	40	122	947	4,398	289	18
Brighton........................	15,304	874	881	....	4	2	36	167	614	51	7
Broomfield......................	26,670	1,043	1,064	....	1	5	67	169	763	38	21
Canon City......................	13,213	697	698	....	11	6	15	155	484	26	1
Castle Rock.....................	10,753	290	294	....	....	1	12	46	221	10	4
Colorado Springs	304,438	19,608	19,717	19	265	389	882	3,645	13,391	1,017	109
Commerce City...................	17,585	2,330	2,344	3	9	32	230	395	1,502	159	14
Denver	498,402	39,796	40,236	74	393	1,863	2,922	9,128	17,858	7,558	440
Durango.........................	13,387	1,130	1,130	1	10	9	31	120	924	35	....
Englewood.......................	31,698	2,704	2,743	....	18	55	191	385	1,872	183	39
Federal Heights.................	10,221	689	691	....	7	12	24	109	489	48	2
Fort Collins	96,055	4,768	4,795	1	68	26	294	760	3,447	172	27
Fountain........................	11,338	442	448	....	3	6	15	67	338	13	6
Golden	13,946	651	663	....	....	3	38	111	451	48	12
Grand Junction	31,089	2,854	2,873	4	11	22	151	448	2,129	89	19
Greeley.........................	63,574	4,332	4,373	3	20	25	86	675	3,352	171	41
Lafayette	16,362	746	753	....	....	6	59	111	542	28	7
Lakewood........................	129,628	7,864	7,937	6	31	174	427	1,256	5,355	615	73
Littleton.......................	37,574	1,137	1,157	....	9	29	70	265	657	107	20
Longmont........................	56,219	2,697	2,698	3	30	20	51	466	2,044	83	1
Louisville	15,351	466	467	....	2	2	50	90	300	22	1
Loveland........................	41,505	1,641	1,653	....	35	8	125	172	1,246	55	12
Northglenn......................	28,691	1,511	1,519	1	11	18	63	209	1,120	89	8
Pueblo..........................	101,424	7,016	7,072	9	87	165	1,474	1,337	3,640	304	56
Sterling........................	10,433	472	474	....	2	1	14	67	374	14	2
Westminster.....................	83,073	4,516	4,533	2	16	48	217	703	3,182	348	17

116

Table 8. — Number of Offenses Known to the Police, Cities and Towns 10,000 and over in Population, 1993 — Continued

City by State	Population	Crime Index total	Modified* Crime Index total	Murder and non-negligent man-slaughter	Forcible rape	Robbery	Aggra-vated assault	Burglary	Larceny-theft	Motor vehicle theft	Arson*
CONNECTICUT											
Ansonia	18,061	594	599	2	2	14	45	86	364	81	5
Avon	13,849	255	256	....	1	3	2	40	201	8	1
Berlin	16,681	427	427	....	....	7	4	78	296	42	....
Bethel	17,551	222	226	....	....	3	14	46	151	8	4
Bloomfield	19,361	885	887	....	4	23	60	175	526	97	2
Branford	27,477	496	496	1	2	7	10	68	350	58	....
Bridgeport	136,865	13,599	13,791	60	72	1,560	848	3,653	3,820	3,586	192
Bristol[1]	61,108			3	5	49		483	1,150	202	11
Brookfield	14,121	358	359	....	....	1	7	58	276	16	1
Cheshire	25,567	570	579	....	1	4	3	123	398	41	9
Clinton	12,876	236	237	....	....	4	5	78	143	6	1
Coventry	10,152	233	238	1	....	....	8	63	155	6	5
Cromwell	12,390	431	431	....	....	10	7	60	306	48	....
Danbury	65,257	3,524	3,536	1	12	71	88	546	2,405	401	12
Darien	18,206	405	405	....	1	4	....	63	293	44	....
Derby	12,212	527	527	....	2	13	8	121	332	51	....
East Hampton	10,516	168	168	....	....	....	6	53	102	7	....
East Hartford	50,139	2,364	2,381	1	12	80	101	415	1,440	315	17
East Haven Town	26,025	1,293	1,295	....	2	21	14	215	916	125	2
East Windsor	10,017	283	285	....	2	4	2	43	192	40	2
Enfield	45,249	1,461	1,468	1	....	23	17	282	906	232	7
Fairfield[1]	53,451			3	1	35		506	1,180	378	4
Farmington	20,480	854	854	....	2	7	5	117	643	80	....
Glastonbury	27,728	547	548	....	4	1	10	92	425	15	1
Greenwich	58,477	1,405	1,411	1	....	18	12	189	1,044	141	6
Groton Town	34,349	1,334	1,337	....	13	16	48	216	1,006	35	3
Guilford	19,757	543	544	....	1	5	3	103	408	23	1
Hamden	52,197	2,210	2,211	2	8	52	32	239	1,646	231	1
Hartford	131,914	17,927	18,154	30	99	1,243	1,470	3,628	8,824	2,633	227
Madison Town	15,414	301	302	....	....	1	9	74	192	25	1
Manchester	51,297	3,112	3,144	....	39	80	118	772	1,913	190	32
Meriden	58,549	2,757	2,766	1	5	93	90	592	1,676	300	9
Middletown	42,577	2,170	2,173	3	5	27	59	323	1,463	290	3
Milford	48,529	2,741	2,746	....	7	44	16	358	1,884	432	5
Monroe	16,905	312	315	....	....	4	13	94	184	17	3
Naugatuck	31,007	844	854	....	6	2	17	141	572	106	10
New Britain	72,874	5,157	5,158	4	21	215	269	1,083	2,865	700	1
New Canaan	17,875	306	306	....	2	2	5	59	223	15	....
New Haven	123,890	15,553	15,687	22	130	1,238	1,154	3,417	7,719	1,873	134
Newington	29,027	1,061	1,062	....	4	3	16	144	784	110	1
New London	24,341	1,631	1,637	8	11	74	69	339	998	132	6
New Milford	23,939	683	684	....	4	2	21	101	517	38	1
Newtown	20,791	395	398	2	....	2	2	129	235	25	3
North Branford	12,937	266	266	....	1	1	5	70	173	16	....
North Haven	22,146	760	763	....	1	8	10	124	555	62	3
Norwalk	78,480	4,233	4,246	9	10	188	118	840	2,516	552	13
Norwich	36,402	1,598	1,611	3	37	57	96	395	926	84	13
Orange	12,771	858	862	....	....	16	2	107	676	57	4
Plainfield	14,438	195	197	....	1	4	12	59	96	23	2
Plainville	17,284	527	527	....	2	5	8	107	351	54	....
Plymouth	11,976	302	303	....	5	1	5	97	156	38	1
Ridgefield Town	20,931	199	200	....	....	....	....	61	131	7	1
Rocky Hill	16,450	567	567	....	1	6	9	79	409	63	....
Seymour	14,222	384	388	....	4	1	26	85	227	41	4
Shelton	36,483	571	575	....	1	10	5	195	268	92	4
Simsbury	21,884	290	294	....	....	2	....	47	233	8	4

See footnotes at end of table.

Table 8. — Number of Offenses Known to the Police, Cities and Towns 10,000 and over in Population, 1993 — Continued

City by State	Population	Crime Index total	Modified* Crime Index total	Murder and non-negligent man-slaughter	Forcible rape	Robbery	Aggra-vated assault	Burglary	Larceny-theft	Motor vehicle theft	Arson*
CONNECTICUT — Continued											
Southington	38,278	1,112	1,115	....	3	11	9	241	743	105	3
South Windsor	21,952	416	417	4	5	5	10	89	276	27	1
Stamford	107,524	5,872	5,903	8	22	270	237	1,105	3,503	727	31
Stonington	16,458	463	464	....	....	7	1	82	360	13	1
Stratford	49,419	2,275	2,293	1	2	77	20	449	1,330	396	18
Suffield	11,356	132	133	....	....	1	4	25	92	10	1
Torrington	33,867	1,061	1,062	....	8	10	63	272	626	82	1
Trumbull	32,035	1,430	1,430	....	2	13	6	155	979	275	....
Vernon	30,111	739	749	....	1	25	36	125	481	71	10
Wallingford	40,638	1,219	1,232	1	5	13	17	224	835	124	13
Waterbury	106,838	8,735	8,747	20	39	288	239	1,815	4,957	1,377	12
Waterford	17,443	896	901	1	4	13	42	93	701	42	5
Watertown	20,725	692	692	....	....	5	38	103	477	69	....
West Hartford	59,737	2,441	2,450	1	1	78	56	580	1,512	213	9
West Haven	54,135	2,860	2,870	....	5	66	80	521	1,721	467	10
Westport	24,424	841	844	....	....	23	7	173	559	79	3
Wethersfield	25,491	739	741	....	3	22	29	116	473	96	2
Willimantic	15,326	834	834	1	10	15	13	175	550	70	....
Wilton	15,998	223	224	....	....	2	5	54	152	10	1
Windsor	27,644	738	740	1	2	10	10	129	540	46	2
Windsor Locks	12,280	288	291	....	....	4	13	61	178	32	3
Wolcott	13,637	406	407	....	11	6	13	83	254	39	1
DELAWARE											
Dover	28,594	2,372	2,383	....	36	78	145	251	1,786	76	11
DISTRICT OF COLUMBIA											
Washington	578,000	67,946	68,146	454	324	7,107	9,003	11,532	31,466	8,060	200
FLORIDA											
Altamonte Springs	36,104	3,171	3,182	3	17	77	176	542	2,103	253	11
Bartow	15,114	1,720	1,722	1	13	51	166	257	1,056	176	2
Belle Glade	16,788	2,338	2,341	3	9	142	274	649	1,128	133	3
Boca Raton	65,273	3,940	3,947	7	21	82	133	919	2,393	385	7
Boynton Beach	49,522	4,458	4,464	4	15	201	486	972	2,358	422	6
Bradenton	45,359	4,172	4,185	3	31	200	448	1,083	2,099	308	13
Cape Coral	82,708	4,162	4,169	1	12	22	227	1,077	2,588	235	7
Casselberry	20,361	1,304	1,307	2	12	31	75	325	762	97	3
Clearwater	99,547	7,610	7,649	3	70	212	886	1,502	4,567	370	39
Cocoa Beach	12,388	1,327	1,328	2	2	20	52	200	992	59	1
Coconut Creek	28,164	1,433	1,439	....	11	26	131	361	731	173	6
Coral Gables	41,617	6,192	6,199	1	8	234	170	1,051	3,886	842	7
Coral Springs	87,560	4,200	4,204	1	18	42	216	689	2,976	258	4
Dania	13,303	2,621	2,628	4	20	140	211	537	1,416	293	7
Davie	52,835	4,231	4,236	1	21	49	241	706	2,819	394	5
Daytona Beach	65,573	7,524	7,553	12	90	349	916	1,848	3,599	710	29
Deerfield Beach	46,789	3,640	3,645	6	25	116	249	636	2,162	446	5
De Land	17,446	2,696	2,700	2	12	85	261	630	1,548	158	4
Delray Beach	49,490	6,458	6,471	6	28	191	500	1,338	3,897	498	13
Dunedin	34,704	1,556	1,561	1	10	28	139	382	934	62	5
Edgewater	17,080	944	946	....	12	4	164	103	637	24	2
Eustis	14,336	469	469	2	8	17	51	63	304	24	....
Fort Lauderdale	150,683	25,775	25,838	31	76	1,270	973	5,822	14,477	3,126	63
Fort Myers	47,041	7,846	7,866	5	39	459	870	1,682	3,672	1,119	20

Table 8. — Number of Offenses Known to the Police, Cities and Towns 10,000 and over in Population, 1993 — Continued

City by State	Population	Crime Index total	Modified* Crime Index total	Murder and non-negligent man-slaughter	Forcible rape	Robbery	Aggra-vated assault	Burglary	Larceny-theft	Motor vehicle theft	Arson*
FLORIDA — Continued											
Fort Pierce	38,086	5,227	5,245	10	50	246	658	1,314	2,188	761	18
Fort Walton Beach	23,057	1,297	1,303	2	16	29	90	247	820	93	6
Gainesville	88,024	10,697	10,721	4	83	368	948	2,313	6,197	784	24
Greenacres City	21,923	1,550	1,553	....	15	25	96	328	927	159	3
Gulfport	11,588	1,178	1,181	....	2	35	117	270	718	36	3
Haines City	12,231	1,425	1,434	2	5	34	96	290	871	127	9
Hallandale	30,521	2,641	2,644	3	14	175	378	655	1,132	284	3
Hialeah Gardens	10,251	782	785	....	....	16	29	141	420	176	3
Hollywood	123,501	11,534	11,555	9	42	475	518	2,287	6,900	1,303	21
Homestead	29,059	4,045	4,053	3	30	254	498	1,084	1,856	320	8
Jacksonville	672,310	67,513	67,900	125	699	3,604	6,989	15,127	31,936	9,033	387
Jacksonville Beach	19,051	1,729	1,731	2	18	65	186	321	1,051	86	2
Key West	25,731	3,826	3,829	3	20	135	224	742	2,356	346	3
Kissimmee	34,098	4,225	4,234	1	18	99	326	1,191	2,365	225	9
Lady Lake	10,314	250	251	....	2	4	16	79	140	9	1
Lake City	10,191	1,540	1,543	1	5	33	177	275	993	56	3
Lakeland	73,684	10,515	10,530	8	45	366	683	2,195	5,805	1,413	15
Lake Wales	10,166	1,159	1,162	1	4	40	67	422	520	105	3
Lake Worth	28,909	4,525	4,525	6	11	205	316	1,046	2,529	412	....
Largo	68,381	3,250	3,265	1	22	57	348	657	2,064	101	15
Lauderdale Lakes	28,043	2,092	2,095	3	21	159	183	331	984	411	3
Lauderhill	50,064	3,779	3,793	5	32	192	388	787	1,765	610	14
Leesburg	17,371	1,708	1,712	2	16	64	316	405	828	77	4
Lighthouse Point	10,330	333	333	....	....	8	11	49	239	26	....
Longwood	14,690	772	774	....	....	21	56	238	405	52	2
Lynn Haven	10,149	303	303	....	....	3	12	55	221	12	....
Margate	45,438	2,456	2,463	2	6	57	115	537	1,531	208	7
Melbourne	65,210	6,398	6,432	9	28	130	742	1,264	3,838	387	34
Miami	372,519	69,828	70,095	127	204	7,082	7,089	12,277	31,871	11,178	267
Miami Beach	92,217	16,517	16,543	13	64	744	993	2,975	9,317	2,411	26
Miami Shores	10,614	1,210	1,211	....	2	106	49	314	526	213	1
Miami Springs	13,468	1,281	1,281	....	1	86	46	312	588	248	....
Miramar	45,080	2,986	2,999	5	10	132	215	681	1,511	432	13
Naples	20,728	1,395	1,396	....	7	38	72	308	882	88	1
New Port Richey	14,467	1,051	1,055	....	....	16	64	288	636	47	4
New Smyrna Beach	17,485	962	962	2	7	25	67	228	552	81	....
Niceville	12,179	262	263	....	1	3	19	50	183	6	1
North Lauderdale	27,271	1,483	1,491	1	3	38	81	310	887	163	8
North Miami	51,999	6,872	6,885	3	28	509	448	1,589	2,870	1,425	13
North Miami Beach	37,398	3,464	3,467	4	21	244	236	918	1,527	514	3
North Palm Beach	11,203	481	484	....	1	12	17	153	272	26	3
Oakland Park	27,711	4,382	4,384	2	27	179	268	970	2,440	496	2
Ocala	44,556	6,466	6,491	4	53	312	508	1,143	4,197	249	25
Ocoee	13,884	976	976	....	7	11	76	181	620	81	....
Opa Locka	15,796	3,458	3,463	4	22	327	452	711	1,436	506	5
Orlando	176,748	21,953	22,026	15	209	1,107	2,809	4,352	11,655	1,806	73
Ormond Beach	31,446	1,365	1,365	....	10	24	12	293	948	78	....
Oviedo	15,443	990	991	....	4	23	89	288	532	54	1
Palatka	10,646	2,092	2,102	1	26	72	196	494	1,238	65	10
Palm Bay	71,138	4,149	4,157	4	22	46	388	952	2,520	217	8
Palm Beach Gardens	26,036	1,998	2,001	....	1	29	68	328	1,378	194	3
Panama City	37,224	3,531	3,548	3	23	74	269	631	2,348	183	17
Pembroke Pines	71,829	4,545	4,556	....	11	103	139	651	3,193	448	11
Pinellas Park	44,367	3,167	3,185	2	22	60	117	554	2,250	162	18
Plantation	72,649	6,919	6,931	4	12	176	189	1,011	4,689	838	12

Table 8. — Number of Offenses Known to the Police, Cities and Towns 10,000 and over in Population, 1993 — Continued

City by State	Population	Crime Index total	Modified* Crime Index total	Murder and non-negligent man-slaughter	Forcible rape	Robbery	Aggra-vated assault	Burglary	Larceny-theft	Motor vehicle theft	Arson*
FLORIDA — Continued											
Plant City	25,306	3,013	3,013	4	18	130	437	665	1,473	286	....
Pompano Beach	73,929	10,534	10,563	7	54	626	1,375	2,231	5,124	1,117	29
Port Orange	37,830	1,098	1,099	....	3	8	63	180	783	61	1
Port St. Lucie	64,383	2,282	2,293	3	13	9	173	617	1,322	145	11
Punta Gorda	11,712	471	471	1	1	21	28	73	332	15	....
Rockledge	17,346	1,111	1,113	....	10	19	72	226	721	63	2
Royal Palm Beach	16,924	839	839	....	1	7	40	156	588	47	....
Safety Harbor	15,646	522	529	....	8	10	48	135	294	27	7
St. Augustine	12,506	1,672	1,674	2	10	61	210	227	1,123	39	2
St. Cloud	14,384	829	831	....	2	5	51	160	570	41	2
St. Petersburg	238,727	23,022	23,163	19	176	1,599	3,379	4,828	11,729	1,292	141
Sanford	34,567	3,663	3,670	3	16	141	344	1,041	1,896	222	7
Sarasota	51,660	6,971	6,995	3	47	441	529	1,596	4,029	326	24
Satellite Beach	10,147	388	389	....	4	....	12	90	270	12	1
Sebastian	11,190	480	480	....	2	1	37	151	277	12	....
South Daytona	11,968	622	624	1	7	11	39	183	308	73	2
South Miami	10,429	1,400	1,402	....	3	96	95	344	683	179	2
Stuart	12,404	1,201	1,208	1	11	31	97	271	706	84	7
Sunrise	71,358	5,103	5,114	3	11	131	249	874	3,271	564	11
Tallahassee	132,252	19,426	19,456	9	137	790	1,754	3,970	10,701	2,065	30
Tamarac	47,183	2,013	2,016	2	8	58	101	283	1,278	283	3
Tampa	288,877	45,373	45,587	43	247	2,965	6,124	8,987	18,534	8,473	214
Tarpon Springs	18,869	985	985	1	9	32	152	198	565	28	....
Temple Terrace	16,641	668	668	2	....	24	9	123	424	86	....
Venice	17,133	700	700	....	....	5	55	111	505	24	....
Vero Beach	17,989	1,487	1,489	1	15	25	80	297	962	107	2
Wilton Manors	11,783	1,233	1,234	2	4	46	49	251	753	128	1
Winter Garden	11,103	870	876	....	2	11	98	169	521	69	6
Winter Haven	25,295	3,324	3,330	2	18	97	244	608	2,053	302	6
Winter Park	22,168	1,977	1,984	....	10	74	123	392	1,245	133	7
GEORGIA											
Albany	81,328	9,377	9,379	22	55	473	578	2,767	4,957	525	2
Alpharetta	16,751	492	492	....	....	....	13	95	340	44	....
Americus	17,103	1,025	1,029	....	....	24	84	146	739	32	4
Athens-Clark County	89,016	7,133	7,154	13	50	240	416	1,284	4,653	477	21
Atlanta	402,877	69,914	70,162	203	492	6,045	9,541	13,168	31,249	9,216	248
Augusta	45,412	4,481	4,497	15	18	209	133	1,259	2,314	533	16
Bainbridge	11,176	1,004	1,005	2	4	33	74	188	675	28	1
Brunswick	17,263	2,157	2,157	7	18	100	253	438	1,225	116	....
Carrollton	16,995	1,516	1,522	3	9	23	105	252	1,038	86	6
Cartersville	13,259	852	859	....	6	11	81	207	470	77	7
College Park	20,335	3,671	3,671	8	27	202	193	578	1,945	718	....
Columbus	190,331	12,266	12,312	32	49	451	631	2,309	7,752	1,042	46
Covington	11,102	1,605	1,606	1	14	43	97	385	944	121	1
Dalton	22,142	1,578	1,586	....	10	13	113	211	1,105	126	8
Decatur	18,160	1,433	1,441	4	4	98	83	383	717	144	8
Douglas	11,216	1,682	1,686	3	3	19	177	432	986	62	4
Dublin	16,999	1,462	1,462	2	11	55	83	241	1,004	66	....
Duluth	11,036	463	468	....	3	3	7	63	358	29	5
East Point	32,847	4,547	4,570	6	27	314	178	932	2,427	663	23
Forest Park	16,702	1,889	1,903	4	13	87	123	285	1,166	211	14

Table 8.—Number of Offenses Known to the Police, Cities and Towns 10,000 and over in Population, 1993—Continued

City by State	Population	Crime Index total	Modified* Crime Index total	Murder and non-negligent man-slaughter	Forcible rape	Robbery	Aggra-vated assault	Burglary	Larceny-theft	Motor vehicle theft	Arson*
GEORGIA—Continued											
Gainesville	18,983	1,782	1,793	3	8	47	187	223	1,175	139	11
Hinesville	24,986	1,692	1,692	1	7	36	40	226	1,326	56	....
Kennesaw	10,336	243	244	....	2	5	8	52	174	2	1
La Grange	26,855	3,027	3,030	4	8	62	240	569	2,009	135	3
Lawrenceville	20,151	1,221	1,228	....	5	14	60	203	838	101	7
Macon	109,537	11,096	11,141	20	102	384	408	1,811	7,533	838	45
Marietta	48,070	5,560	5,580	....	62	158	214	809	3,838	479	20
Monroe	11,572	540	541	1	14	12	40	113	344	16	1
Moultrie	15,343	1,517	1,521	3	14	50	134	301	947	68	4
Newnan	13,929	867	870	....	1	33	15	162	603	53	3
Peachtree City	22,810	237	238	....	....	2	1	18	200	16	1
Perry	10,162	697	700	1	5	12	45	78	530	26	3
Riverdale	10,034	1,183		....	6	50	22	168	826	111	
Rome	31,547	3,498	3,517	6	6	94	494	807	1,926	165	19
Roswell	51,744	2,260	2,270	4	5	41	59	389	1,588	174	10
St. Marys	11,316	643	647	....	1	7	40	93	475	27	4
Savannah	141,861	12,715	12,758	33	89	831	464	2,868	7,297	1,133	43
Smyrna	32,325	2,951	2,951	1	13	72	62	507	2,031	265	....
Snellville	13,894	496	496	....	4	3	5	67	398	19	....
Statesboro	17,109	826	826	....	4	19	43	99	622	39	....
Thomasville	18,191	1,602	1,612	3	5	41	62	446	973	72	10
Tifton	14,845	1,239	1,239	1	3	49	113	180	861	32	....
Union City	10,232	1,266	1,266	2	6	55	37	129	841	196	....
Valdosta	41,660	3,340	3,343	8	17	164	249	754	1,988	160	3
Warner Robins	46,631	2,739	2,740	2	3	40	82	449	2,040	123	1
Waycross	17,401	1,758	1,766	2	11	54	64	235	1,334	58	8
HAWAII											
Hilo	39,321	2,708	2,721	2	16	18	49	639	1,890	94	13
Honolulu	875,455	56,405	56,681	31	286	1,085	1,099	9,296	40,148	4,460	276
IDAHO											
Blackfoot	10,957	472	474	1	7	3	16	84	345	16	2
Boise	139,868	7,683	7,722	3	72	48	494	1,204	5,538	324	39
Caldwell	21,443	1,479	1,493	1	11	5	63	221	1,087	91	14
Coeur d'Alene	27,434	2,281	2,293	2	18	10	122	278	1,756	95	12
Idaho Falls	49,719	3,080	3,106	1	19	12	145	424	2,364	115	26
Lewiston	30,020	1,290	1,313	4	12	4	52	183	980	55	23
Meridian	11,527	574	580	....	1	1	27	77	443	25	6
Moscow	19,714	476	480	....	4	1	26	81	347	17	4
Pocatello	49,397	2,255	2,265	1	34	17	124	349	1,640	90	10
Rexburg	14,945	618	619	....	1	....	7	45	555	10	1
Twin Falls	30,603	2,125	2,137	1	10	14	117	366	1,491	126	12
ILLINOIS[2]											
Algonquin	13,150			....		2	7	46	201	5	6
Arlington Heights	77,071		2		20	42	389	1,441	63	26	
Aurora	106,694		17		304	499	1,465	3,932	389	54	
Bartlett	23,973		2		3	32	89	460	12	3	
Buffalo Grove	40,157			....		2	12	70	532	17	2

See footnotes at end of table.

121

Table 8.—Number of Offenses Known to the Police, Cities and Towns 10,000 and over in Population, 1993—Continued

City by State	Population	Crime Index total	Modified* Crime Index total	Murder and non-negligent man-slaughter	Forcible rape	Robbery	Aggra-vated assault	Burglary	Larceny-theft	Motor vehicle theft	Arson*
ILLINOIS[2]—Continued											
Calumet City	38,467			7		131	166	479	1,880	768	38
Chicago	2,788,996			845		35,189	39,753	45,670	121,314	40,438	1,676
Crystal Lake	26,946			1		6	29	79	800	18	4
Des Plaines	54,427			....		24	66	293	1,436	135	10
Dolton	24,856			....		78	38	215	1,039	317	1
Edwardsville	15,234			1		7	24	88	396	16	2
Elgin	81,693			8		104	254	763	2,369	239	26
Elk Grove Village	34,724			....		10	45	167	973	90	17
Evanston	74,724			1		224	219	1,327	3,853	324	16
Galesburg	33,758			3		32	42	305	1,251	27	4
Glendale Heights	29,229			....		7	21	81	666	38	3
Glenview	37,710			1		4	20	143	733	31	....
Harvey	30,970			18		368	190	840	1,371	897	12
Hazel Crest	13,751			....		27	51	98	347	141	....
Highland Park	30,688			....		7	4	53	420	34	1
Hoffman Estates	47,607			....		23	51	226	945	58	11
Homewood	20,033			....		18	9	68	745	129	2
Joliet	79,487			17		284	453	1,361	3,818	549	84
Lincolnwood	11,693			....		18	12	80	577	42	3
Lisle	20,490			....		9	7	96	564	30	2
Machesney Park	19,806			....		11	39	297	771	37	3
Morton Grove	22,372			1		7	24	140	540	43	4
Mount Prospect	53,700			....		18	55	188	1,369	77	3
Naperville	92,592			2		20	58	293	2,066	66	19
Palatine	46,876			8		10	39	197	999	42	3
Park Forest	25,361			2		25	30	124	523	113	4
Park Ridge	36,658			....		4	24	284	638	62	4
Prospect Heights	15,476			....		7	19	76	309	11	1
Rockford	142,703			22		774	1,177	4,021	8,385	1,125	58
Rolling Meadows	22,980			....		6	35	132	695	53	3
St. Charles	24,351			....		4	25	139	694	19	8
Schaumburg	71,660			1		42	95	567	2,615	219	14
Streamwood	33,152			....		9	39	154	766	37	7
Wheaton	54,145			....		9	24	220	1,050	24	3
Wheeling	30,662			....		6	44	100	701	28	5
Wilmette	27,312			2		3	10	279	430	13	3
Winnetka	12,583			....		3	3	92	214	7	....
INDIANA											
Anderson	60,946	3,251	3,260	8	34	98	128	608	2,250	125	9
Bedford	14,028	741	745	....	4	3	70	104	516	44	4
Beech Grove	13,475	516	518	1	6	10	5	79	375	40	2
Bloomington	62,100	2,826	2,831	....	20	10	485	354	1,797	160	5
Carmel	29,046	578	580	....	3	3	33	46	470	23	2
Clarksville	21,364	1,753	1,755	3	10	26	10	191	1,406	107	2
Connersville	15,845	818	826	....	1	1	46	107	635	28	8
Crawfordsville	14,176	841	847	1	1	3	4	194	616	22	6
Crown Point	18,769	333	336	....	....	4	6	72	228	23	3
Dyer	11,551	359	360	....	1	4	5	67	256	26	1
East Chicago	33,921	3,138	3,142	7	25	146	668	639	1,161	492	4
Elkhart	44,709	4,305	4,343	3	58	122	43	789	3,114	176	38

See footnotes at end of table.

Table 8. — Number of Offenses Known to the Police, Cities and Towns 10,000 and over in Population, 1993 — Continued

City by State	Population	Crime Index total	Modified* Crime Index total	Murder and non-negligent man-slaughter	Forcible rape	Robbery	Aggra-vated assault	Burglary	Larceny-theft	Motor vehicle theft	Arson*
INDIANA — Continued											
Evansville	128,805	7,071	7,136	7	43	151	571	1,580	4,359	360	65
Fort Wayne	175,405	14,857	15,000	28	130	552	317	2,028	10,016	1,786	143
Gary	117,836	11,231	11,734	105	174	934	1,271	2,555	3,589	2,603	503
Goshen	24,647	1,148	1,157	1	13	6	88	160	845	35	9
Greenfield	12,774	289	291	....	....	3	1	37	229	19	2
Greenwood	28,571	1,092	1,092	....	2	2	....	111	916	61	....
Griffith	18,558	779	780	....	....	13	65	80	482	139	1
Hammond	85,074	7,144	7,212	8	53	281	824	1,148	3,517	1,313	68
Highland	23,349	1,081	1,085	....	2	15	56	79	793	136	4
Hobart	21,981	621	621	....	....	11	29	109	384	88	....
Huntington	16,747	676	679	....	3	6	160	93	388	26	3
Indianapolis	377,723	33,530	33,776	68	517	2,050	3,657	7,629	14,383	5,226	246
Jasper	10,648	256	257	....	....	1	26	35	191	3	1
Kokomo	46,405	2,603	2,608	1	28	36	162	413	1,882	81	5
Lafayette	45,585	2,509	2,517	1	18	19	55	445	1,879	92	8
Lake Station	14,561	904	907	....	9	18	72	143	538	124	3
La Porte	22,476	1,396	1,398	1	5	12	277	143	900	58	2
Lawrence	27,860	1,026	1,027	1	8	57	4	250	601	105	1
Logansport	17,203	891	891	....	8	2	4	177	689	11	....
Martinsville	12,383	514	517	....	1	....	26	59	408	20	3
Merrillville	27,663	1,306	1,308	1	2	32	84	117	783	287	2
Michigan City	34,379	2,692	2,699	4	22	92	109	424	1,677	364	7
Munster	20,525	656	657	3	2	6	30	59	498	58	1
New Albany	38,559	2,200	2,235	1	14	21	454	187	1,407	116	35
New Castle	18,265	1,187	1,187	....	6	6	11	217	901	46	....
Noblesville	19,373	658	662	2	4	4	128	75	422	23	4
Plainfield	10,971	450	452	....	7	2	21	69	328	23	2
Portage	30,792	1,160	1,167	1	11	13	59	221	724	131	7
Richmond	39,205	1,809	1,878	3	12	39	12	266	1,389	88	69
Schererville	21,762	676	679	....	1	5	....	85	497	88	3
South Bend	106,971	10,380	10,442	19	104	459	577	2,606	5,825	790	62
Speedway	12,742	866	868	1	2	14	6	66	696	81	2
Terre Haute	59,771	4,353	4,377	6	31	48	110	1,056	2,839	263	24
Valparaiso	25,782	907	920	....	3	7	86	130	634	47	13
Vincennes	19,800	1,371	1,379	....	9	3	16	529	769	45	8
Wabash	12,132	311	312	....	2	1	21	73	190	24	1
Warsaw	11,881	678	680	....	3	1	....	88	551	35	2
IOWA											
Ames	46,854	1,645		1	16	5	21	144	1,389	69	
Ankeny	19,651	581		....	2	1	11	82	475	10	
Bettendorf	29,698	1,228		....	4	13	123	204	860	24	
Boone	12,455	476		1	2	....	13	54	386	20	
Cedar Falls	35,231	1,076		....	9	5	30	121	879	32	
Davenport	97,890	9,328	9,394	4	65	290	1,166	1,837	5,551	415	66
Des Moines	195,485	15,505	15,738	9	84	271	538	1,986	11,763	854	233
Dubuque	58,804	2,721	2,765	....	43	14	123	527	1,876	138	44
Fort Dodge	25,885	1,529		2	2	12	167	244	1,043	59	
Fort Madison	11,910	540		....	3	1	7	79	433	17	
Indianola	11,900	410		....	1	....	1	53	348	7	
Marshalltown	24,834	1,167		1	....	9	90	166	859	42	
Mason City	29,240	2,519		2	4	12	297	440	1,701	63	

Table 8. — Number of Offenses Known to the Police, Cities and Towns 10,000 and over in Population, 1993 — Continued

City by State	Population	Crime Index total	Modified* Crime Index total	Murder and non-negligent man-slaughter	Forcible rape	Robbery	Aggra-vated assault	Burglary	Larceny-theft	Motor vehicle theft	Arson*
IOWA — Continued											
Newton	14,843	575			1	....	13	65	467	29	
Oskaloosa	10,724	230			8	....	10	38	164	10	
Sioux City	82,228	7,333		4	61	121	1,093	1,275	4,523	256	
Spencer	11,170	221		....	....	....	....	9	203	9	
Urbandale	26,110	856		....	....	2	3	131	684	36	
Waterloo	67,387	4,532		9	50	124	259	1,115	2,766	209	
West Des Moines	34,505	1,325		....	5	6	44	210	1,016	44	
KANSAS²											
Wichita	313,597	27,737		48	265	1,327	1,103	5,847	16,264	2,883	
KENTUCKY											
Ashland	24,488	993	993	....	7	5	114	193	625	49	....
Bowling Green	42,408	2,882	2,891	3	36	58	269	582	1,786	148	9
Campbellsville	10,142	220	220	....	1	1	9	60	142	7	....
Covington	42,886	4,288	4,361	5	29	174	473	1,097	2,280	230	73
Danville	13,157	663	664	1	9	4	89	130	402	28	1
Elizabethtown	19,539	985	987	....	2	13	73	149	718	30	2
Erlanger	15,904	593	593	....	4	5	85	64	421	14	....
Florence	20,754	1,264	1,264	....	5	27	70	152	954	56	....
Fort Thomas	16,211	154	154	....	1	....	9	24	110	10	....
Frankfort	27,445	1,463	1,466	3	17	20	138	269	964	52	3
Georgetown	12,359	1,024	1,025	....	9	11	132	153	697	22	1
Glasgow	12,875	95	95	2	....	....	6	29	54	4	....
Henderson	26,699	1,878	1,887	1	20	12	312	272	1,179	82	9
Hopkinsville	31,174	1,814	1,831	3	18	57	196	424	1,035	81	17
Independence	11,031	240	240	....	2	2	6	61	159	10	....
Jeffersontown	23,528	651	652	....	10	11	72	73	465	20	1
Lexington	235,094	15,641	15,691	8	139	558	1,455	3,187	9,684	610	50
Louisville	273,564	17,329	17,586	37	135	1,393	1,159	4,204	8,076	2,325	257
Madisonville	16,642	1,296	1,303	2	....	13	184	184	846	67	7
Mayfield	10,092	365	366	....	6	22	85	81	147	24	1
Middlesboro	11,080	891	897	....	3	11	53	270	520	34	6
Murray	14,406	472	473	....	6	3	39	76	320	28	1
Newport	18,832	1,559	1,563	2	13	32	159	306	946	101	4
Nicholasville	15,046	632	632	....	3	10	58	93	430	38	....
Owensboro	53,863	2,975	2,981	4	30	53	62	610	2,131	85	6
Paducah	27,103	2,531	2,532	4	25	57	364	445	1,493	143	1
Radcliff	20,096	765	766	2	16	14	42	164	502	25	1
St. Matthews	15,911	799	799	1	1	25	23	120	552	77	....
Shively	15,649	727	727	....	11	48	40	178	336	114	....
Somerset	11,400	604	605	....	6	5	58	84	425	26	1
Winchester	16,745	612	613	....	5	6	75	81	413	32	1
LOUISIANA											
Alexandria	49,133	5,937	5,937	21	23	117	1,613	758	3,119	286	....
Baton Rouge	225,544	36,527	36,685	74	177	1,866	4,705	7,543	18,156	4,006	158
Bogalusa	14,783	1,361	1,367	2	13	37	107	325	835	42	6
Bossier City	53,071	3,911	3,929	9	21	75	483	558	2,550	215	18
Crowley	14,044	1,114	1,114	1	7	22	120	232	689	43	....
De Ridder	10,391	369	370	1	4	2	32	63	261	6	1
Eunice	11,264	713	714	....	2	9	160	213	297	32	1
Gretna	17,566	1,587	1,587	....	9	112	157	387	724	198	....
Harahan	10,331	400	402	....	2	6	10	47	313	22	2

See footnotes at end of table.

Table 8. — Number of Offenses Known to the Police, Cities and Towns 10,000 and over in Population, 1993 — Continued

City by State	Population	Crime Index total	Modified* Crime Index total	Murder and non-negligent man-slaughter	Forcible rape	Robbery	Aggra-vated assault	Burglary	Larceny-theft	Motor vehicle theft	Arson*
LOUISIANA — Continued											
Houma	31,360	1,707	1,711	5	14	78	360	296	856	98	4
Jennings	11,408	957	960	2	4	7	131	195	603	15	3
Kenner	74,012	6,244	6,246	8	42	249	584	1,072	3,491	798	2
Lafayette	97,726	8,638	8,690	18	50	245	582	1,493	5,869	381	52
Lake Charles	71,401	4,834	4,848	12	30	165	441	940	2,932	314	14
Monroe	56,384	6,787		17	29	127	950	1,047	4,357	260	
Natchitoches	16,566	1,225	1,225	1	8	35	89	309	727	56	....
New Iberia	32,689	2,127		2	16	49	50	528	1,396	86	
New Orleans	491,619	52,773		395	298	5,179	4,152	11,184	22,019	9,546	
Pineville	12,215	717	719	....	4	1	10	104	574	24	2
Ruston	20,428	2,104	2,108	....	1	38	223	291	1,519	32	4
Shreveport	197,379	22,631	22,851	76	100	842	1,552	4,774	13,784	1,503	220
Slidell	26,269	2,708	2,708	1	1	48	234	364	1,836	224	....
West Monroe	14,929	1,365	1,373	2	6	5	75	133	1,084	60	8
Westwego	11,773	815	817	....	4	34	51	142	440	144	2
MAINE											
Auburn	23,998	714	717	....	3	8	6	116	553	28	3
Augusta	20,570	1,234	1,246	....	12	8	12	251	891	60	12
Bangor	32,223	1,612	1,623	2	18	20	32	162	1,314	64	11
Biddeford	21,296	1,146	1,176	....	12	9	12	206	875	32	30
Brunswick	21,059	468	471	....	....	4	2	100	357	5	3
Gorham	11,942	112	112	....	....	....	2	34	68	8	....
Lewiston	38,123	2,517	2,537	....	7	48	85	534	1,791	52	20
Orono	10,582	137	138	....	....	....	2	9	124	2	1
Portland	62,624	4,808	4,921	2	61	92	261	1,142	2,978	272	113
Presque Isle	10,523	345	346	....	1	....	8	25	298	13	1
Saco	15,488	622	624	....	2	3	5	94	498	20	2
Sanford	20,764	698	698	....	....	3	4	175	486	30	....
Scarborough	12,609	448	448	....	3	2	9	94	321	19	....
South Portland	23,019	1,289	1,296	....	4	7	24	113	1,098	43	7
Waterville	16,754	990	991	....	2	3	30	121	801	33	1
Westbrook	16,237	698	704	....	4	4	5	121	522	42	6
Windham	13,114	418	421	....	2	4	6	102	268	36	3
MARYLAND											
Aberdeen	13,703	850	854	....	12	16	112	142	537	31	4
Annapolis	34,402	2,760	2,835	4	26	201	275	552	1,559	143	75
Baltimore	732,968	91,920	92,465	353	668	12,376	8,548	17,901	41,451	10,623	545
Cambridge	11,737	1,075	1,078	1	6	12	159	211	662	24	3
Cumberland	24,135	1,477	1,477	....	5	15	250	222	934	51	....
Easton	10,098	701	703	1	5	14	105	119	442	15	2
Frederick	43,809	2,762	2,781	3	30	88	461	443	1,587	150	19
Greenbelt	21,575	1,177		1	13	45	56	101	761	200	
Hagerstown	37,938	1,954	1,975	....	12	57	171	422	1,187	105	21
Hyattsville	14,435	911		1	3	59	40	157	547	104	
Laurel	20,821	1,276		1	8	75	52	215	766	159	
Salisbury	21,481	2,988	3,011	1	31	111	351	556	1,799	139	23
Takoma Park (Montgomery County)	12,644	460		1	2	55	27	97	228	50	
Takoma Park (Prince George's County)	5,064	552		....	4	44	39	127	269	69	
Westminster	13,997	1,008	1,021	3	4	19	45	153	747	37	13
MASSACHUSETTS											
Amesbury	15,358	435	435	....	....	....	90	84	218	43	....
Andover	29,856	881	882	....	9	7	16	178	540	131	1

125

Table 8.— Number of Offenses Known to the Police, Cities and Towns 10,000 and over in Population, 1993 — Continued

City by State	Population	Crime Index total	Modified* Crime Index total	Murder and non-negligent man-slaughter	Forcible rape	Robbery	Aggra-vated assault	Burglary	Larceny-theft	Motor vehicle theft	Arson*
MASSACHUSETTS — Continued											
Arlington	45,268	707	710	1	3	11	72	166	357	97	3
Ashland	12,237	141	141	....	....	1	43	25	70	2	....
Athol	11,669	482	482	1	10	5	111	130	216	9	....
Barnstable	41,609	2,179	2,179	2	22	29	723	609	666	128	....
Bedford	13,180	159	159	....	....	1	18	37	96	7	....
Belchertown	10,718	228	229	....	1	....	40	69	109	9	1
Bellingham	15,074	233	255	....	4	3	24	53	129	20	22
Belmont	25,074	352	354	....	....	3	7	66	258	18	2
Beverly	38,499	1,267	1,271	....	4	14	16	538	589	106	4
Boston	553,870	55,555		98	480	4,081	6,184	7,982	24,798	11,932	
Bourne	16,322	786	787	....	6	7	55	212	454	52	1
Braintree	34,287	1,374	1,379	....	2	22	123	196	764	267	5
Bridgewater	21,812	286	286	....	1	2	33	54	155	41	....
Brockton	89,473	6,895		15	54	328	759	1,816	2,089	1,834	
Brookline	55,447	2,371	2,375	1	8	72	187	372	1,379	352	4
Cambridge	93,850	6,388	6,409	2	27	253	643	929	3,566	968	21
Canton	18,777	426	426	....	....	5	20	108	235	58	....
Chelmsford	32,845	1,025	1,027	....	1	11	112	178	578	145	2
Clinton	13,475	342	343	1	5	3	60	48	217	8	1
Concord	17,319	243	243	....	....	....	7	17	216	3	....
Danvers	24,758	1,321	1,321	....	1	9	60	161	810	280	....
Dartmouth	27,801	1,504	1,504	....	1	14	70	263	999	157	....
Dedham	24,098	847	849	2	2	18	46	75	497	207	2
Dennis	14,087	756	765	....	3	3	37	296	387	30	9
Dracut	25,960	1,075	1,075	....	7	15	54	250	497	252	....
Duxbury	14,263	146	146	....	....	....	7	27	106	6	....
East Bridgewater	11,399	377	378	....	1	9	28	81	212	46	1
East Longmeadow	13,551	558	561	....	3	6	29	93	357	70	3
Easton	20,230	497	497	....	....	11	18	150	229	89	....
Everett	35,198	2,036	2,036	1	9	56	510	334	707	419	....
Fall River	91,354	5,283	5,398	4	57	143	501	1,161	2,673	744	115
Fitchburg	39,060	2,570	2,582	1	38	83	506	685	1,050	207	12
Foxborough	14,830	218	218	....	4	1	25	58	110	20	....
Framingham	65,919	2,728	2,732	....	29	36	594	457	1,378	234	4
Franklin	22,389	286	286	....	2	2	14	16	227	25	....
Gardner	20,127	726	727	....	15	7	145	191	319	49	1
Gloucester	28,900	1,120	1,120	....	4	4	342	211	476	83	....
Grafton	13,284	152	152	....	1	....	49	34	60	8	....
Greenfield	18,755	1,095	1,095	....	17	15	286	205	517	55	....
Harvard	12,565	16	16	....	....	....	1	4	10	1	....
Harwich	10,439	334	335	....	....	5	34	79	208	8	1
Haverhill	52,332	2,671	2,701	....	22	58	225	773	1,102	491	30
Hingham	20,347	500	500	....	3	4	1	127	328	37	....
Holbrook	11,187	330	330	....	4	11	10	90	152	63	....
Holliston	13,110	118	118	....	....	....	8	23	83	4	....
Hudson	17,478	269	269	....	2	....	25	57	167	18	....
Hull	10,743	323	326	....	6	....	93	105	101	18	3
Ipswich	12,158	268	268	....	....	....	18	30	207	13	....
Lawrence[4]	65,700			3	33	387	925	1,464			69
Leicester	10,385	173	173	1	....	1	31	39	100	1	....
Leominster	38,379	1,842	1,845	4	13	25	115	458	1,082	145	3
Lexington	29,387	377	379	....	....	1	3	70	288	15	2
Longmeadow	15,681	319	322	....	3	1	3	41	260	11	3
Lowell	100,190	8,562	8,728	6	49	302	874	2,244	3,126	1,961	166
Ludlow	19,081	546	548	....	4	4	56	135	290	57	2
Lynn	78,904	7,081	7,081	8	19	371	994	1,824	2,301	1,564	....

See footnotes at end of table.

Table 8. — Number of Offenses Known to the Police, Cities and Towns 10,000 and over in Population, 1993 — Continued

City by State	Population	Crime Index total	Modified* Crime Index total	Murder and non-negligent man-slaughter	Forcible rape	Robbery	Aggra-vated assault	Burglary	Larceny-theft	Motor vehicle theft	Arson*
MASSACHUSETTS — Continued											
Malden	53,879	2,130	2,130	2	12	76	372	453	822	393	....
Marblehead	20,453	362	362	....	1	1	25	111	205	19	....
Marlborough	32,436	749	750	....	3	1	165	83	430	67	1
Marshfield	22,103	537	537	....	1	2	38	89	372	35	....
Maynard	10,471	185	188	....	2	....	25	62	88	8	3
Medfield	10,670	119	119	....	....	2	1	34	78	4	....
Medford	56,881	2,176	2,180	....	8	36	392	336	1,045	359	4
Medway	10,062	143	143	....	....	....	27	35	68	13	....
Melrose	27,865	467	467	....	2	9	9	100	291	56	....
Methuen	40,957	2,070	2,078	2	20	43	85	258	1,003	659	8
Middleboro	18,340	776	781	....	....	4	145	157	393	77	5
Milford	25,842	260	260	....	2	2	....	56	125	75	....
Milton	26,067	418	418	....	3	15	35	70	247	48	....
Natick	30,946	706	706	....	5	5	49	126	460	61	....
Needham	27,924	505	509	....	3	3	35	92	346	26	4
New Bedford[3]	97,226			3	59	327	974	2,014	2,237		89
Newton	82,386	2,414	2,414	1	11	27	181	479	1,467	248	....
North Adams	16,131	666	666	....	2	2	85	151	406	20	....
Northampton	29,120	1,186	1,189	2	24	18	113	182	717	130	3
North Andover	23,342	561	561	....	7	7	26	84	362	75	....
North Attleboro	25,575	1,119	1,119	....	9	9	133	176	681	111	....
Northborough	12,157	191	192	....	....	1	25	37	115	13	1
Northbridge	13,627	322	322	....	3	1	90	53	163	12	....
North Reading	12,172	204	206	....	....	....	8	38	136	22	2
Norton	14,570	319	319	....	....	....	28	78	195	18	....
Norwood	29,081	579	596	....	4	9	54	110	288	114	17
Oxford	12,829	307	310	....	....	3	55	77	138	34	3
Peabody	47,537	2,008	2,011	....	13	21	41	368	1,246	319	3
Pembroke	14,930	401	401	....	2	4	41	71	248	35	....
Pepperell	10,241	202	202	1	....	....	21	55	119	6	....
Pittsfield	47,253	1,859	1,859	....	2	29	216	530	956	126	....
Plymouth	46,820	1,984	1,985	1	14	11	409	464	1,009	76	1
Quincy	84,724	3,025	3,046	2	24	64	222	653	1,443	617	21
Randolph	30,493	1,061	1,065	....	4	16	44	238	533	226	4
Raynham	10,077	794	794	....	3	6	82	115	474	114	....
Reading	22,861	347	347	....	3	3	19	107	189	26	....
Salem	37,686	2,218	2,221	1	14	31	41	489	1,268	374	3
Sandwich	15,738	447	447	....	2	3	84	98	232	28	....
Saugus[3]	26,166			....	2	19	112	155	107		
Scituate	17,232	218	229	....	1	1	5	62	134	15	11
Sharon	15,723	144	144	1	....	2	15	37	69	20	....
Shrewsbury	24,609	825	825	....	2	7	97	157	522	40	....
Somerset	18,032	393	393	....	4	1	13	71	273	31	....
Somerville	72,532	2,846	2,854	....	10	123	400	604	948	761	8
South Hadley	16,905	288	288	....	2	7	26	36	177	40	....
Springfield[1]	153,952			20	120	676		3,140	4,506	3,770	
Stoughton	27,133	753	755	....	7	19	47	177	328	175	2
Sudbury	14,563	255	255	....	....	1	36	49	161	8	....
Swampscott	13,979	468	469	....	....	4	10	198	230	26	1
Swansea	15,741	340	369	....	....	16	16	20	231	57	29
Taunton	50,857	2,391	2,396	....	14	65	271	528	1,163	350	5
Uxbridge	10,614	179	179	....	10	1	59	38	67	4	....
Wakefield	25,179	564	564	....	3	6	9	140	316	90	....
Walpole	20,480	413	413	1	17	3	42	79	228	43	....
Waltham	56,877	1,995	1,995	....	10	24	217	450	1,118	176	....
Watertown	33,759	1,667	1,667	2	2	15	215	183	1,112	138	....

See footnotes at end of table.

Table 8. — Number of Offenses Known to the Police, Cities and Towns 10,000 and over in Population, 1993 — Continued

City by State	Population	Crime Index total	Modified* Crime Index total	Murder and non-negligent man-slaughter	Forcible rape	Robbery	Aggra-vated assault	Burglary	Larceny-theft	Motor vehicle theft	Arson*
MASSACHUSETTS — Continued											
Webster	16,507	676	677	....	9	4	46	199	379	39	1
Westborough	14,404	364	364	....	3	2	41	59	221	38	....
Westfield	38,288	1,437	1,445	....	11	14	315	292	697	108	8
Westford	16,625	229	229	....	1	1	14	44	155	14	....
Weston	10,345	133	133	....	1	....	12	39	80	1	....
Westport	14,148	273	274	....	3	1	28	79	128	34	1
West Springfield	27,919	2,209	2,224	1	14	23	131	404	1,223	413	15
Westwood	12,724	199	199	....	2	1	6	51	115	24	....
Weymouth	54,783	1,802	1,813	1	6	22	217	339	837	380	11
Wilbraham	12,810	377	383	....	2	3	22	112	178	60	6
Wilmington	17,902	612	618	1	8	5	64	150	300	84	6
Winchester	20,555	301	301	....	2	1	8	63	188	39	....
Woburn	36,522	1,774	1,785	....	6	16	68	269	1,098	317	11
Worcester[1]	163,932			12	77	628		3,404	5,221	1,692	
Yarmouth	21,514	1,028	1,035	....	9	9	82	280	592	56	7
MICHIGAN[4]											
Adrian	22,642			....		8	37	126	946	44	3
Albion	10,271			1		17	88	101	382	9	3
Allen Park	30,857			....		20	41	131	723	182	5
Alpena	11,533			....		2	15	103	480	16	7
Ann Arbor	110,277			2		129	336	1,101	4,032	260	35
Auburn Hills	18,681			....		20	96	188	710	89	5
Battle Creek	54,688			8		194	490	1,172	3,339	271	27
Bay City	39,204			....		54	180	349	1,392	117	10
Bedford Township	10,004			....		9	16	85	92	11	4
Benton Harbor	13,106			5		160	654	663	880	157	23
Benton Township	17,505			5		60	182	431	1,856	124	10
Berkley	16,327			....		11	17	48	286	28	....
Berrien Springs-Oronoko	11,979			1		1	19	40	211	11	1
Beverly Hills	10,507			....		5	6	31	177	11	5
Big Rapids	12,699			....		9	27	94	467	8	3
Birmingham	20,021			....		11	12	70	546	55	....
Bloomfield Township	43,320			....		20	55	190	992	96	12
Bridgeport Township	13,000			....		7	12	64	202	11	1
Brownstown Township	19,185			....		8	57	146	500	123	13
Buena Vista Township	11,116			2		31	116	255	703	33	11
Burton	27,935			2		40	115	272	1,358	118	8
Cadillac	10,330			1		2	24	69	532	17	3
Chesterfield Township	26,421			....		5	64	145	849	72	2
Clawson	13,872			....		8	25	56	304	17	4
Clay-Algonac	13,679			....		1	....	56	244	15	....
Clinton Township	87,580			....		64	240	486	2,193	295	12
Clio-Vienna	16,153			....		7	93	113	584	33	6
Davison Township	14,962			....		6	7	96	290	31	2
Dearborn	88,707			1		187	331	621	5,076	1,157	17
Dearborn Heights	59,798			2		108	138	481	1,926	350	3
Detroit	1,020,062			579		13,591	12,999	23,092	42,818	28,061	1,219
De Witt Township	10,655			....		6	9	49	210	8	2
East Grand Rapids	10,544			....		2	3	26	221	8	2
East Lansing	48,739			2		28	82	252	1,522	161	10
East Pointe	35,986			1		62	356	216	1,328	275	1
Ecorse	11,994			1		36	107	158	200	85	25
Emmett Township	10,977			1		16	53	149	403	35	16
Farmington	10,018			....		4	9	66	337	8	3

See footnotes at end of table.

Table 8. — Number of Offenses Known to the Police, Cities and Towns*10,000 and over in Population, 1993 — Continued

City by State	Population	Crime Index total	Modified* Crime Index total	Murder and non-negligent man-slaughter	Forcible rape	Robbery	Aggra-vated assault	Burglary	Larceny-theft	Motor vehicle theft	Arson*
MICHIGAN[4] — Continued											
Farmington Hills........................	77,250			1		44	166	528	1,907	231	23
Ferndale.............................	24,207			1		80	151	243	990	221	6
Flint................................	139,960			48		1,039	2,507	4,024	7,701	2,307	338
Flint Township.......................	34,761			....		53	107	247	2,088	216	8
Fraser..............................	14,123			....		12	37	75	471	52	4
Garden City..........................	31,610			....		22	53	180	924	85	9
Genesee Township	24,572			2		15	92	278	481	91	9
Grand Blanc Township.................	25,898			1		9	47	150	634	63	5
Grand Haven........................	12,471			....		1	26	83	655	13	2
Grand Rapids	192,121			33		829	1,793	3,161	8,827	1,075	79
Grandville	16,414			2		7	10	90	479	24	3
Green Oak Township..................	11,834			....		1	15	76	179	17	3
Grosse Pointe Farms.................	10,205			....		4	11	21	207	21	....
Grosse Pointe Park...................	12,990			....		8	9	32	301	51	2
Grosse Pointe Woods..................	17,659			....		10	1	21	294	31	....
Hamburg Township	13,343			....		2	11	55	218	21	3
Hamtramck..........................	17,656			5		128	257	476	919	447	11
Harper Woods.......................	14,680			....		43	21	78	1,748	240	5
Hazel Park	19,528			2		57	267	198	813	180	17
Highland Park	20,223			12		281	443	475	833	578	15
Holland.............................	31,640			1		7	122	193	1,424	54	8
Huron Township	10,654			....		1	26	91	189	44	3
Jackson	38,341			5		74	1,245	359	1,769	154	23
Kalamazoo...........................	81,631			8		248	1,112	1,308	4,082	493	85
Kalamazoo Township..................	21,394			1		12	75	179	672	79	9
Kentwood...........................	39,662			1		30	62	205	1,526	78	6
Lansing.............................	127,311			14		302	1,066	1,372	5,295	700	86
Lincoln Township	13,875			....		....	26	62	305	9	2
Lincoln Park.........................	41,859			5		67	126	284	1,417	331	14
Livonia	101,847			1		82	148	622	2,686	444	
Marquette	22,076			....		3	24	55	652	26	2
Melvindale	11,169			....		25	41	150	453	113	5
Midland	39,193			....		10	46	110	945	32	6
Monroe.............................	23,404			....		22	94	200	737	56	13
Mount Clemens......................	18,748			1		62	163	212	743	33	6
Mount Morris Township	25,701			1		70	138	390	709	203	16
Mount Pleasant......................	23,633			....		3	37	140	830	33	6
Mundy Township.....................	11,740			....		6	19	75	388	18	2
Muskegon...........................	41,122			3		142	451	1,139	2,920	295	25
Muskegon Heights	13,683			1		67	250	432	1,109	141	18
Muskegon Township..................	15,606			2		8	101	157	696	18	1
Niles	12,540			....		19	75	166	641	45	5
Niles Township	13,083			....		1	11	51	223	14	5
Northville Township	17,657			....		3	7	71	413	25	2
Norton Shores	22,413			....		9	17	108	554	38	3
Novi................................	37,401			1		8	85	192	1,487	129	4
Oak Park	30,500			1		77	191	324	1,331	358	11
Oscoda-Ausable Township	14,553			....		....	7	93	186	12	5
Owosso.............................	16,491			....		5	77	112	431	32	7
Pittsfield Township....................	18,020			....		43	50	256	1,203	103	7
Plymouth Township	24,118			1		3	9	51	355	51	1
Pontiac.............................	69,673			19		423	1,420	1,470	1,964	874	60
Portage.............................	41,888			....		19	90	278	1,886	64	13
Port Huron	34,140			2		54	201	354	1,441	98	30
River Rouge.........................	11,274			2		41	91	188	459	126	15
Riverview	13,807			1		....	1	37	214	29	....

See footnotes at end of table.

Table 8. — Number of Offenses Known to the Police, Cities and Towns 10,000 and over in Population, 1993 — Continued

City by State	Population	Crime Index total	Modified* Crime Index total	Murder and non-negligent man-slaughter	Forcible rape	Robbery	Aggra-vated assault	Burglary	Larceny-theft	Motor vehicle theft	Arson*
MICHIGAN[4] — Continued											
Romulus	23,215			3		50	148	323	1,147	423	11
Roseville	51,362			1		78	210	309	2,778	384	6
Royal Oak	67,611			1		49	141	332	2,059	249	10
Saginaw	71,048			22		479	1,586	1,817	3,307	245	131
Saginaw Township	38,435			....		21	64	132	1,407	34	7
Sault Ste. Marie	14,871			....		5	7	92	517	28	1
Shelby Township	49,626			1		9	64	204	1,023	108	7
Southfield	81,465			3		204	420	991	3,353	1,201	13
Southgate	30,294			....		34	75	133	1,129	239	14
Sterling Heights	118,865			....		43	312	511	3,464	314	32
Sturgis	10,455			....		2	21	57	310	16	2
Summit Township	21,550			....		6	27	58	218	17	1
Sumpter Township	11,107			....		2	18	88	187	61	4
Taylor	70,577			4		138	435	729	3,078	467	41
Thomas Township	11,188			....		1	12	45	281	11	1
Traverse City	15,489			....		2	32	98	653	13	2
Trenton	20,599			....		3	15	47	318	33	5
Troy	79,085			1		28	185	477	2,572	335	17
Van Buren Township	21,429			....		16	54	118	739	130	4
Wayne	19,811			1		58	111	194	810	163	14
West Bloomfield Township	55,603			....		10	62	205	898	26	12
Westland	85,922			4		96	343	666	2,692	494	48
White Lake Township	23,057			....		3	61	157	618	47	9
Woodhaven	11,534			....		4	15	84	547	70	2
Wyandotte	30,684			....		17	27	102	684	80	....
Wyoming	64,421			1		116	243	625	2,235	264	13
Ypsilanti	24,515			4		110	269	407	833	140	22
MINNESOTA[4]											
Albert Lea	18,174			....		2	28	82	585	39	3
Andover	17,589			....		3	16	183	366	34	1
Anoka	17,193			....		6	21	166	636	53	11
Apple Valley	38,216			....		6	29	216	955	46	17
Austin	21,914			....		5	34	134	646	41	2
Bemidji	11,817			....		4	14	91	1,060	91	5
Blaine	40,858			....		17	50	312	1,972	102	12
Bloomington	86,115			4		65	103	715	3,658	417	
Brainerd	13,068			....		5	17	173	775	64	3
Brooklyn Center	28,311			....		48	56	284	1,851	208	16
Brooklyn Park	58,028			4		70	187	492	1,873	217	17
Burnsville	54,331			....		16	26	255	2,266	157	12
Champlin	19,267			....		5	20	123	391	22	5
Chanhassen	13,753			1		1	8	40	203	9	1
Chaska	12,491			....		2	13	58	372	11	1
Cloquet	11,202			....		4	21	64	396	31	1
Columbia Heights	18,991	1,214	1,231	....	4	37	47	242	792	92	17
Cottage Grove	25,040	811	812	....	3	16	34	108	630	20	1
Crystal	23,682			3		20	31	126	518	52	4
Duluth	86,368			6		53	221	859	3,266	268	14
Eagan	53,466			....		15	33	272	1,382	199	10
Eden Prairie	43,561			....		7	28	254	1,338	80	13
Edina	46,756			1		17	38	346	1,353	84	8
Elk River	12,357			....		2	11	96	348	20	1
Fairmont	11,231			....		1	13	121	496	25	3

See footnotes at end of table.

Table 8. — Number of Offenses Known to the Police, Cities and Towns 10,000 and over in Population, 1993 — Continued

City by State	Population	Crime Index total	Modified* Crime Index total	Murder and non-negligent man-slaughter	Forcible rape	Robbery	Aggra-vated assault	Burglary	Larceny-theft	Motor vehicle theft	Arson*
MINNESOTA[4] — Continued											
Faribault	17,869			....		8	17	178	767	75	10
Fergus Falls	12,534			....		1	16	90	423	12	2
Fridley	27,864			1		27	70	268	1,459	118	4
Golden Valley	21,165			....		9	9	139	440	51	5
Hastings	16,145			....		2	16	120	369	40	1
Hibbing	18,181			....	....		4	41	231	8	....
Hopkins	16,489	799	803	....	10	7	30	113	572	67	4
Hutchinson	12,197			1		1	10	40	492	16	4
Inver Grove Heights	24,164			....		3	30	192	671	78	19
Lakeville	30,323			1		1	27	120	717	63	20
Lino Lakes	10,111			1		2	12	53	138	19	2
Mankato	31,604			....		9	26	329	1,762	108	3
Maple Grove	42,744			....		5	30	235	984	68	5
Maplewood	32,380			....		27	37	226	1,618	159	7
Marshall	11,881			....		3	18	69	303	19	2
Mendota Heights	10,300			....		1	4	44	212	19	1
Minneapolis	366,642	40,463		58	518	3,178	2,727	9,358	19,952	4,672	
Minnetonka	50,645			....		13	17	371	1,137	68	9
Moorhead	33,071			1		4	44	194	1,386	59	6
Mounds View	12,935			....		4	29	68	397	35	4
New Brighton	22,136			....		4	33	184	534	53	4
New Hope	21,687			1		14	27	108	526	39	4
New Ulm	13,283			....	....		9	67	283	25	6
Northfield	15,375	529	535	....	4	1	12	62	425	9	1
North Mankato	10,648			....	....		2	15	287	9	1
North St. Paul	12,677			....		5	15	60	325	34	12
Oakdale	21,120			....		11	48	101	578	31	8
Owatonna	20,002			....		2	13	94	470	39	3
Plymouth	55,435			....		13	55	271	1,468	100	62
Prior Lake	12,273			....		3	3	26	341	15	3
Ramsey	13,817			2		2	9	83	331	33	2
Red Wing	15,516			2		4	22	108	620	38	5
Richfield	35,667			....		39	69	372	1,126	167	5
Robbinsdale	14,304	760	764	....	6	19	27	101	538	69	4
Rochester	74,723			3		22	94	603	2,454	188	4
Roseville	33,671			....		11	19	198	1,730	134	9
St. Cloud	50,412			2		15	68	343	2,344	152	17
St. Louis Park	43,224			....		22	31	344	1,522	119	5
St. Paul	271,208	20,382	20,706	22	242	954	1,486	4,023	11,329	2,326	324
Savage	12,208			....		2	11	97	255	22	2
Shakopee	12,275	692	694	....	4	6	24	96	514	48	2
Shoreview	26,271			2		1	1	61	226	19	3
South Lake Minnetonka	10,764			1		2	13	60	259	14	2
South St. Paul	20,326			....		4	48	145	667	84	5
Stillwater	14,619			....		2	25	69	357	24	....
Vadnais Heights	12,272			....		2	3	35	121	23	1
West St. Paul	19,334			....		19	26	99	927	126	2
White Bear Lake	25,428			1		8	5	195	876	82	14
Willmar	18,257			....		7	44	118	817	30	6
Winona	25,293			....		2	11	127	1,322	36	4
Woodbury	24,812			....		4	13	205	693	28	9
Worthington	10,242			....		1	17	77	307	9	1
MISSISSIPPI											
Brandon	12,525	174	175	1	1	2	24	72	64	10	1
Clinton	22,822	644	649	2	....	14	12	169	435	12	5

See footnotes at end of table.

Table 8. — Number of Offenses Known to the Police, Cities and Towns 10,000 and over in Population, 1993 — Continued

City by State	Population	Crime Index total	Modified* Crime Index total	Murder and non-negligent man-slaughter	Forcible rape	Robbery	Aggra-vated assault	Burglary	Larceny-theft	Motor vehicle theft	Arson*
MISSISSIPPI — Continued											
Columbus	25,995	1,403	1,409	1	15	32	74	233	1,002	46	6
Greenville	44,500	4,811	4,868	16	34	66	133	1,745	2,631	186	57
Greenwood	19,252	2,210	2,217	4	10	46	33	772	1,254	91	7
Grenada	11,142	1,176	1,177	3	15	41	211	195	665	46	1
Gulfport	41,938	3,027	3,048	4	29	86	143	473	2,127	165	21
Hattiesburg	43,226	3,526	3,533	10	26	77	241	948	2,096	128	7
Jackson	198,227	25,508	25,653	83	173	1,505	1,019	7,071	11,603	4,054	145
Laurel[1]	18,866			3	15	55		448	1,179	104	8
McComb	11,692	1,084	1,087	4	3	30	55	271	677	44	3
Meridian	41,332	2,028	2,038	7	19	78	88	495	1,222	119	10
Moss Point	17,952	1,370	1,395	5	19	36	79	470	701	60	25
Natchez	19,519	1,534	1,542	2	15	36	54	283	1,124	20	8
Ocean Springs	15,566	763	764	....	8	13	32	160	515	35	1
Oxford	10,275	551	552	1	3	21	10	93	411	12	1
Pascagoula	28,590	2,993	3,002	9	27	125	159	683	1,736	254	9
Ridgeland	12,877	778	778	1	3	22	10	108	589	45	....
Starkville	18,927	1,185	1,189	3	3	22	112	166	828	51	4
Tupelo	32,276	2,532	2,535	3	6	58	33	411	1,773	248	3
Vicksburg	21,493	2,283	2,283	6	21	57	115	672	1,276	136	....
MISSOURI											
Arnold	19,919	712	716	1	2	10	68	99	501	31	4
Ballwin	24,186	418	418	....	1	8	10	69	317	13	....
Bellefontaine Neighbors	10,891	518	518			21	16	88	338	55	....
Belton	19,593	683	686	1	10	5	26	95	512	34	3
Berkeley	12,792	763	767	3	5	56	45	207	326	121	4
Blue Springs	43,371	1,489	1,498	1	9	23	55	159	1,160	82	9
Bridgeton	17,395	1,243	1,243	1	6	41	43	193	820	139	....
Cape Girardeau	35,337	2,254	2,256	2	10	42	66	266	1,757	111	2
Carthage	10,973	441	442	2	....	3	10	90	323	13	1
Chesterfield	40,213	1,047	1,053	....	4	12	27	177	797	30	6
Clayton	13,931	702	703	....		19	30	137	473	43	1
Columbia	73,683	4,708	4,738	1	30	108	300	571	3,532	166	30
Crestwood	11,209	667	671	....	1	7	6	34	600	19	4
Creve Coeur	12,014	387	387	....	....	9	9	64	274	31	....
Excelsior Springs	10,818	584	587		1	....	12	93	458	20	3
Farmington	12,130	528	530	1	3	2	18	46	435	23	2
Ferguson	22,216	1,297	1,301		10	70	42	239	699	237	4
Florissant	51,882	1,461	1,472		6	37	50	205	1,055	108	11
Fulton	10,281	469	470		5	6	31	80	336	11	1
Gladstone	26,822	723	723		9	26	42	154	419	73	....
Grandview	25,288	985	990	....	5	55	47	296	445	137	5
Hannibal	18,208	1,233	1,243		9	7	104	217	865	31	10
Hazelwood	15,134	787	794	2	3	24	38	176	437	107	7
Independence	113,646	7,199	7,228	4	51	137	463	1,372	4,315	857	29
Jefferson City	37,396	1,647	1,655	....	4	26	51	231	1,274	61	8
Joplin	41,693	2,901	2,924	5	25	55	142	631	1,876	167	23
Kansas City	435,428	55,165	55,692	153	515	3,891	6,402	12,106	23,611	8,487	527
Kennett	11,186	1,227	1,227	1	18	20	110	287	734	57	....
Kirksville	17,124	593	593		4	2	1	93	471	22	....
Kirkwood	27,538	723	728	1	4	17	45	99	518	39	5
Lebanon	10,184	545	549	....	13	3	26	115	347	41	4
Lees Summit	51,751	1,167	1,199	....	9	17	35	292	737	77	32
Marshall	12,401	242	242		3	2	....	39	196	2	....
Maryland Heights	25,499	1,076	1,079	1	4	18	53	187	728	85	3
Maryville	10,521	282	282	....	1	....	11	42	215	13	....

City by State	Population	Crime Index total	Modified* Crime Index total	Murder and non-negligent man-slaughter	Forcible rape	Robbery	Aggra-vated assault	Burglary	Larceny-theft	Motor vehicle theft	Arson*
MISSOURI—Continued											
Mexico	11,330	282	282	1	1	3	12	75	180	10	....
Moberly	12,577	729	730	1	8	5	111	94	489	21	1
O'Fallon	21,727	751	753	1	2	3	13	118	572	42	2
Overland	17,965	1,109	1,111	....	4	24	50	150	823	58	2
Poplar Bluff	17,682	1,492	1,511	2	17	19	42	307	1,045	60	19
Raytown	30,547	1,126	1,129	....	6	40	36	241	671	132	3
Richmond Heights	10,236	1,380	1,381	....	2	37	40	71	1,141	89	1
Rolla	14,448	484	493	....	4	2	19	91	336	32	9
St. Ann	14,283	1,827	1,827	....	7	49	41	118	1,400	212	....
St. Charles	57,748	1,934	1,954	....	17	51	100	382	1,236	148	20
St. Joseph	72,524	5,053	5,084	3	33	54	233	866	3,643	221	31
St. Louis	387,053	64,438	65,244	267	319	6,223	8,189	12,400	26,975	10,065	806
St. Peters	50,345	1,649	1,656	....	9	23	82	172	1,273	90	7
Sedalia	19,992	1,263	1,263	2	8	7	102	188	920	36	....
Springfield	146,642	10,907	11,041	7	77	136	449	2,094	7,690	454	134
University City	39,738	2,627	2,652	5	16	131	110	622	1,479	264	25
Warrensburg	15,939	506	508	1	9	12	13	103	348	20	2
Washington	11,169	505	507	....	2	1	55	63	366	18	2
Webster Groves	23,345	450	456	1	....	11	17	71	316	34	6
MONTANA5											
NEBRASKA											
Beatrice	12,345	530	532	....	5	3	4	54	442	22	2
Bellevue	31,110	1,461	1,463	....	....	12	11	221	1,153	64	2
Columbus	19,892	684	685	1	2	3	25	72	568	13	1
Fremont	23,694	1,006	1,010	....		6	15	175	774	36	4
Grand Island	40,186	2,708	2,708	....	14	21	75	409	2,100	89	....
Hastings	22,825	760	760	1	4	3	15	143	572	22	14
Kearney	24,982	1,201	1,215	....	2	1	15	202	947	34	....
La Vista	10,481	400	400	....	1	4	4	33	331	27	....
Lincoln	198,228	13,561	13,637	4	83	127	911	1,984	10,023	429	76
North Platte	23,349	1,524	1,532	....	8	5	55	222	1,198	36	8
Papillion	10,880	207	209	....	....	2	4	22	169	10	2
Scottsbluff	14,103	965	969	....	8	3	28	90	813	23	4
NEVADA											
Boulder City	13,312	431	437	1	....	2	38	108	241	41	6
Henderson	87,704	3,215	3,248	1	75	109	104	746	1,810	370	33
Las Vegas Metropolitan Police Department Jurisdiction	717,441	48,365	48,824	91	435	3,572	3,183	9,783	23,855	7,446	459
Reno	145,433	11,571	11,643	16	129	432	470	1,837	8,006	681	72
Sparks	58,416	3,966		4	45	101	161	651	2,808	196	
NEW HAMPSHIRE											
Bedford	12,693	130	130	....	....	1	3	19	99	8	....
Berlin	11,629	205	207	....	5	1	10	64	121	4	2
Claremont	13,613	598	600	....	27	....	12	80	461	18	2
Concord	35,955	1,608	1,617	....	20	13	16	264	1,248	47	9
Derry	29,914	1,027	1,058	....	40	7	21	255	602	102	31
Dover	25,058	753	755	....	10	1	14	45	647	36	2
Durham	11,941	257	260	....	9	....	4	44	191	9	3
Exeter	12,612	226	234	....	2	1	5	29	174	15	8
Goffstown	14,775	354	357	2	3	4	14	58	267	6	3
Hudson	19,735	438	443	....	6	3	9	67	318	35	5
Keene	22,509	1,109	1,123	....	23	4	68	155	835	24	14
Laconia	15,448	1,010	1,054	1	62	4	30	144	728	41	44
Lebanon	12,397	691	695	....	1	....	17	64	582	27	4

See footnotes at end of table.

Table 8. — Number of Offenses Known to the Police, Cities and Towns 10,000 and over in Population, 1993 — Continued

City by State	Population	Crime Index total	Modified* Crime Index total	Murder and non-negligent man-slaughter	Forcible rape	Robbery	Aggra-vated assault	Burglary	Larceny-theft	Motor vehicle theft	Arson*
NEW HAMPSHIRE — Continued											
Londonderry	19,988	498	507	....	1	1	6	74	377	39	9
Manchester	98,145	5,480	5,508	5	33	140	41	1,277	3,536	448	28
Merrimack	22,389	283	284	....	1	1	3	64	200	14	1
Milford	11,917	361	366	....	7	4	18	41	283	8	5
Nashua	80,435	2,649	2,684	3	26	13	26	380	1,935	266	35
Portsmouth	20,901	1,021	1,030	....	31	14	34	171	701	70	9
Salem	26,017	1,559	1,563	2	4	29	20	145	1,030	329	4
Somersworth	11,233	350	354	....	4	1	4	66	263	12	4
NEW JERSEY											
Aberdeen Township	17,678	643	643	1	15	10	27	151	392	47	....
Asbury Park	16,395	1,470	1,472	2	19	150	151	221	786	141	2
Atlantic City	37,539	11,142	11,244	10	46	643	618	1,268	8,146	411	102
Barnegat Township	12,495	221	226	....	2	....	11	29	174	5	5
Bayonne	62,270	2,046	2,051	....	6	105	194	335	1,157	249	5
Belleville	34,775	1,578	1,587	1	4	61	103	322	623	464	9
Bellmawr	12,657	195	199	....	1	2	7	7	159	19	4
Bergenfield	24,809	485	486	....	....	12	26	110	312	25	1
Berkeley Heights	12,190	173	175	....	....	1	4	14	138	16	2
Berkeley Township	38,115	809	816	....	3	5	33	173	565	30	7
Bernards Township	18,336	239	239	....	....	....	14	46	170	9	....
Bloomfield	45,801	2,137	2,142	....	3	96	72	449	915	602	5
Branchburg Township	11,607	193	202	....	2	....	7	30	147	7	9
Brick Township	67,891	1,817	1,831	2	9	28	51	415	1,214	98	14
Bridgeton	19,311	1,946	1,961	8	17	135	269	478	987	52	15
Bridgewater Township	34,660	900	905	....	....	16	15	101	698	70	5
Brigantine	11,887	688	691	....	2	4	36	162	463	21	3
Burlington	10,255	596	603	....	9	24	65	171	236	91	7
Burlington Township	12,642	679	687	....	3	10	43	134	431	58	8
Camden	87,582	12,722	13,028	42	90	1,654	1,155	4,039	3,926	1,816	306
Carteret	19,335	758	758	....	14	26	49	321	280	68	....
Cedar Grove Township	12,250	347	358	....	1	8	38	100	169	31	11
Cherry Hill	71,673	3,345	3,350	....	4	70	77	612	2,158	424	5
Cinnaminson Township	14,803	484	484	1	2	22	12	94	271	82	....
Clark	14,885	327	327	1	1	7	7	47	233	31	....
Cliffside Park	20,939	377	377	....	3	6	17	64	231	56	....
Clifton	73,065	2,443	2,448	....	8	72	73	438	1,402	450	5
Clifton Township	10,979	136	136	....	1	3	7	25	89	11	....
Collingswood	14,905	752	754	....	....	27	32	152	405	136	2
Cranford Township	23,031	576	577	....	2	6	16	70	437	45	1
Delran Township	13,377	456	459	1	5	13	32	61	294	50	3
Denville Township	14,190	249	249	....	1	2	20	16	195	15	....
Deptford Township	25,102	1,518	1,524	2	....	41	54	261	1,011	149	6
Dover	14,960	612	616	....	3	9	25	103	397	75	4
Dover Township	78,000	3,087	3,106	1	16	36	109	641	2,150	134	19
Dumont	17,396	305	305	....	....	2	8	64	220	11	....
East Brunswick Township	44,997	1,569	1,576	....	11	18	40	213	1,186	101	7
East Hanover Township	10,197	293	293	....	....	3	4	36	211	39	....
East Orange	72,794	7,305	7,402	15	88	1,129	922	1,732	1,944	1,475	97
East Windsor Township	22,784	462	462	....	2	6	14	87	324	29	....
Eatontown	14,080	737	737	....	....	13	16	74	593	41	....
Edison	91,631	3,353	3,366	2	....	83	48	668	2,162	390	13
Egg Harbor Township	24,916	1,563	1,569	3	15	26	59	320	1,046	94	6
Elizabeth	109,131	9,465	9,488	17	42	878	464	1,851	4,058	2,155	23
Elmwood Park	17,854	835	838	....	2	14	6	82	651	80	3
Englewood	25,024	1,304	1,305	1	9	69	77	323	694	131	1

City by State	Population	Crime Index total	Modified* Crime Index total	Murder and non-negligent man-slaughter	Forcible rape	Robbery	Aggra-vated assault	Burglary	Larceny-theft	Motor vehicle theft	Arson*
NEW JERSEY — Continued											
Evesham Township	35,845	900	905	....	4	9	53	204	581	49	5
Ewing Township	34,844	1,837	1,855	2	11	38	25	220	1,027	514	18
Fair Lawn	31,105	615	616	....	....	13	12	97	444	49	1
Fairview	10,711	326	328	....	....	17	16	68	175	50	2
Florence Township	10,420	263	264	....	1	10	20	54	147	31	1
Fort Lee	32,473	1,226	1,226	2	4	52	79	451	514	124	....
Franklin Lakes	10,197	114	115	....	....	....	3	26	84	1	1
Franklin Township (Gloucester County)	15,060	514	524	1	3	10	25	164	270	41	10
Franklin Township (Somerset County)	45,611	1,848	1,874	1	10	60	89	465	1,082	141	26
Freehold	11,291	604	605	....	12	25	41	86	417	23	1
Freehold Township	25,638	800	800	....	1	10	11	49	664	65	....
Galloway Township	23,684	929	936	1	5	10	44	266	557	46	7
Garfield	26,921	824	831	2	2	19	53	134	471	143	7
Glassboro	16,671	963	969	....	16	23	33	182	667	42	6
Glen Rock	11,151	181	181	....	....	3	6	43	117	12	....
Gloucester City	12,891	412	412	....	5	7	8	104	249	39	....
Gloucester Township	55,600	2,233	2,239	1	35	25	99	361	1,502	210	6
Hackensack	38,116	2,057	2,069	4	12	68	82	164	1,401	326	12
Haddonfield	11,711	398	400	....	1	4	3	60	320	10	2
Haddon Township	15,333	733	741	1	....	25	22	142	482	61	8
Hamilton Township (Atlantic County)	16,254	1,172	1,187	1	23	13	74	240	748	73	15
Hamilton Township (Mercer County)	88,226	2,645	2,665	1	5	64	43	485	1,466	581	20
Hammonton	12,265	449	454	....	1	7	21	135	258	27	5
Hanover Township	11,853	222	223	....	....	4	7	34	162	15	1
Harrison	13,398	763	764	....	5	33	39	168	276	242	1
Hasbrouck Heights	11,659	379	380	....	1	8	1	64	247	58	1
Hawthorne	17,768	403	403	....	5	5	4	84	282	23	....
Hazlet Township	22,802	318	319	....	....	1	15	69	208	25	1
Highland Park	13,074	302	303	....	....	5	6	70	214	7	1
Hillsborough Township	30,714	456	457	....	....	9	1	105	323	18	1
Hillside Township	21,415	1,508	1,513	....	9	139	52	274	674	360	5
Hoboken	33,977	2,667	2,668	2	4	81	172	444	1,311	653	1
Holmdel Township	11,965	268	270	....	2	2	8	43	207	6	2
Hopatcong	15,931	289	291	....	4	....	17	55	206	7	2
Hopewell Township	11,813	149	150	1	1	2	19	28	90	8	1
Howell Township	40,454	882	897	....	10	9	34	183	597	49	15
Irvington	62,021	7,545	7,578	10	60	934	497	1,560	2,061	2,423	33
Jackson Township	33,942	1,467	1,470	....	....	5	18	114	1,296	34	3
Jefferson Township	18,312	260	262	....	....	1	12	81	150	16	2
Jersey City	230,298	18,760	18,819	20	100	2,500	1,964	4,190	6,331	3,655	59
Keansburg	11,609	299	301	2	1	2	70	49	164	11	2
Kearny	35,530	2,202	2,207	1	8	70	77	456	1,233	357	5
Lacey Township	22,613	625	638	....	....	3	15	92	495	20	13
Lakewood	46,009	2,876	2,915	3	23	126	118	723	1,675	208	39
Lawrence Township	26,284	2,027	2,031	1	5	23	41	203	1,154	600	4
Lincoln Park	11,239	159	160	....	....	....	11	24	111	13	1
Linden	36,854	1,897	1,913	1	8	90	96	359	982	361	16
Lindenwold	18,091	1,064	1,069	....	7	47	58	263	532	157	5
Little Egg Harbor Township	13,616	538	540	1	4	....	30	135	352	16	2
Little Falls Township	11,762	566	567	....	2	12	24	70	370	88	1
Little Ferry	10,095	231	232	....	2	2	13	21	154	39	1
Livingston	27,045	956	957	....	....	4	19	73	706	154	1
Lodi	22,723	935	936	....	1	8	38	149	578	161	1
Long Branch	28,620	2,389	2,411	2	13	119	210	623	1,278	144	22
Lower Township	21,136	763	771	....	19	9	24	189	486	36	8
Lyndhurst Township	18,909	698	701	....	6	10	18	88	440	136	3

Table 8.—Number of Offenses Known to the Police, Cities and Towns 10,000 and over in Population, 1993—Continued

City by State	Population	Crime Index total	Modified* Crime Index total	Murder and non-negligent man-slaughter	Forcible rape	Robbery	Aggra-vated assault	Burglary	Larceny-theft	Motor vehicle theft	Arson*
NEW JERSEY – Continued											
Madison	15,837	263	263	....	....	4	4	33	203	19	....
Mahwah Township	18,540	399	405	....	1	7	7	61	307	16	6
Manalapan Township	27,721	469	471	....	2	3	20	88	331	25	2
Manchester Township	36,742	343	359	2	5	1	25	60	239	11	16
Mantua Township	10,475	440	441	1	2	2	13	87	321	14	1
Manville	10,699	224	224	....	....	3	11	18	181	11	....
Maple Shade Township	19,502	820	836	....	3	9	47	161	406	194	16
Maplewood Township	22,007	1,121	1,123	1	3	53	42	198	524	300	2
Marlboro Township	29,026	535	539	....	3	4	42	93	374	19	4
Medford Township	20,837	436	439	2	3	5	14	88	313	11	3
Metuchen	12,950	374	377	....	....	12	12	88	232	30	3
Middlesex	13,190	366	367	....	....	4	15	37	293	17	1
Middle Township	14,995	640	644	....	10	3	22	162	428	15	4
Middletown Township	70,749	1,170	1,171	....	5	13	31	231	846	44	1
Millburn Township	18,934	703	703	....	1	14	7	111	439	131	....
Millville	26,479	1,652	1,669	2	28	69	155	414	907	77	17
Monroe Township (Gloucester County)	27,771	903	910	....	1	17	36	274	499	76	7
Monroe Township (Middlesex County)	22,995	239	240	....	4	3	11	67	145	9	1
Montclair	38,348	2,586	2,591	....	7	70	118	588	1,371	432	5
Montgomery Township	10,248	203	205	....	....	1	6	41	153	2	2
Montville Township	16,026	338	338	1	1	3	1	52	243	37	....
Moorestown Township	16,360	494	498	....	4	8	18	142	286	36	4
Morristown	16,118	1,057	1,057	....	3	48	80	166	710	50	....
Morris Township	20,498	316	317	1	3	1	15	58	217	21	1
Mount Holly	10,799	892	910	2	10	43	101	168	520	48	18
Mount Laurel Township	30,728	696	698	....	4	10	18	200	383	81	2
Mount Olive Township	21,864	378	385	....	8	7	26	87	218	32	7
Neptune Township	29,206	2,129	2,149	....	7	64	120	642	1,197	99	20
Newark	269,892	38,514	38,698	96	257	5,892	3,977	6,879	10,420	10,993	184
New Brunswick	42,706	3,712	3,731	5	18	311	289	797	1,955	337	19
New Milford	16,198	300	303	....	2	3	20	73	185	17	3
New Providence	11,724	129	131	....	....	3	3	12	93	18	2
North Arlington	14,073	395	395	....	2	8	12	75	226	72	....
North Bergen Township	49,872	2,220	2,224	2	9	80	57	508	1,004	560	4
North Brunswick Township	32,327	1,275	1,283	....	7	42	45	258	748	175	8
North Hanover Township	10,144	81	82	....	....	....	5	33	36	7	1
North Plainfield	19,221	1,194	1,198	....	2	30	54	243	717	148	4
Nutley	27,544	753	768	1	3	24	49	198	355	123	15
Oakland	12,114	87	88	....	....	....	3	6	75	3	1
Ocean City	15,670	1,612	1,615	....	4	14	26	410	1,124	34	3
Ocean Township	26,000	1,237	1,245	....	1	27	32	246	882	49	8
Old Bridge	58,354	1,628	1,648	1	3	30	49	318	964	263	20
Orange	30,416	3,612	3,636	3	29	398	359	890	1,037	896	24
Palisades Park	14,552	304	304	....	....	8	9	60	180	47	....
Paramus	24,924	3,529	3,547	....	3	24	76	241	2,494	691	18
Parsippany-Troy Hills Township	49,807	1,379	1,389	3	11	15	45	391	810	104	10
Passaic	57,389	3,726	3,731	3	17	382	204	583	1,864	673	5
Paterson	140,409	11,346	11,459	23	78	1,089	994	3,260	4,079	1,823	113
Pemberton Township	31,817	1,000	1,020	....	22	20	79	323	489	67	20
Pennsauken	35,902	2,147	2,154	2	3	130	66	584	791	571	7
Pennsville Township	14,002	304	306	1	1	4	7	29	249	13	2
Pequannock Township	13,195	322	324	....	....	1	14	60	234	13	2
Perth Amboy	41,661	3,135	3,152	1	18	179	296	831	1,572	238	17
Phillipsburg	15,984	364	366	....	....	4	34	81	230	15	2
Piscataway Township	48,655	1,442	1,445	....	8	44	102	372	802	114	3
Plainfield	45,697	3,667	3,683	9	28	377	296	924	1,609	424	16

Table 8. — Number of Offenses Known to the Police, Cities and Towns 10,000 and over in Population, 1993 — Continued

City by State	Population	Crime Index total	Modified* Crime Index total	Murder and non-negligent man-slaughter	Forcible rape	Robbery	Aggra-vated assault	Burglary	Larceny-theft	Motor vehicle theft	Arson*
NEW JERSEY — Continued											
Plainsboro Township	14,684	394	396	1	2	6	15	74	265	31	2
Pleasantville	17,200	1,233	1,245	3	12	91	191	325	553	58	12
Point Pleasant	18,331	530	530	1	....	4	13	88	405	19	....
Pompton Lakes	10,827	254	254	....	....	....	6	38	191	19	....
Princeton	12,095	610	611	....	....	4	6	97	487	16	1
Princeton Township	13,451	273	274	....	1	1	8	69	182	12	1
Rahway	25,845	1,100	1,104	....	1	61	39	271	555	173	4
Ramsey	13,844	435	435	1	1	3	22	47	317	44	....
Randolph Township	20,520	386	386	....	....	3	6	53	309	15	....
Raritan Township	15,852	367	367	....	1	1	7	49	296	13	....
Readington Township	13,602	168	168	....	....	1	6	23	128	10	....
Red Bank	10,643	730	733	....	6	17	24	93	548	42	3
Ridgefield	10,031	164	164	....	....	2	4	27	98	33	....
Ridgefield Park	12,716	189	190	....	....	2	7	21	127	32	1
Ridgewood	24,572	323	327	....	....	4	9	7	62	222	19	4
Ringwood	12,929	142	143	....	1	....	1	31	101	8	1
River Edge	10,869	182	182	....	1	3	5	29	126	18	....
Rockaway Township	20,108	976	979	....	2	8	25	89	796	56	3
Roselle	20,847	718	727	....	14	47	39	154	355	109	9
Roselle Park	12,825	342	342	....	2	9	8	79	179	65	....
Roxbury Township	20,988	434	437	....	3	6	13	76	310	26	3
Rutherford	17,926	394	396	....	2	5	16	50	246	75	2
Saddle Brook Township	13,767	481	482	....	2	7	3	45	350	74	1
Sayreville	35,781	1,133	1,139	....	5	24	75	208	713	108	6
Scotch Plains Township	21,532	492	494	1	3	12	9	102	276	89	2
Secaucus	14,915	1,117	1,118	....	5	16	21	79	783	213	1
Somers Point	11,470	351	352	1	3	6	14	86	226	15	1
Somerville	11,943	595	598	....	5	13	9	75	467	26	3
South Brunswick Township	26,649	709	712	1	2	9	26	131	474	66	3
South Orange	16,658	1,330	1,330	....	2	82	28	224	498	496	....
South Plainfield	20,873	1,070	1,075	1	4	28	20	121	825	71	5
South River	13,802	281	281	....	3	4	31	77	144	22	....
Sparta Township	15,386	219	220	....	....	1	7	39	160	12	1
Springfield	13,656	509	509	....	2	5	8	40	268	186	....
Stafford Township	13,608	437	440	1	6	1	24	109	286	10	3
Summit	19,697	431	434	....	3	3	12	83	295	35	3
Teaneck Township	39,167	1,419	1,438	4	7	30	60	247	963	108	19
Tenafly	13,386	251	253	....	....	3	3	87	142	16	2
Tinton Falls	13,191	443	444	3	4	5	19	98	296	18	1
Totowa	10,362	530	531	....	1	6	12	54	374	83	1
Trenton	88,468	7,923	7,940	11	109	717	916	1,710	2,608	1,852	17
Union City	57,687	3,102	3,109	1	23	287	182	900	1,171	538	7
Union Township	50,905	2,915	2,924	1	8	140	61	408	1,515	782	9
Ventnor City	11,086	676	676	....	....	10	24	198	425	19	....
Vernon Township	21,532	485	485	1	1	1	22	105	339	16	....
Verona	13,820	298	298	....	1	8	17	43	195	34	....
Vineland	55,076	4,460	4,495	4	46	193	253	971	2,631	362	35
Voorhees Township	25,381	1,292	1,303	2	6	34	27	177	880	166	11
Wallington	10,834	309	313	....	....	3	2	52	201	51	4
Wall Township	21,006	461	463	....	....	7	10	107	326	11	2
Warren Township	11,545	243	244	....	....	1	9	43	181	9	1
Washington Township (Gloucester County)	43,637	1,324	1,336	....	7	27	65	296	804	125	12
Washington Township (Morris County)	16,018	190	192	....	....	2	8	29	140	11	2
Waterford Township	11,306	328	340	....	2	1	12	95	192	26	12
Wayne Township	48,978	2,570	2,575	1	9	16	36	227	1,817	464	5
Weehawken Township	12,757	805	807	2	1	30	42	167	448	115	2

Table 8.—Number of Offenses Known to the Police, Cities and Towns 10,000 and over in Population, 1993—Continued

City by State	Population	Crime Index total	Modified* Crime Index total	Murder and non-negligent man-slaughter	Forcible rape	Robbery	Aggra-vated assault	Burglary	Larceny-theft	Motor vehicle theft	Arson*
NEW JERSEY—Continued											
West Caldwell	10,593	271	271	....	....	5	4	27	213	22	....
West Deptford Township	20,154	660	661	1	2	9	17	146	443	42	....
Westfield	29,276	615	616	....	2	9	15	97	445	47	1
West Milford Township	26,486	485	490	....	4	5	14	123	318	21	5
West New York	37,765	2,122	2,151	1	3	112	93	599	950	364	29
West Orange	39,744	1,664	1,675	....	5	65	48	301	795	450	11
West Paterson	11,300	489	490	....	2	5	20	76	294	92	1
West Windsor Township	16,330	452	452	1	1	7	8	43	270	122	....
Westwood	10,393	222	222	....	3	3	3	38	171	4	....
Willingboro Township	36,842	1,376	1,394	1	10	34	64	273	810	184	18
Winslow Township	31,094	1,000	1,011	1	6	29	119	258	488	99	11
Woodbridge Township	96,184	4,223	4,244	3	15	108	270	665	2,444	718	21
Woodbury	11,056	635	635	....	2	26	27	126	419	35	....
Wyckoff	15,917	171	173	....	1	3	3	58	104	2	2
NEW MEXICO											
Alamogordo	28,151	1,451	1,458	2	7	9	128	294	968	43	7
Albuquerque	407,286	39,025	39,256	50	259	1,552	4,835	8,199	20,552	3,578	231
Artesia	11,578	613	615	....	2	4	29	102	466	10	2
Deming	12,271	861	865	....	2	6	66	233	509	45	4
Farmington	36,982	2,803	2,817	2	50	38	212	367	2,035	99	14
Gallup	20,565	2,751	2,763	5	24	48	250	299	1,992	133	12
Hobbs	29,995	2,673	2,676	4	19	30	346	637	1,581	56	3
Portales	11,515	471	471	3	5	2	27	195	228	11	....
Rio Rancho	37,151	855	861	....	6	9	75	188	526	51	6
Roswell	46,511	3,594	3,618	9	40	31	314	817	2,295	88	24
Silver City	11,453	793	799	....	7	5	58	134	569	20	6
NEW YORK											
Albany	100,192	7,802	7,847	6	59	481	692	2,063	4,030	471	45
Amherst Town[1]	107,404			1	6	56		346	2,210	316	9
Amsterdam	20,535	469		....	3	3	4	128	314	17	
Auburn	31,104	1,195	1,197	2	10	17	30	177	953	6	2
Batavia	16,531	752	758	2	....	14	7	108	611	10	6
Beacon	13,547	396	399	....	5	22	61	89	195	24	3
Bedford Town	17,108	298	298	....	1	1	1	43	232	20	....
Bethlehem Town	27,882	702	704	....	1	4	44	94	549	10	2
Binghamton	52,306	3,133	3,142	3	18	62	62	329	2,653	6	9
Brighton Town	34,868	1,088	1,090	1	1	16	8	182	827	53	2
Buffalo	324,855	31,871	32,305	76	295	2,898	2,772	7,597	12,714	5,519	434
Camillus Town and Village	23,908	250		....	....	1	4	25	217	3	
Canandaigua	11,010	358	358	....	6	2	2	41	304	3	....
Carmel Town	29,162	551	556	....	....	4	13	110	402	22	5
Cheektowaga Town	94,640	3,910		2	19	85	255	656	2,334	559	
Cicero Town	23,907	489	491	....	1	4	32	82	358	12	2
Clarkstown Town	77,465	2,167		....	8	28	122	273	1,553	183	
Clay Town	54,974	669	687	....	3	9	20	115	522	....	18
Cohoes	17,023	463		....	1	3	102	124	219	14	
Colonie Town	73,028	3,376	3,384	2	7	43	27	473	2,726	98	8
Corning	11,914	767		....	5	6	54	104	576	22	
Cortland	19,939	1,047	1,062	....	8	9	24	172	804	30	15
Cortland Town	28,709	401	409	....	2	12	45	64	266	12	8
Depew Village	18,021	616	624	....	1	8	55	99	391	62	8
Dewitt Town	22,065	1,088		....	1	9	4	202	850	22	
Dobbs Ferry Village	10,121	311	312	....	2	3	31	47	216	12	1

See footnotes at end of table.

Table 8.—Number of Offenses Known to the Police, Cities and Towns 10,000 and over in Population, 1993—Continued

City by State	Population	Crime Index total	Modified* Crime Index total	Murder and non-negligent man-slaughter	Forcible rape	Robbery	Aggra-vated assault	Burglary	Larceny-theft	Motor vehicle theft	Arson*
NEW YORK—Continued											
Dunkirk	14,052	660	665	....	3	13	20	106	502	16	5
East Aurora- Aurora Town	13,593	296	296	....	1	....	9	52	215	19	....
Eastchester Town	18,758	411	411	1	1	4	10	46	281	68	....
East Fishkill Town	22,365	301		....	....	2	7	85	197	10	
East Greenbush Town	14,243	432	435	....	1	3	53	53	317	5	3
East Hampton Town	14,157	533		....	....	1	10	172	335	15	
Endicott Village	13,674	773		....	....	1	56	124	579	13	
Evans Town	15,429	463	465	....	2	5	55	83	288	30	2
Fishkill Town	15,885	289		....	2	4	29	41	201	12	
Floral Park Village	16,147	282	286	....	....	23	....	46	172	41	4
Fredonia Village	10,418	310	311	....	....	....	17	13	276	4	1
Freeport Village	40,498	1,914		5	12	141	144	265	1,150	197	
Fulton	13,266	727	731	4	1	11	6	125	565	15	4
Garden City Village	21,722	728		2	....	12	9	84	523	98	
Gates Town	28,925	1,151	1,154	1	4	18	3	198	830	97	3
Geneva	14,387	671		....	2	6	87	108	467	1	
Glens Falls	14,277	1,272		....	10	12	247	196	790	17	
Glenville Town	21,668	370		....	1	2	20	92	235	20	
Gloversville	17,109	1,041		....	10	10	33	225	716	47	
Goshen	11,638	80	81	....	....	....	2	20	54	4	1
Greece Town	91,189	2,980		1	8	26	24	341	2,341	239	
Greenburgh Town	41,066	1,640	1,644	....	2	48	46	188	1,135	221	4
Hamburg Town	40,878	1,959		....	6	16	185	358	1,185	209	
Hamburg Village	10,564	271		....	1	4	33	38	181	14	
Harrison Town	23,401	531		....	3	4	2	86	359	77	
Hempstead Village	49,233	2,323	2,358	6	23	270	414	307	926	377	35
Irondequoit Town	53,006	3,120	3,124	2	7	55	9	492	2,335	220	4
Ithaca	29,531	2,224	2,227	....	12	58	33	434	1,654	33	3
Kenmore Village	16,964	469		....	1	10	29	89	306	34	
Kent Town	13,340	242	243	....	....	3	10	84	135	10	1
Kingston	23,051	1,217		....	10	22	46	173	909	57	
Lackawanna	20,532	1,005		....	3	35	252	192	387	136	
Lancaster Town	14,116	402	404	....	1	5	29	73	268	26	2
Lockport	25,210	1,372	1,376	....	14	30	190	282	792	64	4
Long Beach	34,435	1,168		2	1	57	71	284	547	206	
Lynbrook Village	19,542	392	393	....	1	12	12	65	242	60	1
Mamaroneck Town	11,542	255		....	....	2	....	50	145	58	
Mamaroneck Village	17,595	560	560	....	1	10	4	63	398	84	....
Manlius Town	31,024	591		....	2	5	9	120	442	13	
Middletown	24,684	1,410	1,418	....	17	41	62	264	984	42	8
Mount Pleasant Town	25,353	427	428	1	2	4	6	74	311	29	1
Mount Vernon	67,375	4,462	4,489	5	31	436	479	961	1,628	922	27
Newburgh	26,259	1,715	1,737	5	26	142	226	528	735	53	22
Newburgh Town	24,346	1,334		1	4	9	48	126	1,099	47	
New Castle Town	16,847	180		1	....	....	....	38	128	13	
New Hartford Town and Village	19,953	970	971	....	1	4	19	85	846	15	1
New Paltz Town and Village	11,523	522	524	1	1	5	65	70	362	18	2
New Windsor Town	23,212	559		3	4	8	67	96	345	36	
New York	7,347,257	600,346	604,789	1,946	2,818	86,001	62,778	99,207	235,132	112,464	4,443
Niagara Falls	62,002	4,938		3	39	207	196	1,068	2,932	493	
Niskayuna Town	19,276	546		....	....	4	35	85	409	13	
North Castle Town	10,181	195	195	....	....	2	9	44	132	8	....
North Greenbush Town	11,020	164	166	....	2	1	23	25	104	9	2
North Tonawanda	33,919	870	873	1	1	9	17	177	622	43	3
Ogden Town	17,114	341		....	1	....	4	61	266	9	
Ogdensburg	13,543	618		....	....	....	1	81	524	12	

Table 8. — Number of Offenses Known to the Police, Cities and Towns 10,000 and over in Population, 1993 — Continued

City by State	Population	Crime Index total	Modified* Crime Index total	Murder and non-negligent man-slaughter	Forcible rape	Robbery	Aggra-vated assault	Burglary	Larceny-theft	Motor vehicle theft	Arson*
NEW YORK – Continued											
Olean	17,288	762	764	....	2	7	74	84	587	8	2
Oneida	11,294	543		....	2	1	10	73	444	13	
Oneonta	13,336	361	363	....	2	2	13	71	266	7	2
Orangetown Town	35,253	1,008	1,013		4	25	68	217	652	42	5
Orchard Park Town	24,927	877	881		6	5	34	148	621	63	4
Ossining Village	23,035	672	677		2	62	14	148	409	37	5
Oswego	19,085	898		....	....	1	....	146	707	44	
Peekskill	19,931	877		1	5	33	116	141	508	73	
Port Washington Village	14,953	433	436	....	2	9	8	81	306	27	3
Poughkeepsie	29,202	2,176	2,185	10	11	172	131	520	1,204	128	9
Poughkeepsie Town	39,754	1,872		....	9	28	58	199	1,515	63	
Ramapo Town	63,855	1,476	1,485	3	4	31	19	256	1,139	24	9
Riverhead Town	23,287	1,070	1,074	....	5	29	177	326	511	22	4
Rochester	235,301	25,520	25,868	64	159	1,638	843	6,340	13,522	2,954	348
Rockville Centre Village	25,017	694		....	1	28	18	86	453	108	
Rome	45,358	906	914	....	9	14	39	215	580	49	8
Rotterdam Town	28,735	944	949	1	....	2	1	147	750	43	5
Rye	15,050	299	299	2	....	2	1	55	207	32	....
Saratoga Springs	26,139	1,595	1,602	....	20	13	314	245	963	40	7
Saugerties Town	14,726	326	329	....	....	2	22	102	192	8	3
Schenectady	65,712	4,219		5	40	170	448	1,077	2,237	242	
Schodack Town	10,471	186		....	3	1	8	38	127	9	
Shawangunk Town	10,201	84	84	....	....	....	14	24	37	9	....
Southampton Town	37,569	2,058	2,067	2	10	26	167	545	1,244	64	9
Southold Town	17,978	387	389	....	....	1	....	97	289	....	2
Spring Valley Village	22,064	1,288	1,294	2	5	87	40	185	909	60	6
Stony Point Town	12,967	118	118	1	....	....	3	35	79	....	....
Suffern Village	11,498	273	275	1	2	6	8	49	192	15	2
Syracuse	163,626	11,115	11,231	18	79	561	703	2,824	6,358	572	116
Tarrytown Village	11,627	299	300	....	....	4	20	50	189	36	1
Tonawanda	17,503	592		1	6	7	42	76	418	42	
Tonawanda Town	66,068	1,797	1,801	1	5	33	94	281	1,221	162	4
Ulster Town	12,476	653		....	6	3	39	108	480	17	
Utica	67,173	3,848	3,861	14	24	170	65	681	2,634	260	13
Vestal Town	27,053	447		....	....	4	8	43	377	15	
Wallkill Town	23,292	751	752	1	1	4	11	69	644	21	1
Warwick Town	15,689	217	217	....	....	....	9	39	160	9	....
Webster Town and Village	32,018	869	874	....	1	7	6	130	672	53	5
West Seneca Town	48,405	1,446		....	11	19	73	247	883	213	
White Plains	49,739	2,866	2,870	....	7	84	91	205	2,201	278	4
Yonkers	186,967	9,494	9,583	19	34	852	446	1,682	4,593	1,868	89
Yorktown Town	33,868	799	800	....	....	5	8	112	639	35	1
NORTH CAROLINA											
Albemarle	15,773	1,762	1,767	1	....	37	121	417	1,140	46	5
Asheboro	16,978	1,506	1,509	1	2	47	68	326	992	70	3
Asheville	63,791	5,268	5,276	9	44	142	261	1,148	3,311	353	8
Boone	13,107	426	426	....	1	1	19	55	341	9	....
Burlington	42,621	2,620	2,631	5	17	59	172	530	1,737	100	11
Carrboro	12,351	1,002	1,002	2	2	31	47	173	709	38	....
Cary	52,707	1,899	1,920	....	2	40	58	367	1,366	66	21
Chapel Hill	43,903	2,699	2,713	1	15	100	203	516	1,766	98	14
Charlotte	422,862	49,758	50,147	122	356	3,227	6,020	10,691	26,370	2,972	389
Concord	29,051	1,991	2,004	4	5	59	161	481	1,203	78	13
Durham	143,172	14,980	15,070	26	109	848	724	4,851	7,471	951	90

Table 8.—Number of Offenses Known to the Police, Cities and Towns 10,000 and over in Population, 1993—Continued

City by State	Population	Crime Index total	Modified* Crime Index total	Murder and non-negligent man-slaughter	Forcible rape	Robbery	Aggra-vated assault	Burglary	Larceny-theft	Motor vehicle theft	Arson*
NORTH CAROLINA—Continued											
Eden	15,451	977	980	2	....	19	56	197	651	52	3
Elizabeth City	15,725	1,214	1,220	3	8	35	98	280	761	29	6
Fayetteville	77,872	10,189	10,248	30	92	583	1,081	2,071	5,685	647	59
Garner	16,279	849	857	....	2	14	33	164	600	36	8
Gastonia	57,985	6,138	6,170	19	25	304	546	1,386	3,590	268	32
Goldsboro	43,283	4,208	4,220	6	20	207	444	910	2,419	202	12
Graham	11,284	693	693	1	5	11	106	137	400	33	....
Greensboro	192,951	15,303	15,399	27	105	791	797	3,177	9,657	749	96
Greenville	47,445	5,560	5,568	5	52	244	391	1,322	3,243	303	8
Havelock	21,732	588	591	....	1	11	43	151	357	25	3
Henderson	16,036	2,144	2,154	6	3	73	207	628	1,125	102	10
Hickory	29,134	3,414	3,444	3	25	136	174	707	2,214	155	30
High Point	71,879	7,084	7,132	12	39	291	592	2,060	3,714	376	48
Jacksonville	32,084	3,528	3,536	3	25	101	181	778	2,292	148	8
Kannapolis	31,122	1,140	1,151	5	11	56	76	318	605	69	11
Kernersville	11,556	860	861	1	1	17	43	150	606	42	1
Kinston	25,672	3,036	3,057	5	20	101	217	786	1,800	107	21
Laurinburg	12,488	1,190	1,204	1	8	28	88	284	736	45	14
Lenoir	14,449	1,289	1,296	1	5	37	102	241	848	55	7
Lexington	17,261	1,672	1,680	2	9	49	131	441	968	72	8
Lumberton	19,252	2,274	2,285	4	2	77	105	601	1,351	134	11
Matthews	14,474	608	611	....	4	8	45	133	401	17	3
Monroe	17,648	1,799	1,800	3	12	37	126	387	1,172	62	1
Mooresville	10,355	805	813	3	8	16	78	120	554	26	8
Morganton	15,676	1,250	1,252	....	4	22	63	246	876	39	2
New Bern	18,024	2,774	2,786	1	16	80	310	675	1,582	110	12
Newton	10,339	759	761	1	4	12	49	149	518	26	2
Raleigh	224,057	15,255	15,284	27	94	795	1,114	2,947	9,395	883	29
Reidsville	12,429	1,072	1,077	2	4	27	30	226	744	39	5
Roanoke Rapids	16,375	1,443	1,445	....	1	19	87	299	987	50	2
Rocky Mount	51,201	5,523	5,533	14	25	203	432	1,356	3,259	234	10
Salisbury	23,837	2,894	2,908	7	11	108	192	852	1,615	109	14
Sanford	15,317	2,509	2,521	2	11	46	146	541	1,702	61	12
Shelby	15,682	1,660	1,667	3	12	70	143	454	937	41	7
Tarboro	11,136	791	798	....	2	27	110	154	492	6	7
Thomasville	16,624	1,589	1,596	3	4	42	106	485	901	48	7
Wilmington	60,435	6,829	6,878	7	38	279	443	1,531	4,156	375	49
Wilson	37,942	4,882	4,897	8	19	186	360	1,348	2,695	266	15
Winston-Salem	147,098	18,338	18,499	36	177	1,053	1,566	4,783	9,590	1,133	161
NORTH DAKOTA											
Bismarck	51,400	2,269	2,269	....	7	3	34	369	1,773	83	....
Dickinson	16,289	395	395	....	1	....	5	17	367	5	....
Fargo	77,186	3,872	3,880	....	35	16	41	425	3,149	206	8
Grand Forks	49,409	2,692	2,706	....	19	14	28	234	2,202	195	14
Jamestown	15,319	418	424	....	8	3	9	60	306	32	6
Minot	34,500	1,484	1,493	....	15	5	17	185	1,206	56	9
West Fargo	12,680	451	457	....	4	....	2	72	344	29	6
Williston	13,053	495	495	....	1	2	3	31	432	26	....
OHIO											
Akron[1]	225,040			19	204	840		3,367	8,675	2,043	190
Alliance	23,774	2,418	2,439	....	25	96	120	428	1,600	149	21
Amherst	10,819	377	378	....	6	8	....	28	323	12	1

See footnotes at end of table.

Table 8. — Number of Offenses Known to the Police, Cities and Towns 10,000 and over in Population, 1993 — Continued

City by State	Population	Crime Index total	Modified* Crime Index total	Murder and non-negligent man-slaughter	Forcible rape	Robbery	Aggra-vated assault	Burglary	Larceny-theft	Motor vehicle theft	Arson*
OHIO — Continued											
Ashland	20,678	486	488	....	1	2	4	68	381	30	2
Athens	21,272	657	657	1	9	10	31	70	512	24	....
Barberton	28,062	1,490	1,509	....	7	22	176	206	990	89	19
Beavercreek	36,015	1,336	1,362	....	3	20	13	200	1,030	70	26
Bedford Heights	12,100	475	475	2	5	8	25	63	234	138	....
Bellefontaine	12,639	416	416	....	8	5	20	73	296	14	....
Bexley	13,541	599	603	....	1	33	4	104	426	31	4
Bowling Green	27,607	1,193	1,193	....	23	15	22	171	928	34	....
Brecksville	12,137	119	119	....	1	1	3	16	87	11	....
Brooklyn	11,316	420	421	....	1	11	....	10	309	89	1
Bucyrus	13,361	669	670	....	6	2	14	158	458	31	1
Canton	85,326	7,280	7,356	11	82	537	405	1,700	3,910	635	76
Centerville	21,708	719	724	....	5	7	13	134	525	35	5
Chillicothe	22,316	1,663	1,695	....	10	33	50	258	1,228	84	32
Cincinnati	366,591	30,923	31,504	39	449	2,327	2,806	6,154	17,085	2,063	581
Cleveland	505,730	40,005	40,661	167	834	4,297	3,012	8,031	13,494	10,170	656
Cleveland Heights	53,644	1,353	1,353	....	1	28	2	131	957	234	....
Columbus	646,933	56,322	57,351	105	658	3,887	2,496	13,055	29,051	7,070	1,029
Conneaut	13,305	338	338	1	4	2	6	72	240	13	....
Dayton	184,352	19,637	19,897	49	269	1,475	1,129	4,303	9,473	2,939	260
Delaware	21,289	1,028	1,040	1	24	16	17	202	719	49	12
Delhi Township	30,915	773	778	....	10	6	7	79	661	10	5
Dover	11,706	433	433	....	1	3	4	62	349	14	....
Dublin	18,160	713	713	....	2	8	4	157	506	36	....
Englewood	11,609	661	668	....	2	3	7	55	558	36	7
Fairborn	31,568	1,054	1,058	1	6	9	21	185	777	55	4
Fairfield	41,376	2,050	2,059	2	8	24	162	316	1,422	116	9
Forest Park	18,971	1,191	1,200	1	10	37	14	75	1,027	27	9
Franklin	11,555	574	574	....	1	5	21	130	392	25	....
Fremont	18,164	1,006	1,013	....	5	16	41	148	753	43	7
Gahanna	31,170	866	871	....	6	14	9	146	649	42	5
Garfield Heights	31,435	967	976	5	13	45	51	182	488	183	9
Girard	11,597	253	253	1	1	3	2	51	172	23	....
Goshen Township	12,975	229	230	....	1	1	7	65	139	16	1
Greenville	12,954	605	608	....	5	7	2	101	472	18	3
Grove City	21,068	770	770	....	7	16	5	79	612	51	....
Hamilton	64,232	5,373	5,422	6	81	246	601	1,152	2,889	398	49
Hilliard	13,675	663	675	....	6	4	14	126	480	33	12
Huber Heights	40,309	1,579	1,597	1	22	28	21	227	1,128	152	18
Jackson Township	32,775	1,329	1,333	2	8	34	23	129	1,065	68	4
Kent	28,886	1,117	1,127	....	10	26	78	194	743	66	10
Kettering	60,533	2,564	2,583	....	14	44	22	405	1,906	173	19
Lakewood	59,178	1,413	1,419	....	9	44	11	132	1,063	154	6
Lancaster[1]	35,566			....	3	18		224	1,184	60	....
Lebanon	11,072	597	598	....	20	9	17	118	410	23	1
Liberty Township	13,437	586		2	5	18	7	71	363	120	
Lima	45,530	4,441	4,498	6	48	207	784	1,009	2,182	205	57
Lorain	71,936	2,172	2,180	2	51	84	81	718	1,051	185	8
Loveland	11,026	386	386	1	1	2	6	52	316	8	....
Madison Township (Lake County)	18,348	482	491	....	5	2	44	88	322	21	9
Mansfield	53,563	5,420	5,436	3	50	128	1,151	1,265	2,613	210	16
Marietta	15,223	782	782	1	9	8	15	84	641	24	....
Marion	34,718	2,297	2,300	1	16	37	20	587	1,533	103	3
Marysville	10,452	197	200	....	1	4	7	32	143	10	3
Mason	12,137	348	350	....	4	6	8	52	274	4	2
Massillon	31,397	1,368	1,368	2	11	35	35	260	926	99	....

See footnotes at end of table.

Table 8. — Number of Offenses Known to the Police, Cities and Towns 10,000 and over in Population, 1993 — Continued

City by State	Population	Crime Index total	Modified* Crime Index total	Murder and non-negligent man-slaughter	Forcible rape	Robbery	Aggra-vated assault	Burglary	Larceny-theft	Motor vehicle theft	Arson*
OHIO — Continued											
Maumee	15,890	734	735	....	....	17	37	74	569	37	1
Mentor	49,543	1,462	1,467	....	6	15	19	178	1,126	118	5
Miamisburg	18,090	1,113	1,119	....	6	9	19	182	785	112	6
Miami Township	23,034	718	725	1	12	4	14	99	571	17	7
Middletown	47,620	2,611	2,632	2	23	68	87	612	1,708	111	21
Newark	45,260	2,499		....	29	51	410	444	1,445	120	
New Philadelphia	16,033	485	486	....	3	9	17	45	395	16	1
Niles	21,532	1,003	1,003	....	1	13	78	128	700	83	....
North Canton	14,959	352	352	....	3	11	2	80	241	15	....
North Ridgeville	22,125	368	369	....	1	2	53	76	214	22	1
Norton	11,845	339	343	....	....	5	15	68	241	10	4
Norwalk	15,141	363	363	....	1	1	....	43	317	1	....
Norwood	23,325	1,397	1,403	....	16	61	33	217	1,015	55	6
Oregon	18,394	1,064	1,071	....	7	34	33	134	759	97	7
Perkins Township	11,029	428	428	1	1	14	11	52	341	8	....
Perrysburg	13,148	369	369	....	....	1	2	46	305	15	....
Perry Township	30,973	990	1,000	....	5	19	55	203	647	61	10
Piqua	20,857	1,177	1,180	....	26	10	8	169	921	43	3
Poland Township	11,242	118	119	....	1	....	....	26	79	12	1
Portsmouth	22,824	2,044	2,064	1	30	33	95	560	1,239	86	20
Reading	11,860	331	331	....	6	4	4	59	231	27	....
Salem	12,820	109	110	....	....	....	6	4	89	10	1
Sandusky	30,234	2,138	2,140	3	29	25	31	465	1,465	120	2
Seven Hills	12,240	125	126	....	1	2	4	20	86	12	1
Shaker Heights	31,006	1,304	1,310	2	7	96	19	443	503	234	6
Sharonville	13,957	875	876	....	4	12	8	175	673	3	1
Solon	19,567	406	406	....	....	5	7	50	304	40	....
Springdale	10,694	1,206	1,207	....	2	16	12	79	1,056	41	1
Springfield	70,868	6,527	6,533	6	59	208	786	963	4,048	457	6
Springfield Township	39,356	1,507	1,520	....	15	38	126	324	968	36	13
Steubenville	22,023	1,196		2	6	43	370	189	519	67	
Stow	28,839	732	732	....	4	14	12	74	612	16	....
Streetsboro	10,291	397		....	4	5	9	89	282	8	
Strongsville	37,803	801	810	....	2	16	4	181	535	63	9
Sylvania	17,840	217	217	....	1	5	5	47	147	12	....
Sylvania Township	23,181	1,043	1,046	1	3	14	8	141	787	89	3
Tallmadge	15,271	592	607	....	4	10	18	104	399	57	15
Tiffin	18,646	747	750	1	4	13	12	106	601	10	3
Toledo	331,416	28,461	28,818	45	357	1,594	1,195	5,502	15,251	4,517	357
Troy	20,201	758	770	1	8	11	5	109	600	24	12
Twinsburg	10,759	208	212	....	....	4	2	41	149	12	4
Union Township (Butler County)	40,576	1,322	1,349	2	3	11	42	309	923	32	27
Union Township (Clermont County)	34,101	2,252	2,261	1	15	31	11	182	1,909	103	9
University Heights	14,766	313	313	....	2	14	18	62	186	31	....
Upper Arlington	36,054	978	986	....	11	22	18	132	779	16	8
Urbana	11,537	538	540	....	8	6	19	54	430	21	2
Vandalia	13,909	455	459	....	6	4	6	70	340	29	4
Van Wert	11,281	596	605	....	16	....	38	108	402	32	9
Vermilion	11,433	297	297	....	3	1	4	30	248	11	....
Wadsworth	16,434	301	307	....	4	4	5	40	232	16	6
Warrensville Heights	16,092	781	790	3	9	69	66	114	353	167	9
Washington Court House	13,267	429	430	....	4	12	8	92	303	10	1
West Carrollton	14,669	609	610	2	6	7	18	104	406	66	1
Westerville	32,708	1,121	1,138	....	13	17	14	169	885	23	17
Westlake	28,797	424	425	....	2	7	10	96	249	60	1
Wickliffe	14,237	320	320	....	1	4	13	56	216	30	....

Table 8.—Number of Offenses Known to the Police, Cities and Towns 10,000 and over in Population, 1993—Continued

City by State	Population	Crime Index total	Modified* Crime Index total	Murder and non-negligent man-slaughter	Forcible rape	Robbery	Aggra-vated assault	Burglary	Larceny-theft	Motor vehicle theft	Arson*
OHIO—Continued											
Wilmington	11,534	570	570	1	9	6	33	60	442	19	....
Wooster	22,644	936	943	....	8	7	27	147	718	29	7
Worthington	15,297	548	552	....	2	10	5	99	414	18	4
Xenia	24,676	1,428	1,429	3	7	19	79	162	1,132	26	1
Youngstown	94,986	8,141	8,419	47	79	771	1,223	2,041	2,637	1,343	278
Zanesville	27,210	1,526	1,574	3	14	40	156	228	977	108	48
OKLAHOMA											
Ada	15,664	841	848	....	5	10	70	180	541	35	7
Altus	22,039	1,347	1,348	1	....	16	52	345	904	29	1
Ardmore	23,389	2,413	2,415	3	4	38	127	662	1,440	139	2
Bartlesville	34,714	1,707	1,725	1	13	17	138	359	1,141	38	18
Bethany	20,339	931	938	....	3	7	21	188	648	64	7
Bixby	10,461	167	168	....	1	....	6	56	88	16	1
Broken Arrow	63,238	2,037	2,043	....	13	15	88	386	1,427	108	6
Chickasha	15,221	973	980	4	11	15	143	289	458	53	7
Claremore	14,365	542	543	....	5	2	26	108	370	31	1
Del City	23,953	1,260	1,262	2	19	28	21	296	787	107	2
Duncan	22,469	978	984	....	6	11	34	238	649	40	6
Durant	13,282	845	850	2	3	4	39	173	575	49	5
Edmond	57,591	2,110	2,131	1	13	21	64	375	1,476	160	21
Elk City	10,543	544	545	....	6	5	14	139	349	31	1
El Reno	15,891	775	793	4	12	24	41	184	453	57	18
Enid	45,441	3,763	3,792	1	31	37	347	717	2,486	144	29
Guthrie	10,612	535	541	....	10	8	37	152	291	37	6
Lawton	87,874	6,046	6,079	12	62	161	590	1,262	3,635	324	33
McAlester	17,144	790	799	....	6	6	64	172	494	48	9
Miami	13,173	811	811	....	9	7	38	165	541	51	....
Midwest City	53,273	3,360	3,370	1	36	73	133	713	2,093	311	10
Moore	41,996	1,807	1,815	....	24	18	100	428	1,081	156	8
Muskogee	38,639	3,195	3,215	6	39	109	298	837	1,663	243	20
Mustang	10,973	349	351	....	6	....	14	64	251	14	2
Norman	84,356	4,553	4,563	2	34	38	128	1,040	3,009	302	10
Oklahoma City	457,448	51,335	51,755	80	515	1,724	4,161	10,000	29,316	5,539	420
Okmulgee	13,758	983	990	2	7	19	108	203	575	69	7
Owasso	12,390	379	385	....	5	5	9	84	249	27	6
Ponca City	26,639	1,185	1,209	1	20	6	35	291	774	58	24
Sand Springs	16,168	777	778	....	5	18	42	137	462	113	1
Sapulpa	18,434	968	972	....	3	7	42	226	566	124	4
Shawnee	26,925	1,607	1,621	....	16	14	93	380	1,021	83	14
Stillwater	36,730	1,517	1,535	2	16	15	68	294	1,080	42	18
Tahlequah	11,207	640	641	2	5	8	17	163	419	26	1
The Village	10,730	908	910	....	4	16	46	139	632	71	2
Tulsa	378,350	29,354	29,603	54	339	1,143	3,385	7,196	12,790	4,447	249
Woodward	12,422	438	438	....	4	1	52	109	257	15	....
Yukon	22,054	887	899	....	5	6	18	173	641	44	12
OREGON											
Albany	30,976	2,837	2,873	....	23	26	27	336	2,263	162	36
Ashland	16,908	985	997	1	5	11	8	154	772	34	12
Astoria	10,437	558	561	....	8	3	20	142	353	32	3
Beaverton	58,387	3,235	3,264	....	17	52	122	523	2,234	287	29
Bend	22,968	2,421	2,429	....	10	26	86	353	1,865	81	8
Coos Bay	17,470	1,207	1,213	....	6	15	14	253	852	67	6
Corvallis	45,714	2,380	2,406	1	18	28	57	344	1,856	76	26

Table 8. — Number of Offenses Known to the Police, Cities and Towns 10,000 and over in Population, 1993 — Continued

City by State	Population	Crime Index total	Modified* Crime Index total	Murder and non-negligent man-slaughter	Forcible rape	Robbery	Aggra-vated assault	Burglary	Larceny-theft	Motor vehicle theft	Arson*
OREGON — Continued											
Dallas	10,187	368	368	....	6	....	....	41	304	17	....
Eugene	118,390	8,697	8,754	3	64	166	237	1,381	6,471	375	57
Forest Grove	14,579	655	660	2	3	8	7	117	478	40	5
Gladstone	10,846	579	586	....	5	9	17	99	382	67	7
Grants Pass	18,518	2,003	2,011	....	6	27	9	313	1,542	106	8
Gresham	75,936	4,009	4,038	1	52	110	111	736	2,320	679	29
Hermiston	10,877	687	688	....	4	3	13	101	526	40	1
Hillsboro	42,008	1,594	1,609	....	3	43	50	231	1,138	129	15
Keizer	24,561	1,148	1,159	....	7	13	19	174	838	97	11
Klamath Falls	18,458	919	924	2	10	25	60	244	500	78	5
La Grande	12,372	469	472	2	7	3	10	93	334	20	3
Lake Oswego	32,588	897	913	....	7	10	29	167	629	55	16
Lebanon	11,525	1,183	1,183	....	1	2	75	133	934	38	....
McMinnville	19,652	1,117	1,124	....	9	15	31	161	840	61	7
Medford	50,517	4,584	4,628	1	35	39	206	639	3,471	193	44
Milwaukie	19,559	914	919	1	11	24	15	164	565	134	5
Newberg	14,589	681	687	....	5	3	27	91	527	28	6
North Bend	10,069	677	684	....	5	7	3	116	525	21	7
Ontario	10,394	970	975	....	2	9	44	127	742	46	5
Oregon City	15,753	1,041	1,048	2	3	16	55	169	707	89	7
Portland	454,889	51,765	52,369	58	479	2,305	5,603	7,845	27,016	8,459	604
Roseburg	17,787	1,381	1,396	1	12	30	15	227	1,037	59	15
Salem	114,311	9,802	9,862	7	67	208	109	1,592	7,122	697	60
Springfield	47,215	3,644	3,672	2	20	51	178	624	2,605	164	28
The Dalles	10,067	902	910	....	7	7	30	131	673	54	8
Tigard	32,885	2,286	2,308	3	6	56	14	274	1,797	136	22
Tualatin	17,578	821	831	....	2	11	21	158	565	64	10
West Linn	17,929	419	425	....	5	5	43	66	284	16	6
Woodburn	14,082	1,017	1,029	2	10	22	40	109	756	78	12
PENNSYLVANIA											
Allentown	106,899	7,508	7,550	6	42	324	347	1,682	4,659	448	42
Altoona	52,708	1,566	1,588	....	16	40	107	417	888	98	22
Aston Township	15,307	343	349	....	5	6	30	52	218	32	6
Beaver Falls	10,904	240	241	2	1	24	24	58	117	14	1
Bensalem Township	57,649	2,840	2,865	3	14	93	99	416	1,656	559	25
Berwick	10,869	174	176	....	1	2	6	43	103	19	2
Bethel Park	34,075	445	447	....	3	8	9	56	294	75	2
Bethlehem	72,692	2,877	2,884	1	18	73	134	533	1,944	174	7
Bethlehem Township	16,673	460	461	....	1	4	9	29	405	12	1
Bloomsburg Town	12,324	359	360	....	4	2	3	68	259	23	1
Brentwood	10,748	193	194	....	1	7	17	33	116	19	1
Bristol	10,461	543	552	....	3	27	61	59	327	66	9
Butler	16,300	544	548	1	3	3	29	68	400	40	4
Butler Township (Butler County)	22,140	511	511	....	3	1	10	35	428	34	....
Caln Township	12,178	565	565	....	4	14	37	68	392	50	....
Carlisle	18,999	700	707	3	6	36	22	86	518	29	7
Center Township	10,903	54	54	....	....	2	6	18	22	6	....
Chester	41,278	5,333	5,395	28	53	538	1,309	958	1,494	953	62
Coatesville	11,555	632	635	2	6	76	41	110	331	66	3
Columbia	11,272	529	534	....	8	12	40	91	345	33	5
Cranberry Township	15,039	241	241	....	1	....	....	32	184	24	....
Cumru Township	19,258	591	591	....	....	8	53	63	443	24	....
Doylestown Township	14,728	235	239	....	2	1	40	27	159	6	4
Dunmore	15,240	371	372	....	4	6	12	30	299	20	1

145

Table 8.— Number of Offenses Known to the Police, Cities and Towns 10,000 and over in Population, 1993—Continued

City by State	Population	Crime Index total	Modified* Crime Index total	Murder and non-negligent man-slaughter	Forcible rape	Robbery	Aggra-vated assault	Burglary	Larceny-theft	Motor vehicle theft	Arson*
PENNSYLVANIA—Continued											
East Lampeter Township	12,180	541	541	....	1	8	9	65	432	26	....
East Norriton Township	13,525	367	367	....	1	4	6	40	297	19	....
Elizabethtown	10,400	231	234	....	3	3	12	41	160	12	3
Emmaus	11,630	367	368	....	3	3	11	45	291	14	1
Ephrata	13,020	347	347	....	3	3	10	50	267	14	....
Erie	109,749	5,474	5,537	7	59	426	345	999	3,261	377	63
Falls Township (Buck County)	35,527	1,034	1,038	....	3	22	24	174	676	135	4
Hampden Township	20,693	511	512	....	1	3	32	57	400	18	1
Hampton Township	15,802	215	215	....	....	1	16	25	162	11	....
Hanover	15,273	668	678	2	....	6	12	98	529	21	10
Harrisburg	53,666	4,976	4,998	13	67	539	525	1,043	2,382	407	22
Haverford Township	50,603	601	602	1	2	13	23	103	408	51	1
Hazleton	25,115	616	618	....	5	7	16	222	342	24	2
Hilltown Township	10,741	231	231	....	2	....	4	42	171	12	....
Johnstown	27,806	1,310	1,320	....	19	48	123	296	762	62	10
Kingston	14,255	435	445	....	3	4	11	33	367	17	10
Lancaster	57,423	4,485	4,515	11	45	273	177	882	2,784	313	30
Lancaster Township	13,386	434	437	....	....	7	3	79	307	38	3
Lansdowne	11,780	241	241	....	2	6	19	28	160	26	....
Lebanon	25,364	1,002	1,004	6	11	27	32	155	743	28	2
Logan Township	12,567	323	324	....	3	4	12	42	255	7	1
Lower Allen Township	15,484	419	419	....	2	4	9	34	363	7	....
Lower Gwynedd Township	10,108	196	196	....	1	3	8	46	120	18	....
Lower Makefield Township	25,463	520	520	1	....	1	4	107	359	48	....
Lower Moreland Township	11,945	261	262	....	1	3	6	55	157	39	1
Lower Paxton Township	39,755	1,570	1,574	1	7	37	115	229	1,143	38	4
Lower Salford Township	10,896	153	·154	....	2	....	22	20	103	6	1
Manheim Township	29,317	914	917	....	1	18	18	98	736	43	3
Marple Township	23,473	489	490	....	1	5	24	57	376	26	1
McCandless	29,217	469	469	....	....	2	5	49	384	29	....
Middletown Township	45,097	1,793		....	5	22	21	206	1,319	220	
Mifflin County Regional	17,205	367	368	....	4	4	6	61	286	6	1
Millcreek Township	47,529	1,263	1,279	1	10	14	18	273	900	47	16
Montgomery Township	12,363	636	637	1	....	3	3	45	537	47	1
Moon Township	19,928	382	382	....	3	4	7	43	262	63	....
Morrisville	10,019	342	342	....	3	13	12	41	208	65	....
Muhlenberg Township	12,827	521	522	1	1	8	10	61	388	52	1
Murrysville	17,501	337	340	....	1	3	21	55	249	8	3
Nanticoke	12,210	280	282	....	....	6	12	46	207	9	2
Nazareth Area	10,350	258	258	....	....	3	11	35	200	9	....
Nether Providence Township	13,429	268	269	....	....	2	19	35	182	30	1
Newberry Township	12,649	304	305	....	3	....	4	95	191	11	1
New Castle	28,238	1,105	1,127	3	15	63	60	296	549	119	22
Newtown	13,892	209	209	....	....	....	4	38	139	28	....
Newtown Township (Delaware County)	11,536	156	156	....	3	2	1	32	104	14	....
Northampton Township	35,942	265	267	....	2	1	12	62	165	23	2
North Huntingdon Township	28,584	425	426	....	1	7	21	76	282	38	1
Oil City	11,930	478	486	....	5	2	6	77	366	22	8
Pennridge Regional	21,337	165	165	....	1	....	19	20	116	9	....
Penn Township (York County)	11,834	420	427	....	5	5	2	59	331	18	7
Peters Township	14,685	224	231	....	....	2	1	35	167	19	7
Philadelphia	1,559,534	97,659	99,941	439	785	11,531	6,821	15,117	39,181	23,785	2,282
Philadelphia State Police	....	4	4	....	....	....	1	....	2	1	....
Phoenixville	15,597	517	517	....	3	14	17	63	335	85	....
Pittsburgh	368,473	28,613	28,948	80	226	2,784	1,389	4,611	13,017	6,506	335
Plains Township	11,154	390	391	....	2	4	14	78	271	21	1

146

Table 8. — Number of Offenses Known to the Police, Cities and Towns 10,000 and over in Population, 1993 — Continued

City by State	Population	Crime Index total	Modified* Crime Index total	Murder and non-negligent man-slaughter	Forcible rape	Robbery	Aggra-vated assault	Burglary	Larceny-theft	Motor vehicle theft	Arson*
PENNSYLVANIA – Continued											
Pottsville	16,751	337	337	....	3	3	14	57	248	12	....
Radnor Township	29,137	539	540	1	2	4	10	66	420	36	1
Reading	79,377	6,405	6,457	6	42	555	334	1,521	3,362	585	52
Richland Township	14,146	381	384	....	4	....	72	52	238	15	3
Rostraver Township	11,393	400	401	....	....	2	5	42	308	43	1
Salisbury Township	13,603	461	461	1	1	2	5	36	405	11	....
Scott Township (Allegheny County)	17,377	292	295	1	1	2	3	62	176	47	3
Scranton	80,098	2,829	2,854	2	26	86	117	487	1,870	241	25
Shaler Township	30,995	408	409	....	1	4	20	46	293	44	1
S.W. Mercer County Regional	10,448	449	449	....	4	20	59	76	269	21	....
South Whitehall Township	18,536	850	854	....	2	8	11	81	720	28	4
Springfield Township (Delaware County)	24,525	956	960	....	2	14	68	78	649	145	4
Springfield Township (Montgomery County)	19,909	424	425	2	....	16	12	47	282	65	1
Spring Garden Township	11,376	380	381	....	1	6	1	45	321	6	1
Spring Township (Berk County)	19,185	213	214	....	5	2	5	29	162	10	1
Stroud Township	10,759	605	608	....	2	5	14	45	509	30	3
Swatara Township	19,958	1,443	1,446	....	8	24	73	187	1,064	87	3
Swissvale	10,504	429	438	2	5	18	18	65	200	121	9
Towamencin Township	14,381	319	320	....	1	2	7	58	243	8	1
Tredyffrin Township	28,453	571	577	....	....	10	20	115	384	42	6
Upper Allen Township	13,548	205	205	....	....	....	9	28	165	3	....
Upper Chichester Township	15,231	494	497	....	4	18	21	61	317	73	3
Upper Darby Township	82,408	2,797	2,798	2	12	93	127	298	1,907	358	1
Upper Gwynedd Township	12,381	208	211	....	1	3	3	30	166	5	3
Upper Providence Township (Delaware County)	10,870	93	93	....	1	....	10	19	53	10	....
Warrington Township	12,353	263	268	....	....	1	6	58	177	21	5
Warwick Township (Lancaster County)	11,796	63	63	....	....	....	2	2	58	1	....
West Chester	18,652	914	920	....	4	29	55	118	653	55	6
West Goshen Township	18,354	585	586	....	1	4	34	54	440	52	1
West Hempfield Township	13,137	241	241	1	4	1	15	30	180	10	....
West Hills Regional	11,538	61	61	....	....	....	14	12	30	5	....
West Lampeter Township	10,013	233	237	....	2	....	9	18	194	10	4
West Manchester Township	14,586	773	773	....	....	12	6	55	684	16	....
West Mifflin	23,739	1,118	1,121	2	2	27	79	94	535	379	3
Westtown Township	27,749	462	464	....	....	2	33	80	308	39	2
West Whiteland Township	12,590	517	519	....	1	3	5	45	408	55	2
Whitehall	14,124	125	125	....	3	1	2	9	87	23	....
Whitehall Township	23,123	1,113	1,119	....	2	15	27	162	823	84	6
Wilkes-Barre	47,091	1,887	1,893	2	21	61	134	359	1,176	134	6
Wilkinsburg	20,545	1,639	1,650	6	19	184	317	334	432	347	11
Williamsport	32,469	2,083	2,097	2	8	48	43	439	1,477	66	14
Yeadon	12,120	474	479	....	....	24	19	62	262	107	5
York Township	24,517	598	602	1	5	1	11	105	455	20	4
RHODE ISLAND											
Barrington	15,831	312	314	....	....	5	8	31	263	5	2
Bristol	21,602	399	399	....	....	....	25	72	287	15	....
Burrillville	16,057	207	208	....	1	....	14	63	120	9	1
Central Falls	16,150	985	985	4	8	24	188	214	318	229	....
Coventry	31,313	765	781	....	4	1	34	180	509	37	16
Cranston	76,626	2,733	2,749	....	9	36	83	616	1,650	339	16
Cumberland	28,731	986	987	....	2	6	179	156	583	60	1
East Greenwich	11,952	293	293	....	1	1	8	82	188	13	....
East Providence	50,343	1,516	1,536	....	2	20	53	266	965	210	20
Johnston	26,261	940	945	....	1	7	17	190	577	148	5

City by State	Population	Crime Index total	Modified* Crime Index total	Murder and non-negligent man-slaughter	Forcible rape	Robbery	Aggra-vated assault	Burglary	Larceny-theft	Motor vehicle theft	Arson*
RHODE ISLAND—Continued											
Lincoln	17,854	715	716	....	8	3	3	100	467	134	1
Middletown	19,334	575	579	....	5	5	146	43	353	23	4
Narragansett	15,334	499	499	....	4	1	59	149	263	23	....
Newport	28,045	2,347	2,390	1	16	49	219	499	1,479	84	43
North Kingstown	24,342	576	580	....	....	....	18	131	402	25	4
North Providence	31,751	946	954	....	9	13	58	216	508	142	8
North Smithfield	10,385	274	274	....	1	1	56	64	138	14	....
Pawtucket	71,956	4,207	4,221	2	29	117	166	1,227	1,898	768	14
Portsmouth	16,747	225	226	....	4	2	18	46	135	20	1
Providence	159,178	15,162	15,546	22	114	636	601	4,240	6,433	3,116	384
Smithfield	18,960	282	285	....	4	3	8	54	170	43	3
South Kingstown	25,207	459	459	....	9	2	12	91	323	22	....
Tiverton	14,219	368	370	....	....	5	2	99	228	34	2
Warren	11,372	360	360	....	1	....	....	61	280	18	....
Warwick	86,062	3,960	4,008	3	17	35	308	517	2,444	636	48
Westerly	22,110	329	330	2	....	2	10	84	214	17	1
Woonsocket	42,330	1,124	1,132	1	11	27	104	238	626	117	8
SOUTH CAROLINA											
Aiken	22,677	1,400	1,402	2	9	41	111	263	889	85	2
Anderson	28,241	2,477	2,480	8	15	134	394	568	1,221	137	3
Beaufort	10,097	1,416	1,417	3	9	49	162	201	948	44	1
Cayce	11,465	958	958	....	7	39	90	135	618	69	....
Charleston	82,203	6,661	6,663	12	35	340	602	1,071	4,091	510	2
Clemson	11,535	547	547	....	5	3	32	119	363	25	....
Columbia	99,929	12,363	12,376	22	94	666	1,422	2,090	7,316	753	13
Conway	11,030	1,267	1,268	2	7	37	188	135	842	56	1
Easley	17,297	663	663	2	6	23	81	132	385	34	....
Florence	31,081	3,457	3,463	1	20	180	344	629	2,108	175	6
Gaffney	14,625	551	551	1	3	20	39	162	292	34	....
Georgetown	10,057	1,349	1,350	2	7	35	193	303	746	63	1
Goose Creek	27,288	725	726	1	6	7	50	100	531	30	1
Greenville	59,697	6,381	6,407	9	38	254	752	842	4,126	360	26
Greenwood	22,475	2,055	2,058	5	19	63	583	307	1,012	66	3
Greer	10,961	843	843	2	3	36	119	155	495	33	....
Hanahan	12,812	612	612	....	10	8	45	113	409	27	....
Irmo	12,544	349	349	....	2	7	14	67	245	14	....
Laurens	10,124	682	683	1	5	32	127	141	348	28	1
Mauldin	12,119	314	314	....	1	3	24	41	227	18	....
Mount Pleasant	32,393	1,476	1,476	1	3	8	39	164	1,188	73	....
Myrtle Beach	27,766	5,084	5,084	2	31	129	247	996	3,451	228	....
Newberry	10,714	725	726	....	5	15	142	82	465	16	1
North Augusta	16,567	843	844	....	3	18	78	170	500	74	1
North Charleston	75,204	9,323	9,334	9	98	430	1,000	1,484	5,472	830	11
Orangeburg	14,058	1,669	1,674	1	7	82	157	338	1,012	72	5
Rock Hill	44,876	4,094	4,099	6	23	120	816	710	2,270	149	5
Simpsonville	13,421	317	317	....	4	4	12	65	219	13	....
Spartanburg	45,613	6,893	6,903	10	42	319	1,194	1,158	3,830	340	10
Summerville	23,153	1,811	1,811	1	13	41	103	314	1,244	95	....
Sumter	42,932	3,230	3,232	5	22	179	421	810	1,620	173	2
West Columbia	10,637	1,572	1,575	1	10	62	156	271	1,003	69	3
SOUTH DAKOTA											
Aberdeen	25,199	894	904	1	14	4	33	122	692	28	10
Brookings	16,726	547	547	....	3	2	3	110	403	26	....
Mitchell	13,946	615	619	....	11	1	16	134	434	19	4

Table 8.—Number of Offenses Known to the Police, Cities and Towns 10,000 and over in Population, 1993—Continued

City by State	Population	Crime Index total	Modified* Crime Index total	Murder and non-negligent man-slaughter	Forcible rape	Robbery	Aggra-vated assault	Burglary	Larceny-theft	Motor vehicle theft	Arson*
SOUTH DAKOTA—Continued											
Pierre	13,371	800	803	....	8	....	32	125	610	25	3
Rapid City	57,617	3,793		1	45	25	187	481	2,912	142	
Sioux Falls	106,315	4,875	4,904	2	103	44	326	735	3,470	195	29
Vermillion	10,112	285	285	....	2	1	5	52	218	7	....
Watertown	18,256	760	762	....	9	4	16	95	613	23	2
Yankton	13,337	507	510	....	4	3	19	91	370	20	3
TENNESSEE											
Athens	11,086	741	744	....	6	11	77	111	486	50	3
Bartlett	30,550	1,005		....	2	16	50	181	721	35	
Brentwood	18,811	518	518	1	8	2	3	85	397	22	....
Bristol	24,833	1,089	1,095	....	15	4	61	198	773	38	6
Brownsville	10,442	724	725	....	11	16	132	176	338	51	1
Chattanooga	155,140	16,338	16,434	38	154	709	2,131	3,144	7,907	2,255	96
Clarksville	85,637	4,627	4,627	1	87	112	858	875	2,553	141	....
Cleveland	32,929	1,840	1,841	1	12	23	265	369	1,038	132	1
Collierville	16,862	487	488	1	1	3	11	58	380	33	1
Columbia	32,393	2,359	2,373	5	18	61	220	620	1,342	93	14
Cookeville	24,021	888	895	1	4	7	45	145	631	55	7
Dyersburg	17,205	1,345	1,345	4	19	20	131	240	871	60	....
East Ridge	21,087	1,030	1,030	1	3	23	33	229	649	92	....
Franklin	22,698	1,285	1,289	1	13	28	86	157	925	75	4
Gallatin	19,873	1,148	1,151	1	18	20	159	206	687	57	3
Germantown	34,527	676	678	....	1	6	3	61	573	32	2
Goodlettsville	11,911	1,370	1,371	....	....	26	50	127	1,075	92	1
Greeneville	13,912	836	837	....	6	6	47	273	446	58	1
Hendersonville	34,593	1,082	1,083	....	11	13	125	217	712	4	1
Humboldt	10,231	792	792	1	10	18	179	110	456	18	....
Jackson	51,592	5,955	5,990	19	33	247	630	1,264	3,475	287	35
Johnson City	51,131	2,749	2,776	3	13	30	77	530	1,879	217	27
Kingsport	38,399	2,494	2,509	2	5	32	184	405	1,728	138	15
Knoxville	169,751	13,365	13,538	14	102	596	2,200	2,817	6,027	1,609	173
Lawrenceburg	10,865	570	570	....	2	10	69	101	354	34	....
Maryville	20,228	705	709	....	19	8	111	111	406	50	4
McMinnville	11,465	892	901	1	6	8	108	195	472	102	9
Memphis	618,981	62,150	62,735	198	725	5,366	3,824	15,314	23,434	13,289	585
Millington	18,220	925	926	2	6	20	71	293	449	84	1
Morristown	22,121	1,467	1,485	2	13	18	53	234	1,008	139	18
Murfreesboro	51,139	3,706	3,717	3	11	86	305	619	2,482	200	11
Nashville	513,648	55,500		87	577	2,709	5,791	9,149	32,456	4,731	
Oak Ridge	28,388	1,740	1,747	1	8	35	54	223	1,325	94	7
Red Bank	11,771	712	714	....	6	10	70	123	446	57	2
Shelbyville	15,394	676	679	1	5	13	74	185	376	22	3
Smyrna	15,581	571	576	....	7	19	24	110	387	24	5
Springfield	12,727	1,137	1,137	1	7	22	168	122	795	22	....
Tullahoma	17,489	792		....	4	7	17	150	558	56	
Union City	10,741	1,104	1,111	1	7	12	81	266	706	31	7
TEXAS											
Abilene	110,222	5,474	5,507	8	75	134	673	1,089	3,323	172	33
Alice	20,475	1,532	1,554	....	9	10	122	389	961	41	22
Allen[1]	22,049			....	7	1		149	497	38	3
Alvin	20,835	1,317	1,319	2	5	17	53	178	1,006	56	2

See footnotes at end of table.

Table 8.—Number of Offenses Known to the Police, Cities and Towns 10,000 and over in Population, 1993—Continued

City by State	Population	Crime Index total	Modified* Crime Index total	Murder and non-negligent man-slaughter	Forcible rape	Robbery	Aggra-vated assault	Burglary	Larceny-theft	Motor vehicle theft	Arson*
TEXAS—Continued											
Amarillo	164,234	13,868	13,937	11	89	208	821	2,739	9,351	649	69
Andrews	11,062	347	347	....	....	1	18	71	246	11	....
Angleton	18,713	882	886	1	15	19	69	156	572	50	4
Arlington	281,336	20,202	20,299	7	146	710	1,396	3,977	11,514	2,452	97
Athens	11,141	677	678	1	2	2	142	158	345	27	1
Austin	502,018	51,468	52,078	37	271	1,555	1,148	8,453	35,647	4,357	610
Balch Springs	18,825	1,521	1,544	1	19	36	332	257	743	133	23
Bay City[3]	19,060			2	5	27	80		1,379	65	3
Baytown	67,754	4,554	4,572	10	46	106	227	754	2,898	513	18
Beaumont	117,766	12,577	12,636	23	200	683	560	2,610	6,939	1,562	59
Bedford	45,184	1,637	1,641	....	16	23	47	300	1,148	103	4
Beeville	13,511	767	768	....	2	7	79	192	474	13	1
Bellaire	14,546	603	604	1	2	24	25	149	357	45	1
Belton	12,526	462	463	....	7	10	24	84	316	21	1
Benbrook	20,971	512	513	1	7	9	15	66	357	57	1
Big Spring	23,648	1,325	1,337	2	19	17	107	348	773	59	12
Borger	15,653	551	553	....	3	5	29	91	404	19	2
Brenham	12,347	831	837	....	8	10	77	146	563	27	6
Brownsville	107,838	11,393	11,424	17	28	281	771	2,209	7,291	796	31
Brownwood	18,860	1,242	1,252	....	13	14	106	239	832	38	10
Bryan	57,657	4,368	4,376	2	54	87	369	853	2,719	284	8
Burkburnett	10,167	295	308	....	1	1	14	36	235	8	13
Burleson	17,648	598	606	1	3	6	21	135	399	33	8
Canyon	11,617	238	239	....	2	....	6	37	186	7	1
Carrollton	90,656	3,974	4,001	4	20	65	117	831	2,542	395	27
Cedar Hill	23,034	816	819	1	4	6	16	194	533	62	3
Cleburne	23,140	1,506	1,514	3	1	9	69	208	1,173	43	8
College Station	56,777	2,280	2,281	....	19	25	84	405	1,622	125	1
Colleyville	15,932	274	275	....	1	1	4	31	229	8	1
Conroe	30,056	2,885	2,890	3	30	88	321	378	1,799	266	5
Coppell	20,588	565	567	2	....	1	8	191	353	10	2
Copperas Cove	25,063	1,630	1,642	....	30	13	78	407	1,055	47	12
Corpus Christi	271,654	27,416	27,630	34	194	509	1,488	4,600	18,919	1,672	214
Corsicana	23,258	1,828	1,849	....	28	38	93	383	1,227	59	21
Dallas	1,042,619	110,799	112,123	317	1,000	7,420	9,439	20,975	54,183	17,465	1,324
Deer Park	29,944	710	711	....	....	8	55	210	397	40	1
Del Rio	33,059	1,990	1,996	....	....	4	105	455	1,336	90	6
Denison	21,757	1,720	1,733	2	9	27	138	258	1,228	58	13
Denton	69,167	3,880	3,936	5	41	102	342	676	2,513	201	56
DeSoto	33,996	1,771	1,780	....	9	33	56	411	1,100	162	9
Dickinson	10,273	742	745	....	6	21	39	135	479	62	3
Donna	13,746	1,358	1,358	1	7	8	26	270	961	85	....
Dumas[3]	13,380			....	....	....		186		1	....
Duncanville	39,733	2,037	2,053	....	19	56	98	414	1,188	262	16
Eagle Pass	23,007	2,602	2,608	2	1	15	163	371	1,943	107	6
Edinburg	33,268	2,600	2,616	2	7	40	134	452	1,760	205	16
El Campo	10,540	693	694	1	3	10	52	138	459	30	1
El Paso	554,515	46,738	47,199	47	281	1,561	4,220	5,643	29,440	5,546	461
Ennis	14,371	748	749	5	1	6	26	168	493	49	1
Euless	40,445	1,846	1,863	3	9	31	63	383	1,204	153	17
Farmers Branch	25,259	1,691	1,697	1	....	37	59	326	1,030	238	6
Flower Mound	18,174	557	561	....	3	3	117	123	286	25	4
Forest Hill	12,079	883	896	1	12	56	70	173	474	97	13
Fort Worth	463,373	49,801	50,220	133	507	2,750	3,589	10,505	26,310	6,007	419
Freeport	12,218	708	714	....	1	11	61	140	411	84	6
Friendswood	26,632	610	614	1	8	9	37	110	410	35	4

See footnotes at end of table.

150

Table 8.—Number of Offenses Known to the Police, Cities and Towns 10,000 and over in Population, 1993—Continued

City by State	Population	Crime Index total	Modified* Crime Index total	Murder and non-negligent man-slaughter	Forcible rape	Robbery	Aggra-vated assault	Burglary	Larceny-theft	Motor vehicle theft	Arson*
TEXAS—Continued											
Gainesville	14,428	732	734	1	5	13	21	157	505	30	2
Galena Park	10,522	329	330	....	2	7	43	91	154	32	1
Galveston	60,754	6,650	6,710	24	56	296	684	975	3,844	771	60
Garland[1]	194,930			12	114	293		2,522	7,657	1,033	145
Gatesville	11,775	231	234	....	3	1	12	83	121	11	3
Georgetown	16,073	743	748	....	4	5	41	123	545	25	5
Grand Prairie	106,537	7,036	7,039	9	54	169	502	1,259	4,035	1,008	3
Grapevine	33,332	1,164	1,178	....	16	15	78	210	776	69	14
Greenville	23,706	2,211	2,233	2	27	62	241	506	1,267	106	22
Groves	16,831	888	892	....	....	14	11	180	624	59	4
Haltom City	35,507	2,344	2,360	2	26	51	197	503	1,346	219	16
Harker Heights	13,139	661	664	2	18	12	118	148	331	32	3
Harlingen	52,984	4,971	4,981	6	3	65	355	834	3,325	383	10
Henderson[3]	11,582			2		24	256	251	725	148	....
Hereford	14,782	829	837	1	2	9	57	124	598	38	8
Houston[3]	1,724,327			446	1,109			27,022	61,569	27,519	1,549
Humble	12,974	1,405	1,408	2	11	38	52	160	782	360	3
Huntsville	29,084	1,380	1,381	7	19	49	145	242	851	67	1
Hurst	35,094	2,667	2,674	2	36	63	208	375	1,783	200	7
Irving	164,434	10,818	10,863	8	67	185	415	1,663	7,583	897	45
Jacinto City	10,018	331	334	1	1	9	24	95	153	48	3
Jacksonville	12,825	664	665	4	10	12	50	149	403	36	1
Keller	16,029	335	336	1	7	4	50	59	196	18	1
Kerrville	18,321	887	895	....	3	11	33	151	654	35	8
Kilgore	11,361	1,374	1,378	1	17	21	82	264	892	97	4
Killeen	67,884	4,768	4,904	6	90	223	224	1,142	2,800	283	136
Kingsville	25,932	1,688	1,706	4	15	16	183	448	984	38	18
Lake Jackson	24,813	590	591	1	4	4	8	89	450	34	1
La Marque	15,367	762	763	4	7	16	24	191	455	65	1
Lamesa[3]	10,775			....	2	2	72			4	....
Lancaster	23,609	1,334	1,363	2	11	29	73	334	747	138	29
La Porte	29,987	898	903	1	22	15	83	182	517	78	5
Laredo	139,194	10,059	10,139	21	7	163	862	1,720	6,246	1,040	80
League City	34,299	1,358	1,358	....	9	14	26	333	884	92	....
Leon Valley	10,330	880	882	....	5	14	21	97	666	77	2
Levelland	14,757	567	570	2	4	1	29	62	450	19	3
Lewisville	50,829	3,209	3,229	1	32	50	70	557	2,195	304	20
Live Oak	10,994	462	462	....	2	4	23	56	347	30	...... *
Longview	74,125	6,147	6,169	10	73	198	341	1,317	3,669	539	22
Lubbock	191,639	12,353	12,481	17	136	282	840	2,541	7,927	610	128
Lufkin	31,910	2,287	2,292	6	8	53	190	465	1,418	147	5
Mansfield	17,597	743	744	1	2	11	115	158	428	28	1
Marshall	23,912	1,937	1,947	7	18	35	162	368	1,249	98	10
McAllen	92,028	11,867	11,887	8	28	135	547	2,083	7,706	1,360	20
McKinney	23,728	1,640	1,646	1	25	24	275	354	894	67	6
Mercedes	13,858	562	566	1	9	6	169	166	164	47	4
Mesquite[3]	110,455			5	33	137	481		5,181	761	93
Midland	97,039	5,398	5,424	6	83	91	268	1,126	3,485	339	26
Mineral Wells	14,863	774	799	1	11	3	87	180	446	46	25
Mission	33,394	2,290	2,306	....	2	12	56	456	1,562	202	16
Missouri City	33,394	1,533	1,535	2	10	37	54	460	815	155	2
Mount Pleasant	12,838	753	757	3	3	8	33	164	503	39	4
Nacogdoches	31,281	1,583	1,608	2	13	40	168	300	997	63	25
Nederland	17,050	827	827	....	11	3	9	123	629	52	....
New Braunfels	29,611	2,219	2,228	1	5	22	520	264	1,302	105	9
North Richland Hills	51,349	2,437	2,442	....	28	44	78	389	1,669	229	5

See footnotes at end of table.

Table 8.—Number of Offenses Known to the Police, Cities and Towns 10,000 and over in Population, 1993—Continued

City by State	Population	Crime Index total	Modified* Crime Index total	Murder and non-negligent man-slaughter	Forcible rape	Robbery	Aggra-vated assault	Burglary	Larceny-theft	Motor vehicle theft	Arson*
TEXAS—Continued											
Odessa	95,605	8,848	8,907	9	39	146	577	1,969	5,684	424	59
Orange	20,250	2,466	2,475	2	34	94	124	428	1,675	109	9
Palestine	18,449	1,357	1,362	1	15	34	167	246	833	61	5
Pampa	20,005	874	875	2	31	16	46	209	547	23	1
Paris	25,238	2,863	2,877	3	21	42	380	552	1,725	140	14
Pasadena	127,886	9,139	9,216	10	106	192	1,336	1,701	4,684	1,110	77
Pearland	21,893	855	863	....	1	11	40	163	531	109	8
Pecos	12,131	441	441	....	1	4	23	107	298	8	....
Pharr	36,502	3,706	3,743	2	14	68	244	669	2,383	326	37
Plainview	22,334	1,340	1,347	4	4	20	101	315	857	39	7
Plano	144,902	6,941	6,960	2	32	90	363	1,319	4,714	421	19
Port Arthur	70,589	5,538	5,593	8	18	246	713	1,404	2,401	748	55
Portland	13,111	447	449	2	....	....	10	90	334	11	2
Port Lavaca	11,681	766	772	....	3	8	135	155	437	28	6
Port Neches	13,687	549	553	1	3	5	39	112	348	41	4
Richardson	77,866	4,391	4,402	4	22	94	99	928	2,951	293	11
Richmond	11,322	802	808	1	9	44	115	215	378	40	6
Robstown	13,385	739	747	1	1	3	52	302	324	56	8
Rockwall	12,532	490	497	....	4	10	41	87	321	27	7
Rosenberg	21,596	1,867	1,937	1	6	65	191	258	1,253	93	70
Round Rock	35,705	1,415	1,421	1	22	15	40	214	1,033	90	6
Rowlett	26,061	1,038	1,043	....	8	9	94	251	642	34	5
San Angelo	87,793	4,812		8	43	39	373	842	3,333	174	
San Antonio	985,456	97,671	98,629	220	553	2,979	2,973	17,866	61,284	11,796	958
San Benito	22,030	1,519	1,524	1	12	14	100	251	1,044	97	5
San Juan	11,892	703	705	1	3	8	29	233	359	70	2
San Marcos	30,074	1,644	1,653	2	19	33	92	303	1,112	83	9
Schertz	11,439	411	416	....	2	10	24	89	268	18	5
Seguin	19,495	1,337	1,339	2	14	25	114	398	753	31	2
Sherman	31,766	2,668	2,674	1	29	71	131	468	1,817	151	6
Snyder	12,690	407	408	....	3	....	90	65	245	4	1
South Houston	15,119	1,140	1,143	....	....	21	25	191	694	209	3
Stephenville	13,799	697	698	....	1	3	5	132	546	10	1
Sugar Land	29,699	1,206	1,211	....	....	16	52	224	789	125	5
Sulphur Springs	14,334	981	983	1	13	17	149	176	583	42	2
Sweetwater	11,919	809	814	1	7	9	97	214	451	30	5
Taylor	12,113	608	608	3	5	5	78	134	350	33	....
Temple	45,990	3,570	3,577	5	73	89	451	567	2,089	296	7
Terrell	13,071	962	964	3	13	39	58	202	571	76	2
Texarkana	32,754	3,224	3,244	4	28	102	345	601	1,970	174	20
Texas City	42,542	3,913	3,953	4	36	109	144	674	2,565	381	40
The Colony	25,203	776	801	....	1	5	32	168	527	43	25
Tyler	78,384	8,647	8,682	9	100	229	595	1,797	5,389	528	35
Universal City[1]	13,901			....	1	9		76	433	28	2
University Park	22,812	616	621	1	1	24	5	77	476	32	5
Uvalde	15,609	429	433	....	1	6	47	116	245	14	4
Vernon	11,911	859	868	2	17	12	262	262	294	10	9
Victoria	58,517	4,987	5,008	4	21	82	469	1,116	3,049	246	21
Vidor	11,559	525	528	2	....	7	22	75	391	28	3
Village	12,162	199	199	....	....	6	5	46	131	11	....
Waco	106,043	11,254	11,272	29	141	453	1,043	2,397	6,121	1,070	18
Watauga	22,212	549	549	....	8	17	16	106	380	22	....
Waxahachie	19,252	1,780	1,786	4	5	29	97	365	1,199	81	6
Weatherford	15,982	678	680	1	6	10	51	129	462	19	2
Weslaco	24,033	2,268	2,274	2	2	14	107	506	1,386	251	6
West University Place	13,797	350	351	....	1	10	5	98	208	28	1

See footnotes at end of table.

152

Table 8.—Number of Offenses Known to the Police, Cities and Towns 10,000 and over in Population, 1993—Continued

City by State	Population	Crime Index total	Modified* Crime Index total	Murder and non-negligent man-slaughter	Forcible rape	Robbery	Aggra-vated assault	Burglary	Larceny-theft	Motor vehicle theft	Arson*
TEXAS—Continued											
White Settlement	15,847	820	820	....	9	14	42	103	587	65	....
Wichita Falls	96,887	8,003	8,058	9	69	189	564	1,463	5,307	402	55
UTAH											
American Fork	16,827	741	741	....	7	....	28	90	585	31	....
Bountiful	38,823	1,042	1,053	....	10	6	36	162	791	37	11
Brigham City	16,634	669	669	....	6	1	9	98	547	8	....
Cedar City	14,477	566	566	....	5	1	9	71	460	20	....
Centerville	13,148	452	452	....	7	5	6	175	252	7	....
Clearfield	23,200	712	719	1	5	8	28	91	544	35	7
Kaysville	15,600	398	404	....	3	....	7	85	293	10	6
Logan	34,790	1,356	1,357	1	9	5	18	131	1,162	30	1
Midvale	12,466	1,206	1,211	....	8	16	37	182	912	51	5
Murray	33,318	3,146	3,154	3	15	29	47	410	2,521	121	8
North Ogden	12,490	274	275	....	2	....	4	21	240	7	1
Ogden	68,028	5,700	5,742	6	42	98	254	890	4,156	254	42
Orem	71,315	3,159	3,165	1	11	12	34	386	2,602	113	6
Pleasant Grove	18,622	599	599	....	9	3	10	111	426	40	....
Provo	93,661	3,695	3,705	1	36	18	88	508	2,889	155	10
Roy	26,487	1,094	1,094	....	6	8	89	131	820	40	....
St. George	33,610	1,908	1,910	....	13	7	38	251	1,503	96	2
Salt Lake City	170,380	18,453	18,533	19	204	498	681	2,823	12,831	1,397	80
Sandy	83,194	3,358	3,363	....	13	28	74	679	2,454	110	5
South Jordan	14,511	604	604	....	2	3	28	126	399	46	....
South Ogden	12,853	647	647	....	3	5	15	136	445	43	....
South Salt Lake	11,050	1,681	1,688	....	7	22	40	239	1,253	120	7
Spanish Fork	12,363	523	524	....	4	2	9	63	433	12	1
Springville	14,866	624	625	....	13	3	25	77	476	30	1
Tooele	14,806	724	724	1	3	1	25	114	523	57	....
West Jordan	47,912	1,702	1,709	1	5	2	38	253	1,354	49	7
West Valley	94,215	6,776	6,799	4	65	102	240	852	5,350	163	23
VERMONT											
Burlington	38,906	3,051		1	26	9	34	620	2,269	92	
Colchester	15,050	504		....	3	....	1	117	370	13	
Rutland	17,959	846		1	9	1	13	186	618	18	
South Burlington	13,085	843		....	3	4	9	125	686	16	
VIRGINIA											
Alexandria	114,850	8,324	8,355	9	33	376	334	921	5,682	969	31
Alexandria State Police	....	14	14	....	....	....	....	....	3	11	....
Arlington	174,184	10,133	10,171	4	37	294	265	923	7,484	1,126	38
Arlington State Police	....	22	22	....	3	....	1	....	9	9	....
Blacksburg	35,469	838	838	....	13	4	23	137	647	14	....
Bristol	18,370	839	850	1	6	9	51	134	599	39	11
Bristol State Police	....	2	2	....	....	....	....	....	1	1	....
Charlottesville	41,173	2,752	2,767	....	25	80	180	384	1,934	149	15
Chesapeake	168,523	7,846	7,941	13	61	327	385	1,612	4,958	490	95
Chesapeake State Police	....	20	21	....	....	2	1	2	9	6	1
Christiansburg	16,608	860	860	....	6	4	10	86	716	38	....
Colonial Heights	16,682	888	889	....	6	15	18	88	718	43	1
Colonial Heights State Police	....	1	1	....	....	....	....	....	1	....	....
Danville	54,383	2,303	2,320	10	24	78	99	388	1,622	82	17
Danville State Police	....	1	1	....	....	1	....	....	....	....	....
Fairfax City	20,822	1,287	1,292	....	5	23	28	146	1,016	69	5

153

Table 8. — Number of Offenses Known to the Police, Cities and Towns 10,000 and over in Population, 1993 — Continued

City by State	Population	Crime Index total	Modified* Crime Index total	Murder and non-negligent man-slaughter	Forcible rape	Robbery	Aggra-vated assault	Burglary	Larceny-theft	Motor vehicle theft	Arson*
VIRGINIA — Continued											
Fairfax City State Police		2	2					1		1	
Fredericksburg	21,169	865	877	1	9	27	63	102	631	32	12
Fredericksburg State Police		9	9		1				5	3	
Front Royal	12,932	574	578		3	10	11	70	455	25	4
Hampton	139,127	7,698	7,771	14	49	329	251	962	5,532	561	73
Hampton State Police		16	16				1		6	9	
Harrisonburg	32,643	1,475	1,484	1	7	17	26	166	1,214	44	9
Harrisonburg State Police		3	3				1		2		
Herndon	17,513	642	644		3	10	10	42	556	21	2
Hopewell	23,952	1,451	1,484	2	12	41	120	230	1,009	37	33
Leesburg	17,659	515	516	1	8	4	17	54	408	23	1
Lynchburg	67,099	3,566	3,616	3	45	107	351	560	2,316	184	50
Lynchburg State Police		1	1					1			
Manassas	30,760	1,391	1,397		10	55	32	141	1,067	86	6
Martinsville	16,203	1,307	1,316	2	7	22	78	164	980	54	9
Newport News	179,975	12,230	12,293	22	103	719	1,334	2,101	7,267	684	63
Newport News State Police		11	11		1	3				2	5	
Norfolk	257,617	22,209	22,344	62	204	1,428	1,075	3,732	13,535	2,173	135
Norfolk State Police		28	30			2	2		13	11	2
Petersburg	40,719	3,306	3,314	11	26	221	293	810	1,720	225	8
Petersburg State Police		5	5						4	1	
Poquoson	11,401	216	218		1	1	40	19	150	5	2
Portsmouth	105,944	9,347	9,474	33	56	746	532	1,720	5,008	1,252	127
Portsmouth State Police		9	9						3	6	
Pulaski	10,045	413	418		5	3	41	59	290	15	5
Pulaski State Police		17	17				1	1	15		
Radford	16,364	470	477		4	3	51	59	339	14	7
Radford State Police		1	1						1		
Richmond	205,331	22,142	22,312	112	174	1,578	1,411	5,081	11,571	2,215	170
Richmond State Police		32	32		1	4	1	2	10	14	
Roanoke	98,221	6,458	6,515	11	32	217	305	1,180	4,398	315	57
Roanoke State Police		5	5			2			2	1	
Salem	24,201	740	749	1	2	9	13	85	607	23	9
Salem State Police		1	1					1			
Staunton	24,997	799	801	1	8	4	30	110	625	21	2
Staunton State Police		4	5		1				3		1
Suffolk	54,084	3,384	3,410	9	37	160	304	646	1,974	254	26
Suffolk State Police		2	4						2		2
Vienna	15,680	484	488	1	3	4	7	66	379	24	4
Virginia Beach	423,387	20,516	20,716	22	181	631	414	3,261	14,812	1,195	200
Virginia Beach State Police		35	35			2	1	1	27	4	
Waynesboro	18,998	854	859	4	5	5	50	136	597	57	5
Williamsburg	12,271	494	495		3	19	5	48	390	29	1
Winchester	23,206	1,935	1,942		10	24	137	216	1,494	54	7
Winchester State Police		5	5						1	4	
WASHINGTON											
Aberdeen	17,143	1,564	1,591	1	28	20	41	198	1,234	42	27
Anacortes	12,303	489	497		2		7	35	420	25	8
Auburn	35,327	2,454	2,475	1	24	33	108	297	1,783	208	21
Bellevue	87,491	4,853	4,894	2	32	74	83	641	3,742	279	41
Bellingham	56,499	4,326	4,357	2	45	44	106	689	3,179	261	31
Bothell	13,064	973	988		2	10	16	180	711	54	15
Bremerton	42,569	2,343	2,349		43	63	161	366	1,573	137	6
Centralia	12,649	992	1,000		10	8	51	185	686	52	8

Table 8.—Number of Offenses Known to the Police, Cities and Towns 10,000 and over in Population, 1993—Continued

City by State	Population	Crime Index total	Modified* Crime Index total	Murder and non-negligent man-slaughter	Forcible rape	Robbery	Aggra-vated assault	Burglary	Larceny-theft	Motor vehicle theft	Arson*
WASHINGTON—Continued											
Des Moines	18,314	1,050	1,060	....	42	39	27	191	611	140	10
Edmonds	31,571	1,241	1,245	1	6	27	26	248	852	81	4
Ellensburg	12,674	686	687	....	1	2	24	92	541	26	1
Everett	76,760	6,348	6,408	4	116	161	126	915	4,565	461	60
Federal Way	70,647	5,631	5,644	2	131	128	170	804	3,844	552	13
Kelso	12,509	1,096	1,107	....	30	17	45	191	751	62	11
Kennewick	46,061	2,962	2,967	2	32	24	128	460	2,187	129	5
Kent	41,551	4,065	4,109	5	28	105	85	718	2,645	479	44
Kirkland	41,645	1,754	1,765	1	13	40	41	316	1,169	174	11
Lacey	21,737	1,541	1,543	1	5	14	41	195	1,227	58	2
Longview	32,978	2,415		1	15	38	59	486	1,698	118	
Lynnwood	30,526	3,160	3,173	1	15	55	43	375	2,490	181	13
Mercer Island	21,359	444	451	....	3	6	13	90	313	19	7
Moses Lake	12,771	1,404	1,412	2	20	3	132	217	975	55	8
Mountlake Terrace	20,442	986	995	....	17	16	26	142	678	107	9
Mount Vernon	19,624	1,663	1,676	3	15	18	9	200	1,324	94	13
Oak Harbor	19,029	652	657	....	11	1	7	56	563	14	5
Olympia	37,588	2,924	2,932	....	33	37	60	313	2,342	139	8
Pasco	22,688	1,595	1,601	4	24	42	138	308	931	148	13
Port Angeles	18,833	1,275	1,288	2	14	15	15	177	1,005	47	13
Pullman	23,064	424	426	1	6	2	40	77	285	13	2
Puyallup	25,967	1,995	2,022	....	6	15	58	209	1,578	129	27
Redmond	38,982	1,698	1,714	1	18	18	21	247	1,306	87	16
Renton	44,147	4,483	4,514	3	32	109	120	643	3,093	483	31
Richland	34,945	1,072	1,079	....	23	5	56	153	791	44	7
Sea Tac	23,732	2,069	2,075	1	47	73	89	376	1,173	310	6
Seattle	531,274	62,999	62,999	67	356	2,670	4,344	9,247	39,176	6,819	320
Spokane	191,511	15,952	16,026	13	112	354	1,079	2,699	10,965	730	74
Sunnyside	12,464	1,631	1,636	....	11	11	101	175	1,235	98	5
Tacoma	187,895	21,046	21,206	31	191	1,015	2,204	3,915	11,355	2,335	160
Tukwila	12,586	3,279	3,293	3	41	70	95	301	2,481	288	14
Tumwater	11,266	781	784	....	8	8	18	108	597	42	3
Vancouver	50,654	4,350	4,390	3	43	96	314	629	2,905	360	40
Walla Walla	28,613	2,509	2,530	....	40	25	203	435	1,725	81	21
Wenatchee	23,109	2,087	2,094	....	20	19	76	317	1,573	82	7
Yakima	59,720	7,777	7,808	6	65	175	522	1,443	5,164	402	31
WEST VIRGINIA											
Beckley	18,219	1,709	1,721	3	13	46	160	248	1,175	64	12
Bluefield	12,818	402	402	1	1	14	25	99	249	13	....
Charleston	57,430	6,754	6,838	16	51	290	412	1,293	4,238	454	84
Clarksburg	18,059	480	481	....	5	3	7	73	365	27	1
Fairmont	20,512	870	870	....	1	12	95	119	614	29	....
Huntington	54,422	3,486	3,519	2	61	83	158	787	2,259	136	33
Martinsburg	14,811	1,252	1,267	3	....	20	35	202	927	65	15
Morgantown	26,841	1,362	1,369	....	24	13	59	208	1,008	50	7
Moundsville	10,892	396	396	....	....	1	3	80	278	34	....
Parkersburg	33,854	1,305	1,342	3	12	18	39	347	820	66	37
St. Albans	11,020	333	334	2	....	1	....	52	257	21	1
South Charleston	13,689	419	421	1	2	12	13	51	304	36	2
Vienna	11,036	298	300	....	....	1	2	15	274	6	2
Weirton	22,015	487	490	1	3	4	44	115	288	32	3
Wheeling	34,421	1,215	1,225	1	12	56	113	388	557	88	10

155

Table 8. — Number of Offenses Known to the Police, Cities and Towns 10,000 and over in Population, 1993 — Continued

City by State	Population	Crime Index total	Modified* Crime Index total	Murder and non-negligent man-slaughter	Forcible rape	Robbery	Aggra-vated assault	Burglary	Larceny-theft	Motor vehicle theft	Arson*
WISCONSIN											
Appleton	69,078	2,691	2,716	2	9	11	23	372	2,187	87	25
Ashwaubenon	17,109	876	878	....	2	5	20	68	760	21	2
Beaver Dam	14,801	840	841	....	4	....	35	61	728	12	1
Beloit	36,762	2,216	2,232	....	11	70	46	269	1,688	132	16
Brookfield	36,706	1,485	1,485	....	2	11	53	207	1,142	70	....
Brown Deer	13,086	495	495	....	1	7	9	49	390	39	....
Caledonia	22,385	422	425	....	1	5	5	77	296	38	3
Cedarburg	10,362	208	210	....	2	....	2	20	176	8	2
Chippewa Falls	13,153	458	462	....	2	1	4	50	386	15	4
Cudahy	18,726	700	701	....	4	12	24	105	475	80	1
De Pere	17,507	613	617	....	6	....	24	119	448	16	4
Eau Claire	58,492	2,939	2,977	....	....	8	77	550	2,201	103	38
Everest	14,017	421	422	....	1	2	22	46	341	9	1
Fitchburg	16,554	511	511	....	1	6	33	133	313	25	....
Fond du Lac	39,207	2,783	2,802	....	10	11	137	232	2,302	91	19
Fort Atkinson	10,780	563	567	....	....	2	7	63	482	9	4
Franklin	24,246	508	510	....	1	4	3	103	355	42	2
Germantown	15,236	421	431	....	4	5	1	34	368	9	10
Glendale	14,298	1,051	1,053	....	3	49	2	106	799	92	2
Grand Chute	14,620	863	863	....	2	1	28	75	741	16	....
Green Bay	101,364	4,702	4,711	2	62	46	341	644	3,368	239	9
Greendale	15,027	716	716	1	1	5	4	23	646	36	....
Greenfield	34,309	1,509	1,516	....	2	18	10	233	1,068	178	7
Janesville	54,784	3,826	3,846	....	23	26	64	682	2,888	143	20
Kaukauna	11,989	328	328	....	....	2	7	56	254	9	....
Kenosha	84,258	4,772	4,805	8	53	129	270	859	3,141	312	33
La Crosse	51,809	2,914	2,928	....	7	13	18	183	2,625	68	14
Madison	196,919	10,616	10,672	2	99	316	214	1,606	7,466	913	56
Manitowoc	33,108	1,690	1,696	1	8	3	25	204	1,358	91	6
Marinette	12,226	507	512	....	6	....	9	38	448	6	5
Marshfield	19,581	802	804	....	1	1	28	99	656	17	2
Menasha	15,481	726	727	....	3	....	4	77	628	14	1
Menasha Town	14,277	415	418	....	....	2	2	81	310	20	3
Menomonee Falls	28,319	844	850	1	1	5	19	149	599	70	6
Menomonie	13,848	936	939	....	2	2	2	108	787	35	3
Mequon	20,603	265	267	....	....	....	2	35	211	17	2
Merrill	10,124	475	475	....	....	....	....	38	424	13	....
Middleton	13,748	491	491	....	....	7	4	85	369	26	....
Milwaukee	623,114	50,432	50,944	157	424	4,022	1,411	8,250	25,553	10,615	512
Monroe	10,529	360	365	....	1	3	5	67	269	15	5
Mount Pleasant	21,443	791	793	1	6	22	17	148	559	38	2
Muskego	18,496	250	251	....	1	....	5	56	178	10	1
Neenah	24,178	854	858	....	2	6	35	104	665	42	4
New Berlin	35,219	818	847	....	2	4	35	200	548	29	29
Oak Creek	21,213	894	894	....	6	12	7	107	700	62	....
Oconomowoc	11,473	354	355	....	....	5	15	36	273	25	1
Onalaska	11,909	717	717	....	1	1	5	72	631	7	....
Oshkosh	56,799	3,304	3,314	5	19	7	57	479	2,625	112	10
Pleasant Prairie	12,565	390	390	1	1	4	22	53	292	17	....
Racine	86,896	6,480	6,522	8	18	325	353	1,288	4,014	474	42
River Falls	10,990	702	705	....	....	....	12	26	637	27	3
Sheboygan	50,651	2,842	2,864	1	11	22	40	309	2,368	91	22
Shorewood	14,105	588	588	1	1	14	6	73	462	31	....
South Milwaukee	20,891	866	884	....	5	8	12	145	671	25	18
Stevens Point	23,617	1,422	1,432	1	9	....	42	157	1,182	31	10
Sun Prairie	16,279	770	776	....	4	....	9	69	661	27	6

Table 8.—Number of Offenses Known to the Police, Cities and Towns 10,000 and over in Population, 1993—Continued

City by State	Population	Crime Index total	Modified* Crime Index total	Murder and non-negligent man-slaughter	Forcible rape	Robbery	Aggra-vated assault	Burglary	Larceny-theft	Motor vehicle theft	Arson*
WISCONSIN—Continued											
Superior	27,639	1,926	1,955	1	17	15	43	347	1,403	100	29
Two Rivers	13,320	384	386	....	....	2	4	48	319	11	2
Watertown	19,792	826	831	....	5	9	8	116	658	30	5
Waukesha	59,705	2,064	2,081	1	9	19	55	254	1,618	108	17
Wausau	38,393	1,503	1,509	....	6	9	4	210	1,212	62	6
Wauwatosa	49,791	2,089		3	6	59	12	372	1,436	201	
West Allis	62,708	2,893	2,935	2	8	78	58	423	2,059	265	42
West Bend	25,593	1,265	1,274	....	6	1	28	91	1,095	44	9
Whitefish Bay	14,378	345	345	....	....	3	2	36	286	18	....
Whitewater	13,219	373	376	....	8	2	9	39	305	10	3
Wisconsin Rapids	18,456	1,070	1,072	1	1	2	45	137	868	16	2
WYOMING											
Cheyenne	53,033	2,666	2,678	....	22	17	69	258	2,224	76	12
Evanston	11,821	645	645	1	6	2	24	90	496	26	....
Gillette	18,665	1,014	1,032	....	4	3	64	72	844	27	18
Green River	13,437	493	498	....	2	2	17	66	393	13	5
Laramie	27,156	1,034	1,041	1	5	6	66	90	828	38	7
Rock Springs	20,197	1,303	1,303	1	14	6	111	213	882	76	....
Sheridan	14,357	576	580	....	6	....	14	62	462	32	4

[1]Due to reporting changes, aggravated assault figures are not comparable to previous years.

[2]Complete data for 1993 were not available for the states of Illinois and Kansas. See "Offense Estimation," page 376 for details. Forcible rape figures furnished by the state-level Uniform Crime Reporting (UCR) Program administered by the Illinois Department of State Police under the summary reporting system were not in accordance with national UCR guidelines. Therefore, the figures were excluded from the forcible rape, Crime Index total, and Modified Crime Index total categories.

[3]Due to reporting changes, figures are not comparable to previous years.

[4]Forcible rape figures furnished by the state-level Uniform Crime Reporting (UCR) Programs administered by the Michigan State Police and the Minnesota Department of Public Safety were not in accordance with national UCR guidelines. Therefore, the figures were excluded from the forcible rape, Crime Index total and Modified Crime Index total categories. However, some Minnesota law enforcement agencies verified and/or adjusted their forcible rape figures to comply with national UCR guidelines and are shown in this table.

[5]Twelve months of useable data were not received for any Montana cities over 10,000 in population.

Table 9. — Number of Offenses Known to the Police, Universities and Colleges, 1993

*Arson is shown only if 12 months of arson data were received. Leaders (...) indicate zero data.

University/College	Student enroll-ment[1]	Violent[2] crime total	Murder and non-negligent man-slaughter	Forcible rape	Robbery	Aggra-vated assault	Property[3] crime total	Burglary	Larceny-theft	Motor vehicle theft	Arson[*]
ALABAMA											
Alabama State University	5,488	31	...	...	4	27	167	11	154	2	...
Auburn University:											
Main Campus	21,551	7	...	...	3	4	468	76	388	4	...
Montgomery	6,386	2	...	1	1	...	41	3	38	...	...
Enterprise State Junior College	2,282	...	...	...	...	...	1	...	1	...	...
Jacksonville State University	8,022	6	...	1	...	5	81	8	73	...	...
Livingston University	1,977	1	...	...	...	1	39	1	38	...	...
Troy State University	6,063	2	...	...	1	1	66	...	63	3	...
University of Alabama:											
Huntsville	8,026	1	...	...	...	1	32	4	28	...	...
Tuscaloosa	[4]	19	...	4	5	10	614	32	575	7	...
University of Montevallo	3,246	...	...	...	...	...	23	1	20	2	...
University of South Alabama	12,311	7	...	1	2	4	97	18	76	3	...
ALASKA											
University of Alaska, Fairbanks	8,116	22	1	8	1	12	135	3	129	3	1
ARIZONA											
Arizona State University	43,628	47	...	4	7	36	1,286	157	1,088	41	6
Arizona Western College	5,386	1	...	...	...	1	47	2	44	1	1
Central Arizona College	4,586	1	...	...	...	1	45	21	24	...	...
Northern Arizona University	18,485	27	...	5	2	20	522	37	484	1	...
Pima Community College	30,175	6	...	...	1	5	176	43	127	6	...
University of Arizona	35,118	20	...	5	4	11	1,212	144	1,032	36	14
Yavapai College	4,817	1	...	...	...	1	70	7	63	...	...
ARKANSAS											
University of Arkansas:											
Fayetteville	14,582	11	...	3	2	6	243	104	135	4	...
Little Rock	12,348	7	...	...	2	5	102	11	83	8	1
Medical Science	1,734	3	...	...	2	1	209	23	179	7	...
Pine Bluff	3,709	8	...	1	2	5	110	16	92	2	2
University of Central Arkansas	9,473	11	...	1	3	7	125	22	102	1	1
CALIFORNIA											
Allan Hancock College	7,941	1	...	...	1	...	54	20	34	...	...
Cabrillo College	12,986	2	...	...	1	1	58	21	34	3	...
California State Polytechnic University:											
Pomona	18,294	9	...	...	1	8	412	50	325	37	4
San Luis Obispo	16,373	7	...	2	...	5	452	28	423	1	...
California State University:											
Bakersfield	5,433	3	...	1	...	2	72	25	47	...	...
Chico	15,164	6	...	2	2	2	468	50	413	5	7
Dominguez Hills	10,472	4	...	1	3	...	176	65	88	23	...
Fresno	18,902	6	...	1	3	2	477	54	376	47	...
Fullerton	24,402	6	...	3	3	...	460	18	410	32	...
Hayward	12,981	3	...	1	1	1	148	8	133	7	2
Long Beach	30,067	21	...	3	3	15	488	74	314	100	...
Los Angeles	19,399	12	...	2	7	3	434	5	375	54	3
Northridge	29,088	22	...	1	6	15	697	60	545	92	...
Sacramento	24,466	6	...	...	2	4	474	62	369	43	...
San Bernardino	12,483	4	...	...	...	4	300	58	218	24	...
San Jose	[4]	18	...	3	3	12	408	29	366	13	...
Stanislaus	5,897	1	...	...	...	1	129	3	121	5	...
College of Marin	11,708	3	...	...	...	3	46	1	43	2	2
College of the Sequoias	9,139	2	...	1	...	1	57	23	22	3	...
Contra Costa Community College	7,886	36	...	1	9	26	359	52	269	38	...
Evergreen Valley/San Jose Community College	9,524	1	...	1	...	...	150	5	142	3	1
Foothill-Deanza College	39,226	4	...	...	...	4	193	8	182	3	...
Fresno Community College	18,431	5	...	1	2	2	332	8	262	62	...
Humboldt State University	7,849	2	...	...	...	2	212	2	209	1	1
Kings River Community College	5,440	2	...	1	...	1	63	9	48	6	3
Los Angeles City College	17,017	22	...	3	11	8	149	75	51	23	...

See footnotes at end of table.

Table 9. — Number of Offenses Known to the Police, Universities and Colleges, 1993 — Continued

University/College	Student enrollment[1]	Violent[2] crime total	Violent crime — Murder and nonnegligent manslaughter	Violent crime — Forcible rape	Violent crime — Robbery	Violent crime — Aggravated assault	Property[3] crime total	Property crime — Burglary	Property crime — Larceny-theft	Property crime — Motor vehicle theft	Property crime — Arson*
CALIFORNIA — Continued											
Pasadena City College	22,024	8		1	5	2	341	31	267	43	2
San Bernardino Community College	10,827	4			1	3	94	3	71	20	
San Diego State University	30,887	13		1	2	10	917	58	724	135	2
San Francisco State University	26,528	15		2	6	7	500	59	345	96	10
Santa Rosa Junior College	23,390	3			1	2	204	12	188	4	1
Sonoma State University	7,396	5		1	2	2	133	16	113	4	
University of California:											
Berkeley	30,616	54		4	25	25	1,540	114	1,399	27	19
Davis	22,880	11		3	1	7	1,602	178	1,395	29	5
Hastings College of the Law	1,240	1			1		52	4	47	1	
Irvine	17,181	13		2	3	8	794	104	655	35	1
Lawrence Livermore Laboratory	[4]						36		36		
Los Angeles	35,403	38		1	21	16	1,078	564	402	112	22
Riverside	8,799	28		2	7	19	569	96	411	62	3
Sacramento	3,744	13			4	9	348	19	305	24	
San Diego	18,239	5		2	2	1	915	136	648	131	3
San Francisco	3,746	1				1	787	84	698	5	
Santa Barbara	18,651	2				2	799	87	702	10	4
Santa Cruz	10,251	6		3		3	296	45	247	4	4
West Valley College	12,677						132	53	74	5	2
COLORADO											
Adams State College	5,294	1				1	158	33	124	1	
Arapahoe Community College	7,643						39		39		
Auraria Higher Education Center	[4]	22		1	4	17	508	28	460	20	3
Colorado School of Mines	3,450						50	5	44	1	
Red Rocks Community College	6,888						16	2	14		
University of Colorado:											
Boulder	28,524	8		5		3	928	212	701	15	5
Colorado Springs	6,408						25	1	24		
Health Sciences	2,251						355	11	334	10	
University of Northern Colorado	12,667	4		2	1	1	322	30	290	2	3
University of Southern Colorado	4,867	2		1		1	78	17	61		
CONNECTICUT											
Central Connecticut State University	13,779						106	1	99	6	
Eastern Connecticut State University	4,493	1				1	136	19	115	2	
Southern Connecticut State University	12,415	4		1	1	2	217	89	116	12	
University of Connecticut:											
Avery Point	[4]						11	1	10		
Health Center	[4]						113	8	102	3	
Storrs	[4]	20		4	2	14	449	97	343	9	3
Western Connecticut State University	5,727	2		1		1	113	19	92	2	3
Yale University [5]	10,945	14		1	6	7			587	22	1
FLORIDA											
Florida Atlantic University	14,673	5		2	1	2	237	5	207	25	
Florida International University	23,093	7			3	4	436	27	384	25	
Florida State University:											
Panama City	[4]						1		1		
Tallahassee	28,424	34		6	17	11	816	48	694	74	
University of Central Florida	21,873	2				2	252	32	215	5	
University of Florida	36,447	29		3	8	18	1,410	68	1,265	77	15
University of North Florida	9,073	3		1	1	1	143	26	117		2
University of South Florida:											
St. Petersburg	[4]	1				1	31	4	23	4	
Sarasota	[4]	3		1		2	28	5	22	1	
Tampa	[4]	40		3	2	35	908	65	776	67	
University of West Florida	7,521	4	1			3	109	17	90	2	
GEORGIA											
Abraham Baldwin Agricultural College	2,851	4				4	70	15	55		
Agnes Scott College	619	1			1		27	2	24	1	

See footnotes at end of table.

Table 9. — Number of Offenses Known to the Police, Universities and Colleges, 1993 — Continued

University/College	Student enrollment[1]	Violent[2] crime total	Violent crime — Murder and non-negligent man-slaughter	Violent crime — Forcible rape	Violent crime — Robbery	Violent crime — Aggra-vated assault	Property[3] crime total	Property crime — Burglary	Property crime — Larceny-theft	Property crime — Motor vehicle theft	Property crime — Arson*
GEORGIA – Continued											
Albany State College	3,106	5	....	....	1	4	18	4	14	....	....
Armstrong State College	4,839	....	....	....	....	....	50	1	49	....	....
Berry College	1,745	....	....	....	....	....	50	2	48	....	....
Brunswick College	1,835	....	....	....	....	....	25	13	12	....	....
Clark Atlanta University	4,480	16	....	2	11	3	256	66	181	9	9
Clayton State College	4,862	....	....	....	....	....	41	2	38	1	....
Columbus College	4,998	7	....	....	....	7	39	5	33	1	....
Dalton College	2,883	....	....	....	....	....	9	....	9	....	....
Fort Valley State College	2,537	4	....	1	....	3	21	6	14	1	....
Georgia College	5,501	....	....	....	....	....	54	....	53	1	2
Georgia Institute of Technology	12,814	30	....	3	21	6	1,029	124	844	61	1
Georgia Southern University	14,030	5	....	2	....	3	311	5	304	2	1
Georgia Southwestern College	2,532	3	....	....	1	2	26	3	23	....	....
Georgia State University	24,050	4	....	....	1	3	446	2	437	7	....
Gordon College	1,909	....	....	....	....	....	2	....	2	....	....
Kennesaw College	11,661	....	....	....	....	....	62	12	49	1	....
Medical College of Georgia	4,117	3	....	....	3	....	292	10	267	15	....
Mercer University	6,342	2	....	....	2	....	142	13	124	5	1
Middle Georgia College	1,878	1	....	....	....	1	18	1	16	1	....
North Georgia College	2,794	1	....	....	1	....	18	3	15	....	....
Reinhardt College	864	2	....	1	1	....	16	1	15	....	....
South Georgia College	1,495	1	....	....	....	1	22	4	18	....	....
Southern College of Technology	3,907	1	....	1	....	....	64	24	39	1	....
University of Georgia	28,493	17	....	3	7	7	472	24	439	9	....
Valdosta State University	7,860	2	....	....	1	1	187	34	152	1	1
Wesleyan College	484	....	....	....	....	....	21	2	19	....	....
West Georgia College	7,714	1	....	....	....	1	191	35	152	4	5
ILLINOIS[6]											
INDIANA											
Ball State University	21,235	29	....	5	3	21	814	115	690	9	....
Indiana State University	12,270	10	....	2	1	7	411	19	386	6	1
Indiana University:											
Bloomington	36,071	13	....	6	3	4	1,152	164	960	28	1
Gary	[4]	4	....	....	1	3	56	1	46	9	....
Indianapolis	28,342	9	....	1	6	2	631	8	602	21	....
New Albany	[4]	....	....	....	....	....	39	....	39	....	....
Purdue University	37,746	38	....	2	....	36	913	61	840	12	6
IOWA											
Iowa State University	25,695	15	....	....	3	12	684	91	587	6	....
KANSAS[6]											
KENTUCKY											
Eastern Kentucky University	16,811	13	....	....	....	13	217	10	199	8	....
Jefferson Community College	11,858	....	....	....	....	....	12	....	12	....	....
Kentucky State University	2,541	....	....	....	....	....	19	1	18	....	....
Morehead State University	9,161	8	....	1	....	7	164	9	151	4	....
Murray State University	8,163	2	....	....	1	1	75	13	62	....	1
Northern Kentucky University	11,871	3	....	....	....	3	140	2	137	1	....

See footnotes at end of table.

Table 9.—Number of Offenses Known to the Police, Universities and Colleges, 1993—Continued

University/College	Student enroll-ment[1]	Violent[2] crime total	Violent crime — Murder and non-negligent man-slaughter	Violent crime — Forcible rape	Violent crime — Robbery	Violent crime — Aggra-vated assault	Property[3] crime total	Property crime — Burglary	Property crime — Larceny-theft	Property crime — Motor vehicle theft	Property crime — Arson*
KENTUCKY—Continued											
University of Kentucky	23,699	15	....	3	1	11	805	64	718	23	9
University of Louisville	21,987	23	....	....	14	9	411	25	373	13	....
Western Kentucky University	15,653	11	....	1	3	7	209	8	199	2	2
LOUISIANA											
Grambling State University	7,533	32	....	1	5	26	153	24	127	2	3
Louisiana State University, Baton Rouge	[4]	31	....	1	14	16	765	153	537	75	....
Louisiana Tech. University	10,189	10	....	....	7	3	262	33	228	1	1
McNeese State University	8,438	....	....	....	....	....	96	16	80	....	....
Northeast Louisiana University	11,732	5	....	....	....	5	293	4	289	....	....
Southeastern Louisiana University	12,759	6	....	2	....	4	195	38	156	1	....
Southern University and A & M College, Baton Rouge	10,403	24	....	....	13	11	396	10	356	30	2
MAINE											
University of Maine:											
Farmington	2,265	1	....	....	....	1	24	2	22	....	....
Orono	12,315	4	....	3	....	1	352	11	337	4	1
University of Southern Maine	10,077	....	....	....	....	....	120	15	105	....	....
MARYLAND											
Bowie State University	4,809	4	....	....	....	4	42	22	18	2	....
Coppin State University	2,944	....	....	....	....	....	45	2	37	6	1
Frostburg State University	5,295	3	....	....	1	2	81	8	72	1	....
Morgan State University	5,402	28	....	....	11	17	256	112	139	5	1
St. Mary's College	1,510	....	....	....	....	....	77	7	70	....	....
Salisbury State University	6,022	8	....	1	2	5	214	18	188	8	2
Towson State University	15,230	4	....	1	....	3	384	85	290	9	10
University of Baltimore	5,841	5	....	....	4	1	176	13	155	8	....
University of Maryland:											
Baltimore City	[4]	23	....	....	15	8	869	27	816	26	....
Baltimore County	10,650	6	....	1	2	3	284	61	215	8	3
College Park	32,916	46	....	4	11	31	1,214	179	983	52	9
Eastern Shore	2,430	4	....	1	....	3	90	3	87	....	....
MASSACHUSETTS											
Boston College	14,450	16	....	6	2	8	344	21	310	13	....
Boston University	28,375	28	....	2	6	20	1,020	181	796	43	7
Brandeis University	3,848	4	....	1	....	3	120	9	110	1	....
Emerson College	3,068	1	....	....	1	....	79	2	69	8	....
Framingham State College	5,142	4	....	1	1	2	43	1	42	....	....
Massachusetts College of Art	1,806	3	....	....	1	2	27	....	27	....	....
Massachusetts Institute of Technology	9,798	10	....	1	4	5	866	18	787	61	....
North Adams State College	2,144	6	....	....	....	6	21	5	16	....	....
Northeastern University	27,586	14	....	....	8	6	432	19	395	18	....
University of Massachusetts, Amherst	24,185	26	....	4	....	22	799	238	544	17	....
Wentworth Institute of Technology	3,298	4	....	....	1	3	62	3	58	1	....
MICHIGAN[7]											
Central Michigan University	17,268		....		1	....	426	15	406	5	2
Delta College	11,129		....		....	....	129	1	127	1	....
Eastern Michigan University	24,096		....		5	17	586	20	554	12	11
Ferris State University	12,071		....		2	3	387	16	366	5	4
Grand Valley State University	12,736		....		....	2	95	18	76	1	1
Hope College	2,755		....		....	....	123	3	120	....	2
Lansing Community College	21,204		....		....	1	152	5	146	1	....
Macomb Community College	26,498		....		1	1	133	5	116	12	....
Michigan State University	39,138		....		10	25	1,467	305	1,109	53	17
Michigan Technological University	6,961		....		....	....	176	3	172	1	....
Northern Michigan University	8,820		....		....	4	171	9	162	....	5
Oakland University	13,068		....		1	5	118	3	113	2	....
Saginaw Valley State University	6,705		....		....	3	160	5	154	1	1

See footnotes at end of table.

Table 9. — Number of Offenses Known to the Police, Universities and Colleges, 1993 — Continued

University/College	Student enroll-ment[1]	Violent[2] crime total	Violent crime				Property[3] crime total	Property crime			
			Murder and non-negligent man-slaughter	Forcible rape	Robbery	Aggra-vated assault		Burglary	Larceny-theft	Motor vehicle theft	Arson*
MICHIGAN[7] — Continued											
University of Michigan:											
Ann Arbor	35,476	....	....		7	34	1,845	180	1,631	34	26
Flint	5,947	....	....		1	....	111	1	109	1	
Western Michigan University	27,281	....	....		1	5	578	6	568	4	18
MINNESOTA[7]											
University of Minnesota, Twin Cities	54,671	....	....		6	3	1,275	101	1,171	3	10
MISSISSIPPI											
Itawamba Community College	3,237	1	....	....	....	1	53	12	39	2	....
Jackson State University	6,203	35	1	6	24	4	149	36	99	14	....
Mississippi State University	14,619	35	....	1	2	32	304	22	279	3	1
University of Mississippi	11,038	....	....			....	282	63	217	2	....
University of Mississippi, Medical Center	1,631	....	....			....	181	....	167	14	....
MISSOURI											
Central Missouri State University	11,631	1	....	....	....	1	282	57	224	1	3
Lincoln University	4,030	8	....	....	1	7	89	7	82	....	....
University of Missouri:											
Columbia	23,418	9	....	....	3	6	529	52	472	5	3
St. Louis	14,918	1	....	....	1	....	92	8	79	5	
Washington University	11,572	3	....	....	2	1	278	10	257	11	
MONTANA											
Montana State University	10,537	5	....	2	....	3	160	3	155	2	4
University of Montana	10,612	7	....	1	....	6	302	59	242	1	....
NEBRASKA											
University of Nebraska:											
Kearney	8,371	....	....			....	122	13	107	2	....
Lincoln	24,573	6	....	2	3	1	979	60	909	10	....
NEVADA											
University of Nevada:											
Las Vegas	18,694	7	....	1	4	2	319	96	195	28	1
Reno	11,894	8	....	3	....	5	362	135	219	8	8
NEW HAMPSHIRE											
University of New Hampshire	13,872	10	....	4	1	5	323	44	276	3	2
NEW JERSEY											
Brookdale Community College	12,409	....	....			....	105	2	99	4	....
Burlington County College	7,084	....	....			....	23	....	23	....	....
Essex County College	8,474	10	....	....	5	5	38	....	28	10	....
Kean College	12,497	15	....	2	5	8	281	48	209	24	1
Middlesex County College	11,794	1	....	....	....	1	42	....	39	3	....
Monmouth College	4,195	4	....	1	1	2	122	9	112	1	....
Montclair State College	13,595	9	....	2	....	7	266	17	213	36	1
New Jersey Institute of Technology	7,697	10	....	1	1	8	130	12	103	15	....
Rowan College	9,849	3	....	1	....	2	120	12	98	10	....
Rutgers University:											
Camden	5,214	4	....	....	2	2	142	13	112	17	....
New Brunswick	33,943	25	....	5	8	12	759	38	691	30	....
Newark	9,761	10	....	1	3	6	207	26	166	15	....
Stockton State College	5,683	7	....	2	1	4	84	5	79	....	....
Trenton State College	7,162	....	....			....	199	8	177	14	1
University of Medicine and Dentistry:											
Camden	4		....				16	....	16		....
Newark	4	85	....	2	48	35	757	26	640	91	....
Piscataway	4	5	....	....	....	5	55	2	51	2	....
William Paterson College	9,386	3	....	....	....	3	184	1	180	3	2

See footnotes at end of table.

Table 9.— Number of Offenses Known to the Police, Universities and Colleges, 1993—Continued

University/College	Student enroll-ment[1]	Violent[2] crime total	Murder and non-negligent man-slaughter	Forcible rape	Robbery	Aggra-vated assault	Property[3] crime total	Burglary	Larceny-theft	Motor vehicle theft	Arson*
NEW MEXICO											
Eastern New Mexico University	3,909	2			1	1	83	10	73		1
New Mexico Highlands University	2,807	17				17	54	9	43	2	2
New Mexico State University	15,500	10		1		9	526	48	454	24	
NEW YORK											
Cornell University	[4]	17			1	16	838	118	719	1	1
Ithaca College	6,259						189	15	174		
Rensselaer Polytechnic Institute	6,988	5		1	1	3	325	65	258	2	2
State University of New York:											
Albany	19,001	12		1	4	7	457	108	344	5	
Binghamton	11,966	8	1		2	5	350	90	260		
Buffalo	25,357	12			7	5	732	194	498	40	
College of Technology	[4]						130	37	93		
Downstate Medical Center	[4]	2				2	234	2	232		
Maritime College	899	1				1	53	33	20		
Stony Brook	17,125	7		1	2	4	862	72	770	20	3
Upstate Medical Center	[4]	2		1	1		269	1	268		
State University of New York Agricultural and Technical College:											
Alfred	3,435	3		1		2	135	38	96	1	
Canton	2,278	3		1	1	1	121	8	113		
Cobleskill	[4]	1				1	112	50	62		
Farmingdale	8,799	8	1	1	2	4	195	40	148	7	
Morrisville	[4]	3		1		2	71	12	59		
State University of New York College:											
Brockport	9,227	7		2	2	3	179	28	149	2	
Buffalo	12,104	7		1	2	4	424	80	331	13	
Cortland	6,991	2			1	1	159	14	145		
Environmental Science and Forestry	1,456						25		25		
Fredonia	4,889						123	13	110		
Geneseo	5,651	2				2	133	1	130	2	
New Paltz	8,086	3		1	1	1	109	2	107		
Old Westbury	4,109	6			1	5	101	18	78	5	
Oneonta	5,927	3			2	1	143	21	122		
Optometry	266						9		9		
Oswego	8,555	2			2		192	24	166	2	
Plattsburgh	6,160	2				2	111	6	105		
Potsdam	4,562	2			2		179	3	176		
Purchase	3,949	1				1	140	2	133	5	
Utica-Rome	2,550						42		41	1	
NORTH CAROLINA											
Appalachian State University	12,065	9		1	1	7	181	21	159	1	1
Campbell University	6,102	3				3	55	8	46	1	
Davidson College	1,550	1				1	58	3	54	1	2
Duke University	11,426	16		1	4	11	1,146	106	1,025	15	
East Carolina University	19,264	16		2	3	11	398	45	351	2	1
Elizabeth City State University	2,019	18		1		17	71	37	33	1	1
Fayetteville State University	3,902	10	1		2	7	111	17	91	3	
Mars Hill College	1,354						25	6	19		
North Carolina A & T State University, Greensboro	7,723	23			1	22	285	23	257	5	1
North Carolina Central University, Durham	5,681	17			3	14	185	32	151	2	1
North Carolina School of the Arts	310	1			1		27	8	19		
North Carolina State University, Raleigh	27,766	42		2	11	29	800	125	668	7	3
Pembroke State University	3,041	3				3	58	25	32	1	
Queens College	4,465						20	6	14		
University of North Carolina:											
Asheville	3,240	1		1			41	7	34		
Chapel Hill	23,977	23			3	20	815	83	722	10	
Charlotte	15,781	8			2	6	312	53	252	7	4
Greensboro	13,230	14			5	9	262	32	223	7	4
Wilmington	8,804	2			2		272	15	255	2	5
Wake Forest University	5,630	7				7	277	86	191		2
Western Carolina University	6,837	1		1			115	17	98		
Winston-Salem State University	2,728	2			1	1	36	9	25		

See footnotes at end of table.

Table 9.—Number of Offenses Known to the Police, Universities and Colleges, 1993—Continued

University/College	Student enroll-ment[1]	Violent[2] crime total	Murder and non-negligent man-slaughter	Forcible rape	Robbery	Aggra-vated assault	Property[3] crime total	Burglary	Larceny-theft	Motor vehicle theft	Arson*
NORTH DAKOTA											
University of North Dakota	12,289	2	....	2	....	....	257	6	240	11	3
OHIO											
Bowling Green State University	18,173	10	....	4	....	6	483	60	416	7	....
Kent State University, Main Campus	24,098	4	....	1	1	2	459	5	450	4	1
Lakeland Community College	9,174	....	....	....	....	....	65	1	64	....	....
Marietta College	1,379	1	....	1	....	....	45	4	41	....	....
Miami University, Oxford	16,098	9	....	4	1	4	412	9	403	....	1
Ohio State University	52,179	33	....	1	11	21	1,699	311	1,355	33	8
Ohio University	18,862	7	....	1	2	4	343	23	318	2	....
University of Akron	27,063	14	....	1	7	6	549	25	506	18	2
University of Cincinnati	28,779	29	....	3	7	19	1,108	150	952	6	....
University of Toledo	24,539	22	....	1	3	18	340	25	297	18	1
Wright State University	16,749	7	....	4	....	3	272	13	254	5	2
Youngstown State University	14,806	4	....	....	4	....	106	7	96	3	....
OKLAHOMA											
Cameron University	6,120	1	....	....	1	....	32	1	27	4	....
East Central University	4,451	....	....	....	....	....	40	6	33	1	....
Murray State College	1,491	....	....	....	....	....	7	5	2	....	....
Northeastern Oklahoma State University	9,246	4	....	1	....	3	102	18	82	2	2
Oklahoma State University:											
Main Campus	19,602	6	....	1	1	4	248	66	181	1	5
Okmulgee	2,114	2	....	....	1	1	57	7	47	3	5
Southeastern Oklahoma State University	4,027	5	....	....	....	5	36	1	34	1	....
Tulsa Junior College	19,583	....	....	....	....	....	42	....	42	....	....
University of Central Oklahoma	15,167	4	....	....	....	4	186	14	163	9	....
University of Oklahoma:											
Health Science Center	3,102	....	....	....	....	....	37	....	34	3	....
Norman	21,724	10	....	3	6	1	648	95	538	15	2
PENNSYLVANIA											
Bloomsburg University	7,551	....	....	....	....	....	88	2	86	....	....
California University	6,484	4	....	....	....	4	117	....	112	5	....
Clarion University	1,668	1	....	....	1	....	106	1	105	....	....
East Stroudsburg University	5,352	7	....	....	1	6	104	....	97	7	1
Edinboro University	8,202	2	....	....	....	2	96	3	93	....	....
Elizabethtown College	1,845	1	....	....	....	1	33	....	33	....	....
Kutztown University	7,791	1	....	....	....	1	76	3	72	1	4
Lehigh University	6,349	17	....	2	1	14	199	6	190	3	....
Mansfield University	3,223	3	....	1	....	2	69	4	65	....	....
Millersville University	7,791	4	....	2	....	2	98	2	96	....	....
Pennsylvania State University:											
Behrend College	4	3	....	....	....	3	59	1	57	1	....
Capitol Campus	4	1	....	1	....	....	59	3	56	....	....
University Park	38,446	11	....	4	1	6	790	86	698	6	1
Shippensburg University	6,688	1	....	....	....	1	101	5	95	1	....
Slippery Rock University	7,777	....	....	....	....	....	94	1	91	2	....
University of Pittsburgh, Bradford	1,309	....	....	....	....	....	11	....	11	....	....
West Chester University	11,806	11	....	4	....	7	148	16	122	10	3
RHODE ISLAND											
Brown University	7,593	8	....	....	1	7	606	134	470	2	6
University of Rhode Island	15,449	6	....	....	....	6	254	16	235	3	1
SOUTH CAROLINA											
Clemson University	17,666	16	....	2	2	12	397	35	356	6	....
Francis Marion University	3,975	6	....	1	....	5	54	6	48	....	....
Lander University	2,521	....	....	....	....	....	36	5	31	....	....
Medical University of South Carolina	2,290	2	....	....	1	1	640	25	613	2	1
South Carolina State University	5,071	17	....	....	6	11	123	26	94	3	1
The Citadel	3,633	2	....	....	....	2	70	2	68	....	....
Trident Technical College	9,152	....	....	....	....	....	92	1	87	4	....

See footnotes at end of table.

Table 9. — Number of Offenses Known to the Police, Universities and Colleges, 1993 — Continued

University/College	Student enroll-ment[1]	Violent[2] crime total	Violent crime				Property[3] crime total	Property crime			
			Murder and non-negligent man-slaughter	Forcible rape	Robbery	Aggra-vated assault		Burglary	Larceny-theft	Motor vehicle theft	Arson*
SOUTH CAROLINA — Continued											
University of South Carolina:											
Coastal Carolina	4,023	2	....	1	1	....	77	5	72	....	....
Columbia	26,471	18	....	1	5	12	681	25	628	28	....
Winthrop University	5,025	....	....	....	....	....	95	7	87	1	....
SOUTH DAKOTA											
South Dakota State University	9,260	2	....	....	1	1	220	120	100	....	....
TENNESSEE											
Austin Peay State University	7,816	3	....	....	2	1	100	14	86	....	....
East Tennessee State University	11,711	2	....	1	....	1	177	4	165	8	....
Middle Tennessee State University	16,787	5	....	....	2	3	314	29	281	4	....
The University of Tennessee, Memphis	2,001	1	....	....	....	1	223	8	191	24	....
Knoxville	26,579	24	....	2	9	13	657	41	616	....	8
Martin	5,646	4	....	1	....	3	99	3	96	....	....
TEXAS											
Alamo Community College	4	12	....	....	3	9	479	6	441	32	....
Alvin Community College	3,904	....					15	1	14		
Amarillo College	6,553	....					48	3	45		
Angelo State University	6,102	1				1	50	2	48		
Austin College	1,146						31	1	30		
Baylor University	12,179	7				7	239	33	200	6	2
Baylor University Medical Center	4	9			4	5	259	8	244	7	
Central Texas College	6,217	7		1	1	5	68	3	64	1	
College of the Mainland	3,875	1				1	31	....	31		
Eastfield College	10,151	1				1	108	3	104	1	
East Texas State University, Commerce	4	3			2	1	142	34	105	3	1
Hardin-Simmons University	1,950	....					33	2	31		
Houston Baptist University	2,201	....					33	11	22		
Lamar University, Beaumont	10,687	9			1	8	143	13	114	16	
Laredo Community College	5,943						70	10	56	4	
McLennan Community College	6,006						42		42		
Midwestern State University	5,764	1				1	95	10	85		
North Harris Montgomery Community College	17,537	1				1	61	....	57	4	
North Lake College	7,212	....					39	....	38	1	
Paris Junior College	2,492	4			1	3	24	4	20		2
Prairie View A & M University	5,660	12		5		7	361	108	242	11	2
Rice University	4,251	2			1	1	262	15	231	16	4
Richland College	13,117	....					98	1	94	3	
St. Mary's University	4,006	1				1	119	14	87	18	
Southern Methodist University	8,978	2		1		1	175	12	157	6	1
South Plains College	5,960	....					47	13	34		
Southwestern University	1,204	2				2	26	4	22		
Southwest Texas State University	21,302	22		1	2	19	460	101	353	6	5
Stephen F. Austin State University	12,721	5		2	2	1	353	34	313	6	
Sul Ross State University	2,706	1			1		30	16	14		
Tarleton State University	6,425	2		1		1	65	11	54		
Texas A & M University:											
College Station	4	7		2	1	4	714	53	648	13	2
Corpus Christi	4	....					13	1	10	2	
Galveston	1,278	....					4	....	4		
Kingsville	6,414	....					115	35	80		
Texas Christian University	6,728	4			1	3	131	19	112		
Texas College Osteo. Med.	416						53	2	49	2	
Texas Southern University	10,777	36		1	10	25	233	53	161	19	7
Texas State Technical College:											
Amarillo	560	4		2		2	26	4	20	2	1
Waco	3,379	2		1	1	....	206	54	145	7	2
Texas Tech. University:											
Health Science Center	1,263	3				3	261	22	236	3	
Lubbock	24,154	8		3	1	4	504	84	410	10	9
Texas Woman's University	9,636	1		1			51	1	49	1	
Trinity University	2,511	1				1	181	36	127	18	5
Tyler Junior College	8,367	6				6	69	11	55	3	

See footnotes at end of table.

Table 9. — Number of Offenses Known to the Police, Universities and Colleges, 1993 — Continued

University/College	Student enroll-ment[1]	Violent[2] crime total	Murder and non-negligent man-slaughter	Forcible rape	Robbery	Aggra-vated assault	Property[3] crime total	Burglary	Larceny-theft	Motor vehicle theft	Arson*
TEXAS — Continued											
University of Houston:											
Central Campus	33,022	17			5	12	560	9	512	39	
Clearlake	6,681						24		24		
Downtown Campus	8,092	4				4	106	6	93	7	1
University of North Texas	26,433	11			3	8	336	84	248	4	
University of Texas:											
Arlington	24,729	12		2	4	6	321	20	294	7	
Austin	49,253	18		2	1	15	767	18	721	28	
Brownsville	6,429						69	2	67		
Dallas	8,993	1				1	64	5	59		
El Paso	17,223	6				6	274	20	231	23	1
Galveston	[4]	1			1		227	8	213	6	
Health Science Center, San Antonio	2,573						40		38	2	
Health Science Center, Tyler	3,203	1				1	22		22		
Houston	[4]	3			1	2	324	8	315	1	1
Pan American	[4]	1				1	196	48	136	12	
Permian Basin	2,281	1				1	17		16	1	
San Antonio	16,767	3		2		1	146	8	135	3	
Southwestern Medical School	1,634						147		147		
Tyler	1,613	1				1	26		26		1
West Texas State University	6,040	2		1		1	152	43	105	4	3
UTAH											
Brigham Young University	32,289	5			1	4	488	15	463	10	3
College of Eastern Utah	2,743	2		1		1	28	1	27		
Salt Lake State College	17,024	2				2	104	6	92	6	
Southern Utah University	4,060	4		1		3	50	27	21	2	
University of Utah	26,795	14		3	3	8	870	51	813	6	
Utah State University	16,513	1		1			278	8	267	3	
Utah Valley Community College	9,619	1		1			121	7	113	1	
Weber State University	14,993	5		2		3	126	27	97	2	
VERMONT											
University of Vermont	10,885	4		2		2	322	14	299	9	
VIRGINIA											
Christopher Newport College	4,880						30	1	29		
Clinch Valley College	1,839	6		3		3	28	12	16		
College of William & Mary	7,766	5		1	1	3	331	12	317	2	7
George Mason University	20,829	22				22	571	92	477	2	
Hampton University	5,582	11			2	9	83	19	64		
James Madison University	11,343	2			1	1	201	58	142	1	
Longwood College	3,287	4		2		2	103	1	101	1	1
Mary Washington College	3,696	11		6	1	4	168	32	135	1	1
Norfolk State University	8,624	10			5	5	211	45	161	5	4
Northern Virginia Community College	38,343	7		1		6	130		128	2	1
Old Dominion University	16,507						401	27	362	12	
Radford University	9,470	8				8	165	4	161		3
Thomas Nelson Community College	7,815						38		38		
University of Richmond	4,678	7				7	154	12	140	2	
University of Virginia	21,535	7		1	2	4	649	12	627	10	1
Virginia Commonwealth University	21,939	13		1	4	8	705	13	685	7	
Virginia Military Institute	1,265						7	1	6		
Virginia Polytechnic Institute and State University	26,003	23		1	2	20	477	22	452	3	2
Virginia State University	4,435	13		1	1	11	132	14	117	1	2
Virginia Western Community College	6,626	1				1	7		7		
WASHINGTON											
Central Washington University	7,685	4		2		2	266	23	239	4	1
Eastern Washington University	8,356	3		2		1	104	6	97	1	
University of Washington	34,597	21		3	6	12	1,019	181	830	8	3
Washington State University	17,871	14		6	2	6	411	36	369	6	1
Western Washington University	10,145	2		1		1	247	23	220	4	

See footnotes at end of table.

Table 9. — Number of Offenses Known to the Police, Universities and Colleges, 1993 — Continued

University/College	Student enroll-ment[1]	Violent[2] crime total	Violent crime				Property[3] crime total	Property crime			
			Murder and non-negligent man-slaughter	Forcible rape	Robbery	Aggra-vated assault		Burglary	Larceny-theft	Motor vehicle theft	Arson*
WEST VIRGINIA											
Concord College	2,960	....	....	....	....	....	29	15	14	....	....
Glenville State College	2,346	....	....	....	....	....	19	2	17	....	....
Marshall University	13,093	....	....	....	....	....	149	6	141	2	....
West Liberty State College	2,377	5	....	1	....	4	20	....	20	....	1
West Virginia State College	4,793	6	....	....	....	6	40	11	29	....	....
West Virginia Tech	3,051	1	....	....	....	1	22	9	13	....	....
West Virginia University	22,712	6	....	2	1	3	403	33	362	8	....
WISCONSIN											
University of Wisconsin:											
Eau Claire	10,635	1	....	....	....	1	173	....	172	1	1
Green Bay	5,205	5	....	....	1	4	67	4	62	1	....
La Crosse	8,648	2	....	1	....	1	113	19	93	1	1
Madison	41,824	12	....	....	6	6	906	45	826	35	15
Milwaukee	24,991	2	....	....	2	....	328	20	302	6	....
Oshkosh	11,062	1	....	1	....	....	157	3	152	2	2
Parkside	5,174	6	....	4	....	2	108	5	101	2	....
Platteville	5,532	2	....	1	....	1	100	1	97	2	2
Stout	7,625	4	....	....	....	4	123	....	123	....	....
Superior	2,966	....	....	....	....	....	41	....	41	....	....
Whitewater	11,030	4	....	2	....	2	188	17	169	2	4
WYOMING											
University of Wyoming	12,044	11	....	2	....	9	288	8	277	3	....

[1]The student enrollment figures provided by the United States Department of Education are for 1992, the most recent year available. The enrollment figure includes full-time and part-time students. See Appendix I for details.

[2]Violent crimes are offenses of murder, forcible rape, robbery, and aggravated assault.

[3]Property crimes are offenses of burglary, larceny-theft, and motor vehicle theft. Data are not included for the property crime of arson.

[4]Student enrollment figures were not available.

[5]1993 figures are not comparable to prior years.

[6]Complete data for 1993 were not available for the states of Illinois and Kansas; therefore, it was necessary that their crime counts be estimated. "See Offense Estimation," page 376 for details.

[7]Forcible rape figures furnished by the state-level Uniform Crime Reporting (UCR) Program administered by the Michigan State Police and the Minnesota Department of Public Safety were not in accordance with national UCR guidelines. Therefore, the figures were excluded from the forcible rape and violent crime total categories.

NOTE: Caution should be exercised in making any inter-campus comparisons or ranking schools, as university/college crime statistics are affected by a variety of factors. These include: demographic characteristics of the surrounding community, ratio of male to female students, number of on-campus residents, accessibility of outside visitors, size of enrollment, etc.

Table 10. — Number of Offenses Known to the Police, Suburban Counties, 1993

[The data shown in this table do not reflect county totals but are the number of offenses reported by the sheriff's office, county police department, or state police.]

* Arson is shown only if 12 months of arson data were received. Leaders (...) indicate zero data. The Modified Crime Index total is the sum of the Crime Index offenses, including arson.

County by State	Crime Index total	Modified* Crime Index total	Murder and non-negligent man-slaughter	Forcible rape	Robbery	Aggra-vated assault	Burglary	Larceny-theft	Motor vehicle theft	Arson*
ALABAMA										
Autauga	192		1	...	2	15	71	96	7	
Baldwin	1,292		...	13	13	116	371	725	54	
Blount	490		2	3	3	74	195	179	34	
Calhoun	416		3	6	6	38	157	183	23	
Colbert	148		6	2	...	19	41	64	16	
Dale	127		...	2	...	19	50	53	3	
Elmore	806		2	5	6	92	303	361	37	
Etowah	476		3	4	4	38	145	258	24	
Houston	388		2	2	5	50	112	194	23	
Jefferson	6,619	6,729	10	55	133	898	1,646	3,376	501	110
Lawrence	86		5	...	2	18	19	37	5	
Limestone	193		2	2	1	59	51	60	18	
Madison	1,525	1,528	...	14	25	181	481	761	63	3
Mobile	2,499		8	12	50	280	661	1,389	99	
Montgomery	989	989	2	9	12	149	305	461	51	...
Morgan	322		1	1	2	11	134	161	12	
Russell	415	415	...	6	6	57	156	165	25	...
St. Clair	406		...	5	8	41	148	176	28	
Shelby	248		5	8	13	15	115	58	34	
Tuscaloosa	1,911		2	15	28	322	526	903	115	
ARIZONA										
Maricopa	6,136	6,150	22	21	68	398	1,585	3,328	714	14
Pima	12,854	12,960	19	97	121	464	2,153	8,858	1,142	106
Pinal	1,781	1,783	9	32	17	157	635	790	141	2
ARKANSAS										
Benton	969	969	3	15	3	70	225	622	31	...
Crawford	499	518	...	8	1	80	141	242	27	19
Crittenden	537	538	5	10	15	59	184	223	41	1
Faulkner	459	461	5	1	...	28	149	246	30	2
Jefferson	492	495	1	9	9	20	224	192	37	3
Lonoke	144	144	...	1	2	2	39	59	41	...
Miller	421	422	2	5	...	55	110	216	33	1
Pulaski	2,200	2,217	14	31	65	364	571	1,006	149	17
Saline	1,180	1,184	2	22	6	102	356	627	65	4
Sebastian	270	270	1	3	1	25	81	148	11	...
Washington	400	404	3	3	1	26	190	152	25	4
CALIFORNIA										
Alameda	5,648	5,675	12	48	221	1,101	1,241	2,433	592	27
Alameda Highway Patrol	68		...	...	...	...	...	1	67	
Alameda State Police	198	198	...	1	3	10	28	149	7	...
Butte	3,312	3,441	4	41	50	322	1,335	1,551	9	129
Butte Highway Patrol	276		...	...	...	1	...	59	216	
Butte State Police	38	38	...	...	...	5	4	28	1	...
Contra Costa	6,292	6,350	29	61	234	405	1,923	3,634	6	58
Contra Costa Highway Patrol	799		...	...	...	...	...	95	704	
Contra Costa State Police	16	16	...	...	1	...	2	10	3	...
El Dorado	2,961	2,977	2	23	25	280	1,363	1,239	29	16
El Dorado Highway Patrol	252		...	...	...	...	...	52	200	
Fresno	8,990	9,009	33	92	251	1,095	2,979	3,047	1,493	19
Fresno Highway Patrol	149		...	...	...	2	...	18	129	
Fresno State Police	83	83	...	...	2	...	8	59	14	
Kern	16,895	17,932	37	107	481	1,933	4,844	7,963	1,530	1,037
Kern Highway Patrol	207		...	...	...	...	...	71	136	
Kern State Police	34	34	...	...	...	...	1	33	...	
Los Angeles	45,121	45,673	229	321	4,603	10,901	8,824	11,825	8,418	552
Los Angeles Highway Patrol	630		...	...	...	348	...	32	250	
Los Angeles State Police	408	408	...	...	13	33	84	235	43	...
Madera	2,021	2,072	7	41	26	118	1,042	782	5	51
Madera Highway Patrol	179		...	...	...	...	...	36	143	

Table 10. — Number of Offenses Known to the Police, Suburban Counties, 1993 — Continued

County by State	Crime Index total	Modified* Crime Index total	Murder and non-negligent man-slaughter	Forcible rape	Robbery	Aggra-vated assault	Burglary	Larceny-theft	Motor vehicle theft	Arson*
CALIFORNIA — Continued										
Marin	1,747	1,755	1	10	39	203	410	1,075	9	8
Marin Highway Patrol	102	...	...	...	...	...	...	14	88	...
Merced	2,151	2,157	8	24	37	153	825	1,103	1	6
Merced Highway Patrol	342	...	...	...	...	...	...	44	298	...
Merced State Police	4	4	...	...	...	...	1	3	...	...
Monterey	3,270	3,420	4	23	77	185	1,061	1,905	15	150
Monterey Highway Patrol	195	...	...	...	...	...	...	20	175	...
Napa	890	893	1	8	11	85	267	494	24	3
Napa Highway Patrol	64	...	...	...	...	...	...	23	41	...
Orange	4,685	4,731	8	24	118	478	1,118	2,246	693	46
Orange Highway Patrol	54	...	...	...	...	25	...	6	23	...
Orange State Police	19	19	...	...	...	...	2	15	2	...
Placer	3,695	3,719	7	27	38	305	1,238	2,049	31	24
Placer Highway Patrol	261	...	...	...	...	...	...	73	188	...
Riverside	22,406	22,587	57	93	490	2,882	7,247	8,551	3,086	181
Riverside Highway Patrol	61	...	...	...	...	7	...	6	48	...
Riverside State Police	54	54	...	...	...	1	15	31	7	...
Sacramento	34,340	34,472	60	286	1,565	3,086	10,470	18,549	324	132
Sacramento Highway Patrol	8,605	...	...	...	...	...	...	548	8,057	...
Sacramento State Police	740	741	...	1	11	48	92	516	72	1
San Bernardino	13,484	13,534	59	111	372	1,138	4,958	5,086	1,760	50
San Bernardino Highway Patrol	57	...	...	...	...	4	...	11	42	...
San Bernardino State Police	75	75	...	...	...	5	23	42	5	...
San Diego	26,455	26,630	48	164	886	2,669	7,717	10,657	4,314	175
San Diego Highway Patrol	113	...	...	...	...	5	...	25	83	...
San Diego State Police	92	93	...	1	...	1	13	71	6	1
San Joaquin	6,546	6,617	17	53	191	412	2,469	3,350	54	71
San Joaquin Highway Patrol	907	...	...	...	...	...	...	101	806	...
San Joaquin State Police	45	45	...	...	...	1	3	40	1	...
San Luis Obispo	1,957	1,961	...	19	14	236	598	1,087	3	4
San Luis Obispo Highway Patrol	143	...	...	...	...	1	...	40	102	...
San Mateo	3,346	3,346	5	27	93	85	845	1,682	609	...
San Mateo Highway Patrol	92	...	...	...	...	...	...	2	90	...
San Mateo State Police	12	12	...	...	...	1	1	10	...	...
Santa Barbara	4,086	4,127	5	47	42	359	1,735	1,862	36	41
Santa Barbara Highway Patrol	195	...	...	...	...	3	...	46	146	...
Santa Barbara State Police	1	1	...	...	...	...	...	1	...	...
Santa Clara	3,781	3,784	8	48	43	436	763	2,287	196	3
Santa Clara Highway Patrol	61	...	...	...	...	...	...	10	51	...
Santa Clara State Police	46	46	...	...	...	9	2	33	2	...
Santa Cruz	4,407	4,441	5	32	75	493	1,175	2,615	12	34
Santa Cruz Highway Patrol	341	...	...	...	...	3	...	79	259	...
Shasta	1,941	2,017	3	27	23	171	706	1,000	11	76
Shasta Highway Patrol	252	...	...	...	...	...	...	41	211	...
Shasta State Police	21	21	...	...	...	1	7	11	2	...
Solano	758	765	4	13	18	103	333	284	3	7
Solano Highway Patrol	91	...	...	...	...	...	...	12	79	...
Solano State Police	8	8	...	...	2	1	3	2	...	...
Sonoma	4,480	4,525	14	52	73	489	1,471	2,367	14	45
Sonoma Highway Patrol	563	...	...	...	...	...	...	151	412	...
Sonoma State Police	53	53	...	1	...	4	10	36	2	...
Stanislaus	6,710	6,890	7	69	129	1,410	2,460	2,569	66	180
Stanislaus Highway Patrol	681	...	...	...	...	4	...	75	602	...
Stanislaus State Police	5	5	...	...	...	...	2	3	...	...
Sutter	1,287	1,289	...	13	8	216	494	534	22	2
Sutter Highway Patrol	70	...	...	...	...	...	...	1	69	...
Tulare	5,091	5,580	14	63	86	568	1,695	2,665	...	489
Tulare Highway Patrol	725	...	...	...	...	...	...	87	638	...
Ventura	2,071	2,117	6	25	33	270	628	936	173	46
Ventura Highway Patrol	41	...	...	...	...	3	...	19	19	...
Ventura State Police	2	2	...	...	...	...	1	1	...	...
Yolo	708	720	2	11	15	127	247	297	9	12
Yolo Highway Patrol	84	...	...	...	...	...	...	17	67	...
Yolo State Police	29	31	...	...	...	2	2	14	11	2
Yuba	2,639	2,657	1	22	30	465	793	1,314	14	18
Yuba Highway Patrol	175	...	...	...	...	...	...	3	172	...

Table 10. — Number of Offenses Known to the Police, Suburban Counties, 1993 — Continued

County by State	Crime Index total	Modified* Crime Index total	Murder and non-negligent man-slaughter	Forcible rape	Robbery	Aggra-vated assault	Burglary	Larceny-theft	Motor vehicle theft	Arson*
COLORADO										
Adams	4,171	4,219	8	57	70	262	990	2,279	505	48
Arapahoe	3,096	3,125	9	....	43	48	758	2,073	165	29
Boulder	917	950	2	40	7	57	298	445	68	33
Douglas	1,014	1,027	1	2	6	63	225	690	27	13
Jefferson	4,745	4,795	2	22	40	58	1,008	3,397	218	50
Larimer	1,281	1,288	1	4	7	44	259	902	64	7
Pueblo	658	663	....	4	7	31	190	397	29	5
DELAWARE										
New Castle Police Department	8,462	8,515	5	186	128	814	1,723	4,818	788	53
FLORIDA										
Alachua	5,779	5,789	6	65	154	644	1,585	2,905	420	10
Bay	4,172	4,184	3	45	24	346	895	2,687	172	12
Brevard	8,097	8,148	9	70	111	806	1,755	4,986	360	51
Broward	11,395	11,455	13	96	579	1,406	2,354	5,764	1,183	60
Charlotte	3,246	3,250	5	19	58	252	875	1,847	190	4
Clay	4,136	4,136	7	58	43	482	790	2,568	188	....
Collier	7,986	8,017	11	100	267	803	2,204	3,923	678	31
Dade	139,937	140,054	183	643	7,878	12,057	27,033	70,310	21,833	117
Escambia	14,393	14,484	18	117	513	2,075	3,495	7,534	641	91
Flagler	671	675	....	6	6	38	194	412	15	4
Gadsden	1,213	1,219	5	21	67	165	372	447	136	6
Hernando	4,600	4,620	13	20	38	576	1,052	2,708	193	20
Hillsborough	37,276	37,397	25	290	1,013	3,204	7,982	20,201	4,561	121
Lake	3,174	3,178	4	48	22	402	1,132	1,321	245	4
Lee	9,431	9,449	13	136	217	531	2,274	4,879	1,381	18
Leon	4,109	4,134	2	48	86	524	1,467	1,553	429	25
Manatee	11,140	11,191	9	80	320	1,521	2,832	5,641	737	51
Marion	6,348	6,371	4	135	111	1,253	1,857	2,671	317	23
Martin	4,315	4,320	9	27	113	274	1,096	2,573	223	5
Nassau	1,218	1,224	6	4	11	150	317	670	60	6
Okaloosa	3,690	3,690	5	19	53	294	756	2,376	187	....
Orange	35,445	35,483	19	241	1,161	3,958	8,719	17,992	3,355	38
Osceola	4,735	4,746	6	46	86	421	1,858	2,063	255	11
Palm Beach	30,837	30,985	20	193	632	2,829	7,173	17,179	2,811	148
Pasco	9,425	9,465	4	89	115	830	2,733	5,155	499	40
Pinellas	13,402	13,486	10	121	182	1,331	2,878	8,214	666	84
St. Johns	3,166	3,167	3	16	46	490	762	1,697	152	1
St. Lucie	3,084	3,104	4	27	54	272	959	1,425	343	20
Santa Rosa	3,135	3,144	2	42	26	522	886	1,512	145	9
Sarasota	9,489	9,508	5	44	123	675	2,492	5,669	481	19
Seminole	7,119	7,136	3	64	145	826	1,774	3,824	483	17
GEORGIA										
Barrow	532	538	2	1	5	14	184	281	45	6
Bibb	1,820	1,821	2	3	14	67	412	1,191	131	1
Bryan	153	155	....	1	4	9	51	81	7	2
Butts	207	210	....	3	3	19	79	96	7	3
Carroll	1,361	1,363	3	16	21	75	323	785	138	2
Catoosa	916	918	....	5	3	26	137	588	157	2
Chatham Police Department	3,513	3,522	4	23	60	246	805	2,083	292	9
Chattahoochee	114	115	....	....	1	12	30	64	7	1
Cherokee	2,026	2,064	1	9	8	111	567	1,170	160	38
Clayton Police Department	9,547	9,605	15	60	277	505	2,086	5,664	940	58
Cobb Police Department	15,143	15,204	13	77	336	708	2,857	9,516	1,636	61
Columbia	2,438	2,439	4	39	23	64	391	1,718	199	1
Coweta	1,155	1,167	....	8	11	45	282	660	149	12
Dade	163	163	1	....	1	8	44	97	12	....
DeKalb Police Department	47,236	47,448	66	217	2,477	1,142	10,502	25,799	7,033	212
Dougherty	28	....	....	....	3	1	3	19	2	....
Dougherty Police Department	351	351	....	1	5	7	121	200	17	....
Douglas	1,778	1,795	2	15	27	67	454	1,009	204	17

Table 10.—Number of Offenses Known to the Police, Suburban Counties, 1993—Continued

County by State	Crime Index total	Modified* Crime Index total	Murder and non-negligent man-slaughter	Forcible rape	Robbery	Aggra-vated assault	Burglary	Larceny-theft	Motor vehicle theft	Arson*
GEORGIA—Continued										
Fayette	527	529	1	2	7	5	142	338	32	2
Forsyth	2,447	2,457	4	12	13	168	563	1,485	202	10
Fulton Police Department	9,199	9,237	15	71	372	358	1,830	4,738	1,815	38
Gwinnett Police Department	15,910	16,022	9	58	270	358	3,052	10,970	1,193	112
Harris	358	360	4	1	1	6	165	167	14	2
Henry Police Department	2,556	2,559	2	12	46	143	562	1,627	164	3
Houston	962	964	7	6	3	97	243	567	39	2
Jones	294	295	....	1	4	29	115	126	19	1
Lee	303	303	....	1	1	6	95	196	5	....
Newton	1,623	1,623	2	5	12	56	469	993	86	....
Oconee	428	428	1	3	2	17	129	258	18	....
Paulding	1,178	1,187	....	14	4	24	362	665	109	9
Pickens	262	262	....	....	4	13	117	100	28	....
Richmond	7,360	7,367	22	68	386	796	1,993	3,028	1,067	7
Rockdale	1,972	1,972	....	14	22	190	442	1,147	157	....
Spalding	1,080	1,081	1	11	13	114	295	571	75	1
Twiggs	84	84	....	....	1	....	50	27	6	....
Walton	470	471	....	5	8	12	161	269	15	1
IDAHO										
Ada	1,817	1,826	....	20	6	103	377	1,212	99	9
Canyon	890	892	1	5	3	48	238	511	84	2
ILLINOIS[1]										
Cook			10		55	205	1,051	2,553	360	7
Lake			2		18	160	784	1,625	296	19
McHenry			4		3	31	294	781	62	....
Winnebago			2		40	111	761	1,396	127	4
INDIANA										
Allen	1,976	1,980	6	9	13	50	474	1,198	226	4
Allen State Police	137	137	....	6	....	19	16	81	15	....
Clark	393	395	....	2	2	....	129	229	31	2
Clark State Police	207	207	....	2	3	37	64	75	26	....
Dearborn	359	360	....	....	....	19	126	186	28	1
Dearborn State Police	92	92	....	2	....	17	22	45	6	....
Hancock	415	415	....	2	2	....	140	259	12	....
Hancock State Police	33	33	....	....	....	9	5	15	4	....
Howard	687	687	1	5	2	171	148	331	29	....
Howard State Police	28	28	....	2	....	3	5	14	4	....
Huntington	170	171	....	1	....	34	56	78	1	1
Huntington State Police	25	25	....	....	....	5	4	12	4	....
Lake	2,289	2,289	....	7	19	97	339	1,387	440	....
Lake State Police	258	258	....	3	7	78	13	81	76	....
Marion	20,991	21,077	17	160	436	316	3,726	14,562	1,774	86
Marion State Police	386	386	1	15	7	73	11	154	125	....
Porter	1,094	1,096	1	10	1	43	235	710	94	2
Porter State Police	84	86	....	1	2	24	....	49	8	2
St. Joseph	2,471	2,477	2	15	27	16	471	1,850	90	6
St. Joseph State Police	147	148	....	2	....	25	36	74	10	1
Tippecanoe	1,068	1,073	....	6	8	189	189	652	24	5
Tippecanoe State Police	119	119	....	2	2	25	10	62	18	....
Vanderburgh	698	710	....	4	2	78	100	496	18	12
Vanderburgh State Police	41	41	....	4	....	1	2	27	7	....
Wells	90	90	1	....	....	1	40	42	6	....
Wells State Police	29	30	1	....	....	1	8	18	1	1

See footnotes at end of table.

County by State	Crime Index total	Modified* Crime Index total	Murder and non-negligent man-slaughter	Forcible rape	Robbery	Aggra-vated assault	Burglary	Larceny-theft	Motor vehicle theft	Arson*
IOWA										
Black Hawk	290		....	2	....	24	99	157	8	
Dubuque	400	406	....	19	....	17	185	162	17	6
Johnson	369		....	5	3	58	86	204	13	
Linn	882		....	5	2	84	297	434	60	
Warren	356		....	1	....	27	96	222	10	
Woodbury	266		....	5	1	24	114	112	10	
KANSAS¹										
KENTUCKY										
Boone	168	168	....	2	....	27	21	114	4	....
Boone Police Department	808	808	....	16	6	85	169	492	40	....
Boone State Police	17	17	....	....	1	3	1	12	....	
Bourbon	53	53	....	1	....	5	22	20	....	
Bourbon State Police	94	94	1	7	1	6	33	44	2	
Boyd	98	99	....	....	1	11	36	44	6	1
Boyd Police Department	5	5	....	....	....	....	....	5	....	
Boyd State Police	197	203	....	5	3	24	55	103	7	6
Bullitt	284	284	1	....	3	4	79	167	30	
Bullitt State Police	99	103	2	5	2	19	28	36	7	4
Campbell Police Department	318	318	....	8	1	23	89	182	15	
Campbell State Police	9	9	....	....	....	3	2	3	1	
Carter	2	2	....	....	....	1	....	1	....	
Carter State Police	211	220	3	2	1	62	60	59	24	9
Christian	441	447	1	1	4	87	120	207	21	6
Christian Police Department	48	48	....	5	....	28	4	10	1	
Christian State Police	27	28	1	....	....	8	6	11	1	1
Clark	231	232	....	1	1	8	68	140	13	1
Clark State Police	42	44	....	....	....	4	8	29	1	2
Daviess	389	389	....	1	3	15	115	244	11	
Daviess State Police	196	197	....	5	1	25	96	66	3	1
Fayette State Police	11	11	....	4	....	1	....	6	....	
Gallatin	3	3	....	....	....	3	....	....	....	
Gallatin State Police	60	68	....	1	....	6	23	25	5	8
Grant	10	10	....	....	....	....	6	3	1	
Grant State Police	259	259	....	5	6	28	77	125	18	
Greenup	102	102	....	....	....	2	50	43	7	
Greenup State Police	81	93	2	1	4	16	28	24	6	12
Henderson	221	221	....	....	....	3	63	150	5	
Jefferson Police Department	13,871	13,934	11	72	302	1,710	2,799	8,096	881	63
Jefferson State Police	6	6	....	1	1	....	....	....	4	
Jessamine	270	270	....	1	....	6	86	164	13	
Jessamine State Police	59	63	....	22	1	9	13	8	6	4
Kenton Police Department	269	275	....	3	1	16	98	134	17	6
Kenton State Police	26	26	....	3	....	5	....	17	1	
Oldham	36	37	....	....	....	1	11	24	....	1
Oldham Police Department	486	486	....	2	3	33	145	284	19	
Oldham State Police	52	52	....	3	....	8	11	28	2	
Pendleton State Police	77	81	....	2	....	8	30	35	2	4
Scott	254	255	....	....	1	22	56	160	15	1
Scott State Police	12	13	....	....	....	1	4	7	....	1
Woodford	5	5	....	....	....	....	2	3	....	
Woodford Police Department	169	169	2	....	....	28	45	88	6	....
LOUISIANA										
Ascension	1,248	1,248	3	8	9	24	287	889	28	....
Bossier	887	891	3	8	10	53	205	570	38	4
Caddo	1,661	1,661	7	22	28	232	470	811	91	....

See footnotes at end of table.

Table 10. — Number of Offenses Known to the Police, Suburban Counties, 1993 — Continued

County by State	Crime Index total	Modified* Crime Index total	Murder and non-negligent man-slaughter	Forcible rape	Robbery	Aggra-vated assault	Burglary	Larceny-theft	Motor vehicle theft	Arson*
LOUISIANA — Continued										
Calcasieu	5,128	5,148	3	57	89	630	1,137	3,010	202	20
East Baton Rouge	10,620	10,644	12	46	213	562	1,860	7,217	710	24
Jefferson	30,283	30,427	46	196	1,160	1,879	4,842	18,873	3,287	144
Lafayette	1,920	1,931	2	19	26	217	497	1,072	87	11
Lafourche	1,561	1,572	4	8	28	62	454	920	85	11
Livingston	765	767	13	17	9	80	432	192	22	2
Ouachita	1,848	1,848	4	7	15	179	781	762	100	....
Rapides	2,177	2,180	4	31	15	521	513	939	154	3
St. Charles	2,124	2,131	5	20	49	432	445	1,062	111	7
St. Landry	905	905	4	6	16	85	259	493	42	....
St. Martin	683	685	2	7	7	52	196	400	19	2
St. Tammany	3,749	3,765	9	39	50	326	911	2,179	235	16
Terrebonne	3,077	3,095	1	22	37	290	935	1,616	176	18
Webster	169	169	1	4	6	28	51	72	7	....
West Baton Rouge	938	941	1	10	14	75	176	630	32	3
MAINE										
Androscoggin	364	365	....	1	3	7	113	218	22	1
Androscoggin State Police	55	55	....	2	....	2	17	29	5	....
Cumberland	758	766	....	5	2	20	331	362	38	8
Cumberland State Police	126	127	....	3	....	4	51	62	6	1
MARYLAND										
Allegany	92	92	....	1	....	16	17	55	3	....
Allegany State Police	500	511	1	8	3	49	82	316	41	11
Anne Arundel	2	2	....	....	....	2	....	....	....	....
Anne Arundel Police Department	17,563	17,634	17	110	441	1,090	3,424	10,965	1,516	71
Anne Arundel State Police	960	960	1	5	5	27	50	677	195	....
Baltimore Police Department	43,693	44,075	36	281	2,307	4,827	7,881	22,925	5,436	382
Baltimore State Police	120	120	....	....	2	26	3	70	19	....
Calvert	840	840	....	9	13	89	193	503	33	....
Calvert State Police	433	446	4	5	3	84	81	240	16	13
Carroll	38	38	....	....	....	....	5	29	4	....
Carroll State Police	1,989	2,003	1	29	18	46	573	1,195	127	14
Cecil	601	601	2	6	5	47	179	333	29	....
Cecil State Police	1,352	1,376	3	4	16	212	339	672	106	24
Charles	4,167	4,167	4	18	84	402	631	2,679	349	....
Charles State Police	384	420	1	4	15	32	47	235	50	36
Frederick	778	778	....	7	3	63	193	465	47	....
Frederick State Police	1,157	1,193	1	11	12	180	211	683	59	36
Harford	3,178	3,178	....	30	34	184	770	1,983	177	22
Harford State Police	772	794	....	12	13	43	200	423	81	22
Howard	8,333	8,333	4	26	127	326	1,488	5,284	1,078	....
Howard State Police	99	137	1	....	3	22	2	66	5	38
Montgomery	22	22	....	....	....	22	....	....	....	....
Montgomery Police Department	31,141	31,482	29	205	842	1,034	4,529	21,405	3,097	341
Montgomery State Police	48	48	....	2	....	23	1	19	3	....
Prince George's Police Department	48,314	48,644	133	406	3,875	3,491	8,788	23,423	8,198	330
Prince George's State Police	161	161	....	2	2	35	6	75	41	....
Queen Anne's	420	420	....	5	5	51	110	232	17	....
Queen Anne's State Police	549	563	1	1	6	43	138	323	37	14
Washington	832	832	3	7	9	46	214	502	51	....
Washington State Police	430	456	2	8	4	45	115	234	22	26
MASSACHUSETTS										
Barnstable State Police	79	79	....	2	1	44	2	18	12	....
Berkshire State Police	112	112	....	1	....	15	51	39	6	....
Dukes State Police	11	11	....	....	....	5	1	5	....	....
Franklin State Police	34	34	....	....	....	5	11	14	4	....
Hampden State Police	39	39	....	....	1	11	12	9	6	....
Hampshire State Police	33	33	....	....	....	7	9	15	2	....
Plymouth State Police	116	116	....	1	....	37	1	18	59	....
Worcester State Police	8	8	....	1	....	3	3	1	....	....

Table 10. — Number of Offenses Known to the Police, Suburban Counties, 1993 — Continued

County by State	Crime Index total	Modified* Crime Index total	Murder and non-negligent manslaughter	Forcible rape	Robbery	Aggravated assault	Burglary	Larceny-theft	Motor vehicle theft	Arson*
MICHIGAN[2]										
Allegan			4		3	87	411	825	69	16
Allegan State Police			....		1	45	252	282	31	13
Bay			....		7	21	151	617	50	4
Bay State Police			....		6	21	74	317	28	13
Berrien			....		12	94	294	444	50	
Berrien State Police			....		16	81	176	389	35	22
Calhoun			....		3	42	130	226	25	7
Calhoun State Police			....		3	13	54	97	11	9
Clinton			1		1	9	114	257	20	2
Clinton State Police			....		1	2	7	9	....	
Eaton			3		32	83	352	1,889	122	6
Eaton State Police			....		....	5	16	37	4	2
Ingham			1		7	110	287	842	69	14
Ingham State Police			....		2	8	9	163	19	3
Jackson			2		10	72	182	562	40	14
Jackson State Police			....		5	122	90	233	20	2
Kalamazoo			2		16	67	484	1,634	131	14
Kalamazoo State Police			....		....	5	6	12	3	7
Kent			3		26	191	741	2,731	175	17
Kent State Police			1		3	9	138	417	23	3
Lapeer			....		....	36	180	471	32	7
Lapeer State Police			....		3	16	55	126	20	2
Lenawee			....		5	46	256	430	52	6
Lenawee State Police			....		6	21	103	126	15	3
Livingston			....		4	45	206	549	42	4
Livingston State Police			1		4	46	264	572	45	11
Macomb			....		14	71	319	1,432	152	....
Macomb State Police			3		2	20	37	172	10	10
Midland			....		....	103	168	461	31	4
Midland State Police			....		....	....	5	5	....	
Monroe			....		42	233	625	2,199	264	30
Monroe State Police			2		5	37	104	416	42	12
Muskegon			....		7	46	340	864	87	1
Muskegon State Police			....		2	44	115	310	23	5
Oakland			3		36	478	970	4,464	276	71
Oakland State Police			....		3	64	118	240	21	4
Ottawa			....		15	49	525	1,725	113	20
Ottawa State Police			....		....	10	103	232	14	4
Saginaw			1		25	175	197	906	92	....
Saginaw State Police			4		19	73	129	415	28	4
St. Clair			2		14	80	440	1,187	95	26
St. Clair State Police			....		1	22	97	172	24	12
Van Buren			1		4	42	358	388	62	11
Van Buren State Police			2		12	90	505	516	64	32
Washtenaw			8		80	371	556	1,381	281	19
Washtenaw State Police			1		11	45	97	154	23	15
MINNESOTA[2]										
Anoka			1		2	19	189	265	54	....
Carver			1		....	19	61	213	29	4
Chisago			....		7	20	233	778	78	1
Clay			....		....	6	41	55	14	....
Dakota			....		1	12	69	127	26	2
Hennepin			2		6	8	26	157	23	4
Houston			....		....	2	37	61	3	....
Isanti			....		2	4	105	110	30	1
Olmsted			....		....	13	198	248	34	....
Polk			....		....	6	78	98	17	1
Ramsey			....		....	....	25	87	13	1
Scott			....		....	17	88	192	34	2
Sherburne			1		1	16	98	357	35	....
St. Louis			2		4	22	461	380	66	9
Stearns			....		....	5	120	552	59	1
Washington			1	4	3	13	303	814	89	....

See footnotes at end of table.

Table 10. — Number of Offenses Known to the Police, Suburban Counties, 1993 — Continued

County by State	Crime Index total	Modified* Crime Index total	Murder and non-negligent man-slaughter	Forcible rape	Robbery	Aggra-vated assault	Burglary	Larceny-theft	Motor vehicle theft	Arson*
MISSISSIPPI										
Harrison	2,041	2,051	6	102	63	82	1,003	577	208	10
Madison	648	670	2	7	4	41	261	278	55	22
Rankin	921	929	6	8	15	34	388	413	57	8
MISSOURI										
Andrew	157	157	1	1		14	37	101	3	
Boone	680	682	1	13	9	59	153	415	30	2
Christian	375	375		4	1		130	226	14	
Clay	194	194		2	2	23	76	90	1	
Franklin	1,445	1,447		18	10	119	588	601	109	2
Greene	1,243	1,259		9	12	44	306	800	72	16
Jasper	543	543		9	1		216	283	34	
Jefferson	3,500	3,558	3	32	37	286	966	1,909	267	58
Platte	482	483	1	5	1	83	122	236	34	1
St. Charles	1,950	1,962	1	21	9	210	417	1,175	117	12
St. Louis Police Department	13,686	13,768	27	79	301	568	2,194	9,088	1,429	82
MONTANA										
Yellowstone	730	735	1	1	4	3	181	506	34	5
NEBRASKA										
Cass	318	322				6	90	216	6	4
Cass State Patrol	17	17				1	2	12	2	
Dakota	93	94				3	18	63	9	1
Douglas	1,467		1	12	11	59	247	1,050	87	
Douglas State Patrol	9	9		1		1		6	1	
Lancaster	579	586	3	4	3	9	124	403	33	7
Lancaster State Patrol	28	28				8	2	14	4	
Sarpy	849	850	2	4	8	28	142	624	41	1
Sarpy State Patrol	6	6				1	1	3	1	
Washington	83	83		1		1	24	53	4	
Washington State Patrol	1	1		1						
NEVADA										
Washoe	2,172	2,172	3	14	21	212	535	1,179	208	
NEW HAMPSHIRE										
Rockingham State Police	35	36	1	5	2	6	7	10	4	1
Strafford State Police	31	31	1	1		6	11	9	3	
NEW JERSEY										
Atlantic State Police	1,251	1,268		6	27	44	139	1,000	35	17
Bergen State Police	242	244	1		7	13	18	144	59	2
Burlington State Police	796	807	1	8	13	50	227	407	90	11
Camden State Police	51	51		1	1	7	8	29	5	
Cape May State Police	468	469	1	5	7	46	126	254	29	1
Cumberland State Police	891	917	7	21	20	103	276	393	71	26
Essex Police Department	432	446	3	23	85	26	29	180	86	14
Essex State Police	98	99			24	17	10	40	7	1
Gloucester State Police	23	26		2		3	2	8	8	3
Hudson State Police	34	35			3	3	3	21	4	1
Hunterdon State Police	309	310			1	12	81	198	17	1
Mercer State Police	343	344				7	26	261	49	1
Middlesex State Police	174	174			5	16	15	115	23	
Monmouth State Police	385	385		3	5	32	94	218	33	
Morris State Police	45	45		1	2	11	5	18	8	
Ocean State Police	138	139		1	3	14	17	95	8	1
Passaic State Police	30	30			1	3	4	8	14	
Salem State Police	525	532		6	9	38	146	291	35	7
Somerset State Police	16	16			1	5	3	6	1	
Sussex State Police	631	640		6	11	39	179	340	56	9

County by State	Crime Index total	Modified* Crime Index total	Murder and non-negligent man-slaughter	Forcible rape	Robbery	Aggra-vated assault	Burglary	Larceny-theft	Motor vehicle theft	Arson*
NEW JERSEY — Continued										
Union State Police	60	62	1	....	10	9	2	29	9	2
Warren State Police	295	305	....	4	1	18	63	174	35	10
NEW MEXICO										
Dona Ana	1,770	1,788	3	24	17	170	736	682	138	18
Sandoval	188	189	2	3	1	42	48	79	13	1
NEW YORK										
Albany	138	138	....	3	....	45	32	52	6	....
Albany State Police	347	347	....	4	3	11	86	225	18	....
Broome	1,012		1	3	7	30	248	702	21	
Broome State Police	774	781		4	2	27	232	493	16	7
Cayuga	385			4	3	27	130	211	10	
Cayuga State Police	510	510		2	2	90	82	329	5	
Chautauqua	1,120		1	3	....	130	260	673	53	
Chautauqua State Police	349	350	1	3	1	17	96	223	8	1
Chemung	833		1	13	4	50	114	632	19	
Chemung State Police	285	291		3	....	26	53	191	12	6
Dutchess	1,027		....	4	9	36	260	680	38	
Dutchess State Police	1,175		2	4	12	188	242	677	50	
Erie	1,935		2	5	23	237	292	1,237	139	
Erie State Police	741	749	1	2	5	71	172	442	48	8
Genesee	604	621	1	5	1	16	195	347	39	17
Genesee State Police	177	178		1	2	18	45	98	13	1
Herkimer State Police	412	420		2	2	18	195	184	11	8
Livingston	598	603	1	4	2	48	117	414	12	5
Livingston State Police	161	161	....	5	1	11	17	121	6	....
Madison	91		....	....	....	2	34	53	2	
Madison State Police	484	493	3	9	1	18	127	315	11	9
Montgomery	262	265		1	1	17	59	176	8	3
Montgomery State Police	166	168	....	....	2	2	32	124	6	2
Monroe	6,133		....	17	58	82	718	4,801	457	
Monroe State Police	444	444	....	3	1	11	32	385	12	....
Nassau	29,022	29,376	18	71	1,129	899	4,417	16,101	6,387	354
Nassau State Police	26		1	1	5	1	5	15	2	
Niagara	1,786		....	13	29	156	370	1,074	144	1
Niagara State Police	366	369	....	2	3	20	73	238	30	3
Oneida	890	893	1	27	3	113	281	441	24	3
Oneida State Police	996	997	2	3	3	46	240	673	29	1
Onondaga	3,049	3,074	2	50	38	86	616	2,121	136	25
Onondaga State Police	1,202	1,207	1	3	5	21	229	918	25	5
Ontario	1,029	1,038	1	9	6	17	260	697	39	9
Ontario State Police	471	474	....	1	4	18	80	362	6	3
Orange	29	29	....	....	....	21	3	5	....	
Orange State Police	1,186	1,200	2	11	15	92	214	769	83	14
Orleans	349	350	1	5	....	4	82	248	9	1
Orleans State Police	129	129		1	....	16	68	40	4	....
Oswego	820	853	....	8	2	10	273	489	38	33
Oswego State Police	667	667	1	6	5	29	215	402	9	....
Putnam	375	378	....	3	6	8	119	220	19	3
Putnam State Police	192	193	2	....	3	12	57	109	9	1
Rensselaer	464	485		1	1	85	146	223	8	21
Rensselaer State Police	517	521	2	5	3	29	151	315	12	4
Rockland	96		....	....	....	3	2	91	....	
Rockland State Police	88	89	....	2	2	14	6	57	7	1
Saratoga	1,118	1,133	2	21	8	22	260	782	23	15
Saratoga State Police	697	702	2	4	4	33	153	485	16	5
Schenectady State Police	74	75		1	....	4	21	43	5	1
Schoharie	74	75		....	....	1	30	42	1	1
Schoharie State Police	248	250	....	3	1	15	89	128	12	2
Suffolk	36	36	....	2	4	5	22	2	1	....
Suffolk Police Department	43,999	45,106	44	65	1,697	1,332	10,487	22,394	7,980	1,107
Suffolk State Police	88		1	1	8	21	18	30	9	
Washington	325	332	....	1	1	17	79	209	18	7
Washington State Police	295	305	1	5	....	47	68	162	12	10
Wayne	810		2	12	2	14	223	531	26	

Table 10. — Number of Offenses Known to the Police, Suburban Counties, 1993 — Continued

County by State	Crime Index total	Modified* Crime Index total	Murder and non-negligent manslaughter	Forcible rape	Robbery	Aggravated assault	Burglary	Larceny-theft	Motor vehicle theft	Arson*
NEW YORK – Continued										
Wayne State Police	774	780	....	3	7	41	173	528	22	6
NORTH CAROLINA										
Alamance	1,267	1,269	6	5	9	55	496	638	58	2
Alexander	608	609	3	5	2	22	247	304	25	1
Buncombe	2,021	2,026	6	8	19	103	631	1,138	116	5
Burke	1,215	1,221	3	16	9	80	424	620	63	6
Cabarrus	953	953	1	2	13	21	429	442	45	....
Caldwell	1,377	1,391	....	12	15	100	499	691	60	14
Catawba	1,586	1,587	2	5	15	70	626	793	75	1
Chatham	915	922	6	7	6	97	324	448	27	7
Cumberland	10,879	10,976	27	95	331	495	3,183	5,880	868	97
Currituck	485	485	2	....	1	17	177	278	10	....
Davidson	2,366	2,397	6	19	19	97	951	1,120	154	31
Davie	531	532	1	1	2	17	184	284	42	1
Durham	1,261	1,269	4	5	16	97	383	695	61	8
Edgecombe	657	664	3	6	9	23	298	298	20	7
Forsyth	3,163	3,226	4	13	24	248	1,033	1,698	143	63
Franklin	835	839	....	....	4	37	399	339	56	4
Gaston	2,411	2,436	5	14	30	209	964	1,058	131	25
Guilford	3,550	3,567	3	18	48	213	1,227	1,910	131	17
Johnston	1,832	1,832	3	11	14	86	742	812	164	....
Lincoln	1,304	1,316	3	9	7	54	491	687	53	12
Mecklenburg	3,665	3,694	6	19	38	324	1,289	1,870	119	29
Nash	1,352	1,368	2	4	27	39	497	688	95	16
New Hanover	2,559	2,560	....	19	17	286	591	1,527	119	1
Onslow	2,898	2,914	2	20	34	48	898	1,751	145	16
Orange	1,340	1,345	1	4	8	26	499	737	65	5
Pitt	2,025	2,047	5	17	21	146	889	858	89	22
Randolph	1,907	1,911	3	6	17	112	781	903	85	4
Rowan	1,758	1,778	5	15	27	126	649	795	141	20
Stokes	586	587	....	10	3	63	212	258	40	1
Union	1,700	1,707	2	11	16	124	618	868	61	7
Wake	3,227	3,305	5	32	64	242	1,247	1,434	203	78
Wayne	1,506	1,525	4	9	24	94	622	660	93	19
Yadkin	466	467	2	1	2	2	131	288	40	1
NORTH DAKOTA										
Burleigh	107	107	1	....	....	....	42	56	8	....
Cass	282	....	....	7	....	10	52	184	29	....
Grand Forks	283	291	....	4	....	12	76	173	18	8
Morton	111	111	....	2	....	7	24	75	3	....
OHIO										
Ashtabula	1,503	1,513	....	8	20	20	407	973	75	10
Auglaize	343	343	....	9	2	22	117	179	14	....
Clark	2,025	2,028	2	24	21	77	315	1,439	147	3
Clermont	1,352	1,365	....	31	13	104	224	927	53	13
Columbiana	603	607	....	7	6	49	93	386	62	4
Delaware	615	618	3	8	5	17	169	380	33	3
Franklin	4,158	4,171	4	46	151	99	880	2,639	339	13
Fulton	350	351	2	2	....	14	113	192	27	1
Geauga	535	535	1	5	2	5	87	409	26	....
Greene	383	385	2	8	2	44	131	183	13	2
Hamilton	8,089	8,159	2	53	170	103	1,159	6,260	342	70
Jefferson	401	401	....	....	....	....	140	236	25	....
Lake	778	784	1	3	4	9	156	563	42	6
Licking	850	858	....	6	6	24	204	547	63	8
Loraine	1,240	1,260	1	25	21	194	548	396	55	20
Lucas	1,747	1,762	....	10	12	39	350	1,243	93	15
Miami	435	435	1	13	4	15	155	222	25	....
Montgomery	3,525		3	48	168	102	961	1,805	438	
Pickaway	776	779	....	5	4	25	266	459	17	3
Portage	1,584	1,585	2	16	21	54	414	1,001	76	1
Richland	1,335	1,337	....	....	9	6	368	867	85	2

Table 10. — Number of Offenses Known to the Police, Suburban Counties, 1993 — Continued

County by State	Crime Index total	Modified* Crime Index total	Murder and non-negligent man-slaughter	Forcible rape	Robbery	Aggra-vated assault	Burglary	Larceny-theft	Motor vehicle theft	Arson*
OHIO — Continued										
Stark	3,583	3,591	2	38	99	129	1,170	1,878	267	8
Wood	463	466	1	6	1	6	137	280	32	3
OKLAHOMA										
Canadian	129	133	....	3	1	7	39	68	11	4
Cleveland	233	239	....	4	2	7	126	85	9	6
Comanche	305	313	2	3	3	14	88	164	31	8
Creek	505	509	1	5	4	43	226	191	35	4
Garfield	122	122	....	....	....	3	45	72	2	....
Logan	362	366	5	2	1	48	146	140	20	4
McClain	151	153	....	2	....	8	67	62	12	2
Oklahoma	291	293	....	5	1	26	132	110	17	2
Osage	314	316	....	2	1	36	134	118	23	2
Pottawatomie	508	518	2	3	4	81	171	213	34	10
Rogers	603	617	2	7	3	51	271	226	43	14
Sequoyah	309	315	3	3	1	36	148	101	17	6
Tulsa	1,908	1,929	3	27	35	241	516	865	221	21
Wagoner	480	481	1	....	1	29	193	215	41	1
OREGON										
Clackamas	9,139	9,165	7	80	120	139	1,911	5,645	1,237	26
Clackamas State Police	75	98	....	8	3	12	4	33	15	23
Columbia	428	433	1	....	1	9	131	255	31	5
Columbia State Police	30	31	....	2	....	17	1	5	5	1
Jackson	2,125	2,131	2	22	12	212	475	1,263	139	6
Jackson State Police	184	201	....	17	2	19	40	76	30	17
Lane	1,706	1,716	....	17	23	54	534	979	99	10
Lane State Police	439	450	....	9	6	49	124	216	35	11
Marion	3,400	3,415	5	16	47	138	655	2,114	425	15
Marion State Police	262	274	....	9	....	59	34	129	31	12
Multnomah	2,489	2,510	2	22	45	240	551	1,235	394	21
Multnomah State Police	64	64	....	8	1	11	4	32	8	....
Polk	400	406	....	3	6	12	107	233	39	6
Polk State Police	3	4	1	....	....	2	....	....	....	1
Washington	4,462	4,482	2	34	74	54	1,008	2,790	500	20
Washington State Police	35	44	1	3	....	2	3	22	4	9
Yamhill	759	766	1	11	2	25	197	464	59	7
Yamhill State Police	17	17	....	2	....	4	2	3	6	....
PENNSYLVANIA										
Allegheny Police Department	947	1,042	....	97	45	155	248	388	14	95
Allegheny State Police	169	170	....	3	6	67	32	51	10	1
Beaver State Police	167	171	....	7	2	17	60	60	21	4
Berks State Police	596	598	3	9	5	19	183	314	63	2
Blair State Police	464	490	....	5	....	19	155	234	51	26
Bucks State Police	580	585	1	4	2	48	111	348	66	5
Butler State Police	1,073	1,101	2	11	7	27	380	558	88	28
Cambria State Police	226	241	3	7	1	12	91	77	35	15
Carbon State Police	513	516	1	6	....	21	300	163	22	3
Centre State Police	643	657	4	28	7	53	186	335	30	14
Chester Detective	37	37	6	6	1	....	3	21	....	....
Chester State Police	1,586	1,622	1	26	32	110	461	835	121	36
Columbia State Police	178	180	....	2	1	5	89	71	10	2
Cumberland State Police	562	572	1	4	6	52	178	276	45	10
Dauphin State Police	967	981	3	15	10	92	221	579	47	14
Delaware State Police	1,139	1,157	2	7	15	32	154	766	163	18
Erie State Police	1,734	1,762	....	19	12	55	410	1,124	114	28
Fayette State Police	2,032	2,143	4	31	49	74	765	744	365	111
Lackawanna State Police	245	295	....	7	2	46	66	99	25	50
Lancaster State Police	855	877	2	9	5	36	319	421	63	22
Lebanon State Police	336	338	3	5	5	21	81	175	46	2
Lehigh State Police	1,373	1,377	1	13	17	46	281	947	68	4
Luzerne State Police	789	858	3	18	5	68	255	363	77	69
Lycoming State Police	908	922	....	13	6	32	297	492	68	14
Mercer State Police	408	412	....	3	....	17	164	178	46	4

Table 10. — Number of Offenses Known to the Police, Suburban Counties, 1993 — Continued

County by State	Crime Index total	Modified* Crime Index total	Murder and non-negligent man-slaughter	Forcible rape	Robbery	Aggra-vated assault	Burglary	Larceny-theft	Motor vehicle theft	Arson*
PENNSYLVANIA — Continued										
Montgomery State Police..............	467	471	1	2	8	42	105	258	51	4
Northampton State Police..............	469	472	....	4	2	10	98	326	29	3
Perry State Police.....................	516	525	2	3	1	15	244	219	32	9
Pike State Police......................	833	838	....	7	1	80	426	283	36	5
Somerset State Police.................	574	589	....	6	5	22	255	223	63	15
Washington	1	1	....	....	....	....	1	....	....	....
Washington State Police	838	861	1	13	18	46	344	304	112	23
Westmoreland Detective	56	56	....	....	....	3	....	53	....	....
Westmoreland Park Police..............	15	15	....	....	....	....	3	11	1	....
Westmoreland State Police	2,252	2,318	1	30	34	116	651	1,124	296	66
Wyoming State Police	386	390	....	6	4	12	145	182	37	4
York State Police	773	796	1	8	7	82	235	372	68	23
RHODE ISLAND										
Kent State Police	48	52	3	5	1	2	12	20	5	4
Providence State Police	195	198	....	15	4	28	20	92	36	3
Washington State Police	275	277	....	1	....	29	53	178	14	2
SOUTH CAROLINA										
Aiken	3,342	3,348	10	43	93	478	1,015	1,434	269	6
Anderson	5,486	5,526	11	55	107	752	1,629	2,614	318	40
Berkeley	3,648	3,654	5	58	55	414	894	2,004	218	6
Charleston	5,898	5,903	13	56	205	925	1,679	2,530	490	5
Cherokee	1,250	1,255	4	16	32	206	360	551	81	5
Dorchester	2,275	2,281	....	19	41	245	451	1,412	107	6
Edgefield	294	296	2	5	1	35	102	128	21	2
Florence	3,921	3,950	11	49	57	426	1,190	1,908	280	29
Greenville	9,948	10,031	13	108	339	1,311	2,357	5,238	582	83
Horry Police Department	5,099	5,103	9	47	108	373	1,326	2,852	384	4
Lexington	6,033	6,038	6	55	138	582	1,566	3,330	356	5
Pickens	1,038	1,040	3	27	7	158	261	536	46	2
Richland...........................	9,438	9,468	20	143	471	1,168	2,416	4,282	938	30
Spartanburg........................	10,250	10,273	18	86	263	1,750	2,234	5,288	611	23
Sumter	3,322	3,330	5	28	60	483	1,180	1,339	227	8
York	3,451	3,459	8	38	54	478	948	1,729	196	8
SOUTH DAKOTA										
Lincoln............................	70	70	....	1	1	....	32	36	....	....
Minnehaha..........................	391	392	....	4	1	25	134	212	15	1
Pennington.........................	630	632	3	39	2	45	166	342	33	2
TENNESSEE										
Carter.............................	540	550	1	8	1	8	175	297	50	10
Hamilton	1,259		3	7	11	126	462	568	82	
Hawkins............................	480	493	2	8	2	77	175	177	39	13
Knox..............................	4,724	4,795	5	24	52	387	1,378	2,455	423	71
Madison............................	868	873	....	12	15	98	252	431	60	5
Montgomery.........................	525		....	2	1	62	185	254	21	
Robertson	446	446	1	17	7	53	123	224	21	....
Rutherford..........................	1,416		3	29	11	49	483	731	110	
Shelby.............................	6,145	6,199	7	68	136	365	1,580	3,172	817	54
Sullivan............................	1,611		....	15	13	122	508	826	127	
Sumner............................	936	938	1	16	5	68	288	512	46	2
Unicoi.............................	106	107	....	2	....	10	31	59	4	1
Washington	620	644	1	6	2	27	216	322	46	24
TEXAS										
Archer.............................	32	32	....	....	....	1	11	20	....	....
Bastrop............................	870	874	4	33	4	181	302	300	46	4
Bell...............................	992	1,025	4	25	4	124	309	482	44	33
Bexar..............................	7,986	8,111	21	64	98	301	1,817	4,882	803	125
Bowie	675	688	4	9	12	50	257	298	45	13
Brazoria...........................	1,390	1,393	1	37	11	138	442	633	128	3

Table 10.—Number of Offenses Known to the Police, Suburban Counties, 1993—Continued

County by State	Crime Index total	Modified* Crime Index total	Murder and non-negligent man-slaughter	Forcible rape	Robbery	Aggra-vated assault	Burglary	Larceny-theft	Motor vehicle theft	Arson*
TEXAS—Continued										
Brazos	328	328	1	2	....	10	122	175	18	....
Caldwell	193	194	2	4	....	33	75	77	2	1
Cameron	1,883	1,929	7	2	21	201	958	586	108	46
Chambers	497	499	1	10	8	16	141	292	29	2
Collin	842	852	1	5	4	87	303	393	49	10
Comal	914	933	5	13	1	147	270	446	32	19
Coryell	134	137	1	....	....	11	55	57	10	3
Dallas	629	661	2	2	15	185	135	270	20	32
Denton	597	599	4	2	1	27	166	361	36	2
Ector	1,286	1,289	6	15	4	24	431	743	63	3
Ellis	919	919	2	1	2	33	428	425	28	....
El Paso	2,597	2,613	8	59	59	333	701	1,259	178	16
Fort Bend	2,079	2,145	2	18	51	118	672	1,038	180	66
Galveston	1,212	1,225	2	21	16	138	341	592	102	13
Grayson	863	885	1	10	5	33	353	430	31	22
Gregg	636	637	2	7	21	77	173	295	61	1
Guadalupe	934	935	5	2	6	105	314	465	37	1
Hardin[3]			....	1	7		167	296	30	5
Harris	39,208	39,688	71	930	1,860	2,362	8,778	16,924	8,283	480
Harrison	1,042	1,067	1	3	4	134	358	489	53	25
Hays	858	908	....	21	10	51	358	397	21	50
Henderson	1,091	1,099	4	19	6	70	446	505	41	8
Hidalgo[3]			23	44	110		2,710	1,382	385	69
Hood	507	515	....	....	....	27	161	300	19	8
Hunt	607	614	....	....	1	60	260	248	38	7
Jefferson	697	701	3	23	9	48	215	340	59	4
Johnson	882	888	5	7	6	21	384	394	65	6
Kaufman	950		2	15	2	71	319	454	87	
Liberty	786	787	6	23	1	52	365	302	37	1
Lubbock	763	772	2	11	3	135	182	405	25	9
McLennan	714	722	3	2	17	54	267	328	43	8
Midland	659	659	1	9	10	39	200	377	23	....
Montgomery	4,972	5,048	5	62	40	278	1,630	2,570	387	76
Nueces	299	300	1	36	1	24	95	106	36	1
Orange	844	849	2	5	9	53	302	404	69	5
Parker	1,013	1,020	4	47	4	56	468	404	30	7
Potter	270	273	....	8	5	29	83	131	14	3
Randall	326	328	1	3	....	15	108	162	37	2
Rockwall	239	242	....	4	2	41	71	98	23	3
San Patricio	466	467	1	....	2	35	174	233	21	1
Smith	2,422	2,454	8	21	32	204	786	1,212	159	32
Tarrant	1,328	1,367	3	4	17	150	387	703	64	39
Taylor	183	186	....	3	3	18	74	76	9	3
Tom Green[3]			....	12	....		82	214	8	3
Travis	4,904	4,927	4	88	52	401	1,386	2,619	354	23
Upshur	431	431	....	11	2	65	205	134	14	....
Victoria	562	569	....	10	4	22	173	334	19	7
Waller	152	152	....	1	....	3	111	33	4	....
Webb	336	341	....	3	3	45	145	117	23	5
Wichita	153	161	....	2	2	26	57	62	4	8
Williamson	2,050	2,059	2	17	13	117	453	1,351	97	9
Wilson	249	257	4	....	2	19	105	106	13	8
UTAH										
Davis	221	221	....	24	....	14	63	112	8	....
Salt Lake	15,348	15,422	11	92	135	856	2,157	11,459	638	74
Utah	396	399	1	6	2	22	105	233	27	3
Weber	711	711	....	8	3	30	174	465	31	....
VIRGINIA										
Albemarle Police Department	2,126	2,138	2	21	11	49	402	1,521	120	12
Albemarle State Police	7	7	....	....	1	....	....	6	....	....
Amherst	615	620	....	6	4	46	104	434	21	5
Amherst State Police	11	11	....	....	....	1	1	6	3	....
Bedford	611	613	....	10	2	32	181	366	20	2
Bedford State Police	12	12	....	....	....	1	1	8	2	....

See footnotes at end of table.

Table 10. — Number of Offenses Known to the Police, Suburban Counties, 1993 — Continued

County by State	Crime Index total	Modified* Crime Index total	Murder and non-negligent man-slaughter	Forcible rape	Robbery	Aggra-vated assault	Burglary	Larceny-theft	Motor vehicle theft	Arson*
VIRGINIA — Continued										
Botetourt	274	276	1	3	3	7	62	183	15	2
Botetourt State Police	5	5	....	....	....	....	1	3	1	....
Campbell	928	943	5	18	8	96	150	609	42	15
Campbell State Police	16	16	....	....	1	....	5	8	2	....
Charles City	70	70	....	2	....	8	18	41	1	....
Charles City State Police	9	9	....	1	....	1	5	1	1	....
Chesterfield Police Department	8,005	8,071	10	56	125	134	1,476	5,899	305	66
Chesterfield State Police	33	33	....	....	4	3	....	19	7	....
Clarke	125	126	1	....	....	5	29	78	11	1
Clarke State Police	4	4	....	....	....	....	1	3	....	....
Culpeper	297	299	....	5	7	14	52	203	16	2
Culpeper State Police	20	20	....	1	....	3	1	12	3	....
Dinwiddie	402	404	4	6	9	20	105	234	24	2
Dinwiddie State Police	12	12	....	....	....	1	....	5	6	....
Fairfax Police Department	25,147	25,375	17	100	460	343	2,211	20,295	1,721	228
Fairfax State Police	62	62	....	....	....	6	4	23	29	....
Fauquier	662	686	....	10	5	54	135	421	37	24
Fauquier State Police	32	32	....	....	....	1	4	23	4	....
Fluvanna	221	222	1	1	2	8	63	132	14	1
Fluvanna State Police	1	1	....	....	....	....	....	1	....	....
Gloucester	478	478	2	1	3	19	88	339	26	....
Gloucester State Police	7	8	....	....	....	....	1	3	3	1
Goochland	119	119	....	7	1	7	43	47	14	....
Goochland State Police	12	12	....	....	1	2	2	5	2	....
Greene	152	152	....	3	....	8	39	93	9	....
Greene State Police	1	1	....	....	....	....	1	....	....	....
Hanover	1,287	1,287	7	3	10	21	247	947	52	....
Hanover State Police	43	43	....	....	2	3	....	32	6	....
Henrico Police Department	10,331	10,400	11	68	234	309	1,751	7,360	598	69
Henrico State Police	39	39	....	1	1	2	5	21	9	....
Isle of Wight	452	458	....	2	12	27	84	298	29	6
Isle of Wight State Police	3	5	....	....	....	....	1	2	....	2
James City Police Department	1,102	1,103	5	10	24	57	121	845	40	1
James City State Police	3	3	....	....	....	....	....	3	....	....
King George	232	233	....	2	3	13	51	158	5	1
King George State Police	4	4	....	....	....	....	1	3	....	....
Loudoun	1,767	1,773	1	17	24	103	163	1,356	103	6
Loudoun State Police	23	23	....	....	....	....	2	16	5	....
Mathews	107	108	....	10	1	7	33	53	3	1
Mathews State Police	1	1	....	....	....	....	....	1	....	....
New Kent	286	286	1	4	2	8	65	190	16	....
New Kent State Police	24	24	....	....	2	1	5	12	4	....
Pittsylvania	834	842	7	26	17	25	253	464	42	8
Pittsylvania State Police	30	30	....	1	....	....	1	10	18	....
Powhatan	164	164	....	2	4	4	38	108	8	....
Powhatan State Police	22	22	....	1	....	2	2	17	....	....
Prince George	528	530	....	6	12	14	173	300	23	2
Prince George State Police	5	5	....	....	....	1	....	2	2	....
Prince William Police Department	8,684	8,794	9	87	187	283	1,132	6,515	471	110
Prince William State Police	36	36	1	1	3	5	2	15	9	....
Roanoke Police Department	1,873	1,900	1	16	10	116	385	1,299	46	27
Roanoke State Police	7	7	....	....	....	....	....	5	2	....
Scott	260	263	2	7	1	27	82	117	24	3
Scott State Police	7	15	....	....	....	1	....	2	4	8
Spotsylvania	1,744	1,745	3	4	15	21	175	1,425	101	1
Spotsylvania State Police	52	52	....	2	3	2	1	40	4	....
Stafford	1,556	1,568	2	21	23	55	176	1,190	89	12
Stafford State Police	32	32	....	....	1	1	3	24	3	....
Washington	568	568	....	7	4	16	194	324	23	....
Washington State Police	21	26	....	....	....	1	4	13	3	5
York	1,485	1,486	....	8	39	43	168	1,152	75	1
York State Police	9	9	....	....	....	....	....	8	1	....
WASHINGTON										
Benton	945	959	1	16	4	76	248	564	36	14
Clark	6,552	6,597	7	81	181	297	1,455	3,980	551	45
Franklin	392	394	2	8	....	32	117	204	29	2

Table 10.—Number of Offenses Known to the Police, Suburban Counties, 1993—Continued

County by State	Crime Index total	Modified* Crime Index total	Murder and non-negligent man-slaughter	Forcible rape	Robbery	Aggra-vated assault	Burglary	Larceny-theft	Motor vehicle theft	Arson*
WASHINGTON—Continued										
Island	710	711	....	12	1	29	228	415	25	1
King	21,835	22,069	16	436	394	725	4,409	13,789	2,066	234
Kitsap	4,877	4,915	2	49	61	218	1,043	3,264	240	38
Pierce	17,077	17,196	26	186	386	1,320	3,832	10,133	1,194	119
Spokane	7,137	7,169	4	61	83	200	1,466	4,953	370	32
Thurston	3,096	3,117	....	58	13	113	892	1,849	171	21
Whatcom	1,863	1,878	....	26	13	56	592	1,105	71	15
Yakima	3,525	3,560	7	63	24	123	1,373	1,726	209	35
WEST VIRGINIA										
Brooke	111	111	....	3	2	1	22	80	3	....
Brooke State Police	2	2	....	....	....	....	....	1	1	....
Cabell	828	830	3	7	7	33	206	525	47	2
Cabell State Police	97	97	....	1	1	8	23	51	13	....
Hancock	120	121	2	....	2	7	23	75	11	....
Hancock State Police	7	7	....	....	....	....	2	5	....	....
Kanawha	1,412	1,431	3	1	12	91	495	670	140	19
Kanawha State Police	527	530	1	15	2	28	158	247	76	3
Marshall	246	247	....	1	1	31	96	102	15	1
Marshall State Police	28	28	....	....	....	5	12	7	4	....
Mineral	41	53	....	....	....	2	18	20	1	12
Mineral State Police	185	192	....	....	2	36	54	79	14	7
Ohio	131	131	....	3	1	2	52	58	15	....
Ohio State Police	42	42	....	....	....	1	8	31	2	....
Putnam	626	632	1	....	5	17	154	422	27	6
Putnam State Police	147	147	....	9	1	18	22	86	11	....
Wayne	116	116	6	....	3	9	46	36	16	....
Wayne State Police	203	203	1	4	4	13	66	81	34	....
Wood	437	437	....	....	....	23	119	274	21	....
Wood State Police	67	67	....	3	....	1	24	29	10	....
WISCONSIN										
Brown	1,422	1,425	1	15	4	51	247	1,033	71	3
Calumet	186	187	....	1	....	9	44	121	11	1
Chippewa	362	362	....	1	1	7	88	234	31	....
Dane	1,427	1,438	1	7	9	289	264	798	59	11
Douglas	274	275	....	5	3	5	162	83	16	1
Eau Claire	465	469	....	5	3	4	151	279	23	4
Kenosha	1,322	1,335	....	9	9	51	201	974	78	13
La Crosse	234	236	....	6	1	33	49	126	19	2
Marathon	556	556	1	....	2	4	106	415	28	....
Milwaukee	271	271	....	1	4	11	....	243	12	....
Outagamie	540	540	....	5	1	38	150	328	18	....
Ozaukee	219	220	....	4	1	....	42	155	17	1
Pierce	276	282	1	1	1	5	105	143	20	6
Racine	795	796	....	4	10	10	126	606	39	1
Rock	587	591	....	3	5	77	117	352	33	4
St. Croix	425	428	1	2	....	12	106	267	37	3
Sheboygan	791	798	....	12	1	19	175	559	25	7
Washington	748	757	....	4	1	18	189	494	42	9
Waukesha	1,142	1,149	....	5	2	82	211	763	79	7
Winnebago	543	545	....	3	4	1	148	354	33	2
WYOMING										
Laramie	513	515	....	18	7	28	67	373	20	2
Natrona	508	512	....	6	....	23	156	292	31	4

[1]Complete data for 1993 were not available for the states of Illinois and Kansas; therefore, it was necessary that their crime counts be estimated. See "Offense Estimation," page 376 for details. Forcible rape figures furnished by the state-level Uniform Crime Reporting (UCR) Program administered by the Illinois Department of State Police under the summary reporting system were not in accordance with national UCR guidelines. Therefore, the figures were excluded from the forcible rape, Crime Index total, and Modified Crime Index total categories.

[2]Forcible rape figures furnished by the state-level UCR Program administered by the Michigan State Police and Minnesota Department of Public Safety were not in accordance with national UCR guidelines. Therefore, the figures were excluded from the forcible rape, Crime Index total, and the Modified Crime Index total categories.

[3]1993 figures are not comparable to prior years.

Table 11. — Number of Offenses Known to the Police, Rural Counties 25,000 and over in Population, 1993

[The data shown in this table do not reflect county totals but are the number of offenses reported by the sheriff's office, county police department, or state police.]

* Arson is shown only if 12 months of arson data were received. Leaders (...) indicate zero data. The Modified Crime Index total is the sum of the Crime Index offenses, including arson.

County by State	Crime Index total	Modified* Crime Index total	Murder and non-negligent man-slaughter	Forcible rape	Robbery	Aggra-vated assault	Burglary	Larceny-theft	Motor vehicle theft	Arson*
ALABAMA										
Cullman	1,026		2	14	4	194	298	423	91	
De Kalb	307	308	....	....	...	6	183	114	4	1
Jackson	516	524	2	5	6	58	238	159	48	8
Lee	853		1	6	6	67	323	414	36	
Marshall	250		....	....	1	12	139	87	11	
Walker	289		....	1	4	....	110	142	32	
ARIZONA										
Apache	253	253	1	2	3	34	86	121	6	....
Cochise	1,209	1,217	1	3	12	97	467	549	80	8
Coconino	825	827	3	23	5	70	212	473	39	2
Navajo	493	502	1	8	4	61	162	229	28	9
Yavapai	1,506	1,514	2	3	6	154	634	602	105	8
ARKANSAS										
Garland	298	299	1	4	5	12	125	113	38	1
Independence	1,059	1,059	....	9	6	26	160	812	46	....
Mississippi	599	612	2	10	11	77	218	242	39	13
Pope	352	355	1	4	1	6	148	175	17	3
White	649	650	3	4	3	23	298	265	53	1
CALIFORNIA										
Calaveras	919	930	1	6	7	74	442	389	....	11
Calaveras Highway Patrol	59		....	....	...	1	....	11	47	
Humboldt	2,006	2,026	6	25	30	225	812	891	17	20
Humboldt Highway Patrol	190		....	....	...	....	....	....	190	
Imperial	1,281	1,309	2	6	19	93	506	647	8	28
Imperial Highway Patrol	91		....	....	...	....	....	17	74	
Kings	862	871	3	16	19	130	340	343	11	9
Kings Highway Patrol	104		....	....	...	....	....	20	84	
Lake	978	978	1	15	12	142	459	343	6	....
Lake Highway Patrol	91		....	....	...	....	....	12	79	
Mendocino	1,476	1,489	5	30	21	282	618	508	12	13
Mendocino Highway Patrol	122		....	....	...	6	....	26	90	
Nevada	1,997	2,001	5	15	15	212	552	1,195	3	4
Nevada Highway Patrol	96		....	....	...	....	....	18	78	
Tehama	898	924	1	13	11	113	352	405	3	26
Tehama Highway Patrol	81		....	....	...	1	....	....	80	
Tuolumne	1,388	1,394	4	8	8	53	512	803	....	6
Tuolumne Highway Patrol	103		....	....	...	....	....	19	84	
COLORADO										
Mesa	1,438	1,442	2	16	2	30	342	970	76	4
FLORIDA										
Citrus	1,866	1,899	3	7	14	171	739	857	75	33
Columbia	2,009	2,021	2	30	25	196	550	1,088	118	12
Highlands	2,724	2,731	1	7	26	289	918	1,288	195	7
Indian River	3,365	3,371	2	36	66	248	1,017	1,775	221	6
Monroe	3,423	3,427	4	28	60	388	647	2,119	177	4
Okeechobee	1,214	1,219	....	15	23	223	343	555	55	5
Putnam	3,652	3,663	7	125	43	387	1,440	1,481	169	11
Sumter	918	920	1	9	24	144	347	355	38	2
GEORGIA										
Floyd	15	15	....	....	...	8	....	7	....	....
Floyd Police Department	1,277	1,277	2	8	9	48	508	604	98	....
Glynn Police Department	3,294	3,306	3	17	54	254	621	2,167	178	12
Gordon	777	777	....	4	10	10	219	454	80	....

Table 11.—Number of Offenses Known to the Police, Rural Counties 25,000 and over in Population, 1993—Continued

County by State	Crime Index total	Modified* Crime Index total	Murder and non-negligent man-slaughter	Forcible rape	Robbery	Aggra-vated assault	Burglary	Larceny-theft	Motor vehicle theft	Arson*
GEORGIA—Continued										
Hall	2,719	2,727	....	33	26	173	768	1,458	261	8
Liberty	512	512	1	7	14	37	137	296	20	....
Lowndes	1,260	1,265	8	10	26	59	322	761	74	5
Whitfield	1,323	1,336	1	8	14	54	516	614	116	13
HAWAII										
Hawaii Police Department	4,172	4,197	4	27	29	106	1,128	2,658	220	25
Kauai Police Department	2,346	2,355	3	21	14	66	545	1,562	135	9
Maui Police Department	7,935	7,980	5	44	68	88	1,702	5,654	374	45
IDAHO										
Bonneville	573	577	....	5	3	28	110	388	39	4
Kootenai	949	954	2	25	2	97	264	501	58	5
ILLINOIS[1]										
INDIANA										
Bartholomew	279	279	....	5	3	37	32	185	17	....
Bartholomew State Police	39	40	....	....	....	6	2	22	9	1
Grant	368	369	1	2	....	45	73	235	12	1
Grant State Police	18	18	....	....	....	2	1	10	5	....
La Grange	229	229	....	1	2	31	64	122	9	....
La Grange State Police	108	110	1	....	1	6	31	56	13	2
La Porte	969	970	1	5	4	37	324	564	34	1
La Porte State Police	109	110	....	1	2	38	8	47	13	1
Lawrence	311	311	1	1	1	14	86	179	29	....
Lawrence State Police	18	18	....	2	....	1	4	10	1	....
Wayne	408	411	1	3	3	4	134	243	20	3
Wayne State Police	39	41	....	2	1	6	7	20	3	2
KANSAS[1]										
KENTUCKY										
Floyd	3	3	....	....	....	....	2	1	....	....
Floyd State Police	467	489	10	10	5	76	165	165	36	22
Harlan	4	4	....	....	....	....	1	2	1	....
Harlan State Police	436	438	1	2	6	134	108	165	20	2
Knox	28	28	....	....	....	6	5	16	1	....
Knox State Police	323	326	6	5	4	51	90	132	35	3
Laurel	309	310	....	1	4	21	84	167	32	1
Laurel State Police	466	486	5	15	7	52	130	171	86	20
Madison	141	141	....	....	....	2	40	91	8	....
Madison State Police	288	298	1	17	1	44	104	100	21	10
McCracken	921	923	3	10	10	150	219	489	40	2
Perry State Police	624	636	4	19	8	127	150	276	40	12
Pulaski	653	656	....	8	1	19	232	362	31	3
Pulaski State Police	90	91	....	3	....	1	33	47	6	1
Warren	96	96	....	....	....	....	25	68	3	....
Warren State Police	447	453	1	11	8	94	186	111	36	6
LOUISIANA										
Avoyelles	524	526	2	28	6	201	69	218	....	2
Plaquemines	626	627	9	9	11	75	140	360	22	1
Vermillion	501	501	....	11	3	39	151	267	30	....
Vernon	862	864	2	6	5	185	93	536	35	2
MAINE										
Aroostook	131	131	....	....	....	....	65	64	2	....
Aroostook State Police	442	444	2	12	1	2	197	201	27	2

See footnotes at end of table.

184

Table 11. — Number of Offenses Known to the Police, Rural Counties 25,000 and over in Population, 1993 — Continued

County by State	Crime Index total	Modified* Crime Index total	Murder and non-negligent man-slaughter	Forcible rape	Robbery	Aggra-vated assault	Burglary	Larceny-theft	Motor vehicle theft	Arson*
MAINE — Continued										
Hancock	404	405	....	....	1	6	123	259	15	1
Hancock State Police	69	69	....	5	....	3	38	20	3	....
Kennebec	393	395	....	8	2	2	170	190	21	2
Kennebec State Police	392	392	3	6	....	9	172	173	29	....
Penobscot	632	635	....	2	....	7	228	371	24	3
Penobscot State Police	247	247	1	8	2	4	84	131	17	....
Somerset	387	388	....	10	....	13	141	205	18	1
Somerset State Police	206	206	1	4	2	3	97	80	19	....
Waldo	181	182	....	....	1	3	80	82	15	1
Waldo State Police	61	61	....	1	....	3	33	20	4	....
York	333	335	....	1	4	4	150	151	23	2
York State Police	214	214	4	....	....	7	76	108	19	....
MARYLAND										
Garrett	354	354	....	2	....	26	93	227	6	....
Garrett State Police	273	275	1	1	4	22	74	157	14	2
St. Mary's	1,970	1,991	2	25	37	235	485	1,135	51	21
St. Mary's State Police	386	406	1	10	12	36	89	219	19	20
Wicomico	804	804	1	13	11	77	243	428	31	....
Wicomico State Police	667	687	1	4	10	102	212	288	50	20
MICHIGAN[2]										
Barry			....		1	42	167	183	17	4
Barry State Police			....		1	31	178	238	22	5
Cass			....		4	41	290	339	28	4
Cass State Police			....		1	11	44	63	12	8
Grand Traverse			1		5	24	145	657	31	12
Grand Traverse State Police			1		2	7	80	277	16	4
Hillsdale			3		2	34	116	218	11	3
Hillsdale State Police			....		3	6	33	88	8	5
Ionia			1		1	49	92	268	23	2
Ionia State Police			....		2	26	76	185	12	6
Isabella			....		1	20	72	189	13	2
Isabella State Police			1		1	10	92	185	11	5
Mecosta			1		....	13	177	346	9	4
Mecosta State Police			....		....	9	25	27	2	....
Montcalm			1		2	63	257	474	48	8
Montcalm State Police			....		2	21	94	147	22	7
Newaygo			1		1	59	259	229	25	6
Newaygo State Police			....		....	13	147	160	16	2
St. Joseph			....		6	74	193	313	36	
St. Joseph State Police			1		1	12	102	167	12	8
Sanilac			1		2	35	156	249	35	6
Sanilac State Police			....		....	11	66	115	28	6
Shiawassee			....		3	28	125	281	30	3
Shiawassee State Police			....		2	14	52	117	8	4
Tuscola			1		....	15	101	175	15	7
Tuscola State Police			....		....	30	70	96	22	3
MINNESOTA[2]										
Crow Wing			3		1	24	427	448	87	5
Itasca			....		2	24	310	391	40	9
Otter Tail			1		....	19	317	330	52	2
MISSISSIPPI										
Jones	790		1	5	1	10	429	294	50	
Warren	577	578	1	5	2	22	215	307	25	1
MISSOURI										
Camden	391	393	1	2	1	14	161	202	10	2
Cole	458	461	....	5	3	38	116	279	17	3
Pulaski	233	239	1	4	3	37	84	94	10	6

See footnotes at end of table.

Table 11. — Number of Offenses Known to the Police, Rural Counties 25,000 and over in Population, 1993 — Continued

County by State	Crime Index total	Modified* Crime Index total	Murder and non-negligent man-slaughter	Forcible rape	Robbery	Aggra-vated assault	Burglary	Larceny-theft	Motor vehicle theft	Arson*
MONTANA										
Missoula	1,082	1,094	1	23	2	57	189	698	112	12
Silver Bow	1,960	1,967	1	3	6	37	248	1,580	85	7
NEVADA										
Carson City	2,682	2,695	....	24	27	580	387	1,556	108	13
NEW HAMPSHIRE										
Hillsboro State Police	30	31	....	2	1	6	10	8	3	1
NEW MEXICO										
Grant	297	297	....	....	2	81	106	89	19	....
McKinley	287	287	....	5	9	30	66	145	32	....
San Juan	812	813	1	31	11	108	234	377	50	1
NEW YORK										
Allegany State Police	633	648	....	6	4	45	356	215	7	15
Cattaraugus	662		1	2	2	82	328	217	30	
Cattaraugus State Police	603	606	....	5	4	33	180	369	12	3
Chenango	466	474		1	....	62	143	251	9	8
Chenango State Police	234	234	....	....		34	81	116	3	....
Clinton	26	26		....	....	....		26	....	....
Clinton State Police	1,191	1,199	3	15	....	110	292	745	26	8
Columbia	394	400		2	2	13	127	230	20	6
Columbia State Police	460	463	1	2	1	22	181	238	15	3
Cortland	417		1	1	1	41	110	256	7	
Cortland State Police	378	378	....	1	1	8	60	295	13	....
Delaware	154	154		1	....	5	83	62	3	....
Delaware State Police	504	510	4	2	....	45	219	219	15	6
Franklin State Police	523	534	1	....	3	56	156	296	11	11
Greene	65	65		....		4	15	46	....	
Greene State Police	774	798	....	4		185	238	333	14	24
Jefferson	527		2	11	2	9	164	322	17	
Jefferson State Police	579	581	....	9	1	14	164	382	9	2
Otsego	98		1	....		4	33	59	1	
Otsego State Police	690	696	1	5	1	62	199	413	9	6
St. Lawrence	583	586	....	8	1	50	163	333	28	3
St. Lawrence State Police	713	721	1	12		55	231	391	23	8
Sullivan	803		3	2	6	125	309	322	36	
Sullivan State Police	800	820	1	5	8	84	339	336	27	20
Tompkins	739	742	1	10	3	40	161	493	31	3
Tompkins State Police	419	419	....	4	3	17	117	269	9	....
Ulster	213		1	6	1	20	58	113	14	
Ulster State Police	1,034	1,053	1	13	10	133	286	533	58	19
Wyoming	571		....	1	....	79	193	274	24	
Wyoming State Police	150	150	4	2	....	53	42	45	4	....
NORTH CAROLINA										
Beaufort	922	925	3	5	6	44	530	292	42	3
Carteret	1,001	1,004	2	2	9	13	293	630	52	3
Cleveland	2,209	2,211	11	8	22	93	1,000	981	94	2
Columbus	1,155	1,165	3	9	16	128	463	462	74	10
Craven	1,471	1,472	2	12	13	133	428	793	90	1
Dublin	804	807	6	6	13	106	327	295	51	3
Halifax	999	1,016	2	8	16	65	449	408	51	17
Harnett	1,769	1,791	7	14	28	153	767	696	104	22
Henderson	1,089	1,097	....	8	3	28	392	577	81	8
Iredell	810	816	....	9	13	51	398	265	74	6
Jackson	403	404	....	....	2	16	213	160	12	1
Lee	690	692	2	6	2	45	164	428	43	2
Lenoir	953	959	6	4	11	79	337	451	65	6
McDowell	517	519	2	5	2	46	133	296	33	2

Table 11. — Number of Offenses Known to the Police, Rural Counties 25,000 and over in Population, 1993 — Continued

County by State	Crime Index total	Modified* Crime Index total	Murder and non-negligent man-slaughter	Forcible rape	Robbery	Aggra-vated assault	Burglary	Larceny-theft	Motor vehicle theft	Arson*
NORTH CAROLINA — Continued										
Moore[3]			2	2	11		205	247	54	7
Pender	686	691	4	5	1	153	176	302	45	5
Richmond	504	504	7	1	6	76	152	231	31	....
Robeson	1,240	1,254	19	7	13	142	583	379	97	14
Rockingham	1,532	1,539	4	14	15	176	488	759	76	7
Rutherford	1,032	1,032	5	3	7	80	376	481	80	....
Sampson	1,153	1,164	4	15	15	134	492	406	87	11
Stanly	828	833	4	3	6	52	307	406	50	5
Surry	940	944	2	5	12	37	309	485	90	4
Wilkes	911	921	7	4	12	102	340	391	55	10
Wilson	775	783	2	10	10	49	323	320	61	8
OHIO										
Coshocton	500	518	....	1	....	21	82	383	13	18
Darke	525	534	1	8	2	67	181	227	39	9
Huron	357	362	....	1	....	18	158	158	22	5
Logan	387	387	2	1	2	10	127	237	8	....
Muskingum	1,131	1,135	2	6	5	41	279	771	27	4
Preble	509	515	1	24	2	12	159	283	28	6
Ross	1,006	1,023	4	8	5	22	305	622	40	17
Seneca	286	286	1	3	2	2	114	147	17	....
Shelby	292	294	....	....	....	22	68	174	28	2
Tuscarawas	182	182	....	....	....	....	48	133	1	....
Wayne	546	549		19	2	4	174	304	43	3
OREGON										
Coos	699	703	1	13	7	25	209	389	55	4
Coos State Police	86	86	....	5	1	10	11	45	14	....
Deschutes	1,007	1,014	....	7	2	2	286	644	66	7
Deschutes State Police	93	108	....	2	....	7	37	31	16	15
Douglas	1,439	1,447	5	13	6	89	410	839	77	8
Douglas State Police	83	87	....	5	2	22	12	32	10	4
Josephine	1,182	1,188	3	13	9	27	419	622	89	6
Josephine State Police	70	73	1	14	....	22	10	18	5	3
Klamath	574	576	2	....	2	20	146	349	55	2
Klamath State Police	437	448	1	39	3	92	74	152	76	11
PENNSYLVANIA										
Adams State Police	613	617	1	12	8	101	185	271	35	4
Armstrong State Police	523	529	....	8	....	19	189	261	46	6
Bedford State Police	740	756	....	10	4	34	264	382	46	16
Bradford State Police	483	493	....	8	....	26	210	204	35	10
Clarion State Police	561	577	2	5	1	13	231	266	43	16
Clearfield State Police	465	476	1	7	3	20	174	230	30	11
Crawford State Police	909	921	1	15	3	26	445	358	61	12
Franklin State Police	915	917	2	8	17	26	271	485	106	2
Greene State Police	663	685	....	14	12	41	243	256	97	22
Huntingdon State Police	494	506	3	6	1	30	194	232	28	12
Indiana State Police	834	853	4	8	10	123	280	310	99	19
Lawrence State Police	663	691	2	7	10	34	235	278	97	28
Monroe State Police	1,222	1,232	1	14	7	57	514	542	87	10
Northumberland State Police	307	311	3	7	5	22	79	169	22	4
Schuylkill State Police	901	919	3	12	7	112	228	470	69	18
Snyder State Police	259	264	1	4	3	7	81	148	15	5
Susquehanna State Police	319	327	....	3	3	12	155	118	28	8
Tioga State Police	360	364	1	6	....	17	188	127	21	4
Venango State Police	701	711	2	9	4	24	283	337	42	10
Wayne State Police	661	663	3	5	4	31	251	324	43	2
RHODE ISLAND										
Newport State Police	21	21	....	....	....	1	2	18	....	....

See footnotes at end of table.

Table 11. — Number of Offenses Known to the Police, Rural Counties 25,000 and over in Population, 1993 — Continued

County by State	Crime Index total	Modified* Crime Index total	Murder and non-negligent manslaughter	Forcible rape	Robbery	Aggra-vated assault	Burglary	Larceny-theft	Motor vehicle theft	Arson*
SOUTH CAROLINA										
Beaufort	5,690	5,694	6	38	75	625	1,229	3,493	224	4
Chesterfield	699	700	5	11	15	122	199	291	56	1
Colleton	1,269	1,275	4	12	38	215	378	543	79	6
Darlington	1,652	1,654	7	14	22	210	566	703	130	2
Georgetown	1,425	1,428	2	20	13	194	418	685	93	3
Greenwood	1,219	1,221	1	20	24	194	300	627	53	2
Kershaw	1,276	1,279	2	4	24	83	362	712	89	3
Lancaster	1,822	1,826	5	22	30	150	574	955	86	4
Laurens	1,393	1,394	6	11	20	213	503	564	76	1
Oconee	1,048	1,053	3	5	16	136	288	562	38	5
Orangeburg	3,189	3,198	19	40	125	610	873	1,316	206	9
Williamsburg	805	807	3	14	25	132	263	308	60	2
TENNESSEE										
Bradley	601	601	2	15	6	54	165	296	63	....
Hamblen	450	450	....	1	2	2	169	247	29	....
Jefferson	333	333	....	2	1	3	149	148	30	....
McMinn	625	628	3	4	11	44	244	270	49	3
Roane	721		....	15	2	202	201	255	46	
TEXAS										
Anderson	455	470	2	18	2	57	161	199	16	15
Angelina	747	749	1	9	9	41	205	433	49	2
Polk	702	702	2	....	10	76	304	284	26	....
Rusk	668	681	2	8	6	25	255	310	62	13
Starr	996	1,010	10	9	10	97	335	475	60	14
Van Zandt	499	502	3	7	4	27	193	241	24	3
Wise	639	644	....	7	3	73	244	280	32	5
UTAH										
Cache	688	689	....	7	2	9	109	531	30	1
VIRGINIA										
Accomack	179	179	1	6	....	11	56	92	13	....
Accomack State Police	40	42	....	1	2	2	5	24	6	2
Augusta	859	860	2	8	....	24	156	631	38	1
Augusta State Police	19	20	....	....	2	1	....	12	4	1
Buchanan	319	327	2	2	....	45	104	130	36	8
Buchanan State Police	78	80	....	2	1	3	22	45	5	2
Carroll	305	308	1	10	1	22	121	130	20	3
Carroll State Police	8	8	....	....	....	....	....	7	1	....
Franklin	407	410	....	5	2	42	126	203	29	3
Franklin State Police	5	5	....	....	....	....	....	2	3	....
Frederick	1,226	1,226	2	11	1	75	269	822	46	....
Frederick State Police	41	41	1	....	1	1	4	26	8	....
Halifax	507	514	5	5	4	25	198	259	11	7
Halifax State Police	40	40	2	....	....	1	4	16	17	....
Henry	1,427	1,438	7	12	16	70	433	785	104	11
Henry State Police	24	24	....	....	....	1	....	15	8	....
Rockingham	408	415	4	6	6	19	106	255	12	7
Rockingham State Police	27	27	....	....	....	1	....	9	17	....
Tazewell	331	334	1	10	4	71	70	157	18	3
Tazewell State Police	34	36	....	2	....	3	6	19	4	2
Wise	174	175	1	....	1	....	52	111	9	1
Wise State Police	23	25	....	....	....	2	3	10	8	2
WASHINGTON										
Chelan	1,207	1,208	2	16	3	17	270	836	63	1
Clallam	672	680	2	11	1	27	176	418	37	8
Cowlitz	917	922	1	24	5	34	281	511	61	5
Douglas	476	477	2	28	3	48	119	243	33	1

Table 11. — Number of Offenses Known to the Police, Rural Counties 25,000 and over in Population, 1993 — Continued

County by State	Crime Index total	Modified* Crime Index total	Murder and non-negligent man-slaughter	Forcible rape	Robbery	Aggra-vated assault	Burglary	Larceny-theft	Motor vehicle theft	Arson*
WASHINGTON — Continued										
Grant	813	813	2	18	1	15	283	430	64	....
Grays Harbor	503	506	2	7	4	27	207	231	25	3
Lewis	916	920	3	7	6	33	314	493	60	4
Mason	1,346	1,348	3	14	3	59	512	690	65	2
Skagit	1,260	1,265	2	24	6	23	359	789	57	5
WEST VIRGINIA										
Berkeley	1,011	1,042	1	3	4	77	232	666	28	31
Berkeley State Police	667	667	2	9	6	47	204	334	65	....
Fayette	291	293	4	2	5	18	89	144	29	2
Fayette State Police	250	253	1	4	2	7	63	163	10	3
Harrison	273	277	2	2	4	9	80	159	17	4
Harrison State Police	172	173	1	....	1	3	85	66	16	1
Jefferson	144	144	....	....	3	3	45	91	2	....
Jefferson State Police	342	343	1	....	2	9	136	185	9	1
Logan	164	165	2	....	3	14	63	70	12	1
Logan State Police	472	478	1	....	2	16	117	274	62	6
McDowell	93	94	5	1	2	17	27	35	6	1
McDowell State Police	116	116	1	1	....	6	66	23	19	....
Marion	318	328	3	2	3	23	86	168	33	10
Marion State Police	62	62	....	....	....	....	14	36	12	....
Mercer	585	585	2	....	3	102	195	232	51	....
Mercer State Police	115	116	1	2	3	5	42	33	29	1
Mingo	165	165	1	....	3	20	49	78	14	....
Mingo State Police	234	241	1	3	5	15	72	85	53	7
Monongalia	482	483	1	2	1	9	89	352	28	1
Monongalia State Police	292	294	1	3	1	2	85	143	57	2
Raleigh	1,288	1,289	6	1	18	109	279	808	67	1
Raleigh State Police	207	208	1	....	1	6	31	154	14	1
WISCONSIN										
Barron	467	474	....	7	3	31	164	235	27	7
Clark	357	359	....	3	1	4	133	198	18	2
Columbia	551	556	....	5	2	17	148	354	25	5
Dodge	358	358	....	6	....	11	123	184	34	....
Fond Du Lac	494	495	2	1	1	6	97	356	31	1
Grant	280	282	....	2	1	17	70	170	20	2
Jefferson	546	549	....	5	1	25	132	330	53	3
Manitowoc	434	435	2	3	....	13	122	252	42	1
Marinette	655		....	9	1	1	341	286	17	....
Polk	485	488	....	3	2	9	264	180	27	3
Portage	542	542	2	4	3	31	106	358	38	....
Sauk	215	216	....	....	1	....	48	162	4	1
Shawano	555	559	....	1	1	20	173	345	15	4
Walworth	518	522	1	8	....	16	117	334	42	4
Waupaca	589	589	1	1	....	4	209	347	27	....
Wood	564	567	....	7	2	5	142	376	32	3
STATE AGENCIES										
Alaska State Police	6,991	7,060	16	173	29	877	1,738	3,643	515	69
Arizona Department of Public Safety	50	50	....	....	3	17	1	28	1	....
Connecticut State Police	8,394	8,495	10	118	101	1,162	2,461	3,880	662	101
Minnesota Highway Patrol2			....	....		6	2	95	17	....
Vermont State Police	5,195	5,341	10	58	4	104	2,034	2,766	219	146
OTHER AREAS										
Guam	5,774	5,788	11	89	93	207	1,221	3,758	395	14
Virgin Islands	10,557	10,605	27	78	713	1,875	3,315	3,526	1,023	48

[1]Complete data for 1993 were not available for the states of Illinois and Kansas; therefore, it was necessary that their crime figures be estimated. See "Offense Estimation," page 376 for details.

[2]Forcible rape figures furnished by the state-level Uniform Crime Reporting (UCR) Program administered by the Michigan State Police and the Minnesota Department of Public Safety were not in accordance with national UCR guidelines. Therefore, the figures were excluded from the forcible rape, violent crime, and Crime Index total categories.

[3]1993 figures are not comparable to prior years.

Table 12. — Crime Trends, Offenses Known to the Police, Population Group, 1992-1993

[1993 estimated population]

Population group	Crime Index total	Modified Crime Index total[1]	Violent crime[2]	Property crime[3]	Murder and non-negligent man-slaughter	Forcible rape	Robbery	Aggra-vated assault	Burglary	Larceny-theft	Motor vehicle theft	Arson[1]
TOTAL ALL AGENCIES: 11,943 agencies; population 225,587,000:												
1992	12,914,813	13,011,866	1,722,047	11,192,766	21,416	89,041	609,566	1,002,024	2,669,286	7,043,658	1,479,822	97,053
1993	12,608,201	12,699,961	1,712,629	10,895,572	22,143	85,877	598,033	1,006,576	2,530,745	6,931,689	1,433,138	91,760
Percent change	-2.4	-2.4	-.5	-2.7	+3.4	-3.6	-1.9	+.5	-5.2	-1.6	-3.2	-5.5
TOTAL CITIES: 8,259 cities; population 149,808,000:												
1992	10,386,733	10,462,549	1,434,753	8,951,980	17,150	67,183	548,318	802,102	2,007,614	5,693,265	1,251,101	75,816
1993	10,123,293	10,195,465	1,424,952	8,698,341	17,778	64,461	538,216	804,497	1,899,969	5,597,325	1,201,047	72,172
Percent change	-2.5	-2.6	-.7	-2.8	+3.7	-4.1	-1.8	+.3	-5.4	-1.7	-4.0	-4.8
GROUP I												
63 cities, 250,000 and over; population 43,246,000:												
1992	4,112,347	4,149,701	749,652	3,362,695	10,515	28,574	349,213	361,350	781,789	1,890,325	690,581	37,354
1993	3,978,870	4,013,928	738,654	3,240,216	10,730	27,083	340,185	360,656	728,464	1,859,003	652,749	35,058
Percent change	-3.2	-3.3	-1.5	-3.6	+2.0	-5.2	-2.6	-.2	-6.8	-1.7	-5.5	-6.1
8 cities, 1,000,000 and over; population 18,419,000:												
1992	1,640,966	1,659,293	365,040	1,275,926	5,243	8,730	183,745	167,322	291,261	653,298	331,367	18,327
1993	1,565,615	1,582,006	352,608	1,213,007	5,094	8,325	175,818	163,371	270,845	638,219	303,943	16,391
Percent change	-4.6	-4.7	-3.4	-4.9	-2.8	-4.6	-4.3	-2.4	-7.0	-2.3	-8.3	-10.6
17 cities, 500,000 to 999,999; population 11,158,000:												
1992	1,047,466	1,055,143	152,384	895,082	2,306	8,558	71,702	69,818	198,453	545,905	150,724	7,677
1993	1,017,544	1,025,320	153,586	863,958	2,407	8,323	70,511	72,345	183,796	539,145	141,017	7,776
Percent change	-2.9	-2.8	+.8	-3.5	+4.4	-2.7	-1.7	+3.6	-7.4	-1.2	-6.4	+1.3
38 cities, 250,000 to 499,999; population 13,669,000:												
1992	1,423,915	1,435,265	232,228	1,191,687	2,966	11,286	93,766	124,210	292,075	691,122	208,490	11,350
1993	1,395,711	1,406,602	232,460	1,163,251	3,229	10,435	93,856	124,940	273,823	681,639	207,789	10,891
Percent change	-2.0	-2.0	+.1	-2.4	+8.9	-7.5	+.1	+.6	-6.2	-1.4	-.3	-4.0
GROUP II												
132 cities, 100,000 to 249,999; population 19,614,000:												
1992	1,579,652	1,591,705	206,735	1,372,917	2,331	10,906	73,482	120,016	329,765	864,988	178,164	12,053
1993	1,553,149	1,565,058	210,613	1,342,536	2,570	10,442	73,291	124,310	315,693	853,589	173,254	11,909
Percent change	-1.7	-1.7	+1.9	-2.2	+10.3	-4.3	-.3	+3.6	-4.3	-1.3	-2.8	-1.2
GROUP III												
336 cities, 50,000 to 99,999; population 23,060,000:												
1992	1,475,888	1,485,086	175,932	1,299,956	1,567	9,523	56,405	108,437	294,980	845,140	159,836	9,198
1993	1,448,711	1,457,189	173,895	1,274,816	1,713	9,181	55,794	107,207	280,502	838,728	155,586	8,478
Percent change	-1.8	-1.9	-1.2	-1.9	+9.3	-3.6	-1.1	-1.1	-4.9	-.8	-2.7	-7.8
GROUP IV												
616 cities, 25,000 to 49,999; population 21,377,000:												
1992	1,210,950	1,217,817	124,122	1,086,828	1,019	7,528	33,782	81,793	236,737	748,541	101,550	6,867
1993	1,178,682	1,185,295	122,738	1,055,944	1,113	7,146	33,542	80,937	225,065	730,794	100,085	6,613
Percent change	-2.7	-2.7	-1.1	-2.8	+9.2	-5.1	-.7	-1.0	-4.9	-2.4	-1.4	-3.7

See footnotes at end of table.

190

Table 12.—Crime Trends, Offenses Known to the Police, Population Group, 1992-1993—Continued

Population group	Crime Index total	Modified Crime Index total[1]	Violent crime[2]	Property crime[3]	Murder and non-negligent man-slaughter	Forcible rape	Robbery	Aggra-vated assault	Burglary	Larceny-theft	Motor vehicle theft	Arson[1]
GROUP V												
1,449 cities, 10,000 to 24,999; population 22,785,000:												
1992	1,086,865	1,092,307	99,630	987,235	977	6,149	21,998	70,506	203,715	708,897	74,623	5,442
1993	1,063,306	1,068,670	99,126	964,180	923	6,210	21,825	70,168	194,864	695,351	73,965	5,364
Percent change	-2.2	-2.2	-.5	-2.3	-5.5	+1.0	-.8	-.5	-4.3	-1.9	-.9	-1.4
GROUP VI												
5,663 cities under 10,000; population 19,726,000:												
1992	921,031	925,933	78,682	842,349	741	4,503	13,438	60,000	160,628	635,374	46,347	4,902
1993	900,575	905,325	79,926	820,649	729	4,399	13,579	61,219	155,381	619,860	45,408	4,750
Percent change	-2.2	-2.2	+1.6	-2.6	-1.6	-2.3	+1.0	+2.0	-3.3	-2.4	-2.0	-3.1
SUBURBAN COUNTIES												
1,259 agencies; population 50,784,000:												
1992	1,997,984	2,014,815	231,151	1,766,833	2,938	16,400	56,990	154,823	489,105	1,078,026	199,702	16,831
1993	1,963,126	1,978,574	230,752	1,732,374	2,992	15,905	55,594	156,261	464,199	1,065,820	202,355	15,448
Percent change	-1.7	-1.8	-.2	-2.0	+1.8	-3.0	-2.4	+.9	-5.1	-1.1	+1.3	-8.2
RURAL COUNTIES[4]												
2,425 agencies; population 24,995,000:												
1992	530,096	534,502	56,143	473,953	1,328	5,458	4,258	45,099	172,567	272,367	29,019	4,406
1993	521,782	525,922	56,925	464,857	1,373	5,511	4,223	45,818	166,577	268,544	29,736	4,140
Percent change	-1.6	-1.6	+1.4	-1.9	+3.4	+1.0	-.8	+1.6	-3.5	-1.4	+2.5	-6.0
SUBURBAN AREA[5]												
5,917 agencies: population 95,658,000;												
1992	4,156,498	4,185,171	427,924	3,728,574	4,596	27,714	107,991	287,623	889,122	2,466,053	373,399	28,673
1993	4,063,615	4,090,434	426,046	3,637,569	4,650	26,940	106,355	288,101	845,478	2,418,955	373,136	26,819
Percent change	-2.2	-2.3	-.4	-2.4	+1.2	-2.8	-1.5	+.2	-4.9	-1.9	-.1	-6.5

[1]The number of agency reports used in arson trends is less than used in compiling trends for other Crime Index offenses. It is not necessary to report arson by property classification to be included in this table. The Modified Crime Index total is the sum of the Crime Index offenses, including arson.

[2]Violent crimes are offenses of murder, forcible rape, robbery, and aggravated assault.

[3]Property crimes are offenses of burglary, larceny-theft, and motor vehicle theft. Data are not included for the property crime of arson.

[4]Includes state police agencies with no county breakdowns.

[5]Includes suburban city and county law enforcement agencies within metropolitan areas. Excludes central cities. Suburban cities and counties are also included in other groups.

Forcible rape figures furnished by the state-level Uniform Crime Reporting (UCR) Programs administered by the Michigan State Police and the Minnesota Department of Public Safety were not in accordance with national UCR guidelines and were excluded from the forcible rape, violent crime, Crime Index total, and Modified Crime Index total categories.

Complete data for 1993 were not available for the states of Illinois and Kansas; therefore, it was necessary that their crime counts be estimated. See "Offense Estimation," page 376 for details.

Table 13. — Crime Trends, Offenses Known to the Police, Suburban and Nonsuburban Cities[1], Population Group, 1992-1993

[1993 estimated population]

Population group	Crime Index total	Modified Crime Index total[2]	Violent crime[3]	Property Crime[4]	Murder and non-negligent man-slaughter	Forcible rape	Robbery	Aggra-vated assault	Burglary	Larceny-theft	Motor vehicle theft	Arson[2]
Suburban Cities												
TOTAL SUBURBAN CITIES: 4,658 cities; population 44,874,000:												
1992	2,158,514	2,170,356	196,773	1,961,741	1,658	11,314	51,001	132,800	400,017	1,388,027	173,697	11,842
1993	2,100,489	2,111,860	195,294	1,905,195	1,658	11,035	50,761	131,840	381,279	1,353,135	170,781	11,371
Percent change	-2.7	-2.7	-.8	-2.9	....	-2.5	-.5	-.7	-4.7	-2.5	-1.7	-4.0
GROUP IV												
476 cities, 25,000 to 49,999; population 16,422,000:												
1992	856,062	860,990	85,570	770,492	685	4,931	24,510	55,444	166,359	522,990	81,143	4,928
1993	835,904	840,633	85,081	750,823	717	4,743	24,629	54,992	159,433	510,771	80,619	4,729
Percent change	-2.4	-2.4	-.6	-2.6	+4.7	-3.8	+.5	-.8	-4.2	-2.3	-.6	-4.0
GROUP V												
1,072 cities, 10,000 to 24,999; population 16,924,000:												
1992	740,292	744,104	67,217	673,075	638	3,861	16,514	46,204	138,848	474,460	59,767	3,812
1993	719,150	722,812	65,868	653,282	599	3,847	16,236	45,186	131,039	463,757	58,486	3,662
Percent change	-2.9	-2.9	-2.0	-2.9	-6.1	-.4	-1.7	-2.2	-5.6	-2.3	-2.1	-3.9
GROUP VI												
3,110 cities under 10,000; population 11,527,000:												
1992	562,160	565,262	43,986	518,174	335	2,522	9,977	31,152	94,810	390,577	32,787	3,102
1993	545,435	548,415	44,345	501,090	342	2,445	9,896	31,662	90,807	378,607	31,676	2,980
Percent change	-3.0	-3.0	+.8	-3.3	+2.1	-3.1	-.8	+1.6	-4.2	-3.1	-3.4	-3.9
Nonsuburban Cities												
TOTAL NONSUBURBAN CITIES: 3,070 cities; population 19,014,000:												
1992	1,060,332	1,065,701	105,661	954,671	1,079	6,866	18,217	79,499	201,063	704,785	48,823	5,369
1993	1,042,074	1,047,430	106,496	935,578	1,107	6,720	18,185	80,484	194,031	692,870	48,677	5,356
Percent change	-1.7	-1.7	+.8	-2.0	+2.6	-2.1	-.2	+1.2	-3.5	-1.7	-.3	-.2
GROUP IV												
140 cities, 25,000 to 49,999; population 4,955,000:												
1992	354,888	356,827	38,552	316,336	334	2,597	9,272	26,349	70,378	225,551	20,407	1,939
1993	342,778	344,662	37,657	305,121	396	2,403	8,913	25,945	65,632	220,023	19,466	1,884
Percent change	-3.4	-3.4	-2.3	-3.5	+18.6	-7.5	-3.9	-1.5	-6.7	-2.5	-4.6	-2.8
GROUP V												
377 cities, 10,000 to 24,999; population 5,861,000:												
1992	346,573	348,203	32,413	314,160	339	2,288	5,484	24,302	64,867	234,437	14,856	1,630
1993	344,156	345,858	33,258	310,898	324	2,363	5,589	24,982	63,825	231,594	15,479	1,702
Percent change	-.7	-.7	+2.6	-1.0	-4.4	+3.3	+1.9	+2.8	-1.6	-1.2	+4.2	+4.4
GROUP VI												
2,553 cities under 10,000; population 8,199,000:												
1992	358,871	360,671	34,696	324,175	406	1,981	3,461	28,848	65,818	244,797	13,560	1,800
1993	355,140	356,910	35,581	319,559	387	1,954	3,683	29,557	64,574	241,253	13,732	1,770
Percent change	-1.0	-1.0	+2.6	-1.4	-4.7	-1.4	+6.4	+2.5	-1.9	-1.4	+1.3	-1.7

[1]Suburban places are within Metropolitan Statistical Areas (MSAs) and include suburban city and county law enforcement agencies within the metropolitan area. Central cities are excluded. Nonsuburban places are outside MSAs.

[2]The number of agencies used in arson trends is less than used in compiling trends for other Crime Index offenses. It is not necessary to report arson by property classification to be included in this table. The Modified Crime Index total is the sum of the Crime Index offenses, including arson.

[3]Violent crimes are offenses of murder, forcible rape, robbery, and aggravated assault.

[4]Property crimes are offenses of burglary, larceny-theft, and motor vehicle theft. Data are not included for the property crime of arson.

Forcible rape figures furnished by the state-level Uniform Crime Reporting (UCR) Programs administered by the Michigan State Police and the Minnesota Department of Public Safety were not in accordance with national UCR guidelines and were excluded from the forcible rape, violent crime, Crime Index total, and Modified Crime Index total categories.

Complete data for 1993 were not available for the states of Illinois and Kansas; therefore, it was necessary that their crime counts be estimated. See "Offense Estimation," page 376 for details.

Table 14.—Crime Trends, Offenses Known to the Police, Suburban and Nonsuburban Counties, Population Group 1992-1993

[1993 estimated population]

Population group	Crime Index total	Modified Crime Index total[1]	Violent crime[2]	Property Crime[3]	Murder and non-negligent man-slaughter	Forcible rape	Robbery	Aggra-vated assault	Burglary	Larceny-theft	Motor vehicle theft	Arson[1]
Suburban Counties[4]												
100,000 and over												
123 counties; population 31,034,000:												
1992	1,450,835	1,462,850	175,722	1,275,113	2,019	10,991	50,138	112,574	334,299	786,477	154,337	12,015
1993	1,429,696	1,440,871	176,298	1,253,398	2,082	10,788	49,205	114,223	319,492	779,014	154,892	11,175
Percent change	-1.5	-1.5	+.3	-1.7	+3.1	-1.8	-1.9	+1.5	-4.4	-.9	+.4	-7.0
25,000 to 99,999												
338 counties; population 17,104,000:												
1992	414,695	417,818	40,817	373,878	683	4,153	4,950	31,031	124,399	224,482	24,997	3,123
1993	405,233	408,129	40,444	364,789	689	3,846	4,610	31,299	116,603	222,713	25,473	2,896
Percent change	-2.3	-2.3	-.9	-2.4	+.9	-7.4	-6.9	+.9	-6.3	-.8	+1.9	-7.3
Under 25,000												
794 counties; population 2,566,000:												
1992	130,811	132,503	14,317	116,494	231	1,243	1,872	10,971	29,838	66,386	20,270	1,692
1993	126,453	127,826	13,724	112,729	212	1,254	1,759	10,499	27,531	63,307	21,891	1,373
Percent change	-3.3	-3.5	-4.1	-3.2	-8.2	+.9	-6.0	-4.3	-7.7	-4.6	+8.0	-18.9
Nonsuburban Counties[4]												
25,000 and over												
255 counties; population 10,074,000:												
1992	208,215	209,702	21,363	186,852	445	2,194	1,991	16,733	67,603	107,936	11,313	1,487
1993	206,616	207,912	21,433	185,183	473	2,128	1,979	16,853	65,651	107,883	11,649	1,296
Percent change	-.8	-.9	+.3	-.9	+6.3	-3.0	-.6	+.7	-2.9	[5]	+3.0	-12.8
10,000 to 24,999												
638 counties; population 10,020,000:												
1992	173,688	174,889	18,510	155,178	487	1,532	1,245	15,246	59,331	87,054	8,793	1,201
1993	170,954	172,068	18,956	151,998	432	1,559	1,288	15,677	57,198	85,824	8,976	1,114
Percent change	-1.6	-1.6	+2.4	-2.0	-11.3	+1.8	+3.5	+2.8	-3.6	-1.4	+2.1	-7.2
Under 10,000												
1,438 counties; population 4,351,000:												
1992	118,906	120,430	13,572	105,334	360	1,336	776	11,100	37,715	60,567	7,052	1,524
1993	115,518	117,028	13,613	101,905	426	1,424	750	11,013	35,747	58,826	7,332	1,510
Percent change	-2.8	-2.8	+.3	-3.3	+18.3	+6.6	-3.4	-.8	-5.2	-2.9	+4.0	-.9

[1]The number of agencies used in arson trends is less than used in compiling trends for other Crime Index offenses. It is not necessary to report arsons by property classification to be included in this table. The Modified Crime Index total is the sum of the Crime Index offenses, including arson.

[2]Violent crimes are offenses of murder, forcible rape, robbery, and aggravated assault.

[3]Property crimes are offenses of burglary, larceny-theft, and motor vehicle theft. Data are not included for the property crime of arson.

[4]Crime offenses include sheriffs' and county law enforcement agencies. State police offenses are not included.

[5]Less than one tenth of one percent.

Forcible rape figures furnished by the state-level Uniform Crime Reporting (UCR) Programs administered by the Michigan State Police and the Minnesota Department of Public Safety were not in accordance with national UCR guidelines and were excluded from the forcible rape, violent crime, Crime Index total, and Modified Crime Index total categories.

Complete data for 1993 were not available for the states of Illinois and Kansas; therefore, it was necessary that their crime counts be estimated. See "Offense Estimation," page 376 for details.

Table 15. — Crime Trends, Offenses Known Breakdown, Population Group, 1992-1993
[1993 estimated population]

Population group	Forcible rape — Rape by force	Forcible rape — Assault to rape-attempts	Robbery — Firearm	Robbery — Knife or cutting instrument	Robbery — Other weapon	Robbery — Strong-armed	Aggravated assault — Firearm	Aggravated assault — Knife or cutting instrument	Aggravated assault — Other weapon	Aggravated assault — Hands, fists, feet, etc.	Burglary — Forcible entry	Burglary — Unlawful entry	Burglary — Attempted forcible entry	Motor vehicle theft — Autos	Motor vehicle theft — Trucks and buses	Motor vehicle theft — Other vehicles	Arson[1] — Structure	Arson[1] — Mobile	Arson[1] — Other
TOTAL ALL AGENCIES: 11,717 agencies; population 222,333,000:																			
1992	74,822	12,850	242,375	64,561	58,611	240,071	235,721	175,985	304,700	269,631	1,812,670	609,078	210,732	1,163,812	224,606	81,792	51,135	25,472	17,605
1993	72,508	11,359	251,227	59,093	56,051	226,672	246,428	173,804	303,758	260,442	1,692,162	591,458	198,169	1,124,463	217,994	77,939	47,489	23,590	18,393
Percent change	-3.1	-11.6	+3.7	-8.5	-4.4	-5.6	+4.5	-1.2	-.3	-3.4	-6.6	-2.9	-6.0	-3.4	-2.9	-4.7	-7.1	-7.4	+4.5
TOTAL CITIES: 8,091 cities; population 147,981,000:																			
1992	56,042	10,185	217,661	59,628	50,495	216,881	193,534	146,749	241,678	206,988	1,359,450	453,969	167,378	1,003,939	181,588	57,554	40,217	19,773	13,264
1993	54,213	9,036	225,648	54,664	48,225	205,262	203,134	145,337	241,118	198,187	1,269,951	439,073	158,534	962,392	175,079	54,019	37,859	18,275	13,992
Percent change	-3.3	-11.3	+3.7	-8.3	-4.5	-5.4	+5.0	-1.0	-.2	-4.3	-6.6	-3.3	-5.3	-4.1	-3.6	-6.1	-5.9	-7.6	+5.5
GROUP I																			
63 cities, 250,000 and over; population 43,246,000:																			
1992	24,224	4,350	149,046	39,410	29,837	130,920	109,480	72,821	114,051	64,998	558,415	163,962	59,412	568,117	100,969	21,495	19,488	11,033	5,171
1993	23,169	3,914	154,319	35,800	27,667	122,399	114,161	71,896	113,250	61,349	519,445	152,484	56,535	537,440	96,246	19,063	18,174	10,125	5,429
Percent change	-4.4	-10.0	+3.5	-9.2	-7.3	-6.5	+4.3	-1.3	-.7	-5.6	-7.0	-7.0	-4.8	-5.4	-4.7	-11.3	-6.7	-8.2	+5.0
8 cities, 1,000,000 and over; population 18,419,000:																			
1992	7,289	1,441	79,565	24,124	16,811	63,245	50,085	35,306	49,336	32,595	205,206	60,705	25,350	278,738	45,493	7,136	8,726	5,645	2,618
1993	6,937	1,388	80,054	21,393	15,322	59,049	49,514	34,882	47,844	31,131	189,943	56,248	24,654	255,904	41,809	6,230	7,851	4,713	2,608
Percent change	-4.8	-3.7	+.6	-11.3	-8.9	-6.6	-1.1	-1.2	-3.0	-4.5	-7.4	-7.3	-2.7	-8.2	-8.1	-12.7	-10.0	-16.5	-.4
17 cities, 500,000 to 999,999; population 11,158,000:																			
1992	7,410	1,148	31,905	6,879	4,766	28,152	20,067	14,534	24,405	10,812	143,986	40,851	13,616	123,635	20,906	6,183	4,590	2,318	769
1993	7,280	1,043	32,508	6,394	4,563	27,046	21,696	14,242	25,371	11,036	130,484	41,025	12,287	115,945	19,305	5,767	4,375	2,369	1,032
Percent change	-1.8	-9.1	+1.9	-7.1	-4.3	-3.9	+8.1	-2.0	+4.0	+2.1	-9.4	+.4	-9.8	-6.2	-7.7	-6.7	-4.7	+2.2	+34.2
38 cities, 250,000 to 499,999; population 13,669,000:																			
1992	9,525	1,761	37,576	8,407	8,260	39,523	39,328	22,981	40,310	21,591	209,223	62,406	20,446	165,744	34,570	8,176	6,172	3,070	1,784
1993	8,952	1,483	41,757	8,013	7,782	36,304	42,951	22,772	40,035	19,182	199,018	55,211	19,594	165,591	35,132	7,066	5,948	3,043	1,789
Percent change	-6.0	-15.8	+11.1	-4.7	-5.8	-8.1	+9.2	-.9	-.7	-11.2	-4.9	-11.5	-4.2	-.1	+1.6	-13.6	-3.6	-.9	+.3
GROUP II																			
130 cities, 100,000 to 249,999; population 19,269,000:																			
1992	8,923	1,768	28,298	7,966	6,737	29,481	30,673	21,738	39,285	26,763	229,352	68,974	27,736	140,760	26,473	8,643	6,469	3,113	1,925
1993	8,800	1,419	29,837	7,391	6,599	28,592	33,120	21,528	39,689	28,766	215,906	68,948	26,696	136,748	26,165	8,143	6,387	2,932	2,152
Percent change	-1.4	-19.7	+5.4	-7.2	-2.0	-3.0	+8.0	-1.0	+1.0	+7.5	-5.9	[2]	-3.7	-2.9	-1.2	-5.8	-1.3	-5.8	+11.8

See footnotes at end of table.

Table 15. — Crime Trends, Offenses Known Breakdown, Population Group, 1992-1993 — Continued

[1993 estimated population]

Population group	Forcible rape		Robbery				Aggravated assault				Burglary			Motor vehicle theft			Arson[1]		
	Rape by force	Assault to rape-attempts	Firearm	Knife or cutting instrument	Other weapon	Strong-armed	Firearm	Knife or cutting instrument	Other weapon	Hands, fists, feet, etc.	Forcible entry	Unlawful entry	Attempted forcible entry	Autos	Trucks and buses	Other vehicles	Structure	Mobile	Other
GROUP III 332 cities, 50,000 to 99,999; population 22,792,000:																			
1992	7,897	1,390	18,126	5,459	6,632	25,218	22,759	19,278	34,696	29,625	193,916	68,912	25,451	127,816	21,982	8,800	4,847	2,329	1,866
1993	7,701	1,268	19,163	5,157	6,633	23,783	24,081	19,231	34,378	27,464	182,888	67,421	23,831	124,124	21,466	8,511	4,344	2,093	1,937
Percent change	-2.5	-8.8	+5.7	-5.5	.2[2]	-5.7	+5.8	-.2	-.9	-7.3	-5.7	-2.2	-6.4	-2.9	-2.3	-3.3	-10.4	-10.1	+3.8
GROUP IV 609 cities, 25,000 to 49,999; population 21,129,000:																			
1992	6,273	1,067	11,169	3,189	3,562	15,150	12,922	13,138	23,103	29,786	152,509	55,775	22,242	78,293	13,786	7,656	3,439	1,463	1,900
1993	5,943	886	11,005	2,939	3,509	14,925	13,477	12,861	23,074	27,197	141,324	55,311	20,309	76,746	13,691	7,503	3,346	1,342	1,867
Percent change	-5.3	-17.0	-1.5	-7.8	-1.5	-1.5	+4.3	-2.1	-.1	-8.7	-7.3	-.8	-8.7	-2.0	-.7	-2.0	-2.7	-8.3	-1.7
GROUP V 1,418 cities, 10,000 to 24,999; population 22,291,000:																			
1992	5,175	819	6,934	2,009	2,567	9,904	10,536	11,383	18,104	27,240	129,768	50,274	18,648	56,213	11,021	5,927	3,134	1,055	1,171
1993	5,082	856	7,099	1,872	2,640	9,383	10,720	11,377	17,975	25,332	120,707	49,221	17,818	55,483	10,511	5,876	2,941	1,066	1,281
Percent change	-1.8	+4.5	+2.4	-6.8	+2.8	-5.3	+1.7	-.1	-.7	-7.0	-7.0	-2.1	-4.5	-1.3	-4.6	-.9	-6.2	+1.0	+9.4
GROUP VI 5,539 cities under 10,000; population 19,254,000:																			
1992	3,550	791	4,088	1,595	1,160	6,208	7,164	8,391	12,439	28,576	95,490	46,072	13,889	32,740	7,357	5,033	2,840	780	1,231
1993	3,518	693	4,225	1,505	1,177	6,180	7,575	8,444	12,752	28,079	89,681	45,688	13,345	31,851	7,000	4,923	2,667	717	1,326
Percent change	-.9	-12.4	+3.4	-5.6	+1.5	-.5	+5.7	+.6	+2.5	-1.7	-6.1	-.8	-3.9	-2.7	-4.9	-2.2	-6.1	-8.1	+7.7
SUBURBAN COUNTIES 1,239 agencies; population 50,014,000:																			
1992	14,076	2,079	23,058	4,458	7,667	21,624	33,117	22,929	52,940	44,310	333,419	116,186	34,257	143,725	37,101	18,081	8,136	4,833	3,630
1993	13,865	1,733	23,983	4,023	7,361	19,895	34,694	22,415	52,576	44,450	312,940	113,036	30,897	145,730	37,482	17,654	7,162	4,424	3,716
Percent change	-1.5	-16.6	+4.0	-9.8	-4.0	-8.0	+4.8	-2.2	-.7	+.3	-6.1	-2.7	-9.8	+1.4	+1.0	-2.4	-12.0	-8.5	+2.4
RURAL COUNTIES 2,387 agencies; population 24,338,000:																			
1992	4,704	586	1,656	475	449	1,566	9,070	6,307	10,082	18,333	119,801	38,923	9,097	16,148	5,917	6,157	2,782	866	711
1993	4,430	590	1,596	406	465	1,515	8,600	6,052	10,064	17,805	109,271	39,349	8,738	16,341	5,433	6,266	2,468	891	685
Percent change	-5.8	+.7	-3.6	-14.5	+3.6	-3.3	-5.2	-4.0	-.2	-2.9	-8.8	+1.1	-3.9	+1.2	-8.2	+1.8	-11.3	+2.9	-3.7
SUBURBAN AREA[3] 5,816 agencies; population 94,260,000:																			
1992	23,493	3,754	40,288	9,330	13,328	43,852	52,055	42,872	88,050	99,157	583,038	220,715	72,087	276,976	61,352	31,819	14,287	7,209	6,840
1993	23,001	3,264	41,223	8,558	12,994	41,736	54,557	41,794	87,726	95,955	545,400	215,486	66,399	276,343	61,159	30,927	12,987	6,648	6,952
Percent change	-2.1	-13.1	+2.3	-8.3	-2.5	-4.8	+4.8	-2.5	-.4	-3.2	-6.5	-2.4	-7.9	-.2	-.3	-2.8	-9.1	-7.8	+1.6

[1] The number of agency reports used in arson trends is less than used in compiling trends for the other Crime Index offenses.

[2] Less than one-tenth of one percent.

[3] Includes suburban city and county law enforcement agencies within metropolitan areas. Excludes central cities. Suburban cities and counties are also included in other groups.

Forcible rape figures furnished by the state-level Uniform Crime Reporting (UCR) Programs administered by the Michigan State Police and the Minnesota Department of Public Safety were not in accordance with national UCR guidelines and were excluded from the forcible rape categories.

Complete data for 1993 were not available for the states of Illinois and Kansas; therefore, it was necessary that their crime counts be estimated. See "Offense Estimation," page 376, for details.

Table 16. — Crime Rates, Offenses Known to the Police, Population Group, 1993

[1993 estimated population. Rate: Number of crimes per 100,000 inhabitants]

Population group	Crime Index total	Modified Crime Index total[1]	Violent crime[2]	Property crime[3]	Murder and non-negligent man-slaughter	Forcible rape	Robbery	Aggra-vated assault	Burglary	Larceny-theft	Motor vehicle theft	Arson[1]
TOTAL ALL AGENCIES: 11,212 agencies; population 219,054,000:												
Number of offenses known	12,468,002		1,703,758	10,764,244	21,938	92,801	594,580	994,439	2,501,025	6,840,454	1,422,765	
Rate	5,691.7		777.8	4,914.0	10.0	42.4	271.4	454.0	1,141.7	3,122.7	649.5	
TOTAL CITIES: 7,727 cities; population 145,713,000:												
Number of offenses known	10,037,498		1,420,760	8,616,738	17,656	69,373	535,708	798,023	1,884,331	5,537,857	1,194,550	
Rate	6,888.5		975.0	5,913.5	12.1	47.6	367.6	547.7	1,293.2	3,800.5	819.8	
GROUP I												
63 cities, 250,000 and over; population 43,246,000:												
Number of offenses known....	3,980,534		740,318	3,240,216	10,730	28,747	340,185	360,656	728,464	1,859,003	652,749	
Rate	9,204.5		1,711.9	7,492.6	24.8	66.5	786.6	834.0	1,684.5	4,298.7	1,509.4	
8 cities, 1,000,000 and over; population 18,419,000:												
Number of offenses known....	1,566,662		353,655	1,213,007	5,094	9,372	175,818	163,371	270,845	638,219	303,943	
Rate	8,505.6		1,920.0	6,585.6	27.7	50.9	954.5	887.0	1,470.5	3,465.0	1,650.2	
17 cities, 500,000 to 999,999; population 11,158,000:												
Number of offenses known....	1,017,544		153,586	863,958	2,407	8,323	70,511	72,345	183,796	539,145	141,017	
Rate	9,119.7		1,376.5	7,743.2	21.6	74.6	632.0	648.4	1,647.3	4,832.1	1,263.9	
38 cities, 250,000 to 499,999; population 13,669,000:												
Number of offenses known....	1,396,328		233,077	1,163,251	3,229	11,052	93,856	124,940	273,823	681,639	207,789	
Rate	10,215.4		1,705.2	8,510.2	23.6	80.9	686.6	914.0	2,003.3	4,986.8	1,520.2	
GROUP II												
129 cities, 100,000 to 249,999; population 19,183,000:												
Number of offenses known....	1,541,148		209,691	1,331,457	2,541	11,150	72,848	123,152	312,918	845,803	172,736	
Rate	8,034.0		1,093.1	6,940.9	13.2	58.1	379.8	642.0	1,631.2	4,409.2	900.5	
GROUP III												
325 cities, 50,000 to 99,999; population 22,460,000:												
Number of offenses known....	1,435,289		173,706	1,261,583	1,692	10,138	55,267	106,609	277,644	830,049	153,890	
Rate	6,390.5		773.4	5,617.1	7.5	45.1	246.1	474.7	1,236.2	3,695.7	685.2	

See footnotes at end of table.

Table 16. — Crime Rates, Offenses Known to the Police, Population Group, 1993 — Continued

[1993 estimated population. Rate: Number of crimes per 100,000 inhabitants]

Population group	Crime Index total	Modified Crime Index total[1]	Violent crime[2]	Property crime[3]	Murder and non-negligent man-slaughter	Forcible rape	Robbery	Aggra-vated assault	Burglary	Larceny-theft	Motor vehicle theft	Arson[1]
GROUP IV												
597 cities, 25,000 to 49,999; population 20,713,000:												
Number of offenses known....	1,157,936		120,671	1,037,265	1,081	7,459	32,867	79,264	221,992	716,424	98,849	
Rate	5,590.4		582.3	5,007.8	5.2	36.0	158.7	382.7	1,071.7	3,458.8	477.2	
GROUP V												
1,382 cities, 10,000 to 24,999; population 21,711,000:												
Number of offenses known....	1,039,685		97,438	942,247	902	6,973	21,240	68,323	190,616	679,433	72,198	
Rate	4,788.7		448.8	4,339.9	4.2	32.1	97.8	314.7	878.0	3,129.4	332.5	
GROUP VI												
5,231 cities under 10,000; population 18,401,000:												
Number of offenses known....	882,906		78,936	803,970	710	4,906	13,301	60,019	152,697	607,145	44,128	
Rate	4,798.2		429.0	4,369.2	3.9	26.7	72.3	326.2	829.8	3,299.6	239.8	
SUBURBAN COUNTIES												
1,190 agencies; population 49,181,000:												
Number of offenses known....	1,919,189		226,687	1,692,502	2,949	17,005	54,729	152,004	453,502	1,039,898	199,102	
Rate	3,902.3		460.9	3,441.4	6.0	28.9	111.3	309.1	922.1	2,114.4	404.8	
RURAL COUNTIES[4]												
2,295 agencies; population 24,160,000:												
Number of offenses known....	511,315		56,311	455,004	1,333	6,423	4,143	44,412	163,192	262,699	29,113	
Rate	2,116.3		233.1	1,883.3	5.5	26.6	17.1	183.8	675.5	1,087.3	120.5	
SUBURBAN AREA[5]												
5,556 agencies; population 92,030,000:												
Number of offenses known....	3,983,617		420,303	3,563,314	4,565	29,148	104,610	281,980	828,829	2,367,739	366,746	
Rate	4,328.6		456.7	3,871.9	5.0	31.7	113.7	306.4	900.6	2,572.8	398.5	

[1]Arson rates are not presented in this table because fewer agencies furnished complete reports for arson than for the other seven Crime Index offenses. Independently tabulated arson rates appear on page 54 of this publication.

[2]Violent crimes are offenses of murder, forcible rape, robbery, and aggravated assault.

[3]Property crimes are offenses of burglary, larceny-theft, and motor vehicle theft. Data are not included for the property crime of arson.

[4]Includes state police agencies with no county breakdown.

[5]Includes suburban city and county law enforcement agencies within metropolitian areas. Excludes central cities. Suburban cities and counties are also included in other groups. Population figures were rounded to the nearest thousand. All rates were calculated on the population before rounding.

Forcible rape figures furnished by the state-level Uniform Crime Reporting (UCR) Programs administered by Michigan State Police and Minnesota Department of Public Safety were not in accordance with national UCR guidelines. See Appendix I for details.

Complete data for 1993 were not available for the states of Illinois and Kansas; therefore, it was necessary that their crime counts be estimated. See "Offense Estimation," page 376 for details.

Table 17.-Crime Rates, Offenses Known to the Police, Suburban and Nonsuburban Cities[1], Population Group, 1993

[1993 estimated population. Rate: Number of crimes per 100,000 inhabitants]

Population group	Crime Index total	Modified Crime Index total[2]	Violent crime[3]	Property crime[4]	Murder and non-negligent manslaughter	Forcible rape	Robbery	Aggra-vated assault	Burglary	Larceny-theft	Motor vehicle theft	Arson[2]
Suburban Cities												
TOTAL SUBURBAN CITIES:												
4,366 cities;												
population 42,849,000:												
Number of offenses known	**2,064,456**		**193,644**	**1,870,812**	**1,616**	**12,171**	**49,881**	**129,976**	**375,327**	**1,327,841**	**167,644**	
Rate	**4,818.0**		**451.9**	**4,366.1**	**3.8**	**28.4**	**116.4**	**303.3**	**875.9**	**3,098.9**	**391.2**	
GROUP IV												
466 cities, 25,000 to 49,999;												
population 16,081,000:												
Number of offenses known....	831,195		85,375	745,820	708	5,160	24,401	55,106	158,578	507,115	80,127	
Rate	5,168.9		530.9	4,637.9	4.4	32.1	151.7	342.7	986.1	3,153.5	498.3	
GROUP V												
1,019 cities, 10,000 to 24,999;												
population 16,070,000:												
Number of offenses known....	698,960		64,539	634,421	577	4,290	15,761	43,911	127,426	450,040	56,955	
Rate	4,349.5		401.6	3,947.9	3.6	26.7	98.1	273.3	793.0	2,800.5	354.4	
GROUP VI												
2,881 cities under 10,000;												
population 10,698,000:												
Number of offenses known....	534,301		43,730	490,571	331	2,721	9,719	30,959	89,323	370,686	30,562	
Rate	4,994.3		408.8	4,585.5	3.1	25.4	90.8	289.4	834.9	3,464.9	285.7	
Nonsuburban Cities												
TOTAL NONSUBURBAN CITIES:												
2,884 cities;												
population 17,976,000:												
Number of offenses known	**1,016,151**		**103,481**	**912,670**	**1,077**	**7,247**	**17,527**	**77,630**	**189,978**	**675,161**	**47,531**	
Rate	**5,652.8**		**575.7**	**5,077.2**	**6.0**	**40.3**	**97.5**	**431.9**	**1,056.8**	**3,755.9**	**264.4**	
GROUP IV												
131 cities, 25,000 to 49,999;												
population 4,632,000:												
Number of offenses known....	326,844		35,399	291,445	373	2,402	8,466	24,158	63,414	209,309	18,722	
Rate	7,055.8		764.2	6,291.6	8.1	51.9	182.8	521.5	1,369.0	4,518.5	404.2	
GROUP V												
363 cities, 10,000 to 24,999;												
population 5,641,000:												
Number of offenses known....	340,629		32,803	307,826	325	2,587	5,479	24,412	63,190	229,393	15,243	
Rate	6,038.2		581.5	5,456.7	5.8	45.9	97.1	432.7	1,120.1	4,066.4	270.2	
GROUP VI												
2,350 cities under 10,000;												
population 7,703,000:												
Number of offenses known....	348,678		35,279	313,399	379	2,258	3,582	29,060	63,374	236,459	13,566	
Rate	4,526.9		458.1	4,068.8	4.9	29.3	46.5	377.3	822.8	3,069.9	176.1	

[1]Suburban places are within Metropolitan Statistical Areas (MSAs) and include suburban city and county law enforcement agencies within the metropolitan area. Central cities are excluded. Nonsuburban places are outside MSAs.

[2]Arson rates are not presented in this table because fewer agencies furnished complete reports for arson than for the other seven Crime Index offenses. Independently tabulated arson rates appear on page 54 of this publication.

[3]Violent crimes are offenses of murder, forcible rape, robbery, and aggravated assault.

[4]Property crimes are offenses of burglary, larceny-theft, and motor vehicle theft. Data are not included for the property crime of arson.

Population figures were rounded to the nearest thousand. All rates were calculated on the population before rounding.

Forcible rape figures furnished by the state-level Uniform Crime Reporting (UCR) Programs administered by Michigan State Police and Minnesota Department of Public Safety were not in accordance with national UCR guidelines. See Appendix I for details.

Complete data for 1993 were not available for the states of Illinois and Kansas; therefore, it was necessary that their crime counts be estimated. See "Offense Estimation," page 376 for details.

Table 18.— Crime Rates, Offenses Known to the Police, Suburban and Nonsuburban Counties, Population Group, 1993

[1993 estimated population. Rate: Number of crimes per 100,000 inhabitants]

Population group	Crime Index total	Modified[1] Crime Index total	Violent crime[2]	Property crime[3]	Murder and non-negligent man-slaughter	Forcible rape	Robbery	Aggra-vated assault	Burglary	Larceny-theft	Motor vehicle theft	Arson[1]
Suburban Counties[4]												
100,000 and over												
120 counties; population 30,281,000:												
Number of offenses known....	1,395,920		172,320	1,223,600	2,057	10,895	48,580	110,788	311,304	759,804	152,492	
Rate......................	4,609.8		569.1	4,040.8	6.8	36.0	160.4	365.9	1,028.0	2,509.2	503.6	
25,000 to 99,999												
324 counties; population 16,335,000:												
Number of offenses known....	399,729		40,243	359,486	670	3,923	4,572	31,078	114,953	219,430	25,103	
Rate......................	2,447.1		246.4	2,200.8	4.1	24.0	28.0	190.3	703.7	1,343.3	153.7	
Under 25,000												
746 counties; population 2,565,000:												
Number of offenses known....	122,640		13,224	109,416	222	1,287	1,577	10,138	27,245	60,664	21,507	
Rate......................	4,781.7		515.6	4,266.1	8.7	50.2	61.5	395.3	1,062.3	2,365.3	838.6	
Nonsuburban Counties[4]												
25,000 and over												
250 counties; population 9,883,000:												
Number of offenses known....	205,082		21,257	183,825	474	2,208	1,968	16,607	64,984	107,235	11,606	
Rate......................	2,075.0		215.1	1,859.9	4.8	22.3	19.9	168.0	657.5	1,085.0	117.4	
10,000 to 24,999												
614 counties; population 9,649,000:												
Number of offenses known....	166,388		18,603	147,785	425	1,699	1,247	15,232	55,866	83,196	8,723	
Rate......................	1,724.5		192.8	1,531.7	4.4	17.6	12.9	157.9	579.0	862.3	90.4	
Under 10,000												
1,338 counties; population 4,079,000:												
Number of offenses known....	110,436		12,816	97,620	392	1,401	722	10,301	34,361	56,254	7,005	
Rate......................	2,707.6		314.2	2,393.4	9.6	34.3	17.7	252.5	842.4	1,379.2	171.7	

[1]Arson rates are not presented in this table because fewer agencies furnished complete reports for arson than for the other seven Crime Index offenses. Independently tabulated arson rates appear on page 54 of this publication.

[2]Violent crimes are offenses of murder, forcible rape, robbery, and aggravated assault.

[3]Property crimes are offenses of burglary, larceny-theft, and motor vehicle theft. Data are not included for the property crime of arson.

[4]Offenses include sheriffs' and county law enforcement agencies. State police offenses are not included.

Population figures were rounded to the nearest thousand. All rates were calculated on the population before rounding.

Forcible rape figures furnished by the state-level Uniform Crime Reporting (UCR) Programs administered by Michigan State Police and Minnesota Department of Public Safety were not in accordance with national UCR guidelines. See Appendix I for details.

Complete data for 1993 were not available for the states of Illinois and Kansas; therefore, it was necessary that their crime counts be estimated. See "Offense Estimation," page 376 for details.

Table 19.—Crime Rates, Offenses Known Breakdown, Population Group, 1993

[1993 estimated population. Rate: number of crimes per 100,000 inhabitants]

Population group	Forcible rape: Rape by force	Forcible rape: Assault to rape-attempts	Robbery: Firearm	Robbery: Knife or cutting instrument	Robbery: Other weapon	Robbery: Strong-armed	Aggravated assault: Firearm	Aggravated assault: Knife or cutting instrument	Aggravated assault: Other weapon	Aggravated assault: Hands, fists, feet, etc.	Burglary: Forcible entry	Burglary: Unlawful entry	Burglary: Attempted forcible entry	Motor vehicle theft: Autos	Motor vehicle theft: Trucks and buses	Motor vehicle theft: Other vehicles	Arson[1]: Structure	Arson[1]: Mobile	Arson[1]: Other
TOTAL ALL AGENCIES: 10,917 agencies; population 215,029,000: Number of offenses known	79,674	11,775	250,047	58,848	55,769	225,181	244,679	172,073	302,075	256,676	1,678,636	587,415	196,402	1,118,130	216,984	77,233			
Rate	37.1	5.5	116.3	27.4	25.9	104.7	113.8	80.0	140.5	119.4	780.7	273.4	91.3	520.0	100.9	35.9			
TOTAL CITIES: 7,501 cities; population 143,627,000: Number of offenses known	58,966	9,430	224,882	54,493	48,003	204,094	202,112	144,231	240,342	196,661	1,262,956	437,305	157,240	958,119	174,470	53,595			
Rate	41.1	6.6	156.6	37.9	33.4	142.1	140.7	100.4	167.3	136.9	879.3	304.5	109.5	667.1	121.5	37.3			
GROUP I																			
63 cities, 250,000 and over; population 43,246,000: Number of offenses known	24,561	4,186	154,319	35,800	27,667	122,399	114,161	71,896	113,250	61,349	519,445	152,484	56,535	537,440	96,246	19,063			
Rate	56.8	9.7	356.8	82.8	64.0	283.0	264.0	166.3	261.9	141.9	1,201.2	352.6	130.7	1,242.8	222.6	44.1			
8 cities, 1,000,000 and over; population 18,419,000: Number of offenses known	7,847	1,525	80,054	21,393	15,322	59,049	49,514	34,882	47,844	31,131	189,943	56,248	24,654	255,904	41,809	6,230			
Rate	42.6	8.3	434.6	116.1	83.2	320.6	268.8	189.4	259.8	169.0	1,031.2	305.4	133.9	1,389.3	227.0	33.8			
17 cities, 500,000 to 999,999; population 11,158,000: Number of offenses known	7,280	1,043	32,508	6,394	4,563	27,046	21,696	14,242	25,371	11,036	130,484	41,025	12,287	115,945	19,305	5,767			
Rate	65.2	9.3	291.4	57.3	40.9	242.4	194.5	127.6	227.4	98.9	1,169.5	367.7	110.1	1,039.2	173.0	51.7			
38 cities, 250,000 to 499,999; population 13,669,000: Number of offenses known	9,434	1,618	41,757	8,013	7,782	36,304	42,951	22,772	40,035	19,182	199,018	55,211	19,594	165,591	35,132	7,066			
Rate	69.0	11.8	305.5	58.6	56.9	265.6	314.2	166.6	292.9	140.3	1,456.0	403.9	143.3	1,211.4	257.0	51.7			
GROUP II																			
128 cities, 100,000 to 249,999; population 18,958,000: Number of offenses known	9,477	1,469	29,641	7,408	6,390	28,569	32,546	21,431	39,365	28,744	214,504	68,298	26,749	136,715	25,900	8,078			
Rate	50.0	7.7	156.4	39.1	33.7	150.7	171.7	113.0	207.6	151.6	1,131.5	360.3	141.1	721.2	136.6	42.6			
GROUP III																			
320 cities, 50,000 to 99,999; population 22,094,000: Number of offenses known	8,606	1,296	18,938	5,078	6,570	23,435	23,862	18,862	33,737	27,166	180,631	66,469	23,287	122,345	21,380	8,460			
Rate	39.0	5.9	85.7	23.0	29.7	106.1	108.0	85.4	152.7	123.0	817.5	300.8	105.4	553.7	96.8	38.3			

See footnotes at end of table.

Table 19.-Crime Rates, Offenses Known Breakdown, Population Group, 1993 — Continued

Population group	Forcible rape: Rape by force	Forcible rape: Assault to rape-attempts	Robbery: Firearm	Robbery: Knife or cutting instrument	Robbery: Other weapon	Robbery: Strong-armed	Aggravated assault: Firearm	Aggravated assault: Knife or cutting instrument	Aggravated assault: Other weapon	Aggravated assault: Hands, fists, feet, etc.	Burglary: Forcible entry	Burglary: Unlawful entry	Burglary: Attempted forcible entry	Motor vehicle theft: Autos	Motor vehicle theft: Trucks and buses	Motor vehicle theft: Other vehicles	Arson[1]: Structure	Arson[1]: Mobile	Arson[1]: Other
GROUP IV 589 cities, 25,000 to 49,999; population 20,431,000:																			
Number of offenses known	6,370	879	10,841	2,897	3,561	14,560	13,352	12,566	23,071	26,982	140,243	55,573	20,156	75,932	13,567	7,466			
Rate	31.2	4.3	53.1	14.2	17.4	71.3	65.4	61.5	112.9	132.1	686.4	272.0	98.7	371.6	66.4	36.5			
GROUP V 1,346 cities, 10,000 to 24,999; population 21,142,000:																			
Number of offenses known	5,912	897	7,011	1,837	2,627	9,112	10,582	11,131	18,031	25,049	119,284	48,922	17,446	54,558	10,405	5,761			
Rate	27.9	4.2	33.2	8.7	12.4	43.1	50.1	52.6	85.3	118.5	564.0	231.4	82.5	258.1	49.2	27.2			
GROUP VI 5,055 cities under 10,000; population 17,756,000:																			
Number of offenses known	4,040	703	4,132	1,473	1,188	6,019	7,609	8,345	12,888	27,371	88,849	45,559	13,067	31,129	6,972	4,767			
Rate	22.8	4.0	23.3	8.3	6.7	33.9	42.9	47.0	72.6	154.1	500.4	256.6	73.6	175.3	39.3	26.8			
SUBURBAN COUNTIES 1,164 agencies; population 48,044,000:																			
Number of offenses known	14,983	1,749	23,532	3,943	7,287	19,569	33,591	21,805	51,398	42,050	304,942	110,357	30,465	143,320	36,944	17,350			
Rate	31.2	3.6	49.0	8.2	15.2	40.7	69.9	45.4	107.0	87.5	634.7	229.7	63.4	298.3	76.9	36.1			
RURAL COUNTIES 2,252 agencies; population 23,357,000:																			
Number of offenses known	5,725	596	1,633	412	479	1,518	8,976	6,037	10,335	17,965	110,738	39,753	8,697	16,691	5,570	6,288			
Rate	24.5	2.6	7.0	1.8	2.1	6.5	38.4	25.8	44.2	76.9	474.1	170.2	37.2	71.5	23.8	26.9			
SUBURBAN AREA[2] 5,416 agencies; population 90,064,000:																			
Number of offenses known	25,266	3,318	40,507	8,406	12,952	40,950	53,113	40,773	86,623	93,227	534,220	212,503	65,310	271,599	60,297	30,320			
Rate	28.1	3.7	45.0	9.3	14.4	45.5	59.0	45.3	96.2	103.5	593.2	235.9	72.5	301.6	66.9	33.6			

[1]Arson rates are not presented in this table because fewer agencies furnished complete reports for arson than for the other seven Crime Index offenses. Independently tabulated arson rates appear on page 54 of this publication.
[2]Includes suburban city and county law enforcement agencies within metropolitan areas. Excludes central cities. Suburban cities and counties are also included in other groups.
Population figures were rounded to the nearest thousand. All rates were calculated on the population before rounding.
Forcible rape figures furnished by the state-level Uniform Crime Reporting (UCR) Programs administered by Michigan State Police and Minnesota Department of Public Safety were not in accordance with national UCR guidelines. See Appendix I for details.
Complete data for 1993 were not available for the states of Illinois and Kansas; therefore, it was necessary that their crime counts be estimated. See "Offense Estimation," page 376 for details.

Table 20. — Murder, State, Type of Weapon, 1993

State	Total murders[1]	Total firearms	Handguns	Rifles	Shotguns	Firearms (type unknown)	Knives or cutting instruments	Other weapons	Hands, fists, feet, etc.
Alabama	473	284	234	14	35	1	66	105	18
Alaska	54	27	20	5	1	1	11	14	2
Arizona	330	230	168	15	15	32	45	33	22
Arkansas	244	175	125	17	20	13	26	31	12
California	4,094	3,007	2,609	154	167	77	473	476	138
Colorado	206	132	111	5	6	10	32	30	12
Connecticut	206	139	117	5	2	15	28	30	9
Delaware	20	12	10	1	1	....	4	2	2
District of Columbia	417	350	350	....	....	....	32	35	....
Florida	1,223	753	486	24	36	207	143	270	57
Georgia	750	506	435	24	32	15	114	94	36
Hawaii	43	16	12	2	2	....	12	5	10
Idaho	31	17	14	3	....	....	7	4	3
Illinois[2]									
Indiana	357	260	225	14	17	4	35	46	16
Iowa	45	18	10	1	3	4	13	9	5
Kansas[2]									
Kentucky	236	161	115	10	24	12	17	48	10
Louisiana	721	586	520	39	21	6	52	55	28
Maine	7	5	4	....	....	1	....	2	....
Maryland	632	458	427	2	22	7	80	65	29
Massachusetts	210	110	60	3	2	45	57	33	10
Michigan	922	681	379	49	70	183	90	112	39
Minnesota	131	69	51	8	10	....	29	17	16
Mississippi	218	161	141	8	8	4	32	14	11
Missouri	546	410	324	26	28	32	57	56	23
Montana[3]									
Nebraska	28	13	7	1	5	....	3	8	4
Nevada	129	84	79	2	3	....	17	10	18
New Hampshire	20	10	5	....	2	3	7	2	1
New Jersey	418	213	182	9	15	7	93	68	44
New Mexico	95	49	39	5	5	....	26	9	11
New York	2,415	1,739	1,604	16	50	69	310	262	104
North Carolina	771	493	368	49	71	5	107	126	45
North Dakota	11	5	3	....	1	1	2	3	1
Ohio	599	431	375	12	28	16	62	58	48
Oklahoma	272	170	131	22	16	1	39	48	15
Oregon	143	76	57	7	8	4	31	26	10
Pennsylvania	804	573	486	14	35	38	93	82	56
Rhode Island	39	21	16	2	1	2	7	9	2
South Carolina	375	264	213	18	24	9	53	37	21
South Dakota	18	10	8	2	....	....	....	4	4
Tennessee	450	322	271	13	32	6	58	49	21
Texas	2,142	1,535	1,107	77	133	218	281	234	92
Utah	58	23	17	3	1	2	13	6	16
Vermont	12	8	5	2	1	....	1	3	....
Virginia	539	394	325	17	41	11	71	48	26
Washington	264	155	127	15	10	3	45	49	15
West Virginia	125	85	53	12	17	3	12	18	10
Wisconsin	222	117	88	7	12	10	29	51	25
Wyoming	16	10	6	4	....	....	2	1	3

[1]Total number of murders for which supplemental homicide data were received.

[2]Complete data for 1993 were not available for the states of Illinois and Kansas. See "Offense Estimation," page 376 for details.

[3]No 1993 supplemental homicide data were available for the state of Montana.

Table 21. — Robbery, State, Type of Weapon, 1993

State	Total robberies[1]	Firearms	Knives or cutting instruments	Other weapons	Strong-armed	Agency count	Population
Alabama	3,883	1,046	933	919	985	5	954,000
Alaska	713	266	74	57	316	27	576,000
Arizona	6,267	2,594	585	540	2,548	85	3,738,000
Arkansas	3,017	1,460	232	233	1,092	180	2,415,000
California	126,314	51,890	12,791	15,178	46,455	736	31,154,000
Colorado	4,065	1,429	435	468	1,733	197	3,236,000
Connecticut	6,454	2,518	658	531	2,747	100	2,786,000
Delaware	209	46	17	17	129	3	377,000
District of Columbia	7,107	3,121	521	292	3,173	2	578,000
Florida	46,523	18,580	3,371	3,290	21,282	415	12,622,000
Georgia	15,689	8,401	1,015	2,029	4,244	340	5,849,000
Hawaii	1,214	131	93	25	965	5	1,172,000
Idaho	137	44	28	16	49	69	859,000
Illinois[2]							
Indiana	5,999	2,797	522	388	2,292	219	3,702,000
Iowa	621	129	91	100	301	140	1,814,000
Kansas[2]							
Kentucky	3,006	1,159	338	283	1,226	465	3,325,000
Louisiana	10,764	6,862	648	770	2,484	76	2,954,000
Maine	263	66	29	18	150	140	1,196,000
Maryland	21,580	12,125	1,566	1,279	6,610	150	4,964,000
Massachusetts	9,328	2,298	1,921	912	4,197	221	4,934,000
Michigan	22,028	11,909	1,370	3,163	5,586	555	8,789,000
Minnesota	5,085	1,266	433	423	2,963	294	4,466,000
Mississippi	2,555	1,284	167	169	935	74	1,078,000
Missouri	12,310	6,144	848	863	4,455	208	4,160,000
Montana	34	17	7	1	9	51	377,000
Nebraska	252	54	29	18	151	244	1,209,000
Nevada	4,281	2,180	385	242	1,474	21	1,206,000
New Hampshire	284	45	40	18	181	89	957,000
New Jersey	23,319	8,091	2,397	1,783	11,048	516	7,873,000
New Mexico	1,772	808	252	168	544	39	905,000
New York	101,505	37,650	15,079	9,949	38,827	619	17,238,000
North Carolina	13,110	5,806	1,107	1,299	4,898	432	6,651,000
North Dakota	50	6	6	30	8	83	587,000
Ohio	18,585	7,822	1,122	1,694	7,947	290	7,399,000
Oklahoma	3,933	1,608	306	266	1,753	281	3,188,000
Oregon	3,896	1,237	449	351	1,859	185	2,930,000
Pennsylvania	19,562	8,373	1,527	1,035	8,627	664	9,067,000
Rhode Island	1,007	249	122	86	550	43	971,000
South Carolina	6,785	2,538	718	747	2,782	181	3,587,000
South Dakota	97	25	7	8	57	60	546,000
Tennessee	10,776	5,733	765	695	3,583	141	3,569,000
Texas	40,375	19,257	3,724	3,440	13,954	874	17,980,000
Utah	1,090	350	97	133	510	103	1,791,000
Vermont	23	2	5	10	6	12	366,000
Virginia	9,216	4,429	711	759	3,317	406	6,491,000
Washington	7,076	2,315	686	621	3,454	199	4,897,000
West Virginia	781	284	64	48	385	297	1,818,000
Wisconsin	5,709	3,026	458	297	1,928	319	5,016,000
Wyoming	57	25	7	6	19	61	398,000

[1]The number of robberies for which breakdowns were received for twelve months of 1993.

[2]Complete data for 1993 were not available for the states of Illinois and Kansas. See "Offense Estimation," page 376 for details.

Table 22. — Aggravated Assault, State, Type of Weapon, 1993

State	Total aggravated assaults[1]	Firearms	Knives or cutting instruments	Other weapons	Personal weapons	Agency count	Population
Alabama	23,144	2,593	2,084	2,132	16,335	5	954,010
Alaska	3,124	729	670	685	1,040	27	576,000
Arizona	19,052	7,159	2,940	4,970	3,983	85	3,738,000
Arkansas	9,989	3,141	1,434	2,250	3,164	180	2,415,000
California	193,773	44,855	24,312	52,174	72,432	736	31,154,000
Colorado	13,451	3,972	2,266	4,107	3,106	197	3,236,000
Connecticut	7,507	1,065	1,224	2,701	2,517	100	2,786,000
Delaware	981	186	263	383	149	3	377,000
District of Columbia	9,003	2,170	2,129	3,848	856	2	578,000
Florida	100,977	25,572	18,887	41,111	15,407	415	12,622,000
Georgia	25,710	7,667	5,338	8,032	4,673	340	5,849,000
Hawaii	1,408	175	144	300	789	5	1,172,000
Idaho	2,066	644	415	465	542	69	859,000
Illinois[2]							
Indiana	13,896	2,658	1,776	3,362	6,100	219	3,702,000
Iowa	3,810	530	679	957	1,644	140	1,814,000
Kansas[2]							
Kentucky	9,868	2,340	1,314	3,171	3,043	465	3,325,000
Louisiana	21,222	7,976	3,753	5,783	3,710	76	2,954,000
Maine	927	47	157	252	471	140	1,196,000
Maryland	25,133	6,211	5,183	9,746	3,993	150	4,964,000
Massachusetts	30,122	2,593	5,010	10,218	12,301	221	4,934,000
Michigan	42,800	12,540	7,277	17,329	5,654	555	8,789,000
Minnesota	7,915	2,076	2,044	2,264	1,531	294	4,466,000
Mississippi	3,537	1,463	645	696	733	74	1,078,000
Missouri	21,861	8,550	3,233	6,364	3,714	208	4,160,000
Montana	381	148	52	59	122	51	377,000
Nebraska	1,654	130	318	772	434	244	1,209,000
Nevada	4,912	1,030	678	1,643	1,561	21	1,206,000
New Hampshire	624	72	105	119	328	89	957,000
New Jersey	23,438	4,043	5,398	7,382	6,615	516	7,873,000
New Mexico	7,276	1,962	1,152	2,795	1,367	39	905,000
New York	84,169	16,739	20,312	28,388	18,730	619	17,238,000
North Carolina	29,724	9,413	5,651	8,088	6,572	432	6,651,000
North Dakota	227	18	33	100	76	83	587,000
Ohio	22,660	6,230	3,954	6,120	6,356	290	7,399,000
Oklahoma	14,662	3,999	2,101	4,142	4,420	281	3,188,000
Oregon	9,484	2,237	1,541	3,227	2,479	185	2,930,000
Pennsylvania	19,672	4,131	3,041	4,580	7,920	664	9,067,000
Rhode Island	2,542	340	465	871	866	43	971,000
South Carolina	27,931	7,097	6,291	10,729	3,814	181	3,587,000
South Dakota	881	176	211	160	334	60	546,000
Tennessee	21,839	6,010	3,732	6,812	5,285	141	3,569,000
Texas	84,474	24,756	16,168	20,933	22,617	874	17,980,000
Utah	3,532	664	623	1,267	978	103	1,791,000
Vermont	189	48	35	53	53	12	366,000
Virginia	12,322	2,447	2,767	3,436	3,672	406	6,491,000
Washington	15,837	4,322	2,546	4,850	4,119	199	4,897,000
West Virginia	2,517	427	492	561	1,037	297	1,818,000
Wisconsin	6,076	1,390	937	1,009	2,740	319	5,016,000
Wyoming	893	125	154	196	418	61	398,000

[1]The number of aggravated assaults for which breakdowns were received for twelve months of 1993.

[2]Complete data for 1993 were not available for the states of Illinois and Kansas. See "Offense Estimation," page 376 for details.

Table 23.—Offense Analysis, 1993, and Percent Change from 1992

[11,748 agencies; 1993 estimated population 216,355,000]

Classification	Number of offenses 1993	Percent change over 1992	Percent distribu-tion[1]	Average value
MURDER...	21,211	+4.0	....	$76
FORCIBLE RAPE	80,643	-2.9	....	26
ROBBERY:				
Total	577,925	-1.4	100.0	815
Street/highway.......................................	315,994	-2.2	54.7	628
Commercial house	72,154	+.9	12.5	1,304
Gas or service station............................	13,480	-5.9	2.3	515
Convenience store..................................	30,493	-7.6	5.3	449
Residence...	59,480	+1.0	10.3	1,104
Bank...	10,384	+1.6	1.8	3,308
Miscellaneous	75,940	+.9	13.1	759
BURGLARY:				
Total	2,413,232	-4.8	100.0	1,185
Residence (dwelling):	1,603,748	-4.2	66.5	1,189
Night..	503,455	-5.1	20.9	1,002
Day...	704,638	-3.2	29.2	1,273
Unknown	395,655	-4.9	16.4	1,275
Nonresidence (store, office, etc.):	809,484	-6.0	33.5	1,179
Night..	375,123	-7.1	15.5	1,041
Day...	206,301	-4.8	8.5	1,213
Unknown	228,060	-5.3	9.5	1,375
LARCENY-THEFT (EXCEPT MOTOR VEHICLE THEFT):				
Total	6,635,120	-1.2	100.0	504
By type:				
Pocket-picking....................................	61,741	-5.7	.9	411
Purse-snatching..................................	58,069	-4.2	.9	341
Shoplifting...	1,018,832	-4.9	15.4	109
From motor vehicles (except accessories)	1,550,542	+.8	23.4	531
Motor vehicle accessories	925,459	-3.4	13.9	303
Bicycles...	405,939	-.2	6.1	241
From buildings....................................	872,984	-.6	13.2	831
From coin-operated machines	52,333	-21.4	.8	208
All others..	1,689,221	+1.0	25.5	740
By value:				
Over $200...	2,431,002	-.3	36.6	1,279
$50 to $200	1,551,810	-1.4	23.4	119
Under $50	2,652,308	-2.0	40.0	19
MOTOR VEHICLE THEFT....................................	1,377,238	-5.0	....	4,808

[1]Because of rounding, percentages may not add to totals.

Complete data for 1993 were not available for the states of Kansas and Illinois. See "Offense Estimation," page 376 for details.

Table 24.—Type and Value of Property Stolen and Recovered, 1993

[11,748 agencies; 1993 estimated population 216,355,000]

Type of property	Value of property		Percent recovered
	Stolen	Recovered	
Total[1]	$13,304,578,000	$4,578,141,000	34.4
Currency, notes, etc...	886,252,000	42,394,000	4.8
Jewelry and precious metals	1,145,813,000	55,386,000	4.8
Clothing and furs	328,787,000	47,445,000	14.4
Locally stolen motor vehicles..............................	6,682,729,000	4,125,665,000	61.7
Office equipment...	327,563,000	22,414,000	6.8
Televisions, radios, stereos, etc...........................	1,017,950,000	45,095,000	4.4
Firearms	113,969,000	11,849,000	10.4
Household goods..	223,149,000	12,327,000	5.5
Consumable goods	103,112,000	10,026,000	9.7
Livestock..	36,549,000	4,534,000	12.4
Miscellaneous..	2,438,705,000	201,006,000	8.2

[1]All totals and percentages calculated before rounding.

Complete data for 1993 were not available for the states of Kansas and Illinois. See "Offense Estimation," page 376 for details.

SECTION III

Crime Index Offenses Cleared

For UCR purposes, law enforcement agencies clear or solve an offense when at least one person is arrested, charged with the commission of the offense, and turned over to the court for prosecution. Clearances recorded in 1993 may be for offenses which occurred in prior years. Several crimes may be cleared by the arrest of one person, while the arrest of many persons may clear only one offense. Law enforcement agencies may clear a crime by exceptional means when some element beyond law enforcement control precludes the placing of formal charges against the offender. Examples of circumstances allowing such clearances are the death of the offender (suicide, justifiably killed by police or private citizen, etc.); the victim's refusal to cooperate with prosecution after the offender has been identified; or the denial of extradition because the offender committed another crime and is being prosecuted in a different jurisdiction. In all exceptional clearance cases, law enforcement must have identified the offender, have enough evidence to support arrest, and know the offender's location.

Law enforcement agencies nationwide recorded a 21-percent Crime Index clearance rate for 1993. Collectively, 44 percent of violent crimes were cleared. Among the violent offenses, the rates were 66 percent for murder, 53 percent for forcible rape, 24 percent for robbery, and 56 percent for aggravated assault. Clearances for crimes against persons (murder, forcible rape, and aggravated assault) are generally higher as these offenses are often given more intensive investigative efforts and the victims and/or witnesses can frequently identify the perpetrators.

The overall property crime clearance rate was 17 percent. Thirteen percent of the burglaries, 20 percent of the larceny-thefts, 14 percent of motor vehicle thefts, and 15 percent of arsons were cleared during the year.

When considering the Modified Crime Index total which includes arson, the overall clearance rate remained the same, 21 percent.

The highest total Crime Index clearance rate geographically was registered in the Southern States, with 22 percent. The Western States registered a 21-percent clearance rate, and the Midwestern and Northeastern States each recorded a 20-percent clearance rate. For violent crime overall, the highest clearance rate, 48 percent, was also recorded in the South. In the West, the rate was 46 percent,

in the Northeast, 40 percent, and in the Midwest, 39 percent. Property crime clearance rates were 18 percent in the South and West, 17 percent in the Midwest, and 16 percent in the Northeast.

By community type, city law enforcement agencies showed clearances for 21 percent of the Crime Index offenses brought to their attention. Those in suburban counties cleared 20 percent, and those in rural counties, 23 percent. Among the population groups, cities with 10,000 to 24,999 inhabitants registered the highest total Crime Index clearance rate, 26 percent. The highest violent crime clearance rate was recorded in the rural counties with 61 percent. Like the Crime Index clearance rate, the property crime rate was highest for cities with populations from 10,000 to 24,999, 23 percent. (See Table 25.)

Clearances Involving Only Persons under 18 Years of Age

Involvement of juveniles in crime can be measured by the number of crimes in which they have been identified as the offenders. Even though no physical arrest may have been made, a clearance by arrest is recorded when an offender under 18 years of age is cited to appear in juvenile court or before other juvenile authorities. Since the juvenile clearance percentages shown in this publication indicate only those offenses where no adults were involved, they should be considered a slight underestimation of juvenile involvement in crime. Juveniles (persons under 18 years of age) account for 26 percent of the United States population, according to 1993 Bureau of the Census estimates.

Twenty-one percent of the Crime Index offenses cleared by law enforcement during 1993 involved only young people under age 18. Persons in this age group accounted for 13 percent of the violent crime clearances and 23 percent of those for property crimes. Murder showed the lowest percentage of juvenile involvement (9 percent), while the highest percentage was shown for arson (44 percent).

Geographically, the Midwestern States recorded the largest percentage of Crime Index offense involvement by the under 18 age group—23 percent. Juveniles alone were the offenders in 21 percent of the clearances in the Western States, 20 percent of those in the Southern States, and 19 percent of those in the Northeastern States.

CHART 3.1

CRIMES CLEARED
by ARREST
1993

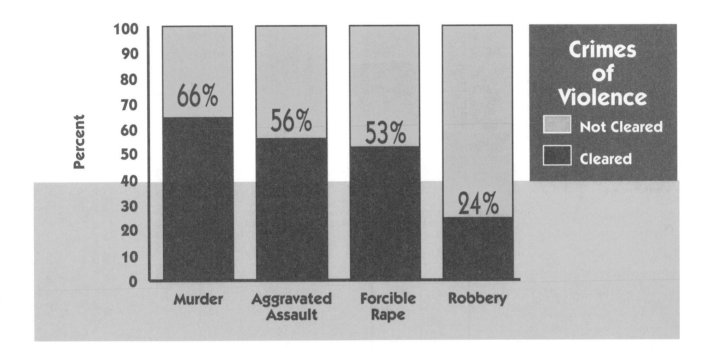

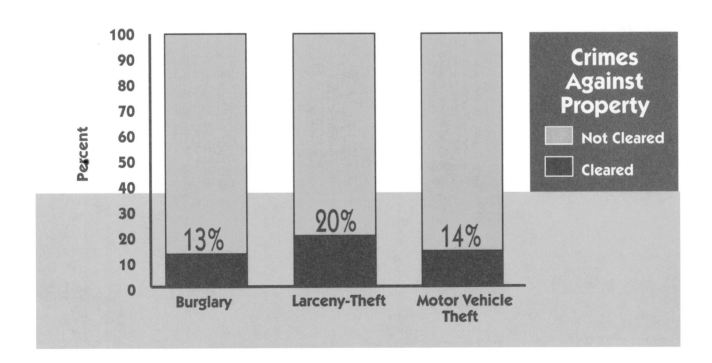

Table 25. — Offenses Known and Percent Cleared by Arrest[1], Population Group, 1993

[1993 estimated population]

Population group	Crime Index total	Modified Crime Index total[2]	Violent crime[3]	Property crime[4]	Murder and non-negligent man-slaughter	Forcible rape	Robbery	Aggra-vated assault	Burglary	Larceny-theft	Motor vehicle theft	Arson[2]
TOTAL ALL AGENCIES: 12,577 agencies; population 229,420,000:												
Offenses known	12,863,631	12,957,051	1,772,279	11,091,352	22,697	84,624	628,332	1,036,626	2,562,566	7,068,072	1,460,714	93,420
Percent cleared by arrest	21.1	21.1	44.2	17.4	65.6	52.8	23.5	55.5	13.1	19.8	13.6	15.4
TOTAL CITIES: 8,813 cities; population 155,971,000:												
Offenses known	10,456,904	10,531,713	1,491,498	8,965,406	18,434	63,811	571,075	838,178	1,950,151	5,774,982	1,240,273	74,809
Percent cleared by arrest	21.2	21.1	42.5	17.6	64.7	52.0	23.2	54.5	12.6	20.4	12.8	14.4
GROUP I												
62 cities, 250,000 and over; population 45,452,000:												
Offenses known	4,202,560	4,239,078	805,019	3,397,541	11,406	26,521	372,341	394,751	761,657	1,949,125	686,759	36,518
Percent cleared by arrest	18.5	18.4	37.6	14.0	62.1	52.4	21.0	51.6	10.7	16.6	10.1	9.7
9 cities, 1,000,000 and over; population 21,208,000:												
Offenses known	1,848,818	1,866,884	428,394	1,420,424	5,939	8,325	211,007	203,123	316,513	759,531	344,380	18,066
Percent cleared by arrest	18.5	18.4	36.6	13.1	60.8	51.2	20.2	52.2	9.8	16.5	8.5	6.0
17 cities, 500,000 to 999,999; population 11,158,000:												
Offenses known	1,017,544	1,025,320	153,586	863,958	2,407	8,323	70,511	72,345	183,796	539,145	141,017	7,776
Percent cleared by arrest	17.9	17.8	37.6	14.3	65.1	55.4	21.0	50.9	12.1	15.7	12.3	13.1
36 cities, 250,000 to 499,999; population 13,086,000:												
Offenses known	1,336,198	1,346,874	223,039	1,113,159	3,060	9,873	90,823	119,283	261,348	650,449	201,362	10,676
Percent cleared by arrest	19.0	19.0	39.6	14.9	62.5	51.0	23.0	50.8	10.8	17.7	11.2	13.5
GROUP II												
129 cities, 100,000 to 249,999; population 18,787,000:												
Offenses known	1,507,133	1,518,968	205,288	1,301,845	2,508	9,796	71,701	121,283	306,784	824,367	170,694	11,835
Percent cleared by arrest	21.1	21.0	45.0	17.3	64.0	52.9	26.3	55.0	12.2	19.9	13.7	16.5
GROUP III												
347 cities, 50,000 to 99,999; population 23,848,000:												
Offenses known	1,471,004	1,479,583	173,987	1,297,017	1,709	9,203	55,861	107,214	283,482	858,476	155,059	8,579
Percent cleared by arrest	22.0	22.0	44.9	18.9	68.3	49.4	25.9	54.1	13.0	22.1	12.4	16.8

See footnotes at end of table.

Table 25. — Offenses Known and Percent Cleared by Arrest[1], Population Group, 1993 — Continued

Population group	Crime Index total	Modified Crime Index total[2]	Violent crime[3]	Property crime[4]	Murder and non-negligent man-slaughter	Forcible rape	Robbery	Aggra-vated assault	Burglary	Larceny-theft	Motor vehicle theft	Arson[2]
GROUP IV												
658 cities, 25,000 to 49,999; population 22,816,000:												
Offenses known	1,226,611	1,233,616	125,448	1,101,163	1,151	7,241	34,795	82,261	233,708	764,589	102,866	7,005
Percent cleared by arrest	23.3	23.3	48.4	20.4	71.2	49.9	28.5	56.4	13.9	23.0	16.5	18.0
GROUP V												
1,531 cities, 10,000 to 24,999; population 24,109,000:												
Offenses known	1,109,996	1,115,704	100,417	1,009,579	926	6,438	22,382	70,671	202,352	729,729	77,498	5,708
Percent cleared by arrest	25.6	25.6	53.3	22.8	73.4	52.5	30.7	60.3	15.4	25.0	21.4	23.2
GROUP VI												
6,086 cities under 10,000; population 20,960,000:												
Offenses known	939,600	944,764	81,339	858,261	734	4,612	13,995	61,998	162,168	648,696	47,397	5,164
Percent cleared by arrest	24.0	24.0	57.3	20.8	76.2	55.0	29.9	63.4	15.8	21.5	28.5	23.6
SUBURBAN COUNTIES												
1,267 agencies; population 48,152,000:												
Offenses known	1,881,052	1,895,162	223,716	1,657,336	2,907	15,234	53,059	152,516	445,345	1,021,209	190,782	14,110
Percent cleared by arrest	20.4	20.3	51.0	16.2	65.0	54.3	25.5	59.3	14.1	17.1	16.2	18.8
RURAL COUNTIES												
2,497 agencies; population 25,296,000:												
Offenses known	525,675	530,176	57,065	468,610	1,356	5,579	4,198	45,932	167,070	271,881	29,659	4,501
Percent cleared by arrest	22.9	22.9	60.7	18.3	79.8	58.6	38.6	62.4	16.3	18.0	32.8	21.3
SUBURBAN AREA[5]												
6,312 agencies; population 96,400,000:												
Offenses known	4,096,662	4,122,989	425,391	3,671,271	4,634	26,679	106,034	288,044	845,039	2,456,566	369,666	26,327
Percent cleared by arrest	21.7	21.7	51.0	18.3	66.9	53.0	26.6	59.6	14.2	19.9	16.9	19.4

[1]Includes offenses cleared by exceptional means.

[2]The number of agency reports used in arson clearance rates is less than used in compiling clearance rates for other Crime Index offenses. It is not necessary to report clearances by detailed property classification to be included in this table. The Modified Crime Index total is the sum of the Crime Index offenses, including arson.

[3]Violent crimes are offenses of murder, forcible rape, robbery, and aggravated assault.

[4]Property crimes are offenses of burglary, larceny-theft, and motor vehicle theft. Data are not included for the property crime of arson.

[5]Includes suburban city and county law enforcement agencies within metropolitan areas. Excludes central cities. Suburban cities and counties are also included in other groups.

Forcible rape figures furnished by the state-level Uniform Crime Reporting (UCR) Programs administered by the Michigan State Police and the Minnesota Department of Public Safety were not in accordance with national UCR guidelines and were excluded from the forcible rape, violent crime, Crime Index total, and Modified Crime Index total categories.

Complete data for 1993 were not available for the states of Illinois and Kansas; therefore, it was necessary that their crime counts be estimated. See "Offense Estimation," page 376 for details.

Table 26. — Offenses Known and Percent Cleared by Arrest[1], Geographic Region and Division, 1993

[1993 estimated population]

Geographic region/ division	Crime Index total	Modified Crime Index total[2]	Violent crime[3]	Property crime[4]	Murder and non-negligent man-slaughter	Forcible rape	Robbery	Aggra-vated assault	Burglary	Larceny-theft	Motor vehicle theft	Arson[2]
TOTAL												
12,577 agencies; population 229,420,000:												
Offenses known	**12,863,631**	**12,957,051**	**1,772,279**	**11,091,352**	**22,697**	**84,624**	**628,332**	**1,036,626**	**2,562,566**	**7,068,072**	**1,460,714**	**93,420**
Percent cleared by arrest	**21.1**	**21.1**	**44.2**	**17.4**	**65.6**	**52.8**	**23.5**	**55.5**	**13.1**	**19.8**	**13.6**	**15.4**
NEW ENGLAND												
646 agencies; population 11,150,000:												
Offenses known	508,242	511,625	61,824	446,418	502	3,556	16,871	40,895	106,678	271,680	68,060	3,383
Percent cleared by arrest	21.7	21.6	51.4	17.5	63.9	53.0	24.7	62.2	13.3	19.7	15.5	16.9
MIDDLE ATLANTIC												
2,204 agencies; population 36,097,000:												
Offenses known	1,702,214	1,716,442	288,776	1,413,438	3,588	10,121	144,505	130,562	312,129	850,942	250,367	14,228
Percent cleared by arrest	19.5	19.4	37.5	15.8	66.5	53.2	22.5	52.2	12.6	19.1	8.8	11.6
NORTHEAST												
2,850 agencies; population 47,248,000:												
Offenses known	**2,210,456**	**2,228,067**	**350,600**	**1,859,856**	**4,090**	**13,677**	**161,376**	**171,457**	**418,807**	**1,122,622**	**318,427**	**17,611**
Percent cleared by arrest	**20.0**	**19.9**	**40.0**	**16.2**	**66.2**	**53.1**	**22.7**	**54.6**	**12.8**	**19.2**	**10.2**	**12.6**
EAST NORTH CENTRAL												
2,087 agencies; population 35,765,000:												
Offenses known	1,820,398	1,834,847	245,560	1,574,838	3,193	8,699	93,553	140,115	334,007	1,049,897	190,934	14,449
Percent cleared by arrest	19.7	19.6	37.7	16.8	58.5	49.3	18.3	49.4	10.6	19.3	14.4	11.7
WEST NORTH CENTRAL												
1,108 agencies; population 13,444,000:												
Offenses known	603,793	608,050	61,911	541,882	828	2,905	19,277	38,901	114,605	377,156	50,121	4,257
Percent cleared by arrest	21.9	21.9	44.9	19.3	72.7	52.9	24.0	54.0	12.3	21.6	18.1	13.7
MIDWEST												
3,195 agencies; population 49,208,000:												
Offenses known	**2,424,191**	**2,442,897**	**307,471**	**2,116,720**	**4,021**	**11,604**	**112,830**	**179,016**	**448,612**	**1,427,053**	**241,055**	**18,706**
Percent cleared by arrest	**20.2**	**20.2**	**39.1**	**17.5**	**61.4**	**50.2**	**19.2**	**50.4**	**11.0**	**19.9**	**15.1**	**12.2**
SOUTH ATLANTIC												
2,485 agencies; population 44,230,000:												
Offenses known	2,788,379	2,801,205	386,425	2,401,954	4,797	18,886	122,490	240,252	597,958	1,551,965	252,031	12,826
Percent cleared by arrest	21.8	21.8	47.3	17.7	71.6	57.6	25.6	57.0	15.0	18.7	18.0	20.9
EAST SOUTH CENTRAL												
715 agencies; population 8,251,000:												
Offenses known	404,238	406,923	56,823	347,415	873	3,854	16,226	35,870	91,301	215,161	40,953	2,685
Percent cleared by arrest	23.1	23.0	47.8	19.0	74.6	54.2	24.8	56.9	15.5	21.1	15.9	16.8
WEST SOUTH CENTRAL												
1,439 agencies; population 26,992,000:												
Offenses known	1,690,241	1,703,198	209,488	1,480,753	3,463	13,990	58,568	133,467	348,772	959,963	172,018	12,957
Percent cleared by arrest	21.8	21.8	48.5	18.1	69.4	54.0	29.0	56.0	13.8	20.0	15.8	19.6

See footnotes at end of table.

Table 26. — Offenses Known and Percent Cleared by Arrest[1], Geographic Region and Division, 1993 — Continued

Geographic region/ division	Crime Index total	Modified Crime Index total[2]	Violent crime[3]	Property crime[4]	Murder and non-negligent man-slaughter	Forcible rape	Robbery	Aggra-vated assault	Burglary	Larceny-theft	Motor vehicle theft	Arson[2]
SOUTH												
4,639 agencies; population 79,473,000:												
Offenses known	**4,882,858**	**4,911,326**	**652,736**	**4,230,122**	**9,133**	**36,730**	**197,284**	**409,589**	**1,038,031**	**2,727,089**	**465,002**	**28,468**
Percent cleared by arrest	**21.9**	**21.9**	**47.7**	**17.9**	**71.0**	**55.9**	**26.5**	**56.7**	**14.6**	**19.3**	**17.0**	**19.9**
MOUNTAIN												
717 agencies; population 13,240,000:												
Offenses known	776,548	780,936	78,124	698,424	874	5,665	17,998	53,587	145,652	482,023	70,749	4,388
Percent cleared by arrest	22.8	22.8	46.9	20.1	68.8	42.9	23.1	55.0	11.9	23.2	16.0	20.2
PACIFIC												
1,176 agencies; population 40,251,000:												
Offenses known	2,569,578	2,593,825	383,348	2,186,230	4,579	16,948	138,844	222,977	511,464	1,309,285	365,481	24,247
Percent cleared by arrest	21.0	20.9	45.4	16.7	57.3	51.2	23.6	58.4	12.5	19.9	10.9	13.6
WEST												
1,893 agencies; population 53,491,000:												
Offenses known	**3,346,126**	**3,374,761**	**461,472**	**2,884,654**	**5,453**	**22,613**	**156,842**	**276,564**	**657,116**	**1,791,308**	**436,230**	**28,635**
Percent cleared by arrest	**21.4**	**21.3**	**45.7**	**17.5**	**59.2**	**49.1**	**23.5**	**57.7**	**12.3**	**20.8**	**11.7**	**14.6**

[1]Includes offenses cleared by exceptional means.

[2]The number of agency reports used in arson clearance rates is less than used in compiling clearance rates for other Crime Index offenses. It is not necessary to report clearances by detailed property classification to be included in this table. The Modified Crime Index total is the sum of the Crime Index offenses, including arson.

[3]Violent crimes are offenses of murder, forcible rape, robbery, and aggravated assault.

[4]Property crimes are offenses of burglary, larceny-theft, and motor vehicle theft. Data are not included for the property crime of arson.

Forcible rape figures furnished by the state-level Uniform Crime Reporting (UCR) Programs administered by Michigan State Police and the Minnesota Department of Public Safety were not in accordance with national UCR guidelines and were excluded from the forcible rape, violent crime, Crime Index total, and Modified Crime Index total categories.

Complete data for 1993 were not available for the states of Illinois and Kansas; therefore, it was necessary that their crime counts be estimated. See "Offense Estimation," page 376 for details.

Table 27.—Offenses Known Breakdown and Percent Cleared by Arrest[1], Population Group, 1993

[1993 estimated population]

Population group	Forcible rape — Rape by force	Forcible rape — Assault to rape-attempts	Robbery — Firearm	Robbery — Knife or cutting instrument	Robbery — Other weapon	Robbery — Strong-armed	Aggravated assault — Firearm	Aggravated assault — Knife or cutting instrument	Aggravated assault — Other weapon	Aggravated assault — Hands, fists, feet, etc.	Burglary — Forcible entry	Burglary — Unlawful entry	Burglary — Attempted forcible entry	Motor vehicle theft — Autos	Motor vehicle theft — Trucks and buses	Motor vehicle theft — Other vehicles	Arson[2] — Structure	Arson[2] — Mobile	Arson[2] — Other
TOTAL ALL AGENCIES: 12,569 agencies; population 229,307,000:																			
Offenses known	73,493	11,095	266,612	61,460	58,857	241,261	262,065	184,140	324,170	265,733	1,746,212	613,307	202,060	1,162,449	221,368	76,619	48,289	23,124	19,166
Percent cleared by arrest	53.4	49.0	19.7	25.0	25.3	26.9	43.5	62.0	54.1	64.7	13.0	14.1	10.7	13.7	12.5	15.5	19.2	8.0	16.7
TOTAL CITIES: 8,807 cities; population 155,944,000:																			
Offenses known	54,967	8,814	241,808	57,277	51,247	220,625	218,091	155,596	261,035	203,274	1,329,169	458,511	161,819	1,008,421	178,599	53,044	39,060	18,463	14,773
Percent cleared by arrest	52.6	48.2	19.5	24.7	25.5	26.4	41.9	61.1	53.2	64.6	12.4	13.8	10.5	12.9	11.5	14.8	18.0	7.4	15.9
GROUP I																			
62 cities, 250,000 and over; population 45,452,000:																			
Offenses known	22,803	3,718	168,992	38,298	29,760	135,291	126,302	79,332	127,876	61,241	547,566	157,342	56,749	569,437	99,216	18,106	19,016	10,095	6,077
Percent cleared by arrest	52.8	50.2	17.3	22.2	24.7	24.5	38.7	60.5	51.8	65.9	10.5	11.2	11.2	10.2	9.0	11.5	12.7	4.9	10.5
9 cities, 1,000,000 and over; population 21,208,000:																			
Offenses known	6,937	1,388	95,805	24,425	17,954	72,823	63,146	43,633	64,148	32,196	225,025	64,187	27,301	291,337	46,480	6,563	8,844	4,741	3,262
Percent cleared by arrest	51.3	50.6	15.9	21.6	23.6	24.6	36.8	58.8	50.4	77.4	9.5	10.1	12.0	8.5	8.1	8.2	8.6	3.0	5.6
17 cities, 500,000 to 999,999; population 11,158,000:																			
Offenses known	7,280	1,043	32,508	6,394	4,563	27,046	21,696	14,242	25,371	11,036	130,484	41,025	12,287	115,945	19,305	5,767	4,375	2,369	1,032
Percent cleared by arrest	55.7	53.1	18.7	20.4	26.5	22.9	43.0	61.2	51.2	52.5	11.7	13.4	11.9	12.7	10.6	9.9	16.7	4.6	17.6
36 cities, 250,000 to 499,999; population 13,086,000:																			
Offenses known	8,586	1,287	40,679	7,479	7,243	35,422	41,460	21,457	38,357	18,009	192,057	52,130	17,161	162,155	33,431	5,776	5,797	2,985	1,783
Percent cleared by arrest	51.5	47.3	19.8	25.9	26.3	25.5	39.5	63.6	54.5	53.4	10.9	10.9	9.4	11.3	9.3	17.0	16.0	8.1	15.4
GROUP II																			
129 cities, 100,000 to 249,999; population 18,787,000:																			
Offenses known	8,497	1,299	29,628	7,044	6,209	28,820	32,641	21,106	39,234	28,302	217,144	65,918	23,722	138,706	25,040	6,948	6,410	2,986	2,167
Percent cleared by arrest	53.9	46.0	24.2	28.2	28.1	27.5	41.9	61.4	55.1	65.3	11.8	14.4	10.3	14.2	11.0	12.4	20.2	8.3	18.6
GROUP III																			
347 cities, 50,000 to 99,999; population 23,848,000:																			
Offenses known	7,908	1,281	19,297	5,243	6,956	24,310	24,323	19,839	34,912	28,140	186,848	71,096	25,147	124,537	21,732	8,675	4,269	2,073	1,980
Percent cleared by arrest	50.2	45.4	23.0	29.4	23.7	28.1	43.1	60.2	51.7	62.4	12.9	14.6	9.4	12.6	11.2	12.7	21.5	7.3	18.6
GROUP IV																			
658 cities, 25,000 to 49,999; population 22,816,000:																			
Offenses known	6,324	917	11,797	3,127	3,965	15,906	14,892	13,910	25,032	28,427	150,746	60,245	22,717	81,007	14,070	7,789	3,442	1,396	1,897
Percent cleared by arrest	51.0	42.3	25.5	30.1	27.7	30.5	48.8	60.7	54.6	60.0	14.1	15.0	9.6	16.6	15.7	17.0	21.6	11.2	19.1

See footnotes at end of table.

212

Table 27.-Offenses Known Breakdown and Percent Cleared by Arrest[1], Population Group, 1993 — Continued

Population group	Forcible rape		Robbery				Aggravated assault				Burglary			Motor vehicle theft			Arson[2]		
	Rape by force	Assault to rape-attempts	Firearm	Knife or cutting instrument	Other weapon	Strong-armed	Firearm	Knife or cutting instrument	Other weapon	Hands, fists, feet, etc.	Forcible entry	Unlawful entry	Attempted forcible entry	Autos	Trucks and buses	Other vehicles	Structure	Mobile	Other
GROUP V																			
1,531 cities, 10,000 to 24,999; population 24,109,000:																			
Offenses known	5,565	872	7,595	2,002	2,925	9,858	11,611	12,291	19,581	27,188	129,383	53,887	19,048	60,123	11,101	6,272	3,075	1,129	1,311
Percent cleared by arrest	53.4	46.7	26.4	34.2	28.1	33.9	52.0	63.2	55.7	65.8	15.8	16.0	11.0	21.8	20.2	19.5	28.1	14.3	22.7
GROUP VI																			
6,080 cities under 10,000; population 20,933,000:																			
Offenses known	3,870	727	4,499	1,563	1,432	6,440	8,322	9,118	14,400	29,976	97,482	50,023	14,436	34,611	7,440	5,254	2,848	784	1,341
Percent cleared by arrest	54.8	56.4	26.1	29.8	27.8	33.1	58.8	65.9	58.5	66.4	16.3	16.2	11.2	29.5	27.2	23.6	27.5	19.5	21.2
SUBURBAN COUNTIES																			
1,266 agencies; population 48,105,000:																			
Offenses known	13,550	1,683	23,102	3,759	7,117	19,081	34,501	22,235	52,211	43,479	301,387	112,637	31,100	136,646	36,961	17,143	6,522	3,704	3,666
Percent cleared by arrest	54.9	49.9	20.7	28.0	23.3	31.6	48.6	67.4	57.6	65.8	14.2	14.7	11.1	16.9	14.0	15.3	25.0	8.8	18.8
RURAL COUNTIES																			
2,496 agencies; population 25,258,000:																			
Offenses known	4,976	598	1,702	424	493	1,555	9,473	6,309	10,924	18,980	115,656	42,159	9,141	17,382	5,808	6,432	2,707	957	727
Percent cleared by arrest	58.8	57.7	36.9	42.2	39.6	39.4	62.8	65.0	58.7	63.9	16.7	16.3	11.9	36.6	33.7	21.8	23.8	16.0	22.0
SUBURBAN AREA[3]																			
6,306 agencies; population 96,329,000:																			
Offenses known	23,378	3,287	41,601	8,552	13,507	42,317	56,405	43,292	90,528	97,557	550,350	224,175	70,082	276,831	61,605	31,115	12,596	6,061	6,980
Percent cleared by arrest	53.7	47.9	22.2	28.6	24.5	31.2	49.0	65.4	56.9	65.7	14.3	15.2	10.6	17.4	15.1	16.5	24.9	10.7	18.8

[1] Includes offenses cleared by exceptional means.

[2] The number of agency reports used in arson clearance rates is less than used in compiling clearance rates for other Crime Index offenses.

[3] Includes suburban city and county law enforcement agencies within metropolitan areas. Excludes central cities. Suburban cities and counties are also included in other groups.

Forcible rape figures furnished by the state-level Uniform Crime Reporting (UCR) Programs administered by Michigan State Police and the Minnesota Department of Public Safety were not in accordance with national UCR guidelines and were excluded from the forcible rape, violent crime, Crime Index total, and Modified Crime Index total categories.

Complete data for 1993 were not available for the states of Illinois and Kansas; therefore, it was necessary that their crime counts be estimated. See "Offense Estimation," page 376 for details.

Table 28. — Offenses Cleared by Arrest[1] of Persons Under 18 Years of Age, 1993

[1993 estimated population]

Population group	Crime Index total	Modified Crime Index total[2]	Violent crime[3]	Property crime[4]	Murder and non-negligent man-slaughter	Forcible rape	Robbery	Aggra-vated assault	Burglary	Larceny-theft	Motor vehicle theft	Arson[2]
TOTAL ALL AGENCIES:												
12,422 agencies;												
population 218,221,000:												
Total clearances	**2,584,717**	**2,598,765**	**718,370**	**1,866,347**	**13,164**	**42,128**	**126,681**	**536,397**	**319,705**	**1,356,952**	**189,690**	**14,048**
Percent under 18	**20.5**	**20.6**	**13.4**	**23.3**	**9.3**	**14.5**	**16.6**	**12.7**	**20.6**	**23.7**	**24.6**	**43.7**
TOTAL CITIES: 8,781 cities;												
population 146,279,000:												
Total clearances	**2,089,593**	**2,100,069**	**571,747**	**1,517,846**	**10,245**	**30,761**	**111,669**	**419,072**	**231,182**	**1,136,662**	**150,002**	**10,476**
Percent under 18	**20.5**	**20.7**	**13.2**	**23.3**	**9.7**	**12.9**	**16.3**	**12.5**	**19.9**	**23.7**	**25.2**	**46.0**
GROUP I												
59 cities: 250,000 and over;												
population 36,908,000:												
Total clearances	669,769	673,138	244,081	425,688	5,482	11,872	58,159	168,568	69,503	294,397	61,788	3,369
Percent under 18	16.7	16.8	11.8	19.5	10.4	11.5	14.7	10.9	15.6	18.5	28.2	39.2
8 cities, 1,000,000 and over;												
population 13,861,000:												
Total clearances	262,026	263,107	109,248	152,778	2,403	3,034	24,648	79,163	23,479	105,406	23,893	1,081
Percent under 18	14.0	14.0	10.0	16.8	9.8	10.5	14.3	8.7	14.0	15.3	26.0	34.5
15 cities, 500,000 to 999,999;												
population 9,961,000:												
Total clearances	153,694	154,537	46,438	107,256	1,167	3,805	12,607	28,859	17,716	74,104	15,436	843
Percent under 18	16.8	17.0	13.3	18.3	8.3	13.1	14.4	13.1	13.5	17.6	27.3	40.0
36 cities, 250,000 to 499,999;												
population 13,086,000:												
Total clearances	254,049	255,494	88,395	165,654	1,912	5,033	20,904	60,546	28,308	114,887	22,459	1,445
Percent under 18	19.4	19.5	13.3	22.6	12.4	10.9	15.5	12.8	18.3	22.1	31.0	42.4
GROUP II												
127 cities, 100,000 to 249,999;												
population 18,439,000:												
Total clearances	312,699	314,597	90,771	221,928	1,568	5,068	18,495	65,640	36,773	162,157	22,998	1,898
Percent under 18	18.3	18.5	12.3	20.8	9.6	12.0	15.3	11.5	16.6	21.3	23.8	49.4
GROUP III												
341 cities, 50,000 to 99,999;												
population 23,462,000:												
Total clearances	318,793	320,212	77,133	241,660	1,158	4,409	14,294	57,272	36,447	186,348	18,865	1,419
Percent under 18	22.9	23.0	14.6	25.5	9.1	13.0	18.7	13.8	20.6	26.5	25.0	49.9

See footnotes at end of table.

Table 28. — Offenses Cleared by Arrest[1] of Persons Under 18 Years of Age, 1993 — Continued

Population group	Crime Index total	Modified Crime Index total[2]	Violent crime[3]	Property crime[4]	Murder and non-negligent man-slaughter	Forcible rape	Robbery	Aggra-vated assault	Burglary	Larceny-theft	Motor vehicle theft	Arson[2]
GROUP IV												
651 cities, 25,000 to 49,999; population 22,574,000:												
Total clearances	282,485	283,738	60,270	222,215	808	3,572	9,773	46,117	31,999	173,706	16,510	1,253
Percent under 18	23.7	23.8	15.5	25.9	8.4	14.6	19.0	14.9	22.0	26.9	22.7	48.4
GROUP V												
1,523 cities, 10,000 to 24,999; population 23,964,000:												
Total clearances	280,556	281,873	53,005	227,551	670	3,309	6,775	42,251	30,840	180,356	16,355	1,317
Percent under 18	23.5	23.6	15.2	25.4	7.8	15.3	20.3	14.5	24.2	26.1	21.0	46.8
GROUP VI												
6,080 cities under 10,000; population 20,933,000:												
Total clearances	225,291	226,511	46,487	178,804	559	2,531	4,173	39,224	25,620	139,698	13,486	1,220
Percent under 18	24.1	24.2	15.1	26.4	8.9	14.9	21.1	14.6	26.9	26.7	22.8	51.1
SUBURBAN COUNTIES												
1,216 agencies; population 47,174,000:												
Total clearances	378,002	380,630	113,003	264,999	1,866	8,176	13,438	89,523	61,992	172,731	30,276	2,628
Percent under 18	21.3	21.5	15.3	23.9	8.4	20.3	19.9	14.3	22.5	24.6	22.6	41.1
RURAL COUNTIES												
2,425 agencies; population 24,768,000:												
Total clearances	117,122	118,066	33,620	83,502	1,053	3,191	1,574	27,802	26,531	47,559	9,412	944
Percent under 18	17.8	17.9	10.2	20.8	7.3	15.5	13.3	9.6	22.2	20.0	21.5	25.3
SUBURBAN AREA[5]												
6,249 agencies; population 95,190,000:												
Total clearances	882,270	887,346	215,591	666,679	3,068	13,999	28,049	170,475	118,858	485,992	61,829	5,076
Percent under 18	22.3	22.5	15.8	24.4	8.0	18.5	20.5	15.0	22.9	25.1	21.8	46.0

[1]Includes offenses cleared by exceptional means.

[2]The number of agency reports used in arson clearance rates is less than those used in compiling clearance rates for other Crime Index offenses. It is not necessary to report clearances by detailed property classification to be included in this table. The Modified Crime Index total is the sum of the Crime Index offenses, including arson.

[3]Violent crimes are offenses of murder, forcible rape, robbery, and aggravated assault.

[4]Property crimes are offenses of burglary, larceny-theft, and motor vehicle theft. Data are not included for the property crime of arson.

[5]Includes suburban city and county law enforcement agencies within metropolitan areas. Excludes central cities. Suburban cities are also included in other groups.

Forcible rape figures furnished by the state-level Uniform Crime Reporting (UCR) Programs administered by Michigan State Police and the Minnesota Department of Public Safety were not in accordance with national UCR guidelines and were excluded from the forcible rape, violent crime, Crime Index total, and Modified Crime Index total categories.

Complete data for 1993 were not available for the states of Illinois and Kansas; therefore, it was necessary that their crime counts be estimated. See "Offense Estimation," page 376 for details.

SECTION IV

Persons Arrested

Primarily a gauge of law enforcement's response to crime, arrest counts also provide definitive data concerning the age, sex, and race of perpetrators. Arrest practices, policies, and enforcement emphases vary from place to place and even within a community from time to time as, for example, during a local police campaign against residential burglary. While the practices for certain unlawful conduct such as drunkenness, disorderly conduct, vagrancy, and related violations may differ among agencies, those for robbery, burglary, and other serious crime arrests are more likely to be uniform and consistent throughout all jurisdictions. The Program's procedures require that an arrest be counted on each separate occasion a person is taken into custody, notified, or cited. Annual arrest figures do not measure the number of individuals arrested since one person may be arrested several times during the year for the same or different offenses.

Nationwide, law enforcement agencies made an estimated 14 million arrests in 1993 for all criminal infractions except traffic violations. The highest arrest counts among the specific crime categories were for driving under the influence and larceny-theft, both 1.5 million; and simple assault and drug abuse violations, each 1.1 million. (See Table 29.)

When the overall arrest volume was related to the total United States population, the rate was 5,490 arrests per 100,000 inhabitants. Among the city population groupings, those with more than 250,000 inhabitants recorded the highest rate, 7,103, while those with populations from 25,000 to 49,999 recorded the lowest rate, 5,255. (See Table 31.) For suburban county agencies overall, the arrest rate was 4,010, and for rural county law enforcement, it was 3,989 per 100,000 inhabitants. Regionally, the arrest rates per 100,000 population ranged from 5,020 in the Northeast to 5,773 in the South. (See Table 30.)

Due to NIBRS conversion efforts, no arrest data for Kansas law enforcement agencies were available for 1993. Therefore, tables showing the age, sex, or race of persons arrested contain no Kansas data. Arrest totals were, however, estimated for inclusion in Table 29, "Total Estimated Arrests, United States, 1993."

Arrest Trends

The national total number of arrests for all offenses except traffic violations declined 1 percent in 1993 as compared to the 1992 volume. Overall Crime Index arrests fell 2 percent, and those for property crimes declined 3 percent. An increase of 1 percent was reported for violent crime arrests. During the same time period, adult arrests for all offenses declined 3 percent, while those of juveniles were up 5 percent. (See Table 36.) Violent crime arrests were down less than 1 percent for adults but up 6 percent for juveniles. (See Table 36.)

Two-year arrest trends for rural county agencies showed a 2-percent increase, 1993 over 1992, while a 2-percent decrease was recorded for city and suburban county agencies. (See Tables 44, 50, and 56.)

For the 5-year period, 1989 versus 1993, total arrests increased less than 1 percent and juvenile arrests were up 13 percent, while adult arrests declined 2 percent. (See Table 34.) Total Crime Index arrests declined 1 percent, and those of adults, 5 percent; but those of juveniles rose 7 percent. During the same years, 1989-1993, total violent crime arrests increased 13 percent, and property crime arrests fell 6 percent.

For the decade, 1984-1993, arrests for all offenses were up 18 percent; Crime Index arrests, 21 percent; violent crime arrests, 50 percent; and property crime arrests, 13 percent. (See Table 32.)

The 1993 drug abuse violation arrest total was up 4 percent from the 1992 level, 14 percent lower than in 1989, and 56 percent higher than in 1984. The following table shows the types of drugs involved in violations resulting in arrests during 1993 by geographic region.

Table 4.1 – Arrests for Drug Abuse Violations, 1993
[Percent distribution]

	United States total	North-eastern States	Mid-western States	South-ern States	West-ern States
Total[1]	100.0	100.0	100.0	100.0	100.0
Sale/manufacture:	29.7	40.8	29.4	26.5	24.7
Heroin or cocaine and their derivatives	19.2	33.1	10.2	18.0	13.3
Marijuana	6.2	6.0	8.2	5.9	5.9
Synthetic or manufactured drugs ...	.6	.6	.5	.7	.4
Other dangerous nonnarcotic drugs	3.7	1.1	10.4	1.9	5.1
Possession:	70.3	59.2	70.6	73.5	75.3
Heroin or cocaine and their derivatives	31.1	31.7	20.1	32.4	33.1
Marijuana	27.6	24.4	38.0	35.0	18.8
Synthetic or manufactured drugs ...	1.2	.9	1.0	1.8	.9
Other dangerous nonnarcotic drugs	10.4	2.2	11.5	4.3	22.4

[1]Because of rounding, percentages may not add to totals.

Age

Six percent of all persons arrested nationally in 1993 were under the age of 15; 17 percent were under 18; 30 percent were under 21; and 45 percent were under 25. Persons in the under-25 age group accounted for 46 percent of arrests in the cities, 40 percent of those in the suburban counties, and 39 percent of those in the rural counties.

Age distribution figures for persons arrested for Crime Index offenses showed 29 percent were under the age of 18; 43 percent, under 21; and 55 percent, under 25. The under-25 age group was also responsible for 47 percent of the violent crime arrests and 58 percent of property crime arrests in 1993.

Larceny-theft was the offense resulting in the most arrests of persons under age 18, while adults were most often arrested for driving under the influence. (See Table 38.)

Sex

Eighty-one percent of the persons arrested in the Nation during 1993 were males. (See Table 42.) They accounted for 77 percent of Index crime arrests, 87 percent of those for violent crimes, and 74 percent of the property crime arrests.

Men were most often arrested for driving under the influence, which accounted for 11 percent of all male arrests.

As in past years, larceny-theft was the crime for which females were most often arrested. This single offense accounted for 74 percent of arrests of women for Index crimes and 18 percent of all female arrests. Fifty-three percent of all female larceny-theft arrestees were under 25 years of age.

Two-year trends showed a 2-percent decline in total male arrests from 1992 to 1993, while female arrests were up 1 percent for the same period. (See Table 37.) Arrests of males were down 1 percent, and those of females, up 8 percent for the 5-year period from 1989 to 1993.

Race

Race distribution figures for the total number of arrests in the United States during 1993 showed 67 percent of the arrestees were white, 31 percent were black, and the remainder were of other races. (See Table 43.) Whites accounted for 61 percent of the Index crime arrests, 53 percent of the arrests for violent crimes, and 64 percent of those for property crimes.

Table 29. – Total Estimated Arrests[1], United States, 1993

Total[2]...............................	**14,036,300**	Embezzlement	12,900
Murder and nonnegligent manslaughter	23,400	Stolen property; buying, receiving, possessing	158,100
Forcible rape	38,420	Vandalism	313,000
Robbery	173,620	Weapons; carrying, possessing, etc.	262,300
Aggravated assault	518,670	Prostitution and commercialized vice	97,800
Burglary	402,700	Sex offenses (except forcible rape and prostitution)	104,100
Larceny-theft	1,476,300	Drug abuse violations	1,126,300
Motor vehicle theft	195,900	Gambling	17,300
Arson	19,400	Offenses against family and children	109,100
		Driving under the influence	1,524,800
Violent crime[3]	754,110	Liquor laws	518,500
Property crime[4]	2,094,300	Drunkenness	726,600
Crime Index total[5]	2,848,400	Disorderly conduct	727,000
		Vagrancy	28,200
		All other offenses	3,518,700
Other assaults	1,144,900	Suspicion (not included in totals)	14,100
Forgery and counterfeiting	106,900	Curfew and loitering law violations	100,200
Fraud	410,700	Runaways	180,500

[1]Arrest totals are based on all reporting agencies and estimates for unreported areas.
[2]Because of rounding, figures may not add to totals.
[3]Violent crimes are offenses of murder, forcible rape, robbery, and aggravated assault.
[4]Property crimes are offenses of burglary, larceny-theft, motor vehicle theft, and arson.
[5]Includes arson.

Table 30. — Arrests, Number and Rate, Regions, 1993

[Rate: Number of arrests per 100,000 inhabitants]

Offense charged	United States Total (10,512 agencies; population 214,099,000)	Northeast (2,257 agencies; population 42,417,000)	Midwest (2,469 agencies; population 41,875,000)	South (4,165 agencies; population 78,141,000)	West (1,621 agencies; population 51,666,000)
TOTAL	**11,753,628**	**2,129,481**	**2,183,251**	**4,510,817**	**2,930,079**
Rate	**5,489.8**	**5,020.4**	**5,213.7**	**5,772.7**	**5,671.2**
Murder and nonnegligent manslaughter	20,285	2,988	4,068	8,847	4,382
Rate	9.5	7.0	9.7	11.3	8.5
Forcible rape	32,523	5,867	7,013	12,747	6,896
Rate	15.2	13.8	16.7	16.3	13.3
Robbery	153,533	49,140	18,766	48,511	37,116
Rate	71.7	115.9	44.8	62.1	71.8
Aggravated assault	442,075	80,951	55,018	166,451	139,655
Rate	206.5	190.8	131.4	213.0	270.3
Burglary	338,238	53,549	46,218	131,843	106,628
Rate	158.0	126.2	110.4	168.7	206.4
Larceny-theft	1,251,277	197,828	241,909	467,406	344,134
Rate	584.4	466.4	577.7	598.2	666.1
Motor vehicle theft	168,795	27,865	23,884	56,048	60,998
Rate	78.8	65.7	57.0	71.7	118.1
Arson	16,113	2,872	3,332	5,518	4,391
Rate	7.5	6.8	8.0	7.1	8.5
Violent crime[1]	648,416	138,946	84,865	236,556	188,049
Rate	302.9	327.6	202.7	302.7	364.0
Property crime[2]	1,774,423	282,114	315,343	660,815	516,151
Rate	828.8	665.1	753.1	845.7	999.0
Crime Index total[3]	2,422,839	421,060	400,208	897,371	704,200
Rate	1,131.6	992.7	955.7	1,148.4	1,363.0
Other assaults	965,318	163,683	191,855	390,661	219,119
Rate	450.9	385.9	458.2	499.9	424.1
Forgery and counterfeiting	89,487	11,510	12,647	42,207	23,123
Rate	41.8	27.1	30.2	54.0	44.8
Fraud	335,580	72,966	53,188	187,244	22,182
Rate	156.7	172.0	127.0	239.6	42.9
Embezzlement	10,916	693	1,496	6,203	2,524
Rate	5.1	1.6	3.6	7.9	4.9
Stolen property; buying, receiving, possessing	134,864	32,927	24,950	37,759	39,228
Rate	63.0	77.6	59.6	48.3	75.9
Vandalism	261,282	59,837	59,469	67,491	74,485
Rate	122.0	141.1	142.0	86.4	144.2
Weapons; carrying, possessing, etc.	224,395	33,121	41,275	88,888	61,111
Rate	104.8	78.1	98.6	113.8	118.3
Prostitution and commercialized vice	88,850	21,413	14,908	24,918	27,611
Rate	41.5	50.5	35.6	31.9	53.4
Sex offenses (except forcible rape and prostitution)	87,712	13,842	16,429	29,175	28,266
Rate	41.0	32.6	39.2	37.3	54.7
Drug abuse violations	968,606	222,804	108,765	329,729	307,308
Rate	452.4	525.3	259.7	422.0	594.8
Gambling	15,336	5,370	2,026	5,946	1,994
Rate	7.2	12.7	4.8	7.6	3.9
Offenses against family and children	89,157	26,025	22,234	30,906	9,992
Rate	41.6	61.4	53.1	39.6	19.3
Driving under the influence	1,229,971	125,916	238,281	470,925	394,849
Rate	574.5	296.9	569.0	602.7	764.2
Liquor laws	419,082	48,891	138,973	121,920	109,298
Rate	195.7	115.3	331.9	156.0	211.5
Drunkenness	604,979	29,066	46,975	392,644	136,294
Rate	282.6	68.5	112.2	502.5	263.8
Disorderly conduct	607,472	184,337	156,423	190,081	76,631
Rate	283.7	434.6	373.5	243.3	148.3
Vagrancy	24,806	10,795	2,228	3,637	8,146
Rate	11.6	25.4	5.3	4.7	15.8
All other offenses (except traffic)	2,935,490	616,947	586,141	1,119,648	612,754
Rate	1,371.1	1,454.5	1,399.7	1,432.9	1,186.0
Suspicion (not included in totals)	12,136	1,395	2,474	8,016	251
Rate	5.7	3.3	5.9	10.3	.5
Curfew and loitering law violations	85,354	8,604	26,693	15,384	34,673
Rate	39.9	20.3	63.7	19.7	67.1
Runaways	152,132	19,674	38,087	58,080	36,291
Rate	71.1	46.4	91.0	74.3	70.2

[1]Violent crimes are offenses of murder, forcible rape, robbery, and aggravated assault.

[2]Property crimes are offenses of burglary, larceny-theft, motor vehicle theft, and arson.

[3]Includes arson. Population figures were rounded to the nearest thousand. All rates were calculated before rounding.

Table 31.—Arrest, Number and Rate, Population Group, 1993
[Rate: Number of arrests per 100,000 inhabitants]

Offense charged	Total (10,512 agencies; population 214,099,000)	Cities — Total cities (7,446 cities; population 145,549,000)	Group I (62 cities, 250,000 and over; population 42,742,000)	Group II (129 cities, 100,000 to 249,999; population 19,156,000)	Group III (327 cities, 50,000 to 99,999; population 22,502,000)	Group IV (603 cities, 25,000 to 49,999; population 20,982,000)	Group V (1,408 cities, 10,000 to 24,999; population 22,238,000)	Group VI (4,917 cities under 10,000; population 17,929,000)	Counties — Suburban counties[1] (1,007 agencies; population 46,243,000)	Rural counties (2,059 agencies; population 22,306,000)	Suburban area[2] (5,327 agencies; population 92,137,000)
TOTAL.	11,753,628	9,009,580	3,036,057	1,219,236	1,200,152	1,102,678	1,202,136	1,249,321	1,854,231	889,817	4,271,595
Rate.	5,489.8	6,190.0	7,103.2	6,364.7	5,333.6	5,255.4	5,405.7	6,968.2	4,009.8	3,989.1	4,636.1
Murder and nonnegligent manslaughter	20,285	15,756	9,478	2,146	1,580	1,030	876	646	3,083	1,446	4,789
Rate.	9.5	10.8	22.2	11.2	7.0	4.9	3.9	3.6	6.7	6.5	5.2
Forcible rape.	32,523	24,125	9,926	3,815	3,194	2,613	2,546	2,031	5,349	3,049	10,195
Rate.	15.2	16.6	23.2	19.9	14.2	12.5	11.4	11.3	11.6	13.7	11.1
Robbery.	153,533	136,203	78,764	19,025	15,619	10,190	7,646	4,959	14,812	2,518	32,738
Rate.	71.7	93.6	184.3	99.3	69.4	48.6	34.4	27.7	32.0	11.3	35.5
Aggravated assault.	442,075	340,401	135,444	56,390	49,221	37,800	32,639	28,907	72,186	29,488	143,087
Rate.	206.5	233.9	316.9	294.4	218.7	180.2	146.8	161.2	156.1	132.2	155.3
Burglary.	338,238	249,485	79,019	40,585	41,186	31,666	30,644	26,385	58,430	30,323	119,869
Rate.	158.0	171.4	184.9	211.9	183.0	150.9	137.8	147.2	126.4	135.9	130.1
Larceny-theft.	1,251,277	1,053,135	292,894	157,600	173,151	154,493	158,820	116,177	151,903	46,239	442,000
Rate.	584.4	723.6	685.3	822.7	769.5	736.3	714.2	648.0	328.5	207.3	479.7
Motor vehicle theft.	168,795	134,296	65,537	18,917	17,627	11,807	10,608	9,800	26,567	7,932	50,037
Rate.	78.8	92.3	153.3	98.8	78.3	56.3	47.7	54.7	57.5	35.6	54.3
Arson.	16,113	11,944	3,582	1,713	1,745	1,571	1,724	1,609	2,801	1,368	6,145
Rate.	7.5	8.2	8.4	8.9	7.8	7.5	7.8	9.0	6.1	6.1	6.7
Violent crime[3]	648,416	516,485	233,612	81,376	69,614	51,633	43,707	36,543	95,430	36,501	190,809
Rate.	302.9	354.9	546.6	424.8	309.4	246.1	196.5	203.8	206.4	163.6	207.1
Property crime[4]	1,774,423	1,448,860	441,032	218,815	233,709	199,537	201,796	153,971	239,701	85,862	618,051
Rate.	828.8	995.4	1,031.8	1,142.3	1,038.6	951.0	907.4	858.8	518.4	384.9	670.8
Crime Index total[5]	2,422,839	1,965,345	674,644	300,191	303,323	251,170	245,503	190,514	335,131	122,363	808,860
Rate.	1,131.6	1,350.3	1,578.4	1,567.1	1,348.0	1,197.1	1,104.0	1,062.6	724.7	548.6	877.9

See footnotes at end of table.

Table 31.—Arrest, Number and Rate, Population Group, 1993—Continued

Offense charged	Total (10,512 agencies; population 214,099,000)	Total cities; (7,446 cities; population 145,549,000)	Cities — Group I (62 cities, 250,000 and over; population 42,742,000)	Group II (129 cities, 100,000 to 249,999; population 19,156,000)	Group III (327 cities, 50,000 to 99,999; population 22,502,000)	Group IV (603 cities, 25,000 to 49,999; population 20,982,000)	Group V (1,408 cities, 10,000 to 24,999; population 22,238,000)	Group VI (4,917 cities under 10,000; population 17,929,000)	Counties — Suburban counties[1] (1,007 agencies; population 46,243,000)	Rural counties (2,059 agencies; population 22,306,000)	Suburban area[2] (5,327 agencies; population 92,137,000)
Other assaults	965,318	755,369	249,552	123,160	101,896	92,254	101,203	87,304	141,996	67,953	326,804
Rate	450.9	519.0	583.9	642.9	452.8	439.7	455.1	486.9	307.1	304.6	354.7
Forgery and counterfeiting	89,487	67,120	19,500	10,578	9,899	8,932	9,903	8,308	15,092	7,275	32,209
Rate	41.8	46.1	45.6	55.2	44.0	42.6	44.5	46.3	32.6	32.6	35.0
Fraud	335,580	205,752	57,868	26,220	22,821	30,090	33,242	35,511	84,273	45,555	149,173
Rate	156.7	141.4	135.4	136.9	101.4	143.4	149.5	198.1	182.2	204.2	161.9
Embezzlement	10,916	7,874	1,859	2,120	1,349	1,003	854	689	2,171	871	3,838
Rate	5.1	5.4	4.3	11.1	6.0	4.8	3.8	3.8	4.7	3.9	4.2
Stolen property; buying, receiving, possessing	134,864	108,162	37,449	17,413	16,569	14,386	13,061	9,284	20,324	6,378	48,910
Rate	63.0	74.3	87.6	90.9	73.6	68.6	58.7	51.8	44.0	28.6	53.1
Vandalism	261,282	209,805	58,350	28,361	30,885	28,686	32,521	31,002	33,121	18,356	96,612
Rate	122.0	144.1	136.5	148.1	137.3	136.7	146.2	172.9	71.6	82.3	104.9
Weapons; carrying, possessing, etc.	224,395	182,359	77,513	26,961	23,566	18,891	18,361	17,067	30,841	11,195	70,122
Rate	104.8	125.3	181.4	140.7	104.7	90.0	82.6	95.2	66.7	50.2	76.1
Prostitution and commercialized vice	88,850	83,996	59,634	12,842	6,563	3,452	1,189	316	4,692	162	9,307
Rate	41.5	57.7	139.5	67.0	29.2	16.5	5.3	1.8	10.1	.7	10.1
Sex offenses (except forcible rape and prostitution)	87,712	63,604	25,200	9,046	8,948	7,242	6,977	6,191	15,979	8,129	30,006
Rate	41.0	43.7	59.0	47.2	39.8	34.5	31.4	34.5	34.6	36.4	32.6
Drug abuse violations	968,606	762,947	352,730	123,183	99,119	74,410	60,836	52,669	148,327	57,332	291,059
Rate	452.4	524.2	825.3	643.0	440.5	354.6	273.6	293.8	320.8	257.0	315.9
Gambling	15,336	13,238	9,290	1,189	816	955	597	391	1,589	509	2,962
Rate	7.2	9.1	21.7	6.2	3.6	4.6	2.7	2.2	3.4	2.3	3.2
Offenses against family and children	89,157	49,607	11,075	6,236	6,423	8,656	9,864	7,353	28,473	11,077	45,074
Rate	41.6	34.1	25.9	32.6	28.5	41.3	44.4	41.0	61.6	49.7	48.9
Driving under the influence	1,229,971	753,463	169,014	81,279	97,196	110,998	137,006	157,970	278,799	197,709	549,668
Rate	574.5	517.7	395.4	424.3	431.9	529.0	616.1	881.1	602.9	886.3	596.6
Liquor laws	419,082	333,528	68,161	31,537	38,203	42,110	66,672	86,845	46,189	39,365	153,318
Rate	195.7	229.2	159.5	164.6	169.8	200.7	299.8	484.4	99.9	176.5	166.4
Drunkenness	604,979	507,479	130,043	68,398	79,873	68,849	76,276	84,040	56,860	40,640	191,630
Rate	282.6	348.7	304.2	357.1	355.0	328.1	343.0	468.7	123.0	182.2	208.0
Disorderly conduct	607,472	530,697	162,661	57,381	71,538	65,932	83,073	90,112	46,386	30,389	203,870
Rate	283.7	364.6	380.6	299.5	317.9	314.2	373.6	502.6	100.3	136.2	221.3
Vagrancy	24,806	22,598	14,271	2,318	1,922	1,270	1,370	1,447	1,721	487	4,596
Rate	11.6	15.5	33.4	12.1	8.5	6.1	6.2	8.1	3.7	2.2	5.0
All other offenses (except traffic)	2,935,490	2,185,498	796,739	262,830	248,097	245,751	272,739	359,342	537,258	212,734	1,173,409
Rate	1,371.1	1,501.6	1,864.1	1,372.0	1,102.6	1,171.3	1,226.4	2,004.3	1,161.8	953.7	1,273.5
Suspicion (not included in totals)	12,136	10,021	6,163	328	525	877	760	1,368	1,859	256	3,783
Rate	5.7	6.9	14.4	1.7	2.3	4.2	3.4	7.6	4.0	1.1	4.1
Curfew and loitering law violations	85,354	81,125	29,969	7,946	9,212	10,395	13,364	10,239	2,540	1,689	26,045
Rate	39.9	55.7	70.1	41.5	40.9	49.5	60.1	57.1	5.5	7.6	28.3
Runaways	152,132	120,014	30,535	20,047	21,934	17,246	17,525	12,727	22,469	9,649	54,123
Rate	71.1	82.5	71.4	104.6	97.5	82.2	78.8	71.0	48.6	43.3	58.7

[1]Includes only suburban county law enforcement agencies.
[2]Includes suburban city and county law enforcement agencies within metropolitan areas. Excludes central cities. Suburban cities and counties are also included in other groups.
[3]Violent crimes are offenses of murder, forcible rape, robbery, and aggravated assault.
[4]Property crimes are offenses of burglary, larceny-theft, motor vehicle theft, and arson.
[5]Includes arson. Population figures were rounded to the nearest thousand. All rates were calculated before rounding.

Table 32. — Total Arrest Trends, 1984-1993

[7,978 agencies; 1993 estimated population 190,781,000; 1984 estimated population 174,077,000]

Offense charged	Number of persons arrested								
	Total all ages			Under 18 years of age			18 years of age and over		
	1984	1993	Percent change	1984	1993	Percent change	1984	1993	Percent change
TOTAL..............................	8,828,447	10,448,491	+ 18.4	1,466,212	1,791,083	+ 22.2	7,362,235	8,657,408	+ 17.6
Murder and nonnegligent manslaughter	15,126	18,856	+ 24.7	1,154	3,092	+ 167.9	13,972	15,764	+ 12.8
Forcible rape	28,565	29,432	+ 3.0	4,357	4,750	+ 9.0	24,208	24,682	+ 2.0
Robbery...................................	115,522	143,877	+ 24.5	29,018	40,499	+ 39.6	86,504	103,378	+ 19.5
Aggravated assault...........................	241,664	408,148	+ 68.9	31,315	62,039	+ 98.1	210,349	346,109	+ 64.5
Burglary...................................	338,737	308,849	-8.8	125,718	104,901	-16.6	213,019	203,948	-4.3
Larceny-theft	981,812	1,131,768	+ 15.3	320,960	352,866	+ 9.9	660,852	778,902	+ 17.9
Motor vehicle theft	96,975	156,711	+ 61.6	33,771	69,465	+ 105.7	63,204	87,246	+ 38.0
Arson.....................................	14,288	14,504	+ 1.5	5,978	7,183	+ 20.2	8,310	7,321	-11.9
Violent crime[1]	400,877	600,313	+ 49.7	65,844	110,380	+ 67.6	335,033	489,933	+ 46.2
Property crime[2]	1,431,812	1,611,832	+ 12.6	486,427	534,415	+ 9.9	945,385	1,077,417	+ 14.0
Crime Index total[3]........................	1,832,689	2,212,145	+ 20.7	552,271	644,795	+ 16.8	1,280,418	1,567,350	+ 22.4
Other assaults................................	423,258	870,146	+ 105.6	65,444	138,713	+ 112.0	357,814	731,433	+ 104.4
Forgery and counterfeiting	65,486	80,989	+ 23.7	6,300	5,858	-7.0	59,186	75,131	+ 26.9
Fraud.....................................	230,346	296,737	+ 28.8	17,356	13,301	-23.4	212,990	283,436	+ 33.1
Embezzlement	7,315	10,092	+ 38.0	477	586	+ 22.9	6,838	9,506	+ 39.0
Stolen property; buying, receiving, possessing	96,632	122,256	+ 26.5	22,783	32,485	+ 42.6	73,849	89,771	+ 21.6
Vandalism..................................	182,347	235,170	+ 29.0	80,885	105,866	+ 30.9	101,462	129,304	+ 27.4
Weapons; carrying, possessing, etc...............	139,928	204,433	+ 46.1	21,000	47,369	+ 125.6	118,928	157,064	+ 32.1
Prostitution and commercialized vice	96,262	83,346	-13.4	2,524	923	-63.4	93,738	82,423	-12.1
Sex offenses (except forcible rape and prostitution)	77,653	80,332	+ 3.4	13,104	15,038	+ 14.8	64,549	65,294	+ 1.2
Drug abuse violations	568,032	884,771	+ 55.8	66,425	84,902	+ 27.8	501,607	799,869	+ 59.5
Gambling..................................	29,532	14,121	-52.2	744	1,020	+ 37.1	28,788	13,101	-54.5
Offenses against family and children..............	37,842	71,119	+ 87.9	1,439	3,034	+ 110.8	36,403	68,085	+ 87.0
Driving under the influence.....................	1,362,499	1,059,517	-22.2	18,635	9,289	-50.2	1,343,864	1,050,228	-21.9
Liquor laws.................................	354,861	357,116	+ .6	90,650	77,866	-14.1	264,211	279,250	+ 5.7
Drunkenness	839,256	558,833	-33.4	22,050	12,588	-42.9	817,206	546,245	-33.2
Disorderly conduct...........................	480,469	542,837	+ 13.0	67,814	106,779	+ 57.5	412,655	436,058	+ 5.7
Vagrancy...................................	28,519	23,000	-19.4	1,914	2,969	+ 55.1	26,605	20,031	-24.7
All other offenses (except traffic)................	1,806,754	2,531,244	+ 40.1	245,630	277,415	+ 12.9	1,561,124	2,253,829	+ 44.4
Suspicion (not included in totals)................	15,230	7,412	-51.3	2,448	1,093	-55.4	12,782	6,319	-50.6
Curfew and loitering law violations	62,487	73,502	+ 17.6	62,487	73,502	+ 17.6	....	....	....
Runaways	106,280	136,785	+ 28.7	106,280	136,785	+ 28.7	....	....	....

[1]Violent crimes are offenses of murder, forcible rape, robbery, and aggravated assault.
[2]Property crimes are offenses of burglary, larceny-theft, motor vehicle theft, and arson.
[3]Includes arson.

Table 33. — Total Arrest Trends, Sex, 1984-1993

[7,978 agencies; 1993 estimated population 190,781,000; 1984 estimated population 174,077,000]

Offense charged	Males Total 1984	Males Total 1993	Males Total Percent change	Males Under 18 1984	Males Under 18 1993	Males Under 18 Percent change	Females Total 1984	Females Total 1993	Females Total Percent change	Females Under 18 1984	Females Under 18 1993	Females Under 18 Percent change
TOTAL....................	7,342,459	8,413,026	+14.6	1,144,694	1,364,103	+19.2	1,485,988	2,035,465	+37.0	321,518	426,980	+32.8
Murder and nonnegligent manslaughter	13,154	17,096	+30.0	1,054	2,914	+176.5	1,972	1,760	-10.8	100	178	+78.0
Forcible rape....................	28,315	29,052	+2.6	4,301	4,669	+8.6	250	380	+52.0	56	81	+44.6
Robbery........................	107,259	131,381	+22.5	27,144	36,949	+36.1	8,263	12,496	+51.2	1,874	3,550	+89.4
Aggravated assault.............	208,618	343,758	+64.8	26,059	51,060	+95.9	33,046	64,390	+94.8	5,256	10,979	+108.9
Burglary.......................	313,340	277,871	-11.3	116,529	94,734	-18.7	25,397	30,978	+22.0	9,189	10,167	+10.6
Larceny-theft	686,332	762,014	+11.0	234,599	242,028	+3.2	295,480	369,754	+25.1	86,361	110,838	+28.3
Motor vehicle theft............	88,216	138,400	+56.9	30,050	60,098	+100.0	8,759	18,311	+109.1	3,721	9,367	+151.7
Arson.........................	12,521	12,353	-1.3	5,444	6,299	+15.7	1,767	2,151	+21.7	534	884	+65.5
Violent crime[1]................	357,346	521,287	+45.9	58,558	95,592	+63.2	43,531	79,026	+81.5	7,286	14,788	+103.0
Property crime[2]	1,100,409	1,190,638	+8.2	386,622	403,159	+4.3	331,403	421,194	+27.1	99,805	131,256	+31.5
Crime Index total[3]	1,457,755	1,711,925	+17.4	445,180	498,751	+12.0	374,934	500,220	+33.4	107,091	146,044	+36.4
Other assaults..................	359,385	714,891	+98.9	50,321	102,675	+104.0	63,873	155,255	+143.1	15,123	36,038	+138.3
Forgery and counterfeiting.......	43,631	52,905	+21.3	4,296	3,804	-11.5	21,855	28,084	+28.5	2,004	2,054	+2.5
Fraud.........................	134,806	175,909	+30.5	13,395	9,675	-27.8	95,540	120,828	+26.5	3,961	3,626	-8.5
Embezzlement	4,665	5,990	+28.4	316	347	+9.8	2,650	4,102	+54.8	161	239	+48.4
Stolen property; buying, receiving, possessing	85,469	106,598	+24.7	20,542	28,948	+40.9	11,163	15,658	+40.3	2,241	3,537	+57.8
Vandalism.....................	164,005	206,389	+25.8	73,898	95,663	+29.5	18,342	28,781	+56.9	6,987	10,203	+46.0
Weapons; carrying, possessing, etc.	129,438	189,010	+46.0	19,653	43,601	+121.9	10,490	15,423	+47.0	1,347	3,768	+179.7
Prostitution and commercialized vice	29,572	29,462	-.4	770	405	-47.4	66,690	53,884	-19.2	1,754	518	-70.5
Sex offenses (except forcible rape and prostitution).........	72,138	73,296	+1.6	12,246	13,737	+12.2	5,515	7,036	+27.6	858	1,301	+51.6
Drug abuse violations	488,987	740,595	+51.5	56,364	75,535	+34.0	79,045	144,176	+82.4	10,061	9,367	-6.9
Gambling......................	25,562	12,130	-52.5	680	972	+42.9	3,970	1,991	-49.8	64	48	-25.0
Offenses against family and children	33,372	57,705	+72.9	948	1,974	+108.2	4,470	13,414	+200.1	491	1,060	+115.9
Driving under the influence.......	1,203,973	911,265	-24.3	16,054	7,936	-50.6	158,526	148,252	-6.5	2,581	1,353	-47.6
Liquor laws	297,528	288,899	-2.9	67,348	55,776	-17.2	57,333	68,217	+19.0	23,302	22,090	-5.2
Drunkenness...................	766,830	497,229	-35.2	18,521	10,567	-42.9	72,426	61,604	-14.9	3,529	2,021	-42.7
Disorderly conduct..............	397,301	430,485	+8.4	55,107	82,168	+49.1	83,168	112,352	+35.1	12,707	24,611	+93.7
Vagrancy......................	25,614	20,488	-20.0	1,556	2,499	+60.6	2,905	2,512	-13.5	358	470	+31.3
All other offenses (except traffic)..	1,529,772	2,076,503	+35.7	194,843	217,718	+11.7	276,982	454,741	+64.2	50,787	59,697	+17.5
Suspicion (not included in totals)..	13,213	6,265	-52.6	1,943	909	-53.2	2,017	1,147	-43.1	505	184	-63.6
Curfew and loitering law violations	47,921	52,821	+10.2	47,921	52,821	+10.2	14,566	20,681	+42.0	14,566	20,681	+42.0
Runaways......................	44,735	58,531	+30.8	44,735	58,531	+30.8	61,545	78,254	+27.1	61,545	78,254	+27.1

[1]Violent crimes are offenses of murder, forcible rape, robbery, and aggravated assault.

[2]Property crimes are offenses of burglary, larceny-theft, motor vehicle theft, and arson.

[3]Includes arson.

222

Table 34. — Total Arrest Trends, 1989-1993

[8,383 agencies; 1993 estimated population 181,355,000; 1989 estimated population 175,072,000]

Offense charged	Number of persons arrested								
	Total all ages			Under 18 years of age			18 years of age and over		
	1989	1993	Percent change	1989	1993	Percent change	1989	1993	Percent change
TOTAL.....................................	9,991,357	10,017,787	+.3	1,532,987	1,738,465	+13.4	8,458,370	8,279,322	-2.1
Murder and nonnegligent manslaughter	16,146	17,886	+10.8	2,039	2,950	+44.7	14,107	14,936	+5.9
Forcible rape	27,461	27,837	+1.4	4,125	4,515	+9.5	23,336	23,322	-.1
Robbery......................................	123,317	134,506	+9.1	27,789	38,153	+37.3	95,528	96,353	+.9
Aggravated assault.............................	320,749	369,807	+15.3	41,736	57,287	+37.3	279,013	312,520	+12.0
Burglary......................................	320,470	283,111	-11.7	100,448	96,059	-4.4	220,022	187,052	-15.0
Larceny-theft	1,102,112	1,064,882	-3.4	317,042	334,052	+5.4	785,070	730,830	-6.9
Motor vehicle theft	165,317	145,475	-12.0	67,808	64,586	-4.8	97,509	80,889	-17.0
Arson.......................................	13,048	14,092	+8.0	5,676	7,029	+23.8	7,372	7,063	-4.2
Violent crime[1]	487,673	550,036	+12.8	75,689	102,905	+36.0	411,984	447,131	+8.5
Property crime[2]	1,600,947	1,507,560	-5.8	490,974	501,726	+2.2	1,109,973	1,005,834	-9.4
Crime Index total[3].......................	2,088,620	2,057,596	-1.5	566,663	604,631	+6.7	1,521,957	1,452,965	-4.5
Other assaults................................	667,907	834,771	+25.0	95,337	136,970	+43.7	572,570	697,801	+21.9
Forgery and counterfeiting	70,875	75,790	+6.9	5,459	5,670	+3.9	65,416	70,120	+7.2
Fraud..	258,769	285,592	+10.4	8,789	12,849	+46.2	249,980	272,743	+9.1
Embezzlement................................	11,577	9,115	-21.3	850	533	-37.3	10,727	8,582	-20.0
Stolen property; buying, receiving, possessing......	129,491	118,727	-8.3	32,564	32,281	-.9	96,927	86,446	-10.8
Vandalism....................................	213,158	231,734	+8.7	85,444	105,939	+24.0	127,714	125,795	-1.5
Weapons; carrying, possessing, etc...............	159,263	199,004	+25.0	28,148	46,883	+66.6	131,115	152,121	+16.0
Prostitution and commercialized vice	81,164	78,246	-3.6	1,133	847	-25.2	80,031	77,399	-3.3
Sex offenses (except forcible rape and prostitution)	73,739	76,616	+3.9	11,948	14,629	+22.4	61,791	61,987	+.3
Drug abuse violations	974,620	840,393	-13.8	80,089	81,742	+2.1	894,531	758,651	-15.2
Gambling....................................	13,972	13,383	-4.2	619	1,045	+68.8	13,353	12,338	-7.6
Offenses against family and children..............	48,965	75,064	+53.3	1,870	3,185	+70.3	47,095	71,879	+52.6
Driving under the influence.....................	1,182,471	1,031,660	-12.8	13,428	9,016	-32.9	1,169,043	1,022,644	-12.5
Liquor laws...................................	434,383	350,483	-19.3	100,319	80,331	-19.9	334,064	270,152	-19.1
Drunkenness	619,300	561,498	-9.3	16,373	12,714	-22.3	602,927	548,784	-9.0
Disorderly conduct............................	533,495	524,695	-1.6	83,507	105,509	+26.3	449,988	419,186	-6.8
Vagrancy.....................................	27,737	23,319	-15.9	2,153	3,014	+40.0	25,584	20,305	-20.6
All other offenses (except traffic)................	2,225,845	2,418,740	+8.7	222,288	269,316	+21.2	2,003,557	2,149,424	+7.3
Suspicion (not included in totals)................	13,351	8,685	-34.9	2,305	1,164	-49.5	11,046	7,521	-31.9
Curfew and loitering law violations	58,488	78,056	+33.5	58,488	78,056	+33.5	....	....	....
Runaways	117,518	133,305	+13.4	117,518	133,305	+13.4	....	....	....

[1]Violent crimes are offenses of murder, forcible rape, robbery, and aggravated assault.
[2]Property crimes are offenses of burglary, larceny-theft, motor vehicle theft, and arson.
[3]Includes arson.

Table 35. — Total Arrest Trends, Sex, 1989-1993

[8,383 agencies; 1993 estimated population 181,355,000; 1989 estimated population 175,072,000]

Offense charged	Males						Females					
	Total			Under 18			Total			Under 18		
	1989	1993	Percent change	1989	1993	Percent change	1989	1993	Percent change	1989	1993	Percent change
TOTAL	8,173,575	8,060,456	-1.4	1,194,083	1,323,462	+10.8	1,817,782	1,957,331	+7.7	338,904	415,003	+22.5
Murder and nonnegligent manslaughter....	14,222	16,208	+14.0	1,911	2,777	+45.3	1,924	1,678	-12.8	128	173	+35.2
Forcible rape.........................	27,150	27,457	+1.1	4,035	4,434	+9.9	311	380	+22.2	90	81	-10.0
Robbery	112,654	122,684	+8.9	25,402	34,737	+36.7	10,663	11,822	+10.9	2,387	3,416	+43.1
Aggravated assault	277,550	312,521	+12.6	35,539	47,280	+33.0	43,199	57,286	+32.6	6,197	10,007	+61.5
Burglary............................	291,515	254,080	-12.8	92,248	86,587	-6.1	28,955	29,031	+.3	8,200	9,472	+15.5
Larceny-theft........................	763,135	715,226	-6.3	231,198	229,862	-.6	338,977	349,656	+3.2	85,844	104,190	+21.4
Motor vehicle theft	148,691	128,452	-13.6	60,979	55,831	-8.4	16,626	17,023	+2.4	6,829	8,755	+28.2
Arson	11,248	12,018	+6.8	5,110	6,162	+20.6	1,800	2,074	+15.2	566	867	+53.2
Violent crime[1]	431,576	478,870	+11.0	66,887	89,228	+33.4	56,097	71,166	+26.9	8,802	13,677	+55.4
Property crime[2]....................	1,214,589	1,109,776	-8.6	389,535	378,442	-2.8	386,358	397,784	+3.0	101,439	123,284	+21.5
Crime Index total[3]	1,646,165	1,588,646	-3.5	456,422	467,670	+2.5	442,455	468,950	+6.0	110,241	136,961	+24.2
Other assaults	562,585	685,350	+21.8	73,615	101,398	+37.7	105,322	149,421	+41.9	21,722	35,572	+63.8
Forgery and counterfeiting	46,792	48,890	+4.5	3,715	3,684	-.8	24,083	26,900	+11.7	1,744	1,986	+13.9
Fraud.............................	140,259	169,377	+20.8	6,225	9,426	+51.4	118,510	116,215	-1.9	2,564	3,423	+33.5
Embezzlement	6,995	5,352	-23.5	509	317	-37.7	4,582	3,763	-17.9	341	216	-36.7
Stolen property; buying, receiving, possessing..........................	114,312	103,496	-9.5	29,631	28,703	-3.1	15,179	15,231	+.3	2,933	3,578	+22.0
Vandalism	189,673	203,639	+7.4	77,853	95,836	+23.1	23,485	28,095	+19.6	7,591	10,103	+33.1
Weapons; carrying, possessing, etc	146,964	183,759	+25.0	26,288	43,173	+64.2	12,299	15,245	+24.0	1,860	3,710	+99.5
Prostitution and commercialized vice	24,884	27,168	+9.2	429	376	-12.4	56,280	51,078	-9.2	704	471	-33.1
Sex offenses (except forcible rape and prostitution)........................	67,930	69,806	+2.8	11,083	13,321	+20.2	5,809	6,810	+17.2	865	1,308	+51.2
Drug abuse violations..................	813,706	703,082	-13.6	70,721	72,562	+2.6	160,914	137,311	-14.7	9,368	9,180	-2.0
Gambling...........................	11,824	11,493	-2.8	587	998	+70.0	2,148	1,890	-12.0	32	47	+46.9
Offenses against family and children	40,434	60,233	+49.0	1,190	2,085	+75.2	8,531	14,831	+73.8	680	1,100	+61.8
Driving under the influence	1,038,129	887,094	-14.5	11,558	7,718	-33.2	144,342	144,566	+.2	1,870	1,298	-30.6
Liquor laws..........................	351,765	281,477	-20.0	72,204	57,390	-20.5	82,618	69,006	-16.5	28,115	22,941	-18.4
Drunkenness.........................	559,247	499,643	-10.7	13,658	10,667	-21.9	60,053	61,855	+3.0	2,715	2,047	-24.6
Disorderly conduct	428,484	414,093	-3.4	66,224	81,196	+22.6	105,011	110,602	+5.3	17,283	24,313	+40.7
Vagrancy...........................	24,152	20,536	-15.0	1,834	2,508	+36.8	3,585	2,783	-22.4	319	506	+58.6
All other offenses (except traffic)	1,864,034	1,984,316	+6.5	175,096	211,428	+20.7	361,811	434,424	+20.1	47,192	57,888	+22.7
Suspicion (not included in totals)	11,229	7,367	-34.4	1,838	954	-48.1	2,122	1,318	-37.9	467	210	-55.0
Curfew and loitering law violations	43,627	56,124	+28.6	43,627	56,124	+28.6	14,861	21,932	+47.6	14,861	21,932	+47.6
Runaways...........................	51,614	56,882	+10.2	51,614	56,882	+10.2	65,904	76,423	+16.0	65,904	76,423	+16.0

[1]Violent crimes are offenses of murder, forcible rape, robbery, and aggravated assault.

[2]Property crimes are offenses of burglary, larceny-theft, motor vehicle theft, and arson.

[3]Includes arson.

Table 36. — Total Arrest Trends, 1992-1993
[9,337 agencies; 1993 estimated population 200,200,000; 1992 estimated population 198,147,000]

Offense charged	Number of persons arrested											
	Total all ages			Under 15 years of age			Under 18 years of age			18 years of age and over		
	1992	1993	Percent change	1992	1993	Percent change	1992	1993	Percent change	1992	1993	Percent change
TOTAL....................	11,203,780	11,046,849	-1.4	644,961	662,983	+2.8	1,820,335	1,904,763	+4.6	9,383,445	9,142,086	-2.6
Murder and nonnegligent manslaughter	18,755	19,416	+3.5	297	369	+24.2	2,770	3,150	+13.7	15,985	16,266	+1.8
Forcible rape...................	31,507	30,742	-2.4	1,903	1,962	+3.1	5,023	5,026	+.1	26,484	25,716	-2.9
Robbery......................	150,600	148,480	-1.4	11,354	11,989	+5.6	39,764	42,011	+5.7	110,836	106,469	-3.9
Aggravated assault..............	415,529	421,385	+1.4	19,486	20,415	+4.8	60,921	64,405	+5.7	354,608	356,980	+.7
Burglary......................	341,516	323,084	-5.4	47,295	44,587	-5.7	115,394	110,512	-4.2	226,122	212,572	-6.0
Larceny-theft	1,214,778	1,179,716	-2.9	169,815	166,226	-2.1	373,948	368,907	-1.3	840,830	810,809	-3.6
Motor vehicle theft..............	166,617	160,910	-3.4	21,230	21,174	-.3	73,398	71,444	-2.7	93,219	89,466	-4.0
Arson	15,265	15,170	-.6	4,820	4,942	+2.5	7,401	7,513	+1.5	7,864	7,657	-2.6
Violent crime[1]..............	616,391	620,023	+.6	33,040	34,735	+5.1	108,478	114,592	+5.6	507,913	505,431	-.5
Property crime[2]	1,738,176	1,678,880	-3.4	243,160	236,929	-2.6	570,141	558,376	-2.1	1,168,035	1,120,504	-4.1
Crime Index total[3]	2,354,567	2,298,903	-2.4	276,200	271,664	-1.6	678,619	672,968	-.8	1,675,948	1,625,935	-3.0
Other assaults...................	855,585	901,411	+5.4	56,929	61,288	+7.7	135,613	147,604	+8.8	719,972	753,807	+4.7
Forgery and counterfeiting........	81,988	84,533	+3.1	1,144	1,005	-12.2	6,359	6,128	-3.6	75,629	78,405	+3.7
Fraud	321,706	321,045	-.2	4,186	4,088	-2.3	14,739	15,846	+7.5	306,967	305,199	-.6
Embezzlement	11,086	10,516	-5.1	96	72	-25.0	614	599	-2.4	10,472	9,917	-5.3
Stolen property; buying, receiving, possessing	131,192	127,861	-2.5	10,305	9,795	-4.9	34,864	34,542	-.9	96,328	93,319	-3.1
Vandalism	240,883	244,133	+1.3	53,799	53,645	-.3	108,036	111,817	+3.5	132,847	132,316	-.4
Weapons; carrying, possessing, etc.	197,347	213,132	+8.0	13,383	15,240	+13.9	44,550	50,006	+12.2	152,797	163,126	+6.8
Prostitution and commercialized vice	85,779	83,751	-2.4	164	140	-14.6	1,085	942	-13.2	84,694	82,809	-2.2
Sex offenses (except forcible rape and prostitution)	86,260	83,160	-3.6	7,973	8,091	+1.5	15,651	15,619	-.2	70,609	67,541	-4.3
Drug abuse violations	894,898	931,695	+4.1	10,467	14,285	+36.5	72,064	89,832	+24.7	822,834	841,863	+2.3
Gambling......................	15,102	14,976	-.8	197	213	+8.1	1,107	1,139	+2.9	13,995	13,837	-1.1
Offenses against family and children	75,809	82,287	+8.5	1,234	1,101	-10.8	3,569	3,547	-.6	72,240	78,740	+9.0
Driving under the influence.......	1,220,573	1,156,198	-5.3	308	279	-9.4	10,757	10,086	-6.2	1,209,816	1,146,112	-5.3
Liquor laws	407,084	389,944	-4.2	8,635	8,861	+2.6	87,826	85,133	-3.1	319,258	304,811	-4.5
Drunkenness...................	625,965	583,907	-6.7	1,783	1,865	+4.6	14,121	13,402	-5.1	611,844	570,505	-6.8
Disorderly conduct..............	562,831	571,750	+1.6	34,635	38,536	+11.3	101,755	114,797	+12.8	461,076	456,953	-.9
Vagrancy	29,724	23,664	-20.4	1,138	878	-22.8	3,408	3,100	-9.0	26,316	20,564	-21.9
All other offenses (except traffic)..	2,799,922	2,697,311	-3.7	80,409	82,477	+2.6	280,119	300,984	+7.4	2,519,803	2,396,327	-4.9
Suspicion (not included in totals)..	15,076	11,705	-22.4	1,835	407	-77.8	4,856	1,287	-73.5	10,220	10,418	+1.9
Curfew and loitering law violations	68,274	81,652	+19.6	20,595	24,782	+20.3	68,274	81,652	+19.6	....	....	....
Runaways......................	137,205	145,020	+5.7	61,381	64,678	+5.4	137,205	145,020	+5.7	....	....	....

[1]Violent crimes are offenses of murder, forcible rape, robbery, and aggravated assault.

[2]Property crimes are offenses of burglary, larceny-theft, motor vehicle theft, and arson.

[3]Includes arson.

Table 37. — Total Arrest Trends, Sex, 1992-1993

[9,337 agencies; 1993 estimated population 200,200,000; 1992 estimated population 198,147,000]

Offense charged	Males						Females					
	Total			Under 18			Total			Under 18		
	1992	1993	Percent change	1992	1993	Percent change	1992	1993	Percent change	1992	1993	Percent change
TOTAL........................	9,080,300	8,900,790	-2.0	1,402,738	1,450,633	+3.4	2,123,480	2,146,059	+1.1	417,597	454,130	+8.7
Murder and nonnegligent manslaughter	16,946	17,585	+3.8	2,614	2,966	+13.5	1,809	1,831	+1.2	156	184	+17.9
Forcible rape	31,154	30,363	-2.5	4,928	4,941	+.3	353	379	+7.4	95	85	-10.5
Robbery...........................	137,728	135,525	-1.6	36,345	38,274	+5.3	12,872	12,955	+.6	3,419	3,737	+9.3
Aggravated assault.................	352,898	355,050	+.6	50,773	52,981	+4.3	62,631	66,335	+5.9	10,148	11,424	+12.6
Burglary	309,528	290,798	-6.1	104,913	99,785	-4.9	31,988	32,286	+.9	10,481	10,727	+2.3
Larceny-theft	824,654	794,164	-3.7	263,121	253,587	-3.6	390,124	385,552	-1.2	110,827	115,320	+4.1
Motor vehicle theft	148,877	141,989	-4.6	64,453	61,763	-4.2	17,740	18,921	+6.7	8,945	9,681	+8.2
Arson.............................	13,200	12,938	-2.0	6,595	6,587	-.1	2,065	2,232	+8.1	806	926	+14.9
Violent crime[1]	538,726	538,523	[2]	94,660	99,162	+4.8	77,665	81,500	+4.9	13,818	15,430	+11.7
Property crime[3]	1,296,259	1,239,889	-4.3	439,082	421,722	-4.0	441,917	438,991	-.7	131,059	136,654	+4.3
Crime Index total[4]..............	1,834,985	1,778,412	-3.1	533,742	520,884	-2.4	519,582	520,491	+.2	144,877	152,084	+5.0
Other assaults	708,776	739,418	+4.3	102,413	109,225	+6.7	146,809	161,993	+10.3	33,200	38,379	+15.6
Forgery and counterfeiting	53,721	55,288	+2.9	4,147	3,999	-3.6	28,267	29,245	+3.5	2,212	2,129	-3.8
Fraud............................	187,504	190,893	+1.8	10,894	11,650	+6.9	134,202	130,152	-3.0	3,845	4,196	+9.1
Embezzlement	6,723	6,237	-7.2	364	350	-3.8	4,363	4,279	-1.9	250	249	-.4
Stolen property; buying, receiving, possessing.......................	114,849	111,575	-2.9	31,140	30,734	-1.3	16,343	16,286	-.3	3,724	3,808	+2.3
Vandalism........................	213,432	214,493	+.5	98,637	101,076	+2.5	27,451	29,640	+8.0	9,399	10,741	+14.3
Weapons; carrying, possessing, etc.....	182,507	196,838	+7.9	41,321	45,999	+11.3	14,840	16,294	+9.8	3,229	4,007	+24.1
Prostitution and commercialized vice..............................	29,571	29,296	-.9	531	403	-24.1	56,208	54,455	-3.1	554	539	-2.7
Sex offenses (except forcible rape and prostitution)	79,249	75,986	-4.1	14,516	14,249	-1.8	7,011	7,174	+2.3	1,135	1,370	+20.7
Drug abuse violations	747,978	780,126	+4.3	64,203	79,890	+24.4	146,920	151,569	+3.2	7,861	9,942	+26.5
Gambling	13,052	12,876	-1.3	1,031	1,088	+5.5	2,050	2,100	+2.4	76	51	-32.9
Offenses against family and children.........................	62,066	66,631	+7.4	2,314	2,300	-.6	13,743	15,656	+13.9	1,255	1,247	-.6
Driving under the influence...........	1,052,539	994,312	-5.5	9,258	8,622	-6.9	168,034	161,886	-3.7	1,499	1,464	-2.3
Liquor laws.......................	329,660	314,934	-4.5	62,759	60,944	-2.9	77,424	75,010	-3.1	25,067	24,189	-3.5
Drunkenness	558,910	519,366	-7.1	11,790	11,203	-5.0	67,055	64,541	-3.7	2,331	2,199	-5.7
Disorderly conduct	445,782	452,854	+1.6	79,358	88,536	+11.6	117,049	118,896	+1.6	22,397	26,261	+17.3
Vagrancy.........................	26,818	20,855	-22.2	2,916	2,603	-10.7	2,906	2,809	-3.3	492	497	+1.0
All other offenses (except traffic)	2,322,708	2,219,935	-4.4	221,934	236,413	+6.5	477,214	477,376	[2]	58,185	64,571	+11.0
Suspicion (not included in totals)......	12,442	9,886	-20.5	3,748	1,073	-71.4	2,634	1,819	-30.9	1,108	214	-80.7
Curfew and loitering law violations	50,064	58,578	+17.0	50,064	58,578	+17.0	18,210	23,074	+26.7	18,210	23,074	+26.7
Runaways	59,406	61,887	+4.2	59,406	61,887	+4.2	77,799	83,133	+6.9	77,799	83,133	+6.9

[1]Violent crimes are offenses of murder, forcible rape, robbery, and aggravated assault.
[2]Less than one-tenth of 1 percent.
[3]Property crimes are offenses of burglary, larceny-theft, motor vehicle theft, and arson.
[4]Includes arson.

226

Table 38. — Total Arrests, Distribution by Age, 1993

[10,512 agencies; 1993 estimated population 214,099,000]

Offense charged	Total all ages	Ages under 15	Ages under 18	Ages 18 and over	Under 10	10-12	13-14	15	16	17	18	19	20	21
TOTAL.....................	11,765,764	701,129	2,014,472	9,751,292	35,572	162,495	503,062	386,163	454,004	473,176	513,323	496,764	471,617	457,570
Percent distribution[1]........	100.0	6.0	17.1	82.9	.3	1.4	4.3	3.3	3.9	4.0	4.4	4.2	4.0	3.9
Murder and nonnegligent manslaughter	20,285	380	3,284	17,001	8	26	346	575	992	1,337	1,573	1,493	1,322	1,170
Forcible rape....................	32,523	2,078	5,303	27,220	99	519	1,460	941	1,138	1,146	1,437	1,264	1,201	1,291
Robbery........................	153,533	12,376	43,340	110,193	223	2,298	9,855	8,977	10,874	11,113	10,702	9,088	7,477	6,762
Aggravated assault..............	442,075	21,546	67,751	374,324	1,024	4,995	15,527	12,854	16,054	17,297	18,069	17,039	16,746	17,271
Burglary........................	338,238	46,861	116,024	222,214	3,018	11,979	31,864	22,416	23,938	22,809	22,260	17,296	13,457	12,227
Larceny-theft	1,251,277	176,851	391,950	859,327	9,589	50,616	116,646	71,956	74,612	68,531	62,911	50,791	41,060	37,410
Motor vehicle theft..............	168,795	22,345	75,315	93,480	214	2,618	19,513	18,555	18,940	15,475	11,870	9,014	7,145	5,945
Arson	16,113	5,202	7,949	8,164	921	1,664	2,617	1,156	873	718	595	479	395	368
Violent crime[2]..............	648,416	36,380	119,678	528,738	1,354	7,838	27,188	23,347	29,058	30,893	31,781	28,884	26,746	26,494
Percent distribution[1].........	100.0	5.6	18.5	81.5	.2	1.2	4.2	3.6	4.5	4.8	4.9	4.5	4.1	4.1
Property crime[3]	1,774,423	251,259	591,238	1,183,185	13,742	66,877	170,640	114,083	118,363	107,533	97,636	77,580	62,057	55,950
Percent distribution[1].........	100.0	14.2	33.3	66.7	.8	3.8	9.6	6.4	6.7	6.1	5.5	4.4	3.5	3.2
Crime Index total[4]	2,422,839	287,639	710,916	1,711,923	15,096	74,715	197,828	137,430	147,421	138,426	129,417	106,464	88,803	82,444
Percent distribution[1]	100.0	11.9	29.3	70.7	.6	3.1	8.2	5.7	6.1	5.7	5.3	4.4	3.7	3.4
Other assaults..................	965,318	64,830	156,268	809,050	3,354	17,143	44,333	29,106	31,417	30,915	31,407	31,446	31,991	35,316
Forgery and counterfeiting.......	89,487	1,058	6,506	82,981	24	232	802	1,026	1,726	2,696	3,940	4,421	4,483	4,162
Fraud	335,580	4,146	16,158	319,422	114	669	3,363	3,700	3,466	4,846	8,339	11,317	13,120	14,319
Embezzlement	10,916	79	616	10,300	6	26	47	54	161	322	492	578	576	558
Stolen property; buying, receiving, possessing	134,864	10,425	36,440	98,424	246	1,915	8,264	7,608	8,992	9,415	9,884	8,274	6,953	6,048
Vandalism......................	261,282	57,154	119,142	142,140	5,875	16,834	34,445	21,089	22,153	18,746	14,631	10,788	8,675	8,251
Weapons; carrying, possessing, etc.	224,395	15,950	52,352	172,043	574	3,157	12,219	10,072	12,503	13,827	15,352	13,464	11,890	11,623
Prostitution and commercialized vice	88,850	152	994	87,856	2	23	127	128	232	482	1,437	2,100	2,534	2,987
Sex offenses (except forcible rape and prostitution)	87,712	8,505	16,393	71,319	715	2,305	5,485	2,815	2,630	2,443	2,514	2,219	2,305	2,376
Drug abuse violations	968,606	14,787	93,316	875,290	174	1,443	13,170	16,612	26,779	35,138	48,198	47,051	45,374	43,588
Gambling.......................	15,336	220	1,167	14,169	9	26	185	213	304	430	599	496	489	452
Offenses against family and children	89,157	1,266	3,940	85,217	148	244	874	794	916	964	1,959	2,120	2,400	2,850
Driving under the influence.......	1,229,971	319	10,722	1,219,249	103	33	183	513	2,737	7,153	18,617	25,288	31,943	46,922
Liquor laws	419,082	9,488	91,701	327,381	128	735	8,625	13,820	26,591	41,802	62,571	60,831	49,542	15,572
Drunkenness....................	604,979	1,929	13,887	591,092	86	182	1,661	2,075	3,514	6,369	13,310	14,697	15,889	21,156
Disorderly conduct..............	607,472	40,532	121,212	486,260	1,700	9,186	29,646	23,860	27,474	29,346	30,527	27,361	25,744	27,696
Vagrancy	24,806	915	3,235	21,571	21	152	742	743	801	776	1,079	862	707	689
All other offenses (except traffic)..	2,935,490	87,750	320,636	2,614,854	5,301	18,051	64,398	54,490	78,409	99,987	118,577	126,471	127,716	130,097
Suspicion	12,136	451	1,385	10,751	31	125	295	323	296	315	473	516	483	464
Curfew and loitering law violations	85,354	25,885	85,354	....	349	3,778	21,758	20,091	22,973	16,405	....	....	....	....
Runaways.......................	152,132	67,649	152,132	....	1,516	11,521	54,612	39,601	32,509	12,373	....	....	....	....

See footnotes at end of table.

Table 38. — Total Arrests, Distribution by Age, 1993 — Continued

Offense charged	Age											
	22	23	24	25-29	30-34	35-39	40-44	45-49	50-54	55-59	60-64	65 and over
TOTAL	457,217	434,225	404,678	1,856,055	1,724,659	1,256,231	759,580	412,742	224,409	122,983	74,140	85,099
Percent distribution[1]	3.9	3.7	3.4	15.8	14.7	10.7	6.5	3.5	1.9	1.0	.6	.7
Murder and nonnegligent manslaughter	1,087	938	784	2,874	2,000	1,446	892	553	364	203	122	180
Forcible rape	1,189	1,152	1,139	5,346	4,915	3,539	2,075	1,153	611	351	294	263
Robbery	6,486	5,902	5,291	23,525	17,574	10,041	4,433	1,724	659	233	128	168
Aggravated assault	17,221	16,519	15,579	74,413	68,167	49,004	28,862	15,913	8,482	4,729	2,868	3,442
Burglary	11,252	10,429	9,482	43,368	37,703	24,525	11,677	4,850	1,983	853	383	469
Larceny-theft	36,076	33,349	31,758	151,420	147,266	111,911	67,942	35,725	19,469	11,185	7,842	13,212
Motor vehicle theft	5,471	4,689	4,247	17,435	13,204	7,671	3,843	1,596	719	293	140	198
Arson	345	299	263	1,292	1,415	1,091	714	353	248	128	80	99
Violent crime[2]	25,983	24,511	22,793	106,158	92,656	64,030	36,262	19,343	10,116	5,516	3,412	4,053
Percent distribution[1]	4.0	3.8	3.5	16.4	14.3	9.9	5.6	3.0	1.6	.9	.5	.6
Property crime[3]	53,144	48,766	45,750	213,515	199,588	145,198	84,176	42,524	22,419	12,459	8,445	13,978
Percent distribution[1]	3.0	2.7	2.6	12.0	11.2	8.2	4.7	2.4	1.3	.7	.5	.8
Crime Index total[4]	79,127	73,277	68,543	319,673	292,244	209,228	120,438	61,867	32,535	17,975	11,857	18,031
Percent distribution[1]	3.3	3.0	2.8	13.2	12.1	8.6	5.0	2.6	1.3	.7	.5	.7
Other assaults	37,050	36,494	35,421	168,929	158,628	109,633	62,731	32,888	17,038	8,978	5,074	6,026
Forgery and counterfeiting	4,272	4,220	3,865	17,267	15,188	10,783	5,621	2,590	1,125	515	269	260
Fraud	15,209	15,068	14,634	65,920	58,858	44,567	28,016	15,051	7,376	3,683	1,987	1,958
Embezzlement	601	469	449	1,961	1,685	1,186	809	455	237	118	82	44
Stolen property; buying, receiving, possessing	5,489	4,744	4,396	17,846	14,629	9,814	5,346	2,642	1,170	558	324	307
Vandalism	7,718	7,109	6,172	26,612	22,452	14,265	7,509	3,871	1,810	942	565	770
Weapons; carrying, possessing, etc.	10,827	9,505	7,813	30,095	22,481	15,598	9,629	5,899	3,331	1,901	1,188	1,447
Prostitution and commercialized vice	3,736	4,328	4,158	21,887	20,756	12,515	5,835	2,646	1,267	699	459	512
Sex offenses (except forcible rape and prostitution)	2,516	2,447	2,484	12,224	12,786	10,144	6,753	4,514	2,841	1,855	1,400	1,941
Drug abuse violations	44,061	42,248	38,789	180,947	164,688	113,872	61,234	25,932	10,994	4,557	2,147	1,610
Gambling	403	390	346	1,767	1,668	1,699	1,495	1,259	1,070	780	590	666
Offenses against family and children	3,164	3,293	3,528	17,370	18,444	14,161	8,123	4,103	1,878	930	450	444
Driving under the influence	50,700	51,225	48,782	233,197	233,491	179,689	119,843	75,599	45,330	26,267	16,432	15,924
Liquor laws	11,894	9,653	7,728	28,724	25,810	20,144	13,887	8,539	5,283	3,262	1,985	1,956
Drunkenness	21,149	20,343	19,588	97,641	109,091	93,497	66,039	40,206	25,162	15,127	9,182	9,015
Disorderly conduct	26,918	24,146	21,971	90,478	80,574	56,448	33,295	18,461	9,986	5,311	3,291	4,053
Vagrancy	634	653	650	2,990	4,059	3,514	2,412	1,488	980	387	246	221
All other offenses (except traffic)	131,274	124,097	114,917	518,333	465,088	333,963	199,723	104,324	54,803	29,049	16,561	19,861
Suspicion	475	516	444	2,194	2,039	1,511	842	408	193	89	51	53
Curfew and loitering law violations	....	....	....	....	....	....	....	....	....	....	....	....
Runaways	....	....	....	....	....	....	....	....	....	....	....	....

[1]Because of rounding, the percentages may not add to total.
[2]Violent crimes are offenses of murder, forcible rape, robbery, and aggravated assault.
[3]Property crimes are offenses of burglary, larceny-theft, motor vehicle theft, and arson.
[4]Includes arson.

Table 39. — Male Arrests, Distribution by Age, 1993

[10,512 agencies; 1993 estimated population 214,099,000]

Offense charged	Total all ages	Ages under 15	Ages under 18	Ages 18 and over	Under 10	10-12	13-14	15	16	17	18	19	20	21
TOTAL	9,475,344	509,935	1,534,356	7,940,988	29,666	124,359	355,910	284,281	352,720	387,420	431,622	415,885	393,642	381,078
Percent distribution[1]	100.0	5.4	16.2	83.8	.3	1.3	3.8	3.0	3.7	4.1	4.6	4.4	4.2	4.0
Murder and nonnegligent manslaughter	18,375	339	3,093	15,282	5	19	315	538	953	1,263	1,501	1,398	1,256	1,103
Forcible rape	32,107	2,025	5,212	26,895	97	500	1,428	926	1,125	1,136	1,420	1,245	1,183	1,277
Robbery	140,128	10,929	39,493	100,635	205	2,075	8,649	8,124	10,033	10,407	10,111	8,526	7,000	6,366
Aggravated assault	372,557	17,005	55,731	316,826	917	4,112	11,976	10,338	13,451	14,937	15,855	14,841	14,443	14,896
Burglary	304,702	41,543	104,871	199,831	2,694	10,646	28,203	20,353	21,977	20,998	20,744	16,047	12,335	11,174
Larceny-theft	842,658	122,198	269,690	572,968	7,669	36,546	77,983	48,384	51,036	48,072	44,650	35,250	27,558	24,935
Motor vehicle theft	148,932	18,363	65,117	83,815	193	2,201	15,969	15,878	16,813	14,063	10,970	8,305	6,609	5,419
Arson................................	13,738	4,544	6,975	6,763	851	1,458	2,235	1,007	767	657	537	431	357	330
Violent crime[2]	563,167	30,298	103,529	459,638	1,224	6,706	22,368	19,926	25,562	27,743	28,887	26,010	23,882	23,642
Percent distribution[1]..............	100.0	5.4	18.4	81.6	.2	1.2	4.0	3.5	4.5	4.9	5.1	4.6	4.2	4.2
Property crime[3]...................	1,310,030	186,648	446,653	863,377	11,407	50,851	124,390	85,622	90,593	83,790	76,901	60,033	46,859	41,858
Percent distribution[1]..............	100.0	14.2	34.1	65.9	.9	3.9	9.5	6.5	6.9	6.4	5.9	4.6	3.6	3.2
Crime Index total[4]...............	1,873,197	216,946	550,182	1,323,015	12,631	57,557	146,758	105,548	116,155	111,533	105,788	86,043	70,741	65,500
Percent distribution[1]..............	100.0	11.6	29.4	70.6	.7	3.1	7.8	5.6	6.2	6.0	5.6	4.6	3.8	3.5
Other assaults	792,848	46,593	115,714	677,134	2,828	13,053	30,712	20,980	23,729	24,412	25,685	25,775	26,225	29,233
Forgery and counterfeiting	58,425	669	4,243	54,182	10	156	503	635	1,143	1,796	2,666	2,934	3,067	2,763
Fraud...............................	199,297	2,843	11,847	187,450	81	439	2,323	2,760	2,630	3,614	5,516	7,134	7,888	8,379
Embezzlement......................	6,493	63	366	6,127	6	17	40	31	93	179	276	315	319	315
Stolen property; buying, receiving, possessing........................	117,531	8,999	32,404	85,127	211	1,676	7,112	6,741	8,094	8,570	9,035	7,481	6,220	5,355
Vandalism..........................	229,424	51,308	107,701	121,723	5,433	15,208	30,667	19,068	20,234	17,091	13,226	9,679	7,714	7,213
Weapons; carrying, possessing, etc.	206,990	14,117	48,159	158,831	534	2,764	10,819	9,262	11,679	13,101	14,677	12,835	11,316	10,970
Prostitution and commercialized vice.	31,712	75	443	31,269	1	17	57	61	92	215	521	687	821	1,022
Sex offenses (except forcible rape and prostitution)	80,211	7,680	14,969	65,242	633	2,059	4,988	2,588	2,431	2,270	2,318	2,003	2,065	2,072
Drug abuse violations.................	811,493	12,312	82,968	728,525	147	1,139	11,026	14,630	24,129	31,897	43,525	42,215	40,392	38,167
Gambling...........................	13,186	204	1,115	12,071	9	24	171	207	292	412	560	468	463	408
Offenses against family and children......................	71,967	739	2,538	69,429	93	142	504	485	606	708	1,560	1,662	1,907	2,270
Driving under the influence	1,056,544	251	9,170	1,047,374	90	23	138	413	2,312	6,194	16,273	22,139	28,224	41,018
Liquor laws.........................	338,276	5,288	65,586	272,690	100	411	4,777	8,831	19,130	32,337	49,622	49,339	40,924	13,329
Drunkenness	537,690	1,339	11,599	526,091	78	133	1,128	1,630	2,940	5,690	12,151	13,368	14,525	19,197
Disorderly conduct	481,553	29,694	93,472	388,081	1,445	7,025	21,224	17,953	21,698	24,127	25,397	22,649	21,182	23,008
Vagrancy...........................	21,765	739	2,698	19,067	17	129	593	599	689	671	943	714	600	589
All other offenses (except traffic)	2,410,082	64,676	2,158,448	251,634	3,964	14,045	46,667	41,046	62,614	83,298	101,460	108,000	108,612	109,866
Suspicion..........................	10,266	365	1,154	9,112	26	100	239	264	245	280	423	445	437	404
Curfew and loitering law violations..........................	61,343	17,276	61,343	....	287	2,627	14,362	14,207	17,100	12,760	....	....	....	....
Runaways	65,051	27,759	65,051	....	1,042	5,615	21,102	16,342	14,685	6,265	....	....	....	....

See footnotes at end of table.

Table 39. — Male Arrests, Distribution by Age, 1993 — Continued

Offense charged	Age											
	22	23	24	25-29	30-34	35-39	40-44	45-49	50-54	55-59	60-64	65 and over
TOTAL	376,869	354,748	328,256	1,484,220	1,368,671	1,008,938	623,345	344,401	190,267	105,400	63,409	70,237
Percent distribution[1]	4.0	3.7	3.5	15.7	14.4	10.6	6.6	3.6	2.0	1.1	.7	.7
Murder and nonnegligent manslaughter	1,010	871	709	2,541	1,708	1,198	770	469	313	168	108	159
Forcible rape	1,183	1,138	1,120	5,282	4,854	3,496	2,042	1,141	611	348	294	261
Robbery	5,961	5,426	4,838	21,240	15,632	8,883	3,994	1,574	602	214	122	146
Aggravated assault	14,814	14,074	13,174	62,101	56,388	40,763	24,506	13,766	7,384	4,148	2,577	3,096
Burglary	10,188	9,336	8,433	38,618	33,404	21,708	10,338	4,280	1,732	744	328	422
Larceny-theft	23,589	21,570	20,485	97,980	97,557	76,522	47,273	23,954	12,674	6,778	4,565	7,628
Motor vehicle theft	4,939	4,144	3,795	15,334	11,469	6,742	3,402	1,444	663	269	132	179
Arson	290	262	226	1,056	1,111	859	567	278	208	97	71	83
Violent crime[2]	22,968	21,509	19,841	91,164	78,582	54,340	31,312	16,950	8,910	4,878	3,101	3,662
Percent distribution[1]	4.1	3.8	3.5	16.2	14.0	9.6	5.6	3.0	1.6	.9	.6	.7
Property crime[3]	39,006	35,312	32,939	152,988	143,541	105,831	61,580	29,956	15,277	7,888	5,096	8,312
Percent distribution[1]	3.0	2.7	2.5	11.7	11.0	8.1	4.7	2.3	1.2	.6	.4	.6
Crime Index total[4].	61,974	56,821	52,780	244,152	222,123	160,171	92,892	46,906	24,187	12,766	8,197	11,974
Percent distribution[1]	3.3	3.0	2.8	13.0	11.9	8.6	5.0	2.5	1.3	.7	.4	.6
Other assaults	30,780	30,216	29,445	140,858	132,504	92,387	53,587	28,358	14,691	7,783	4,429	5,178
Forgery and counterfeiting	2,669	2,773	2,436	11,001	7,130	3,758	1,786	823	389	207	201
Fraud................................	8,633	8,641	8,286	37,702	33,962	25,926	16,502	9,363	4,634	2,331	1,327	1,226
Embezzlement	346	260	273	1,180	1,041	718	482	287	147	82	53	33
Stolen property; buying, receiving, possessing...........................	4,795	4,109	3,768	15,046	12,234	8,126	4,563	2,273	1,034	517	296	275
Vandalism...........................	6,700	6,061	5,240	22,264	18,664	11,884	6,329	3,268	1,538	791	504	648
Weapons; carrying, possessing, etc.	10,196	8,827	7,234	27,511	20,116	13,900	8,670	5,342	3,036	1,759	1,119	1,323
Prostitution and commercialized vice.................................	1,190	1,252	1,262	6,724	6,176	4,465	2,819	1,745	1,045	640	424	476
Sex offenses (except forcible rape and prostitution)	2,207	2,138	2,184	10,729	11,506	9,409	6,344	4,362	2,771	1,832	1,380	1,922
Drug abuse violations.................	38,254	36,065	32,541	147,335	130,553	90,677	50,206	21,829	9,489	4,005	1,872	1,400
Gambling	365	343	299	1,464	1,367	1,387	1,228	1,043	878	671	528	599
Offenses against family and children............................	2,548	2,646	2,835	13,978	14,827	11,538	6,919	3,561	1,632	819	369	358
Driving under the influence	44,039	44,590	42,276	199,566	196,337	151,640	102,311	65,628	40,132	23,709	14,997	14,495
Liquor laws..........................	10,369	8,320	6,708	24,519	21,768	17,049	12,028	7,485	4,713	2,971	1,805	1,741
Drunkenness	19,202	18,308	17,527	85,549	94,143	81,994	58,999	36,359	23,285	14,291	8,681	8,512
Disorderly conduct	21,861	19,389	17,550	69,590	61,954	44,281	26,889	15,217	8,367	4,557	2,815	3,375
Vagrancy............................	545	483	543	2,457	3,578	3,186	2,265	1,408	946	376	241	193
All other offenses (except traffic)	109,779	103,078	94,688	420,782	374,568	271,803	165,833	87,820	46,752	25,026	14,118	16,263
Suspicion	417	428	381	1,813	1,671	1,267	721	361	167	85	47	45
Curfew and loitering law violations..........................	....	....	....	....	....	....	....	....	....	....	....	....
Runaways	....	....	....	....	....	....	....	....	....	....	....	....

[1]Because of rounding, the percentages may not add to total.

[2]Violent crimes are offenses of murder, forcible rape, robbery, and aggravated assault.

[3]Property crimes are offenses of burglary, larceny-theft, motor vehicle theft, and arson.

[4]Includes arson.

Table 40. — Female Arrests, Distribution by Age, 1993

[10,512 agencies; 1993 estimated population 214,099,000]

Offense charged	Total all ages	Ages under 15	Ages under 18	Ages 18 and over	Under 10	10-12	13-14	15	16	17	18	19	20	21
														Age
TOTAL	2,290,420	191,194	480,116	1,810,304	5,906	38,136	147,152	101,882	101,284	85,756	81,701	80,879	77,975	76,492
Percent distribution[1]	100.0	8.3	21.0	79.0	.3	1.7	6.4	4.4	4.4	3.7	3.6	3.5	3.4	3.3
Murder and nonnegligent manslaughter........................	1,910	41	191	1,719	3	7	31	37	39	74	72	95	66	67
Forcible rape	416	53	91	325	2	19	32	15	13	10	17	19	18	14
Robbery	13,405	1,447	3,847	9,558	18	223	1,206	853	841	706	591	562	477	396
Aggravated assault	69,518	4,541	12,020	57,498	107	883	3,551	2,516	2,603	2,360	2,214	2,198	2,303	2,375
Burglary	33,536	5,318	11,153	22,383	324	1,333	3,661	2,063	1,961	1,811	1,516	1,249	1,122	1,053
Larceny-theft..........................	408,619	54,653	122,260	286,359	1,920	14,070	38,663	23,572	23,576	20,459	18,261	15,541	13,502	12,475
Motor vehicle theft	19,863	3,982	10,198	9,665	21	417	3,544	2,677	2,127	1,412	900	709	536	526
Arson	2,375	658	974	1,401	70	206	382	149	106	61	58	48	38	38
Violent crime[2]	85,249	6,082	16,149	69,100	130	1,132	4,820	3,421	3,496	3,150	2,894	2,874	2,864	2,852
Percent distribution[1]	100.0	7.1	18.9	81.1	.2	1.3	5.7	4.0	4.1	3.7	3.4	3.4	3.4	3.3
Property crime[3]	464,393	64,611	144,585	319,808	2,335	16,026	46,250	28,461	27,770	23,743	20,735	17,547	15,198	14,092
Percent distribution[1]	100.0	13.9	31.1	68.9	.5	3.5	10.0	6.1	6.0	5.1	4.5	3.8	3.3	3.0
Crime Index total[4]	549,642	70,693	160,734	388,908	2,465	17,158	51,070	31,882	31,266	26,893	23,629	20,421	18,062	16,944
Percent distribution[1]	100.0	12.9	29.2	70.8	.4	3.1	9.3	5.8	5.7	4.9	4.3	3.7	3.3	3.1
Other assaults	172,470	18,237	40,554	131,916	526	4,090	13,621	8,126	7,688	6,503	5,722	5,671	5,766	6,083
Forgery and counterfeiting	31,062	389	2,263	28,799	14	76	299	391	583	900	1,274	1,487	1,416	1,399
Fraud.................................	136,283	1,303	4,311	131,972	33	230	1,040	940	836	1,232	2,823	4,183	5,232	5,940
Embezzlement.........................	4,423	16	250	4,173	....	9	7	23	68	143	216	263	257	243
Stolen property; buying, receiving, possessing.........................	17,333	1,426	4,036	13,297	35	239	1,152	867	898	845	849	793	733	693
Vandalism	31,858	5,846	11,441	20,417	442	1,626	3,778	2,021	1,919	1,655	1,405	1,109	961	1,038
Weapons; carrying, possessing, etc.	17,405	1,833	4,193	13,212	40	393	1,400	810	824	726	675	629	574	653
Prostitution and commercialized vice	57,138	77	551	56,587	1	6	70	67	140	267	916	1,413	1,713	1,965
Sex offenses (except forcible rape and prostitution).....................	7,501	825	1,424	6,077	82	246	497	227	199	173	196	216	240	304
Drug abuse violations..................	157,113	2,475	10,348	146,765	27	304	2,144	1,982	2,650	3,241	4,673	4,836	4,982	5,421
Gambling	2,150	16	52	2,098	....	2	14	6	12	18	39	28	26	44
Offenses against family and children	17,190	527	1,402	15,788	55	102	370	309	310	256	399	458	493	580
Driving under the influence	173,427	68	1,552	171,875	13	10	45	100	425	959	2,344	3,149	3,719	5,904
Liquor laws...........................	80,806	4,200	26,115	54,691	28	324	3,848	4,989	7,461	9,465	12,949	11,492	8,618	2,243
Drunkenness	67,289	590	2,288	65,001	8	49	533	445	574	679	1,159	1,329	1,364	1,959
Disorderly conduct	125,919	10,838	27,740	98,179	255	2,161	8,422	5,907	5,776	5,219	5,130	4,712	4,562	4,688
Vagrancy.............................	3,041	176	537	2,504	4	23	149	144	112	105	136	148	107	100
All other offenses (except traffic)	525,408	23,074	69,002	456,406	1,337	4,006	17,731	13,444	15,795	16,689	17,117	18,471	19,104	20,231
Suspicion	1,870	86	231	1,639	5	25	56	59	51	35	50	71	46	60
Curfew and loitering law violations.........................	24,011	8,609	24,011	....	62	1,151	7,396	5,884	5,873	3,645	....	....	....	....
Runaways.............................	87,081	39,890	87,081	....	474	5,906	33,510	23,259	17,824	6,108	....	....	....	....

See footnotes at end of table.

Table 40. — Female Arrests, Distribution by Age, 1993 — Continued

Offense charged	Age											
	22	23	24	25-29	30-34	35-39	40-44	45-49	50-54	55-59	60-64	65 and over
TOTAL	80,348	79,477	76,422	371,835	355,988	247,293	136,235	68,341	34,142	17,583	10,731	14,862
Percent distribution[1]	3.5	3.5	3.3	16.2	15.5	10.8	5.9	3.0	1.5	.8	.5	.6
Murder and nonnegligent manslaughter......................	77	67	75	333	292	248	122	84	51	35	14	21
Forcible rape	6	14	19	64	61	43	33	12	....	3	....	2
Robbery	525	476	453	2,285	1,942	1,158	439	150	57	19	6	22
Aggravated assault	2,407	2,445	2,405	12,312	11,779	8,241	4,356	2,147	1,098	581	291	346
Burglary	1,064	1,093	1,049	4,750	4,299	2,817	1,339	570	251	109	55	47
Larceny-theft........................	12,487	11,779	11,273	53,440	49,709	35,889	20,669	11,771	6,795	4,407	3,277	5,584
Motor vehicle theft..................	532	545	452	2,101	1,735	929	441	152	56	24	8	19
Arson	55	37	37	236	304	232	147	75	40	31	9	16
Violent crime[2].....................	3,015	3,002	2,952	14,994	14,074	9,690	4,950	2,393	1,206	638	311	391
Percent distribution[1]	3.5	3.5	3.5	17.6	16.5	11.4	5.8	2.8	1.4	.7	.4	.5
Property crime[3]....................	14,138	13,454	12,811	60,527	56,047	39,367	22,596	12,568	7,142	4,571	3,349	5,666
Percent distribution[1]	3.0	2.9	2.8	13.0	12.1	8.5	4.9	2.7	1.5	1.0	.7	1.2
Crime Index total[4]	17,153	16,456	15,763	75,521	70,121	49,057	27,546	14,961	8,348	5,209	3,660	6,057
Percent distribution[1]	3.1	3.0	2.9	13.7	12.8	8.9	5.0	2.7	1.5	.9	.7	1.1
Other assaults	6,270	6,278	5,976	28,071	26,124	17,246	9,144	4,530	2,347	1,195	645	848
Forgery and counterfeiting	1,603	1,447	1,429	6,266	5,609	3,653	1,863	804	302	126	62	59
Fraud...............................	6,576	6,427	6,348	28,218	24,896	18,641	11,514	5,688	2,742	1,352	660	732
Embezzlement.......................	255	209	176	781	644	468	327	168	90	36	29	11
Stolen property; buying, receiving, possession...........................	694	635	628	2,800	2,395	1,688	783	369	136	41	28	32
Vandalism...........................	1,018	1,048	932	4,348	3,788	2,381	1,180	603	272	151	61	122
Weapons; carrying, possessing, etc.	631	678	579	2,584	2,365	1,698	959	557	295	142	69	124
Prostitution and commercialized vice	2,546	3,076	2,896	15,163	14,580	8,050	3,016	901	222	59	35	36
Sex offenses (except forcible rape and prostitution).....................	309	309	300	1,495	1,280	735	409	152	70	23	20	19
Drug abuse violations...................	5,807	6,183	6,248	33,612	34,135	23,195	11,028	4,103	1,505	552	275	210
Gambling............................	38	47	47	303	301	312	267	216	192	109	62	67
Offenses against family and children.........................	616	647	693	3,392	3,617	2,623	1,204	542	246	111	81	86
Driving under the influence	6,661	6,635	6,506	33,631	37,154	28,049	17,532	9,971	5,198	2,558	1,435	1,429
Liquor laws..........................	1,525	1,333	1,020	4,205	4,042	3,095	1,859	1,054	570	291	180	215
Drunkenness	1,947	2,035	2,061	12,092	14,948	11,503	7,040	3,847	1,877	836	501	503
Disorderly conduct	5,057	4,757	4,421	20,888	18,620	12,167	6,406	3,244	1,619	754	476	678
Vagrancy............................	89	170	107	533	481	328	147	80	34	11	5	28
All other offenses (except traffic)	21,495	21,019	20,229	97,551	90,520	62,160	33,890	16,504	8,051	4,023	2,443	3,598
Suspicion	58	88	63	381	368	244	121	47	26	4	4	8
Curfew and loitering law violations..........................	....	....	....	....	....	....	....	....	....	....	....	....
Runaways............................	....	....	....	....	....	....	....	....	....	....	....	....

[1]Because of rounding, the percentages may not add to total.
[2]Violent crimes are offenses of murder, forcible rape, robbery, and aggravated assault.
[3]Property crimes are offenses of burglary, larceny-theft, motor vehicle theft, and arson.
[4]Includes arson.

Table 41.—Total Arrests of Persons under 15, 18, 21, and 25 Years of Age, 1993

[10,512 agencies; 1993 estimated population 214,099,000]

Offense charged	Total all ages	Number of persons arrested				Percent of total all ages			
		Under 15	Under 18	Under 21	Under 25	Under 15	Under 18	Under 21	Under 25
TOTAL.................................	11,765,764	701,129	2,014,472	3,496,176	5,249,866	6.0	17.1	29.7	44.6
Murder and nonnegligent manslaughter..................	20,285	380	3,284	7,672	11,651	1.9	16.2	37.8	57.4
Forcible rape............................	32,523	2,078	5,303	9,205	13,976	6.4	16.3	28.3	43.0
Robbery................................	153,533	12,376	43,340	70,607	95,048	8.1	28.2	46.0	61.9
Aggravated assault..................................	442,075	21,546	67,751	119,605	186,195	4.9	15.3	27.1	42.1
Burglary...............................	338,238	46,861	116,024	169,037	212,427	13.9	34.3	50.0	62.8
Larceny-theft..........................	1,251,277	176,851	391,950	546,712	685,305	14.1	31.3	43.7	54.8
Motor vehicle theft....................	168,795	22,345	75,315	103,344	123,696	13.2	44.6	61.2	73.3
Arson.................................	16,113	5,202	7,949	9,418	10,693	32.3	49.3	58.4	66.4
Violent crime[1]........................	648,416	36,380	119,678	207,089	306,870	5.6	18.5	31.9	47.3
Property crime[2].......................	1,774,423	251,259	591,238	828,511	1,032,121	14.2	33.3	46.7	58.2
Crime Index total[3]........................	2,422,839	287,639	710,916	1,035,600	1,338,991	11.9	29.3	42.7	55.3
Other assaults........................	965,318	64,830	156,268	251,112	395,393	6.7	16.2	26.0	41.0
Forgery and counterfeiting........................	89,487	1,058	6,506	19,350	35,869	1.2	7.3	21.6	40.1
Fraud.................................	335,580	4,146	16,158	48,934	108,164	1.2	4.8	14.6	32.2
Embezzlement........................	10,916	79	616	2,262	4,339	.7	5.6	20.7	39.7
Stolen property; buying, receiving, possessing............	134,864	10,425	36,440	61,551	82,228	7.7	27.0	45.6	61.0
Vandalism.............................	261,282	57,154	119,142	153,236	182,486	21.9	45.6	58.6	69.8
Weapons; carrying, possessing, etc.	224,395	15,950	52,352	93,058	132,826	7.1	23.3	41.5	59.2
Prostitution and commercialized vice....................	88,850	152	994	7,065	22,274	.2	1.1	8.0	25.1
Sex offenses (except forcible rape and prostitution)........	87,712	8,505	16,393	23,431	33,254	9.7	18.7	26.7	37.9
Drug abuse violations..........................	968,606	14,787	93,316	233,939	402,625	1.5	9.6	24.2	41.6
Gambling.............................	15,336	220	1,167	2,751	4,342	1.4	7.6	17.9	28.3
Offenses against family and children....................	89,157	1,266	3,940	10,419	23,254	1.4	4.4	11.7	26.1
Driving under the influence........................	1,229,971	319	10,722	86,570	284,199	[4]	.9	7.0	23.1
Liquor laws...........................	419,082	9,488	91,701	264,645	309,492	2.3	21.9	63.1	73.8
Drunkenness...........................	604,979	1,929	13,887	57,783	140,019	.3	2.3	9.6	23.1
Disorderly conduct.....................	607,472	40,532	121,212	204,844	305,575	6.7	20.0	33.7	50.3
Vagrancy.............................	24,806	915	3,235	5,883	8,509	3.7	13.0	23.7	34.3
All other offenses (except traffic).....................	2,935,490	87,750	320,636	693,400	1,193,785	3.0	10.9	23.6	40.7
Suspicion.............................	12,136	451	1,385	2,857	4,756	3.7	11.4	23.5	39.2
Curfew and loitering law violations.....................	85,354	25,885	85,354	85,354	85,354	30.3	100.0	100.0	100.0
Runaways.............................	152,132	67,649	152,132	152,132	152,132	44.5	100.0	100.0	100.0

[1]Violent crimes are offenses of murder, forcible rape, robbery, and aggravated assault.

[2]Property crimes are offenses of burglary, larceny-theft, motor vehicle theft, and arson.

[3]Includes arson.

[4]Less than one-tenth of 1 percent.

233

Table 42. — Total Arrests, Distribution by Sex, 1993
[10,512 agencies; 1993 estimated population 214,099,000]

Offense charged	Number of persons arrested			Percent male	Percent female	Percent distribution[1]		
	Total	Male	Female			Total	Male	Female
TOTAL...	11,765,764	9,475,344	2,290,420	80.5	19.5	100.0	100.0	100.0
Murder and nonnegligent manslaughter.............................	20,285	18,375	1,910	90.6	9.4	.2	.2	.1
Forcible rape...	32,523	32,107	416	98.7	1.3	.3	.3	....
Robbery...	153,533	140,128	13,405	91.3	8.7	1.3	1.5	.6
Aggravated assault..	442,075	372,557	69,518	84.3	15.7	3.8	3.9	3.0
Burglary...	338,238	304,702	33,536	90.1	9.9	2.9	3.2	1.5
Larceny-theft...	1,251,277	842,658	408,619	67.3	32.7	10.6	8.9	17.8
Motor vehicle theft..	168,795	148,932	19,863	88.2	11.8	1.4	1.6	.9
Arson..	16,113	13,738	2,375	85.3	14.7	.1	.1	.1
Violent crime[2]...	648,416	563,167	85,249	86.9	13.1	5.5	5.9	3.7
Property crime[3]..	1,774,423	1,310,030	464,393	73.8	26.2	15.1	13.8	20.3
Crime Index total[4].......................................	2,422,839	1,873,197	549,642	77.3	22.7	20.6	19.8	24.0
Other assaults..	965,318	792,848	172,470	82.1	17.9	8.2	8.4	7.5
Forgery and counterfeiting..................................	89,487	58,425	31,062	65.3	34.7	.8	.6	1.4
Fraud..	335,580	199,297	136,283	59.4	40.6	2.9	2.1	6.0
Embezzlement..	10,916	6,493	4,423	59.5	40.5	.1	.1	.2
Stolen property; buying, receiving, possessing	134,864	117,531	17,333	87.1	12.9	1.1	1.2	.8
Vandalism...	261,282	229,424	31,858	87.8	12.2	2.2	2.4	1.4
Weapons; carrying, possessing, etc.	224,395	206,990	17,405	92.2	7.8	1.9	2.2	.8
Prostitution and commercialized vice.........................	88,850	31,712	57,138	35.7	64.3	.8	.3	2.5
Sex offenses (except forcible rape and prostitution)	87,712	80,211	7,501	91.4	8.6	.7	.8	.3
Drug abuse violations	968,606	811,493	157,113	83.8	16.2	8.2	8.6	6.9
Gambling..	15,336	13,186	2,150	86.0	14.0	.1	.1	.1
Offenses against family and children	89,157	71,967	17,190	80.7	19.3	.8	.8	.8
Driving under the influence	1,229,971	1,056,544	173,427	85.9	14.1	10.5	11.2	7.6
Liquor laws..	419,082	338,276	80,806	80.7	19.3	3.6	3.6	3.5
Drunkenness...	604,979	537,690	67,289	88.9	11.1	5.1	5.7	2.9
Disorderly conduct..	607,472	481,553	125,919	79.3	20.7	5.2	5.1	5.5
Vagrancy..	24,806	21,765	3,041	87.7	12.3	.2	.2	.1
All other offenses (except traffic)............................	2,935,490	2,410,082	525,408	82.1	17.9	24.9	25.4	22.9
Suspicion	12,136	10,266	1,870	84.6	15.4	.1	.1	.1
Curfew and loitering law violations...........................	85,354	61,343	24,011	71.9	28.1	.7	.6	1.0
Runaways..	152,132	65,051	87,081	42.8	57.2	1.3	.7	3.8

[1]Because of rounding, the percentages may not add to total.
[2]Violent crimes are offenses of murder, forcible rape, robbery, and aggravated assault.
[3]Property crimes are offenses of burglary, larceny-theft, motor vehicle theft, and arson.
[4]Includes arson.

Table 43. — Total Arrests, Distribution by Race, 1993

[10,509 agencies; 1993 estimated population 213,093,000]

Offense charged	Total arrests					Percent distribution[1]				
	Total	White	Black	American Indian or Alaskan Native	Asian or Pacific Islander	Total	White	Black	American Indian or Alaskan Native	Asian or Pacific Islander
TOTAL	11,741,751	7,855,287	3,647,174	126,017	113,273	100.0	66.9	31.1	1.1	1.0
Murder and nonnegligent manslaughter....	20,243	8,243	11,656	131	213	100.0	40.7	57.6	.6	1.1
Forcible rape	32,469	18,473	13,419	321	256	100.0	56.9	41.3	1.0	.8
Robbery	153,281	55,893	95,164	635	1,589	100.0	36.5	62.1	.4	1.0
Aggravated assault	441,455	257,628	175,827	3,801	4,199	100.0	58.4	39.8	.9	1.0
Burglary	337,810	226,857	104,473	2,969	3,511	100.0	67.2	30.9	.9	1.0
Larceny-theft.........................	1,249,303	806,511	411,705	13,110	17,977	100.0	64.6	33.0	1.0	1.4
Motor vehicle theft....................	168,591	96,328	67,938	1,509	2,816	100.0	57.1	40.3	.9	1.7
Arson	16,073	11,990	3,784	147	152	100.0	74.6	23.5	.9	.9
Violent crime[2]	647,448	340,237	296,066	4,888	6,257	100.0	52.6	45.7	.8	1.0
Property crime[3]	1,771,777	1,141,686	587,900	17,735	24,456	100.0	64.4	33.2	1.0	1.4
Crime Index total[4]	2,419,225	1,481,923	883,966	22,623	30,713	100.0	61.3	36.5	.9	1.3
Other assaults	963,427	606,211	336,360	11,516	9,340	100.0	62.9	34.9	1.2	1.0
Forgery and counterfeiting	89,377	56,315	31,634	506	922	100.0	63.0	35.4	.6	1.0
Fraud................................	335,051	208,601	122,614	1,597	2,239	100.0	62.3	36.6	.5	.7
Embezzlement........................	10,914	7,357	3,380	45	132	100.0	67.4	31.0	.4	1.2
Stolen property; buying, receiving, possessing.........................	134,579	75,432	56,889	806	1,452	100.0	56.1	42.3	.6	1.1
Vandalism	260,724	194,940	59,820	2,890	3,074	100.0	74.8	22.9	1.1	1.2
Weapons; carrying, possessing, etc.	223,940	124,135	96,189	1,204	2,412	100.0	55.4	43.0	.5	1.1
Prostitution and commercialized vice	88,792	55,081	31,913	506	1,292	100.0	62.0	35.9	.6	1.5
Sex offenses (except forcible rape and prostitution)........................	87,581	67,435	18,304	888	954	100.0	77.0	20.9	1.0	1.1
Drug abuse violations..................	967,722	578,214	380,460	3,901	5,147	100.0	59.8	39.3	.4	.5
Gambling...........................	15,320	7,382	7,178	56	704	100.0	48.2	46.9	.4	4.6
Offenses against family and children	88,608	58,137	27,605	1,138	1,728	100.0	65.6	31.2	1.3	2.0
Driving under the influence	1,227,289	1,069,632	130,026	16,158	11,473	100.0	87.2	10.6	1.3	.9
Liquor laws..........................	417,340	352,567	52,533	9,658	2,582	100.0	84.5	12.6	2.3	.6
Drunkenness	604,462	481,885	107,863	12,869	1,845	100.0	79.7	17.8	2.1	.3
Disorderly conduct	606,586	391,969	203,533	7,975	3,109	100.0	64.6	33.6	1.3	.5
Vagrancy............................	24,654	13,945	10,148	459	102	100.0	56.6	41.2	1.9	.4
All other offenses (except traffic)	2,927,662	1,833,220	1,039,100	28,252	27,090	100.0	62.6	35.5	1.0	.9
Suspicion	12,125	5,690	6,304	70	61	100.0	46.9	52.0	.6	.5
Curfew and loitering law violations	85,156	67,091	15,382	949	1,734	100.0	78.8	18.1	1.1	2.0
Runaways............................	151,217	118,125	25,973	1,951	5,168	100.0	78.1	17.2	1.3	3.4

See footnotes at the end of table.

Table 43. — Total Arrests, Distribution by Race, 1993 — Continued

Offense charged	Arrests under 18					Percent distribution[1]				
	Total	White	Black	American Indian or Alaskan Native	Asian or Pacific Islander	Total	White	Black	American Indian or Alaskan Native	Asian or Pacific Islander
TOTAL	2,009,019	1,387,847	564,635	21,622	34,915	100.0	69.1	28.1	1.1	1.7
Murder and nonnegligent manslaughter....	3,281	1,181	2,043	16	41	100.0	36.0	62.3	.5	1.2
Forcible rape	5,290	2,921	2,299	38	32	100.0	55.2	43.5	.7	.6
Robbery	43,241	15,693	26,720	173	655	100.0	36.3	61.8	.4	1.5
Aggravated assault	67,662	37,328	28,964	580	790	100.0	55.2	42.8	.9	1.2
Burglary	115,818	86,046	26,656	1,360	1,756	100.0	74.3	23.0	1.2	1.5
Larceny-theft..........................	391,100	277,616	100,314	4,978	8,192	100.0	71.0	25.6	1.3	2.1
Motor vehicle theft.....................	75,201	42,326	30,479	862	1,534	100.0	56.3	40.5	1.1	2.0
Arson	7,938	6,360	1,401	73	104	100.0	80.1	17.6	.9	1.3
Violent crime[2].......................	119,474	57,123	60,026	807	1,518	100.0	47.8	50.2	.7	1.3
Property crime [3]	590,057	412,348	158,850	7,273	11,586	100.0	69.9	26.9	1.2	2.0
Crime Index total[4]	709,531	469,471	218,876	8,080	13,104	100.0	66.2	30.8	1.1	1.8
Other assaults	155,511	96,061	55,328	1,649	2,473	100.0	61.8	35.6	1.1	1.6
Forgery and counterfeiting	6,499	5,205	1,142	62	90	100.0	80.1	17.6	1.0	1.4
Fraud.................................	16,151	8,797	6,937	104	313	100.0	54.5	43.0	.6	1.9
Embezzlement.........................	615	450	157	1	7	100.0	73.2	25.5	.2	1.1
Stolen property; buying, receiving, possession..........................	36,417	20,796	14,731	328	562	100.0	57.1	40.5	.9	1.5
Vandalism	118,811	96,255	19,607	1,160	1,789	100.0	81.0	16.5	1.0	1.5
Weapons; carrying, possessing, etc.	52,303	32,218	19,050	312	723	100.0	61.6	36.4	.6	1.4
Prostitution and commercialized vice	993	666	309	5	13	100.0	67.1	31.1	.5	1.3
Sex offenses (except forcible rape and prostitution).........................	16,337	11,666	4,359	140	172	100.0	71.4	26.7	.9	1.1
Drug abuse violations....................	93,171	52,736	39,289	438	708	100.0	56.6	42.2	.5	.8
Gambling	1,166	230	922	2	12	100.0	19.7	79.1	.2	1.0
Offenses against family and children	3,921	2,951	820	41	109	100.0	75.3	20.9	1.0	2.8
Driving under the influence	10,706	9,783	594	241	88	100.0	91.4	5.5	2.3	.8
Liquor laws...........................	91,429	83,737	4,926	2,210	556	100.0	91.6	5.4	2.4	.6
Drunkenness	13,873	12,225	1,371	218	59	100.0	88.1	9.9	1.6	.4
Disorderly conduct	121,045	79,063	40,265	962	755	100.0	65.3	33.3	.8	.6
Vagrancy.............................	3,234	2,303	874	8	49	100.0	71.2	27.0	.2	1.5
All other offenses (except traffic)	319,549	217,018	93,363	2,747	6,421	100.0	67.9	29.2	.9	2.0
Suspicion	1,384	1,000	360	14	10	100.0	72.3	26.0	1.0	.7
Curfew and loitering law violations	85,156	67,091	15,382	949	1,734	100.0	78.8	18.1	1.1	2.0
Runaways.............................	151,217	118,125	25,973	1,951	5,168	100.0	78.1	17.2	1.3	3.4

See footnotes at the end of table.

Table 43. — Total Arrests, Distribution by Race, 1993 — Continued

Offense charged	Arrests 18 and over					Percent distribution[1]				
	Total	White	Black	American Indian or Alaskan Native	Asian or Pacific Islander	Total	White	Black	American Indian or Alaskan Native	Asian or Pacific Islander
TOTAL	9,732,732	6,467,440	3,082,539	104,395	78,358	100.0	66.5	31.7	1.1	.8
Murder and nonnegligent manslaughter....	16,962	7,062	9,613	115	172	100.0	41.6	56.7	.7	1.0
Forcible rape	27,179	15,552	11,120	283	224	100.0	57.2	40.9	1.0	.8
Robbery	110,040	40,200	68,444	462	934	100.0	36.5	62.2	.4	.8
Aggravated assault	373,793	220,300	146,863	3,221	3,409	100.0	58.9	39.3	.9	.9
Burglary..............................	221,992	140,811	77,817	1,609	1,755	100.0	63.4	35.1	.7	.8
Larceny-theft.........................	858,203	528,895	311,391	8,132	9,785	100.0	61.6	36.3	.9	1.1
Motor vehicle theft	93,390	54,002	37,459	647	1,282	100.0	57.8	40.1	.7	1.4
Arson	8,135	5,630	2,383	74	48	100.0	69.2	29.3	.9	.6
Violent crime[2]	527,974	283,114	236,040	4,081	4,739	100.0	53.6	44.7	.8	.9
Property crime [3]	1,181,720	729,338	429,050	10,462	12,870	100.0	61.7	36.3	.9	1.1
Crime Index total[4]	1,709,694	1,012,452	665,090	14,543	17,609	100.0	59.2	38.9	.9	1.0
Other assaults	807,916	510,150	281,032	9,867	6,867	100.0	63.1	34.8	1.2	.8
Forgery and counterfeiting	82,878	51,110	30,492	444	832	100.0	61.7	36.8	.5	1.0
Fraud..................................	318,900	199,804	115,677	1,493	1,926	100.0	62.7	36.3	.5	.6
Embezzlement.........................	10,299	6,907	3,223	44	125	100.0	67.1	31.3	.4	1.2
Stolen property; buying, receiving, possessing.	98,162	54,636	42,158	478	890	100.0	55.7	42.9	.5	.9
Vandalism	141,913	98,685	40,213	1,730	1,285	100.0	69.5	28.3	1.2	.9
Weapons; carrying, possessing, etc.	171,637	91,917	77,139	892	1,689	100.0	53.6	44.9	.5	1.0
Prostitution and commercialized vice	87,799	54,415	31,604	501	1,279	100.0	62.0	36.0	.6	1.5
Sex offenses (except forcible rape and prostitution).........................	71,244	55,769	13,945	748	782	100.0	78.3	19.6	1.0	1.1
Drug abuse violations...................	874,551	525,478	341,171	3,463	4,439	100.0	60.1	39.0	.4	.5
Gambling	14,154	7,152	6,256	54	692	100.0	50.5	44.2	.4	4.9
Offenses against family and children	84,687	55,186	26,785	1,097	1,619	100.0	65.2	31.6	1.3	1.9
Driving under the influence	1,216,583	1,059,849	129,432	15,917	11,385	100.0	87.1	10.6	1.3	.9
Liquor laws............................	325,911	268,830	47,607	7,448	2,026	100.0	82.5	14.6	2.3	.6
Drunkenness	590,589	469,660	106,492	12,651	1,786	100.0	79.5	18.0	2.1	.3
Disorderly conduct	485,541	312,906	163,268	7,013	2,354	100.0	64.4	33.6	1.4	.5
Vagrancy.............................	21,420	11,642	9,274	451	53	100.0	54.4	43.3	2.1	.2
All other offenses (except traffic)	2,608,113	1,616,202	945,737	25,505	20,669	100.0	62.0	36.3	1.0	.8
Suspicion	10,741	4,690	5,944	56	51	100.0	43.7	55.3	.5	.5
Curfew and loitering law violations	....	....	....	....	....	....	....	....	....	....
Runaways.............................	....	....	....	....	....	....	....	....	....	....

[1]Because of rounding, the percentages may not add to total.
[2]Violent crimes are offenses of murder, forcible rape, robbery, and aggravated assault.
[3]Property crimes are offenses of burglary, larceny-theft, motor vehicle theft, and arson.
[4]Includes arson.

Table 44. — City Arrest Trends, 1992-1993

[6,571 agencies; 1993 estimated population 137,365,000; 1992 population 136,319,000]

Offense charged	Number of persons arrested								
	Total all ages			Under 18 years of age			18 years of age and over		
	1992	1993	Percent change	1992	1993	Percent change	1992	1993	Percent change
TOTAL..........................	8,643,239	8,512,382	-1.5	1,516,942	1,594,654	+5.1	7,126,297	6,917,728	-2.9
Murder and nonnegligent manslaughter	14,666	15,215	+3.7	2,326	2,672	+14.9	12,340	12,543	+1.6
Forcible rape................................	23,868	22,882	-4.1	3,906	3,838	-1.7	19,962	19,044	-4.6
Robbery....................................	133,423	132,384	-.8	36,175	38,446	+6.3	97,248	93,938	-3.4
Aggravated assault...........................	325,438	327,446	+.6	49,734	52,830	+6.2	275,704	274,616	-.4
Burglary...................................	254,476	239,651	-5.8	84,769	80,877	-4.6	169,707	158,774	-6.4
Larceny-theft..............................	1,026,885	996,174	-3.0	321,728	317,645	-1.3	705,157	678,529	-3.8
Motor vehicle theft	133,567	128,199	-4.0	59,946	58,349	-2.7	73,621	69,850	-5.1
Arson.....................................	11,175	11,243	+.6	5,805	6,017	+3.7	5,370	5,226	-2.7
Violent crime[1]	497,395	497,927	+.1	92,141	97,786	+6.1	405,254	400,141	-1.3
Property crime [2].........................	1,426,103	1,375,267	-3.6	472,248	462,888	-2.0	953,855	912,379	-4.3
Crime Index total[3]	1,923,498	1,873,194	-2.6	564,389	560,674	-.7	1,359,109	1,312,520	-3.4
Other assaults..............................	675,673	706,399	+4.5	112,705	122,380	+8.6	562,968	584,019	+3.7
Forgery and counterfeiting....................	60,955	63,891	+4.8	5,191	5,024	-3.2	55,764	58,867	+5.6
Fraud......................................	196,186	200,911	+2.4	13,163	14,368	+9.2	183,023	186,543	+1.9
Embezzlement	8,122	7,681	-5.4	491	499	+1.6	7,631	7,182	-5.9
Stolen property; buying, receiving, possessing	107,028	103,968	-2.9	29,770	29,494	-.9	77,258	74,474	-3.6
Vandalism..................................	192,617	195,494	+1.5	86,905	90,754	+4.4	105,712	104,740	-.9
Weapons; carrying, possessing, etc.	161,251	173,810	+7.8	38,283	42,814	+11.8	122,968	130,996	+6.5
Prostitution and commercialized vice............	82,111	79,705	-2.9	988	875	-11.4	81,123	78,830	-2.8
Sex offenses (except forcible rape and prostitution)	63,561	60,423	-4.9	11,536	11,279	-2.2	52,025	49,144	-5.5
Drug abuse violations	705,871	738,713	+4.7	61,751	76,806	+24.4	644,120	661,907	+2.8
Gambling..................................	13,338	12,996	-2.6	1,048	1,061	+1.2	12,290	11,935	-2.9
Offenses against family and children............	42,344	45,172	+6.7	2,840	2,782	-2.0	39,504	42,390	+7.3
Driving under the influence...................	742,489	703,888	-5.2	6,803	6,315	-7.2	735,686	697,573	-5.2
Liquor laws................................	321,377	310,858	-3.3	66,028	64,835	-1.8	255,349	246,023	-3.7
Drunkenness................................	529,055	493,200	-6.8	12,171	11,655	-4.2	516,884	481,545	-6.8
Disorderly conduct..........................	499,137	501,000	+.4	92,512	103,540	+11.9	406,625	397,460	-2.3
Vagrancy..................................	28,020	21,816	-22.1	3,017	2,644	-12.4	25,003	19,172	-23.3
All other offenses (except traffic)...............	2,116,405	2,026,073	-4.3	233,150	253,665	+8.8	1,883,255	1,772,408	-5.9
Suspicion (not included in totals)...............	13,620	9,663	-29.1	4,640	1,133	-75.6	8,980	8,530	-5.0
Curfew and loitering law violations.............	64,511	77,629	+20.3	64,511	77,629	+20.3	....	....	....
Runaways..................................	109,690	115,561	+5.4	109,690	115,561	+5.4	....	....	....

[1]Violent crimes are offenses of murder, forcible rape, robbery, and aggravated assault.

[2]Property crimes are offenses of burglary, larceny-theft, motor vehicle theft, and arson.

[3]Includes arson.

Table 45. — City Arrest Trends, Sex, 1992-1993

[6,571 agencies; 1993 estimated population 137,365,000; 1992 estimated population 136,319,000]

Offense charged	Males						Females					
	Total			Under 18			Total			Under 18		
	1992	1993	Percent change	1992	1993	Percent change	1992	1993	Percent change	1992	1993	Percent change
TOTAL	6,981,435	6,830,856	-2.2	1,164,333	1,209,876	+3.9	1,661,804	1,681,526	+1.2	352,609	384,778	+9.1
Murder and nonnegligent manslaughter...	13,321	13,847	+3.9	2,201	2,516	+14.3	1,345	1,368	+1.7	125	156	+24.8
Forcible rape	23,613	22,597	-4.3	3,835	3,772	-1.6	255	285	+11.8	71	66	-7.0
Robbery	121,931	120,692	-1.0	33,030	34,959	+5.8	11,492	11,692	+1.7	3,145	3,487	+10.9
Aggravated assault	274,843	274,178	-.2	41,267	43,212	+4.7	50,595	53,268	+5.3	8,467	9,618	+13.6
Burglary	229,419	214,752	-6.4	76,590	72,753	-5.0	25,057	24,899	-.6	8,179	8,124	-.7
Larceny-theft	690,241	663,826	-3.8	223,744	215,598	-3.6	336,644	332,348	-1.3	97,984	102,047	+4.1
Motor vehicle theft	119,393	113,286	-5.1	52,750	50,662	-4.0	14,174	14,913	+5.2	7,196	7,687	+6.8
Arson..............................	9,643	9,596	-.5	5,174	5,281	+2.1	1,532	1,647	+7.5	631	736	+16.6
Violent crime[1]	433,708	431,314	-.6	80,333	84,459	+5.1	63,687	66,613	+4.6	11,808	13,327	+12.9
Property crime [2]	1,048,696	1,001,460	-4.5	358,258	344,294	-3.9	377,407	373,807	-1.0	113,990	118,594	+4.0
Crime Index total[3]	1,482,404	1,432,774	-3.3	438,591	428,753	-2.2	441,094	440,420	-.2	125,798	131,921	+4.9
Other assaults	559,184	578,989	+3.5	84,631	90,119	+6.5	116,489	127,410	+9.4	28,074	32,261	+14.9
Forgery and counterfeiting	39,925	41,895	+4.9	3,404	3,283	-3.6	21,030	21,996	+4.6	1,787	1,741	-2.6
Fraud..............................	122,846	128,505	+4.6	9,888	10,672	+7.9	73,340	72,406	-1.3	3,275	3,696	+12.9
Embezzlement.......................	4,852	4,452	-8.2	283	293	+3.5	3,270	3,229	-1.3	208	206	-1.0
Stolen property; buying, receiving, possessing.........................	93,571	90,585	-3.2	26,608	26,267	-1.3	13,457	13,383	-.5	3,162	3,227	+2.1
Vandalism..........................	170,517	171,389	+.5	79,275	81,878	+3.3	22,100	24,105	+9.1	7,630	8,876	+16.3
Weapons; carrying, possessing, etc.	149,036	160,657	+7.8	35,479	39,330	+10.9	12,215	13,153	+7.7	2,804	3,484	+24.3
Prostitution and commercialized vice	28,059	27,448	-2.2	478	369	-22.8	54,052	52,257	-3.3	510	506	-.8
Sex offenses (except forcible rape and prostitution)........................	57,649	54,558	-5.4	10,707	10,357	-3.3	5,912	5,865	-.8	829	922	+11.2
Drug abuse violations..................	590,517	619,355	+4.9	55,285	68,629	+24.1	115,354	119,358	+3.5	6,466	8,177	+26.5
Gambling	11,571	11,172	-3.4	976	1,011	+3.6	1,767	1,824	+3.2	72	50	-30.6
Offenses against family and children	31,984	33,481	+4.7	1,793	1,764	-1.6	10,360	11,691	+12.8	1,047	1,018	-2.8
Driving under the influence	635,950	600,745	-5.5	5,860	5,382	-8.2	106,539	103,143	-3.2	943	933	-1.1
Liquor laws.........................	261,308	251,925	-3.6	47,590	46,635	-2.0	60,069	58,933	-1.9	18,438	18,200	-1.3
Drunkenness	472,360	438,662	-7.1	10,188	9,716	-4.6	56,695	54,538	-3.8	1,983	1,939	-2.2
Disorderly conduct	393,843	395,806	+.5	72,143	79,777	+10.6	105,294	105,194	-.1	20,369	23,763	+16.7
Vagrancy...........................	25,367	19,290	-24.0	2,572	2,234	-13.1	2,653	2,526	-4.8	445	410	-7.9
All other offenses (except traffic)	1,756,569	1,664,788	-5.2	184,659	199,027	+7.8	359,836	361,285	+.4	48,491	54,638	+12.7
Suspicion (not included in totals)	11,173	8,090	-27.6	3,554	932	-73.8	2,447	1,573	-35.7	1,086	201	-81.5
Curfew and loitering law violations	47,435	55,829	+17.7	47,435	55,829	+17.7	17,076	21,800	+27.7	17,076	21,800	+27.7
Runaways	46,488	48,551	+4.4	46,488	48,551	+4.4	63,202	67,010	+6.0	63,202	67,010	+6.0

[1]Violent crimes are offenses of murder, forcible rape, robbery, and aggravated assault.
[2]Property crimes are offenses of burglary, larceny-theft, motor vehicle theft, and arson.
[3]Includes arson.

Table 46. — City Arrests, Distribution by Age, 1993

[7,446 agencies; 1993 estimated population 145,550,000]

Offense charged	Total all ages	Ages under 15	Ages under 18	Ages 18 and over	Age								
					Under 10	10-12	13-14	15	16	17	18	19	20
TOTAL........................	9,019,601	596,288	1,681,821	7,337,780	30,013	139,541	426,734	322,957	375,679	386,897	402,495	386,248	363,521
Percent distribution[1]...............	100.0	6.6	18.6	81.4	.3	1.5	4.7	3.6	4.2	4.3	4.5	4.3	4.0
Murder and nonnegligent manslaughter....	15,756	323	2,766	12,990	4	19	300	483	826	1,134	1,299	1,260	1,078
Forcible rape..........................	24,125	1,622	4,052	20,073	78	414	1,130	736	829	865	1,007	919	886
Robbery..............................	136,203	11,506	39,543	96,660	208	2,157	9,141	8,222	9,899	9,916	9,381	7,965	6,478
Aggravated assault....................	340,401	17,686	55,287	285,114	820	4,091	12,775	10,625	13,116	13,860	14,096	13,410	13,155
Burglary.............................	249,485	35,476	84,757	164,728	2,315	9,108	24,053	16,416	17,213	15,652	14,771	11,690	9,139
Larceny—theft.......................	1,053,135	156,060	337,513	715,622	8,726	45,386	101,948	61,580	62,939	56,934	51,050	41,248	33,442
Motor vehicle theft...................	134,296	18,563	61,513	72,783	176	2,227	16,160	15,164	15,365	12,421	9,323	7,049	5,591
Arson...............................	11,944	4,268	6,389	5,555	757	1,353	2,158	911	680	530	416	322	253
Violent crime[2]....................	516,485	31,137	101,648	414,837	1,110	6,681	23,346	20,066	24,670	25,775	25,783	23,554	21,597
Percent distribution[1]...............	100.0	6.0	19.7	80.3	.2	1.3	4.5	3.9	4.8	5.0	5.0	4.6	4.2
Property crime[3]..................	1,448,860	214,367	490,172	958,688	11,974	58,074	144,319	94,071	96,197	85,537	75,560	60,309	48,425
Percent distribution[1]...............	100.0	14.8	33.8	66.2	.8	4.0	10.0	6.5	6.6	5.9	5.2	4.2	3.3
Crime Index total[4]..................	1,965,345	245,504	591,820	1,373,525	13,084	64,755	167,665	114,137	120,867	111,312	101,343	83,863	70,022
Percent distribution[1]...............	100.0	12.5	30.1	69.9	.7	3.3	8.5	5.8	6.1	5.7	5.2	4.3	3.6
Other assaults.........................	755,369	54,729	129,587	625,782	2,758	14,555	37,416	24,286	25,805	24,767	24,672	24,973	25,491
Forgery and counterfeiting..............	67,120	868	5,322	61,798	15	198	655	831	1,406	2,217	2,971	3,410	3,424
Fraud................................	205,752	3,889	14,616	191,136	94	631	3,164	3,537	3,074	4,116	6,247	7,905	8,688
Embezzlement........................	7,874	65	511	7,363	6	21	38	43	135	268	382	465	449
Stolen property; buying, receiving, possessing...........................	108,162	9,123	30,868	77,294	214	1,735	7,174	6,474	7,500	7,771	7,942	6,541	5,473
Vandalism...........................	209,805	47,736	96,837	112,968	4,831	14,099	28,806	17,285	17,265	14,551	11,173	8,240	6,780
Weapons; carrying, possessing, etc.	182,359	13,531	44,583	137,776	472	2,625	10,434	8,579	10,684	11,789	12,792	11,279	9,967
Prostitution and commercialized vice	83,996	135	920	83,076	2	18	115	117	214	454	1,368	1,995	2,413
Sex offenses (except forcible rape and prostitution).........................	63,604	6,218	11,819	51,785	507	1,716	3,995	2,037	1,851	1,713	1,728	1,590	1,657
Drug abuse violations..................	762,947	12,820	79,483	683,464	150	1,240	11,430	14,422	22,905	29,336	38,648	37,263	35,602
Gambling............................	13,238	202	1,088	12,150	8	25	169	198	283	405	531	451	449
Offenses against family and children	49,607	968	2,972	46,635	98	189	681	606	683	715	1,360	1,366	1,516
Driving under the influence	753,463	226	6,746	746,717	72	22	132	343	1,756	4,421	10,962	15,673	19,787
Liquor laws..........................	333,528	7,660	70,065	263,463	95	603	6,962	10,700	20,214	31,491	48,461	47,794	39,350
Drunkenness.........................	507,479	1,715	12,018	495,461	76	161	1,478	1,799	3,043	5,461	10,571	11,817	12,891
Disorderly conduct....................	530,697	36,923	109,319	421,378	1,522	8,434	26,967	21,619	24,621	26,156	27,060	24,298	22,869
Vagrancy............................	22,598	761	2,740	19,858	21	130	610	624	683	672	965	751	609
All other offenses (except traffic)	2,185,498	73,513	268,154	1,917,344	4,300	15,041	54,172	45,159	65,668	83,814	92,941	96,147	95,694
Suspicion	10,021	413	1,214	8,807	30	116	267	306	250	245	378	427	390
Curfew and loitering law violations	81,125	24,378	81,125	....	332	3,554	20,492	19,055	21,921	15,771	....	....	....
Runaways............................	120,014	54,911	120,014	....	1,326	9,673	43,912	30,800	24,851	9,452	....	....	....

See footnotes at end of table.

Table 46.—City Arrests, Distribution by Age, 1993 — Continued

Offense charged	Age												
	21	22	23	24	25-29	30-34	35-39	40-44	45-49	50-54	55-59	60-64	65 and over
TOTAL....................	349,124	346,797	327,883	303,726	1,392,058	1,288,761	938,215	564,966	302,020	163,838	89,686	54,404	64,038
Percent distribution[1]..............	3.9	3.8	3.6	3.4	15.4	14.3	10.4	6.3	3.3	1.8	1.0	.6	.7
Murder and nonnegligent manslaughter....	932	872	739	585	2,224	1,456	1,024	602	358	241	126	76	118
Forcible rape..........................	954	884	870	859	4,093	3,762	2,607	1,474	807	392	232	170	157
Robbery.............................	5,909	5,655	5,147	4,607	20,687	15,612	8,823	3,896	1,482	570	196	110	142
Aggravated assault.....................	13,511	13,317	12,888	11,962	57,090	51,613	36,750	21,763	11,459	6,135	3,380	2,096	2,489
Burglary............................	8,496	7,900	7,485	6,990	33,064	29,806	19,490	9,390	3,744	1,516	625	281	341
Larceny-theft........................	30,630	29,648	27,572	26,167	126,195	124,083	94,639	57,427	29,719	16,294	9,344	6,694	11,470
Motor vehicle theft....................	4,630	4,251	3,665	3,315	13,550	10,390	5,992	2,910	1,178	527	191	89	132
Arson...............................	259	224	181	165	883	982	765	495	246	165	82	55	62
Violent crime[2].....................	21,306	20,728	19,644	18,013	84,094	72,443	49,204	27,735	14,106	7,338	3,934	2,452	2,906
Percent distribution[1]...............	4.1	4.0	3.8	3.5	16.3	14.0	9.5	5.4	2.7	1.4	.8	.5	.6
Property crime[3]...................	44,015	42,023	38,903	36,637	173,692	165,261	120,886	70,222	34,887	18,502	10,242	7,119	12,005
Percent distribution[1]...............	3.0	2.9	2.7	2.5	12.0	11.4	8.3	4.8	2.4	1.3	.7	.5	.8
Crime Index total[4].................	65,321	62,751	58,547	54,650	257,786	237,704	170,090	97,957	48,993	25,840	14,176	9,571	14,911
Percent distribution[1]...............	3.3	3.2	3.0	2.8	13.1	12.1	8.7	5.0	2.5	1.3	.7	.5	.8
Other assaults........................	28,167	29,548	28,968	27,853	132,545	122,386	83,403	47,033	24,112	12,282	6,397	3,598	4,354
Forgery and counterfeiting..............	3,165	3,233	3,132	2,837	12,852	11,272	7,904	4,212	1,861	821	339	192	173
Fraud................................	8,822	9,209	9,111	8,926	39,431	34,772	25,780	16,016	8,282	3,862	1,909	1,046	1,130
Embezzlement........................	455	455	367	323	1,421	1,174	777	531	273	137	76	50	28
Stolen property; buying, receiving, possessing..........................	4,767	4,296	3,743	3,351	13,937	11,595	7,735	4,184	2,012	842	410	230	236
Vandalism...........................	6,604	6,168	5,728	4,908	21,469	18,197	11,627	6,020	3,011	1,386	693	420	544
Weapons; carrying, possessing, etc.	9,633	8,939	7,693	6,334	24,026	17,625	11,984	7,293	4,392	2,435	1,439	863	1,082
Prostitution and commercialized vice	2,849	3,563	4,149	3,966	20,826	19,668	11,793	5,431	2,417	1,134	638	397	469
Sex offenses (except forcible rape and prostitution)	1,749	1,853	1,831	1,872	9,270	9,492	7,390	4,877	3,155	1,913	1,248	901	1,259
Drug abuse violations...................	34,053	34,187	32,815	30,366	140,408	127,802	88,944	48,255	20,275	8,549	3,511	1,610	1,176
Gambling............................	405	364	355	305	1,555	1,448	1,482	1,264	1,008	858	624	488	563
Offenses against family and children	1,763	1,909	1,885	1,918	9,624	9,769	7,446	4,125	2,004	930	488	239	293
Driving under the influence	29,603	31,811	31,716	30,276	143,814	142,946	109,810	72,234	45,500	27,095	15,790	9,911	9,789
Liquor laws..........................	12,568	9,740	7,910	6,308	23,344	21,256	16,884	11,882	7,297	4,504	2,819	1,705	1,641
Drunkenness.........................	17,458	17,515	16,692	16,088	81,199	91,435	79,217	56,149	34,278	21,630	12,943	7,862	7,716
Disorderly conduct	24,595	23,880	21,440	19,246	78,491	69,067	48,028	28,165	15,537	8,248	4,353	2,714	3,387
Vagrancy............................	599	555	588	579	2,683	3,777	3,329	2,298	1,411	940	371	229	174
All other offenses (except traffic)	96,163	96,431	90,793	83,257	375,594	335,683	243,344	146,335	75,878	40,286	21,396	12,336	15,066
Suspicion	385	390	420	363	1,783	1,693	1,248	705	324	146	66	42	47
Curfew and loitering law violations........	....	....	....	....	....	....	....	....	....	....	....	....	....
Runaways............................	....	....	....	....	....	....	....	....	....	....	....	....	....

[1]Because of rounding, the percentages may not add to total.
[2]Violent crimes are offenses of murder, forcible rape, robbery, and aggravated assault.
[3]Property crimes are offenses of burglary, larceny-theft, motor vehicle theft, and arson.
[4]Includes arson.

Table 47. — City Arrests of Persons under 15, 18, 21, and 25 Years of Age, 1993

[7,446 agencies; estimated population 145,550,000]

Offense charged	Total all ages	Number of persons arrested				Percent of total all ages			
		Under 15	Under 18	Under 21	Under 25	Under 15	Under 18	Under 21	Under 25
TOTAL..........................	9,019,601	596,288	1,681,821	2,834,085	4,161,615	6.6	18.6	31.4	46.1
Murder and nonnegligent manslaughter...................	15,756	323	2,766	6,403	9,531	2.1	17.6	40.6	60.5
Forcible rape...........................	24,125	1,622	4,052	6,864	10,431	6.7	16.8	28.5	43.2
Robbery..............................	136,203	11,506	39,543	63,367	84,685	8.4	29.0	46.5	62.2
Aggravated assault	340,401	17,686	55,287	95,948	147,626	5.2	16.2	28.2	43.4
Burglary..............................	249,485	35,476	84,757	120,357	151,228	14.2	34.0	48.2	60.6
Larceny-theft..........................	1,053,135	156,060	337,513	463,253	577,270	14.8	32.0	44.0	54.8
Motor vehicle theft.....................	134,296	18,563	61,513	83,476	99,337	13.8	45.8	62.2	74.0
Arson	11,944	4,268	6,389	7,380	8,209	35.7	53.5	61.8	68.7
Violent crime[1].........................	516,485	31,137	101,648	172,582	252,273	6.0	19.7	33.4	48.8
Property crime[2]........................	1,448,860	214,367	490,172	674,466	836,044	14.8	33.8	46.6	57.7
Crime Index total[3]	1,965,345	245,504	591,820	847,048	1,088,317	12.5	30.1	43.1	55.4
Other assaults........................	755,369	54,729	129,587	204,723	319,259	7.2	17.2	27.1	42.3
Forgery and counterfeiting..............	67,120	868	5,322	15,127	27,494	1.3	7.9	22.5	41.0
Fraud	205,752	3,889	14,616	37,456	73,524	1.9	7.1	18.2	35.7
Embezzlement.........................	7,874	65	511	1,807	3,407	.8	6.5	22.9	43.3
Stolen property; buying, receiving, possessing	108,162	9,123	30,868	50,824	66,981	8.4	28.5	47.0	61.9
Vandalism	209,805	47,736	96,837	123,030	146,438	22.8	46.2	58.6	69.8
Weapons; carrying, possessing, etc.	182,359	13,531	44,583	78,621	111,220	7.4	24.4	43.1	61.0
Prostitution and commercialized vice....................	83,996	135	920	6,696	21,223	.2	1.1	8.0	25.3
Sex offenses (except forcible rape and prostitution)	63,604	6,218	11,819	16,794	24,099	9.8	18.6	26.4	37.9
Drug abuse violations.................	762,947	12,820	79,483	190,996	322,417	1.7	10.4	25.0	42.3
Gambling.............................	13,238	202	1,088	2,519	3,948	1.5	8.2	19.0	29.8
Offenses against family and children	49,607	968	2,972	7,214	14,689	2.0	6.0	14.5	29.6
Driving under the influence	753,463	226	6,746	53,168	176,574	[4]	.9	7.1	23.4
Liquor laws	333,528	7,660	70,065	205,670	242,196	2.3	21.0	61.7	72.6
Drunkenness..........................	507,479	1,715	12,018	47,297	115,050	.3	2.4	9.3	22.7
Disorderly conduct....................	530,697	36,923	109,319	183,546	272,707	7.0	20.6	34.6	51.4
Vagrancy.............................	22,598	761	2,740	5,065	7,386	3.4	12.1	22.4	32.7
All other offenses (except traffic).....................	2,185,498	73,513	268,154	552,936	919,580	3.4	12.3	25.3	42.1
Suspicion	10,021	413	1,214	2,409	3,967	4.1	12.1	24.0	39.6
Curfew and loitering law violations....................	81,125	24,378	81,125	81,125	81,125	30.0	100.0	100.0	100.0
Runaways.............................	120,014	54,911	120,014	120,014	120,014	45.8	100.0	100.0	100.0

[1]Violent crimes are offenses of murder, forcible rape, robbery, and aggravated assault.
[2]Property crimes are offenses of burglary, larceny-theft, motor vehicle theft, and arson.
[3]Includes arson.
[4]Less than one-tenth of 1 percent.

242

Table 48. — City Arrests, Distribution by Sex, 1993

[7,446 agencies; 1993 estimated population 145,550,000]

Offense charged	Number of persons arrested			Percent male	Percent female	Percent distribution[1]		
	Total	Male	Female			Total	Male	Female
TOTAL..	9,019,601	7,234,404	1,785,197	80.2	19.8	100.0	100.0	100.0
Murder and nonnegligent manslaughter...............................	15,756	14,344	1,412	91.0	9.0	.2	.2	.1
Forcible rape...	24,125	23,809	316	98.7	1.3	.3	.3	[2]
Robbery...	136,203	124,146	12,057	91.1	8.9	1.5	1.7	.7
Aggravated assault.......................................	340,401	285,196	55,205	83.8	16.2	3.8	3.9	3.1
Burglary..	249,485	223,766	25,719	89.7	10.3	2.8	3.1	1.4
Larceny-theft..	1,053,135	702,071	351,064	66.7	33.3	11.7	9.7	19.7
Motor vehicle theft......................................	134,296	118,649	15,647	88.3	11.7	1.5	1.6	.9
Arson..	11,944	10,191	1,753	85.3	14.7	.1	.1	.1
Violent crime[3]...	516,485	447,495	68,990	86.6	13.4	5.7	6.2	3.9
Property crime[4]...	1,448,860	1,054,677	394,183	72.8	27.2	16.1	14.6	22.1
Crime Index total[5]....................................	1,965,345	1,502,172	463,173	76.4	23.6	21.8	20.8	25.9
Other assaults..	755,369	619,815	135,554	82.1	17.9	8.4	8.6	7.6
Forgery and counterfeiting.................................	67,120	43,878	23,242	65.4	34.6	.7	.6	1.3
Fraud...	205,752	131,457	74,295	63.9	36.1	2.3	1.8	4.2
Embezzlement...	7,874	4,575	3,299	58.1	41.9	.1	.1	.2
Stolen property; buying, receiving, possessing	108,162	94,119	14,043	87.0	13.0	1.2	1.3	.8
Vandalism...	209,805	183,820	25,985	87.6	12.4	2.3	2.5	1.5
Weapons; carrying, possessing, etc	182,359	168,328	14,031	92.3	7.7	2.0	2.3	.8
Prostitution and commercialized vice.........................	83,996	29,386	54,610	35.0	65.0	.9	.4	3.1
Sex offenses (except forcible rape and prostitution)	63,604	57,572	6,032	90.5	9.5	.7	.8	.3
Drug abuse violations	762,947	639,957	122,990	83.9	16.1	8.5	8.8	6.9
Gambling..	13,238	11,387	1,851	86.0	14.0	.1	.2	.1
Offenses against family and children	49,607	36,856	12,751	74.3	25.7	.5	.5	.7
Driving under the influence	753,463	642,113	111,350	85.2	14.8	8.4	8.9	6.2
Liquor laws..	333,528	270,130	63,398	81.0	19.0	3.7	3.7	3.6
Drunkenness...	507,479	451,122	56,357	88.9	11.1	5.6	6.2	3.2
Disorderly conduct.......................................	530,697	419,623	111,074	79.1	20.9	5.9	5.8	6.2
Vagrancy..	22,598	19,981	2,617	88.4	11.6	.3	.3	.1
All other offenses (except traffic)...........................	2,185,498	1,790,662	394,836	81.9	18.1	24.2	24.8	22.1
Suspicion..	10,021	8,406	1,615	83.9	16.1	.1	.1	.1
Curfew and loitering law violations..........................	81,125	58,454	22,671	72.1	27.9	.9	.8	1.3
Runaways..	120,014	50,591	69,423	42.2	57.8	1.3	.7	3.9

[1]Because of rounding, the percentages may not add to total.
[2]Less than one-tenth of 1 percent.
[3]Violent crimes are offenses of murder, forcible rape, robbery, and aggravated assault.
[4]Property crimes are offenses of burglary, larceny-theft, motor vehicle theft, and arson.
[5]Includes arson.

Table 49. — City Arrests, Distribution by Race, 1993

[7,444 agencies; 1993 estimates population 145,549,000]

Offense charged	Total arrests					Percent distribution[1]				
	Total	White	Black	American Indian or Alaskan Native	Asian or Pacific Islander	Total	White	Black	American Indian or Alaskan Native	Asian or Pacific Islander
TOTAL	**9,000,265**	**5,776,804**	**3,039,675**	**91,007**	**92,779**	**100.0**	**64.2**	**33.8**	**1.0**	**1.0**
Murder and nonnegligent manslaughter...	15,718	5,381	10,070	89	178	100.0	34.2	64.1	.6	1.1
Forcible rape	24,089	12,350	11,353	167	219	100.0	51.3	47.1	.7	.9
Robbery	135,966	47,892	86,082	538	1,454	100.0	35.2	63.3	.4	1.1
Aggravated assault	339,932	185,214	148,566	2,434	3,718	100.0	54.5	43.7	.7	1.1
Burglary	249,229	157,248	87,400	1,774	2,807	100.0	63.1	35.1	.7	1.1
Larceny-theft	1,051,437	668,103	355,988	11,545	15,801	100.0	63.5	33.9	1.1	1.5
Motor vehicle theft	134,170	72,115	58,525	1,075	2,455	100.0	53.7	43.6	.8	1.8
Arson................................	11,913	8,473	3,206	96	138	100.0	71.1	26.9	.8	1.2
Violent crime[2]	515,705	250,837	256,071	3,228	5,569	100.0	48.6	49.7	.6	1.1
Property crime[3]	1,446,749	905,939	505,119	14,490	21,201	100.0	62.6	34.9	1.0	1.5
Crime Index total[4]	1,962,454	1,156,776	761,190	17,718	26,770	100.0	58.9	38.8	.9	1.4
Other assaults	753,880	449,734	287,932	8,601	7,613	100.0	59.7	38.2	1.1	1.0
Forgery and counterfeiting	67,036	40,488	25,353	396	799	100.0	60.4	37.8	.6	1.2
Fraud................................	205,458	120,209	82,406	932	1,911	100.0	58.5	40.1	.5	.9
Embezzlement........................	7,873	5,128	2,625	31	89	100.0	65.1	33.3	.4	1.1
Stolen property; buying, receiving, possessing..........................	107,897	56,773	49,273	592	1,259	100.0	52.6	45.7	.5	1.2
Vandalism............................	209,359	151,148	53,372	2,165	2,674	100.0	72.2	25.5	1.0	1.3
Weapons; carrying, possessing, etc.	181,949	95,167	83,835	889	2,058	100.0	52.3	46.1	.5	1.1
Prostitution and commercialized vice	83,942	51,347	30,876	493	1,226	100.0	61.2	36.8	.6	1.5
Sex offenses (except forcible rape and prostitution)........................	63,531	46,645	15,478	591	817	100.0	73.4	24.4	.9	1.3
Drug abuse violations..................	762,246	427,212	328,317	2,577	4,140	100.0	56.0	43.1	.3	.5
Gambling............................	13,230	5,963	6,609	44	614	100.0	45.1	50.0	.3	4.6
Offenses against family and children	49,366	32,802	14,422	593	1,549	100.0	66.4	29.2	1.2	3.1
Driving under the influence	752,102	653,472	83,008	9,330	6,292	100.0	86.9	11.0	1.2	.8
Liquor laws..........................	331,934	275,215	47,087	7,578	2,054	100.0	82.9	14.2	2.3	.6
Drunkenness	507,068	396,429	98,022	11,077	1,540	100.0	78.2	19.3	2.2	.3
Disorderly conduct	529,910	332,596	188,664	5,916	2,734	100.0	62.8	35.6	1.1	.5
Vagrancy............................	22,446	12,368	9,563	437	78	100.0	55.1	42.6	1.9	.3
All other offenses (except traffic)	2,178,532	1,308,874	827,972	18,920	22,766	100.0	60.1	38.0	.9	1.0
Suspicion	10,014	3,934	6,015	13	52	100.0	39.3	60.1	.1	.5
Curfew and loitering law violations	80,931	63,933	15,010	778	1,210	100.0	79.0	18.5	1.0	1.5
Runaways............................	119,107	90,591	22,646	1,336	4,534	100.0	76.1	19.0	1.1	3.8

See footnotes at end of table.

Table 49. — City Arrests, Distribution by Race, 1993 — Continued

Offense charged	Arrests under 18					Percent distribution[1]				
	Total	White	Black	American Indian or Alaskan Native	Asian or Pacific Islander	Total	White	Black	American Indian or Alaskan Native	Asian or Pacific Islander
TOTAL	1,677,142	1,130,523	500,179	16,464	29,976	100.0	67.4	29.8	1.0	1.8
Murder and nonnegligent manslaughter...	2,766	915	1,804	8	39	100.0	33.1	65.2	.3	1.4
Forcible rape	4,048	2,038	1,969	19	22	100.0	50.3	48.6	.5	.5
Robbery	39,450	14,108	24,580	157	605	100.0	35.8	62.3	.4	1.5
Aggravated assault	55,231	29,296	24,837	394	704	100.0	53.0	45.0	.7	1.3
Burglary	84,654	60,436	22,013	811	1,394	100.0	71.4	26.0	1.0	1.6
Larceny-theft.........................	336,780	237,288	87,839	4,454	7,199	100.0	70.5	26.1	1.3	2.1
Motor vehicle theft	61,433	32,855	26,675	630	1,273	100.0	53.5	43.4	1.0	2.1
Arson................................	6,380	5,006	1,225	53	96	100.0	78.5	19.2	.8	1.5
Violent crime[2]	101,495	46,357	53,190	578	1,370	100.0	45.7	52.4	.6	1.3
Property crime[3]..................	489,247	335,585	137,752	5,948	9,962	100.0	68.6	28.2	1.2	2.0
Crime Index total[4]	590,742	381,942	190,942	6,526	11,332	100.0	64.7	32.3	1.1	1.9
Other assaults	128,941	77,461	48,128	1,250	2,102	100.0	60.1	37.3	1.0	1.6
Forgery and counterfeiting	5,318	4,234	962	50	72	100.0	79.6	18.1	.9	1.4
Fraud................................	14,610	7,535	6,680	96	299	100.0	51.6	45.7	.7	2.0
Embezzlement.......................	511	369	135	1	6	100.0	72.2	26.4	.2	1.2
Stolen property; buying, receiving, possessing.........................	30,851	16,932	13,158	281	480	100.0	54.9	42.7	.9	1.6
Vandalism...........................	96,594	76,586	17,629	841	1,538	100.0	79.3	18.3	.9	1.6
Weapons; carrying, possessing, etc.	44,549	26,929	16,738	256	626	100.0	60.4	37.6	.6	1.4
Prostitution and commercialized vice	919	604	297	5	13	100.0	65.7	32.3	.5	1.4
Sex offenses (except forcible rape and prostitution).......................	11,788	7,947	3,623	70	148	100.0	67.4	30.7	.6	1.3
Drug abuse violations..................	79,366	42,938	35,568	312	548	100.0	54.1	44.8	.4	.7
Gambling	1,088	211	866	2	9	100.0	19.4	79.6	.2	.8
Offenses against family and children	2,961	2,112	729	24	96	100.0	71.3	24.6	.8	3.2
Driving under the influence	6,734	6,181	379	131	43	100.0	91.8	5.6	1.9	.6
Liquor laws..........................	69,830	63,451	4,399	1,568	412	100.0	90.9	6.3	2.2	.6
Drunkenness	12,005	10,523	1,248	186	48	100.0	87.7	10.4	1.5	.4
Disorderly conduct	109,189	70,207	37,535	783	664	100.0	64.3	34.4	.7	.6
Vagrancy............................	2,739	1,903	800	7	29	100.0	69.5	29.2	.3	1.1
All other offenses (except traffic)	267,156	177,054	82,383	1,959	5,760	100.0	66.3	30.8	.7	2.2
Suspicion	1,213	880	324	2	7	100.0	72.5	26.7	.2	.6
Curfew and loitering law violations	80,931	63,933	15,010	778	1,210	100.0	79.0	18.5	1.0	1.5
Runaways............................	119,107	90,591	22,646	1,336	4,534	100.0	76.1	19.0	1.1	3.8

See footnotes at end of table.

Table 49. — City Arrests, Distribution by Race, 1993 — Continued

Offense charged	Arrests 18 and over					Percent distribution[1]				
	Total	White	Black	American Indian or Alaskan Native	Asian or Pacific Islander	Total	White	Black	American Indian or Alaskan Native	Asian or Pacific Islander
TOTAL	7,323,123	4,646,281	2,539,496	74,543	62,803	100.0	63.4	34.7	1.0	.9
Murder and nonnegligent manslaughter...	12,952	4,466	8,266	81	139	100.0	34.5	63.8	.6	1.1
Forcible rape	20,041	10,312	9,384	148	197	100.0	51.5	46.8	.7	1.0
Robbery	96,516	33,784	61,502	381	849	100.0	35.0	63.7	.4	.9
Aggravated assault	284,701	155,918	123,729	2,040	3,014	100.0	54.8	43.5	.7	1.1
Burglary	164,575	96,812	65,387	963	1,413	100.0	58.8	39.7	.6	.9
Larceny-theft.........................	714,657	430,815	268,149	7,091	8,602	100.0	60.3	37.5	1.0	1.2
Motor vehicle theft	72,737	39,260	31,850	445	1,182	100.0	54.0	43.8	.6	1.6
Arson................................	5,553	3,467	1,981	43	42	100.0	62.7	35.8	.8	.8
Violent crime[2]	414,210	204,480	202,881	2,650	4,199	100.0	49.4	49.0	.6	1.0
Property crime[3]	957,502	570,354	367,367	8,542	11,239	100.0	59.6	38.4	.9	1.2
Crime Index total[4]	1,371,712	774,834	570,248	11,192	15,438	100.0	56.5	41.6	.8	1.1
Other assaults	624,939	372,273	239,804	7,351	5,511	100.0	59.6	38.4	1.2	.9
Forgery and counterfeiting	61,718	36,254	24,391	346	727	100.0	58.7	39.5	.6	1.2
Fraud................................	190,848	112,674	75,726	836	1,612	100.0	59.0	39.7	.4	.8
Embezzlement........................	7,362	4,759	2,490	30	83	100.0	64.6	33.8	.4	1.1
Stolen property; buying, receiving, possession.........................	77,046	39,841	36,115	311	779	100.0	51.7	46.9	.4	1.0
Vandalism............................	112,765	74,562	35,743	1,324	1,136	100.0	66.1	31.7	1.2	1.0
Weapons; carrying, possessing, etc.	137,400	68,238	67,097	633	1,432	100.0	49.7	48.8	.5	1.0
Prostitution and commercialized vice	83,023	50,743	30,579	488	1,213	100.0	61.1	36.8	.6	1.5
Sex offenses (except forcible rape and prostitution)........................	51,743	38,698	11,855	521	669	100.0	74.8	22.9	1.0	1.3
Drug abuse violations..................	682,880	384,274	292,749	2,265	3,592	100.0	56.3	42.9	.3	.5
Gambling	12,142	5,752	5,743	42	605	100.0	47.4	47.3	.3	5.0
Offenses against family and children	46,405	30,690	13,693	569	1,453	100.0	66.1	29.5	1.2	3.1
Driving under the influence	745,368	647,291	82,629	9,199	6,249	100.0	86.8	11.1	1.2	.8
Liquor laws..........................	262,104	211,764	42,688	6,010	1,642	100.0	80.8	16.3	2.3	.6
Drunkenness.........................	495,063	385,906	96,774	10,891	1,492	100.0	78.0	19.5	2.2	.3
Disorderly conduct	420,721	262,389	151,129	5,133	2,070	100.0	62.4	35.9	1.2	.5
Vagrancy............................	19,707	10,465	8,763	430	49	100.0	53.1	44.5	2.2	.2
All other offenses (except traffic)	1,911,376	1,131,820	745,589	16,961	17,006	100.0	59.2	39.0	.9	.9
Suspicion	8,801	3,054	5,691	11	45	100.0	34.7	64.7	.1	.5
Curfew and loitering law violations	....	....	....	....	....	....	....	....	....	....
Runaways	....	....	....	....	....	....	....	....	....	....

[1]Because of rounding the percentages may not add to total.
[2]Violent crimes are offenses of murder, forcible rape, robbery, and aggravated assault.
[3]Property crimes are offenses of burglary, larceny-theft, motor vehicle theft, and arson.
[4]Includes arson.

Table 50. — Suburban County Arrest Trends, 1992-1993

[918 agencies; 1993 estimated population 42,794,000; 1992 estimated population 41,879,000]

| Offense charged | Number of persons arrested | | | | | | | | |
| | Total all ages | | | Under 18 years of age | | | 18 years of age and over | | |
	1992	1993	Percent change	1992	1993	Percent change	1992	1993	Percent change
TOTAL...	1,747,164	1,708,794	-2.2	222,828	223,614	+.4	1,524,336	1,485,180	-2.6
Murder and nonnegligent manslaughter	2,770	2,869	+3.6	352	369	+4.8	2,418	2,500	+3.4
Forcible rape...........................	5,066	5,034	-.6	818	843	+3.1	4,248	4,191	-1.3
Robbery................................	14,802	13,824	-6.6	3,279	3,234	-1.4	11,523	10,590	-8.1
Aggravated assault........................	64,745	66,407	+2.6	9,002	9,035	+.4	55,743	57,372	+2.9
Burglary...............................	58,963	55,266	-6.3	21,240	19,778	-6.9	37,723	35,488	-5.9
Larceny-theft...........................	145,011	140,733	-3.0	42,119	40,368	-4.2	102,892	100,365	-2.5
Motor vehicle theft........................	25,626	25,273	-1.4	10,459	10,159	-2.9	15,167	15,114	-.3
Arson	2,827	2,664	-5.8	1,235	1,125	-8.9	1,592	1,539	-3.3
Violent crime[1].................................	87,383	88,134	+.9	13,451	13,481	+.2	73,932	74,653	+1.0
Property crime[2]	232,427	223,936	-3.7	75,053	71,430	-4.8	157,374	152,506	-3.1
Crime Index total[3]...............................	319,810	312,070	-2.4	88,504	84,911	-4.1	231,306	227,159	-1.8
Other assaults...........................	124,114	131,762	+6.2	17,974	19,194	+6.8	106,140	112,568	+6.1
Forgery and counterfeiting...................	14,393	13,961	-3.0	805	768	-4.6	13,588	13,193	-2.9
Fraud.................................	80,996	76,737	-5.3	1,022	899	-12.0	79,974	75,838	-5.2
Embezzlement	2,133	2,034	-4.6	86	70	-18.6	2,047	1,964	-4.1
Stolen property; buying, receiving, possessing	18,251	17,998	-1.4	4,120	4,038	-2.0	14,131	13,960	-1.2
Vandalism..............................	32,043	31,691	-1.1	14,804	14,587	-1.5	17,239	17,104	-.8
Weapons; carrying, possessing, etc.	26,798	28,717	+7.2	5,270	5,881	+11.6	21,528	22,836	+6.1
Prostitution and commercialized vice.....................	3,494	3,897	+11.5	83	60	-27.7	3,411	3,837	+12.5
Sex offenses (except forcible rape and prostitution)	15,277	15,093	-1.2	2,817	2,969	+5.4	12,460	12,124	-2.7
Drug abuse violations	136,348	139,870	+2.6	8,060	10,137	+25.8	128,288	129,733	+1.1
Gambling..............................	1,322	1,497	+13.2	42	63	+50.0	1,280	1,434	+12.0
Offenses against family and children	24,783	27,002	+9.0	490	471	-3.9	24,293	26,531	+9.2
Driving under the influence...........................	283,536	264,597	-6.7	1,977	1,922	-2.8	281,559	262,675	-6.7
Liquor laws	46,759	43,326	-7.3	12,087	11,072	-8.4	34,672	32,254	-7.0
Drunkenness............................	57,643	52,694	-8.6	1,198	1,100	-8.2	56,445	51,594	-8.6
Disorderly conduct........................	36,928	42,470	+15.0	6,477	7,735	+19.4	30,451	34,735	+14.1
Vagrancy..............................	1,393	1,511	+8.5	300	393	+31.0	1,093	1,118	+2.3
All other offenses (except traffic).......................	499,558	478,974	-4.1	35,127	34,451	-1.9	464,431	444,523	-4.3
Suspicion (not included in totals)	1,251	1,841	+47.2	163	115	-29.4	1,088	1,726	+58.6
Curfew and loitering law violations........................	2,314	2,423	+4.7	2,314	2,423	+4.7	....	....	....
Runaways..............................	19,271	20,470	+6.2	19,271	20,470	+6.2	....	....	....

[1]Violent crimes are offenses of murder, forcible rape, robbery, and aggravated assault.
[2]Property crimes are offenses of burglary, larceny-theft, motor vehicle theft, and arson.
[3]Includes arson.

Table 51. — Suburban County Arrest Trends, Sex, 1992-1993

[918 agencies; 1993 estimated population 42,794,000; 1992 estimated population 41,879,000]

Offense charged	Males						Females					
	Total			Under 18			Total			Under 18		
	1992	1993	Percent change	1992	1993	Percent change	1992	1993	Percent change	1992	1993	Percent change
TOTAL...	1,425,830	1,388,847	-2.6	175,486	173,761	-1.0	321,334	319,947	-.4	47,342	49,853	+5.3
Murder and nonnegligent manslaughter	2,481	2,577	+3.9	330	355	+7.6	289	292	+1.0	22	14	-36.4
Forcible rape..	5,008	4,973	-.7	800	831	+3.9	58	61	+5.2	18	12	-33.3
Robbery...	13,616	12,755	-6.3	3,020	3,000	-.7	1,186	1,069	-9.9	259	234	-9.7
Aggravated assault....................................	56,013	56,906	+1.6	7,643	7,625	-.2	8,732	9,501	+8.8	1,359	1,410	+3.8
Burglary..	54,162	50,356	-7.0	19,652	18,030	-8.3	4,801	4,910	+2.3	1,588	1,748	+10.1
Larceny-theft...	101,479	97,207	-4.2	31,225	29,212	-6.4	43,532	43,526	1	10,894	11,156	+2.4
Motor vehicle theft....................................	22,939	22,324	-2.7	9,190	8,730	-5.0	2,687	2,949	+9.8	1,269	1,429	+12.6
Arson	2,460	2,251	-8.5	1,099	979	-10.9	367	413	+12.5	136	146	+7.4
Violent crime[2].......................................	77,118	77,211	+.1	11,793	11,811	+.2	10,265	10,923	+6.4	1,658	1,670	+.7
Property crime[3]	181,040	172,138	-4.9	61,166	56,951	-6.9	51,387	51,798	+.8	13,887	14,479	+4.3
Crime Index total[4]	258,158	249,349	-3.4	72,959	68,762	-5.8	61,652	62,721	+1.7	15,545	16,149	+3.9
Other assaults..	102,776	107,856	+4.9	13,926	14,520	+4.3	21,338	23,906	+12.0	4,048	4,674	+15.5
Forgery and counterfeiting............................	9,424	9,020	-4.3	517	480	-7.2	4,969	4,941	-.6	288	288	.....
Fraud..	41,475	39,770	-4.1	656	611	-6.9	39,521	36,967	-6.5	366	288	-21.3
Embezzlement	1,347	1,286	-4.5	61	41	-32.8	786	748	-4.8	25	29	+16.0
Stolen property; buying, receiving, possessing	16,093	15,852	-1.5	3,688	3,617	-1.9	2,158	2,146	-.6	432	421	-2.5
Vandalism..	28,615	28,145	-1.6	13,645	13,304	-2.5	3,428	3,546	+3.4	1,159	1,283	+10.7
Weapons; carrying, possessing, etc.	24,770	26,251	+6.0	4,899	5,426	+10.8	2,028	2,466	+21.6	371	455	+22.6
Prostitution and commercialized vice..................	1,434	1,772	+23.6	49	30	-38.8	2,060	2,125	+3.2	34	30	-11.8
Sex offenses (except forcible rape and prostitution)	14,520	14,132	-2.7	2,629	2,622	-.3	757	961	+26.9	188	347	+84.6
Drug abuse violations	112,835	115,772	+2.6	7,014	8,796	+25.4	23,513	24,098	+2.5	1,046	1,341	+28.2
Gambling...	1,118	1,283	+14.8	40	62	+55.0	204	214	+4.9	2	1	-50.0
Offenses against family and children	22,568	24,378	+8.0	340	308	-9.4	2,215	2,624	+18.5	150	163	+8.7
Driving under the influence............................	246,907	230,312	-6.7	1,718	1,648	-4.1	36,629	34,285	-6.4	259	274	+5.8
Liquor laws	37,172	34,761	-6.5	8,424	7,974	-5.3	9,587	8,565	-10.7	3,663	3,098	-15.4
Drunkenness...	51,390	46,833	-8.9	982	929	-5.4	6,253	5,861	-6.3	216	171	-20.8
Disorderly conduct....................................	29,828	34,217	+14.7	5,079	6,049	+19.1	7,100	8,253	+16.2	1,398	1,686	+20.6
Vagrancy...	1,184	1,281	+8.2	266	318	+19.5	209	230	+10.0	34	75	+120.6
All other offenses (except traffic)......................	413,606	395,636	-4.3	27,984	27,323	-2.4	85,952	83,338	-3.0	7,143	7,128	-.2
Suspicion (not included in totals)	1,098	1,625	+48.0	152	108	-28.9	153	216	+41.2	11	7	-36.4
Curfew and loitering law violations.....................	1,685	1,731	+2.7	1,685	1,731	+2.7	629	692	+10.0	629	692	+10.0
Runaways..	8,925	9,210	+3.2	8,925	9,210	+3.2	10,346	11,260	+8.8	10,346	11,260	+8.8

[1]Less than one-tenth of 1 percent.
[2]Violent crimes are offenses of murder, forcible rape, robbery, and aggravated assault.
[3]Property crimes are offenses of burglary, larceny-theft, motor vehicle theft, and arson.
[4]Includes arson.

Table 52. — Suburban County Arrests, Distribution by Age, 1993

[1,007 agencies; 1993 estimated population 46,243,000]

Offense charged	Total all ages	Ages under 15	Ages under 18	Ages 18 and over	Age								
					Under 10	10-12	13-14	15	16	17	18	19	20
TOTAL....................	1,856,090	78,766	239,826	1,616,264	3,818	16,968	57,980	46,820	55,324	58,916	73,451	72,768	70,799
Percent distribution[1]	100.0	4.2	12.9	87.1	.2	.9	3.1	2.5	3.0	3.2	4.0	3.9	3.8
Murder and nonnegligent manslaughter	3,083	32	396	2,687	2	5	25	73	134	157	210	150	172
Forcible rape....................	5,349	351	891	4,458	15	82	254	143	222	175	267	211	185
Robbery.......................	14,812	819	3,432	11,380	13	132	674	691	885	1,037	1,135	930	840
Aggravated assault...............	72,186	3,169	9,781	62,405	171	724	2,274	1,802	2,254	2,556	2,776	2,533	2,461
Burglary.......................	58,430	7,775	20,848	37,582	415	1,884	5,476	4,131	4,443	4,499	4,537	3,416	2,566
Larceny-theft	151,903	16,798	42,978	108,925	647	4,157	11,994	8,317	9,043	8,820	8,709	6,904	5,409
Motor vehicle theft..............	26,567	2,923	10,702	15,865	21	295	2,607	2,632	2,826	2,321	1,959	1,480	1,189
Arson.........................	2,801	745	1,171	1,630	124	251	370	170	128	128	111	98	75
Violent crime[2]...............	95,430	4,371	14,500	80,930	201	943	3,227	2,709	3,495	3,925	4,388	3,824	3,658
Percent distribution[1]	100.0	4.6	15.2	84.8	.2	1.0	3.4	2.8	3.7	4.1	4.6	4.0	3.8
Property crime[3]	239,701	28,241	75,699	164,002	1,207	6,587	20,447	15,250	16,440	15,768	15,316	11,898	9,239
Percent distribution[1]	100.0	11.8	31.6	68.4	.5	2.7	8.5	6.4	6.9	6.6	6.4	5.0	3.9
Crime Index total[4]	335,131	32,612	90,199	244,932	1,408	7,530	23,674	17,959	19,935	19,693	19,704	15,722	12,897
Percent distribution[1]	100.0	9.7	26.9	73.1	.4	2.2	7.1	5.4	5.9	5.9	5.9	4.7	3.8
Other assaults..................	141,996	8,071	20,276	121,720	456	2,013	5,602	3,775	4,071	4,359	4,423	4,289	4,137
Forgery and counterfeiting.......	15,092	144	829	14,263	8	27	109	141	220	324	633	660	672
Fraud	84,273	147	946	83,327	16	22	109	113	230	456	1,316	2,164	2,714
Embezzlement	2,171	9	72	2,099	....	5	4	9	17	37	85	87	98
Stolen property; buying, receiving, possessing	20,324	1,071	4,512	15,812	24	150	897	941	1,199	1,301	1,464	1,292	1,099
Vandalism.....................	33,121	6,646	15,292	17,829	652	1,855	4,139	2,700	3,238	2,708	2,025	1,569	1,153
Weapons; carrying, possessing, etc.	30,841	2,044	6,374	24,467	86	434	1,524	1,267	1,470	1,593	2,015	1,680	1,451
Prostitution and commercialized vice	4,692	15	67	4,625	....	5	10	9	16	27	60	99	118
Sex offenses (except forcible rape and prostitution)	15,979	1,608	3,145	12,834	139	408	1,061	526	543	468	481	393	381
Drug abuse violations	148,327	1,560	10,738	137,589	9	139	1,412	1,776	2,991	4,411	7,096	7,079	7,000
Gambling......................	1,589	11	64	1,525	....	....	11	12	19	22	56	37	34
Offenses against family and children	28,473	204	616	27,857	31	44	129	115	153	144	385	506	611
Driving under the influence.......	278,799	41	2,026	276,773	6	9	26	88	450	1,447	4,609	5,448	7,078
Liquor laws	46,189	915	11,576	34,613	10	70	835	1,630	3,395	5,636	7,553	6,870	5,390
Drunkenness...................	56,860	151	1,173	55,687	....	15	136	179	302	541	1,576	1,607	1,647
Disorderly conduct..............	46,386	2,554	8,190	38,196	110	519	1,925	1,619	1,926	2,091	2,196	1,912	1,704
Vagrancy	1,721	135	429	1,292	....	20	115	109	100	85	89	81	70
All other offenses (except traffic)..	537,258	10,749	38,166	499,092	724	2,241	7,784	7,021	9,030	11,366	17,602	21,195	22,468
Suspicion.....................	1,859	19	127	1,732	1	7	11	14	30	64	83	78	77
Curfew and loitering law violations	2,540	822	2,540	....	9	103	710	636	677	405	....	....	....
Runaways.....................	22,469	9,238	22,469	....	129	1,352	7,757	6,181	5,312	1,738	....	....	....

See footnotes at end of table.

Table 52. — Suburban County Arrests, Distribution by Age, 1993 — Continued

Offense charged	21	22	23	24	25-29	30-34	35-39	40-44	45-49	50-54	55-59	60-64	65 and over
TOTAL	72,251	74,457	71,793	68,199	318,548	296,733	214,692	127,956	72,149	37,916	20,567	11,860	12,125
Percent distribution[1]	3.9	4.0	3.9	3.7	17.2	16.0	11.6	6.9	3.9	2.0	1.1	.6	.7
Murder and nonnegligent manslaughter	177	156	126	134	440	353	281	175	118	84	43	28	40
Forcible rape	204	182	184	177	807	733	594	370	235	124	73	59	53
Robbery	713	698	632	593	2,398	1,636	1,019	456	193	71	28	16	22
Aggravated assault	2,628	2,672	2,448	2,488	12,332	11,876	8,644	4,849	3,082	1,599	931	517	569
Burglary	2,341	2,143	1,946	1,593	6,898	5,555	3,603	1,620	738	315	155	65	91
Larceny-theft	4,911	4,715	4,299	4,128	19,370	18,087	13,611	8,248	4,634	2,370	1,379	875	1,276
Motor vehicle theft	999	972	795	712	2,991	2,166	1,297	690	320	137	69	40	49
Arson	66	72	68	61	257	269	221	140	73	57	24	15	23
Violent crime[2]	3,722	3,708	3,390	3,392	15,977	14,598	10,538	5,850	3,628	1,878	1,075	620	684
Percent distribution[1]	3.9	3.9	3.6	3.6	16.7	15.3	11.0	6.1	3.8	2.0	1.1	.6	.7
Property crime[3]	8,317	7,902	7,108	6,494	29,516	26,077	18,732	10,698	5,765	2,879	1,627	995	1,439
Percent distribution[1]	3.5	3.3	3.0	2.7	12.3	10.9	7.8	4.5	2.4	1.2	.7	.4	.6
Crime Index total[4]	12,039	11,610	10,498	9,886	45,493	40,675	29,270	16,548	9,393	4,757	2,702	1,615	2,123
Percent distribution[1]	3.6	3.5	3.1	2.9	13.6	12.1	8.7	4.9	2.8	1.4	.8	.5	.6
Other assaults	4,501	4,814	4,936	4,937	24,461	24,597	17,764	10,414	5,846	3,026	1,616	926	1,033
Forgery and counterfeiting	657	690	711	685	3,057	2,640	1,986	947	513	191	117	47	57
Fraud	3,435	3,839	3,857	3,712	17,412	16,022	12,503	7,692	4,418	2,162	1,067	548	466
Embezzlement	75	107	81	93	408	354	264	194	122	67	28	25	11
Stolen property; buying, receiving, possessing	945	902	741	807	2,967	2,296	1,560	861	450	228	99	51	50
Vandalism	919	938	826	742	3,186	2,700	1,673	904	561	264	151	85	133
Weapons; carrying, possessing, etc.	1,468	1,412	1,345	1,091	4,365	3,349	2,451	1,506	969	607	299	219	240
Prostitution and commercialized vice	135	164	174	186	1,043	1,057	698	391	221	128	58	55	38
Sex offenses (except forcible rape and prostitution)	394	436	419	394	1,959	2,272	1,846	1,251	920	582	409	292	405
Drug abuse violations	6,792	7,018	6,670	5,969	29,221	26,395	17,963	9,245	3,992	1,711	761	378	299
Gambling	40	32	29	29	170	175	169	156	174	154	119	73	78
Offenses against family and children	741	880	1,001	1,174	5,693	6,292	4,927	2,889	1,542	680	323	132	81
Driving under the influence	10,148	11,371	11,980	11,351	54,555	53,168	40,316	26,846	17,209	10,284	5,776	3,557	3,077
Liquor laws	1,580	1,187	926	795	3,092	2,622	1,877	1,117	686	401	217	152	148
Drunkenness	2,176	2,113	2,108	2,022	9,751	10,521	8,383	5,786	3,429	1,945	1,204	719	700
Disorderly conduct	1,808	1,762	1,568	1,564	7,072	6,881	5,000	2,928	1,654	977	512	301	357
Vagrancy	54	65	44	46	239	213	134	90	59	34	15	13	46
All other offenses (except traffic)	24,276	25,040	23,796	22,642	104,030	94,188	65,672	38,073	19,914	9,678	5,075	2,664	2,779
Suspicion	68	77	83	74	374	316	236	118	77	40	19	8	4
Curfew and loitering law violations	....	....	....	....	....	....	....	....	....	....	....	....	....
Runaways	....	....	....	....	....	....	....	....	....	....	....	....	....

[1]Because of rounding, the percentages may not add to total.
[2]Violent crimes are offenses of murder, forcible rape, robbery, and aggravated assault.
[3]Property crimes are offenses of burglary, larceny-theft, motor vehicle theft, and arson.
[4]Includes arson.

Table 53. — Suburban County Arrests of Persons under 15, 18, 21, and 25 Years of Age, 1993

[1,007 agencies; 1993 estimated population 46,243,000]

Offense charged	Total all ages	Number of persons arrested				Percent of total all ages			
		Under 15	Under 18	Under 21	Under 25	Under 15	Under 18	Under 21	Under 25
TOTAL..	1,856,090	78,766	239,826	456,844	743,544	4.2	12.9	24.6	40.1
Murder and nonnegligent manslaughter..................	3,083	32	396	928	1,521	1.0	12.8	30.1	49.3
Forcible rape...	5,349	351	891	1,554	2,301	6.6	16.7	29.1	43.0
Robbery..	14,812	819	3,432	6,337	8,973	5.5	23.2	42.8	60.6
Aggravated assault....................................	72,186	3,169	9,781	17,551	27,787	4.4	13.5	24.3	38.5
Burglary...	58,430	7,775	20,848	31,367	39,390	13.3	35.7	53.7	67.4
Larceny-theft..	151,903	16,798	42,978	64,000	82,053	11.1	28.3	42.1	54.0
Motor vehicle theft...................................	26,567	2,923	10,702	15,330	18,808	11.0	40.3	57.7	70.8
Arson	2,801	745	1,171	1,455	1,722	26.6	41.8	51.9	61.5
Violent crime[1]....................................	95,430	4,371	14,500	26,370	40,582	4.6	15.2	27.6	42.5
Property crime[2]..................................	239,701	28,241	75,699	112,152	141,973	11.8	31.6	46.8	59.2
Crime Index total[3]	335,131	32,612	90,199	138,522	182,555	9.7	26.9	41.3	54.5
Other assaults.......................................	141,996	8,071	20,276	33,125	52,313	5.7	14.3	23.3	36.8
Forgery and counterfeiting............................	15,092	144	829	2,794	5,537	1.0	5.5	18.5	36.7
Fraud	84,273	147	946	7,140	21,983	.2	1.1	8.5	26.1
Embezzlement..	2,171	9	72	342	698	.4	3.3	15.8	32.2
Stolen property; buying, receiving, possessing	20,324	1,071	4,512	8,367	11,762	5.3	22.2	41.2	57.9
Vandalism...	33,121	6,646	15,292	20,039	23,464	20.1	46.2	60.5	70.8
Weapons; carrying, possessing, etc.	30,841	2,044	6,374	11,520	16,836	6.6	20.7	37.4	54.6
Prostitution and commercialized vice....................	4,692	15	67	344	1,003	.3	1.4	7.3	21.4
Sex offenses (except forcible rape and prostitution)	15,979	1,608	3,145	4,400	6,043	10.1	19.7	27.5	37.8
Drug abuse violations.................................	148,327	1,560	10,738	31,913	58,362	1.1	7.2	21.5	39.3
Gambling..	1,589	11	64	191	321	.7	4.0	12.0	20.2
Offenses against family and children	28,473	204	616	2,118	5,914	.7	2.2	7.4	20.8
Driving under the influence	278,799	41	2,026	19,161	64,011	4	.7	6.9	23.0
Liquor laws	46,189	915	11,576	31,389	35,877	2.0	25.1	68.0	77.7
Drunkenness...	56,860	151	1,173	6,003	14,422	.3	2.1	10.6	25.4
Disorderly conduct...................................	46,386	2,554	8,190	14,002	20,704	5.5	17.7	30.2	44.6
Vagrancy..	1,721	135	429	669	878	7.8	24.9	38.9	51.0
All other offenses (except traffic)......................	537,258	10,749	38,166	99,431	195,185	2.0	7.1	18.5	36.3
Suspicion..	1,859	19	127	365	667	1.0	6.8	19.6	35.9
Curfew and loitering law violations.....................	2,540	822	2,540	2,540	2,540	32.4	100.0	100.0	100.0
Runaways..	22,469	9,238	22,469	22,469	22,469	41.1	100.0	100.0	100.0

[1]Violent crimes are offenses of murder, forcible rape, robbery, and aggravated assault.
[2]Property crimes are offenses of burglary, larceny-theft, motor vehicle theft, and arson.
[3]Includes arson.
[4]Less than one-tenth of 1 percent.

Table 54. — Suburban County Arrests, Distribution by Sex, 1993
[1,007 agencies; 1993 estimated population 46,243,000]

Offense charged	Number of persons arrested			Percent male	Percent female	Percent distribution[1]		
	Total	Male	Female			Total	Male	Female
TOTAL...	**1,856,090**	**1,506,992**	**349,098**	**81.2**	**18.8**	**100.0**	**100.0**	**100.0**
Murder and nonnegligent manslaughter	3,083	2,771	312	89.9	10.1	.2	.2	.1
Forcible rape...	5,349	5,285	64	98.8	1.2	.3	.4	[2]
Robbery...	14,812	13,677	1,135	92.3	7.7	.8	.9	.3
Aggravated assault...	72,186	61,723	10,463	85.5	14.5	3.9	4.1	3.0
Burglary...	58,430	53,288	5,142	91.2	8.8	3.1	3.5	1.5
Larceny-theft...	151,903	104,762	47,141	69.0	31.0	8.2	7.0	13.5
Motor vehicle theft..	26,567	23,464	3,103	88.3	11.7	1.4	1.6	.9
Arson...	2,801	2,368	433	84.5	15.5	.2	.2	.1
Violent crime[3]...	95,430	83,456	11,974	87.5	12.5	5.1	5.5	3.4
Property crime[4]	239,701	183,882	55,819	76.7	23.3	12.9	12.2	16.0
Crime Index total[5]	335,131	267,338	67,793	79.8	20.2	18.1	17.7	19.4
Other assaults...	141,996	116,536	25,460	82.1	17.9	7.7	7.7	7.3
Forgery and counterfeiting..................................	15,092	9,746	5,346	64.6	35.4	.8	.6	1.5
Fraud...	84,273	44,041	40,232	52.3	47.7	4.5	2.9	11.5
Embezzlement	2,171	1,378	793	63.5	36.5	.1	.1	.2
Stolen property; buying, receiving, possessing	20,324	17,854	2,470	87.8	12.2	1.1	1.2	.7
Vandalism...	33,121	29,397	3,724	88.8	11.2	1.8	2.0	1.1
Weapons; carrying, possessing, etc.	30,841	28,182	2,659	91.4	8.6	1.7	1.9	.8
Prostitution and commercialized vice...........................	4,692	2,240	2,452	47.7	52.3	.3	.1	.7
Sex offenses (except forcible rape and prostitution)	15,979	14,884	1,095	93.1	6.9	.9	1.0	.3
Drug abuse violations.......................................	148,327	122,934	25,393	82.9	17.1	8.0	8.2	7.3
Gambling...	1,589	1,353	236	85.1	14.9	.1	.1	.1
Offenses against family and children	28,473	25,545	2,928	89.7	10.3	1.5	1.7	.8
Driving under the influence...................................	278,799	242,521	36,278	87.0	13.0	15.0	16.1	10.4
Liquor laws...	46,189	37,066	9,123	80.2	19.8	2.5	2.5	2.6
Drunkenness...	56,860	50,442	6,418	88.7	11.3	3.1	3.3	1.8
Disorderly conduct...	46,386	37,424	8,962	80.7	19.3	2.5	2.5	2.6
Vagrancy...	1,721	1,403	318	81.5	18.5	.1	.1	.1
All other offenses (except traffic).............................	537,258	443,207	94,051	82.5	17.5	28.9	29.4	26.9
Suspicion...	1,859	1,642	217	88.3	11.7	.1	.1	.1
Curfew and loitering law violations.............................	2,540	1,819	721	71.6	28.4	.1	.1	.2
Runaways...	22,469	10,040	12,429	44.7	55.3	1.2	.7	3.6

[1]Because of rounding, the percentages may not add to total.
[2]Less than one-tenth of 1 percent.
[3]Violent crimes are offenses of murder, forcible rape, robbery, and aggravated assault.
[4]Property crimes are offenses of burglary, larceny-theft, motor vehicle theft, and arson.
[5]Includes arson.

Table 55. — Suburban County Arrests, Distribution by Race, 1993

[1,006 agencies; 1993 estimated population 46,243,000]

Offense charged	Total arrests					Percent distribution[1]				
	Total	White	Black	American Indian or Alaskan Native	Asian or Pacific Islander	Total	White	Black	American Indian or Alaskan Native	Asian or Pacific Islander
TOTAL	1,853,147	1,374,757	461,590	8,245	8,555	100.0	74.2	24.9	.4	.5
Murder and nonnegligent manslaughter....	3,080	1,945	1,103	7	25	100.0	63.1	35.8	.2	.8
Forcible rape	5,331	3,811	1,489	12	19	100.0	71.5	27.9	.2	.4
Robbery	14,800	6,724	7,933	49	94	100.0	45.4	53.6	.3	.6
Aggravated assault	72,069	51,278	20,090	360	341	100.0	71.2	27.9	.5	.5
Burglary	58,314	45,237	12,558	198	321	100.0	77.6	21.5	.3	.6
Larceny - theft........................	151,744	102,494	47,500	561	1,189	100.0	67.5	31.3	.4	.8
Motor vehicle theft	26,502	17,837	8,389	94	182	100.0	67.3	31.7	.4	.7
Arson	2,795	2,328	429	26	12	100.0	83.3	15.3	.9	.4
Violent crime[2]	95,280	63,758	30,615	428	479	100.0	66.9	32.1	.4	.5
Property crime[3]	239,355	167,896	68,876	879	1,704	100.0	70.1	28.8	.4	.7
Crime Index total[4]	334,635	231,654	99,491	1,307	2,183	100.0	69.2	29.7	.4	.7
Other assaults	141,634	105,445	34,760	749	680	100.0	74.4	24.5	.5	.5
Forgery and counterfeiting	15,085	10,493	4,478	34	80	100.0	69.6	29.7	.2	.5
Fraud................................	84,080	55,201	28,498	202	179	100.0	65.7	33.9	.2	.2
Embezzlement........................	2,170	1,498	655	7	10	100.0	69.0	30.2	.3	.5
Stolen property; buying, receiving, possessing...........................	20,312	13,668	6,388	99	157	100.0	67.3	31.4	.5	.8
Vandalism	33,031	28,194	4,488	146	203	100.0	85.4	13.6	.4	.6
Weapons; carrying, possessing, etc.	30,807	20,747	9,770	101	189	100.0	67.3	31.7	.3	.6
Prostitution and commercialized vice	4,688	3,600	1,011	11	66	100.0	76.8	21.6	.2	1.4
Sex offenses (except forcible rape and prostitution).........................	15,940	13,555	2,247	55	83	100.0	85.0	14.1	.3	.5
Drug abuse violations...................	148,241	106,043	41,341	353	504	100.0	71.5	27.9	.2	.3
Gambling............................	1,581	1,129	426	5	21	100.0	71.4	26.9	.3	1.3
Offenses against family and children	28,194	17,276	10,782	58	78	100.0	61.3	38.2	.2	.3
Driving under the influence	277,835	250,885	24,157	1,211	1,582	100.0	90.3	8.7	.4	.6
Liquor laws..........................	46,159	41,709	3,680	485	285	100.0	90.4	8.0	1.1	.6
Drunkenness	56,858	49,851	6,345	441	221	100.0	87.7	11.2	.8	.4
Disorderly conduct	46,312	35,319	10,527	275	191	100.0	76.3	22.7	.6	.4
Vagrancy............................	1,721	1,249	446	3	23	100.0	72.6	25.9	.2	1.3
All other offenses (except traffic)	536,998	363,999	168,795	2,508	1,696	100.0	67.8	31.4	.5	.3
Suspicion	1,859	1,564	266	20	9	100.0	84.1	14.3	1.1	.5
Curfew and loitering law violations	2,538	2,193	316	10	19	100.0	86.4	12.5	.4	.7
Runaways............................	22,469	19,485	2,723	165	96	100.0	86.7	12.1	.7	.4

See footnotes at end of table.

Table 55.—Suburban County Arrests, Distribution by Race, 1993—Continued

Offense charged	Arrests under 18					Percent distribution[1]				
	Total	White	Black	American Indian or Alaskan Native	Asian or Pacific Islander	Total	White	Black	American Indian or Alaskan Native	Asian or Pacific Islander
TOTAL	239,184	181,108	54,829	1,270	1,977	100.0	75.7	22.9	.5	.8
Murder and nonnegligent manslaughter....	393	196	193	2	2	100.0	49.9	49.1	.5	.5
Forcible rape	882	602	270	2	8	100.0	68.3	30.6	.2	.9
Robbery	3,427	1,418	1,958	12	39	100.0	41.4	57.1	.4	1.1
Aggravated assault	9,748	6,189	3,425	63	71	100.0	63.5	35.1	.6	.7
Burglary	20,755	16,832	3,672	87	164	100.0	81.1	17.7	.4	.8
Larceny - theft........................	42,872	30,858	11,362	169	483	100.0	72.0	26.5	.4	1.1
Motor vehicle theft	10,671	6,963	3,523	43	142	100.0	65.3	33.0	.4	1.3
Arson	1,169	1,005	144	12	8	100.0	86.0	12.3	1.0	.7
Violent crime[2]	14,450	8,405	5,846	79	120	100.0	58.2	40.5	.5	.8
Property crime[3]	75,467	55,658	18,701	311	797	100.0	73.8	24.8	.4	1.1
Crime Index total[4]	89,917	64,063	24,547	390	917	100.0	71.2	27.3	.4	1.0
Other assaults	20,169	13,968	5,921	115	165	100.0	69.3	29.4	.6	.8
Forgery and counterfeiting	826	655	155	2	14	100.0	79.3	18.8	.2	1.7
Fraud...............................	945	738	200	....	7	100.0	78.1	21.2	....	.7
Embezzlement	71	52	19	....	....	100.0	73.2	26.8	....	....
Stolen property; buying, receiving, possessing...........................	4,508	2,957	1,453	27	71	100.0	65.6	32.2	.6	1.6
Vandalism	15,217	13,383	1,638	59	137	100.0	87.9	10.8	.4	.9
Weapons; carrying, possessing, etc.	6,359	4,223	2,041	26	69	100.0	66.4	32.1	.4	1.1
Prostitution and commercialized vice	67	57	10	....	....	100.0	85.1	14.9	....	....
Sex offenses (except forcible rape and prostitution)........................	3,122	2,479	620	9	14	100.0	79.4	19.9	.3	.4
Drug abuse violations....................	10,712	7,450	3,171	48	43	100.0	69.5	29.6	.4	.4
Gambling	63	11	52	....	....	100.0	17.5	82.5	....	....
Offenses against family and children	609	530	74	4	1	100.0	87.0	12.2	.7	.2
Driving under the influence	2,024	1,894	105	19	6	100.0	93.6	5.2	.9	.3
Liquor laws...........................	11,563	10,980	375	142	66	100.0	95.0	3.2	1.2	.6
Drunkenness..........................	1,172	1,060	92	10	10	100.0	90.4	7.8	.9	.9
Disorderly conduct	8,154	5,918	2,149	31	56	100.0	72.6	26.4	.4	.7
Vagrancy.............................	429	347	63	....	19	100.0	80.9	14.7	....	4.4
All other offenses (except traffic)	38,123	28,577	9,069	213	264	100.0	75.0	23.8	.6	.7
Suspicion	127	88	36	....	3	100.0	69.3	28.3	....	2.4
Curfew and loitering law violations	2,538	2,193	316	10	19	100.0	86.4	12.5	.4	.7
Runaways.............................	22,469	19,485	2,723	165	96	100.0	86.7	12.1	.7	.4

See footnotes at end of table.

254

Table 55.—Suburban County Arrests, Distribution by Race, 1993—Continued

Offense charged	Arrests 18 and over					Percent distribution[1]				
	Total	White	Black	American Indian or Alaskan Native	Asian or Pacific Islander	Total	White	Black	American Indian or Alaskan Native	Asian or Pacific Islander
TOTAL	1,613,963	1,193,649	406,761	6,975	6,578	100.0	74.0	25.2	.4	.4
Murder and nonnegligent manslaughter....	2,687	1,749	910	5	23	100.0	65.1	33.9	.2	.9
Forcible rape	4,449	3,209	1,219	10	11	100.0	72.1	27.4	.2	.2
Robbery	11,373	5,306	5,975	37	55	100.0	46.7	52.5	.3	.5
Aggravated assault	62,321	45,089	16,665	297	270	100.0	72.3	26.7	.5	.4
Burglary	37,559	28,405	8,886	111	157	100.0	75.6	23.7	.3	.4
Larceny - theft.........................	108,872	71,636	36,138	392	706	100.0	65.8	33.2	.4	.6
Motor vehicle theft	15,831	10,874	4,866	51	40	100.0	68.7	30.7	.3	.3
Arson	1,626	1,323	285	14	4	100.0	81.4	17.5	.9	.2
Violent crime[2].....................	80,830	55,353	24,769	349	359	100.0	68.5	30.6	.4	.4
Property crime[3]....................	163,888	112,238	50,175	568	907	100.0	68.5	30.6	.3	.6
Crime Index total[4]	244,718	167,591	74,944	917	1,266	100.0	68.5	30.6	.4	.5
Other assaults	121,465	91,477	28,839	634	515	100.0	75.3	23.7	.5	.4
Forgery and counterfeiting	14,259	9,838	4,323	32	66	100.0	69.0	30.3	.2	.5
Fraud...............................	83,135	54,463	28,298	202	172	100.0	65.5	34.0	.2	.2
Embezzlement........................	2,099	1,446	636	7	10	100.0	68.9	30.3	.3	.5
Stolen property; buying, receiving, possessing........................	15,804	10,711	4,935	72	86	100.0	67.8	31.2	.5	.5
Vandalism	17,814	14,811	2,850	87	66	100.0	83.1	16.0	.5	.4
Weapons; carrying, possessing, etc.	24,448	16,524	7,729	75	120	100.0	67.6	31.6	.3	.5
Prostitution and commercialized vice	4,621	3,543	1,001	11	66	100.0	76.7	21.7	.2	1.4
Sex offenses (except forcible rape and prostitution)........................	12,818	11,076	1,627	46	69	100.0	86.4	12.7	.4	.5
Drug abuse violations....................	137,529	98,593	38,170	305	461	100.0	71.7	27.8	.2	.3
Gambling	1,518	1,118	374	5	21	100.0	73.6	24.6	.3	1.4
Offenses against family and children	27,585	16,746	10,708	54	77	100.0	60.7	38.8	.2	.3
Driving under the influence	275,811	248,991	24,052	1,192	1,576	100.0	90.3	8.7	.4	.6
Liquor laws..........................	34,596	30,729	3,305	343	219	100.0	88.8	9.6	1.0	.6
Drunkenness	55,686	48,791	6,253	431	211	100.0	87.6	11.2	.8	.4
Disorderly conduct	38,158	29,401	8,378	244	135	100.0	77.1	22.0	.6	.4
Vagrancy............................	1,292	902	383	3	4	100.0	69.8	29.6	.2	.3
All other offenses (except traffic)	498,875	335,422	159,726	2,295	1,432	100.0	67.2	32.0	.5	.3
Suspicion	1,732	1,476	230	20	6	100.0	85.2	13.3	1.2	.3
Curfew and loitering law violations	....	....	....	....	....	....	....	....	....	....
Runaways............................	....	....	....	....	....	....	....	....	....	....

[1]Because of rounding, the percentages may not add to total.
[2]Violent crimes are offenses of murder, forcible rape, robbery, and aggravated assault.
[3]Property crimes are offenses of burglary, larceny-theft, motor vehicle theft, and arson.
[4]Includes arson.

Table 56.—Rural County Arrest Trends, 1992-1993

[1,848 agencies; 1993 estimated population 20,041,000; 1992 estimated population 19,950,000]

Offense charged	Number of persons arrested								
	Total all ages			Under 18 years of age			18 years of age and over		
	1992	1993	Percent change	1992	1993	Percent change	1992	1993	Percent change
TOTAL	813,377	825,673	+1.5	80,565	86,495	+7.4	732,812	739,178	+.9
Murder and nonnegligent manslaughter...........................	1,319	1,332	+1.0	92	109	+18.5	1,227	1,223	-.3
Forcible rape	2,573	2,826	+9.8	299	345	+15.4	2,274	2,481	+9.1
Robbery	2,375	2,272	-4.3	310	331	+6.8	2,065	1,941	-6.0
Aggravated assault	25,346	27,532	+8.6	2,185	2,540	+16.2	23,161	24,992	+7.9
Burglary	28,077	28,167	+.3	9,385	9,857	+5.0	18,692	18,310	-2.0
Larceny-theft	42,882	42,809	-.2	10,101	10,894	+7.9	32,781	31,915	-2.6
Motor vehicle theft	7,424	7,438	+.2	2,993	2,936	-1.9	4,431	4,502	+1.6
Arson..	1,263	1,263	....	361	371	+2.8	902	892	-1.1
Violent crime[1]	31,613	33,962	+7.4	2,886	3,325	+15.2	28,727	30,637	+6.6
Property crime[2]	79,646	79,677	[3]	22,840	24,058	+5.3	56,806	55,619	-2.1
Crime Index total[4]	111,259	113,639	+2.1	25,726	27,383	+6.4	85,533	86,256	+.8
Other assaults	55,798	63,250	+13.4	4,934	6,030	+22.2	50,864	57,220	+12.5
Forgery and counterfeiting	6,640	6,681	+.6	363	336	-7.4	6,277	6,345	+1.1
Fraud..	44,524	43,397	-2.5	554	579	+4.5	43,970	42,818	-2.6
Embezzlement...	831	801	-3.6	37	30	-18.9	794	771	-2.9
Stolen property; buying, receiving, possessing..........................	5,913	5,895	-.3	974	1,010	+3.7	4,939	4,885	-1.1
Vandalism..	16,223	16,948	+4.5	6,327	6,476	+2.4	9,896	10,472	+5.8
Weapons; carrying, possessing, etc.	9,298	10,605	+14.1	997	1,311	+31.5	8,301	9,294	+12.0
Prostitution and commercialized vice	174	149	-14.4	14	7	-50.0	160	142	-11.3
Sex offenses (except forcible rape and prostitution)	7,422	7,644	+3.0	1,298	1,371	+5.6	6,124	6,273	+2.4
Drug abuse violations....................................	52,679	53,112	+.8	2,253	2,889	+28.2	50,426	50,223	-.4
Gambling	442	483	+9.3	17	15	-11.8	425	468	+10.1
Offenses against family and children	8,682	10,113	+16.5	239	294	+23.0	8,443	9,819	+16.3
Driving under the influence	194,548	187,713	-3.5	1,977	1,849	-6.5	192,571	185,864	-3.5
Liquor laws...	38,948	35,760	-8.2	9,711	9,226	-5.0	29,237	26,534	-9.2
Drunkenness	39,267	38,013	-3.2	752	647	-14.0	38,515	37,366	-3.0
Disorderly conduct	26,766	28,280	+5.7	2,766	3,522	+27.3	24,000	24,758	+3.2
Vagrancy...	311	337	+8.4	91	63	-30.8	220	274	+24.5
All other offenses (except traffic)	183,959	192,264	+4.5	11,842	12,868	+8.7	172,117	179,396	+4.2
Suspicion (not included in totals)	205	201	-2.0	53	39	-26.4	152	162	+6.6
Curfew and loitering law violations	1,449	1,600	+10.4	1,449	1,600	+10.4	....	....	....
Runaways..	8,244	8,989	+9.0	8,244	8,989	+9.0	....	....	....

[1]Violent crimes are offenses of murder, forcible rape, robbery, and aggravated assault.
[2]Property crimes are offenses of burglary, larceny-theft, motor vehicle theft, and arson.
[3]Less than one-tenth of 1 percent.
[4]Includes arson.

Table 57. — Rural County Arrest Trends, Sex, 1992-1993

[1,848 agencies; 1993 estimated population 20,041,000; 1992 estimated population 19,950,000]

Offense charged	Males Total 1992	1993	Percent change	Males Under 18 1992	1993	Percent change	Females Total 1992	1993	Percent change	Females Under 18 1992	1993	Percent Change
TOTAL...................................	673,035	681,087	+1.2	62,919	66,996	+6.5	140,342	144,586	+3.0	17,646	19,499	+10.5
Murder and nonnegligent manslaughter	1,144	1,161	+1.5	83	95	+14.5	175	171	-2.3	9	14	+55.6
Forcible rape	2,533	2,793	+10.3	293	338	+15.4	40	33	-17.5	6	7	+16.7
Robbery..................................	2,181	2,078	-4.7	295	315	+6.8	194	194	....	15	16	+6.7
Aggravated assault.........................	22,042	23,966	+8.7	1,863	2,144	+15.1	3,304	3,566	+7.9	322	396	+23.0
Burglary..................................	25,947	25,690	-1.0	8,671	9,002	+3.8	2,130	2,477	+16.3	714	855	+19.7
Larceny-theft	32,934	33,131	+.6	8,152	8,777	+7.7	9,948	9,678	-2.7	1,949	2,117	+8.6
Motor vehicle theft	6,545	6,379	-2.5	2,513	2,371	-5.7	879	1,059	+20.5	480	565	+17.7
Arson....................................	1,097	1,091	-.5	322	327	+1.6	166	172	+3.6	39	44	+12.8
Violent crime[1]	27,900	29,998	+7.5	2,534	2,892	+14.1	3,713	3,964	+6.8	352	433	+23.0
Property crime[2]	66,523	66,291	-.3	19,658	20,477	+4.2	13,123	13,386	+2.0	3,182	3,581	+12.5
Crime Index total[3]	94,423	96,289	+2.0	22,192	23,369	+5.3	16,836	17,350	+3.1	3,534	4,014	+13.6
Other assaults................................	46,816	52,573	+12.3	3,856	4,586	+18.9	8,982	10,677	+18.9	1,078	1,444	+34.0
Forgery and counterfeiting	4,372	4,373	[4]	226	236	+4.4	2,268	2,308	+1.8	137	100	-27.0
Fraud....................................	23,183	22,618	-2.4	350	367	+4.9	21,341	20,779	-2.6	204	212	+3.9
Embezzlement	524	499	-4.8	20	16	-20.0	307	302	-1.6	17	14	-17.6
Stolen property; buying, receiving, possessing..................................	5,185	5,138	-.9	844	850	+.7	728	757	+4.0	130	160	+23.1
Vandalism................................	14,300	14,959	+4.6	5,717	5,894	+3.1	1,923	1,989	+3.4	610	582	-4.6
Weapons; carrying, possessing, etc.	8,701	9,930	+14.1	943	1,243	+31.8	597	675	+13.1	54	68	+25.9
Prostitution and commercialized vice	78	76	-2.6	4	4	....	96	73	-24.0	10	3	-70.0
Sex offenses (except forcible rape and prostitution)	7,080	7,296	+3.1	1,180	1,270	+7.6	342	348	+1.8	118	101	-14.4
Drug abuse violations	44,626	44,999	+.8	1,904	2,465	+29.5	8,053	8,113	+.7	349	424	+21.5
Gambling	363	421	+16.0	15	15	....	79	62	-21.5	2	....	....
Offenses against family and children.............	7,514	8,772	+16.7	181	228	+26.0	1,168	1,341	+14.8	58	66	+13.8
Driving under the influence....................	169,682	163,255	-3.8	1,680	1,592	-5.2	24,866	24,458	-1.6	297	257	-13.5
Liquor laws................................	31,180	28,248	-9.4	6,745	6,335	-6.1	7,768	7,512	-3.3	2,966	2,891	-2.5
Drunkenness	35,160	33,871	-3.7	620	558	-10.0	4,107	4,142	+.9	132	89	-32.6
Disorderly conduct...........................	22,111	22,831	+3.3	2,136	2,710	+26.9	4,655	5,449	+17.1	630	812	+28.9
Vagrancy..................................	267	284	+6.4	78	51	-34.6	44	53	+20.5	13	12	-7.7
All other offenses (except traffic).................	152,533	159,511	+4.6	9,291	10,063	+8.3	31,426	32,753	+4.2	2,551	2,805	+10.0
Suspicion (not included in totals).................	171	171	....	42	33	-21.4	34	30	-11.8	11	6	-45.5
Curfew and loitering law violations	944	1,018	+7.8	944	1,018	+7.8	505	582	+15.2	505	582	+15.2
Runaways..................................	3,993	4,126	+3.3	3,993	4,126	+3.3	4,251	4,863	+14.4	4,251	4,863	+14.4

[1]Violent crimes are offenses of murder, forcible rape, robbery, and aggravated assault.
[2]Property crimes are offenses of burglary, larceny-theft, motor vehicle theft, and arson.
[3]Includes arson.
[4]Less than one-tenth of 1 percent.

Table 58. — Rural County Arrests, Distribution by Age, 1993

[2,059 agencies; 1993 estimated population 22,307,000]

Offense charged	Total all ages	Ages under 15	Ages under 18	Ages 18 and over	Under 10	10-12	13-14	15	16	17	18	19	20
TOTAL..........................	890,073	26,075	92,825	797,248	1,741	5,986	18,348	16,386	23,001	27,363	37,377	37,748	37,297
Percent distribution[1].......................	100.0	2.9	10.4	89.6	.2	.7	2.1	1.8	2.6	3.1	4.2	4.2	4.2
Murder and nonnegligent manslaughter	1,446	25	122	1,324	2	2	21	19	32	46	64	83	72
Forcible rape	3,049	105	360	2,689	6	23	76	62	87	106	163	134	130
Robbery.....................................	2,518	51	365	2,153	2	9	40	64	90	160	186	193	159
Aggravated assault............................	29,488	691	2,683	26,805	33	180	478	427	684	881	1,197	1,096	1,130
Burglary....................................	30,323	3,610	10,419	19,904	288	987	2,335	1,869	2,282	2,658	2,952	2,190	1,752
Larceny-theft	46,239	3,993	11,459	34,780	216	1,073	2,704	2,059	2,630	2,777	3,152	2,639	2,209
Motor vehicle theft	7,932	859	3,100	4,832	17	96	746	759	749	733	588	485	365
Arson......................................	1,368	189	389	979	40	60	89	75	65	60	68	59	67
Violent crime[2]	36,501	872	3,530	32,971	43	214	615	572	893	1,193	1,610	1,506	1,491
Percent distribution[1]......................	100.0	2.4	9.7	90.3	.1	.6	1.7	1.6	2.4	3.3	4.4	4.1	4.1
Property crime[3]	85,862	8,651	25,367	60,495	561	2,216	5,874	4,762	5,726	6,228	6,760	5,373	4,393
Percent distribution[1]......................	100.0	10.1	29.5	70.5	.7	2.6	6.8	5.5	6.7	7.3	7.9	6.3	5.1
Crime Index total[4].........................	122,363	9,523	28,897	93,466	604	2,430	6,489	5,334	6,619	7,421	8,370	6,879	5,884
Percent distribution[1].......................	100.0	7.8	23.6	76.4	.5	2.0	5.3	4.4	5.4	6.1	6.8	5.6	4.8
Other assaults...............................	67,953	2,030	6,405	61,548	140	575	1,315	1,045	1,541	1,789	2,312	2,184	2,363
Forgery and counterfeiting	7,275	46	355	6,920	1	7	38	54	100	155	336	351	387
Fraud......................................	45,555	110	596	44,959	4	16	90	50	162	274	776	1,248	1,718
Embezzlement	871	5	33	838	....	....	5	2	9	17	25	26	29
Stolen property; buying, receiving, possessing	6,378	231	1,060	5,318	8	30	193	193	293	343	478	441	381
Vandalism...................................	18,356	2,772	7,013	11,343	392	880	1,500	1,104	1,650	1,487	1,433	979	742
Weapons; carrying, possessing, etc.	11,195	375	1,395	9,800	16	98	261	226	349	445	545	505	472
Prostitution and commercialized vice	162	2	7	155	....	....	2	2	2	1	9	6	3
Sex offenses (except forcible rape and prostitution)	8,129	679	1,429	6,700	69	181	429	252	236	262	305	236	267
Drug abuse violations	57,332	407	3,095	54,237	15	64	328	414	883	1,391	2,454	2,709	2,772
Gambling	509	7	15	494	1	1	5	3	2	3	12	8	6
Offenses against family and children.............	11,077	94	352	10,725	19	11	64	73	80	105	214	248	273
Driving under the influence.....................	197,709	52	1,950	195,759	25	2	25	82	531	1,285	3,046	4,167	5,078
Liquor laws.................................	39,365	913	10,060	29,305	23	62	828	1,490	2,982	4,675	6,557	6,167	4,802
Drunkenness	40,640	63	696	39,944	10	6	47	97	169	367	1,163	1,273	1,351
Disorderly conduct...........................	30,389	1,055	3,703	26,686	68	233	754	622	927	1,099	1,271	1,151	1,171
Vagrancy...................................	487	19	66	421	....	2	17	10	18	19	25	30	28
All other offenses (except traffic)...............	212,734	3,488	14,316	198,418	277	769	2,442	2,310	3,711	4,807	8,034	9,129	9,554
Suspicion...................................	256	19	44	212	....	2	17	3	16	6	12	11	16
Curfew and loitering law violations	1,689	685	1,689	....	8	121	556	400	375	229	....	....	....
Runaways	9,649	3,500	9,649	....	61	496	2,943	2,620	2,346	1,183	....	....	....

See footnotes at end of table.

Table 58.—Rural County Arrests, Distribution by Age, 1993—Continued

Offense charged	Age												
	21	22	23	24	25-29	30-34	35-39	40-44	45-49	50-54	55-59	60-64	65 and over
TOTAL	36,195	35,963	34,549	32,753	145,449	139,165	103,324	66,658	38,573	22,655	12,730	7,876	8,936
Percent distribution[1]	4.1	4.0	3.9	3.7	16.3	15.6	11.6	7.5	4.3	2.5	1.4	.9	1.0
Murder and nonnegligent manslaughter	61	59	73	65	210	191	141	115	77	39	34	18	22
Forcible rape	133	123	98	103	446	420	338	231	111	95	46	65	53
Robbery	140	133	123	91	440	326	199	81	49	18	9	2	4
Aggravated assault	1,132	1,232	1,183	1,129	4,991	4,678	3,610	2,250	1,372	748	418	255	384
Burglary	1,390	1,209	998	899	3,406	2,342	1,432	667	368	152	73	37	37
Larceny-theft	1,869	1,713	1,478	1,463	5,855	5,096	3,661	2,267	1,372	805	462	273	466
Motor vehicle theft	316	248	229	220	894	648	382	243	98	55	33	11	17
Arson	43	49	50	37	152	164	105	79	34	26	22	10	14
Violent crime[2]	1,466	1,547	1,477	1,388	6,087	5,615	4,288	2,677	1,609	900	507	340	463
Percent distribution[1]	4.0	4.2	4.0	3.8	16.7	15.4	11.7	7.3	4.4	2.5	1.4	.9	1.3
Property crime[3]	3,618	3,219	2,755	2,619	10,307	8,250	5,580	3,256	1,872	1,038	590	331	534
Percent distribution[1]	4.2	3.7	3.2	3.1	12.0	9.6	6.5	3.8	2.2	1.2	.7	.4	.6
Crime Index total[4]	5,084	4,766	4,232	4,007	16,394	13,865	9,868	5,933	3,481	1,938	1,097	671	997
Percent distribution[1]	4.2	3.9	3.5	3.3	13.4	11.3	8.1	4.8	2.8	1.6	.9	.5	.8
Other assaults	2,648	2,688	2,590	2,631	11,923	11,645	8,466	5,284	2,930	1,730	965	550	639
Forgery and counterfeiting	340	349	377	343	1,358	1,276	893	462	216	113	59	30	30
Fraud	2,062	2,161	2,100	1,996	9,077	8,064	6,284	4,308	2,351	1,352	707	393	362
Embezzlement	28	39	21	33	132	157	145	84	60	33	14	7	5
Stolen property; buying, receiving, possessing	336	291	260	238	942	738	519	301	180	100	49	43	21
Vandalism	728	612	555	522	1,957	1,555	965	585	299	160	98	60	93
Weapons; carrying, possessing, etc.	522	476	467	388	1,704	1,507	1,163	830	538	289	163	106	125
Prostitution and commercialized vice	3	9	5	6	18	31	24	13	8	5	3	7	5
Sex offenses (except forcible rape and prostitution)	233	227	197	218	995	1,022	908	625	439	346	198	207	277
Drug abuse violations	2,743	2,856	2,763	2,454	11,318	10,491	6,965	3,734	1,665	734	285	159	135
Gambling	7	7	6	12	42	45	48	75	77	58	37	29	25
Offenses against family and children	346	375	407	436	2,053	2,383	1,788	1,109	557	268	119	79	70
Driving under the influence	7,171	7,518	7,529	7,155	34,828	37,377	29,563	20,763	12,890	7,951	4,701	2,964	3,058
Liquor laws	1,424	967	817	625	2,288	1,932	1,383	888	556	378	226	128	167
Drunkenness	1,522	1,521	1,543	1,478	6,691	7,135	5,897	4,104	2,499	1,587	980	601	599
Disorderly conduct	1,293	1,276	1,138	1,161	4,915	4,626	3,420	2,202	1,270	761	446	276	309
Vagrancy	36	14	21	25	68	69	51	24	18	6	1	4	1
All other offenses (except traffic)	9,658	9,803	9,508	9,018	38,709	35,217	24,947	15,315	8,532	4,839	2,578	1,561	2,016
Suspicion	11	8	13	7	37	30	27	19	7	7	4	1	2
Curfew and loitering law violations	....	....	....	....	....	....	....	....	....	....	....	....	....
Runaways	....	....	....	....	....	....	....	....	....	....	....	....	....

[1]Because of rounding, the percentages may not add to total.
[2]Violent crimes are offenses of murder, forcible rape, robbery, and aggravated assault.
[3]Property crimes are offenses of burglary, larceny-theft, motor vehicle theft, and arson.
[4]Includes arson.

Table 59. — Rural County Arrests of Persons under 15, 18, 21, and 25 Years of Age, 1993

[2,059 agencies; 1993 estimated population 22,307,000]

Offense charged	Total all ages	Number of persons arrested				Percent of total all ages			
		Under 15	Under 18	Under 21	Under 25	Under 15	Under 18	Under 21	Under 25
TOTAL...............................	890,073	26,075	92,825	205,247	344,707	2.9	10.4	23.1	38.7
Murder and nonnegligent manslaughter	1,446	25	122	341	599	1.7	8.4	23.6	41.4
Forcible rape................................	3,049	105	360	787	1,244	3.4	11.8	25.8	40.8
Robbery......................................	2,518	51	365	903	1,390	2.0	14.5	35.9	55.2
Aggravated assault..........................	29,488	691	2,683	6,106	10,782	2.3	9.1	20.7	36.6
Burglary.....................................	30,323	3,610	10,419	17,313	21,809	11.9	34.4	57.1	71.9
Larceny-theft...............................	46,239	3,993	11,459	19,459	25,982	8.6	24.8	42.1	56.2
Motor vehicle theft	7,932	859	3,100	4,538	5,551	10.8	39.1	57.2	70.0
Arson..	1,368	189	389	583	762	13.8	28.4	42.6	55.7
Violent crime[1]	36,501	872	3,530	8,137	14,015	2.4	9.7	22.3	38.4
Property crime[2]	85,862	8,651	25,367	41,893	54,104	10.1	29.5	48.8	63.0
Crime Index total[3]	122,363	9,523	28,897	50,030	68,119	7.8	23.6	40.9	55.7
Other assaults...............................	67,953	2,030	6,405	13,264	23,821	3.0	9.4	19.5	35.1
Forgery and counterfeiting...................	7,275	46	355	1,429	2,838	.6	4.9	19.6	39.0
Fraud..	45,555	110	596	4,338	12,657	.2	1.3	9.5	27.8
Embezzlement	871	5	33	113	234	.6	3.8	13.0	26.9
Stolen property; buying, receiving, possessing	6,378	231	1,060	2,360	3,485	3.6	16.6	37.0	54.6
Vandalism....................................	18,356	2,772	7,013	10,167	12,584	15.1	38.2	55.4	68.6
Weapons; carrying, possessing, etc.	11,195	375	1,395	2,917	4,770	3.3	12.5	26.1	42.6
Prostitution and commercialized vice......................	162	2	7	25	48	1.2	4.3	15.4	29.6
Sex offenses (except forcible rape and prostitution)	8,129	679	1,429	2,237	3,112	8.4	17.6	27.5	38.3
Drug abuse violations	57,332	407	3,095	11,030	21,846	.7	5.4	19.2	38.1
Gambling....................................	509	7	15	41	73	1.4	2.9	8.1	14.3
Offenses against family and children........................	11,077	94	352	1,087	2,651	.8	3.2	9.8	23.9
Driving under the influence....................	197,709	52	1,950	14,241	43,614	[4]	1.0	7.2	22.1
Liquor laws..................................	39,365	913	10,060	27,586	31,419	2.3	25.6	70.1	79.8
Drunkenness.................................	40,640	63	696	4,483	10,547	.2	1.7	11.0	26.0
Disorderly conduct...........................	30,389	1,055	3,703	7,296	12,164	3.5	12.2	24.0	40.0
Vagrancy....................................	487	19	66	149	245	3.9	13.6	30.6	50.3
All other offenses (except traffic)........................	212,734	3,488	14,316	41,033	79,020	1.6	6.7	19.3	37.1
Suspicion....................................	256	19	44	83	122	7.4	17.2	32.4	47.7
Curfew and loitering law violations.......................	1,689	685	1,689	1,689	1,689	40.6	100.0	100.0	100.0
Runaways....................................	9,649	3,500	9,649	9,649	9,649	36.3	100.0	100.0	100.0

[1]Violent crimes are offenses of murder, forcible rape, robbery, and aggravated assault.
[2]Property crimes are offenses of burglary, larceny-theft, motor vehicle theft, and arson.
[3]Includes arson.
[4]Less than one-tenth of 1 percent.

Table 60.—Rural County Arrests, Distribution by Sex, 1993

[2,059 agencies; 1993 estimated population 22,307,000]

Offense charged	Number of persons arrested			Percent male	Percent female	Percent distribution[1]		
	Total	Male	Female			Total	Male	Female
TOTAL..	890,073	733,948	156,125	82.5	17.5	100.0	100.0	100.0
Murder and nonnegligent manslaughter..............................	1,446	1,260	186	87.1	12.9	.2	.2	.1
Forcible rape...	3,049	3,013	36	98.8	1.2	.3	.4	[2]
Robbery...	2,518	2,305	213	91.5	8.5	.3	.3	.1
Aggravated assault..	29,488	25,638	3,850	86.9	13.1	3.3	3.5	2.5
Burglary...	30,323	27,648	2,675	91.2	8.8	3.4	3.8	1.7
Larceny-theft...	46,239	35,825	10,414	77.5	22.5	5.2	4.9	6.7
Motor vehicle theft..	7,932	6,819	1,113	86.0	14.0	.9	.9	.7
Arson..	1,368	1,179	189	86.2	13.8	.2	.2	.1
Violent crime[3]..	36,501	32,216	4,285	88.3	11.7	4.1	4.4	2.7
Property crime[4]	85,862	71,471	14,391	83.2	16.8	9.6	9.7	9.2
Crime Index total[5]	122,363	103,687	18,676	84.7	15.3	13.7	14.1	12.0
Other assaults...	67,953	56,497	11,456	83.1	16.9	7.6	7.7	7.3
Forgery and counterfeiting.................................	7,275	4,801	2,474	66.0	34.0	.8	.7	1.6
Fraud..	45,555	23,799	21,756	52.2	47.8	5.1	3.2	13.9
Embezzlement...	871	540	331	62.0	38.0	.1	.1	.2
Stolen property; buying, receiving, possessing	6,378	5,558	820	87.1	12.9	.7	.8	.5
Vandalism...	18,356	16,207	2,149	88.3	11.7	2.1	2.2	1.4
Weapons; carrying, possessing, etc.	11,195	10,480	715	93.6	6.4	1.3	1.4	.5
Prostitution and commercialized vice.........................	162	86	76	53.1	46.9	....	....	[2]
Sex offenses (except forcible rape and prostitution)	8,129	7,755	374	95.4	4.6	.9	1.1	.2
Drug abuse violations	57,332	48,602	8,730	84.8	15.2	6.4	6.6	5.6
Gambling...	509	446	63	87.6	12.4	.1	.1	[2]
Offenses against family and children	11,077	9,566	1,511	86.4	13.6	1.2	1.3	1.0
Driving under the influence	197,709	171,910	25,799	87.0	13.0	22.2	23.4	16.5
Liquor laws	39,365	31,080	8,285	79.0	21.0	4.4	4.2	5.3
Drunkenness...	40,640	36,126	4,514	88.9	11.1	4.6	4.9	2.9
Disorderly conduct.......................................	30,389	24,506	5,883	80.6	19.4	3.4	3.3	3.8
Vagrancy..	487	381	106	78.2	21.8	.1	.1	.1
All other offenses (except traffic)...........................	212,734	176,213	36,521	82.8	17.2	23.9	24.0	23.4
Suspicion	256	218	38	85.2	14.8	....	....	[2]
Curfew and loitering law violations..........................	1,689	1,070	619	63.4	36.6	.2	.1	.4
Runaways...	9,649	4,420	5,229	45.8	54.2	1.1	.6	3.3

[1]Because of rounding, the percentages may not add to total.
[2]Less than one-tenth of 1 percent.
[3]Violent crimes are offenses of murder, forcible rape, robbery, and aggravated assault.
[4]Property crimes are offenses of burglary, larceny-theft, motor vehicle theft, and arson.
[5]Includes arson.

Table 61. — Rural County Arrests, Distribution by Race, 1993

[2,059 agencies; 1993 estimated population 22,307,000]

Offense charged	Total arrests					Percent distribution[1]				
	Total	White	Black	American Indian or Alaskan Native	Asian or Pacific Islander	Total	White	Black	American Indian or Alaskan Native	Asian or Pacific Islander
TOTAL............................	888,339	703,726	145,909	26,765	11,939	100.0	79.2	16.4	3.0	1.3
Murder and nonnegligent manslaughter.....	1,445	917	483	35	10	100.0	63.5	33.4	2.4	.7
Forcible rape............................	3,049	2,312	577	142	18	100.0	75.8	18.9	4.7	.6
Robbery...............................	2,515	1,277	1,149	48	41	100.0	50.8	45.7	1.9	1.6
Aggravated assault......................	29,454	21,136	7,171	1,007	140	100.0	71.8	24.3	3.4	.5
Burglary..............................	30,267	24,372	4,515	997	383	100.0	80.5	14.9	3.3	1.3
Larceny-theft..........................	46,122	35,914	8,217	1,004	987	100.0	77.9	17.8	2.2	2.1
Motor vehicle theft.....................	7,919	6,376	1,024	340	179	100.0	80.5	12.9	4.3	2.3
Arson.................................	1,365	1,189	149	25	2	100.0	87.1	10.9	1.8	.1
Violent crime[2]......................	36,463	25,642	9,380	1,232	209	100.0	70.3	25.7	3.4	.6
Property crime[3]....................	85,673	67,851	13,905	2,366	1,551	100.0	79.2	16.2	2.8	1.8
Crime Index total[4]..................	122,136	93,493	23,285	3,598	1,760	100.0	76.5	19.1	2.9	1.4
Other assaults..........................	67,913	51,032	13,668	2,166	1,047	100.0	75.1	20.1	3.2	1.5
Forgery and counterfeiting................	7,256	5,334	1,803	76	43	100.0	73.5	24.8	1.0	.6
Fraud.................................	45,513	33,191	11,710	463	149	100.0	72.9	25.7	1.0	.3
Embezzlement..........................	871	731	100	7	33	100.0	83.9	11.5	.8	3.8
Stolen property; buying, receiving, possessing..........................	6,370	4,991	1,228	115	36	100.0	78.4	19.3	1.8	.6
Vandalism.............................	18,334	15,598	1,960	579	197	100.0	85.1	10.7	3.2	1.1
Weapons; carrying, possessing, etc.	11,184	8,221	2,584	214	165	100.0	73.5	23.1	1.9	1.5
Prostitution and commercialized vice	162	134	26	2	....	100.0	82.7	16.0	1.2	....
Sex offenses (except forcible rape and prostitution).................	8,110	7,235	579	242	54	100.0	89.2	7.1	3.0	.7
Drug abuse violations....................	57,235	44,959	10,802	971	503	100.0	78.6	18.9	1.7	.9
Gambling.............................	509	290	143	7	69	100.0	57.0	28.1	1.4	13.6
Offenses against family and children	11,048	8,059	2,401	487	101	100.0	72.9	21.7	4.4	.9
Driving under the influence	197,352	165,275	22,861	5,617	3,599	100.0	83.7	11.6	2.8	1.8
Liquor laws............................	39,247	35,643	1,766	1,595	243	100.0	90.8	4.5	4.1	.6
Drunkenness...........................	40,536	35,605	3,496	1,351	84	100.0	87.8	8.6	3.3	.2
Disorderly conduct	30,364	24,054	4,342	1,784	184	100.0	79.2	14.3	5.9	.6
Vagrancy	487	328	139	19	1	100.0	67.4	28.5	3.9	.2
All other offenses (except traffic)	212,132	160,347	42,333	6,824	2,628	100.0	75.6	20.0	3.2	1.2
Suspicion	252	192	23	37	....	100.0	76.2	9.1	14.7	....
Curfew and loitering law violations	1,687	965	56	161	505	100.0	57.2	3.3	9.5	29.9
Runaways..............................	9,641	8,049	604	450	538	100.0	83.5	6.3	4.7	5.6

See footnotes at end of table.

Table 61. — Rural County Arrests, Distribution by Race, 1993 — Continued

Offense charged	Arrests under 18					Percent distribution[1]				
	Total	White	Black	American Indian or Alaskan Native	Asian or Pacific Islander	Total	White	Black	American Indian or Alaskan Native	Asian or Pacific Islander
TOTAL	92,693	76,216	9,627	3,888	2,962	100.0	82.2	10.4	4.2	3.2
Murder and nonnegligent manslaughter.....	122	70	46	6	....	100.0	57.4	37.7	4.9	....
Forcible rape...........................	360	281	60	17	2	100.0	78.1	16.7	4.7	.6
Robbery	364	167	182	4	11	100.0	45.9	50.0	1.1	3.0
Aggravated assault	2,683	1,843	702	123	15	100.0	68.7	26.2	4.6	.6
Burglary..............................	10,409	8,778	971	462	198	100.0	84.3	9.3	4.4	1.9
Larceny-theft..........................	11,448	9,470	1,113	355	510	100.0	82.7	9.7	3.1	4.5
Motor vehicle theft.....................	3,097	2,508	281	189	119	100.0	81.0	9.1	6.1	3.8
Arson	389	349	32	8	....	100.0	89.7	8.2	2.1	....
Violent crime[2]......................	3,529	2,361	990	150	28	100.0	66.9	28.1	4.3	.8
Property crime[3].....................	25,343	21,105	2,397	1,014	827	100.0	83.3	9.5	4.0	3.3
Crime Index total[4]	28,872	23,466	3,387	1,164	855	100.0	81.3	11.7	4.0	3.0
Other assaults	6,401	4,632	1,279	284	206	100.0	72.4	20.0	4.4	3.2
Forgery and counterfeiting	355	316	25	10	4	100.0	89.0	7.0	2.8	1.1
Fraud	596	524	57	8	7	100.0	87.9	9.6	1.3	1.2
Embezzlement	33	29	3	....	1	100.0	87.9	9.1	....	3.0
Stolen property; buying, receiving, possessing..........................	1,058	907	120	20	11	100.0	85.7	11.3	1.9	1.0
Vandalism	7,000	6,286	340	260	114	100.0	89.8	4.9	3.7	1.6
Weapons; carrying, possessing, etc.	1,395	1,066	271	30	28	100.0	76.4	19.4	2.2	2.0
Prostitution and commercialized vice	7	5	2	....	....	100.0	71.4	28.6	....	....
Sex offenses (except forcible rape and prostitution)	1,427	1,240	116	61	10	100.0	86.9	8.1	4.3	.7
Drug abuse violations....................	3,093	2,348	550	78	117	100.0	75.9	17.8	2.5	3.8
Gambling	15	8	4	....	3	100.0	53.3	26.7	....	20.0
Offenses against family and children	351	309	17	13	12	100.0	88.0	4.8	3.7	3.4
Driving under the influence	1,948	1,708	110	91	39	100.0	87.7	5.6	4.7	2.0
Liquor laws...........................	10,036	9,306	152	500	78	100.0	92.7	1.5	5.0	.8
Drunkenness..........................	696	642	31	22	1	100.0	92.2	4.5	3.2	.1
Disorderly conduct	3,702	2,938	581	148	35	100.0	79.4	15.7	4.0	.9
Vagrancy	66	53	11	1	1	100.0	80.3	16.7	1.5	1.5
All other offenses (except traffic)	14,270	11,387	1,911	575	397	100.0	79.8	13.4	4.0	2.8
Suspicion	44	32	....	12	....	100.0	72.7	....	27.3	....
Curfew and loitering law violations	1,687	965	56	161	505	100.0	57.2	3.3	9.5	29.9
Runaways.............................	9,641	8,049	604	450	538	100.0	83.5	6.3	4.7	5.6

See footnotes at end of table.

Table 61. — Rural County Arrests, Distribution by Race, 1993 — Continued

Offense charged	Arrests 18 and over					Percent distribution[1]				
	Total	White	Black	American Indian or Alaskan Native	Asian or Pacific Islander	Total	White	Black	American Indian or Alaskan Native	Asian or Pacific Islander
TOTAL	795,646	627,510	136,282	22,877	8,977	100.0	78.9	17.1	2.9	1.1
Murder and nonnegligent manslaughter.....	1,323	847	437	29	10	100.0	64.0	33.0	2.2	.8
Forcible rape..........................	2,689	2,031	517	125	16	100.0	75.5	19.2	4.6	.6
Robbery	2,151	1,110	967	44	30	100.0	51.6	45.0	2.0	1.4
Aggravated assault	26,771	19,293	6,469	884	125	100.0	72.1	24.2	3.3	.5
Burglary..............................	19,858	15,594	3,544	535	185	100.0	78.5	17.8	2.7	.9
Larceny-theft..........................	34,674	26,444	7,104	649	477	100.0	76.3	20.5	1.9	1.4
Motor vehicle theft	4,822	3,868	743	151	60	100.0	80.2	15.4	3.1	1.2
Arson	976	840	117	17	2	100.0	86.1	12.0	1.7	.2
Violent crime[2].......................	32,934	23,281	8,390	1,082	181	100.0	70.7	25.5	3.3	.5
Property crime[3]......................	60,330	46,746	11,508	1,352	724	100.0	77.5	19.1	2.2	1.2
Crime Index total[4]	93,264	70,027	19,898	2,434	905	100.0	75.1	21.3	2.6	1.0
Other assaults	61,512	46,400	12,389	1,882	841	100.0	75.4	20.1	3.1	1.4
Forgery and counterfeiting	6,901	5,018	1,778	66	39	100.0	72.7	25.8	1.0	.6
Fraud	44,917	32,667	11,653	455	142	100.0	72.7	25.9	1.0	.3
Embezzlement..........................	838	702	97	7	32	100.0	83.8	11.6	.8	3.8
Stolen property; buying, receiving, possessing..........................	5,312	4,084	1,108	95	25	100.0	76.9	20.9	1.8	.5
Vandalism	11,334	9,312	1,620	319	83	100.0	82.2	14.3	2.8	.7
Weapons; carrying, possessing, etc.	9,789	7,155	2,313	184	137	100.0	73.1	23.6	1.9	1.4
Prostitution and commercialized vice	155	129	24	2	....	100.0	83.2	15.5	1.3	....
Sex offenses (except forcible rape and prostitution)	6,683	5,995	463	181	44	100.0	89.7	6.9	2.7	.7
Drug abuse violations.....................	54,142	42,611	10,252	893	386	100.0	78.7	18.9	1.6	.7
Gambling..............................	494	282	139	7	66	100.0	57.1	28.1	1.4	13.4
Offenses against family and children	10,697	7,750	2,384	474	89	100.0	72.5	22.3	4.4	.8
Driving under the influence	195,404	163,567	22,751	5,526	3,560	100.0	83.7	11.6	2.8	1.8
Liquor laws............................	29,211	26,337	1,614	1,095	165	100.0	90.2	5.5	3.7	.6
Drunkenness...........................	39,840	34,963	3,465	1,329	83	100.0	87.8	8.7	3.3	.2
Disorderly conduct	26,662	21,116	3,761	1,636	149	100.0	79.2	14.1	6.1	.6
Vagrancy	421	275	128	18	....	100.0	65.3	30.4	4.3	....
All other offenses (except traffic)	197,862	148,960	40,422	6,249	2,231	100.0	75.3	20.4	3.2	1.1
Suspicion	208	160	23	25	....	100.0	76.9	11.1	12.0	....
Curfew and loitering law violations	....	....	....	....	....	....	....	....	....	....
Runaways	....	....	....	....	....	....	....	....	....	....

[1]Because of rounding, the percentages may not add to total.

[2]Violent crimes are offenses of murder, forcible rape, robbery, and aggravated assault.

[3]Property crimes are offenses of burglary, larceny-theft, motor vehicle theft, and arson.

[4]Includes arson.

Table 62. — Suburban Area[1] Arrest Trends, 1992-1993
[4,668 agencies; 1993 estimated population 82,383,000; 1992 population 80,682,000]

Offense charged	Number of persons arrested								
	Total all ages			Under 18 years of age			18 years of age and over		
	1992	1993	Percent change	1992	1993	Percent change	1992	1993	Percent change
TOTAL.........................	3,791,344	3,774,453	-.4	631,611	647,990	+2.6	3,159,733	3,126,463	-1.1
Murder and nonnegligent manslaughter	4,057	4,281	+5.5	556	566	+1.8	3,501	3,715	+6.1
Forcible rape	9,169	9,126	-.5	1,573	1,640	+4.3	7,596	7,486	-1.4
Robbery.............................	30,046	28,770	-4.2	7,784	7,758	-.3	22,262	21,012	-5.6
Aggravated assault......................	123,672	126,939	+2.6	19,484	20,317	+4.3	104,188	106,622	+2.3
Burglary.............................	114,169	108,854	-4.7	43,651	41,333	-5.3	70,518	67,521	-4.2
Larceny-theft.........................	402,738	388,834	-3.5	131,564	126,162	-4.1	271,174	262,672	-3.1
Motor vehicle theft	46,330	45,891	-.9	20,606	20,204	-2.0	25,724	25,687	-.1
Arson..............................	5,859	5,573	-4.9	3,134	2,971	-5.2	2,725	2,602	-4.5
Violent crime[2]	166,944	169,116	+1.3	29,397	30,281	+3.0	137,547	138,835	+.9
Property crime[3]	569,096	549,152	-3.5	198,955	190,670	-4.2	370,141	358,482	-3.1
Crime Index total[4]...................	736,040	718,268	-2.4	228,352	220,951	-3.2	507,688	497,317	-2.0
Other assaults.........................	273,232	287,896	+5.4	46,901	50,910	+8.5	226,331	236,986	+4.7
Forgery and counterfeiting	28,653	28,800	+.5	2,115	2,045	-3.3	26,538	26,755	+.8
Fraud...............................	140,275	137,360	-2.1	4,869	4,753	-2.4	135,406	132,607	-2.1
Embezzlement	3,583	3,520	-1.8	191	185	-3.1	3,392	3,335	-1.7
Stolen property; buying, receiving, possessing.....................	43,370	43,123	-.6	12,257	12,089	-1.4	31,113	31,034	-.3
Vandalism............................	87,231	85,246	-2.3	44,694	43,854	-1.9	42,537	41,392	-2.7
Weapons; carrying, possessing, etc.	57,956	62,374	+7.6	14,329	15,862	+10.7	43,627	46,512	+6.6
Prostitution and commercialized vice	7,621	7,069	-7.2	185	162	-12.4	7,436	6,907	-7.1
Sex offenses (except forcible rape and prostitution)	28,172	27,381	-2.8	5,675	5,651	-.4	22,497	21,730	-3.4
Drug abuse violations	250,578	262,578	+4.8	18,969	25,050	+32.1	231,609	237,528	+2.6
Gambling	2,351	2,565	+9.1	179	181	+1.1	2,172	2,384	+9.8
Offenses against family and children.............	36,836	40,197	+9.1	1,262	1,475	+16.9	35,574	38,722	+8.8
Driving under the influence..................	532,950	501,480	-5.9	4,450	4,110	-7.6	528,500	497,370	-5.9
Liquor laws...........................	144,642	136,493	-5.6	37,755	35,091	-7.1	106,887	101,402	-5.1
Drunkenness	175,652	164,323	-6.4	4,645	4,463	-3.9	171,007	159,860	-6.5
Disorderly conduct.......................	163,242	173,144	+6.1	35,794	41,513	+16.0	127,448	131,631	+3.3
Vagrancy............................	4,132	3,989	-3.5	1,011	1,085	+7.3	3,121	2,904	-7.0
All other offenses (except traffic)...............	1,010,279	1,018,313	+.8	103,429	108,226	+4.6	906,850	910,087	+.4
Suspicion (not included in totals)...............	3,221	3,424	+6.3	833	734	-11.9	2,388	2,690	+12.6
Curfew and loitering law violations	20,025	22,656	+13.1	20,025	22,656	+13.1	....	....	....
Runaways	44,524	47,678	+7.1	44,524	47,678	+7.1	....	....	....

[1]Includes suburban city and county law enforcement agencies within metropolitan areas. Excludes central cities. Suburban cities and counties are also included in other groups.
[2]Violent crimes are offenses of murder, forcible rape, robbery, and aggravated assault.
[3]Property crimes are offenses of burglary, larceny-theft, motor vehicle theft, and arson.
[4]Includes arson.

Table 63. — Suburban Area[1] Arrest Trends, Sex, 1992-1993

[4,668 agencies; 1993 estimated population 82,383,000; 1992 estimated population 80,682,000]

Offense charged	Males						Females					
	Total			Under 18			Total			Under 18		
	1992	1993	Percent change	1992	1993	Percent change	1992	1993	Percent change	1992	1993	Percent change
TOTAL....................	3,072,315	3,042,106	-1.0	494,249	500,091	+1.2	719,029	732,347	+1.9	137,362	147,899	+7.7
Murder and nonnegligent manslaughter	3,636	3,846	+5.8	518	531	+2.5	421	435	+3.3	38	35	-7.9
Forcible rape	9,052	9,026	-.3	1,535	1,619	+5.5	117	100	-14.5	38	21	-44.7
Robbery........................	27,588	26,357	-4.5	7,175	7,136	-.5	2,458	2,413	-1.8	609	622	+2.1
Aggravated assault................	106,699	108,543	+1.7	16,501	17,032	+3.2	16,973	18,396	+8.4	2,983	3,285	+10.1
Burglary	104,285	98,705	-5.4	40,138	37,596	-6.3	9,884	10,149	+2.7	3,513	3,737	+6.4
Larceny-theft	275,558	263,239	-4.5	96,400	90,518	-6.1	127,180	125,595	-1.2	35,164	35,644	+1.4
Motor vehicle theft	41,070	40,272	-1.9	17,831	17,243	-3.3	5,260	5,619	+6.8	2,775	2,961	+6.7
Arson...........................	5,145	4,798	-6.7	2,816	2,602	-7.6	714	775	+8.5	318	369	+16.0
Violent crime[2]	146,975	147,772	+.5	25,729	26,318	+2.3	19,969	21,344	+6.9	3,668	3,963	+8.0
Property crime[3]	426,058	407,014	-4.5	157,185	147,959	-5.9	143,038	142,138	-.6	41,770	42,711	+2.3
Crime Index total[4].............	573,033	554,786	-3.2	182,914	174,277	-4.7	163,007	163,482	+.3	45,438	46,674	+2.7
Other assaults	225,056	234,440	+4.2	36,132	38,252	+5.9	48,176	53,456	+11.0	10,769	12,658	+17.5
Forgery and counterfeiting	18,762	18,489	-1.5	1,381	1,334	-3.4	9,891	10,311	+4.2	734	711	-3.1
Fraud...........................	76,446	75,565	-1.2	3,559	3,426	-3.7	63,829	61,795	-3.2	1,310	1,327	+1.3
Embezzlement	2,176	2,100	-3.5	127	110	-13.4	1,407	1,420	+.9	64	75	+17.2
Stolen property; buying, receiving, possessing......................	37,713	37,417	-.8	10,966	10,726	-2.2	5,657	5,706	+.9	1,291	1,363	+5.6
Vandalism.......................	78,306	75,688	-3.3	41,145	39,816	-3.2	8,925	9,558	+7.1	3,549	4,038	+13.8
Weapons; carrying, possessing, etc.....	53,798	57,416	+6.7	13,409	14,715	+9.7	4,158	4,958	+19.2	920	1,147	+24.7
Prostitution and commercialized vice......................	3,633	3,379	-7.0	121	93	-23.1	3,988	3,690	-7.5	64	69	+7.8
Sex offenses (except forcible rape and prostitution)	26,656	25,623	-3.9	5,305	5,096	-3.9	1,516	1,758	+16.0	370	555	+50.0
Drug abuse violations	208,457	218,699	+4.9	16,530	21,773	+31.7	42,121	43,879	+4.2	2,439	3,277	+34.4
Gambling	2,007	2,210	+10.1	170	177	+4.1	344	355	+3.2	9	4	-55.6
Offenses against family and children......................	32,398	34,826	+7.5	875	967	+10.5	4,438	5,371	+21.0	387	508	+31.3
Driving under the influence...........	457,821	429,931	-6.1	3,838	3,520	-8.3	75,129	71,549	-4.8	612	590	-3.6
Liquor laws........................	115,604	109,396	-5.4	26,980	25,430	-5.7	29,038	27,097	-6.7	10,775	9,661	-10.3
Drunkenness	156,488	145,878	-6.8	3,904	3,733	-4.4	19,164	18,445	-3.8	741	730	-1.5
Disorderly conduct	132,481	139,677	+5.4	28,604	32,716	+14.4	30,761	33,467	+8.8	7,190	8,797	+22.4
Vagrancy........................	3,573	3,454	-3.3	881	901	+2.3	559	535	-4.3	130	184	+41.5
All other offenses (except traffic)	833,229	835,510	+.3	82,730	85,407	+3.2	177,050	182,803	+3.2	20,699	22,819	+10.2
Suspicion (not included in totals)......	2,783	2,950	+6.0	722	601	-16.8	438	474	+8.2	111	133	+19.8
Curfew and loitering law violations	14,669	16,419	+11.9	14,669	16,419	+11.9	5,356	6,237	+16.4	5,356	6,237	+16.4
Runaways	20,009	21,203	+6.0	20,009	21,203	+6.0	24,515	26,475	+8.0	24,515	26,475	+8.0

[1]Includes suburban city and county law enforcement agencies within metropolitan areas. Excludes central cities. Suburban cities and counties are also included in other groups.

[2]Violent crimes are offenses of murder, forcible rape, robbery, and aggravated assault.

[3]Property crimes are offenses of burglary, larceny-theft, motor vehicle theft, and arson.

[4]Includes arson.

Table 64. — Suburban Area[1] Arrests, Distribution by Age, 1993

[5,327 agencies; 1993 estimated population 92,137,000]

Offense charged	Total all ages	Ages under 15	Ages under 18	Ages 18 and over	Under 10	10-12	13-14	15	16	17	18	19	20	21
TOTAL	4,275,378	253,929	731,478	3,543,900	13,368	58,299	182,262	140,951	164,807	171,791	194,936	184,915	172,893	167,055
Percent distribution[2]	100.0	5.9	17.1	82.9	.3	1.4	4.3	3.3	3.9	4.0	4.6	4.3	4.0	3.9
Murder and nonnegligent manslaughter	4,789	61	644	4,145	4	8	49	121	205	257	329	286	274	257
Forcible rape	10,195	721	1,819	8,376	31	180	510	296	425	377	518	415	365	413
Robbery	32,738	2,483	8,842	23,896	52	476	1,955	1,738	2,268	2,353	2,459	1,979	1,729	1,452
Aggravated assault	143,087	7,544	22,897	120,190	385	1,729	5,430	4,352	5,293	5,708	5,965	5,441	5,192	5,443
Burglary	119,869	17,902	45,644	74,225	1,009	4,429	12,464	8,997	9,555	9,190	8,946	6,846	4,940	4,503
Larceny-theft	442,000	62,504	143,317	298,683	3,220	16,948	42,336	26,573	28,013	26,227	24,707	19,241	14,971	13,367
Motor vehicle theft	50,037	6,317	22,210	27,827	59	671	5,587	5,590	5,665	4,638	3,584	2,693	2,088	1,750
Arson	6,145	2,057	3,238	2,907	310	687	1,060	499	352	330	250	189	151	138
Violent crime[3]	190,809	10,809	34,202	156,607	472	2,393	7,944	6,507	8,191	8,695	9,271	8,121	7,560	7,565
Percent distribution[2]	100.0	5.7	17.9	82.1	.2	1.3	4.2	3.4	4.3	4.6	4.9	4.3	4.0	4.0
Property crime[4]	618,051	88,780	214,409	403,642	4,598	22,735	61,447	41,659	43,585	40,385	37,487	28,969	22,150	19,758
Percent distribution[2]	100.0	14.4	34.7	65.3	.7	3.7	9.9	6.7	7.1	6.5	6.1	4.7	3.6	3.2
Crime Index total[5]	808,860	99,589	248,611	560,249	5,070	25,128	69,391	48,166	51,776	49,080	46,758	37,090	29,710	27,323
Percent distribution[2]	100.0	12.3	30.7	69.3	.6	3.1	8.6	6.0	6.4	6.1	5.8	4.6	3.7	3.4
Other assaults	326,804	23,190	57,151	269,653	1,358	5,882	15,950	10,760	11,631	11,570	11,170	10,597	10,347	11,132
Forgery and counterfeiting	32,209	382	2,309	29,900	12	87	283	376	609	942	1,461	1,616	1,651	1,426
Fraud	149,173	1,330	5,000	144,173	64	199	1,067	1,098	1,015	1,557	3,302	4,675	5,614	6,461
Embezzlement	3,838	28	200	3,638	4	9	15	19	58	95	177	201	222	176
Stolen property; buying, receiving, possessing	48,910	3,868	13,607	35,303	94	748	3,026	2,815	3,392	3,532	3,712	3,101	2,486	2,167
Vandalism	96,612	23,456	49,362	47,250	2,430	6,819	14,207	8,744	9,441	7,721	5,874	4,220	3,114	2,792
Weapons; carrying, possessing, etc.	70,122	5,976	17,958	52,164	216	1,201	4,559	3,594	4,108	4,280	4,784	3,913	3,351	3,196
Prostitution and commercialized vice	9,307	34	195	9,112	......	9	25	34	51	76	162	210	259	275
Sex offenses (except forcible rape and prostitution)	30,006	3,136	6,180	23,826	269	807	2,060	1,049	1,046	949	965	818	799	812
Drug abuse violations	291,059	4,203	27,872	263,187	43	401	3,759	4,812	7,764	11,093	15,999	15,324	14,517	13,603
Gambling	2,962	84	281	2,681	6	17	61	67	63	67	115	83	85	98
Offenses against family and children	45,074	609	1,854	43,220	76	112	421	381	454	410	778	901	1,061	1,305
Driving under the influence	549,668	123	4,464	545,204	32	18	73	181	1,032	3,128	8,660	11,123	14,137	20,765
Liquor laws	153,318	3,696	38,810	114,508	52	261	3,383	5,751	11,323	18,040	26,385	24,226	19,107	5,214
Drunkenness	191,630	738	5,195	186,435	30	76	632	795	1,352	2,310	4,955	5,266	5,574	7,431
Disorderly conduct	203,870	16,214	47,702	156,168	767	3,757	11,690	9,639	10,603	11,246	11,073	9,379	8,315	9,028
Vagrancy	4,596	349	1,197	3,399	15	59	275	261	334	253	293	225	194	164
All other offenses (except traffic)	1,173,409	35,409	122,588	1,050,821	2,259	7,652	25,498	21,629	29,227	36,323	48,126	51,756	52,172	53,549
Suspicion	3,783	255	774	3,009	21	81	153	186	164	169	187	191	178	138
Curfew and loitering law violations	26,045	7,999	26,045	....	93	1,215	6,691	6,307	7,175	4,564	....	....	....	....
Runaways	54,123	23,261	54,123	....	457	3,761	19,043	14,287	12,189	4,386	....	....	....	....

See footnotes at end of table.

Table 64. — Suburban Area[1] Arrests, Distribution by Age, 1993 — Continued

Offense charged	Age											
	22	23	24	25-29	30-34	35-39	40-44	45-49	50-54	55-59	60-64	65 and over
TOTAL	168,435	159,855	148,036	677,800	622,215	449,350	268,228	149,644	80,659	43,748	26,263	29,868
Percent distribution[2]	3.9	3.7	3.5	15.9	14.6	10.5	6.3	3.5	1.9	1.0	.6	.7
Murder and nonnegligent												
manslaughter	240	212	202	699	535	424	240	171	124	53	43	56
Forcible rape	369	360	357	1,581	1,407	1,039	655	392	200	116	98	91
Robbery	1,450	1,296	1,189	5,011	3,668	2,090	936	377	135	63	25	37
Aggravated assault	5,327	5,117	4,974	23,795	22,257	15,915	9,078	5,399	2,759	1,562	905	1,061
Burglary	4,171	3,737	3,180	13,893	11,082	7,133	3,230	1,393	597	279	130	165
Larceny-theft	12,880	11,699	11,040	51,530	48,955	37,380	22,408	12,237	6,705	3,941	2,828	4,794
Motor vehicle theft	1,698	1,430	1,238	5,113	3,795	2,240	1,179	539	242	106	54	78
Arson	121	122	87	449	480	384	225	126	89	37	25	34
Violent crime[3]	7,386	6,985	6,722	31,086	27,867	19,468	10,909	6,339	3,218	1,794	1,071	1,245
Percent distribution[2]	3.9	3.7	3.5	16.3	14.6	10.2	5.7	3.3	1.7	.9	.6	.7
Property crime[4]	18,870	16,988	15,545	70,985	64,312	47,137	27,042	14,295	7,633	4,363	3,037	5,071
Percent distribution[2]	3.1	2.7	2.5	11.5	10.4	7.6	4.4	2.3	1.2	.7	.5	.8
Crime Index total[5]	26,256	23,973	22,267	102,071	92,179	66,605	37,951	20,634	10,851	6,157	4,108	6,316
Percent distribution[2]	3.2	3.0	2.8	12.6	11.4	8.2	4.7	2.6	1.3	.8	.5	.8
Other assaults	11,754	11,794	11,481	54,825	52,825	37,285	21,364	11,807	6,082	3,169	1,865	2,156
Forgery and counterfeiting	1,484	1,474	1,414	6,201	5,478	4,028	1,940	955	367	217	89	99
Fraud	6,964	7,064	6,445	30,267	26,815	20,369	12,471	6,918	3,386	1,702	877	843
Embezzlement	188	149	175	683	593	403	300	178	98	38	38	19
Stolen property; buying, receiving,												
possessing	2,007	1,732	1,638	6,428	5,084	3,434	1,800	907	438	179	93	97
Vandalism	2,627	2,302	1,972	8,256	6,899	4,278	2,248	1,247	605	324	213	279
Weapons; carrying,												
possessing, etc.	3,127	2,812	2,250	9,056	6,979	4,892	3,090	1,989	1,180	633	403	509
Prostitution and												
commercialized vice	358	380	356	2,047	2,048	1,343	724	405	239	125	92	89
Sex offenses (except forcible												
rape and prostitution)	845	809	808	3,871	4,143	3,333	2,191	1,567	977	668	492	728
Drug abuse violations	13,851	13,039	11,610	54,881	48,938	32,542	16,703	6,961	2,966	1,208	572	473
Gambling	69	67	58	295	295	283	266	260	264	190	127	126
Offenses against family and												
children	1,492	1,612	1,807	8,869	9,540	7,372	4,284	2,241	1,044	514	219	181
Driving under the influence	22,790	23,451	22,240	105,976	104,796	79,980	52,715	33,724	20,000	11,369	6,999	6,479
Liquor laws	4,079	3,194	2,454	9,242	7,562	5,279	3,182	1,951	1,124	629	439	441
Drunkenness	7,183	6,805	6,471	31,716	34,466	28,428	19,579	11,852	7,239	4,232	2,648	2,590
Disorderly conduct	8,464	7,569	6,788	28,565	25,515	17,720	10,377	5,916	3,326	1,765	1,107	1,261
Vagrancy	174	132	132	549	550	396	254	137	67	38	36	58
All other offenses (except												
traffic)	54,595	51,349	47,553	213,397	186,993	131,015	76,588	39,880	20,353	10,564	5,829	7,102
Suspicion	128	148	117	605	517	365	201	115	53	27	17	22
Curfew and loitering law												
violations	......	......	......	......	......	......	......	......	......	......	......	......
Runaways	......	......	......	......	......	......	......	......	......	......	......	......

[1]Includes suburban city and county law enforcement agencies within metropolitan areas. Excludes central cities. Suburban cities and counties are also included in other groups.
[2]Because of rounding, the percentages may not add to total.
[3]Violent crimes are offenses of murder, forcible rape, robbery, and aggravated assault.
[4]Property crimes are offenses of burglary, larceny-theft, motor vehicle theft, and arson.
[5]Includes arson.

Table 65. — Suburban Area[1] Arrests of Persons under 15, 18, 21, and 25 Years of Age, 1993

[5,327 agencies; 1993 estimated population 92,137,000]

Offense charged	Total all ages	Number of persons arrested				Percent of total all ages			
		Under 15	Under 18	Under 21	Under 25	Under 15	Under 18	Under 21	Under 25
TOTAL	4,275,378	253,929	731,478	1,284,222	1,927,603	5.9	17.1	30.0	45.1
Murder and nonnegligent manslaughter................	4,789	61	644	1,533	2,444	1.3	13.4	32.0	51.0
Forcible rape	10,195	721	1,819	3,117	4,616	7.1	17.8	30.6	45.3
Robbery	32,738	2,483	8,842	15,009	20,396	7.6	27.0	45.8	62.3
Aggravated assault	143,087	7,544	22,897	39,495	60,356	5.3	16.0	27.6	42.2
Burglary	119,869	17,902	45,644	66,376	81,967	14.9	38.1	55.4	68.4
Larceny-theft...........................	442,000	62,504	143,317	202,236	251,222	14.1	32.4	45.8	56.8
Motor vehicle theft.....................	50,037	6,317	22,210	30,575	36,691	12.6	44.4	61.1	73.3
Arson	6,145	2,057	3,238	3,828	4,296	33.5	52.7	62.3	69.9
Violent crime[2]	190,809	10,809	34,202	59,154	87,812	5.7	17.9	31.0	46.0
Property crime[3]	618,051	88,780	214,409	303,015	374,176	14.4	34.7	49.0	60.5
Crime Index total[4]	808,860	99,589	248,611	362,169	461,988	12.3	30.7	44.8	57.1
Other assaults	326,804	23,190	57,151	89,265	135,426	7.1	17.5	27.3	41.4
Forgery and counterfeiting	32,209	382	2,309	7,037	12,835	1.2	7.2	21.8	39.8
Fraud..	149,173	1,330	5,000	18,591	45,525	.9	3.4	12.5	30.5
Embezzlement..	3,838	28	200	800	1,488	.7	5.2	20.8	38.8
Stolen property; buying, receiving, possessing...........	48,910	3,868	13,607	22,906	30,450	7.9	27.8	46.8	62.3
Vandalism	96,612	23,456	49,362	62,570	72,263	24.3	51.1	64.8	74.8
Weapons; carrying, possessing, etc....................	70,122	5,976	17,958	30,006	41,391	8.5	25.6	42.8	59.0
Prostitution and commercialized vice	9,307	34	195	826	2,195	.4	2.1	8.9	23.6
Sex offenses (except forcible rape and prostitution)	30,006	3,136	6,180	8,762	12,036	10.5	20.6	29.2	40.1
Drug abuse violations...............................	291,059	4,203	27,872	73,712	125,815	1.4	9.6	25.3	43.2
Gambling	2,962	84	281	564	856	2.8	9.5	19.0	28.9
Offenses against family and children	45,074	609	1,854	4,594	10,810	1.4	4.1	10.2	24.0
Driving under the influence	549,668	123	4,464	38,384	127,630	[5]	.8	7.0	23.2
Liquor laws...	153,318	3,696	38,810	108,528	123,469	2.4	25.3	70.8	80.5
Drunkenness..	191,630	738	5,195	20,990	48,880	.4	2.7	11.0	25.5
Disorderly conduct	203,870	16,214	47,702	76,469	108,318	8.0	23.4	37.5	53.1
Vagrancy...	4,596	349	1,197	1,909	2,511	7.6	26.0	41.5	54.6
All other offenses (except traffic)	1,173,409	35,409	122,588	274,642	481,688	3.0	10.4	23.4	41.1
Suspicion	3,783	255	774	1,330	1,861	6.7	20.5	35.2	49.2
Curfew and loitering law violations	26,045	7,999	26,045	26,045	26,045	30.7	100.0	100.0	100.0
Runaways...	54,123	23,261	54,123	54,123	54,123	43.0	100.0	100.0	100.0

[1]Includes suburban city and county law enforcement agencies within metropolitan areas. Excludes central cities. Suburban cities and counties are also included in other groups.

[2]Violent crimes are offenses of murder, forcible rape, robbery, and aggravated assault.

[3]Property crimes are offenses of burglary, larceny-theft, motor vehicle theft, and arson.

[4]Includes arson.

[5]Less than one-tenth of 1 percent.

Table 66. — Suburban Area[1] Arrests, Distribution by Sex, 1993

[5,327 agencies; 1993 estimated population 92,137,000]

Offense charged	Number of persons arrested			Percent male	Percent female	Percent distribution[2]		
	Total	Male	Female			Total	Male	Female
TOTAL	4,275,378	3,443,071	832,307	80.5	19.5	100.0	100.0	100.0
Murder and nonnegligent manslaughter.........................	4,789	4,311	478	90.0	10.0	.1	.1	.1
Forcible rape...	10,195	10,075	120	98.8	1.2	.2	.3	3
Robbery..	32,738	29,943	2,795	91.5	8.5	.8	.9	.3
Aggravated assault.......................................	143,087	122,062	21,025	85.3	14.7	3.3	3.5	2.5
Burglary..	119,869	108,871	10,998	90.8	9.2	2.8	3.2	1.3
Larceny-theft...	442,000	298,898	143,102	67.6	32.4	10.3	8.7	17.2
Motor vehicle theft......................................	50,037	43,894	6,143	87.7	12.3	1.2	1.3	.7
Arson..	6,145	5,293	852	86.1	13.9	.1	.2	.1
Violent crime[4]	190,809	166,391	24,418	87.2	12.8	4.5	4.8	2.9
Property crime[5]	618,051	456,956	161,095	73.9	26.1	14.5	13.3	19.4
Crime Index total[6]	808,860	623,347	185,513	77.1	22.9	18.9	18.1	22.3
Other assaults	326,804	266,505	60,299	81.5	18.5	7.6	7.7	7.2
Forgery and counterfeiting	32,209	20,648	11,561	64.1	35.9	.8	.6	1.4
Fraud.................................	149,173	82,405	66,768	55.2	44.8	3.5	2.4	8.0
Embezzlement	3,838	2,310	1,528	60.2	39.8	.1	.1	.2
Stolen property; buying, receiving, possessing.	48,910	42,385	6,525	86.7	13.3	1.1	1.2	.8
Vandalism	96,612	85,704	10,908	88.7	11.3	2.3	2.5	1.3
Weapons; carrying, possessing, etc.........	70,122	64,339	5,783	91.8	8.2	1.6	1.9	.7
Prostitution and commercialized vice	9,307	4,493	4,814	48.3	51.7	.2	.1	.6
Sex offenses (except forcible rape and prostitution).....................	30,006	28,013	1,993	93.4	6.6	.7	.8	.2
Drug abuse violations....................	291,059	242,867	48,192	83.4	16.6	6.8	7.1	5.8
Gambling	2,962	2,534	428	85.6	14.4	.1	.1	.1
Offenses against family and children	45,074	38,789	6,285	86.1	13.9	1.1	1.1	.8
Driving under the influence	549,668	470,498	79,170	85.6	14.4	12.9	13.7	9.5
Liquor laws............................	153,318	122,910	30,408	80.2	19.8	3.6	3.6	3.7
Drunkenness	191,630	169,880	21,750	88.7	11.3	4.5	4.9	2.6
Disorderly conduct	203,870	164,027	39,843	80.5	19.5	4.8	4.8	4.8
Vagrancy..............................	4,596	3,933	663	85.6	14.4	.1	.1	.1
All other offenses (except traffic)	1,173,409	961,420	211,989	81.9	18.1	27.4	27.9	25.5
Suspicion	3,783	3,272	511	86.5	13.5	.1	.1	.1
Curfew and loitering law violations	26,045	18,969	7,076	72.8	27.2	.6	.6	.9
Runaways	54,123	23,823	30,300	44.0	56.0	1.3	.7	3.6

[1]Includes suburban city and county law enforcement agencies within metropolitan areas. Excludes central cities. Suburban cities and counties are also included in other groups.

[2]Because of rounding, the percentages may not add to total.

[3]Less than one-tenth of 1 percent.

[4]Violent crimes are offenses of murder, forcible rape, robbery, and aggravated assault.

[5]Property crimes are offenses of burglary, larceny-theft, motor vehicle theft, and arson.

[6]Includes arson.

Table 67. — Suburban Area[1] Arrests, Distribution by Race, 1993

[5,324 agencies; 1993 estimated population 92,137,000]

Offense charged	Total arrests					Percent distribution[2]				
	Total	White	Black	American Indian or Alaskan Native	Asian or Pacific Islander	Total	White	Black	American Indian or Alaskan Native	Asian or Pacific Islander
TOTAL	4,262,526	3,191,923	1,027,787	19,505	23,311	100.0	74.9	24.1	.5	.5
Murder and nonnegligent manslaughter....	4,786	2,799	1,923	14	50	100.0	58.5	40.2	.3	1.0
Forcible rape	10,168	7,132	2,958	28	50	100.0	70.1	29.1	.3	.5
Robbery	32,715	14,479	17,887	112	237	100.0	44.3	54.7	.3	.7
Aggravated assault	142,881	100,094	41,231	687	869	100.0	70.1	28.9	.5	.6
Burglary	119,701	91,152	27,343	422	784	100.0	76.1	22.8	.4	.7
Larceny-theft	441,167	303,894	130,985	1,915	4,373	100.0	68.9	29.7	.4	1.0
Motor vehicle theft....................	49,922	34,032	15,268	191	431	100.0	68.2	30.6	.4	.9
Arson	6,128	5,163	894	38	33	100.0	84.3	14.6	.	.5
Violent crime[3]	190,550	124,504	63,999	841	1,206	100.0	65.3	33.6	.4	.6
Property crime[4]....................	616,918	434,241	174,490	2,566	5,621	100.0	70.4	28.3	.4	.9
Crime Index total[5]	807,468	558,745	238,489	3,407	6,827	100.0	69.2	29.5	.4	.8
Other assaults	326,151	239,885	82,672	1,728	1,866	100.0	73.6	25.3	.5	.6
Forgery and counterfeiting	32,156	22,342	9,527	80	207	100.0	69.5	29.6	.2	.6
Fraud.................................	148,888	99,584	48,297	346	661	100.0	66.9	32.4	.2	.4
Embezzlement........................	3,837	2,733	1,065	11	28	100.0	71.2	27.8	.3	.7
Stolen property; buying, receiving, possessing.........................	48,817	32,034	16,105	212	466	100.0	65.6	33.0	.4	1.0
Vandalism	96,422	80,707	14,707	341	667	100.0	83.7	15.3	.4	.7
Weapons; carrying, possessing, etc.........	69,931	47,538	21,636	234	523	100.0	68.0	30.9	.3	.7
Prostitution and commercialized vice	9,302	6,791	2,360	32	119	100.0	73.0	25.4	.3	1.3
Sex offenses (except forcible rape and prostitution).........................	29,945	25,199	4,457	104	185	100.0	84.2	14.9	.3	.6
Drug abuse violations....................	290,529	210,931	77,916	701	981	100.0	72.6	26.8	.2	.3
Gambling	2,950	1,730	1,180	11	29	100.0	58.6	40.0	.4	1.0
Offenses against family and children	44,711	30,536	13,914	121	140	100.0	68.3	31.1	.3	.3
Driving under the influence	547,514	498,517	43,559	2,649	2,789	100.0	91.1	8.0	.5	.5
Liquor laws...........................	152,078	137,767	12,357	1,152	802	100.0	90.6	8.1	.8	.5
Drunkenness	191,580	167,891	21,364	1,750	575	100.0	87.6	11.2	.9	.3
Disorderly conduct	203,429	155,175	46,589	863	802	100.0	76.3	22.9	.4	.4
Vagrancy.............................	4,594	3,401	1,137	13	43	100.0	74.0	24.7	.3	.9
All other offenses (except traffic)	1,168,437	798,758	359,374	5,329	4,976	100.0	68.4	30.8	.5	.4
Suspicion	3,780	2,842	889	29	20	100.0	75.2	23.5	.8	.5
Curfew and loitering law violations	25,925	22,319	3,309	78	219	100.0	86.1	12.8	.3	.8
Runaways.............................	54,082	46,498	6,884	314	386	100.0	86.0	12.7	.6	.7

See footnotes at end of table.

Table 67. — Suburban Area[1] Arrests, Distribution by Race, 1993 — Continued

Offense charged	Arrests under 18					Percent distribution[2]				
	Total	White	Black	American Indian or Alaskan Native	Asian or Pacific Islander	Total	White	Black	American Indian or Alaskan Native	Asian or Pacific Islander
TOTAL	729,422	560,951	158,735	3,225	6,511	100.0	76.9	21.8	.4	.9
Murder and nonnegligent manslaughter....	641	303	330	3	5	100.0	47.3	51.5	.5	.8
Forcible rape	1,807	1,245	547	5	10	100.0	68.9	30.3	.3	.6
Robbery	8,833	3,722	4,974	32	105	100.0	42.1	56.3	.4	1.2
Aggravated assault	22,857	14,838	7,720	115	184	100.0	64.9	33.8	.5	.8
Burglary	45,515	36,388	8,546	176	405	100.0	79.9	18.8	.4	.9
Larceny-theft	142,948	106,889	33,457	647	1,955	100.0	74.8	23.4	.5	1.4
Motor vehicle theft	22,153	14,891	6,859	93	310	100.0	67.2	31.0	.4	1.4
Arson	3,227	2,817	366	19	25	100.0	87.3	11.3	.6	.8
Violent crime[3]	34,138	20,108	13,571	155	304	100.0	58.9	39.8	.5	.9
Property crime[4]	213,843	160,985	49,228	935	2,695	100.0	75.3	23.0	.4	1.3
Crime Index total[5]	247,981	181,093	62,799	1,090	2,999	100.0	73.0	25.3	.4	1.2
Other assaults	56,957	40,444	15,816	282	415	100.0	71.0	27.8	.5	.7
Forgery and counterfeiting	2,304	1,935	339	5	25	100.0	84.0	14.7	.2	1.1
Fraud...............................	4,994	2,889	2,032	11	62	100.0	57.8	40.7	.2	1.2
Embezzlement.......................	199	155	42	1	1	100.0	77.9	21.1	.5	.5
Stolen property; buying, receiving, possessing......................	13,587	9,022	4,273	81	211	100.0	66.4	31.4	.6	1.6
Vandalism	49,233	42,651	5,996	152	434	100.0	86.6	12.2	.3	.9
Weapons; carrying, possessing, etc.........	17,916	12,673	4,985	63	195	100.0	70.7	27.8	.4	1.1
Prostitution and commercialized vice	194	149	43	1	1	100.0	76.8	22.2	.5	.5
Sex offenses (except forcible rape and prostitution).....................	6,149	4,872	1,237	13	27	100.0	79.2	20.1	.2	.4
Drug abuse violations..................	27,784	20,368	7,202	85	129	100.0	73.3	25.9	.3	.5
Gambling	280	100	180	....	....	100.0	35.7	64.3	....	....
Offenses against family and children	1,837	1,539	284	9	5	100.0	83.8	15.5	.5	.3
Driving under the influence	4,454	4,209	196	33	16	100.0	94.5	4.4	.7	.4
Liquor laws..........................	38,636	36,579	1,592	286	179	100.0	94.7	4.1	.7	.5
Drunkenness	5,187	4,828	292	43	24	100.0	93.1	5.6	.8	.5
Disorderly conduct	47,584	35,452	11,754	105	273	100.0	74.5	24.7	.2	.6
Vagrancy............................	1,196	1,006	160	1	29	100.0	84.1	13.4	.1	2.4
All other offenses (except traffic)	122,170	91,618	29,108	570	874	100.0	75.0	23.8	.5	.7
Suspicion	773	552	212	2	7	100.0	71.4	27.4	.3	.9
Curfew and loitering law violations	25,925	22,319	3,309	78	219	100.0	86.1	12.8	.3	.8
Runaways............................	54,082	46,498	6,884	314	386	100.0	86.0	12.7	.6	.7

See footnotes at end of table.

Table 67.—Suburban Area[1] Arrests, Distribution by Race, 1993—Continued

Offense charged	Arrests 18 and over					Percent distribution[2]				
	Total	White	Black	American Indian or Alaskan Native	Asian or Pacific Islander	Total	White	Black	American Indian or Alaskan Native	Asian or Pacific Islander
TOTAL	3,533,104	2,630,972	869,052	16,280	16,800	100.0	74.5	24.6	.5	.5
Murder and nonnegligent manslaughter....	4,145	2,496	1,593	11	45	100.0	60.2	38.4	.3	1.1
Forcible rape	8,361	5,887	2,411	23	40	100.0	70.4	28.8	.3	.5
Robbery	23,882	10,757	12,913	80	132	100.0	45.0	54.1	.3	.6
Aggravated assault	120,024	85,256	33,511	572	685	100.0	71.0	27.9	.5	.6
Burglary	74,186	54,764	18,797	246	379	100.0	73.8	25.3	.3	.5
Larceny-theft.........................	298,219	197,005	97,528	1,268	2,418	100.0	66.1	32.7	.4	.8
Motor vehicle theft.....................	27,769	19,141	8,409	98	121	100.0	68.9	30.3	.4	.4
Arson	2,901	2,346	528	19	8	100.0	80.9	18.2	.7	.3
Violent crime[3]	156,412	104,396	50,428	686	902	100.0	66.7	32.2	.4	.6
Property crime[4].....................	403,075	273,256	125,262	1,631	2,926	100.0	67.8	31.1	.4	.7
Crime Index total[5]	559,487	377,652	175,690	2,317	3,828	100.0	67.5	31.4	.4	.7
Other assaults	269,194	199,441	66,856	1,446	1,451	100.0	74.1	24.8	.5	.5
Forgery and counterfeiting	29,852	20,407	9,188	75	182	100.0	68.4	30.8	.3	.6
Fraud................................	143,894	96,695	46,265	335	599	100.0	67.2	32.2	.2	.4
Embezzlement.........................	3,638	2,578	1,023	10	27	100.0	70.9	28.1	.3	.7
Stolen property; buying, receiving, possessing.........................	35,230	23,012	11,832	131	255	100.0	65.3	33.6	.4	.7
Vandalism	47,189	38,056	8,711	189	233	100.0	80.6	18.5	.4	.5
Weapons; carrying, possessing, etc........	52,015	34,865	16,651	171	328	100.0	67.0	32.0	.3	.6
Prostitution and commercialized vice	9,108	6,642	2,317	31	118	100.0	72.9	25.4	.3	1.3
Sex offenses (except forcible rape and prostitution).....................	23,796	20,327	3,220	91	158	100.0	85.4	13.5	.4	.7
Drug abuse violations...................	262,745	190,563	70,714	616	852	100.0	72.5	26.9	.2	.3
Gambling	2,670	1,630	1,000	11	29	100.0	61.0	37.5	.4	1.1
Offenses against family and children	42,874	28,997	13,630	112	135	100.0	67.6	31.8	.3	.3
Driving under the influence	543,060	494,308	43,363	2,616	2,773	100.0	91.0	8.0	.5	.5
Liquor laws...........................	113,442	101,188	10,765	866	623	100.0	89.2	9.5	.8	.5
Drunkenness.........................	186,393	163,063	21,072	1,707	551	100.0	87.5	11.3	.9	.3
Disorderly conduct	155,845	119,723	34,835	758	529	100.0	76.8	22.4	.5	.3
Vagrancy.............................	3,398	2,395	977	12	14	100.0	70.5	28.8	.4	.4
All other offenses (except traffic)	1,046,267	707,140	330,266	4,759	4,102	100.0	67.6	31.6	.5	.4
Suspicion	3,007	2,290	677	27	13	100.0	76.2	22.5	.9	.4
Curfew and loitering law violations	....	....	....	....	....	....	....	....	....	....
Runaways.............................	....	....	....	....	....	....	....	....	....	....

[1]Includes suburban city and county law enforcement agencies within metropolitan areas. Excludes central cities. Suburban cities and counties are also included in other groups.
[2]Because of rounding, the percentages may not add to total.
[3]Violent crimes are offenses of murder, forcible rape, robbery, and aggravated assault.
[4]Property crimes are offenses of burglary, larceny-theft, motor vehicle theft, and arson.
[5]Includes arson.

Table 68. — Arrests by State, 1993

[1993 estimated population] Leaders indicate zero data.

State	Total[1] all classes	Crime[2] Index total	Violent[3] crime	Property[4] crime	Murder and non-negligent man-slaughter	Forcible rape	Robbery	Aggra-vated assault	Burglary	Larceny-theft	Motor vehicle theft	Arson	Other assaults	Forgery and counter-feiting	Fraud
ALABAMA: 255 agencies; population 3,956,000															
Under 18	13,719	5,791	920	4,871	43	59	268	550	776	3,594	477	24	846	45	93
Total all ages	186,681	34,942	11,347	23,595	450	644	1,948	8,305	3,941	17,870	1,637	147	25,288	1,572	12,821
ALASKA: 26 agencies; population 567,000															
Under 18	6,155	3,373	250	3,123	5	20	55	170	604	2,229	267	23	413	16	14
Total all ages	37,959	8,300	1,606	6,694	22	163	174	1,247	1,123	5,056	476	39	4,358	93	150
ARIZONA: 84 agencies; population 3,730,000															
Under 18	60,361	18,803	2,256	16,547	46	39	495	1,676	3,263	11,286	1,771	227	4,282	151	119
Total all ages	251,159	55,035	9,657	45,378	245	297	1,563	7,552	7,061	34,762	3,198	357	25,297	1,408	1,840
ARKANSAS: 180 agencies; population 2,415,000															
Under 18	17,365	6,197	818	5,379	48	78	217	475	1,147	3,850	342	40	782	71	117
Total all ages	177,421	23,476	5,123	18,353	282	477	990	3,374	3,387	14,110	719	137	7,141	1,709	20,960
CALIFORNIA: 610 agencies; population 31,080,000															
Under 18	254,585	107,736	21,046	86,690	621	532	8,254	11,639	23,228	45,237	16,827	1,398	21,434	918	783
Total all ages	1,621,970	422,796	146,320	276,476	3,297	3,570	29,568	109,885	74,564	155,343	44,172	2,397	77,806	14,524	9,669
COLORADO: 191 agencies; population 2,974,000															
Under 18	52,887	16,053	1,752	14,301	35	82	299	1,336	1,735	11,081	1,275	210	3,961	155	178
Total all ages	236,309	45,300	8,760	36,540	208	530	1,002	7,020	3,774	29,977	2,459	330	23,285	1,257	3,169
CONNECTICUT: 99 agencies; population 2,773,000															
Under 18	29,043	9,365	1,458	7,907	26	77	401	954	1,605	4,989	1,196	117	2,454	32	39
Total all ages	182,472	39,701	8,803	30,898	153	438	2,003	6,209	5,548	22,588	2,475	287	18,224	1,021	2,773
DELAWARE: 2 agencies; population 373,000															
Under 18	1,810	700	164	536	......	34	39	91	167	300	63	6	347	7	27
Total all ages	10,026	2,305	762	1,543	2	101	111	548	433	997	100	13	3,020	84	418
DISTRICT OF COLUMBIA: 2 agencies; population 578,000															
Under 18	4,391	1,642	746	896	34	26	232	454	47	183	666	......	407	7	......
Total all ages	51,805	11,676	5,485	6,191	283	134	1,275	3,793	1,038	3,152	1,969	32	5,461	267	122
FLORIDA: 289 agencies; population 12,812,000															
Under 18	83,605	48,733	8,947	39,786	205	403	2,930	5,409	10,400	23,125	6,027	234	5,344	219	397
Total all ages	613,331	171,877	52,229	119,648	1,177	2,253	10,682	38,117	27,391	79,087	12,563	607	46,124	4,912	6,944
GEORGIA: 343 agencies; population 5,600,000															
Under 18	41,626	14,323	2,853	11,470	91	111	774	1,877	2,402	7,343	1,623	102	3,479	180	254
Total all ages	382,825	70,176	20,208	49,968	718	841	4,174	14,475	9,380	36,218	3,971	399	28,833	5,443	13,877
HAWAII: 5 agencies; population 1,172,000															
Under 18	19,246	4,762	272	4,490	1	11	150	110	678	3,187	587	38	1,479	34	29
Total all ages	63,805	12,632	1,233	11,399	52	129	460	592	1,549	8,137	1,653	60	4,825	329	597
IDAHO: 78 agencies; population 867,000															
Under 18	13,523	4,819	362	4,457	1	14	34	313	530	3,517	362	48	904	50	45
Total all ages	46,760	8,725	1,147	7,578	15	80	55	997	875	6,138	503	62	4,528	158	608
ILLINOIS[6]															
INDIANA: 118 agencies; population 3,452,000															
Under 18	37,293	11,451	1,820	9,631	20	49	230	1,521	1,338	7,161	1,064	68	2,140	55	54
Total all ages	156,497	32,204	8,501	23,703	221	243	963	7,074	3,133	18,385	2,041	144	10,458	741	1,648

See footnotes at end of table.

274

Table 68. — Arrests by State, 1993 — Continued

Embezzlement	Stolen property; buying, receiving; possessing	Vandalism	Weapons; carrying, possessing, etc.	Prostitution and commercialized vice	Sex offenses (except forcible rape and prostitution)	Drug abuse violations	Gambling	Offenses against family and children	Driving under the influence	Liquor laws	Drunkenness[5]	Disorderly conduct	Vagrancy	All other offenses (except traffic)	Suspicion	Curfew and loitering law violations	Runaways
1	413	508	565	3	27	674	22	5	149	837	221	725	32	1,418	......	160	1,184
22	2,137	3,583	2,660	405	520	9,774	97	1,057	19,708	9,149	15,653	5,260	210	40,479	......	160	1,184
......	15	363	99	1	58	121	......	3	57	594	1	58	......	938	......	31	......
3	43	1,067	607	99	364	1,120	3	129	5,366	2,178	4	978	......	13,066	......	31	......
20	775	3,151	974	14	390	2,790	6	......	243	4,842	......	3,396	58	4,682	......	8,775	6,890
204	2,387	8,596	4,243	1,792	2,188	18,232	29	1,497	25,980	22,853	......	20,397	1,051	42,465	......	8,775	6,890
......	589	462	473	16	44	659	21	7	202	626	313	905	83	3,509	118	799	1,372
9	2,545	1,479	3,054	477	409	7,931	144	784	19,567	3,822	21,120	6,812	638	52,554	619	799	1,372
74	6,879	22,858	10,476	197	2,669	17,557	126	16	1,696	4,292	3,254	6,353	905	28,701	......	9,706	7,955
1,127	28,137	37,257	41,803	17,657	16,323	234,475	1,373	586	230,329	15,702	125,778	14,004	4,552	310,411	......	9,706	7,955
15	265	2,854	1,129	6	395	1,638	4	41	366	3,966	7	3,108	29	10,094	6	4,163	4,454
296	704	6,988	4,158	1,485	1,892	10,223	78	1,736	28,769	15,805	493	18,256	1,199	62,592	7	4,163	4,454
10	113	2,035	964	9	228	2,232	7	103	74	442	2	4,230	77	5,577	3	139	908
66	440	4,838	3,208	879	967	18,092	125	2,072	10,503	1,704	8	27,163	506	49,130	5	139	908
......	54	111	21	......	13	72	3	......	......	114	......	112	2	213	......	14	......
......	113	348	112	69	91	556	9	40	......	339	170	443	42	1,853	......	14	......
......	32	96	263	10	14	732	8	......	......	9	......	407	......	219	......	......	545
1	489	802	1,737	1,352	134	8,234	213	16	3,560	46	......	7,272	......	6,067	3,811	......	545
38	1,002	2,393	1,902	81	572	5,245	41	16	123	1,152	......	2,730	......	13,617	......	......	......
794	5,044	4,936	8,649	6,119	4,480	63,721	632	1,289	36,969	20,698	......	19,888	......	210,255	......	......	......
7	1,123	1,433	1,559	20	401	1,996	86	206	433	1,592	238	2,870	50	8,081	29	718	2,548
490	6,098	4,047	8,365	1,684	3,808	29,298	882	3,615	52,048	12,148	12,776	31,156	218	94,361	236	718	2,548
2	49	569	85	6	118	479	7	131	36	239	......	138	......	4,885	......	1,228	4,970
76	239	1,208	703	628	576	3,372	422	2,096	5,177	1,076	......	1,303	......	22,348	......	1,228	4,970
9	87	676	152	1	80	98	1	5	87	1,115	1	259	......	2,031	......	773	2,330
88	167	1,099	450	5	244	749	5	123	8,982	3,560	97	1,274	12	12,783	......	773	2,330
2	497	1,654	444	12	255	747	10	58	103	2,421	388	1,717	1	6,494	58	2,576	6,156
14	1,130	2,643	2,032	998	1,442	6,336	285	765	18,106	8,938	17,619	7,051	9	35,254	92	2,576	6,156

Table 68.—Arrests by State, 1993—Continued

State	Total[1] all classes	Crime[2] Index total	Violent[3] crime	Property[4] crime	Murder and non-negligent man-slaughter	Forcible rape	Robbery	Aggra-vated assault	Burglary	Larceny-theft	Motor vehicle theft	Arson	Other assaults	Forgery and counter-feiting	Fraud
IOWA: 145 agencies; population 1,998,000															
Under 18	13,977	4,980	584	4,396	7	28	62	487	834	3,195	300	67	1,254	115	39
Total all ages	71,555	13,453	2,638	10,815	21	110	241	2,266	1,740	8,377	579	119	6,598	498	1,536
KANSAS:[6]															
KENTUCKY: 248 agencies; population 1,823,000															
Under 18	13,056	5,893	971	4,922	16	32	274	649	1,089	3,279	468	86	315	105	132
Total all ages	124,556	22,486	7,716	14,770	156	344	1,191	6,025	3,095	10,297	1,170	208	7,951	1,997	8,584
LOUISIANA: 58 agencies; population 2,579,000															
Under 18	24,547	9,244	2,005	7,239	103	63	548	1,291	1,472	5,119	558	90	2,577	59	35
Total all ages	181,388	39,893	11,266	28,627	497	462	2,322	7,985	5,539	21,623	1,256	209	15,865	1,642	2,470
MAINE: 127 agencies; population 1,052,000															
Under 18	7,490	3,643	114	3,529	....	16	11	87	861	2,422	172	74	849	38	20
Total all ages	37,662	8,357	826	7,531	2	95	90	639	1,658	5,360	406	107	5,089	221	529
MARYLAND: 147 agencies; population 4,962,000															
Under 18	42,814	17,701	3,495	14,206	138	181	1,069	2,107	2,663	7,877	3,403	263	5,218	64	108
Total all ages	270,465	64,492	14,433	50,059	632	958	4,693	8,150	10,907	32,060	6,611	481	29,470	1,203	3,612
MASSACHUSETTS: 200 agencies; population 4,451,000															
Under 18	19,392	7,312	2,503	4,809	26	95	468	1,914	1,340	2,511	891	67	1,037	27	6
Total all ages	146,305	38,596	16,450	22,146	146	730	2,237	13,337	5,714	14,094	2,169	169	12,221	524	302
MICHIGAN: 450 agencies; population 8,387,000															
Under 18	53,269	21,937	3,849	18,088	208	321	1,069	2,251	3,342	12,839	1,649	258	3,215	76	719
Total all ages	367,814	71,946	22,759	49,187	1,704	1,982	4,819	14,254	9,377	35,932	3,210	668	24,521	1,381	11,749
MINNESOTA: 291 agencies; population 4,440,000															
Under 18	51,849	18,887	2,196	16,691	34	204	437	1,521	2,101	12,236	2,129	225	4,049	368	1,115
Total all ages	195,717	42,513	8,533	33,980	231	1,070	1,426	5,806	4,762	25,322	3,555	341	20,298	2,323	11,345
MISSISSIPPI: 54 agencies; population 854,000															
Under 18	7,798	3,165	334	2,831	25	28	91	190	617	1,855	345	14	658	18	13
Total all ages	61,591	12,571	2,153	10,418	189	203	524	1,237	1,892	7,745	706	75	6,411	564	1,102
MISSOURI: 182 agencies; population 3,303,000															
Under 18	32,594	10,750	1,841	8,909	142	133	558	1,008	1,346	5,985	1,457	121	3,434	128	51
Total all ages	261,934	45,267	10,251	35,016	547	786	2,582	6,336	5,294	25,740	3,601	381	33,310	1,650	2,482
MONTANA: 51 agencies; population 377,000															
Under 18	2,387	729	33	696	1	2	1	29	99	505	76	16	106	18	9
Total all ages	9,677	1,738	194	1,544	10	11	9	164	238	1,147	135	24	1,179	62	200
NEBRASKA: 242 agencies; population 1,489,000															
Under 18	14,909	5,685	300	5,385	5	37	132	126	559	4,499	262	65	1,321	94	104
Total all ages	72,944	13,097	1,499	11,598	49	221	360	869	1,306	9,700	474	118	7,282	523	2,047
NEVADA: 20 agencies; population 1,203,000															
Under 18	15,412	4,588	473	4,115	12	36	182	243	857	2,975	258	25	994	34	57
Total all ages	91,696	16,761	3,003	13,758	133	300	1,081	1,489	2,892	10,141	659	66	10,011	766	1,510
NEW HAMPSHIRE: 72 agencies; population 738,000															
Under 18	5,329	1,632	112	1,520	....	14	9	89	173	1,224	75	48	411	....	5
Total all ages	24,368	4,331	583	3,748	4	80	59	440	461	3,090	135	62	2,753	108	316

See footnotes at end of table.

Table 68. — Arrests by State, 1993 — Continued

Embezzle-ment	Stolen property; buying, receiving; possessing	Vandalism	Weapons; carrying, possessing, etc.	Prostitution and commercialized vice	Sex offenses (except forcible rape and prostitution)	Drug abuse violations	Gambling	Offenses against family and children	Driving under the influence	Liquor laws	Drunken-ness[5]	Disorderly conduct	Vagrancy	All other offenses (except traffic)	Suspicion	Curfew and loitering law violations	Runaways
4	78	935	125	1	56	96	......	2	165	2,131	219	832	......	1,535	......	438	972
75	173	1,825	597	256	268	1,243	7	157	12,577	8,782	7,069	3,554	23	11,454	......	438	972
3	921	488	226	8	90	630	10	10	191	518	543	1,026	......	1,901	......	11	35
295	2,457	2,118	1,929	490	1,080	9,744	166	1,873	16,516	1,731	19,809	8,192	1	17,091	......	11	35
2	980	1,138	752	9	131	1,242	41	149	83	289	132	1,304	71	3,963	120	776	1,450
9	4,044	3,773	3,654	359	958	14,105	313	1,187	10,984	1,013	8,789	9,023	639	59,952	490	776	1,450
	100	623	43	......	79	174	......	4	77	291	4	146	......	1,035	......	51	312
14	336	1,572	237	12	369	1,622	2	187	6,581	1,446	17	1,463	......	9,245	......	51	312
19	69	2,505	1,216	16	679	4,631	76	7	178	956	......	1,024	31	5,921	72	628	1,695
524	281	4,820	5,161	1,383	1,959	35,647	367	1,927	23,198	5,094	21	5,749	280	82,739	215	628	1,695
1	1,141	733	383	38	71	1,804	4	163	108	781	314	1,546	32	2,722	34	85	1,050
7	4,182	2,554	1,543	2,993	878	18,558	105	3,590	12,471	3,060	7,927	9,896	65	25,319	379	85	1,050
60	1,701	3,062	1,809	27	540	2,646	48	......	409	2,065	37	2,615	57	6,516	......	1,780	3,950
1,075	8,341	7,750	8,950	2,737	2,696	27,499	559	2,419	46,380	18,510	347	21,835	365	103,024	......	1,780	3,950
......	1,118	4,112	1,147	24	345	1,360	12	22	350	5,461	......	3,443	21	4,571	......	2,931	2,513
5	2,538	7,412	2,718	1,367	1,069	9,234	77	524	32,261	15,345	......	11,798	205	29,241	......	2,931	2,513
5	51	189	201	3	34	361	30	13	54	201	103	916	2	1,234	4	126	417
222	265	535	1,151	99	206	4,560	248	476	6,278	1,869	5,918	5,270	11	13,232	60	126	417
3	310	1,960	1,084	18	354	1,414	18	83	196	1,131	39	935	117	6,032	97	1,453	2,987
42	1,681	7,464	6,573	2,714	2,237	14,130	107	2,257	23,118	6,340	1,458	9,275	627	94,862	1,900	1,453	2,987
......	8	228	19	......	51	39	1	......	50	686	......	131	......	197	......	115	......
1	23	493	44	1	122	278	3	83	2,043	1,803	......	892	......	597	......	115	......
5	591	1,073	282	1	129	345	2	15	185	1,951	......	599	1	1,748	......	368	410
61	1,272	2,492	1,156	316	749	4,346	50	1212	11,858	7,437	......	3,942	10	14,305	11	368	410
25	579	574	280	17	56	464	3	42	33	922	9	271	48	1,786	2	3,404	1,224
439	2,187	1,275	1,696	2,691	717	7,129	25	846	6,236	3,411	533	2,949	898	26,980	8	3,404	1,224
......	125	338	33	2	40	220	......	1	50	463	301	164	5	808	55	95	581
4	410	735	116	14	224	1,701	......	46	4,220	1,893	1,356	958	101	4,351	55	95	581

Table 68. — Arrests by State, 1993 — Continued

State	Total[1] all classes	Crime[2] Index total	Violent[3] crime	Property[4] crime	Murder and non-negligent man-slaughter	Forcible rape	Robbery	Aggra-vated assault	Burglary	Larceny-theft	Motor vehicle theft	Arson	Other assaults	Forgery and counter-feiting	Fraud
NEW JERSEY: 542 agencies; population 7,633,000															
Under 18	82,454	23,251	5,438	17,813	63	220	1,999	3,156	3,824	12,211	1,516	262	9,457	47	178
Total all ages	363,846	74,435	20,757	53,678	368	1,151	5,930	13,308	10,389	40,083	2,690	516	40,044	999	5,695
NEW MEXICO: 34 agencies; population 806,000															
Under 18	9,437	3,673	383	3,290	9	17	75	282	506	2,595	164	25	619	20	51
Total all ages	54,263	10,518	1,851	8,667	58	73	242	1,478	1,013	7,321	294	39	4,684	197	421
NEW YORK: 493 agencies; population 15,532,000															
Under 18	157,215	42,293	17,504	24,789	264	309	11,389	5,542	4,794	16,476	3,162	357	9,542	302	8,613
Total all ages	1,004,521	170,313	67,467	102,846	1,612	1,978	31,284	32,593	18,209	72,000	11,822	815	50,508	6,277	55,538
NORTH CAROLINA: 433 agencies; population 6,757,000															
Under 18	44,251	15,811	3,110	12,701	96	95	673	2,246	3,669	8,085	754	193	4,785	192	513
Total all ages	484,583	85,610	27,195	58,415	876	847	3,960	21,512	15,847	39,779	2,266	523	44,293	5,191	50,472
NORTH DAKOTA: 70 agencies; population 535,000															
Under 18	6,459	2,152	52	2,100	1	8	14	29	195	1,729	163	13	340	49	19
Total all ages	21,105	3,973	173	3,800	7	40	21	105	421	3,099	265	15	1,138	189	3,672
OHIO: 260 agencies; population 6,654,000															
Under 18	64,180	18,915	2,854	16,061	76	274	1,218	1,286	3,013	10,477	2,242	329	5,751	117	112
Total all ages	335,272	57,480	13,981	43,499	516	1,198	4,548	7,719	8,058	30,918	3,889	634	26,316	1,921	6,241
OKLAHOMA: 278 agencies; population 3,170,000															
Under 18	24,909	11,724	1,270	10,454	43	56	353	818	1,889	6,824	1,430	311	874	114	106
Total all ages	143,221	26,915	5,868	21,047	243	429	1,032	4,164	4,069	14,131	2,389	458	5,783	1,047	1,896
OREGON: 185 agencies; population 2,930,000															
Under 18	40,899	15,258	1,122	14,136	13	81	379	649	2,000	10,350	1,468	318	3,103	265	111
Total all ages	150,584	40,040	4,533	35,507	136	497	1,315	2,585	4,579	26,958	3,509	461	19,730	1,733	1,336
PENNSYLVANIA: 675 agencies; population 8,994,000															
Under 18	76,406	22,564	5,120	17,444	82	220	1,939	2,879	3,190	10,581	3,373	300	5,098	160	247
Total all ages	327,567	75,987	21,480	54,507	672	1,208	7,259	12,341	10,239	36,031	7,469	768	29,849	2,120	6,474
RHODE ISLAND: 43 agencies; population 971,000															
Under 18	8,746	2,793	530	2,263	11	21	68	430	412	1,523	245	83	792	2	26
Total all ages	39,900	8,199	2,395	5,804	25	112	274	1,984	1,103	3,928	654	119	4,890	216	1,200
SOUTH CAROLINA: 205 agencies; population 3,554,000															
Under 18	20,397	9,106	1,505	7,601	43	127	311	1,024	2,086	4,897	563	55	2,664	75	155
Total all ages	173,194	35,135	10,092	25,043	411	735	1,692	7,254	5,906	17,757	1,205	175	17,856	1,764	28,315
SOUTH DAKOTA: 52 agencies; population 498,000															
Under 18	8,922	2,646	129	2,517	1	18	10	100	361	1,976	140	40	445	43	18
Total all ages	32,380	5,234	578	4,656	10	87	27	454	671	3,729	199	57	2,342	189	610
TENNESSEE: 118 agencies; population 2,960,000															
Under 18	20,749	5,981	589	5,392	24	29	126	410	840	3,998	497	57	1,477	153	51
Total all ages	177,697	33,724	8,876	24,848	379	532	1,866	6,099	4,303	18,960	1,387	198	13,275	1,891	2,521
TEXAS: 855 agencies; population 17,449,000															
Under 18	185,336	60,876	8,796	52,080	367	.383	2,983	5,063	10,622	34,267	6,688	503	13,319	653	497
Total all ages	1,032,728	189,257	39,526	149,731	1,898	2,653	8,994	25,981	25,956	108,529	14,019	1,227	82,594	7,597	12,064
UTAH: 99 agencies; population 1,717,000															
Under 18	41,591	16,222	1,040	15,182	6	91	138	805	1,766	12,112	1,179	125	2,811	243	128
Total all ages	110,511	28,354	2,592	25,762	50	251	389	1,902	2,707	21,315	1,549	191	9,936	830	926

See footnotes at end of table.

Table 68. — Arrests by State, 1993 — Continued

Embezzlement	Stolen property; buying, receiving; possessing	Vandalism	Weapons; carrying, possessing, etc.	Prostitution and commercialized vice	Sex offenses (except forcible rape and prostitution)	Drug abuse violations	Gambling	Offenses against family and children	Driving under the influence	Liquor laws	Drunkenness[5]	Disorderly conduct	Vagrancy	All other offenses (except traffic)	Suspicion	Curfew and loitering law violations	Runaways
4	3,648	6,271	2,888	36	443	5,538	18	17	179	2,707	2	9,979	43	9,820	......	2,187	5,741
73	9,760	10,892	7,197	3,047	2,141	42,105	245	15,524	24,640	8,391	40	37,186	454	73,050	......	2,187	5,741
10	179	255	145	16	21	419	......	73	168	983	6	359	2	1,741	29	273	395
97	540	529	572	602	153	2,344	2	1,052	9,612	3,295	489	1,981	8	16,412	87	273	395
16	2,682	8,463	3,386	65	1,230	10,173	89	297	195	1,642	......	8,852	940	52,933	......	......	5,502
341	13,573	23,782	15,838	12,310	6,182	111,096	4,522	2,994	36,716	14,385	......	53,844	9,325	411,475	......	......	5,502
105	1,143	2,506	1,405	20	253	2,248	15	85	955	1,408	......	2,299	26	9,070	......	75	1,337
1,790	6,254	10,166	8,948	1,254	2,662	26,931	726	6,329	70,863	10,492	......	15,166	154	135,870	......	75	1,337
1	105	447	62	......	31	46	......	85	55	882	1	299	......	649	......	375	861
5	152	676	136	1	80	429	3	215	2,398	2,997	328	1,109	......	2,368	......	375	861
4	2,446	2,857	1,316	37	390	2,634	77	1,017	314	2,691	377	3,425	44	12,901	48	4,164	4,543
32	6,957	5,300	6,468	4,301	2,263	25,091	487	9,663	26,738	16,027	18,766	19,143	701	92,488	182	4,164	4,543
49	552	799	609	9	103	774	4	33	273	947	637	376	......	2,644	......	1,242	3,040
489	1,860	1,434	2,884	362	1,006	10,140	70	719	24,635	5,062	29,224	2,502	......	22,911	......	1,242	3,040
4	177	2,678	491	23	413	978	10	8	202	4,092	......	1,036	......	4,617	......	3,827	3,606
55	580	5,406	2,367	968	1,750	11,390	19	311	21,067	13,942	......	4,705	......	17,752	......	3,827	3,606
14	1,053	5,996	1,555	25	597	3,064	4	66	170	5,350	248	10,959	62	8,478	......	5,927	4,769
90	3,436	13,635	4,392	1,902	2,562	26,032	318	996	27,521	16,620	19,673	50,714	339	34,211	......	5,927	4,769
2	227	775	244	3	59	403	3	50	19	163	19	593	4	1,220	419	120	810
86	693	1,623	587	254	417	3,251	53	424	2,309	1,277	43	3,060	5	9,427	956	120	810
1	408	912	672	10	153	229	6	62	164	931	224	2,023	......	1,627	......	28	947
26	1,573	2,819	2,737	455	765	2,415	242	916	18,428	9,751	14,869	17,058	205	16,890	......	28	947
7	109	472	87	......	46	105	3	3	70	1,471	17	281	......	1,622	6	414	1,057
27	198	745	204	8	188	842	13	109	5,293	6,162	135	2,156	......	6,447	7	414	1,057
2	64	779	581	5	62	808	56	3	104	918	267	1,309	102	3,999	6	2,348	1,674
83	290	2,342	3,888	1,136	635	12,178	645	1,057	21,802	4,008	25,546	8,742	149	37,337	2,426	2,348	1,674
33	497	8,572	5,011	99	1,097	8,004	108	570	816	4,725	4,749	11,701	149	24,340	97	5,200	34,223
319	1,874	16,136	24,204	7,311	6,740	72,103	807	7,780	101,978	21,550	180,965	35,890	1,058	222,919	159	5,200	34,223
4	325	3,025	818	28	507	1,170	......	24	186	2,983	135	1,469	150	7,729	8	1,975	1,651
48	702	4,199	1,463	732	1,378	5,421	14	546	8,004	9,699	7,531	4,054	161	22,877	10	1,975	1,651

Table 68. — Arrests by State, 1993 — Continued

State	Total[1] all classes	Crime[2] Index total	Violent[3] crime	Property[4] crime	Murder and non-negligent man-slaughter	Forcible rape	Robbery	Aggra-vated assault	Burglary	Larceny-theft	Motor vehicle theft	Arson	Other assaults	Forgery and counter-feiting	Fraud
VERMONT: 6 agencies; population 272,000															
Under 18	467	248	19	229	1	9	....	9	45	166	16	2	45	3	3
Total all ages	4,235	1,141	185	956	6	75	4	100	228	654	45	29	105	24	139
VIRGINIA: 403 agencies; population 6,488,000															
Under 18	49,401	15,570	1,572	13,998	77	118	579	798	2,313	9,822	1,645	218	4,532	201	189
Total all ages	387,552	63,543	12,771	50,772	534	1,001	2,797	8,439	7,351	39,341	3,583	497	45,240	4,812	16,181
WASHINGTON: 177 agencies; population 3,837,000															
Under 18	45,612	20,990	1,665	19,325	28	214	431	992	3,150	14,549	1,411	215	5,254	255	53
Total all ages .:..............	231,989	50,980	6,672	44,308	147	954	1,239	4,332	5,963	35,762	2,236	347	32,057	1,645	1,569
WEST VIRGINIA: 295 agencies; population 1,812,000															
Under 18	6,742	2,449	145	2,304	10	14	55	66	479	1,559	220	46	495	25	55
Total all ages	59,769	9,293	1,506	7,787	120	133	260	993	1,408	5,750	497	132	6,056	512	4.885
WISCONSIN: 318 agencies; population 5,003,000															
Under 18	121,288	31,534	2,305	29,229	118	135	876	1,176	3,644	21,963	3,257	365	5,341	368	367
Total all ages	402,491	68,042	7,947	60,095	521	689	2,300	4,437	6,922	47,674	4,953	546	27,919	1,914	10,438
WYOMING: 61 agencies; population 406,000															
Under 18	5,164	1,276	66	1,210	3	6	3	54	109	1,015	78	8	182	26	16
Total all ages	23,648	3,021	481	2,540	9	41	19	412	290	2,077	155	18	1,423	121	187

[1]Does not include traffic arrests.

[2]Includes arson.

[3]Violent crime includes offenses of murder, forcible rape, robbery, and aggravated assault.

[4]Property crime includes offenses of burglary, larceny-theft, motor vehicle theft, and arson.

[5]Drunkenness is not considered a crime in some states; therefore, the figures vary widely from state to state.

[6]Complete data for 1993 were not available for the states of Illinois and Kansas.

NOTE: Direct comparisons of arrest totals listed in this table should not be made with prior years' issues. Some Part II offenses are not considered crimes in some states; therefore figures may vary widely.

Table 68. — Arrests by State, 1993 — Continued

Embezzle- ment	Stolen property; buying, receiving; possessing	Vandalism	Weapons; carrying, possessing, etc.	Prosti- tution and commer- cialized vice	Sex offenses (except forcible rape and prostitution)	Drug abuse violations	Gambling	Offenses against family and children	Driving under the influence	Liquor laws	Drunken- ness[5]	Disorderly conduct	Vagrancy	All other offenses (except traffic)	Suspicion	Curfew and loitering law violations	Runaways
. . . . . .	17	28	. . . .	. . . .	10	13	. . . .	4	17	27	1	8	. . . .	42	. . . .	. . . .	1
12	97	206	3	2	102	347	. . . .	192	955	115	2	53	. . . .	739	. . . .	. . . .	1
15	430	2,409	1,562	6	462	1,800	104	22	198	1,778	614	1,544	. . . .	8,391	. . . .	2,779	6,795
1,039	1,981	6,877	8,353	1,834	3,426	20,227	331	1,652	35,304	14,053	47,668	9,689	1	95,767	. . . .	2,779	6,795
5	1,350	2,909	911	27	477	1,183	. . . .	21	261	3,254	6	595	31	5,445	20	170	2,395
78	3,455	6,053	2,880	948	2,431	11,804	19	650	38,785	12,843	59	4,397	260	58,389	122	170	2,395
. . . . . .	73	409	161	1	31	171	1	. . . .	71	103	253	223	5	918	. . . .	480	818
91	454	1,276	1,402	129	296	2,165	54	189	9,087	1,095	10,116	1,969	31	9,371	. . . .	480	818
34	829	6,748	2,620	27	1,882	1,822	70	361	385	9,943	74	17,815	50	21,068	144	7,083	12,723
156	1,570	13,616	8,265	1,556	4,630	12,600	317	4,564	35,073	32,813	267	63,570	193	94,922	260	7,083	12,723
. . . . . .	22	130	38	. . . .	19	90	. . . .	13	58	1,039	40	415	1	1,136	9	233	421
12	64	315	125	3	128	771	2	337	4,499	3,131	1,310	1,441	5	6,082	17	233	421

Table 69.—Police Disposition of Juvenile Offenders Taken into Custody, 1993

[1993 estimated population]

Population group	Total[1]	Handled within department and released	Referred to juvenile court jurisdiction	Referred to welfare agency	Referred to other police agency	Referred to criminal or adult court
TOTAL ALL AGENCIES: 8,805 agencies; population 172,804,000:						
Number	1,286,903	329,166	865,630	19,307	11,149	61,651
Percent[2]	100.0	25.6	67.3	1.5	.9	4.8
TOTAL CITIES: 6,289 cities; population 118,989,000:						
Number	1,091,890	285,795	729,947	15,659	9,121	51,368
Percent[2]	100.0	26.2	66.9	1.4	.8	4.7
GROUP I						
51 cities, 250,000 and over; population 31,737,000:						
Number	278,301	74,268	197,560	2,387	1,670	2,416
Percent[2]	100.0	26.7	71.0	.9	.6	.9
GROUP II						
112 cities, 100,000 to 249,999; population 16,147,000:						
Number	142,679	32,584	99,886	2,943	1,077	6,189
Percent[2]	100.0	22.8	70.0	2.1	.8	4.3
GROUP III						
285 cities, 50,000 to 99,999; population 19,545,000:						
Number	178,468	52,753	110,818	3,220	1,832	9,845
Percent[2]	100.0	29.6	62.1	1.8	1.0	5.5
GROUP IV						
506 cities, 25,000 to 49,999; population 17,548,000:						
Number	154,944	40,793	103,512	1,952	1,993	6,694
Percent[2]	100.0	26.3	66.8	1.3	1.3	4.3
GROUP V						
1,198 cities, 10,000 to 24,999; population 18,989,000:						
Number	179,196	46,064	117,110	2,384	1,304	12,334
Percent[2]	100.0	25.7	65.4	1.3	.7	6.9
GROUP VI						
4,137 cities under 10,000; population 15,024,000:						
Number	158,302	39,333	101,061	2,773	1,245	13,890
Percent[2]	100.0	24.8	63.8	1.8	.8	8.8
SUBURBAN COUNTIES						
862 agencies; population 35,995,000:						
Number	140,672	32,877	97,858	2,153	1,452	6,332
Percent[2]	100.0	23.4	69.6	1.5	1.0	4.5
RURAL COUNTIES						
1,654 agencies; population 17,820,000:						
Number	54,341	10,494	37,825	1,495	576	3,951
Percent[2]	100.0	19.3	69.6	2.8	1.1	7.3
SUBURBAN AREA[3]						
4,706 agencies; population 86,879,000:						
Number	577,143	160,331	369,033	6,966	6,450	34,363
Percent[2]	100.0	27.8	63.9	1.2	1.1	6.0

[1]Includes all offenses except traffic and neglect cases.

[2]Because of rounding, the percentages may not add to total.

[3]Includes suburban city and county law enforcement agencies within metropolitan areas. Excludes central cities. Suburban cities and counties are also included in other groups.

SECTION V

Homicide Patterns: Past and Present

Murder has always been regarded as the most serious of all crimes. Today, the prevailing public perception is that homicides, in general, are more vicious and senseless than ever before. In an effort to address this issue, the following study examines the changing nature of murder from 1965 to 1992.

While the Nation's homicide rate per 100,000 residents was 9.3 in 1992, the historical high actually occurred 13 years prior (10.2 in 1980). What, then, has spurred the current national debate on how to curtail murders and violent crime? Ostensibly, something has changed in the constitution of murder to bring about the unparalleled level of concern and fear confronting the Nation.

A historical review of the U.S. murder rate trend reveals that after a rapid escalation from 5.1 in 1965 to 9.4 in 1973, the rate stabilized in subsequent years, ranging from 8.0 to 10.2, as shown in Chart 5.1. This study focuses on significant changes in the types of victims, arrestees, related circumstances, and weapons usage as possible contributing factors for the current trepidation associated with homicides.

Victim Profile

The most striking change in murder victimization since the 1980s is the youthfulness of the victims. Of particular note are the increases in the number of murder victims in the age groups "under 1" and "10 to 14" as indicated by Table 5.1. The number of victims in these two age groups, while remaining relatively small overall, increased 46 percent and 64 percent, respectively, from 1975 to 1992. Further, the number of victims in the "15 to 24" age group, the most murder prone, increased nearly 50 percent. These three age groups were primarily responsible for the 16-percent increase in total homicides nationwide between

Table 5.1

Estimated Number of Murder Victims, Selected Age Groups, United States, 1975-1992

Age	1975	1980	1985	1992
Under 1	183	222	206	268
1 to 9	516	495	514	563
10 to 14	226	233	233	370
15 to 24	4,993	6,008	4,415	7,412
25 to 49	10,207	11,729	10,112	12,073
50 and over	4,033	3,956	3,087	2,748
Unknown	351	395	414	326
Total	20,509	23,038	18,981	23,760

1975 and 1992. The same held true for the 25-percent increase in homicides from 1985-1992.

Conversely, the number of murder victims aged 50 and over decreased 32 percent between 1975 and 1992. As this population segment is among the Nation's fastest growing, an increase in the number of victims contained in it was expected. The decline confirms a definitive trend toward more youthful murder victims.

Victim data by race and age reveal that blacks aged 24 or younger constituted 41 percent of black murder victims during 1992, up from 29 percent in 1975. The 1992 statistic is in concert with the finding of the U.S. Department of Health and Human Services that homicide is now the leading cause of death for young black males. The corresponding percentage for whites rose only slightly from 28 percent to 31 percent, 1975 versus 1992. These data indicate that black victims are, on average, more youthful than white victims.

The gender distribution for murder victims has remained virtually unchanged from 1975 to 1992 as shown in Table 5.2. Homicide victims are predominantly male.

Table 5.2

Sex of Murder Victims, Percent Distribution, United States, 1975-1992

Year	Male	Female
1975	76%	24%
1980	77	23
1985	74	26
1992	77	23

Circumstances/Relationships

Nationally, the circumstances/relationships associated with homicides have changed significantly since the 1960s. Historically, the vast majority of murders have been between people with some type of relationship or acquaintance. During the 1990s, however, there is evidence that this is no longer the case. For example, in 1965, only 5 percent of murder circumstances were unknown, while in 1992, this figure rose to 28 percent. When addressing victim/offender relationships, murders by strangers and unknown persons represented 53 percent of the murders in the Nation during 1992. This percentage represents a historical high.

The prevalence of murder among family members as a percentage of all murders also experienced a prominent

MURDER RATES

CHART 5.1
UNITED STATES
1965 - 1992

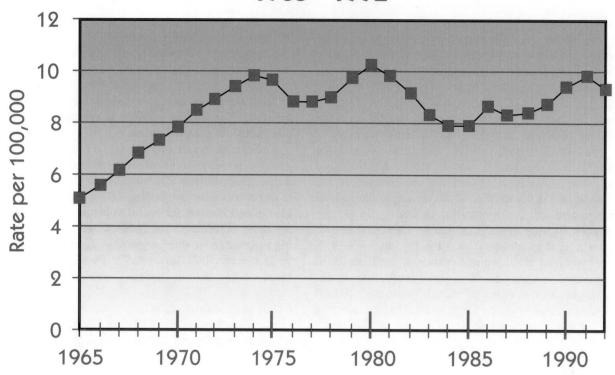

284

shift. In 1965, nearly 1 out of 3 (31 percent) murder victims was killed by a person or persons within his or her family. In 1992, however, the figure fell to only 12 percent, (see Table 5.3) supporting the trend of murders becoming less family-oriented. The Nation's drug trade is widely considered to be a major contributing factor to the rise in murders whose circumstances are unknown.

Table 5.3

Estimated Number and Percent of Murder Victims Killed Within Family, United States, 1965-1992

	1965	1970	1975	1980	1985	1992
Number of Victims	3,063	4,408	5,128	3,685	3,227	2,851
Percent of Murder Total ..	31%	25%	25%	16%	17%	12%

From a longitudinal perspective, after peaking in the mid-1970s, felony murders and suspected felony murders have been relatively stable in spite of some minor variations as shown in Table 5.4. This trend also holds true when considering the percentage of the total these murders represent. It should be cautioned, however, that from 1985 to 1992, known felony-related murders increased 47 percent. This increase was primarily driven by a 147-percent rise in narcotics felony-related homicides.

Table 5.4

Estimated Felony-Type or Suspected Felony-Type Murders, Percent of Total, United States, 1965-1992

	1965	1970	1975	1980	1985	1992
Number of Victims	1,580	4,599	6,563	5,520	3,796	5,569
Percent of Murder Total ..	16%	29%	32%	24%	20%	23%

While murder has traditionally been called a crime of passion resulting from romantic triangles and lovers' quarrels, recent statistics reveal that these types of murders have been declining as a percentage of total homicides. (See Table 5.5.) In fact, the number of murder victims killed under these circumstances declined 22 percent from 1975 to 1992.

Table 5.5

Estimated Murder Victims Due to Romantic Triangles and Lovers' Quarrels, Percent of Total, United States, 1965-1992

	1965	1970	1975	1980	1985	1992
Number of Victims	996	1,126	1,497	1,244	1,177	1,164
Percent of Murder Total ..	10.1%	7.1%	7.3%	5.4%	6.2%	4.9%

The fastest growing murder circumstance is juvenile gang killings. It should be noted that in a juvenile gang killing the perpetrator is associated with a juvenile gang but may be of any age, i.e., an adult gang leader. The victim, whether juvenile or adult, is not necessarily associated with a gang. Prior to 1980, the number of murders in this category was well below 200 per year. As shown in Table 5.6, from 1980 to 1992, juvenile gang killings increased 371 percent. Further, 95 percent of victims of juvenile gang killings in 1992 were slain with firearms. When considering the race of the victims, 68 percent were white and 27 percent were black. Sixty-nine percent of the victims killed by juvenile gangs were age 18 and older.

Table 5.6

Estimated Juvenile Gang Killings, Percent of Total, United States, 1980-1992

	1980	1985	1992
Number of Victims	181	231	852
Percent of Murder Total	.8%	1.2%	3.6%

Homicide is one of the most intraracial crimes when considering victims and offenders. This dimension of murder has been constant throughout time. A review of homicide incidents during 1992 which involved one victim and one offender showed that 94 percent of black murder victims were killed by black offenders, and 83 percent of white murder victims were killed by white offenders.

Weapons Usage

The Nation experienced an increase in the percentage of homicides committed with guns during the period 1985 to 1992, as shown in Table 5.7. Conversely, the percentage of knives/cutting instruments used in murders has declined since 1965. The use of other types of weapons, e.g., blunt objects, poison, explosives, has been relatively stable.

Table 5.7

Murder Weapons, Percent Distribution, United States, 1965-1992

Weapon Type	1965	1970	1975	1980	1985	1992
Firearms	57%	65%	66%	62%	59%	68%
Knives	23	19	18	19	21	15
Other	20	16	16	19	20	17
Total	100%	100%	100%	100%	100%	100%

An examination of weapons used against victims of various ages showed the leading weapon used against those under the age of 5 from 1975 through 1992 was personal weapons (hands, fists, and feet). The gun category was the leading weapon type for all remaining age groups, especially the "15 to 19" age group. In 1975, 66 percent of the murders of persons in this group were attributable to guns, while in 1992 the figure rose to 85 percent. This increase supports the theory that today's high school-aged youths are exposed to an environment that includes guns.

The level of gun usage in homicides varies by type of circumstance, particularly for felonies. Table 5.8 delineates the percent of murders by firearm for selected felonies during 1992.

285

Table 5.8

Estimated Felony-Type Murders, Percent by Gun, United States, 1992

Felony Circumstances	Number of Murders	Percent Killed With Guns
Rape	141	17%
Robbery	2,329	67%
Burglary	215	47%
Motor Vehicle Theft	69	59%
Narcotic Drug Laws	1,360	89%

Profile of Arrestees

As with other aspects of homicide, the profile of the murder arrestee has changed somewhat since 1970. The most notable difference relates to white murder arrestees. Table 5.9 reveals that the number of whites arrested for homicide rose 67 percent from 1970 to 1992, accounting for most of the overall increase in the national murder arrest total. Moreover, the number of white juvenile murder arrestees increased 204 percent and the number of white adult murder arrestees was up 56 percent for the 23-year period as shown in Tables 5.10 and 5.11. The increase in the number of white juvenile arrestees was the largest among all racial groups by age classification (adult and juvenile).

Table 5.9

Estimated Total of Murder Arrests by Race, Percent Distribution, United States, 1970-1992

Year	Total Arrests	Arrests by Race			Percent Distribution			
		White	Black	Other	Total	White	Black	Other
1970	15,230	5,853	9,026	351	100.0	38.4	59.3	2.3
1975	20,180	8,748	10,981	451	100.0	43.3	54.4	2.2
1980	20,040	10,138	9,601	301	100.0	50.6	47.9	1.5
1985	18,330	9,171	8,873	286	100.0	50.0	48.4	1.6
1992	22,510	9,791	12,400	319	100.0	43.5	55.1	1.4
Percent Change 1992/1970	+47.8	+67.3	+37.4	-9.1				

Table 5.10

Estimated Adult Murder Arrests by Race, Percent Distribution, United States, 1970-1992

Year	Total Arrests	Arrests by Race			Percent Distribution			
		White	Black	Other	Total	White	Black	Other
1970	13,631	5,412	7,933	286	100.0	39.7	58.2	2.1
1975	18,263	7,926	9,917	420	100.0	43.4	54.3	2.3
1980	18,176	9,124	8,779	273	100.0	50.2	48.3	1.5
1985	16,809	8,438	8,102	269	100.0	50.2	48.2	1.6
1992	19,246	8,449	10,526	271	100.0	43.9	54.7	1.4
Percent Change 1992/1970	+41.2	+56.1	+32.7	-5.2				

Adults = Arrestees 18 and over.

When considering black murder arrestees, there have been significant increases for both adults and juveniles, but not at the rate experienced by their white counterparts (see Tables 5.10 and 5.11). It should be mentioned, however, that

after falling to less than 50 percent of homicide arrests in 1980, blacks constituted 55 percent of the murder arrest total in 1992 (see Table 5.9).

Table 5.11

Estimated Juvenile Murder Arrests by Race, Percent Distribution, United States, 1970-1992

Year	Total Arrests	Arrests by Race			Percent Distribution			
		White	Black	Other	Total	White	Black	Other
1970	1,599	441	1,093	65	100.0	27.6	68.3	4.1
1975	1,917	822	1,064	31	100.0	42.9	55.5	1.6
1980	1,864	1,014	822	28	100.0	54.4	44.1	1.5
1985	1,521	733	771	17	100.0	48.2	50.7	1.1
1992	3,264	1,342	1,874	48	100.0	41.1	57.4	1.5
Percent Change 1992/1970	+104.1	+204.3	+72.5	-26.2				

Juveniles = Arrestees under the age of 18.

In conjunction with the youthfulness of murder victims, as earlier discussed, the average age of murder arrestees has fallen significantly since 1965 as well (see Table 5.12). The decline from 1985 to 1992 is particularly noteworthy. This latter decline tends to indicate that the surge in the number of youthful murder offenders commenced during the latter part of the 1980s.

Table 5.12

Average Age of Murder Arrestees, United States, 1965-1992

Year	Average Age of Murder Arrestees
1965	32.5
1970	30.7
1975	29.7
1980	29.3
1985	29.8
1992	27.0

Although the total number of murder arrests has risen substantially over time, this increase does not reflect the movement of the Nation's murder clearance rate. Specifically, as shown in Table 5.13, the percent of murders cleared by arrest has fallen from 91 percent in 1965 to an all-time low of 65 percent in 1992. The primary reason for this trend may be that circumstances and victim/offender relationships composing today's murders are more likely to be unknown.

Table 5.13

Murder Clearance Rates, United States, 1965-1992

	1965	1970	1975	1980	1985	1992
Number of Murders	9,880	15,860	20,510	23,040	18,980	23,760
Percent Cleared	91%	86%	78%	72%	72%	65%

Conclusions

The typical assumptions associated with homicides throughout this century must be reevaluated in view of the unprecedented shift in national homicide patterns as evidenced during the 1990s. Every American now has a realistic chance of murder victimization in view of the random nature the crime has assumed. This notion is somewhat supported by the fact that a majority of the Nation's murder victims are now killed by strangers or unknown persons. The advent of this trend has generated a profound fear of murder victimization in that the circumstances surrounding homicides are perceived to be more irrational. In the past, the accepted normality was based upon clearly defined circumstances such as felonies, passion, and arguments among family members or acquaintances. The concern about homicide is further perpetuated by youthfulness of both victims and offenders, as illustrated by the rise in juvenile gang killings during the past decade. The reasons for these changes in homicide patterns are multidimensional. Some suggested causal factors are related to the illicit drug trade, the disintegration of the family unit, and weapon proliferation.

SECTION VI

Law Enforcement Personnel

The Nation's law enforcement community employed an average of 2.3 full-time officers for every 1,000 inhabitants as of October 31, 1993. Considering full-time civilians, the overall law enforcement employee rate was 3.1 per 1,000 inhabitants according to 13,041 city, county, and state police agencies reporting in 1993. These agencies collectively offered law enforcement service to a population of over 244 million, employing 553,773 officers and 212,353 civilians. A listing of reported full-time law enforcement officers and civilian employees by state is shown in Table 77.

Varying demographic and other jurisdictional characteristics greatly affect the requirements for law enforcement service from one locale to another. The needs of a community having a highly mobile or seasonal population, for example, may be very different from those of a city whose population is relatively stable. Similarly, a small community situated between two large cities may require a greater number of law enforcement personnel than a community of the same size which has no urban centers nearby.

The functions of law enforcement are also significantly diverse throughout the Nation. In certain areas, sheriffs' responsibilities are limited almost exclusively to civil functions and/or the administration of the county jail facilities. Likewise, the responsibilities of state police and highway patrol agencies vary from one jurisdiction to another.

In view of these differing service requirements and responsibilities, care should be used when attempting any comparison of law enforcement employee rates. The rates presented in the following tables represent national averages; they should be viewed as guides or indicators, not as recommended or desirable police strengths. Adequate personnel for a specific locale can be determined only after careful study and analysis of the various conditions affecting service requirements in that jurisdiction.

The law enforcement employee average for all cities nationwide in 1993 was 2.8 per 1,000 inhabitants. The Nation's smallest cities, those with fewer than 10,000 inhabitants, employed an average of 3.5 employees per 1,000 population, while for the largest cities (over 250,000 population) the rate was 3.6 per 1,000. Cities with populations between 10,000 and 249,999 registered lesser rates ranging from 2.2 to 2.4 employees per 1,000 inhabitants. Rural and suburban counties averaged full-time law enforcement employee rates of 3.9 and 3.6 per 1,000 population, respectively. (See Table 70.)

Regionally, the law enforcement employee rate was highest in the South with 3.3, and lowest in the West, 2.4. (See Table 70.)

Sworn Personnel

Rates based solely on sworn law enforcement personnel (excluding civilians) showed the national average for all cities was 2.2 officers per 1,000 inhabitants. By population grouping, the rates ranged from 1.7 for cities with populations of 25,000 to 99,999 to 2.8 in cities with 250,000 or more inhabitants. Suburban county law enforcement agencies averaged 2.3 officers per 1,000 population, while agencies in rural counties averaged 2.6. (See Table 71.)

Geographically, the highest rates of officers to population were recorded in the Northeastern and Southern States where there were 2.5 officers per 1,000 inhabitants. Following were the Midwestern States with 2.1 and the Western States with 1.7.

Males comprised 91 percent of all sworn employees both nationally and in cities. Ninety-three percent of those in rural counties and 88 percent in suburban counties were males.

Civilian Employees

Civilians made up 28 percent of the total United States law enforcement employee force in 1993. They represented 22 percent of the police employees in cities, 34 percent in rural counties, and 37 percent of the suburban county law enforcement strength. Thirty-seven percent of all civilian employees were males.

Law Enforcement Officers Killed and Assaulted

Seventy law enforcement officers were feloniously slain in the line of duty during 1993, 7 more than in 1992. Accidents occurring while performing official duties claimed the lives of an additional 59 officers in 1993. The 1993 total for officers accidentally killed was 7 fewer than the 1992 total of 66.

Extensive data on line-of-duty deaths and assaults on city, county, state, and federal officers can be found in the Uniform Crime Reporting publication, *Law Enforcement Officers Killed and Assaulted.*

Table 70. — Full-time Law Enforcement Employees[1], Number and Rate per 1,000 Inhabitants, Geographic Region and Division by Population Group, October 31, 1993

[1993 estimated population]

Geographic region/division	Total (9,903 cities; population 162,619,000)	Population group					
		Group I (64 cities, 250,000 and over; population 45,870,000)	Group II (133 cities, 100,000 to 249,999; population 19,676,000)	Group III (344 cities, 50,000 to 99,999; population 23,610,000)	Group IV (680 cities, 25,000 to 49,999; population 23,522,000)	Group V (1,662 cities, 10,000 to 24,999; population 26,149,000)	Group VI (7,020 cities, under 10,000; population 23,793,000)
TOTAL: 9,903 cities; population 162,619,000:							
Number of employees	461,655	166,997	47,827	52,497	51,739	59,022	83,573
Average number of employees per 1,000 inhabitants	2.8	3.6	2.4	2.2	2.2	2.3	3.5
New England: 700 cities; population 11,714,000:							
Number of employees	28,889	2,604	3,858	5,772	5,734	6,245	4,676
Average number of employees per 1,000 inhabitants	2.5	4.7	3.3	2.3	2.1	2.1	2.6
Middle Atlantic: 1,659 cities; population 28,370,000:							
Number of employees	92,059	49,927	3,851	6,561	9,562	11,548	10,610
Average number of employees per 1,000 inhabitants	3.2	5.1	3.1	2.4	2.3	2.1	2.2
NORTHEAST: 2,359 cities; population 40,085,000:							
Number of employees	120,948	52,531	7,709	12,333	15,296	17,793	15,286
Average number of employees per 1,000 inhabitants	3.0	5.0	3.2	2.4	2.2	2.1	2.3
East North Central: 1,894 cities; population 28,907,000:							
Number of employees	76,816	26,168	6,040	9,048	9,849	12,521	13,190
Average number of employees per 1,000 inhabitants	2.7	4.3	2.3	2.1	2.0	2.1	2.8
West North Central: 855 cities; population 11,054,000:							
Number of employees	25,591	7,063	2,635	2,772	2,868	4,310	5,943
Average number of employees per 1,000 inhabitants	2.3	3.3	2.1	1.6	1.7	2.0	2.7
MIDWEST: 2,749 cities; population 39,961,000:							
Number of employees	102,407	33,231	8,675	11,820	12,717	16,831	19,133
Average number of employees per 1,000 inhabitants	2.6	4.0	2.2	1.9	1.9	2.1	2.8
South Atlantic: 1,680 cities; population 18,853,000:							
Number of employees	73,243	18,277	9,630	9,243	7,636	8,672	19,785
Average number of employees per 1,000 inhabitants	3.9	4.4	3.0	3.2	3.0	3.2	6.1
East South Central: 759 cities; population 7,899,000:							
Number of employees	24,423	5,090	3,752	1,302	2,650	4,282	7,347
Average number of employees per 1,000 inhabitants	3.1	3.0	2.8	2.7	2.6	2.7	4.0
West South Central: 1,048 cities; population 18,696,000:							
Number of employees	52,049	20,968	5,529	5,269	3,955	5,915	10,413
Average number of employees per 1,000 inhabitants	2.8	2.9	2.3	2.3	2.2	2.3	4.1
SOUTH: 3,487 cities; population 45,447,000:							
Number of employees	149,715	44,335	18,911	15,814	14,241	18,869	37,545
Average number of employees per 1,000 inhabitants	3.3	3.4	2.7	2.8	2.7	2.7	5.0
Mountain: 566 cities; population 10,208,000:							
Number of employees	25,527	9,742	3,299	2,980	2,673	1,914	4,919
Average number of employees per 1,000 inhabitants	2.5	2.6	2.2	1.8	2.1	2.3	3.8
Pacific: 742 cities; population 26,918,000:							
Number of employees	63,058	27,158	9,233	9,550	6,812	3,615	6,690
Average number of employees per 1,000 inhabitants	2.3	2.6	1.9	1.9	2.0	2.1	4.7
WEST: 1,308 cities; population 37,127,000:							
Number of employees	88,585	36,900	12,532	12,530	9,485	5,529	11,609
Average number of employees per 1,000 inhabitants	2.4	2.6	2.0	1.9	2.0	2.1	4.3

Suburban and County

Suburban[2]: 6,278 agencies; population 103,103,000:		County: 3,138 agencies; population 81,701,000:	
Number of employees	323,403	Number of employees	304,471
Average number of employees per 1,000 inhabitants	3.1	Average number of employees per 1,000 inhabitants	3.7

[1]Includes civilians.

[2]Includes suburban city and county law enforcement agencies within metropolitan areas. Excludes central cities. Suburban cities and counties are also included in other groups. Population figures were rounded to the nearest thousand. All rates were calculated before rounding.

Table 71.—Full-time Law Enforcement Officers, Number and Rate per 1,000 Inhabitants, Geographic Region and Division by Population Group, October 31, 1993

[1993 estimated population]

Geographic region/division	Total (9,903 cities; population 162,619,000)	Population group					
		Group I (64 cities, 250,000 and over; population 45,870,000)	Group II (133 cities, 100,000 to 249,999; population 19,676,000)	Group III (344 cities, 50,000 to 99,999; population 23,610,000)	Group IV (680 cities, 25,000 to 49,999; population 23,522,000)	Group V (1,662 cities, 10,000 to 24,999; population 26,149,000)	Group VI (7,020 cities under 10,000; population 23,793,000)
TOTAL: 9,903 cities; population 162,619,000:							
Number of officers...........................	358,152	129,491	36,407	40,232	40,591	47,211	64,220
Average number of officers per 1,000 inhabitants	2.2	2.8	1.9	1.7	1.7	1.8	2.7
New England: 700 cities; population 11,714,000:							
Number of officers...........................	23,980	1,944	3,228	4,955	4,983	5,267	3,603
Average number of officers per 1,000 inhabitants	2.0	3.5	2.7	2.0	1.8	1.8	2.0
Middle Atlantic: 1,659 cities; population 28,370,000:							
Number of officers...........................	74,354	38,729	3,323	5,440	8,009	9,814	9,039
Average number of officers per 1,000 inhabitants	2.6	3.9	2.6	2.0	2.0	1.8	1.9
NORTHEAST: 2,359 cities; population 40,085,000:							
Number of officers...........................	98,334	40,673	6,551	10,395	12,992	15,081	12,642
Average number of officers per 1,000 inhabitants	2.5	3.9	2.7	2.0	1.9	1.8	1.9
East North Central: 1,894 cities; population 28,907,000:							
Number of officers...........................	62,421	22,129	4,896	7,166	7,723	9,973	10,534
Average number of officers per 1,000 inhabitants	2.2	3.6	1.9	1.6	1.5	1.7	2.2
West North Central: 855 cities; population 11,054,000:							
Number of officers...........................	19,862	5,159	1,997	2,202	2,253	3,402	4,849
Average number of officers per 1,000 inhabitants	1.8	2.4	1.6	1.3	1.4	1.6	2.2
MIDWEST: 2,749 cities; population 39,961,000:							
Number of officers...........................	82,283	27,288	6,893	9,368	9,976	13,375	15,383
Average number of officers per 1,000 inhabitants	2.1	3.3	1.8	1.5	1.5	1.6	2.2
South Atlantic: 1,680 cities; population 18,853,000:							
Number of officers...........................	55,818	14,249	7,312	6,944	5,851	6,753	14,709
Average number of officers per 1,000 inhabitants	3.0	3.4	2.2	2.4	2.3	2.5	4.6
East South Central: 759 cities; population 7,899,000:							
Number of officers...........................	18,835	3,933	2,690	1,023	2,045	3,377	5,767
Average number of officers per 1,000 inhabitants	2.4	2.3	2.0	2.1	2.0	2.1	3.2
West South Central: 1,048 cities; population 18,696,000:							
Number of officers...........................	39,300	16,013	4,292	3,966	2,983	4,581	7,465
Average number of officers per 1,000 inhabitants	2.1	2.2	1.8	1.7	1.7	1.8	2.9
SOUTH: 3,487 cities; population 45,447,000:							
Number of officers...........................	113,953	34,195	14,294	11,933	10,879	14,711	27,941
Average number of officers per 1,000 inhabitants	2.5	2.6	2.1	2.1	2.0	2.1	3.7
Mountain: 566 cities; population 10,208,000:							
Number of officers...........................	18,730	7,262	2,370	2,145	1,954	1,401	3,598
Average number of officers per 1,000 inhabitants	1.8	2.0	1.6	1.3	1.6	1.7	2.8
Pacific: 742 cities; population 26,918,000:							
Number of officers...........................	44,852	20,073	6,299	6,391	4,790	2,643	4,656
Average number of officers per 1,000 inhabitants	1.7	1.9	1.3	1.3	1.4	1.5	3.3
WEST: 1,308 cities; population 37,127,000:							
Number of officers...........................	63,582	27,335	8,669	8,536	6,744	4,044	8,254
Average number of officers per 1,000 inhabitants	1.7	1.9	1.4	1.3	1.4	1.6	3.0

Suburban and County

Suburban[1]: 6,278 agencies; population 103,103,000:		County: 3,138 agencies; population 81,701,000:	
Number of officers..	224,372	Number of officers..	195,621
Average number of officers per 1,000 inhabitants	2.2	Average number of officers per 1,000 inhabitants	2.4

[1]Includes suburban city and county law enforcement agencies within metropolitan areas. Excludes central cities. Suburban cities and counties are also included in other groups. Population figures were rounded to the nearest thousand. All rates were calculated before rounding.

Table 72.-Full-time Law Enforcement Employees, October 31, 1993

[Range in rate per 1,000 inhabitants]

Rate range		Total[1] (9,237 cities; population 162,619,000)	Group I (64 cities, 250,000 and over; population 45,870,000)	Group II (133 cities, 100,000 to 249,999; population 19,676,000)	Group III (344 cities, 50,000 to 99,999; population 23,610,000)	Group IV (680 cities, 25,000 to 49,999; population 23,522,000)	Group V (1,662 cities, 10,000 to 24,999; population 26,149,000)	Group VI (6,354 cities under 10,000; population 23,793,000)
.1-.5	Number	134	....	....	1	....	12	121
	Percent	1.5	....	....	.3	....	.7	1.9
.6-1.0	Number	564	....	2	2	15	67	478
	Percent	6.1	....	1.5	.6	2.2	4.0	7.5
1.1-1.5	Number	1,231	....	7	41	99	187	897
	Percent	13.3	....	5.3	11.9	14.6	11.3	14.1
1.6-2.0	Number	1,910	8	39	134	207	450	1,072
	Percent	20.7	12.5	29.3	39.0	30.4	27.1	16.9
2.1-2.5	Number	1,796	14	40	81	206	439	1,016
	Percent	19.4	21.9	30.1	23.5	30.3	26.4	16.0
2.6-3.0	Number	1,208	16	21	46	80	246	799
	Percent	13.1	25.0	15.8	13.4	11.8	14.8	12.6
3.1-3.5	Number	789	9	12	20	36	149	563
	Percent	8.5	14.1	9.0	5.8	5.3	9.0	8.9
3.6-4.0	Number	480	7	9	7	22	66	369
	Percent	5.2	10.9	6.8	2.0	3.2	4.0	5.8
4.1-4.5	Number	299	2	2	4	6	26	259
	Percent	3.2	3.1	1.5	1.2	.9	1.6	4.1
4.6-5.0	Number	230	4	1	7	6	11	201
	Percent	2.5	6.3	.8	2.0	.9	.7	3.2
5.1 and over	Number	596	4	....	1	3	9	579
	Percent	6.5	6.3	....	.3	.4	.5	9.1
Total		9,237	64	133	344	680	1,662	6,354
Percent[2]		100.0	100.0	100.0	100.0	100.0	100.0	100.0

[1]The number of agencies used to compile these figures differs from the other Law Enforcement Employee tables because small agencies with no resident population are excluded from this table.

[2]Because of rounding, percentages may not add to totals.

Table 73. — Law Enforcement Officers, October 31, 1993

[Range in rate per 1,000 inhabitants]

Rate range		Total[1] (9,237 cities; population 162,619,000)	Group I (64 cities, 250,000 and over; population 45,870,000)	Group II (133 cities, 100,000 to 249,999; population 19,676,000)	Group III (344 cities, 50,000 to 99,999; population 23,610,000)	Group IV (680 cities, 25,000 to 49,999; population 23,522,000)	Group V (1,662 cities, 10,000 to 24,999; population 26,149,000)	Group VI (6,354 cities under 10,000; population 23,793,000)
.1-.5	Number	154	....	....	1	2	15	136
	Percent	1.7	....	....	.3	.3	.9	2.1
.6-1.0	Number	781	....	4	27	59	120	571
	Percent	8.5	....	3.0	7.8	8.7	7.2	9.0
1.1-1.5	Number	2,175	12	46	133	227	460	1,297
	Percent	23.5	18.8	34.6	38.7	33.4	27.7	20.4
1.6-2.0	Number	2,467	16	43	111	239	571	1,487
	Percent	26.7	25.0	32.3	32.3	35.1	34.4	23.4
2.1-2.5	Number	1,488	13	19	42	97	295	1,022
	Percent	16.1	20.3	14.3	12.2	14.3	17.7	16.1
2.6-3.0	Number	821	11	12	18	38	126	616
	Percent	8.9	17.2	9.0	5.2	5.6	7.6	9.7
3.1-3.5	Number	464	3	8	7	11	50	385
	Percent	5.0	4.7	6.0	2.0	1.6	3.0	6.1
3.6-4.0	Number	258	6	1	4	5	16	226
	Percent	2.8	9.4	.8	1.2	.7	1.0	3.6
4.1-4.5	Number	187	2	....	1	1	6	177
	Percent	2.0	3.1	....	.3	.1	.4	2.8
4.6-5.0	Number	100	....	....	....	....	3	97
	Percent	1.0	....	....	....	....	.2	1.5
5.1 and over	Number	342	1	....	....	1	....	340
	Percent	3.7	1.6	....	....	.1	....	5.4
Total		9,237	64	133	344	680	1,662	6,354
Percent[2]		100.0	100.0	100.0	100.0	100.0	100.0	100.0

[1]The number of agencies used to compile these figures differs from the other Law Enforcement Officer tables because small agencies with no resident population are excluded from this table.

[2]Because of rounding, percentages may not add to totals.

Table 74. — Law Enforcement Employees, Percent Male and Female, October 31, 1993

[1993 estimated population]

Population group	Total police employees			Police officers (sworn)			Civilian employees		
	Total	Percent male	Percent female	Total	Percent male	Percent female	Total	Percent male	Percent female
TOTAL AGENCIES: 13,041 agencies;									
population 244,320,000:	**766,126**	**75.7**	**24.3**	**553,773**	**90.6**	**9.4**	**212,353**	**36.9**	**63.1**
TOTAL CITIES: 9,903 cities;									
population 162,619,000:	**461,655**	**77.2**	**22.8**	**358,152**	**90.9**	**9.1**	**103,503**	**30.0**	**70.0**
GROUP I									
64 cities, 250,000 and over;									
population 45,870,000:	166,997	73.8	26.2	129,491	86.3	13.7	37,506	30.7	69.3
9 cities, 1,000,000 and over;									
population 21,208,000:	90,600	73.0	27.0	70,522	85.0	15.0	20,078	30.9	69.1
16 cities, 500,000 to 999,999;									
population 10,652,000:	35,492	75.6	24.4	27,685	87.7	12.3	7,807	32.3	67.7
39 cities, 250,000 to 499,999;									
population 14,010,000:	40,905	73.9	26.1	31,284	87.7	12.3	9,621	28.8	71.2
GROUP II									
133 cities, 100,000 to 249,999;									
population 19,676,000:	47,827	75.4	24.6	36,407	91.0	9.0	11,420	25.8	74.2
GROUP III									
344 cities, 50,000 to 99,999;									
population 23,610,000:	52,497	77.5	22.5	40,232	93.2	6.8	12,265	26.0	74.0
GROUP IV									
680 cities, 25,000 to 49,999;									
population 23,522,000:	51,739	79.6	20.4	40,591	94.2	5.8	11,148	26.4	73.6
GROUP V									
1,662 cities, 10,000 to 24,999;									
population 26,149,000:	59,022	81.2	18.8	47,211	94.9	5.1	11,811	26.4	73.6
GROUP VI									
7,020 cities, under 10,000;									
population 23,793,000:	83,573	80.8	19.2	64,220	93.8	6.2	19,353	37.7	62.3
SUBURBAN COUNTIES									
870 agencies; population 52,459,000:	190,075	72.4	27.6	120,417	88.4	11.6	69,658	44.7	55.3
RURAL COUNTIES									
2,268 agencies; population 29,242,000:	114,396	75.2	24.8	75,204	93.0	7.0	39,192	41.2	58.8
SUBURBAN AREA[1]									
6,278 agencies; population 103,103,000:	323,403	75.8	24.2	224,372	91.0	9.0	99,031	41.2	58.8

[1]Includes suburban city and county law enforcement agencies within metropolitan areas. Excludes central cities. Suburban cities and counties are also included in other groups.

Table 75. — Civilian Law Enforcement Employees, Percent of Total, Population Group, October 31, 1993

[1993 estimated population]

Population group	Percent civilian employees	Population group	Percent civilian employees
TOTAL AGENCIES: 13,041 agencies;		GROUP IV	
population 244,320,000:	**27.8**	680 cities, 25,000 to 49,999;	
		population 23,522,000:	21.5
TOTAL CITIES: 9,903 cities;		GROUP V	
population 162,619,000:	**22.4**	1,662 cities, 10,000 to 24,999;	
		population 26,149,000:	20.0
GROUP I		GROUP VI	
64 cities, 250,000 and over;		7,020 cities under 10,000;	
population 45,870,000:	22.5	population 23,793,000:	23.2
9 cities, 1,000,000 and over;			
population 21,208,000:	22.2	SUBURBAN COUNTIES	
16 cities, 500,000 to 999,999;		870 agencies;	
population 10,652,000:	22.0	population 52,459,000:	36.7
39 cities, 250,000 to 499,999;			
population 14,010,000:	23.5	RURAL COUNTIES	
		2,268 agencies;	
GROUP II		population 29,242,000:	34.6
133 cities, 100,000 to 249,999;			
population 19,676,000:	23.9	SUBURBAN AREA[1]	
		6,278 agencies;	
GROUP III		population 103,103,000:	30.6
344 cities, 50,000 to 99,999;			
population 23,610,000:	23.4		

[1]Includes suburban city and county law enforcement agencies within metropolitan areas. Excludes central cities. Suburban cities and counties are also included in other groups.

Table 76. — Full-time State Law Enforcement Employees, October 31, 1993

State	Number of law enforcement employees					State	Number of law enforcement employees				
	TOTAL	Officers		Civilians			Total	Officers		Civilians	
		Male	Female	Male	Female			Male	Female	Male	Female
TOTAL	91,262	57,132	3,579	12,195	18,356	**MISSOURI:**					
						State Highway Patrol	1,880	851	15	565	449
ALABAMA:						**MONTANA:**					
Department of Public						Highway Patrol	246	174	15	20	37
Safety	1,285	628	11	218	428	Other state agencies.....	339	244	22	32	41
Other state agencies......	190	159	6	4	21	**NEBRASKA:**					
ALASKA:						State Patrol............	625	462	20	54	89
State Police	535	337	19	48	131	**NEVADA:**					
ARIZONA:						Highway Patrol	484	299	22	38	125
Department of Public						**NEW HAMPSHIRE:**					
Safety	1,572	842	52	326	352	State Police	341	231	21	34	55
Other state agencies......	32	22	....	6	4	**NEW JERSEY:**					
ARKANSAS:						State Police	3,576	2,545	62	413	556
State Police	677	461	19	69	128	**NEW MEXICO:**					
CALIFORNIA:						State Police	573	415	10	49	99
Highway Patrol	8,251	5,246	480	1,012	1,513	**NEW YORK:**					
Other state agencies.....	934	585	86	132	131	State Police	4,636	3,651	287	244	454
COLORADO:						Other state agencies....	416	310	15	69	22
State Patrol............	752	519	18	71	144	**NORTH CAROLINA:**					
Other state agencies.....	214	117	22	27	48	Highway Patrol	1,586	1,237	9	198	142
CONNECTICUT:						Other state agencies....	1,860	1,265	114	178	303
State Police	1,449	908	56	215	270	**NORTH DAKOTA:**					
DELAWARE:						Highway Patrol	188	119	2	39	28
State Police	667	459	30	72	106	**OHIO:**					
Other state agencies......	180	136	12	16	16	State Highway Patrol	2,431	1,342	84	462	543
FLORIDA:						**OKLAHOMA:**					
Highway Patrol	2,097	1,435	153	179	330	Department of Public					
Other state agencies.....	2,606	1,138	106	503	859	Safety	1,271	711	6	266	288
GEORGIA:						**OREGON:**					
Department of Public						State Police	1,002	752	39	51	160
Safety	1,976	818	27	398	733	**PENNSYLVANIA:**					
Other state agencies......	1,406	850	105	138	313	State Police	5,160	3,957	143	479	581
IDAHO:						Other state agencies.....	305	233	26	8	38
State Police	224	171	6	8	39	**RHODE ISLAND:**					
Other state agencies......	58	41	4	1	12	State Police	223	167	13	25	18
ILLINOIS:						**SOUTH CAROLINA:**					
State Police	3,331	1,716	161	423	1,031	Highway Patrol	1,188	959	20	52	157
Other state agencies......	249	205	15	9	20	Other state agencies.....	999	705	88	36	170
INDIANA:						**SOUTH DAKOTA:**					
State Police	1,683	995	45	273	370	Highway Patrol	240	155	2	61	22
IOWA:						**TENNESSEE:**					
Department of Public						Department of Public					
Safety	807	557	27	95	128	Safety	1,568	720	22	175	651
KANSAS:						**TEXAS:**					
Highway Patrol	804	538	39	113	114	Department of Public					
KENTUCKY:						Safety	5,594	2,426	65	888	2,215
State Police	1,582	894	20	347	321	**UTAH:**					
Other state agencies......	875	664	21	69	121	Highway Patrol	398	350	19	8	21
LOUISIANA:						**VERMONT:**					
State Police	1,022	711	8	88	215	State Police	406	259	10	52	85
MAINE:						**VIRGINIA:**					
State Police	482	330	13	77	62	State Police	2,315	1,646	50	201	418
Other state agencies......	128	44	2	36	46	Other state agencies.....	1,267	314	29	558	366
MARYLAND:						**WASHINGTON:**					
State Police	2,232	1,485	120	269	358	State Patrol............	1,931	943	40	502	446
Other state agencies......	1,209	748	120	191	150	**WEST VIRGINIA:**					
MASSACHUSETTS:						State Police	804	478	13	99	214
State Police	2,514	2,084	201	123	106	Other state agencies	116	110	1	....	5
MICHIGAN:						**WISCONSIN:**					
State Police	2,916	1,749	189	469	509	State Patrol............	660	433	62	81	84
MINNESOTA:						Other state agencies.....	63	37	11	7	8
State Patrol.............	683	460	19	121	83	**WYOMING:**					
MISSISSIPPI:						Highway Patrol	290	141	2	52	95
Highway Safety Patrol	691	461	8	59	163						

NOTE: The responsibilities of the various state police, highway patrol, and departments of public safety agencies range from full law enforcement duties to traffic patrol only. Any comparison of these data from state to state must take these factors and those on page iv into consideration.

Table 77. — Full-time Law Enforcement Employees, State, 1993

[1993 estimated population]

State	Total employees	Officers Male	Officers Female	Civilians Male	Civilians Female	State	Total employees	Officers Male	Officers Female	Civilians Male	Civilians Female
ALABAMA: 309 agencies; Population 4,181,000:	12,429	7,906	676	1,494	2,353	**MONTANA:** 98 agencies; Population 838,000:	2,061	1,278	58	248	477
ALASKA: 36 agencies; Population 599,000:	1,653	974	69	167	443	**NEBRASKA:** 161 agencies; Population 1,599,000:	3,982	2,670	220	283	809
ARIZONA: 99 agencies; Population 3,927,000:	13,461	7,194	683	2,586	2,998	**NEVADA:** 32 agencies; Population 1,380,000:	4,739	2,959	358	279	1,143
ARKANSAS: 183 agencies; Population 2,419,000:	5,208	3,180	193	815	1,020	**NEW HAMPSHIRE:** 111 agencies; Population 929,000:	2,492	1,814	87	160	431
CALIFORNIA: 481 agencies; Population 27,959,000:	85,750	52,878	5,891	8,940	18,041	**NEW JERSEY:** 530 agencies; Population 7,603,000:	34,059	25,836	1,339	2,255	4,629
COLORADO: 235 agencies; Population 3,563,000:	11,278	7,334	964	788	2,192	**NEW MEXICO:** 93 agencies; Population 1,536,000:	4,701	3,045	223	444	989
CONNECTICUT: 100 agencies; Population 2,786,000:	8,862	6,710	455	534	1,163	**NEW YORK:** 392 agencies; Population 16,139,000:	65,591	45,394	5,702	4,417	10,078
DELAWARE: 45 agencies; Population 693,000:	2,622	1,898	157	212	355	**NORTH CAROLINA:** 499 agencies; Population 6,935,000:	20,942	14,146	1,622	2,087	3,087
DISTRICT OF COLUMBIA: 2 agencies; Population 578,000:	5,222	3,425	965	283	549	**NORTH DAKOTA:** 99 agencies; Population 634,000:	1,335	930	65	123	217
FLORIDA: 357 agencies; Population 13,449,000:	56,328	29,187	3,519	9,784	13,838	**OHIO:** 491 agencies; Population 10,130,000:	24,835	16,625	1,530	2,621	4,059
GEORGIA: 603 agencies; Population 6,721,000:	25,474	16,588	2,314	2,148	4,424	**OKLAHOMA:** 284 agencies; Population 3,176,000:	8,916	5,644	420	1,223	1,629
HAWAII: 5 agencies; Population 1,172,000:	3,384	2,528	175	221	460	**OREGON:** 169 agencies; Population 2,948,000:	6,160	4,282	355	290	1,233
IDAHO: 109 agencies; Population 1,098,000:	2,683	1,828	188	130	537	**PENNSYLVANIA:** 875 agencies; Population 9,090,000:	25,123	19,790	1,848	1,324	2,161
ILLINOIS: 715 agencies; Population 11,643,000:	39,058	26,789	3,129	3,179	5,961	**RHODE ISLAND:** 41 agencies; Population 994,000:	2,739	2,127	103	239	270
INDIANA: 231 agencies; Population 5,546,000:	13,404	8,192	627	2,013	2,572	**SOUTH CAROLINA:** 241 agencies; Population 3,624,000:	9,762	6,874	575	757	1,556
IOWA: 225 agencies; Population 2,789,000:	6,093	4,209	230	502	1,152	**SOUTH DAKOTA:** 80 agencies; Population 620,000:	1,152	781	39	124	208
KANSAS: 338 agencies; Population 2,466,000:	8,092	5,425	458	753	1,456	**TENNESSEE:** 252 agencies; Population 4,705,000:	14,144	8,816	828	1,759	2,741
KENTUCKY: 392 agencies; Population 3,743,000:	8,938	6,266	588	851	1,233	**TEXAS:** 880 agencies; Population 18,025,000:	62,829	35,380	3,542	10,434	13,473
LOUISIANA: 173 agencies; Population 4,293,000:	15,901	11,216	2,294	758	1,633	**UTAH:** 121 agencies; Population 1,852,000:	4,232	3,161	280	157	634
MAINE: 134 agencies; Population 1227,000:	2,641	1,900	81	305	355	**VERMONT:** 51 agencies; Population 576,000:	1,144	789	46	98	211
MARYLAND: 125 agencies; Population 4,852,000:	16,426	11,336	1,410	1,364	2,316	**VIRGINIA:** 270 agencies; Population 6,478,000:	18,219	12,274	1,258	1,573	3,114
MASSACHUSETTS: 296 agencies; Population 5,890,000:	16,915	13,634	853	938	1,490	**WASHINGTON:** 221 agencies; Population 5,157,000:	11,640	7,613	597	1,122	2,308
MICHIGAN: 569 agencies; Population 9,438,000:	24,905	16,730	1,950	2,417	3,808	**WEST VIRGINIA:** 242 agencies; Population 1,514,000:	3,646	2,492	93	525	536
MINNESOTA: 250 agencies; Population 4,172,000:	9,351	6,190	460	1,038	1,663	**WISCONSIN:** 318 agencies; Population 4,897,000:	14,321	9,933	1,120	1,016	2,252
MISSISSIPPI: 164 agencies; Population 2,144,000:	5,420	3,531	259	616	1,014	**WYOMING:** 66 agencies; Population 469,000:	1,678	1,051	58	158	411
MISSOURI: 288 agencies; Population 5,124,000:	14,186	9,231	836	1,707	2,412						

Table 78. — Number of Full-time Law Enforcement Employees, Cities, October 31, 1993

City	Total police employees	Total officers	Total civilians	City	Total police employees	Total officers	Total civilians
ALABAMA				**ALABAMA — Continued**			
				Greensboro	11	8	3
Abbeville	14	10	4	Greenville	31	24	7
Adamsville	13	9	4	Guin	4	4	....
Alabaster	27	23	4	Gulf Shores	30	23	7
Albertville	37	28	9	Guntersville	28	23	5
Alexander City	53	43	10	Gurley	5	5	....
Aliceville	9	5	4	Haleyville	19	18	1
Andalusia	33	26	7	Hamilton	10	9	1
Anniston	120	90	30	Hanceville	10	6	4
Arab	23	18	5	Hartford	15	9	6
Ardmore	10	5	5	Hartselle	26	22	4
Ashford	11	6	5	Headland	14	9	5
Ashland	10	7	3	Heflin	7	7	....
Athens	42	33	9	Helena	11	7	4
Atmore	24	19	5	Hokes Bluff	5	5	....
Attalla	24	17	7	Hollywood	5	2	3
Auburn	85	65	20	Homewood	79	57	22
Bay Minette	25	20	5	Hoover	104	83	21
Bayou La Batre	17	12	5	Hueytown	27	21	6
Bear Creek	4	4	....	Huntsville	458	340	118
Bessemer	93	76	17	Hurtsboro	4	4	....
Birmingham	999	770	229	Irondale	29	24	5
Blountsville	10	6	4	Jackson	19	15	4
Boaz	30	24	6	Jacksonville	26	20	6
Brewton	23	19	4	Jasper	60	41	19
Bridgeport	11	7	4	Jemison	2	2	....
Brundidge	13	9	4	Killen	4	3	1
Calera	12	8	4	Kimberly	3	3	....
Camp Hill	5	5	....	Kinston	4	2	2
Carbon Hill	12	6	6	Lafayette	16	12	4
Cedar Bluff	2	2	....	Lanett	30	24	6
Centre	12	8	4	Leeds	26	21	5
Cherokee	5	4	1	Leighton	4	4	....
Chickasaw	18	18	....	Level Plains	4	4	....
Childersburg	16	12	4	Lincoln	14	9	5
Citronelle	12	8	4	Linden	6	6	....
Clanton	16	15	1	Lineville	9	5	4
Clayton	3	3	....	Lipscomb	7	3	4
Columbiana	11	7	4	Littleville	8	5	3
Cordova	5	3	2	Livingston	14	9	5
Cottonwood	3	3	....	Louisville	3	3	....
Courtland	4	4	....	Luverne	22	16	6
Creola	11	9	2	Madison	45	32	13
Cullman	48	39	9	Marion	14	8	6
Dadeville	8	8	....	Midfield	14	10	4
Daleville	21	16	5	Midland	7	4	3
Daphne	37	26	11	Millbrook	16	12	4
Decatur	125	99	26	Mobile	560	425	135
Demopolis	25	18	7	Monroeville	25	20	5
Dora	8	4	4	Montevallo	12	8	4
Dothan	160	108	52	Montgomery	553	412	141
East Brewton	6	4	2	Moody	14	10	4
Eclectic	8	4	4	Morris	2	2	....
Elba	22	17	5	Moulton	9	8	1
Enterprise	54	41	13	Moundville	7	4	3
Eufaula	36	35	1	Mountain Brook	63	48	15
Eutaw	11	7	4	Muscle Shoals	31	31	....
Evergreen	16	12	4	New Brockton	5	5	....
Fairfield	39	33	6	New Hope	3	3	....
Fairhope	16	15	1	Newton	6	3	3
Falkville	4	4	....	Northport	51	41	10
Fayette	10	10	....	Notasulga	7	4	3
Flomaton	12	8	4	Oneonta	13	13	....
Florala	7	3	4	Opelika	86	73	13
Florence	113	85	28	Opp	25	19	6
Foley	24	20	4	Orange Beach	20	15	5
Fort Payne	42	28	14	Oxford	42	33	9
Fultondale	16	12	4	Ozark	60	44	16
Gadsden	128	101	27	Pelham	43	34	9
Gardendale	24	18	6	Pell City	21	21	....
Geneva	15	12	3	Phenix City	75	61	14
Glencoe	5	5	....	Phil Campbell	4	4	....
Goodwater	8	4	4	Piedmont	17	13	4
Gordo	4	4	....	Pleasant Grove	15	11	4
Graysville	6	6	....	Prattville	51	46	5

Table 78. — Number of Full-time Law Enforcement Employees, Cities, October 31, 1993 — Continued

City	Total police employees	Total officers	Total civilians	City	Total police employees	Total officers	Total civilians
ALABAMA — Continued				**ARIZONA — Continued**			
Priceville	4	4	....	Avondale	36	29	7
Prichard	73	54	19	Benson	16	10	6
Rainbow City	24	16	8	Bisbee	20	14	6
Rainsville	12	8	4	Buckeye	27	15	12
Reform	4	4	....	Bullhead City	87	57	30
Roanoke	22	17	5	Camp Verde	21	13	8
Robertsdale	12	8	4	Casa Grande	65	46	19
Russellville	23	19	4	Chandler	156	112	44
Samson	10	6	4	Chino Valley	15	10	5
Saraland	32	27	5	Clarkdale	8	8	....
Satsuma	13	9	4	Coolidge	23	17	6
Scottsboro	50	33	17	Cottonwood	29	17	12
Selma	92	60	32	Douglas	46	35	11
Sheffield	29	25	4	Eagar	7	6	1
Slocomb	6	4	2	El Mirage	14	9	5
Somerville	4	2	2	Eloy	32	20	12
Southside	10	5	5	Flagstaff	111	80	31
Stevenson	11	7	4	Florence	19	13	6
Sulligent	3	3	....	Gilbert	68	48	20
Sumiton	10	5	5	Glendale	303	205	98
Sylacauga	44	38	6	Globe	24	17	7
Talladega	53	40	13	Goodyear	22	17	5
Tallassee	20	16	4	Hayden	7	6	1
Tarrant City	22	17	5	Holbrook	20	15	5
Thomaston	1	1	....	Huachuca City	9	4	5
Thorsby	2	2	....	Jerome	3	3	....
Town Creek	6	6	....	Kearny	10	6	4
Trinity	3	3	....	Kingman	50	35	15
Troy	55	43	12	Lake Havasu City	71	51	20
Trussville	22	17	5	Mammoth	5	5	....
Tuscaloosa	251	196	55	Marana	30	24	6
Tuscumbia	21	21	....	Mesa	699	467	232
Tuskegee	44	35	9	Miami	7	5	2
Union Springs	14	11	3	Nogales	68	51	17
Valley	29	22	7	Paradise Valley	40	31	9
Vance	1	1	....	Parker	16	11	5
Vestavia Hills	36	35	1	Payson	29	19	10
Warrior	10	6	4	Peoria	94	66	28
Weaver	10	9	1	Phoenix	2,658	1,978	680
Wetumpka	20	15	5	Pima	2	2	....
Wilmer	3	1	2	Pinetop-Lakeside	21	13	8
Winfield	8	8	....	Prescott	73	46	27
York	10	7	3	Prescott Valley	23	16	7
				Quartzsite	4	3	1
ALASKA				Safford	16	14	2
				St. Johns	7	6	1
Anchorage	401	267	134	San Luis	18	13	5
Bethel	21	11	10	Scottsdale	330	218	112
Bristol Bay Borough	10	4	6	Sedona	24	17	7
Cordova	10	5	5	Show Low	23	15	8
Craig	8	4	4	Sierra Vista	50	36	14
Dillingham	21	6	15	Snowflake-Taylor	12	10	2
Fairbanks	49	33	16	Somerton	16	11	5
Haines	9	5	4	South Tucson	27	20	7
Homer	16	10	6	Springerville	5	5	....
Hoonah	4	3	1	Superior	11	7	4
Juneau	63	39	24	Surprise	19	18	1
Kenai	25	16	9	Tempe	347	241	106
Ketchikan	28	20	8	Thatcher	7	7	....
Klawock	2	2	....	Tolleson	19	14	5
Kodiak	32	16	16	Tombstone	5	4	1
Kotzebue	18	8	10	Tucson	1,006	759	247
North Pole	11	7	4	Wellton	3	3	....
North Slope Borough	87	49	38	Wickenburg	15	10	5
Palmer	21	9	12	Willcox	15	10	5
Petersburg	9	5	4	Winslow	30	19	11
Seward	20	9	11	Youngtown	16	10	6
Skagway	4	4	....				
Soldotna	13	10	3	**ARKANSAS**			
Wasilla	11	10	1				
Wrangell	13	7	6	Alma	11	5	6
				Arkadelphia	20	16	4
ARIZONA				Ashdown	10	9	1
				Bald Knob	8	4	4
Apache Junction	56	36	20	Barling	8	7	1

Table 78. — Number of Full-time Law Enforcement Employees, Cities, October 31, 1993 — Continued

City	Total police employees	Total officers	Total civilians	City	Total police employees	Total officers	Total civilians
ARKANSAS — Continued				**ARKANSAS — Continued**			
Beebe	8	4	4	Pocahontas	18	13	5
Benton	37	29	8	Prescott	11	7	4
Bentonville	33	24	9	Rogers	63	49	14
Berryville	9	8	1	Russellville	45	35	10
Blytheville	56	44	12	Searcy	41	30	11
Booneville	9	5	4	Sheridan	7	6	1
Bradford	2	2	....	Sherwood	65	56	9
Brinkley	16	11	5	Siloam Springs	33	20	13
Bryant	13	11	2	Smackover	5	4	1
Bull Shoals	2	2	....	Springdale	73	52	21
Cabot	16	12	4	Star City	3	3	....
Camden	40	29	11	Stuttgart	27	18	9
Carlisle	9	5	4	Texarkana	85	64	21
Clarksville	18	11	7	Trumann	15	10	5
Conway	70	58	12	Van Buren	30	24	6
Corning	12	8	4	Vilonia	2	1	1
Crossett	19	12	7	Waldron	6	6	....
Danville	3	3	....	Walnut Ridge	12	8	4
Dardanelle	8	5	3	Warren	18	11	7
De Queen	11	9	2	West Fork	3	3	....
Dermott	11	6	5	West Helena	24	19	5
Des Arc	3	3	....	West Memphis	84	65	19
De Witt	15	10	5	Wynne	18	17	1
Dumas	19	13	6				
Earle	7	5	2	**CALIFORNIA**			
Elaine	1	1	....				
El Dorado	53	44	9	Adelanto	30	19	11
England	10	5	5	Alameda	134	92	42
Eudora	9	5	4	Albany	33	28	5
Eureka Springs	15	9	6	Alhambra	144	86	58
Fayetteville	93	64	29	Alturas	9	8	1
Fordyce	13	9	4	Anaheim	511	347	164
Forrest City	36	26	10	Anderson	23	13	10
Fort Smith	152	115	37	Angels Camp	5	4	1
Greenbrier	2	2	....	Antioch	116	81	35
Green Forest	7	5	2	Arcadia	99	77	22
Greenwood	6	6	....	Arcata	28	20	8
Gurdon	5	4	1	Arroyo Grande	28	20	8
Hamburg	6	5	1	Arvin	17	11	6
Harrison	32	23	9	Atascadero	35	27	8
Hazen	8	4	4	Atherton	25	20	5
Heber Springs	18	11	7	Atwater	29	22	7
Helena	20	17	3	Auburn	27	20	7
Hope	29	22	7	Azusa	82	56	26
Horseshoe Bend	7	6	1	Bakersfield	318	234	84
Hot Springs	89	72	17	Baldwin Park	92	71	21
Hoxie	10	5	5	Banning	42	28	14
Jacksonville	73	56	17	Barstow	51	38	13
Jonesboro	85	67	18	Bear Valley Springs	10	6	4
Judsonia	4	3	1	Beaumont	23	16	7
Kensett	3	3	....	Bell	56	40	16
Lake Village	10	6	4	Bell Gardens	80	56	24
Lincoln	5	5	....	Belmont	43	31	12
Little Rock	488	395	93	Belvedere	9	7	2
Lonoke	11	6	5	Benicia	48	33	15
Magnolia	21	17	4	Berkeley	316	187	129
Malvern	20	13	7	Beverly Hills	210	128	82
Marianna	14	11	3	Bishop	22	14	8
Marion	10	10	....	Blue Lake	3	3	....
Marked Tree	12	9	3	Blythe	25	16	9
Maumelle	36	22	14	Brawley	37	27	10
McGehee	10	7	3	Brea	132	106	26
Mena	10	10	....	Brentwood	19	15	4
Monticello	21	15	6	Brisbane	20	15	5
Morrilton	18	12	6	Broadmoor	11	10	1
Mountain Home	24	18	6	Buena Park	132	86	46
Nashville	10	9	1	Burbank	235	150	85
Newport	16	15	1	Burlingame	64	45	19
North Little Rock	200	145	55	Calexico	48	29	19
Osceola	32	23	9	California City	20	13	7
Ozark	9	6	3	Calipatria	6	5	1
Paragould	33	28	5	Calistoga	12	9	3
Paris	12	7	5	Campbell	56	38	18
Piggott	7	6	1	Capitola	34	23	11
Pine Bluff	142	116	26	Carlsbad	105	77	28

Table 78. — Number of Full-time Law Enforcement Employees, Cities, October 31, 1993 — Continued

City	Total police employees	Total officers	Total civilians	City	Total police employees	Total officers	Total civilians
CALIFORNIA — Continued				**CALIFORNIA — Continued**			
Carmel	25	15	10	Greenfield	10	9	1
Cathedral City	64	41	23	Gridley	17	11	6
Ceres	59	32	27	Grover City	24	17	7
Chico	99	62	37	Guadalupe	7	6	1
China Lake	63	38	25	Gustine	9	8	1
Chino	112	78	34	Half Moon Bay	14	13	1
Chowchilla	24	12	12	Hanford	49	36	13
Chula Vista	248	162	86	Hawthorne	145	94	51
Claremont	57	38	19	Hayward	263	161	102
Clayton	10	9	1	Healdsburg	25	16	9
Clearlake	23	16	7	Hemet	63	48	15
Cloverdale	14	10	4	Hercules	20	17	3
Clovis	100	69	31	Hermosa Beach	55	36	19
Coachella	32	22	10	Hillsborough	32	25	7
Coalinga	23	16	7	Hollister	28	23	5
Colfax	5	5	....	Holtville	11	7	4
Colma	16	13	3	Hughson	8	7	1
Colton	83	60	23	Huntington Beach	378	231	147
Colusa	9	8	1	Huntington Park	105	65	40
Compton	249	125	124	Huron	12	7	5
Concord	188	137	51	Imperial	13	13	....
Corcoran	20	13	7	Indio	62	41	21
Corning	17	12	5	Inglewood	286	207	79
Corona	166	114	52	Ione	4	4	....
Coronado	57	40	17	Irvine	187	129	58
Costa Mesa	201	139	62	Irwindale	26	20	6
Cotati	17	12	5	Isleton	2	2	....
Covina	79	52	27	Jackson	13	10	3
Crescent City	13	12	1	Kensington	9	8	1
Culver City	162	117	45	Kerman	15	13	2
Cypress	80	53	27	King City	20	14	6
Daly City	140	107	33	Kingsburg	15	10	5
Davis	70	50	20	Laguna Beach	79	46	33
Delano	50	41	9	La Habra	90	63	27
Del Rey Oaks	3	3	....	Lakeport	14	12	2
Dinuba	24	18	6	Lake Shastina	3	3	....
Dixon	19	16	3	La Mesa	84	61	23
Dorris	3	2	1	La Palma	30	24	6
Dos Palos	5	5	....	La Verne	56	40	16
Downey	152	119	33	Lemoore	26	20	6
East Palo Alto	44	36	8	Lincoln	17	13	4
El Cajon	195	123	72	Lindsay	21	15	6
El Centro	79	49	30	Livermore	95	60	35
El Cerrito	38	33	5	Livingston	20	15	5
El Monte	156	125	31	Lodi	101	69	32
El Segundo	83	63	20	Lompoc	56	41	15
Emeryville	42	29	13	Long Beach	1,203	791	412
Escalon	13	8	5	Los Alamitos	30	24	6
Escondido	215	147	68	Los Altos	45	28	17
Etna	1	1	....	Los Angeles	10,099	7,637	2,462
Eureka	64	45	19	Los Banos	36	23	13
Exeter	14	13	1	Los Gatos	61	40	21
Fairfax	14	10	4	Madera	58	43	15
Fairfield	138	80	58	Mammoth Lakes	18	15	3
Farmersville	11	10	1	Manhattan Beach	97	60	37
Ferndale	2	2	....	Manteca	61	42	19
Firebaugh	12	8	4	Marina	29	24	5
Folsom	42	33	9	Martinez	53	42	11
Fontana	165	112	53	Marysville	33	21	12
Fort Bragg	26	18	8	Maywood	36	26	10
Fortuna	19	14	5	Menlo Park	66	46	20
Foster City	54	41	13	Merced	105	73	32
Fountain Valley	84	61	23	Millbrae	28	21	7
Fowler	6	6	....	Mill Valley	35	21	14
Fremont	269	180	89	Milpitas	104	74	30
Fresno	668	432	236	Modesto	281	196	85
Fullerton	216	146	70	Monrovia	74	54	20
Galt	26	17	9	Montclair	73	51	22
Gardena	111	89	22	Montebello	119	87	32
Garden Grove	226	160	66	Monterey	72	56	16
Gilroy	77	45	32	Monterey Park	122	80	42
Glendale	315	216	99	Moraga	12	11	1
Glendora	74	52	22	Morgan Hill	33	20	13
Gonzales	10	9	1	Morro Bay	24	18	6
Grass Valley	26	18	8	Mountain View	109	79	30

Table 78.—Number of Full-time Law Enforcement Employees, Cities, October 31, 1993—Continued

City	Total police employees	Total officers	Total civilians	City	Total police employees	Total officers	Total civilians
CALIFORNIA—Continued				**CALIFORNIA—Continued**			
Mount Shasta	14	9	5	San Marino	31	25	6
Murrieta	30	23	7	San Mateo	143	101	42
Napa	106	66	40	San Pablo	44	37	7
National City	94	67	27	San Rafael	93	67	26
Nevada City	10	8	2	Santa Ana	616	387	229
Newark	68	49	19	Santa Barbara	214	134	80
Newman	9	8	1	Santa Clara	178	143	35
Newport Beach	212	143	69	Santa Cruz	115	77	38
Novato	75	52	23	Santa Maria	99	75	24
Oakdale	29	21	8	Santa Monica	427	188	239
Oakland	1,089	719	370	Santa Paula	37	29	8
Oceanside	236	160	76	Santa Rosa	213	140	73
Ontario	298	188	110	Sausalito	24	19	5
Orange	175	140	35	Scotts Valley	28	20	8
Orland	10	9	1	Seal Beach	48	33	15
Oroville	31	21	10	Seaside	50	39	11
Oxnard	239	146	93	Sebastopol	20	14	6
Pacifica	53	41	12	Selma	33	21	12
Pacific Grove	37	26	11	Shafter	20	14	6
Palm Springs	120	77	43	Sierra Madre	18	13	5
Palo Alto	167	92	75	Signal Hill	41	30	11
Palos Verdes Estates	35	23	12	Simi Valley	160	108	52
Paradise	37	23	14	Soledad	14	11	3
Parlier	9	8	1	Sonoma	21	13	8
Pasadena	347	223	124	Sonora	14	10	4
Paso Robles	35	29	6	South Gate	120	90	30
Patterson	16	14	2	South Lake Tahoe	70	51	19
Perris	65	42	23	South Pasadena	52	31	21
Petaluma	78	52	26	South San Francisco	115	75	40
Piedmont	27	20	7	Stallion Springs	4	4	....
Pinole	41	22	19	Stockton	489	324	165
Pismo Beach	35	24	11	Suisun City	31	21	10
Pittsburg	81	66	15	Sunnyvale	172	118	54
Placentia	67	51	16	Susanville	15	14	1
Placerville	22	18	4	Sutter Creek	6	5	1
Pleasant Hill	61	41	20	Taft	20	14	6
Pleasanton	95	66	29	Tiburon	17	14	3
Pomona	287	174	113	Torrance	318	238	80
Porterville	62	40	22	Tracy	60	42	18
Port Hueneme	26	19	7	Trinidad	3	3	....
Red Bluff	36	23	13	Tulare	65	45	20
Redding	173	89	84	Turlock	74	51	23
Redlands	94	68	26	Tustin	119	84	35
Redondo Beach	168	96	72	Twin Cities	40	31	9
Redwood City	106	72	34	Ukiah	33	24	9
Reedley	31	22	9	Union City	89	62	27
Rialto	134	93	41	Upland	110	79	31
Richmond	257	179	78	Vacaville	102	55	47
Ridgecrest	40	31	9	Vallejo	187	125	62
Rio Dell	6	6	....	Ventura	179	119	60
Rio Vista	9	8	1	Vernon	73	55	18
Ripon	18	11	7	Visalia	130	84	46
Riverbank	21	16	5	Walnut Creek	108	78	30
Riverside	444	302	142	Waterford	12	10	2
Rocklin	41	27	14	Watsonville	71	53	18
Rohnert Park	77	50	27	Weed	12	8	4
Roseville	113	67	46	West Covina	160	114	46
Ross	9	8	1	Westminster	148	102	46
Sacramento	889	578	311	Westmorland	4	4	....
St. Helena	16	12	4	West Sacramento	71	50	21
Salinas	181	138	43	Wheatland	7	6	1
San Anselmo	23	17	6	Whittier	134	93	41
San Bernardino	393	251	142	Williams	6	6	....
San Bruno	58	47	11	Willits	18	12	6
San Carlos	46	34	12	Willows	10	8	2
Sand City	5	5	....	Winters	9	8	1
San Diego	2,613	1,861	752	Woodlake	10	9	1
San Fernando	47	33	14	Woodland	68	49	19
San Francisco	2,193	1,804	389	Yreka	21	14	7
San Gabriel	64	53	11	Yuba City	56	39	17
Sanger	30	22	8				
San Jacinto	38	26	12	**COLORADO**			
San Jose	1,624	1,203	421				
San Leandro	125	83	42	Alamosa	22	19	3
San Luis Obispo	77	53	24	Alma	1	1	....

Table 78. — Number of Full-time Law Enforcement Employees, Cities, October 31, 1993 — Continued

City	Total police employees	Total officers	Total civilians	City	Total police employees	Total officers	Total civilians
COLORADO — Continued				**COLORADO — Continued**			
Antonito	4	4	....	Idaho Springs	9	8	1
Arvada	167	117	50	Ignacio	4	4	....
Aspen	31	22	9	Johnstown	4	4	....
Ault	3	3	....	Kersey	2	2	....
Aurora	575	391	184	Kremmling	4	4	....
Avon	11	9	2	Lafayette	29	23	6
Basalt	5	4	1	La Jara	3	3	....
Bayfield	3	3	....	La Junta	19	16	3
Berthoud	5	4	1	Lakeside	5	4	1
Black Hawk	20	16	4	Lakewood	320	216	104
Boulder	199	131	68	Lamar	27	20	7
Bow Mar	2	2	....	La Salle	5	5	....
Breckenridge	22	15	7	Las Animas	6	6	....
Brighton	38	28	10	Leadville	8	7	1
Broomfield	55	41	14	Limon	6	5	1
Brush	12	10	2	Littleton	72	56	16
Buena Vista	6	5	1	Lochbuie	5	4	1
Burlington	7	7	....	Log Lane Village	2	2	....
Canon City	34	24	10	Longmont	125	82	43
Carbondale	9	8	1	Louisville	28	22	6
Castle Rock	22	17	5	Loveland	79	52	27
Cedaredge	3	3	....	Manassa	2	2	....
Center	5	5	....	Manitou Springs	19	14	5
Central City	14	12	2	Manzanola	1	1	....
Cherry Hills Village	25	22	3	Meeker	4	4	....
Colorado Springs	655	468	187	Milliken	3	3	....
Columbine Valley	3	3	....	Minturn	4	4	....
Commerce City	62	42	20	Monte Vista	19	14	5
Cortez	33	22	11	Montrose	29	25	4
Craig	24	16	8	Monument	3	3	....
Crested Butte	5	5	....	Morrison	1	1	....
Cripple Creek	23	16	7	Mountain View	2	2	....
Dacono	4	4	....	Mount Crested Butte	6	5	1
De Beque	1	1	....	Nederland	5	4	1
Del Norte	5	4	1	New Castle	2	2	....
Delta	15	12	3	Northglenn	59	43	16
Denver	1,569	1,394	175	Olathe	4	4	....
Dillon	6	5	1	Pagosa Springs	5	5	....
Durango	49	29	20	Palisade	5	4	1
Eagle	4	4	....	Palmer Lake	3	3	....
Eaton	5	4	1	Paonia	3	3	....
Edgewater	17	14	3	Parachute	8	3	5
Elizabeth	2	2	....	Parker	23	17	6
Empire	1	1	....	Platteville	4	4	....
Englewood	83	63	20	Pueblo	219	174	45
Erie	4	3	1	Rangely	9	5	4
Estes Park	24	14	10	Ridgway	2	2	....
Evans	16	13	3	Rifle	18	12	6
Fairplay	2	2	....	Rocky Ford	8	7	1
Federal Heights	28	19	9	Salida	14	13	1
Firestone	3	3	....	Sheridan	28	19	9
Flagler	1	1	....	Silt	3	3	....
Florence	11	6	5	Silverthorne	13	12	1
Fort Collins	167	108	59	Snowmass Village	11	8	3
Fort Lupton	18	12	6	Springfield	3	3	....
Fort Morgan	27	22	5	Steamboat Springs	25	18	7
Fountain	24	15	9	Sterling	36	23	13
Fowler	3	2	1	Stratton	3	1	2
Frederick	3	3	....	Telluride	7	7	....
Frisco	9	8	1	Thornton	115	87	28
Fruita	8	7	1	Trinidad	27	20	7
Georgetown	4	4	....	Vail	52	33	19
Glendale	38	30	8	Victor	3	3	....
Glenwood Springs	23	20	3	Walsenburg	16	11	5
Golden	36	26	10	Westminster	163	113	50
Grand Junction	106	71	35	Wheat Ridge	82	58	24
Greeley	150	87	63	Wiggins	1	1	....
Green Mountain Falls	2	2	....	Windsor	10	9	1
Greenwood Village	56	41	15	Woodland Park	20	13	7
Gunnison	23	14	9	Wray	10	6	4
Haxtun	3	3	....	Yuma	7	6	1
Hayden	3	3	....				
Holly	1	1	....	**CONNECTICUT**			
Holyoke	4	3	1				
Hotchkiss	2	2	....	Ansonia	39	32	7

Table 78. – Number of Full-time Law Enforcement Employees, Cities, October 31, 1993 – Continued

City	Total police employees	Total officers	Total civilians	City	Total police employees	Total officers	Total civilians
CONNECTICUT – Continued				**CONNECTICUT – Continued**			
Avon	37	30	7	Waterbury	341	289	52
Berlin	46	37	9	Waterford	51	45	6
Bethel	36	30	6	Watertown	39	32	7
Bloomfield	52	43	9	West Hartford	143	118	25
Branford	43	41	2	West Haven	125	110	15
Bridgeport	496	422	74	Weston	14	13	1
Bristol	111	104	7	Westport	74	66	8
Brookfield	35	29	6	Wethersfield	53	42	11
Canton	19	14	5	Willimantic	40	35	5
Cheshire	50	42	8	Wilton	42	40	2
Clinton	31	24	7	Windsor	58	48	10
Coventry	15	11	4	Windsor Locks	29	22	7
Cromwell	27	21	6	Winsted	25	21	4
Danbury	134	128	6	Wolcott	33	22	11
Darien	57	50	7	Woodbridge	25	19	6
Derby	28	27	1				
East Hampton	15	13	2	**DELAWARE**			
East Hartford	150	117	33				
East Haven Town	55	51	4	Bethany Beach	9	7	2
Easton	19	14	5	Bethel	1	1	....
East Windsor	23	16	7	Blades	1	1	....
Enfield	102	84	18	Bridgeville	5	4	1
Fairfield	103	98	5	Camden-Wyoming	7	6	1
Farmington	54	42	12	Clayton	2	2	....
Glastonbury	68	51	17	Dagsboro	1	1	....
Granby	17	12	5	Delmar	9	8	1
Greenwich	170	154	16	Dewey Beach	9	8	1
Groton	38	32	6	Dover	100	80	20
Groton Long Point	5	5	....	Elsmere	13	12	1
Groton Town	69	62	7	Fenwick Island	5	5	....
Guilford	40	33	7	Frankford	1	1	....
Hamden	120	97	23	Frederica	2	2	....
Hartford	549	426	123	Georgetown	10	10	....
Jewett City	9	7	2	Greenwood	4	4	....
Madison Town	42	33	9	Harrington	12	9	3
Manchester	125	98	27	Laurel	10	8	2
Meriden	120	102	18	Lewes	8	8	....
Middlebury	11	9	2	Milford	33	25	8
Middletown	118	96	22	Millsboro	8	7	1
Milford	123	107	16	Milton	5	5	....
Monroe	41	34	7	Newark	65	51	14
Naugatuck	58	49	9	New Castle	11	10	1
New Britain	166	150	16	Newport	6	6	....
New Canaan	49	45	4	Ocean View	2	2	....
New Haven	490	378	112	Rehoboth Beach	24	18	6
Newington	52	41	11	Seaford	27	21	6
New London	81	69	12	Selbyville	3	3	....
New Milford	53	41	12	Smyrna	21	16	5
Newtown	44	33	11	South Bethany	6	6	....
North Branford	25	20	5	Wilmington	312	265	47
North Haven	55	46	9				
Norwalk	198	169	29	**DISTRICT OF COLUMBIA**			
Norwich	92	78	14				
Old Saybrook	25	23	2	Washington	5,203	4,372	831
Orange	42	34	8				
Plainfield	16	15	1	**FLORIDA**			
Plainville	35	28	7				
Plymouth	21	17	4	Alachua	19	14	5
Putnam	19	15	4	Altamonte Springs	121	87	34
Ridgefield Town	41	36	5	Apalachicola	5	5	....
Rocky Hill	36	29	7	Apopka	55	47	8
Seymour	28	27	1	Arcadia	25	17	8
Shelton	57	52	5	Atlantis	16	11	5
Simsbury	38	32	6	Auburndale	31	22	9
Southington	63	56	7	Avon Park	23	16	7
South Windsor	41	33	8	Bal Harbour	27	22	5
Stamford	331	283	48	Bartow	60	43	17
Stonington	42	33	9	Bay Harbor Islands	27	22	5
Stratford	115	99	16	Belleair	15	10	5
Suffield	19	14	5	Belleair Beach	6	5	1
Thomaston	14	11	3	Belleair Bluffs	8	7	1
Torrington	75	69	6	Belle Glade	67	49	18
Trumbull	72	63	9	Belleview	13	11	2
Vernon	53	40	13	Biscayne Park	7	7	....
Wallingford	90	71	19	Blountstown	12	7	5

Table 78. — Number of Full-time Law Enforcement Employees, Cities, October 31, 1993 — Continued

City	Total police employees	Total officers	Total civilians	City	Total police employees	Total officers	Total civilians
FLORIDA — Continued				**FLORIDA — Continued**			
Boca Raton	207	129	78	Holly Hill	32	23	9
Bonifay	9	5	4	Hollywood	472	303	169
Bowling Green	4	4	....	Holmes Beach	16	9	7
Boynton Beach	159	127	32	Homestead	108	83	25
Bradenton	109	90	19	Howey-in-the-Hills	4	4	....
Bradenton Beach	9	8	1	Indialantic	16	11	5
Brooksville	26	18	8	Indian Harbour Beach	23	16	7
Bunnell	9	8	1	Indian River Shores	19	18	1
Bushnell	7	6	1	Indian Rocks Beach	12	11	1
Cape Coral	161	113	48	Indian Shores	12	11	1
Casselberry	66	45	21	Inverness	15	13	2
Cedar Grove	4	4	....	Jacksonville	2,200	1,253	947
Center Hill	1	1	....	Jacksonville Beach	73	50	23
Chattahoochee	11	10	1	Jasper	9	7	2
Chiefland	11	8	3	Juno Beach	16	13	3
Chipley	8	7	1	Jupiter	96	76	20
Clearwater	346	233	113	Jupiter Inlet Colony	5	4	1
Clermont	24	17	7	Jupiter Island	18	14	4
Clewiston	21	11	10	Kenneth City	13	11	2
Cocoa	72	54	18	Key West	106	78	28
Cocoa Beach	44	35	9	Kissimmee	128	82	46
Coconut Creek	88	56	32	Lady Lake	23	18	5
Coleman	2	2	....	Lake Alfred	12	8	4
Cooper City	60	45	15	Lake City	35	28	7
Coral Gables	192	139	53	Lake Clarke Shores	10	10	....
Coral Springs	220	141	79	Lake Hamilton	8	5	3
Crescent City	8	7	1	Lake Helen	5	5	....
Crestview	25	18	7	Lakeland	289	210	79
Cross City	4	4	....	Lake Mary	29	21	8
Crystal River	22	19	3	Lake Park	35	27	8
Dade City	20	17	3	Lake Wales	41	31	10
Davenport	6	5	1	Lake Worth	134	94	40
Davie	137	104	33	Lantana	38	26	12
Daytona Beach	303	221	82	Largo	164	112	52
Daytona Beach Shores	41	28	13	Lauderdale-by-the-Sea	16	14	2
De Funiak Springs	13	12	1	Leesburg	63	48	15
De Land	74	54	20	Lighthouse Point	39	30	9
Delray Beach	199	131	68	Longboat Key	25	19	6
Dundee	12	8	4	Longwood	34	30	4
Dunedin	67	52	15	Lynn Haven	17	12	5
Dunnellon	10	8	2	Madeira Beach	16	15	1
Eagle Lake	5	5	....	Madison	13	12	1
Eatonville	11	10	1	Maitland	46	32	14
Edgewater	40	29	11	Manalapan	13	9	4
Edgewood	8	7	1	Mangonia Park	14	14	....
El Portal	5	5	....	Margate	144	102	42
Eustis	41	31	10	Marianna	20	16	4
Fellesmere	5	5	....	Mascotte	5	5	....
Fernandina Beach	32	25	7	Medley	38	30	8
Flagler Beach	7	7	....	Melbourne	185	137	48
Florida City	40	22	18	Melbourne Beach	9	8	1
Fort Lauderdale	690	442	248	Mexico Beach	4	4	....
Fort Meade	18	13	5	Miami	1,495	1,062	433
Fort Myers	193	138	55	Miami Beach	423	298	125
Fort Pierce	123	98	25	Miami Shores	41	33	8
Fort Walton Beach	64	50	14	Miami Springs	50	41	9
Frostproof	13	8	5	Miccosukee	14	10	4
Fruitland Park	9	8	1	Milton	23	17	6
Gainesville	350	238	112	Minneola	5	5	....
Golden Beach	14	13	1	Miramar	99	83	16
Graceville	10	6	4	Monticello	12	9	3
Greenacres City	76	38	38	Mount Dora	33	24	9
Green Cove Springs	18	13	5	Mulberry	14	8	6
Groveland	12	7	5	Naples	107	75	32
Gulf Breeze	18	16	2	Neptune Beach	21	15	6
Gulfport	34	27	7	New Port Richey	38	29	9
Gulf Stream	9	9	....	New Smyrna Beach	60	43	17
Haines City	49	36	13	Niceville	20	15	5
Hallandale	119	83	36	North Bay Village	29	22	7
Havana	11	8	3	North Lauderdale	63	47	16
Hialeah	435	320	115	North Miami	127	104	23
Hialeah Gardens	29	21	8	North Miami Beach	140	99	41
Highland Beach	11	11	....	North Palm Beach	44	35	9
High Springs	10	6	4	North Port	38	22	16
Hillsboro Beach	16	12	4	Oak Hill	3	3	....

Table 78. — Number of Full-time Law Enforcement Employees, Cities, October 31, 1993 — Continued

City	Total police employees	Total officers	Total civilians	City	Total police employees	Total officers	Total civilians
FLORIDA — Continued				**FLORIDA — Continued**			
Oakland	3	3	....	Valparaiso	10	8	2
Oakland Park	102	72	30	Venice	61	41	20
Ocala	180	119	61	Vero Beach	88	61	27
Ocean Ridge	17	12	5	Virginia Gardens	7	6	1
Ocoee	40	32	8	Waldo	5	5	....
Okeechobee	22	16	6	Wauchula	13	11	2
Opa Locka	64	45	19	Webster	3	3	....
Orange City	22	16	6	West Melbourne	22	20	2
Orange Park	27	21	6	West Miami	19	15	4
Orlando	799	552	247	West Palm Beach	344	226	118
Ormond Beach	81	62	19	White Springs	3	3	....
Oviedo	42	32	10	Wildwood	16	11	5
Pahokee	19	13	6	Williston	14	9	5
Palatka	41	29	12	Wilton Manors	40	29	11
Palm Bay	154	99	55	Windermere	7	7	....
Palm Beach	113	68	45	Winter Garden	35	28	7
Palm Beach Gardens	94	70	24	Winter Haven	93	59	34
Palm Beach Shores	8	7	1	Winter Park	94	68	26
Palmetto	39	29	10	Winter Springs	55	39	16
Palm Springs	34	25	9	Zephyrhills	34	25	9
Panama City	104	79	25	Zolfo Spring	2	2	....
Panama City Beach	42	33	9				
Parker	8	7	1	**GEORGIA**			
Parkland	19	17	2	Abbeville	3	3	....
Pembroke Pines	184	141	43	Acworth	24	20	4
Pensacola	201	144	57	Adairsville	9	7	2
Perry	23	21	2	Adel	18	15	3
Pinellas Park	106	70	36	Adrian	1	1	....
Plantation	218	140	78	Alamo	2	2	....
Plant City	75	57	18	Albany	237	212	25
Pompano Beach	313	246	67	Alma	18	13	5
Ponce Inlet	13	8	5	Alpharetta	52	34	18
Port Orange	72	54	18	Americus	54	43	11
Port Richey	13	9	4	Aragon	9	4	5
Port St. Joe	16	11	5	Arcade	1	1	....
Port St. Lucie	125	95	30	Ashburn	18	13	5
Punta Gorda	37	25	12	Athens-Clarke County	225	179	46
Quincy	66	42	24	Atlanta	2,104	1,626	478
Redington Beach	8	7	1	Attapulgus	2	1	1
Riviera Beach	127	94	33	Auburn	9	8	1
Rockledge	45	34	11	Augusta	202	168	34
Royal Palm Beach	44	31	13	Austell	14	11	3
St. Augustine	47	37	10	Avondale Estates	9	9	....
St. Augustine Beach	11	10	1	Bainbridge	51	37	14
St. Cloud	43	31	12	Baldwin	6	5	1
St. Petersburg	713	508	205	Ball Ground	2	2	....
St. Petersburg Beach	49	30	19	Barnesville	13	12	1
Sanford	102	82	20	Baxley	14	12	2
Sanibel	35	24	11	Berlin	2	2	....
Sarasota	271	186	85	Blackshear	10	9	1
Satellite Beach	22	16	6	Blakely	21	16	5
Sea Ranch Lakes	10	7	3	Bloomingdale	7	6	1
Sebastian	31	23	8	Bowdon	11	7	4
Sebring	33	26	7	Braselton	1	1	....
Sewall's Point	8	8	....	Bremen	16	16	....
Sneads	4	3	1	Brooklet	3	3	....
South Bay	18	10	8	Brunswick	17	14	3
South Daytona	31	23	8	Buchanan	5	5	....
South Miami	56	46	10	Buena Vista	5	5	....
South Palm Beach	9	9	....	Butler	4	4	....
Springfield	20	15	5	Byron	15	9	6
Starke	21	15	6	Cairo	25	20	5
Stuart	56	42	14	Calhoun	36	31	5
Sunrise	183	139	44	Camilla	24	16	8
Surfside	28	23	5	Canton	24	21	3
Sweetwater	21	18	3	Carrollton	62	51	11
Tallahassee	440	308	132	Cartersville	50	42	8
Tampa	1,040	771	269	Cave Spring	3	3	....
Tarpon Springs	57	41	16	Cedartown	27	23	4
Tavares	21	16	5	Chamblee	35	31	4
Temple Terrace	54	37	17	Chatsworth	17	13	4
Tequesta	21	16	5	Chauncey	1	1	....
Titusville	103	74	29	Chickamauga	6	5	1
Treasure Island	24	20	4	Clarkesville	5	5	....
Umatilla	8	7	1				

Table 78. — Number of Full-time Law Enforcement Employees, Cities, October 31, 1993 — Continued

City	Total police employees	Total officers	Total civilians	City	Total police employees	Total officers	Total civilians
GEORGIA — Continued				**GEORGIA — Continued**			
Clarkston	13	12	1	Hazlehurst	15	10	5
Claxton	9	8	1	Helen	12	9	3
Clayton	8	8	....	Helena	3	3	....
Cleveland	7	7	....	Hephzibah	2	2	....
Cochran	11	10	1	Hiawassee	5	3	2
Cohutta	1	1	....	Hinesville	63	56	7
Coolidge	3	3	....	Hiram	5	5	....
College Park	95	75	20	Hoboken	2	1	1
Collins	1	1	....	Hogansville	12	8	4
Columbus	471	369	102	Holly Springs	4	4	....
Comer	3	3	....	Homerville	9	6	3
Commerce	19	14	5	Hoschton	1	1	....
Conyers	50	36	14	Ideal	1	1	....
Cornelia	16	15	1	Ivey	4	3	1
Covington	56	47	9	Jackson	20	14	6
Crawfordville	1	1	....	Jasper	8	8	....
Cumming	12	8	4	Jefferson	15	11	4
Cusseta	8	4	4	Jeffersonville	7	6	1
Cuthbert	12	8	4	Jesup	34	27	7
Dallas	16	12	4	Jonesboro	9	9	....
Dalton	69	56	13	Kennesaw	41	25	16
Danielsville	1	1	....	Kingsland	21	18	3
Darien	5	5	....	Kingston	1	1	....
Davisboro	1	1	....	Lafayette	21	17	4
Dawson	23	17	6	La Grange	87	79	8
Decatur	54	40	14	Lake City	19	17	2
Dillard	1	1	....	Lakeland	7	7	....
Doerun	7	6	1	Lake Park	2	2	....
Donalsonville	9	9	....	Lavonia	11	8	3
Doraville	37	26	11	Lawrenceville	50	40	10
Douglas	45	36	9	Leary	3	3	....
Dublin	53	45	8	Leesburg	3	3	....
Duluth	36	25	11	Leslie	4	4	....
East Dublin	7	6	1	Lilburn	26	20	6
East Ellijay	7	6	1	Lincolnton	4	4	....
Eastman	18	13	5	Lithonia	12	8	4
East Point	111	90	21	Locust Grove	8	7	1
Edison	4	4	....	Lookout Mountain	8	7	1
Elberton	25	20	5	Louisville	8	8	....
Ellaville	4	4	....	Ludowici	8	4	4
Ellijay	13	11	2	Lumpkin	10	8	2
Emerson	2	2	....	Lyerly	1	1	....
Enigma	1	1	....	Macon	327	295	32
Eton	1	1	....	Manchester	18	13	5
Euharlee	1	1	....	Marietta	141	116	25
Fairburn	21	15	6	Marshallville	4	4	....
Fairmount	6	3	3	Maysville	1	1	....
Fayetteville	30	22	8	McCaysville	4	4	....
Fitzgerald	29	24	5	McDonough	11	11	....
Folkston	6	6	....	McIntyre	3	3	....
Forest Park	65	43	22	McRae	9	6	3
Forsyth	21	16	5	Milan	1	1	....
Fort Gaines	6	4	2	Millen	10	10	....
Fort Oglethorpe	24	20	4	Monroe	38	29	9
Fort Valley	29	24	5	Montezuma	14	12	2
Franklin	5	5	....	Monticello	17	12	5
Franklin Springs	1	1	....	Morrow	32	25	7
Gainesville	99	80	19	Morven	1	1	....
Garden City	21	19	2	Moultrie	52	43	9
Georgetown	3	2	1	Mountain City	2	2	....
Glennville	13	8	5	Mount Airy	3	3	....
Glenwood	3	3	....	Nahunta	3	3	....
Gordon	9	5	4	Nashville	15	10	5
Gray	2	2	....	Nelson	1	1	....
Greensboro	10	10	....	Newington	1	1	....
Greenville	6	5	1	Newnan	38	37	1
Griffin	83	69	14	Newton	2	2	....
Grovetown	11	8	3	Nicholls	4	3	1
Hahira	7	4	3	Norcross	29	21	8
Hamilton	1	1	....	Oakwood	8	7	1
Hampton	9	8	1	Ocilla	16	11	5
Hapeville	29	25	4	Oglethorpe	6	5	1
Harlem	12	10	2	Oxford	1	1	....
Hartwell	21	17	4	Palmetto	10	10	....
Hawkinsville	9	8	1	Patterson	2	2	....

Table 78. — Number of Full-time Law Enforcement Employees, Cities, October 31, 1993 — Continued

City	Total police employees	Total officers	Total civilians	City	Total police employees	Total officers	Total civilians
GEORGIA — Continued				**GEORGIA — Continued**			
Peachtree City	42	32	10	Warrenton	7	7	....
Pearson	4	4	....	Watkinsville	4	4	....
Pelham	15	10	5	Waycross	7	6	1
Pembroke	7	6	1	Waynesboro	20	16	4
Perry	34	30	4	West Point	19	14	5
Pine Lake	2	2	....	Whigham	4	3	1
Pine Mountain	5	5	....	White	1	1	....
Pineview	2	1	1	Whitesburg	3	3	....
Pooler	16	14	2	Winder	35	29	6
Porterdale	9	8	1	Winterville	2	2	....
Port Wentworth	15	13	2	Woodbury	9	7	2
Powder Springs	20	16	4	Woodstock	23	21	2
Preston	1	1	....	Wrens	15	14	1
Quitman	18	14	4	Zebulon	4	4	....
Reidsville	10	5	5				
Remerton	3	3	....	**HAWAII**			
Richland	6	4	2				
Richmond Hill	16	10	6	Hilo	236	140	96
Rincon	7	6	1	Honolulu	2,370	1,921	449
Ringgold	4	4	....				
Riverdale	35	27	8	**IDAHO**			
Roberta	3	3	....				
Rockmart	20	15	5	Aberdeen	8	5	3
Rome	88	76	12	American Falls	9	8	1
Rossville	13	9	4	Bellevue	3	3	....
Roswell	139	87	52	Blackfoot	21	18	3
Royston	13	9	4	Boise	207	182	25
St. Marys	29	27	2	Bonners Ferry	7	6	1
Sandersville	31	20	11	Buhl	8	7	1
Sardis	4	4	....	Caldwell	42	31	11
Savannah	464	372	92	Cascade	3	3	....
Senoia	7	7	....	Chubbuck	16	13	3
Shellman	4	4	....	Coeur d'Alene	56	46	10
Shiloh	2	2	....	Emmett	9	9	....
Smyrna	107	78	29	Filer	4	4	....
Snellville	30	24	6	Firth	1	1	....
Soperton	10	6	4	Fruitland	6	5	1
Sparks	1	1	....	Garden City	20	17	3
Sparta	10	5	5	Glenns Ferry	4	3	1
Springfield	5	5	....	Gooding	6	6	....
Statham	3	3	....	Grangeville	5	5	....
Stone Mountain	20	14	6	Hailey	9	7	2
Stone Mountain Park	19	17	2	Heyburn	6	5	1
Summerville	21	21	....	Homedale	5	5	....
Suwanee	14	10	4	Idaho Falls	100	76	24
Swainsboro	24	17	7	Jerome	12	11	1
Sycamore	2	2	....	Kamiah	3	3	....
Sylvania	15	11	4	Kellogg	7	6	1
Sylvester	18	14	4	Ketchum	15	11	4
Tallapoosa	13	10	3	Kimberly	4	4	....
Tallulah Falls	2	1	1	Lewiston	59	41	18
Thomaston	44	36	8	McCall	9	7	2
Thomasville	45	39	6	Meridian	21	18	3
Thomson	19	18	1	Montpelier	5	5	....
Thunderbolt	10	7	3	Moscow	37	28	9
Tifton	52	42	10	Mountain Home	24	16	8
Tignall	3	2	1	Nampa	54	38	16
Toccoa	31	26	5	New Plymouth	4	4	....
Trenton	6	6	....	Orofino	7	6	1
Trion	7	7	....	Osburn	2	2	....
Tunnel Hill	4	4	....	Parma	4	4	....
Tybee Island	21	14	7	Payette	11	10	1
Tyrone	9	8	1	Pinehurst	2	2	....
Unadilla	7	4	3	Pocatello	94	71	23
Union City	34	25	9	Post Falls	33	20	13
Union Point	12	7	5	Preston	4	4	....
Uvalda	4	1	3	Priest River	6	5	1
Valdosta	97	85	12	Rexburg	29	25	4
Varnell	8	7	1	Rigby	5	5	....
Vidalia	38	29	9	Rupert	14	13	1
Vienna	6	6	....	St. Anthony	6	6	....
Villa Rica	19	15	4	St. Maries	4	4	....
Wadley	10	7	3	Salmon	7	6	1
Warm Springs	2	2	....	Sandpoint	21	14	7
Warner Robins	98	84	14	Shelley	6	6	....

Table 78.—Number of Full-time Law Enforcement Employees, Cities, October 31, 1993—Continued

City	Total police employees	Total officers	Total civilians	City	Total police employees	Total officers	Total civilians
IDAHO—Continued				**ILLINOIS—Continued**			
Soda Springs	8	7	1	Burnham	11	7	4
Spirit Lake	3	3	....	Burr Ridge	22	19	3
Sun Valley	8	8	....	Byron	6	5	1
Twin Falls	60	43	17	Cahokia	38	27	11
Wallace	3	2	1	Cairo	17	12	5
Weiser	10	9	1	Calumet City	92	64	28
Wendell	4	4	....	Calumet Park	21	15	6
Wilder	2	2	....	Camp Point	1	1	....
				Canton	28	20	8
ILLINOIS				Carbon Cliff	2	2	....
				Carbondale	72	57	15
Abingdon	9	5	4	Carlinville	14	10	4
Addison	82	64	18	Carlyle	7	6	1
Albany	1	1	....	Carmi	9	8	1
Albion	2	2	....	Carol Stream	62	46	16
Aledo	8	7	1	Carpentersville	47	42	5
Alexis	1	1	....	Carrollton	5	5	....
Algonquin	30	23	7	Carterville	4	4	....
Alorton	4	3	1	Carthage	2	2	....
Alsip	51	40	11	Cary	25	20	5
Altamont	5	5	....	Casey	6	6	....
Alton	75	63	12	Caseyville	14	6	8
Amboy	1	1	....	Central City	2	2	....
Andalusia	2	2	....	Centralia	37	29	8
Anna	7	7	....	Centreville	17	12	5
Antioch	24	15	9	Campaign	135	108	27
Arcola	4	4	....	Channahon	9	8	1
Argenta	3	2	1	Charleston	37	29	8
Arlington Heights	140	105	35	Chatham	9	8	1
Arthur	5	5	....	Chenoa	2	2	....
Ashland	1	1	....	Cherry Valley	11	11	....
Astoria	1	1	....	Chester	10	7	3
Atkinson	2	2	....	Chicago	14,196	12,093	2,103
Atlanta	1	1	....	Chicago Heights	130	78	52
Auburn	8	4	4	Chicago Ridge	30	27	3
Aurora	277	213	64	Chillicothe	13	9	4
Avon	1	1	....	Christopher	3	3	....
Bannockburn	7	7	....	Cicero	121	95	26
Barrington	41	29	12	Clarendon Hills	13	13	....
Barrington Hills	26	18	8	Clinton	16	12	4
Bartlett	44	32	12	Coal City	9	5	4
Bartonville	12	8	4	Coal Valley	6	6	....
Batavia	39	33	6	Cobden	2	2	....
Beardstown	13	9	4	Collinsville	44	34	10
Bedford Park	32	26	6	Colona	4	4	....
Beecher	5	5	....	Columbia	15	8	7
Belleville	77	63	14	Cordova	1	1	....
Bellwood	51	45	6	Coulterville	2	2	....
Belvidere	27	25	2	Country Club Hills	30	23	7
Benld	8	3	5	Countryside	27	21	6
Bensenville	50	40	10	Crest Hill	25	18	7
Benton	10	5	5	Crestwood	5	4	1
Berkeley	18	14	4	Crete	17	12	5
Berwyn	98	73	25	Creve Coeur	8	7	1
Bethalto	18	12	6	Crystal Lake	59	42	17
Bloomingdale	59	42	17	Cuba	1	1	....
Bloomington	101	88	13	Dallas City	1	1	....
Blue Island	46	34	12	Danvers	1	1	....
Blue Mound	1	1	....	Danville	77	61	16
Bolingbrook	94	66	28	Darien	42	27	15
Bourbonnais	22	16	6	Decatur	145	141	4
Bradley	25	17	8	Deerfield	48	37	11
Braidwood	10	7	3	De Kalb	63	52	11
Breese	8	5	3	Depue	1	1	....
Bridgeport	2	2	....	De Soto	4	3	1
Bridgeview	46	39	7	Des Plaines	111	98	13
Brighton	4	3	1	Dixmoor	9	7	2
Broadview	36	29	7	Dixon	25	22	3
Brookfield	31	26	5	Dolton	56	41	15
Brooklyn	10	5	5	Downers Grove	90	67	23
Buda	1	1	....	Dupo	6	6	....
Buffalo Grove	76	64	12	Du Quoin	13	9	4
Bull Valley	1	1	....	Durand	1	1	....
Bunker Hill	3	2	1	Dwight	9	5	4
Burbank	51	44	7	Earlville	2	2	....

Table 78. — Number of Full-time Law Enforcement Employees, Cities, October 31, 1993 — Continued

City	Total police employees	Total officers	Total civilians	City	Total police employees	Total officers	Total civilians
ILLINOIS — Continued				**ILLINOIS — Continued**			
East Alton	18	12	6	Hampton	1	1	....
East Carondelet	1	1	....	Hampshire	4	4	....
East Dubuque	6	6	....	Hanover	1	1	....
East Dundee	12	11	1	Hanover Park	62	43	19
East Hazel Crest	8	8	....	Harrisburg	17	14	3
East Moline	42	32	10	Hartford	6	5	1
East Peoria	45	34	11	Harvard	20	12	8
East St. Louis	104	70	34	Harvey	70	54	16
Edwardsville	32	23	9	Harwood Heights	30	22	8
Effingham	34	24	10	Havana	8	8	....
Elburn	5	4	1	Hawthorn Woods	6	6	....
Eldorado	10	6	4	Hazel Crest	33	25	8
Elgin	169	127	42	Hebron	2	2	....
Elizabeth	2	2	....	Henry	3	3	....
Elk Grove Village	108	95	13	Herrin	16	12	4
Elmhurst	84	63	21	Herscher	2	2	....
Elmwood Park	42	33	9	Hickory Hills	26	25	1
El Paso	4	4	....	Highland	20	14	6
Energy	3	3	....	Highland Park	73	57	16
Erie	2	2	....	Highwood	12	8	4
Eureka	3	3	....	Hillsboro	7	7	....
Evanston	201	152	49	Hillside	41	33	8
Evergreen Park	65	54	11	Hinckley	2	2	....
Fairbury	6	6	....	Hinsdale	38	28	10
Fairfield	12	12	....	Hodgkins	17	16	1
Fairmont City	7	5	2	Hoffman Estates	112	88	24
Fairview	1	1	....	Homer	1	1	....
Fairview Heights	47	36	11	Hometown	5	1	4
Farmer City	6	3	3	Homewood	47	36	11
Farmington	5	4	1	Hoopeston	14	9	5
Fisher	2	2	....	Hopedale	1	1	....
Flora	16	11	5	Huntley	8	8	....
Flossmoor	22	16	6	Illiopolis	1	1	....
Ford Heights	12	6	6	Indian Head Park	14	10	4
Forest Park	52	37	15	Island Lake	15	10	5
Forest View	11	8	3	Itasca	37	26	11
Fox Lake	22	16	6	Jacksonville	43	35	8
Fox River Grove	9	9	....	Jerome	4	4	....
Fox River Valley Gardens	1	1	....	Jerseyville	17	11	6
Frankfort	22	20	2	Johnsburg	7	6	1
Franklin Park	65	50	15	Johnston City	5	5	....
Freeburg	5	5	....	Joliet	242	198	44
Freeport	69	50	19	Jonesboro	3	3	....
Fulton	5	5	....	Justice	37	29	8
Galena	11	9	2	Kankakee	92	67	25
Galesburg	70	48	22	Kenilworth	13	10	3
Galva	4	4	....	Kewanee	22	17	5
Gardner	1	1	....	Kildeer	7	7	....
Geneseo	16	10	6	Kincaid	1	1	....
Geneva	35	25	10	Kirkland	3	3	....
Genoa	6	5	1	Knoxville	4	4	....
Gibson City	9	7	2	Lacon	2	2	....
Gifford	2	2	....	La Grange	39	28	11
Gilberts	1	1	....	La Grange Park	29	24	5
Gillespie	8	5	3	Lake Bluff	14	12	2
Gilman	3	3	....	Lake Forest	54	40	14
Girard	3	3	....	Lake-in-the-Hills	22	16	6
Glen Carbon	15	10	5	Lakemoor	5	5	....
Glencoe	42	33	9	Lake Villa	8	7	1
Glendale Heights	70	49	21	Lakewood	5	5	....
Glen Ellyn	42	33	9	Lake Zurich	42	29	13
Glenview	85	62	23	Lanark	1	1	....
Glenwood	21	15	6	Lansing	67	50	17
Golf	1	1	....	La Salle	21	17	4
Grafton	1	1	....	Lebanon	10	6	4
Granite City	57	49	8	Leland Grove	5	5	....
Grayslake	16	11	5	Lemont	22	19	3
Grayville	6	3	3	Leroy	4	4	....
Greenfield	2	2	....	Lewistown	3	3	....
Green Rock	3	3	....	Libertyville	45	36	9
Greenup	3	3	....	Lincoln	27	24	3
Greenview	1	1	....	Lincolnshire	24	16	8
Greenville	13	9	4	Lincolnwood	45	33	12
Gurnee	52	36	16	Lindenhurst	13	11	2
Hamilton	4	4	....	Lisle	48	35	13

Table 78. — Number of Full-time Law Enforcement Employees, Cities, October 31, 1993 — Continued

City	Total police employees	Total officers	Total civilians	City	Total police employees	Total officers	Total civilians
ILLINOIS — Continued				**ILLINOIS — Continued**			
Litchfield	17	13	4	Nauvoo	2	2	....
Livingston	1	1	....	Neoga	2	2	....
Loami	1	1	....	New Athens	3	3	....
Lockport	28	20	8	New Baden	4	4	....
Lombard	80	64	16	New Lenox	17	16	1
London Mills	1	1	....	Newton	7	6	1
Loves Park	32	23	9	Niles	62	50	12
Ludlow	1	1	....	Nokomis	7	4	3
Lynwood	15	12	3	Normal	62	53	9
Lyons	26	21	5	Norridge	46	33	13
Mackinaw	1	1	....	North Aurora	15	14	1
Macomb	28	23	5	Northbrook	83	60	23
Madison	15	11	4	North Chicago	58	45	13
Mahomet	4	4	....	Northfield	26	20	6
Manhattan	5	5	....	Northlake	36	31	5
Manito	2	2	....	North Pekin	1	1	....
Manteno	8	8	....	North Riverside	36	28	8
Marengo	15	11	4	Oak Brook	52	40	12
Marion	24	18	6	Oakbrook Terrace	24	18	6
Marissa	3	3	....	Oak Forest	47	35	12
Markham	37	31	6	Oak Lawn	148	108	40
Maroa	2	2	....	Oak Park	154	115	39
Marquette Heights	3	3	....	Oakwood Hills	2	2	....
Marseilles	6	6	....	Oblong	1	1	....
Marshall	12	11	1	O'Fallon	37	27	10
Martinsville	2	2	....	Ogden	1	1	....
Maryville	10	6	4	Oglesby	10	7	3
Mascoutah	10	9	1	Okawville	2	2	....
Mason City	4	4	....	Olney	16	11	5
Matteson	45	34	11	Olympia Fields	17	16	1
Mattoon	48	40	8	Oregon	5	5	....
Maywood	67	59	8	Orion	3	3	....
McCook	20	15	5	Orland Hills	8	7	1
McCullom Lake	1	1	....	Orland Park	85	64	21
McHenry	39	28	11	Oswego	16	14	2
McLean	1	1	....	Ottawa	31	26	5
McLeansboro	5	5	....	Palatine	94	73	21
Melrose Park	72	59	13	Palestine	3	3	....
Mendota	15	12	3	Palos Heights	26	24	2
Meredosia	1	1	....	Palos Hills	29	25	4
Metamora	3	3	....	Palos Park	10	8	2
Metropolis	19	15	4	Pana	13	9	4
Midlothian	28	23	5	Paris	20	15	5
Milan	15	11	4	Park City	12	7	5
Milledgeville	1	1	....	Park Forest	45	37	8
Millstadt	4	4	....	Park Ridge	63	50	13
Minier	1	1	....	Pawnee	5	5	....
Minonk	1	1	....	Paxton	6	6	....
Minooka	7	6	1	Pecatonica	1	1	....
Mokena	16	15	1	Pekin	51	45	6
Moline	94	70	24	Peoria	266	218	48
Momence	6	6	....	Peoria Heights	13	9	4
Monee	4	4	....	Peotone	10	6	4
Monmouth	25	19	6	Peru	21	18	3
Montgomery	17	11	6	Petersburg	4	4	....
Monticello	9	8	1	Phoenix	11	5	6
Morris	25	19	6	Pinckneyville	6	5	1
Morrison	5	5	....	Pittsfield	6	6	....
Morton	20	15	5	Plainfield	15	13	2
Morton Grove	61	45	16	Plano	13	13	....
Mount Carmel	18	13	5	Pleasant Plains	1	1	....
Mount Carroll	2	2	....	Plymouth	1	1	....
Mount Morris	7	4	3	Polo	3	3	....
Mount Olive	2	2	....	Pontiac	23	17	6
Mount Prospect	93	73	20	Pontoon Beach	15	10	5
Mount Pulaski	4	3	1	Port Byron	3	3	....
Mount Sterling	8	4	4	Posen	8	8	....
Mount Vernon	37	30	7	Princeton	10	10	....
Mount Zion	8	7	1	Prophetstown	4	3	1
Moweaqua	2	2	....	Prospect Heights	25	22	3
Mundelein	41	31	10	Quincy	85	71	14
Murphysboro	21	14	7	Rantoul	34	28	6
Naperville	213	124	89	Raymond	1	1	....
Nashville	6	5	1	Red Bud	4	4	....
National City	1	1	....	Richmond	5	5	....

Table 78. — Number of Full-time Law Enforcement Employees, Cities, October 31, 1993 — Continued

City	Total police employees	Total officers	Total civilians	City	Total police employees	Total officers	Total civilians
ILLINOIS — Continued				**ILLINOIS — Continued**			
Richton Park	23	19	4	Sumner	1	1	....
Ridgway	1	1	....	Swansea	16	13	3
Riverdale	40	30	10	Sycamore	27	19	8
River Forest	38	29	9	Tampico	1	1	....
River Grove	23	17	6	Taylorville	22	16	6
Riverside	23	19	4	Thomasboro	1	1	....
Robbins	11	6	5	Thornton	11	9	2
Robinson	12	11	1	Tinley Park	62	51	11
Rochelle	22	17	5	Tolono	2	2	....
Rochester	6	6	....	Tonica	1	1	....
Rockdale	4	4	....	Tower Lakes	2	2	....
Rock Falls	24	17	7	Tremont	3	2	1
Rockford	293	260	33	Trenton	3	3	....
Rock Island	113	83	30	Troy	14	10	4
Rockton	6	5	1	Tuscola	7	6	1
Rolling Meadows	76	56	20	University Park	24	17	7
Romeoville	37	28	9	Urbana	57	45	12
Roodhouse	4	4	....	Vandalia	15	10	5
Roscoe	9	8	1	Venice	16	11	5
Roselle	42	31	11	Vernon Hills	51	33	18
Rosemont	79	64	15	Vienna	2	2	....
Rosiclare	2	2	....	Villa Grove	5	4	1
Rossville	14	9	5	Villa Park	50	35	15
Round Lake	9	8	1	Virden	9	5	4
Round Lake Beach	37	30	7	Wamac	2	2	....
Round Lake Heights	3	3	....	Warren	2	2	....
Round Lake Park	7	7	....	Warrensburg	1	1	....
Roxana	7	6	1	Warrenville	22	17	5
Royalton	3	3	....	Washington	18	13	5
Rushville	5	5	....	Washington Park	18	13	5
St. Anne	2	2	....	Waterloo	8	7	1
St. Charles	58	47	11	Watseka	15	10	5
Salem	18	13	5	Wauconda	24	15	9
Sandwich	16	10	6	Waukegan	183	134	49
Sauget	8	8	....	Wayne	4	4	....
Sauk Village	20	14	6	Westchester	45	35	10
Savanna	9	9	....	West Chicago	32	27	5
Schaumburg	193	137	56	West City	8	4	4
Schiller Park	38	29	9	West Dundee	17	15	2
Seneca	6	3	3	Western Springs	24	18	6
Sesser	5	5	....	West Frankfort	16	12	4
Shawneetown	4	4	....	Westmont	49	35	14
Shelbyville	7	6	1	West Salem	1	1	....
Sherman	4	4	....	Wheaton	81	58	23
Shiloh	5	5	....	Wheeling	74	52	22
Shorewood	16	14	2	White Hall	4	4	....
Silvis	16	10	6	Williamsville	1	1	....
Skokie	135	107	28	Willowbrook	27	23	4
Sleepy Hollow	6	5	1	Willow Springs	16	12	4
Smithton	4	3	1	Wilmette	59	43	16
Somonauk	3	3	....	Wilmington	18	11	7
South Barrington	7	6	1	Winchester	2	2	....
South Beloit	12	8	4	Winfield	16	14	2
South Chicago Heights	12	8	4	Winnebago	2	2	....
South Elgin	21	16	5	Winnetka	38	27	11
South Holland	44	33	11	Winthrop Harbor	16	11	5
South Jacksonville	7	5	2	Witt	1	1	....
South Pekin	2	2	....	Wood Dale	45	32	13
South Roxana	3	3	....	Woodhull	1	1	....
Sparta	13	9	4	Woodridge	59	44	15
Springfield	263	214	49	Wood River	25	18	7
Spring Grove	8	7	1	Woodstock	35	24	11
Spring Valley	10	6	4	Worth	26	25	1
Staunton	9	6	3	Yorkville	11	11	....
Steger	15	12	3	Zeigler	5	4	1
Sterling	36	25	11	Zion	55	39	16
Stickney	21	14	7				
Stockton	3	3	....	**INDIANA**			
Stone Park	20	13	7				
Stonington	1	1	....	Alexandria	14	10	4
Streamwood	69	48	21	Anderson	163	125	38
Streator	27	21	6	Angola	17	13	4
Sugar Grove	5	4	1	Auburn	22	17	5
Sullivan	9	8	1	Batesville	11	7	4
Summit	32	26	6	Bedford	37	31	6

City	Total police employees	Total officers	Total civilians	City	Total police employees	Total officers	Total civilians
INDIANA — Continued				**INDIANA — Continued**			
Beech Grove	35	26	9	Princes Lakes	2	2	....
Berne	5	5	....	Rensselaer	12	8	4
Bloomington	82	61	21	Richmond	100	76	24
Bluffton	21	17	4	Schererville	42	33	9
Boonville	12	12	....	Scottsburg	13	9	4
Brazil	16	12	4	Sellersburg	16	11	5
Burns Harbor	9	5	4	South Bend	304	242	62
Carmel	61	51	10	Speedway	34	26	8
Cedar Lake	18	13	5	Tell City	15	10	5
Chesterfield	6	5	1	Terre Haute	127	110	17
Chesterton	21	15	6	Valparaiso	55	39	16
Clarksville	40	33	7	Vincennes	35	30	5
Connersville	33	32	1	Wabash	31	25	6
Corydon	6	6	....	Warsaw	40	32	8
Crawfordsville	45	31	14	West Lafayette	46	35	11
Crown Point	31	24	7	West Terre Haute	4	4	....
Culver	4	4	....	Winchester	15	11	4
Decatur	19	16	3				
Dunkirk	7	4	3	**IOWA**			
Dyer	22	17	5				
East Chicago	135	100	35	Albia	7	7	....
Edinburgh	14	9	5	Algona	13	9	4
Elkhart	126	99	27	Altoona	12	11	1
Elwood	20	16	4	Ames	68	50	18
Evansville	270	249	21	Anamosa	6	5	1
Fairmount	8	4	4	Ankeny	31	24	7
Fort Wayne	373	322	51	Atlantic	15	13	2
Frankfort	39	27	12	Belle Plaine	3	3	....
Garrett	14	9	5	Belmond	4	4	....
Gary	324	213	111	Bettendorf	47	36	11
Gas City	13	9	4	Bloomfield	7	7	....
Georgetown	2	2	....	Boone	15	14	1
Goshen	45	40	5	Burlington	50	36	14
Greenfield	29	23	6	Camanche	7	7	....
Greenwood	60	43	17	Carlisle	5	5	....
Griffith	35	26	9	Carroll	18	13	5
Hammond	229	188	41	Carter Lake	7	6	1
Hartford City	16	11	5	Cedar Falls	52	45	7
Highland	45	38	7	Centerville	16	11	5
Hobart	55	44	11	Chariton	8	7	1
Huntingburg	8	8	....	Charles City	17	12	5
Huntington	39	32	7	Cherokee	9	7	2
Indianapolis	1,329	967	362	Clarinda	13	8	5
Jasper	24	16	8	Clarion	10	5	5
Kendallville	20	15	5	Clear Lake	16	11	5
Kokomo	136	100	36	Clive	16	12	4
Kouts	2	2	....	Council Bluffs	101	87	14
Lafayette	112	82	30	Cresco	8	8	....
Lake Station	23	18	5	Creston	16	11	5
La Porte	44	38	6	Davenport	179	144	35
Lawrence	39	36	3	Decorah	16	12	4
Logansport	43	34	9	Denison	15	11	4
Long Beach	5	5	....	Des Moines	463	353	110
Lowell	16	11	5	De Witt	7	7	....
Madison	27	22	5	Dubuque	84	77	7
Marion	74	64	10	Dyersville	8	5	3
Martinsville	21	16	5	Eagle Grove	7	7	....
Merrillville	55	46	9	Eldora	6	6	....
Mishawaka	91	80	11	Eldridge	5	5	....
Monticello	13	9	4	Emmetsburg	7	6	1
Mooresville	18	13	5	Estherville	11	11	....
Mount Vernon	14	13	1	Evansdale	6	5	1
Muncie	128	119	9	Fairfield	18	12	6
Munster	40	31	9	Forest City	8	8	....
Nappanee	15	11	4	Fort Dodge	47	41	6
New Albany	71	56	15	Fort Madison	27	22	5
New Castle	38	35	3	Garner	6	6	....
New Chicago	6	2	4	Grinnell	14	13	1
New Haven	17	12	5	Grundy Center	4	4	....
Noblesville	44	33	11	Hampton	12	7	5
North Manchester	15	11	4	Hawarden	4	4	....
North Vernon	17	13	4	Humboldt	7	7	....
Petersburg	7	4	3	Independence	15	11	4
Portage	52	38	14	Indianola	20	14	6
Portland	18	14	4	Iowa City	76	59	17

Table 78. — Number of Full-time Law Enforcement Employees, Cities, October 31, 1993 — Continued

City	Total police employees	Total officers	Total civilians	City	Total police employees	Total officers	Total civilians
IOWA — Continued				**KANSAS — Continued**			
Iowa Falls	15	11	4	Bushton	1	1	....
Johnston	10	9	1	Caldwell	4	4	....
Lamoni	3	3	....	Caney	9	5	4
Le Claire	7	4	3	Canton	1	1	....
Le Mars	13	12	1	Carbondale	2	2	....
Manchester	12	8	4	Cawker City	1	1	....
Maquoketa	14	10	4	Cedar Vale	1	1	....
Marion	36	30	6	Chanute	22	19	3
Marshalltown	53	38	15	Chapman	2	2	....
Mason City	56	41	15	Chase	1	1	....
Missouri Valley	5	5	....	Cheney	3	3	....
Monticello	8	5	3	Cherokee	2	2	....
Mount Pleasant	15	13	2	Cherryvale	5	5	....
Muscatine	43	35	8	Chetopa	4	4	....
Nevada	8	8	....	Cimarron	2	2	....
New Hampton	6	6	....	Clay Center	7	7	....
Newton	33	26	7	Clearwater	5	5	....
Norwalk	8	7	1	Clyde	1	1	....
Onawa	4	4	....	Coffeyville	30	22	8
Orange City	5	5	....	Colby	16	16	....
Osage	6	6	....	Coldwater	1	1	....
Oskaloosa	20	18	2	Columbus	8	7	1
Pella	13	11	2	Colwich	2	2	....
Perry	14	10	4	Concordia	13	9	4
Pleasant Hill	8	8	....	Conway Springs	3	3	....
Red Oak	14	10	4	Council Grove	5	4	1
Rock Rapids	3	3	....	Derby	32	23	9
Sac City	5	5	....	Dodge City	47	36	11
Sergeant Bluff	6	5	1	Douglass	4	3	1
Sheldon	11	7	4	Downs	2	2	....
Shenandoah	12	9	3	Eastborough	6	6	....
Sioux City	135	113	22	Edgerton	3	3	....
Spencer	25	18	7	Edwardsville	12	11	1
Spirit Lake	7	6	1	El Dorado	40	35	5
Storm Lake	19	16	3	Elkhart	3	3	....
Story City	4	4	....	Ellinwood	5	5	....
Tama	4	4	....	Ellis	4	4	....
Tipton	5	5	....	Ellsworth	6	6	....
Urbandale	40	33	7	Elwood	3	3	....
Vinton	7	7	....	Emporia	58	41	17
Waterloo	137	118	19	Enterprise	1	1	....
Waukee	7	6	1	Erie	3	3	....
Waverly	14	13	1	Eudora	4	4	....
Webster City	20	14	6	Fairway	7	7	....
West Burlington	8	7	1	Florence	1	1	....
West Des Moines	52	45	7	Fort Scott	21	15	6
West Union	4	4	....	Frankfort	1	1	....
Windsor Heights	12	11	1	Fredonia	7	6	1
Winterset	8	7	1	Frontenac	7	4	3
				Galena	9	9	....
KANSAS				Garden City	77	50	27
				Garden Plain	1	1	....
Abilene	20	11	9	Gardner	13	11	2
Andale	1	1	....	Garnett	13	9	4
Andover	12	7	5	Girard	4	4	....
Anthony	4	4	....	Goddard	3	3	....
Arcadia	1	1	....	Goodland	14	11	3
Argonia	1	1	....	Grandview Plaza	3	3	....
Arkansas City	28	22	6	Great Bend	40	28	12
Arma	4	4	....	Halstead	5	5	....
Atchison	33	23	10	Harper	3	3	....
Attica	2	2	....	Hays	35	25	10
Augusta	25	20	5	Haysville	23	14	9
Baldwin City	7	6	1	Herington	10	5	5
Basehor	3	3	....	Hesston	5	5	....
Baxter Springs	9	8	1	Hiawatha	7	6	1
Belle Plaine	4	3	1	Highland	2	2	....
Belleville	5	5	....	Hill City	4	4	....
Beloit	11	8	3	Hillsboro	4	3	1
Blue Rapids	1	1	....	Hoisington	9	6	3
Bonner Springs	19	16	3	Holcomb	3	3	....
Buhler	3	3	....	Holton	9	9	....
Burden	1	1	....	Holyrood	2	2	....
Burlingame	2	2	....	Hope	1	1	....
Burlington	8	6	2	Horton	9	5	4

Table 78. — Number of Full-time Law Enforcement Employees, Cities, October 31, 1993 — Continued

City	Total police employees	Total officers	Total civilians	City	Total police employees	Total officers	Total civilians
KANSAS — Continued				**KANSAS — Continued**			
Hoxie	2	2	....	Roeland Park	14	11	3
Hugoton	6	5	1	Rose Hill	4	4	....
Humboldt	5	5	....	Rossville	1	1	....
Hutchinson	92	62	30	Russell	13	7	6
Independence	27	20	7	Sabetha	5	5	....
Inman	2	2	....	St. Francis	1	1	....
Iola	20	15	5	St. John	4	4	....
Junction City	66	49	17	St. Marys	4	4	....
Kanopolis	2	1	1	Salina	78	62	16
Kansas City	443	327	116	Scott City	11	6	5
Kingman	10	6	4	Scranton	1	1	....
Kinsley	4	4	....	Sedan	4	4	....
Kiowa	2	2	....	Sedgwick	3	3	....
La Crosse	3	3	....	Seneca	5	5	....
La Cygne	2	2	....	Shawnee	70	55	15
Lake Quivira	2	2	....	Silver Lake	1	1	....
Lansing	9	8	1	Smith Center	3	3	....
Larned	11	7	4	South Haven	2	2	....
Lawrence	133	96	37	South Hutchinson	6	5	1
Leavenworth	69	51	18	Spearville	1	1	....
Leawood	59	41	18	Spring Hill	5	5	....
Lebo	2	2	....	Stafford	4	4	....
Lenexa	97	59	38	Sterling	4	4	....
Leon	1	1	....	Stockton	4	4	....
Le Roy	1	1	....	Tonganoxie	4	4	....
Liberal	33	28	5	Topeka	343	248	95
Lindsborg	4	3	1	Towanda	1	1	....
Louisburg	4	4	....	Udall	1	1	....
Lyndon	2	2	....	Ulysses	6	6	....
Lyons	7	6	1	Valley Center	10	6	4
Maize	3	2	1	Valley Falls	1	1	....
Marion	7	7	....	Wa Keeney	5	5	....
Marquette	1	1	....	Wakefield	1	1	....
Marysville	7	6	1	Wamego	11	6	5
McLouth	1	1	....	Waterville	1	1	....
McPherson	27	27	....	Waverly	1	1	....
Meade	3	3	....	Weir	1	1	....
Medicine Lodge	4	4	....	Wellington	16	12	4
Melvern	1	1	....	Wellsville	3	3	....
Merriam	27	24	3	Westwood	8	7	1
Minneapolis	5	5	....	Wichita	662	496	166
Mission	21	19	2	Wilson	1	1	....
Moundridge	3	3	....	Winfield	25	20	5
Mound Valley	1	1	....	Yates Center	4	3	1
Mount Hope	2	2	....				
Mulberry	2	2	....	**KENTUCKY**			
Mulvane	13	8	5				
Neodesha	7	6	1	Adairville	1	1	....
Ness City	1	1	....	Albany	8	5	3
Newton	24	22	2	Alexandria	6	6	....
North Newton	1	1	....	Anchorage	13	9	4
Norton	6	5	1	Ashland	56	49	7
Oakley	10	10	....	Auburn	2	2	....
Oberlin	4	4	....	Audubon Park	8	7	1
Olathe	107	77	30	Augusta	2	2	....
Osage City	5	5	....	Barbourville	15	12	3
Osawatomie	13	8	5	Bardstown	19	17	2
Osborne	3	3	....	Beattyville	6	4	2
Oswego	5	5	....	Beaver Dam	4	4	....
Ottawa	27	21	6	Bellevue	10	9	1
Overbrook	1	1	....	Benham	1	1	....
Overland Park	180	137	43	Benton	8	6	2
Oxford	2	2	....	Berea	24	17	7
Paola	16	11	5	Bloomfield	1	1	....
Park City	11	10	1	Bowling Green	106	87	19
Parsons	34	23	11	Brandenburg	3	3	....
Pawnee Rock	1	1	....	Brooksville	2	2	....
Peabody	2	2	....	Brownsville	1	1	....
Perry	1	1	....	Burkesville	7	4	3
Pittsburg	37	31	6	Burnside	2	2	....
Plainville	4	4	....	Cadiz	5	5	....
Pleasanton	1	1	....	Calvert City	5	4	1
Prairie Village	48	38	10	Campbellsville	14	12	2
Pratt	20	19	1	Carlisle	6	6	....
Quinter	1	1	....	Carrollton	10	10	....

Table 78. — Number of Full-time Law Enforcement Employees, Cities, October 31, 1993 — Continued

City	Total police employees	Total officers	Total civilians	City	Total police employees	Total officers	Total civilians
KENTUCKY — Continued				**KENTUCKY — Continued**			
Catlettsburg	8	8	....	Liberty	9	6	3
Cave City	7	6	1	Livermore	1	1	....
Centertown	1	1	....	London	16	16	....
Central City	8	8	....	Louisa	9	6	3
Clay City	2	2	....	Louisville	843	627	216
Cloverport	2	2	....	Ludlow	8	7	1
Cold Springs	6	5	1	Lynch	2	2	....
Columbia	7	7	....	Madisonville	49	41	8
Corbin	20	16	4	Manchester	13	9	4
Covington	121	98	23	Marion	6	6	....
Crescent Springs	11	9	2	Mayfield	34	27	7
Crittenden	1	1	....	Maysville	27	23	4
Cumberland	8	6	2	Middlesboro	25	21	4
Cynthiana	20	16	4	Millersburg	1	1	....
Danville	25	22	3	Minor Lane Heights	1	1	....
Dawson Springs	9	5	4	Monticello	12	8	4
Dayton	8	8	....	Morehead	24	16	8
Devondale	2	2	....	Morganfield	15	8	7
Dry Ridge	3	3	....	Morgantown	5	5	....
Edgewood	10	9	1	Mount Sterling	20	16	4
Edmonton	11	6	5	Mount Vernon	8	5	3
Elizabethtown	44	33	11	Mount Washington	8	8	....
Elkton	6	6	....	Muldraugh	1	1	....
Elsmere	10	9	1	Munfordville	1	1	....
Eminence	6	6	....	Murray	28	23	5
Erlanger	32	26	6	Neon	1	1	....
Evarts	5	4	1	Newport	54	44	10
Falmouth	11	7	4	Nicholasville	36	29	7
Flatwoods	12	8	4	Nortonville	1	1	....
Flemingsburg	6	6	....	Oak Grove	9	8	1
Florence	47	43	4	Olive Hill	6	5	1
Fort Mitchell	12	12	....	Owensboro	124	97	27
Fort Thomas	23	22	1	Owenton	3	3	....
Fort Wright	7	7	....	Owingsville	6	4	2
Frankfort	58	52	6	Paducah	75	69	6
Franklin	25	18	7	Paintsville	11	11	....
Fulton	14	10	4	Paris	22	17	5
Georgetown	43	30	13	Park Hills	6	5	1
Glasgow	32	25	7	Pembroke	1	1	....
Grayson	7	7	....	Perryville	1	1	....
Greensburg	9	5	4	Pewee Valley	4	4	....
Greenup	2	2	....	Pikeville	20	16	4
Greenville	7	7	....	Pineville	9	7	2
Guthrie	4	4	....	Pioneer Village	2	2	....
Hardinsburg	4	4	....	Prestonsburg	15	15	....
Harlan	14	9	5	Princeton	14	13	1
Harrodsburg	24	16	8	Prospect	7	7	....
Hartford	4	4	....	Raceland	4	4	....
Hazard	28	22	6	Radcliff	37	28	9
Henderson	56	49	7	Ravenna	2	2	....
Hickman	10	6	4	Richmond	52	42	10
Highland Heights	6	6	....	Russell	11	11	....
Hillview	10	9	1	Russell Springs	5	5	....
Hodgenville	5	5	....	Russellville	28	20	8
Hopkinsville	54	48	6	St. Matthews	33	27	6
Horse Cave	5	5	....	Salyersville	4	4	....
Independence	12	11	1	Scottsville	17	13	4
Indian Hills	5	5	....	Sebree	1	1	....
Irvine	6	6	....	Shelbyville	16	15	1
Irvington	2	2	....	Shepherdsville	8	8	....
Jackson	11	9	2	Shively	26	21	5
Jamestown	5	5	....	Somerset	31	26	5
Jeffersontown	45	39	6	Southgate	5	5	....
Jenkins	4	4	....	Springfield	11	7	4
Junction City	4	4	....	Stamping Ground	1	1	....
La Grange	8	7	1	Stanford	7	7	....
Lakeside Park	7	7	....	Stanton	6	6	....
Lancaster	10	6	4	Sturgis	5	5	....
Land between-the-Lakes	17	16	1	Taylor Mill	6	6	....
Lawrenceburg	18	14	4	Taylorsville	2	2	....
Lebanon	19	13	6	Tompkinsville	11	8	3
Lebanon Junction	3	3	....	Uniontown	2	2	....
Leitchfield	16	11	5	Vanceburg	4	4	....
Lewisport	1	1	....	Versailles	20	15	5
Lexington	531	387	144	Villa Hills	8	7	1

Table 78.—Number of Full-time Law Enforcement Employees, Cities, October 31, 1993—Continued

City	Total police employees	Total officers	Total civilians	City	Total police employees	Total officers	Total civilians
KENTUCKY—Continued				**LOUISIANA—Continued**			
Vine Grove	6	5	1	Rayne	20	20	....
Walton	4	4	....	Ruston	40	33	7
Warsaw	4	2	2	Shreveport	584	452	132
Wayland	1	1	....	Simmesport	3	2	1
West Buechel	10	9	1	Slidell	86	59	27
West Liberty	10	6	4	Springhill	12	12	....
West Point	4	2	2	Vidalia	17	17	....
Wheelwright	2	2	....	Ville Platte	27	27	....
Whitesburg	3	3	....	Vinton	13	13	....
Wilder	5	5	....	Vivian	14	14	....
Williamsburg	9	9	....	Welsh	11	11	....
Williamstown	8	4	4	Westlake	15	15	....
Wilmore	7	5	2	West Monroe	62	56	6
Winchester	37	27	10	Westwego	14	13	1
Wingo	1	1	....	Winnfield	20	20	....
Worthington	2	2	....	Winnsboro	9	8	1
Wurtland	1	1	....	Zachary	24	22	2
LOUISIANA				**MAINE**			
Abbeville	33	33	....	Ashland	3	3	....
Alexandria	162	131	31	Auburn	55	45	10
Baldwin	5	4	1	Augusta	48	36	12
Ball	6	5	1	Baileyville	5	5	....
Bastrop	49	43	6	Bangor	78	65	13
Baton Rouge	778	649	129	Bar Harbor	13	9	4
Berwick	10	10	....	Bath	26	17	9
Bogalusa	44	37	7	Belfast	14	10	4
Bossier City	151	126	25	Berwick	10	9	1
Breaux Bridge	13	13	....	Bethel	3	3	....
Church Point	12	12	....	Biddeford	52	42	10
Covington	33	26	7	Boothbay Harbor	7	6	1
Crowley	32	30	2	Brewer	20	15	5
Dequincy	10	10	....	Bridgton	11	7	4
De Ridder	21	21	....	Brownville	2	2	....
Eunice	35	34	1	Brunswick	39	30	9
Farmerville	12	12	....	Bucksport	9	7	2
Ferriday	19	18	1	Buxton	8	4	4
Franklinton	12	12	....	Calais	12	8	4
Golden Meadow	6	4	2	Camden	14	9	5
Gonzales	28	28	....	Cape Elizabeth	17	12	5
Gretna	75	67	8	Caribou	15	14	1
Hammond	66	66	....	Carrabassett Valley	2	1	1
Harahan	25	25	....	Cumberland	14	10	4
Haynesville	7	7	....	Damariscotta	3	3	....
Houma	65	52	13	Dexter	5	5	....
Iowa	8	8	....	Dixfield	3	3	....
Jackson	4	4	....	Dover-Foxcroft	4	4	....
Jeanerette	17	17	....	East Millinocket	5	5	....
Jena	5	5	....	Eastport	5	4	1
Jennings	40	38	2	Eliot	8	7	1
Jonesboro	17	15	2	Ellsworth	14	10	4
Jonesville	6	6	....	Fairfield	10	9	1
Kaplan	16	16	....	Falmouth	17	12	5
Kenner	157	112	45	Farmington	13	12	1
Kentwood	10	10	....	Fort Fairfield	6	5	1
Kinder	6	6	....	Fort Kent	7	4	3
Lafayette	243	187	56	Freeport	16	11	5
Lake Charles	143	142	1	Fryeburg	4	4	....
Leesville	26	26	....	Gardiner	10	10	....
Lockport	4	4	....	Gorham	21	15	6
Mamou	13	10	3	Gouldsboro - Winter Harbor	1	1	....
Mandeville	30	30	....	Hallowell	5	5	....
Mansfield	17	17	....	Hampden	14	9	5
Many	12	12	....	Houlton	18	13	5
Minden	27	26	1	Jay	11	7	4
Monroe	214	154	60	Kennebunk	20	15	5
Natchitoches	49	48	1	Kennebunkport	16	11	5
New Iberia	70	52	18	Kittery	23	17	6
New Orleans	1,869	1,513	356	Lewiston	95	79	16
Opelousas	50	41	9	Limestone	2	2	....
Patterson	14	14	....	Lincoln	8	7	1
Pineville	39	35	4	Lisbon	18	13	5
Plaquemine	27	26	1	Livermore Falls	11	6	5
Port Allen	21	21	....	Machias	5	4	1

Table 78. — Number of Full-time Law Enforcement Employees, Cities, October 31, 1993 — Continued

City	Total police employees	Total officers	Total civilians	City	Total police employees	Total officers	Total civilians
MAINE — Continued				**MARYLAND — Continued**			
Madawaska	7	6	1	District Heights	8	8	....
Madison	6	5	1	Easton	45	33	12
Mechanic Falls	4	4	....	Edmonston	5	5	....
Medway	2	2	....	Elkton	23	16	7
Mexico	4	4	....	Federalsburg	9	8	1
Millinocket	17	13	4	Forest Heights	5	4	1
Milo	3	3	....	Frederick	103	85	18
Monmouth	2	2	....	Frostburg	19	15	4
Mount Desert	9	5	4	Fruitland	9	8	1
Newport	4	4	....	Glenarden	12	10	2
North Berwick	8	7	1	Great Oaks	11	6	5
Norway	6	6	....	Greenbelt	60	44	16
Oakland	7	6	1	Greensboro	3	3	....
Ogunquit	12	7	5	Hagerstown	108	85	23
Old Orchard Beach	21	16	5	Hampstead	4	4	....
Old Town	17	13	4	Hancock	5	4	1
Orono	18	13	5	Havre de Grace	30	22	8
Oxford	4	3	1	Hurlock	7	7	....
Paris	7	6	1	Hyattsville	34	26	8
Phippsburg	1	1	....	Landover Hills	4	4	....
Pittsfield	9	5	4	La Plata	5	5	....
Portland	191	144	47	Laurel	60	43	17
Presque Isle	23	18	5	Luke	2	2	....
Richmond	4	4	....	Manchester	3	3	....
Rockland	25	18	7	Morningside	6	5	1
Rockport	4	4	....	Mount Ranier	19	13	6
Rumford	17	16	1	North Beach	3	3	....
Sabattus	5	5	....	North East	6	6	....
Saco	32	26	6	Oakland	5	4	1
Sanford	47	34	13	Ocean City	109	86	23
Scarborough	36	24	12	Ocean Pines	15	11	4
Searsport	3	3	....	Oxford	3	3	....
Skowhegan	17	13	4	Pocomoke City	15	11	4
South Berwick	10	6	4	Preston	2	2	....
South Portland	55	51	4	Princess Anne	7	7	....
Southwest Harbor	9	5	4	Ridgely	3	3	....
Thomaston	7	4	3	Rising Sun	4	2	2
Topsham	14	10	4	Riverdale	17	12	5
Van Buren	3	3	....	Rock Hall	3	3	....
Veazie	1	1	....	St. Michaels	7	7	....
Waldoboro	5	4	1	Salisbury	97	74	23
Washburn	1	1	....	Seat Pleasant	11	10	1
Waterville	37	29	8	Smithsburg	1	1	....
Wells	24	19	5	Snow Hill	6	6	....
Westbrook	33	28	5	Sykesville	6	5	1
Wilton	5	5	....	Takoma Park	52	35	17
Windham	22	18	4	Taneytown	6	6	....
Winslow	7	6	1	Thurmont	7	7	....
Winthrop	12	8	4	University Park	7	7	....
Wiscasset	8	7	1	Upper Marlboro	1	1	....
Yarmouth	14	9	5	Westernport	5	5	....
York	27	19	8	Westminster	42	33	9
MARYLAND				**MASSACHUSETTS**			
Aberdeen	44	35	9	Acton	34	29	5
Annapolis	159	116	43	Adams	21	20	1
Baltimore	3,500	2,947	553	Amesbury	29	24	5
Baltimore City Sheriff	115	110	5	Andover	57	44	13
Bel Air	41	30	11	Arlington	71	63	8
Berlin	17	11	6	Ashburnham	6	5	1
Berwyn Heights	7	7	....	Ashfield	1	1	....
Bladensburg	22	17	5	Ashland	20	19	1
Brunswick	12	11	1	Athol	22	18	4
Cambridge	52	39	13	Auburn	30	24	6
Capitol Heights	7	6	1	Avon	16	13	3
Centreville	6	6	....	Ayer	20	15	5
Chesapeake City	1	1	....	Barnstable	90	81	9
Chestertown	7	6	1	Bedford	27	26	1
Cheverly	12	10	2	Belchertown	15	11	4
Cottage City	4	4	....	Bellingham	25	21	4
Crisfield	9	7	2	Belmont	57	47	10
Cumberland	57	52	5	Berkley	5	3	2
Delmar	9	8	1	Berlin	5	4	1
Denton	11	10	1	Beverly	87	84	3

Table 78. — Number of Full-time Law Enforcement Employees, Cities, October 31, 1993 — Continued

City	Total police employees	Total officers	Total civilians	City	Total police employees	Total officers	Total civilians
MASSACHUSETTS — Continued				**MASSACHUSETTS — Continued**			
Blackstone	15	12	3	Lowell	212	181	31
Bolton	10	6	4	Ludlow	32	31	1
Boston	2,604	1,944	660	Lynn	160	141	19
Bourne	33	28	5	Lynnfield	24	19	5
Boxborough	7	6	1	Malden	109	99	10
Boxford	11	11	....	Manchester	16	14	2
Boylston	11	7	4	Marblehead	39	37	2
Braintree	87	77	10	Marion	12	10	2
Brewster	21	16	5	Marlborough	65	62	3
Bridgewater	30	29	1	Marshfield	37	35	2
Brockton	178	157	21	Mattapoisett	16	16	....
Brookline	144	133	11	Maynard	24	22	2
Cambridge	288	253	35	Medfield	21	17	4
Canton	42	40	2	Medford	111	105	6
Carlisle	13	9	4	Medway	17	16	1
Charlton	13	9	4	Melrose	47	45	2
Chatham	21	20	1	Mendon	6	6	....
Chelmsford	49	40	9	Merrimac	7	4	3
Clinton	23	22	1	Methuen	79	66	13
Cohasset	18	18	....	Middleboro	38	32	6
Concord	38	32	6	Middleton	11	10	1
Dalton	10	9	1	Milford	43	42	1
Danvers	54	44	10	Millis	12	12	....
Dartmouth	60	50	10	Milton	54	52	2
Dedham	49	46	3	Montague	15	14	1
Deerfield	6	5	1	Nahant	11	11	....
Dennis	39	31	8	Nantucket	28	23	5
Dighton	10	7	3	Natick	56	50	6
Douglas	11	8	3	Needham	54	50	4
Dover	15	15	....	New Bedford	272	233	39
Dracut	32	31	1	Newton	190	173	17
Dudley	17	13	4	North Adams	30	27	3
East Bridgewater	21	20	1	Northampton	61	53	8
Eastham	21	15	6	North Andover	41	31	10
East Longmeadow	23	21	2	North Attleborough	50	40	10
Easton	28	27	1	Northborough	23	17	6
Edgartown	13	12	1	Northbridge	18	15	3
Everett	89	84	5	North Reading	23	22	1
Fall River	282	226	56	Norton	16	14	2
Fitchburg	82	76	6	Norwood	72	62	10
Foxborough	25	25	....	Orleans	25	21	4
Framingham	105	95	10	Oxford	22	17	5
Franklin	38	31	7	Peabody	91	83	8
Freetown	18	13	5	Pembroke	26	25	1
Gardner	33	31	2	Pepperell	14	13	1
Georgetown	11	8	3	Pittsfield	94	83	11
Gloucester	45	43	2	Plymouth	93	81	12
Grafton	20	15	5	Plympton	5	2	3
Granby	10	8	2	Princeton	6	3	3
Great Barrington	14	14	....	Provincetown	21	16	5
Greenfield	39	35	4	Quincy	176	145	31
Hadley	8	6	2	Randolph	53	51	2
Hamilton	18	14	4	Raynham	24	21	3
Hampden	13	9	4	Reading	39	37	2
Hanson	19	16	3	Rehoboth	26	21	5
Hardwick	2	2	....	Revere	97	89	8
Harvard	11	7	4	Rockport	18	17	1
Harwich	33	26	7	Rowley	9	7	2
Haverhill	87	80	7	Rutland	1	1	....
Hingham	47	43	4	Salem	100	90	10
Holbrook	20	19	1	Sandwich	28	27	1
Hollinston	20	20	....	Saugus	51	49	2
Hopedale	10	9	1	Scituate	37	30	7
Hudson	33	28	5	Sharon	26	22	4
Hull	28	24	4	Shelburne	2	2	....
Ipswich	24	23	1	Sherborn	16	15	1
Lancaster	8	7	1	Shirley	14	9	5
Lawrence	129	109	20	Shrewsbury	39	32	7
Lee	10	10	....	Somerset	33	30	3
Leicester	17	14	3	Somerville	132	127	5
Leominster	65	61	4	Southboro	12	12	....
Lexington	55	48	7	South Hadley	26	25	1
Lincoln	16	12	4	Spencer	9	6	3
Littleton	18	13	5	Springfield	539	482	57
Longmeadow	31	31	....	Sterling	14	9	5

Table 78. — Number of Full-time Law Enforcement Employees, Cities, October 31, 1993 — Continued

City	Total police employees	Total officers	Total civilians	City	Total police employees	Total officers	Total civilians
MASSACHUSETTS — Continued				**MICHIGAN — Continued**			
Stockbridge	6	6	....	Birmingham	54	35	19
Stoughton	52	50	2	Blackman Township	22	21	1
Stow	13	11	2	Blissfield	5	4	1
Sudbury	30	25	5	Bloomfield Hills	27	23	4
Sutton	12	10	2	Bloomfield Township	85	67	18
Swampscott	34	33	1	Bloomingdale	1	1	....
Swansea	32	27	5	Boyne City	10	6	4
Taunton	97	93	4	Breckenridge	3	3	....
Tewksbury	49	47	2	Bridgeport Township	6	5	1
Tisbury	13	11	2	Bridgman	4	4	....
Topsfield	14	10	4	Brighton	12	11	1
Uxbridge	20	15	5	Bronson	6	5	1
Wakefield	48	46	2	Brown City	1	1	....
Walpole	40	37	3	Brownstown Township	38	29	9
Waltham	136	128	8	Buchanan	10	9	1
Ware	14	14	....	Buena Vista Township	18	16	2
Wareham	42	39	3	Burr Oak	1	1	....
Watertown	77	66	11	Burton	42	37	5
Webster	28	24	4	Cadillac	21	17	4
Wellesley	53	45	8	Calumet	2	2	....
Wellfleet	15	10	5	Cambridge Township	1	1	....
Wenham	11	10	1	Camp Grayling	1	1	....
Westborough	31	26	5	Canton Township	80	58	22
West Bridgewater	19	18	1	Capac	5	4	1
Westfield	71	66	5	Carleton	4	3	1
Westford	33	26	7	Caro	8	7	1
Weston	29	25	4	Carrollton Township	6	5	1
Westport	25	24	1	Carson City	2	2	....
West Springfield	76	69	7	Carsonville	1	1	....
Westwood	32	29	3	Caseville	2	2	....
Weymouth	106	94	12	Cass City	3	3	....
Wilbraham	26	25	1	Cassopolis	5	5	....
Wilmington	42	40	2	Cedar Springs	5	5	....
Winchendon	12	11	1	Center Line	31	25	6
Winchester	44	37	7	Centreville	2	2	....
Woburn	72	67	5	Charleston Township	1	1	....
Worcester	450	357	93	Charlevoix	7	6	1
Wrentham	15	14	1	Charlotte	21	20	1
Yarmouth	52	42	10	Cheboygan	9	9	....
				Chelsea	10	7	3
MICHIGAN				Chesaning	5	5	....
				Chesterfield Township	17	13	4
Adrian	38	32	6	Chikaming Township	3	3	....
Albion	36	30	6	Chocolay Township	4	3	1
Allegan	11	9	2	Clare	8	7	1
Allen Park	55	49	6	Clarkston	4	4	....
Alma	14	13	1	Clawson	25	23	2
Almont	4	4	....	Clay-Algonac	23	18	5
Alpena	23	18	5	Clinton	3	3	....
Ann Arbor	216	174	42	Clinton Township	117	86	31
Armada	3	3	....	Clio-Vienna	10	9	1
Atlas Township	2	2	....	Coldwater	17	15	2
Auburn	3	2	1	Coleman	2	2	....
Auburn Hills	54	42	12	Coloma	3	3	....
Augusta	1	1	....	Coloma Township	5	5	....
Bad Axe	7	7	....	Colon	2	2	....
Bangor	4	4	....	Columbia Township	4	4	....
Baraga	2	2	....	Concord Township	2	2	....
Barry Township	2	2	....	Constantine	4	4	....
Bath Township	7	6	1	Coopersville	7	6	1
Battle Creek	154	114	40	Corunna	5	5	....
Bay City	79	73	6	Covert Township	6	6	....
Beaverton	1	1	....	Croswell	5	5	....
Bedford Township	8	7	1	Crystal Falls	5	5	....
Belding	9	8	1	Davison	9	7	2
Bellaire	1	1	....	Davison Township	11	9	2
Belleville	8	7	1	Dearborn	220	197	23
Benton Harbor	27	20	7	Dearborn Heights	117	89	28
Benton Township	28	20	8	Decatur	4	4	....
Berkley	34	31	3	Deckerville	1	1	....
Berrien Springs-Oronoko Township	9	8	1	Denmark Township	1	1	....
Beulah	1	1	....	Denton Township	3	3	....
Beverly Hills	31	27	4	Detour Village	1	1	....
Big Rapids	16	15	1	Detroit	4,398	3,860	538
Birch Run	3	3	....	De Witt	7	6	1

Table 78. — Number of Full-time Law Enforcement Employees, Cities, October 31, 1993 — Continued

City	Total police employees	Total officers	Total civilians	City	Total police employees	Total officers	Total civilians
MICHIGAN — Continued				**MICHIGAN — Continued**			
De Witt Township	11	10	1	Highland Park	77	66	11
Douglas	3	3	....	Hillsdale	20	15	5
Dowagiac	13	12	1	Holland	68	56	12
Dryden Township	2	2	....	Holly	12	8	4
Durand	6	5	1	Homer	2	2	....
East Grand Rapids	33	30	3	Hopkins	3	3	....
East Jordan	4	4	....	Houghton	8	8	....
East Lansing	84	56	28	Howard City	1	1	....
East Pointe	57	51	6	Howard Township	2	2	....
East Tawas	4	4	....	Howell	16	15	1
Eaton Rapids	9	8	1	Hudson	3	3	....
Ecorse	37	32	5	Hudsonville	6	5	1
Edmore-Home	2	2	....	Huntington Woods	21	16	5
Elk Rapids	3	3	....	Huron Township	14	10	4
Elkton	2	2	....	Imlay City	9	8	1
Elsie	1	1	....	Inkster	71	49	22
Emmett Township	7	6	1	Ionia	18	16	2
Erie Township	2	2	....	Iron Mountain	12	12	....
Escanaba	41	34	7	Iron River	4	4	....
Essexville	11	9	2	Ironwood	21	16	5
Evart	3	3	....	Ishpeming	12	11	1
Fairhaven Township	1	1	....	Ishpeming Township	1	1	....
Farmington	28	22	6	Ithaca	5	4	1
Farmington Hills	143	100	43	Jackson	79	65	14
Fenton	18	13	5	Jonesville	4	4	....
Ferndale	62	53	9	Kalamazoo	327	247	80
Flat Rock	23	21	2	Kalamazoo Township	35	26	9
Flint	342	289	53	Kalkaska	6	5	1
Flint Township	33	30	3	Keego Harbor	6	5	1
Flushing	12	11	1	Kentwood	53	47	6
Flushing Township	7	6	1	Kingsford	18	18	....
Forsyth Township	6	6	....	Kinross Township	3	3	....
Frankenmuth	6	6	....	Laingsburg	1	1	....
Frankfort	4	4	....	Lake Angelus	2	2	....
Franklin	11	10	1	Lake Linden	1	1	....
Fraser	48	40	8	Lake Odessa	3	3	....
Fremont	8	7	1	Lake Orion	7	4	3
Frost Township	1	1	....	L'Anse	4	4	....
Galesburg	1	1	....	Lansing	342	256	86
Garden City	50	40	10	Lansing Township	16	15	1
Gaylord	9	7	2	Lapeer	19	16	3
Genesee Township	17	15	2	Lathrup Village	13	10	3
Gerrish Township	3	3	....	Laurium	4	4	....
Gibraltar	14	13	1	Lawrence	3	3	....
Gladstone	11	11	....	Lawton	5	5	....
Gladwin	3	3	....	Leoni Township	3	2	1
Gobles	1	1	....	Leslie	2	2	....
Grand Beach	2	2	....	Lexington	3	3	....
Grand Blanc	21	16	5	Lincoln Township	11	9	2
Grand Blanc Township	31	24	7	Lincoln Park	64	60	4
Grand Haven	28	25	3	Linden	4	4	....
Grand Ledge	13	12	1	Litchfield	4	4	....
Grand Rapids	373	275	98	Livonia	185	164	21
Grandville	21	18	3	Lowell	7	6	1
Grayling	7	6	1	Ludington	15	14	1
Green Oak Township	12	11	1	Luna Pier	4	4	....
Greenville	27	17	10	Mackinac Island	5	4	1
Grosse Ile Township	22	17	5	Mackinaw City	5	5	....
Grosse Pointe	30	25	5	Madison Heights	78	61	17
Grosse Pointe Farms	39	31	8	Madison Township	1	1	....
Grosse Pointe Park	46	43	3	Mancelona	3	3	....
Grosse Pointe Shores	20	18	2	Manchester Township	1	1	....
Grosse Pointe Woods	43	41	2	Manistee	15	14	1
Hamburg Township	11	10	1	Manistique	11	10	1
Hampton Township	11	10	1	Manton	2	2	....
Hamtramck	50	50	....	Marcellus	3	3	....
Hancock	6	6	....	Marenisco Township	1	1	....
Harbor Beach	4	4	....	Marine City	10	8	2
Harbor Springs	6	5	1	Marion	1	1	....
Harper Woods	41	35	6	Marlette	3	3	....
Hart	3	3	....	Marquette	41	34	7
Hartford	6	6	....	Marshall	19	14	5
Hastings	14	13	1	Martin	1	1	....
Hazel Park	41	35	6	Marysville	15	13	2
Hesperia	2	2	....	Mason	10	9	1

Table 78. — Number of Full-time Law Enforcement Employees, Cities, October 31, 1993 — Continued

City	Total police employees	Total officers	Total civilians	City	Total police employees	Total officers	Total civilians
MICHIGAN — Continued				**MICHIGAN — Continued**			
Mattawan	3	3	....	Portage	64	51	13
Mayville	1	1	....	Port Austin	1	1	....
Melvindale	26	24	2	Port Huron	59	51	8
Memphis	2	2	....	Portland	6	6	....
Mendon	1	1	....	Port Sanilac	1	1	....
Menominee	21	16	5	Potterville	2	2	....
Meridian Township	41	35	6	Prairieville Township	1	1	....
Michiana	2	2	....	Quincy	4	4	....
Middleville	3	3	....	Reading	1	1	....
Midland	53	50	3	Reed City	5	5	....
Midland Township	2	2	....	Reese	2	2	....
Milan	12	8	4	Republic Township	1	1	....
Milford	18	12	6	Richfield Township (Roscommon County)	3	3	....
Millington	3	3	....	Richfield Township (Genesee County)	7	6	1
Monroe	51	45	6	Richland	1	1	....
Montague	5	5	....	Richland Township	4	4	....
Montrose	3	3	....	Richmond	10	7	3
Montrose Township	8	6	2	Richmond Township	2	1	1
Morenci	3	3	....	River Rouge	37	33	4
Morrice	1	1	....	Riverview	30	26	4
Mount Clemens	43	33	10	Rochester	20	14	6
Mount Morris	7	5	2	Rockford	10	8	2
Mount Morris Township	27	25	2	Rockwood	8	8	....
Mount Pleasant	26	22	4	Rogers City	7	7	....
Mundy Township	10	8	2	Romeo	10	7	3
Munising	5	5	....	Romulus	72	57	15
Muskegon	88	78	10	Roosevelt Park	7	6	1
Muskegon Heights	31	28	3	Roscommon Township	1	1	....
Muskegon Township	13	12	1	Rose City	1	1	....
Napoleon Township	3	3	....	Roseville	96	83	13
Nashville	1	1	....	Ross Township	2	2	....
Negaunee	12	11	1	Royal Oak	108	90	18
New Baltimore	11	10	1	Royal Oak Township	12	10	2
Newberry	4	4	....	Saginaw	157	140	17
New Buffalo	5	5	....	Saginaw Township	43	40	3
New Haven	6	5	1	St. Charles	3	3	....
New Lothrop	1	1	....	St. Clair	10	9	1
Niles	27	20	7	St. Clair Shores	96	79	17
Niles Township	8	8	....	St. Ignace	6	5	1
Northfield Township	6	5	1	St. Johns	14	12	2
North Muskegon	7	6	1	St. Joseph	25	20	5
Northville	15	13	2	St. Joseph Township	10	9	1
Northville Township	24	20	4	St. Louis	6	5	1
Norton Shores	26	24	2	Saline	17	12	5
Norvell Township	2	2	....	Sand Lake	3	1	2
Norway	6	6	....	Sandusky	4	4	....
Novi	75	50	25	Saugatuck	3	2	1
Oak Park	78	71	7	Sault Ste. Marie	27	21	6
Olivet	2	2	....	Schoolcraft	2	2	....
Onaway	2	2	....	Scottville	3	3	....
Ontonagon	1	1	....	Sebewaing	4	4	....
Ontwa Township-Edwardsburgh	7	6	1	Shelby	3	3	....
Orchard Lake	9	8	1	Shelby Township	59	46	13
Oscoda-Ausable Township	13	10	3	Shepherd	2	2	....
Otisville	1	1	....	Somerset Township	1	1	....
Otsego	8	7	1	Southfield	197	155	42
Ovid	3	3	....	Southgate	52	42	10
Owosso	21	19	2	South Haven	22	17	5
Oxford	17	12	5	South Lyon	10	9	1
Parchment	4	4	....	South Rockwood	1	1	....
Parma	2	2	....	Sparta	9	8	1
Paw Paw	10	7	3	Spaulding Township	1	1	....
Pennfield Township	6	5	1	Spring Arbor Township	2	2	....
Pentwater	3	3	....	Springfield	11	10	1
Perry	4	4	....	Spring Lake-Ferrysburg	10	9	1
Petoskey	15	12	3	Springport Township	2	2	....
Pigeon	1	1	....	Stanton	1	1	....
Pinckney	4	3	1	Sterling Heights	222	165	57
Pinconning	4	4	....	Sturgis	19	16	3
Pittsfield Township	31	22	9	Summit Township	4	4	....
Plainwell	7	7	....	Sumpter Township	16	11	5
Pleasant Ridge	8	7	1	Sunfield	1	1	....
Plymouth	20	15	5	Swartz Creek	8	7	1
Plymouth Township	31	21	10	Sylvan Lake	5	5	....
Pontiac	182	138	44	Taylor	130	108	22

Table 78. — Number of Full-time Law Enforcement Employees, Cities, October 31, 1993 — Continued

City	Total police employees	Total officers	Total civilians	City	Total police employees	Total officers	Total civilians
MICHIGAN — Continued				**MINNESOTA — Continued**			
Tecumseh	14	13	1	Cloquet	17	16	1
Thomas Township	4	3	1	Cold Spring	3	3	....
Three Oaks	4	4	....	Columbia Heights	30	22	8
Three Rivers	15	13	2	Coon Rapids	60	52	8
Tittabawassee Township	3	3	....	Corcoran	3	3	....
Traverse City	33	32	1	Cottage Grove	36	28	8
Trenton	52	47	5	Crookston	15	13	2
Troy	180	130	50	Crosby	8	5	3
Tuscarora Township	4	4	....	Crystal	30	25	5
Twin City	4	4	....	Dawson	3	3	....
Ubly	1	1	....	Deephaven	8	7	1
Union City	4	3	1	Detroit Lakes	14	12	2
Unionville	2	2	....	Dilworth	3	3	....
Utica	17	13	4	Duluth	152	130	22
Van Buren Township	14	12	2	Eagan	62	47	15
Vassar	4	4	....	East Grand Forks	22	21	1
Vicksburg	5	4	1	Eden Prairie	65	44	21
Walker	36	29	7	Edina	54	45	9
Walled Lake	16	12	4	Elk River	22	17	5
Warren	269	227	42	Eveleth	9	9	....
Watertown Township	1	1	....	Fairmont	16	14	2
Watervliet	3	3	....	Faribault	33	23	10
Wayland	4	4	....	Farmington	8	7	1
Wayne	54	37	17	Fergus Falls	22	18	4
Webberville	3	2	1	Forest Lake	11	10	1
West Bloomfield Township	74	56	18	Fridley	40	33	7
West Branch	3	3	....	Gilbert	5	5	....
Westland	116	100	16	Glencoe	9	8	1
White Cloud	1	1	....	Glenwood	3	3	....
Whitehall	6	6	....	Golden Valley	40	29	11
White Lake Township	25	18	7	Goodview	4	4	....
White Pigeon	2	2	....	Grand Rapids	17	12	5
Williamston	4	4	....	Granite Falls	5	5	....
Wixom	17	14	3	Hastings	23	20	3
Wolverine Lake	9	7	2	Hermantown	7	6	1
Woodhaven	33	29	4	Hibbing	29	28	1
Woodstock Township	1	1	....	Hopkins	34	23	11
Wyandotte	60	47	13	Hoyt Lakes	5	5	....
Wyoming	108	79	29	Hutchinson	24	18	6
Yale	3	3	....	International Falls	14	14	....
Ypsilanti	62	51	11	Inver Grove Heights	30	24	6
Zeeland	8	7	1	Jackson	6	6	....
Zilwaukee	3	3	....	Jordan	3	3	....
				Kasson	4	4	....
				Kenyon	3	3	....
MINNESOTA				La Crescent	6	5	1
				Lake City	8	7	1
Albert Lea	37	29	8	Lakefield	3	3	....
Alexandria	22	15	7	Lakeville	40	28	12
Anoka	35	27	8	Le Sueur	10	5	5
Apple Valley	49	34	15	Lino Lakes	11	9	2
Austin	32	29	3	Litchfield	10	9	1
Babbitt	4	4	....	Little Falls	12	10	2
Baxter	6	5	1	Long Prairie	5	5	....
Bayport	5	5	....	Luverne	5	5	....
Bemidji	23	20	3	Madison	3	3	....
Benson	5	5	....	Mankato	45	39	6
Big Lake	5	4	1	Maple Grove	41	34	7
Blaine	43	36	7	Maplewood	51	40	11
Bloomington	126	97	29	Marshall	21	17	4
Blue Earth	6	6	....	Medina	7	6	1
Brainerd	23	19	4	Melrose	4	4	....
Breckenridge	11	7	4	Mendota Heights	17	15	2
Brooklyn Center	54	40	14	Minneapolis	1,038	876	162
Brooklyn Park	76	64	12	Minnetonka	60	46	14
Buffalo	10	9	1	Montevideo	8	8	....
Burnsville	70	57	13	Moorhead	47	41	6
Caledonia	3	3	....	Mora	7	6	1
Cambridge	9	8	1	Morris	8	7	1
Cannon Falls	5	4	1	Mound	14	13	1
Champlin	20	19	1	Mounds View	16	15	1
Chanhassen	7	2	5	New Brighton	23	21	2
Chaska	16	13	3	New Hope	33	28	5
Chisholm	12	11	1	Newport	7	7	....
Circle Pines-Lexington	12	10	2	New Prague	7	6	1

Table 78. — Number of Full-time Law Enforcement Employees, Cities, October 31, 1993 — Continued

City	Total police employees	Total officers	Total civilians	City	Total police employees	Total officers	Total civilians
MINNESOTA — Continued				**MISSISSIPPI — Continued**			
New Ulm	21	18	3	Brandon	25	16	9
Northfield	21	16	5	Brookhaven	32	25	7
North Mankato	10	9	1	Calhoun City	6	6	....
North St. Paul	16	14	2	Clinton	44	33	11
Oakdale	25	22	3	Columbus	66	57	9
Oak Park Heights	9	8	1	Corinth	37	32	5
Olivia	4	4	....	Decatur	3	3	....
Ortonville	5	4	1	De Kalb	3	3	....
Osseo	3	3	....	Edwards	3	3	....
Owatonna	25	23	2	Eupora	8	6	2
Park Rapids	6	6	....	Flowood	23	17	6
Pipestone	5	5	....	Fulton	7	7	....
Plainview	3	3	....	Gloster	7	5	2
Plymouth	62	46	16	Goodman	3	3	....
Princeton	8	7	1	Greenville	130	91	39
Prior Lake	17	16	1	Greenwood	58	42	16
Proctor	6	5	1	Grenada	40	31	9
Ramsey	12	10	2	Gulfport	102	71	31
Red Wing	27	25	2	Hattiesburg	135	89	46
Redwood Falls	10	9	1	Heidelberg	3	3	....
Richfield	52	43	9	Hernando	13	11	2
Robbinsdale	27	19	8	Horn Lake	25	19	6
Rochester	125	97	28	Indianola	29	24	5
Roseau	4	4	....	Inverness	4	4	....
Rosemount	14	13	1	Jackson	749	413	336
Roseville	52	46	6	Laurel	70	50	20
St. Anthony	12	11	1	Leakesville	2	2	....
St. Bonifacius-Minnetrista	10	8	2	Long Beach	27	19	8
St. Cloud	80	65	15	Lucedale	13	9	4
St. James	7	6	1	Macon	5	5	....
St. Joseph	5	5	....	Madison	18	13	5
St. Louis Park	64	51	13	Magee	15	12	3
St. Paul	675	521	154	Marks	7	5	2
St. Paul Park	7	7	....	McComb	47	29	18
St. Peter	16	11	5	Mendenhall	10	7	3
Sartell	7	7	....	Meridian	124	94	30
Sauk Centre	8	5	3	Morton	14	10	4
Sauk Rapids	9	8	1	Moss Point	43	37	6
Savage	16	14	2	Natchez	67	54	13
Shakopee	21	18	3	Newton	13	8	5
Silver Bay	4	4	....	Ocean Springs	37	28	9
Slayton	3	3	....	Pascagoula	80	53	27
Sleepy Eye	5	5	....	Pass Christian	21	16	5
South Lake Minnetonka	14	13	1	Pelahatchie	5	4	1
South St. Paul	29	24	5	Petal	17	12	5
Springfield	4	4	....	Picayune	35	22	13
Spring Lake Park	11	10	1	Purvis	7	6	1
Stillwater	19	16	3	Ridgeland	46	30	16
Thief River Falls	15	14	1	Rolling Fork	5	5	....
Virginia	25	24	1	Shaw	9	5	4
Wabasha	3	3	....	Starkville	45	34	11
Wadena	9	8	1	Stonewall	4	3	1
Waite Park	7	6	1	Tupelo	102	87	15
Warroad	5	4	1	Tylertown	7	5	2
Waseca	11	9	2	Utica	5	5	....
Wayzata	9	7	2	Vaiden	1	1	....
Wells	4	4	....	Verona	12	12	....
West Hennepin	7	7	....	Vicksburg	89	73	16
West St. Paul	32	23	9	Waveland	21	15	6
White Bear Lake	33	27	6	Waynesboro	18	15	3
Willmar	30	26	4	Wiggins	13	9	4
Windom	8	7	1	Winona	15	10	5
Winona	38	35	3				
Woodbury	26	23	3	**MISSOURI**			
				Arnold	49	38	11
MISSISSIPPI				Aurora	14	10	4
				Ballwin	50	40	10
Aberdeen	21	16	5	Bellefontaine Neighbors	23	23	....
Ackerman	5	5	....	Bel-Nor	8	7	1
Amory	19	15	4	Bel-Ridge	19	14	5
Batesville	29	21	8	Belton	35	26	9
Bay St. Louis	30	24	6	Berkeley	54	43	11
Belzoni	11	6	5	Blue Springs	78	55	23
Biloxi	122	84	38	Bolivar	15	10	5
Booneville	23	17	6				

Table 78. — Number of Full-time Law Enforcement Employees, Cities, October 31, 1993 — Continued

City	Total police employees	Total officers	Total civilians	City	Total police employees	Total officers	Total civilians
MISSOURI — Continued				**MISSOURI — Continued**			
Bonne Terre	6	6	....	Maryland Heights	70	56	14
Boonville	20	14	6	Mexico	33	28	5
Branson	42	31	11	Moberly	37	32	5
Breckenridge Hills	14	13	1	Moline Acres	7	7	....
Brentwood	27	21	6	Monett	23	16	7
Bridgeton	67	56	11	Neosho	26	19	7
Brookfield	16	9	7	Nevada	24	17	7
Buckner	7	5	2	Normandy	19	18	1
Butler	10	6	4	North Kansas City	42	34	8
Calverton Park	5	5	....	Northwoods	19	17	2
Cameron	14	10	4	Oakview	4	4	....
Canton	6	3	3	Odessa	6	6	....
Cape Girardeau	85	61	24	O'Fallon	45	31	14
Carthage	26	20	6	Olivette	26	21	5
Centralia	11	6	5	Osage Beach	27	19	8
Chaffee	1	1	....	Overland	61	47	14
Charlack	10	8	2	Pacific	16	11	5
Chesterfield	63	58	5	Pagedale	16	15	1
Claycomo	8	7	1	Parkville	7	6	1
Clayton	61	48	13	Pevely	17	12	5
Clinton	16	15	1	Pine Lawn	15	14	1
Columbia	131	103	28	Pleasant Hill	11	6	5
Cool Valley	9	8	1	Poplar Bluff	48	35	13
Country Club Hills	9	7	2	Potosi	14	14	....
Crestwood	35	29	6	Raytown	74	58	16
Creve Coeur	46	37	9	Republic	15	15	....
Crystal City	16	12	4	Rich Hill	3	3	....
Dellwood	14	13	1	Richland	7	4	3
De Soto	18	13	5	Richmond	15	10	5
Des Peres	39	33	6	Richmond Heights	36	31	5
Edmundson	9	8	1	Riverside	18	13	5
Ellisville	21	20	1	Riverview	7	7	....
Eureka	18	15	3	Rolla	34	22	12
Excelsior Springs	28	19	9	St. Ann	44	38	6
Farmington	26	16	10	St. Charles	113	90	23
Fayette	6	6	....	Ste. Genevieve	9	8	1
Fenton	28	22	6	St. George	4	4	....
Ferguson	58	51	7	St. John	18	16	2
Festus	28	20	8	St. Joseph	136	104	32
Flat River	13	12	1	St. Louis	2,148	1,448	700
Florissant	87	72	15	St. Peters	66	52	14
Frontenac	23	19	4	St. Robert	14	10	4
Fulton	29	21	8	Salem	18	11	7
Garden City	2	2	....	Sedalia	48	39	9
Gladstone	63	52	11	Shrewsbury	19	16	3
Glendale	13	10	3	Sikeston	54	48	6
Grandview	57	47	10	Slater	9	5	4
Hannibal	45	32	13	Smithville	9	8	1
Harrisonville	22	14	8	Springfield	256	199	57
Hazelwood	50	38	12	Sugar Creek	14	12	2
Hillsdale	10	9	1	Sullivan	19	12	7
Independence	225	161	64	Sunset Hills	23	17	6
Ironton	5	5	....	Town and Country	33	30	3
Jackson	18	18	....	Trenton	15	10	5
Jefferson City	92	70	22	Union	14	12	2
Jennings	63	39	24	University City	94	75	19
Joplin	67	61	6	Valley Park	11	10	1
Kansas City	1,758	1,191	567	Vandalia	8	5	3
Kearney	6	6	....	Vinita Park	10	10	....
Kennett	23	22	1	Warrensburg	24	22	2
Kirksville	31	23	8	Warrenton	13	9	4
Kirkwood	68	55	13	Warson Woods	7	6	1
Ladue	35	29	6	Washington	26	21	5
Lake Lotawana	4	4	....	Webb City	16	16	....
Lake St. Louis	22	14	8	Webster Groves	51	42	9
Lake Winnebago	4	4	....	Wentzville	25	19	6
Lamar	9	8	1	Weston	4	4	....
Lebanon	23	17	6	West Plains	18	18	....
Lees Summit	96	68	28	Winchester	2	1	1
Lexington	6	6	....	Windsor	5	5	....
Macon	10	9	1	Woodson Terrace	15	13	2
Manchester	22	20	2				
Maplewood	27	22	5	**MONTANA**			
Marceline	6	5	1				
Marshall	31	22	9	Baker	4	4	....

Table 78. — Number of Full-time Law Enforcement Employees, Cities, October 31, 1993 — Continued

City	Total police employees	Total officers	Total civilians	City	Total police employees	Total officers	Total civilians
MONTANA — Continued				**NEBRASKA — Continued**			
Belgrade	8	6	2	Norfolk	49	35	14
Billings	129	105	24	North Platte	53	34	19
Boulder	2	2	....	Ogallala	12	10	2
Columbia Falls	13	8	5	O'Neill	12	7	5
Conrad	5	5	....	Ord	8	4	4
Dillon	8	7	1	Papillion	19	18	1
East Helena	4	4	....	Pierce	3	3	....
Eureka	2	2	....	Plainview	4	2	2
Fort Benton	3	3	....	Plattsmouth	9	8	1
Glasgow	8	7	1	Ralston	12	11	1
Glendive	16	11	5	Schuyler	6	6	....
Great Falls	96	65	31	Scottsbluff	32	28	4
Hamilton	12	10	2	Seward	12	8	4
Havre	20	17	3	Sidney	13	10	3
Helena	60	42	18	South Sioux City	18	17	1
Kalispell	38	24	14	Stanton	2	2	....
Laurel	12	8	4	Superior	5	5	....
Lewistown	14	11	3	Syracuse	3	3	....
Livingston	17	12	5	Tecumseh	4	3	1
Manhattan	1	1	....	Tekamah	4	4	....
Miles City-Custer County	16	12	4	Valentine	4	4	....
Missoula	81	66	15	Valley	4	4	....
Plentywood	4	3	1	Wahoo	6	6	....
Polson	7	7	....	Wayne	11	7	4
Red Lodge	5	5	....	West Point	6	6	....
Ronan City	4	4	....	Wilber	4	4	....
St. Ignatius	1	1	....	Wymore	3	3	....
Sidney	11	10	1	York	16	12	4
Thompson Falls	2	2	....				
Three Forks	2	2	....	**NEVADA**			
Troy	2	2	....				
West Yellowstone	9	4	5	Boulder City	27	22	5
Whitefish	17	12	5	Carlin	7	6	1
Whitehall	3	2	1	Fallon	27	18	9
				Henderson	157	98	59
NEBRASKA				Las Vegas Metropolitan Police Department Jurisdiction	2,102	1,445	657
Albion	3	3	....	Lovelock	7	6	1
Alliance	27	20	7	Mesquite	13	9	4
Ashland	5	4	1	North Las Vegas	164	116	48
Auburn	5	5	....	Reno	421	282	139
Aurora	8	7	1	Sparks	114	71	43
Beatrice	26	20	6	Wells	5	5	....
Bellevue	64	49	15	Winnemucca	17	14	3
Blair	11	10	1				
Broken Bow	9	8	1	**NEW HAMPSHIRE**			
Central City	6	5	1				
Chadron	18	12	6	Amherst	13	12	1
Columbus	35	25	10	Ashland	6	5	1
Cozad	10	6	4	Atkinson	2	2	....
Crete	14	9	5	Auburn	7	5	2
David City	6	5	1	Barrington	7	6	1
Elkhorn	5	5	....	Bedford	30	22	8
Fairbury	7	6	1	Berlin	23	21	2
Falls City	13	9	4	Boscawen	6	5	1
Fremont	37	29	8	Bow	11	7	4
Geneva	3	3	....	Bristol	7	6	1
Gering	17	14	3	Candia	5	4	1
Gordon	7	5	2	Charlestown	7	4	3
Gothenburg	10	6	4	Chesterfield	4	4	....
Grand Island	64	57	7	Claremont	29	24	5
Hastings	54	37	17	Colebrook	3	3	....
Holdrege	13	9	4	Concord	82	63	19
Imperial	4	4	....	Conway	28	19	9
Kearney	45	37	8	Derry	54	44	10
Kimball	6	5	1	Dover	56	47	9
La Vista	22	19	3	Durham	16	14	2
Lexington	15	13	2	Enfield	7	6	1
Lincoln	340	256	84	Epping	5	4	1
McCook	17	14	3	Exeter	30	23	7
Milford	5	5	....	Farmington	12	11	1
Minden	5	4	1	Fitzwilliam	3	2	1
Mitchell	5	5	....	Franklin	23	17	6
Nebraska City	12	11	1	Gilford	18	12	6
Neligh	3	3	....	Goffstown	33	23	10

Table 78.— Number of Full-time Law Enforcement Employees, Cities, October 31, 1993 — Continued

City	Total police employees	Total officers	Total civilians	City	Total police employees	Total officers	Total civilians
NEW HAMPSHIRE — Continued				**NEW JERSEY — Continued**			
Gorham	8	8	....	Audubon	18	17	1
Greenfield	1	1	....	Audubon Park	4	4	....
Hampstead	3	3	....	Avalon	31	21	10
Hampton	40	32	8	Avon-by-the-Sea	10	10	....
Hanover	24	15	9	Barnegat Township	25	21	4
Henniker	7	6	1	Barrington	16	15	1
Hinsdale	5	4	1	Bay Head	9	8	1
Holderness	6	5	1	Bayonne	190	171	19
Hollis	8	7	1	Beach Haven	17	13	4
Hooksett	33	20	13	Beachwood	16	14	2
Hudson	37	28	9	Bedminster Township	15	14	1
Jaffrey	13	11	2	Belleville	97	93	4
Keene	55	42	13	Bellmawr	25	19	6
Kingston	6	5	1	Belmar	27	22	5
Laconia	42	33	9	Belvidere	6	6	....
Lancaster	6	6	....	Bergenfield	54	49	5
Lebanon	35	30	5	Berkeley Heights	31	26	5
Lincoln	13	9	4	Berkeley Township	75	59	16
Litchfield	9	8	1	Berlin	16	15	1
Littleton	10	9	1	Berlin Township	18	16	2
Londonderry	43	32	11	Bernards Township	35	26	9
Manchester	229	178	51	Bernardsville	21	15	6
Meredith	14	11	3	Beverly	7	7	....
Merrimack	42	31	11	Blairstown Township	10	6	4
Milford	22	19	3	Bloomfield	136	117	19
Milton	4	3	1	Bloomingdale	13	13	....
Moultonboro	7	6	1	Bogota	20	20	....
Nashua	191	139	52	Boonton	25	18	7
New Castle	2	2	....	Boonton Township	10	10	....
Newington	10	9	1	Bordentown	11	10	1
Newmarket	11	10	1	Bordentown Township	25	19	6
Newport	16	12	4	Bound Brook	23	18	5
Newton	5	4	1	Bradley Beach	19	16	3
Northfield	7	6	1	Branchburg Township	19	18	1
North Hampton	10	9	1	Brick Township	117	91	26
Northumberland	4	4	....	Bridgeton	68	59	9
Northwood	4	3	1	Bridgewater Township	72	58	14
Orford	1	1	....	Brielle	16	14	2
Pembroke	9	8	1	Brigantine	41	33	8
Peterboro	12	10	2	Brooklawn	6	6	....
Pittsfield	5	4	1	Buena	14	9	5
Plaistow	17	11	6	Burlington	35	31	4
Plymouth	17	10	7	Burlington Township	42	34	8
Portsmouth	87	66	21	Butler	15	13	2
Raymond	10	9	1	Byram Township	15	13	2
Rindge	6	5	1	Caldwell	24	22	2
Rochester	48	37	11	Califon	2	2	....
Rye	9	8	1	Camden	410	314	96
Salem	62	47	15	Cape May	23	17	6
Seabrook	26	19	7	Carlstadt	31	27	4
Somersworth	26	19	7	Carney's Point Township	23	18	5
Swanzey	6	5	1	Carteret	61	51	10
Tilton	9	8	1	Cedar Grove Township	31	30	1
Troy	2	2	....	Chatham	25	19	6
Wakefield	8	7	1	Chatham Township	31	25	6
Webster	2	2	....	Cherry Hill Township	152	122	30
Wilton	6	5	1	Chesilhurst	8	7	1
Winchester	5	4	1	Chester	9	8	1
Windham	20	15	5	Chesterfield Township	1	1	....
Wolfeboro	12	9	3	Chester Township	18	17	1
Woodstock	4	4	....	Cinnaminson Township	30	25	5
				Clark Township	51	44	7
NEW JERSEY				Clayton	22	12	10
				Clementon	12	11	1
Aberdeen Township	35	28	7	Cliffside Park	40	35	5
Absecon	29	27	2	Clifton	149	130	19
Allendale	17	13	4	Clinton	7	7	....
Allenhurst	12	8	4	Clinton Township	19	17	2
Allentown	6	6	....	Closter	21	19	2
Alpha	3	3	....	Collingswood	29	25	4
Alpine	11	11	....	Colts Neck Township	18	16	2
Andover Township	11	7	4	Cranbury Township	12	11	1
Asbury Park	68	62	6	Cranford Township	66	49	17
Atlantic City	562	420	142	Cresskill	25	22	3
Atlantic Highlands	16	13	3	Deal	17	13	4

Table 78. — Number of Full-time Law Enforcement Employees, Cities, October 31, 1993 — Continued

City	Total police employees	Total officers	Total civilians	City	Total police employees	Total officers	Total civilians
NEW JERSEY — Continued				**NEW JERSEY — Continued**			
Delanco Township	8	7	1	Hammonton	31	25	6
Delaware Township	6	6	....	Hanover Township	36	28	8
Delran Township	28	22	6	Harding Township	16	15	1
Demarest	12	12	....	Hardyston Township	20	14	6
Denville Township	34	26	8	Harrington Park	11	11	....
Deptford Township	61	51	10	Harrison	50	49	1
Dover	36	33	3	Harrison Township	9	9	....
Dover Township	158	125	33	Harvey Cedars	8	7	1
Dumont	37	33	4	Hasbrouck Heights	33	31	2
Dunellen	18	14	4	Haworth	14	12	2
Eastampton Township	16	14	2	Hawthorne	30	29	1
East Brunswick Township	119	87	32	Hazlet Township	53	45	8
East Greenwich Township	13	12	1	Helmetta	3	3	....
East Hanover Township	33	27	6	High Bridge	6	6	....
East Newark	8	8	....	Highland Park	37	30	7
East Orange	290	272	18	Highlands	18	13	5
East Rutherford	26	25	1	Hightstown	16	11	5
East Windsor Township	56	43	13	Hillsborough Township	47	38	9
Eatontown	42	32	10	Hillsdale	22	21	1
Edgewater	25	24	1	Hillside Township	83	71	12
Edgewater Park Township	14	13	1	Hi Nella	3	3	....
Edison Township	230	183	47	Hoboken	154	142	12
Egg Harbor City	22	14	8	Ho-Ho-Kus	13	13	....
Egg Harbor Township	85	65	20	Holland Township	6	5	1
Elizabeth	421	339	82	Holmdel Township	36	26	10
Elk Township	7	6	1	Hopatcong	29	22	7
Elmer	3	3	....	Hopewell Township	33	25	8
Elmwood Park	35	32	3	Howell Township	77	62	15
Emerson	19	19	....	Independence Township	4	4	....
Englewood	94	78	16	Interlaken	5	5	....
Englewood Cliffs	26	25	1	Irvington	199	165	34
Englishtown	2	2	....	Island Heights	6	6	....
Essex Fells	13	11	2	Jackson Township	73	54	19
Evesham Township	47	42	5	Jamesburg	10	9	1
Ewing Township	83	74	9	Jefferson Township	38	32	6
Fairfield	38	34	4	Jersey City	902	821	81
Fair Haven	14	13	1	Keansburg	34	28	6
Fair Lawn	64	54	10	Kearny	130	124	6
Fairview	27	27	....	Kenilworth	26	25	1
Fanwood	22	21	1	Keyport	24	18	6
Far Hills	4	4	....	Kinnelon	16	15	1
Flemington	11	10	1	Lacey Township	45	37	8
Florence Township	25	20	5	Lakehurst	10	8	2
Florham Park	28	27	1	Lakewood	113	94	19
Fort Lee	115	97	18	Lambertville	12	10	2
Franklin	13	12	1	Laurel Springs	8	7	1
Franklin Lakes	26	21	5	Lavallette	16	11	5
Franklin Township (Gloucester County)	28	22	6	Lawnside	7	6	1
Franklin Township (Hunterdon County)	6	6	....	Lawrence Township	64	54	10
Franklin Township (Somerset County)	100	81	19	Lebanon Township	8	7	1
Freehold	31	23	8	Leonia	24	18	6
Freehold Township	56	45	11	Lincoln Park	27	25	2
Frenchtown	4	4	....	Linden	138	122	16
Galloway Township	44	40	4	Lindenwold	35	32	3
Garfield	57	50	7	Linwood	21	17	4
Garwood	18	16	2	Little Egg Harbor Township	37	28	9
Gibbsboro	2	2	....	Little Falls Township	25	20	5
Glassboro	49	39	10	Little Ferry	28	25	3
Glen Ridge	33	27	6	Little Silver	18	14	4
Glen Rock	24	20	4	Livingston	65	57	8
Gloucester City	28	24	4	Lodi	44	41	3
Gloucester Township	89	71	18	Logan Township	12	12	....
Green Brook	19	14	5	Long Beach Township	41	35	6
Greenwich Township (Gloucester County)	20	14	6	Long Branch	93	75	18
Greenwich Township (Warren County)	3	3	....	Long Hill Township	26	19	7
Guttenberg	24	21	3	Longport	15	11	4
Hackensack	130	106	24	Lopatcong Township	14	9	5
Hackettstown	22	17	5	Lower Alloways Creek Township	18	13	5
Haddonfield	27	21	6	Lower Township	53	41	12
Haddon Heights	21	16	5	Lumberton Township	20	18	2
Haddon Township	26	23	3	Lyndhurst Township	52	48	4
Haledon	21	16	5	Madison	38	34	4
Hamburg	7	6	1	Magnolia	8	8	....
Hamilton Township (Atlantic County)	51	38	13	Mahwah Township	56	50	6
Hamilton Township (Mercer County)	208	171	37	Manalapan Township	57	45	12

Table 78. — Number of Full-time Law Enforcement Employees, Cities, October 31, 1993 — Continued

City	Total police employees	Total officers	Total civilians	City	Total police employees	Total officers	Total civilians
NEW JERSEY — Continued				**NEW JERSEY — Continued**			
Manasquan	23	17	6	Oceanport	19	14	5
Manchester Township	79	64	15	Ocean Township (Monmouth County)	69	55	14
Mansfield Township (Burlington County)	3	3	....	Ocean Township (Ocean County)	16	12	4
Mansfield Township (Warren County)	11	11	....	Ogdensburg	7	7	....
Mantoloking	8	7	1	Old Bridge	114	81	33
Mantua Township	28	18	10	Old Tappan	13	12	1
Manville	24	23	1	Oradell	22	21	1
Maple Shade Township	38	30	8	Orange	119	105	14
Maplewood Township	66	56	10	Oxford Township	5	5	....
Margate City	40	31	9	Palisades Park	32	28	4
Marlboro Township	70	53	17	Palmyra	16	15	1
Matawan	27	21	6	Paramus	114	89	25
Maywood	25	24	1	Park Ridge	21	18	3
Medford Lakes	9	8	1	Parsippany-Troy Hills Township	133	111	22
Medford Township	42	33	9	Passaic	146	136	10
Mendham	11	10	1	Paterson	404	364	40
Mendham Township	16	14	2	Paulsboro	20	14	6
Merchantville	13	12	1	Peapack and Gladstone	9	8	1
Metuchen	36	30	6	Pemberton	3	3	....
Middlesex	33	31	2	Pemberton Township	53	46	7
Middle Township	53	40	13	Pennsauken	122	92	30
Middletown Township	119	95	24	Penns Grove	22	17	5
Midland Park	15	11	4	Pennsville Township	33	26	7
Milford	1	1	....	Pequannock Township	32	27	5
Millburn Township	63	58	5	Perth Amboy	134	120	14
Milltown	15	12	3	Phillipsburg	35	29	6
Millville	74	61	13	Pine Beach	7	6	1
Mine Hill Township	9	8	1	Pine Hill	17	15	2
Monmouth Beach	11	10	1	Pine Valley	7	6	1
Monroe Township (Gloucester County)	61	47	14	Piscataway Township	100	84	16
Monroe Township (Middlesex County)	44	31	13	Pitman	18	13	5
Montclair	118	102	16	Plainfield	182	146	36
Montgomery Township	27	19	8	Plainsboro Township	35	26	9
Montvale	23	21	2	Pleasantville	51	43	8
Montville Township	36	34	2	Plumsted Township	5	4	1
Moonachie	18	15	3	Pohatcong Township	7	6	1
Moorestown Township	40	31	9	Point Pleasant	34	26	8
Morris Plains	23	18	5	Point Pleasant Beach	28	21	7
Morristown	66	57	9	Pompton Lakes	25	18	7
Morris Township	53	45	8	Princeton	41	33	8
Mountain Lakes	15	12	3	Princeton Township	37	30	7
Mountainside	26	21	5	Prospect Park	10	10	....
Mount Arlington	9	8	1	Rahway	83	76	7
Mount Ephraim	12	11	1	Ramsey	33	28	5
Mount Holly	26	23	3	Randolph Township	45	37	8
Mount Laurel Township	62	48	14	Raritan	18	16	2
Mount Olive Township	46	39	7	Raritan Township	31	28	3
Mullica Township	14	13	1	Readington Township	17	15	2
National Park	6	6	....	Red Bank	48	40	8
Neptune	21	15	6	Ridgefield	31	28	3
Neptune Township	79	64	15	Ridgefield Park	33	30	3
Netcong	8	7	1	Ridgewood	51	44	7
Newark	1,299	1,151	148	Ringwood	28	22	6
New Brunswick	155	123	32	Riverdale	14	10	4
Newfield	4	4	....	River Edge	27	24	3
New Hanover Township	2	2	....	Riverside	13	12	1
New Milford	35	32	3	Riverton	6	6	....
New Providence	28	23	5	River Vale	19	19	....
Newton	24	18	6	Rochelle Park Township	20	20	....
North Arlington	47	40	7	Rockaway	14	13	1
North Bergen Township	127	114	13	Rockaway Township	65	50	15
North Brunswick Township	92	77	15	Roseland	23	22	1
North Caldwell	19	17	2	Roselle	66	54	12
Northfield	26	19	7	Roselle Park	34	30	4
North Haledon	16	12	4	Roxbury Township	42	35	7
North Hanover Township	6	5	1	Rumson	19	17	2
North Plainfield	46	40	6	Runnemede	16	14	2
Northvale	13	12	1	Rutherford	48	42	6
North Wildwood	35	31	4	Saddle Brook Township	35	33	2
Norwood	14	14	....	Saddle River	15	13	2
Nutley	67	59	8	Salem	25	19	6
Oakland	34	29	5	Sayreville	100	83	17
Oaklyn	9	8	1	Scotch Plains	46	41	5
Ocean City	76	62	14	Sea Bright	13	9	4
Ocean Gate	6	6	....	Sea Girt	13	11	2

Table 78.—Number of Full-time Law Enforcement Employees, Cities, October 31, 1993—Continued

City	Total police employees	Total officers	Total civilians	City	Total police employees	Total officers	Total civilians
NEW JERSEY—Continued				**NEW JERSEY—Continued**			
Sea Isle City	27	21	6	West Paterson	21	20	1
Seaside Heights	35	26	9	Westville	12	8	4
Seaside Park	16	13	3	West Wildwood	4	4	....
Secaucus	74	65	9	West Windsor Township	47	36	11
Ship Bottom	10	9	1	Westwood	26	25	1
Shrewsbury	19	14	5	Wharton	10	9	1
Somerdale	11	10	1	Wildwood	48	39	9
Somers Point	30	24	6	Wildwood Crest	26	21	5
Somerville	42	35	7	Willingboro Township	82	68	14
South Amboy	32	30	2	Winfield Township	11	8	3
South Belmar	9	9	....	Winslow Township	73	64	9
South Bound Brook	13	13	....	Woodbridge Township	234	194	40
South Brunswick Township	88	65	23	Woodbury	34	26	8
South Hackensack	19	19	....	Woodbury Heights	8	7	1
South Harrison Township	4	3	1	Woodcliff Lake	17	16	1
South Orange	58	50	8	Woodlynne	8	7	1
South Plainfield	66	54	12	Wood Ridge	21	19	2
South River	35	29	6	Woodstown	8	7	1
South Toms River	7	6	1	Woolwich Township	6	5	1
Sparta Township	36	29	7	Wyckoff	25	22	3
Spotswood	22	18	4				
Springfield	47	43	4	**NEW MEXICO**			
Springfield Township	3	3	....				
Spring Lake	17	13	4	Alamogordo	79	58	21
Spring Lake Heights	14	12	2	Albuquerque	1,053	751	302
Stafford Township	50	38	12	Artesia	36	22	14
Stanhope	7	6	1	Aztec	22	13	9
Stillwater Township	2	2	....	Bayard	7	6	1
Stone Harbor	23	19	4	Belen	24	17	7
Stratford	13	12	1	Bernalillo	17	11	6
Summit	55	42	13	Bloomfield	20	14	6
Surf City	14	10	4	Capitan	1	1	....
Swedesboro	5	5	....	Clayton	14	5	9
Teaneck Township	111	96	15	Corrales	15	10	5
Tenafly	32	29	3	Cuba	6	2	4
Tewksbury Township	8	8	....	Deming	32	26	6
Tinton Falls	39	30	9	Eunice	9	5	4
Totowa	26	24	2	Farmington	143	92	51
Trenton	438	385	53	Gallup	109	59	50
Tuckerton	8	7	1	Grants	38	19	19
Union Beach	17	14	3	Hobbs	106	67	39
Union City	201	175	26	Hurley	4	4	....
Union Township	165	116	49	Jal	9	5	4
Upper Saddle River	21	17	4	Los Lunas	30	23	7
Ventnor City	46	36	10	Lovington	27	18	9
Vernon Township	35	26	9	Milan	13	8	5
Verona	33	29	4	Mountainair	5	3	2
Vineland	136	120	16	Portales	32	23	9
Voorhees Township	53	41	12	Questa	4	3	1
Waldwick	23	19	4	Raton	22	16	6
Wallington	19	19	....	Red River	9	4	5
Wall Township	63	50	13	Rio Rancho	108	68	40
Wanaque	20	17	3	Roswell	103	83	20
Warren Township	29	22	7	Ruidoso	31	20	11
Washington	19	12	7	Ruidoso Downs	10	6	4
Washington Township (Bergen County)	21	21	....	San Ildefonso Pueblo	4	3	1
Washington Township (Gloucester County)	80	66	14	Silver City	31	24	7
Washington Township (Mercer County)	21	16	5	Socorro	26	15	11
Washington Township (Morris County)	35	27	8	Taos	31	18	13
Washington Township (Warren County)	11	10	1	Taos Pueblo Tribal	12	7	5
Watchung	28	21	7	Tatum	7	3	4
Waterford Township	20	18	2	Truth or Consequences	19	12	7
Wayne Township	135	110	25	Tucumcari	27	21	6
Weehawken Township	48	46	2	Tularosa	13	8	5
Wenonah	6	5	1	Wagon Mound	1	1	....
Westampton Township	21	18	3				
West Amwell Township	6	4	2	**NEW YORK**			
West Caldwell	31	29	2				
West Cape May	6	6	....	Addison Town and Village	1	1	....
West Deptford Township	36	29	7	Albany	380	314	66
Westfield	69	59	10	Albion Village	12	11	1
West Long Branch	21	17	4	Alexandria Bay Village	4	4	....
West Milford Township	50	43	7	Alfred Village	6	6	....
West New York	105	102	3	Altamont Village	1	1	....
West Orange	110	98	12	Amherst Town	174	147	27

Table 78. — Number of Full-time Law Enforcement Employees, Cities, October 31, 1993 — Continued

City	Total police employees	Total officers	Total civilians	City	Total police employees	Total officers	Total civilians
NEW YORK — Continued				**NEW YORK — Continued**			
Amity Town and Belmont Village	1	1	....	Eastchester Town	62	52	10
Amityville Village	25	23	2	East Fishkill Town	28	20	8
Amsterdam	34	32	2	East Greenbush Town	24	17	7
Angola Village	3	3	....	East Hampton Town	57	46	11
Ardsley	17	17	....	East Hampton Village	23	22	1
Asharoken Village	3	3	....	East Rochester Village	9	8	1
Auburn	64	56	8	East Syracuse Village	11	8	3
Avon Village	3	3	....	Eden Town	5	4	1
Baldwinsville Village	15	12	3	Ellenville Village	14	12	2
Ballston Spa Village	11	6	5	Ellicott Town	12	11	1
Batavia	35	29	6	Ellicottville	1	1	....
Bath Village	15	11	4	Elmira	81	75	6
Beacon	36	34	2	Elmira Heights Village	9	9	....
Bedford Town	39	36	3	Elmira Town	4	4	....
Bethlehem Town	46	34	12	Elmsford Village	15	15	....
Binghamton	151	142	9	Endicott Village	37	36	1
Blooming Grove Town	12	11	1	Evans Town	24	19	5
Bolivar Village	1	1	....	Fairport Village	12	11	1
Boonville Village	3	3	....	Fallsburg Town	24	20	4
Brant Town	1	1	....	Floral Park Village	45	36	9
Briarcliff Manor Village	18	18	....	Florida Village	1	1	....
Brighton Town	47	38	9	Fort Edward Village	4	4	....
Brockport Village	10	10	....	Fort Plain Village	3	3	....
Bronxville Village	22	22	....	Frankfort Village	4	4	....
Buchanan Village	7	7	....	Fredonia Village	17	16	1
Buffalo	1,065	931	134	Freeport Village	104	88	16
Cairo Town	1	1	....	Fulton	36	33	3
Caledonia Village	2	2	....	Garden City Village	67	53	14
Cambridge Village	2	2	....	Gates Town	35	29	6
Camden Village	2	2	....	Geddes Town	16	15	1
Camillus Town and Village	18	17	1	Geneseo Village	6	6	....
Canajoharie Village	4	4	....	Geneva	35	31	4
Canandaigua	32	26	6	Glen Cove	56	50	6
Canastota Village	5	5	....	Glens Falls	41	33	8
Canisteo Village	2	2	....	Glenville Town	28	19	9
Canton Village	12	10	2	Gloversville	35	33	2
Carmel Town	40	37	3	Goshen	2	2	....
Carroll Town	1	1	....	Goshen Village	13	12	1
Carthage Village	7	6	1	Gouverneur Village	12	8	4
Catskill Village	15	15	....	Gowanda Village	4	4	....
Cayuga Heights Village	7	6	1	Granville Village	6	6	....
Cazenovia Village	5	5	....	Great Neck Estates Village	14	13	1
Centre Island Village	5	5	....	Greece Town	94	88	6
Chatham Village	1	1	....	Greenburgh Town	121	100	21
Chester Town	3	3	....	Greene Village	2	2	....
Chester Village	7	7	....	Green Island Village	4	4	....
Chittenango Village	6	5	1	Greenport Town	1	1	....
Clayton Village	4	4	....	Greenport Village	9	9	....
Clay Town	24	19	5	Greenwich Village	1	1	....
Clifton Springs Village	1	1	....	Greenwood Lake Village	13	10	3
Clyde Village	2	2	....	Groton Village	2	2	....
Cobleskill Village	9	9	....	Guilderland Town	33	23	10
Coeymans Town	6	3	3	Hamburg Town	77	63	14
Cohocton Town	1	1	....	Hamburg Village	21	15	6
Cohoes	36	33	3	Hamilton Village	5	4	1
Cold Spring Village	2	2	....	Harriman Village	5	5	....
Colonie Town	149	107	42	Harrison Town	68	60	8
Cooperstown Village	7	6	1	Hastings-on-Hudson Village	21	21	....
Corinth Village	4	4	....	Haverstraw Town	29	28	1
Corning	25	25	....	Haverstraw Village	21	21	....
Cornwall-on-the-Hudson Village	5	5	....	Head of the Harbor Village	2	2	....
Cornwall Town	15	10	5	Hempstead Village	128	99	29
Cortland	42	39	3	Herkimer Village	21	20	1
Cortlandt Town	17	10	7	Highland Falls Village	11	7	4
Coxsackie Village	1	1	....	Holley Village	3	3	....
Dansville Village	11	8	3	Homer Village	5	4	1
Delhi Village	4	4	....	Hoosick Falls Village	3	3	....
Depew Village	39	31	8	Hornell	21	20	1
Deposit Village	3	3	....	Horseheads Village	14	10	4
Dewitt Town	35	32	3	Hudson	21	20	1
Dobbs Ferry Village	24	23	1	Hudson Falls Village	15	11	4
Dolgeville Village	4	4	....	Ilion Village	18	16	2
Dryden Village	4	3	1	Inlet Town	6	3	3
Dunkirk	32	32	....	Irondequoit Town	63	53	10
East Aurora-Aurora Town	19	15	4	Irvington Village	20	20	....

Table 78. — Number of Full-time Law Enforcement Employees, Cities, October 31, 1993 — Continued

City	Total police employees	Total officers	Total civilians	City	Total police employees	Total officers	Total civilians
NEW YORK — Continued				**NEW YORK — Continued**			
Ithaca.	82	70	12	Oneida.	23	20	3
Jamestown.	82	68	14	Oneonta.	27	24	3
Johnson City Village.	43	38	5	Orchard Park Town.	31	30	1
Johnstown.	23	23	....	Ossining Town.	13	13	....
Kenmore Village.	27	26	1	Ossining Village.	54	49	5
Kensington Village.	6	6	....	Oswego.	54	48	6
Kent Town.	19	14	5	Owego Village.	9	7	2
Kings Point Village.	24	24	....	Oxford Village.	1	1	....
Kingston.	79	74	5	Oyster Bay Cove Village.	10	10	....
Lackawanna.	59	41	18	Painted Post Village.	4	4	....
Lake Placid Village.	17	14	3	Pawling Village.	3	3	....
Lake Success Village.	25	22	3	Pelham Village.	26	23	3
Lakewood-Busti.	10	9	1	Penn Yan Village.	12	11	1
Lancaster Town.	34	29	5	Perry Village.	5	5	....
Lancaster Village.	21	15	6	Phoenix Village.	3	3	....
Larchmont Village.	30	27	3	Piermont Village.	7	7	....
Laurel Hollow Village.	8	8	....	Plattsburgh.	48	43	5
Le Roy Village.	12	9	3	Pleasantville Village.	24	22	2
Lewiston Village.	2	2	....	Port Chester Village.	58	54	4
Liberty Village.	17	14	3	Port Dickinson Village.	4	3	1
Liverpool Village.	9	8	1	Port Jervis.	25	25	....
Lloyd Harbor Village.	12	11	1	Port Washington Village.	63	54	9
Lloyd Town.	8	8	....	Potsdam Village.	19	15	4
Lockport.	51	49	2	Poughkeepsie.	94	81	13
Lowville Village.	6	6	....	Poughkeepsie Town.	86	75	11
Lynbrook Village.	49	42	7	Pound Ridge Town.	2	2	....
Lyons Village.	12	10	2	Pulaski Village.	2	2	....
Macedon Town and Village.	2	2	....	Putnam Valley Town.	17	11	6
Malone Village.	17	17	....	Quogue Village.	13	13	....
Malverne Village.	22	22	....	Ramapo Town.	114	102	12
Mamaroneck Town.	41	40	1	Rensselaer.	32	26	6
Mamaroneck Village.	53	48	5	Rhinebeck Village.	3	2	1
Manlius Town.	42	37	5	Riverhead Town.	81	67	14
Marcellus Village.	1	1	....	Rochester.	810	670	140
Massena Village.	21	20	1	Rockville Centre Village.	59	49	10
Medina Village.	14	11	3	Rome.	70	66	4
Menands Village.	10	10	....	Rosendale Town.	3	3	....
Middleport Village.	2	2	....	Rotterdam Town.	52	41	11
Middletown.	65	58	7	Rouses Point Village.	3	3	....
Mohawk Village.	4	4	....	Rye.	40	35	5
Monroe Village.	16	13	3	Rye Brook Village.	24	23	1
Montgomery Town.	2	1	1	Sag Harbor Village.	14	13	1
Monticello Village.	23	20	3	St. Johnsville Village.	3	3	....
Moriah Town.	1	1	....	Salamanca.	13	13	....
Mount Hope Town.	1	1	....	Saltaire Village.	1	1	....
Mount Kisco Village.	34	32	2	Sands Point Village.	20	20	....
Mount Pleasant Town.	47	43	4	Saranac Lake Village.	13	13	....
Mount Vernon.	240	166	74	Saratoga Springs.	68	62	6
Newark Village.	19	18	1	Saugerties Town.	17	13	4
Newburgh.	80	70	10	Saugerties Village.	11	10	1
Newburgh Town.	49	37	12	Schenectady.	167	146	21
New Castle Town.	37	35	2	Schodack Town.	8	7	1
New Hartford Town and Village.	25	14	11	Schoharie Village.	1	1	....
New Paltz Town and Village.	26	20	6	Scotia Village.	15	14	1
New Rochelle.	215	177	38	Seneca Falls Village.	16	12	4
New Windsor Town.	44	31	13	Shawangunk Town.	2	2	....
New York.	39,442	29,327	10,115	Shelter Island Town.	9	7	2
New York Mills Village.	2	1	1	Sherburne Village.	1	1	....
Niagara Falls.	182	162	20	Sherrill.	4	4	....
Niagara Town.	5	4	1	Sidney Village.	8	8	....
Niskayuna Town.	34	27	7	Silver Creek Village.	6	5	1
Nissequogue Village.	4	4	....	Skaneateles Village.	5	5	....
North Castle Town.	31	28	3	Solvay Village.	13	13	....
North Greenbush Town.	10	9	1	Southampton Town.	112	87	25
Northport Village.	19	16	3	Southampton Village.	35	24	11
North Syracuse Village.	13	10	3	South Glens Falls Village.	6	6	....
North Tarrytown Village.	24	24	....	South Nyack-Grandview.	6	6	....
North Tonawanda.	59	56	3	Southold Town.	52	39	13
Norwich.	21	20	1	Southport Town.	1	1	....
Norwood Village.	1	1	....	Spring Valley Village.	56	52	4
Ocean Beach Village.	2	2	....	Stony Point Town.	28	27	1
Ogdensburg.	29	24	5	Suffern Village.	31	26	5
Ogden Town.	13	10	3	Syracuse.	522	432	90
Old Brookville Village.	52	41	11	Tarrytown Village.	38	32	6
Olean.	37	35	2	Ticonderoga Town.	7	7	....

Table 78.—Number of Full-time Law Enforcement Employees, Cities, October 31, 1993—Continued

City	Total police employees	Total officers	Total civilians	City	Total police employees	Total officers	Total civilians
NEW YORK—Continued				**NORTH CAROLINA—Continued**			
Tonawanda	35	31	4	Bryson City	5	5	....
Tonawanda Town	150	105	45	Bunn	3	3	....
Trumansburg Village	1	1	....	Burgaw	6	6	....
Tuckahoe Village	28	24	4	Burlington	115	87	28
Tupper Lake Village	12	11	1	Butner	44	38	6
Tuxedo Park Village	7	3	4	Candor	4	4	....
Tuxedo Town	10	10	....	Canton	17	14	3
Ulster Town	23	19	4	Cape Carteret	5	5	....
Vernon Village	1	1	....	Carolina Beach	25	19	6
Vestal Town	41	33	8	Carrboro	29	27	2
Walden Village	11	8	3	Cary	79	62	17
Wallkill Town	23	18	5	Catawba	1	1	....
Walton Village	6	5	1	Chadbourn	8	6	2
Warwick Town	30	26	4	Chapel Hill	94	72	22
Washingtonville Village	9	8	1	Charlotte	1,152	940	212
Waterford Town and Village	11	8	3	Cherryville	18	15	3
Waterloo Village	9	8	1	China Grove	6	6	....
Watertown	66	62	4	Claremont	5	5	....
Watervliet	25	25	....	Clayton	26	20	6
Watkins Glen Village	5	5	....	Clinton	33	25	8
Waverly Village	15	10	5	Clyde	3	3	....
Wayland Village	1	1	....	Coats	5	5	....
Webb Town	4	4	....	Concord	90	72	18
Webster Town and Village	41	29	12	Conover	19	18	1
Wellsville Village	15	11	4	Conway	1	1	....
Westfield Village	5	5	....	Cooleemee	3	3	....
Westhampton Beach Village	16	14	2	Cornelius	22	15	7
West Seneca Town	71	66	5	Cramerton	8	8	....
Whitehall Village	3	3	....	Creedmoor	10	7	3
White Plains	243	200	43	Dallas	12	9	3
Whitesboro Village	6	6	....	Davidson	13	9	4
Whitestown Town	5	5	....	Dobson	4	4	....
Windham Town	2	2	....	Drexel	5	5	....
Woodbury Town	16	13	3	Dunn	38	30	8
Woodridge Village	1	1	....	Durham	352	297	55
Yonkers	588	506	82	East Spencer	4	4	....
Yorktown Town	57	50	7	Eden	49	44	5
Yorkville Village	2	2	....	Edenton	18	16	2
				Elizabeth City	43	36	7
NORTH CAROLINA				Elizabethtown	13	12	1
				Elkin	20	18	2
Aberdeen	19	17	2	Elm City	3	3	....
Ahoskie	21	16	5	Elon College	10	9	1
Albemarle	48	42	6	Emerald Isle	18	14	4
Andrews	4	4	....	Enfield	14	10	4
Angier	12	8	4	Erwin	13	9	4
Apex	23	17	6	Eureka	1	1	....
Archdale	20	15	5	Fair Bluff	4	4	....
Asheboro	50	45	5	Fairmont	15	11	4
Asheville	195	151	44	Farmville	20	16	4
Atlantic Beach	27	23	4	Fayetteville	296	229	67
Aulander	2	2	....	Forest City	27	22	5
Aurora	1	1	....	Four Oaks	3	3	....
Ayden	19	15	4	Foxfire Village	2	2	....
Bailey	2	2	....	Franklinton	9	8	1
Banner Elk	4	4	....	Fremont	3	3	....
Battleboro	3	3	....	Fuquay-Varina	17	12	5
Beaufort	12	12	....	Garner	39	36	3
Beech Mountain	13	9	4	Garysburg	3	3	....
Belhaven	12	9	3	Gastonia	189	155	34
Belmont	25	20	5	Gibsonville	13	10	3
Benson	19	15	4	Goldsboro	109	87	22
Bessemer City	16	11	5	Graham	23	21	2
Bethel	5	5	....	Granite Falls	12	11	1
Beulaville	4	4	....	Greensboro	543	422	121
Biscoe	6	6	....	Greenville	145	116	29
Black Creek	2	2	....	Grifton	6	5	1
Black Mountain	17	13	4	Hamlet	22	17	5
Bladenboro	5	5	....	Havelock	29	22	7
Blowing Rock	12	8	4	Hazelwood	6	6	....
Boiling Springs	4	4	....	Henderson	59	51	8
Boiling Springs Lake	4	4	....	Hendersonville	47	35	12
Boone	38	33	5	Hertford	8	8	....
Brevard	20	18	2	Hickory	110	88	22
Broadway	3	3	....	Highlands	9	9	....

Table 78. — Number of Full-time Law Enforcement Employees, Cities, October 31, 1993 — Continued

City	Total police employees	Total officers	Total civilians	City	Total police employees	Total officers	Total civilians
NORTH CAROLINA — Continued				**NORTH CAROLINA — Continued**			
High Point	192	171	21	Newton Grove	2	2	....
Hillsborough	16	15	1	Norlina	5	4	1
Holden Beach	6	6	....	North Topsail Beach	7	6	1
Holly Ridge	3	3	....	North Wilkesboro	19	16	3
Holly Springs	3	3	....	Norwood	5	5	....
Hope Mills	21	14	7	Oakboro	3	3	....
Hudson	11	10	1	Oak City	1	1	....
Huntersville	13	12	1	Ocean Isle Beach	7	7	....
Indian Beach	4	4	....	Old Fort	5	5	....
Jacksonville	115	92	23	Oxford	34	28	6
Jefferson	3	3	....	Parkton	2	2	....
Jonesville	6	6	....	Pembroke	14	11	3
Kannapolis	77	70	7	Pilot Mountain	9	8	1
Kenansville	3	3	....	Pinehurst	22	17	5
Kenly	6	6	....	Pine Knoll Shores	8	8	....
Kernersville	46	37	9	Pine Level	2	2	....
Kill Devil Hills	26	21	5	Pinetops	8	5	3
King	11	10	1	Pineville	18	17	1
Kings Mountain	31	25	6	Pink Hill	1	1	....
Kinston	89	77	12	Pittsboro	7	7	....
Kitty Hawk	15	13	2	Plymouth	14	10	4
Knightdale	9	8	1	Princeton	3	3	....
La Grange	5	5	....	Raeford	15	14	1
Lake Lure	7	7	....	Raleigh	518	461	57
Lake Waccamaw	1	1	....	Ramseur	6	6	....
Landis	4	4	....	Randleman	9	9	....
Laurel Park	4	4	....	Ranlo	6	6	....
Laurinburg	31	26	5	Red Springs	17	13	4
Leland	2	2	....	Reidsville	50	43	7
Lenoir	56	48	8	Rhodhiss	1	1	....
Lewiston	3	2	1	Richlands	4	4	....
Lexington	82	65	17	River Bend	4	4	....
Liberty	8	8	....	Roanoke Rapids	42	34	8
Lillington	8	8	....	Robbins	6	6	....
Lincolnton	28	24	4	Robersonville	7	7	....
Locust	4	4	....	Rockingham	28	23	5
Long Beach	16	12	4	Rocky Mount	157	122	35
Longview	13	12	1	Rolesville	5	4	1
Louisburg	11	10	1	Rose Hill	4	4	....
Lowell	6	6	....	Rowland	9	5	4
Lucama	2	2	....	Roxboro	24	23	1
Lumberton	75	65	10	Rutherfordton	12	11	1
Madison	15	14	1	St. Pauls	13	9	4
Maggie Valley	3	3	....	Salisbury	88	68	20
Maiden	13	12	1	Saluda	2	2	....
Manteo	7	6	1	Sanford	81	67	14
Marion	22	19	3	Scotland Neck	15	8	7
Mars Hill	5	5	....	Selma	23	18	5
Marshville	6	6	....	Shelby	65	51	14
Matthews	32	24	8	Siler City	21	13	8
Maxton	12	8	4	Smithfield	35	28	7
Mayodan	13	11	2	Southern Pines	33	28	5
McAdenville	4	4	....	Southern Shores	9	9	....
Mebane	14	11	3	Southport	9	8	1
Middlesex	3	3	....	Sparta	6	6	....
Mocksville	12	11	1	Spencer	7	7	....
Monroe	81	75	6	Spindale	11	11	....
Montreat	5	5	....	Spring Hope	6	6	....
Mooresville	31	26	5	Spring Lake	22	15	7
Morehead City	26	20	6	Spruce Pine	13	9	4
Morganton	94	76	18	Stanfield	1	1	....
Morrisville	12	9	3	Stanley	12	8	4
Morven	1	1	....	Stantonsburg	3	3	....
Mount Airy	47	35	12	Star	4	4	....
Mount Gilead	5	5	....	Stoneville	4	4	....
Mount Holly	24	19	5	Sugar Mountain	6	6	....
Mount Olive	16	11	5	Surf City	8	7	1
Murfreesboro	13	9	4	Swansboro	4	4	....
Murphy	12	8	4	Sylva	8	8	....
Nags Head	20	17	3	Tarboro	34	26	8
Nashville	8	7	1	Taylortown	1	1	....
New Bern	87	67	20	Taylorsville	9	9	....
Newland	5	4	1	Thomasville	60	51	9
Newport	4	4	....	Topsail Beach	6	6	....
Newton	42	33	9	Trent Woods	3	3	....

Table 78. — Number of Full-time Law Enforcement Employees, Cities, October 31, 1993 — Continued

City	Total police employees	Total officers	Total civilians	City	Total police employees	Total officers	Total civilians
NORTH CAROLINA — Continued				**NORTH DAKOTA — Continued**			
Troutman............................	5	5	....	Thompson	1	1	....
Troy	8	8	....	Valley City........................	14	12	2
Tryon	13	9	4	Watford City.......................	3	3	....
Valdese	13	12	1	West Fargo.........................	20	14	6
Vanceboro...........................	2	2	....	Williston...........................	25	20	5
Vass	3	3	....	Wishek	2	2	....
Wadesboro	21	16	5				
Wake Forest	20	15	5	**OHIO**			
Wallace	14	12	2				
Walnut Cove	4	4	....	Akron	558	455	103
Warrenton...........................	3	3	....	Alliance	52	40	12
Warsaw	14	11	3	Amberley	17	15	2
Washington..........................	36	30	6	Amherst	20	15	5
Waxhaw	3	3	....	Archbold	7	7	....
Waynesville	24	24	....	Ashland	40	29	11
Weaverville	6	6	....	Athens	28	22	6
Weldon..............................	10	6	4	Aurora	21	16	5
Wendell	12	8	4	Bainbridge Township...............	21	15	6
West Jefferson	5	5	....	Barberton...........................	49	41	8
Whispering Pines....................	6	6	....	Bath Township	21	17	4
Whitakers	3	3	....	Bazetta Township...................	8	7	1
White Lake..........................	4	4	....	Beavercreek.........................	49	39	10
Whiteville	29	23	6	Beaver Township....................	12	8	4
Wilkesboro	16	15	1	Bedford Heights	39	33	6
Williamston.........................	18	17	1	Bellaire.............................	13	13	....
Wilmington..........................	178	148	30	Bellbrook	12	8	4
Wilson	98	81	17	Bellefontaine	29	22	7
Windsor.............................	6	6	....	Bellevue	15	12	3
Winfall..............................	1	1	....	Belpre..............................	15	10	5
Wingate.............................	4	4	....	Berea	38	30	8
Winston-Salem.......................	531	407	124	Bexley	32	24	8
Winterville	5	5	....	Blanchester	9	5	4
Winton..............................	1	1	....	Blue Ash	43	34	9
Woodfin.............................	7	7	....	Bowling Green	39	28	11
Woodland	1	1	....	Bradford............................	3	3	....
Wrightsville Beach...................	25	19	6	Brady Lake	1	1	....
Yadkinville	8	8	....	Brecksville	40	26	14
Yaupon Beach	4	4	....	Brewster............................	4	4	....
Youngsville	4	4	....	Briarwood Beach	3	3	....
Zebulon.............................	17	16	1	Bridgeport	9	6	3
				Broadview Heights	26	21	5
NORTH DAKOTA				Brooklyn............................	34	28	6
				Brookville...........................	14	9	5
Beulah..............................	7	6	1	Bryan	22	17	5
Bismarck............................	94	70	24	Bucyrus	23	17	6
Bowman.............................	3	3	....	Cadiz...............................	4	4	....
Carrington	4	4	....	Cambridge	29	23	6
Casselton............................	1	1	....	Canal Fulton	6	5	1
Cavalier.............................	3	3	....	Canfield	15	10	5
Cooperstown.........................	1	1	....	Canton	184	166	18
Crosby	3	3	....	Carlisle	6	6	....
Devils Lake..........................	16	14	2	Carrollton...........................	6	6	....
Dickinson	35	24	11	Centerville	39	31	8
Elgin	1	1	....	Chardon	13	8	5
Emerado	1	1	....	Chillicothe	57	50	7
Fargo	110	84	26	Cincinnati	1,155	933	222
Grafton.............................	12	10	2	Clear Creek Township...............	9	8	1
Grand Forks.........................	76	64	12	Cleveland...........................	1,863	1,699	164
Harvey	3	3	....	Cleveland Heights...................	117	101	16
Hazen	4	4	....	Clinton Township...................	12	8	4
Jamestown...........................	32	28	4	Clyde...............................	13	9	4
Larimore	2	2	....	Columbus...........................	1,900	1,543	357
Lehr	1	1	....	Conneaut	25	20	5
Linton	1	1	....	Cortland............................	8	8	....
Lisbon	2	2	....	Covington...........................	6	5	1
Mandan.............................	31	27	4	Crestline............................	13	9	4
Mayville.............................	3	3	....	Cuyahoga Falls	93	81	12
Minot	71	54	17	Dayton	585	486	99
Napoleon............................	1	1	....	Deer Park...........................	10	9	1
New Rockford........................	3	3	....	Delaware	40	28	12
Northwood	2	2	....	Delhi Township......................	27	24	3
Oakes...............................	2	2	....	Delta...............................	5	5	....
Rugby...............................	4	4	....	Dennison	5	5	....
Stanton	1	1	....	Dover	22	19	3
Steele...............................	1	1	....	Dublin	55	41	14

333

Table 78. — Number of Full-time Law Enforcement Employees, Cities, October 31, 1993 — Continued

City	Total police employees	Total officers	Total civilians	City	Total police employees	Total officers	Total civilians
OHIO — Continued				**OHIO — Continued**			
East Canton	2	2	....	Marlboro Township	3	3	....
East Cleveland	81	74	7	Marysville	18	14	4
Eastlake	38	30	8	Mason	19	18	1
East Palestine	10	6	4	Massillon	50	48	2
Eaton	16	11	5	Maumee	51	40	11
Elmwood Place	8	7	1	Mayfield Village	19	14	5
Elyria	101	85	16	Mayfield Heights	43	34	9
Englewood	21	16	5	McConnelsville	4	4	....
Evendale	19	18	1	Mentor	93	65	28
Fairborn	54	42	12	Mentor-on-the-Lake	13	8	5
Fairfax	8	8	....	Miamisburg	42	33	9
Fairfield	62	48	14	Miami Township	27	25	2
Fairfield Township	6	6	....	Middleburg Heights	35	29	6
Fairlawn	23	17	6	Middlefield	7	7	....
Fairport Harbor	6	6	....	Middletown	114	83	31
Fairview Park	30	29	1	Milford	15	12	3
Fayette	3	3	....	Minerva	12	8	4
Forest Park	37	31	6	Mingo Junction	12	10	2
Fort Shawnee	4	3	1	Mogadore	7	7	....
Franklin	23	18	5	Monroe	5	1	4
Fremont	37	32	5	Montgomery	19	18	1
Gahanna	43	38	5	Montpelier	7	7	....
Gallipolis	17	13	4	Moraine	34	27	7
Garfield Heights	70	55	15	Mount Sterling	8	5	3
Gates Mills	16	12	4	Munroe Falls	7	6	1
Geneva-on-the-Lake	4	4	....	Navarre	4	4	....
Germantown	11	7	4	Nelsonville	7	6	1
German Township	5	5	....	Newark	65	57	8
Gibsonburg	4	4	....	Newcomerstown	11	6	5
Girard	23	19	4	New Lebanon	8	7	1
Glendale	7	6	1	New Lexington	10	6	4
Goshen Township	7	6	1	New Paris	2	2	....
Grand Rapids	1	1	....	New Philadelphia	23	19	4
Granville	13	10	3	Newtown	5	5	....
Greenfield	11	10	1	Niles	36	30	6
Greenville	28	23	5	North Baltimore	5	5	....
Grove City	47	35	12	North Canton	30	19	11
Hamilton	118	101	17	North Kingsville	4	4	....
Harrison	19	17	2	North Olmsted	66	52	14
Hartville	4	4	....	North Ridgeville	35	27	8
Hicksville	7	6	1	North Royalton	46	29	17
Hilliard	42	31	11	Northwood	17	13	4
Howland	18	14	4	Norton	18	13	5
Hubbard	16	12	4	Norwalk	26	22	4
Huber Heights	46	42	4	Norwood	45	45	....
Hudson	14	9	5	Oak Harbor	5	4	1
Hunting Valley	12	11	1	Oakwood Village	19	15	4
Huron	14	10	4	Oberlin	18	14	4
Indian Hill	24	19	5	Ontario	18	14	4
Jackson Township	29	24	5	Oregon	53	43	10
Jefferson	6	5	1	Orrville	20	15	5
Kent	53	39	14	Ottawa Hills	15	11	4
Kettering	105	79	26	Parma Heights	42	34	8
Kirtland Hills	10	10	....	Pataskala	6	5	1
Lakemore	6	5	1	Pepper Pike	19	15	4
Lake Township	12	11	1	Perkins Township	15	11	4
Lakewood	107	86	21	Perrysburg	28	21	7
Lancaster	87	63	24	Perry Township (Stark County)	25	18	7
Lawrence Township	5	5	....	Pierce Township	13	12	1
Lebanon	29	22	7	Piqua	31	28	3
Lexington	10	6	4	Plain City	4	3	1
Liberty Township	20	19	1	Poland	4	4	....
Lima	105	85	20	Poland Township	8	8	....
Logan	19	13	6	Port Clinton	17	12	5
Lorain	125	97	28	Portsmouth	45	41	4
Lordstown	12	8	4	Randolph Township	12	11	1
Louisville	14	11	3	Reading	23	19	4
Loveland	14	13	1	Reynoldsburg	54	41	13
Lyndhurst	37	29	8	Richmond Heights	24	18	6
Madeira	12	11	1	Rittman	11	8	3
Madison Township (Lake County)	15	13	2	Riverside	5	5	....
Mansfield	128	90	38	Rossford	15	14	1
Mariemont	9	8	1	St. Marys	18	14	4
Marietta	35	28	7	Salem	20	19	1
Marion	70	51	19	Sandusky	54	48	6

Table 78. — Number of Full-time Law Enforcement Employees, Cities, October 31, 1993 — Continued

City	Total police employees	Total officers	Total civilians	City	Total police employees	Total officers	Total civilians
OHIO — Continued				**OHIO — Continued**			
Sebring	9	6	3	Worthington	38	30	8
Seven Hills	16	15	1	Wyoming	18	14	4
Seville	6	5	1	Xenia	67	45	22
Shadyside	7	5	2	Yellow Springs	12	8	4
Shaker Heights	99	66	33	Youngstown	240	210	30
Sharonville	43	32	11	Zanesville	74	57	17
Shawnee Township	16	10	6				
Sheffield Lake	12	9	3	**OKLAHOMA**			
Shelby	16	13	3				
Silverton	12	9	3	Ada	45	32	13
Solon	51	40	11	Altus	51	41	10
South Euclid	43	36	7	Alva	10	6	4
South Russell	8	8	....	Anadarko	22	15	7
Spencerville	4	4	....	Antlers	8	4	4
Springboro	18	12	6	Apache	8	4	4
Springdale	37	30	7	Ardmore	58	42	16
Springfield	158	124	34	Arkoma	6	2	4
Springfield Township (Hamilton County)	43	31	12	Atoka	14	13	1
Springfield Township (Mahoning County)	6	5	1	Barnsdall	6	4	2
Steubenville	56	47	9	Bartlesville	78	50	28
Stow	39	30	9	Beggs	6	3	3
Streetsboro	20	14	6	Bethany	33	23	10
Strongsville	63	53	10	Bixby	20	14	6
Sunbury	6	6	....	Blackwell	20	14	6
Swanton	4	4	....	Blanchard	8	4	4
Sylvania	35	29	6	Boise City	3	3	....
Sylvania Township	31	25	6	Bristow	16	13	3
Tallmadge	34	23	11	Broken Arrow	99	73	26
Tiffin	39	27	12	Broken Bow	16	11	5
Tipp City	14	13	1	Burns Flat	2	2	....
Toledo	709	654	55	Carnegie	4	4	....
Toronto	10	10	....	Catoosa	11	10	1
Trenton	11	7	4	Chandler	12	8	4
Trotwood	26	23	3	Checotah	12	8	4
Troy	37	35	2	Chelsea	4	4	....
Twinsburg	28	20	8	Cherokee	6	3	3
Uniontown	7	6	1	Chickasha	43	33	10
Union Township (Butler County)	49	38	11	Choctaw	15	13	2
Union Township (Clermont County)	43	30	13	Chouteau	5	4	1
University Heights	37	29	8	Claremore	47	31	16
Upper Arlington	61	52	9	Clayton	7	4	3
Upper Sandusky	10	8	2	Cleveland	8	8	....
Urbana	21	17	4	Clinton	28	20	8
Valley View	16	14	2	Coalgate	4	3	1
Vandalia	37	28	9	Collinsville	10	6	4
Van Wert	27	21	6	Comanche	4	4	....
Vermilion	23	18	5	Commerce	3	3	....
Village of Highland Hills	5	5	....	Cordell	7	6	1
Wadsworth	27	22	5	Coweta	12	8	4
Waite Hill	5	5	....	Crescent	7	4	3
Walbridge	7	3	4	Cushing	21	17	4
Walton Hills	15	11	4	Davis	12	9	3
Wapakoneta	18	14	4	Del City	45	34	11
Warren	98	73	25	Dewey	9	8	1
Warrensville Heights	36	32	4	Drumright	8	4	4
Washington Court House	22	16	6	Duncan	50	44	6
Waterville	11	10	1	Durant	34	27	7
Waterville Township	7	7	....	Edmond	101	83	18
Wauseon	11	9	2	Elk City	32	16	16
Waverly	17	11	6	Elmore City	6	2	4
Wellington	6	4	2	El Reno	29	24	5
West Carrollton	32	25	7	Enid	106	84	22
Westerville	68	54	14	Erick	2	2	....
West Jefferson	11	8	3	Eufaula	12	7	5
Westlake	51	40	11	Fairfax	8	4	4
Wickliffe	35	31	4	Fairview	9	5	4
Willard	18	14	4	Forest Park	3	2	1
Willoughby	46	36	10	Fort Gibson	5	5	....
Willoughby Hills	22	15	7	Frederick	16	10	6
Wilmington	18	16	2	Geary	6	2	4
Windham	4	3	1	Glenpool	17	10	7
Woodlawn	16	15	1	Goodwell	2	2	....
Woodsfield	5	5	....	Gore	3	3	....
Woodville	4	3	1	Granite	3	3	....
Wooster	42	38	4	Grove	18	11	7

City	Total police employees	Total officers	Total civilians	City	Total police employees	Total officers	Total civilians
OKLAHOMA — Continued				**OKLAHOMA — Continued**			
Guthrie	28	23	5	Prague	18	7	11
Guymon	18	13	5	Pryor	25	22	3
Harrah	6	6	....	Purcell	23	17	6
Hartshorne	5	5	....	Ringling	2	2	....
Haskell	6	6	....	Roland	10	6	4
Healdton	6	4	2	Rush Springs	3	3	....
Heavener	9	5	4	Sallisaw	19	15	4
Hennessey	8	4	4	Sand Springs	41	31	10
Henryetta	13	9	4	Sapulpa	45	35	10
Hobart	16	10	6	Sayre	8	5	3
Holdenville	12	8	4	Seiling	2	2	....
Hollis	9	5	4	Seminole	20	14	6
Hominy	11	5	6	Shattuck	6	2	4
Hugo	16	12	4	Shawnee	72	52	20
Hulbert	5	4	1	Skiatook	15	9	6
Idabel	21	15	6	Snyder	3	3	....
Inola	5	2	3	Spencer	14	12	2
Jay	11	6	5	Spiro	5	5	....
Jenks	16	12	4	Stigler	13	8	5
Jones	4	4	....	Stillwater	87	60	27
Keyes	1	1	....	Stilwell	17	11	6
Kingfisher	9	7	2	Stratford	3	3	....
Kingston	4	4	....	Stroud	13	9	4
Konawa	7	4	3	Sulphur	13	9	4
Krebs	4	4	....	Tahlequah	36	25	11
Laverne	5	2	3	Talihina	7	4	3
Lawton	183	145	38	Tecumseh	16	11	5
Lexington	9	5	4	The Village	30	24	6
Lindsay	10	7	3	Tishomingo	10	6	4
Locust Grove	8	4	4	Tonkawa	11	7	4
Lone Grove	3	3	....	Tulsa	851	738	113
Luther	2	2	....	Tuttle	8	5	3
Madill	9	9	....	Valliant	8	4	4
Mangum	10	6	4	Vian	3	3	....
Mannford	9	5	4	Vinita	17	11	6
Marietta	6	6	....	Wagoner	16	12	4
Marlow	11	11	....	Walters	4	4	....
Maud	3	3	....	Warner	4	3	1
Maysville	3	2	1	Warr Acres	30	22	8
McAlester	47	37	10	Watonga	10	7	3
McLoud	8	4	4	Waukomis	2	2	....
Meeker	4	4	....	Waurika	5	2	3
Miami	35	28	7	Waynoka	3	3	....
Midwest City	108	88	20	Weatherford	27	18	9
Minco	3	3	....	Weleetka	5	5	....
Moore	55	40	15	Westville	6	3	3
Mooreland	2	2	....	Wetumka	5	5	....
Morris	3	3	....	Wewoka	16	11	5
Muldrow	7	5	2	Wilburton	8	5	3
Muskogee	110	82	28	Woodward	29	20	9
Mustang	19	14	5	Wright City	3	3	....
Newcastle	12	8	4	Wynnewood	9	5	4
Newkirk	5	5	....	Yale	7	3	4
Nichols Hills	21	15	6	Yukon	34	26	8
Nicoma Park	5	5	....				
Noble	15	10	5	**OREGON**			
Norman	162	108	54				
Nowata	8	6	2	Albany	61	45	16
Oilton	2	2	....	Amity	1	1	....
Okeene	6	2	4	Ashland	35	24	11
Okemah	10	6	4	Astoria	23	16	7
Oklahoma City	1,284	988	296	Athena	1	1	....
Okmulgee	32	25	7	Aumsville	5	4	1
Oologah	4	4	....	Aurora	1	1	....
Owasso	28	21	7	Baker	15	11	4
Pauls Valley	20	14	6	Bandon	8	7	1
Pawhuska	12	8	4	Beaverton	89	68	21
Pawnee	6	6	....	Bend	56	43	13
Perkins	4	4	....	Boardman	3	3	....
Perry	17	13	4	Brookings	16	11	5
Piedmont	6	5	1	Burns	9	4	5
Pocola	9	6	3	Butte Falls	1	1	....
Ponca City	68	55	13	Canby	22	16	6
Porum	2	2	....	Cannon Beach	8	7	1
Poteau	19	14	5	Canyonville	4	3	1

Table 78. — Number of Full-time Law Enforcement Employees, Cities, October 31, 1993 — Continued

City	Total police employees	Total officers	Total civilians	City	Total police employees	Total officers	Total civilians
OREGON – Continued				**OREGON – Continued**			
Carlton	1	1	....	Reedsport	16	11	5
Central Point	19	13	6	Rockaway	3	3	....
Clatskanie	6	5	1	Rogue River	5	5	....
Coburg	2	2	....	Roseburg	35	32	3
Coos Bay	43	30	13	St. Helens	18	15	3
Coquille	10	8	2	Salem	228	147	81
Cornelius	13	11	2	Sandy	9	8	1
Corvallis	72	49	23	Scappoose	8	6	2
Cottage Grove	22	14	8	Seaside	22	16	6
Culver	1	1	....	Shady Cove	3	2	1
Dallas	16	15	1	Sherwood	5	5	....
Dundee	5	5	....	Silverton	13	11	2
Eagle Point	6	5	1	Sisters	6	5	1
Elgin	2	2	....	Springfield	76	53	23
Enterprise	4	4	....	Stanfield	3	3	....
Eugene	254	148	106	Stayton	13	11	2
Florence	19	12	7	Sutherlin	10	8	2
Forest Grove	28	22	6	Sweet Home	19	13	6
Garibaldi	2	2	....	Talent	6	5	1
Gaston	1	1	....	The Dalles	18	16	2
Gearhart	2	2	....	Tigard	51	43	8
Gervais	2	2	....	Tillamook	10	9	1
Gladstone	17	12	5	Toledo	12	8	4
Gold Beach	6	5	1	Troutdale	16	13	3
Gold Hill	1	1	....	Tualatin	27	24	3
Grants Pass	43	30	13	Turner	2	2	....
Gresham	124	90	34	Umatilla	7	6	1
Heppner	2	2	....	Union	2	2	....
Hermiston	22	15	7	Vale	4	4	....
Hillsboro	61	50	11	Vernonia	4	4	....
Hines	2	2	....	Waldport	4	3	1
Hood River	13	10	3	Warrenton	6	6	....
Hubbard	4	4	....	West Linn	23	18	5
Independence	11	10	1	Weston	1	1	....
Jacksonville	3	3	....	Winston	11	7	4
Jefferson	2	2	....	Woodburn	33	20	13
John Day	8	4	4	Yamhill	1	1	....
Junction City	10	6	4				
Keizer	27	23	4	**PENNSYLVANIA**			
King City	3	3	....				
Klamath Falls	32	30	2	Adams Township	3	3	....
La Grande	30	15	15	Akron	4	4	....
Lake Oswego	59	39	20	Albion	2	2	....
Lakeview	5	5	....	Alburtis	2	2	....
Lebanon	24	18	6	Aldan	5	5	....
Lincoln City	26	19	7	Aleppo Township	5	5	....
Madras	9	8	1	Aliquippa	19	19	....
McMinnville	29	23	6	Allegheny Township (Blair County)	5	5	....
Medford	103	72	31	Allegheny Township (Westmoreland County)	6	5	1
Milton-Freewater	13	9	4	Allentown	230	207	23
Milwaukie	34	24	10	Altoona	90	71	19
Molalla	9	8	1	Ambler	13	12	1
Monmouth	12	10	2	Ambridge	10	10	....
Mount Angel	6	5	1	Amity Township	5	5	....
Myrtle Creek	14	8	6	Annville Township	4	4	....
Myrtle Point	6	5	1	Archbald	7	7	....
Nehalem Bay	1	1	....	Armagh Township	2	2	....
Newberg	28	19	9	Arnold	11	10	1
Newport	25	21	4	Ashley	3	3	....
North Bend	22	17	5	Aspinwall	6	5	1
North Plains	2	2	....	Aston Township	19	17	2
Nyssa	8	7	1	Athens	5	5	....
Oakland	2	2	....	Athens Township	7	6	1
Oakridge	11	6	5	Avalon	5	5	....
Ontario	27	20	7	Avoca	2	2	....
Oregon City	27	23	4	Baden	2	2	....
Philomath	7	6	1	Baldwin	27	22	5
Phoenix	5	4	1	Baldwin Township	5	5	....
Pilot Rock	3	2	1	Bally	1	1	....
Portland	1,133	881	252	Bangor	6	6	....
Powers	2	2	....	Barrett Township	5	5	....
Prairie City	2	2	....	Beaver	11	7	4
Prineville	20	14	6	Beaver Falls	21	17	4
Rainier	6	5	1	Bedford	6	5	1
Redmond	22	18	4	Bedminister Township	5	5	....

Table 78. — Number of Full-time Law Enforcement Employees, Cities, October 31, 1993 — Continued

City	Total police employees	Total officers	Total civilians	City	Total police employees	Total officers	Total civilians
PENNSYLVANIA — Continued				**PENNSYLVANIA — Continued**			
Belle Acres	1	1	....	Christiana	1	1	....
Bellefonte	12	9	3	Churchill	9	9	....
Bellevue	16	13	3	Clairton	9	9	....
Bellwood	1	1	....	Clarks Summit	6	5	1
Bensalem Township	90	74	16	Clearfield	8	8	....
Benton	2	1	1	Cleona	2	2	....
Benzinger Township	7	6	1	Clifton Heights	11	9	2
Berlin	1	1	....	Coaldale	3	3	....
Bern Township	7	7	....	Coal Township	16	12	4
Berwick	15	11	4	Coatesville	22	19	3
Bethel Park	43	35	8	Cochranton	2	2	....
Bethlehem	155	131	24	Colebrookdale Township	10	10	....
Bethlehem Township	21	20	1	Collegeville	6	6	....
Big Beaver	3	3	....	Collier Township	9	9	....
Birdsboro	6	6	....	Collingdale	10	8	2
Birmingham Township	1	1	....	Columbia	16	14	2
Blair Township	3	3	....	Conemaugh Township (Cambria County)	1	1	....
Blairsville	4	4	....	Conemaugh Township (Somerset County)	5	5	....
Blakely	6	6	....	Conestoga Township	3	3	....
Blawnox	4	4	....	Conewago Township	5	5	....
Bloomsburg Town	14	11	3	Conewango Township	3	3	....
Boyertown	6	6	....	Conyngham	2	2	....
Brackenridge	5	5	....	Connellsville	18	16	2
Braddock Hills	3	3	....	Conshohocken	12	11	1
Bradford	18	17	1	Conway	3	3	....
Bradford Township	6	5	1	Coolbaugh Township	10	9	1
Brecknock Township	3	3	....	Coopersburg	5	5	....
Brentwood	18	14	4	Coplay	3	3	....
Briar Creek Township	2	2	....	Coraopolis	12	9	3
Bridgeport	10	9	1	Cornwall	4	3	1
Bridgeville	9	8	1	Corry	16	12	4
Bridgewater	2	2	....	Coudersport	3	2	1
Brighton Township	4	4	....	Covington Township	1	1	....
Bristol	14	13	1	Crafton	13	9	4
Bristol Township	71	62	9	Cranberry Township	17	15	2
Brockway	2	2	....	Crescent Township	1	1	....
Brookhaven	10	9	1	Cresson	2	2	....
Brookville	7	6	1	Cressona	2	2	....
Brownsville	10	5	5	Cresson Township	1	1	....
Bryn Athyn	5	5	....	Cumberland Township (Adams County)	4	4	....
Buckingham Township	16	15	1	Cumru Township	23	21	2
Burgettstown	2	2	....	Curwensville	3	3	....
Bushkill Township	5	5	....	Dale	1	1	....
Butler	23	22	1	Dallas	5	5	....
Butler Township (Butler County)	22	20	2	Dallas Township	8	8	....
Butler Township (Luzerne County)	4	4	....	Dalton	2	2	....
Butler Township (Schuylkill County)	2	2	....	Danville	8	7	1
Caernarvon Township (Lancaster County)	1	1	....	Darby	15	13	2
California	10	6	4	Darby Township	14	13	1
Caln Township	15	13	2	Daugherty Township	1	1	....
Cambria Township	2	2	....	Denver	4	4	....
Camp Hill	8	8	....	Derry	2	2	....
Canonsburg	17	15	2	Derry Township (Dauphin County)	37	30	7
Canton	2	2	....	Dickson City	9	9	....
Carlisle	36	30	6	Donegal Township	1	1	....
Carmichaels	2	1	1	Donora	5	5	....
Carnegie	17	12	5	Dormont	13	12	1
Carroll Township (Washington County)	4	4	....	Douglass Township (Montgomery County)	9	8	1
Carroll Township (York County)	4	4	....	Downingtown	14	11	3
Carrolltown	1	1	....	Doylestown	17	15	2
Castle Shannon	10	9	1	Doylestown Township	20	17	3
Catasauqua	9	8	1	Du Bois	14	10	4
Catawissa	3	3	....	Duboistown	1	1	....
Cecil Township	10	10	....	Duncansville	1	1	....
Center Township	8	8	....	Dunmore	13	12	1
Centerville	4	4	....	Dupont	1	1	....
Central City	2	2	....	Duquesne	11	11	....
Chalfont	5	5	....	Duryea	7	4	3
Chambersburg	29	26	3	East Berlin	1	1	....
Charleroi	11	10	1	East Bethlehem Township	3	3	....
Chartiers Township	9	9	....	East Brandywine Township	8	7	1
Cheltenham Township	82	75	7	East Buffalo Township	7	7	....
Chester	96	86	10	East Cocalico Township	15	14	1
Cheswick	3	3	....	East Conemaugh	2	2	....
Chippewa Township	8	7	1	East Coventry Township	3	3	....

Table 78. — Number of Full-time Law Enforcement Employees, Cities, October 31, 1993 — Continued

City	Total police employees	Total officers	Total civilians	City	Total police employees	Total officers	Total civilians
PENNSYLVANIA – Continued				**PENNSYLVANIA – Continued**			
East Donegal Township	4	4	....	Greensburg	31	27	4
East Earl Township	5	5	....	Green Tree	11	10	1
East Fallowfield Township	2	2	....	Greenville	12	11	1
East Franklin Township	2	2	....	Grove City	8	8	....
East Hempfield Township	28	24	4	Hamburg	6	6	....
East Lampeter Township	26	23	3	Hampden Township	17	16	1
East Lansdowne	3	3	....	Hampton Township	17	16	1
East McKeesport	3	2	1	Hanover	20	18	2
East Norriton Township	25	21	4	Hanover Township (Luzerne County)	20	15	5
Easton	58	49	9	Harmar Township	5	5	....
East Pennsboro Township	16	15	1	Harmony Township	4	4	....
East Petersburg	58	44	14	Harrisburg	223	177	46
East Pikeland Township	6	6	....	Harrison Township	16	12	4
East Stroudsburg	14	13	1	Hatboro	18	13	5
East Taylor Township	2	2	....	Hatfield Township	27	22	5
Easttown Township	14	13	1	Haverford Township	72	60	12
East Vincent Township	5	5	....	Hazleton	27	23	4
East Washington	2	2	....	Hegins Township	2	2	....
East Whiteland Township	15	13	2	Heidelberg	3	3	....
Ebensburg	5	5	....	Heidelberg Township (Berks County)	1	1	....
Economy	10	9	1	Heidelberg Township (Lebanon County)	2	2	....
Eddystone	6	5	1	Hellam Township	7	7	....
Edgewood	7	7	....	Hellertown	10	9	1
Edgeworth	6	5	1	Hemlock Township	2	2	....
Edinboro	8	7	1	Hempfield Township	7	6	1
Edwardsville	5	5	....	Hermitage	27	24	3
Elizabeth	1	1	....	Highspire	6	6	....
Elizabethtown	15	13	2	Hilltown Township	16	13	3
Elizabethville	1	1	....	Hollidaysburg	12	7	5
Elkland	2	2	....	Homer City	1	1	....
Ellwood City	18	14	4	Homestead	8	8	....
Emmaus	16	14	2	Honesdale	6	6	....
Emporium	3	1	2	Hooversville	1	1	....
Ephrata	22	20	2	Hopewell Township	10	10	....
Ephrata Township	9	8	1	Horsham Township	44	36	8
Erie	230	193	37	Houtzdale	1	1	....
Etna	6	4	2	Hughesville	2	2	....
Evans City	2	2	....	Hummelstown	6	6	....
Everett	2	2	....	Huntingdon	14	11	3
Exeter Township (Berks County)	20	19	1	Independence Township	2	2	....
Fairview	1	1	....	Indiana	23	17	6
Fairview Township (Luzerne County)	3	3	....	Indiana Township	8	8	....
Fairview Township (York County)	14	13	1	Industry	4	4	....
Falls Township (Bucks County)	58	49	9	Ingram	6	6	....
Ferguson Township	13	11	2	Irwin	4	4	....
Ferndale	2	2	....	Jackson Township (Butler County)	3	3	....
Findlay Township	18	12	6	Jackson Township (York County)	9	8	1
Fleetwood	5	5	....	Jeannette	17	16	1
Folcroft	9	9	....	Jefferson	15	14	1
Ford City	4	4	....	Jefferson Township	3	3	....
Forest City	2	2	....	Jenkins Township	3	3	....
Forks Township	11	10	1	Jenkintown	11	11	....
Forty Fort	5	5	....	Jermyn	2	2	....
Forward Township	5	5	....	Jersey Shore	7	6	1
Foster Township	6	5	1	Jim Thorpe	6	5	1
Fountain Hill	6	6	....	Johnsonburg	3	3	....
Fox Chapel	11	11	....	Johnstown	45	37	8
Frackville	5	5	....	Jones Township	1	1	....
Franconia Township	8	7	1	Kane	4	4	....
Franklin (Cambria County)	2	2	....	Kennedy Township	10	9	1
Franklin (Venango County)	21	16	5	Kennett Square	9	7	2
Franklin Park	8	7	1	Kidder Township	7	7	....
Franklin Township (Beaver County)	1	1	....	Kilbuck Township	3	3	....
Franklin Township (Carbon County)	4	4	....	Kingston	23	20	3
Freedom-Greenfield Township	2	2	....	Kingston Township	8	8	....
Freeland	5	5	....	Kittanning	9	8	1
Freemansburg	2	2	....	Kline Township	2	2	....
Freeport	2	2	....	Kutztown	10	9	1
Gallitzin Township	1	1	....	Lake City	3	3	....
Geistown	2	2	....	Lake Township	1	1	....
Gettysburg	14	12	2	Lancaster	151	126	25
Girard	4	4	....	Lansdale	29	22	7
Glenolden	9	8	1	Lansdowne	18	15	3
Granville Township	4	4	....	Lansford	3	2	1
Greencastle	4	4	....	Larksville	4	4	....

Table 78. — Number of Full-time Law Enforcement Employees, Cities, October 31, 1993 — Continued

City	Total police employees	Total officers	Total civilians	City	Total police employees	Total officers	Total civilians
PENNSYLVANIA — Continued				**PENNSYLVANIA — Continued**			
Latrobe	13	12	1	Middlesex Township (Cumberland County)	7	7	....
Laureldale	4	4	....	Middletown	14	13	1
Lawrence Park Township	7	6	1	Middletown Township	57	46	11
Lawrence Township	7	7	....	Midland	5	5	....
Lebanon	45	38	7	Mifflin County Regional	24	22	2
Leetsdale	5	5	....	Mifflin Town	1	1	....
Leet Township	4	4	....	Milford	2	2	....
Lehighton	9	8	1	Millbourne	3	3	....
Lehigh Township (Northampton County)	7	7	....	Millcreek Township	62	51	11
Lehman Township	2	2	....	Millersburg	4	4	....
Lewisburg	8	7	1	Millersville	10	9	1
Liberty	1	1	....	Millville	1	1	....
Ligonier Township	2	2	....	Milton	11	10	1
Lilly	1	1	....	Minersville	6	5	1
Limerick Township	11	9	2	Mohnton	3	3	....
Lincoln	1	1	....	Monaca	5	5	....
Linesville	1	1	....	Monessen	13	12	1
Lititz	12	10	2	Monongahela	12	8	4
Littlestown	6	6	....	Montgomery	2	2	....
Lock Haven	12	11	1	Montgomery Township	36	28	8
Logan Township	21	15	6	Montoursville	5	5	....
Lower Allen Township	20	17	3	Montrose	2	2	....
Lower Alsace Township	13	12	1	Moon Township	32	27	5
Lower Burrell	13	13	....	Moore Township	6	5	1
Lower Chichester Township	5	4	1	Moosic	2	2	....
Lower Gwynedd Township	21	17	4	Morrisville	13	11	2
Lower Heidelberg Township	5	5	....	Morton	5	5	....
Lower Makefield Township	28	25	3	Mountaintop Regional	4	4	....
Lower Merion Township	159	132	27	Mount Holly Springs	3	3	....
Lower Moreland Township	28	21	7	Mount Jewett	1	1	....
Lower Paxton Township	48	43	5	Mount Joy	10	9	1
Lower Pottsgrove Township	10	9	1	Mount Joy Township	6	5	1
Lower Providence Township	31	24	7	Mount Lebanon	55	44	11
Lower Salford Township	13	12	1	Mount Oliver	4	4	....
Lower Saucon Township	14	10	4	Mount Penn	4	4	....
Lower Southampton Township	28	25	3	Mount Pleasant	3	3	....
Lower Swatara Township	12	11	1	Mount Union	5	5	....
Lower Yoder Township	4	4	....	Muhlenberg Township	25	23	2
Luzerne	2	2	....	Munhall	21	17	4
Luzerne Township	1	1	....	Murrysville	21	17	4
Lykens	1	1	....	Myerstown	4	4	....
Macungie	4	4	....	Nanticoke	14	11	3
Mahoning Township (Carbon County)	4	4	....	Nanty Glo	2	2	....
Mahoning Township (Montour County)	6	6	....	Narberth	6	6	....
Malvern	6	5	1	Nazareth Area	13	11	2
Manheim	7	6	1	Neshannock Township	5	4	1
Manheim Township	58	44	14	Nesquehoning	3	3	....
Manor	2	2	....	Nether Providence Township	13	13	....
Manor Township	16	15	1	Neville Township	8	6	2
Mansfield	5	5	....	Newberry Township	10	9	1
Marcus Hook	5	4	1	New Brighton	12	10	2
Marietta	2	2	....	New Britain	2	2	....
Marlborough Township	4	3	1	New Britain Township	13	12	1
Marple Township	38	30	8	New Castle	32	32	....
Mars	2	2	....	New Cumberland	8	7	1
Martinsburg	2	2	....	New Eagle	3	3	....
Marysville	4	4	....	New Hanover Township	4	4	....
Masontown	5	5	....	New Holland	9	8	1
Matamoras	2	2	....	New Hope	8	7	1
Mayfield	1	1	....	New Kensington	32	24	8
McAdoo	4	4	....	New Oxford	2	2	....
McCandless	32	26	6	Newport	2	2	....
McConnellsburg	2	2	....	New Sewickley Township	6	5	1
McDonald	2	2	....	Newtown	5	5	....
McKeesport	29	27	2	Newtown Township (Bucks County)	18	16	2
McKees Rocks	12	8	4	Newtown Township (Delaware County)	14	13	1
McSherrystown	4	4	....	Newville	2	2	....
Meadville	29	22	7	New Wilmington	4	4	....
Mechanicsburg	15	14	1	Norristown	93	73	20
Mechanicsville	1	1	....	Northampton	14	10	4
Media	21	14	7	Northampton Township	41	36	5
Mercer	3	3	....	North Belle Vernon	2	2	....
Mercersburg	2	2	....	North Bethlehem Township	1	1	....
Meyersdale	4	4	....	North Braddock	8	5	3
Middlesex Township (Butler County)	6	6	....	North Charleroi	2	2	....

Table 78.—Number of Full-time Law Enforcement Employees, Cities, October 31, 1993—Continued

City	Total police employees	Total officers	Total civilians	City	Total police employees	Total officers	Total civilians
PENNSYLVANIA—Continued				**PENNSYLVANIA—Continued**			
North Cornwall Township	8	8	....	Prospect Park	8	8	....
North Coventry Township	9	8	1	Punxsutawney	12	7	5
North East	7	6	1	Pymatuning Township	4	4	....
Northeastern Berks Regional	7	7	....	Quakertown	15	13	2
Northeastern Regional	7	6	1	Radnor Township	52	46	6
Northern York Regional	37	33	4	Ralpho Township	4	4	....
North Fayette Township	17	12	5	Reading	225	193	32
North Franklin Township	8	8	....	Red Lion	9	8	1
North Huntingdon Township	26	20	6	Redstone Township	1	1	....
North Lebanon Township	8	7	1	Reserve Township	3	3	....
North Londonderry Township	6	6	....	Reynoldsville	2	2	....
North Middleton Township	6	6	....	Richland	1	1	....
North Sewickley Township	2	2	....	Richland Township (Allegheny County)	11	10	1
North Strabane Township	8	8	....	Richland Township (Cambria County)	18	17	1
Northumberland	4	4	....	Ridgway	6	6	....
North Versailles Township	10	10	....	Ridley Township	43	33	10
North Wales	3	3	....	Riverside	3	3	....
Norwegian Township	1	1	....	Roaring Spring	1	1	....
Norwood	7	6	1	Robesonia-Heidelberg	2	2	....
Oakdale	1	1	....	Robeson Township	3	2	1
Oakmont	8	7	1	Rochester	11	9	2
O'Hara Township	12	12	....	Rochester Township	1	1	....
Ohio Township	4	4	....	Rosslyn Farms	2	2	....
Ohioville	2	2	....	Ross Township	48	39	9
Oil City	22	17	5	Rostraver Township	10	9	1
Old Forge	7	6	1	Royersford	5	4	1
Old Lycoming Township	8	7	1	Rush Township	1	1	....
Oley Township	1	1	....	Rye Township	1	1	....
Olyphant	6	6	....	St. Clair	5	5	....
Orangeville	1	1	....	St. Marys	8	7	1
Orwigsburg	4	4	....	Salisbury Township	11	10	1
Oxford	9	9	....	Sandy Lake	1	1	....
Paint Township	2	2	....	Sandy Township	6	6	....
Palmerton	9	8	1	Saxonburg	1	1	....
Palmer Township	23	19	4	Saxton	1	1	....
Palmyra	8	8	....	Sayre	10	8	2
Parkside	2	2	....	Schuylkill Haven	12	8	4
Parks Township	1	1	....	Schuylkill Township	6	5	1
Patterson	4	4	....	Scottsdale	7	7	....
Patton	1	1	....	Scott Township (Allegheny County)	21	16	5
Patton Township	11	10	1	Scott Township (Lackawanna County)	3	3	....
Paxtang	3	3	....	Scranton	161	140	21
Pen Argyl	3	3	....	Selinsgrove	4	3	1
Penbrook	6	6	....	Seven Springs	6	5	1
Penn Hills	64	56	8	Sewickley	13	9	4
Pennridge Regional	14	13	1	Shaler Township	40	30	10
Penn Township (Butler County)	5	4	1	Shamokin	17	13	4
Penn Township (Lancaster County)	5	5	....	Shamokin Dam	3	3	....
Penn Township (Westmoreland County)	18	16	2	Sharon	30	25	5
Penn Township (York County)	18	17	1	Sharon Hill	9	8	1
Pequea Township	2	2	....	Sharpsburg	6	5	1
Perkasie	11	10	1	Sharpsville	6	5	1
Perryopolis	2	2	....	Shenandoah	9	8	1
Peters Township	21	17	4	Shenango Township (Lawrence County)	6	5	1
Philadelphia	6,969	6,225	744	Shenango Township (Mercer County)	4	3	1
Philipsburg	2	2	....	Shillington	8	7	1
Phoenixville	23	21	2	Shippensburg	11	10	1
Pine Grove	3	3	....	Shippingport	2	2	....
Pine Township	12	11	1	Shiremanstown	2	2	....
Pitcavin	3	3	....	Silver Spring Township	12	11	1
Pittsburgh	1,152	1,095	57	Sinking Spring	4	4	....
Pittston	11	8	3	Slatington	6	6	....
Plainfield Township	6	6	....	Slippery Rock	5	5	....
Plains Township	8	8	....	Smith Township	1	1	....
Pleasant Hills	18	14	4	Solebury Township	9	8	1
Plumstead Township	8	8	....	Somerset	7	6	1
Plymouth	6	6	....	Souderton	7	6	1
Plymouth Township	40	32	8	South Abington Township	10	9	1
Pocono Township	11	10	1	South Beaver Township	3	3	....
Point Township	4	4	....	South Centre Township	5	5	....
Portage	2	2	....	South Coatesville	2	2	....
Port Allegany	3	3	....	Southern	7	6	1
Port Carbon	3	3	....	South Fayette Township	15	14	1
Pottstown	46	38	8	South Fork	1	1	....
Pottsville	33	29	4	South Greensburg	2	2	....

Table 78.—Number of Full-time Law Enforcement Employees, Cities, October 31, 1993—Continued

City	Total police employees	Total officers	Total civilians	City	Total police employees	Total officers	Total civilians
PENNSYLVANIA—Continued				**PENNSYLVANIA—Continued**			
South Lebanon Township	6	6	....	Upper Yoder Township	5	5	....
South Londonderry Township	3	3	....	Uwchlan Township	19	17	2
South Park Township	16	15	1	Valley Township	6	6	....
South Waverly	2	2	....	Vandergrift	8	8	....
S.W. Mercer County Regional	15	13	2	Vanport Township	3	3	....
South Whitehall Township	38	34	4	Vernon Township	4	4	....
South Williamsport	6	6	....	Verona	3	2	1
Spring City	5	4	1	Versailles	2	2	....
Springdale	2	2	....	Walnutport	3	3	....
Springettbury Township	28	25	3	Warminster Township	50	45	5
Springfield Township (Bucks County)	4	4	....	Warren	20	17	3
Springfield Township (Montgomery County)	31	30	1	Warrington Township	16	14	2
Spring Garden Township	18	17	1	Warwick Township (Bucks County)	9	8	1
Spring Township (Berks County)	20	19	1	Warwick Township (Lancaster County)	14	12	2
Spring Township (Centre County)	4	4	....	Washington	27	26	1
State College	70	53	17	Washington Township (Franklin County)	10	9	1
Steelton	11	10	1	Washington Township (Northampton County)	2	2	....
Stoneycreek Township	3	3	....	Washington Township (Westmoreland County)	3	3	....
Stowe Township	9	7	2	Waynesboro	16	15	1
Strasburg	3	3	....	Waynesburg	7	7	....
Stroudsburg	17	13	4	Weatherly	3	3	....
Stroud Township	16	14	2	Wellsboro	6	6	....
Sugarcreek	4	4	....	Wernersville	2	2	....
Sugarloaf Township	2	2	....	Wesleyville	3	3	....
Summit Hill	2	2	....	West Brandywine Township	6	6	....
Sunbury	20	14	6	West Chester	50	33	17
Susquehanna Township (Cambria County)	1	1	....	West Deer Township	10	9	1
Susquehanna Township (Dauphin County)	32	30	2	West Donegal Township	6	6	....
Swarthmore	9	9	....	West Earl Township	3	3	....
Swatara Township	34	31	3	West Fairview	2	2	....
Swissvale	13	9	4	Westfall Township	2	2	....
Swoyersville	5	4	1	West Goshen Township	25	22	3
Tamaqua	10	9	1	West Grove	3	3	....
Tarentum	12	7	5	West Hempfield Township	16	14	2
Taylor	5	5	....	West Hills Regional	9	9	....
Telford	6	5	1	West Homestead	9	5	4
Temple	2	2	....	West Lampeter Township	9	9	....
Throop	6	6	....	West Manchester Township	23	21	2
Tinicum Township (Bucks County)	4	4	....	West Manheim Township	6	6	....
Tinicum Township (Delaware County)	13	11	2	West Mayfield	1	1	....
Titusville	14	13	1	West Mifflin	33	28	5
Tobyhanna Township	9	8	1	West Norriton Township	28	23	5
Towamencin Township	19	17	2	West Pittston	8	4	4
Towanda	4	4	....	West Pottsgrove Township	7	7	....
Trafford	1	1	....	West Reading	8	7	1
Trainer	4	4	....	Westtown Township	17	15	2
Tredyffrin Township	61	50	11	West View	12	9	3
Troy	3	3	....	West Whiteland Township	21	19	2
Tunkhannock	4	4	....	West Wyoming	2	2	....
Tunkhannock Township	1	1	....	West York	6	6	....
Turtle Creek	8	6	2	Whitehall	23	18	5
Tyrone	6	5	1	Whitehall Township	51	40	11
Union City	7	4	3	White Haven	1	1	....
Union Township (Mifflin County)	2	2	....	Whitemarsh Township	32	29	3
Union Township (Washington County)	6	6	....	White Oak	10	10	....
Upland	2	2	....	Whitpain Township	28	25	3
Upper Allen Township	15	14	1	Wiconisco Township	1	1	....
Upper Chichester Township	22	20	2	Wilkes-Barre Township	13	9	4
Upper Darby Township	118	104	14	Wilkinsburg	26	19	7
Upper Dublin Township	41	35	6	Wilkins Township	10	10	....
Upper Gwynedd Township	16	15	1	Williamsburg	1	1	....
Upper Makefield Township	6	6	....	Williamsport	58	54	4
Upper Merion Township	70	53	17	Willistown Township	15	14	1
Upper Moreland Township	45	36	9	Wilmerding	2	2	....
Upper Mount Bethel Township	6	6	....	Wilson	7	7	....
Upper Nazareth Township	2	2	....	Windber	3	2	1
Upper Perkiomen	8	7	1	Wind Gap	3	3	....
Upper Pottsgrove Township	4	4	....	Windsor Township	9	8	1
Upper Providence Township (Delaware County)	11	11	....	Wormleysburg	5	4	1
				Wrightsville	2	2	....
Upper Providence Township (Montgomery County)	11	10	1	Wyomissing	23	17	6
Upper Saucon Township	14	13	1	Wyomissing Hills	4	4	....
Upper Southampton Township	24	21	3	Yardley	3	3	....
Upper Uwchlan Township	6	5	1	Yeadon	17	16	1
				York	104	94	10

Table 78. — Number of Full-time Law Enforcement Employees, Cities, October 31, 1993 — Continued

City	Total police employees	Total officers	Total civilians	City	Total police employees	Total officers	Total civilians
PENNSYLVANIA – Continued				**SOUTH CAROLINA – Continued**			
York Springs-Latimore	3	3	....	Chapin	1	1	....
York Township	26	23	3	Charleston	388	277	111
Youngsville	2	2	....	Cheraw	26	21	5
Zelienople	6	6	....	Chesnee	5	5	....
				Chester	25	21	4
RHODE ISLAND				Chesterfield	5	4	1
				Clemson	28	22	6
Barrington	29	23	6	Clinton	30	24	6
Bristol	44	35	9	Clover	18	14	4
Burrillville	24	18	6	Columbia	317	257	60
Central Falls	39	37	2	Conway	40	32	8
Charlestown	22	17	5	Cowpens	8	7	1
Coventry	63	50	13	Darlington	25	21	4
Cranston	174	144	30	Denmark	8	8	....
Cumberland	52	43	9	Dillon	18	14	4
East Greenwich	36	34	2	Due West	4	4	....
East Providence	111	91	20	Duncan	5	5	....
Foster	10	6	4	Easley	31	26	5
Glocester	13	9	4	Edgefield	14	11	3
Hopkinton	15	10	5	Edisto Beach	4	3	1
Jamestown	16	13	3	Ehrhardt	1	1	....
Johnston	76	59	17	Elloree	4	4	....
Lincoln	37	32	5	Estill	6	5	1
Little Compton	12	8	4	Eutawville	1	1	....
Middletown	41	38	3	Fairfax	4	4	....
Narragansett	44	34	10	Florence	88	71	17
Newport	108	87	21	Folly Beach	14	8	6
New Shoreham	7	3	4	Forest Acres	33	27	6
North Kingstown	60	49	11	Fort Lawn	2	2	....
North Providence	71	53	18	Fort Mill	18	13	5
North Smithfield	24	19	5	Fountain Inn	18	13	5
Pawtucket	178	150	28	Gaffney	31	24	7
Portsmouth	30	27	3	Gaston	1	1	....
Providence	450	410	40	Georgetown	41	34	7
Richmond	10	5	5	Goose Creek	40	31	9
Scituate	21	15	6	Great Falls	8	6	2
Smithfield	44	36	8	Greenville	183	148	35
South Kingstown	57	43	14	Greenwood	61	52	9
Tiverton	30	21	9	Greer	42	31	11
Warren	27	21	6	Hampton	8	7	1
Warwick	222	167	55	Hanahan	29	21	8
Westerly	47	37	10	Hardeeville	13	9	4
West Greenwich	12	7	5	Harleyville	4	4	....
West Warwick	61	55	6	Hartsville	40	36	4
Woonsocket	113	105	8	Hemingway	8	5	3
				Holly Hill	9	5	4
SOUTH CAROLINA				Honea Path	15	11	4
				Inman	5	5	....
Abbeville	20	14	6	Irmo	17	16	1
Aiken	100	85	15	Isle of Palms	24	17	7
Allendale	10	10	....	Iva	6	5	1
Anderson	87	64	23	Jackson	4	4	....
Andrews	15	11	4	Jamestown	2	2	....
Atlantic Beach	3	3	....	Jefferson	5	5	....
Aynor	9	4	5	Johnsonville	9	5	4
Bamberg	9	8	1	Johnston	11	7	4
Barnwell	11	10	1	Jonesville	3	3	....
Batesburg-Leesville	23	18	5	Kershaw	10	5	5
Beaufort	37	33	4	Kingstree	18	13	5
Belton	19	14	5	Lake City	27	22	5
Bennettsville	26	23	3	Lake View	4	2	2
Bishopville	18	13	5	Lamar	2	2	....
Blacksburg	7	6	1	Lancaster	42	36	6
Blackville	6	5	1	Landrum	9	8	1
Bluffton	4	4	....	Latta	10	7	3
Bonneau	1	1	....	Laurens	30	25	5
Bowman	3	1	2	Lexington	19	17	2
Branchville	1	1	....	Liberty	13	9	4
Briarcliffe Acres	1	1	....	Loris	12	7	5
Brunson	1	1	....	Lyman	6	5	1
Calhoun Falls	7	6	1	Manning	12	11	1
Camden	29	22	7	Marion	30	24	6
Campobello	1	1	....	Mauldin	34	28	6
Cayce	44	37	7	Mayesville	1	1	....
Central	4	4	....	McBee	3	2	1

Table 78. — Number of Full-time Law Enforcement Employees, Cities, October 31, 1993 — Continued

City	Total police employees	Total officers	Total civilians	City	Total police employees	Total officers	Total civilians
SOUTH CAROLINA — Continued				**SOUTH DAKOTA — Continued**			
McColl	8	3	5	Brookings	28	24	4
McCormick	6	6	....	Burke	2	2	....
Moncks Corner	19	17	2	Canton	4	4	....
Mount Pleasant	87	62	25	Chamberlain	9	5	4
Mullins	26	21	5	Deadwood	11	10	1
Myrtle Beach	137	104	33	Eagle Butte	3	3	....
Newberry	29	27	2	Fort Pierre	3	3	....
New Ellenton	5	5	....	Harrisburg	1	1	....
Ninety Six	6	6	....	Hot Springs	6	5	1
North	2	2	....	Kadoka	1	1	....
North Augusta	58	44	14	Lead	8	7	1
North Charleston	231	168	63	Madison	13	10	3
North Myrtle Beach	65	50	15	McLaughlin	3	3	....
Norway	5	2	3	Miller	4	4	....
Orangeburg	76	65	11	Mitchell	30	22	8
Pacolet	3	2	1	Mobridge	9	5	4
Pageland	15	11	4	Parker	1	1	....
Pamplico	8	1	7	Parkston	2	2	....
Pendleton	7	7	....	Pierre	30	22	8
Pickens	11	9	2	Rapid City	114	87	27
Pine Ridge	1	1	....	Salem	2	2	....
Pinewood	3	2	1	Sioux Falls	173	148	25
Port Royal	12	12	....	Spearfish	16	11	5
Prosperity	4	4	....	Sturgis	11	10	1
Ridgeland	7	7	....	Vermillion	22	16	6
Ridge Spring	2	2	....	Watertown	30	26	4
Ridgeway	2	2	....	Winner	16	7	9
Rock Hill	108	88	20	Yankton	37	22	15
St. George	10	9	1				
St. Matthews	6	6	....	**TENNESSEE**			
St. Stephens	3	3	....				
Saluda	8	8	....	Adamsville	8	5	3
Santee	6	4	2	Alcoa	23	21	2
Sellers	3	2	1	Ardmore	8	5	3
Seneca	26	22	4	Ashland City	7	7	....
Simpsonville	34	27	7	Athens	28	26	2
Society Hill	7	5	2	Bartlett	64	44	20
South Congaree	4	3	1	Benton	6	4	2
Spartanburg	145	123	22	Bethel Springs	1	1	....
Springdale	8	7	1	Bolivar	23	18	5
Sullivans Island	8	6	2	Brentwood	45	35	10
Summerton	7	5	2	Bristol	62	53	9
Summerville	40	37	3	Brownsville	30	23	7
Sumter	104	72	32	Bruceton	4	4	....
Surfside Beach	13	9	4	Carthage	11	7	4
Tega Cay	13	9	4	Centerville	14	10	4
Timmonsville	9	6	3	Chattanooga	509	390	119
Travelers Rest	17	11	6	Church Hill	6	6	....
Union	40	31	9	Clarksville	153	137	16
Vance	2	1	1	Cleveland	80	64	16
Varnville	5	3	2	Collegedale	9	9	....
Wagener	4	4	....	Collierville	45	32	13
Walhalla	13	10	3	Collinwood	3	3	....
Walterboro	31	20	11	Columbia	62	53	9
Ware Shoals	9	8	1	Cookeville	73	59	14
Wellford	5	5	....	Cornersville	1	1	....
West Columbia	39	30	9	Cowan	4	4	....
Westminster	9	9	....	Crossville	25	20	5
West Pelzer	3	3	....	Cumberland Gap	2	2	....
West Union	2	1	1	Dandridge	3	3	....
Whitmire	11	5	6	Dayton	13	12	1
Whitten Center	4	4	....	Dickson	45	30	15
Williamston	19	19	....	Dyer	6	5	1
Williston	7	7	....	Dyersburg	61	46	15
Winnsboro	24	18	6	East Ridge	38	31	7
Woodruff	13	9	4	Elkton	1	1	....
Yemassee	3	3	....	Erwin	10	10	....
York	23	19	4	Estill Springs	4	4	....
				Etowah	12	9	3
SOUTH DAKOTA				Fairview	15	10	5
				Fayetteville	24	18	6
Aberdeen	51	38	13	Franklin	63	51	12
Belle Fourche	7	7	....	Friendsville	1	1	....
Beresford	8	4	4	Gallatin	49	39	10
Box Elder	6	5	1	Gallaway	1	1	....

344

City	Total police employees	Total officers	Total civilians	City	Total police employees	Total officers	Total civilians
TENNESSEE—Continued				**TENNESSEE—Continued**			
Gatlinburg	39	31	8	Town of Decaturville	1	1	....
Germantown	64	51	13	Trenton	19	13	6
Gleason	4	4	....	Trimble	4	4	....
Goodlettsville	41	30	11	Tullahoma	35	31	4
Grand Junction	3	3	....	Union City	33	25	8
Greeneville	43	41	2	Waverly	13	9	4
Halls	6	6	....	Winchester	22	17	5
Hartsville	12	8	4	Woodbury	9	7	2
Henderson	12	12	....				
Hendersonville	68	51	17	**TEXAS**			
Hohenwald	11	11	....				
Humboldt	31	25	6	Abernathy	4	4	....
Huntingdon	15	11	4	Abilene	224	169	55
Jacksboro	1	1	....	Addison	65	49	16
Jackson	214	163	51	Alamo	22	16	6
Jasper	11	8	3	Alamo Heights	25	18	7
Jefferson City	12	11	1	Alice	43	33	10
Jellico	7	7	....	Allen	39	26	13
Johnson City	153	127	26	Alpine	11	7	4
Jonesborough	15	11	4	Alto	2	2	....
Kenton	5	5	....	Alvarado	9	5	4
Kimball	9	5	4	Alvin	43	32	11
Kingsport	131	91	40	Amarillo	321	247	74
Knoxville	392	323	69	Andrews	16	14	2
Lafayette	15	12	3	Angleton	37	28	9
La Follette	23	17	6	Anson	6	5	1
Lake City	9	7	2	Anthony	8	7	1
La Vergne	24	18	6	Aransas Pass	22	17	5
Lawrenceburg	44	29	15	Arlington	495	381	114
Lexington	27	22	5	Arp	2	2	....
Livingston	18	13	5	Athens	28	22	6
Manchester	24	23	1	Atlanta	17	12	5
Martin	28	20	8	Austin	1,242	881	361
Maryville	39	34	5	Azle	26	20	6
McKenzie	16	12	4	Balch Springs	27	21	6
McMinnville	40	33	7	Balcones Heights	24	18	6
Memphis	1,810	1,437	373	Ballinger	8	5	3
Milan	21	17	4	Bangs	1	1	....
Millersville	8	5	3	Bastrop	12	10	2
Millington	29	23	6	Bay City	46	35	11
Minor Hill	4	2	2	Bayou Vista	5	5	....
Morristown	66	63	3	Baytown	142	109	33
Mount Carmel	5	5	....	Beaumont	337	266	71
Mount Juliet	17	12	5	Bedford	89	64	25
Mount Pleasant	10	9	1	Beeville	25	18	7
Murfreesboro	122	96	26	Bellaire	52	37	15
Nashville	1,438	1,099	339	Bellmead	18	13	5
Newbern	14	9	5	Bellville	10	8	2
New Johnsonville	4	4	....	Belton	28	19	9
New Tazewell	6	6	....	Benbrook	40	32	8
Oak Ridge	59	47	12	Bertram	1	1	....
Obion	3	3	....	Beverly Hills	7	6	1
Oliver Springs	12	12	....	Big Sandy	3	3	....
Pigeon Forge	39	31	8	Big Spring	62	39	23
Portland	19	13	6	Bishop	8	4	4
Pulaski	27	21	6	Blanco	3	3	....
Red Bank	22	19	3	Blue Mound	8	4	4
Rockwood	17	17	....	Boerne	14	12	2
Rutherford	4	4	....	Bonham	21	15	6
Savannah	22	14	8	Borger	28	20	8
Sevierville	38	30	8	Bovina	2	2	....
Sewanee	12	8	4	Bowie	16	11	5
Sharon	3	3	....	Brady	13	7	6
Shelbyville	34	29	5	Brazoria	12	7	5
Signal Mountain	16	14	2	Breckenridge	14	8	6
Soddy-Daisy	19	16	3	Brenham	37	25	12
Somerville	11	9	2	Bridge City	19	14	5
South Carthage	4	4	....	Bridgeport	12	7	5
South Fulton	8	6	2	Brookshire	12	8	4
Sparta	20	15	5	Brownfield	22	16	6
Spring City	6	6	....	Brownsville	222	165	57
Springfield	40	28	12	Brownwood	41	29	12
Spring Hill	8	8	....	Bryan	105	86	19
Sweetwater	15	14	1	Burkburnett	18	13	5
Tazewell	8	7	1	Burleson	42	32	10

Table 78. — Number of Full-time Law Enforcement Employees, Cities, October 31, 1993 — Continued

City	Total police employees	Total officers	Total civilians	City	Total police employees	Total officers	Total civilians
TEXAS — Continued				**TEXAS — Continued**			
Burnet	10	9	1	El Campo	30	22	8
Caddo Mills	3	2	1	Electra	9	5	4
Caldwell	8	7	1	Elgin	18	13	5
Cameron	13	8	5	El Paso	1,053	850	203
Caney City	3	3	....	Elsa	18	11	7
Canton	11	7	4	Ennis	31	26	5
Canyon	17	15	2	Euless	88	60	28
Carrollton	178	130	48	Everman	17	12	5
Carthage	19	12	7	Fairfield	6	6	....
Castle Hills	23	19	4	Fair Oaks Ranch	5	5	....
Cedar Hill	34	28	6	Falfurrias	11	10	1
Cedar Park	18	12	6	Farmers Branch	77	63	14
Celina	4	4	....	Farmersville	4	4	....
Center	17	12	5	Ferris	15	10	5
Childress	14	9	5	Florence	1	1	....
Cisco	8	7	1	Floresville	9	8	1
Clarksville	12	8	4	Flower Mound	41	31	10
Cleburne	49	37	12	Floydada	4	4	....
Cleveland	23	15	8	Forest Hill	29	21	8
Clifton	6	5	1	Forney	12	10	2
Clute	27	19	8	Fort Stockton	25	15	10
Cockrell Hill	14	10	4	Fort Worth	1,390	1,074	316
Coleman	14	9	5	Frankston	8	4	4
College Station	96	72	24	Fredericksburg	19	17	2
Colleyville	29	21	8	Freeport	31	24	7
Colorado City	13	7	6	Freer	8	4	4
Columbus	8	7	1	Friendswood	41	30	11
Comanche	6	6	....	Friona	9	5	4
Combes	3	3	....	Frisco	23	17	6
Commerce	24	19	5	Gainesville	38	28	10
Conroe	76	60	16	Galena Park	23	18	5
Converse	15	14	1	Galveston	202	159	43
Coppell	30	24	6	Garland	331	240	91
Copperas Cove	65	49	16	Gatesville	15	10	5
Corinth	9	8	1	Georgetown	43	28	15
Corpus Christi	536	385	151	Giddings	14	9	5
Corrigan	10	6	4	Gilmer	9	8	1
Corsicana	46	38	8	Gladewater	20	14	6
Crane	11	6	5	Glenn Heights	12	7	5
Crockett	18	12	6	Gonzales	13	8	5
Crowley	23	17	6	Graham	16	14	2
Crystal City	11	7	4	Granbury	19	16	3
Cuero	10	9	1	Grand Prairie	248	163	85
Cuney	1	1	....	Grand Saline	5	5	....
Daingerfield	6	5	1	Granite Shoals	3	3	....
Dalhart	15	9	6	Grapevine	80	54	26
Dallas	3,525	2,807	718	Greenville	63	48	15
Dalworthington Gardens	7	7	....	Groesbeck	6	5	1
Dayton	17	11	6	Groves	16	15	1
Decatur	15	10	5	Gruver	2	2	....
Deer Park	57	45	12	Gun Barrel City	14	10	4
De Kalb	5	4	1	Hale Center	3	3	....
Del Rio	67	57	10	Hallettsville	5	4	1
Denison	49	40	9	Haltom City	68	51	17
Denton	131	104	27	Hamlin	8	4	4
Denver City	13	7	6	Harker Heights	32	23	9
DeSoto	63	45	18	Harlingen	112	91	21
Devine	11	6	5	Hawkins	4	4	....
Diboll	14	10	4	Hearne	17	11	6
Dickinson	22	17	5	Heath	6	6	....
Dimmitt	8	7	1	Hedwig Village	22	16	6
Donna	26	17	9	Helotes	5	5	....
Dublin	8	6	2	Hemphill	3	3	....
Dumas	27	21	6	Hempstead	10	9	1
Duncanville	77	50	27	Henderson	30	24	6
Eagle Lake	5	4	1	Hereford	31	24	7
Eagle Pass	57	43	14	Hewitt	21	15	6
Early	6	5	1	Hico	3	3	....
Earth	3	2	1	Hidalgo	36	26	10
Eastland	10	8	2	Highland Park	64	51	13
Edcouch	7	7	....	Highland Village	18	12	6
Eden	1	1	....	Hill Country	14	14	....
Edgewood	5	5	....	Hillsboro	23	17	6
Edinburg	64	43	21	Hitchcock	15	9	6
Edna	10	9	1	Hollywood Park	7	7	....

Table 78. — Number of Full-time Law Enforcement Employees, Cities, October 31, 1993 — Continued

City	Total police employees	Total officers	Total civilians	City	Total police employees	Total officers	Total civilians
TEXAS — Continued				**TEXAS — Continued**			
Hondo	14	12	2	Llano	7	6	1
Hooks	4	4	....	Lockhart	14	14	....
Horizon City	5	5	....	Lockney	2	2	....
Horseshoe Bay	7	6	1	Lone Star	3	3	....
Houston	6,700	4,734	1,966	Longview	177	128	49
Hubbard	3	3	....	Lorena	3	3	....
Humble	51	41	10	Los Fresnos	11	6	5
Huntington	4	4	....	Lubbock	355	312	43
Huntsville	47	34	13	Lufkin	80	61	19
Hurst	89	59	30	Luling	13	7	6
Hutchins	15	10	5	Lumberton	10	9	1
Hutto	4	4	....	Madisonville	7	6	1
Idalou	3	3	....	Malakoff	3	3	....
Ingleside	15	11	4	Manor	4	3	1
Ingram	3	3	....	Mansfield	35	23	12
Iowa Colony	4	4	....	Manvel	5	5	....
Iowa Park	15	10	5	Marble Falls	18	11	7
Irving	368	267	101	Marlin	15	10	5
Jacinto City	20	14	6	Marshall	59	43	16
Jacksboro	7	5	2	Mart	4	4	....
Jacksonville	33	24	9	Martindale	2	2	....
Jamaica Beach	5	5	....	Mathis	11	6	5
Jasper	22	15	7	McAllen	261	171	90
Jefferson	5	5	....	McGregor	13	8	5
Jersey Village	19	13	6	McKinney	49	37	12
Johnson City	2	2	....	Meadows	11	10	1
Joshua	8	8	....	Memphis	3	2	1
Jourdanton	6	6	....	Mercedes	28	19	9
Junction	4	4	....	Merkel	3	3	....
Katy	23	18	5	Mesquite	229	168	61
Kaufman	19	14	5	Mexia	21	14	7
Keene	11	7	4	Midland	188	151	37
Keller	33	22	11	Midlothian	20	16	4
Kemah	9	5	4	Mineola	13	10	3
Kemp	4	4	....	Mineral Wells	31	24	7
Kennedale	16	12	4	Mission	72	53	19
Kermit	14	9	5	Missouri City	52	38	14
Kerrville	50	40	10	Monahans	21	14	7
Kilgore	33	26	7	Mont Belvieu	9	8	1
Killeen	164	128	36	Morgans Point Resort	5	5	....
Kingsville	62	44	18	Mount Pleasant	26	19	7
Kirby	16	12	4	Muleshoe	11	5	6
Kirbyville	3	3	....	Munday	2	2	....
Kyle	4	4	....	Mustang Ridge	1	1	....
Lacy-Lakeview	14	9	5	Nacogdoches	65	51	14
La Feria	12	8	4	Naples	2	2	....
Lago Vista	12	7	5	Nassau Bay	20	15	5
La Grange	6	5	1	Navasota	21	12	9
La Joya	9	6	3	Nederland	26	18	8
Lake Dallas	14	8	6	Needville	6	5	1
Lake Jackson	44	32	12	New Boston	11	7	4
Lakeside	3	2	1	New Braunfels	61	44	17
Lakeview	15	11	4	New Deal	2	1	1
Lakeway Village	17	12	5	Nocona	9	5	4
Lake Worth	23	17	6	Nolanville	2	2	....
La Marque	28	21	7	Northcrest	3	3	....
Lamesa	22	15	7	North Richland Hills	104	74	30
Lampasas	16	11	5	Oak Ridge North	8	7	1
Lancaster	44	32	12	Odessa	230	168	62
La Porte	70	50	20	Olmos Park	11	11	....
Laredo	265	216	49	Olney	10	5	5
La Vernia	2	2	....	Olton	3	3	....
La Villa	2	1	1	Onalaska	4	4	....
Lavon	5	5	....	Orange	53	41	12
League City	60	46	14	Orange Grove	3	3	....
Leander	11	6	5	Ore City	3	3	....
Leon Valley	33	25	8	Overton	8	5	3
Levelland	26	19	7	Oyster Creek	9	5	4
Lewisville	114	79	35	Palacios	8	5	3
Lexington	1	1	....	Palestine	40	30	10
Liberty	18	12	6	Palmer	3	3	....
Lindale	10	6	4	Pampa	32	26	6
Littlefield	16	11	5	Panhandle	4	4	....
Live Oak	25	19	6	Pantego	15	10	5
Livingston	17	10	7	Paris	65	44	21

City	Total police employees	Total officers	Total civilians	City	Total police employees	Total officers	Total civilians
TEXAS — Continued				**TEXAS — Continued**			
Parker	1	1	....	Seagoville	16	12	4
Pasadena	262	206	56	Seagraves	5	3	2
Pearland	53	38	15	Sealy	11	10	1
Pearsall	8	7	1	Seguin	54	35	19
Pecos	24	17	7	Selma	7	6	1
Pelican Bay	1	1	....	Seminole	13	11	2
Perryton	15	9	6	Seven Points	10	5	5
Pflugerville	17	11	6	Seymour	6	5	1
Pharr	81	65	16	Shallowater	3	3	....
Pilot Point	4	4	....	Shamrock	3	2	1
Pinehurst	11	6	5	Shavano Park	38	38	....
Pittsburg	9	8	1	Shenandoah	5	5	....
Plainview	40	33	7	Sherman	75	55	20
Plano	261	192	69	Silsbee	19	14	5
Pleasanton	15	11	4	Sinton	10	9	1
Port Aransas	16	10	6	Slaton	12	7	5
Port Arthur	143	108	35	Smithville	11	6	5
Port Isabel	23	15	8	Snyder	22	16	6
Portland	27	17	10	Somerset	2	2	....
Port Lavaca	26	20	6	Somerville	5	5	....
Port Neches	20	17	3	Sonora	8	6	2
Poteet	4	4	....	Sour Lake	7	6	1
Pottsboro	5	4	1	South Houston	40	30	10
Premont	3	3	....	Southlake	30	21	9
Primera	3	3	....	South Padre Island	25	19	6
Princeton	5	4	1	Southside Place	9	5	4
Quanah	3	3	....	Spearman	10	5	5
Quinlan	5	4	1	Springtown	8	4	4
Quitman	7	6	1	Spring Valley	21	15	6
Ranger	4	4	....	Spur	2	2	....
Ransom Canyon	1	1	....	Stafford	32	24	8
Raymondville	19	10	9	Stamford	9	7	2
Red Oak	14	10	4	Stanton	3	3	....
Refugio	6	5	1	Stephenville	36	29	7
Richardson	221	144	77	Stratford	2	2	....
Richland Hills	25	18	7	Sugar Land	74	58	16
Richmond	21	15	6	Sulphur Springs	41	34	7
Richwood	7	6	1	Sunset Valley	3	3	....
River Oaks	21	15	6	Surfside Beach	6	6	....
Roanoke	6	5	1	Sweeny	5	5	....
Robinson	17	11	6	Sweetwater	26	21	5
Robstown	30	23	7	Taft	5	5	....
Rockdale	14	9	5	Tahoka	4	4	....
Rockport	23	17	6	Tatum	4	2	2
Rockwall	42	28	14	Taylor	22	16	6
Rollingwood	9	8	1	Teague	5	5	....
Roma	22	16	6	Temple	114	95	19
Roman Forest	1	1	....	Terrell	39	30	9
Ropesville	1	1	....	Terrell Hills	16	16	....
Roscoe	1	1	....	Texarkana	86	77	9
Rosebud	3	3	....	Texas City	87	75	12
Rose City	2	1	1	The Colony	33	24	9
Rosenberg	58	44	14	Tomball	25	20	5
Round Rock	62	48	14	Trinity	8	5	3
Rowlett	53	40	13	Trophy Club	8	7	1
Royse City	7	5	2	Troup	6	4	2
Rusk	10	9	1	Tulia	11	6	5
Sabinal	2	2	....	Tye	2	2	....
Sachse	17	12	5	Tyler	183	133	50
Saginaw	21	15	6	Universal City	32	25	7
St. Jo	1	1	....	University Park	42	34	8
San Angelo	196	158	38	Uvalde	23	18	5
San Angelo Park	2	2	....	Van	4	4	....
San Antonio	2,023	1,662	361	Vernon	29	22	7
San Augustine	5	5	....	Victoria	131	97	34
San Benito	39	32	7	Vidor	28	21	7
Sanger	7	7	....	Village	32	27	5
San Juan	28	21	7	Village of Jones Creek	4	4	....
San Marcos	66	51	15	Waco	256	185	71
Sansom Park Village	11	7	4	Wake Village	5	5	....
Santa Anna	1	1	....	Waller	8	7	1
Santa Fe	20	14	6	Wallis	3	3	....
Schertz	25	18	7	Watauga	41	31	10
Seabrook	25	22	3	Waxahachie	44	34	10
Seadrift	1	1	....	Weatherford	49	35	14

Table 78. — Number of Full-time Law Enforcement Employees, Cities, October 31, 1993 — Continued

City	Total police employees	Total officers	Total civilians	City	Total police employees	Total officers	Total civilians
TEXAS — Continued				**UTAH — Continued**			
Webster	40	27	13	Pleasant Grove	16	15	1
Weimar	5	5	....	Pleasant View	5	4	1
Weslaco	48	39	9	Price	17	15	2
West	4	4	....	Provo	102	69	33
West Columbia	11	7	4	Richfield	11	9	2
West Lake Hills	17	12	5	Riverdale	17	15	2
West Orange	9	8	1	Roosevelt	9	8	1
Westover Hills	13	12	1	Roy	31	23	8
West Tawakoni	4	3	1	St. George	57	43	14
West University Place	28	21	7	Salem	5	4	1
Westworth	8	4	4	Salina	3	3	....
Wharton	26	18	8	Salt Lake City	421	349	72
Whitehouse	9	7	2	Sandy	90	78	12
White Oak	15	11	4	Santaquin	3	3	....
Whitesboro	11	7	4	South Jordan	13	11	2
White Settlement	34	25	9	South Ogden	23	19	4
Whitney	6	5	1	South Salt Lake	42	33	9
Wichita Falls	244	170	74	Spanish Fork	16	15	1
Willow Park	3	3	....	Springville	19	14	5
Wills Point	7	6	1	Stockton	1	1	....
Wilmer	13	8	5	Sunset	9	8	1
Windcrest	23	17	6	Syracuse	4	4	....
Winnsboro	12	9	3	Tooele	21	19	2
Winters	5	5	....	Tremonton	8	7	1
Wolfforth	3	3	....	Vernal	16	14	2
Woodville	6	5	1	Washington Terrace	12	10	2
Woodway	27	16	11	Wellington	2	2	....
Wylie	18	14	4	Wendover	6	5	1
Yoakum	15	9	6	West Bountiful	6	5	1
Yorktown	3	3	....	West Jordan	59	54	5
				West Valley	137	118	19
UTAH				Willard	2	2	....
				Woods Cross	7	6	1
Alpine	5	5	....				
Alta	9	4	5	**VERMONT**			
American Fork	21	18	3				
Beaver	3	3	....	Barre	22	17	5
Bountiful	39	30	9	Barre Town	6	6	....
Brian Head	3	3	....	Bellows Falls	11	7	4
Brigham City	27	22	5	Bennington	29	24	5
Cedar City	20	17	3	Brandon	7	6	1
Centerville	13	11	2	Brattleboro	43	28	15
Clearfield	26	24	2	Bristol	2	2	....
Clinton	7	7	....	Burlington	117	88	29
East Carbon	5	3	2	Castleton	1	1	....
Ephraim	4	4	....	Chester	5	4	1
Farmington	8	7	1	Colchester	27	23	4
Grantsville	5	5	....	Dover	6	5	1
Gunnison	2	2	....	Essex	32	26	6
Harrisville	5	4	1	Fair Haven	2	2	....
Heber City	9	7	2	Hardwick	7	6	1
Hildale	5	4	1	Hartford	26	20	6
Hurricane	7	6	1	Ludlow	8	4	4
Kanab	4	4	....	Lyndonville	1	1	....
Kaysville	12	10	2	Manchester	13	8	5
Layton	58	47	11	Middlebury	13	11	2
Lehi	11	10	1	Milton	12	10	2
Logan	51	42	9	Montpelier	20	13	7
Mapleton	5	5	....	Morristown	7	6	1
Midvale	26	23	3	Newport	12	10	2
Minersville	1	1	....	Northfield	3	3	....
Moab	10	9	1	Norwich	5	4	1
Monticello	3	3	....	Randolph	4	4	....
Moroni	2	1	1	Richmond	4	4	....
Mount Pleasant	4	4	....	Rutland	44	36	8
Murray	65	55	10	St. Albans	19	13	6
Naples	6	4	2	St. Johnsbury	15	10	5
Nephi	7	6	1	Shelburne	15	10	5
North Ogden	13	11	2	South Burlington	35	30	5
North Salt Lake	9	8	1	Springfield	20	15	5
Ogden	122	105	17	Stowe	12	11	1
Orem	82	60	22	Swanton	4	3	1
Park City	24	18	6	Vergennes	4	4	....
Parowan	2	2	....	Vernon	3	3	....
Perry	1	1	....	Waterbury	3	3	....

Table 78. — Number of Full-time Law Enforcement Employees, Cities, October 31, 1993 — Continued

City	Total police employees	Total officers	Total civilians	City	Total police employees	Total officers	Total civilians
VERMONT — Continued				**VIRGINIA — Continued**			
Weathersfield	1	1	....	Haysi	1	1	....
Williston	3	3	....	Herndon	41	32	9
Wilmington	7	5	2	Hillsville	6	6	....
Windsor	11	7	4	Honaker	3	3	....
Winhall	4	4	....	Hopewell	53	42	11
Winooski	16	12	4	Hurt	4	3	1
Woodstock	6	5	1	Independence	2	2	....
				Iron Gate	1	1	....
VIRGINIA				Jonesville	3	3	....
				Kenbridge	5	5	....
Abingdon	18	16	2	Kilmarnock	4	4	....
Alexandria	372	261	111	La Crosse	1	1	....
Altavista	15	11	4	Lawrenceville	5	5	....
Amherst	4	4	....	Lebanon	8	7	1
Appalachia	7	6	1	Leesburg	36	33	3
Arlington	400	320	80	Lexington	20	15	5
Ashland	22	19	3	Louisa	3	3	....
Bedford	25	19	6	Luray	14	13	1
Berryville	8	7	1	Lynchburg	176	134	42
Big Stone Gap	21	14	7	Manassas	80	63	17
Blacksburg	65	50	15	Manassas Park	19	12	7
Blackstone	16	11	5	Marion	20	16	4
Bluefield	15	11	4	Martinsville	55	49	6
Bowling Green	1	1	....	McKenney	1	1	....
Bridgewater	6	6	....	Middleburg	3	3	....
Bristol	60	44	16	Middletown	1	1	....
Brookneal	3	3	....	Mount Jackson	3	3	....
Buena Vista	14	10	4	Narrows	5	5	....
Burkeville	3	3	....	New Market	3	3	....
Cape Charles	4	4	....	Newport News	423	318	105
Cedar Bluff	2	2	....	Norfolk	759	664	95
Charlottesville	115	94	21	Norton	19	14	5
Chase City	12	8	4	Onancock	3	3	....
Chatham	4	4	....	Onley	1	1	....
Chesapeake	334	262	72	Orange	13	13	....
Chilhowie	6	6	....	Parksley	3	3	....
Chincoteague	10	7	3	Pearisburg	6	6	....
Christiansburg	36	29	7	Pembroke	1	1	....
Clarkesville	8	5	3	Pennington Gap	10	4	6
Clifton Forge	13	10	3	Petersburg	134	93	41
Clintwood	2	2	....	Pocahontas	2	2	....
Coeburn	8	7	1	Poquoson	21	16	5
Colonial Beach	12	8	4	Portsmouth	284	213	71
Colonial Heights	49	38	11	Pound	4	4	....
Courtland	3	1	2	Pulaski	35	26	9
Covington	20	14	6	Purcellville	6	6	....
Crewe	5	5	....	Quantico	3	3	....
Culpeper	36	27	9	Radford	36	25	11
Damascus	2	2	....	Rich Creek	1	1	....
Danville	131	113	18	Richlands	21	16	5
Dayton	3	2	1	Richmond	758	659	99
Dublin	8	7	1	Roanoke	298	255	43
Dumfries	12	10	2	Rocky Mount	12	12	....
Edinburg	2	2	....	Rural Retreat	1	1	....
Elkton	9	5	4	St. Paul	5	5	....
Emporia	26	19	7	Salem	77	58	19
Exmore	2	2	....	Saltville	5	5	....
Fairfax City	73	58	15	Shenandoah	4	4	....
Falls Church	38	28	10	Smithfield	16	10	6
Farmville	26	17	9	South Boston	20	16	4
Franklin	32	24	8	South Hill	21	16	5
Fredericksburg	78	57	21	Stanley	3	3	....
Fries	1	1	....	Staunton	62	45	17
Front Royal	39	30	9	Stephens City	2	2	....
Galax	28	22	6	Strasburg	11	9	2
Gate City	3	3	....	Suffolk	131	102	29
Glade Springs	2	2	....	Tappahannock	5	5	....
Glen Lyn	1	1	....	Tazewell	12	10	2
Gordonsville	5	5	....	Urbanna	1	1	....
Gretna	3	3	....	Victoria	4	4	....
Grottoes	3	3	....	Vienna	48	38	10
Grundy	4	4	....	Vinton	24	17	7
Halifax	4	4	....	Virginia Beach	824	614	210
Hampton	304	223	81	Warrenton	25	19	6
Harrisonburg	63	49	14	Warsaw	2	2	....

Table 78.—Number of Full-time Law Enforcement Employees, Cities, October 31, 1993—Continued

City	Total police employees	Total officers	Total civilians	City	Total police employees	Total officers	Total civilians
VIRGINIA—Continued				**WASHINGTON—Continued**			
Waverly	5	5	....	La Conner	4	4	....
Waynesboro	50	46	4	Lake Forest Park	11	6	5
Weber City	3	3	....	Lake Stevens	7	7	....
Williamsburg	41	29	12	Long Beach	7	6	1
Winchester	65	49	16	Longview	55	49	6
Wise	12	11	1	Lummi Tribal	22	17	5
Woodstock	12	11	1	Lynden	12	9	3
Wytheville	32	23	9	Lynnwood	60	48	12
				Marysville	39	23	16
WASHINGTON				McCleary	4	4	....
				Medina	8	7	1
Aberdeen	48	36	12	Mercer Island	39	30	9
Algona	7	6	1	Mill Creek	18	14	4
Anacortes	28	18	10	Milton	10	9	1
Arlington	11	10	1	Monroe	19	16	3
Auburn	91	67	24	Montesano	9	7	2
Bainbridge Island	19	16	3	Morton	3	2	1
Battle Ground	10	9	1	Moses Lake	33	22	11
Bellevue	230	149	81	Mossyrock	2	2	....
Bellingham	154	94	60	Mountlake Terrace	32	29	3
Black Diamond	6	5	1	Mount Vernon	37	31	6
Blaine	14	12	2	Mukilteo	23	20	3
Bonney Lake	20	14	6	Napavine	3	2	1
Bothell	44	30	14	Newport	4	4	....
Bremerton	78	62	16	Normandy Park	13	12	1
Brewster	6	5	1	Oak Harbor	38	24	14
Brier	9	7	2	Ocean Shores	10	7	3
Buckley	17	8	9	Olympia	86	65	21
Burlington	23	16	7	Omak	10	9	1
Camas	17	14	3	Oroville	9	5	4
Carnation	6	5	1	Othello	13	9	4
Castle Rock	5	4	1	Pacific	9	8	1
Centralia	27	24	3	Palouse	1	1	....
Chehalis	22	17	5	Pasco	49	39	10
Chelan	10	9	1	Pomeroy	3	3	....
Cheney	13	11	2	Port Angeles	50	27	23
Chewelah	6	5	1	Port Orchard	12	11	1
Clarkston	15	12	3	Port Townsend	12	10	2
Cle Elum	7	6	1	Poulsbo	15	13	2
Clyde Hill	8	7	1	Prosser	13	9	4
Colfax	5	5	....	Pullman	33	24	9
College Place	12	8	4	Puyallup	58	52	6
Colville	10	9	1	Quincy	10	8	2
Connell	5	5	....	Raymond	7	6	1
Cosmopolis	6	5	1	Redmond	75	55	20
Coulee Dam	3	3	....	Renton	107	78	29
Davenport	2	2	....	Republic	2	2	....
Dayton	4	3	1	Richland	50	44	6
Des Moines	38	27	11	Ridgefield	3	3	....
East Wenatchee	12	10	2	Ritzville	3	3	....
Eatonville	5	5	....	Ruston	2	2	....
Edmonds	53	37	16	Seattle	1,749	1,245	504
Ellensburg	25	19	6	Sedro Woolley	17	10	7
Elma	6	5	1	Selah	13	11	2
Enumclaw	27	16	11	Sequim	13	10	3
Ephrata	17	10	7	Shelton	31	18	13
Everett	184	146	38	Snohomish	19	17	2
Ferndale	13	11	2	Snoqualmie	7	6	1
Fife	24	15	9	Soap Lake	4	4	....
Fircrest	10	8	2	South Bend	5	4	1
Forks	11	6	5	Spokane	356	261	95
Gig Harbor	11	9	2	Stanwood	9	7	2
Goldendale	5	5	....	Steilacoom	11	10	1
Grand Coulee	3	3	....	Sumner	22	14	8
Grandview	18	14	4	Sunnyside	28	20	8
Hoquiam	26	21	5	Swinomish Tribal	9	8	1
Issaquah	28	19	9	Tacoma	394	350	44
Kalama	5	5	....	Toledo	3	3	....
Kelso	28	24	4	Tonasket	4	4	....
Kennewick	76	60	16	Toppenish	20	14	6
Kent	126	81	45	Tukwila	73	62	11
Kettle Falls	4	4	....	Tumwater	24	21	3
Kirkland	74	55	19	Twisp	4	3	1
La Center	4	4	....	Union Gap	18	13	5
Lacey	38	33	5	Vader	1	1	....

Table 78. — Number of Full-time Law Enforcement Employees, Cities, October 31, 1993 — Continued

City	Total police employees	Total officers	Total civilians	City	Total police employees	Total officers	Total civilians
WASHINGTON — Continued				**WEST VIRGINIA — Continued**			
Vancouver	114	95	19	Matewan	3	3	....
Waitsburg	1	1	....	McMechen	4	4	....
Walla Walla	54	36	18	Middlebourne	1	1	....
Wapato	20	14	6	Mill Creek	1	1	....
Washougal	9	8	1	Milton	2	2	....
Wenatchee	51	37	14	Mitchell Heights	1	1	....
Westport	8	7	1	Monongah	1	1	....
West Richland	11	10	1	Montgomery	11	10	1
White Salmon	4	4	....	Moorefield	5	5	....
Wilbur	2	2	....	Morgantown	53	46	7
Winlock	1	1	....	Moundsville	18	13	5
Winthrop	2	2	....	Mount Hope	6	5	1
Woodland	5	5	....	Mullens	5	5	....
Yakima	141	105	36	New Cumberland	4	4	....
Zillah	6	5	1	New Haven	3	2	1
				New Martinsville	14	10	4
WEST VIRGINIA				Nitro	14	10	4
				North Fork	3	3	....
Alderson	3	3	....	Nutter Fort	5	5	....
Anmoore	2	2	....	Oak Hill	12	8	4
Ansted	4	3	1	Oceana	5	5	....
Barboursville	12	11	1	Paden City	6	4	2
Beckley	55	40	15	Parkersburg	74	58	16
Belington	2	2	....	Parsons	2	2	....
Belle	4	4	....	Pennsboro	1	1	....
Benwood	4	4	....	Petersburg	4	4	....
Bethlehem	4	4	....	Philippi	6	6	....
Bluefield	34	27	7	Piedmont	2	2	....
Bridgeport	18	16	2	Pineville	4	4	....
Buckhannon	6	6	....	Poca	1	1	....
Cameron	4	4	....	Point Pleasant	8	7	1
Cedar Grove	3	3	....	Princeton	27	21	6
Ceredo	9	5	4	Rainelle	2	2	....
Chapmanville	5	5	....	Ranson	9	8	1
Charleston	179	155	24	Ravenswood	11	7	4
Charles Town	10	8	2	Reedsville	1	1	....
Chesapeake	3	3	....	Richwood	8	5	3
Chester	5	5	....	Ripley	8	7	1
Clarksburg	40	34	6	Romney	4	3	1
Clendenin	3	3	....	Ronceverte	3	3	....
Danville	3	2	1	St. Albans	21	14	7
Delbarton	2	2	....	St. Marys	7	3	4
Dunbar	17	12	5	Salem	3	3	....
Elkins	15	9	6	Shepherdstown	6	5	1
Fairmont	39	29	10	Shinnston	5	5	....
Fayetteville	5	4	1	Sistersville	3	3	....
Follansbee	9	9	....	Smithers	2	2	....
Fort Gay	2	2	....	Sophia	3	3	....
Gauley Bridge	2	2	....	South Charleston	31	29	2
Glen Dale	6	5	1	Spencer	8	5	3
Glenville	5	5	....	Star City	5	5	....
Grafton	13	8	5	Stonewood	2	2	....
Grantsville	1	1	....	Summersville	11	11	....
Granville	5	4	1	Sutton	3	3	....
Harpers Ferry-Bolivar	3	3	....	Vienna	21	13	8
Harrisville	1	1	....	War	4	4	....
Hinton	4	4	....	Wayne	3	1	2
Huntington	105	98	7	Weirton	46	39	7
Hurricane	14	9	5	Welch	13	11	2
Kenova	10	8	2	Wellsburg	3	3	....
Kermit	2	2	....	Weston	10	8	2
Keyser	13	8	5	Westover	7	7	....
Kimball	2	2	....	Wheeling	81	80	1
Kingwood	4	4	....	White Sulphur Springs	8	7	1
Lewisburg	10	8	2	Whitesville	2	2	....
Logan	12	9	3	Williamson	8	6	2
Lumberport	2	2	....	Williamstown	5	4	1
Mabscott	2	2	....				
Madison	7	6	1	**WISCONSIN**			
Man	6	4	2				
Mannington	4	4	....	Adams	3	3	....
Marlinton	1	1	....	Algoma	5	5	....
Marmet	5	5	....	Altoona	9	8	1
Martinsburg	48	37	11	Amery	7	6	1
Mason	3	3	....	Antigo	18	17	1

Table 78. — Number of Full-time Law Enforcement Employees, Cities, October 31, 1993 — Continued

City	Total police employees	Total officers	Total civilians	City	Total police employees	Total officers	Total civilians
WISCONSIN — Continued				**WISCONSIN — Continued**			
Appleton	117	93	24	Hartland	13	12	1
Ashland	25	19	6	Hayward	6	5	1
Ashwaubenon	38	33	5	Hillsboro	2	2	....
Bangor	1	1	....	Holmen	5	5	....
Baraboo	26	23	3	Horicon	11	9	2
Barron	5	5	....	Hudson	19	16	3
Bayfield	3	3	....	Hurley	8	7	1
Bayside	16	13	3	Jackson	5	4	1
Beaver Dam	37	28	9	Janesville	104	87	17
Belleville	3	3	....	Jefferson	14	12	2
Beloit	90	73	17	Juneau	3	3	....
Beloit Town	9	9	....	Kaukauna	21	20	1
Berlin	16	12	4	Kenosha	178	166	12
Black Earth	2	2	....	Kewaskum	6	5	1
Black River Falls	8	8	....	Kewaunee	6	6	....
Boscobel	6	6	....	Kiel	10	5	5
Brillion	4	4	....	Kimberly	10	9	1
Brodhead	11	7	4	Kohler	5	5	....
Brookfield	84	63	21	La Crosse	110	88	22
Brookfield Township	9	8	1	Ladysmith	7	6	1
Brown Deer	36	27	9	Lake Delton	10	9	1
Burlington	28	22	6	Lake Geneva	21	17	4
Burlington Town	7	7	....	Lake Mills	8	7	1
Butler	11	8	3	Lancaster	7	6	1
Caledonia	30	24	6	Little Chute	14	12	2
Campbell Township	5	5	....	Lodi	5	4	1
Cedarburg	26	18	8	Madison	358	302	56
Chenequa	8	8	....	Manitowoc	71	61	10
Chilton	6	6	....	Maple Bluff	5	5	....
Chippewa Falls	33	25	8	Marinette	29	23	6
Clear Lake	2	2	....	Markesan	3	3	....
Clintonville	13	11	2	Marshfield	52	38	14
Columbus	12	8	4	Mauston	7	6	1
Combined Locks	4	4	....	Mayville	10	8	2
Cornell	8	4	4	Mazomanie	3	3	....
Crandon	2	2	....	McFarland	9	8	1
Cross Plains	4	4	....	Medford	9	8	1
Cuba City	3	3	....	Menasha	33	28	5
Cudahy	48	34	14	Menasha Town	23	19	4
Dane	1	1	....	Menomonee Falls	72	55	17
Darlington	4	4	....	Menomonie	38	26	12
De Forest	9	8	1	Mequon	37	36	1
Delafield	10	9	1	Merrill	25	21	4
Delavan	17	13	4	Middleton	32	26	6
Delavan Town	7	7	....	Milton	7	7	....
De Pere	30	25	5	Milwaukee	2,481	2,079	402
Dodgeville	10	9	1	Minocqua	14	9	5
Durand	4	4	....	Mondovi	4	4	....
Eagle River	6	6	....	Monona	21	18	3
East Troy	7	6	1	Monroe	31	24	7
Eau Claire	113	85	28	Montello	3	2	1
Edgerton	10	9	1	Mosinee	6	5	1
Eleva	1	1	....	Mount Horeb	8	7	1
Elkhorn	13	11	2	Mount Pleasant	30	22	8
Elm Grove	21	16	5	Mukwonago	15	10	5
Elroy	3	3	....	Muskego	36	27	9
Evansville	9	6	3	Neenah	49	41	8
Everest	20	18	2	Neillsville	7	6	1
Fitchburg	27	21	6	New Berlin	76	59	17
Fond Du Lac	74	62	12	New Glarus	4	4	....
Fort Atkinson	23	18	5	New Holstein	6	6	....
Fox Lake	1	1	....	New Lisbon	3	3	....
Fox Point	22	16	6	New London	17	17	....
Franklin	42	32	10	New Richmond	9	8	1
Germantown	33	24	9	North Fond du Lac	10	8	2
Glendale	48	41	7	Oak Creek	47	40	7
Grafton	25	19	6	Oconomowoc	27	21	6
Grand Chute	11	9	2	Oconomowoc Town	10	9	1
Green Bay	220	172	48	Oconto	8	8	....
Greendale	33	26	7	Oconto Falls	5	5	....
Greenfield	75	51	24	Omro	6	5	1
Green Lake	3	3	....	Onalaska	24	22	2
Hales Corners	21	17	4	Oregon	9	8	1
Hallie	7	6	1	Osceola	3	3	....
Hartford	23	18	5	Oshkosh	97	82	15

Table 78. — Number of Full-time Law Enforcement Employees, Cities, October 31, 1993 — Continued

City	Total police employees	Total officers	Total civilians	City	Total police employees	Total officers	Total civilians
WISCONSIN — Continued				**WISCONSIN — Continued**			
Palmyra	4	4	....	Waunakee	10	9	1
Park Falls	7	6	1	Waupaca	16	12	4
Peshtigo	6	6	....	Waupun	21	14	7
Pewaukee	13	13	....	Wausau	67	55	12
Pewaukee Township	8	7	1	Wauwatosa	104	83	21
Phillips	5	5	....	West Allis	154	130	24
Platteville	22	17	5	West Bend	59	45	14
Pleasant Prairie	16	16	....	West Milwaukee	24	19	5
Plover	11	10	1	West Salem	5	5	....
Plymouth	14	13	1	Whitefish Bay	27	22	5
Portage	27	21	6	Whitehall	3	3	....
Port Washington	22	17	5	Whitewater	33	23	10
Prairie du Chien	16	11	5	Williams Bay	6	5	1
Prescott	7	6	1	Winneconne	5	4	1
Pulaski	6	6	....	Wisconsin Dells	14	10	4
Racine	238	205	33	Wisconsin Rapids	49	39	10
Reedsburg	17	12	5	Wonewoc	1	1	....
Rhinelander	25	18	7				
Rice Lake	21	15	6				
Richland Center	12	10	2	**WYOMING**			
Ripon	18	13	5				
River Falls	20	17	3	Afton	4	4	....
River Hills	13	13	....	Basin	4	4	....
Rome Town	4	4	....	Buffalo	12	8	4
Rothschild	7	7	....	Casper	83	68	15
St. Croix Falls	3	3	....	Cheyenne	97	77	20
St. Francis	20	19	1	Cody	16	14	2
Sauk Prairie	11	10	1	Diamondville	4	3	1
Saukville	8	7	1	Douglas	18	11	7
Shawano	23	18	5	Encampment	2	1	1
Sheboygan	112	85	27	Evanston	28	23	5
Sheboygan Falls	8	8	....	Evansville	12	6	6
Shorewood	31	26	5	Gillette	54	38	16
Shorewood Hills	8	5	3	Glenrock	8	5	3
Slinger	3	2	1	Green River	29	25	4
Somerset	4	3	1	Greybull	4	4	....
South Milwaukee	34	32	2	Guernsey	4	4	....
Sparta	18	13	5	Hanna	5	2	3
Spring Green	4	4	....	Jackson	22	17	5
Stanley	4	4	....	Kemmerer	11	8	3
Stevens Point	53	42	11	Lander	15	14	1
Stoughton	18	14	4	Laramie	41	38	3
Strum	1	1	....	Lovell	9	4	5
Sturgeon Bay	19	18	1	Lusk	3	3	....
Sturtevant	11	9	2	Lyman	11	7	4
Summit	7	7	....	Mills	7	6	1
Sun Prairie	40	29	11	Moorcroft	4	3	1
Superior	59	55	4	Newcastle	12	7	5
Thiensville	8	7	1	Pine Bluffs	5	2	3
Tomah	23	17	6	Powell	18	11	7
Tomahawk	7	6	1	Rawlins	30	19	11
Town Of Madison	18	16	2	Riverton	32	21	11
Twin Lakes	11	7	4	Rock Springs	59	32	27
Two Rivers	29	24	5	Saratoga	9	4	5
Verona	11	10	1	Sheridan	42	27	15
Viroqua	11	8	3	Sundance	4	4	....
Washburn	5	5	....	Thermopolis	15	10	5
Washington Island	1	1	....	Torrington	19	13	6
Waterloo	6	6	....	Upton	4	3	1
Watertown	45	33	12	Wheatland	10	9	1
Waukesha	130	97	33	Worland	11	11	....

Table 79. — Number of Full-time Law Enforcement Employees, Universities and Colleges, October 31, 1993

University/College	Total police employees	Total officers	Total civilians	University/College	Total police employees	Total officers	Total civilians
ALABAMA				**CALIFORNIA – Continued**			
				Hastings College of Law	12	7	5
Alabama State University	28	25	3	Irvine	30	22	8
Auburn University:				Lawrence Livermore Laboratory	220	2	218
Main Campus	48	25	23	Los Angeles	69	54	15
Montgomery	20	13	7	Riverside	19	19	....
Enterprise State Junior College	2	2	....	San Diego	49	26	23
Jacksonville State University	19	15	4	San Francisco Medical School	61	24	37
Livingston University	7	5	2	Santa Barbara	24	24	....
Troy State University	9	8	1	Santa Cruz	26	17	9
University of Alabama:				West Valley College	12	9	3
Birmingham	87	56	31				
Huntsville	16	10	6	**COLORADO**			
Tuscaloosa	38	31	7				
University of Montevallo	14	9	5	Adams State College	3	3	....
University of South Alabama	33	23	10	Arapahoe Community College	3	3	....
				Auraria Higher Education Center	34	17	17
ALASKA				Colorado School of Mines	8	7	1
				Colorado State University	27	19	8
University of Alaska, Fairbanks	42	9	33	Pike's Peak Community College	6	5	1
				Red Rocks Community College	10	6	4
ARIZONA				University of Colorado:			
				Boulder	75	35	40
Arizona State University	63	41	22	Colorado Springs	13	9	4
Arizona Western College	8	7	1	Health Sciences	37	23	14
Central Arizona College	5	5	....	University of Northern Colorado	17	11	6
Northern Arizona University	32	20	12	University of Southern Colorado	10	3	7
Pima Community College	31	21	10				
University of Arizona	62	37	25	**CONNECTICUT**			
Yavapai College	5	5	....				
				Central Connecticut State University	26	23	3
ARKANSAS				Eastern Connecticut State University	15	13	2
				Southern Connecticut State University	27	23	4
University of Arkansas:				University of Connecticut:			
Fayetteville	31	24	7	Avery Point	5	5	....
Little Rock	22	20	2	Health Center	23	17	6
Medical Science	45	31	14	Storrs	42	36	6
Pine Bluff	20	13	7	Western Connecticut State University	20	15	5
University of Central Arkansas	19	18	1	Yale University	85	70	15
CALIFORNIA				**DELAWARE**			
Allen Hancock College	8	2	6	University of Delaware	72	42	30
Cabrillo College	9	7	2				
California State Polytechnic University:				**FLORIDA**			
Pomona	26	12	14	Florida A&M University	29	23	6
San Luis Obispo	21	11	10	Florida Atlantic University	30	25	5
California State University:				Florida International University	49	31	18
Bakersfield	15	9	6	Florida State University:			
Chico	14	10	4	Panama City	3	2	1
Dominguez Hills	19	11	8	Tallahassee	60	44	16
Fresno	29	15	14	University of Central Florida	50	32	18
Fullerton	33	14	19	University of Florida	125	76	49
Hayward	26	11	15	University of North Florida	26	18	8
Long Beach	23	18	5	University of South Florida:			
Los Angeles	31	16	15	St. Petersburg	13	9	4
Northridge	20	15	5	Sarasota	16	12	4
Sacramento	19	13	6	Tampa	59	40	19
San Bernardino	15	9	6	University of West Florida	25	19	6
San Diego	33	20	13				
San Jose	44	22	22	**GEORGIA**			
Stanislaus	13	9	4				
College of Marin	9	8	1	Abraham Baldwin Agricultural College	12	11	1
College of the Sequoias	1	1	....	Agnes Scott College	17	11	6
Contra Costa Community College	23	18	5	Albany State College	19	15	4
Evergreen Valley/San Jose Community College	16	8	8	Armstrong State College	12	9	3
Foothill-Deanza College	11	10	1	Berry College	15	12	3
Fresno Community College	12	11	1	Brunswick College	6	5	1
Humboldt State University	17	10	7	Cherokee College	5	5	....
King's River Community College	5	4	1	Clark Atlanta University	55	24	31
Pasadena City College	19	10	9	Clayton State College	14	12	2
San Francisco State University	32	20	12	Columbus College	9	8	1
Santa Rosa Junior College	9	7	2	Dalton College	5	5	....
Sonoma State University	20	12	8	DeKalb College	32	14	18
University of California:				Emory University	45	33	12
Berkeley	118	76	42	Fort Valley State College	20	17	3
Davis	79	47	32				

Table 79. — Number of Full-time Law Enforcement Employees, Universities and Colleges, October 31, 1993 — Continued

University/College	Total police employees	Total officers	Total civilians	University/College	Total police employees	Total officers	Total civilians
GEORGIA — Continued				**KANSAS — Continued**			
Georgia College	12	10	2	Pittsburg State University	15	12	3
Georgia Institute of Technology	48	35	13	University of Kansas:			
Georgia Southern University	36	28	8	Lawrence	53	33	20
Georgia Southwestern College	10	9	1	Medical Center	44	29	15
Georgia State University	69	62	7	Wichita State University	30	22	8
Gordon College	5	2	3	**KENTUCKY**			
Kennesaw College	25	19	6				
Medical College of Georgia	62	43	19	Eastern Kentucky University	29	18	11
Mercer University	31	23	8	Jefferson Community College	6	6	....
Middle Georgia College	11	7	4	Kentucky State University	12	9	3
North Georgia College	9	7	2	Morehead State University	18	11	7
Reinhardt College	3	3	....	Murray State University	19	12	7
Savannah State College	31	14	17	Northern Kentucky University	26	16	10
Southern College of Technology	16	12	4	University of Kentucky	58	34	24
South Georgia College	7	7	....	University of Louisville	34	24	10
University of Georgia	71	61	10	Western Kentucky University	28	21	7
Valdosta State	35	22	13	**LOUISIANA**			
Wesleyan College	6	5	1				
West Georgia College	30	18	12	Grambling State University	34	33	1
Young Harris College	1	1	....	Louisiana State University, Baton Rouge	59	57	2
ILLINOIS				Louisiana Tech. University	22	20	2
				McNeese State University	13	12	1
Black Hawk College	5	4	1	Nichols State University	15	12	3
Chicago State University	27	21	6	Northeast Louisiana University	22	18	4
College of DuPage	14	10	4	Northwestern State University	17	14	3
College of Lake County	6	6	....	Southeastern Louisiana University	24	20	4
Eastern Illinois University	29	20	9	Southern University and A&M College,	36	34	2
Governors State University	13	10	3	Baton Rouge			
Illinois State University	37	25	12	**MAINE**			
John A. Logan College	2	1	1	University of Maine:			
Joliet Junior College	7	6	1	Farmington	4	4	....
Loyola University of Chicago	46	38	8	Orono	36	24	12
Morton College	11	8	3	University of Southern Maine	24	18	6
Northeastern Illinois University	23	17	6	**MARYLAND**			
Northern Illinois University	40	26	14				
Oakton Community College	7	6	1	Bowie State University	22	16	6
Rock Valley College	6	5	1	Coppin State University	13	10	3
Sangamon State University	13	1	12	Frostburg State University	19	15	4
Southern Illinois University:				Morgan State University	41	32	9
Carbondale	55	43	12	St. Mary's College	11	3	8
Edwardsville	25	17	8	Salisbury State University	18	17	1
School of Medicine	13	2	11	Towson State University	48	32	16
South Suburban College	17	12	5	University of Baltimore	32	11	21
State Community College	4	4	....	University of Maryland:			
Triton College	18	13	5	Baltimore City	115	60	55
University of Illinois:				Baltimore County	27	19	8
Chicago	87	64	23	College Park	75	65	10
Urbana	57	43	14	Eastern Shore	15	13	2
Waubonsee College	2	2	....	**MASSACHUSETTS**			
Western Illinois University	34	23	11				
William Rainey Harper College	14	7	7	Boston College	48	45	3
INDIANA				Boston University	44	40	4
				Brandeis University	23	22	1
Ball State University	42	30	12	Emerson College	15	14	1
Indiana State University	30	23	7	Framingham State College	17	12	5
Indiana University:				Massachusetts Institute of Technology	67	55	12
Bloomington	57	47	10	North Adams State College	11	8	3
Gary	14	10	4	Northeastern University	70	41	29
Indianapolis	60	36	24	University of Massachusetts:			
New Albany	8	7	1	Amherst	89	48	41
Purdue University	43	37	6	Boston	40	26	14
IOWA				Worcester	40	30	10
				Wentworth Institute of Technology	25	10	15
Iowa State University	31	25	6	Westfield State College	40	14	26
University of Iowa	47	27	20	**MICHIGAN**			
University of Northern Iowa	26	19	7				
KANSAS				Central Michigan University	25	15	10
				Delta College	11	8	3
Emporia State University	11	9	2	Eastern Michigan University	28	23	5
Fort Hays State University	11	10	1	Ferris State University	21	15	6
Garden City Community College	2	2	....				
Kansas State University, Manhattan	31	19	12				

Table 79. — Number of Full-time Law Enforcement Employees, Universities and Colleges, October 31, 1993 — Continued

University/College	Total police employees	Total officers	Total civilians	University/College	Total police employees	Total officers	Total civilians
MICHIGAN — Continued				**NEW JERSEY — Continued**			
Grand Valley State University	9	8	1	Trenton State College	23	19	4
Hope College	8	5	3	University of Medicine and Dentistry:			
Lansing Community College	10	8	2	Camden	20	19	1
Macomb Community College	33	22	11	Newark	124	55	69
Michigan State University	54	48	6	Piscataway	33	26	7
Michigan Technological University	13	9	4	William Paterson College	34	26	8
Northern Michigan University	17	14	3				
Oakland Community College	21	18	3				
Oakland University	19	15	4	**NEW MEXICO**			
Saginaw Valley State University	7	6	1				
University of Michigan:				Eastern New Mexico University	7	6	1
Ann Arbor	76	33	43	New Mexico State University	28	19	9
Flint	14	5	9	University of New Mexico	41	25	16
Western Michigan University	34	24	10				
				NEW YORK			
MINNESOTA							
				Cornell University	51	39	12
University of Minnesota:				Ithaca College	36	15	21
Duluth	9	8	1	Rensselaer Polytechnic Institute	19	17	2
Minneapolis	45	38	7	State University of New York:			
				Albany	41	34	7
MISSISSIPPI				Downstate Medical Center	109	32	77
				Maritime College	13	9	4
Hinds Community College	15	12	3	Stony Brook	100	60	40
Itawamba Community College	3	2	1	Upstate Medical Center	63	2	61
Mississippi State University	42	26	16	State University of New York Agricultural and			
University of Mississippi:				Technical College:			
Medical Center	65	58	7	Alfred	17	14	3
Oxford	46	24	22	Canton	11	10	1
				Cobleskill	11	10	1
MISSOURI				Delhi	11	9	2
				Farmingdale	18	16	2
Central Missouri State University	25	16	9	Morrisville	13	11	2
Lincoln University	11	9	2	State University of New York College:			
University of Missouri:				Brockport	21	18	3
Columbia	44	30	14	Buffalo	34	28	6
St. Louis	24	17	7	Cortland	18	16	2
Washington University	25	18	7	Fredonia	16	15	1
				Geneseo	18	16	2
MONTANA				New Paltz	23	21	2
				Old Westbury	22	20	2
Montana State University	14	10	4	Oneonta	18	17	1
University of Montana	15	11	4	Optometry	4	2	2
				Oswego	26	21	5
NEBRASKA				Plattsburgh	20	14	6
				Potsdam	14	11	3
University of Nebraska:				Purchase	18	14	4
Kearney	6	5	1	Utica-Rome	17	12	5
Lincoln	42	23	19				
				NORTH CAROLINA			
NEVADA							
				Appalachian State University	23	18	5
University of Nevada:				Campbell University	13	9	4
Las Vegas	30	18	12	Davidson College	10	9	1
Reno	18	16	2	Duke University	129	58	71
				East Carolina University	50	32	18
NEW HAMPSHIRE				Elizabeth City State University	14	11	3
				Fayetteville State University	23	15	8
University of New Hampshire	33	16	17	Mars Hill College	5	4	1
				North Carolina A&T State University,			
NEW JERSEY				Greensboro	48	26	22
				North Carolina Central University, Durham	35	21	14
Brookdale Community College	19	13	6	North Carolina School of the Arts	8	8	....
Burlington County College	21	20	1	North Carolina State University, Raleigh	47	35	12
Essex County College	44	12	32	Pembroke State University	13	10	3
Kean College	32	19	13	Queens College	10	9	1
Middlesex County College	17	11	6	University of North Carolina:			
Monmouth College	15	11	4	Asheville	9	7	2
Montclair State College	31	12	19	Chapel Hill	46	30	16
New Jersey Institute of Technology	59	21	38	Charlotte	33	27	6
Rowan College	25	5	20	Greensboro	36	25	11
Rutgers University:				Wilmington	27	20	7
Camden	34	18	16	Wake Forest University	23	13	10
Newark	58	29	29	Western Carolina University	16	13	3
New Brunswick	124	62	62	Winston-Salem State University	11	11	....
Stockton State College	22	17	5				

357

Table 79. — Number of Full-time Law Enforcement Employees, Universities and Colleges, October 31, 1993

University/College	Total police employees	Total officers	Total civilians
NORTH DAKOTA			
University of North Dakota	12	11	1
OHIO			
Baldwin-Wallace College	10	8	2
Bowling Green State University	26	17	9
Cleveland State University	37	30	7
Cuyahoga Community College	33	30	3
Kent State University	37	27	10
Lakeland Community College	11	6	5
Marietta College	4	4	....
Miami University	37	29	8
Ohio State University	62	51	11
Ohio University	28	22	6
University of Akron	36	29	7
University of Cincinnati	98	49	49
University of Toledo	31	28	3
Wright State University	24	17	7
Youngstown State University	21	18	3
OKLAHOMA			
Cameron University	7	6	1
Central State University	21	15	6
East Central University	5	4	1
Murray State College	3	3	....
Northeastern Oklahoma State University	13	11	2
Oklahoma State University:			
Main Campus	33	25	8
Okmulgee	8	8	....
Southeastern State College	7	7	....
Tulsa Junior College	14	7	7
University of Oklahoma:			
Health Science Center	24	16	8
Norman	36	26	10
PENNSYLVANIA			
Beaver County Community College	6	2	4
Bloomsburg University	18	17	1
California University	18	14	4
Cheyney University	14	12	2
Clarion University	14	10	4
East Stroudsburg University	14	12	2
Edinboro University	15	14	1
Elizabethtown College	13	8	5
Kutztown University	19	12	7
Lehigh University	27	14	13
Lincoln University	14	1	13
Lock Haven University	9	8	1
Millersville University	18	13	5
Moravian College	11	7	4
Pennsylvania State University:			
Altoona Campus	6	5	1
Behrend College	5	4	1
Capital Campus	5	4	1
University Park	63	49	14
Shippensburg University	16	14	2
Slippery Rock University	16	15	1
University of Pittsburgh, Bradford	6	5	1
West Chester University	30	17	13
RHODE ISLAND			
Brown University	55	19	36
University of Rhode Island	31	20	11
SOUTH CAROLINA			
Clemson University	47	33	14
Denmark Technical College	6	6	....
Francis Marion University	11	11	....
Lander University	17	10	7
Medical University of South Carolina	155	79	76
South Carolina State University	30	24	6

University/College	Total police employees	Total officers	Total civilians
SOUTH CAROLINA – Continued			
The Citadel	17	14	3
Trident Technical College	18	17	1
University of South Carolina:			
Aiken	3	2	1
Coastal Carolina	16	9	7
Columbia	74	56	18
Spartanburg	9	8	1
Winthrop College	22	16	6
SOUTH DAKOTA			
South Dakota State University	13	7	6
TENNESSEE			
Austin Peay State University	19	11	8
East Tennessee State University	26	18	8
Middle Tennessee State University	22	19	3
University of Tennessee:			
Knoxville	58	50	8
Martin	15	12	3
Memphis	50	37	13
TEXAS			
Alamo Community College	32	22	10
Alvin Community College	10	7	3
Amarillo College	5	3	2
Angelo State University	11	9	2
Austin College	9	8	1
Baylor University	28	18	10
Baylor University Medical Center	67	46	21
Central Texas College	10	9	1
College of the Mainland	8	7	1
Eastfield College	8	7	1
East Texas State University	19	14	5
Hardin-Simmons University	6	4	2
Houston Baptist University	8	8	....
Lamar University	20	11	9
Laredo Junior College	10	9	1
McLennan Community College	6	3	3
Midwestern State University	8	7	1
North Harris Montgomery Community College	7	7	....
North Lake College	8	7	1
Paris Junior College	3	2	1
Prairie View A&M University	23	16	7
Rice University	35	16	19
Richland College	10	10	....
St. Mary's University	15	11	4
Southern Methodist University	31	16	15
South Plains College	4	4	....
Southwestern University	4	4	....
Southwest Texas State University	34	20	14
Stephen F. Austin State University	32	17	15
Sul Ross State University	8	6	2
Tarleton State University	12	10	2
Texas A&M University:			
College Station	105	42	63
Corpus Christi	11	9	2
Galveston	7	7	....
Kingsville	20	14	6
Texas Christian University	30	17	13
Texas College Osteo. Med	20	12	8
Texas Southern University	31	16	15
Texas State Technical College:			
Amarillo	12	8	4
Waco	13	11	2
Texas Tech. University:			
Health Science Center	28	11	17
Lubbock	59	28	31
Texas Woman's University	23	16	7
Trinity University	29	12	17
Tyler Junior College	8	7	1
University of Houston:			
Central Campus	44	31	13
Clearlake	12	6	6
Downtown Campus	24	14	10

Table 79. — Number of Full-time Law Enforcement Employees, Universities and Colleges, October 31, 1993 — Continued

University/College	Total police employees	Total officers	Total civilians	University/College	Total police employees	Total officers	Total civilians
TEXAS — Continued				**VIRGINIA — Continued**			
University of North Texas	42	25	17	Thomas Nelson Community College	8	7	1
University of Texas:				University of Richmond	30	16	14
Arlington	57	25	32	University of Virginia	108	55	53
Austin	160	64	96	Virginia Commonwealth University	116	49	67
Brownsville	10	5	5	Virginia Military Institute	6	6	....
Dallas	28	9	19	Virginia Polytechnic Institute and State			
El Paso	46	15	31	University	41	30	11
Galveston	87	30	57	Virginia State University	13	9	4
Health Science Center, San Antonio	50	14	36	Virginia Western Community College	5	5	....
Health Science Center, Tyler	11	4	7				
Houston	181	58	123	**WASHINGTON**			
Pan American	17	12	5				
Permian Basin	11	5	6	Central Washington University	11	10	1
San Antonio	51	21	30	Eastern Washington University	6	5	1
Southwest Medical School	52	23	29	University of Washington	75	54	21
Tyler	18	4	14	Washington State University	20	17	3
West Texas State University	12	8	4	Western Washington University	16	12	4
UTAH				**WEST VIRGINIA**			
Brigham Young University	36	25	11	Concord College	5	5	....
College of Eastern Utah	2	2	....	Glenville State College	3	3	....
Salt Lake Community College	10	10	....	Marshall University	37	20	17
Southern Utah University	4	3	1	West Liberty State College	6	6	....
University of Utah	44	35	9	West Virginia State College	10	9	1
Utah State University	16	10	6	West Virginia Tech	8	8	....
Utah Valley State College	27	4	23	West Virginia University	60	42	18
Weber State University	16	11	5				
				WISCONSIN			
VERMONT				University of Wisconsin:			
				Eau Claire	12	10	2
University of Vermont	28	17	11	Green Bay	11	3	8
				La Crosse	9	8	1
VIRGINIA				Madison	98	41	57
				Milwaukee	36	32	4
Christopher Newport College	9	9	....	Oshkosh	13	12	1
Clinch Valley College	5	5	....	Parkside	8	6	2
College of William and Mary	24	18	6	Platteville	7	7	....
George Mason University	40	32	8	Stout	9	7	2
Hampton University	29	22	7	Superior	5	4	1
James Madison University	28	18	10	Whitewater	13	10	3
Longwood College	12	11	1				
Mary Washington College	18	13	5	**WYOMING**			
Norfolk State University	39	21	18				
Northern Virginia Community College	32	29	3	University of Wyoming	23	13	10
Old Dominion University	29	26	3				
Radford University	21	16	5				

Table 80. — Number of Full-time Law Enforcement Employees, Suburban Counties, October 31, 1993 — Continued

County by State	Total police employees	Total officers	Total civilians
ALABAMA			
Autauga	22	22	....
Baldwin	110	52	58
Blount	28	18	10
Calhoun	56	23	33
Colbert	31	19	12
Dale	25	12	13
Elmore	36	17	19
Etowah	71	46	25
Houston	106	39	67
Jefferson	579	461	118
Lauderdale	36	24	12
Lawrence	36	19	17
Limestone	41	26	15
Madison	159	90	69
Mobile	433	143	290
Montgomery	197	166	31
Morgan	68	41	27
Russell	64	21	43
St. Clair	20	18	2
Shelby	80	57	23
Tuscaloosa	101	64	37
ARIZONA			
Maricopa	1,914	497	1,417
Mohave	214	84	130
Pima	948	367	581
Pinal	235	126	109
ARKANSAS			
Benton	76	34	42
Crawford	34	14	20
Crittenden	53	25	28
Faulkner	47	13	34
Jefferson	39	30	9
Lonoke	21	11	10
Miller	40	20	20
Pulaski	269	76	193
Saline	37	24	13
Sebastian	62	24	38
Washington	68	28	40
CALIFORNIA			
Alameda	1,203	721	482
Butte	122	90	32
Contra Costa	810	572	238
El Dorado	257	126	131
Fresno	460	314	146
Kern	480	305	175
Los Angeles	7,295	5,127	2,168
Madera	75	56	19
Marin	248	172	76
Merced	85	64	21
Monterey	353	277	76
Napa	83	66	17
Orange	2,088	1,190	898
Placer	305	195	110
Riverside	1,869	1,044	825
Sacramento	1,493	1,062	431
San Bernardino	1,612	1,186	426
San Diego	2,520	1,533	987
San Joaquin	318	165	153
San Luis Obispo	297	220	77
San Mateo	448	292	156
Santa Barbara	340	241	99
Santa Clara	504	407	97
Santa Cruz	125	96	29
Shasta	228	138	90
Solano	328	75	253
Sonoma	281	196	85
Stanislaus	385	147	238
Sutter	75	55	20
Tulare	357	263	94
Ventura	867	565	302

County by State	Total police employees	Total officers	Total civilians
CALIFORNIA — Continued			
Yolo	203	72	131
Yuba	62	44	18
COLORADO			
Adams	345	228	117
Arapahoe	449	309	140
Boulder	234	158	76
Douglas	110	80	30
El Paso	146	100	46
Jefferson	532	384	148
Larimer	221	144	77
Pueblo	71	60	11
Weld	152	127	25
DELAWARE			
New Castle Police Department	303	274	29
FLORIDA			
Alachua	339	206	133
Bay	174	134	40
Brevard	703	301	402
Broward	2,921	841	2,080
Charlotte	297	166	131
Clay	230	138	92
Collier	686	356	330
Dade	3,848	2,696	1,152
Escambia	438	297	141
Flagler	88	45	43
Gadsden	80	29	51
Hernando	206	134	72
Hillsborough	2,319	883	1,436
Lake	404	130	274
Lee	701	326	375
Leon	505	291	214
Manatee	624	248	376
Marion	547	181	366
Martin	417	174	243
Nassau	116	76	40
Okaloosa	165	128	37
Orange	1,324	896	428
Osceola	381	212	169
Palm Beach	2,254	895	1,359
Pasco	720	293	427
Pinellas	1,819	610	1,209
Polk	977	383	594
Santa Rosa	195	93	102
Sarasota	647	311	336
Seminole	539	367	172
St. Johns	326	132	194
St. Lucie	475	193	282
Volusia	448	302	146
GEORGIA			
Barrow	70	64	6
Bibb	222	196	26
Bryan	28	18	10
Butts	31	19	12
Carroll	77	47	30
Catoosa	79	47	32
Chatham Police Department	172	135	37
Chattahoochee	3	2	1
Cherokee	166	152	14
Cherokee Police Department	1	1	....
Clarke	154	133	21
Clayton Police Department	229	204	25
Cobb	372	280	92

County by State	Total police employees	Total officers	Total civilians
GEORGIA — Continued			
Cobb Police Department	565	406	159
Columbia	127	115	12
Coweta	123	49	74
Dade	34	15	19
DeKalb	391	309	82
DeKalb Police Department	753	646	107
Dougherty	113	110	3
Dougherty Police Department	54	54	....
Fayette	102	72	30
Forsyth	91	70	21
Fulton	740	653	87
Fulton Police Department	325	220	105
Gwinnett	265	201	64
Gwinnett Police Department	465	316	149
Harris	42	27	15
Henry	75	65	10
Henry Police Department	121	107	14
Houston	112	73	39
Jones	41	20	21
Lee	25	17	8
McDuffie	21	12	9
Newton	68	41	27
Oconee	38	22	16
Paulding	77	62	15
Peach	47	22	25
Pickens	25	15	10
Richmond	345	321	24
Rockdale	113	104	9
Spalding	104	88	16
Twiggs	9	6	3
Walker	80	71	9
Walker Police Department	3	2	1
Walton	89	41	48
IDAHO			
Ada	178	89	89
Canyon	67	42	25
ILLINOIS			
Boone	23	21	2
Champaign	57	50	7
Clinton	25	18	7
Cook	615	533	82
De Kalb	58	46	12
Du Page	193	139	54
Grundy	44	34	10
Henry	40	40	....
Jersey	16	15	1
Kane	194	135	59
Kankakee	95	53	42
Kendall	39	32	7
Lake	374	177	197
Macon	141	43	98
Madison	130	73	57
McHenry	219	184	35
McLean	129	47	82
Menard	11	6	5
Monroe	20	9	11
Ogle	51	37	14
Peoria	163	61	102
Rock Island	83	51	32
Sangamon	240	72	168
St. Clair	59	59	....
Tazewell	54	33	21
Will	398	301	97
Winnebago	234	122	112
Woodford	24	15	9

Table 80. — Number of Full-time Law Enforcement Employees, Suburban Counties, October 31, 1993 — Continued

County by State	Total police employees	Total officers	Total civilians	County by State	Total police employees	Total officers	Total civilians	County by State	Total police employees	Total officers	Total civilians
INDIANA				**KENTUCKY— Continued**				**MICHIGAN— Continued**			
Adams	32	11	21	Oldham	9	9	....	Clinton	59	24	35
Allen	214	116	98	Oldham Police				Eaton	119	70	49
Clark	73	26	47	Department	17	16	1	Genesee	235	100	135
Clay	19	9	10	Pendleton	3	2	1	Ingham	204	106	98
Dearborn	59	17	42	Scott	20	17	3	Jackson	101	48	53
Elkhart	145	62	83	Shelby	12	12	....	Kalamazoo	150	118	32
Hancock	55	29	26	Woodford	5	5	....	Kent	150	123	27
Harrison	27	10	17	Woodford Police				Lapeer	62	46	16
Howard	88	33	55	Department	19	18	1	Lenawee	57	40	17
Huntington	24	8	16					Livingston	87	68	19
Johnson	74	56	18	**LOUISIANA**				Macomb	354	162	192
Lake	354	168	186					Midland	55	37	18
Marion	813	421	392	Acadia	99	73	26	Monroe	159	88	71
Monroe	45	29	16	Ascension	147	146	1	Muskegon	40	34	6
Porter	103	46	57	Bossier	99	99	....	Oakland	708	575	133
Posey	20	8	12	Caddo	487	360	127	Ottawa	101	68	33
St. Joseph	174	128	46	Calcasieu	409	407	2	Saginaw	122	81	41
Tippecanoe	102	38	64	East Baton Rouge	590	590	....	St. Clair	89	64	25
Tipton	15	6	9	Jefferson	1,243	823	420	Van Buren	56	32	24
Vanderburgh	157	98	59	Lafayette	412	412	....	Washtenaw	225	119	106
Vermillion	17	6	11	Lafourche	205	152	53	Wayne	1,383	690	693
Wells	30	10	20	Livingston	116	116	....				
				Ouachita	236	236	....	**MINNESOTA**			
IOWA				Rapides	270	270	....				
Black Hawk	87	72	15	St. Charles	218	135	83	Anoka	168	77	91
Dubuque	45	38	7	St. John the Baptist	143	141	2	Benton	21	13	8
Johnson	67	45	22	St. Landry	97	97	....	Carver	76	43	33
Linn	123	88	35	St. Martin	132	131	1	Chisago	46	22	24
Polk	211	169	42	St. Tammany	315	315	....	Clay	43	18	25
Pottawattamie	58	34	24	Terrebonne	238	238	....	Dakota	138	65	73
Scott	115	39	76	Webster	58	58	....	Hennepin	579	280	299
Warren	29	20	9	West Baton Rouge	62	45	17	Houston	17	11	6
Woodbury	87	69	18					Isanti	30	13	17
				MAINE				Polk	29	17	12
KANSAS								Ramsey	301	249	52
Butler	48	29	19	Androscoggin	17	11	6	St. Louis	114	95	19
Douglas	70	30	40	Cumberland	51	37	14	Scott	86	30	56
Harvey	19	19	....					Sherburne	56	24	32
Johnson	300	236	64					Stearns	98	42	56
Leavenworth	44	32	12	**MARYLAND**				Washington	184	72	112
Miami	25	15	10					Wright	113	63	50
Sedgwick	308	139	169	Allegany	50	20	30				
Shawnee	119	98	21	Anne Arundel	36	29	7	**MISSISSIPPI**			
Wyandotte	172	139	33	Anne Arundel Police							
				Department	730	542	188	De Soto	70	62	8
KENTUCKY				Baltimore	73	52	21	Harrison	168	168	....
Boone	21	19	2	Baltimore Police				Madison	48	20	28
Boone Police				Department	1,563	1,382	181	Rankin	70	30	40
Department	52	48	4	Calvert	59	53	6				
Bourbon	8	8	....	Carroll	34	28	6	**MISSOURI**			
Boyd	17	14	3	Cecil	44	39	5				
Boyd Police				Charles	218	129	95	Andrew	11	7	4
Department	15	15	....	Frederick	87	68	19	Boone	87	65	22
Bullitt	16	13	3	Harford	266	150	116	Christian	23	19	4
Campbell	11	11	....	Howard	40	25	15	Clay	120	87	33
Campbell Police				Howard Police				Franklin	81	74	7
Department	32	22	10	Department	357	296	61	Greene	125	111	14
Christian	19	18	1	Montgomery	111	100	11	Jackson	116	89	27
Christian Police				Montgomery Police				Jasper	80	76	4
Department	19	18	1	Department	1,124	861	263	Jefferson	190	146	44
Clark	9	9	....	Prince George's	285	208	77	Lafayette	24	21	3
Daviess	31	31	....	Prince George's Police				Platte	58	46	12
Fayette	59	50	9	Department	1,442	1,140	302	St. Charles	211	112	99
Gallatin	3	3	....	Queen Anne's	28	26	2	St. Louis Police			
Grant	5	5	....	Washington	137	52	85	Department	723	521	202
Greenup	8	8	....					Warren	17	17	....
Henderson	13	13	....	**MICHIGAN**				Webster	13	13	....
Jefferson	223	221	2								
Jefferson Police				Allegan	87	48	39	**MONTANA**			
Department	550	414	136	Bay	34	28	6				
Jessamine	10	10	....	Berrien	162	57	105	Cascade	49	31	18
Kenton	29	29	....	Calhoun	87	50	37	Yellowstone	104	44	60
Kenton Police											
Department	46	33	13								

Table 80.—Number of Full-time Law Enforcement Employees, Suburban Counties, October 31, 1993—Continued

County by State	Total police employees	Total officers	Total civilians
NEBRASKA			
Cass	29	15	14
Dakota	21	8	13
Douglas	150	105	45
Lancaster	77	60	17
Sarpy	128	93	35
Washington	21	10	11
NEVADA			
Washoe	482	321	161
NEW JERSEY			
Atlantic	126	101	25
Atlantic Prosecutor	148	63	85
Bergen	453	379	74
Bergen Police Department	112	85	27
Bergen Prosecutor	257	114	143
Burlington	61	49	12
Burlington Prosecutor	117	44	73
Camden	254	224	30
Camden Prosecutor	211	98	113
Cape May	127	107	20
Cape May Prosecutor	34	13	21
Cumberland	171	147	24
Cumberland Prosecutor	49	17	32
Essex	462	415	47
Essex Police Department	61	58	3
Essex Prosecutor	440	303	137
Gloucester	215	150	65
Gloucester Prosecutor	73	42	31
Hudson	168	138	30
Hudson Police Department	110	95	15
Hudson Prosecutor	276	105	171
Hunterdon	30	22	8
Hunterdon Prosecutor	43	24	19
Mercer	117	90	27
Mercer Prosecutor	120	78	42
Middlesex	220	176	44
Middlesex Prosecutor	226	136	90
Monmouth	303	265	38
Monmouth Prosecutor	237	108	129
Morris	307	224	83
Morris Prosecutor	139	92	47
Ocean	187	79	108
Ocean Prosecutor	127	60	67
Passaic	566	442	124
Passaic Prosecutor	177	79	98
Salem	132	111	21
Salem Prosecutor	34	10	24
Somerset	194	140	54
Somerset Prosecutor	109	73	36
Sussex	103	91	12
Sussex Prosecutor	45	29	16
Union	170	150	20
Union Prosecutor	214	123	91
Warren	19	16	3
Warren Prosecutor	52	32	20
NEW MEXICO			
Dona Ana	87	76	11
Sandoval	32	23	9
Valencia	30	20	10

County by State	Total police employees	Total officers	Total civilians
NEW YORK			
Broome	55	45	10
Cayuga	30	21	9
Chautauqua	99	78	21
Chemung	48	40	8
Dutchess	137	111	26
Erie	633	530	103
Genesee	50	36	14
Herkimer	47	40	7
Livingston	58	46	12
Monroe	275	234	41
Montgomery	24	19	5
Nassau	3,444	2,809	635
Oneida	159	125	34
Onondaga	281	250	31
Ontario	77	54	23
Orange	100	91	9
Orleans	32	24	8
Oswego	72	61	11
Putnam	76	63	13
Rensselaer	59	36	23
Rockland	58	53	5
Saratoga	96	69	27
Schoharie	21	11	10
Suffolk	157	119	38
Suffolk Police Department	2,910	2,386	524
Tioga	52	36	16
Warren	81	63	18
Washington	28	19	9
Wayne	72	47	25
NORTH CAROLINA			
Alamance	109	69	40
Alexander	25	17	8
Brunswick	73	61	12
Buncombe	212	129	83
Burke	91	51	40
Cabarrus	115	107	8
Caldwell	72	40	32
Catawba	97	91	6
Chatham	51	37	14
Cumberland	386	312	74
Currituck	31	23	8
Davidson	119	73	46
Davie	38	34	4
Durham	281	94	187
Edgecombe	61	34	27
Forsyth	336	220	116
Franklin	54	27	27
Gaston Rural Police	213	169	44
Guilford	332	179	153
Johnston	53	42	11
Lincoln	65	55	10
Mecklenburg Rural Police	692	578	114
Nash	59	35	24
New Hanover	222	175	47
Onslow	123	72	51
Orange	86	75	11
Pitt	173	82	91
Randolph	91	71	20
Rowan	99	93	6
Stokes	37	31	6
Union	104	81	23
Wake	434	204	230
Wayne	63	35	28
Yadkin	41	19	22
NORTH DAKOTA			
Burleigh	45	33	12
Cass	64	40	24

County by State	Total police employees	Total officers	Total civilians
NORTH DAKOTA—Continued			
Grand Forks	26	20	6
Morton	30	16	14
OHIO			
Ashtabula	75	38	37
Auglaize	30	16	14
Clark	113	94	19
Clermont	154	75	80
Columbiana	59	31	28
Cuyahoga	881	151	730
Delaware	78	34	44
Fulton	29	18	11
Geauga	44	30	14
Greene	90	79	11
Hamilton	930	707	223
Jefferson	50	42	8
Lake	147	37	110
Licking	129	94	35
Lorain	136	47	89
Lucas	313	232	81
Mehoning	142	131	11
Miami	71	39	32
Montgomery	317	178	139
Pickaway	81	35	46
Richland	90	41	49
Stark	180	95	85
Trumbull	73	32	41
Washington	59	30	29
Wood	97	89	8
OKLAHOMA			
Canadian	31	17	14
Cleveland	78	28	50
Comanche	47	28	19
Creek	24	14	10
Garfield	17	10	7
Logan	13	6	7
McClain	11	7	4
Oklahoma	415	107	308
Osage	22	22	....
Pottawatomie	21	9	12
Rogers	19	12	7
Sequoyah	13	7	6
Tulsa	273	167	106
Wagoner	14	9	5
OREGON			
Clackamas	166	126	40
Columbia	14	12	2
Jackson	61	45	16
Lane	110	69	41
Marion	95	71	24
Multnomak	192	140	52
Polk	23	17	6
Washington	186	138	48
Yamhill	43	38	5
PENNSYLVANIA			
Allegheny	134	115	19
Allegheny Police Department	300	257	43
Blair	14	12	2
Cambria	20	16	4
Centre	10	10	....
Chester Detective	19	16	3
Cumberland	17	16	1
Lebanon Detective	5	4	1
Washington	27	23	4
Westmoreland Detective	12	12	....
Westmoreland Park Police	16	16	....

Table 80.—Number of Full-time Law Enforcement Employees, Suburban Counties, October 31, 1993—Continued

County by State	Total police employees	Total officers	Total civilians	County by State	Total police employees	Total officers	Total civilians	County by State	Total police employees	Total officers	Total civilians
SOUTH CAROLINA				**TEXAS—Continued**				**VIRGINIA—Continued**			
Aiken	100	77	23	Hidalgo	323	136	187	New Kent	19	12	7
Anderson	120	98	22	Hood	45	17	28	Pittsylvania	78	39	39
Berkeley	100	64	36	Hunt	45	21	24	Powhatan	19	16	3
Charleston	506	213	293	Jefferson	411	156	255	Prince George	48	39	9
Cherokee	43	33	10	Johnson	108	30	78	Prince William Police Department	404	286	118
Dorchester	80	55	25	Kaufman	56	25	31	Roanoke Police Department	116	88	28
Edgefield	24	13	11	Liberty	129	27	102	Scott	37	37	......
Florence	86	68	18	Lubbock	248	143	105	Spotsylvania	61	46	15
Greenville	337	272	65	McLennan	177	54	123	Stafford	104	79	25
Horry	15	12	3	Midland	161	86	75	Washington	56	44	12
Horry Police Department	128	117	11	Montgomery	333	202	131	York	71	64	7
Lexington	243	155	88	Nueces	353	194	159				
Pickens	73	55	18	Orange	100	44	56	**WASHINGTON**			
Richland	304	265	39	Parker	71	30	41	Benton	57	44	13
Spartanburg	201	182	19	Potter	154	120	34	Clark	199	130	69
Sumter	87	80	7	Randall	73	59	14	Franklin	20	18	2
York	106	83	23	Rockwall	35	14	21	Island	48	31	17
				San Patricio	60	33	27	King	845	599	246
SOUTH DAKOTA				Smith	205	63	142	Kitsap	104	83	21
				Tarrant	1,325	682	643	Pierce	286	246	40
Lincoln	4	3	1	Taylor	132	80	52	Snohomish	238	166	72
Minnehaha	99	66	33	Tom Green	83	35	48	Spokane	217	163	54
Pennington	49	37	12	Travis	972	350	622	Thurston	106	75	31
				Upshur	36	15	21	Whatcom	65	53	12
TENNESSEE				Victoria	81	61	20	Yakima	99	68	31
				Waller	39	15	24				
Carter	46	30	16	Webb	258	168	90	**WEST VIRGINIA**			
Hawkins	47	44	3	Wichita	106	33	73				
Knox	520	200	320	Williamson	158	99	59	Brooke	19	14	5
Madison	57	57	......	Wilson	23	10	13	Cabell	81	30	51
Robertson	59	45	14					Hancock	31	21	10
Shelby	1,407	473	934	**UTAH**				Kanawha	70	59	11
Sullivan	186	163	23					Marshall	30	18	12
Sumner	111	55	56	Davis	166	124	42	Mineral	12	6	6
Unicoi	30	17	13	Salt Lake	727	578	149	Ohio	32	19	13
Washington	76	40	36	Utah	149	98	51	Putnam	30	19	11
				Weber	136	101	35	Wayne	38	11	27
TEXAS								Wood	67	30	37
				VIRGINIA							
Archer	11	7	4	Albermarle Police Department	94	77	17	**WISCONSIN**			
Bastrop	83	21	62	Amherst	48	40	8				
Bell	237	75	162	Bedford	83	83	......	Brown	199	128	71
Bexar	1,511	338	1,173	Botetourt	47	36	11	Calumet	31	23	8
Bowie	121	37	84	Campbell	56	46	10	Chippewa	49	45	4
Brazoria	201	126	75	Charles City	14	8	6	Dane	344	303	41
Brazos	123	56	67	Chesterfield Police Department	395	341	54	Eau Claire	76	51	25
Caldwell	51	10	41	Clarke	15	10	5	Kenosha	156	60	54
Cameron	200	56	144	Culpepper	63	51	12	La Crosse	79	32	47
Chambers	51	19	32	Dinwiddie	47	39	8	Marathon	127	63	64
Collin	303	99	204	Fairfax Police Department	1,241	957	284	Milwaukee	715	535	180
Comal	100	41	59	Fauquier	86	68	18	Outagamie	172	68	104
Coryell	37	14	23	Fluvanna	13	11	2	Ozaukee	83	66	17
Dallas	1,799	441	1,358	Gloucester	61	50	11	Pierce	36	35	1
Denton	420	126	294	Goochland	18	14	4	Racine	243	178	65
Ector	111	54	57	Greene	29	11	18	Rock	163	90	73
Ellis	98	36	62	Hanover	115	108	7	Sheboygan	123	74	49
El Paso	561	193	368	Henrico Police Department	561	401	160	St. Croix	53	48	5
Fort Bend	215	157	58	Isle of Wight	27	21	6	Washington	102	53	49
Galveston	299	254	45	James City Police Department	51	48	3	Waukesha	295	145	150
Grayson	68	55	13	King George	25	24	1	Winnebago	146	93	53
Gregg	96	56	40	Loudoun	196	158	38				
Guadalupe	68	23	45	Mathews	14	8	6	**WYOMING**			
Hardin	34	27	7								
Harris	3,361	2,167	1,194					Laramie	64	37	27
Harrison	76	28	48					Natrona	49	39	10
Hays	179	53	126								
Henderson	86	30	56								

Table 81. — Number of Full-time Law Enforcement Employees, Rural Counties, October 31, 1993

County by State	Total police employees	Total officers	Total civilians	County by State	Total police employees	Total officers	Total civilians	County by State	Total police employees	Total officers	Total civilians
ALABAMA				**ARKANSAS—** Continued				**COLORADO—** Continued			
Barbour	16	9	7	Grant	10	6	4	Baca	9	5	4
Chambers	50	17	33	Greene	18	10	8	Bent	9	5	4
Chilton	13	11	2	Hempstead	18	8	10	Chaffee	24	14	10
Choctaw	14	4	10	Hot Spring	20	11	9	Cheyenne	9	5	4
Cleburne	10	5	5	Howard	16	6	10	Clear Creek	30	24	6
Coffee	11	9	2	Independence	55	33	22	Conejos	9	8	1
Conecuh	19	7	12	Izard	12	7	5	Costilla	12	7	5
Coosa	9	4	5	Jackson	15	9	6	Crowley	12	12	....
Covington	15	11	4	Johnson	13	7	6	Custer	4	4	....
Crenshaw	12	5	7	Lafayette	11	5	6	Delta	36	15	21
Cullman	58	38	20	Lawrence	16	8	8	Dolores	6	3	3
Dallas	43	39	4	Lee	10	5	5	Eagle	50	43	7
De Kalb	36	19	17	Lincoln	14	3	11	Elbert	11	10	1
Escambia	31	12	19	Little River	15	6	9	Fremont	51	45	6
Fayette	10	9	1	Logan	16	6	10	Garfield	34	14	20
Franklin	27	14	13	Madison	14	7	7	Gilpin	17	9	8
Geneva	15	6	9	Marion	14	5	9	Grand	41	26	15
Greene	15	6	9	Mississippi	44	21	23	Gunnison	19	18	1
Hale	11	5	6	Monroe	12	5	7	Hinsdale	4	3	1
Henry	13	7	6	Montgomery	11	5	6	Huerfano	20	19	1
Jackson	39	27	12	Nevada	12	6	6	Kiowa	4	3	1
Lee	68	33	35	Newton	7	4	3	Kit Carson	12	12	....
Lowndes	18	5	13	Quachita	24	13	11	Lake	17	9	8
Macon	20	12	8	Perry	10	5	5	La Plata	70	29	41
Marengo	18	9	9	Phillips	31	8	23	Las Animas	17	15	2
Marion	17	7	10	Pike	9	5	4	Lincoln	16	16	....
Marshall	36	20	16	Poinsett	18	9	9	Logan	21	10	11
Monroe	28	14	14	Polk	17	7	10	Mesa	167	131	36
Perry	13	6	7	Pope	40	19	21	Mineral	4	4	....
Pickens	10	7	3	Prairie	12	6	6	Moffat	29	25	4
Pike	16	10	6	Randolph	10	9	1	Montezuma	35	30	5
Randolph	21	19	2	St. Francis	34	14	20	Montrose	44	36	8
Sumter	4	3	1	Scott	11	4	7	Morgan	38	33	5
Tallapoosa	15	15	....	Searcy	8	5	3	Otero	16	16	....
Walker	37	19	18	Sevier	14	8	6	Ouray	5	4	1
Wilcox	14	6	8	Sharp	15	7	8	Park	24	15	9
Winston	16	8	8	Stone	14	7	7	Phillips	2	2	....
				Union	48	19	29	Pitkin	36	32	4
ARIZONA				Van Buren	12	8	4	Prowers	28	22	6
				White	41	19	22	Rio Blanco	17	12	5
Apache	49	22	27	Woodruff	12	6	6	Rio Grande	17	14	3
Cochise	148	62	86	Yell	16	8	8	Routt	32	29	3
Coconino	115	61	54					Saguache	10	10	....
Gila	112	51	61	**CALIFORNIA**				San Juan	4	3	1
Graham	28	13	15					San Miguel	14	12	2
Greenlee	23	15	8	Alpine	12	9	3	Sedgwick	10	5	5
Lapaz	34	29	5	Amador	49	36	13	Summit	38	32	6
Navajo	67	39	28	Calaveras	69	38	31	Teller	35	17	18
Santa Cruz	58	32	26	Colusa	52	40	12	Washington	11	8	3
Yavapai	157	69	88	Del Norte	36	28	8	Yuma	10	5	5
				Glenn	51	21	30				
ARKANSAS				Humboldt	95	70	25	**FLORIDA**			
				Imperial	222	129	93				
Arkansas	8	8	....	Inyo	59	39	20	Baker	48	22	26
Ashley	23	11	12	Kings	158	65	93	Bradford	23	14	9
Baxter	29	19	10	Lake	140	106	34	Calhoun	18	10	8
Boone	21	12	9	Lassen	77	22	55	Citrus	262	106	156
Bradley	5	4	1	Mariposa	39	27	12	Columbia	144	65	79
Calhoun	7	4	3	Mendocino	81	63	18	De Soto	61	30	31
Carroll	23	11	12	Modoc	10	10	....	Dixie	32	19	13
Chicot	7	5	2	Mono	42	25	17	Franklin	33	22	11
Clark	23	11	12	Nevada	107	51	56	Gilchrist	18	16	2
Clay	13	7	6	Plumas	62	34	28	Glades	44	21	23
Cleburne	19	11	8	San Benito	18	16	2	Gulf	28	15	13
Cleveland	8	4	4	Sierra	16	11	5	Hamilton	47	14	33
Columbia	21	11	10	Siskiyou	89	72	17	Hardee	75	30	45
Conway	16	8	8	Tehama	80	57	23	Hendry	94	41	53
Craighead	42	16	26	Trinity	26	20	6	Highlands	194	90	104
Cross	22	10	12	Tuolumne	66	46	20	Holmes	25	10	15
Dallas	10	5	5					Indian River	331	137	194
Desha	11	6	5	**COLORADO**				Jackson	45	30	15
Drew	6	6	....					Jefferson	33	15	18
Franklin	12	6	6	Alamosa	31	26	5	Lafayette	14	6	8
Fulton	8	4	4	Archuleta	27	14	13	Levy	99	36	63
Garland	74	29	45								

Table 81. — Number of Full-time Law Enforcement Employees, Rural Counties, October 31, 1993 — Continued

County by State	Total police employees	Total officers	Total civilians	County by State	Total police employees	Total officers	Total civilians	County by State	Total police employees	Total officers	Total civilians
FLORIDA — Continued				**GEORGIA — Continued**				**IDAHO — Continued**			
Liberty	14	9	5	Liberty	57	34	23	Boise	12	7	5
Madison	37	19	18	Lincoln	19	14	5	Bonner	47	40	7
Monroe	445	180	265	Long	8	7	1	Bonneville	83	83	....
Okeechobee	119	49	70	Lowndes	144	69	75	Boundary	20	20	....
Putman	174	110	64	Lumpkin	30	23	7	Butte	10	5	5
Sumter	82	33	49	Macon	8	7	1	Camas	5	5	....
Suwannee	59	29	30	Marion	7	4	3	Caribou	13	7	6
Taylor	65	26	39	McIntosh	28	22	6	Cassia	40	30	10
Union	17	9	8	Meriwether	24	12	12	Clark	5	2	3
Wakulla	64	24	40	Miller	13	13	....	Clearwater	23	17	6
Walton	77	41	36	Mitchell	22	13	9	Custer	10	6	4
Washington	39	32	7	Monroe	53	46	7	Elmore	27	26	1
				Morgan	29	29	....	Franklin	13	6	7
GEORGIA				Murray	40	18	22	Fremont	13	13	....
				Pierce	14	7	7	Gem	17	15	2
Appling	16	15	1	Pike	16	11	5	Gooding	20	8	12
Atkinson	10	4	6	Polk	44	42	2	Idaho	31	15	16
Bacon	13	6	7	Polk Police Department	22	15	7	Jefferson	19	12	7
Baker	4	4	....	Pulaski	16	7	9	Jerome	20	11	9
Baldwin	56	32	24	Putnam	72	17	55	Kootenai	86	60	26
Banks	25	16	9	Quitman	2	2	....	Latah	29	20	9
Ben Hill	22	16	6	Rabun	20	19	1	Lemhi	9	5	4
Berrien	16	10	6	Schley	3	2	1	Lewis	16	6	10
Bleckley	13	7	6	Screven	15	14	1	Lincoln	6	2	4
Brantley	13	12	1	Seminole	11	8	3	Madison	19	18	1
Brooks	24	14	10	Stephens	21	16	5	Minidoka	17	8	9
Bulloch	47	44	3	Stewart	3	3	....	Nez Perce	29	17	12
Calhoun	12	6	6	Talbot	10	5	5	Oneida	11	6	5
Camden	55	28	27	Taliaferro	2	2	...	Owyhee	15	8	7
Candler	9	4	5	Tattnall	14	8	6	Payette	26	10	16
Chattooga	42	42	....	Taylor	11	10	1	Power	11	7	4
Clay	8	4	4	Telfair	11	7	4	Shoshone	29	29	....
Clinch	10	6	4	Terrell	16	9	7	Teton	6	6	....
Coffee	45	21	24	Thomas	49	43	6	Twin Falls	42	29	13
Colquitt	63	24	39	Tift	56	28	28	Valley	29	12	17
Cook	15	10	5	Toombs	12	12	....	Washington	19	19	....
Crawford	20	9	11	Towns	12	9	3				
Crisp	55	40	15	Treutlen	10	7	3	**ILLINOIS**			
Dawson	23	12	11	Troup	69	64	5				
Decatur	28	16	12	Turner	17	9	8	Adams	65	36	29
Dodge	19	11	8	Union	22	16	6	Alexander	7	7	....
Dooly	23	10	13	Upson	36	35	1	Bond	15	7	8
Early	23	15	8	Ware	51	26	25	Brown	4	3	1
Elbert	21	17	4	Ware Police Department	13	2	11	Bureau	27	27	....
Emanuel	17	16	1	Warren	2	2	....	Calhoun	5	2	3
Fannin	18	12	6	Washington	21	15	6	Carroll	16	7	9
Floyd	74	58	16	Wayne	19	18	1	Cass	6	5	1
Floyd Police Department	58	55	3	Webster	4	3	1	Christian	14	14	....
Franklin	21	17	4	Wheeler	4	3	1	Clark	11	11	....
Glascock	3	2	1	White	24	23	1	Clay	12	7	5
Glynn	27	20	7	Whitfield	113	64	49	Coles	39	34	5
Glynn Police Department	121	98	23	Wilcox	9	5	4	Crawford	17	12	5
Gordon	55	27	28	Wilkes	18	10	8	Cumberland	10	5	5
Grady	26	10	16	Wilkinson	15	7	8	De Witt	31	25	6
Habersham	32	32	....	Worth	24	13	11	Douglas	19	10	9
Hall	251	184	67					Edgar	17	17	....
Hancock	28	10	18	**HAWAII**				Edwards	3	3	...
Hancock Police Department	1	1	....	Hawaii Police Department	231	209	22	Effingham	26	9	17
Haralson	36	24	12	Kauai Police Department	157	132	25	Fayette	21	8	13
Hart	30	30	....	Maui Police Department	390	301	89	Ford	16	14	2
Heard	17	15	2					Franklin	43	18	25
Irwin	6	6	....	**IDAHO**				Fulton	36	29	7
Jackson	46	35	11					Gallatin	3	3	....
Jasper	14	9	5	Adams	13	13	....	Greene	11	5	6
Jeff Davis	11	9	2	Bannock	44	31	13	Hamilton	8	4	4
Jefferson	21	17	4	Bear Lake	10	4	6	Hancock	16	8	8
Jenkins	6	3	3	Benewah	14	14	....	Hardin	4	2	2
Johnson	16	16	....	Bingham	51	38	13	Henderson	11	10	1
Lamar	32	9	23	Blaine	34	34	....	Iroquois	24	16	8
Lanier	10	5	5					Jackson	62	18	44
Laurens	70	34	36					Jasper	18	8	10
								Jefferson	32	16	16
								Jo Daviess	24	17	7
								Johnson	10	5	5

County by State	Total police employees	Total officers	Total civilians	County by State	Total police employees	Total officers	Total civilians	County by State	Total police employees	Total officers	Total civilians
ILLINOIS— Continued				**IOWA— Continued**				**IOWA— Continued**			
Knox	45	43	2	Appanoose	14	9	5	Winnebago	10	5	5
La Salle	58	47	11	Audubon	8	5	3	Winneshiek	16	10	6
Lawrence	9	9	....	Benton	19	7	12	Worth	11	5	6
Lee	27	27	....	Boone	13	8	5	Wright	7	6	1
Livingston	44	26	18	Bremer	11	10	1				
Logan	24	19	5	Buchanan	21	13	8	**KANSAS**			
Macoupin	47	41	6	Buena Vista	12	8	4				
Marion	24	21	3	Butler	12	8	4	Allen	13	7	6
Marshall	18	8	10	Calhoun	11	6	5	Anderson	4	4	....
Mason	10	9	1	Carroll	12	9	3	Atchison	9	5	4
Massac	16	8	8	Cass	7	6	1	Barber	10	5	5
McDonough	19	13	6	Cedar	17	6	11	Barton	34	27	7
Mercer	22	12	10	Cerro Gordo	28	14	14	Bourbon	6	6	....
Montgomery	19	11	8	Cherokee	12	5	7	Brown	17	17	....
Morgan	30	14	16	Chickasaw	13	8	5	Chase	7	3	4
Moultrie	15	9	6	Clarke	8	4	4	Chautauqua	8	8	....
Perry	29	14	15	Clay	11	6	5	Cherokee	19	19	....
Piatt	19	10	9	Clayton	18	10	8	Cheyenne	4	3	1
Pike	18	9	9	Crawford	15	8	7	Clark	8	4	4
Pope	4	2	2	Davis	4	3	1	Clay	13	6	7
Pulaski	11	6	5	Decatur	8	4	4	Cloud	13	11	2
Putnam	9	5	4	Delaware	12	10	2	Coffey	21	9	12
Randolph	18	9	9	Dickinson	13	8	5	Comanche	6	3	3
Richland	18	12	6	Emmet	13	6	7	Cowley	23	22	1
Saline	39	37	2	Fayette	19	9	10	Crawford	21	9	12
Schuyler	10	4	6	Floyd	12	6	6	Decatur	7	3	4
Scott	3	3	....	Franklin	8	7	1	Dickinson	24	13	11
Shelby	20	10	10	Greene	17	5	12	Doniphan	8	4	4
Stark	8	3	5	Grundy	11	7	4	Edwards	9	5	4
Stephenson	48	30	18	Guthrie	8	5	3	Elk	7	3	4
Union	13	12	1	Hamilton	11	9	2	Ellis	17	15	2
Vermilion	70	30	40	Hancock	8	6	2	Ellsworth	9	5	4
Wabash	10	5	5	Hardin	13	8	5	Finney	52	49	3
Warren	19	12	7	Harrison	13	5	8	Ford	25	14	11
Washington	20	5	15	Henry	16	9	7	Franklin	30	12	18
Wayne	13	7	6	Howard	8	7	1	Geary	46	44	2
White	7	7	....	Iowa	12	8	4	Gove	3	2	1
Whiteside	48	21	27	Jackson	14	8	6	Graham	7	7	....
Williamson	48	21	27	Jasper	24	7	17	Grant	12	6	6
				Jefferson	12	6	6	Gray	8	5	3
INDIANA				Jones	16	8	8	Greeley	7	3	4
				Keokuk	8	5	3	Greenwood	19	10	9
Bartholomew	66	36	30	Kossuth	11	9	2	Hamilton	8	4	4
Benton	15	4	11	Lee	30	15	15	Harper	13	5	8
Blackford	11	7	4	Louisa	18	10	8	Haskell	14	14	....
Carroll	17	7	10	Lucas	11	5	6	Hodgeman	8	4	4
Daviess	16	8	8	Lyon	14	8	6	Jackson	12	12	....
Decatur	20	7	13	Madison	11	5	6	Jefferson	25	14	11
Gibson	27	10	17	Mahaska	15	8	7	Jewell	8	8	....
Grant	83	37	46	Marion	19	10	9	Kearny	14	9	5
Jackson	25	11	14	Marshall	27	13	14	Kingman	6	5	1
Jefferson	22	11	11	Mills	18	8	10	Kiowa	13	13	....
Jennings	17	7	10	Mitchell	7	6	1	Labette	26	14	12
LaGrange	23	13	10	Monona	14	7	7	Lane	9	5	4
La Porte	96	50	46	Monroe	10	5	5	Lincoln	10	6	4
Lawrence	42	17	25	Muscatine	35	16	19	Linn	12	6	6
Martin	14	5	9	O'Brien	21	10	11	Logan	2	2	....
Miami	27	10	17	Osceola	13	9	4	Lyon	36	10	26
Montgomery	26	13	13	Page	10	5	5	Marion	11	5	6
Newton	18	9	9	Palo Alto	9	6	3	Marshall	13	6	7
Pulaski	20	8	12	Plymouth	17	8	9	McPherson	20	10	10
Putnam	16	8	8	Pocahontas	11	6	5	Meade	10	10	....
Ripley	21	8	13	Poweshiek	11	7	4	Mitchell	5	5	....
Rush	22	10	12	Ringgold	8	3	5	Montgomery	22	16	6
Spencer	26	8	18	Sac	9	6	3	Morris	7	4	3
Steuben	21	17	4	Sioux	22	12	10	Morton	8	4	4
Wabash	25	10	15	Story	49	33	16	Nemaha	10	10	....
Wayne	69	53	16	Tama	16	9	7	Neosho	19	19	....
White	23	9	14	Taylor	8	4	4	Ness	10	5	5
				Union	8	3	5	Norton	8	3	5
IOWA				Van Buren	9	5	4	Osage	25	24	1
				Wapello	19	6	13	Osborne	10	5	5
Adair	6	5	1	Washington	24	17	7	Ottawa	9	5	4
Adams	7	3	4	Wayne	8	4	4	Pawnee	10	9	1

Table 81. — Number of Full-time Law Enforcement Employees, Rural Counties, October 31, 1993 — Continued

County by State	Total police employees	Total officers	Total civilians	County by State	Total police employees	Total officers	Total civilians	County by State	Total police employees	Total officers	Total civilians
KANSAS—Continued				**KENTUCKY—Continued**				**LOUISIANA—Continued**			
Phillips	13	8	5	Johnson	10	10	....	Grant	34	34	....
Pottawatomie	27	16	11	Knott	4	4	....	Iberia	123	27	96
Pratt	11	10	1	Knox	7	6	1	Iberville	99	52	47
Rawlins	7	2	5	Larue	6	5	1	Jackson	31	31	....
Reno	54	47	7	Laurel	10	10	....	Jefferson Davis	59	35	24
Republic	9	5	4	Lawrence	5	4	1	La Salle	42	41	1
Rice	9	9	...	Lee	3	3	....	Lincoln	46	46	...
Riley Police Department	116	82	34	Leslie	5	5	....	Morehouse	71	36	35
Rooks	10	5	5	Letcher	8	8	....	Natchitoches	55	55	...
Rush	10	4	6	Lewis	4	4	....	Plaquemines	141	141	...
Russell	13	5	8	Lincoln	6	6	....	Pointe Coupee	81	80	1
Saline	51	51	....	Livingston	6	6	....	Red River	40	38	2
Scott	5	4	1	Logan	10	9	1	Sabine	42	40	2
Seward	13	7	6	Lyon	3	3	....	St. Helena	32	28	4
Sheridan	4	3	1	Lyon Police Department	3	3	....	St. James	89	70	19
Sherman	11	11	....	Madison	14	11	3	St. Mary	103	79	24
Smith	7	2	5	Magoffin	4	2	2	Tensas	23	23	....
Stafford	3	3	....	Marion	3	2	1	Union	38	24	14
Stanton	10	6	4	Marshall	12	11	1	Vermilion	91	91	...
Stevens	12	6	6	Martin	6	4	2	Vernon	84	52	32
Sumner	18	10	8	Mason	11	8	3	Washington	85	77	8
Thomas	9	9	....	McCracken	31	30	1	West Carroll	25	25	...
Trego	6	2	4	McCreary	10	10	....	Winn	28	28	...
Wabaunsee	9	5	4	McCreary Police Department	1	1	....				
Wallace	6	4	2	McLean	3	3	....	**MAINE**			
Washington	9	6	3	Meade	6	6	....	Aroostook	15	10	5
Wichita	8	4	4	Menifee	2	2	....	Franklin	17	12	5
Wilson	15	6	9	Mercer	5	5	....	Hancock	20	13	7
Woodson	8	4	4	Metcalfe	4	4	....	Kennebec	24	17	7
				Monroe	7	7	....	Knox	19	14	5
KENTUCKY				Montgomery	10	10	....	Lincoln	26	16	10
Adair	4	3	1	Morgan	4	3	1	Oxford	19	13	6
Allen	5	4	1	Muhlenberg	10	9	1	Penobscot	27	17	10
Anderson	5	5	....	Nelson	8	5	3	Piscataquis	10	6	4
Anderson Police Department	2	2	....	Nelson Police Department	6	6	....	Sagadahoc	17	13	4
Ballard	6	6	....	Nicholas	3	3	....	Somerset	20	14	6
Barren	7	7	....	Ohio	5	3	2	Waldo	14	9	5
Bath	4	3	1	Owen	4	4	....	Washington	14	9	5
Bell	9	6	3	Owsley	3	3	....	York	21	12	9
Boyle	7	7	....	Perry	11	10	1				
Breathitt	2	1	1	Pike	67	50	17	**MARYLAND**			
Breckinridge	6	6	....	Powell	5	5	....	Caroline	40	19	21
Butler	4	4	....	Pulaski	27	15	12	Dorchester	30	22	8
Caldwell	6	6	....	Robertson	2	2	....	Garrett	29	16	13
Calloway	5	5	....	Rockcastle	5	5	....	Kent	19	18	1
Carlisle	2	2	....	Rowan	7	5	2	St. Mary's	133	68	65
Carroll	4	3	1	Russell	8	6	2	Somerset	13	12	1
Carter	7	3	4	Simpson	7	5	2	Talbot	13	10	3
Casey	4	4	....	Spencer	3	2	1	Wicomico	67	54	13
Clay	6	6	....	Todd	3	3	....	Worcester	28	23	5
Clinton	2	2	....	Trigg	5	5	....				
Crittenden	3	2	1	Trimble	3	3	....	**MICHIGAN**			
Cumberland	2	2	....	Union	7	5	2	Alcona	21	12	9
Edmonson	3	2	1	Warren	25	22	3	Alger	8	8	....
Elliott	4	4	....	Washington	4	4	....	Alpena	23	13	10
Estill	6	5	1	Wayne	6	4	2	Antrim	31	17	14
Fleming	6	6	....	Webster	4	4	....	Arenac	12	11	1
Floyd	19	11	8	Whitley	8	8	....	Baraga	5	5	....
Franklin	9	9	....	Wolfe	2	1	1	Barry	36	20	16
Fulton	3	3	....					Benzie	35	13	22
Garrard	3	3	....	**LOUISIANA**				Branch	39	18	21
Graves	11	8	3	Allen	47	40	7	Cass	60	24	36
Grayson	5	5	....	Avoyelles	188	188	....	Charlevoix	23	14	9
Green	4	4	....	Beauregard	62	43	19	Cheboygan	25	13	12
Hancock	5	5	....	Caldwell	30	30	....	Chippewa	26	12	14
Hardin	18	18	....	Cameron	80	79	1	Clare	27	20	7
Harlan	9	7	2	Claiborne	23	22	1	Crawford	23	14	9
Harrison	5	5	....	Concordia	37	36	1	Delta	26	13	13
Hart	4	4	....	East Feliciana	35	35	....	Dickinson	15	12	3
Henry	5	5	....	Evangeline	49	49	....	Emmet	24	14	10
Hickman	2	2	....	Franklin	77	77	....	Gladwin	25	17	8
Hopkins	13	13	....								

Table 81.—Number of Full-time Law Enforcement Employees, Rural Counties, October 31, 1993—Continued

County by State	Total police employees	Total officers	Total civilians	County by State	Total police employees	Total officers	Total civilians	County by State	Total police employees	Total officers	Total civilians
MICHIGAN— Continued				**MINNESOTA— Continued**				**MISSOURI— Continued**			
Gogebic	19	14	5	Mille Lacs	27	13	14	Cedar	8	4	4
Grand Traverse	74	45	29	Morrison	36	13	23	Chariton	8	7	1
Gratiot	28	16	12	Mower	39	18	21	Clark	7	5	2
Hillsdale	35	24	11	Murray	9	5	4	Cole	37	35	2
Houghton	31	21	10	Nobles	15	15	......	Cooper	5	5	......
Huron	43	21	22	Norman	7	4	3	Crawford	12	12	......
Ionia	21	16	5	Otter Tail	55	22	33	Dallas	13	9	4
Iosco	22	11	11	Pennington	14	6	8	Daviess	5	3	2
Iron	9	9	......	Pine	31	18	13	Dent	7	6	1
Isabella	39	20	19	Pipestone	15	6	9	Douglas	6	3	3
Kalkaska	34	16	18	Pope	11	5	6	Dunklin	13	11	2
Keweenaw	4	4	......	Red Lake	10	8	2	Gasconade	10	10	......
Lake	36	11	25	Redwood	16	8	8	Gentry	7	3	4
Leelanau	19	10	9	Renville	14	8	6	Grundy	7	3	4
Luce	4	3	1	Rice	36	33	3	Harrison	8	3	5
Mackinac	17	7	10	Rock	10	5	5	Hickory	12	6	6
Manistee	23	10	13	Roseau	12	7	5	Holt	12	5	7
Marquette	22	21	1	Sibley	12	7	5	Lewis	6	4	2
Mason	30	30	......	Steele	30	16	14	Linn	4	3	1
Mecosta	42	22	20	Stevens	9	4	5	Livingston	8	8	......
Menominee	18	8	10	Swift	10	4	6	Macon	9	9	......
Missaukee	18	7	11	Todd	23	12	11	Maries	8	5	3
Montcalm	49	23	26	Traverse	7	4	3	Marion	32	25	7
Montmorency	21	10	11	Wabasha	20	11	9	McDonald	12	12	......
Newaygo	27	21	6	Wadena	14	6	8	Mercer	7	3	4
Oceana	29	16	13	Watonwan	14	7	7	Montgomery	15	10	5
Ogemaw	21	13	8	Wilkin	6	5	1	Morgan	14	11	3
Ontonagon	9	9	......	Winona	63	18	45	New Madrid	21	18	3
Osceola	20	6	14	Yellow Medicine	11	6	5	Nodaway	13	12	1
Oscoda	16	10	6					Oregon	8	4	4
Otsego	19	10	9	**MISSISSIPPI**				Ozark	8	5	3
Presque Isle	27	12	15					Pemiscot	15	14	1
Roscommon	21	15	6	Bolivar	33	14	19	Perry	18	14	4
St. Joseph	44	22	22	Chickasaw	11	10	1	Pike	22	13	9
Sanilac	46	28	18	Claiborne	17	8	9	Polk	17	13	4
Schoolcraft	2	2	......	Clarke	12	7	5	Pulaski	16	16	......
Shiawassee	52	31	21	Coahoma	29	10	19	Reynolds	8	5	3
Tuscola	47	28	19	Copiah	20	9	11	Ripley	6	6	......
Wexford	41	17	24	Covington	13	6	7	St. Clair	25	12	13
				Forrest	70	62	8	St. Francois	31	27	4
MINNESOTA				Franklin	7	3	4	Ste. Genevieve	29	23	6
				Humphreys	8	6	2	Saline	15	14	1
Aitkin	23	10	13	Issaquena	4	4	......	Scotland	9	7	2
Becker	36	14	22	Itawamba	6	5	1	Shelby	8	3	5
Beltrami	46	19	27	Jones	34	32	2	Sullivan	6	4	2
Big Stone	6	3	3	Lawrence	3	3	......	Vernon	15	13	2
Blue Earth	42	21	21	Lee	36	25	11	Washington	24	12	12
Brown	18	10	8	Monroe	19	16	3	Wayne	8	4	4
Carlton	24	17	7	Prentiss	16	8	8	Worth	5	3	2
Cass	43	28	15	Simpson	27	10	17				
Chippewa	8	7	1	Tishomingo	13	7	6	**MONTANA**			
Cook	10	8	2	Tunica	18	14	4				
Dodge	25	16	9	Walthall	4	4	..	Beaverhead	11	6	5
Douglas	31	30	1	Warren	44	35	9	Big Horn	28	14	14
Faribault	17	8	9	Washington	37	32	5	Blaine	13	5	8
Fillmore	20	13	7	Wayne	9	4	5	Broadwater	6	3	3
Freeborn	32	17	15	Webster	8	4	4	Carbon	10	6	4
Goodhue	54	30	24	Winston	9	4	5	Chouteau	15	9	6
Grant	9	4	5	Yalobusha	10	5	5	Custer	10	5	5
Hubbard	19	9	10					Daniels	7	3	4
Jackson	14	7	7	**MISSOURI**				Dawson	7	5	2
Kanabec	14	7	7					Deer Lodge	26	19	7
Kandiyohi	35	25	10	Atchison	10	10	......	Fallon	9	2	7
Kittson	9	5	4	Audrain	18	18	......	Fergus	16	8	8
Koochiching	15	9	6	Barry	12	7	5	Flathead	82	40	42
Lac Qui Parle	7	3	4	Barton	10	10	......	Gallatin	55	29	26
Lake	17	11	6	Bates	10	9	1	Golden Valley	2	2	......
Lake-of-the-Woods	8	4	4	Benton	13	13	......	Granite	7	3	4
Le Sueur	21	12	9	Bollinger	9	4	5	Hill	17	9	8
Lincoln	8	4	4	Caldwell	9	3	6	Jefferson	17	9	8
Lyon	19	8	11	Camden	31	31	......	Lake	24	12	12
Marshall	13	8	5	Cape Girardeau	39	28	11	Lewis and Clark	45	25	20
Martin	22	8	14	Carroll	13	7	6	Liberty	8	4	4
Meeker	19	8	11	Carter	5	3	2	Lincoln	33	21	12

Table 81. — Number of Full-time Law Enforcement Employees, Rural Counties, October 31, 1993 — Continued

County by State	Total police employees	Total officers	Total civilians	County by State	Total police employees	Total officers	Total civilians	County by State	Total police employees	Total officers	Total civilians
MONTANA— Continued				**NEBRASKA— Continued**				**NEW MEXICO— Continued**			
Madison	10	7	3	Kearney	11	6	5	Sierra	22	9	13
McCone	3	3	....	Keith	15	9	6	Socorro	17	9	8
Meagher	6	3	3	Keya Paha	1	1	....	Taos	17	14	3
Mineral	11	6	5	Kimball	7	3	4	Torrance	16	14	2
Missoula	80	45	35	Knox	12	4	8				
Musselshell	12	6	6	Lincoln	39	21	18	**NEW YORK**			
Park	16	10	6	Logan	4	4	....	Allegany	35	30	5
Phillips	13	7	6	Loup	1	1	....	Cattaraugus	55	37	18
Pondera	9	6	3	Madison	25	16	9	Chenango	33	20	13
Powder River	3	3	....	McPherson	1	1	....	Clinton	35	30	5
Powell	9	5	4	Merrick	10	5	5	Columbia	45	35	10
Ravalli	29	16	13	Morrill	8	3	5	Delaware	15	10	5
Richland	15	6	9	Nance	11	7	4	Essex	23	23	....
Roosevelt	35	17	18	Nemaha	8	4	4	Franklin	14	12	2
Rosebud	37	17	20	Nuckolls	6	4	2	Fulton	35	34	1
Sanders	15	6	9	Otoe	18	9	9	Greene	24	22	2
Sheridan	10	5	5	Pawnee	4	3	1	Jefferson	49	31	18
Silver Bow	65	41	24	Phelps	10	4	6	Otsego	16	13	3
Stillwater	11	7	4	Pierce	8	4	4	Seneca	33	23	10
Sweet Grass	8	4	4	Platte	12	11	1	Steuben	40	26	14
Teton	10	6	4	Polk	12	6	6	Sullivan	50	33	17
Toole	19	12	7	Red Willow	5	4	1	Tompkins	40	31	9
Treasure	2	2	....	Richardson	8	3	5	Ulster	50	46	4
Valley	16	8	8	Rock	8	3	5	Wyoming	38	27	11
Wheatland	8	3	5	Saline	15	9	6	Yates	29	19	10
				Saunders	19	9	10				
NEBRASKA				Scotts Bluff	18	14	4	**NORTH CAROLINA**			
Adams	18	16	2	Seward	22	9	13	Alleghany	21	10	11
Antelope	10	6	4	Sheridan	5	4	1	Anson	24	19	5
Arthur	1	1	....	Sherman	3	2	1	Ashe	26	15	11
Banner	1	1	....	Sioux	2	2	....	Avery	30	25	5
Blaine	1	1	....	Stanton	5	4	1	Beaufort	62	36	26
Boone	8	4	4	Thayer	10	7	3	Bertie	18	12	6
Box Butte	14	4	10	Thomas	2	1	1	Bladen	45	25	20
Boyd	2	2	....	Thurston	11	3	8	Camden	6	6	....
Brown	7	3	4	Valley	6	2	4	Carteret	49	33	16
Buffalo	46	16	30	Wayne	5	4	1	Caswell	28	22	6
Burt	7	4	3	Webster	9	5	4	Cherokee	21	13	8
Butler	8	4	4	Wheeler	1	1	....	Chowan	21	14	7
Cedar	8	4	4	York	18	8	10	Clay	16	8	8
Chase	6	2	4					Cleveland	94	56	38
Cherry	11	4	7	**NEVADA**				Columbus	62	43	19
Cheyenne	11	4	7	Carson City	100	75	25	Craven	90	50	40
Clay	9	4	5	Churchill	35	29	6	Dare	99	45	54
Colfax	11	4	7	Elko	52	44	8	Duplin	53	36	17
Cuming	9	4	5	Esmeralda	14	10	4	Gates	5	5	....
Custer	7	6	1	Lander	34	34	....	Granville	44	29	15
Dawes	7	3	4	Lincoln	24	23	1	Greene	24	21	3
Dawson	18	16	2	Mineral	32	25	7	Halifax	70	35	35
Deuel	7	4	3	Pershing	15	10	5	Harnett	89	54	35
Dixon	8	4	4	Storey	19	19	....	Haywood	31	30	1
Dodge	19	16	3	White Pine	31	26	5	Henderson	99	74	25
Dundy	8	4	4					Hertford	37	13	24
Fillmore	7	4	3	**NEW HAMPSHIRE**				Hoke	40	32	8
Franklin	6	2	4	Belknap	16	8	8	Hyde	13	9	4
Frontier	9	5	4	Carroll	15	9	6	Iredell	91	84	7
Furnas	13	8	5	Cheshire	9	7	2	Jackson	30	25	5
Gage	15	9	6	Sullivan	7	5	2	Jones	13	8	5
Garden	10	5	5					Lee	47	26	21
Garfield	1	1	....	**NEW MEXICO**				Lenoir	65	42	23
Gosper	5	4	1	Curry	17	13	4	Macon	28	27	1
Grant	2	2	....	Eddy	45	23	22	Martin	16	13	3
Greeley	2	1	1	Grant	41	26	15	McDowell	40	28	12
Hall	29	24	5	Guadalupe	11	5	6	Montgomery	33	21	12
Hamilton	12	6	6	Hidalgo	24	10	14	Moore	65	48	17
Harlan	10	5	5	Lincoln	24	18	6	Northampton	32	15	17
Hayes	2	2	....	Luna	28	24	4	Pamlico	20	11	9
Hitchcock	7	4	3	McKinley	47	32	15	Pasquotank	16	14	2
Holt	10	4	6	Otero	32	22	10	Pender	48	29	19
Hooker	1	1	....	Roosevelt	10	9	1	Perquimans	7	6	1
Howard	4	3	1	San Juan	71	52	19	Person	50	25	25
Jefferson	9	5	4					Polk	33	20	13
Johnson	8	2	6								

Table 81. — Number of Full-time Law Enforcement Employees, Rural Counties, October 31, 1993 — Continued

County by State	Total police employees	Total officers	Total civilians	County by State	Total police employees	Total officers	Total civilians	County by State	Total police employees	Total officers	Total civilians
NORTH CAROLINA — Continued				**OHIO — Continued**				**OKLAHOMA — Continued**			
Richmond	51	33	18	Darke	46	20	26	Muskogee	15	12	3
Robeson	82	69	13	Defiance	22	17	5	Noble	9	9	......
Rockingham	90	71	19	Erie	65	30	35	Nowata	11	6	5
Rutherford	38	35	3	Fayette	26	23	3	Okfuskee	10	5	5
Sampson	72	48	24	Hardin	21	11	10	Okmulgee	18	11	7
Scotland	45	32	13	Harrison	11	10	1	Ottawa	15	13	2
Stanly	43	33	10	Henry	21	21	......	Pawnee	13	7	6
Surry	57	40	17	Highland	25	24	1	Payne	21	14	7
Swain	23	10	13	Hocking	18	12	6	Pittsburg	24	18	6
Transylvania	46	30	16	Holmes	30	21	9	Pontotoc	17	8	9
Tyrrell	11	6	5	Huron	29	21	8	Pushmataha	11	5	6
Vance	27	27	......	Jackson	22	20	2	Roger Mills	10	4	6
Warren	13	13	......	Logan	56	45	11	Seminole	13	12	1
Washington	18	12	6	Monroe	25	20	5	Stephens	18	10	8
Watauga	36	25	11	Morgan	22	17	5	Texas	12	6	6
Wilkes	66	45	21	Muskingum	82	49	33	Tillman	11	6	5
Wilson	90	51	39	Paulding	20	9	11	Washita	9	8	1
Yancey	13	7	6	Preble	35	22	13	Washington	20	18	2
				Ross	71	65	6	Woods	7	3	4
NORTH DAKOTA				Seneca	30	13	17	Woodward	12	8	4
				Shelby	38	36	2				
Adams	5	4	1	Tuscarawas	66	23	43	**OREGON**			
Barnes	11	9	2	Union	40	25	15				
Benson	3	3	......	Van Wert	20	14	6	Baker	7	6	1
Billings	4	3	1	Vinton	9	4	5	Benton	32	25	7
Bottineau	12	8	4	Wayne	71	61	10	Clatsop	17	14	3
Bowman	1	1	......	Williams	19	17	2	Coos	47	32	15
Burke	4	4	......	Wyandot	18	10	8	Crook	9	7	2
Cavalier	9	5	4					Curry	27	21	6
Dickey	5	4	1	**OKLAHOMA**				Deschutes	56	42	14
Divide	4	4	......					Douglas	83	67	16
Dunn	4	3	1	Adair	12	7	5	Gilliam	4	3	1
Eddy	3	2	1	Alfalfa	8	4	4	Grant	5	4	1
Emmons	2	2	......	Atoka	9	5	4	Harney	9	8	1
Foster	3	2	1	Beaver	11	7	4	Hood River	17	14	3
Golden Valley	7	3	4	Beckham	14	12	2	Jefferson	17	11	6
Grant	2	2	......	Blaine	6	6	......	Josephine	60	44	16
Hettinger	3	3	......	Bryan	20	8	12	Klamath	20	16	4
Kidder	3	2	1	Caddo	17	7	10	Lake	6	6	......
Lamoure	4	3	1	Carter	43	15	28	Lincoln	26	23	3
Logan	5	2	3	Cherokee	23	14	9	Linn	70	51	19
McHenry	3	3	......	Choctaw	10	4	6	Malheur	16	10	6
McIntosh	2	2	......	Cimarron	8	4	4	Morrow	14	9	5
McKenzie	9	5	4	Coal	8	3	5	Sherman	5	4	1
McLean	25	21	4	Cotton	9	4	5	Tillamook	22	19	3
Mercer	18	18	......	Craig	9	7	2	Umatilla	22	12	10
Mountrail	8	4	4	Custer	18	8	10	Umatilla Tribal	13	8	5
Oliver	3	3	......	Delaware	13	7	6	Union	6	4	2
Pembina	16	13	3	Dewey	7	4	3	Wallowa	10	5	5
Pierce	7	3	4	Ellis	7	3	4	Wasco	28	20	8
Ramsey	6	5	1	Garvin	15	7	8	Wheeler	2	2	......
Ransom	5	5	......	Grady	17	8	9				
Renville	4	3	1	Grant	9	5	4	**PENNSYLVANIA**			
Richland	13	7	6	Greer	5	4	1				
Rolette	12	9	3	Harmon	3	3	......	Clarion	6	4	2
Sargent	3	2	1	Harper	7	3	4	Jefferson	4	4	......
Sheridan	2	2	......	Haskell	12	7	5	Warren	39	33	6
Slope	1	1	......	Hughes	8	4	4				
Stark	12	9	3	Jackson	13	8	5	**SOUTH CAROLINA**			
Steele	3	3	......	Jefferson	7	4	3				
Stutsman	10	8	2	Johnston	10	6	4	Abbeville	33	24	9
Towner	2	1	1	Kay	27	11	16	Allendale	9	8	1
Traill	6	3	3	Kingfisher	11	7	4	Bamberg	11	9	2
Walsh	13	7	6	Kiowa	9	7	2	Barnwell	19	11	8
Ward	37	17	20	Latimer	10	7	3	Beaufort	125	114	11
Wells	2	2	......	Le Flore	19	9	10	Calhoun	13	12	1
Williams	26	25	1	Lincoln	14	7	7	Chester	34	31	3
				Love	14	6	8	Chesterfield	29	19	10
OHIO				Major	7	3	4	Clarendon	49	25	24
				Marshall	11	7	4	Colleton	59	31	28
Ashland	45	38	7	Mayes	17	11	6	Darlington	42	38	4
Champaign	32	30	2	McCurtain	13	9	4	Dillon	27	16	11
Clinton	32	28	4	McIntosh	11	6	5	Fairfield	44	31	13
Coshocton	54	46	8	Murray	9	4	5	Georgetown	45	41	4

County by State	Total police employees	Total officers	Total civilians	County by State	Total police employees	Total officers	Total civilians	County by State	Total police employees	Total officers	Total civilians
SOUTH CAROLINA — Continued				**TENNESSEE —** Continued				**TEXAS —** Continued			
Greenwood	63	50	13	Henry	32	28	4	Edwards	10	5	5
Hampton	18	10	8	Hickman	17	9	8	Erath	41	13	28
Jasper	33	17	16	Humphreys	16	7	9	Falls	12	7	5
Kershaw	40	32	8	Jefferson	32	18	14	Fannin	19	11	8
Lancaster	66	40	26	Lawrence	40	23	17	Fayette	26	12	14
Laurens	49	32	17	Lincoln	37	14	23	Fisher	10	6	4
Lee	21	19	2	McMinn	46	42	4	Floyd	13	5	8
Marion	18	17	1	McNairy	16	9	7	Foard	5	4	1
Marlboro	19	14	5	Meigs	13	8	5	Franklin	17	7	10
McCormick	18	7	11	Monroe	28	17	11	Freestone	21	14	7
Newberry	39	25	14	Perry	13	8	5	Frio	16	7	9
Oconee	49	36	13	Putnam	73	57	16	Gaines	17	8	9
Orangeburg	66	50	16	Roane	40	30	10	Garza	13	9	4
Saluda	20	10	10	Stewart	13	8	5	Gillespie	21	11	10
Union	30	26	4	Trousdale	15	6	9	Glasscock	4	2	2
Williamsburg	42	20	22	Warren	52	30	22	Goliad	14	7	7
				Wayne	13	8	5	Gonzales	22	12	10
SOUTH DAKOTA				Weakley	29	.21	8	Gray	29	13	16
				White	21	14	7	Grimes	26	11	15
Aurora	4	3	1					Hale	46	18	28
Beadle	14	5	9	**TEXAS**				Hall	7	3	4
Bennett	10	6	4					Hamilton	18	7	11
Bon Homme	4	3	1	Anderson	49	22	27	Hansford	7	3	4
Brookings	14	7	7	Andrews	24	12	12	Hardeman	8	4	4
Brown	25	11	14	Angelina	62	32	30	Hartley	5	3	2
Charles Mix	9	3	6	Aransas	30	15	15	Haskell	6	3	3
Clay	6	5	1	Armstrong	4	1	3	Hemphill	14	8	6
Custer	14	9	5	Atascosa	59	20	39	Hill	31	19	12
Day	7	3	4	Austin	31	14	17	Hockley	18	8	10
Deuel	7	4	3	Bailey	9	4	5	Hopkins	44	22	22
Douglas	2	2	....	Bandera	24	13	11	Houston	16	8	8
Edmunds	6	4	2	Baylor	12	3	9	Howard	15	10	5
Fall River	12	4	8	Bee	36	14	22	Hudspeth	28	8	20
Faulk	5	3	2	Blanco	10	6	4	Hutchinson	28	12	16
Haakon	2	2	....	Borden	3	2	1	Irion	7	3	4
Hand	3	2	1	Bosque	20	10	10	Jack	12	8	4
Hanson	1	1	....	Brewster	13	5	8	Jackson	20	10	10
Harding	2	1	1	Briscoe	3	2	1	Jasper	27	15	12
Hughes	19	9	10	Brooks	23	8	15	Jeff Davis	4	4	....
Hutchinson	2	2	....	Brown	31	12	19	Jim Hogg	30	15	15
Hyde	1	1	....	Burleson	18	8	10	Jim Wells	28	14	14
Jackson	1	1	....	Burnet	41	23	18	Jones	22	10	12
Jerauld	1	1	....	Calhoun	36	21	15	Karnes	15	7	8
Lake	7	4	3	Callahan	12	6	6	Kendall	29	12	17
Lawrence	34	10	24	Camp	14	5	9	Kenedy	6	6	....
Lyman	4	3	1	Carson	11	5	6	Kent	2	2	....
Marshall	8	4	4	Cass	34	12	22	Kerr	42	20	22
McCook	3	2	1	Castro	14	9	5	Kimble	8	3	5
McPherson	1	1	....	Cherokee	44	20	24	King	3	2	1
Meade	14	11	3	Childress	8	5	3	Kinney	11	3	8
Miner	3	3	....	Clay	16	10	6	Kleberg	37	23	14
Moody	10	7	3	Cochran	14	8	6	Knox	7	6	1
Perkins	3	2	1	Coke	5	4	1	La Salle	16	10	6
Potter	7	2	5	Coleman	12	6	6	Lamar	57	16	41
Sanborn	3	2	1	Collingsworth	10	6	4	Lamb	14	8	6
Spink	13	8	5	Colorado	22	12	10	Lampasas	18	9	9
Turner	3	2	1	Comanche	27	8	19	Lavaca	16	10	6
Union	7	4	3	Concho	8	3	5	Lee	13	9	4
Yankton	7	6	1	Cooke	32	17	15	Leon	21	9	12
				Cottle	4	2	2	Limestone	36	14	22
TENNESSEE				Crane	10	6	4	Lipscomb	9	5	4
				Crockett	11	10	1	Live Oak	19	11	8
Bradley	87	85	2	Crosby	16	8	8	Llano	24	11	13
Chester	18	7	11	Culberson	13	6	7	Loving	4	2	2
Cocke	32	19	13	Dallam	9	3	6	Lynn	10	5	5
Crockett	20	9	11	Dawson	12	7	5	Madison	23	12	11
Fentress	19	9	10	Deaf Smith	31	16	15	Marion	13	7	6
Gibson	28	23	5	Delta	11	7	4	Martin	8	3	5
Giles	24	14	10	Dewitt	20	8	12	Mason	5	3	2
Grainger	18	9	9	Dickens	6	2	4	Matagorda	67	46	21
Greene	39	29	10	Dimmit	21	11	10	Maverick	41	18	23
Hamblen	46	42	4	Donley	8	6	2	McCulloch	7	6	1
Hardeman	21	12	9	Duval	26	15	11	McMullen	3	3	....
Henderson	22	15	7	Eastland	15	7	8	Medina	23	11	12

Table 81.—Number of Full-time Law Enforcement Employees, Rural Counties, October 31, 1993—Continued

County by State	Total police employees	Total officers	Total civilians	County by State	Total police employees	Total officers	Total civilians	County by State	Total police employees	Total officers	Total civilians
TEXAS—Continued				**UTAH—Continued**				**VIRGINIA—Continued**			
Menard	7	3	4	Box Elder	34	26	8	Patrick	27	14	13
Milam	21	7	14	Cache	56	51	5	Prince Edward	16	16	....
Mills	8	4	4	Carbon	21	20	1	Pulaski	65	52	13
Mitchell	11	5	6	Daggett	4	3	1	Rappahannock	17	7	10
Montague	18	7	11	Duchesne	17	16	1	Richmond	16	11	5
Moore	23	9	14	Emery	37	30	7	Rockbridge	24	16	8
Morris	21	8	13	Garfield	8	8	....	Rockingham	72	51	21
Motley	2	2	....	Grand	18	13	5	Russell	40	38	2
Nacogdoches	47	18	29	Iron	17	15	2	Shenandoah	59	59	....
Navarro	63	23	40	Juab	11	11	....	Smyth	39	39	....
Newton	13	9	4	Kane	16	10	6	Southampton	42	33	9
Nolan	19	10	9	Millard	31	24	7	Surry	13	8	5
Ochiltree	16	7	9	Morgan	7	6	1	Sussex	33	31	2
Oldham	13	8	5	Piute	2	2	....	Tazewell	52	44	8
Palo Pinto	49	25	24	Rich	9	8	1	Warren	48	47	1
Panola	32	15	17	San Juan	27	19	8	Westmoreland	32	25	7
Parmer	13	5	8	Sanpete	19	14	5	Wise	56	43	13
Pecos	22	14	8	Sevier	33	28	5	Wythe	40	32	8
Polk	44	23	21	Summit	31	23	8				
Presidio	10	4	6	Tooele	44	32	12	**WASHINGTON**			
Rains	17	6	11	Uintah	31	23	8				
Reagan	9	5	4	Wasatch	16	15	1	Adams	25	16	9
Real	6	3	3	Washington	40	36	4	Asotin	20	9	11
Red River	16	10	6	Wayne	4	3	1	Chelan	50	38	12
Reeves	44	14	30					Clallam	38	29	9
Refugio	23	11	12	**VERMONT**				Columbia	9	4	5
Roberts	4	3	1					Cowlitz	49	45	4
Robertson	19	7	12	Lamoille	15	11	4	Douglas	34	24	10
Runnels	12	7	5	Orleans	8	6	2	Ferry	15	9	6
Rusk	48	26	22	Windham	20	14	6	Garfield	7	3	4
Sabine	16	8	8					Grant	48	31	17
San Augustine	9	3	6	**VIRGINIA**				Grays Harbor	49	40	9
San Jacinto	20	10	10					Jefferson	22	18	4
San Saba	10	3	7	Accomack	44	41	3	Kittitas	27	23	4
Schleicher	8	4	4	Alleghany	33	30	3	Klickitat	26	17	9
Scurry	12	6	6	Amelia	13	7	6	Lewis	55	43	12
Shackelford	14	5	9	Augusta	83	72	11	Lincoln	12	11	1
Shelby	24	8	16	Bath	17	17	....	Mason	40	34	6
Sherman	9	5	4	Bland	20	13	7	Okanogan	33	27	6
Somervell	25	12	13	Brunswick	27	20	7	Pacific	19	11	8
Starr	72	37	35	Buchanan	44	34	10	Pend Oreille	19	12	7
Stephens	9	7	2	Buckingham	14	10	4	San Juan	24	16	8
Sterling	4	3	1	Caroline	36	29	7	Skagit	51	37	14
Stonewall	6	2	4	Carroll	39	31	8	Skamania	21	18	3
Sutton	13	5	8	Charlotte	22	20	2	Stevens	28	24	4
Swisher	9	3	6	Craig	10	5	5	Wahkiakum	9	5	4
Terrell	5	3	2	Cumberland	12	8	4	Walla Walla	21	18	3
Terry	15	7	8	Dickenson	25	25	....	Whitman	16	13	3
Throckmorton	8	2	6	Essex	13	8	5				
Titus	26	12	14	Floyd	20	15	5	**WEST VIRGINIA**			
Trinity	12	7	5	Franklin	61	50	11				
Tyler	26	12	14	Frederick	62	51	11	Barbour	10	6	4
Upton	15	8	7	Giles	31	24	7	Berkeley	30	23	7
Uvalde	22	9	13	Grayson	27	21	6	Boone	19	18	1
Val Verde	73	18	55	Greensville	28	26	2	Braxton	5	4	1
Van Zandt	46	21	25	Halifax	38	31	7	Calhoun	1	1	....
Walker	60	27	33	Henry	88	77	11	Clay	4	4	....
Ward	30	15	15	Highland	13	8	5	Doddridge	2	2	....
Washington	46	15	31	King and Queen	10	6	4	Fayette	29	29	....
Wharton	48	29	19	King William	19	13	6	Gilmer	4	4	....
Wheeler	10	6	4	Lancaster	22	19	3	Grant	8	5	3
Wilbarger	17	7	10	Lee	43	41	2	Greenbrier	31	16	15
Willacy	31	16	15	Louisa	27	20	7	Hampshire	10	5	5
Winkler	13	9	4	Lunenburg	13	7	6	Hardy	6	6	....
Wise	55	24	31	Madison	15	10	5	Harrison	24	23	1
Wood	44	21	23	Mecklenburg	54	21	33	Jackson	11	10	1
Yoakum	20	9	11	Middlesex	12	7	5	Jefferson	11	9	2
Young	26	14	12	Montgomery	51	40	11	Lewis	10	9	1
Zapata	30	20	10	Nelson	22	22	....	Lincoln	6	5	1
Zavala	20	8	12	Northampton	35	31	4	Logan	46	18	28
				Northumberland	18	17	1	Marion	51	23	28
UTAH				Nottoway	16	9	7	Mason	27	12	15
				Orange	27	17	10	McDowell	13	9	4
Beaver	11	10	1	Page	36	36	....	Mercer	35	17	18

372

Table 81. — Number of Full-time Law Enforcement Employees, Rural Counties, October 31, 1993 — Continued

County by State	Total police employees	Total officers	Total civilians	County by State	Total police employees	Total officers	Total civilians	County by State	Total police employees	Total officers	Total civilians
WEST VIRGINIA — Continued				**WISCONSIN —** Continued				**WISCONSIN —** Continued			
Mingo	33	13	20	Florence	11	11	....	Walworth	160	77	83
Monongalia	44	20	24	Fond Du Lac	79	73	6	Washburn	22	22	....
Monroe	6	2	4	Forest	13	12	1	Waupaca	38	35	3
Morgan	6	6	....	Grant	39	22	17	Waushara	25	25	....
Nicholas	21	15	6	Green	31	24	7	Wood	69	42	27
Pendleton	5	2	3	Green Lake	25	25	....				
Pleasants	10	7	3	Iowa	21	21	....	**WYOMING**			
Pocahontas	13	5	8	Iron	10	10	....	Albany	22	18	4
Preston	26	12	14	Jackson	30	18	12	Big Horn	11	7	4
Raleigh	42	34	8	Jefferson	97	79	18	Campbell	49	30	19
Randolph	10	4	6	Juneau	29	27	2	Carbon	22	14	8
Ritchie	10	4	6	Kewaunee	25	23	2	Converse	17	10	7
Roane	5	5	....	Lafayette	18	12	6	Crook	12	6	6
Summers	10	3	7	Langlade	23	15	8	Fremont	42	25	17
Taylor	15	6	9	Lincoln	34	26	8	Goshen	8	7	1
Tucker	3	3	....	Manitowoc	96	53	43	Hot Springs	13	12	1
Tyler	7	3	4	Marinette	47	26	21	Johnson	11	10	1
Upshur	16	7	9	Marquette	24	23	1	Lincoln	31	13	18
Webster	4	4	....	Menominee	11	10	1	Niobrara	9	3	6
Wetzel	16	6	10	Menominee Tribal	17	15	2	Park	24	17	7
Wirt	2	2	....	Monroe	36	34	2	Platte	11	6	5
Wyoming	25	13	12	Oconto	40	20	20	Sheridan	15	13	2
				Oneida	40	26	14	Sublette	15	13	2
WISCONSIN				Pepin	10	10	....	Sweetwater	59	36	23
Adams	31	29	2	Polk	32	29	3	Teton	50	29	21
Ashland	19	15	4	Portage	70	40	30	Uinta	40	25	15
Barron	31	31	....	Price	22	19	3	Washakie	7	6	1
Bayfield	25	23	2	Richland	25	24	1	Weston	6	6	....
Buffalo	18	9	9	Rusk	20	20	....				
Clark	37	35	2	Sauk	74	65	9	**OTHER AREAS**			
Columbia	65	31	34	Sawyer	28	22	6	American Samoa	207	116	91
Crawford	20	19	1	Shawano	46	39	7	Guam	469	374	95
Dodge	72	39	33	Taylor	23	17	6	Puerto Rico	15,072	13,158	1,914
Door	38	35	3	Trempealeau	33	31	2	Virgin Islands	625	478	147
Dunn	30	18	12	Vernon	23	22	1				
				Vilas	40	26	14				

SECTION VII
APPENDIX I
Methodology

The information compiled by UCR contributors is forwarded to the FBI either directly from local law enforcement agencies or through state-level UCR Programs in 44 states and the District of Columbia. Agencies submitting directly to the FBI are provided continuing guidance and support on an individual basis.

State-level UCR Programs are very effective intermediaries between local contributors and the FBI. Many of the Programs have mandatory reporting requirements and collect data beyond the national UCR scope to address crime problems germane to their particular locales. In most cases, these agencies are also able to provide more direct and frequent service to participating law enforcement agencies, to make information more readily available for use at the state level, and to contribute to more streamlined operations at the national level.

With the development of a state UCR Program, the FBI ceases direct collection of data from individual law enforcement agencies within the state. Instead, information from local agencies is forwarded to the national Program through the state data collection agency.

The conditions under which these systems are developed ensure consistency and comparability in the data submitted to the national Program, as well as provide for regular and timely reporting of national crime data. These conditions are: (1) The state Program must conform to national Uniform Crime Reports' standards, definitions, and information requirements. The states are not, of course, prohibited from collecting other statistical data beyond the national requirements. (2) The state criminal justice agency must have a proven, effective, statewide Program and have instituted acceptable quality control procedures. (3) Coverage within the state by a state agency must be, at least, equal to that attained by the national Uniform Crime Reports. (4) The state agency must have adequate field staff assigned to conduct audits and to assist contributing agencies in record practices and crime reporting procedures. (5) The state agency must furnish to the FBI all of the detailed data regularly collected by the FBI in the form of duplicate returns, computer printouts, and/or magnetic tapes. (6) The state agency must have the proven capability (tested over a period of time) to supply all the statistical data required in time to meet national Uniform Crime Reports' publication deadlines.

To fulfill its responsibilities in connection with the UCR Program, the FBI continues to edit and review individual agency reports for both completeness and quality; has direct contact with individual contributors within the state when necessary in connection with crime reporting matters, coordinating such contact with the state agency; and upon request, conducts training programs within the state on law enforcement records and crime reporting procedures. Should circumstances develop whereby the state agency does not comply with the aforementioned requirements, the national Program may reinstitute a direct collection of Uniform Crime Reports from law enforcement agencies within the state.

Reporting Procedures

Based on records of all reports of crime received from victims, officers who discover infractions, or other sources, law enforcement agencies across the country tabulate the number of Crime Index or Part I offenses brought to their attention each month. Specifically, the crimes reported to the FBI are murder and nonnegligent manslaughter, forcible rape, robbery, aggravated assault, burglary, larceny-theft, motor vehicle theft, and arson.

Whenever complaints of crime are determined through investigation to be unfounded or false, they are eliminated from an agency's count. The number of "actual offenses known" is reported to the FBI regardless of whether anyone is arrested for the crime, stolen property is recovered, or prosecution is undertaken.

Another integral part of the monthly submission is the total number of actual Crime Index offenses cleared. Crimes are "cleared" in one of two ways: (1) at least one person is arrested, charged, and turned over to the court for prosecution; or (2) by exceptional means when some element beyond law enforcement control precludes the arrest of an offender. Law enforcement agencies also report the number of Index crime clearances which involve only offenders under the age of 18; the value of property stolen and recovered in connection with the offenses; and detailed information pertaining to criminal homicide and arson.

In addition to its primary collection on Crime Index (Part I) offenses, the UCR Program solicits monthly data on persons arrested for all crimes except traffic violations.

The age, sex, and race of arrestees are reported by crime category, both Part I and Part II. Part II offenses include all crimes not classified as Part I.

Various data on law enforcement officers killed or assaulted are collected on a monthly basis. The number of full-time sworn and civilian personnel are reported as of October 31 each year.

Editing Procedures

Each report submitted to the UCR Program is thoroughly examined for arithmetical accuracy and for deviations which may indicate errors. To identify any unusual fluctuations in an agency's crime counts, monthly reports are compared with previous submissions of the agency and with those for similar agencies. Large variations in crime levels may indicate modified records procedures, incomplete reporting, or changes in the jurisdiction's geopolitical structure.

Data reliability is a high priority of the Program and noted deviations or arithmetical adjustments are brought to the attention of the state UCR Program or the submitting agency through correspondence. A standard procedure of the FBI is to study the monthly reports and to evaluate periodic trends prepared for individual reporting units. Any significant increase or decrease is made the subject of a special inquiry. When it is found that changes in crime reporting procedures or annexations are influencing the level of crime, the figures for specific crime categories, or if necessary, totals are excluded from trend tabulations.

To assist contributors in complying with UCR standards, the national Program provides training seminars and instructional materials in crime reporting procedures. Throughout the country, liaison with state Programs and law enforcement personnel is maintained, and training sessions are held to explain the purpose of the Program, the rules of uniform classification and scoring, and the methods of assembling the information for reporting. When an individual agency has specific problems in compiling its crime statistics and remedial efforts are unsuccessful, FBI Headquarters' personnel may visit the contributor to aid in resolving the difficulties.

The *Uniform Crime Reporting Handbook*, which details procedures for classifying and scoring offenses, is supplied to all contributors as the basic resource document for preparing reports. Since a good records system is essential for accurate crime reporting, the FBI also furnishes the *Manual of Law Enforcement Records*.

To enhance communication among Program participants, letters to UCR contributors and State UCR Program "Bulletins" are utilized. They address Program policy, as well as present information and instructional material, and are produced as needed.

The final responsibility for data submissions rests with the individual contributing law enforcement agency.

Although the Program makes every effort through its editing procedures, training practices, and correspondence to assure the validity of the data it receives, the statistics' accuracy depends primarily on the adherence of each contributor to the established standards of reporting. Deviations from these established standards which cannot be resolved by the national UCR Program may be brought to the attention of the Committee on Uniform Crime Records of the International Association of Chiefs of Police or the Committee on Uniform Crime Reporting of the National Sheriffs' Association.

NIBRS Conversion

Several states provided their UCR data in the expanded NIBRS format. For presentation in this book, NIBRS data were converted to the historical summary UCR formats. The NIBRS data base was constructed to allow for such conversion so that UCR's long-running time series could continue.

Offense Estimation

Tables 1 through 5 and 7 of this publication contain statistics for the entire United States. Because not all law enforcement agencies provide data for complete reporting periods, estimated crime counts are included in these presentations. Offense estimation occurs within each of three areas: Metropolitan Statistical Areas (MSAs), cities outside MSAs, and rural counties. Using the known crime experiences of similar areas within a state, the estimates are computed by assigning the same proportional crime volumes to nonreporting agencies. The size of agency; type of jurisdiction, e.g., police department versus sheriff's office; and geographic location are considered in the estimation process.

Because of efforts to convert to the National Incident-Based Reporting System, it has become necessary to estimate totals for some states during the transitional period. Crime counts for the states of Iowa in 1991 and Kansas and Illinois in 1993 were estimated using procedures based on data availability specific to each state. The Iowa conversion was successful and state figures for 1992 and 1993 were available. Kansas and Illinois are continuing conversion efforts. Within these two states, 1993 jurisdictional data are only available for Wichita, Kansas, and approximately 60 Illinois agencies still reporting under the summary format. These figures are shown in Tables 8 through 11.

For Iowa (1991) and Kansas (1993), state totals were estimated by updating previous valid annual totals for individual jurisdictions, subdivided by population group. For the year in question, percent changes for each offense within each population group of the geographic division in which the state resides were applied to the previous annual valid figures. The state totals were compiled from the sums of the population group estimates. (This same method was used to estimate Florida and Kentucky totals for 1988 when there were reporting problems at the state levels.)

A different method was used to estimate 1993 Illinois totals. Since valid figures were available for some Illinois individual jurisdictions, those counts were maintained. The counts for the remaining jurisdictions were replaced with the most recent valid annual totals for previous years or were generated using standard estimation procedures. The results of all sources were then combined to arrive at the 1993 state total for Illinois.

The inability of some state UCR Programs to provide forcible rape figures in accordance with the UCR guidelines also required unique estimation procedures. The 1985 through 1993 Illinois and 1993 Michigan and Minnesota forcible rape totals were estimated using national rates per 100,000 inhabitants within the eight population groups and assigning the forcible rape volumes proportionally to each state. Forcible rape figures are shown for a limited number of Minnesota agencies in this book's Tables 6 and 8 through 11.

Crime Trends

Showing fluctuations from year to year, trend statistics offer the data user an added perspective from which to study crime. Percent change tabulations in this publication are computed only for reporting units which have provided comparable data for the periods under consideration. Exclusions from trend computations are made when figures from a reporting agency are not received for comparable timeframes or when it is ascertained that unusual fluctuations are due to such variables as improved records procedures, annexations, etc.

Care should be exercised in any direct comparison between data in this publication and those in prior issues of *Crime in the United States*. Valid percent changes for 2-, 5-, and 10-year periods are presented in this book's tabular portions.

Variation from Monthly Average

For the overall Crime Index, violent crime, property crime, and each Crime Index offense, charts titled "variation from monthly average" are shown in Section II. These charts present monthly seasonal indices and describe varia-

tions that arise from seasonal factors by eliminating the impact of crime trends or random factors. In order to stabilize the seasonal indices, the variations are based on the means of UCR data covering the most recent 10-year interval.

The variations are different from the data in the tables entitled "By Month, Percent of Annual Total" in two major respects: the latter is a percent distribution of a single year's statistics and 12 figures add to 100, whereas the former adds to zero. The second difference is that the latter (by month, percent of annual total) is not strictly a seasonal indicator because crime trend, for example, will have an impact on the monthly distribution.

Table Methodology

Although most law enforcement agencies submit crime reports to the UCR Program, data are sometimes not received for complete annual periods. To be included in this publication's Tables 8 through 11, showing specific jurisdictional statistics, figures for all 12 months of the current year must have been received at the FBI prior to established publication deadlines. Other tabular presentations are aggregated on varied levels of submission. Unless consisting of estimates for the total United States population, each table in this publication shows the number of agencies reporting and the extent of population coverage.

Designed to assist the reader, this appendix explains the construction of many of this book's tabular presentations. The following key refers to the columnar headings used throughout the appendix.

Key: A) Column 1 shows the table numbers. Included are Tables 1 through 69, *Crime in the United States - 1993*.

B) Column 2 indicates the level of submission necessary for an agency's statistics to be included in a table.

C) Column 3 explains how each table was constructed. Data adjustments, if any, are discussed along with various definitions of data aggregation.

D) Column 4 contains general comments regarding the potential use and misuse of the statistics presented.

(1) Table	(2) Data Base	(3) Table Construction	(4) General Comments
1	All law enforcement agencies in the UCR Program (including those submitting less than 12 months).	The 1993 statistics are consistent with Table 2. Pre-1993 crime statistics may have been updated, and hence, may not be consistent with prior publications. Crime statistics include estimated offense totals for agencies submitting less than 12 months of offense reports for each year. Population statistics represent July 1 provisional estimations for each year except 1970, 1980, and 1990, which are Bureau of the Census decennial census data (see App. III). Crime volume statistics are rounded to the nearest 10 for violent crime and the nearest 100 for property crime. Percent changes and rates are computed prior to rounding.	Represents an estimation of national reported crime activity from 1974 to 1993.
2	All law enforcement agencies in the UCR Program (including those submitting less than 12 months in 1993).	Statistics are aggregated from individual state statistics as shown in Table 5. Crime statistics include estimated offense totals for agencies submitting less than 12 months of offense reports. Population statistics represent July 1, 1993, Bureau of the Census provisional estimates. See Appendix III for UCR population breakdowns.	Represents an estimation of national reported crime activity in 1993.
3	All law enforcement agencies in the UCR Program (including those submitting less than 12 months in 1993).	Regional offense distributions are computed from volume figures as shown in Table 4. Population distributions are based on July 1, 1993, Bureau of the Census provisional estimates (see App. III).	Represents the 1993 geographical distribution of estimated Crime Index offenses and population.
4	All law enforcement agencies in the UCR Program (including those submitting less than 12 months).	The 1993 statistics are aggregated from individual state statistics as shown in Table 5. Crime statistics include estimated offense totals for agencies submitting less than 12 months of offense reports for 1992 and 1993. Population statistics represent July 1 provisional estimates for 1992 and 1993 (see App. III).	Represents an estimation of reported crime activity for Index offenses at the: 1. national level 2. regional level 3. division level 4. state level Any comparison of UCR statistics should take into consideration demographic factors.
5	All law enforcement agencies in the UCR Program (including those submitting less than 12 months in 1993).	Crime statistics include estimated offense totals for agencies submitting less than 12 months of offense reports. Population statistics represent 1993 estimates (see App. III). Statistics under the heading "Area Actually Reporting" represent reported offense totals for agencies submitting 12 months of offense reports and estimated totals for agencies submitting less than 12 but more than 2 months of offense reports. The statistics under the heading "Estimated Totals" represent the above plus estimated offense totals for agencies having less than 3 months of offense reports.	Represents an estimation of reported crime activity for Index offenses at the state level. Any comparison of UCR statistics should take into consideration demographic factors.
6	All law enforcement agencies in the UCR Program (including those submitting less than 12 months in 1993).	Statistics are published for all Metropolitan Statistical Areas (MSAs) having at least 75% reporting and for which the central city/cities submitted 12 months of data in 1993. Crime statistics include estimated offense totals for agencies submitting less than 12 months of offense statistics for 1993. Population statistics represent July 1, 1993, Bureau of the Census provisional estimates. The statistics under the heading "Area Actually Reporting" represent reported offense totals for agencies submitting all 12 months of offense reports plus estimated offense totals for agencies submitting less than 12 but more than 2 months of offense reports. The statistics under the heading "Estimated Total" represent the above plus the estimated offense totals for agencies submitting less than 3 months of offense reports. The tabular breakdowns are according to UCR definitions (see App. II).	Represents an estimation of the reported crime activity for Index offenses at individual MSA level. Any comparison of UCR statistics should take into consideration demographic factors.
7	All law enforcement agencies in the UCR Program (including those submitting less than 12 months in 1993).	Offense totals are for all Index offense categories other than aggravated assault. Crime statistics include estimated offense totals for agencies submitting less than 12 months of offense reports for each year.	Represents an estimation of national reported crime activity from 1989 to 1993. Aggravated assault is excluded from Table 7, because if money or property is taken in connection with an assault the offense is robbery.
8	All law enforcement agencies submitting complete reports for 12 months in 1993.	"Cities and Towns" are defined to be agencies in Population Groups I through V (App. III). The agency populations are 1993 estimates for each agency (see App. III).	Represents reported crime activity of individual agencies in cities and towns 10,000 and over in population. Any comparison of UCR statistics should take into consideration demographic factors.

(1) Table	(2) Data Base	(3) Table Construction	(4) General Comments
9	All university/college law enforcement agencies submitting complete reports for 12 months in 1993.	The 1992 student enrollment figures, which are provided by the U.S. Department of Education, are the most recent available. They include full- and part-time students. No adjustments to equate part-time enrollments into full-time equivalents have been made.	Represents reported crime from those individual university/college law enforcement agencies contributing to the UCR Program. These agencies are listed alphabetically by state. Any comparison of these UCR statistics should take into consideration size of enrollment, number of on-campus residents, and other demographic factors.
10	All law enforcement agencies submitting complete reports for 12 months in 1993.	"Suburban Counties" are defined as the areas covered by noncity agencies within an MSA (App. III). Population estimates of suburban counties are as of July 1, 1993 (see App. III).	Represents crime reported to individual law enforcement agencies in suburban counties, i.e., the individual sheriff's office, county police department, highway patrol, and/or state police. These figures do not represent the county totals since they exclude city crime counts. Any comparison of UCR statistics should take into consideration demographic factors.
11	All law enforcement agencies submitting complete reports for 12 months in 1993.	"Rural Counties" are those outside MSAs and whose jurisdictions are not covered by city police agencies (App. III). Population classifications of rural counties are based on 1993 estimates for individual agencies (see App. III).	Represents crime reported to individual rural county law enforcement agencies covering populations 25,000 and over, i.e., the individual sheriff's office, county police department, highway patrol, and/or state police. These figures do not represent the county totals since they exclude city crime counts. Any comparion of UCR statistics should take into consideration demographic factors.
12-15	All law enforcement agencies submitting complete reports for at least 6 common months in 1992 and 1993.	The 1993 crime trend statistics are 2-year comparisons based on 1993 reported crime activity. Only common reported months for individual agencies are included in 1993 trend calculations. Populations represent July 1, 1993, estimates for individual agencies. See Appendix III for UCR population breakdowns. Note that "Suburban and Nonsuburban Cities" are all municipal agencies other than central cities in MSAs.	Slight decrease in national coverage for Table 15 due to editing procedure and lower submission rate.
16-19	All law enforcement agencies submitting complete reports for 12 months in 1993.	The 1993 crime rates are the ratios of the aggregated 1993 crime volumes and the aggregated 1993 populations of the contributing agencies. Population statistics represent 1993 estimates for individual agencies. See Appendix III for UCR population breakdowns. Note that "Suburban and Nonsuburban Cities" are all municipal agencies other than central cities in MSAs.	The forcible rape figures furnished by the Illinois, Michigan, and Minnesota state-level UCR Programs were not in accordance with national guidelines. For inclusion in these tables, the forcible rape figures for these states were estimated by using the national rates for each population group applied to each state's population by group for agencies supplying all 12 months of data. Slight decrease in national coverage for Table 19 due to editing procedure and lower submission rate.
20	All law enforcement agencies submitting Supplementary Homicide Report (SHR) data in 1993.	The weapon totals are the aggregate for each murder victim recorded on the SHRs for calendar year 1993.	The SHR is the monthly report form concerning homicides. It details victim and offender characteristics, circumstances, weapons used, etc.
21, 22	All law enforcement agencies submitting complete reports for 12 months in 1993.	The weapon totals are aggregated 1993 totals. Population statistics represent 1993 estimates.	
23, 24	All law enforcement agencies submitting complete reports for at least 6 months in 1993.	Offense total and value lost total are computed for all Index offense categories other than aggravated assault. Percent distribution is derived based on offense total of each Index offense. Trend statistics are derived based on agencies with at least 6 common months complete for 1992 and 1993.	Aggravated assault is excluded from Table 23. For UCR Program purposes, the taking of money or property in connection with an assault is reported as a robbery.
25-28	All law enforcement agencies submitting complete reports for at least 6 months in 1993.	The 1993 clearance rates are based on offense and clearance volume totals of the contributing agencies for 1993. Population statistics represents 1993 estimates. See Appendix III for UCR population breakdowns.	
29	All law enforcement agencies in the UCR Program (including those submitting less than 12 months in 1993).	The arrest totals presented are national estimates based on the arrest statistics of all law enforcement agencies in the UCR Program (including those submitting less than 12 months). The "Total Estimated Arrests" statistic is the sum of estimated arrest volumes for each of the 29 offenses. Each individual arrest total is the sum of the estimated volumes within each of the eight population groups (App. III). Each group's estimate is the reported volume (as shown in Table 26) divided by the percent of total group population reporting (according to 1993 Bureau of the Census provisional estimates; see App. III).	

(1) Table	(2) Data Base	(3) Table Construction	(4) General Comments
30, 31	All law enforcement agencies submitting complete reports for 12 months in 1993.	The 1993 arrest rates are the ratios, per 100,000 inhabitants, of the aggregated 1993 reported arrest statistics and population. The population statistics represent July 1, 1993, estimates. See Appendix III for UCR population classifications/geographical configuration.	
32, 33	All law enforcement agencies submitting complete reports for 12 months in 1984 and 1993.	The arrest trends are the percentage differences between 1984 and 1993 arrest volumes aggregated from all common agencies. Population statistics represent July 1, 1993, estimates (see App. III).	
34, 35	All law enforcement agencies submitting complete reports for 12 months in 1989 and 1993.	The arrest trends are the percentage differences between 1989 and 1993 arrest volumes aggregated from common agencies. Population statistics represent 1993 estimates (see App. III).	
36, 37	All law enforcement agencies submitting complete reports for 12 months in 1992 and 1993.	The arrest trends are 2-year comparisons between 1992 and 1993 arrest volumes aggregated from common agencies. Population statistics represent 1993 estimates (see App. III).	
38-43	All law enforcement agencies submitting complete reports for 12 months in 1993.		Slight decrease in coverage for Table 43 due to editing procedure and lower submission of race data.
44, 45	All city law enforcement agencies submitting complete reports for 12 months in 1992 and 1993.	The 1993 city arrest trends represent the percentage differences between 1992 and 1993 arrest volumes aggregated from common city agencies. "City Agencies" are defined to be all agencies within Population Groups I-VI (App. III).	
46-49	All city law enforcement agencies submitting complete reports for 12 months in 1992 and 1993.	"City Agencies" are defined as agencies within Population Groups I-VI (App. III).	Slight decrease in coverage for Table 49 due to editing procedure and lower submission of race data.
50, 51	All suburban county law enforcement agencies submtting complete reports for 12 months in 1992 and 1993.	The 1993 suburban county arrest trends represent percentage differences between 1992 and 1993 volumes aggregated from contributing agencies. "Suburban Counties" are defined as the areas covered by noncity agencies within an MSA (App. III).	
52-55	All suburban county law enforcement agencies submitting complete reports for 12 months in 1993.	"Suburban Counties" are defined as the areas covered by noncity agencies within an MSA (App. III).	Slight decrease in coverage for Table 55 due to editing procedure and lower submission of race data.
56, 57	All rural county law enforcement agencies submitting complete reports for 12 months in 1992 and 1993.	The 1993 rural county arrest trends represent percentage differences between 1992 and 1993 volumes aggregated from contributing agencies. "Rural Counties" are defined as noncity agencies outside MSAs (App. III).	Slight decrease in coverage for Table 55 due to editing procedure and lower submission of race data.
58-61	All rural county law enforcement agencies submitting complete reports for 12 months in 1993.	"Rural Counties" are defined as noncity agencies outside MSAs (App. III).	Slight decrease in coverage for Table 61 due to editing procedure and lower submission of race data.
62, 63	All suburban area law enforcement agencies submitting complete reports for 12 months in 1992 and 1993.	The 1993 suburban area arrest trends represent percentage differences between 1992 and 1993 arrest volumes aggregated from contributing agencies. "Suburban Area" is defined as cities with fewer than 50,000 inhabitants and all counties within MSAs (App. III).	
64-67	All suburban area law enforcement agencies submitting complete reports for 12 months in 1993.	"Suburban Area" is defined as cities with fewer than 50,000 inhabitants and all counties within MSAs (App. III).	Slight decrease in coverage for Table 67 due to editing procedure and lower submission of race data.
68	All law enforcement agencies submitting complete reports for 12 months in 1993.	Arrest totals are aggregated for individual agencies within each state. Population figures represent July 1, 1993, estimates (see App. III).	Any comparison of statistics should take into consideration variances in arrest practices, particularly for Part II crimes.
69	All law enforcement agencies submitting complete reports for 12 months in 1993.	Population statistics represent July 1, 1993, estimates for individual agencies. See Appendix III for definitions of the population classifications presented.	Data furnished are based upon individual state age definitions for juveniles.

APPENDIX II

Offenses in Uniform Crime Reporting

Offenses in Uniform Crime Reporting are divided into two groupings, Part I and Part II. Information on the volume of Part I offenses known to law enforcement, those cleared by arrest or exceptional means, and the number of persons arrested is reported monthly. Only arrest data are reported for Part II offenses.

The Part I offenses are:

Criminal homicide. — a. Murder and nonnegligent manslaughter: the willful (nonnegligent) killing of one human being by another. Deaths caused by negligence, attempts to kill, assaults to kill, suicides, accidental deaths, and justifiable homicides are excluded. Justifiable homicides are limited to: (1) the killing of a felon by a law enforcement officer in the line of duty; and (2) the killing of a felon by a private citizen. b. Manslaughter by negligence: the killing of another person through gross negligence. Traffic fatalities are excluded. While manslaughter by negligence is a Part I crime, it is not included in the Crime Index.

Forcible rape. — The carnal knowledge of a female forcibly and against her will. Included are rapes by force and attempts or assaults to rape. Statutory offenses (no force used — victim under age of consent) are excluded.

Robbery. — The taking or attempting to take anything of value from the care, custody, or control of a person or persons by force or threat of force or violence and/or by putting the victim in fear.

Aggravated assault. — An unlawful attack by one person upon another for the purpose of inflicting severe or aggravated bodily injury. This type of assault usually is accompanied by the use of a weapon or by means likely to produce death or great bodily harm. Simple assaults are excluded.

Burglary-breaking or entering. — The unlawful entry of a structure to commit a felony or a theft. Attempted forcible entry is included.

Larceny-theft (except motor vehicle theft). — The unlawful taking, carrying, leading, or riding away of property from the possession or constructive possession of another. Examples are thefts of bicycles or automobile accessories, shoplifting, pocket-picking, or the stealing of any property or article which is not taken by force and violence or by fraud. Attempted larcenies are included. Embezzlement, "con" games, forgery, worthless checks, etc., are excluded.

Motor vehicle theft. — The theft or attempted theft of a motor vehicle. A motor vehicle is self-propelled and runs on the surface and not on rails. Specifically excluded from this

category are motorboats, construction equipment, airplanes, and farming equipment.

Arson. — Any willful or malicious burning or attempt to burn, with or without intent to defraud, a dwelling house, public building, motor vehicle or aircraft, personal property of another, etc .

The Part II offenses are:

Other assaults (simple). — Assaults and attempted assaults where no weapon is used and which do not result in serious or aggravated injury to the victim.

Forgery and counterfeiting. — Making, altering, uttering, or possessing, with intent to defraud, anything false in the semblance of that which is true. Attempts are included.

Fraud. — Fraudulent conversion and obtaining money or property by false pretenses. Included are confidence games and bad checks, except forgeries and counterfeiting.

Embezzlement. — Misappropriation or misapplication of money or property entrusted to one's care, custody, or control.

Stolen property; buying, receiving, possessing. — Buying, receiving, and possessing stolen property, including attempts.

Vandalism. — Willful or malicious destruction, injury, disfigurement, or defacement of any public or private property, real or personal, without consent of the owner or persons having custody or control.

Weapons; carrying, possessing, etc. — All violations of regulations or statutes controlling the carrying, using, possessing, furnishing, and manufacturing of deadly weapons or silencers. Included are attempts.

Prostitution and commercialized vice. — Sex offenses of a commercialized nature, such as prostitution, keeping a bawdy house, procuring, or transporting women for immoral purposes. Attempts are included.

Sex offenses (except forcible rape, prostitution, and commercialized vice). — Statutory rape and offenses against chastity, common decency, morals, and the like. Attempts are included.

Drug abuse violations. — State and local offenses relating to the unlawful possession, sale, use, growing, and manufacturing of narcotic drugs. The following drug categories are specified: Opium or cocaine and their derivatives (morphine, heroin, codeine); marijuana; synthetic narcotics — manufactured narcotics that can cause true addiction (demerol, methadone); and dangerous nonnarcotic drugs (barbiturates, benzedrine).

Gambling. — Promoting, permitting, or engaging in illegal gambling.

Offenses against the family and children. — Nonsupport, neglect, desertion, or abuse of family and children.

Driving under the influence. — Driving or operating any vehicle or common carrier while drunk or under the influence of liquor or narcotics.

Liquor laws. — State or local liquor law violations, except "drunkenness" and "driving under the influence." Federal violations are excluded.

Drunkenness. — Offenses relating to drunkenness or intoxication. Excluded is "driving under the influence."

Disorderly conduct. — Breach of the peace.

Vagrancy. — Vagabondage, begging, loitering, etc.

All other offenses. — All violations of state or local laws, except those listed above and traffic offenses.

Suspicion. — No specific offense; suspect released without formal charges being placed.

Curfew and loitering laws (persons under age 18). — Offenses relating to violations of local curfew or loitering ordinances where such laws exist.

Runaways (persons under age 18). — Limited to juveniles taken into protective custody under provisions of local statutes.

APPENDIX III

Uniform Crime Reporting Area Definitions

The presentation of statistics by reporting area facilitates analyzing local crime counts in conjunction with those for areas of similar geographical location or population size. Geographically, the United States is divisible by regions, divisions, and states. Further breakdowns rely on population figures and proximity to metropolitan areas. As a general rule, sheriffs, county police, and state police report crimes committed within the limits of counties but outside cities, while local police report crimes committed within the city limits.

Community Types

UCR data are often presented in aggregations representing three types of communities:

1. Metropolitan Statistical Areas (MSAs) — Each MSA includes a central city of at least 50,000 people or an urbanized area of at least 50,000. The county containing the central city and other contiguous counties having strong economic and social ties to the central city and county are also included. Counties in an MSA are designated "suburban" for UCR purposes. An MSA may cross state lines. The MSA concept facilitates the analysis and presentation of uniform statistical data on metropolitan areas by establishing reporting units which represent major population centers. Due to changes in the geographic composition of MSAs, no year-to-year comparisons of data for those areas should be attempted.

New England MSAs are comprised of cities and towns instead of counties. In this publication's tabular presentations, New England cities and towns are assigned to the proper MSA. Some counties, however, have both suburban and rural portions. Data for state police and sheriffs in those jurisdictions are included in statistics for the rural area.

MSAs made up approximately 79 percent of the total United States population in 1993. Some presentations in this book refer to "suburban area." A suburban area includes cities with less than 50,000 inhabitants in addition to counties (unincorporated areas) within the MSA. The central cities are, of course, excluded. The concept of suburban area is especially important because of the particular crime conditions which exist in the communities surrounding the Nation's largest cities.

2. Cities Outside MSAs — Cities outside of MSAs are mostly incorporated. They comprised 8 percent of the 1993 population of the United States.

3. Rural Counties Outside MSAs — Rural counties are comprised of mostly unincorporated areas. Law enforcement agencies in rural counties cover areas that are not under the jurisdiction of city police departments. Rural county law enforcement agencies serviced 12 percent of the national population in 1993.

The following is an illustration of the community types:

	MSA	NON-MSA
CITIES	CENTRAL CITIES 50,000 AND OVER	CITIES OUTSIDE METROPOLITAN AREAS
	SUBURBAN CITIES	
COUNTIES (including unincorporated areas)	SUBURBAN COUNTIES	RURAL COUNTIES

Population Groups

The population group classifications used by the UCR Program are:

Population Group	Political Label	Population Range
I	City	250,000 and over
II	City	100,000 to 249,999
III	City	50,000 to 99,999
IV	City	25,000 to 49,999
V	City	10,000 to 24,999
VI	City[1]	Less than 10,000
VIII (Rural County)	County[2]	N/A
IX (Suburban County)	County[2]	N/A

[1]Includes universities and colleges to which no population is attributed.
[2]Includes state police to which no population is attributed.

The major source of UCR data is the individual law enforcement agency. The number of agencies included in each population group will vary slightly from year to year due to population growth, geopolitical consolidation, municipal incorporation, etc. Population figures for individual jurisdictions are estimated by the UCR Program in noncensus years. In this edition, the state and national population figures are 1993 Bureau of the Census provisional estimates. Population figures for individual jurisdictions were updated by applying 1993 state growth rates to 1992 city and county estimates supplied by Census. The United States population estimate showed a 1-percent increase in 1993 over 1992.

The following table shows the number of UCR contributing agencies within each population group for 1993.

Population Group	Number of Agencies	Population Covered
I	65	46,376,045
II	139	20,492,390
III	374	25,590,699
IV	718	24,853,627
V	1,733	27,271,751
VI[1]	7,889	25,251,795
VIII (Rural County)[2] ...	3,615	31,835,208
IX (Suburban County)[2] ..	1,974	55,962,485
Total[3]	16,507	257,908,000

[1]Includes universities and colleges to which no population is attributed.
[2]Includes state police to which no population is attributed.
[3]Because of Bureau of the Census rounding, the population covered does not add to total.

Regions and Divisions

As shown in the accompanying map, the United States is comprised of four regions: the Northeastern States, the Midwestern States, the Southern States, and the Western States. These regions are further divided into nine divisions. The following table delineates the regional, divisional, and state configuration of the country.

NORTHEASTERN STATES

New England
  Connecticut
  Maine
  Massachusetts
  New Hampshire
  Rhode Island
  Vermont

Middle Atlantic
  New Jersey
  New York
  Pennsylvania

MIDWESTERN STATES

East North Central
  Illinois
  Indiana
  Michigan
  Ohio
  Wisconsin

West North Central
  Iowa
  Kansas
  Minnesota
  Missouri
  Nebraska
  North Dakota
  South Dakota

SOUTHERN STATES

South Atlantic
  Delaware
  District of Columbia
  Florida
  Georgia
  Maryland
  North Carolina
  South Carolina
  Virginia
  West Virginia

East South Central
  Alabama
  Kentucky
  Mississippi
  Tennessee
West South Central
  Arkansas
  Louisiana
  Oklahoma
  Texas

WESTERN STATES

Mountain
  Arizona
  Colorado
  Idaho
  Montana
  Nevada
  New Mexico
  Utah
  Wyoming

Pacific
  Alaska
  California
  Hawaii
  Oregon
  Washington

REGIONS
AND DIVISIONS
OF THE UNITED STATES

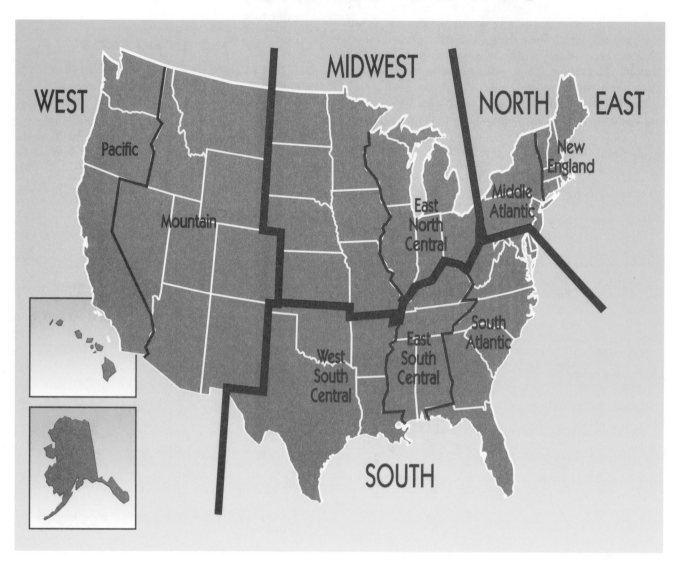

WEST

MIDWEST

NORTH

EAST

Pacific

Mountain

East
North
Central

New
England

Middle
Atlantic

West
South
Central

East
South
Central

South
Atlantic

SOUTH

APPENDIX IV

The Nation's Two Crime Measures

The U.S. Department of Justice administers two statistical programs to measure the magnitude, nature, and impact of crime in the Nation: the Uniform Crime Reporting (UCR) Program and the National Crime Victimization Survey (NCVS). Because of differences in methodology and crime coverage, the results from the two programs are not strictly comparable nor consistent. By complementing each other's findings, the two programs enhance our understanding of the Nation's crime problem.

Uniform Crime Reports

The FBI's UCR Program, which began in 1929, collects information on the following crimes reported to law enforcement authorities: homicide, forcible rape, robbery, aggravated assault, burglary, larceny-theft, motor vehicle theft, and arson.

The UCR data are compiled from monthly law enforcement reports made directly to the FBI or to centralized state agencies that then report to the FBI. Each report submitted to the UCR Program is examined thoroughly for reasonableness, accuracy, and deviations that may indicate errors. Large variations in crime levels may indicate modified records procedures, incomplete reporting, or changes in a jurisdiction's boundaries. To identify any unusual fluctuations in an agency's crime counts, monthly reports are compared with previous submissions of the agency and with those for similar agencies.

In 1993, law enforcement agencies active in the UCR Program represent approximately 245 million United States inhabitants — 95 percent of the total U.S. population.

The UCR Program provides crime counts for the Nation as a whole, as well as for regions, states, counties, cities, and towns. This permits studies among neighboring jurisdictions and among those with similar populations and other common characteristics.

UCR findings for each calendar year are published initially in a preliminary release in the spring followed by a detailed annual report, *Crime in the United States*, issued in the following calendar year. In addition to information on crime counts and trends, this report includes detailed data on crimes cleared, persons arrested (age, sex, race) for a wide range of crimes, law enforcement personnel (including the number of sworn officers killed or assaulted), and the characteristics of homicides (including age, sex, and race of victims and offenders, victim-offender relationships,

weapons used, and circumstances surrounding the homicides). Other special reports are also available from the UCR Program.

Following a 5-year redesign effort, the UCR Program is currently converting to a more comprehensive and detailed reporting system, called the National Incident-Based Reporting System (NIBRS). NIBRS will provide detailed information about each criminal incident in 22 broad categories of offenses.

National Crime Victimization Survey

The Bureau of Justice Statistics' (BJS) NCVS, which began in 1973, collects detailed information on the frequency and nature of the crimes of rape, personal robbery, aggravated and simple assault, household burglary, personal and household theft, and motor vehicle theft. It does not measure homicide or commercial crimes (such as burglaries of stores).

Interviews are conducted by U.S. Census Bureau personnel with all household members at least 12 years old in a nationally representative sample of approximately 49,000 households (about 101,000 persons). Households stay in the sample for 3 years and are interviewed at 6-month intervals. New households rotate into the sample on an ongoing basis.

The NCVS collects information on crimes suffered by individuals and households, whether or not those crimes were reported to law enforcement. It estimates the proportion of each crime type reported to law enforcement, and it details the reasons given by victims for reporting or not reporting.

The survey provides information about victims (age, sex, race, ethnicity, marital status, income, and educational level), their offenders (sex, race, approximate age, and victim-offender relationship), and the crimes (time and place of occurrence, use of weapons, nature of injury, and economic consequences). Questions also cover the experiences of victims with the criminal justice system, details on self-protective measures used by victims, and possible substance abuse by offenders. Periodically, supplements are added to the survey to obtain detailed information on special topics such as school crime.

Findings from the NCVS for each calendar year are published in a press release the following April (preliminary data), in a BJS Bulletin in the fall presenting summary final data, and in a detailed report the following June covering all NCVS variables. Each year BJS staff develop Special and Technical Reports on specific crime topics.

Comparing UCR and NCVS

As the previous description illustrates, there are significant differences between the two programs. The NCVS, for example, includes crimes both reported and not reported to law enforcement, but it excludes homicide, arson, commercial crimes, and crimes against children under age 12 (all of which are included in the UCR Program). The UCR captures crimes reported to law enforcement, but it excludes simple assaults from the Crime Index. Moreover, even when the same crimes are included in the UCR and NCVS, the definitions vary.

Another difference is the way that rate measures are presented for crimes such as burglary, household theft, and motor vehicle theft in the two programs. The UCR rates for these crimes are largely per-capita (number of crimes per 100,000 persons), whereas the NCVS rates for these crimes are per-household (number of crimes per 1,000 households). Because the number of households may not grow at the same rate each year as the total population, trend data for rates of household crimes measured by the two programs may not be comparable.

In any large-scale data collection program, there are many possible sources of error. For example, in the UCR Program, a police officer may classify a crime incorrectly, and in the NCVS, a Census Bureau interviewer may incorrectly record the responses given by a crime victim. Crime data may also be affected by how the victim perceives and recalls the event. Moreover, as data are compiled and processed, clerical errors may be introduced at any stage. Both the UCR and NCVS programs employ extensive accuracy checks at various stages in the data collection process to minimize errors.

As noted above, the NCVS is based on an extensive, scientifically selected sample of American households. Thus, every crime measure presented in NCVS reports is an estimate for the Nation based on results obtained from the sample. Estimates based on a sample have sampling variation, or a margin of error (which defines a confidence interval) associated with each estimate. This means that if another sample is drawn, there is a certain probability that the resulting estimate would be somewhat different from the original one. If the survey were repeated many times with different samples, the resulting estimates would cluster around the actual measure for the entire population. Rigorous statistical methods are used for calculating the magnitude of the sampling variation associated with the NCVS estimates. Trend data in NCVS reports are described as genuine year-to-year changes only if there is at least a 90% certainty that the measured changes are not the result of sampling variation. The UCR data are based on the actual count of offenses reported by law enforcement jurisdictions. In some circumstances, UCR data are estimated for nonparticipating jurisdictions or those reporting partial data.

Some differences in data from the two programs may result from the fact that NCVS estimates are subject to sampling variation. Apparent discrepancies between statistics from the two programs can usually be resolved by comparing NCVS sampling variations (confidence intervals) with UCR statistics. Year-to-year changes in individual crime categories reported by the UCR usually fall within the confidence intervals of the NCVS estimates, indicating no statistically significant differences between the output of the two programs. Even should the UCR changes fall outside the intervals, incompatibility of statistics should not be assumed. To illustrate, when differences between UCR and NCVS occur, there is a 10% chance they are due to sampling variation because of the 90% confidence level established by NCVS. It should also be noted that definitional and procedural differences between the UCR and NCVS programs can account for apparent discrepancies in data output.

As has been discussed throughout, the results of UCR and NCVS are not strictly comparable for a variety of reasons. Data users, however, possessing the basic understanding of each program's objectives, methodology, and coverage, can use the output from each in a complementary manner to better assess crime occurrence, losses, law enforcement involvement, arrestee descriptive information, and victimization data. By properly utilizing both programs in tandem, the crime issues in this country can be viewed in a much broader, more complete scope.

APPENDIX V

Directory of State Uniform Crime Reporting Programs

Alabama

Alabama Criminal Justice Information Center
Suite 350
770 Washington Avenue
Montgomery, Alabama 36130
(205) 242-4900 x 225

Alaska

Uniform Crime Reporting Section
Department of Public Safety Information System
5700 East Tudor Road
Anchorage, Alaska 99507
(907) 269-5659

American Samoa

Commissioner
Department of Public Safety
Post Office Box 1086
Pago
American Samoa 96799
(684) 633-1111

Arizona

Uniform Crime Reporting
Arizona Department of Public Safety
Post Office Box 6638
Phoenix, Arizona 85005
(602) 223-2263

Arkansas

Arkansas Crime Information Center
One Capitol Mall, 4D-200
Little Rock, Arkansas 72201
(501) 682-2222

California

Bureau of Criminal Statistics
Department of Justice
Post Office Box 903427
Sacramento, California 94203
(916) 227-3554

Colorado

Uniform Crime Reporting
Colorado Bureau of Investigation
690 Kipling Street
Denver, Colorado 80215
(303) 239-4300

Connecticut

Uniform Crime Reporting Program
294 Colony Street
Meriden, Connecticut 06450
(203) 238-6653

Delaware

State Bureau of Identification
Post Office Box 430
Dover, Delaware 19903
(302) 739-5875

District of Columbia

Data Processing Division
Metropolitan Police Department
300 Indiana Avenue, Northwest
Washington, D.C. 20001
(202) 727-4301

Florida	Uniform Crime Reports Section Special Services Bureau Florida Department of Law Enforcement Post Office Box 1489 Tallahassee, Florida 32302 (904) 487-1179
Georgia	Georgia Crime Information Center Georgia Bureau of Investigation Post Office Box 370748 Decatur, Georgia 30037 (404) 244-2614
Guam	Guam Police Department Planning, Research and Development Pedro's Plaza 287 West O'Brien Drive Agana, Guam 96910 (671) 472-8911 x 418
Hawaii	Uniform Crime Reporting Program Crime Prevention Program Department of the Attorney General Suite 701 810 Richards Street Honolulu, Hawaii 96813 (808) 586-1416
Idaho	Criminal Identification Bureau Department of Law Enforcement 700 South Stratford Drive Meridian, Idaho 83680 (208) 327-7130
Illinois	Bureau of Identification Illinois State Police 726 South College Street Springfield, Illinois 62704 (217) 782-8263
Iowa	Iowa Department of Public Safety Wallace State Office Building Des Moines, Iowa 50319 (515) 281-8422
Kansas	Kansas Bureau of Investigation 1620 Southwest Tyler Street Topeka, Kansas 66612 (913) 232-6000
Kentucky	Kentucky State Police Information Services Branch 1250 Louisville Road Frankfort, Kentucky 40601 (502) 227-8783
Louisiana	Louisiana Commission on Law Enforcement 12th Floor 1885 Wooddale Boulevard Baton Rouge, Louisiana 70806 (504) 925-4440

Maine

Uniform Crime Reporting Division
Maine State Police
Station #42
36 Hospital Street
Augusta, Maine 04333
(207) 624-7004

Maryland

Central Records Division
Maryland State Police Department
1711 Belmont Avenue
Baltimore, Maryland 21244
(410) 298-3883

Massachusetts

Uniform Crime Reports
Crime Reporting Unit
CIS Fifth Floor
Massachusetts State Police
1010 Commonwealth Avenue
Boston, Massachusetts 02215
(617) 566-4500

Michigan

Uniform Crime Reporting Section
Michigan State Police
7150 Harris Drive
Lansing, Michigan 48913
(517) 322-5542

Minnesota

Office of Information Systems Management
Minnesota Department of Public Safety
Suite 100-H, Town Square
444 Cedar Street
St. Paul, Minnesota 55101
(612) 296-7589

Montana

Montana Board of Crime Control
303 North Roberts
Helena, Montana 59620
(406) 444-3604

Nebraska

Uniform Crime Reporting Section
The Nebraska Commission on Law Enforcement
    and Criminal Justice
Post Office Box 94946
Lincoln, Nebraska 68509
(402) 471-3982

Nevada

Criminal Information Services
Nevada Highway Patrol
555 Wright Way
Carson City, Nevada 89711
(702) 687-5713

New Hampshire

Uniform Crime Report
Division of State Police
10 Hazen Drive
Concord, New Hampshire 03305
(603) 271-2509

New Jersey

Uniform Crime Reporting
Division of State Police
Post Office Box 7068
West Trenton, New Jersey 08628-0068
(609) 882-2000 x 2392

New York

Statistical Services
New York State Division of Criminal Justice Services
8th Floor, Mail Room
Executive Park Tower Building
Stuyvesant Plaza
Albany, New York 12203
(518) 457-8381

North Carolina

Crime Reporting and Field Services
State Bureau of Investigation
Division of Criminal Information
407 North Blount Street
Raleigh, North Carolina 27601
(919) 733-3171

North Dakota

Information Services Section
Bureau of Criminal Investigation
Attorney General's Office
Post Office Box 1054
Bismarck, North Dakota 58502
(701) 221-5500

Oklahoma

Uniform Crime Reporting Section
Oklahoma State Bureau of Investigation
Suite 300
6600 North Harvey
Oklahoma City, Oklahoma 73116
(405) 848-6724

Oregon

Law Enforcement Data Systems Division
Oregon Department of State Police
400 Public Service Building
Salem, Oregon 97310
(503) 378-3057

Pennsylvania

Bureau of Research and Development
Pennsylvania State Police
1800 Elmerton Avenue
Harrisburg, Pennsylvania 17110
(717) 783-5536

Puerto Rico

Superintendent
Puerto Rico Police
Post Office Box 70166
Puerto Nuevo Hato Rey
San Juan, Puerto Rico 00936
(809) 782-1540

Rhode Island

Rhode Island State Police
Post Office Box 185
North Scituate, Rhode Island 02857
(401) 647-3311

South Carolina

South Carolina Law Enforcement Division
Post Office Box 21398
Columbia, South Carolina 29221-1398
(803) 896-7162

South Dakota

South Dakota Statistical Analysis Center
c/o 500 East Capitol Avenue
Pierre, South Dakota 57501
(605) 773-6310

Texas

Uniform Crime Reporting Bureau
Crime Records Division
Texas Department of Public Safety
Post Office Box 4143
Austin, Texas 78765-4143
(512) 465-2091

Utah

Uniform Crime Reporting
Utah Department of Public Safety
4501 South 2700 West
Salt Lake City, Utah 84119
(801) 965-4445

Vermont

Vermont Department of Public Safety
Post Office Box 189
Waterbury, Vermont 05676
(802) 244-8786

Virginia

Records Management Division
Department of State Police
Post Office Box 27472
Richmond, Virginia 23261-7472
(804) 674-2023

Virgin Islands

Records Bureau
Department of Public Safety
Post Office Box 210
Charlotte Amalie
Saint Thomas, Virgin Islands 00801
(809) 774-2211

Washington

Uniform Crime Reporting Program
Washington Association of Sheriffs and Police Chiefs
Post Office Box 826
Olympia, Washington 98507
(206) 586-3221

West Virginia

Uniform Crime Reporting Program
725 Jefferson Road
South Charleston, West Virginia 25309
(304) 746-2159

Wisconsin

Office of Justice Assistance
2nd Floor
222 State Street
Madison, Wisconsin 53703
(608) 266-3323

Wyoming

Uniform Crime Reporting
Criminal Records Section
Division of Criminal Investigation
316 West 22nd Street
Cheyenne, Wyoming 82002
(307) 777-7625

APPENDIX VI

National Uniform Crime Reporting Program Directory

Administration . . . .(202) 324-2614
    Program administration; management; policy

Information Dissemination . . . .(202) 324-5015
    Requests for published and unpublished data; printouts, magnetic tapes, books

    Send correspondence to: Uniform Crime Reports
                          Criminal Justice Information Services Division
                          FBI/GRB
                          Washington, D.C. 20535

Training/Education . . . .(202) 324-5038
    Requests for training of law enforcement; information on police reporting systems;
    technical assistance

Statistical Analysis/Processing . . . .(202) 324-3821
    Statistical models; special studies and analyses; crime forecasting; processing of summary and
    incident-based reports from data contributors; reporting problems; requests for reporting forms;
    data processing; data quality

APPENDIX VII

Uniform Crime Reporting Publications List

Crime in the United States (annual)

Law Enforcement Officers Killed and Assaulted (annual)

Hate Crime Statistics (annual)

Killed in the Line of Duty: A Study of Selected Felonious Killings of Law Enforcement Officers (special report)

UCR Preliminary Release, January-June (semiannual)

UCR Preliminary Annual Report (semiannual)

Uniform Crime Reporting Handbook:
Summary System
National Incident-Based Reporting System (NIBRS)

NIBRS:
Volume 1 — Data Collection Guidelines
Volume 2 — Data Submission Specifications
Volume 3 — Approaches to Implementing an Incident-Based Reporting (IBR) System
Volume 4 — Error Message Manual
Supplemental Guidelines for Federal Participation

Manual of Law Enforcement Records

Hate Crimes:
Hate Crime Data Collection Guidelines
Training Guide for Hate Crime Data Collection
Hate Crime Statistics, 1990: A Resource Book

Age-Specific Arrest Rates and Race-Specific Arrest Rates for Selected Offenses

Population-at-Risk Rates and Selected Crime Indicators

Periodic Press Releases:
Crime Trends (semiannual)
Law Enforcement Officers Killed (semiannual)
Hate Crime (annual)

Evaluation Form For
Crime in the United States - 1993

1. For what purpose did you use this issue of *Crime in the United States?*

2. Was the publication adequate for that purpose?

    ____ Quite adequate   ____ Somewhat adequate   ____ Quite inadequate

    ____ Adequate   ____ Not Adequate

3. Are there presentations not included that you would find particularly useful?

4. What changes, if any, would you recommend for subsequent issues?

5. Can you point our specific table notes or presentations which are not clear or additional terms which need to be defined?

6. In what capacity did you use *Crime in the United States?*

    ____ Criminal justice/law enforcement   ____ Researcher

           agency employee *(specify functional area)*   ____ Student

           ____ Legislator

    ____ Other government employee   ____ Media

    ____ Private citizen   ____ Other *(specify)*

    ____ Educator

7. Add any additional comments you care to make.

OPTIONAL

Name	Telephone ( )
Number and street	
City	State	Zip Code

– – – –(Fold here)– – – –

U.S. Department of Justice
Federal Bureau of Investigation
Washington, D.C. 20535

Uniform Crime Reports
Federal Bureau of Investigation
Washington, D.C. 20535

– – – –(Fold here)– – – –